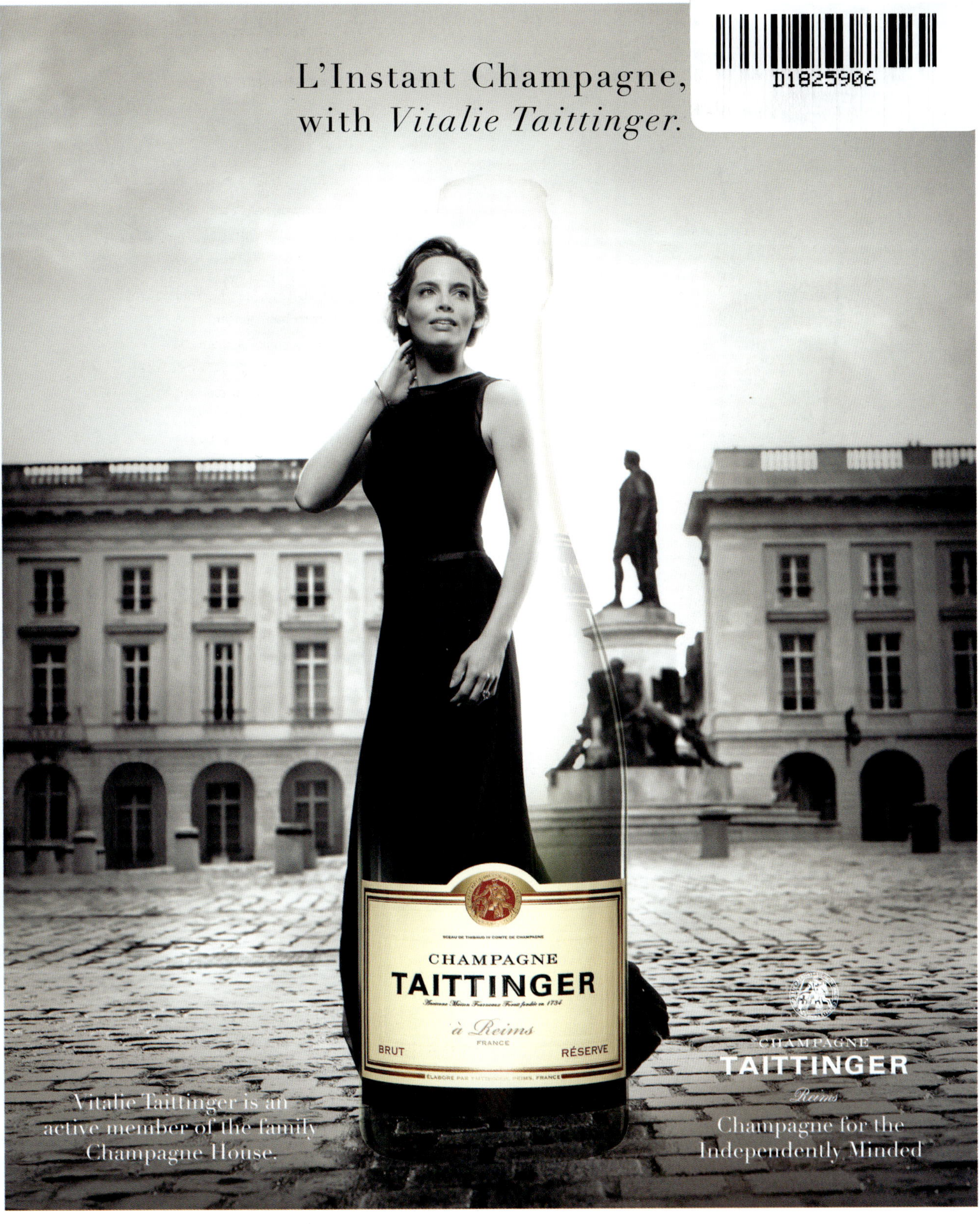

L'Instant Champagne, with *Vitalie Taittinger*.

CHAMPAGNE
TAITTINGER
à Reims
FRANCE

BRUT   RÉSERVE

Vitalie Taittinger is an active member of the family Champagne House.

CHAMPAGNE
TAITTINGER
Reims

Champagne for the Independently Minded

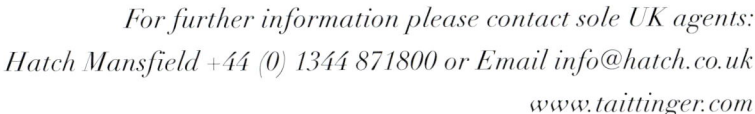
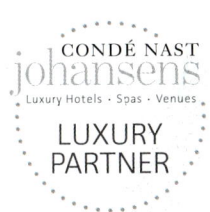

Luxury Partner for fine linens and towelling to Condé Nast Johansens

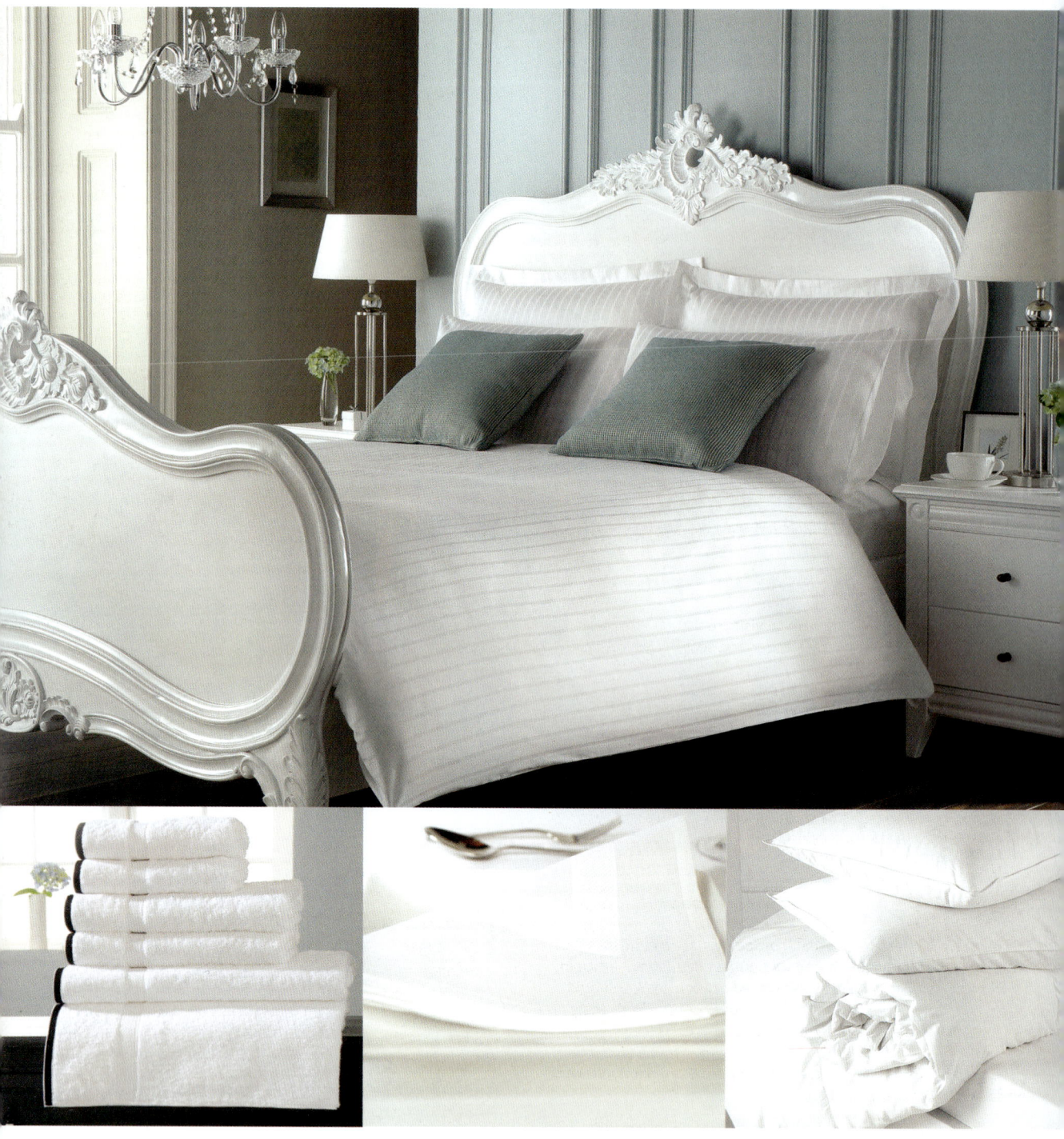

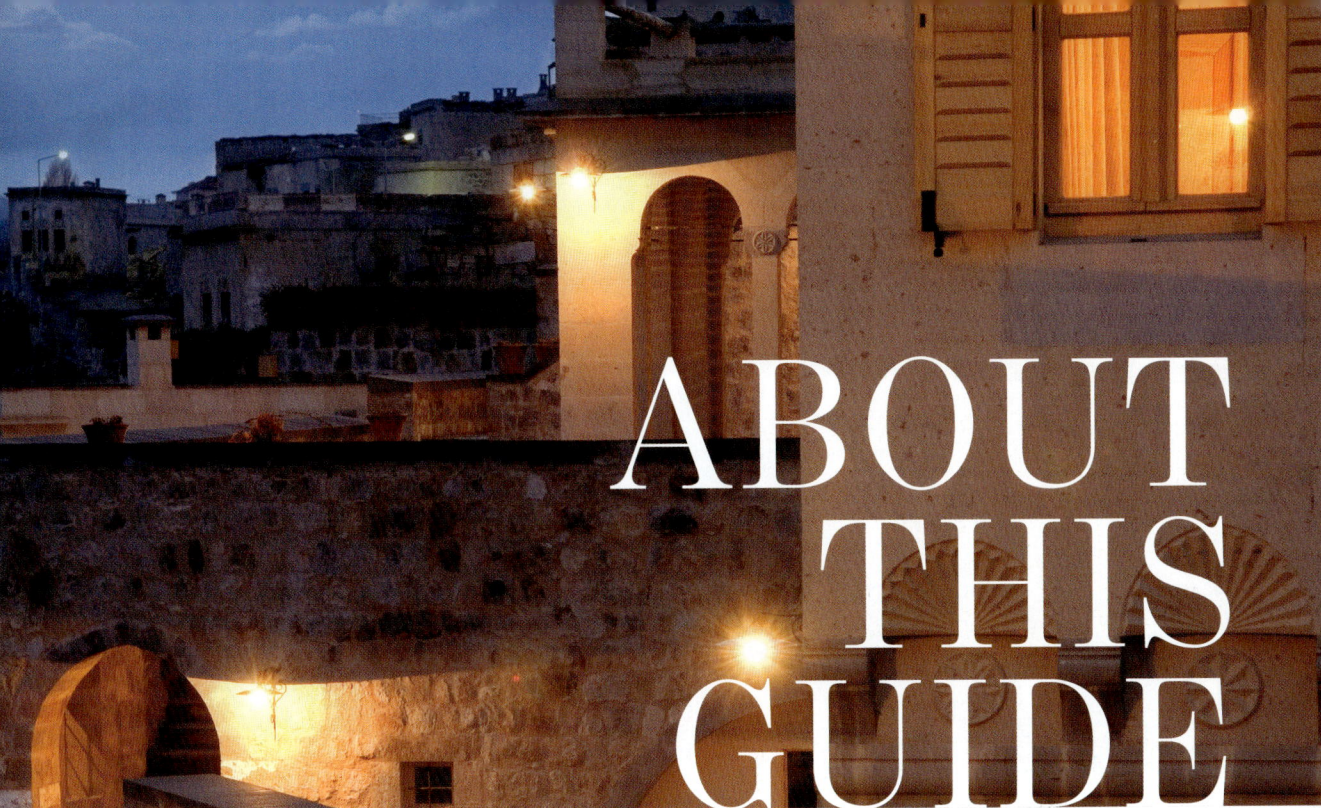

ABOUT THIS GUIDE

Choosing a property:

· Choose the country you wish to visit from the list opposite.
· Turn to the relevant page number and search alphabetically by region.
· Alternatively, turn to the map on pages 316-317 and locate a country marked by its corresponding page number.
· The index starting on page 313 provides a full list of all the properties featured within this Guide, ordered by country and then by property.
· Once you have chosen a property, visit **condenastjohansens.com** where you may send a booking enquiry or call directly using the telephone number on each page.

The information in this Guide is for reference only.

The "Price From" featured on each property's page indicates the lowest room rate available based on double occupancy per room, including tax and breakfast unless stated otherwise. You should always confirm the price and any terms and conditions directly with the property at the time of booking.

When making a booking, please remember to mention you're a Condé Nast Johansens reader!

Top image: argos in Cappadocia, Turkey, page 197

2013 WINNERS OF AWARDS FOR EXCELLENCE

Created to acknowledge, reward and celebrate excellence across our collection of properties, our world-renowned Awards for Excellence are a trusted mark of quality recognised by consumers and travel professionals alike.

The Condé Nast Johansens 2013 Awards were presented at The May Fair Hotel, London, on 5th November 2012. Awards were given to properties throughout the UK, Europe and The Mediterranean that represent the finest quality and service in luxury independent travel.

An important source of information for our Awards is the feedback provided by our readers. Please continue to help us identify who really is the best in the business by nominating the property you think deserves to win one of our Awards by voting online at **condenastjohansens.com/awards**.

THE WINNERS: UK & IRELAND

SERVICE:
The Manor House Hotel, Gloucestershire, page 236

VALUE FOR MONEY:
Ashdown Park Hotel and Country Club, East Sussex, page 275

FAMILY FRIENDLY HOTEL:
Carlyon Bay Hotel, Cornwall, page 212

WATERSIDE HOTEL:
The Atlantic Hotel, Jersey, page 13

ROMANTIC HOTEL:
Park House, West Sussex, page 280

NEWCOMER:
The Arch London, page 263

LONDON HOTEL:
Corinthia Hotel London, page 250

DESTINATION HOTEL:
Chewton Glen, Hampshire, page 239

HOTEL SPA:
Ockenden Manor Hotel, West Sussex, page 279

COUNTRY HOUSE HOTEL:
Gilpin Hotel & Lake House, Cumbria, page 219

APARTMENT:
Cheval Knightsbridge, London, page 259

HOTEL
Barnsley House, Gloucestershire, page 234

Top image: Chewton Glen, England, page 239

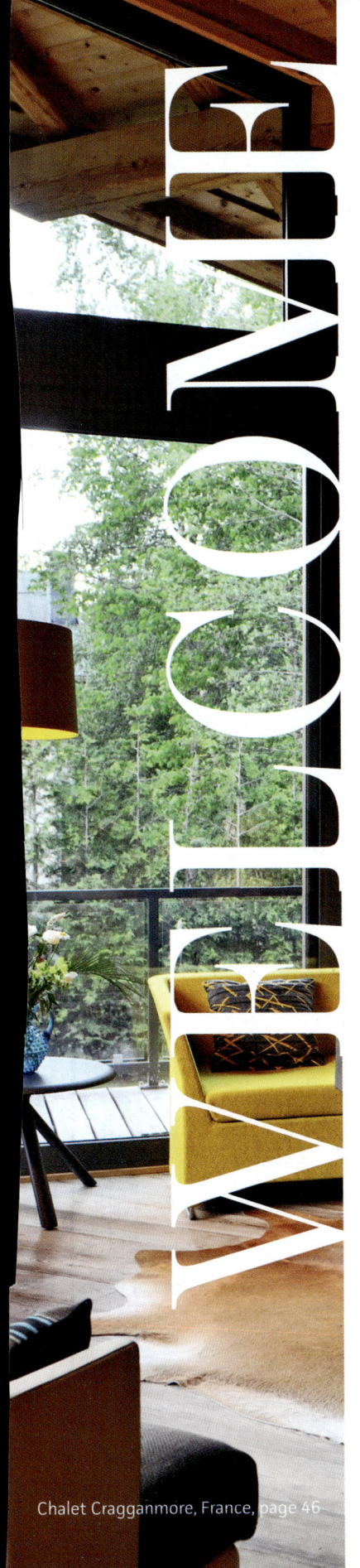

WELCOME

Welcome to our 2014 edition of Luxury Hotels & Spas, UK, Europe & The Mediterranean.

As you browse through, you'll notice some changes... the fresh layout, friendly property reviews containing destination info, travel trivia and the need-to-know facts that all aim to help you choose your ideal getaway.

From beach-side resorts, utterly private villas and country retreats to city escapes and luxury hotel spas, we're proud to share our selection of the finest places to stay in the UK, Europe & The Mediterranean. Eclectic and sometimes a little quirky, our collection showcases edgy designer flair, classic elegance and home-from-home comfort.

Rest assured, each property in this Guide has been approved by one of our team of local experts, so you can trust you'll have an exceptional experience.

This Guide is complemented by our redesigned website: **condenastjohansens.com**, where you can plan your itinerary and send booking enquiries directly to each property.

While visiting our site please remember to tell us about your stay by completing one of our feedback forms or write to us at info@johansens.com. And, if you think a property is deserving, cast your vote for our Annual Awards for Excellence at **condenastjohansens.com/awards**.

Share the Condé Nast Johansens love of independent travel by giving our Gift Vouchers as a gift. They can be redeemed at any of the properties featured within this Guide and on our website. For more information please go to **condenastjohansens.com/gift-shop** or telephone +44 (0)800 035 1449.

Best wishes and happy travels,

Charlotte

Charlotte Evans, Group Publishing Director

Chalet Cragganmore, France, page 46

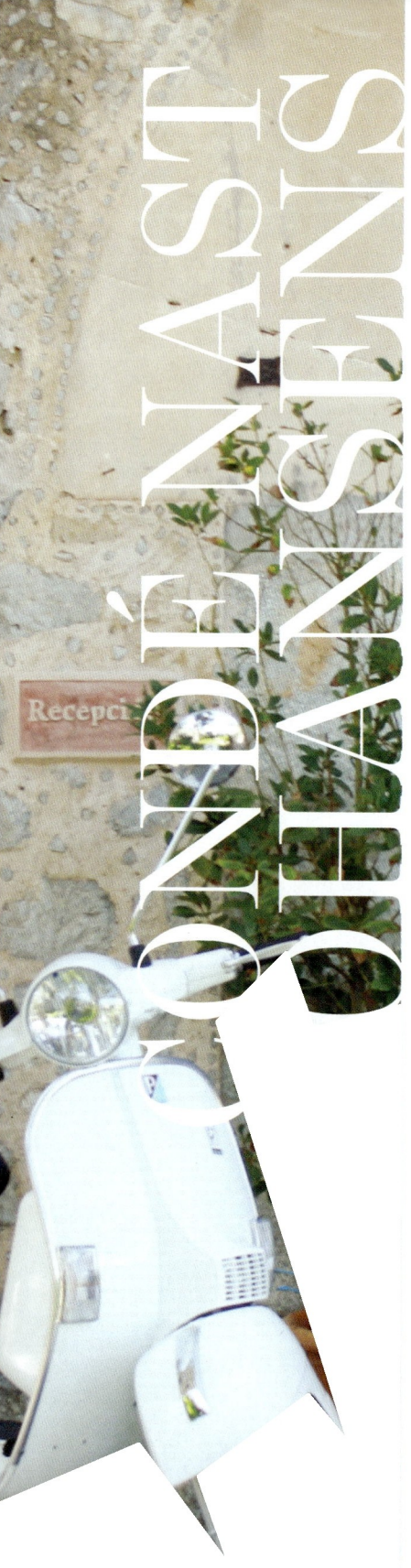

Group Publishing Director:
Charlotte Evans

Account Director - UK & Ireland: Tim Fay

Assistant to Group Publishing Director: Laura Kennedy

Local Experts:
Sharla Ault, Ana María Brebner, Joe Cawley, Michèle Cooren-Lahaye, Stéphanie Court,
Gianna Illari, Núria Llàcer Pascual, Tunde Longmore, Barbara Marcotulli,
Murat Özgüç, Olga Papadaki, Seamus Shortt, Danielle Taljaardt, Christopher Terleski

Client Services Director: Fiona Patrick

Managing Editor: Laura Kerry

Copywriters:
Sasha Creed, Helen Crockett, Catherine Dow, Sarah Heron,
Debra O'Sullivan, Eleanor Sharman, Stefanie Young

Production Director: Sarah Jenson

Production Manager: Joanne Packham

Production Controllers: Samantha Dearden, Frances Seal

Marketing Manager: Adam Crabtree

Digital Marketing Manager: Doug Walker

Digital Marketing Assistant: Kelly Jenkins

Management Accountant: Louise Park

Designer: Lorna Morris

Can't find Condé Nast Johansens in the shops? To order a copy, call +44 (0)800 035 1449.

Copyright © 2013 Condé Nast Johansens Ltd.
Condé Nast Johansens Ltd is part of The Condé Nast Publications Ltd.
ISBN 978-1-903665-69-5
Printed in England by Wyndeham Group.
Internationally distributed by Roundhouse Group.

Condé Nast Publications Ltd

International Director of Communications: Nicky Eaton

Marketing Director: Jean Faulkner

Financial Control Director: Penny Scott-Bayfield

Finance Director: Pam Raynor

Deputy Managing Director: Albert Read

Managing Director:
Nicholas Coleridge

Chairman Condé Nast International:
Jonathan Newhouse

Condé Nast Johansens Ltd, 13 Hanover Square, London W1S 1HN
Enquiries: tel: +44 (0)20 7499 9080; fax +44 (0)20 7152 3565
E-mail: info@johansens.com Web: condenastjohansens.com

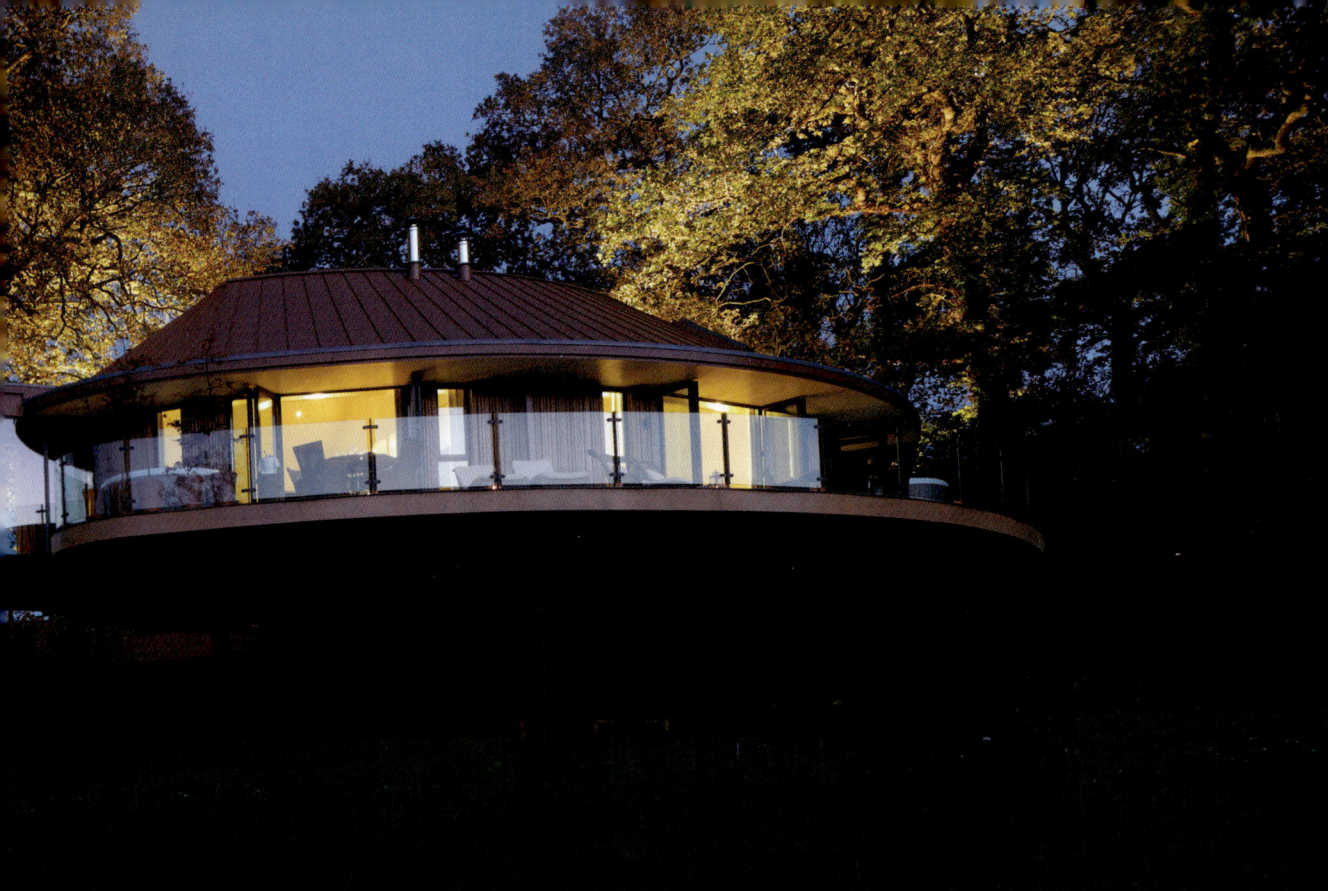

THE WINNERS:
EUROPE & THE MEDITERRANEAN

SERVICE:
Relais San Maurizio, Luxury Spa Resort, Italy, page 90

VALUE FOR MONEY:
Color Hotel style & design, Italy, page 132

FAMILY FRIENDLY HOTEL:
Parkhotel Holzner, Italy, page 101

WATERSIDE HOTEL:
Gran Hotel Atlantis Bahía Real, Spain, page 177

ROMANTIC HOTEL:
Astra Suites, Greece, page 54

NEWCOMER:
Hotel Brunelleschi, Italy, page 109

CITY HOTEL:
The Yeatman Hotel, Portugal, page 163

DESTINATION HOTEL:
Kempinski Hotel Barbaros Bay, Turkey, page 196

**SUSTAINABLE HOSPITALITY
& CORPORATE SOCIAL RESPONSIBILITY:**
argos in Cappadocia, Turkey, page 197

LUXURY GUEST HOUSE:
La Borde, France, page 32

HOTEL SPA:
L'Albereta, Italy, page 85

VILLA/APARTMENT:
Camperio House Suites & Apartments, Italy, page 87

CHARMING HOTEL:
Hotel Byron, Italy, page 115

HOTEL:
Gran Hotel Son Net, Spain, page 174

CONDÉ NAST JOHANSENS READERS' AWARD:
Palazzo Magnani Feroni - all-suites Florence, Italy, page 111

THE KNIGHT FRANK AWARDS
FOR EXCELLENCE
AND INNOVATION

UNITED KINGDOM:
Linthwaite House Hotel, England, page 221

EUROPE & THE MEDITERRANEAN:
Cornelia Diamond Golf Resort and Spa, Turkey, page 193

MEETINGS, INCENTIVES,
CONFERENCES AND EVENTS
(MICE) AWARDS

EUROPE & THE MEDITERRANEAN:
Gran Hotel Bahía del Duque Resort, Spain, page 179
La Posta Vecchia, Italy, page 74

N.B. Winners appearing in this Guide only.

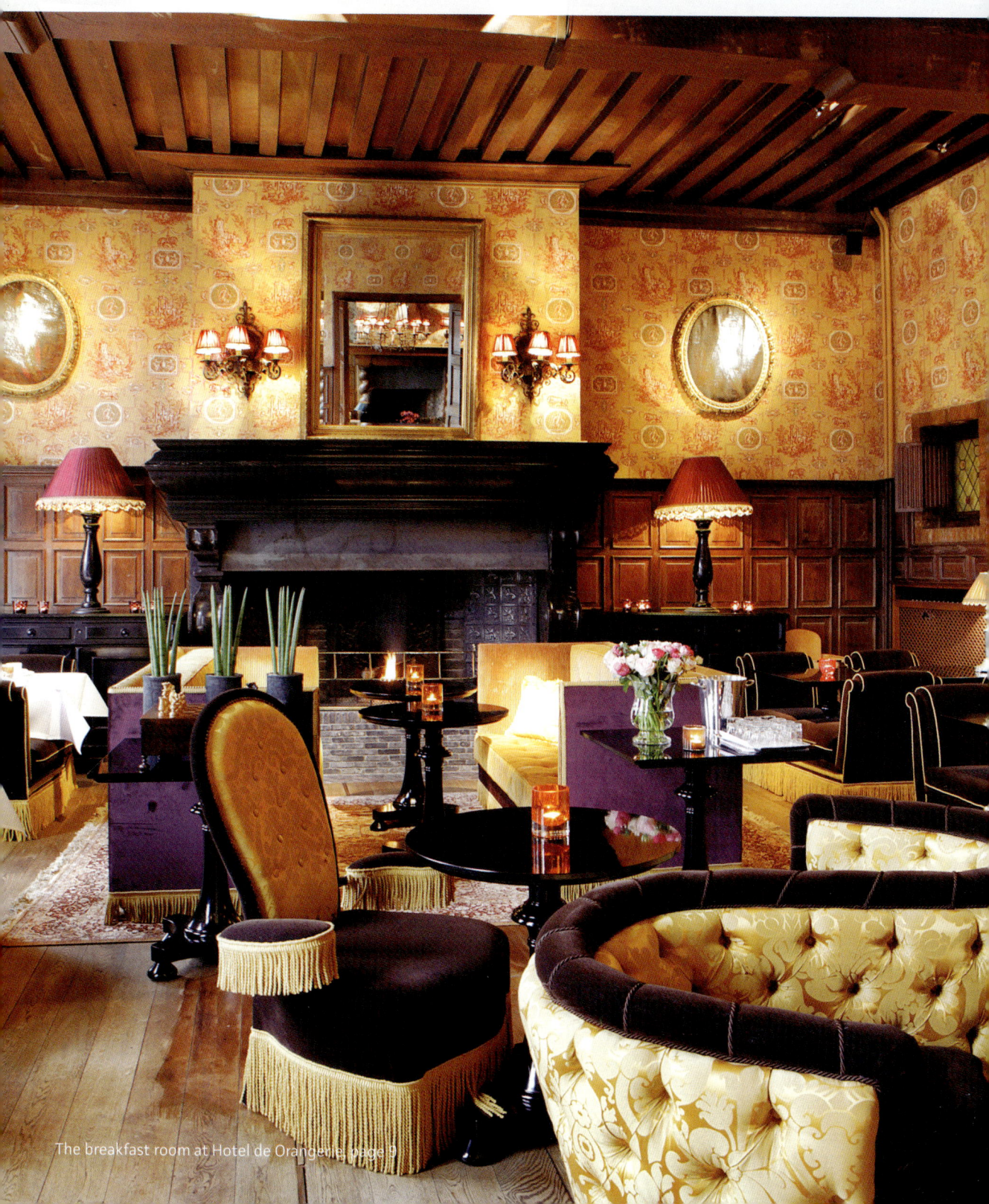

Belgium

Please go to condenastjohansens.com/belgium

The breakfast room at Hotel de Orangerie, page 9

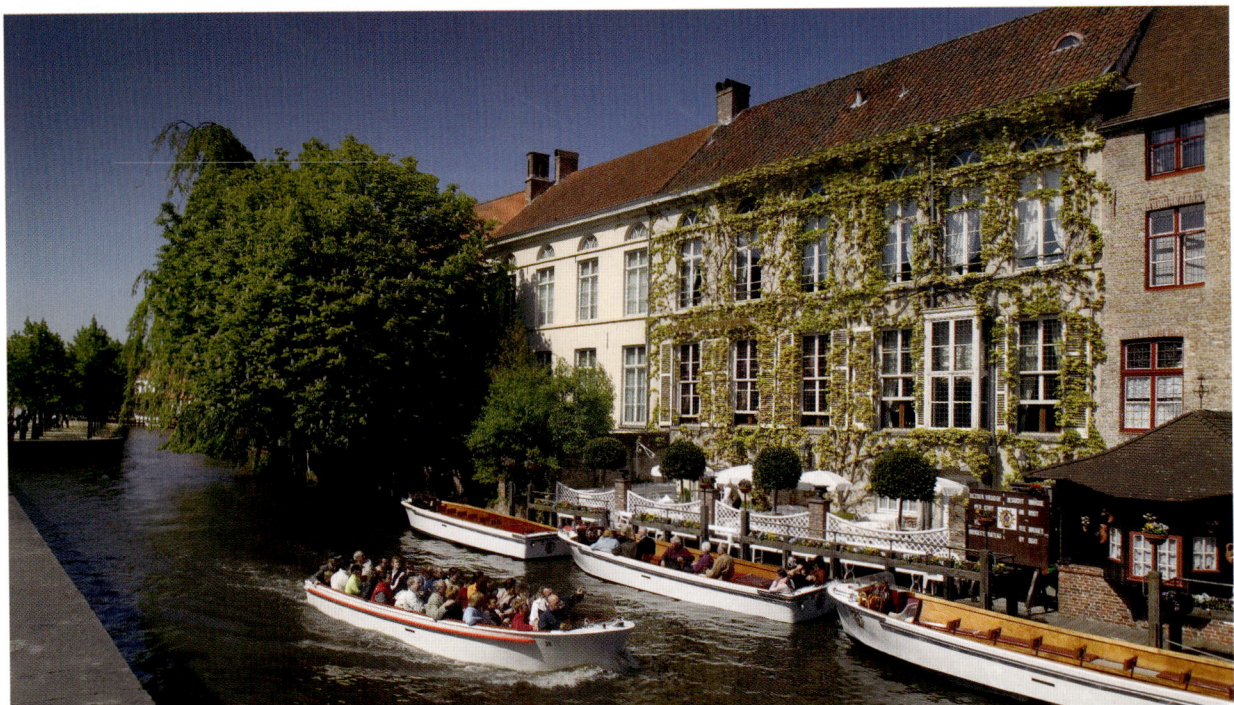

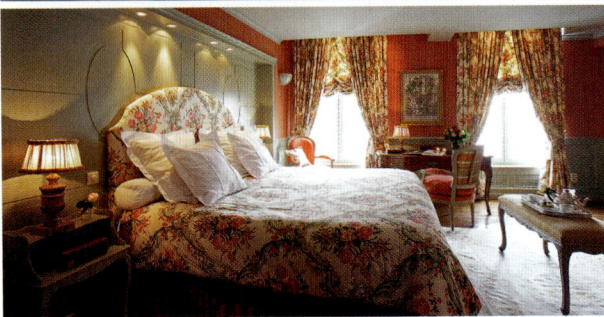

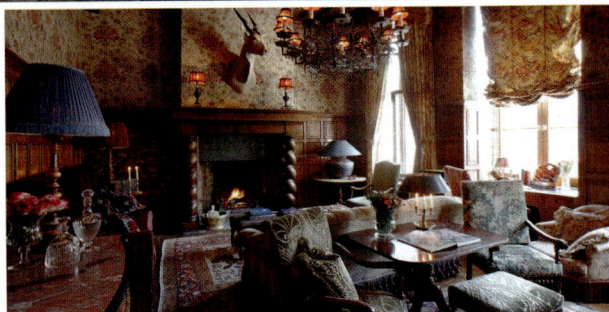

Hotel de Orangerie

Plush, romantic canal-side hotel in Bruges old town

PRICE FROM:
€225

FEATURES:
Family friendly; Lake views; Pet friendly; Wheelchair access

ACTIVITIES:
Cycling; Shopping; Sightseeing

NEARBY:
Horse-drawn carriage rides; Boating; Museums; Basilica of the Holy Blood; Belfry

GETTING THERE:
Lille Airport, France; Brussels Airport

Hotel de Orangerie resides in the cobbled streets of Bruges' old town in the heart of one of Europe's most picturesque medieval cities. A short stroll from Markt and Burg Squares, the setting is implausibly enchanting. Formerly a 15th-century Carthusian convent, pretty creeper devotedly clings to the façade that overlooks the willow-lined Den Dyver canal. It all makes an extremely romantic scene. Inside, a perfume of fresh flowers permeates the air from the generous bunches and delicate posies dotted about the beautifully dressed living rooms and delightfully deluxe bedrooms and suites. Hotel de Orangerie encourages you to really indulge. In the mood for a Champagne breakfast and afternoon tea? Both can be taken on the ritzy canal-side terrace. Want to see the city in sophisticated style? Then hire the hotel's "Bentley service" (more Champagne!) complete with chauffeur. Luxurious comfort of the wood-panelled lounge with its crackling fires and cosy bar await at the end of the day. Whether you want to visit Bruges' Christmas market or stroll along the canals in the sunshine, the divine boutique Hotel de Orangerie won't disappoint.

☎ +32 50 341649
🌐 condenastjohansens.com/hotelorangerie
🏠 Kartuizerinnenstraat 10, 8000 Bruges, Belgium

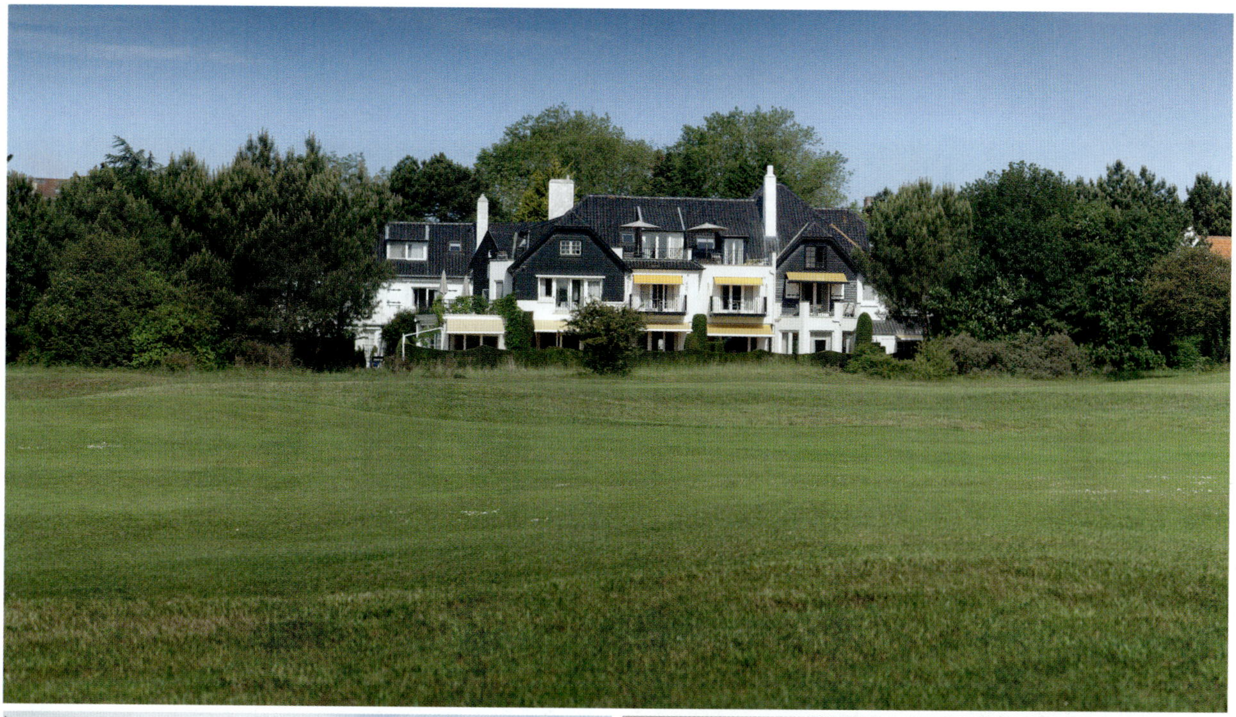

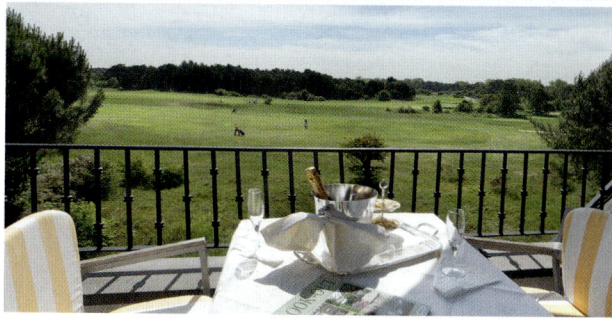

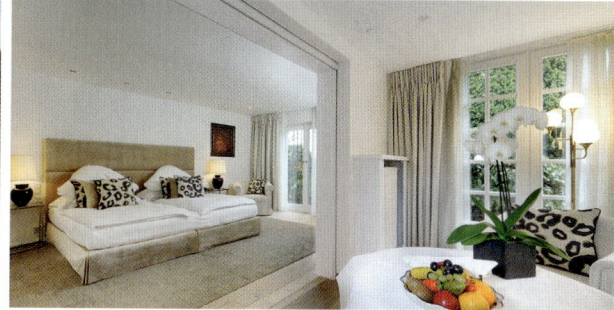

Manoir du Dragon

Romantic coastal manor house overlooking Royal Zoute Golf Course

Manoir du Dragon is that rare thing: a golf hotel adored by golfers and non-golfers alike. It's an elegant, cosy, 1920s manor house in the heart of Knokke with interiors straight out of a glossy magazine and a breakfast that guests rave about. The owner, Ms Van Hollebeke, is the design mastermind behind the 16 chic rooms and suites and she's very much in residence, welcoming guests with smiles, fresh fruit and beautiful flowers. Royal Zoute Golf Course is literally on the doorstep and rooms have pretty terraces overlooking its immaculate greens. Stroll 15 minutes from Manoir du Dragon's gorgeous gardens and discover the beach, all seven kilometres of it, complete with beach cabins fully equipped for a day's coastal loafing. However, for adrenaline junkies there's every kind of water sport available from water-skiing to kite surfing but of course you can always take it easy and explore the stunning seashore by bicycle. Manoir du Dragon's unique location in a peaceful part of town means finding the best restaurants and bars is effortless with the help of the wonderfully friendly staff. And should the thrill of teeing off overlooking the coastline wear thin (surely not!), the designer boutiques of Knokke are just a short walk away.

PRICE FROM:
€250

FEATURES:
Wheelchair access

ACTIVITIES:
Golf; Horse riding; Water sports

NEARBY:
Sluis (Holland/Belgium border); Bruges; Ghent; Le Zoute; Zwin Nature Reserve

GETTING THERE:
Brussels Airport; Lille Eurostar Terminal, France; Calais Eurotunnel Terminal, France

+32 50 63 05 80 ☎
condenastjohansens.com/dudragon 🌐
Albertlaan 73, 8300 Knokke~Heist, Belgium 🏠

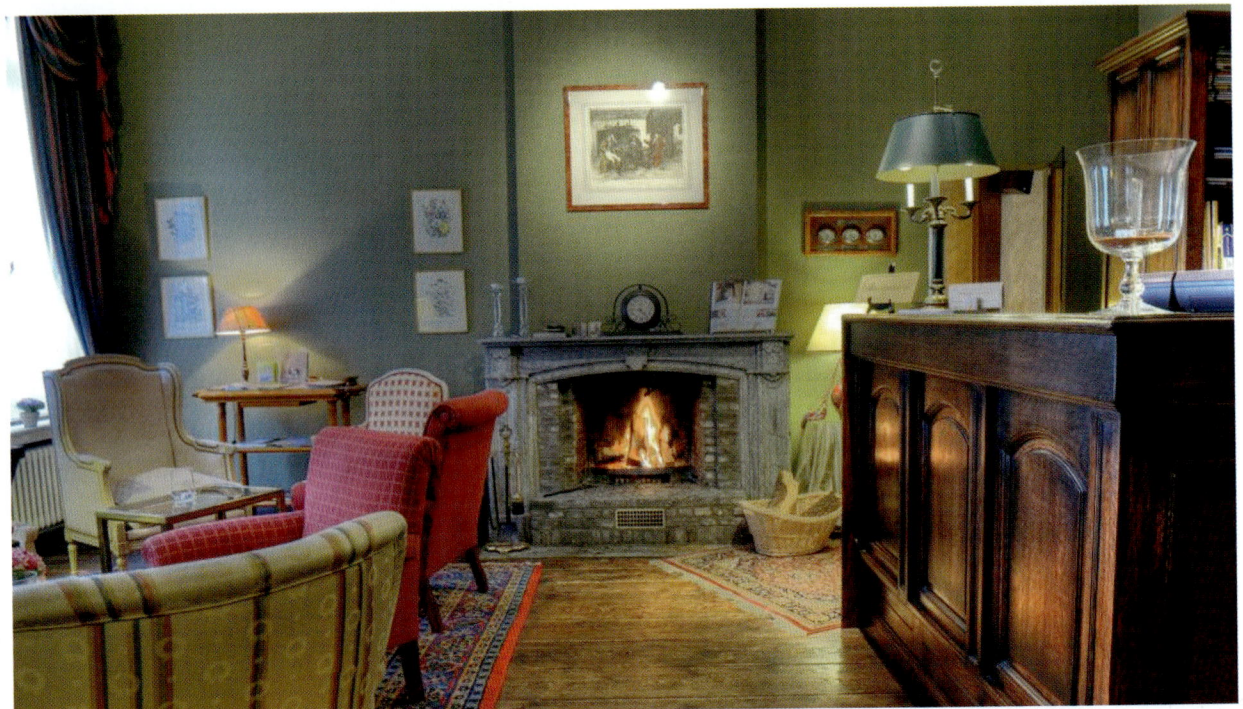

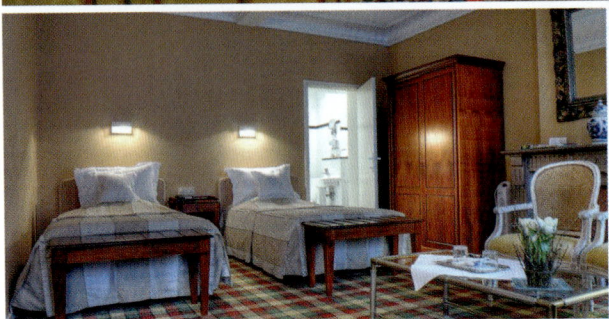

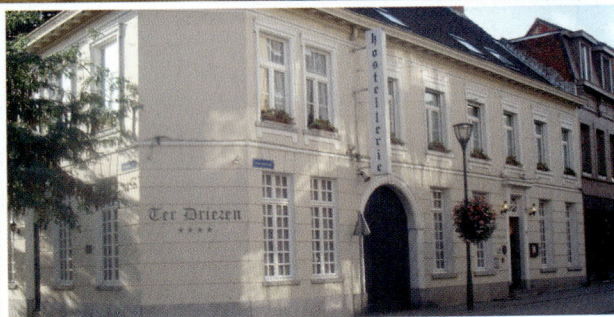

Hostellerie Ter Driezen

Home-sweet-home in Turnhout

PRICE FROM:
€144

FEATURES:
Pet friendly; Restaurant; Wheelchair access

ACTIVITIES:
Sightseeing

NEARBY:
Eindhoven; The Old Convent; The Dukes of Brabant Castle;
Breda city centre; Lower Kempen Park

GETTING THERE:
Eindhoven Airport; Antwerp Airport; Rotterdam Airport

Ever heard a carillon? It's a beautifully melodic peal of dozens of bells heard regularly in Turnhout, a pretty town whose fascinating and far-reaching past can be seen on every street corner from the 12th-century moated castle to the elegant town houses. And one of the best town houses in this little-known region is Hostellerie Ter Driezen, a stylish 18th-century beauty packed with mod cons found right in the epicentre of this cultured and sophisticated place. Great for business travellers and history-buffs, Turnhout is your oyster from these age-old walls. Relax with a coffee on Ter Driezen's chic terrace with its elegant topiary while you plan your day of sightseeing. Ter Driezen is a culture vulture's dream, just a short stroll from the museums, galleries and breathtaking historic buildings that make up so much of this intriguing town. Shopaholics can rest easy and get their fix in Turnhout's numerous boutiques found nearby, and foodies won't be disappointed either. Hostellerie Ter Driezen's restaurant serves a fabulous breakfast of local and international treats. Consider this your Belgian home-from-home.

☎ +32 14 41 87 57
🌐 condenastjohansens.com/terdriezen
🏠 18 Herentalsstraat, 2300 Turnhout, Belgium

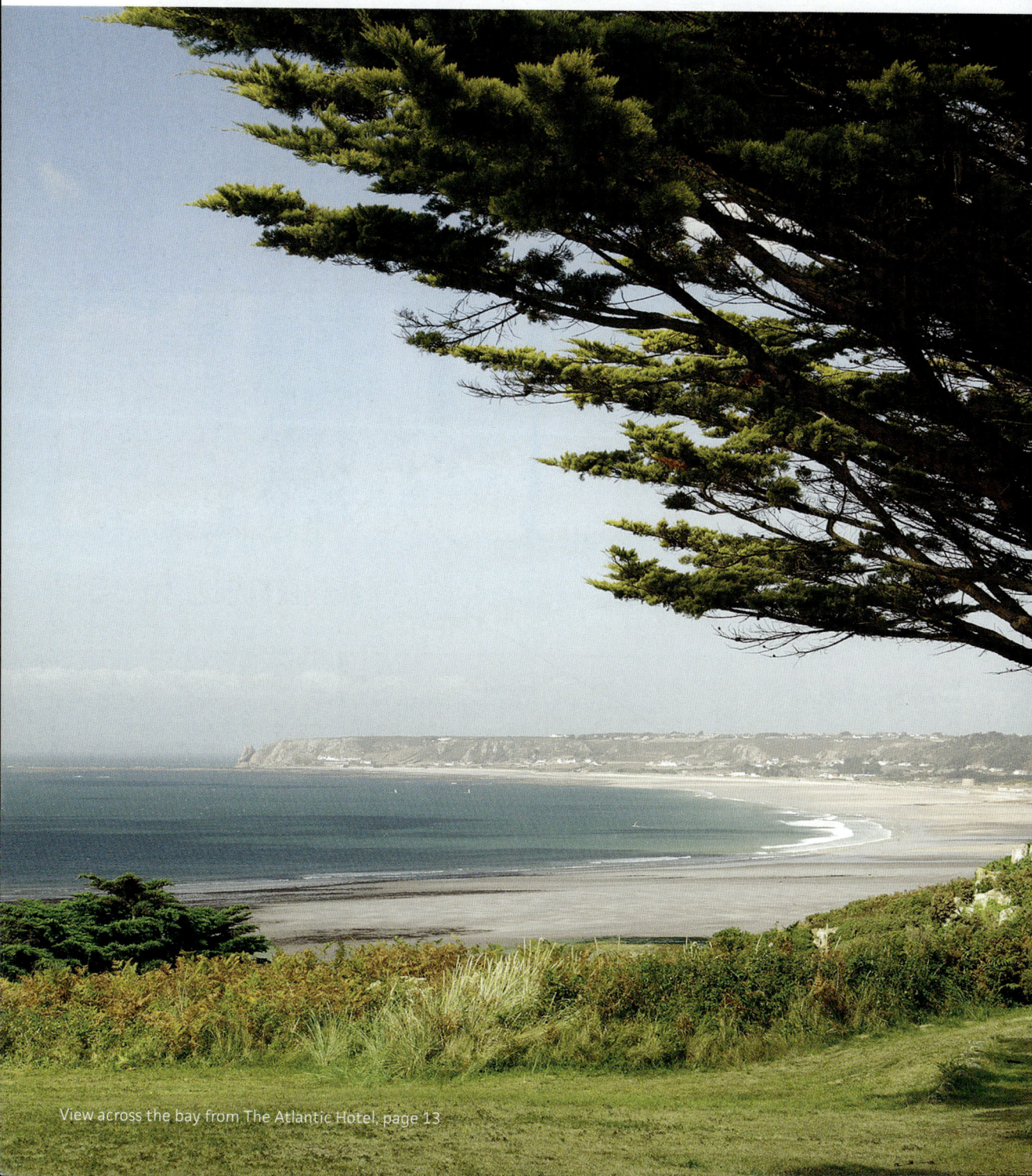

Channel Islands

Please go to condenastjohansens.com/channel-islands

View across the bay from The Atlantic Hotel, page 13

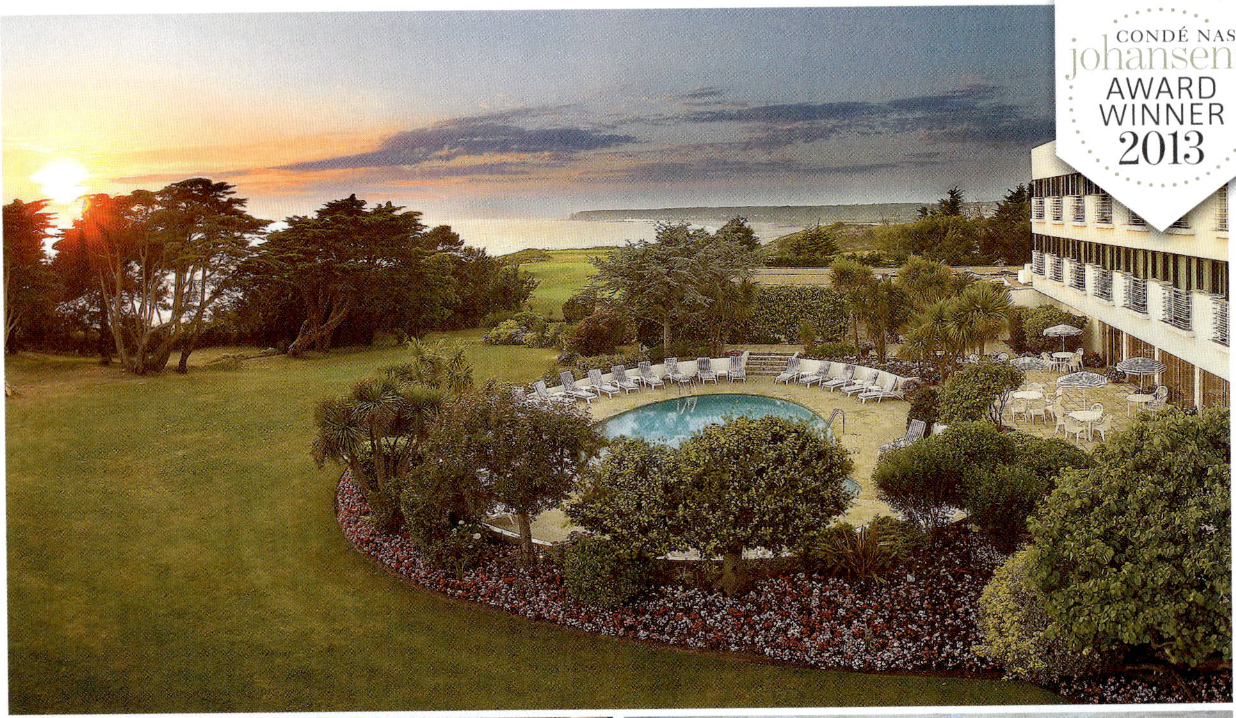

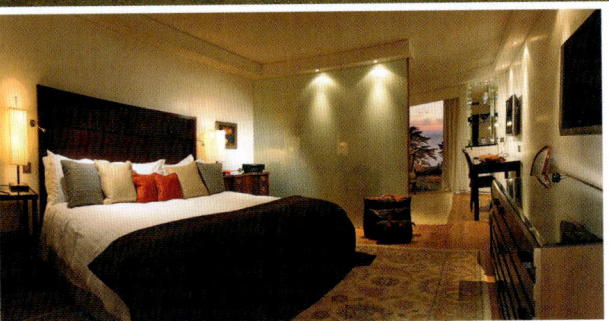

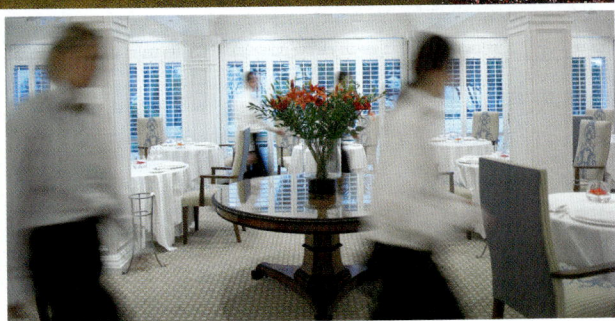

The Atlantic Hotel

Spoiling service plus Jersey charm equals something special

PRICE FROM:
£150

FEATURES:
Family friendly; Gym; Michelin Starred restaurant; Pool; Sea views

ACTIVITIES:
Cycling; Golf; Water sports

NEARBY:
St Helier; La Mare Wine Estate; Jersey War Tunnels; Eric Young Orchid Foundation; Durrell Wildlife Conservation Trust

GETTING THERE:
Jersey Airport

☎ +44 (0)1534 744101
🌐 condenastjohansens.com/atlantic
🏨 Le Mont de la Pulente, St Brelade, Jersey JE3 8HE, Channel Islands

Get yourself off the beaten track and into this beachy-chic spot tucked away in the warmest corner of the British Isles. The Atlantic Hotel and Michelin-Starred Ocean Restaurant is a Channel Islands hideaway perfect for a nature lover's retreat of a weekend. Decorated in hues of blue, white and sand, The Atlantic Hotel at St Ouen's Bay echoes the dramatic natural setting that surrounds it, looking out to crystal clear waters and a sprawling stretch of beach. Rocking a relaxed Hamptons-à-la-Jersey vibe, its façade is bedecked in white-shuttered windows while inside, eye-catching modern art adorns its walls brought to life by the abundance of natural light. Kick off the heels/brogues and embrace the low-key elegance, for it's all about smart, unstuffy hospitality here. Enjoy the natural highs of surfing then relax, restore and unwind in a cosseting bedroom where the only sound is the lapping waves from the beach below and the views are breathtaking ocean vistas (sunsets just like the Caribbean). It's easy to understand how The Ocean Restaurant has retained its Michelin Star since 2007 with highly qualified Restaurant Manager Martinho de Sousa and Executive Chef Mark Jordan at the helm. Only the best in fresh and local produce is served including island treats such as lobster and sole artistically presented. The Atlantic is understated luxury at its best; a Med-esque spot with a British heart.

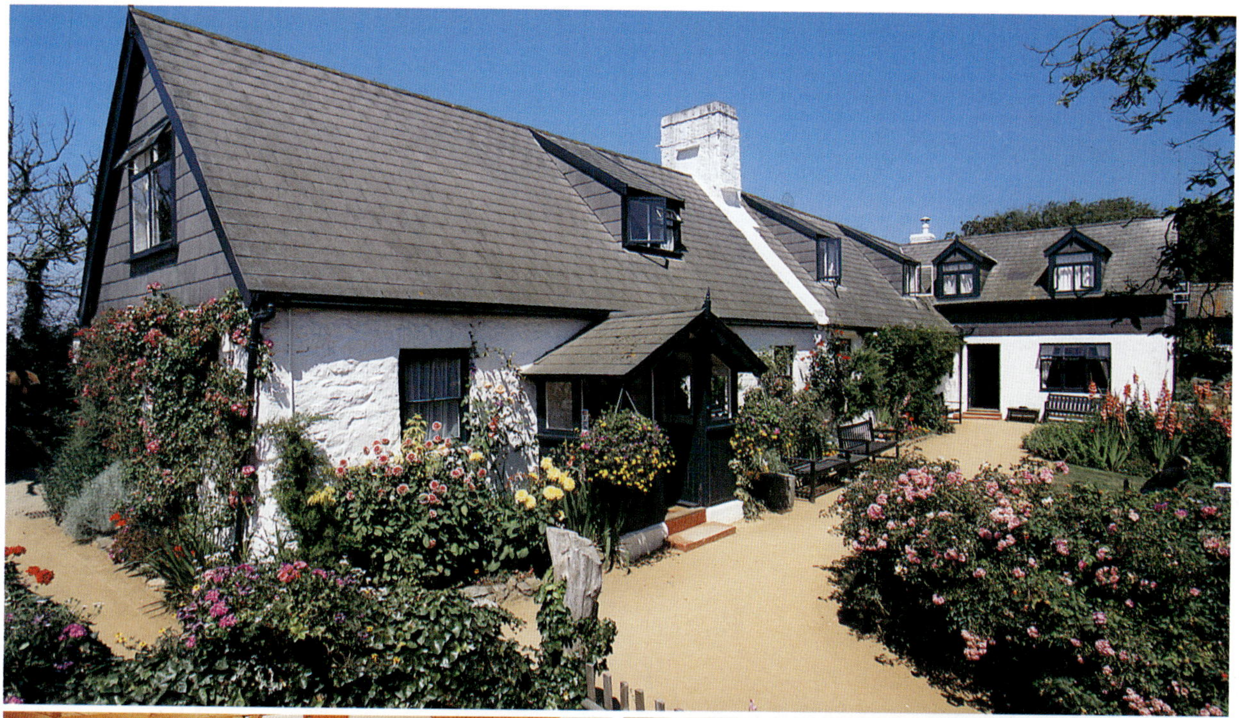

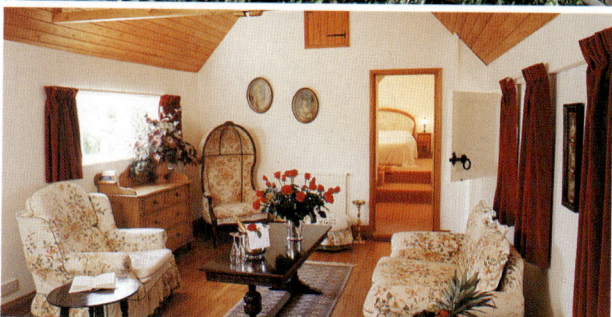

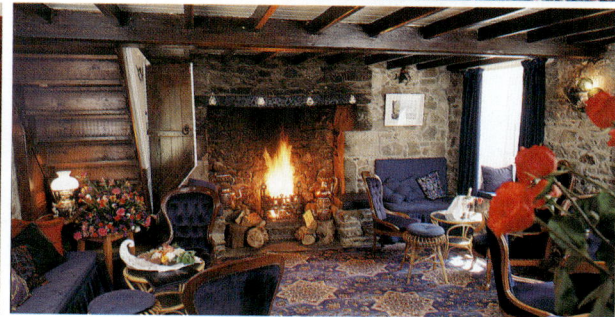

La Sablonnerie

Little Sark's little gem with a big personality

Just three miles long and a mile and a half wide, car-free, leisurely Sark is a whimsical place where horse-drawn carriages and tractor-drawn buses kick up dust from the road. It's the smallest of the four main Channel Islands and the only way to arrive here is by sea. Completely serene and naturally stunning, this is the setting for La Sablonnerie located in Little Sark, the southern, particularly remote part of the island. Hands-on owner and manager Elizabeth Perrée describes her pocket of peace as "an oasis of good living and courtesy," and with her rare passion and quirky charm, La Sablonnerie is a one-of-a-kind gem. You can't help but embrace the unhurried pace and all-encompassing cosiness that characterise this hotel whose low ceilings and 400-year-old oak beams add further personality. Elizabeth has extended and discreetly modernised the bedrooms, which over time have spread across from the original farmhouse and into nearby houses and cottages. Before dining in the restaurant guests often gather in the lounge for a drink then tuck into dishes prepared from produce grown on La Sablonnerie's farm and gardens whenever possible. The locally caught lobster and oysters are a must. Proud to be: a 2013 finalist for Condé Nast Johansens Sustainable Hospitality & Corporate Social Responsibility Award and 2012 finalist for Most Romantic Hotel Award.

PRICE FROM:
£156 (including dinner)

FEATURES:
Restaurant

ACTIVITIES:
Fishing; Horse riding; Walking

NEARBY:
George's boat trip around the island; Bird-watching; Carriage rides; La Seigneurie Gardens; Scuba diving

GETTING THERE:
Ferry from Guernsey, Jersey, Poole, Weymouth and France; Guernsey Airport; Jersey Airport

+44 (0)1481 832061 ☎
condenastjohansens.com/lasablonnerie 🌐
Little Sark, Sark, Guernsey GY10 1SD, Channel Islands 🏠

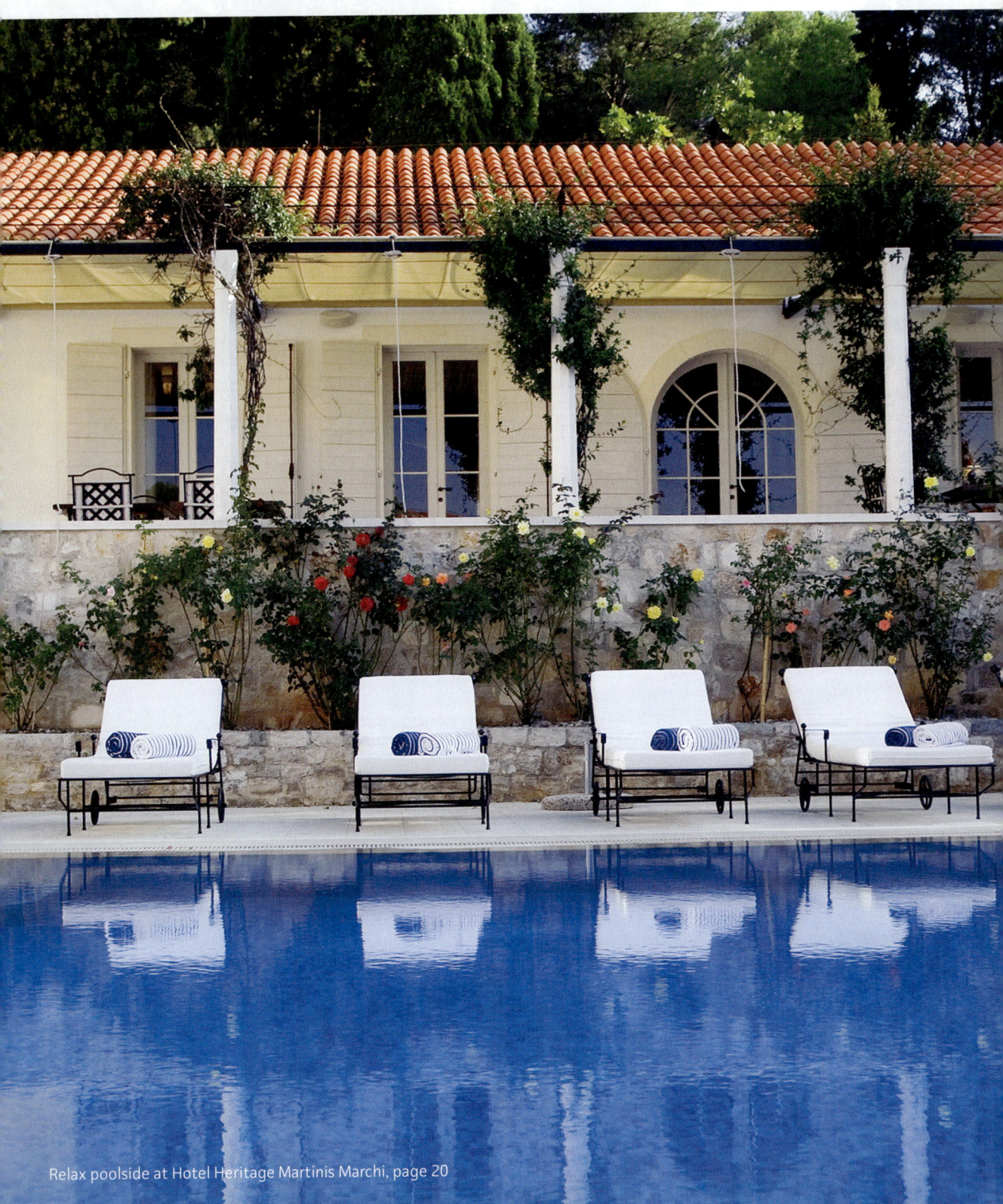

Croatia

Please go to condenastjohansens.com/croatia

Relax poolside at Hotel Heritage Martinis Marchi, page 20

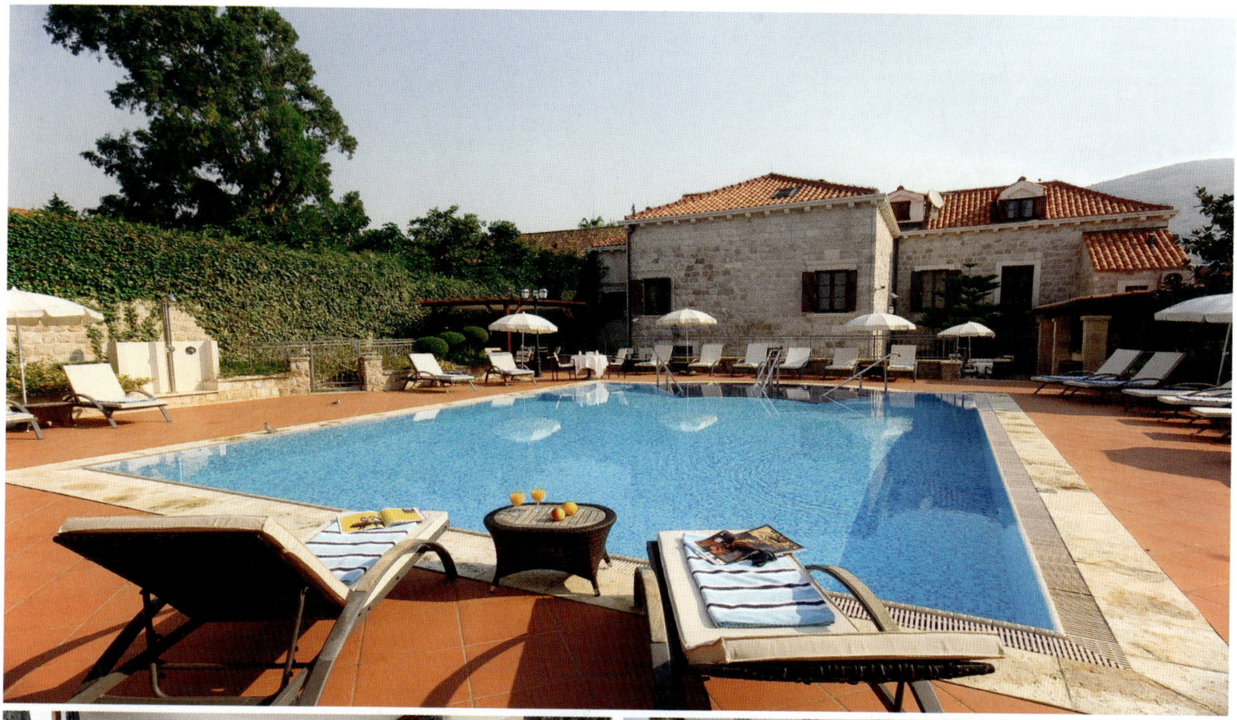

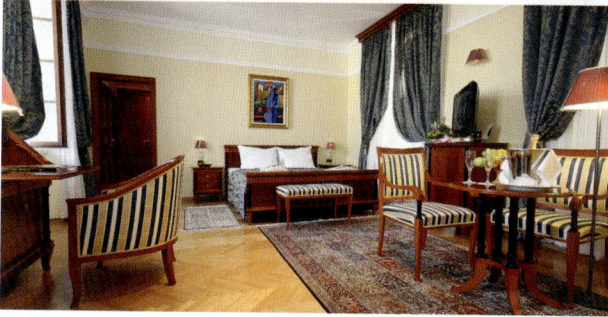
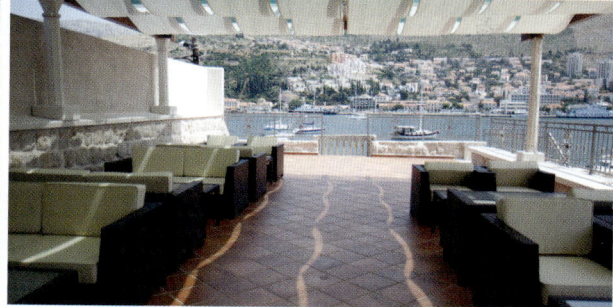

Kazbek

Discreet, private Dubrovnik villa located on the bay of Gruz

Kazbek could be Dubrovnik's best-kept secret. This 16th-century villa set on the waterfront in the bay of Gruz has history, colour and character in spades. A former summer residence to nobility, today it's a 12-room, one-suite boutique hotel that's been lavished with attention (and money) by its Swedish owners. They've created a laid-back-luxe hideaway in a superb location, just three kilometres from Dubrovnik's Old Town. Much of the original features remain so you can expect vaulted rooms, narrow passageways and soaring, beamed ceilings. All the furniture has been handmade locally and lashings of dark-wood panelling, overstuffed armchairs and embroidered drapes, rugs and throws adorn the private and public spaces. The sun-drenched Courtyard Terrace is a lovely spot for breakfast, while an old stone vault is the romantic setting for dinner where deftly prepared Croatian classics crowd the menu. The pool (be careful fair-skinned ones, this is a fantastic suntrap) is the perfect place to while away an afternoon but it's hard to top a trip to the nearby islands on Kazbek's yacht moored in the marina directly opposite the hotel. That is, if you prefer a more relaxing jaunt rather than the high-octane pace of the speedboat...

PRICE FROM:
€189

FEATURES:
Pet friendly; Pool; Restaurant; Sea views

ACTIVITIES:
Sightseeing; Walking; Water sports

NEARBY:
UNESCO Dubrovnik Old Town; ACI Yacht Marina; Elafiti Islands; Mljet National Park; Cavtat

GETTING THERE:
Dubrovnik Airport

+385 20 362 900 ☎
condenastjohansens.com/kazbek 🌐
Lapadska Obala 25, 20000 Dubrovnik, Croatia 🏠

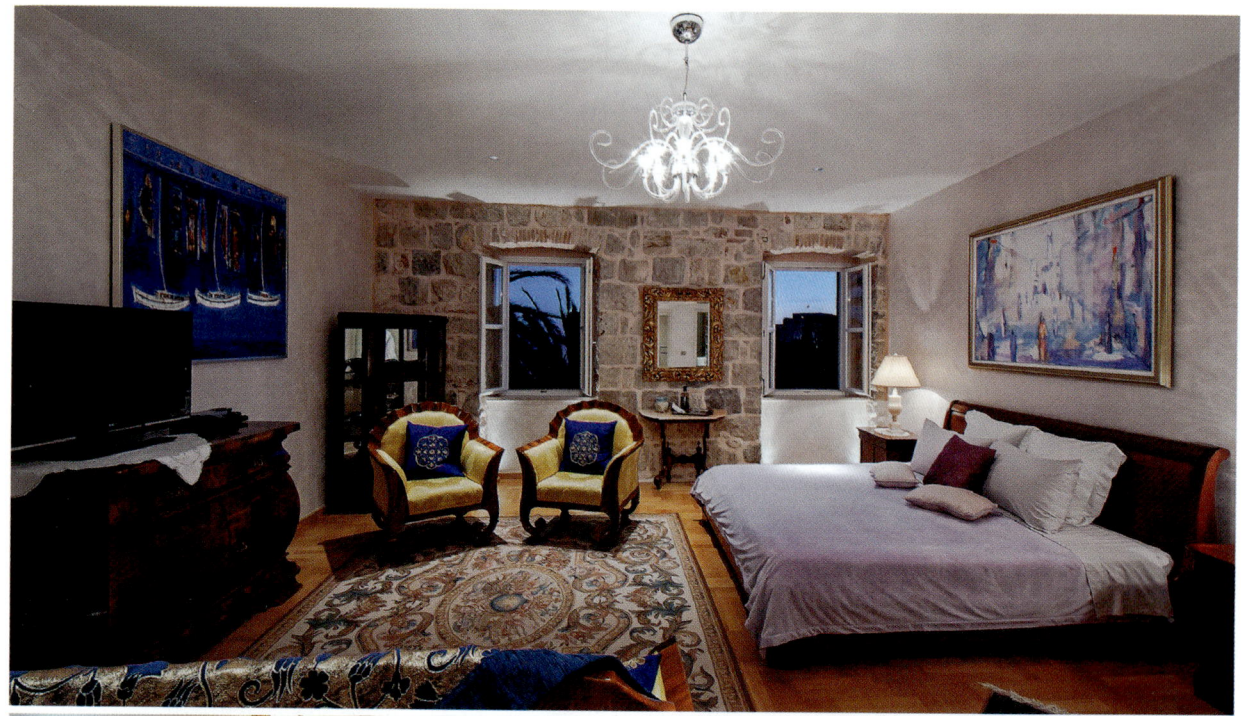

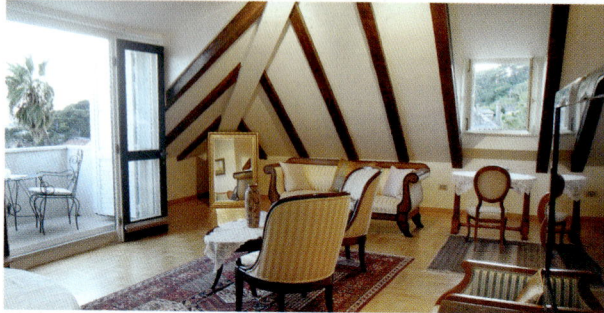
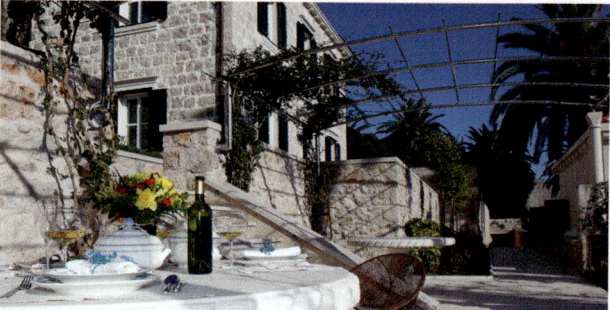

Villa Anastasia

Fully-hosted Croatian villa beside Dubrovnik's ancient Old Town walls

PRICE FROM:
€200

FEATURES:
Family friendly; Sea views

ACTIVITIES:
Fishing; Sightseeing; Water sports

NEARBY:
Kayaking; Dubrovnik's Old Town walls; Cable car; Botanical gardens on Lokrum

GETTING THERE:
Dubrovnik Airport

☎ +385 91 400 4042
🌐 condenastjohansens.com/villaanastasia
🏠 Ulica uz Posat 5, 20 000 Dubrovnik, Croatia

Just like its boundlessly positive, effervescent owner Gordana Barlé MD, Villa Anastasia provides a supercharge of joy. "Anastasia" meaning "revival" in Greek is the principle behind this three-suite villa set in tiered gardens (enticing outdoor Jacuzzi included). It's Gordana's passion for spreading the concept of a healthy, preventative-care lifestyle that led her to create this piece of serenity beside Dubrovnik's UNESCO Old Town. A qualified physician and psychiatrist, Gordana aimed to create a wholesome, relaxing getaway for guests to rejuvenate and regain perspective. Her success is a fusion of many factors. One is her keen eye for comfortable yet refined interior design (each antique and Croatian painting carefully handpicked). Another is the incredible locale, steps from the ancient city entrance (put your walking shoes on, the steep, often cobbled terrain ruins heels) and views across the Adriatic Sea. The attentive service also makes for a special stay with someone always on hand to deal with special requests, to serve breakfast and snacks. Villa Anastasia can be hired in its entirety or on a suite-basis but when booked exclusively, you'll have access to the fully-equipped kitchen, garden kitchen, lounge/dining area, office and wine cellar.

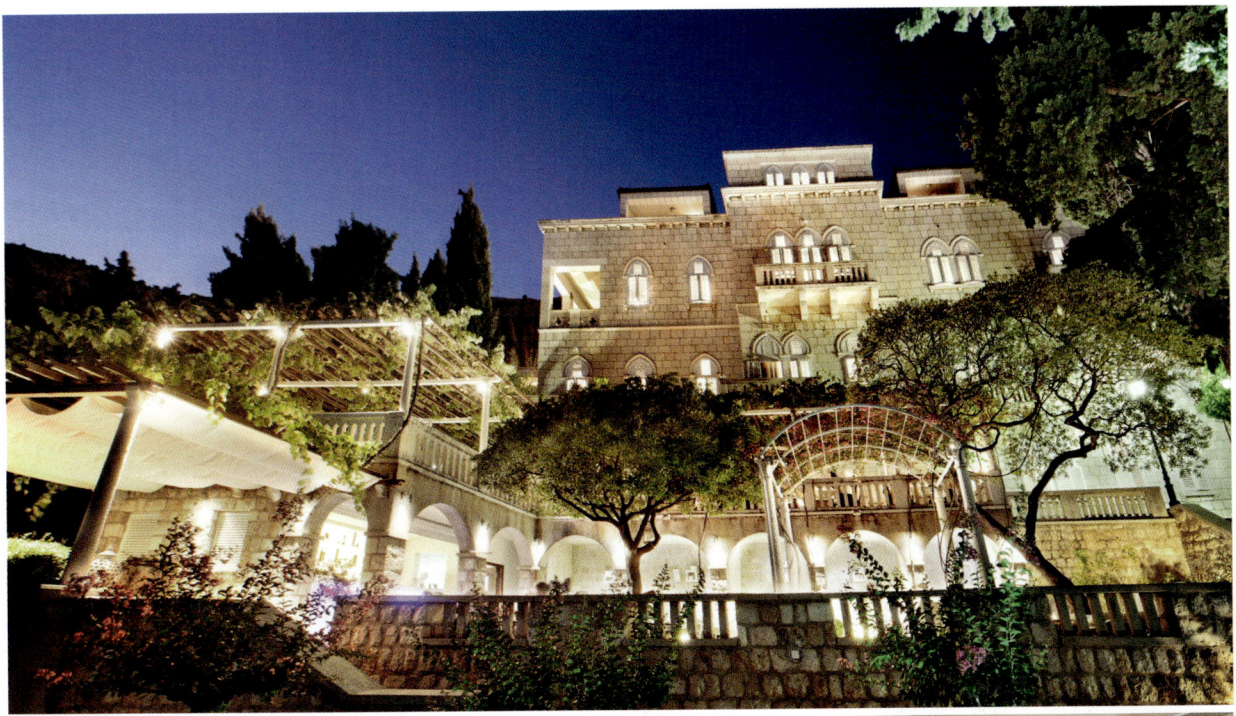

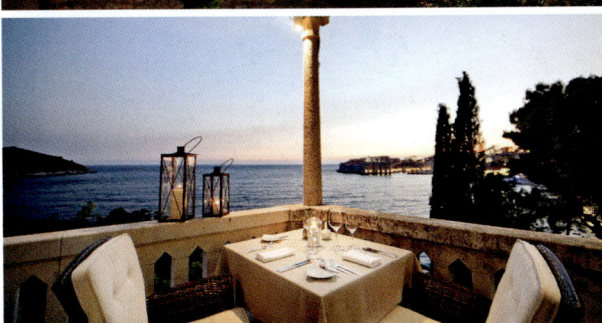
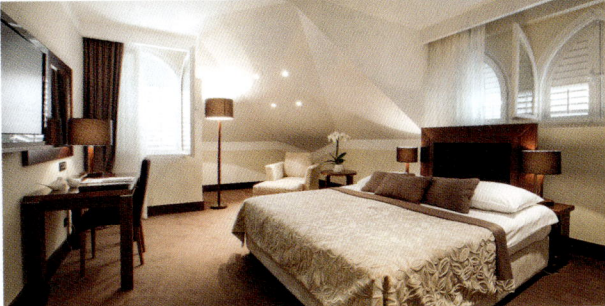

Villa Orsula

Watch out Dubrovnik, this new seaside villa is here to stay

New to the Adriatic Coast's hotel scene, Villa Orsula, Dubrovnik, is everything a leading boutique retreat should be: intimate, stylish and utterly comfortable with personal service. Its plum position beside the sea, five minutes from the Old Town, also means that the city's sites are oh-so convenient to access. Villa Orsula's columned, curved Ottoman façade brilliantly contradicts the clean lines, muted colour schemes and contemporary design within. Funky elements such as surrealist artwork by Roberto Matta and Victor Vasarely's op-art dress the walls while an eclectic collection of objets d'art are purposefully dotted about. Many of the 13 bedrooms have picture windows of the seascape and small balconies, although for a special occasion (a honeymoon, anniversary, celebration with friends…) book the spacious, ultra private Deluxe or Royal Suite. More dazzling views are viewed from the Lounge Bar whose menu of cocktails can be served inside or outside beside the gardens that lead down to the private beach below. Next door to the Lounge Bar is Victoria Restaurant where Mediterranean and international flavours come together alongside a global wine list. Its Executive Chef Thierry Caruel, cooked for Prince William and Kate Middleton's wedding. Beauty bonus: guests of Villa Orsula receive complimentary access to Hotel Excelsior's Spa & Beauty Centre located two minutes away.

PRICE FROM:
€360

FEATURES:
Beach access; Restaurant; Sea views

ACTIVITIES:
Shopping; Sightseeing; Water sports

NEARBY:
Dubrovnik's Old Town; Island of Lokrum

GETTING THERE:
Dubrovnik Airport

+385 20 430 830 ☎
condenastjohansens.com/villaorsula 🌐
Frana Supila 14, 20 000 Dubrovnik, Croatia 🏠

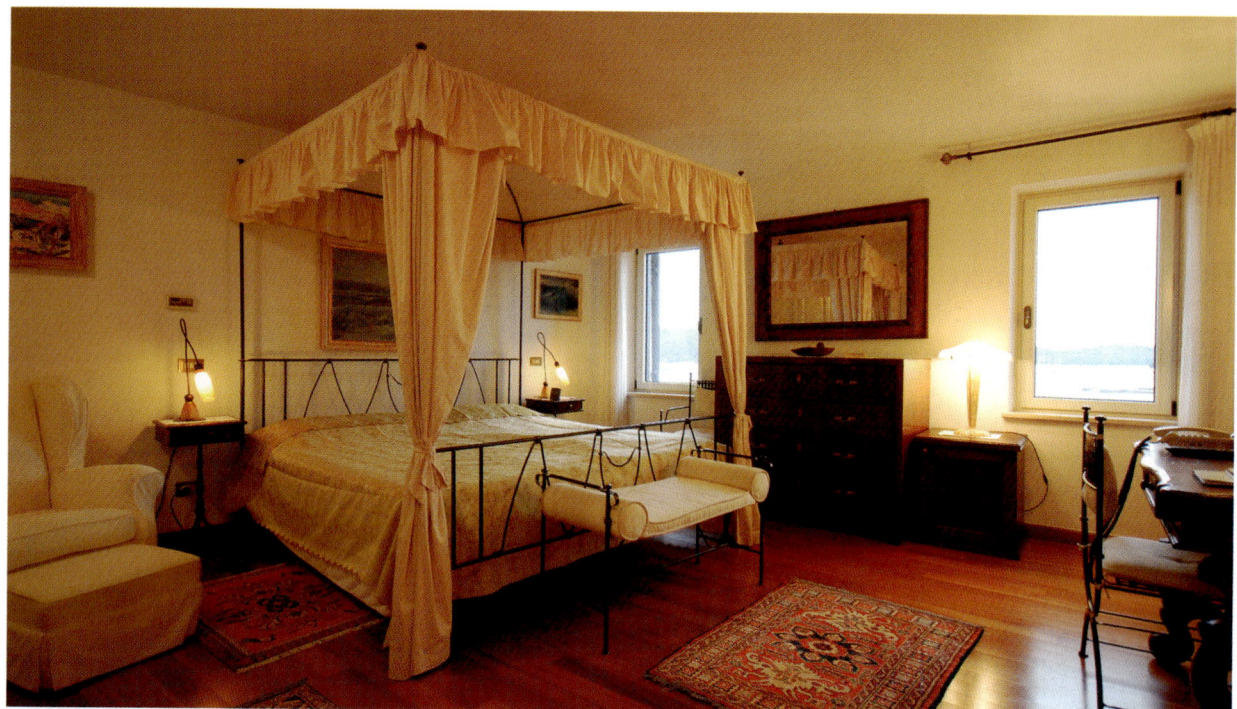

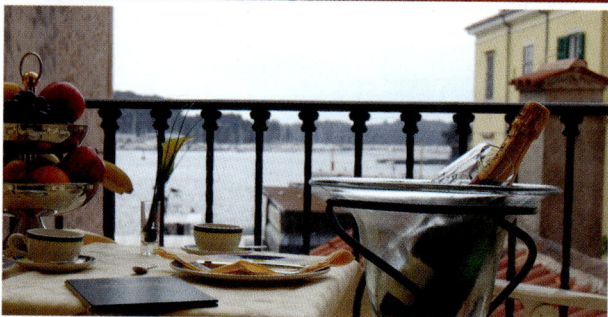

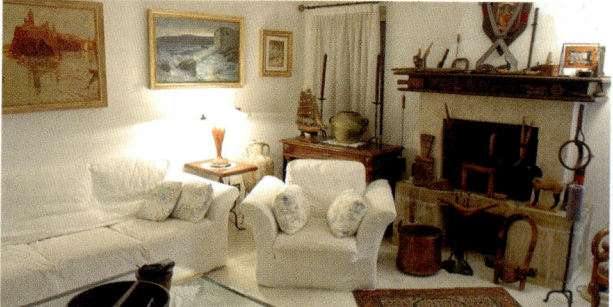

Villa Tuttorotto

Historic waterside villa at the gateway to Istria County

PRICE FROM:
€140

FEATURES:
Sea views

ACTIVITIES:
Fishing; Sightseeing; Water sports

NEARBY:
Umag; Trieste; Brioni Island; Pula Roman ruins

GETTING THERE:
Pula Airport

The unmistakable brushstroke of Italian flair has made its mark on the Croatian coastal city of Rovinj. The Republic of Venice governed here for 500 years and as a lasting reminder of its rule, there's the Baroque tower of St Euphemia's Cathedral - a copy of St Mark's tower in Venice. Today, Rovinj is a tourist gateway to Istria County for those hankering the Mediterranean climate and superior diving spots in the north Adriatic Sea. Facing the sea, in Rovinj's pedestrianised old town is Villa Tuttorotto. A testimony to the city's history, a dizzying array of age-old antiques, paintings and sculptures decorate the rooms. Even its waterfront walls hold historic significance as part of the original fortress. The Villa's basement crypts were once sanctuary for stowaways and a safe haven for supplies in fear of thieving pirates. Bedrooms and the knockout suite are far from antiquated though. They're classically-styled and equipped with all mod-cons and each one has harbour views. Breakfast is served in the dining room and can be brought to your room. And in the evening, a spread containing local and international apéritifs alongside a shelf chock-full of spirits are yours to whet your appetite before heading out for dinner.

☎ +385 52 815 181
🌐 condenastjohansens.com/villatuttorotto
🏠 Dvor Massatto 4, 52210 Rovinj, Croatia

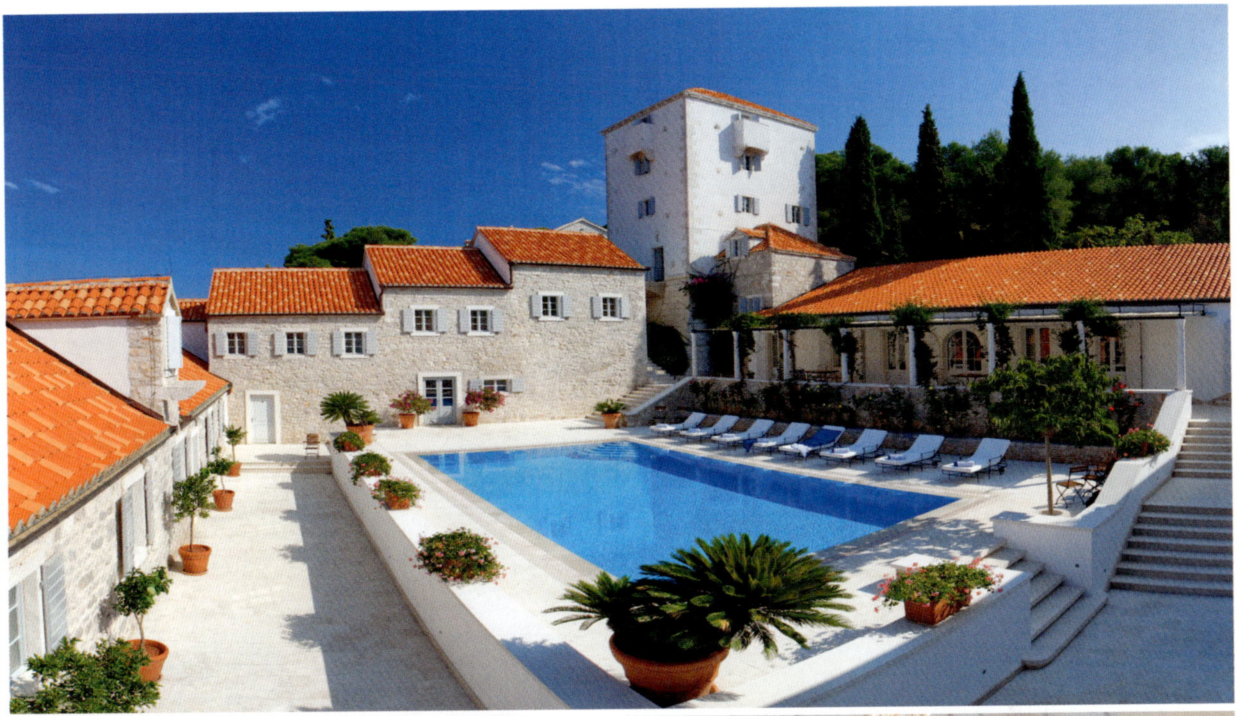

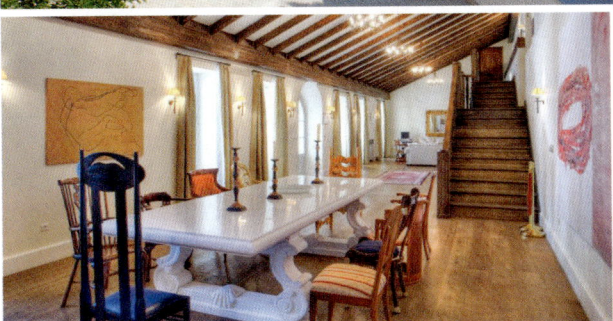

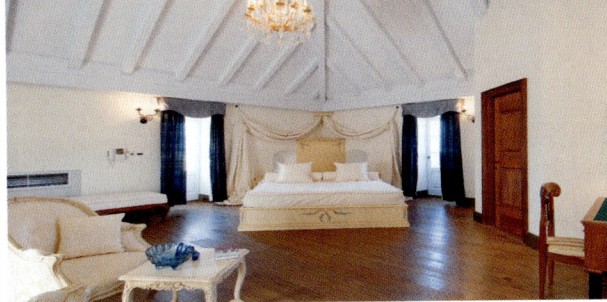

Hotel Heritage Martinis Marchi

Fantasy Mediterranean lifestyle becomes a reality at lush Solta Island

Unhurried, wholesome and traditional, the Dalmatian fishing town of Maslinica is home to the impossibly immaculate Hotel Heritage Martinis Marchi. Flanked by crystal blue waters and lush greenery (lemon trees galore!) Martinis Marchi is a collection of stone-walled buildings frosted with luminescent terracotta tiling. It all looks so new, as if it were built yesterday (despite its 17th-century beginnings) and inside, the rooms are equally fresh and brand-spankingly glossy. Martinis Marchi transports you back in time offering an insight into traditional Mediterranean life and staff regularly organises trips to age-old olive groves, classes in wine and olive oil production and tours through surrounding ancient villages. There'll even be the chance to sample wild honey and try your hand at the traditional production of it too. But back at Martinis Marchi, the restaurant's exceptional seafood menu will have you waxing lyrical about its incredible freshness (try the lemon cake with wild lemon and orange from Šolta island) and sun terrace where you can enjoy the balmy evening temperatures. The fantastic marine-side location of Martinis Marchi means that boat rentals and watery excursions are a cinch to organise and events held at the marina throughout the year provide an interesting flurry of visitors to its shores. The marina also has a theatre, art gallery, numerous taverns, restaurants and cafés.

PRICE FROM:
€200

FEATURES:
Beach access; Pet friendly; Pool; Restaurant; Sea views

ACTIVITIES:
Fishing; Water sports

NEARBY:
UNESCO Split; Solin; Kaštela; UNESCO Trogir; UNESCO Diocletian's Palace

GETTING THERE:
Split Airport

+385 21 572 768 ☎
condenastjohansens.com/martinismarchi 🌐
Maslinica, Solta Island, Croatia 📷

Egypt

Please go to condenastjohansens.com/egypt

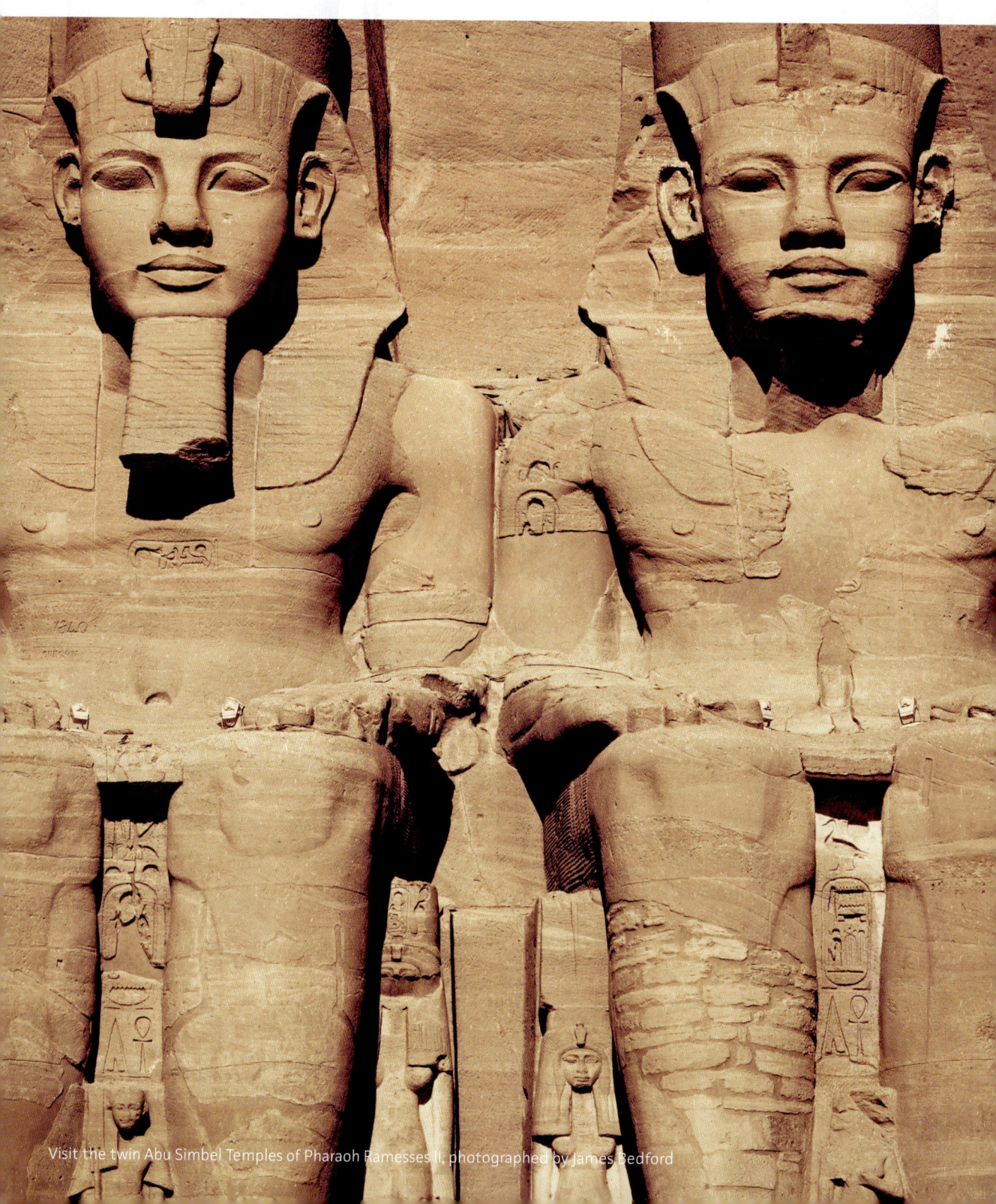

Visit the twin Abu Simbel Temples of Pharaoh Ramesses II, photographed by James Bedford

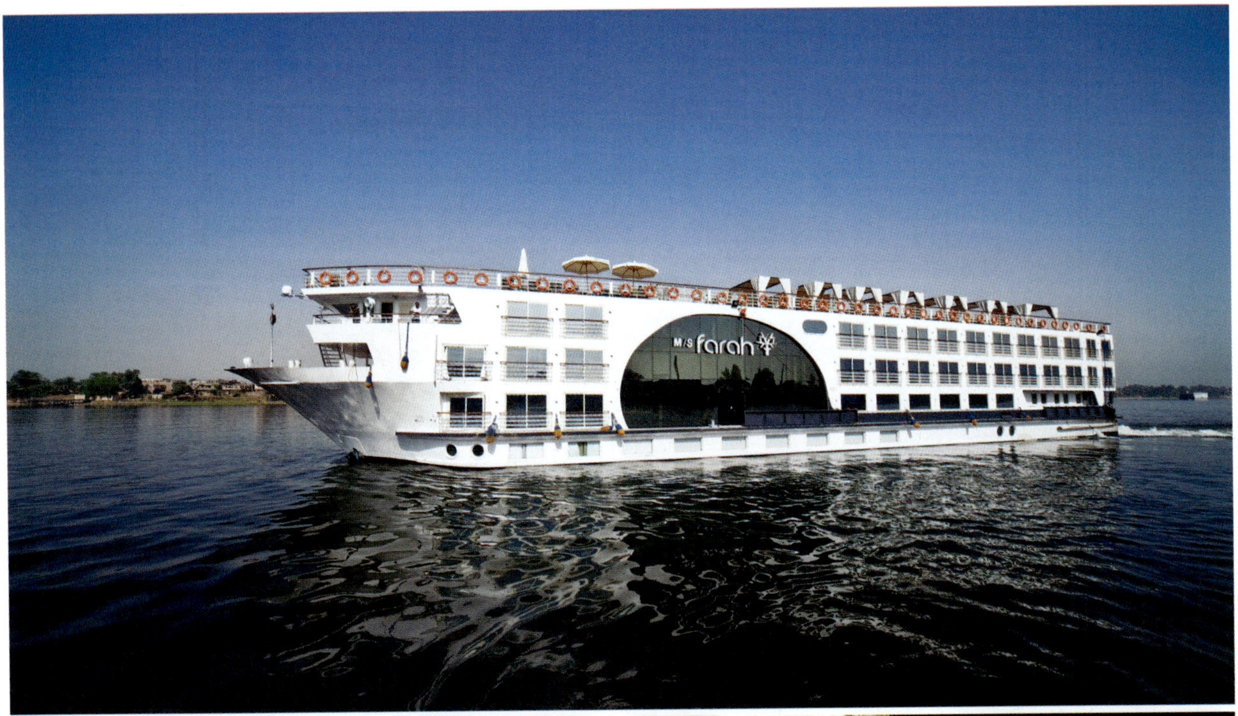

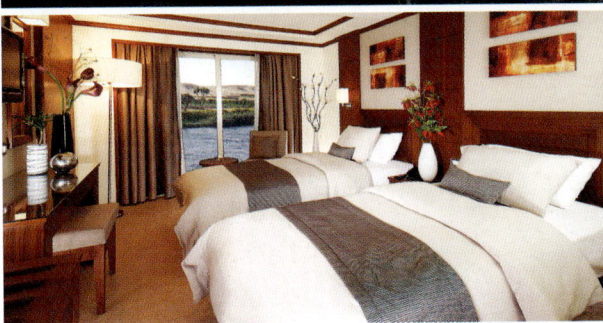

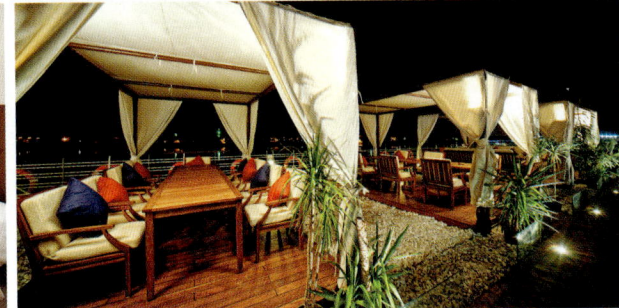

Farah Nile Cruise

Lavish Luxor to Aswan floating boutique hotel

Aboard an architectural wonder, the chrome and glass design of MS Farah is simply stunning. It's a honeymoon destination like no other where guest-of-honour treatment is the only kind of treatment. Farah Nile Cruise's friendly crew will carefully craft your three or seven-night itinerary to include all the awe-inspiring sights of the Nile. One glimpse from your cabin window and you'll witness the River Nile's incredible beauty - the staff's inside knowledge guarantees you'll miss nothing. Your biggest responsibility will be choosing your favourite pillow type. Everything is thoughtfully delivered and personalised; luxuriously spacious cabins feature special touches such as soft Egyptian linens and modern conveniences. As you fall in love with the towns you pass by, it's inevitable you'll be waxing lyrical about the fabulous food, if not enthusing about Farah spa's massages and beauty treatments. From massage bed to sun bed, you can also chill-out in the lounge bar and find quiet time in the library. And when feeling a little restless, there's a medley of boutiques to discover on the boat and an outfit to choose for the traditional on-board Galabia party. You really don't want this ship to sail without you.

PRICE FROM:
US$1,281 (for 3-day cruise)

FEATURES:
Gym; Pool; Restaurant; Spa

ACTIVITIES:
Sightseeing

ROUTE HIGHLIGHTS:
Various temples; Valley of the Kings; The High Dam; The Unfinished Obelisk of Aswan; Kitchener's Island

GETTING THERE:
Luxor Airport; Aswan Airport

+20 2 22731921 ☎
condenastjohansens.com/farahnilecruise 🌐
Platinum Cruise Management 12, Moaez Al Dawla St, 🏠
Makram Ebeid, Nasr City, Cairo, Egypt

France

Please go to condenastjohansens.com/france

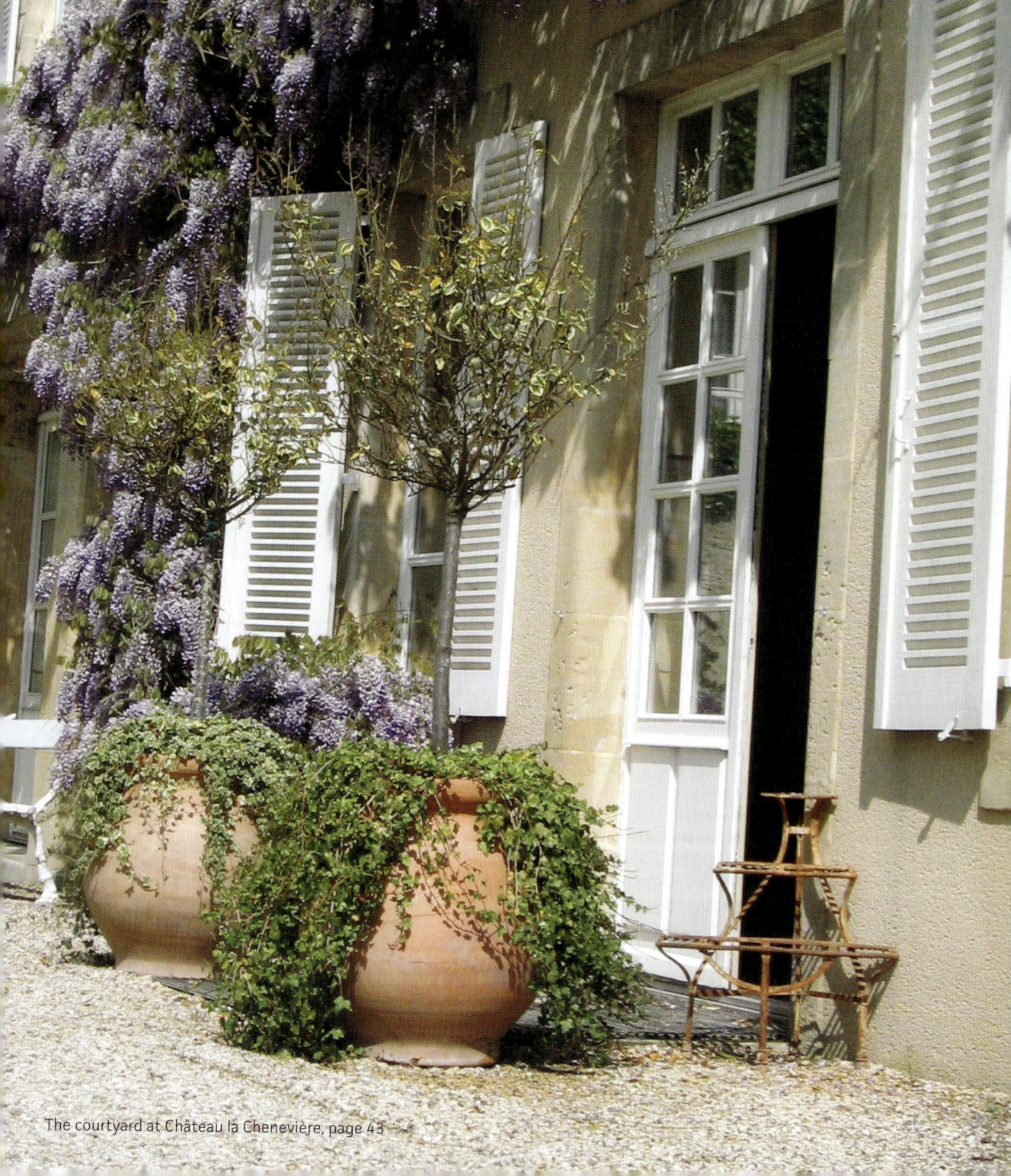

The courtyard at Château la Chenevière, page 43

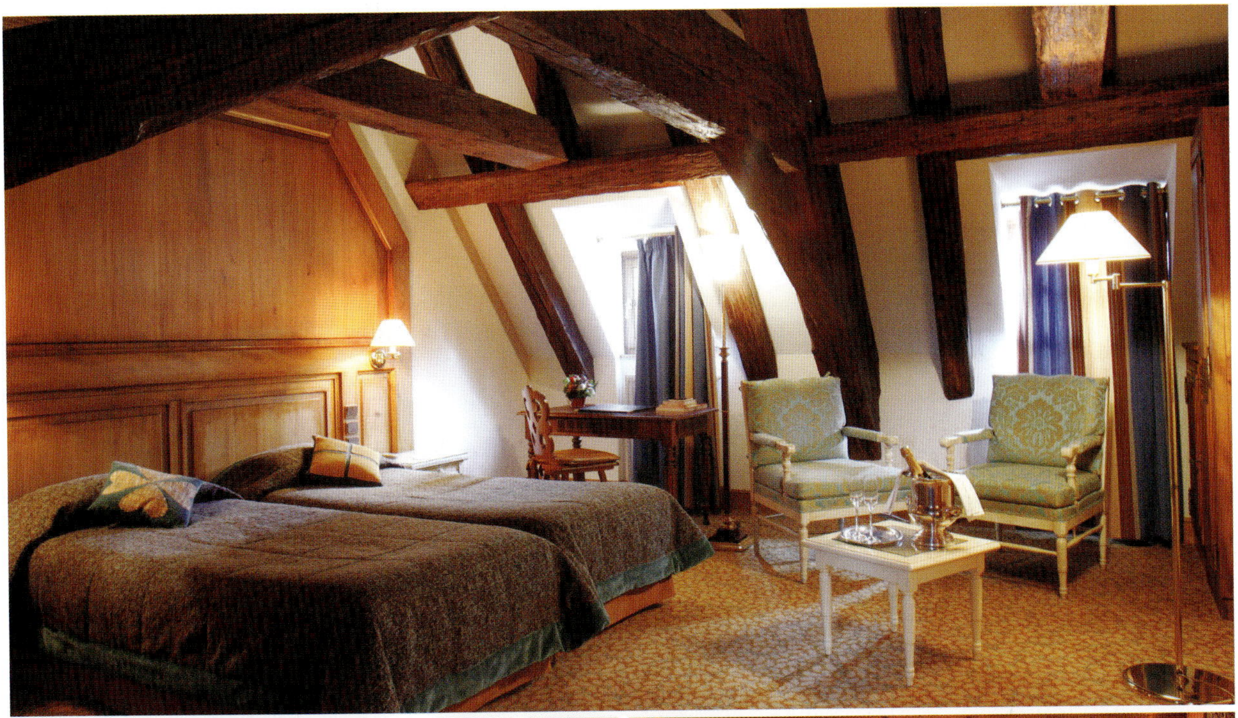

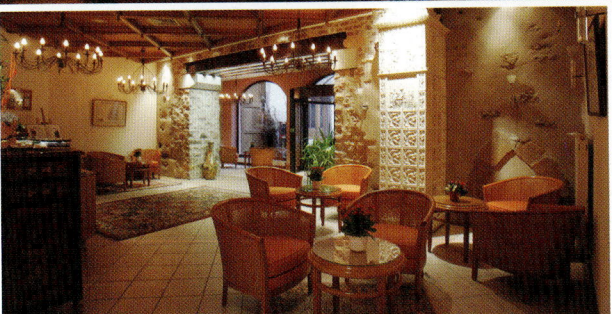
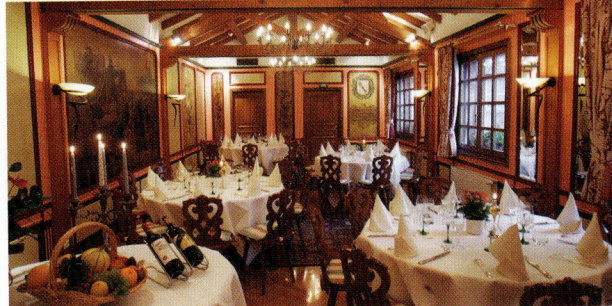

Hôtel Les Têtes

Heartfelt hospitality in kitschy Colmar

Make a date at Hôtel Les Têtes, Colmar, to capture the intoxicating personality of this bustling Alsace town. Historic, artistic and a wine capital of the world, it also happens to be picture-postcard pretty. And Hôtel Les Têtes' Baroque façade, with sculpted heads and vine-shaded courtyard, lures you in from the thick of Colmar's jumbled streets with a glass of something delicious. Hosts Carmen and Marc Rohfritsch run a good old fashioned service with multi-lingual staff and provide rooms with plenty of space for a hotel of this diminuitive number (21). Each one fitted with well needed air-con to keep you cool in the balmy months when the heat rises. Check into a Duplex or Luxe for extra space and a Jacuzzi pick-me-up. In the hotel's wood-beamed restaurant Marc's team whips up gourmet plates of foie gras, scallop and langoustine salad, frogs legs and fillet of beef, and it's never too precious to adapt dishes to your taste. Ever seen small children tuck into delicious home-made broccoli soup with gusto? Here you will! Take a wander outside after dinner to experience Colmar's flower-festooned, canal-lined walkways, the birthplace of Auguste Bartholdi, designer of the iconic Statue of Liberty.

PRICE FROM:
€130

FEATURES:
Family friendly; Pet friendly; Restaurant; Wheelchair access

ACTIVITIES:
Cycling; Golf; Shopping

NEARBY:
Strasbourg; Mulhouse; Colmar Old Town; Little Venice; Alsace vineyards

GETTING THERE:
Basel - Mulhouse Airport

+33 3 89 24 43 43 ☎
condenastjohansens.com/lestetes ⊕
19 Rue des Têtes, 68000 Colmar, Alsace~Lorraine, France ▤

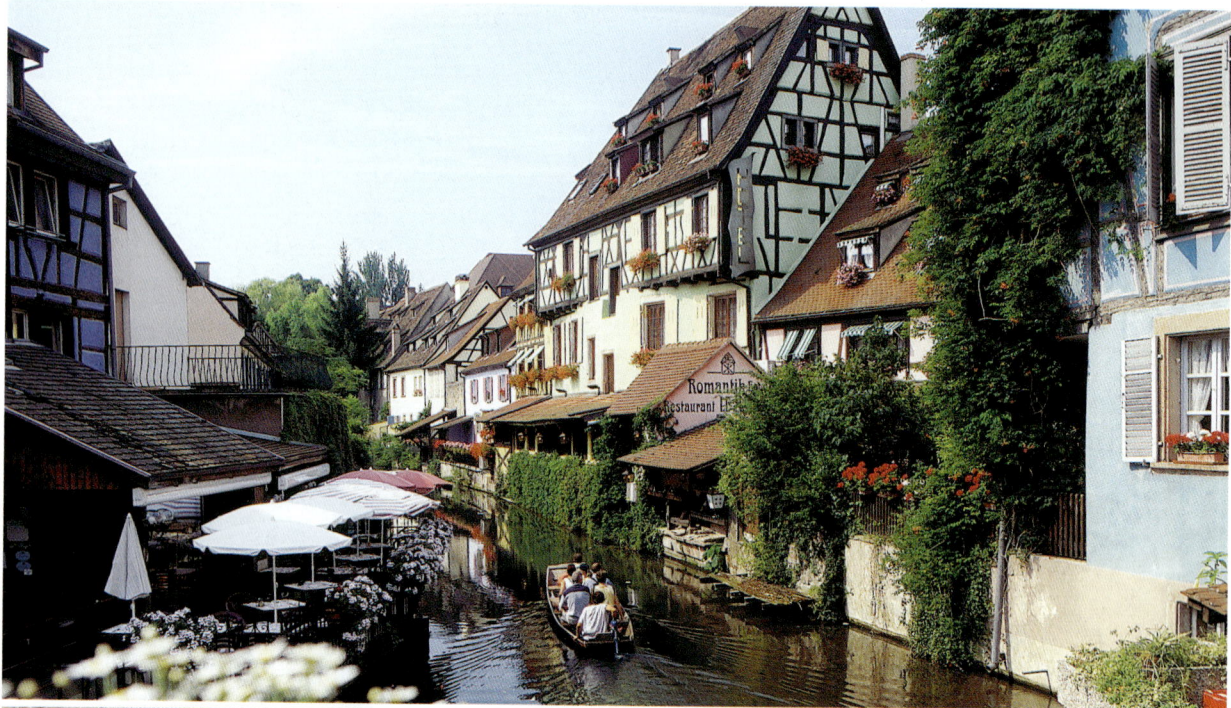

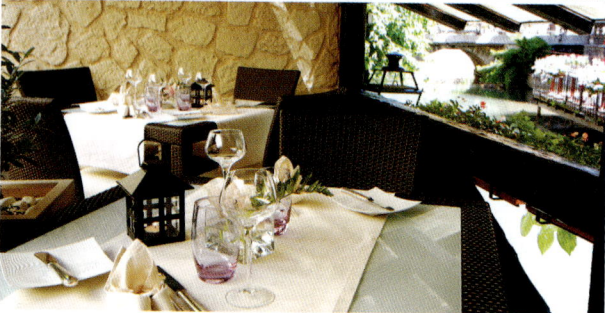
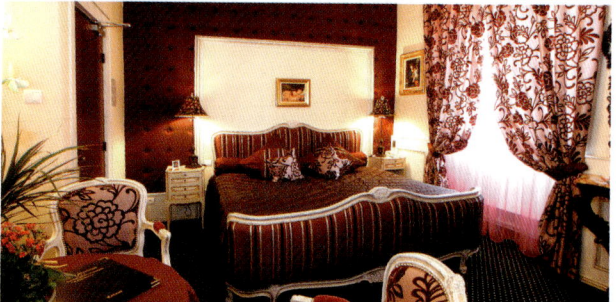

Romantik Hôtel le Maréchal

Romance in Alsace-Lorraine's magical Colmar

PRICE FROM:
€110

FEATURES:
Family friendly; Lake views; Pet friendly; Restaurant

ACTIVITIES:
Cycling; Golf; Sightseeing

NEARBY:
Colmar Old Town; Ancient and traditional Alsace villages; Alsace wine route

GETTING THERE:
Mulhouse Airport; Strasbourg Entzheim Airport

Romantik Hôtel le Maréchal is an ancient, irresistibly charming hostellerie. Set in the middle of Little Venice in the French region of Colmar, it's particularly well located for weekend getaways to the winter markets. Its fascinating Franco-German history means that your stay here is an undeniably European affair where you're warmly welcomed. A beautiful 30-room town house, it's a tastefully decorated, spacious and comfortable haven, just where you want to relax after a day's sightseeing. Soak tired limbs in a bath of bubbles (while being entertained by the bathroom tv if you wish) before sauntering into L'Echevin, Hôtel le Maréchal's restaurant. Dining on the terrace beside the canal is a particularly special setting for enjoying the tasty selection of fine local delicacies such as German snails and French calf. The menu ingeniously fuses both cultures and cuisines with skilful flair; even the wine list aligns Riesling with Côte de Provence. This is a family-friendly hotel whose knowledgeable staff can organise a whole range of excursions such as cycling, which is one of the best ways of getting about this picturesque little town.

☎ +33 3 89 41 60 32
🌐 condenastjohansens.com/marechal
🏠 4 Place Six Montagnes Noires, Petite Venise, 68000 Colmar, Alsace~Lorraine, France

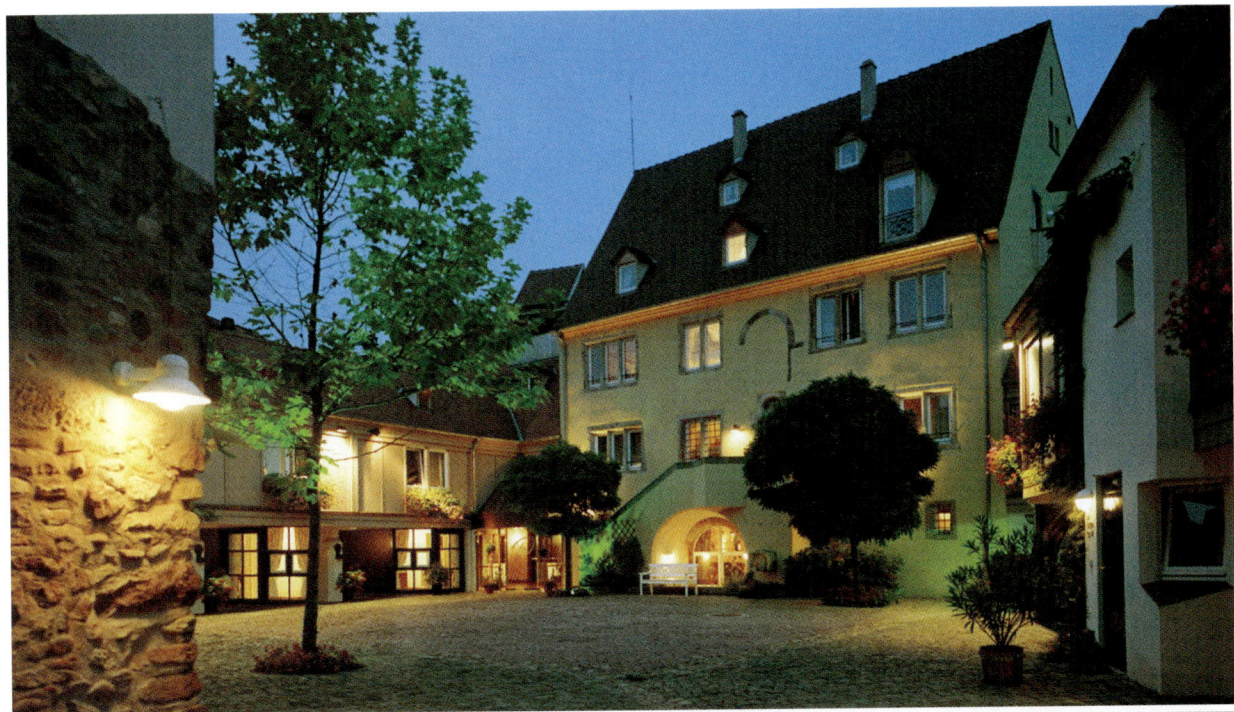

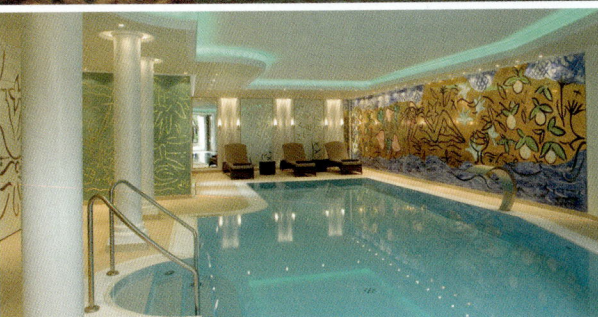

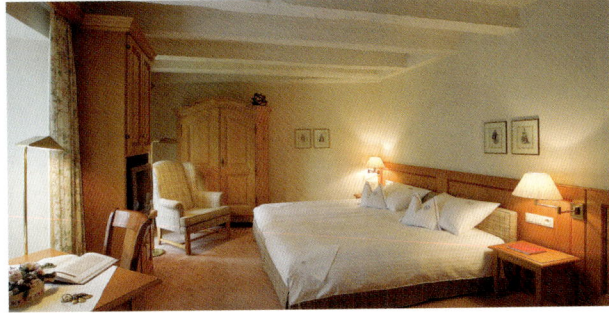

Hôtel à la Cour d'Alsace

Modern Alsatian living in medieval Obernai's walls

Chocolate-box pretty, Hôtel à la Cour d'Alsace, Obernai, has taken a cluster of traditional houses and wrapped them up into a shiny gift of Alsatian delight. Matching the crazy-pretty town that sits at the foot of the Vosges, the hotel blends and merges into Obernai's medieval walls. However, its ethos is fresh and modern Europe and its passion is food. Eat at the Jardin des Remparts for an über gastronomic treat or more casually in the brasserie-style restaurant. Unsurprisingly, for a restored manor house and cellar on a wine route, there's a wine list as thick as a novella! Interiors strike a balance between traditional and contemporary featuring warm wood-panelled walls, half timber frames and large windows that drink in views of the garden. White linens in the guest rooms are crisp and clean as the mountain air and suites are particularly spoiling with space. A sparkling new pool and steam room make a welcome addition, enhancing Hôtel à la Cour d'Alsace's escapist feel that's a great base for wandering into town or braving the undulating landscape by bicycle. Make a bee-line for the hotel's secluded, mountainous spot then turn up, switch off and chill out...

PRICE FROM:
€149

FEATURES:
Family friendly; Pet friendly; Pool; Restaurant; Wheelchair access

ACTIVITIES:
Cycling; Golf; Skiing

NEARBY:
Strasbourg; Colmar; Alsace wine tour; Vosges Lake; The Black Forest

GETTING THERE:
Strasbourg Entzheim Airport; Basel Airport, Switzerland; Frankfurt Airport, Germany

+33 3 88 95 07 00 ☎
condenastjohansens.com/couralsace 🌐
3 Rue de Gail, 67212 Obernai, Alsace~Lorraine, France 🏠

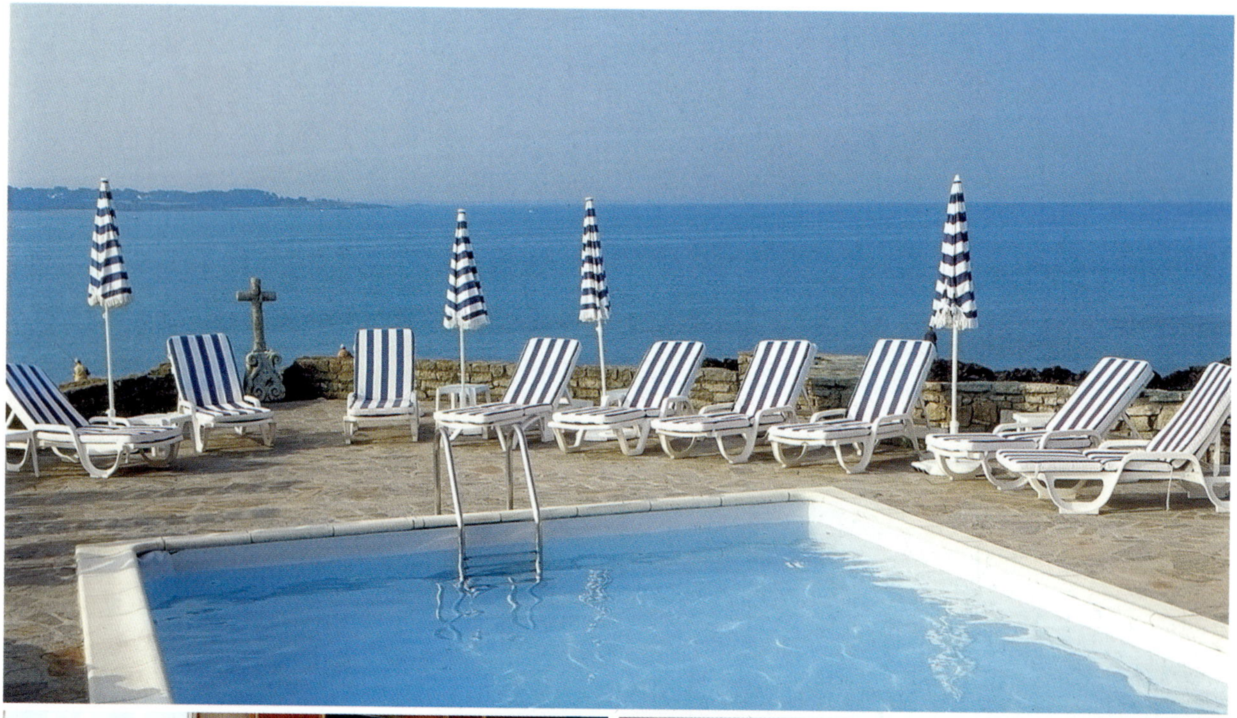

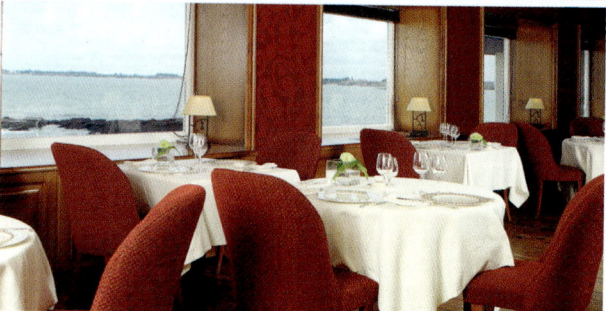
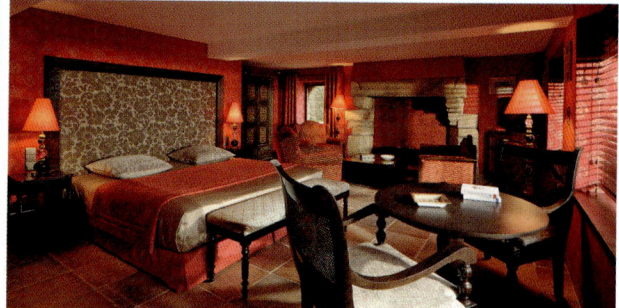

Domaine de Rochevilaine

Photo-pretty Brittany seaside manor

PRICE FROM:
€170

FEATURES:
Beach access; Pool; Restaurant; Sea views; Spa

ACTIVITIES:
Fishing; Golf; Horse riding

NEARBY:
Vannes; Brittany coastline; The Morbihan Gulf

GETTING THERE:
Nantes Airport

Domaine de Rochevilaine, Brittany, is jaw-dropping. Sitting atop craggy rocks and the pounding surf of the Atlantic on its own promontory, it's not so much on the coast as part of the coast. Sea views are a given at Domaine de Rochevilaine. Each sea-facing room is individually and luxuriously decorated; a sacred sanctuary where you can soak in your own private Jacuzzi on your terrace overlooking the dramatic Brittany coast. Wannabe sea captains should book the Admiral's Room complete with sea charts and breathtaking 270° views. It's the closest thing to sailing on a luxury yacht without getting wet! There's no ship's rations here though. Food is utterly delicious. Seafood is the speciality dished up with the backdrop of yet more distracting views of the ocean from Domaine de Rochevilaine's restaurant windows. Even the spa, Aqua Phenicia, is named after the ultimate ocean-going ancients, the Phoenicians. The watch words here are "massage" and "balneation" (the art of bathing). After a blissful morning of treatments, lie back by the elegant pool where natural light pours in through the skylight and relax to the soothing sound of the waves.

☎ +33 2 97 41 61 61
🌐 condenastjohansens.com/domainerochevilaine
🏠 Pointe de Pen Lan, F-56190 Billiers, Brittany, France

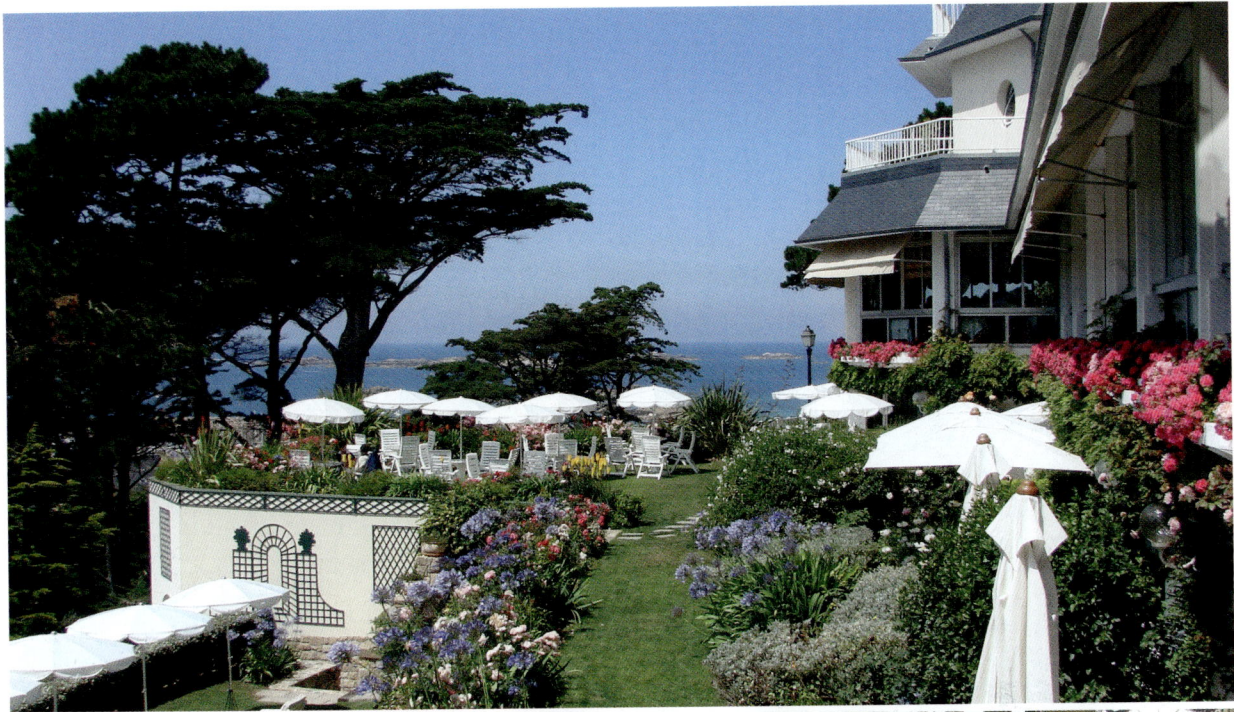

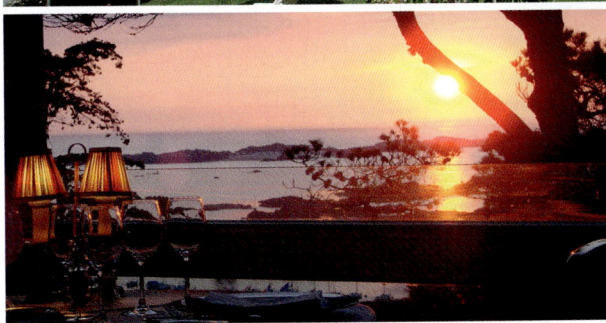

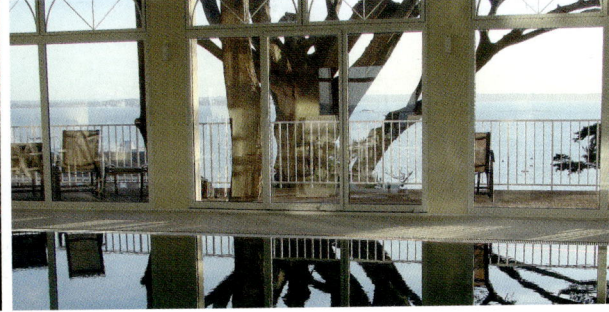

Ti al Lannec & Spa

Brittany coastal manor as pretty as its view

Dramatic coastal setting; fabulous spa; top-notch food and wine. What's not to love about Ti al Lannec & Spa in Trébeurden on Brittany's Pink Granite Coast? On a cliff overlooking rosy, rocky coves, sandy beaches and glimmering clear water, this beautiful Edwardian country manor, run by the quite wonderful Jouanny family, really celebrates its spectacular setting. Views of the sea abound from the restaurant (stunning at sunrise, romantic at sunset), pool and leafy, tiered terraces peppered with sun loungers. Stepping inside Ti al Lannec is like entering a wealthy friend's mansion lavished with English antiques, contemporary chandeliers, heavy drapes, gilt mirrors, paintings and overstuffed sofas with 33 rooms and suites varying in size, shape and décor. Some have writing tables and four posters, terraces, balconies with panoramas of the English Channel or views of the tranquil cypress groves and flower gardens. But all have bags of character. (Very) Fine French cuisine is the order of the day at the à la carte restaurant, while the spa lures you in with its hammam-sauna-Jacuzzi combo after a day spent exploring the sleepy fishing villages, castles and medieval towns of the rugged Côtes-d'Armor.

PRICE FROM:
€196

FEATURES:
Pool; Restaurant; Sea views; Spa

ACTIVITIES:
Sightseeing; Walking

NEARBY:
The centre of Trébeurden; Perros-Guirec; Lannion; Brittany coastline

GETTING THERE:
Brest Bretagne Airport; Lannion Airport; Dinard Airport

+33 2 96 15 01 01 ☎
condenastjohansens.com/tiallannec 🌐
14 Allée de Mezo~Guen, 22560 Trébeurden, Brittany, France 📧

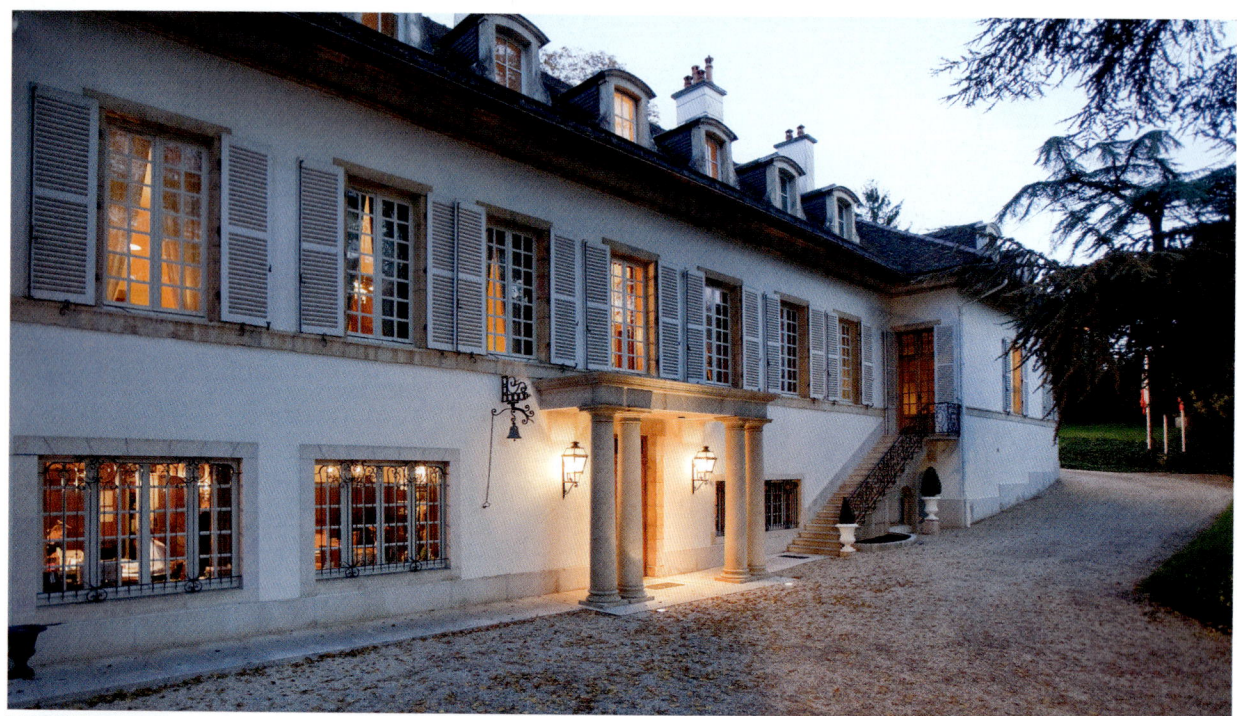

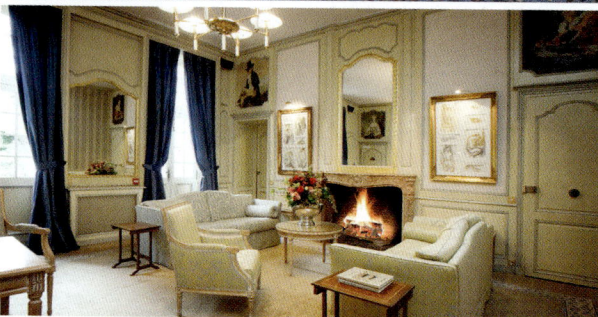

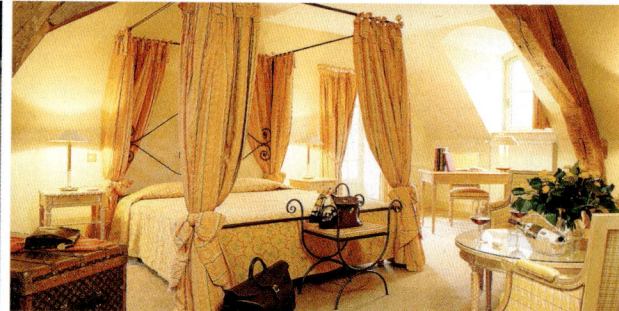

Château Hôtel André Ziltener

Burgundy château with a passion for wine and the good life

PRICE FROM:
€250

FEATURES:
Pet friendly; Wheelchair access

ACTIVITIES:
Cycling; Golf; Horse riding

NEARBY:
Dijon; Beaune; Burgundy vineyards; Abbaye de Citeaux; Hospices de Beaune

GETTING THERE:
Dijon Airport

☎ +33 3 80 62 41 62
🌐 condenastjohansens.com/ziltener
🏠 Rue de la Fontaine, 21220 Chambolle~Musigny, Burgundy, France

Château Hôtel André Ziltener in Chambolle-Musigny brings you bang into the heart of picture-perfect French wine country. The surrounding vineyards of Dijon and Beaune appear to line the land as far as the eye can see and the château itself is THE romantic escape at its epicentre. This is a family-run operation whose staff is a collection of serious oenophiles, however, wine isn't made on Château Hôtel André Ziltener's soil but there is ample opportunity to try a drop of its own label and various other famous Burgundies. In fact, tours offering inside knowledge of the château's Wine Cellar and on-site Wine Museum are a great initiation into the local Burgundy producing business. Proudly embracing its glorious product and heritage, each of its apartments, suites and rooms has been named after a Grand Cru. Serene and incredibly elegant, they're dressed in crisp, natural and pastel tones offset with gleaming marble bathrooms. It's tempting to take advantage of the room service and savour a plentiful continental breakfast in your room, although if you're feeling particularly sociable, breakfast is served around a large dining table each morning. No restaurant at the Château means you get to explore regional restaurants recommended by the hotel. Top tip: be sure to ask a member of staff for a personalised itinerary to get the most out of your visit.

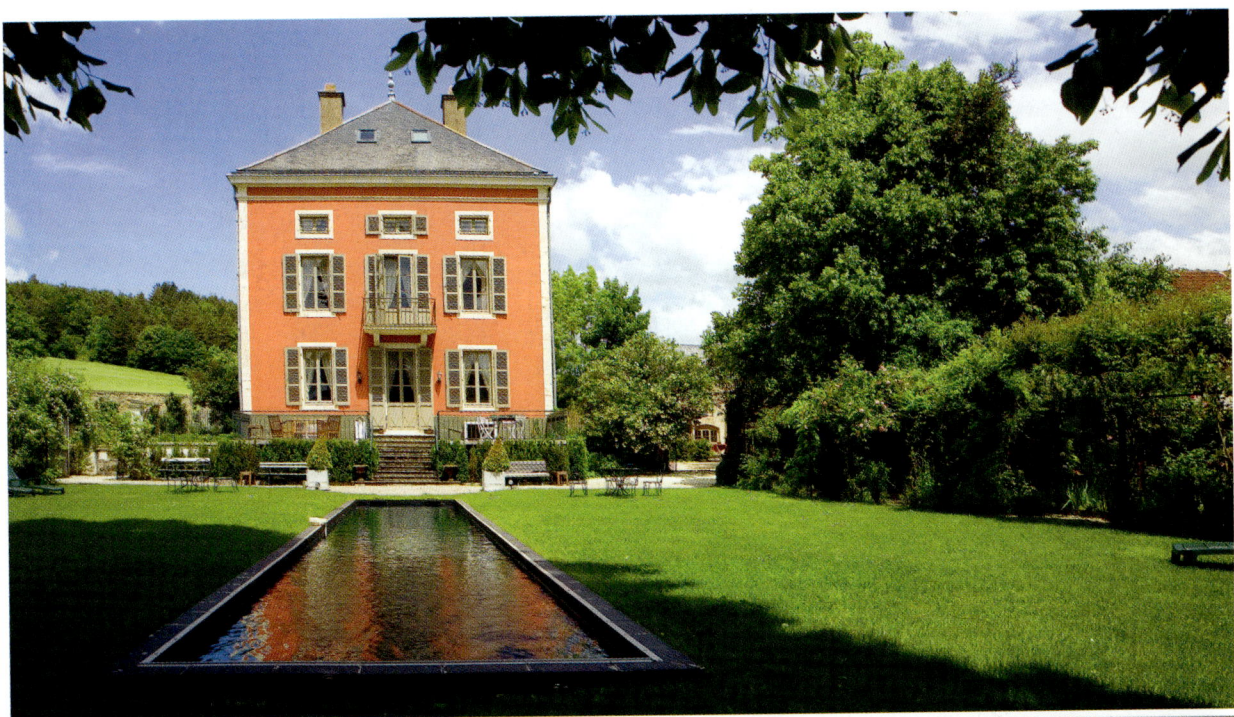

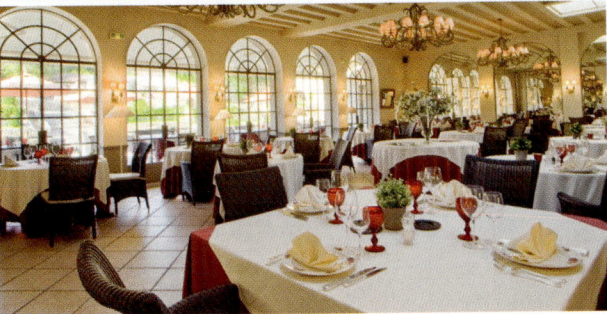

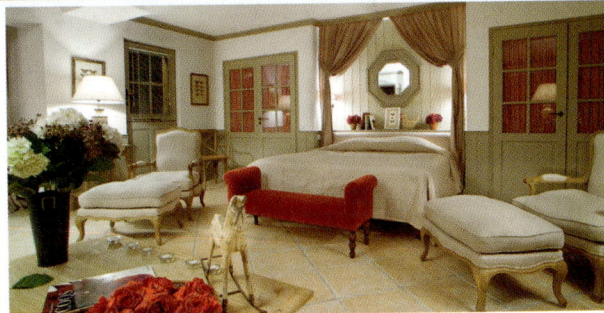

Château de Courban & Spa

Beckoning bolthole in the rolling hills of Burgundy

Owner and interior designer Pierre Vandendriessche has created the quintessential French country manor house in the family-run Château de Courban & Spa, Burgundy. Complete with painted window shutters and beautifully manicured gardens, ladies and gentlemen set your "out of office," it's time for some rest and relaxation. With their high ceilings the luxury suites are incredibly spacious while the lavish furnishings create a comfort that is both tasteful and peaceful. Easily reached from the Alps and the Riviera, you're in the midst of the Champagne and Chablis wine regions here, so red, white and bubble varieties of the potent potion are available to sample by the dozen. Being spoilt for choice is a running theme at Château de Courban whose public rooms (a library, piano room and living room with fireplace) provide pockets of peace for a quiet read on cosy sofas. And there's always Château de Courban's wonderful spa facilities to melt any remaining tension away. Once refreshed, enter the dining room whose outstanding cuisine of La Table du Colombier is undoubtedly the pièce-de-résistance of the château. Its dishes are regional and traditional with a creative spin from Head Chef Ismail Yilmaz. His favourite dish of lobster and truffle is outrageously decadent and the violet sorbet is beyond belief, all enjoyed to the backdrop of the illuminated Italian gardens.

PRICE FROM:
€99 (room only, excluding tax)

FEATURES:
Family friendly; Pet friendly; Pool; Restaurant; Spa

ACTIVITIES:
Cycling; Golf; Sightseeing

NEARBY:
Champagne vineyards; Chablis vineyards; Chatillon sur Seine

GETTING THERE:
Troyes Airport; Dijon Airport; Montbard Railway Station

+33 3 80 93 78 69 ☎
condenastjohansens.com/chateaudecourban 🌐
7 Rue du Lavoir, 21520 Courban, Burgundy, France 🌐

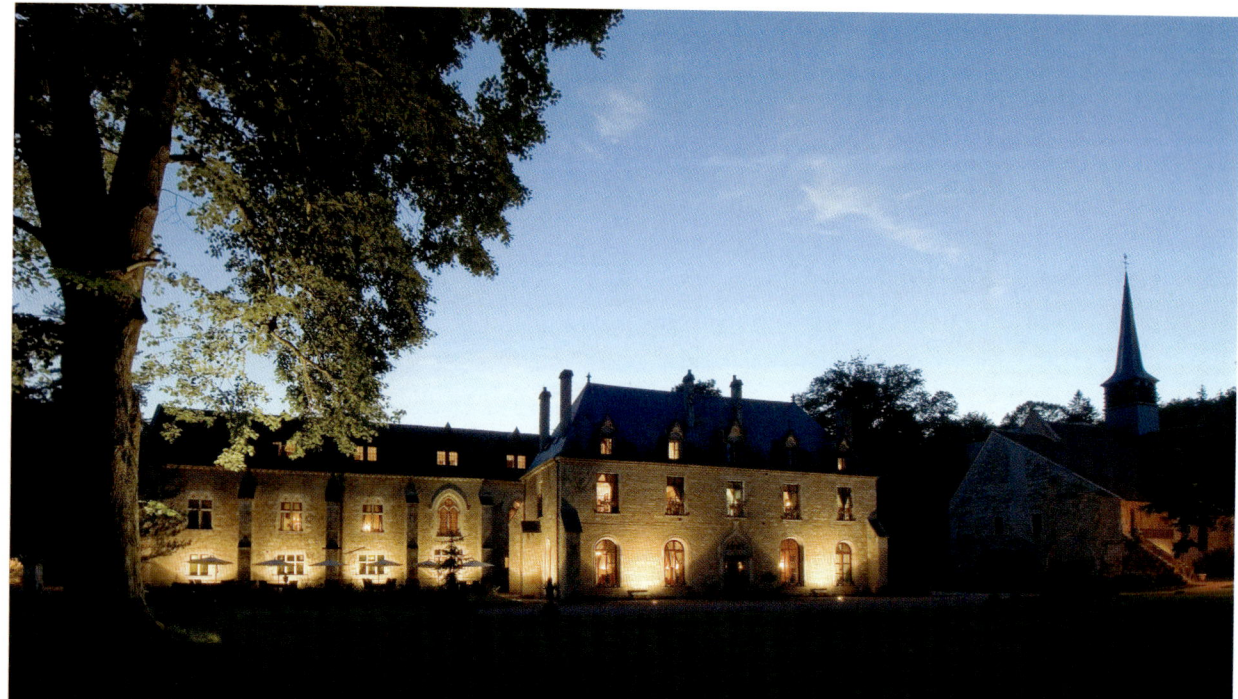

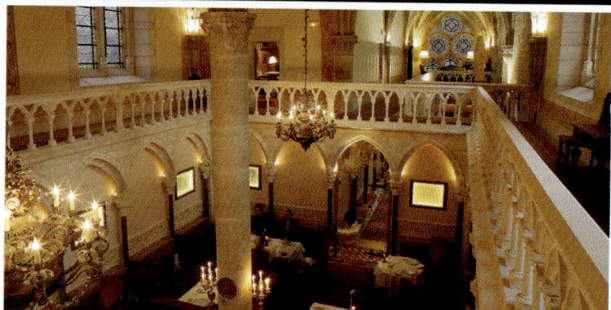
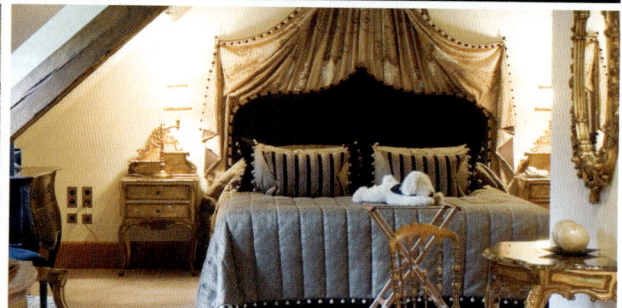

Abbaye de la Bussière

Lavishly resurrected Burgundy abbey enveloped by pin-drop serenity

English owners Tanith and Clive Cummings have done their French cousins proud at Abbaye de la Bussière, Dijon. Not only have they kept the quiet, reflective air of this 12th-century abbey (you can almost hear the echo of chanting monks reverberating off the walls) they've also retained the architectural features that make it so jaw-droppingly beautiful. The Cummings' eye for carefully chosen antiques means that each room looks a million dollars, however, the suites offer something a little extra special. Sumptuous swagged fabrics dress the walls and super-soft cushions add extra squashability to sofas; each one has a whirlpool bath and looks out over the gardens and lake. As opulent and wonderful as the interior is, outside, nature does the talking. Getting lost in the Abbaye's botanical gardens is a meditative experience and cycling along the canal path is made memorable with one of Clive's picnic lunches in a backpack. It's worth making a pilgrimage to Abbaye de la Bussière for the food alone: Michelin-Starred Chef Emmanuel Hébrard's Burgundian cuisine speaks for itself. And of course, you're amidst some of the world's finest vineyards so the wine list is something to behold.

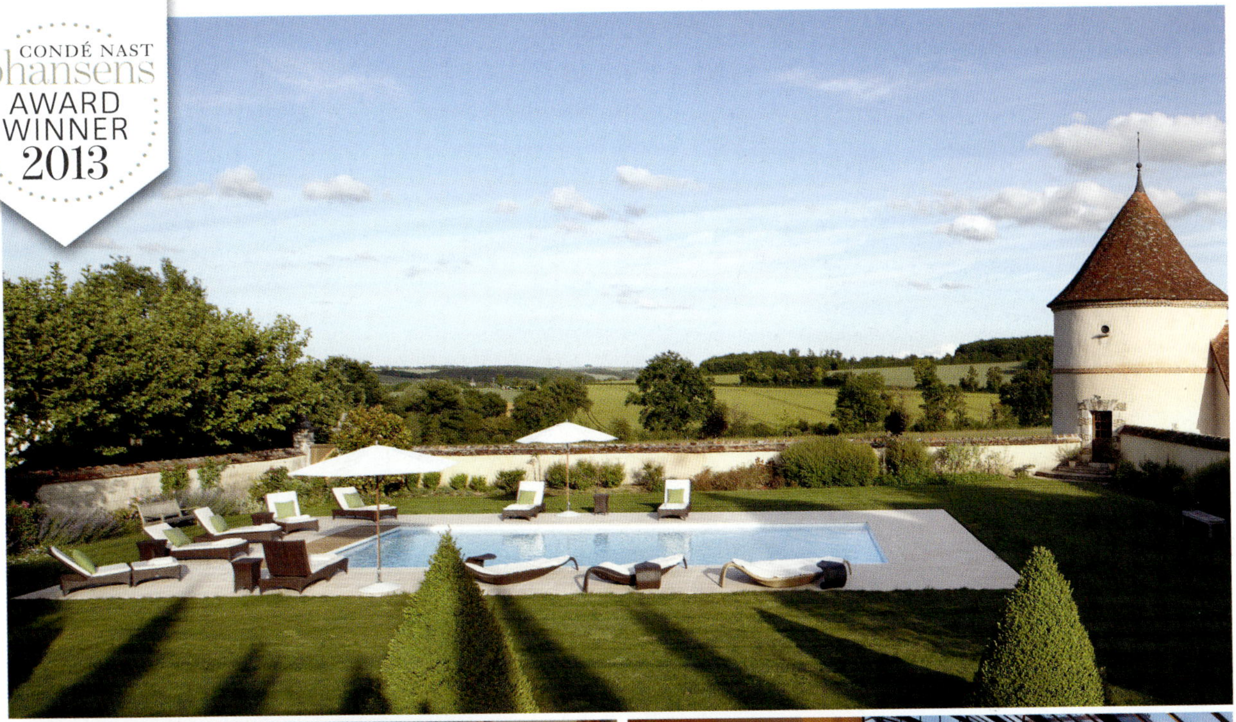

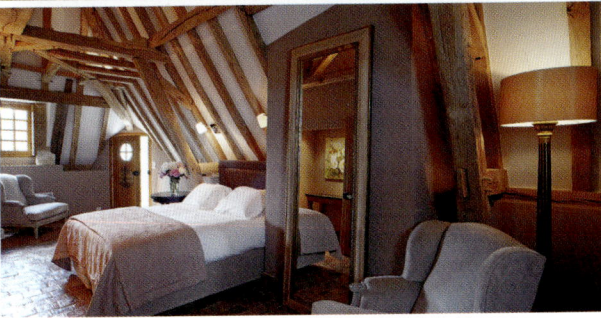

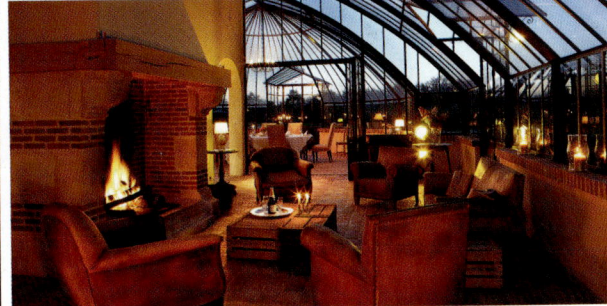

La Borde

A lesson in Burgundy countryside sophistication

The most fabulous way to arrive at La Borde is by helicopter. It's also the best way to see the patchwork Burgundy countryside surrounding this exclusive 16th-century walled manor just outside the village of Leugny, Yonne. Cocooned in wide open acres of fragrant gardens, meadows and orchards, it's fairy-tale pretty with buildings festooned with fragrant climbing roses, towers, an orangery and a dovecote. Lazy days are spent around the sun-drenched pool or in the spa, while cosying up with a good book in the shaded porch adorned with period furniture and antique armchairs, is hard to beat. La Borde's five rooms are pure château-chic. They're all about French country-style décor, exposed beams and waiting-to-be-stroked velvets with sink-into beds, and in some, fireplaces and free-standing baths. With so much space and the laid-back pace, La Borde is a place to lose yourself and nowhere more so than in the tranquil arboretum, home to 50 species of tree. To match the area's famous wines, the hotel's fresh French food is created from fruit, veg and herbs grown in the house's very own organic gardens. Châteaux, vineyards and nature parks are all waiting to be explored nearby but you might find yourself so relaxed that even an unhurried spot of sightseeing feels like too much effort.

PRICE FROM:
€310

FEATURES:
Gym; Helipad; Pool; Restaurant; Spa

ACTIVITIES:
Cycling; Golf; Tennis

NEARBY:
Vézelay; Chablis vineyards; Auxerre Abbey and Cathedral; Guédelon

GETTING THERE:
Auxerre-Branches (private charters only) Airport; Paris Airports; Railways stations Joigny and Auxerre

+33 3 86 47 69 01 ☎
condenastjohansens.com/laborde 🌐
89130 Leugny, Burgundy, France 🏠

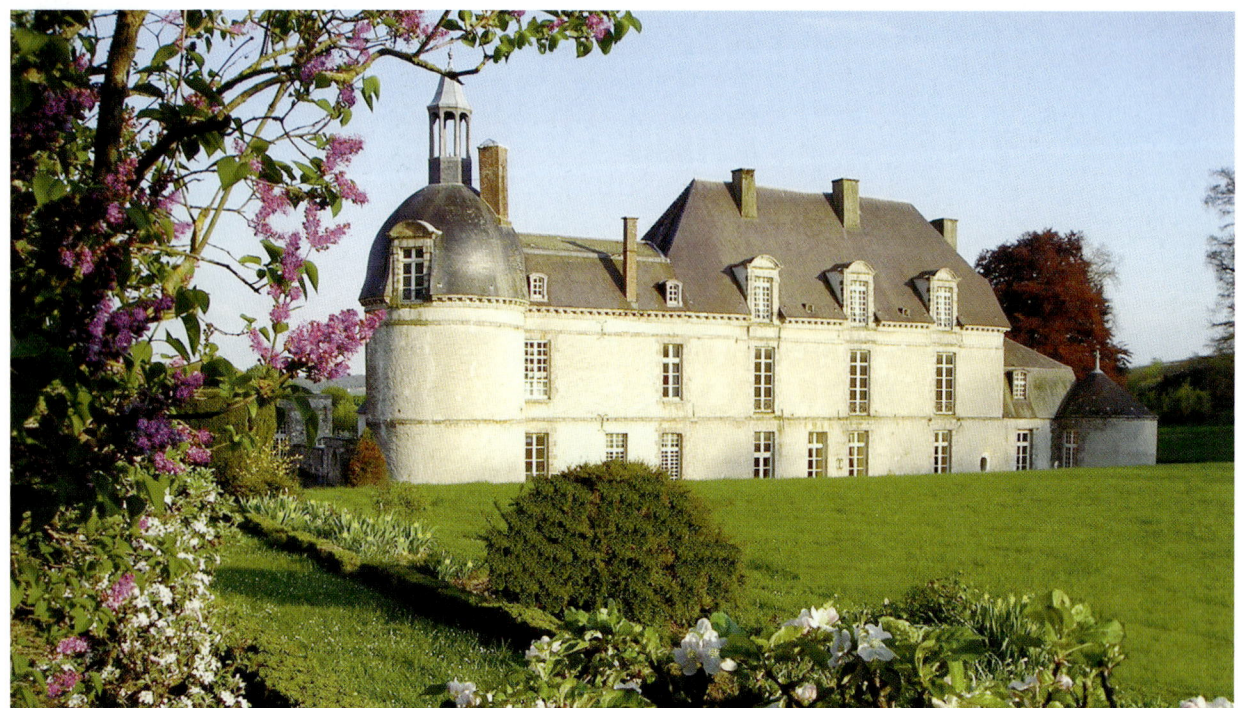

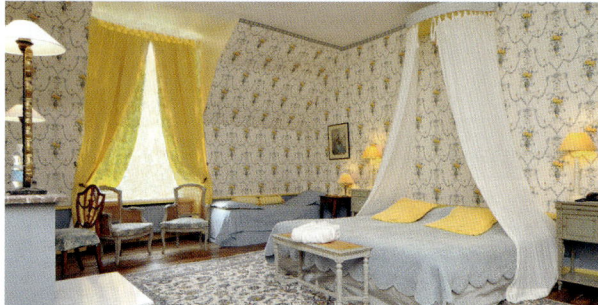

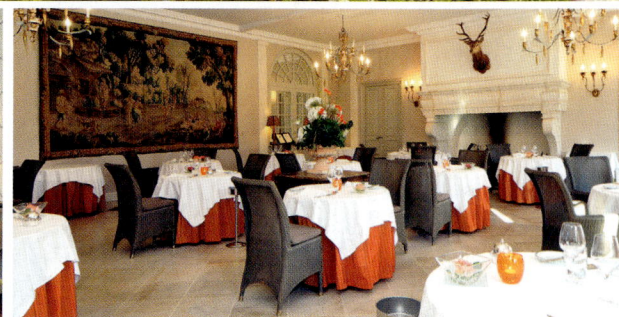

Château d'Etoges

Beautifully renovated Champagne~Ardenne château

PRICE FROM:
€120

FEATURES:
Helipad; Restaurant; Spa; Wheelchair access

ACTIVITIES:
Cycling; Sightseeing; Walking

NEARBY:
Epernay; Reims; Troyes; Champagne houses

GETTING THERE:
Paris-Charles de Gaulle (Roissy) Airport; Paris-Orly Airport

Château splendour. Gourmet French cuisine. Fine Champagne. Indulgent spa. Four fabulous reasons to spend a weekend or even a week at Château d'Etoges. This stunning 17th-century château is straight out of a fairy tale set in a rural idyll of rolling lawns and vineyards. Epernay and Rheims are minutes away where you can take cellar tours of wineries that read like a who's who of the world's finest fizz. Think Taittinger, Moët & Chandon, Dom Perignon and Veuve Clicquot but it's not just about the bubbles here. Each tour of the area takes in some of the region's finest produce from fois gras to flamiche (local leek pie). And after this gastronomic extravaganza, recover chez Château d'Etoges and channel your inner Marie-Antoinette in a sumptuous room complete with grand canopy and views of the grounds. Alternatively, keep it simple, elegant and chic and stay in an Orangerie Room, just a moment's walk down to the restaurant. Gluttons take note: Château d'Etoges' chefs create the finest in French cuisine. It's a gourmet's dream, packed with French classics and a cheese trolley to die for.

☎ +33 3 26 59 30 08
🌐 condenastjohansens.com/etoges
🏠 51270 Etoges~en~Champagne, Champagne~Ardenne, France

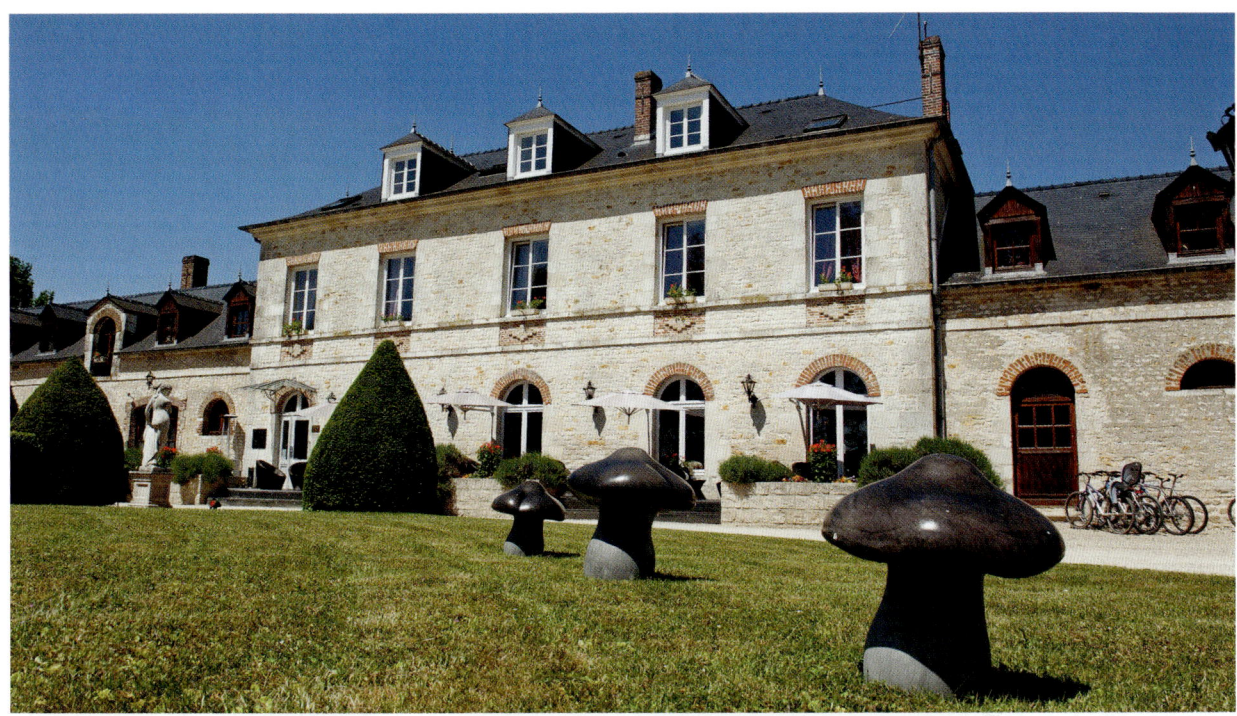

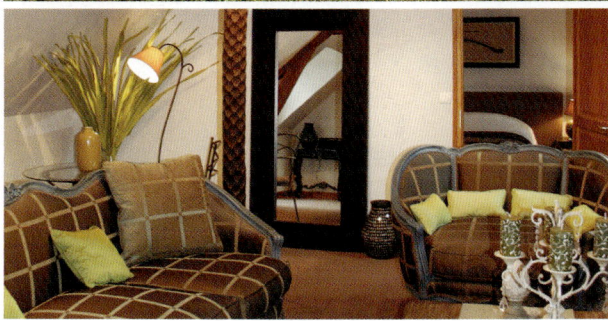
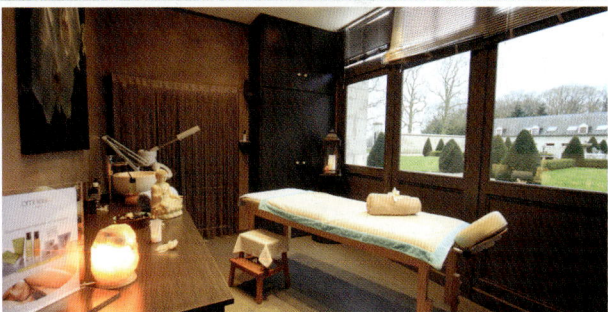

Domaine de Barive

Picture-book château in France's Champagne region

For the ultimate in French farmhouse chic, no-one does it better than Domaine de Barive located just outside Rheims. Former farm it may be but there's nothing rustic about this chic hideaway. It's a country pad to die for and counts the head of Veuve Clicquot amongst its previous owners. Step into one of the stylish bedrooms complete with exposed farmhouse beams and simply enjoy the view. There's over 1,000 acres of parkland and elegant formal gardens to drink in and it's all on your doorstep to explore on foot, bicycle, pony or quad bike. Domaine de Barive is an adventure playground. Take a dip in the heated pool, play some tennis or unwind in the beautiful TranSPArence with an endless array of treatments, all tailored to your needs and guaranteed to bliss you out. What could be more French than a drink over a game of petanque before heading to Les Epicuriens, the Domaine's stylish, contemporary restaurant with sweeping views of the park. Alain Ducasse is a big fan of their seasonal cuisine and no-one should leave without trying the seven-course Menu Gourmande. If you can't get enough of the fabulous food, there's an all-day snack menu for gourmet-loving guests.

PRICE FROM:
€120

FEATURES:
Gym; Helipad; Pool; Restaurant; Spa

ACTIVITIES:
Fishing; Golf; Horse riding

NEARBY:
Laon; Rheims; Chemin des Dames; Champagne vineyards; Cathedrals of Picardy

GETTING THERE:
Paris-Charles de Gaulle (Roissy) Airport

+33 3 23 22 15 15 ☎
condenastjohansens.com/barive 🌐
02350 Sainte~Preuve, Champagne~Ardenne, France 🏠

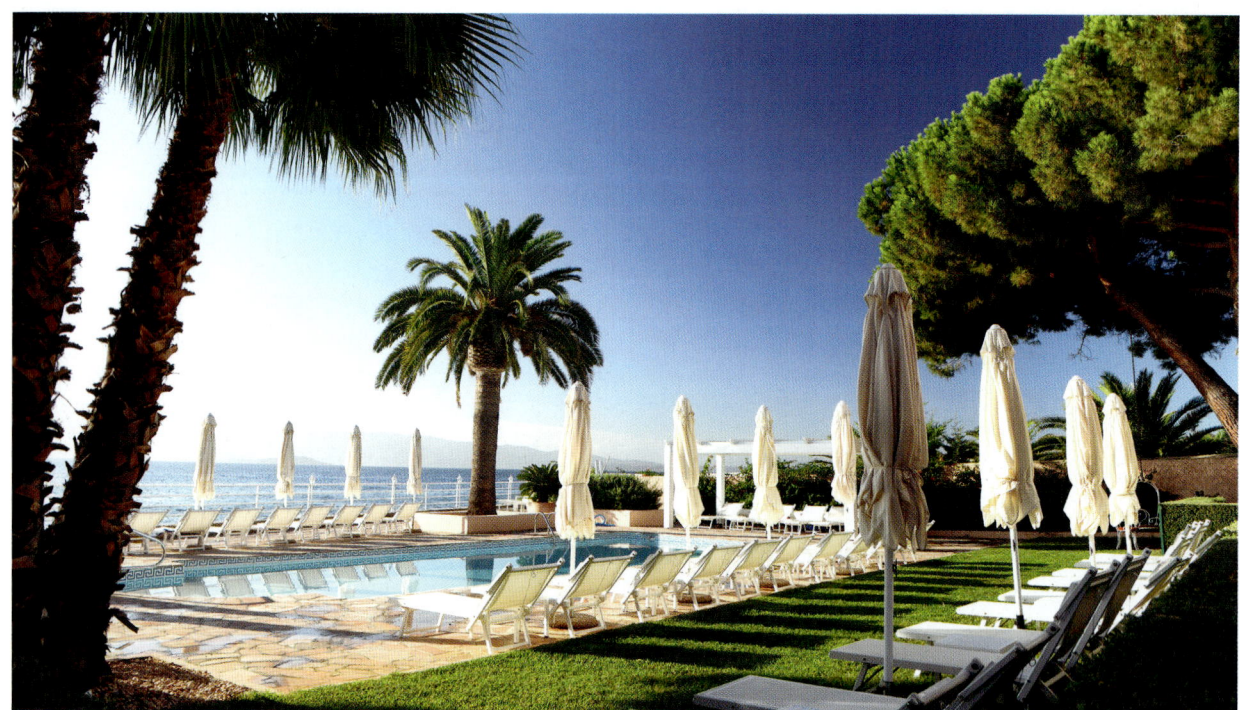

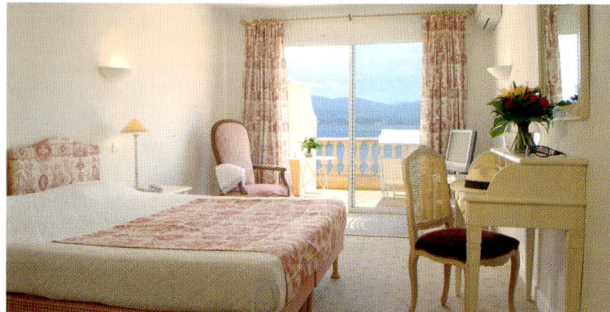

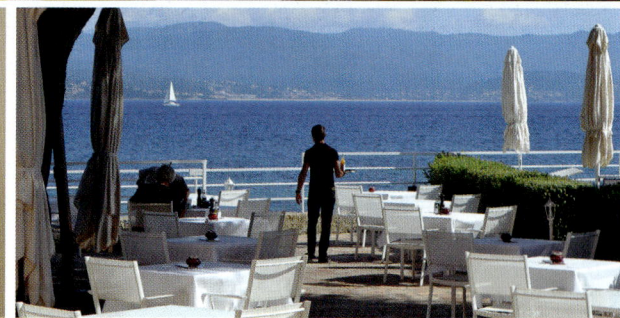

Les Mouettes Hôtel Demeure

Mediterranean enchantment on Corsica's coast

PRICE FROM:
€115

FEATURES:
Beach access; Pool; Sea views; Spa

ACTIVITIES:
Sightseeing; Walking; Water sports

NEARBY:
Ajaccio; West coast of Corsica; Hiking trails; Wine producers; Pristine beaches

GETTING THERE:
Ajaccio Airport; Ajaccio Harbour

From late 19th-century holiday home to turn-of-the-century inn, Les Mouettes Hôtel Demeure is now a well-loved coastal bolthole. Guests return time and again to the Pieri family's pride and joy near Ajaccio in the western corner of Corsica facing the celestial waters of the Mediterranean. This is a convenient base for exploring the Calanques de Piana World Heritage Site (just an hour away), the Sanguinaires Islands and the Parata (a 16th-century Genovese tower) as well as enjoying endless water sports and hiking trails. Plus, the island's capital (Napolean Bonaparte's birthplace) is only a few minutes' drive away with plenty of sites, eateries and shopping to fill the days when not soaking up the comfort and charisma of Les Mouettes. When the sea views are this pretty it seems foolish not to book a room or suite overlooking the azure scene and nowhere beats the lookout from The Blue Suite's large double terrace. Interconnecting rooms are a sure-fire winner with families and the two sizeable suites are complete with dining tables, living rooms and sofa beds. Each morning, breakfast on the beach-side terrace is a continental feast of organic produce such as Corsican cheese, locally farmed cuts of pork and homemade cakes. Snacks including salads and cold dishes are available until 8pm, although wine, beer and cocktails are served until a little later.

☎ +33 4 95 50 40 40
🌐 condenastjohansens.com/hotellesmouettes
🏠 9 Cours Lucien Bonaparte, 20000 Ajaccio, Corsica, France

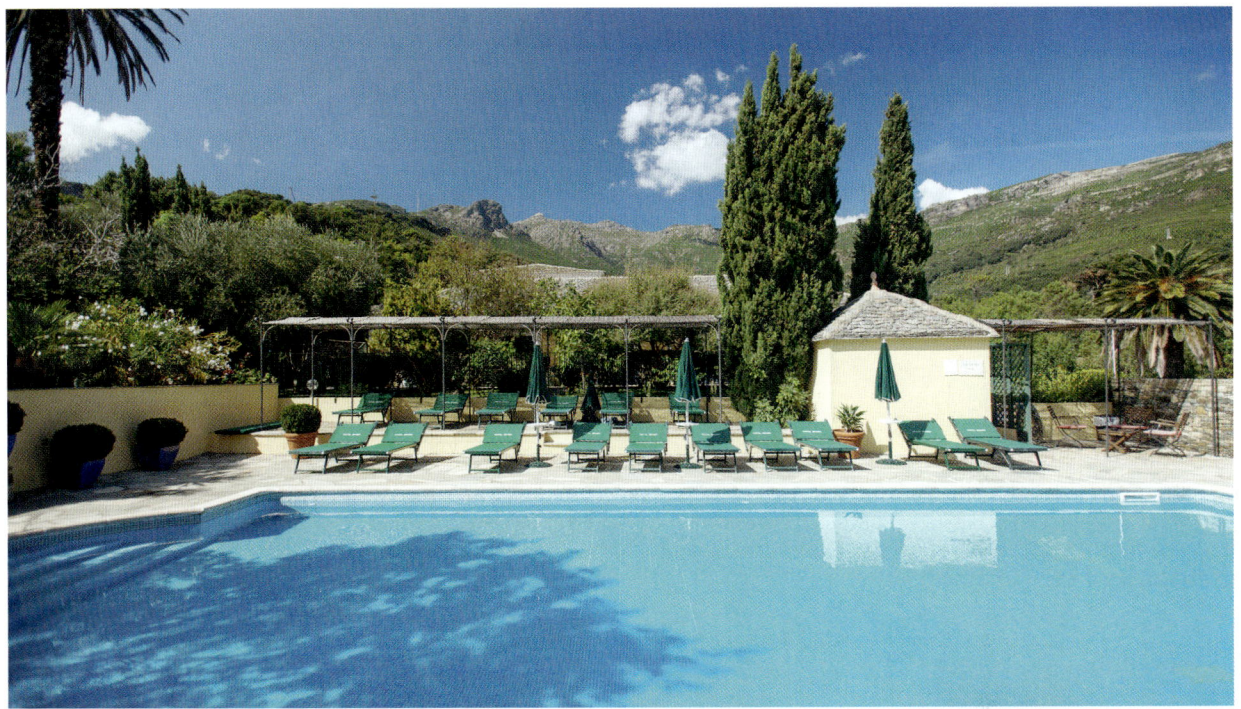

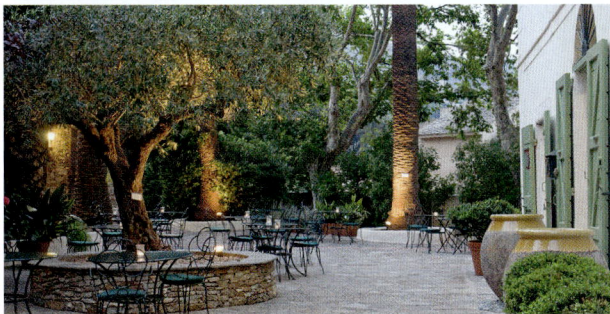
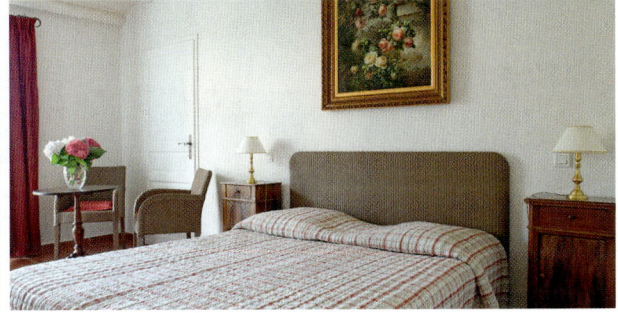

Castel Brando Hôtel demeure

19th-century mansion house in the medieval fishing village of Erbalunga

Corsica's Castel Brando Hôtel demeure in Erbalunga is the French home of your dreams. Set in blossoming gardens with a palm-tree courtyard and two pools, the interior reveals vaulted ceilings, terracotta flooring and elegant antique furnishings. This is one of the many 19th-century "Maisons Américaines" that pepper the island's northerly Cap Corse peninsula built by local families returning home from making their fortunes overseas. It's now the Pieri family's beguiling hotel (they built three villas beside the original house) attracting visitors hankering for a taste of coastal Mediterranean life. For just outside Castel Brando's walls is the fishing village of Erbalunga, a maze of squares and narrow roads leading to a bustling harbour. Castel's two pools (one heated) and Jacuzzi looking across the Corsican Maquis with mountain backdrop, encourage doing very little. The inner courtyard built around a century-old olive tree is a place for contemplation (and breakfast in the summer) while its sprawling park of tropical trees has you meditatively breathing in the exotic scents that permeate the air. Spa treatments can take place out here. Inside the main house and into the Lounge, a small library and display of artwork by the original owners provide a glimpse into a bygone era. Yet the fresh, Mediterranean-styled rooms and suites deliver contemporary comfort.

PRICE FROM:
€96

FEATURES:
Pet friendly; Pool; Sea views; Spa; Wheelchair access

ACTIVITIES:
Horse riding; Sightseeing; Walking

NEARBY:
Bastia; Erbalunga; Corte

GETTING THERE:
Bastia Airport; Bastia Harbour

+33 4 95 30 10 30 ☎
condenastjohansens.com/castelbrando 🌐
Erbalunga 20222, Corsica, France 🏢

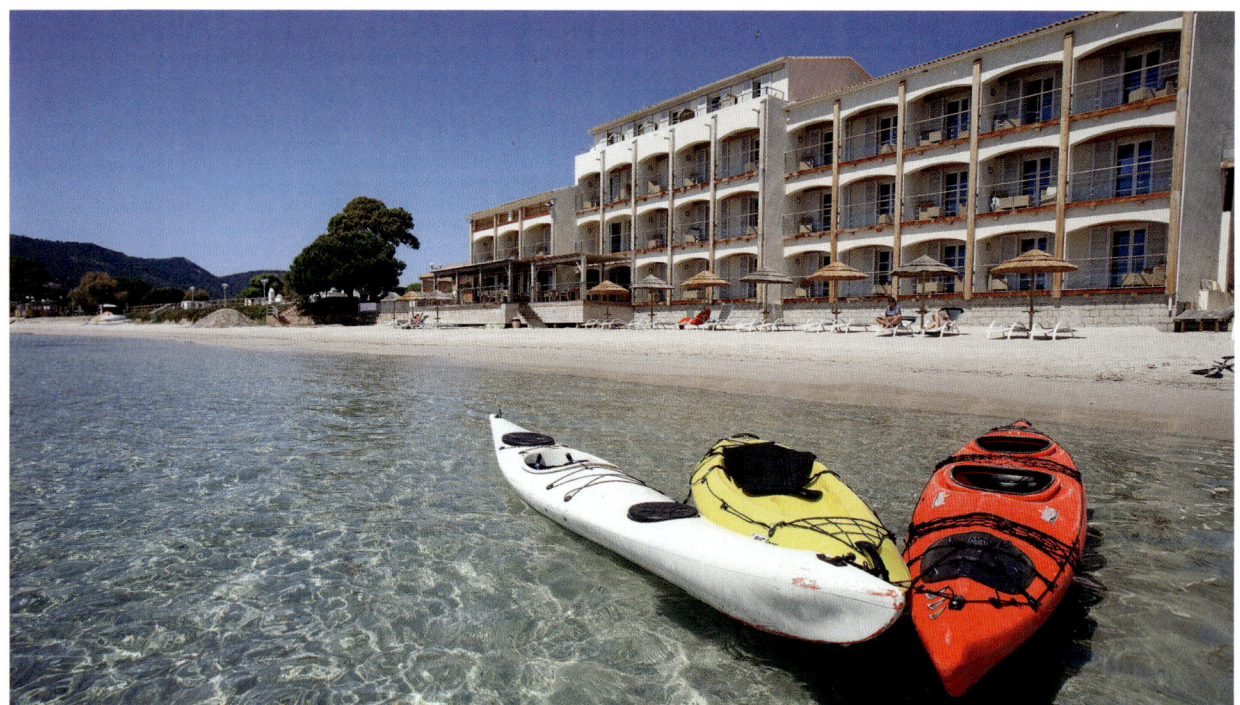

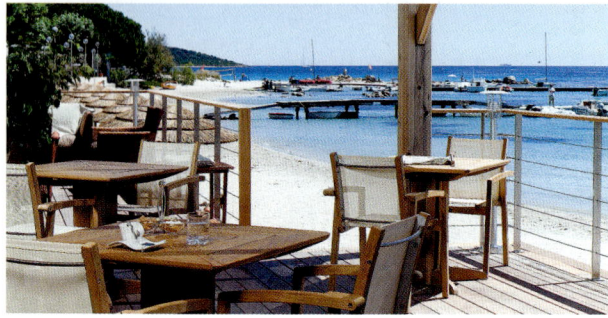

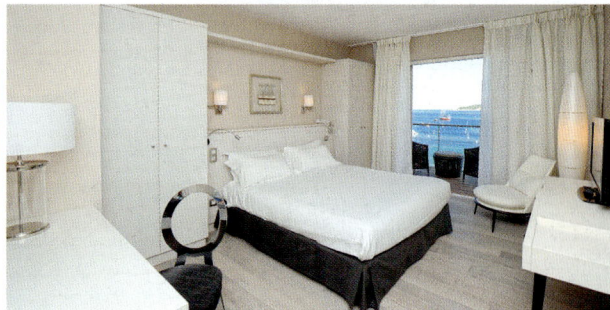

Hôtel Le Pinarello

Unadulterated Corsica alongside the Med

PRICE FROM:
€271

FEATURES:
Beach access; Family friendly; Gym; Restaurant; Sea views

ACTIVITIES:
Horse riding; Sightseeing; Water sports

NEARBY:
Porto Vecchio; Bonifacio; Bavella Needles mountains

GETTING THERE:
Figari Airport; Bastia Airport

☎ +33 4 95 71 44 39
🌐 condenastjohansens.com/lepinarello
🏠 Sainte Lucie de Porto Vecchio, 20144 Porto Vecchio, Corsica, France

Italy and France's love child, Corsica, is a fabulous blend of both countries. This is paradise for the luxury seeking explorer and Hôtel Le Pinarello, a short drive from Porto Vecchio (hidden away on the southern coast), is the perfect place to experience the heavenly Mediterranean cooking, stunning mountain-scapes and laid-back coastal life of this gorgeous island. Low rise Hôtel Le Pinarello is decorated in bleached-out, driftwood tones with chic, cosy rooms each leading to a balcony overlooking Pinarello beach dotted with stylish parasols in a sheltered, beautiful bay. From your balcony you can gaze over the calm waters and contemplate wakeboarding, water-skiing, sailing or even windsurfing. Beginners needn't worry as the flat waters of the bay remain calm and novice-friendly. Delicious snacks and drinks at the bar keep you fed and watered while its open terrace provides yet more pretty-as-a-picture scenes of brightly painted fishing boats and the wide, blue bay. Hôtel Le Pinarello is the ultimate place to kick back and relax. Be sure not to miss the fabulous Anne Semonin beauty centre, complete with a hammam and regular yoga sessions, whose professional therapists and beauticians specifically design treatments for the individual.

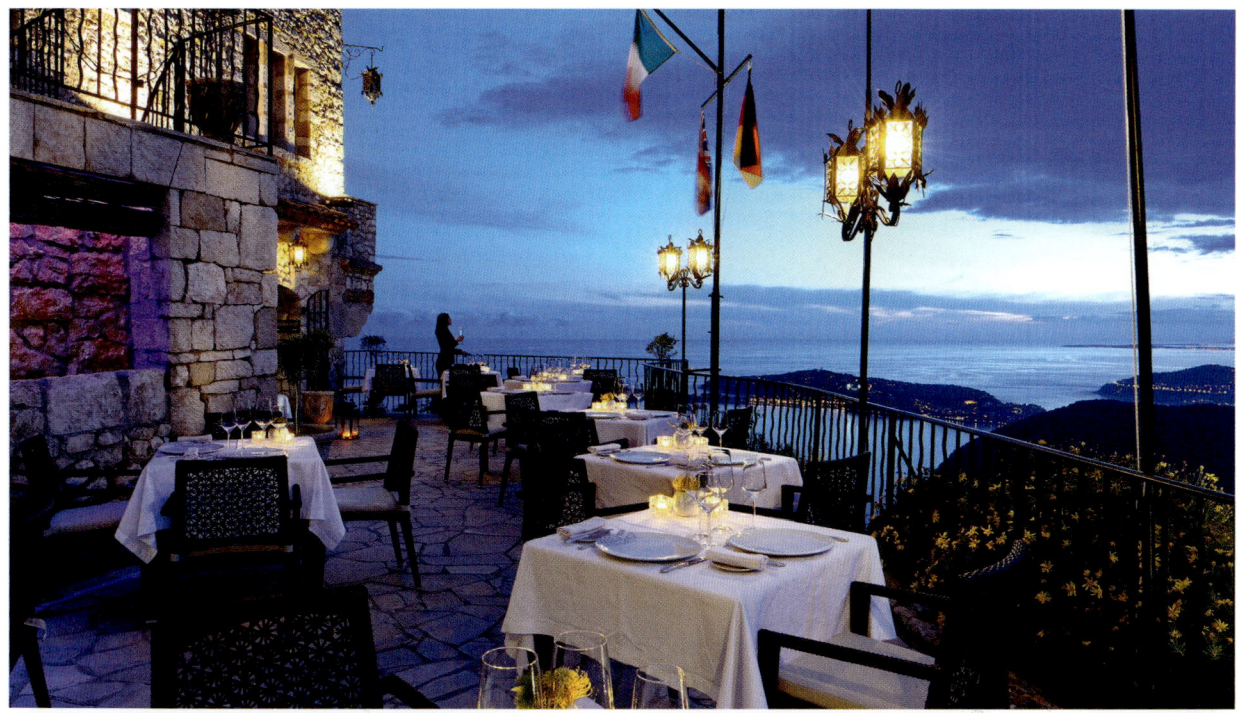

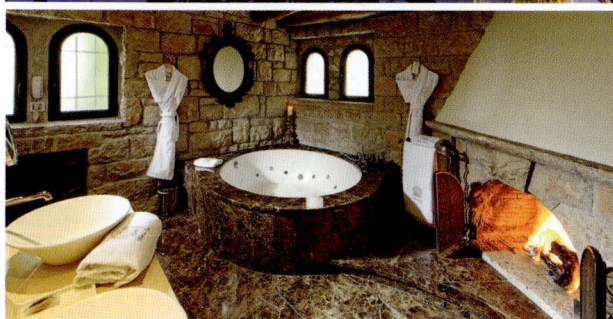
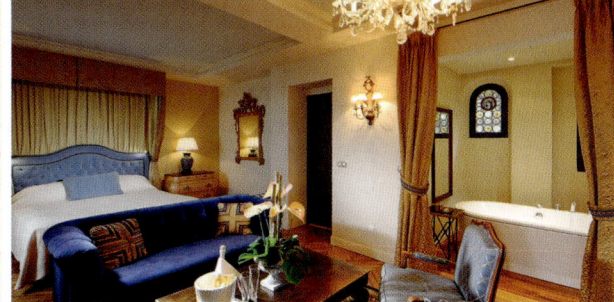

Château Eza

Centuries-old Côte d'Azur hilltop château infused with contemporary style

Old school chic, super-yachts, St Tropez, the French Riviera has effortless glamour by the Hermès bag-full. Add in peaceful seclusion on a luxurious scale and a heavenly sea breeze and you have the intimate, five-star Château Eza, a short hop from Nice and Monaco. With only 12 rooms this is the ultimate boutique hotel de luxe, perched high on a rocky cliff overlooking the sleepy, terracotta tiled medieval village of Èze 400 metres below. The ancient stone Château Eza is all about the views. Everywhere you look there's a 180 of the Côte d'Azur and the startling blue of the Med, from the balcony of your opulent, chic room to the restaurant's terrace where you can feast on Michelin-Starred food with the stunning coastline as your backdrop. By day, enjoy lunch on the outside terrace so you can top up your tan while sampling the delights of Château Eza's fabulous French meets Mediterranean food. By night, watch the lights of the super-yachts twinkling from the secluded bay below.

PRICE FROM:
€180

FEATURES:
Michelin Starred restaurant; Pet friendly; Sea views

ACTIVITIES:
Fishing; Golf; Walking

NEARBY:
Monaco; Nice; Saint-Jean Cap Ferrat; Villa Ephrussi de Rothschild; Cannes

GETTING THERE:
Nice Airport

+33 4 93 41 12 24 ☎
condenastjohansens.com/eza 🌐
Rue de la Pise, 06360 Èze Village, Côte d'Azur, France 🏠

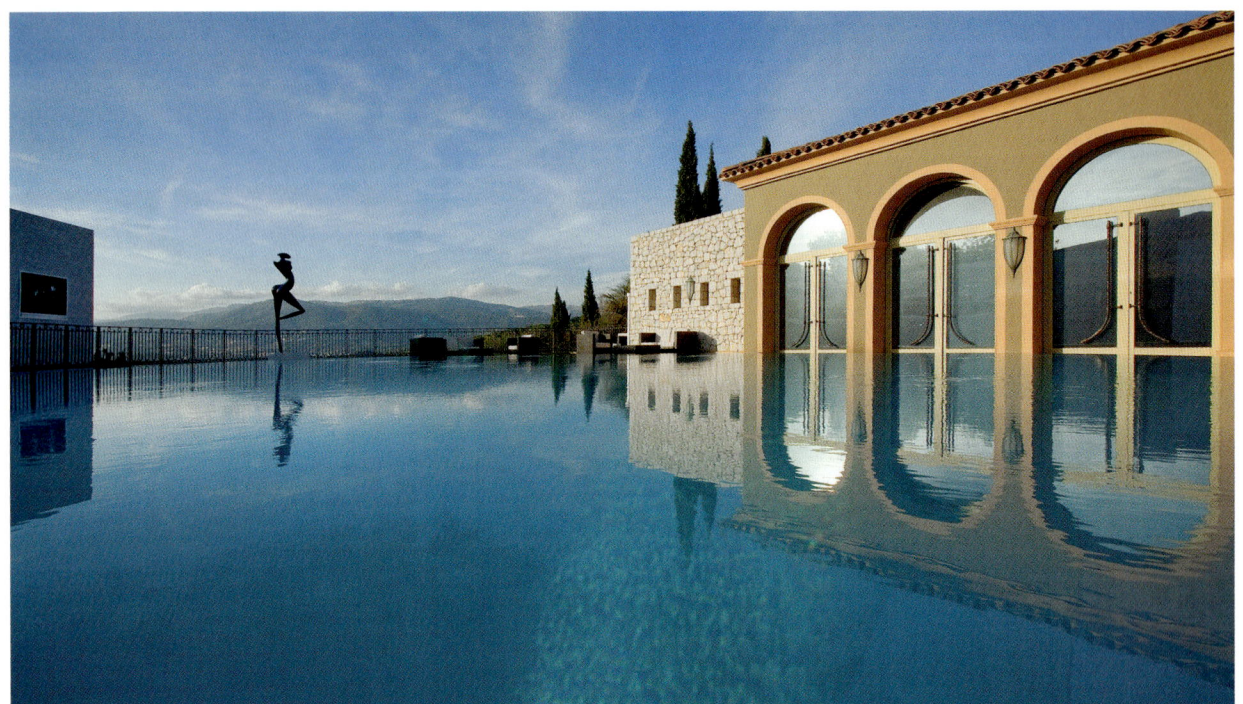

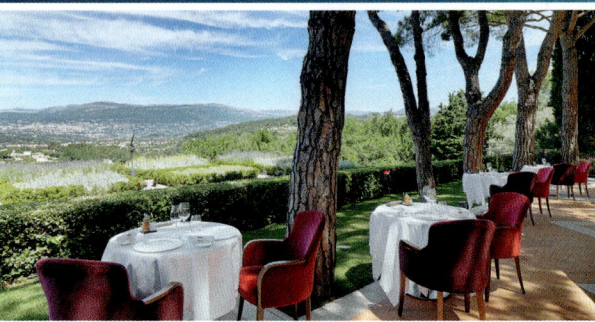
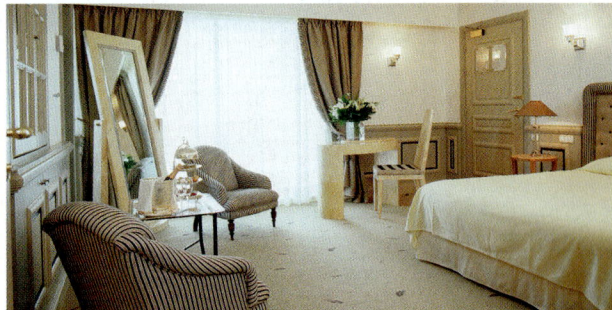

Le Mas Candille

Pure French sophistication and effortless style on the Côte d'Azur

PRICE FROM:
€310

FEATURES:
Gym; Michelin Starred restaurant; Pet friendly; Pool; Spa

ACTIVITIES:
Golf; Skiing; Water sports

NEARBY:
Cannes; Grasse; Nice; Monaco; Mougins

GETTING THERE:
Nice Airport

Jump in a cab from Cannes' glamorous Croisette, make your way through steep, winding roads and the pretty French village of Mougins, and 10 minutes later you'll uncover the small but perfectly formed Le Mas Candille. A former 18th-century farmhouse concealed in 10 acres of ancient olive groves, Le Mas Candille is now a chic 45-room boutique hideaway. It's no surprise that Picasso kept a studio in Mougins for 15 years; the views are spectacular and the living is easy. It's also a gastronomic delight. "Chef Celebre" Serge Gouloumes has created "Le Candille," a unique taste of Italian and Provençal cooking via Los Angeles and his hometown of Gascony. Eat beneath the shady terrace or take a seat in the opulent dining room. Informal but no less fabulous cuisine is served at (the summer restaurant) La Pergola, next to the stunning pool overlooking the cypress-strewn valley where by night the lights of the villages below and legendary French Riviera coastline twinkle into life. For a taste of Japan in the heart of Provence, head to Le Mas Candille's Spa Shiseido. Very chic and very Zen, this is where Qi is aligned, skin smoothed and souls restored, ready to luxuriate in this Provençal paradise.

☎ +33 4 92 28 43 43
🌐 condenastjohansens.com/lemascandille
🏠 Boulevard Clément Rebuffel, 06250 Mougins, Côte d'Azur, France

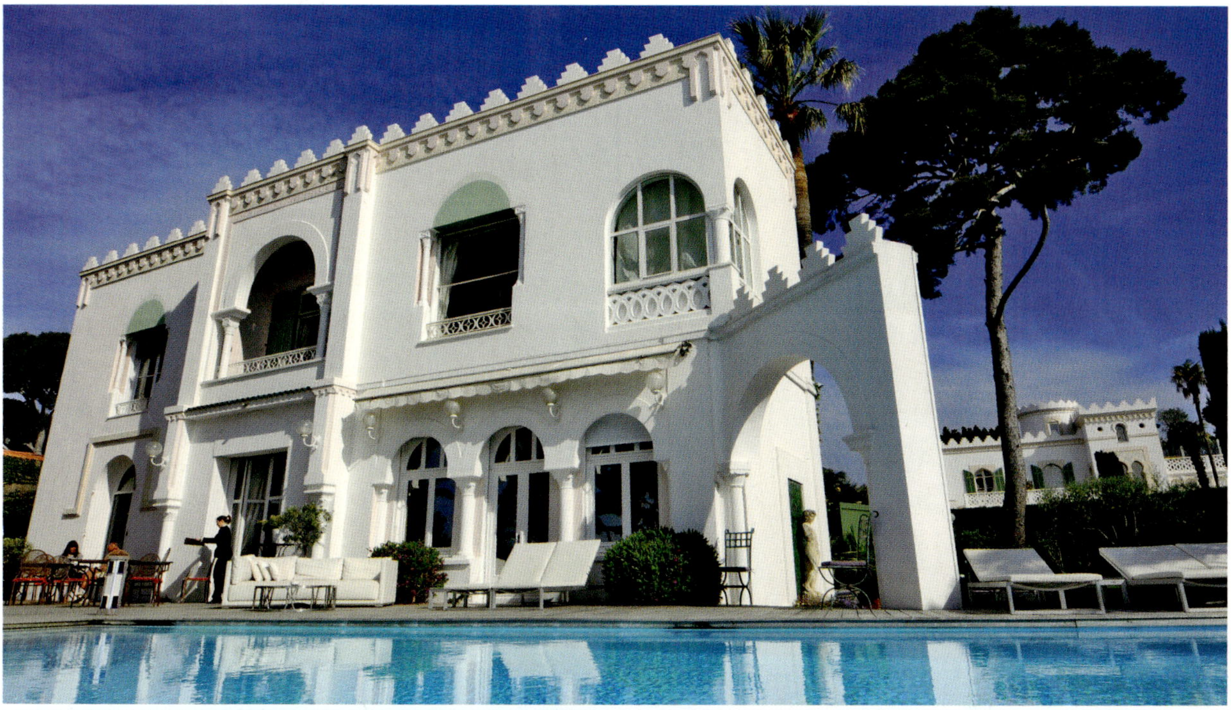

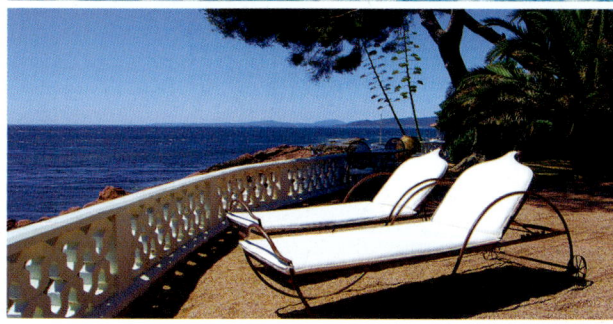

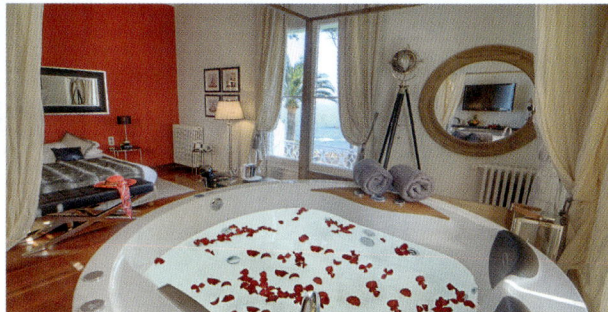

La Villa Mauresque

Intimacy and romance on the dreamy Côte d'Azur

Staying at La Villa Mauresque in St Raphaël on the French Riviera leaves you with just one concern: which fabulous nearby town to visit first? St Maxime, St Tropez or Cannes? This is certainly a superb spot to ruminate the decision in style. Luxuriously boutique, this 19th-century villa soaks up plenty of sunshine in its swoon-worthy seaside location that eagle-eyed TV fans will recognise as the twice-used location for The Bachelor (UK) reality show. Romance comes guaranteed! Rooms are affectionately named in memory of great writers and artists (Shakespeare, Monet, Baudelaire) and many cluster around the pool and terrace. Interiors update the villa with a subtle Moorish feel, keeping it airy and chic where in-room coffee machines, fresh fruit and a complimentary half bottle of Champagne welcome you. Outside, there's a hottub overlooking the Med and of course, the sea itself to explore. La Villa Mauresque happily rents out boats. Tip: stop off along the bay and go snorkelling in the crystal blue waters. By night, the Villa's Michelin-Starred Chef Philippe Nogier takes centre-stage in Le Bougainvillier restaurant. Blissfully beach-side, it captures the heady taste of the Riviera perfectly.

PRICE FROM:
€175

FEATURES:
Beach access; Gym; Pool; Restaurant

ACTIVITIES:
Fishing; Golf; Water sports

NEARBY:
Fréjus; Saint-Tropez; Cannes; Valescure Golf Course; Fréjus Roman theatre

GETTING THERE:
Nice Airport; Toulon-Hyères Airport; Marseille Airport

+33 494 83 02 42 ☎
condenastjohansens.com/mauresque 🌐
1792 route de la Corniche, 83700 Saint~Raphaël, 🏠
Côte d'Azur, France

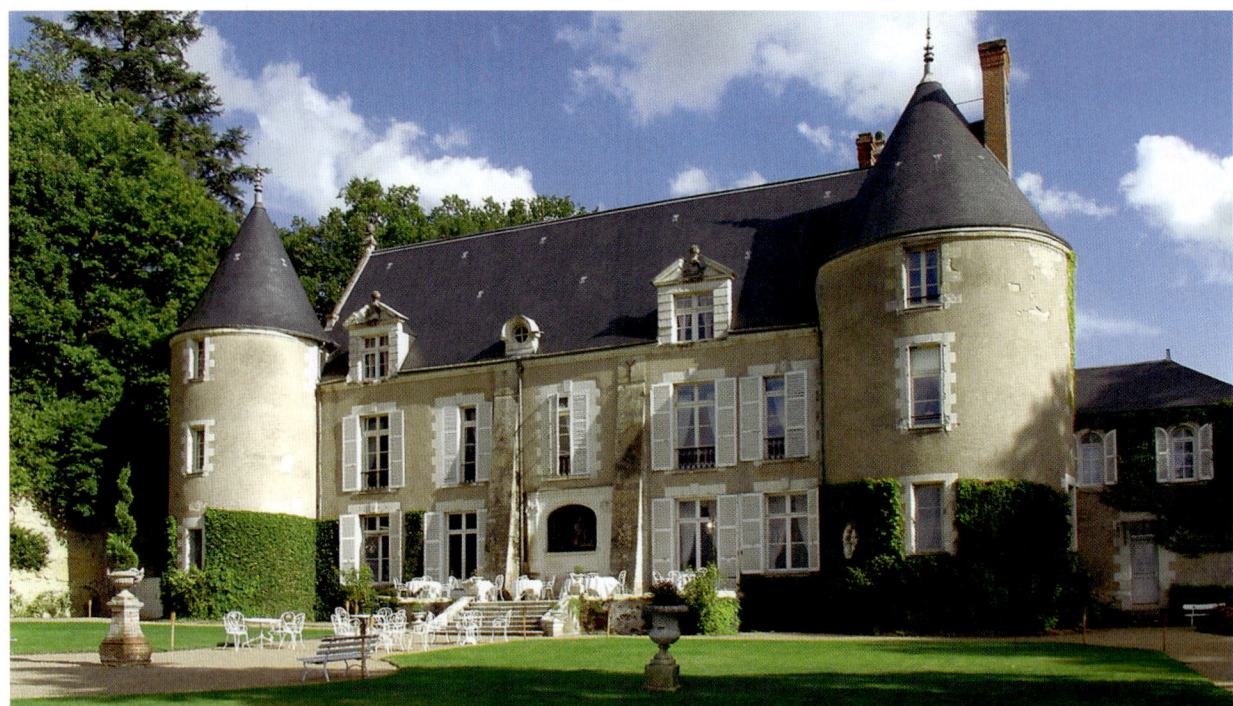

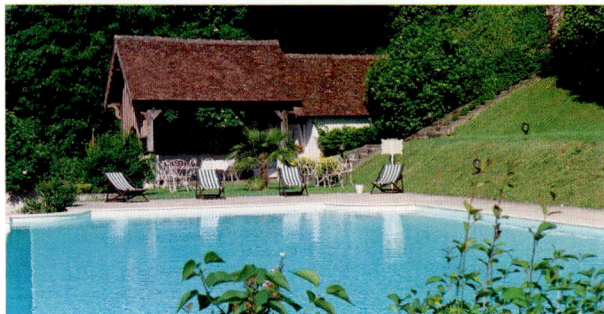

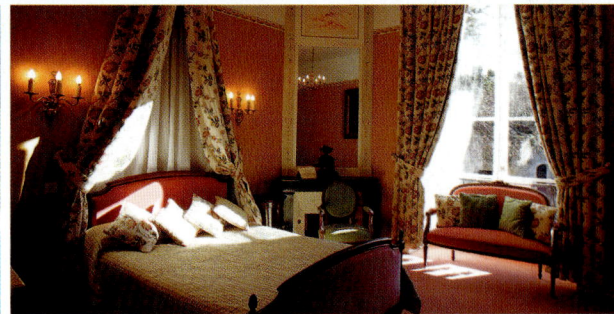

Château de Pray

Quintessential Loire Valley château

PRICE FROM:
€139

FEATURES:
Family friendly; Helipad; Michelin Starred restaurant; Pool

ACTIVITIES:
Fishing; Golf; Horse riding

NEARBY:
Amboise; Tours; Blois; Château d'Amboise; Loire Valley vineyards

GETTING THERE:
Tours Airport; Paris-Orly Airport

Love French château splendour but like a more boutique vibe? Take the best parts of the Loire Valley's finest châteaux, distil them into the perfect petite retreat and you have the miniature gem that is Château de Pray. With grey turreted towers, fairy-tale gardens and only 19 rooms, each guest is made to feel like a visiting dauphin. The staff is so thoughtful and attentive you feel they would lose sleep if your Champagne wasn't perfectly chilled! Which of course it is. Château de Pray is a beautifully preserved reminder of life in aristocratic France. As you walk by suits of armour and ancient coats of arms, you'll catch glimpses of the restaurant, a grand, baronial room where the Michelin-Starred food is served. Before sampling the gourmet delights of this gastronomic paradise, have a drink on the stone terrace overlooking the gardens or check out the walled kitchen gardens. Spend your days exploring the forests and enjoy the activities available at nearby Amboise from riding to sailing. It's the Château's pleasure to arrange adventures for even the smallest of guests with children enjoying their own thoughtfully designed activities menu while parents taste-test the delicious local wine.

☎ +33 247 57 23 67
🌐 condenastjohansens.com/chateaudepray
🏠 Rue du Cèdre, 37530 Chargé~Amboise, Loire Valley, France

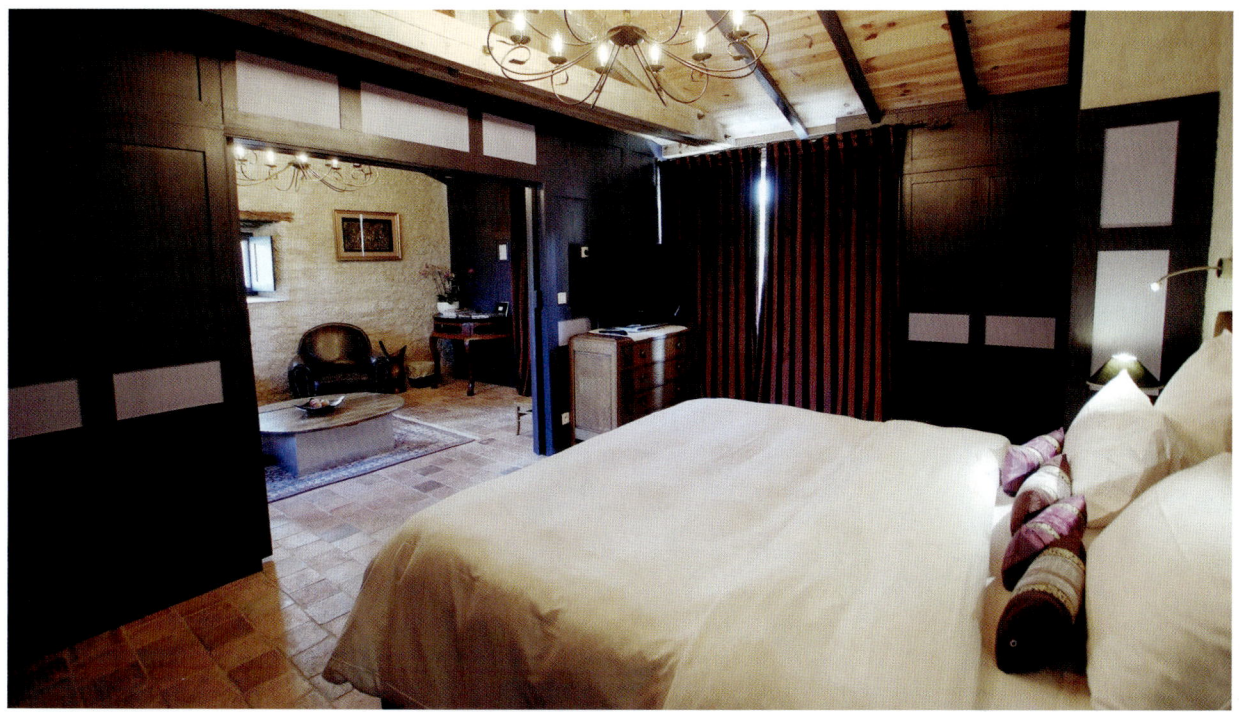

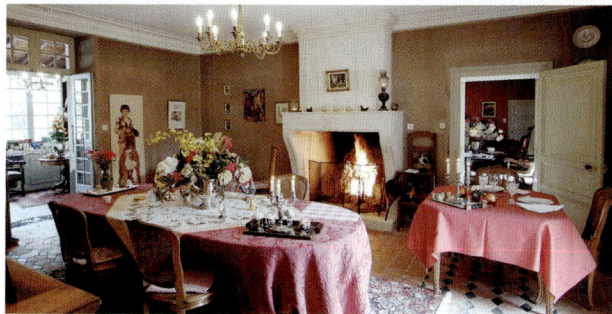

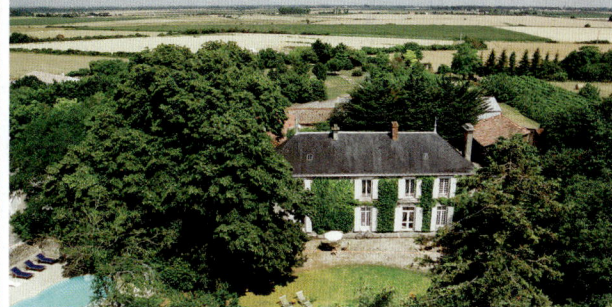

Château de l'Abbaye de Moreilles

Kicking back in La Rochelle made effortlessly easy

A cheeky little number this, the Château de l'Abbaye, Moreilles. Travellers swing by as they head south to Bordeaux or the Dordogne and depart wistfully. What first appears as a modest country château with a spirited host in Madame Renard reveals itself as a bewitching rustic bolthole with a seriously laid-back attitude. Madame and her family draw you into their home where you'll eat off-menu so it's rather like having a wonderful personal chef who conjures up regional or delicate Thai-infused flavours on a nightly basis. And the rooms and suites are beautifully designed with space and style to suit couples and families alike. A slightly off-beat room choice is the purely fantastical Richelieu Suite (a former outbuilding of the Cistercian abbey) with immense circular bed, star-studded bathroom ceiling and private outdoor sitting area while others beckon with Jacuzzis made for two. The children are welcome here, free to run wild in the gardens' lush green acres. But if you're travelling à deux "adult love games" discretely placed in wardrobes are yours to discover. Take a swim in the heated outdoor pool, spend some time checking out nearby Marais Poitevin with canal trips and antique shopping or nip across the water to Île de Ré for some delicious moules and huîtres. There's something for everyone.

PRICE FROM:
€99

FEATURES:
Family friendly; Pet friendly; Pool; Restaurant

ACTIVITIES:
Cycling; Golf; Sightseeing

NEARBY:
Île de Ré; La Rochelle; Les Sables d'Olonne; Le Marais Poitevin; Atlantic Coast beaches

GETTING THERE:
La Rochelle Airport; Nantes Airport; Bordeaux Airport

+33 251 56 17 56 ☎
condenastjohansens.com/chateaulabbaye 🌐
85450 Moreilles, Loire Valley, France 🏠

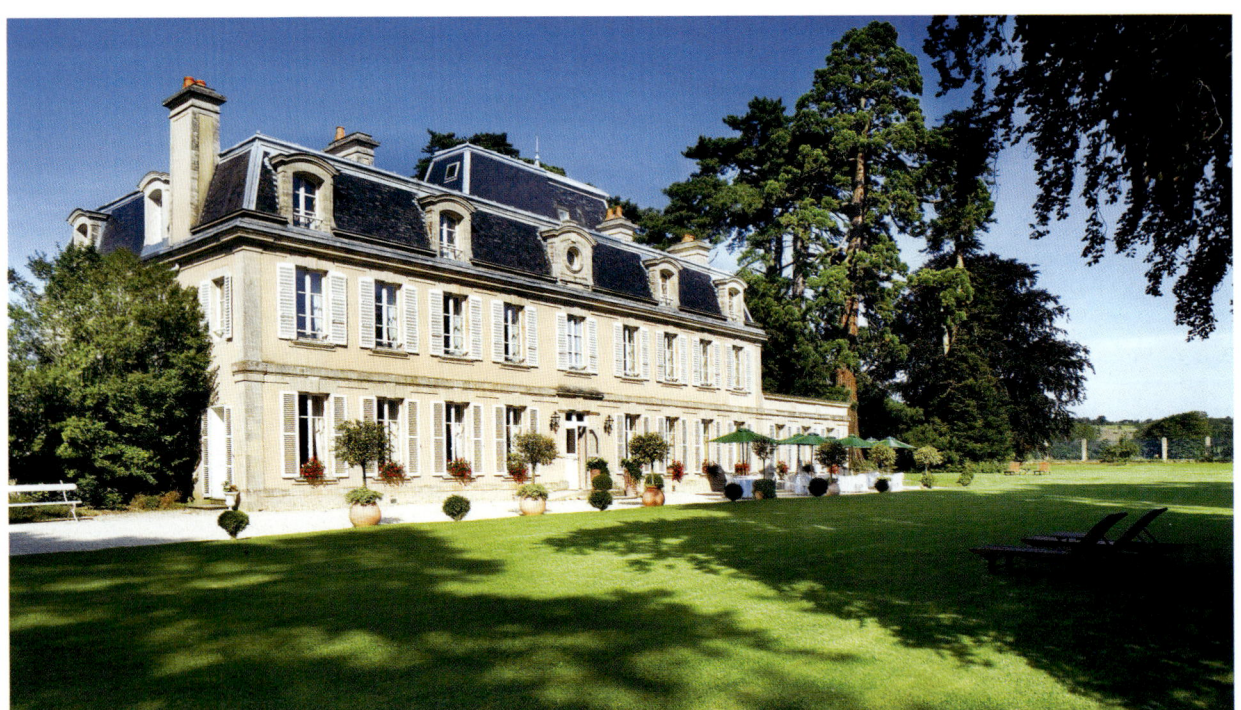

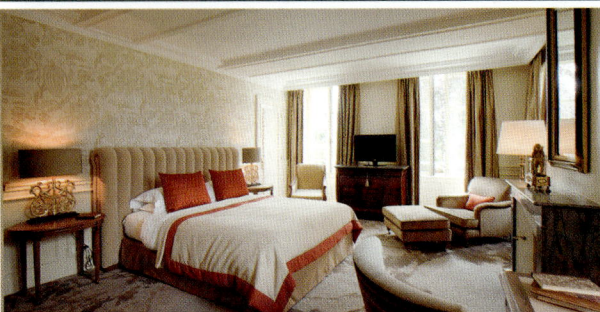

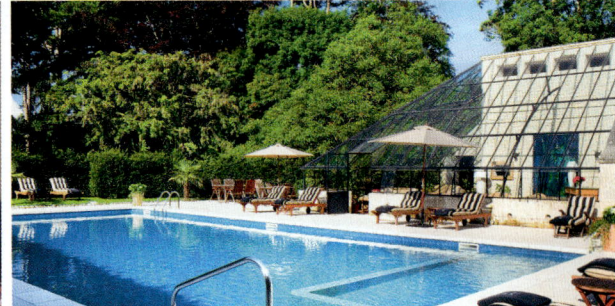

Château la Chenevière

Pretty-as-a-picture Normandy château

PRICE FROM:
€270

FEATURES:
Helipad; Pet friendly; Pool; Restaurant; Wheelchair access

ACTIVITIES:
Cycling; Golf; Sightseeing

NEARBY:
Normandy coast; Omaha beach and the D-Day Landing Beaches; Port en Bessin; Golf Club; The Bayeux Tapestry

GETTING THERE:
Caen Airport; Paris-Charles de Gaulle (Roissy) Airport; Paris-Orly Airport

An 18th-century stunner, Château la Chenevière in Normandy ticks all the boxes. Grand yet welcoming... fabulous morning coffee and pastries... comfy yet elegant furnishings... It's the epitome of Gallic country house charm. Following check-in (the easiest on record) you'll no doubt want to explore. Smiley staff will very sweetly equip you with a chart detailing the acres of landscaped grounds. Or there's the tennis court and heated pool beside the startlingly modern Orangery (a grand homage to the Louvre's glass pyramids when lit up) to keep you busy on-site. History hounds will be in their element here. Château la Chenevière's own history reads like a novel: occupied by the Germans during WWII; in 1944 the Americans then took residence. And the surrounding areas of Caen and Bayeux are awash with things to see and do; the Normandy American cemetery at Omaha beach being just one of them. For active types, the Château can pinpoint the perfect sand yachting, horse riding and golfing spots. But you're in France, so be sure to enjoy the good food accompanied by great wine in the chic surroundings at the Château's dazzling restaurant.

☎ +33 2 31 51 25 25
🌐 condenastjohansens.com/lacheneviere
🏠 Escures - Commes, 14520 Port~en~Bessin, Normandy, France

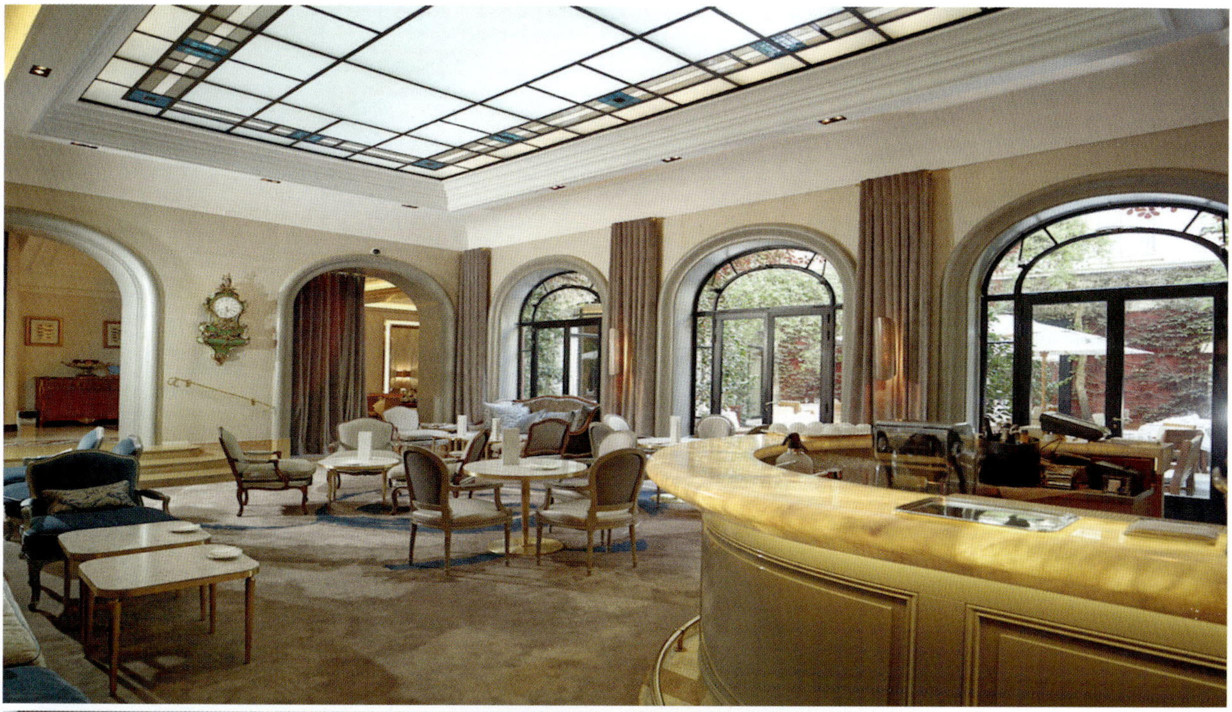

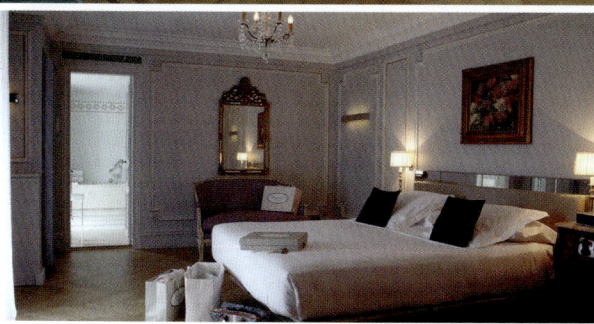
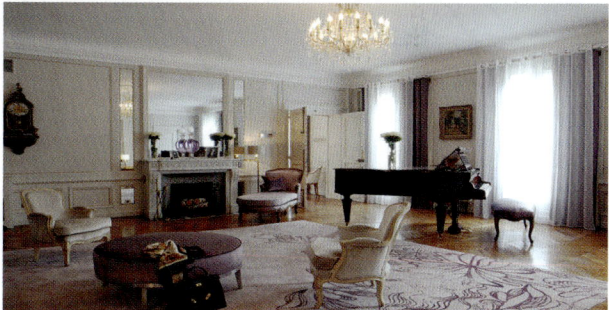

Hôtel Lancaster

Gasp-worthy Parisian town house hotel in the Golden Triangle

Located in one of the most famous and fashionable areas of Paris (and possibly the world), Hôtel Lancaster regally stands tall a stone's throw from Champs-Elysées. Where luxury, grandeur and genteel glamour meet in the most romantic city of the world, Hôtel Lancaster is a lesson in refinement and good taste. Ornate antiquities and just-picked flowers effortlessly feature alongside every much-needed mod con whilst culinary magic is cast at the Michelin-Starred restaurant, La Table du Lancaster. Hôtel Lancaster's Chef Julien Roucheteau whips up an artistic, seasonal menu in intimate surrounds, enjoyed perhaps after an expertly prepared cocktail in the 1930s-inspired bar where plush velvet armchairs welcome tired feet after a day's sightseeing and shopping. Perfect for a romantic weekend break or for those who want to experience the real Paris, Hôtel Lancaster really does offer it all. This is prime city location with iconic Parisian landmarks such as the Avenue Montaigne, Avenue George V and Rue du Faubourg Saint-Honoré all within a short stroll. A favourite haunt with the 1930s "A" list, (Marlene Dietrich loved Hotel Lancaster), this is THE destination for experiencing timeless Parisian decadence and style by the Louis Vuitton bag-full.

PRICE FROM:
€390

FEATURES:
Family friendly; Gym; Michelin Starred restaurant; Pet friendly

ACTIVITIES:
Shopping; Sightseeing

NEARBY:
Avenue des Champs-Elysées; Arc de Triomphe; Place de la Concorde; Louvre Museum; Eiffel Tower

GETTING THERE:
Paris-Orly Airport; Paris-Charles de Gaulle (Roissy) Airport

+33 1 40 76 40 76 ☎
condenastjohansens.com/hotellancaster 🌐
7 Rue de Berri, Champs~Elysées, 75008 Paris, France 🏠

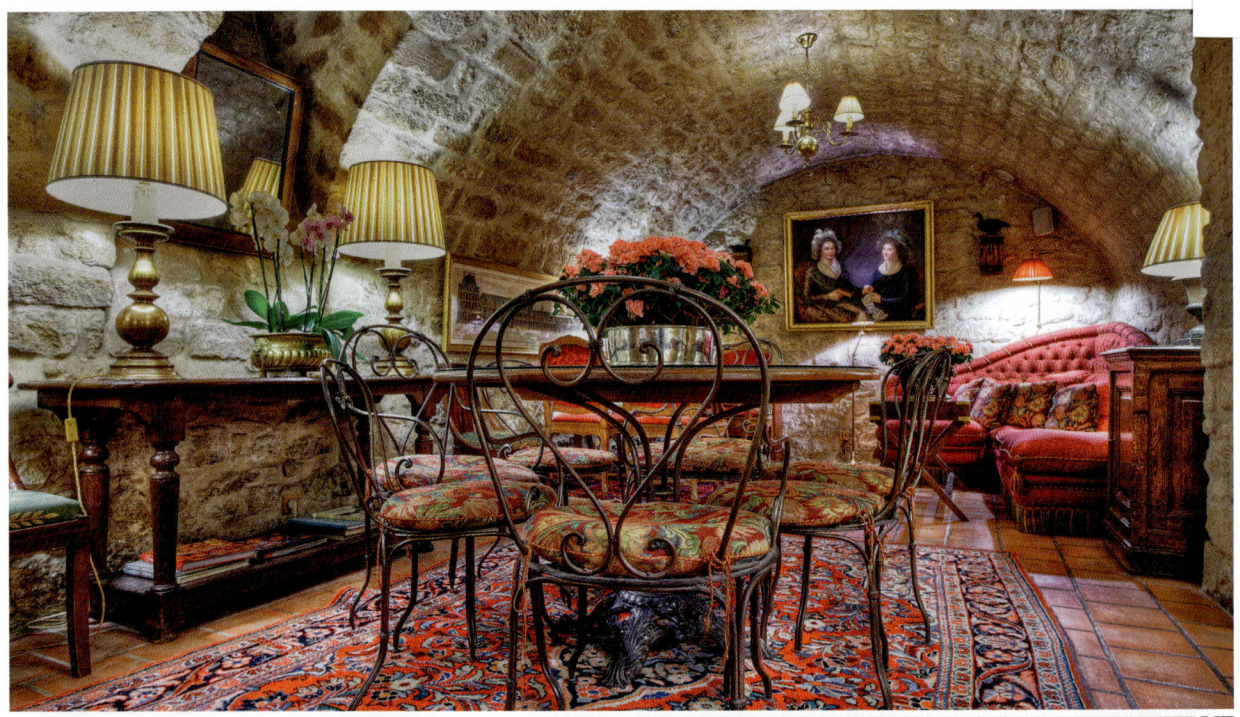

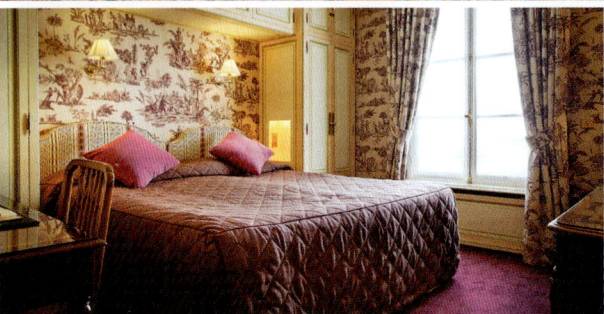
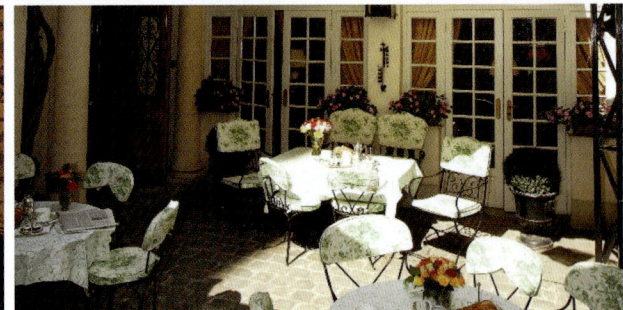

Hôtel Duc de Saint~Simon

Quintessential French sanctuary in peaceful, central Paris

PRICE FROM:
€275

ACTIVITIES:
Shopping; Sightseeing

NEARBY:
Saint-Germain-des-Prés; Musée d'Orsay; Notre-Dame de Paris

GETTING THERE:
Paris-Orly Airport; Paris-Charles de Gaulle (Roissy) Airport

Hôtel Duc de Saint-Simon is that rare find: a serene spot amid the ebullience of Saint-Germain's buzzing bars, bistros and bakeries. This 18th-century town house nestles discreetly in Paris' über-chic Left Bank, a short stroll from the Musée d'Orsay and a multitude of architectural glories and literary hotspots. The dedication to relaxation at Duc de Saint-Simon is beguiling. Exhausted explorers are rewarded with obliging service and splendid surroundings. Plush fabrics and exquisite antiques in the deep-chaired salon, birdsong in the courtyard, vaulted stone ceiling in the breakfast room – this is Parisian comfort at its most charming (fear not tech-lovers, complimentary WiFi is all around). Bedrooms are bijoux but deliciously deluxe, decorated in rich Jouy prints and tones, with splashes of gingham or leopard-print. Sleek en-suite bathrooms contain luxuriant bathrobes and plenty of character. For more space opt for a sumptuous suite but wherever you lay your head at Hôtel Duc de Saint-Simon, you'll get a restorative night's sleep. Tranquillity in such an animated city is precious indeed.

☎ +33 1 44 39 20 20
🌐 condenastjohansens.com/saintsimon
🏠 14 rue de Saint~Simon, 75007 Paris, France

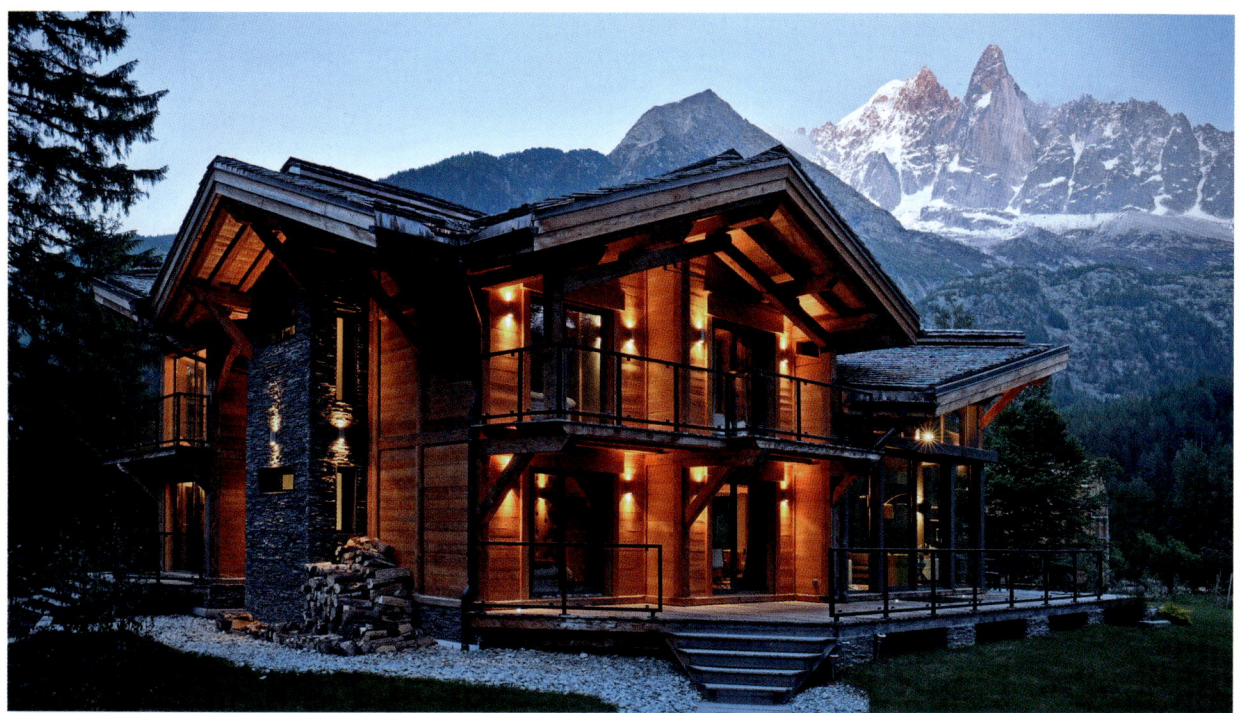

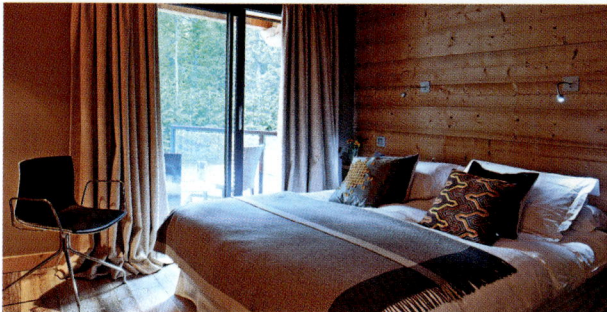
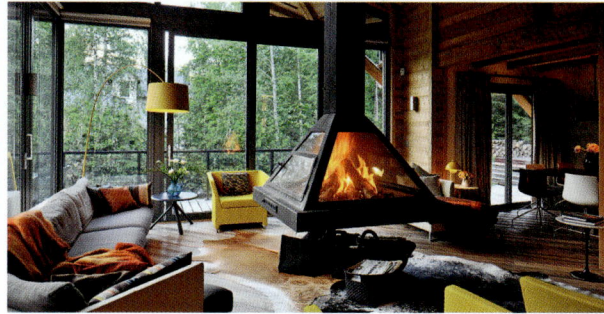

Chalet Cragganmore

The ultimate fully-hosted Alpine mountain chalet

Odes of appreciation for Chalet Cragganmore, Chamonix should be penned. At the very least a little ditty in honour of its mere existence should be composed. Simply put, it's worth shouting about. Available on an all-or-nothing basis, (the Chalet sleeps 12 people so choose your companions carefully – those not invited may hold a grudge) it goes one step beyond. Nothing's average here. Jennifer Martin is the force behind its creation, a regular skier to this age-old snowy playground (Chamonix was host to the first Winter Olympics in 1924) who discovered a fellow-spirit in local architect Renaud Chevallier. Jennifer's vision of a high-end chalet resort offering bespoke packages in both winter and summer was realised in 2008. With Renaud's left-field thinking, he took Jennifer's concept and turned the traditional chalet design on its head. No bombardment of wooden walls and enclosed spaces but rather a mass of floor-to-ceiling windows (triple glazed!) and über-cool interior design. A stay at Chalet Cragganmore means all your activities are taken care of - as adrenaline-pumping or as lazy as you wish – tailored meals are prepared by professional chefs and discrete staff are on-hand whenever desired.

PRICE FROM:
£5,000 (per week)

FEATURES:
Family friendly; Gym

ACTIVITIES:
Golf; Skiing; Walking

NEARBY:
Cormayeur, Italy; Geneva, Switzerland; Chamonix Ski Resort; Chamonix Golf Club; Viewpoint from Aiguille du Midi Cable Car

GETTING THERE:
Geneva Airport, Switzerland

+44 (0)131 556 3296 ☎
condenastjohansens.com/chaletcragganmore 🌐
355 Chemin des Glieres, 74400 Chamonix, Rhône~Alpes, France 🏠

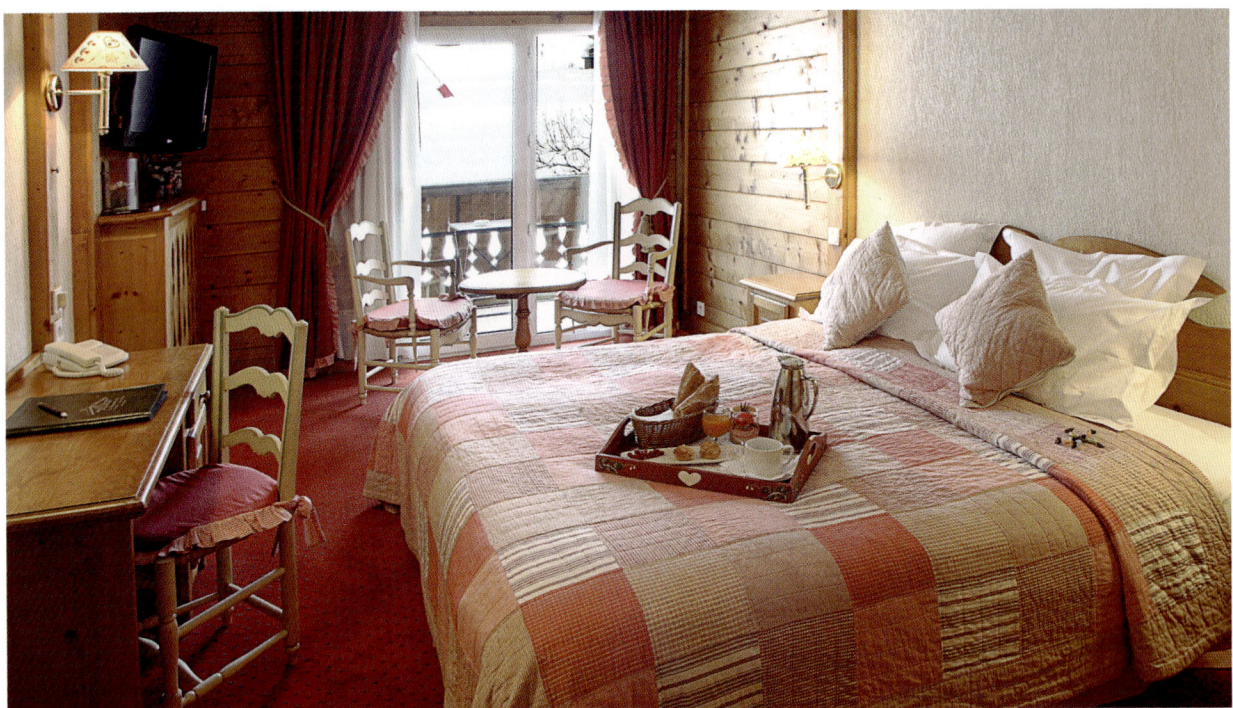

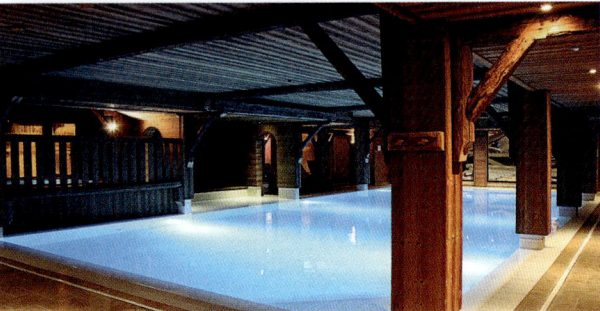

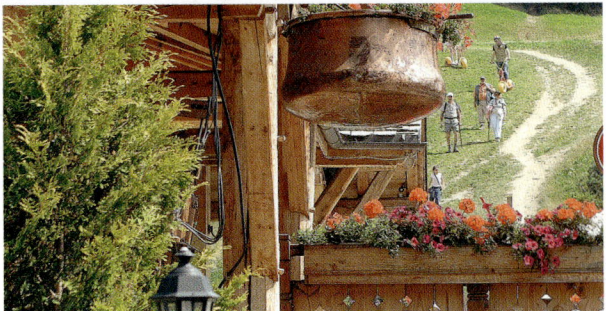

Chalet Hôtel La Marmotte, Ski, Golf & Spa

Rhône~Alpes getaway for outdoor loving families

PRICE FROM:
€244

FEATURES:
Family friendly; Pet friendly; Pool; Restaurant; Spa

ACTIVITIES:
Cycling; Golf; Skiing

NEARBY:
Geneva, Switzerland; Portes du Soleil Ski Area; Bike park; Lac de Baignade; Golf des Gêts

GETTING THERE:
Geneva Airport, Switzerland; Lyon Saint-Exupéry Airport

Chalet Hôtel La Marmotte, Ski, Golf & Spa delivers a quintessential French Alps experience; a refined rusticity in a supreme location by snowcapped mountains. Located in part of the charming Haute-Savoie village of Les Gêts, which hosts events including age-old French festivals and chocolate workshops, this is a mountain escape that's a provincial wonderland for relaxation and respite. At the foot of the Mount Blanc slopes there's La Marmotte whose hallmarks are its unquestionable comfort and intimate ambience. A reinvigorating revamp to its lounge, bar, reception area, kitchen and playroom is bringing a welcome freshness to the interior. While most-spoiling guest rooms in reds, ambers and traditional Savoyard architecture have cloud-like beds, thick cushiony throws and a whole mass of carved, cosy wood furnishings. Soft lighting in these snuggly bedrooms make for relaxing at the end of a day's skiing, golfing or spa-ing extra easy. The recently renovated restaurant champions local produce within its traditional favourites and modern dishes whilst overlooking a sweeping panoramic view of the glistening slopes (pick a spot by the crackling fire for a supremely sublime experience). A sense of peaceful opulence envelops you when you dine here by candlelight while the kids are busy having fun in the children's dining room (complimentary until 9:30pm).

☎ +33 4 50 75 80 33
🌐 condenastjohansens.com/marmotte
🏠 61 Rue du Chêne, 74260 Les Gêts, Rhône~Alpes, France

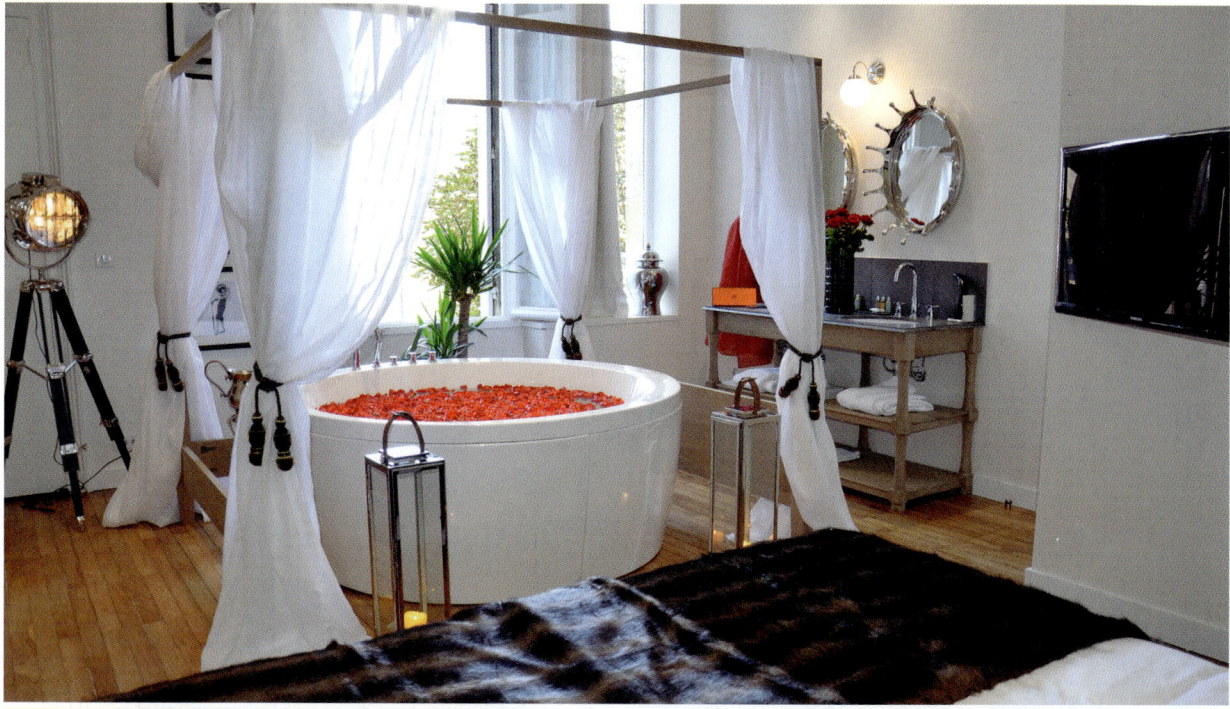

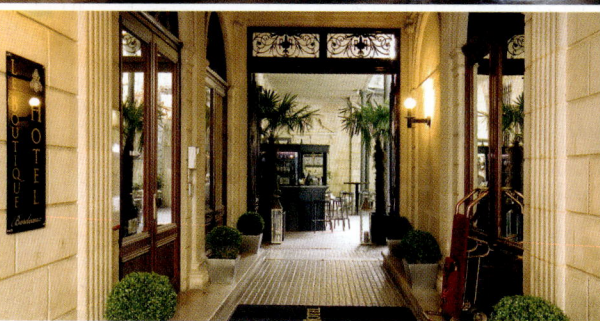
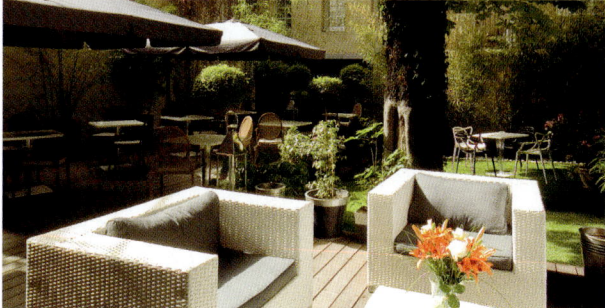

Le Boutique Hotel Bordeaux

Boutique Bordeaux B&B with the kooky factor

Bringing brave new design to the grande dame of the wine world, Le Boutique Hotel Bordeaux mixes a fine vintage with a modern finish. Tucked into Bordeaux's wonderful old city, this inviting town house is not afraid to have fun with plenty of contemporary curios to prove it. White spaces with high ceilings and lofty windows are scattered with Philippe Starck chairs, lit by cinematic-style lamps, and feature fluffy cushions alongside natural skin throws. Le Boutique Hotel Bordeaux is never too cool for its own good (well ok, one suite's Jacuzzi has coloured lighting and an underwater sound system) and it seems to have thought of everything. You can even request a comforting hot water bottle on cooler evenings! But there's no mistaking you're in vino-heaven with rooms named after wine-producing châteaux and wine-themed artwork adorning the walls. So where better to taste a drop of the red/white potion than in Le Boutique Hotel's wine bar? The enthusiastic sommelier will recommend glass by glass for you and enhance your choice with a careful selection from a range of cheeses and charcuterie. Nearby you'll find an endless number of great restaurants, so take the opportunity to stroll out to dine and wander Bordeaux's wide boulevards and the banks of the Garonne.

PRICE FROM:
€169

FEATURES:
Pet friendly; Restaurant; Wheelchair access

ACTIVITIES:
Fishing; Golf

NEARBY:
Historic city centre; Bordeaux vineyards; Bay of Arcachon; Dune of Pyla

GETTING THERE:
Bordeaux Airport

+33 5 56 48 80 40
condenastjohansens.com/hotelbordeaux
3 Rue Lafaurie de Monbadon, 33000 Bordeaux, South West, France

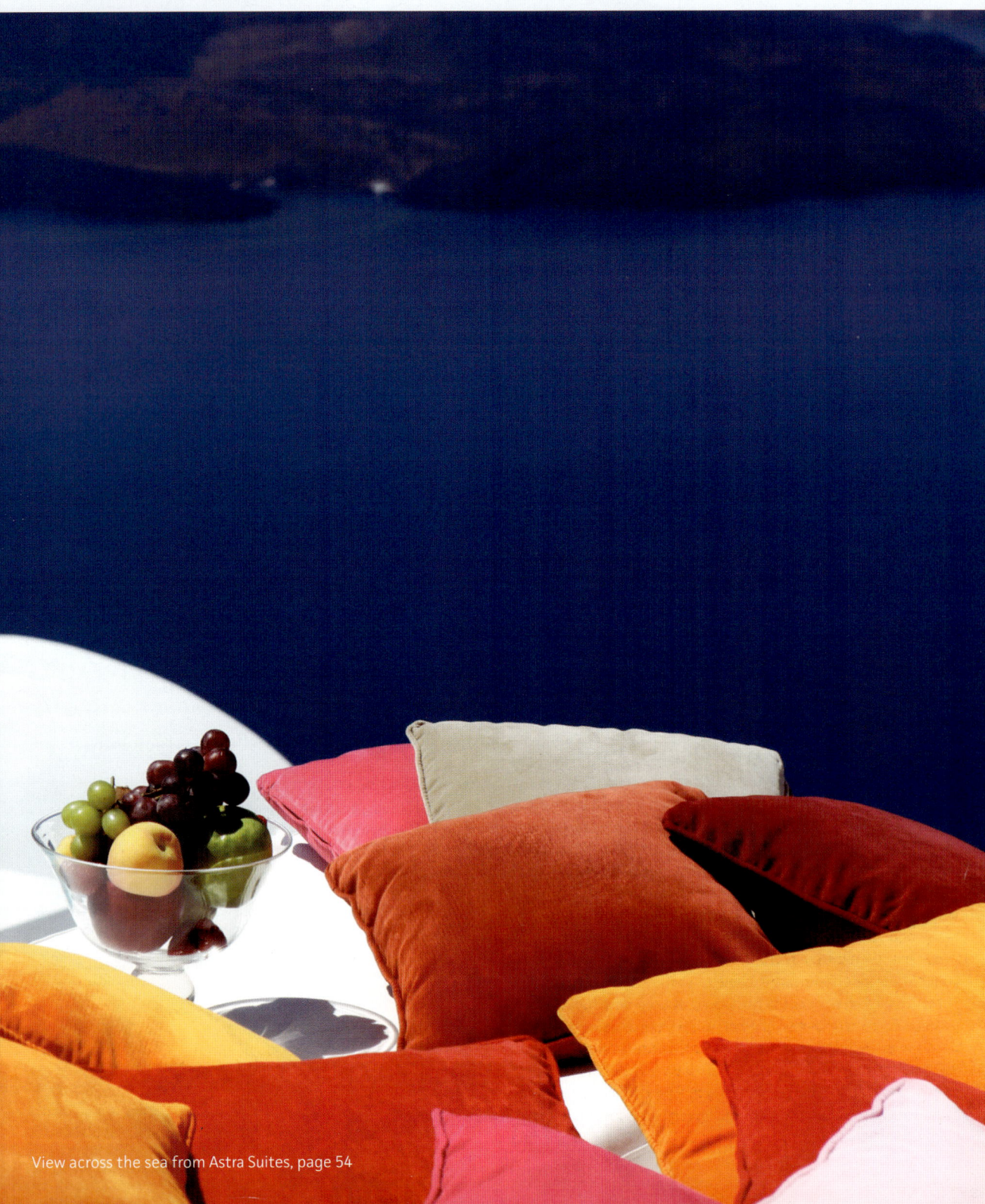

Greece

Please go to condenastjohansens.com/greece

View across the sea from Astra Suites, page 54

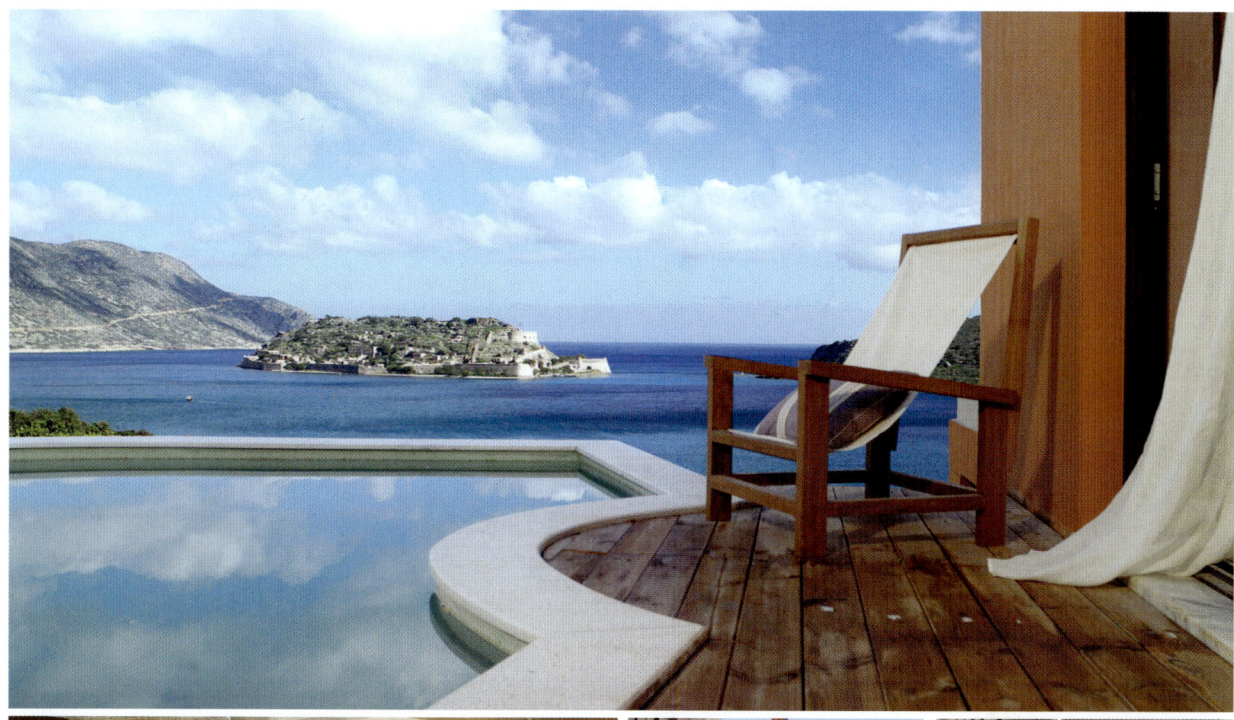

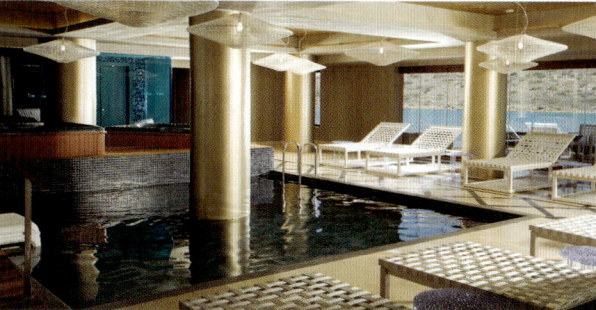
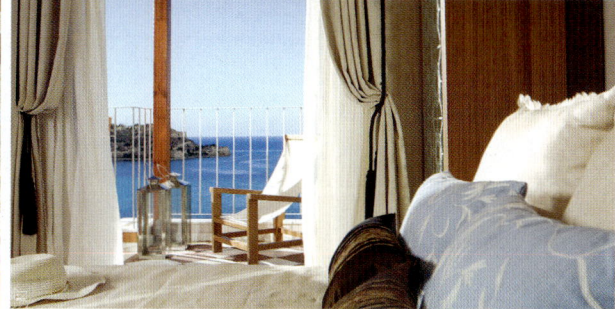

Domes of Elounda Boutique Beach Resort

Glorious villa resort on the bright Cretan coast

A peach and white confection of Moorish inspired architecture, Domes of Elounda Boutique Beach Resort is a Cretan villa complex with romance and relaxation on tap. Its fresh, Greek chic style indulges all your senses with views of Spinalonga Island from suites that take your breath away. Some accommodations are higher up on the hillside reached by nifty golf buggies, and large balconies and terraces max out on sights of Elounda Bay. Some have their own pool out to these blistering views with the private beach below that rarely that gets overcrowded. Children are hugely welcomed here and utterly spoilt by the friendly staff who will willingly fetch buckets and spades for the little darlings and keep them entertained at the UK Ofsted standard crèche and Kids Club. While the children are occupied, mum and dad can enjoy precious time together and in the spa or savour a dinner for two (the babysitting service takes care of the children during the evening). The Domes' alfresco restaurants ooze laid-back sophistication whether you dine at Topos 1910 seafood restaurant or the à la carte Anthos. Scents of the delicious cuisine mingled with the gentle swaying of olive groves in the Cretan breeze will stay with you long after you've left. Top tip: visit during July and August to experience the Domes' annual gastronomic festival when internationally renowned chefs impart their knowledge.

PRICE FROM:
€230

FEATURES:
Beach access; Family friendly; Restaurant; Sea views; Spa

ACTIVITIES:
Fishing; Tennis; Water sports

NEARBY:
Aghios Nikolaos; Heraklion; Archaeological Museum of Aghios Nikolaos; Aghios Nikolaos port and lake; Spinalonga Island

GETTING THERE:
Heraklion Airport

+30 2310 810624 ☎
condenastjohansens.com/domesofelounda 🌐
Elounda, 72053 Crete, Greece 🏠

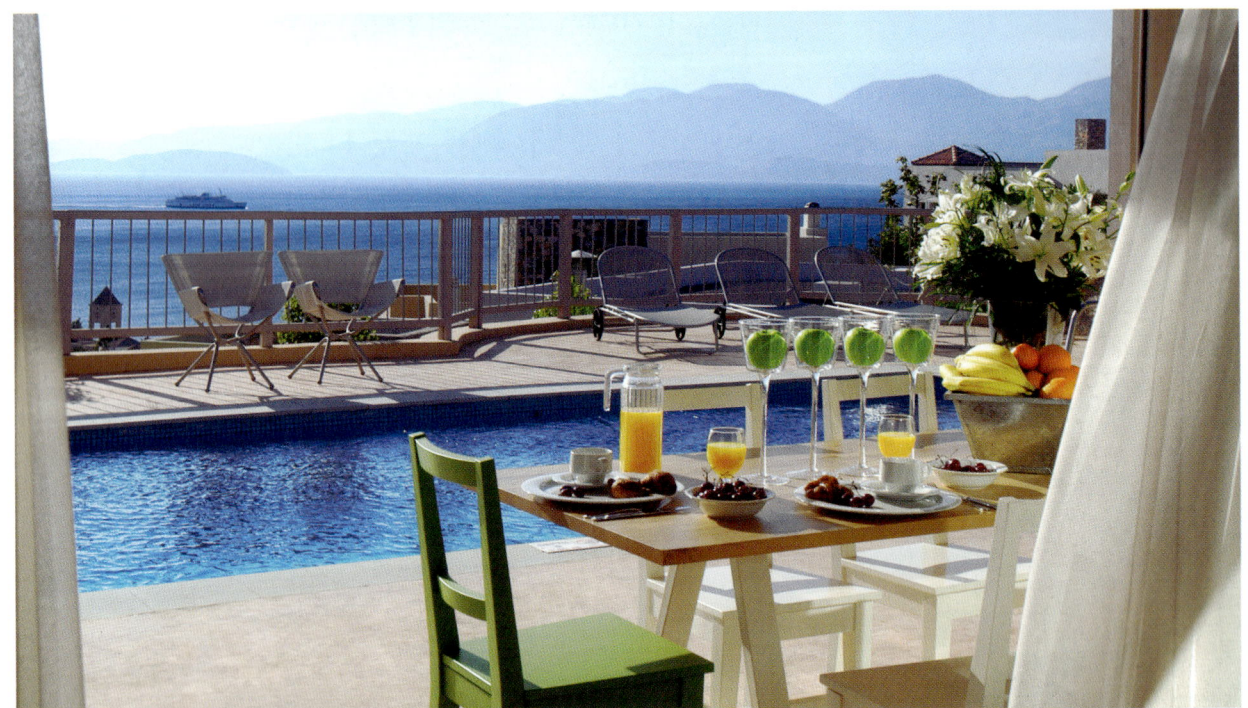

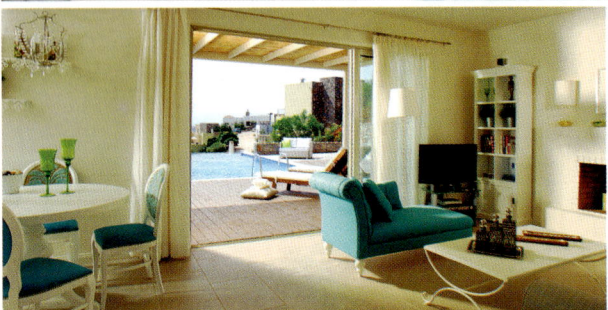

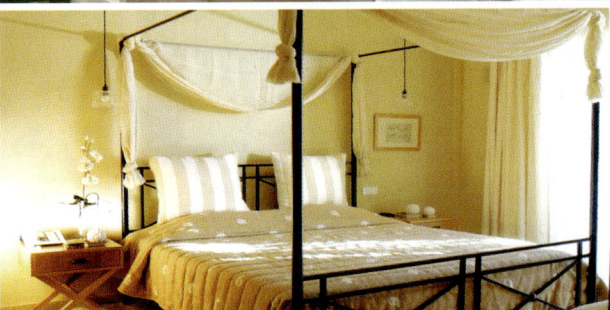

Pleiades Luxurious Villas

Your indulgent Cretan home-from-home

PRICE FROM:
€326 (self catering)

FEATURES:
Family friendly; Gym; Pet friendly; Pool; Sea views

ACTIVITIES:
Fishing; Golf; Horse riding

NEARBY:
Aghios Nikolaos; Elounda; Heraklion; Spinalonga Island; Aquaworld at Hersonissos

GETTING THERE:
Heraklion Airport

Paradise at the island's edge, Pleiades Luxurious Villas cling to Crete's hillside overlooking Mirabello Gulf. Spankingly plush and individually created by renowned designer Olyvia Siskou, each of the nine villas has its own pool, is beautifully furnished and comes spotlessly clean. Enjoy fully-hosted service (breakfasts can be booked, groceries delivered), set up home and feel thoroughly spoiled. Pleiades is fantastic for families or parties of friends holidaying together looking for villa accommodation with extra special touches. Split over two levels, Standard and Superior Villas have ample space for dining, relaxing and well, living. Their cool cocooning interiors open out onto large terraces so you can fire up the barbecue, take a swim or idly admire the dazzling views all in your own time. The Pleiades team is always on hand for recommendations on what to do and where to eat or you can simply head on into bustling Aghios Nikolaos or quieter Elounda and take your pick. (Greek meze and the local seafood are top-notch.) If you do manage to tear yourself from your terrace during the day, its worth going off the tourist track to explore Crete's little beaches and mountains or whizz away on a boat trip from Plaka to Spinalonga Island.

☎ +30 2310 810624
🌐 condenastjohansens.com/pleiades
🏠 72100 Aghios Nikolaos, Crete, Greece

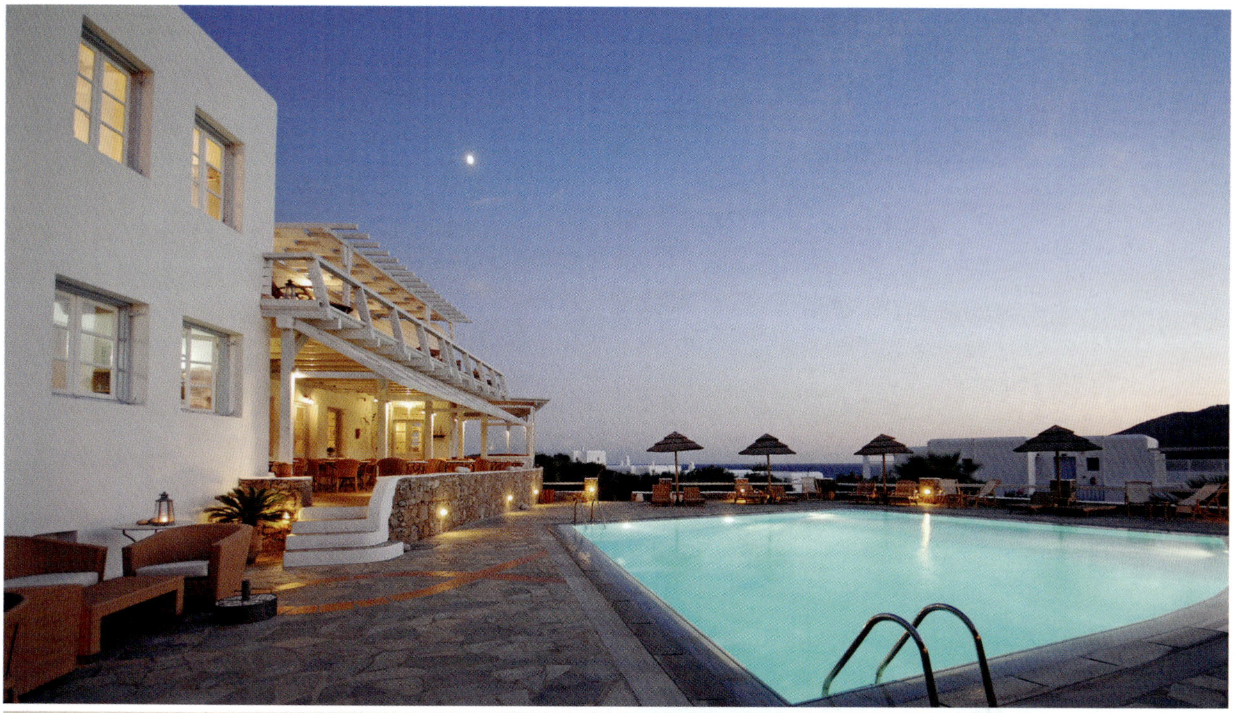

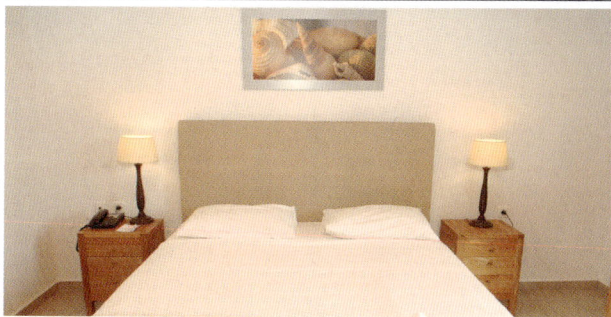

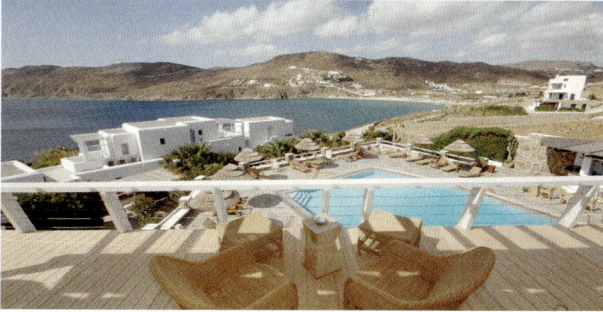

Archipelagos

Home-from-home Cycladic hotel moments from Kalo Livadi beach

Mykonos is a go-to destination for those hankering unadulterated Mediterranean magic. The tantastic can't get enough of the annual 300 days of sunny climes. Beach lovers adore the sandy shores. And hopeless romantics fall for its sugar-cube white building charm. Along the island's longest stretch of sandy beach is Archipelagos hotel, Mykonos, where every guest room and suite faces the Aegean and Kalo Livadi beach. Surprisingly peaceful considering its beauty, the beach is managed with unobtrusive efficiency (you'll never be without an umbrella or sun lounger) and from here water sport fiends can spend their days diving, jet-skiing, windsurfing and water-skiing. Just ask the staff at Archipelagos to help with arrangements. If horse riding is more your style enquire about taking a trot around the island on one of the hotel's horses. Then refuel at Archipelagos' restaurant where fine Greek dishes and Mediterranean classics are prepared from ingredients carefully selected from local producers. However, honeymooners might prefer to take advantage of the room service - and possibly enjoy butler assistance during their stay. After all, each sea-view room has a balcony or terrace with startlingly gorgeous vistas.

PRICE FROM:
€100

FEATURES:
Family friendly; Gym; Pool; Restaurant; Sea views

ACTIVITIES:
Horse riding; Water sports

NEARBY:
Ano Mera; Kalo Livadi beach; Byzantine Monastery of Ano Mera; Shopping in Mykonos town

GETTING THERE:
Mykonos Airport

+30 228 907 2012 ☎
condenastjohansens.com/archipelagos 🌐
Kalo Livadi, 84600 Mykonos, Greece 🏠

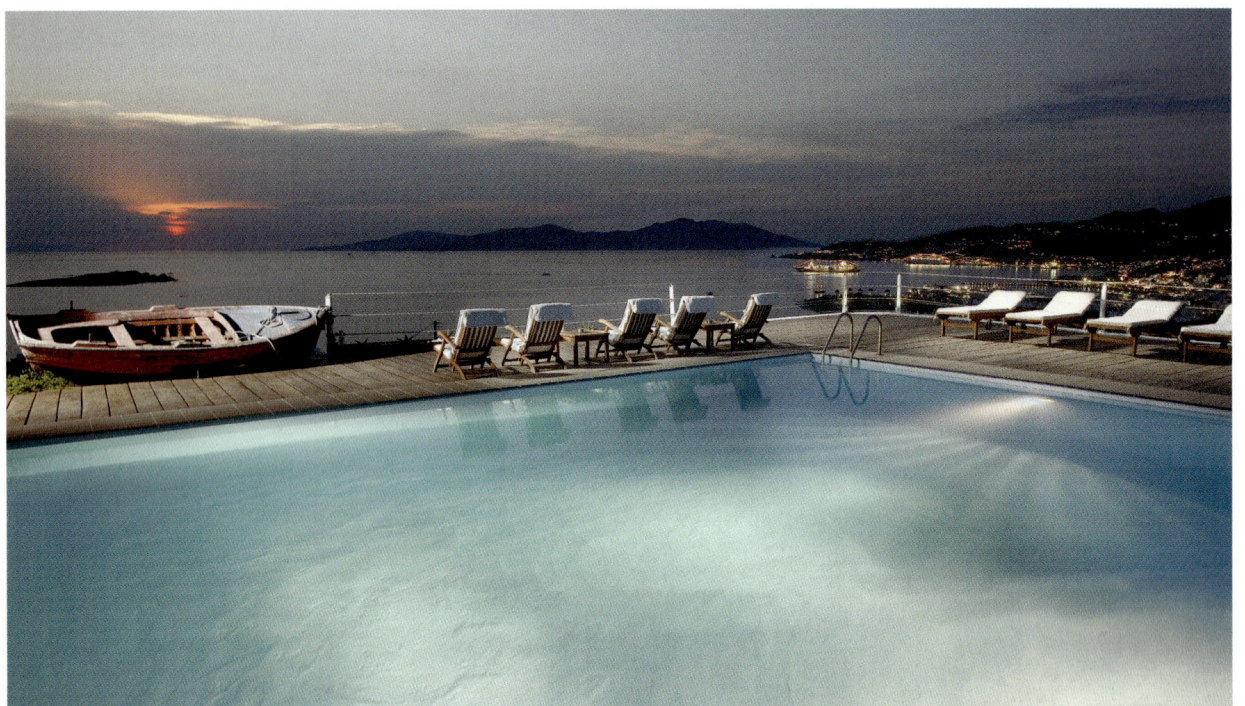

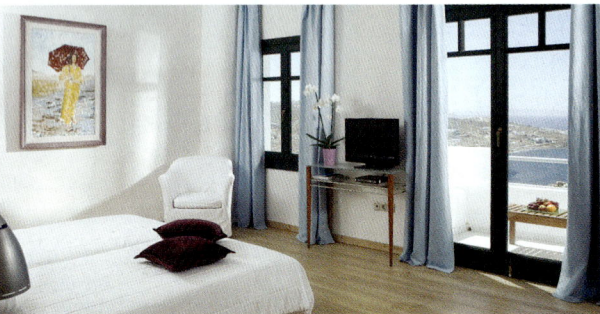

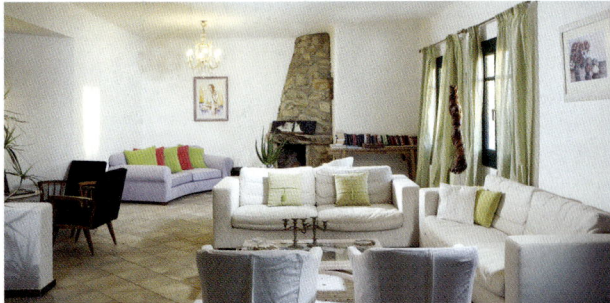

Tharroe of Mykonos

Traditional Mykonos marries contemporary flair

PRICE FROM:
€125

FEATURES:
Beach access; Family friendly; Pool; Restaurant; Sea views

ACTIVITIES:
Fishing; Horse riding; Water sports

NEARBY:
Delos Island; Tinos Island; Fabrika Square; Ornos beaches; Little Venice

GETTING THERE:
Mykonos Airport

☎ +30 22890 27370
🌐 condenastjohansens.com/tharroe
🏠 Mykonos Town, Angelica, 84600 Mykonos, Greece

Pitch up at boutique hotel Tharroe of Mykonos to escape or get the party started. Oozing laid-back, arty sophistication, the Tharroe is the perfect base to explore Mykonos that's reinvented itself as a Greek chic boho hangout for those in the know. Celeb-watch at Paradise or Psarou beaches or simply enjoy spectacular poolside views back at the hotel. Tharroe of Mykonos sits atop a small hill gazing over the Aegean and captures traditional Myconian romance with contemporary edge. Rooms and suites are light and airy, mixing fresh, colourful fabrics with classic furniture. Some raise the modern stakes even higher with mid-century design touches and Jacuzzi baths; most feature patios or balconies. The hotel is also a testament to good old fashioned Greek hospitality. Whether they're serving delicious Mediterranean dishes in the Barbarossa restaurant, booking you a spin in a convertible or mixing a mean cocktail on the glamorous pool terrace, the Tharroe team cannot help enough. Check out the wine-tastings, tête-à-tête dinners and book a pampering alfresco massage. A trip to Mykonos town is worth it for the shopping, famous windmills and nightlife. Then return to Tharroe in time for breakfast and those glorious sunrise vistas...

CONDÉ NAST johansens AWARD WINNER 2013

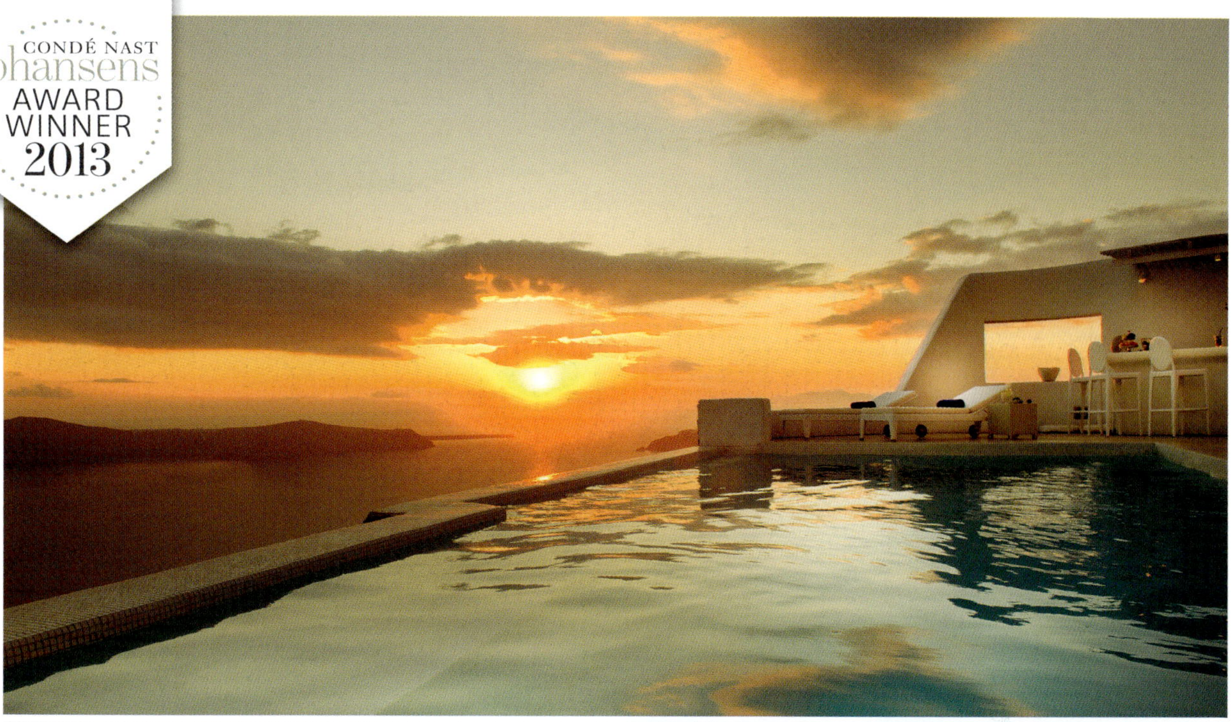

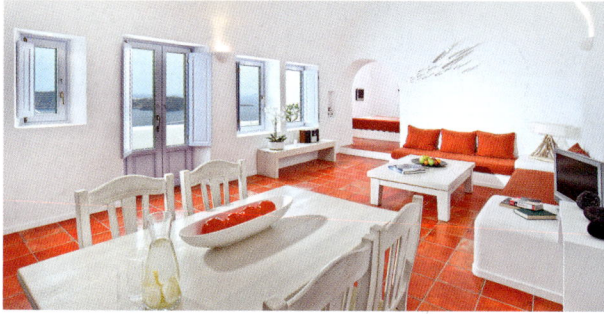

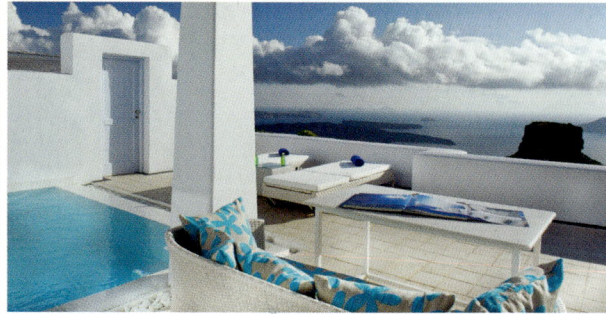

Astra Suites

Vertiginous, sultry Santorini suites

The divinity of Astra Suites, Imerovigli, is no Greek myth. For starters it's located on Santorini, rumoured to be the prettiest Greek island of them all. Then there's the bells and whistles that include relaxing spa treatments, crazy-comfy beds, above-and-beyond service and the most romantic atmosphere. All this and there's a heartbeat-skipping view of the caldera and Aegean at every turn. Whether staying in a standard or luxury suite, the flawlessly blue Santorini skyline and sea is your stunning view. Everything here impassions love. George the manager, and his staff, welcome you into this heavenly retreat where champagne flows, rose petals are sprinkled, chocolates offer temptation and a Jacuzzi bubbles in anticipation. And if that's not enough, Astra chef's culinary delights deliver Greek and Mediterranean flavour in the bucket-load. It doesn't matter where you choose to dine, in the restaurant or on your own balcony, you're guaranteed the best seat in the house at sunset. Astra will have you believe in Utopia after all.

PRICE FROM:
€250

FEATURES:
Pool; Restaurant; Sea views

ACTIVITIES:
Sightseeing

NEARBY:
Fira; Oia; Caldera; Beaches; Akrotiri excavation site

GETTING THERE:
Santorini Airport

+30 22860 23641
condenastjohansens.com/astrasuites
Imergovigli, 84700 Santorini, Greece

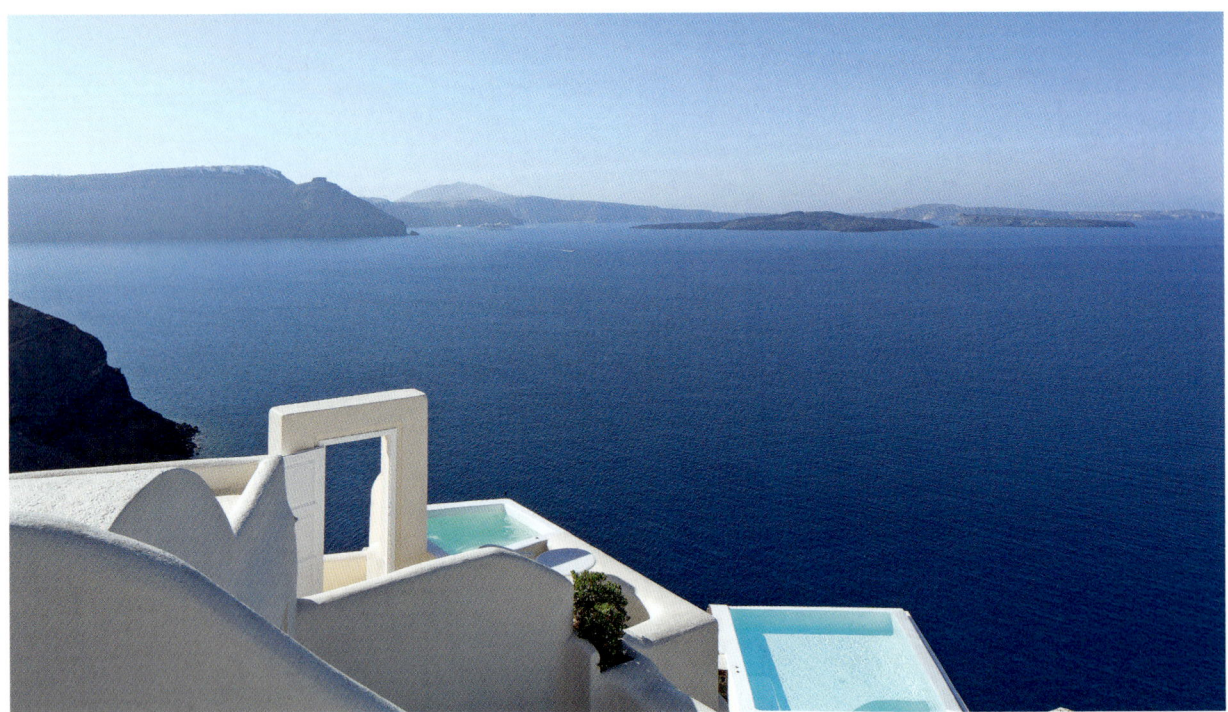

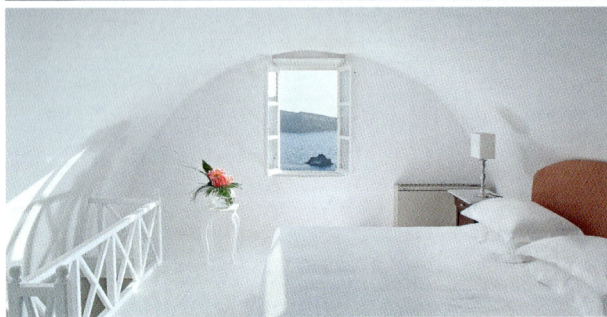

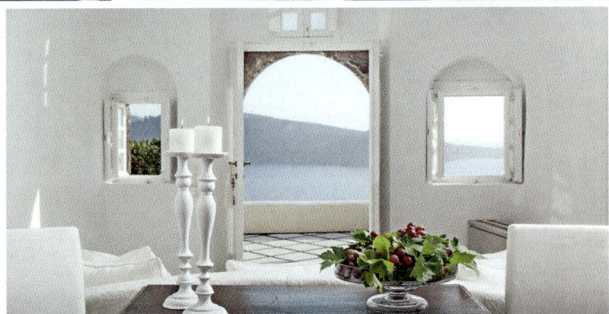

Canaves Oia Suites

All-suite, all-singing, all-dancing Santorini stunner

PRICE FROM:
€380

FEATURES:
Pool; Restaurant; Sea views; Wheelchair access

ACTIVITIES:
Shopping; Sightseeing; Water sports

NEARBY:
Fira; Pyrgos; Caldera; Traditional vineyards; Ancient sites of Thira and Akrotiri

GETTING THERE:
Santorini Airport

All the flattering superlatives describing Santorini are true. But what's not commonly known is that the best scenic spot on this Aegean island is arguably its north-west corner looking down to the famous caldera from the village of Oia. More specifically, Canaves Oia Suites whose collection of 22 suites doesn't miss an inch of this poetic panorama. Part of the luxury Canaves Hotel Oia, the Canaves Oia Suites complex resides next door with its very own infinity pool, bar, poolside restaurant and utterly romantic Petra Gourmet Restaurant (just three tables). It also has the only hotel lift on this undulating island. From junior and superior to the honeymoon suites, a recent renovation has given each space a refreshing boost with splashes of colour and antique furnishings in bold contrast against the pure white walls. However, the property's pride and joy is the split-level Canaves Suite accommodating up to five adults. This two-bedroom, two-bathroom deluxe den features bonus luxuries such as a sauna, private pool, dining area, living room and spacious veranda with unparalleled views. When gazing out to the rippling waves has you itching to be riding them, ask reception about Canaves' private motor yacht and speed boat. Both are available for excursions. Catamarn sailing trips too.

☎ +30 22860 71453
🌐 condenastjohansens.com/canavesoiasuites
📍 84702 Oia, Santorini, Greece

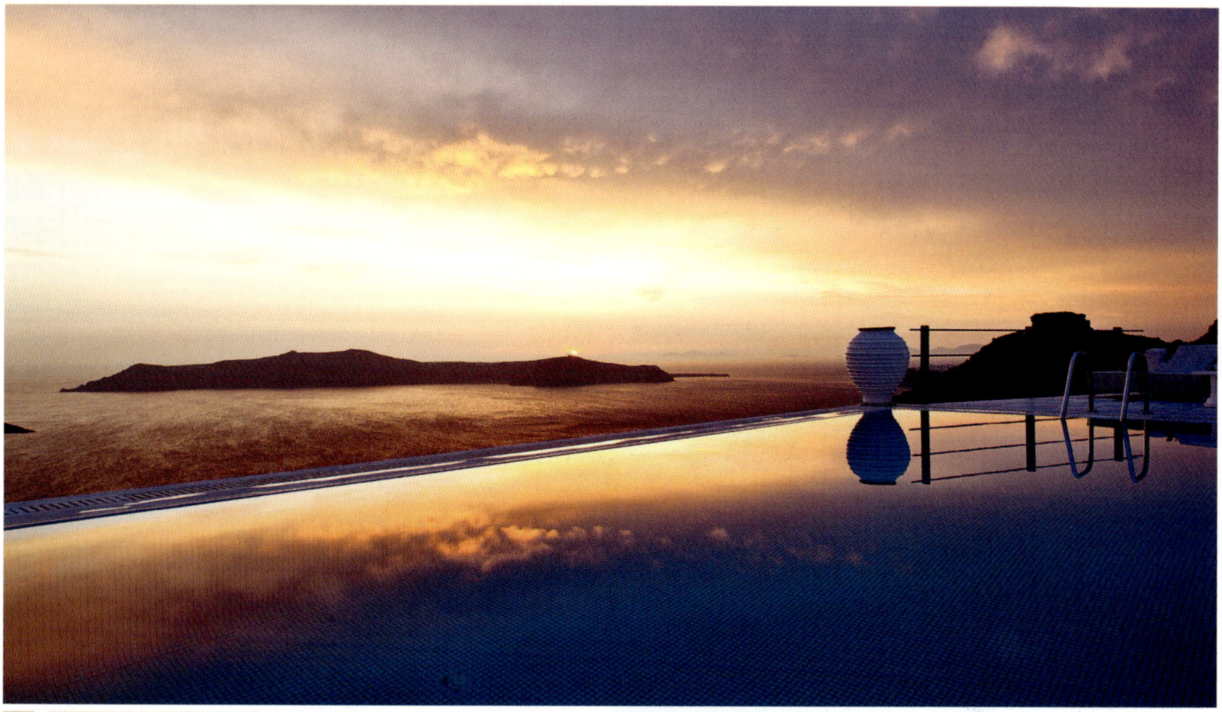

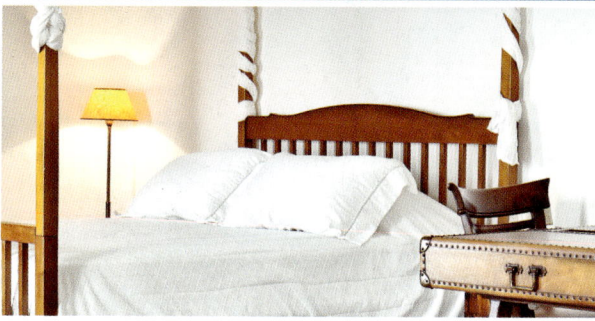

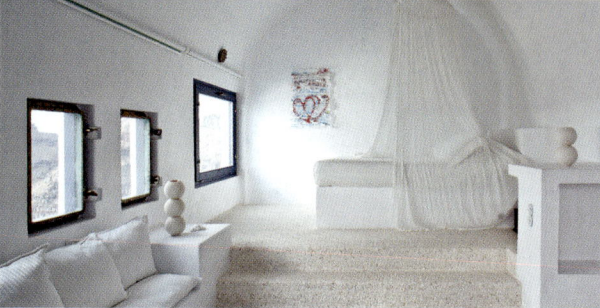

Homeric Poems

Exclusive, contemporary Santorini cliff-side living

Homer + epic = Homeric. It's the only word big enough to describe the views from this minimalist masterpiece carved from the cliff face of Firostefani. Overlooking nothing but the calm, blue Aegean and famous caldera of stunning Santorini, the boutique Homeric Poems is opulent, stylish and more than worthy to bear the name of the only man able to encapsulate the beauty of Santorini in words. Start your own Greek odyssey as you choose your room. Clean, modern lines and a strong focus on comfort is the order of the day here, whether you choose an apartment or a Grand Suite complete with private pool. Buzzing nearby Fira is the island's capital and party hub, whilst the utterly chilled-out Homeric Poems provides relaxed drinks at the bar and Greek specialities at Tastes of Homer, the Poems' restaurant. The chef is so talented he moonlights as a judge on Greece's Masterchef. The gorgeous Greek cuisine can be served on your own private terrace as you gaze into the endless Aegean. Who knows, you may inspired to pen a few lines of your own...

PRICE FROM:
€334

FEATURES:
Family friendly; Pool; Sea views

ACTIVITIES:
Shopping; Sightseeing; Walking

NEARBY:
Fira; Oia; Traditional wineries; Traditional village of Pyrgos; Ancient site of Akrotiri

GETTING THERE:
Santorini Airport; Santorini Port

+30 22860 24661 ☎
condenastjohansens.com/homericpoems 🌐
Firofestani, 84700 Santorini, Greece 📁

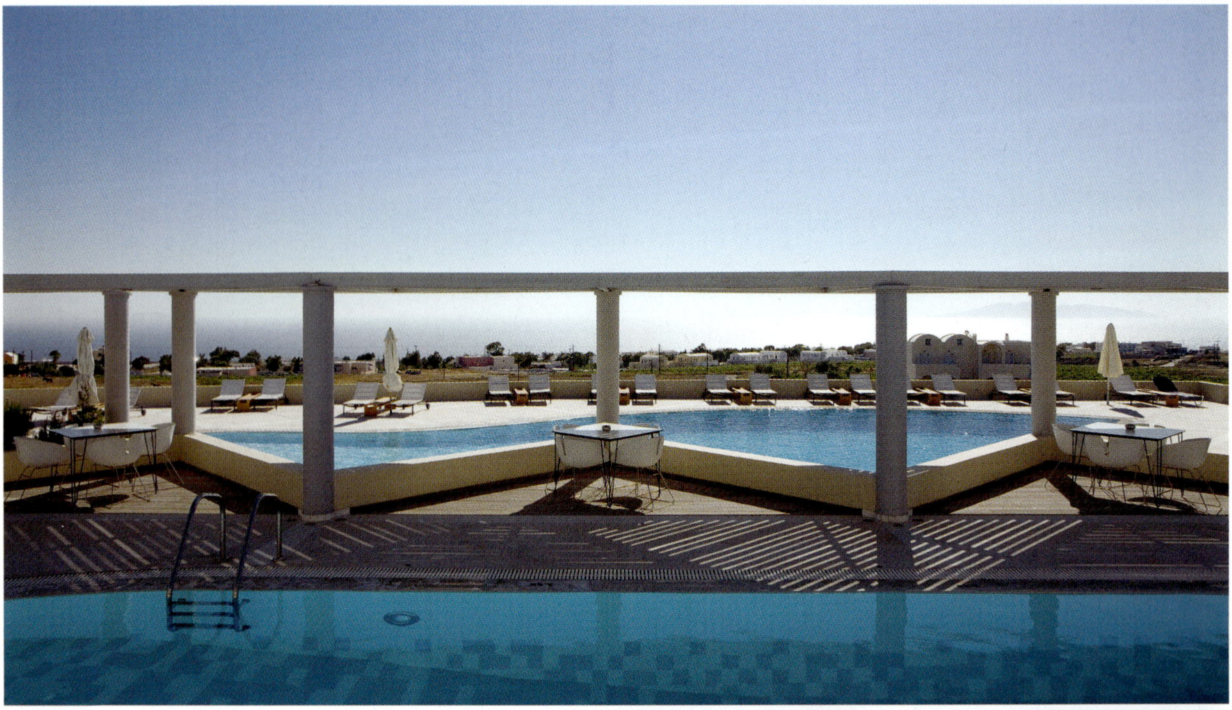

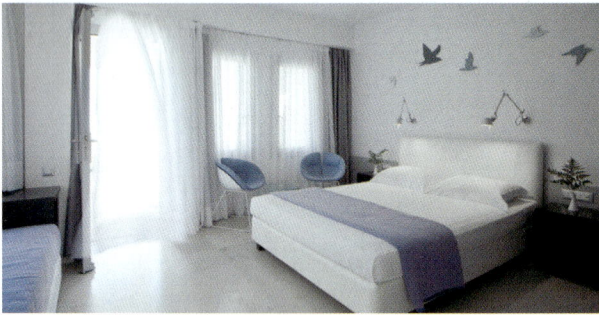
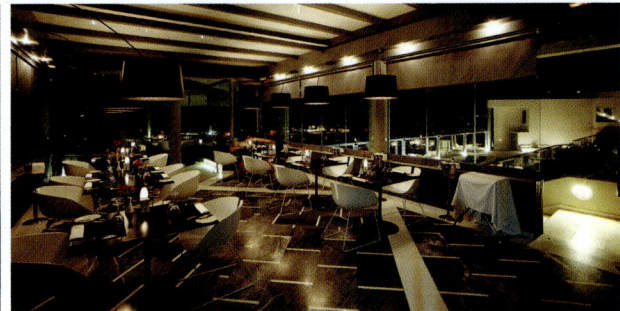

Hotel Majestic

A breath of fresh air in Santorini's fashionable Fira

PRICE FROM:
€160

FEATURES:
Family friendly; Gym; Restaurant; Sea views; Wheelchair access

ACTIVITIES:
Fishing; Horse riding; Water sports

NEARBY:
Pyrgos; Oia; Traditional vineyards; Ancient sites of Thira and Akrotiri

GETTING THERE:
Santorini Airport

Seemingly sponsored by angels, Santorini's Hotel Majestic deserves every twinkle of its five-star rating. A heaven-on-earth nestled in the heart of the Mediterranean, your divine journey begins with complimentary limo pick-up followed by a rest in accommodation so sprawling there's space for an in-room Jacuzzi. Pampering - maybe a massage or beauty therapy - before dinner at the Majestic's gourmet restaurant Crocus, completes the indulgent picture. Alternatively, there's locally sourced, organically-grown gastronomic delights on the à la carte menu at Capparis and the ultimate chilled-out Grand Lounge. The hotel is located a short walk from the lively island capital, Fira where shabby meets chic and old befriends new in a medley of artisan shops, quaint cafés and picturesque backdrops. It's no surprise Santorini is Greece's most photographed island. Back at base, the Majestic's technogym and choice of pools can see off any guilt felt after a relaxing afternoon at one of Santorini's cherished vineyards or days spent enjoying sea or volcano views from the veranda of your luxury room. Soundproofed, rooms are kitted out with free WiFi, flatscreen tvs and iPod docking stations. Top tip: hire a quad bike to see the island.

☎ +30 22860 25972
🌐 condenastjohansens.com/hotelmajestic
🏠 Fira, 84700 Santorini, Greece

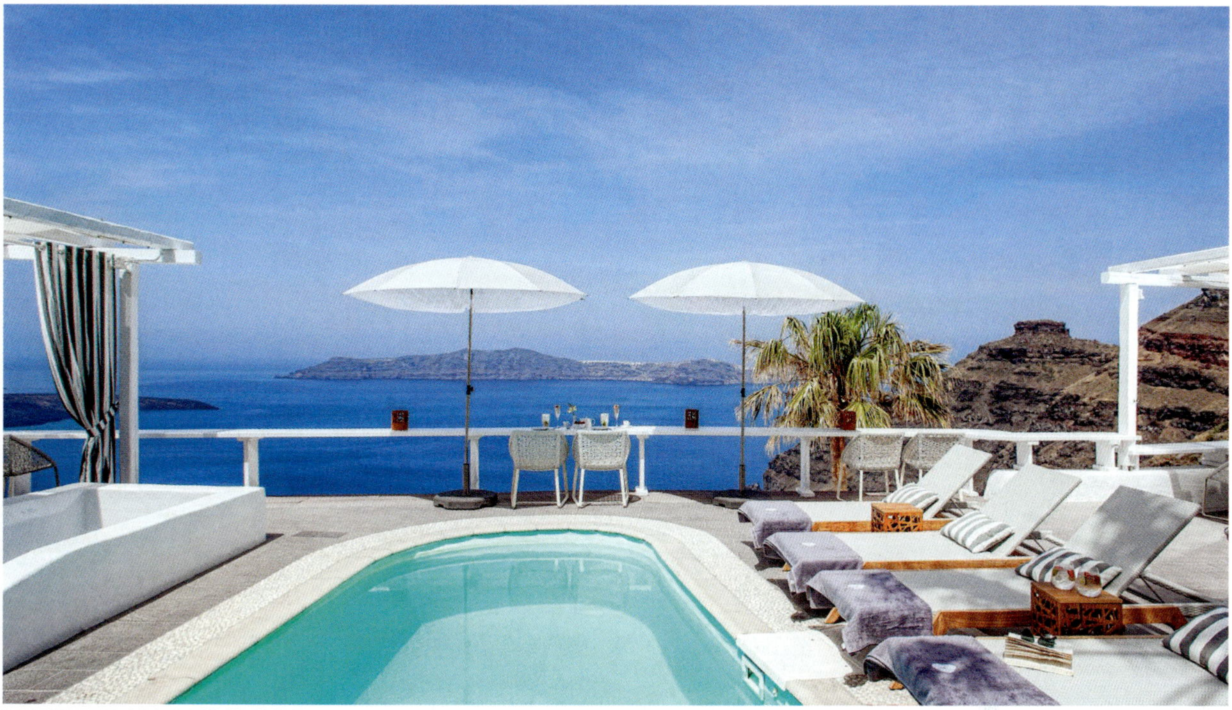

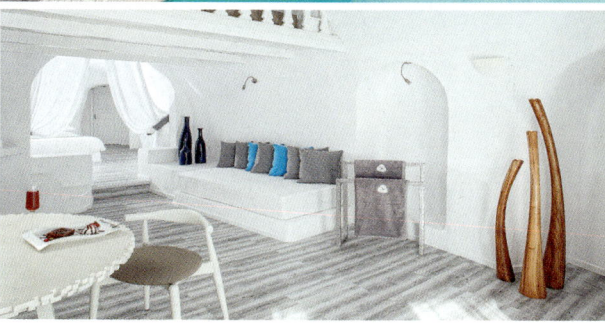
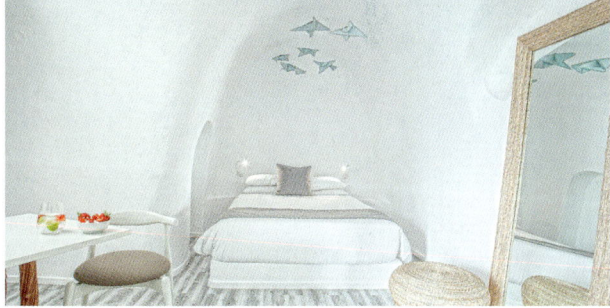

Mill Houses elegant suites

Sultry and seriously spectacular Santorini honeymoon haven

300 metres above the dazzling azure blue of the Aegean are the whitewashed Mill Houses elegant suites perched on the volcanic cliffs of serene Santorini. Pack your sunglasses because you're in for a sensory overload of bright white buildings, intense blue sea and luminous multi-coloured sunsets. There's nothing drab about this Greek island. Everywhere you look there's a picture-perfect view, whether it's the Aegean, the famous caldera of Santorini or the surrounding green islands. And at Mill Houses elegant suites the selection of studios and suites deliver the best of both worlds: the chance to explore the nearby Fira and Firostefani's buzzing nightlife while enjoying fabulous full hotel services and feasts packed with flavour at the quirky Mylos Café (a converted windmill serving sophisticated international food and Santorini specialities). A candlelit supper overlooking the caldera is just about the most romantic experience possible, and don't forget to sample the local wines. 5,000 years in the making, Santorini's wine is rightly celebrated. With every 21st-century luxury provided, it's easy to forget how ancient this island is with monuments, churches and ancient sites everywhere you look. Luckily there's a team of Mill Houses therapists on hand to provide a fabulously indulgent, in-room massage after a hard day's exploring.

PRICE FROM:
€110

FEATURES:
Pool; Restaurant; Sea views

ACTIVITIES:
Fishing; Horse riding; Water sports

NEARBY:
Pyrgos; Fira to Imerovigli caldera walking path; Traditional vineyards; Oia village; Ancient sites of Thira and Akrotiri

GETTING THERE:
Santorini Airport

+30 22860 27117 ☎
condenastjohansens.com/millhouses 🌐
Firostefani, 84700 Santorini, Greece 🏠

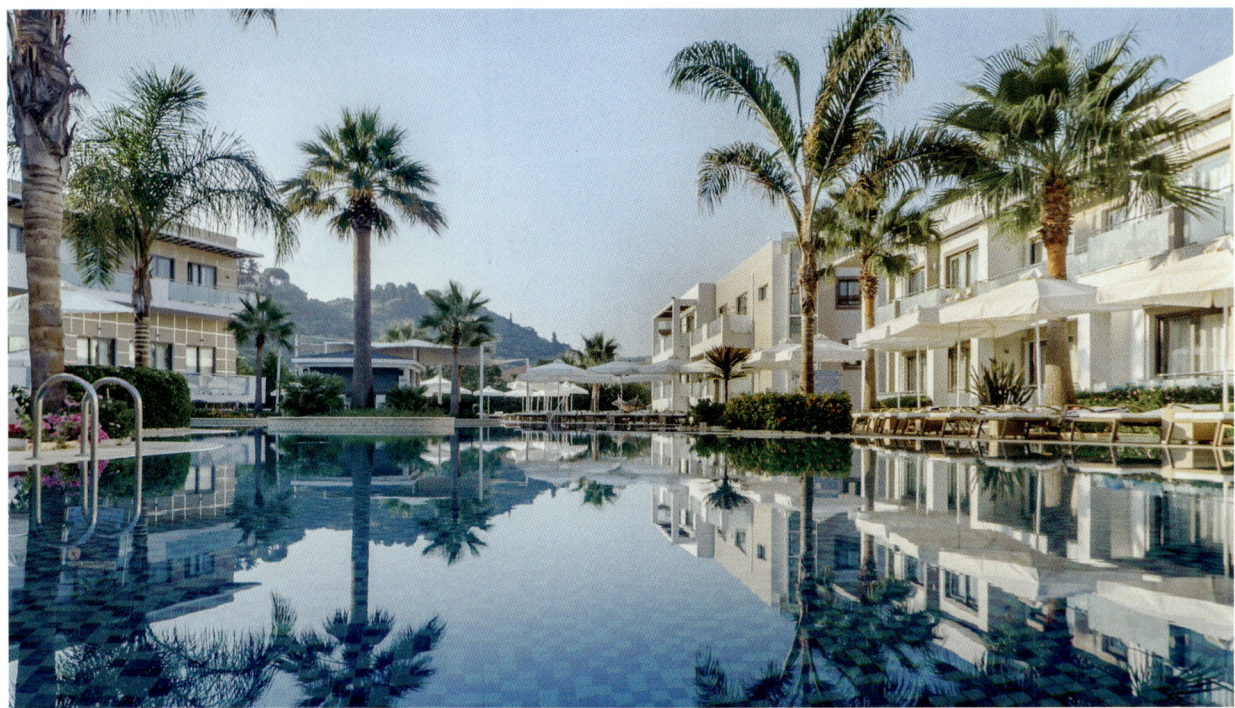

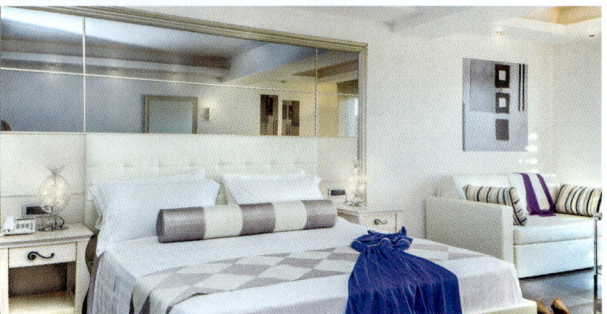

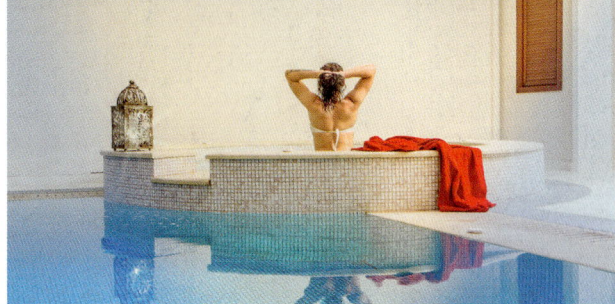

Lesante Luxury Hotel & Spa

One for die-hard romantics and nature lovers in the seaside resort of Tsilivi

PRICE FROM:
€120

FEATURES:
Family friendly; Pool; Restaurant; Sea views; Spa

ACTIVITIES:
Fishing; Water sports

NEARBY:
Zakynthos (Zante); Tsilivi beach; Bohali village; The famous Shipwreck beach

GETTING THERE:
Zakynthos (Zante) Airport

☎ +30 2 69 50 41 330
🌐 condenastjohansens.com/lesante
🏠 Tsilivi, 29100 Zakynthos, Greece

Lesante Luxury Hotel & Spa hits the mark for a stylish beach escape. Situated on the Greek island of Zakynthos' north-east coast – all white-sand bays, rocky coves and clear, calm water – it's a lesson in contemporary cool with trendy décor and fashionable furniture with pops of mint green and fuchsia. The minimalist rooms are predominantly white with huge beds, marble bathrooms and high-tech gadgetry at every turn. The Grand Suites live up to their name with huge terraces complete with hot tubs, daybeds and Ionian sea vistas. Landscaped gardens sweep through the resort, at the centre of which are curvaceous, palm-studded pools, but whatever you do, don't miss a zingy fruit cocktail at the Nectar pool bar. Lesante's spa is the biggest on the island so allow plenty of time delight in the pool, Jacuzzi, hammam, sauna, mood shower and treatments. Top and tail your days at the Ambrosia restaurant where indulgent American breakfasts and Mediterranean dinners are the order of the day. And at lunchtime, it's all about the poolside Neptune restaurant, which is great for seafood under the stars. Packing tip: think pared-back luxe by day, glam at night. There's a jewellery shop on-site if you need a touch more bling.

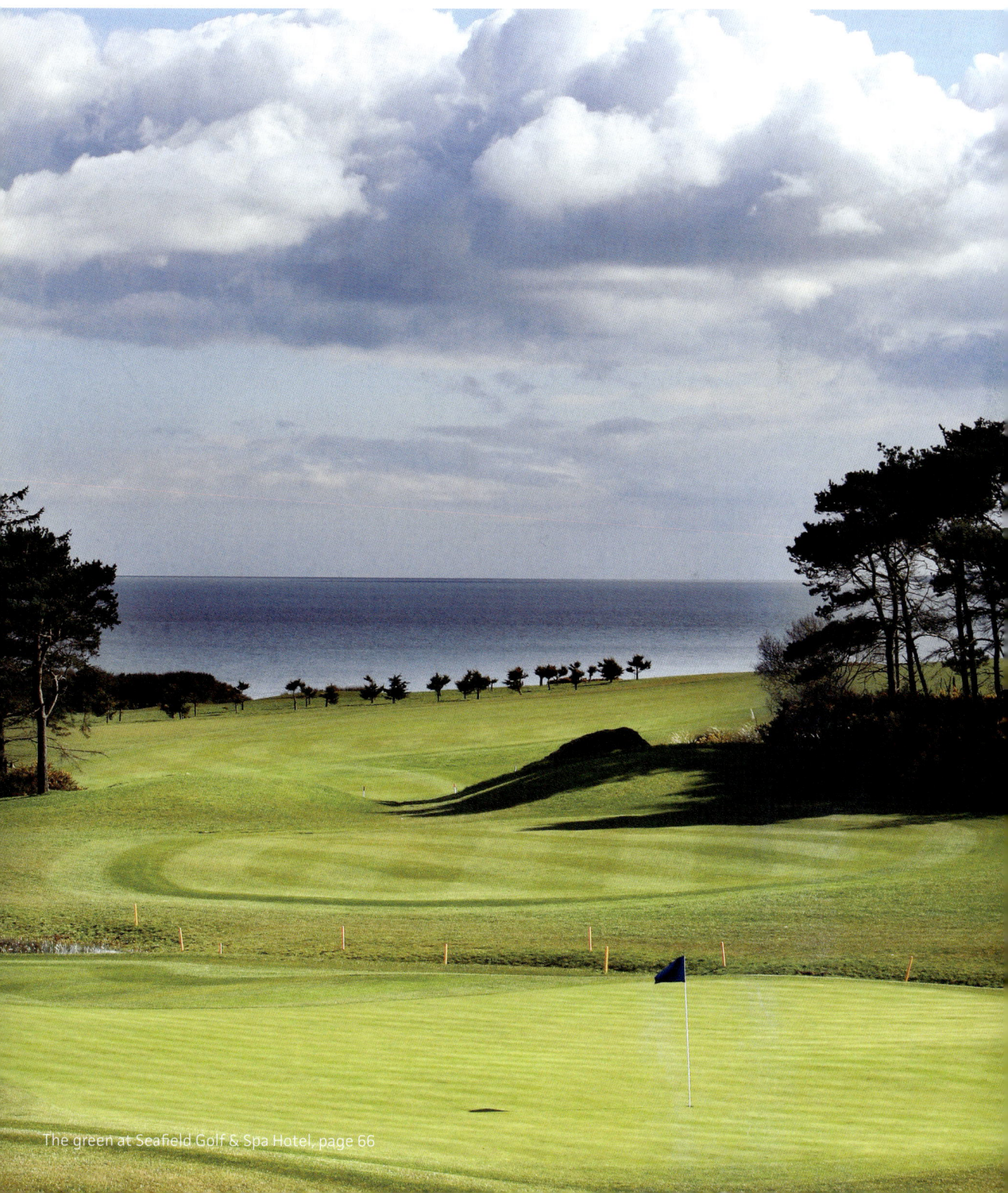

Ireland

Please go to condenastjohansens.com/ireland

The green at Seafield Golf & Spa Hotel, page 66

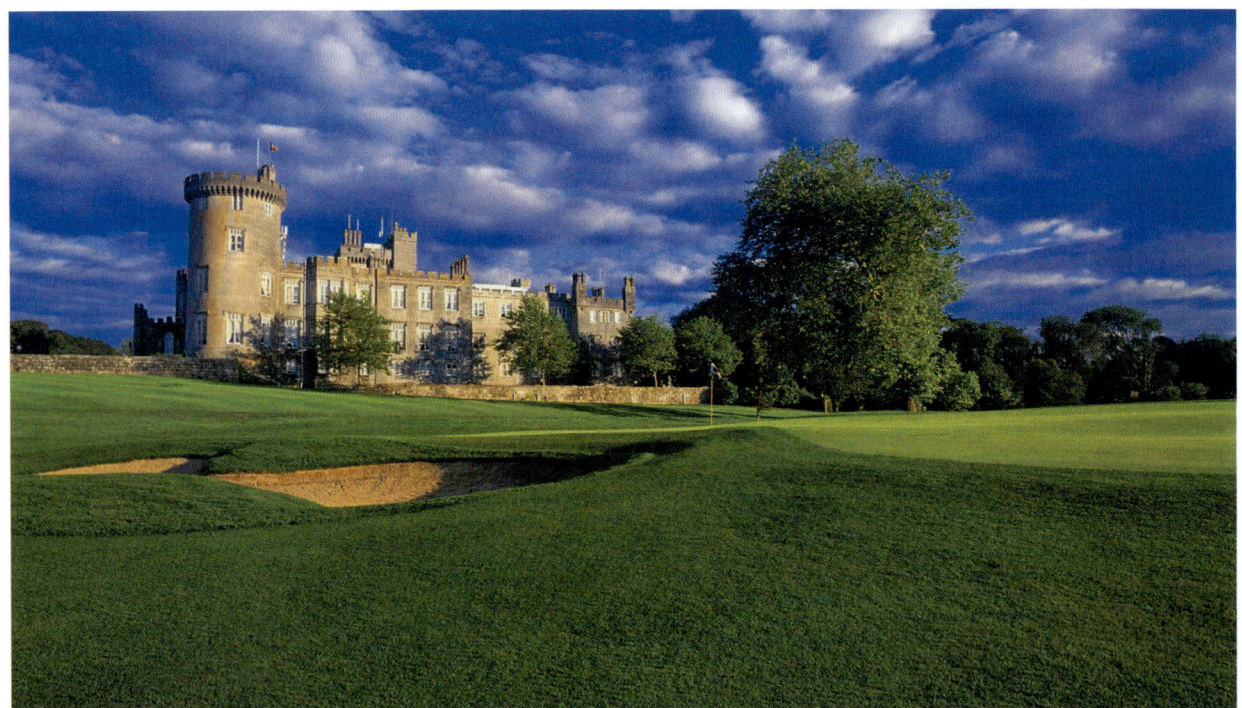

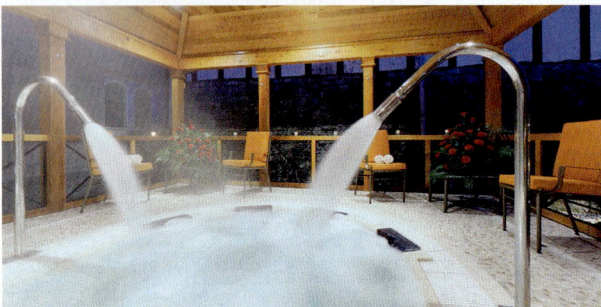
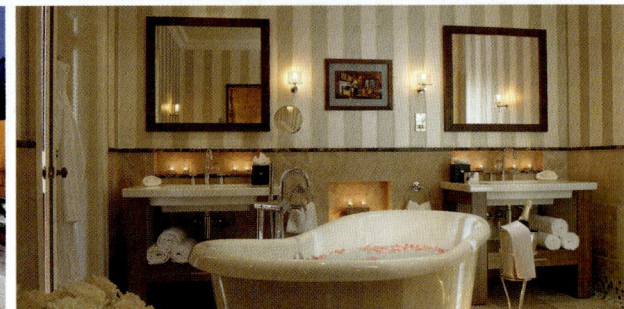

Dromoland Castle Hotel & Country Estate

County Clare's magnificent country pile fit for royalty

PRICE FROM:
€225 (room only)

FEATURES:
Gym; Lake views; Pool; Restaurant; Spa

ACTIVITIES:
Cycling; Fishing; Golf

NEARBY:
The Cliffs of Moher; The Buren region; Galway City; The Aran Islands; Bunratty Castle

GETTING THERE:
Just off the M18; Emis/Limerick Railway Stations; Shannon Airport

Dromoland Castle Hotel & Country Estate in County Clare has to be seen to be believed. Built in the 16th century, this is one of Ireland's most famous baronial castles presiding over hundreds of acres. The ancestral home of the O'Brien clan (direct descendants of Brian Boru, the High King of Ireland) for 18 generations, Dromoland is a perfectly preserved slice of Irish history. Its majesty and epic beauty have been brilliantly transformed into one of Europe's finest resorts where charmed peace, top-class hospitality, tremendous golf, luxury spa-ing and fine dining all come together. The sumptuous interior design befits Dromoland's inherent elegance and grandeur with custom furnishings, marble bathrooms and an artistic use of colour, florals, stripes and lighting alongside contemporary conveniences. Feeling pampered and relaxed is encouraged here where you can unwind in a comfy chair by the fireside or visit the boutique spa complete with indoor pool and sauna. But Dromoland's championship golf course, fishing on Dromoland Lough, falconry, clay shooting and horse riding on the estate might have you reconsidering your day's agenda. Delicious dishes inspired by seasonal produce and Irish tradition are served in various rooms including the refined Earl of Thomond, relaxed Fig Tree and lounge-style Gallery; luxury picnic baskets can be prepared too.

☎ +353 61368144
🌐 condenastjohansens.com/dromolandcastle
🏠 Newmarket on Fergus, Co Clare, Ireland

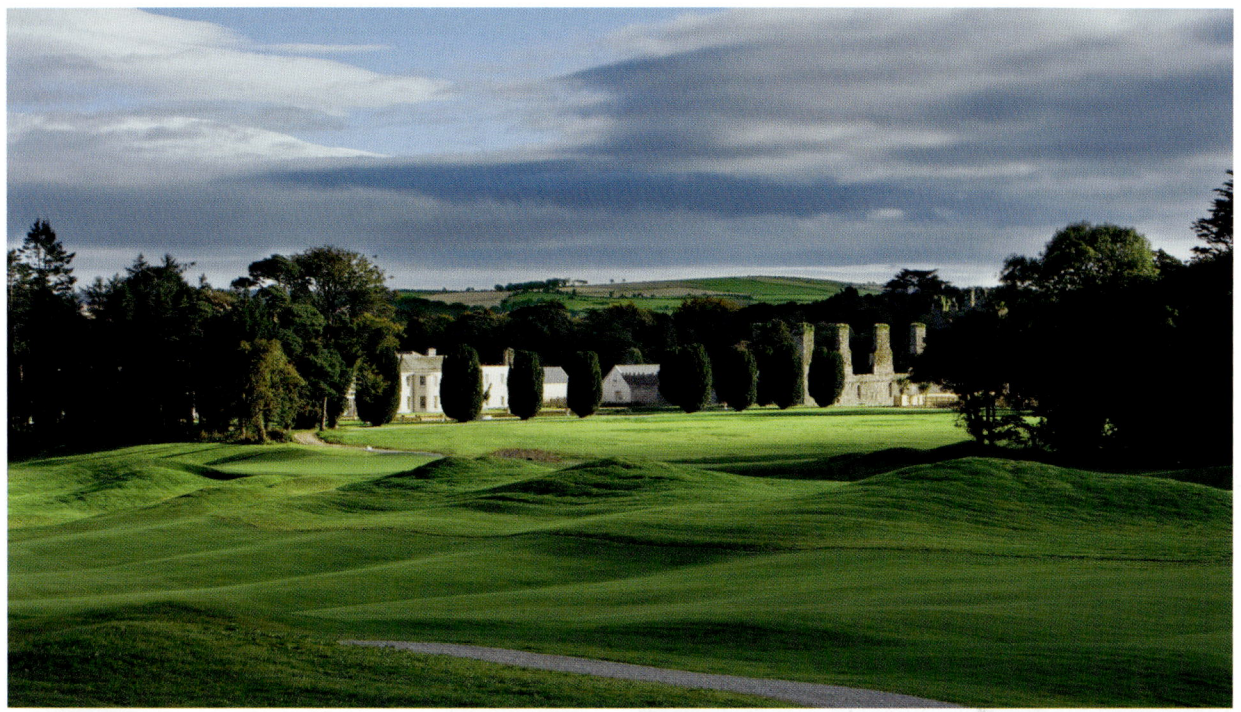

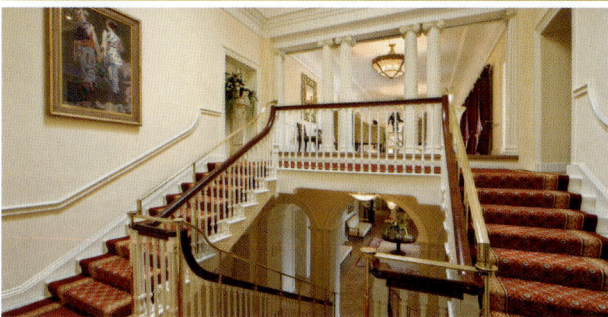

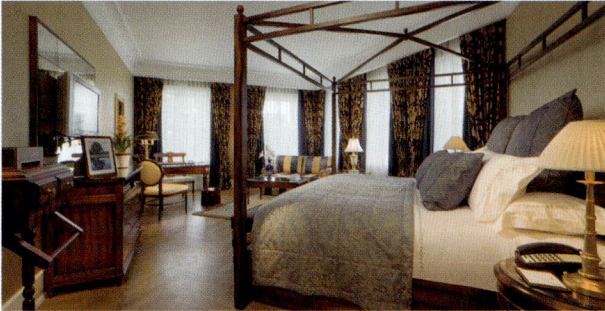

Castlemartyr Resort

Utterly arresting resort with the wow-factor near Cork

Hundreds of acres of emerald green land, a gently meandering river, rich woodland and the ruins of an 800-year-old castle complete the cinematic scene of Castlemartyr Resort near Cork. Suffice to say, there's nothing average about this country manor house-come-premier resort steeped in history dating back to the 17th century. Famous owners of Castlemartyr include Sir Walter Raleigh and Richard Boyle, the first Earl of Cork, and today, it's every bit the aristocratic playground drenched in luxury and elegance complemented by an outstanding level of service. Lavished with opulence and impeccable style, guest rooms and suites are spacious, filled with antiques, elegant fabrics and modern touches (check out the electronic touch panels operating the lights and drapes). A contemporary theme also runs through Castlemartyr's style of cooking served in three venues: the fine dining Bell Tower; lounge-style Knights Bar; and the golf club's casual Club House. Franchini's is the new Italian option dishing up plates of pizza, pasta and risotto. A spa like no other, Castlemartyr's spacious and naturally-lit idyll presents a holistic approach to complete well-being with ESPA treatments and therapies. While outside, there are countless activities such as the 18-hole golf course par 72, cycling routes (tandem bikes available), archery, laser clay pigeon shooting, horse riding and carriage rides.

PRICE FROM:
€150

FEATURES:
Family friendly; Gym; Pool; Restaurant; Spa

ACTIVITIES:
Fishing; Golf; Horse riding

NEARBY:
Kinsale; Titanic Trail, Cobh; Old Jameson Distillery; Fota Wildlife Park

GETTING THERE:
N25; M8; Cork International Airport

+353 21 4219000 ☎
condenastjohansens.com/castlemartyr 🌐
Castlemartyr, Co Cork, Ireland 🏠

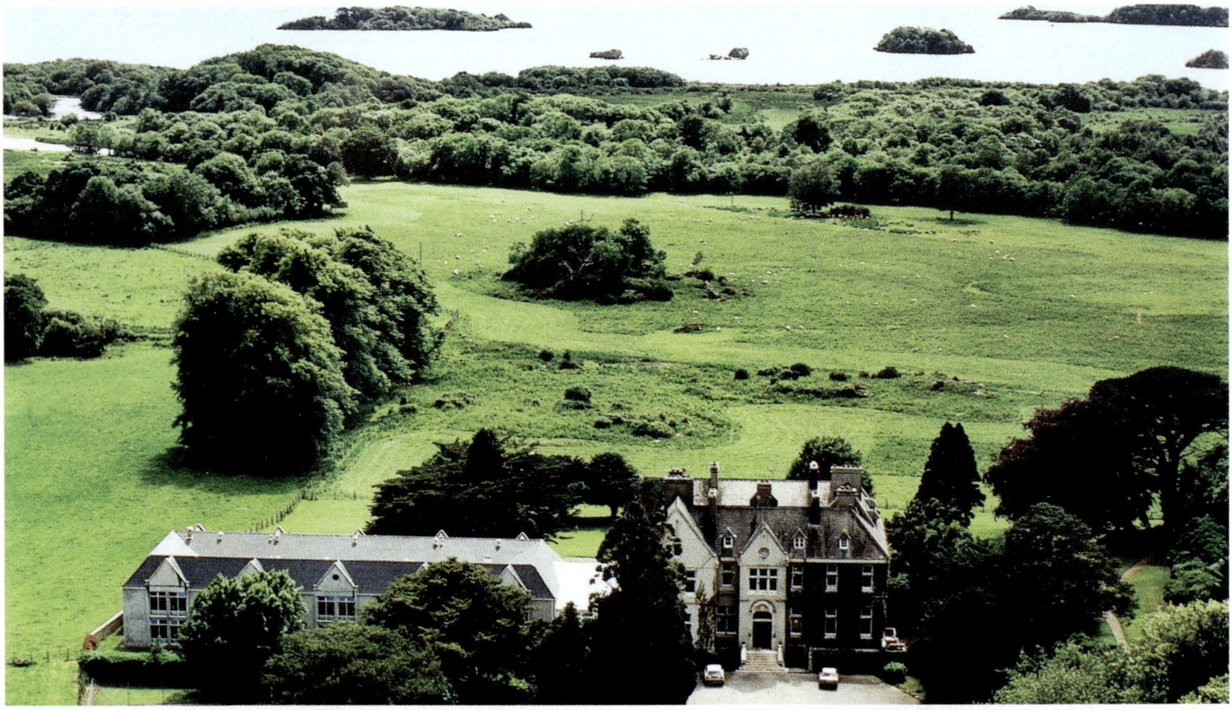

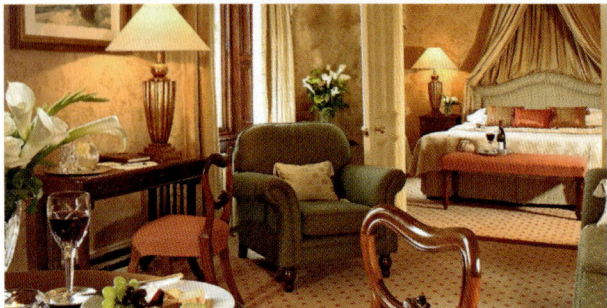

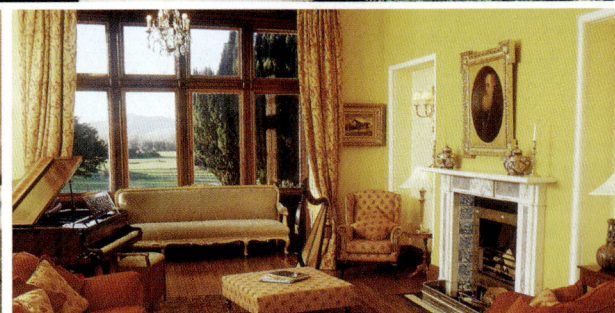

Cahernane House Hotel

Irish splendour, history and beauty in Co Kerry

PRICE FROM:
€130

FEATURES:
Family friendly; Lake views; Restaurant; Wheelchair access

ACTIVITIES:
Fishing; Golf; Walking

NEARBY:
Killarney; Killarney National Park; Ring of Kerry; Muckross House; Killarney Golf Club

GETTING THERE:
N71; Killarney Railway Station; Kerry Airport

With the unspoilt beauty of Killarney National Park one way and Killarney town centre in the other, Cahernane House Hotel enjoys the best of both rural escape and urban convenience. In its own private estate beside Lough Leane, Cahernane is reached by a shady tree-lined driveway. A striking 19th-century manor, time seems to move at a wonderfully sedate pace here, whose parkland, mountain-scape and watery scenes have you stepping back mouth open. Cahernane's life began as the home to the Earls of Pembroke and today, it's the Browne family who welcome you to their 38-room country pile. The Brownes pride themselves on their warm hospitality and will be keen to ensure you make the most of your stay. With so much to do in the area (golfing, tennis, croquet, fishing, deep-sea angling, lake boating, cycling, walking, water sports) their knowledge is extremely helpful. They've also captured the essence of Victorian grandeur to perfection. Guest rooms are full of individual personality and have private patio gardens whilst the suites are utterly indulgent with Jacuzzi baths, fireplaces and sitting rooms. Spoil yourself even further at the Herbert Room restaurant where Chef David Norris conjures up seasonally led dishes. Or there's always the more informal Cellar Bar's bistro-style menu and its highly impressive wine list.

☎ +353 64 6631895
🌐 condenastjohansens.com/cahernane
🏠 Muckross Road, Killarney, Co Kerry, Ireland

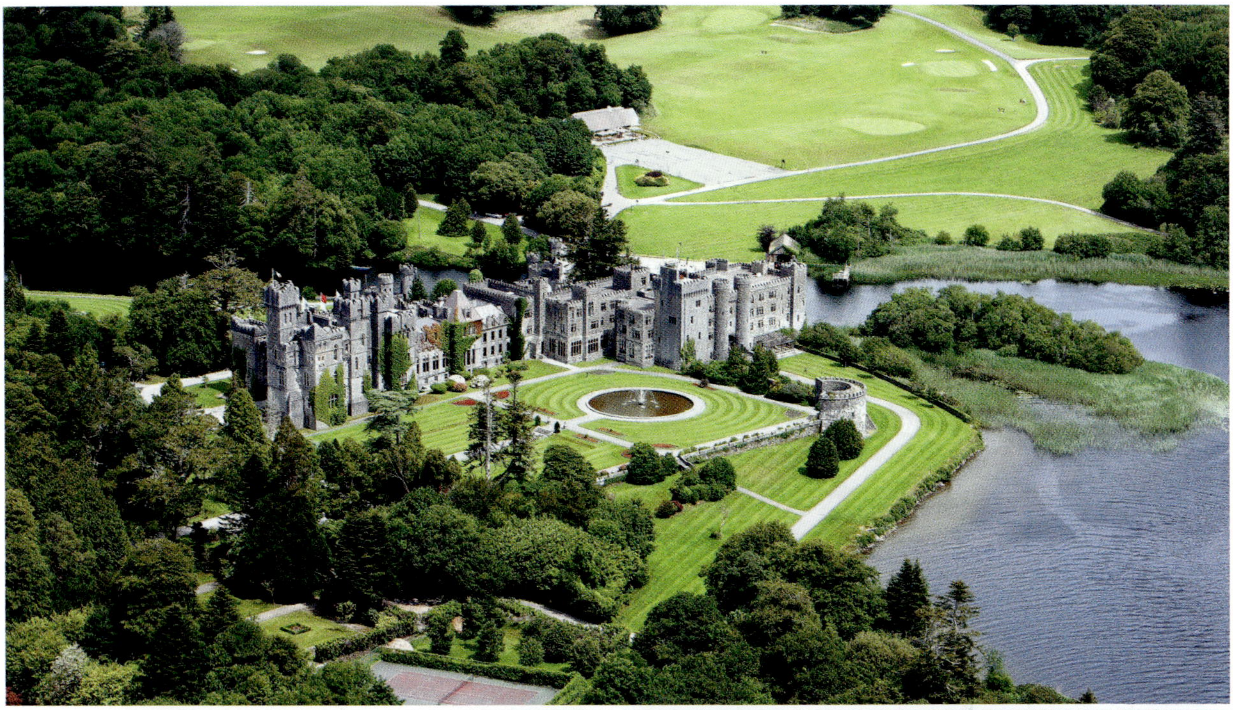

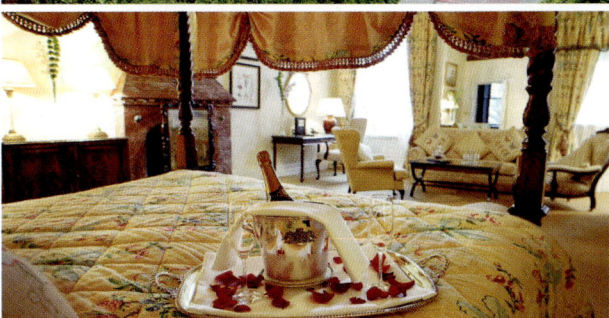

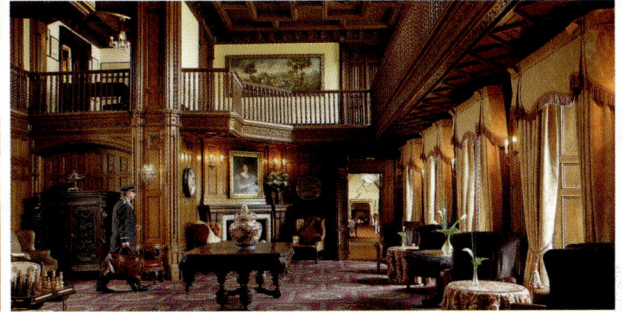

Ashford Castle

Spectacular timepiece of Co Mayo history and majesty

Beside the peaceful Lough Corrib, the staggeringly impressive Ashford Castle near Cong is the image of fairy-tale fantasies. Spanning hundreds of acres of stunning leafy estate, this is one of Ireland's greatest castle hotels brimming with history, tall tales and a guest list crammed with famous names (King George V, Oscar Wilde, Omar Sharif, Brad Pitt…). On the borders of County Galway and Mayo, the first recorded brick on this site was laid in 1228 and from the mid-1800s until 1921 it was the prolific Guinness family's country retreat. Since becoming a hotel in 1939, Ashford developed into the pre-eminent countryside playground it is today. Days are filled with falconry, golf, horse riding, clay pigeon shooting, pampering at the health and beauty centre, leisurely cruises on Lough Corrib and fishing with an Orvis endorsed guide. Ashford Castle is also a mecca for food lovers. Chef Stefan Matz's exceptional cuisine showcases Ireland's seasonal, organic produce in a variety of ways: the fine dining five-course table d'hôte evening menu in the George V Dining Room (the heartbeat of the castle adorned with 11 Waterford crystal chandeliers); casual bistro-style à la carte meals at Cullen's at the Cottage (a short walk away); and daily snacks in the Drawing Room. There's also nightly entertainment you can't afford to miss.

PRICE FROM:
€195

FEATURES:
Family friendly; Helipad; Lake views; Pet friendly; Restaurant

ACTIVITIES:
Cycling; Fishing; Horse riding

NEARBY:
Galway City; Connemara National Park; Westport: Ceidhe Fields

GETTING THERE:
N84; Galway Railway Station; Galway Airport

+353 94 95 46003 ☎
condenastjohansens.com/ashfordcastle 🌐
Cong, Co Mayo, Ireland 🧳

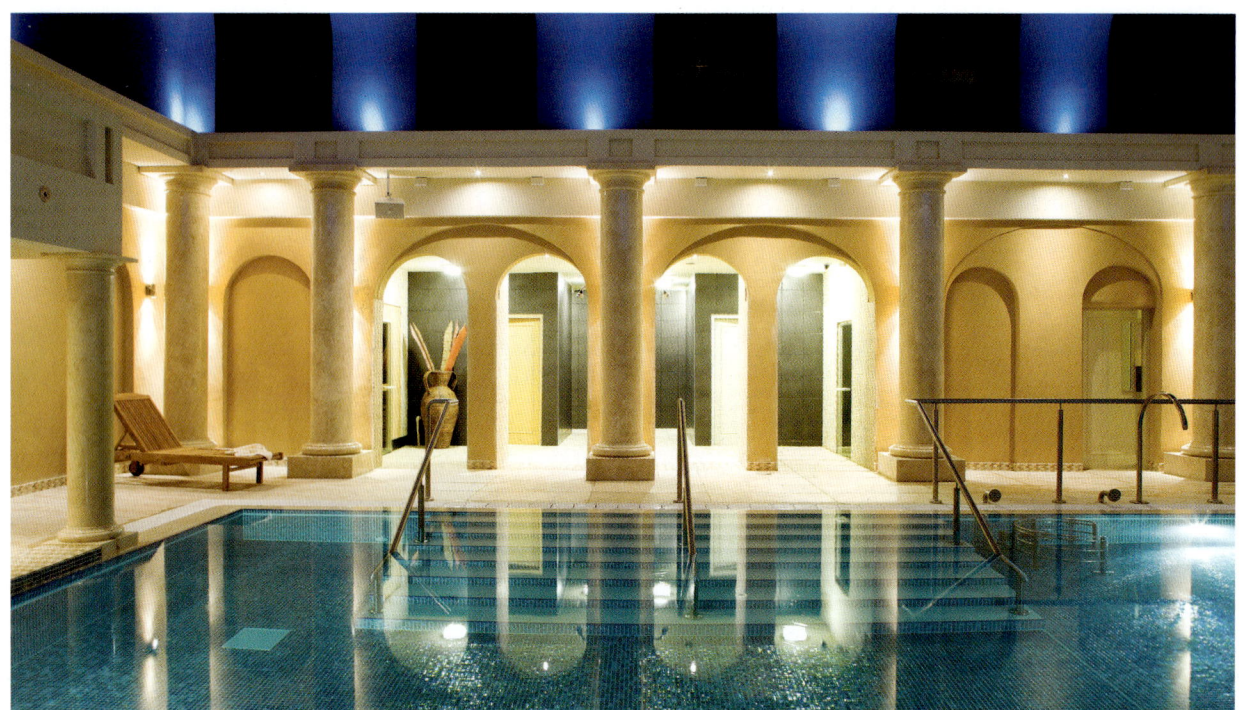

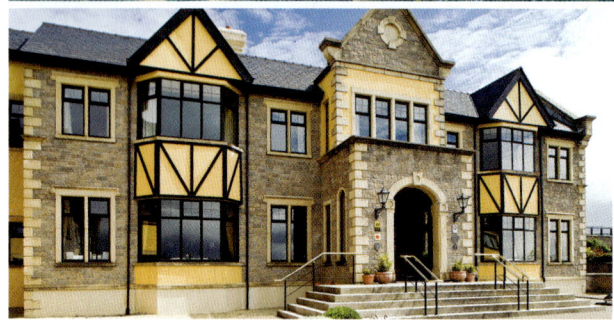

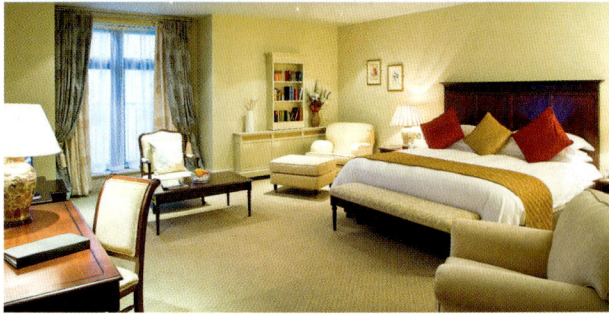

Knockranny House Hotel & Spa

Westport's top rated hotel and spa

PRICE FROM:
€140

FEATURES:
Family friendly; Gym; Pool; Restaurant; Spa

ACTIVITIES:
Fishing; Golf; Walking

NEARBY:
Westport House Estate; Great Western Greenway walking and cycling trail: Croagh Patrick mountain; Clew Bay; Clare Island

GETTING THERE:
Just off the N5; Westport Railway Station; Knock Airport

☎ +353 98 28600
🌐 condenastjohansens.com/knockranny
🏠 Westport, Co Mayo, Ireland

Rising into view against Croagh Patrick mountain, the Victorian designed Knockranny House Hotel & Spa in Westport, County Mayo, is drawing some prize-winning attention as it continues to do what it does best: outstanding hospitality. With the grace of a bygone era and the facilities demanded by today's traveller, this secluded gem looks out to lively Westport (visit during Westport Festival of Music & Food to see music legends and newcomers) offering utter comfort and Irish charm. Knockranny's variety of bedrooms with courtyard or mountain views includes the Penthouse and Presidential Suites with kitchenettes, computers and some of the hotel's best views. However, all rooms are spacious and Executive Rooms list king-size beds, large flat-screen tvs, surround-sound systems, free WiFi and oversized bathrooms with spa baths as standard fixtures. Antique furnishings keep a classical ambience throughout Knockranny while the magnificent scenery from rooms such as the restaurant, conservatory and bar bring the outside beauty in. Modern Irish cuisine and fresh fish dishes are La Fougère Restaurant's speciality and its superb wine cellar is regularly recognised on the award ceremony circuit for good reason. Spa Salveo is also achieving some accolades for its hydrotherapy treatments and amenities such as vitality pool and serail mud chamber.

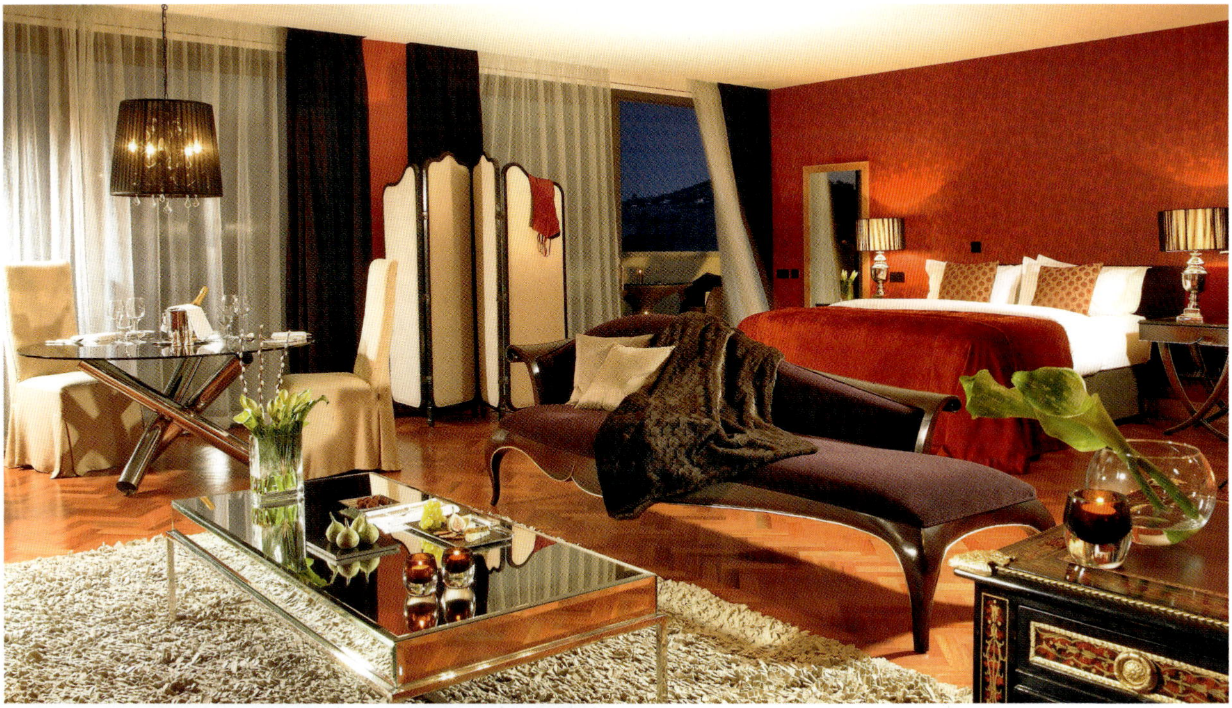

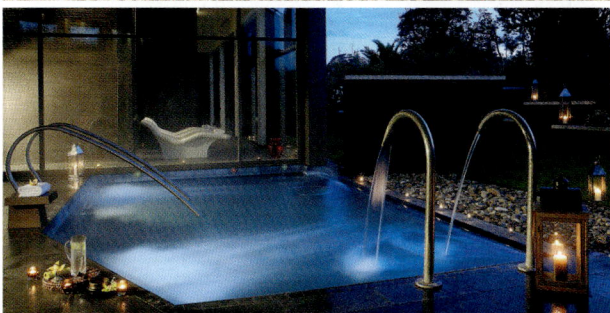
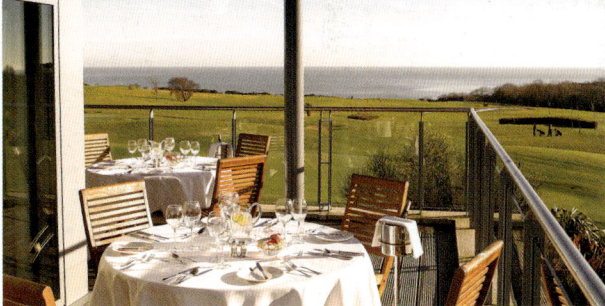

Seafield Golf & Spa Hotel

Golf and spa enthusiasts' haven on the sands of Ballymoney shore

Style and luxury are key at Seafield Golf & Spa Hotel, County Wexford, as is the warm Irish welcome it extends to each guest. Surrounded by a blanket of far-reaching green acres, this trend-setting golf and spa hotel sits on the Ballymoney Shore, just one hour from Dublin. Italian architect Francesco Beia designed its plush, sultry interiors that fully make the most of the enveloping views and natural light. Choose a Deluxe Room for its sink-into mattress, crisp linens and sea views of Ballymoney Beach or an Executive Suite for extra space (with lounge or dining area) and a balcony overlooking the championship golf course. Families are more than welcome at Seafield and are invited to stay in Courtyard Family Suites located adjacent to the main hotel. Seafield Kids Club provides a schedule of activities for the little ones to enjoy - even evening entertainment and special dinners - which means mum and dad can have some precious time to dine and relax together. Back outside and private nature tours through woodland paths and onto the beach can be organised or there's Seafield Golf Club's 18-hole cliff-top golf course created to the highest specifications to keep that swing in check. However, the extraordinary Oceo Spa with its thermal suite, ice grotto and hydrotherapy pool may be the biggest distraction of all.

PRICE FROM:
€170

FEATURES:
Family friendly; Gym; Pool; Restaurant; Spa

ACTIVITIES:
Fishing; Golf; Walking

NEARBY:
12th-century city of Kilkenny; Medieval site of Glendalough; Wexford; Wicklow; Dublin

GETTING THERE:
N11; Gorey Railway Station; Dublin International Airport

+353 53 9424000
condenastjohansens.com/seafieldhotel
Ballymoney, Gorey, Co Wexford, Ireland

Italy

Please go to condenastjohansens.com/italy

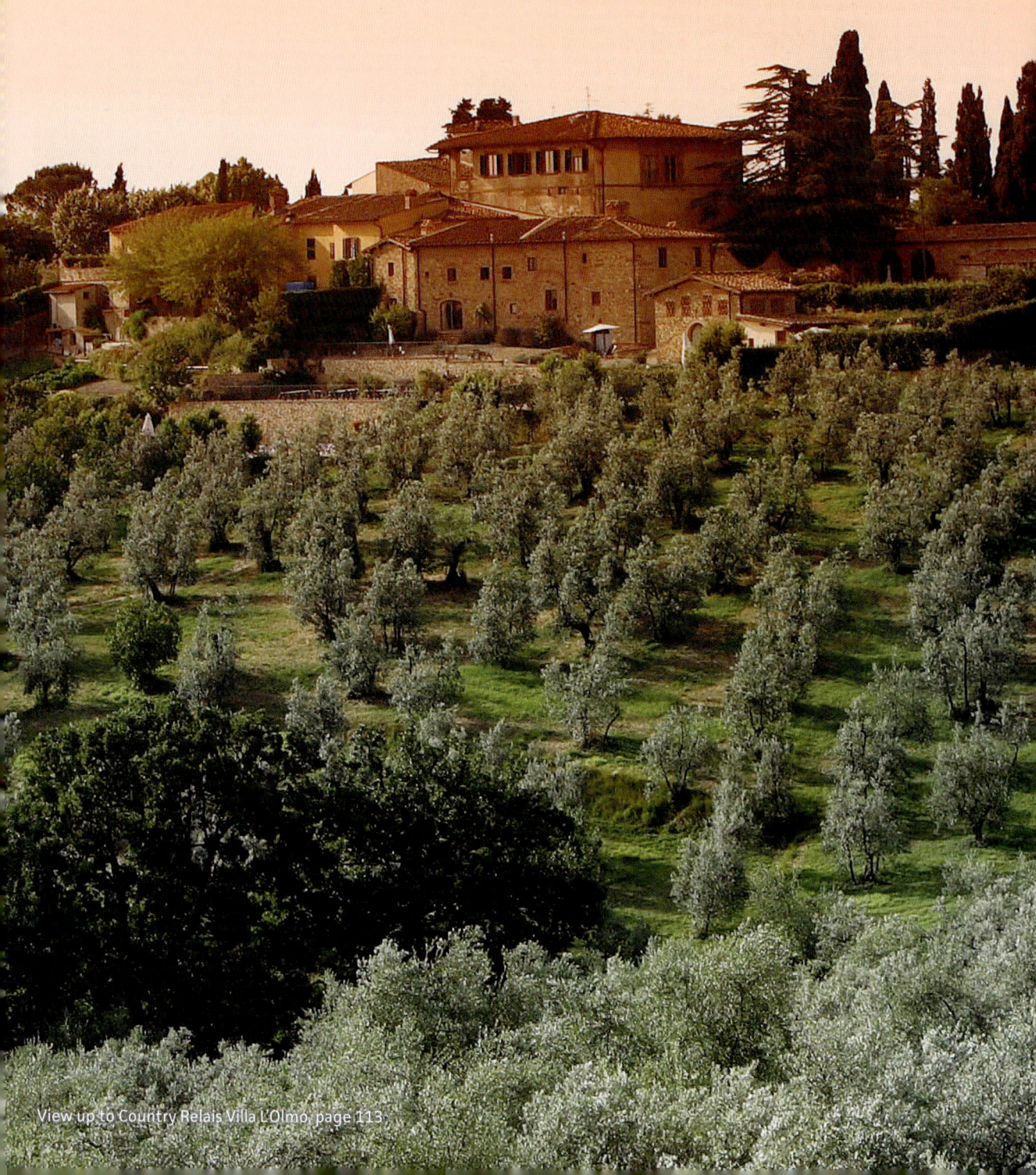

View up to Country Relais Villa L'Olmo, page 113

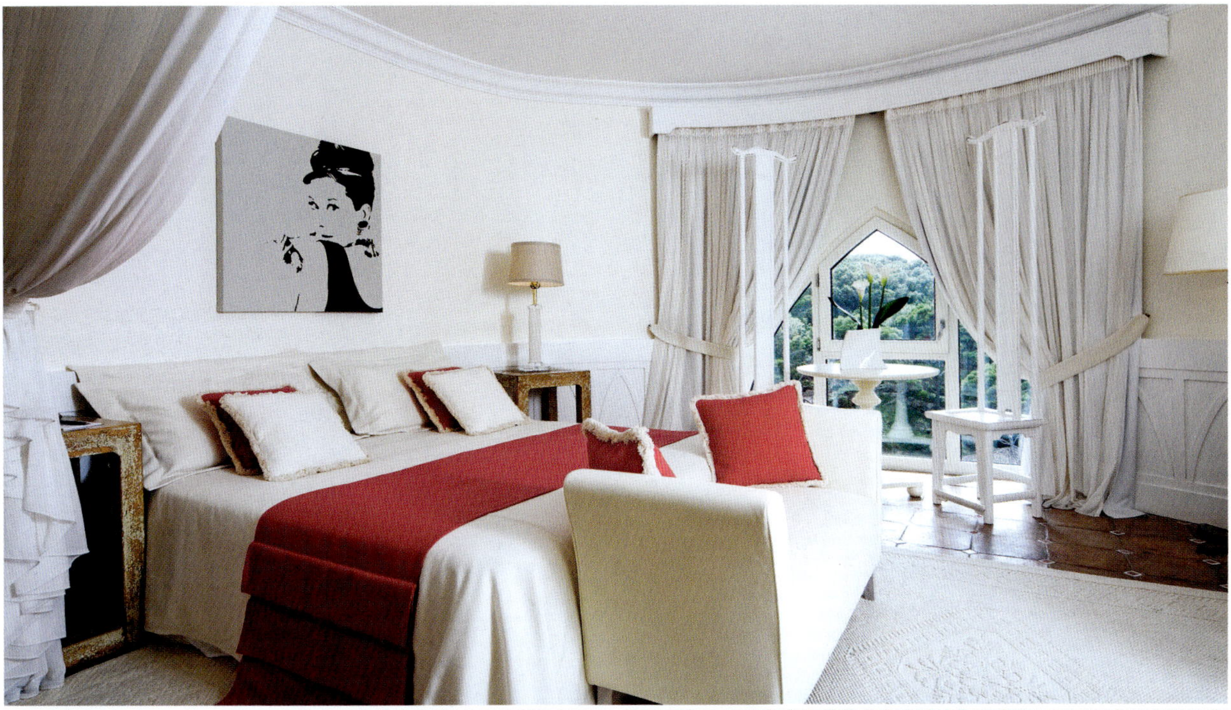

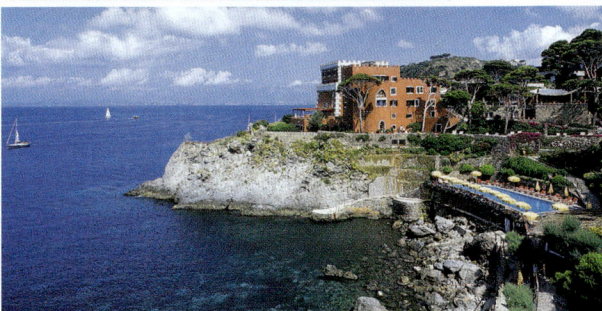
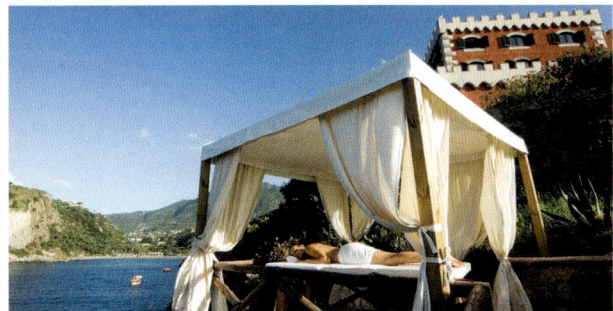

Mezzatorre Resort & Spa

Keeping guard of life's indulgent pleasures on Ischia's coast

Centuries ago the tower of Mezzatorre was built as a look-out on the dramatic, rocky coastline of Ischia. Fast-forward to the 21st century and it's now home to one of Italy's most strikingly beautiful boutique hotels. Standing in several acres of Mediterranean pine forest, Mezzatorre Resort & Spa's tower has been meticulously restored and perches on the edge of a promontory overlooking the Bay of Naples, Epomeo Mountain and Vesuvius. Outside, you can still see the battlements of this ancient fort. Inside, it's a grand, sophisticated affair. Whitewashed walls are the backdrop for opulent décor from the chic bar and sea-viewing suites to the Chandelier restaurant named after the elegant silver candelabra that creates the romantic dining room's only light. Food here is refined Mediterranean on a gastronomic scale. And down below is the spa; a modern, immaculate space where soft lighting and artfully arranged hangings create an atmosphere of almost celestial calm. Grouped around Mezzatorre's tower, several buildings designed to blend seamlessly into the pinewood forest host more rooms, suites and Sciue-Sciue restaurant with palm-frond roof. This is where informal and delicious Campania foodie delights are served overlooking the breathtaking views of the Mediterranean and pool on the pretty terrace below.

PRICE FROM:
€340

FEATURES:
Family friendly; Restaurant; Sea views; Spa

ACTIVITIES:
Fishing; Horse riding; Water sports

NEARBY:
Capri; Naples; Negombo Thermal Gardens; La Mortella Botanical Gardens; Ischia villages

GETTING THERE:
Naples Airport

+39 081 986111
condenastjohansens.com/mezzatorre
Via Mezzatorre 23, 80075 Ischia (NA), Campania, Italy

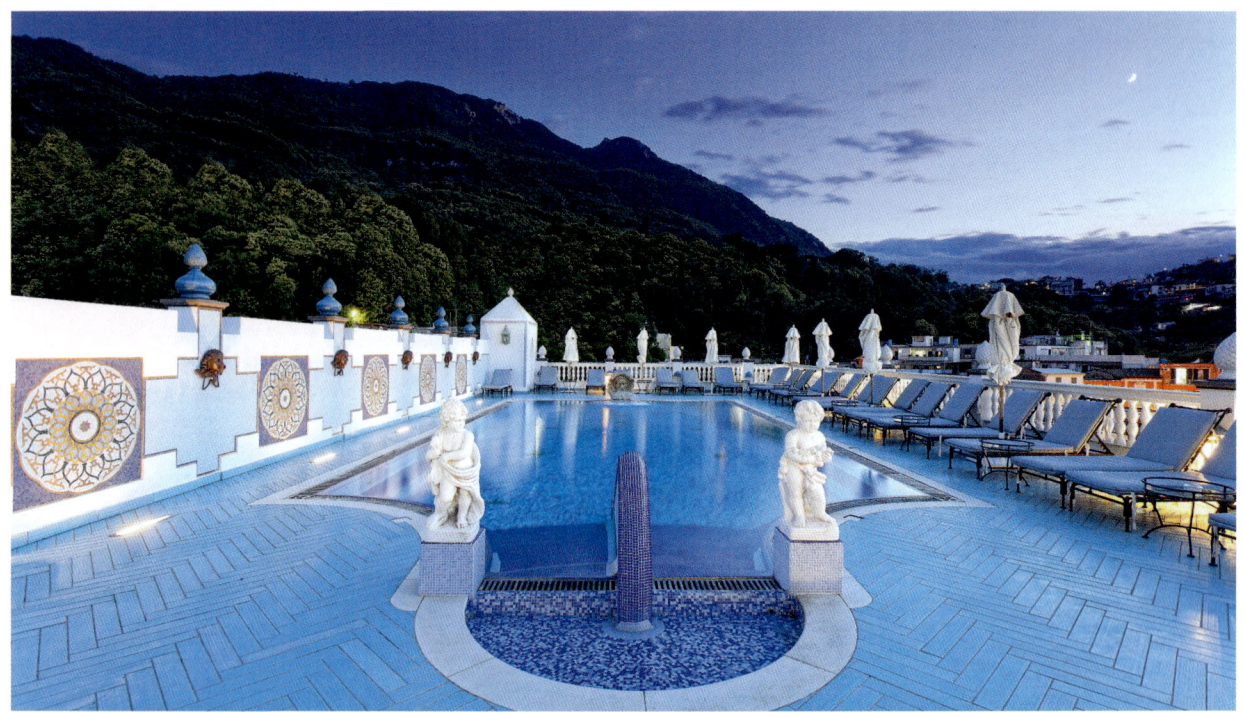

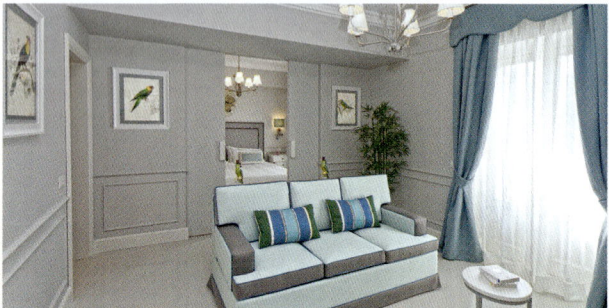
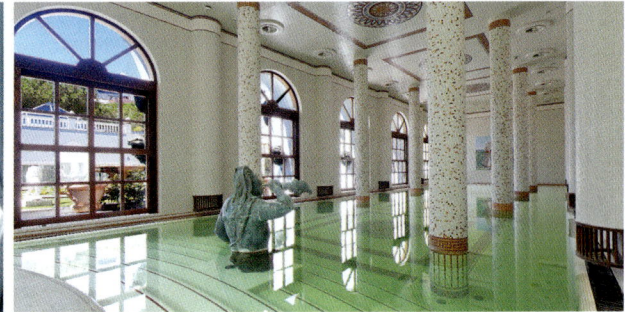

Terme Manzi Hotel & Spa

Classic luxury spa hotel in northern Ischia

PRICE FROM:
€229

FEATURES:
Michelin Starred restaurant; Pool; Spa

ACTIVITIES:
Fishing; Tennis

NEARBY:
Negombo botanical and thermal garden; La Mortella gardens; Ancient castle; Capri; Naples

GETTING THERE:
Naples Ferry Port; Pozzuoli Ferry Port; Naples Airport

☎ +39 081 99 47 22
🌐 condenastjohansens.com/termemanzi
🏠 Piazza Bagni, Casamicciola Terme, 80074 Ischia (NA), Campania, Italy

Ever since Luigi Manzi's discovery of Ischia's hot springs in 1863, the rich, famous and privileged have been coming to this offshore wellness retreat to sample its therapeutic thermal powers. And when Italian editor and filmmaker, Angelo Rizzoli (producer of Federico Fellini's La Dolce Vita), purchased the property in 1960, a soupcon of cinematic drama brought a touch of glamour to its mountainous shores. Today, the Polito family is the proud owner of Terme Manzi Hotel & Spa, now a world-renowned spa, hotel and 2 Michelin-Starred restaurant. The subject of a recent revamp, its Moorish architecture has been given an Oriental gloss while inside, a myriad of cultural influences is expressed by antiques and colourful tapestries. Pastel colours, warming golds and timeless elegance rule the day in the rooms and suites. Most have views of the gardens or countryside. Named after one of its most famous guests, the Garibaldi Suite is Terme Manzi's jewel in the crown with a ceiling covered in gold leaf and walls dressed in silk. Reached by hydrofoil or ferry via Naples or Pozzuoli, a stay at Terme Manzi Hotel & Spa is a real feast for the soul. Personalised spa programmes take care of your physical, aesthetic and spiritual needs whilst the local/Campania dishes at Gli Ulivi Restaurant and Michelin-Starred Mediterranean cuisine, courtesy of Chef Nino Di Costanzo's skilled hands, take care of your appetite.

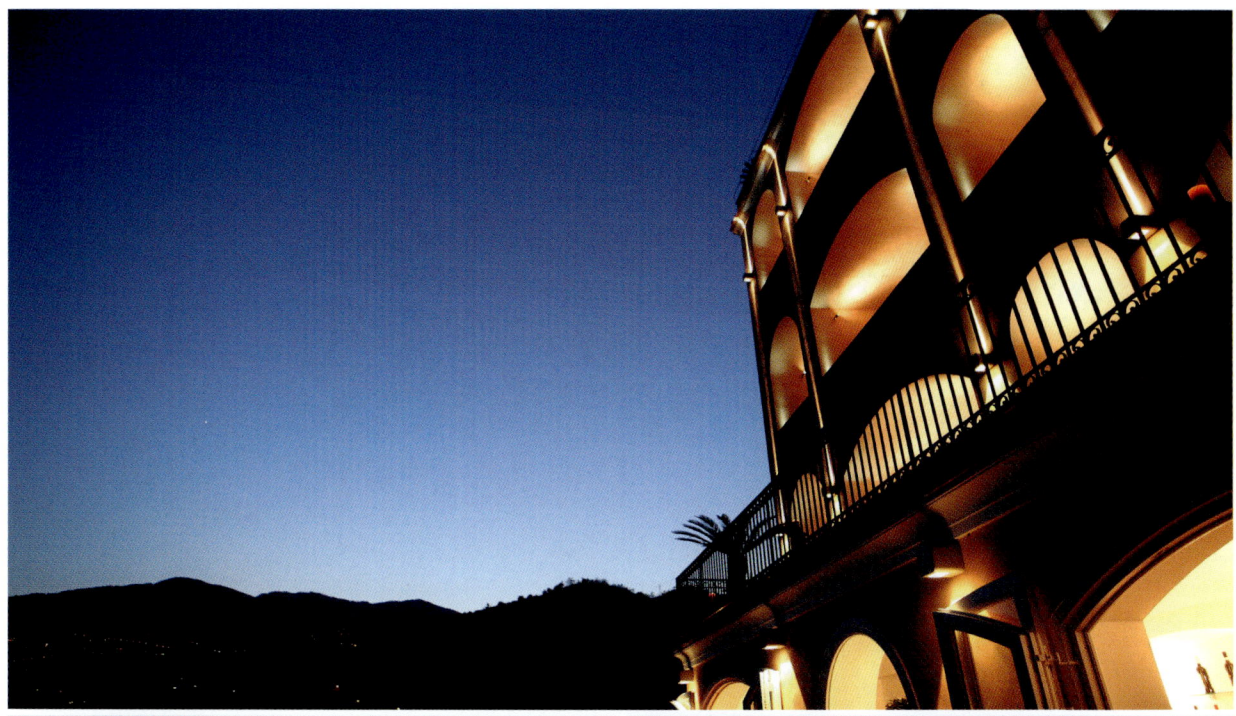

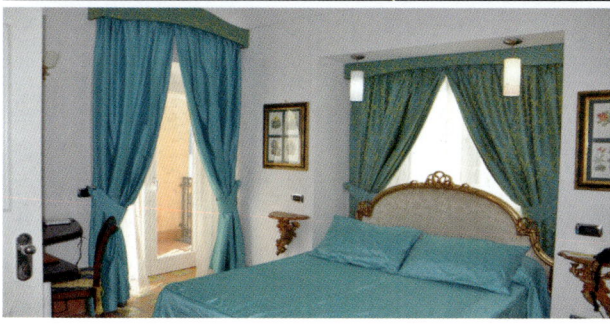
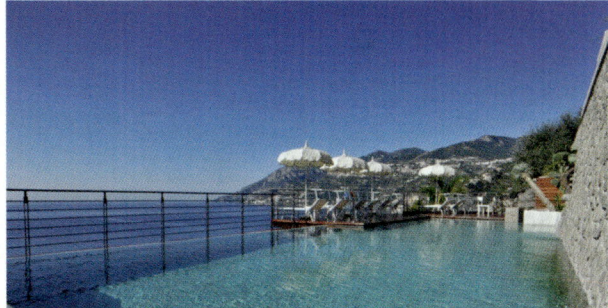

Hotel Botanico San Lazzaro

Ornate Amalfi Coast jewel overlooking the Med

Rugged and winding, dotted with secret coves and hidden beaches, the Amalfi Coast is a spectacular stretch of awesome beauty. Perched on a vertiginous terrace (good news: a lift to the hotel is due for completion very soon) leading down to the Bay of Maiori, Hotel Botanico San Lazzaro commands swoon-inducing views of this romantic Med scene. And as you take in this view from the hotel terraces, guest rooms and suites, the heady scent of citrus and grape fills the air from the surrounding lemon groves and vineyards. Each bedroom is an artistic display of hand-painted furniture, precious Vietri terracotta tiles and pure linen sheets cleverly juxtaposed alongside modern technological amenities. All have outside areas (balconies to private gardens) that make the most of this magical setting. Maiori has the longest beach on the Amalfi Coast, however, there's Botanico San Lazzaro's heavenly infinity pool and huge cliff-side Jacuzzi (cue another breathtaking seascape) to enjoy if swimming in the salty water's not your bag. Botanico San Lazzaro's outdoor gym with stunning views is a unique revelation and the heavily perfumed terrace gardens (six no less!) include exotic, botanical and organic variations; products from which are utilised by the hotel's kitchen. Feast on seafood and spaghetti, homegrown veg and perhaps some limoncello on restaurant Donna Clelia's picturesque terrace.

PRICE FROM:
€260

FEATURES:
Gym; Pet friendly; Restaurant; Sea views

ACTIVITIES:
Fishing; Horse riding; Water sports

NEARBY:
Amalfi; Ravello; Positano; Sorrento; Trekking and walking excursions

GETTING THERE:
Salerno Airport; Naples Airport; Rome Fiumicino Airport

+39 089 877750 ☎
condenastjohansens.com/hbsl 🌐
Via Lazzaro 25, 84010 Maiori -Salerno, Amalfi Coast, Campania, Italy 🏠

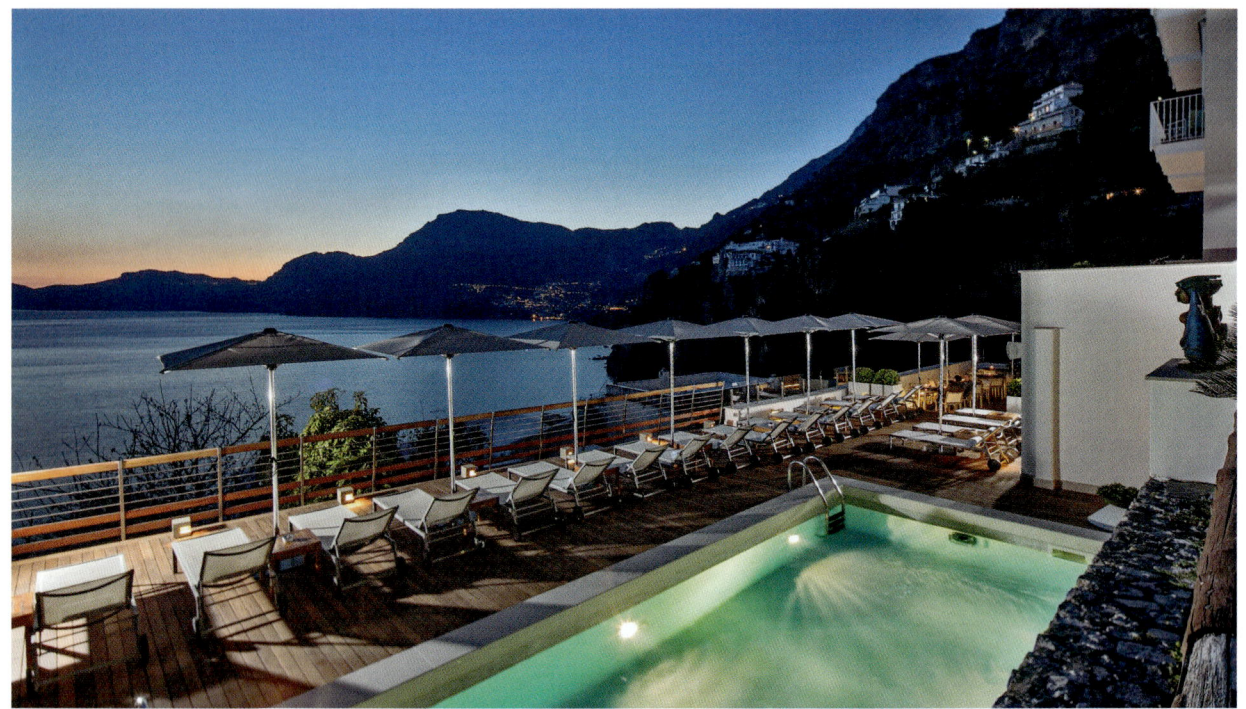

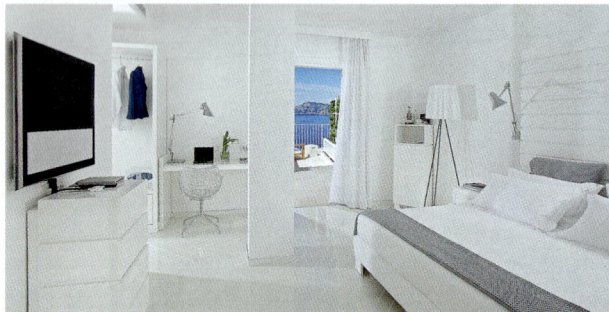

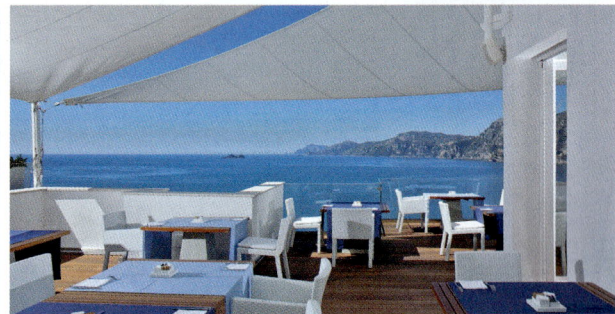

Casa Angelina Lifestyle

Barefoot luxury on the romantic Amalfi Coast

PRICE FROM:
€285

FEATURES:
Beach access; Gym; Pool; Restaurant; Sea views

ACTIVITIES:
Fishing; Sightseeing; Water sports

NEARBY:
Positano; Amalfi; Capri; Sorrento; Pompeii

GETTING THERE:
Naples Capodichino Airport

The town of Praiano is the middle child of the Amalfi Coast with the overachieving Positano and Amalfi to contend with. Its equidistant position between the two world-famous haunts means that the pretty-as-a-picture Praiano sometimes gets overlooked. But not by the shrewd travel contingent desiring a pocket of peace that's central for all the action. For them, Casa Angelina Lifestyle, perched above Praiano's Gavitella Beach, is just the ticket. There are taxis, water taxis, chauffeur-driven cars, trains, hydrofoils and even a private boat all at your service for exploring this coastal wonderland (not to mention a complimentary shuttle bus service to/from Positano), although there's plenty to keep you amused at Casa Angelina. First of all, breakfast beckons. Forget the calorie counting and dive into the homemade pastries, cakes and/or hot, freshly cooked options all washed down with just-squeezed juices and expertly prepared cappuccinos. And if the pang of guilt is too unbearable, take a trip to the Wellness Centre. But take heed, time by the pool sundeck is time well spent. The preposterously beautiful views are pinch-me dreamy. The nibbles and light meals available here are also delicious. However, it's advisable to save some room for evening feasts at the panoramic Un Piano nel Cielo Restaurant.

☎ +39 089 8131333
🌐 condenastjohansens.com/casangelina
🏠 Via Capriglione 147, 84010 Praiano (SA), Amalfi Coast, Campania, Italy

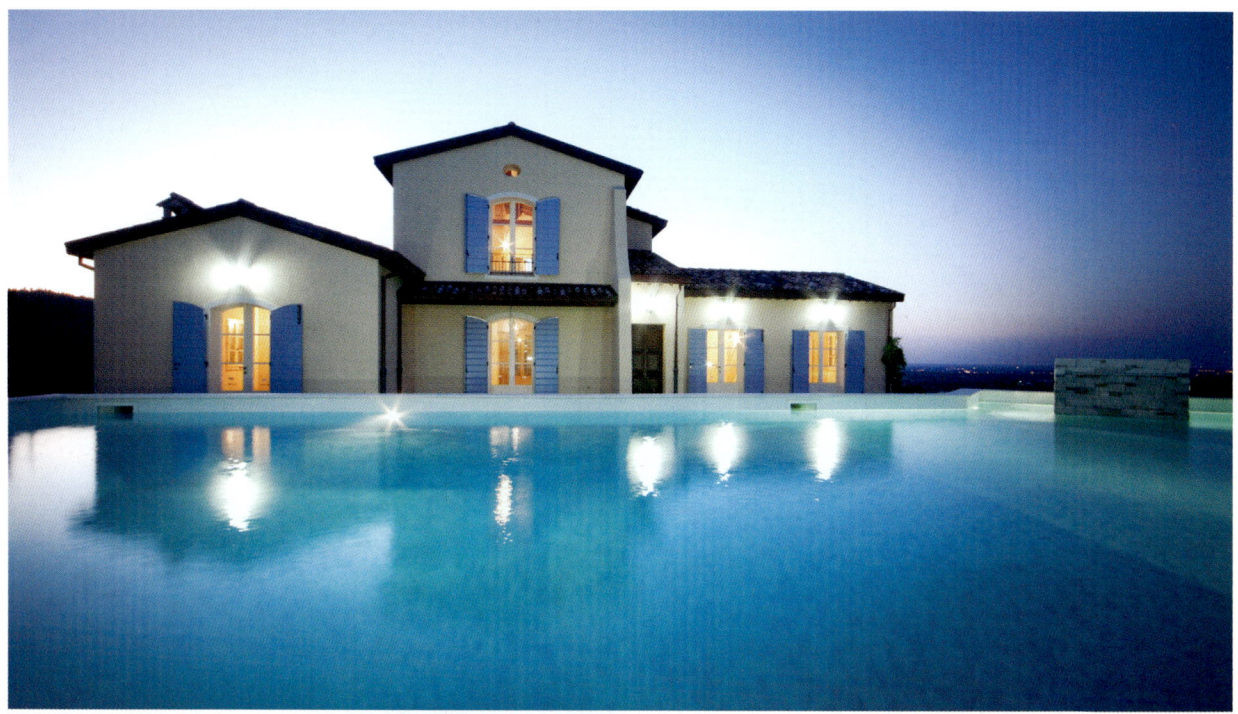

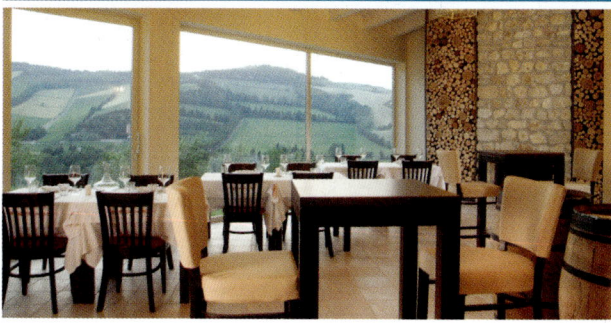

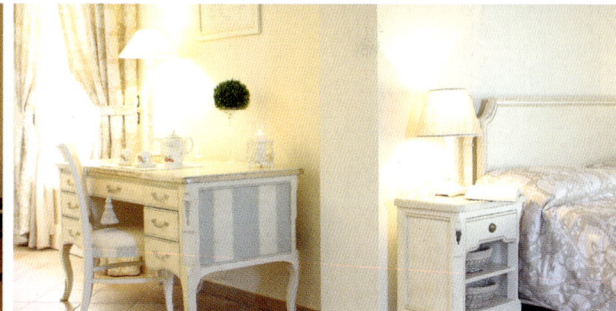

Condé Wine Resort

Mad about wine in Emilia Romagna

Love wine, love Condé Wine Resort in Emilia Romagna. Producing the intoxicating elixir (specifically Sangiovese varieties) for more than six centuries, this is a ferociously fertile land of vineyards as far as the eye can see. And right at its heart in the Predappio Hills is Condé Wine Resort, a magnet for those passionate about all things wine. A family-run enterprise, the estate has three distinct areas: the classic Italian borgo, the villa complex and La Cittadella. The borgo houses most of the guest rooms whose views of the vineyards are a magical wake-up-call. This is also where the indoor and outdoor pools, the spa, breakfast room, Ristorante Alto, conference rooms and wine cellar reside. The villas allow for a little more privacy and can be hired exclusively, making them popular with business events and wedding celebrations. Some have a private pool. Then there's La Cittadella with the Osteria (Romagnole recipes with a modern twist), Il Ristorante (an ever-changing menu dictated by local produce) and Wine Shop. Tours of the cellar, wine-tasting sessions and activities on the vineyard including help with the harvesting (fun for the children), are all yours to experience. Even the spa uses the anti-oxidant properties of the grape in its treatments.

PRICE FROM:
€180

FEATURES:
Gym; Pool; Restaurant; Spa; Wheelchair access

ACTIVITIES:
Cycling; Golf; Horse riding

NEARBY:
Forlì; Sangiovese wine region; Faenza ceramic museum; Ravenna; Romagna coast

GETTING THERE:
A14; Forlì Airport; Bologna Airport

+39 0543 940 860 ☎
condenastjohansens.com/condewineresort 🌐
Via Lucchina 27, 47016 Fiumana Di Predappio (FC), Emilia 🏠
Romagna, Italy

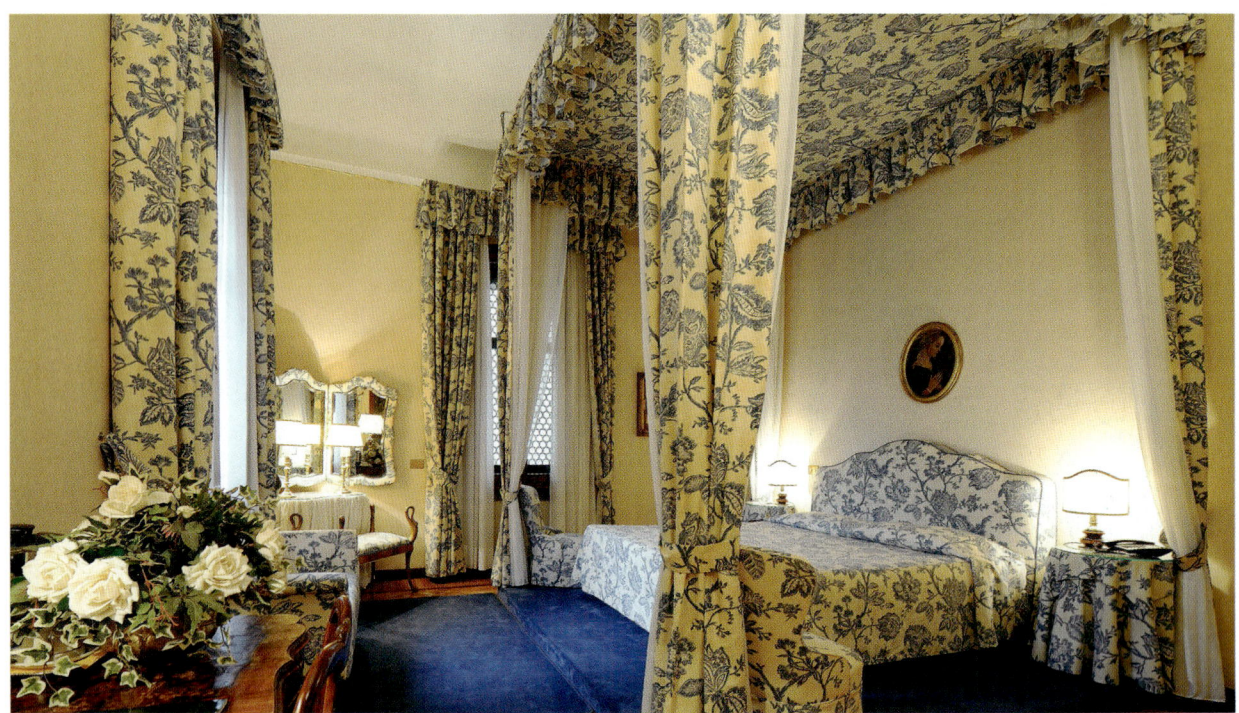

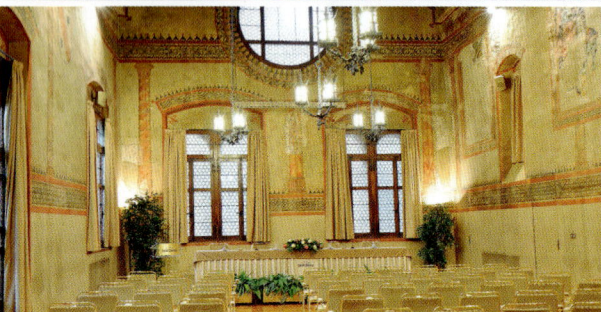
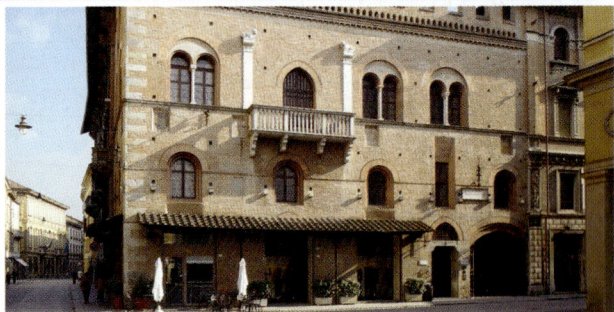

Hotel Posta (Historical Residence)

Ancient Reggio Emilia residence with significant artistic presence

PRICE FROM:
€99

FEATURES:
Gym

ACTIVITIES:
Golf; Shopping; Sightseeing

NEARBY:
Modena; Parma; Balsamic vinegar and Parmesan cheese factories; Enogastronomic tours

GETTING THERE:
Parma Airport; Bologna Airport; Milan Linate Airport

If the thought of staying in a palace excites you, here's one of Italy's oldest: Hotel Posta in Reggio Emilia dating back to 1280. The elder statesman of this 16th/17th-century neighbourhood, the hotel resides in Palazzo del Capitano del Popolo, opposite Piazza Pramplini just a hop, skip and a jump from the city's Romanesque cathedral. If only Hotel Posta's palatial walls could talk to regale dramas to outromance Shakespeare. Instead, it's left to over 700 years of documented tales and art adorning the walls to express its centuries-old history. What's blantantly evident is Hotel Posta's emphasis on amore as the essential ingredient of both art and food. It's also at the heart of the family who have run the property with warmth and generous hospitality since the 1920s. Art influences everything about the hotel, from the scrumptious breakfast in the art-nouveau dining room and frescoes in the age-old Salone del Capitano to the 38 beautifully decorated suites full of old world charm, luxury and comfort. Of course, modern conveniences are at your disposal and helpful staff can arrange discounted excursions. Surprising bonus: the hotel's farmhouse produces balsamic vinegar that's traditionally produced and aged to perfection.

☎ +39 05 22 43 29 44
🌐 condenastjohansens.com/hotelposta
🏠 Piazza del Monte, 2, 42121 Reggio Emilia, Emilia Romagna, Italy

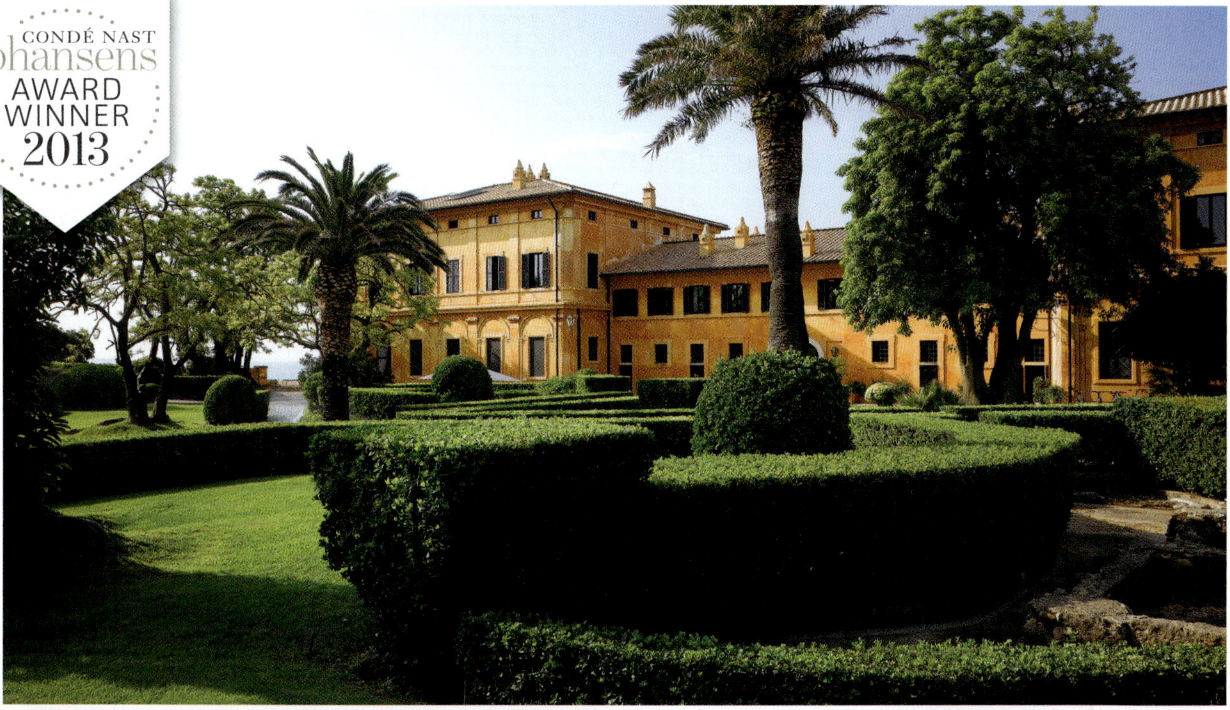

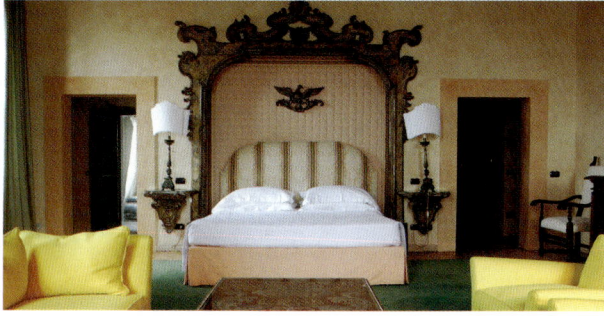
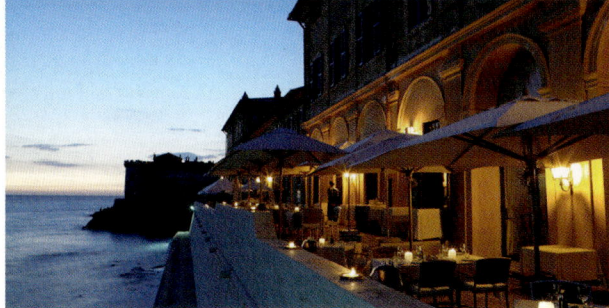

La Posta Vecchia

Lavishly adorned escape on Rome's coast

Live and breathe the Renaissance at La Posta Vecchia near Rome, a stunning villa where the city's beautiful people escape to dine ocean side. Once home to US oil tycoon and art lover J Paul Getty, its staggering collection of 15th and 17th-century artwork, antiques and tapestries are a fitting homage to his life's passion. Beg, steal or borrow to bag the Master Getty Suite, used by the man himself whenever he stayed. From the delicate oak ceiling to the marble bathroom its sheer understated luxury is humbling! Many rooms and suites bring the outside in and once you've been met at the door by a charming member of staff it's effortlessly easy to sink into La Posta's warm terracotta-hued glow. The genius addition of The Cesar restaurant (Michelin Starred no less) means stupendously fresh flavours of herbs and vegetables - many courtesy of the organic garden - sing on your taste buds along with locally sourced fish and meat. Drift into the intimate spa (just one or two at a time), explore the basement Roman ruins or the lounge and chill-out with a drink on the private beach or terrace. Stunning views of nearby Odescalchi Castle will have you goggle-eyed and forgetting that the bustle of Rome is only a short drive away.

PRICE FROM:
€328

FEATURES:
Beach access; Family friendly; Michelin Starred restaurant; Pool; Sea views

ACTIVITIES:
Golf; Horse riding; Water sports

NEARBY:
Ceri Etruscan city; Lake Bracciano; Rome city centre; 2nd-century BC Roman villa museum; Etruscan Necropolis

GETTING THERE:
Civitavecchia Port Airport; Rome Fiumicino Airport

+39 06 9949501 ☎
condenastjohansens.com/lapostavecchia 🌐
Palo Laziale, 00055 Rome, Lazio, Italy 🏠

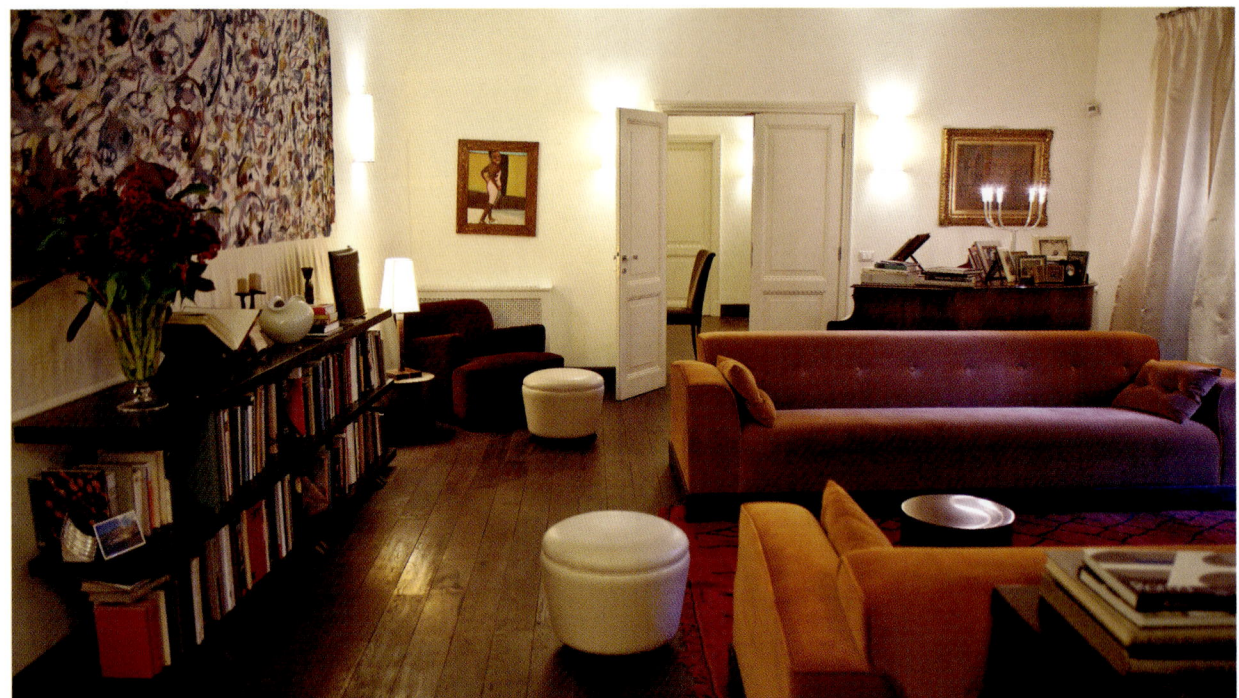

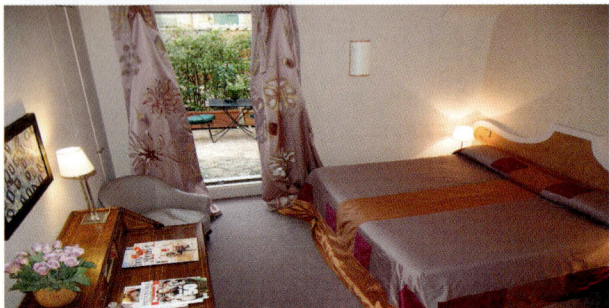

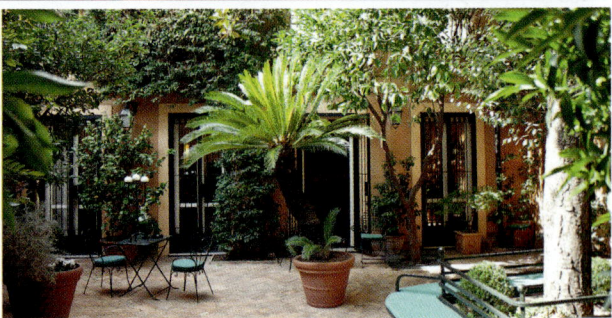

Buonanotte Garibaldi

Welcome to the charming world of Luisa Longo in Rome's bohemian Trastevere

PRICE FROM:
€230

FEATURES:
Pet friendly

ACTIVITIES:
Shopping; Sightseeing; Walking

NEARBY:
Trastereve district; Piazza Trilussa; Pantheon; Navona Square; Campo de' Fiori Square

GETTING THERE:
Rome Fiumicino Airport; Rome Ciampino Airport

☎ +39 06 58 330 733
🌐 condenastjohansens.com/garibaldi
📍 Via Garibaldi 83, 00153 Rome, Lazio, Italy

Buonanotte Garibaldi could be Rome's best-kept secret. Nestled behind ivy-clad walls in arty Trastevere – all narrow cobbled streets and medieval houses – this gorgeous guest house is the home and studio of artist and textile designer Luisa Longo whose graceful fabrics pretty-up the walls and furniture througout. (If you like what you see, there are workshops at which you can learn Longo's craft.) This urban oasis, built around a fragrant courtyard strewn with orange and palm trees, is the stuff of boho-luxe fantasies. The three rooms (yes, just three boutique chic retreats) are sprinkled with 19th and 20th-century antiques while drapes, throws and upholstery carrying Longo's distinctive prints add character and verve. The first-floor Rome Room combines a warm sunset palette with a huge terrace overlooking the courtyard (talk about romantic) while luxurious bathrooms and big, sink-into beds are the standout features of the Chocolate and Orange Rooms; both open onto the sun-drenched patio. Days begin in fine style with a breakfast of homemade pastries, tarts and jams served in the elegant white dining room while the shaded courtyard is a welcome respite from the blazing afternoon sun. Garibaldi is the ultimate intimate, bohemian bolthole.

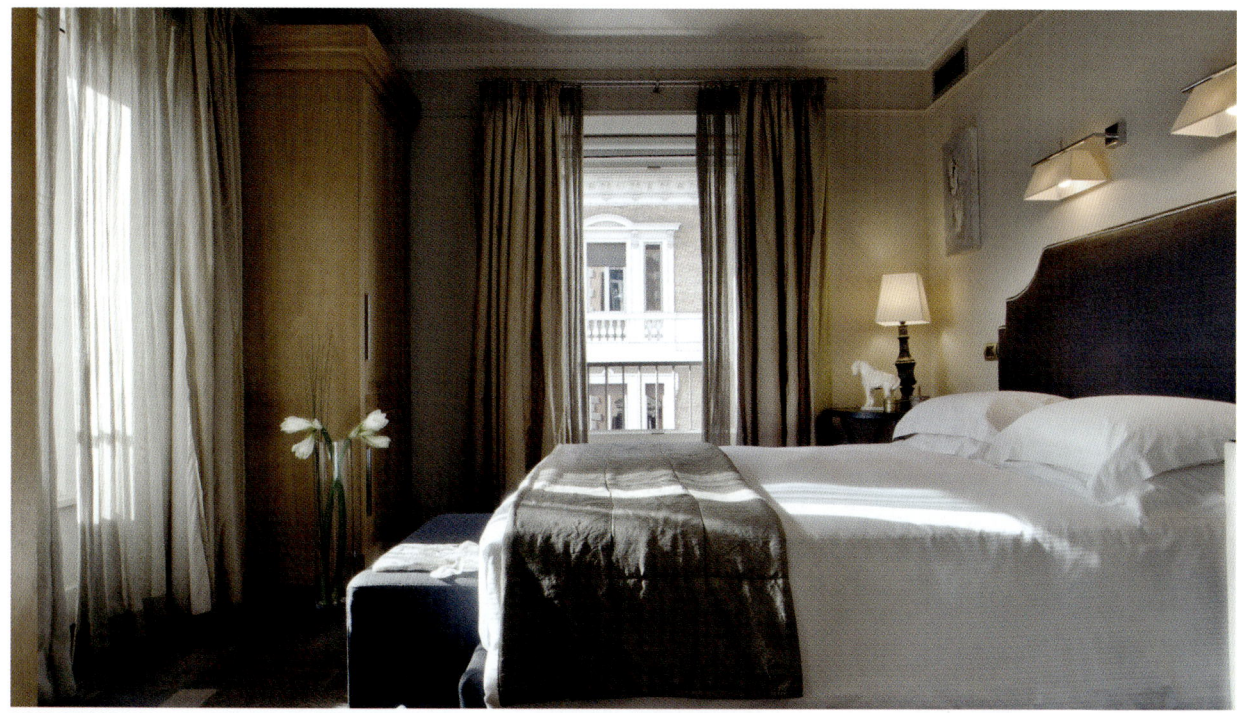

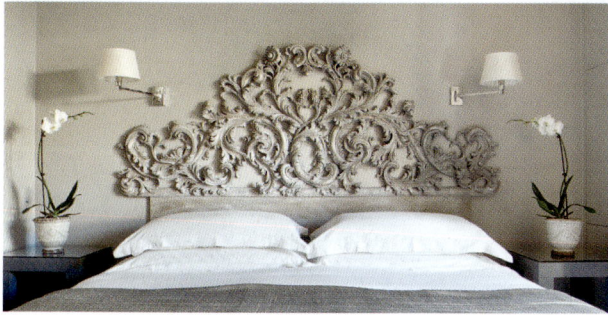
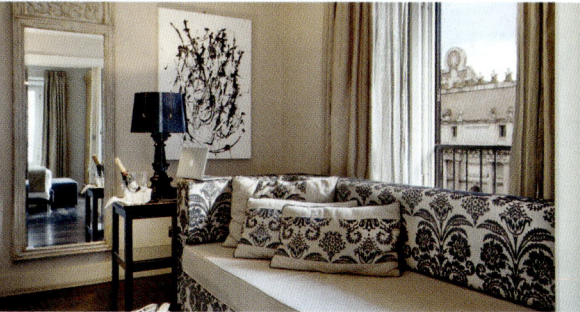

Casa Montani - Luxury Town House

Chic town house B&B in the heart of Rome

Just like the ancient entrance to the city (Porta del Popolo) that Casa Montani overlooks, this urban oasis is a gateway to Rome. Within seconds you're at Piazza del Popolo, Villa Borghese and Via Babuino. In just five minutes you're fighting for a photo opportunity at the Spanish Steps. A further five and you'll be rummaging for your copy of the Da Vinci Code to pinpoint references to the Pantheon and Vatican City. This is what's so fantastic about Casa Montani: so many of Rome's treasures are on your doorstep. You'll feel like a local socialite going about your business from your exclusive city cubbyhole complete with staff who'll bring continental breakfast to your room each morning. Owner Giuseppe Montani has put everything into his family business (the Montanis have owned the third floor of this towering flamingo-pink building since 1916) to create an upscale town house vacation spot. The man himself is often on hand, plus co-owner Charlotte Bontemps, to offer local, inside info on where to eat, shop and visit. They know this city inside/out and their unquestionable taste and penchant for superior quality is evident by the swanky custom-made furnishings and finest Italian/French fabrics in each room and suite. The city may be outside your window but there's nothing but peace and quiet inside. Sound-proofed windows guarantee an undisturbed night's sleep.

PRICE FROM:
€180

ACTIVITIES:
Golf; Shopping; Sightseeing

NEARBY:
Spanish Steps; Vatican; Trevi Fountain; Navona Square; Pantheon

GETTING THERE:
Port of Civitavecchia; Rome Fiumicino Airport; Rome Ciampino Airport

+39 06 3260 0421 ☎
condenastjohansens.com/casamontani 🌐
Piazzale Flaminio 9, 00196 Rome, Lazio, Italy 🏠

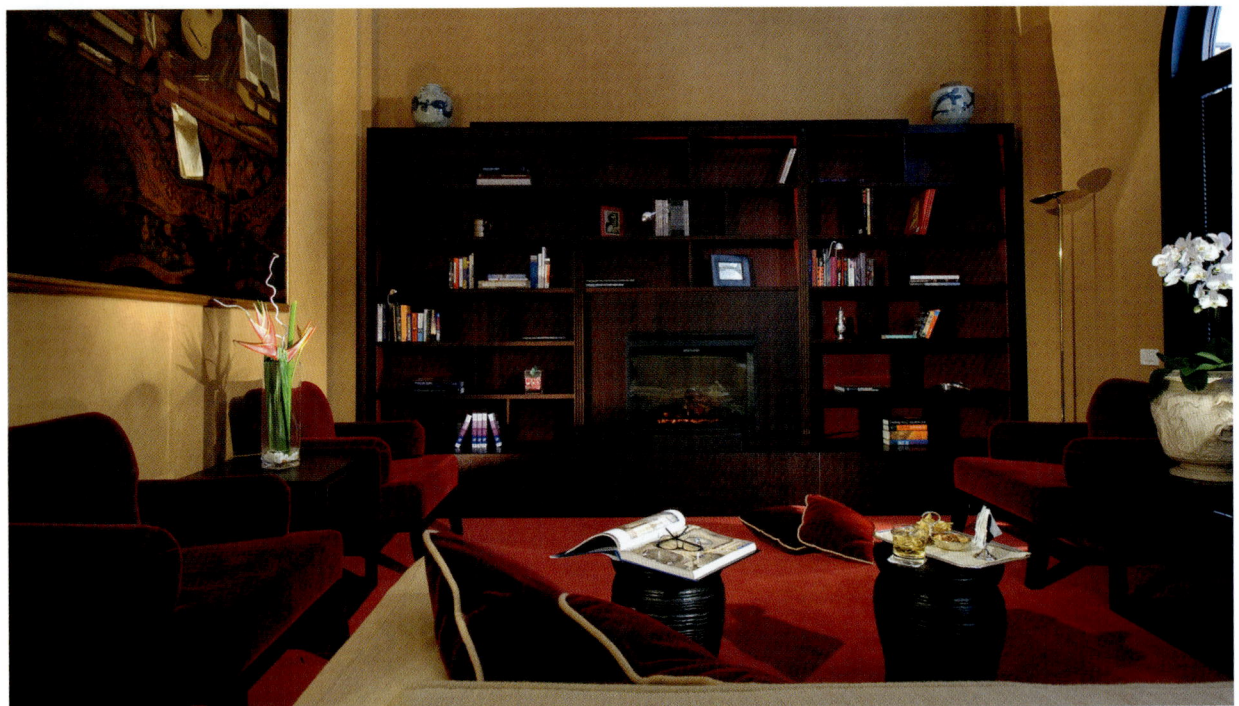

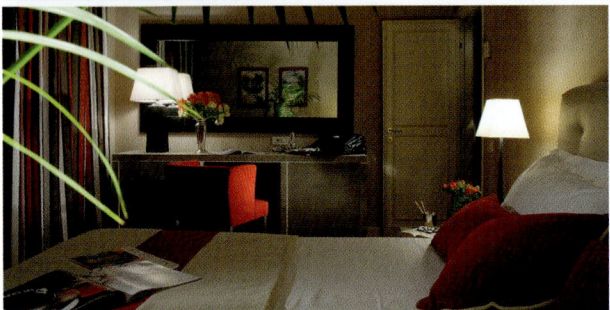
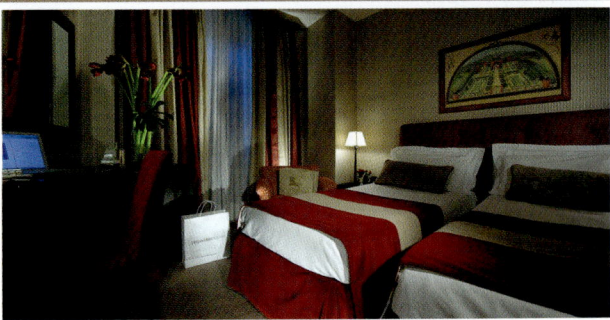

Hotel dei Borgognoni

Sophisticated sleek hideaway a few steps from Rome's popular sites

PRICE FROM:
€225

FEATURES:
Pet friendly

ACTIVITIES:
Golf; Shopping; Sightseeing

NEARBY:
Trevi Fountain; Spanish Steps; Navona Square; Campo dè Fiori

GETTING THERE:
Rome Ciampino Airport; Rome Fiumicino Airport

☎ +39 06 6994 1505
🌐 condenastjohansens.com/borgognoni
🏠 Via del Bufalo 126 (Piazza di Spagna), 00187 Rome, Lazio,
Italy

You know you're in Rome when the hotel welcomes small dogs amongst their guests (mention your pooch upon booking and they'll be provided with their very own bed). Hotel dei Borgognoni provides an exceptional location for your "Roman Holiday" just a three-minute saunter from the Spanish Steps and Trevi Fountain, close to Villa Borghese and the Pantheon. It's perfectly placed to observe that wonderful Italian tradition: the passeggiata (when residents take a gentle evening stroll through the centro storico). However, your wallet won't thank you for the proximity to Rome's famous shopping streets! Despite being at the centre of it all, Hotel dei Borgognoni benefits from the coveted commodity of a garage, and is surprisingly secluded. The enclosed terrace garden of this 19th-century mansion house is a pin-drop quiet spot to soak up the sun after a hectic day. Choose a room with a private terrace to enjoy this utter serenity and spoil yourself even further with a massage in your room or within an equally private area in the hotel. Bedrooms are pleasantly bright and inviting with splashes of red velvet and dark wood that characterise the sleek décor of Hotel dei Borgognoni. Before heading out for the evening, speak to the friendly staff who will assist with restaurant recommendations and directions to the city's hottest nightlife.

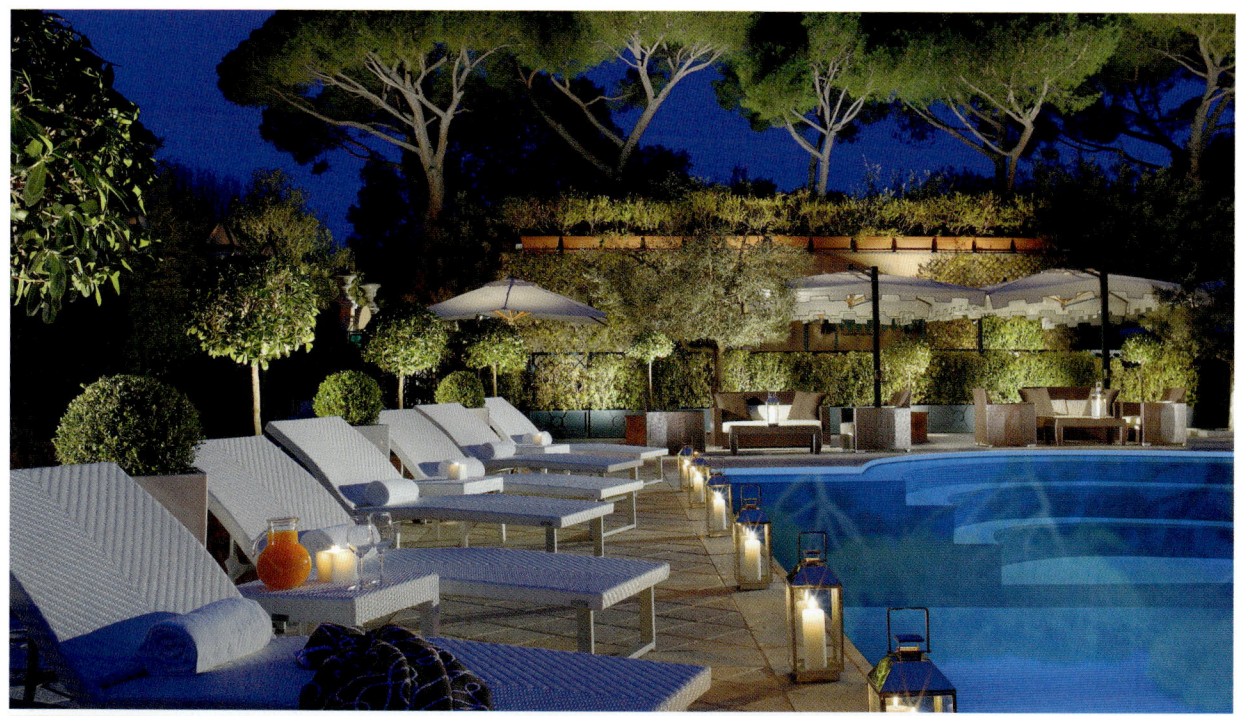

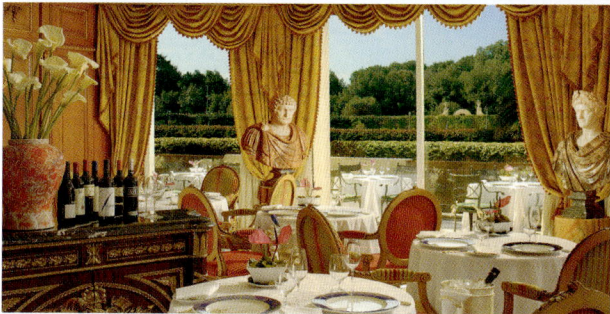

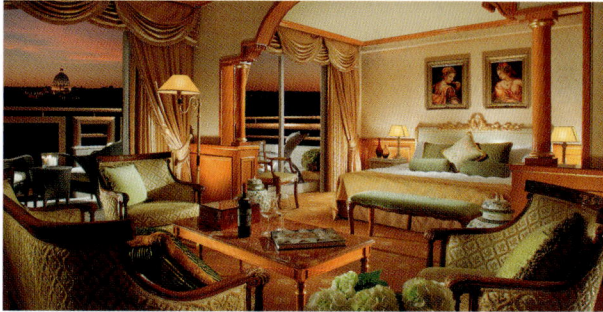

Parco dei Principi Grand Hotel & Spa

A bejewelled, brazen and bold hedonistic slice of Rome

Cool off in the eternal city of historic romance at Rome's Parco dei Principi Grand Hotel & Spa. This oasis of calm next to the Villa Borghese Park is a white-glove service stunner with an outdoor summer pool. Designed by architect Giò Ponti, Parco dei Principi was built in 1964 and has recently been subject to a facelift. Taking inspiration from 17th-century style mavens, rooms are sumptuous and swagged with rich wood panelling, classic furnishings and a liberal sprinkling of artwork and antiques. Minimalist it is not. At the behest of each and every guest, cocktails can be shaken to specific tastes; chaise longues or a chi-chi gazebo can be acquired for extra privacy. The staff await your command! This anything-is-possible attitude is also present at Prince Spa where wellness and soul rejuvenation is the ultimate goal. Serious thought has gone into the materials that create its elegant spaces: natural stone, untreated wood in the Finnish sauna and jewelled mosaics. It's rock-star, OTT opulence at every turn. How about kicking back in the bubbling Jacuzzi with Swarovski-starred ceiling above, followed by dinner at the well-renowned restaurant, Pauline Borghese? It's a done deal. And best of all, you can be in the centre of Rome in a heartbeat - just hop on the complimentary bus to downtown Veneto Street.

PRICE FROM:
€275

FEATURES:
Gym; Pet friendly; Pool; Restaurant; Spa

ACTIVITIES:
Golf; Shopping; Sightseeing

NEARBY:
Galleria Borghese Canova Museum; Via Veneto; Spanish Steps; Vatican City; Trevi Fountain

GETTING THERE:
Rome Fiumicino Airport; Rome Ciampino Airport

+39 06 854421 ☎
condenastjohansens.com/parcodeiprincipi ⊕
Via G Frescobaldi 5, 00198 Rome, Lazio, Italy ⌂

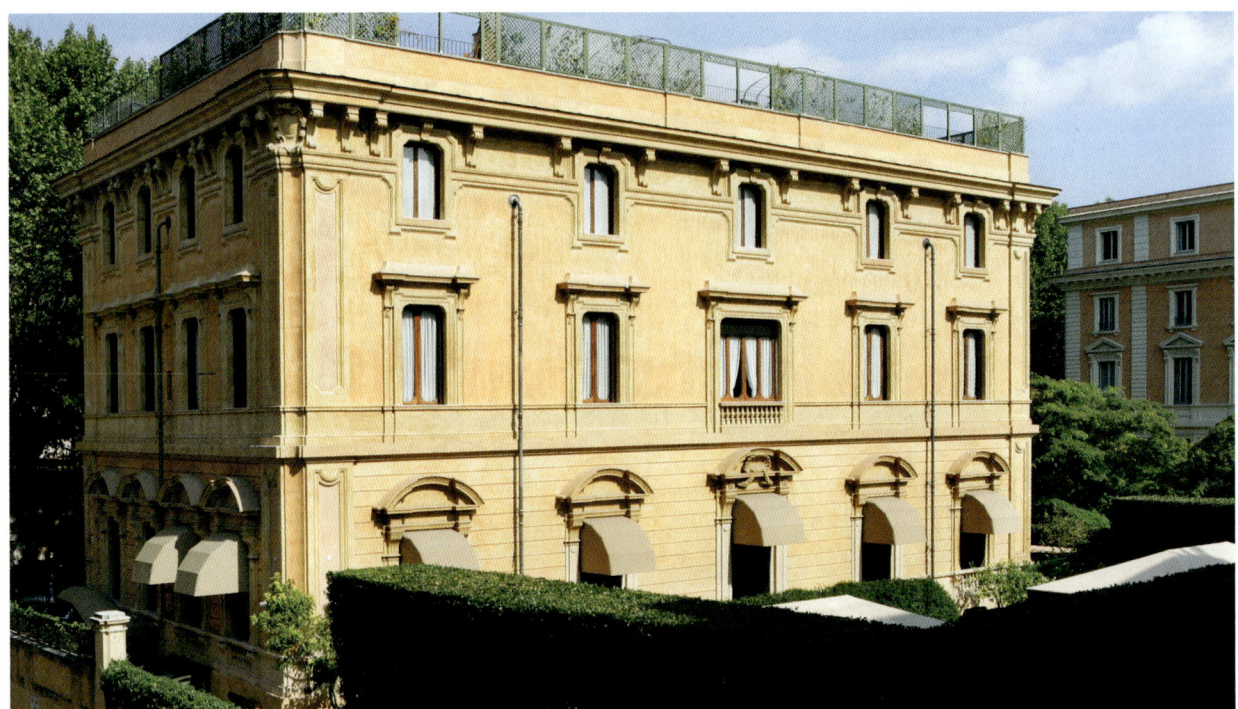

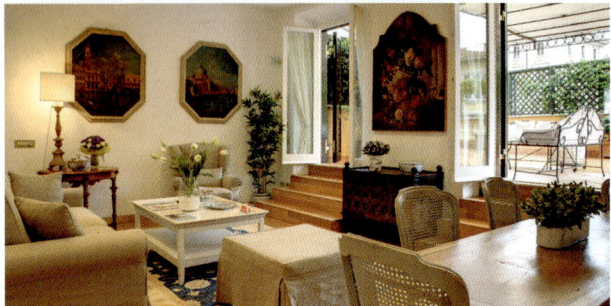
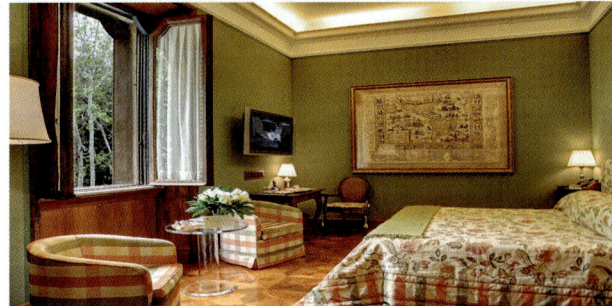

Villa Spalletti Trivelli

The quintessential Roman urban villa

PRICE FROM:
€880

FEATURES:
Family friendly; Gym; Restaurant; Spa

ACTIVITIES:
Shooting; Shopping; Sightseeing

NEARBY:
Trevi Fountain; Spanish Steps; The Coliseum; Roman Forum; Navona Square

GETTING THERE:
Rome Fiumicino Airport; Rome Ciampino Airport

Live like nobility at Villa Spalletti Trivelli, an early 20th-century Neoclassical palazzo, former home to the aristocratic Spalletti-Trivelli family. Occupying a prime position in the heart of Rome, steps from the Piazza del Quirinale (beautiful at sunset), minutes from the Coliseum and Trevi Fountain, the Villa is perfectly located for exploring the city. Inside, opulent interiors are fashioned with art, antiques and tapestries. Marble fireplaces, tall ceilings and wooden floors appear throughout the grand reception rooms while the cosy wood-panelled library is a little slice of Roman history; listed by the Italian Heritage Ministry. A wellness centre (gym, Turkish bath, hammam) completes the relaxed-luxe vibe. First-floor bedrooms overlook the Villa's private gardens (THE dining spot du jour in the summer) or those of the Quirinale. They're big, bright and quite beautiful, with pastel-coloured décor, marble bathrooms, wooden shutters and cashmere throws. But for longer stays and family getaways, the two recently revamped Garden Suites located next door to the Villa are perfect. The day at Villa Spalletti Trivelli begins with breakfast of just-made breads and pastries, unctuous mozzarella and melt-in-the-mouth prosciutto served on the sun-drenched terrace. Lunch and dinner are upon request with dishes featuring olive oil and varieties of white wine from the owners' Umbrian vineyard.

☎ +39 06 48907934
🌐 condenastjohansens.com/villaspallettitrivelli
🏠 Via Piacenza 4, 00184 Rome, Lazio, Italy

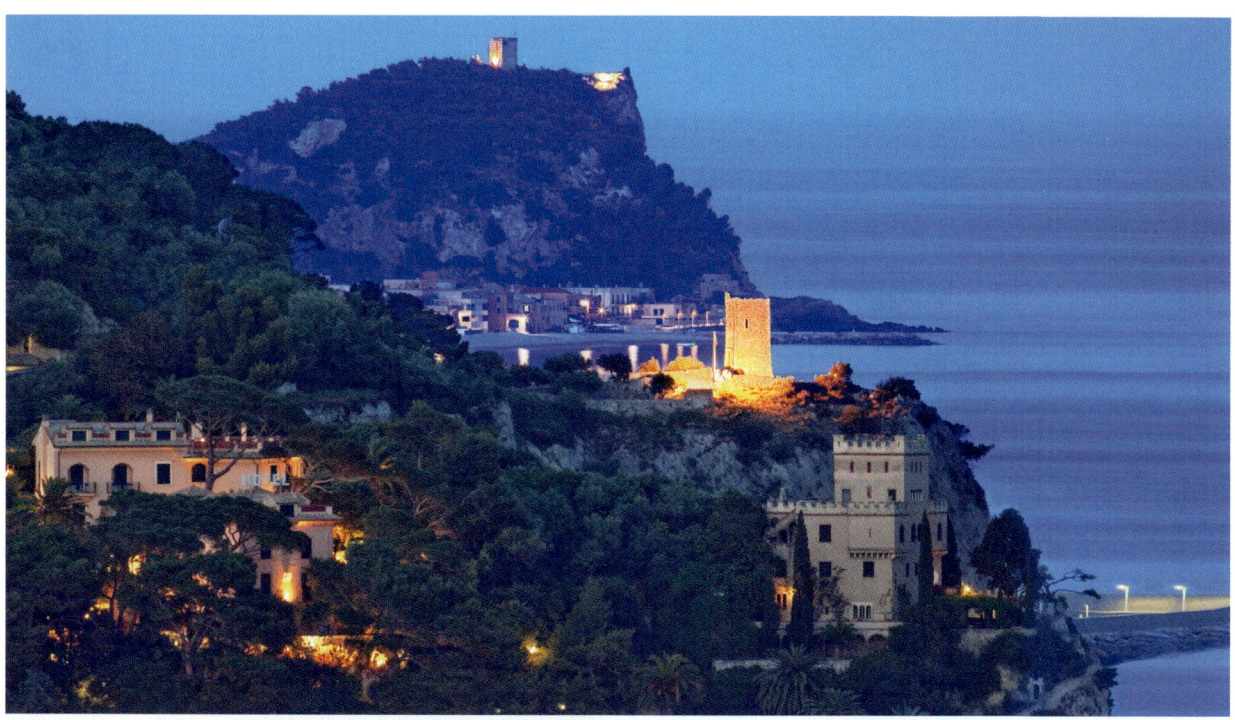

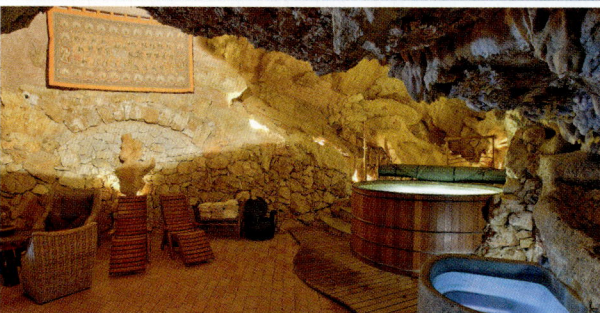

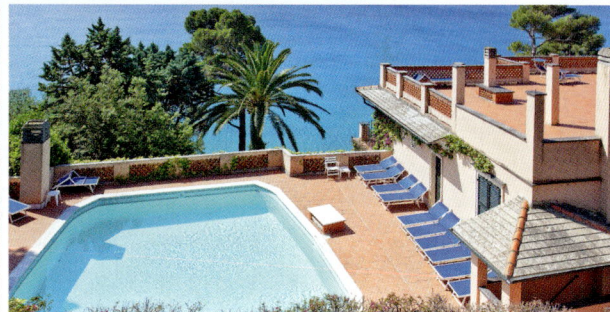

Hotel Punta Est

Classic Italian villa on the hilly Ligurian coast

Follow those in-the-know and holiday at Hotel Punta Est, Liguria, where you'll find many of your fellow guests are Italian (locals know best). A pretty little dame on a green covered hillside, guests are drawn back year after year attracted by its frosted pink façade with cheery blue shutters and dreamy setting. Hotel Punta Est was an 18th-century summer residence for a prolific composer and musician for Milan's Teatro Allo Scala. And today, it's reassuringly traditional with modern touches thrown in with French doors and balconies framing Mediterranean vistas. Hotel Punta's surrounding olive grove is a golden sunshine scene in the day, and vibrant blooming gardens dress the terraces overlooking Finale Bay. Paths and steps from the hotel lead down to the beach (be sure to book your lounger first) but the glistening, sun-dappled pool may well beckon you to stay in this elevated platform to soak up the views from on high. No visit to Hotel Punta Est is complete without some time spent at the grotto spa. Fed by hot and cold springs and cut into the granite, its mellow mood draws you in to while away the hours. Just as the restaurant's super-fresh food, packed with herbs and vegetables grown at the hotel, lure you to try its lovely Ligurian dishes. Social buffets and barbecues are hosted at the weekends. Note for the diary: the hotel is closed from mid-October to mid-April.

PRICE FROM:
€200

FEATURES:
Beach access; Family friendly; Pool; Restaurant; Sea views

ACTIVITIES:
Cycling; Golf; Tennis

NEARBY:
Genova Harbour and Aquarium; Sanremo Casino; Portofino; Monte Carlo, Monaco; Langhe, Piemonte

GETTING THERE:
Genova Airport; Nice Airport, France

+39 019 600611 ☎
condenastjohansens.com/puntaest 🌐
Via Aurelia 1, 17024 Finale Ligure (SV), Liguria, Italy 🏠

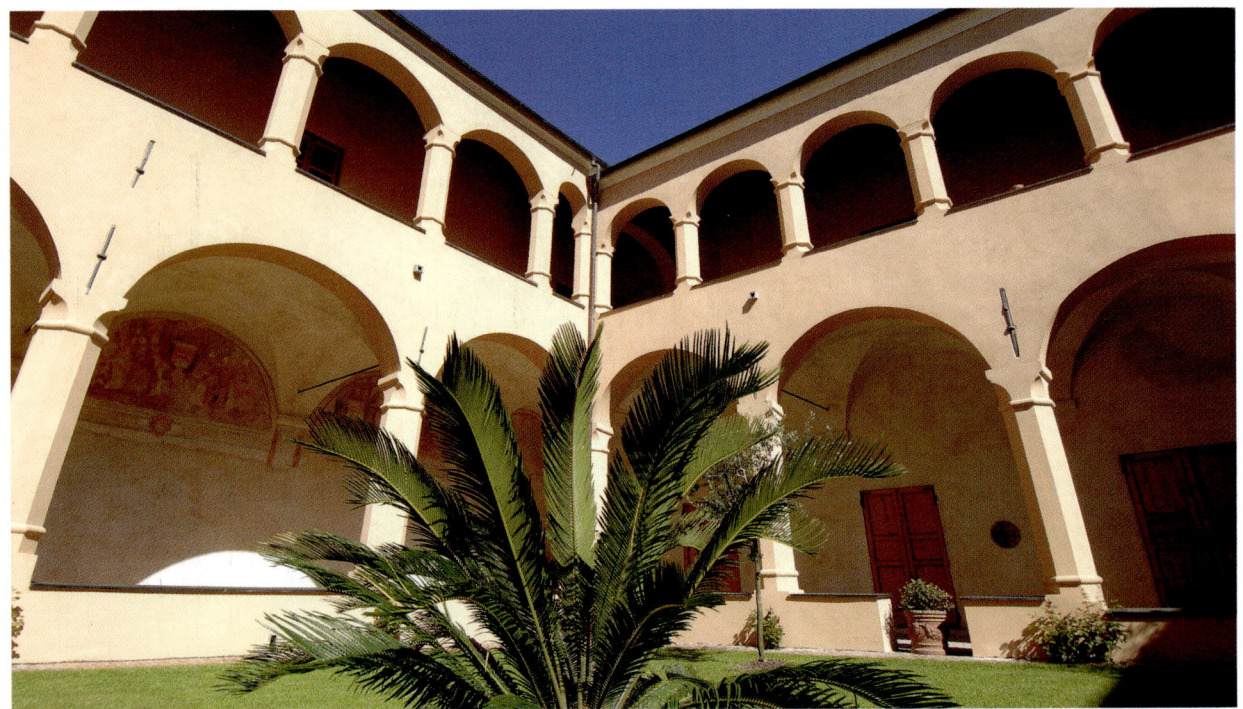

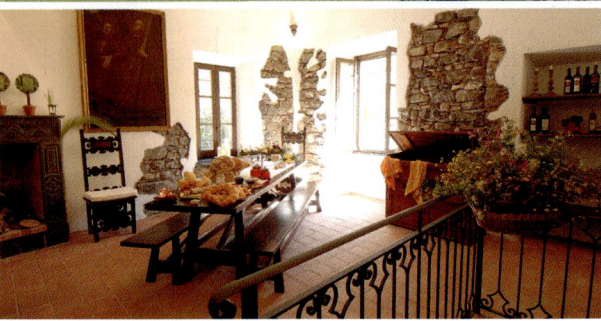
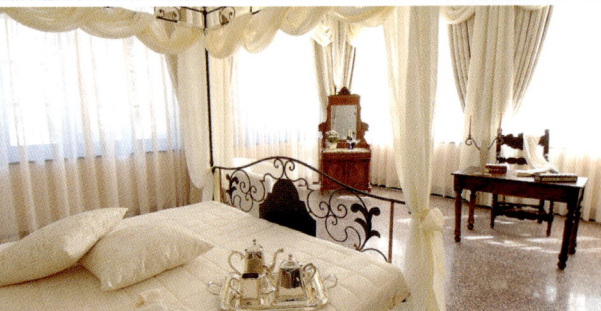

Abbadia San Giorgio - Historical Residence

Romance, history and wine converge at Moneglia, Cinque Terre

PRICE FROM:
€195

ACTIVITIES:
Fishing; Horse riding; Water sports

NEARBY:
Cinque Terre; Portofino; Portofino Natural Park; Genova

GETTING THERE:
Genova Airport; Pisa Airport

Nothing beats the Italian Riviera for good old fashioned romance and glamour: the backdrop for 1960s starlets in silk headscarves and dashing Romeos in lightweight sports jackets still resonates even today. After a day soaking up the scenery along the flower-filled Ligurian coast road, why not park up your classic cabriolet at the wonderfully tucked away Abbadia San Giorgio in Moneglia. Romans referred to this spot as "Monilia" (that's "jewel" to you and me) and no wonder. It sits between the mountains, sea and sky and the precious Abbadia itself is heavenly. Despite its beginnings as a monastery, frugal living is strictly off the menu. Rooms and suites are seriously sumptuous, clustered around the peaceful restored cloisters. Like walking into the artistic creation of an Old Master, lavish wrought-iron four posters, frothy drapes and rich wood tones paint the picture. Awoken at a respectable 8.30am by gentle church bells, the day starts with marvellous breakfasts of organic honey, Monterosso lemon marmalade and local salamis and cheeses created by the fair hand of Chef Suzana. These have you raring to go for exploring the pastel patchwork of Portofino and Cinque Terre just a walk away. Otherwise, you can always kick back beside sister Hotel Villa Edera's pool or on the private sandy beach.

☎ +39 0185 491119
🌐 condenastjohansens.com/abbadiasangiorgio
🏠 Piazzale San Giorgio, 16030 Moneglia (GE), Liguria, Italy

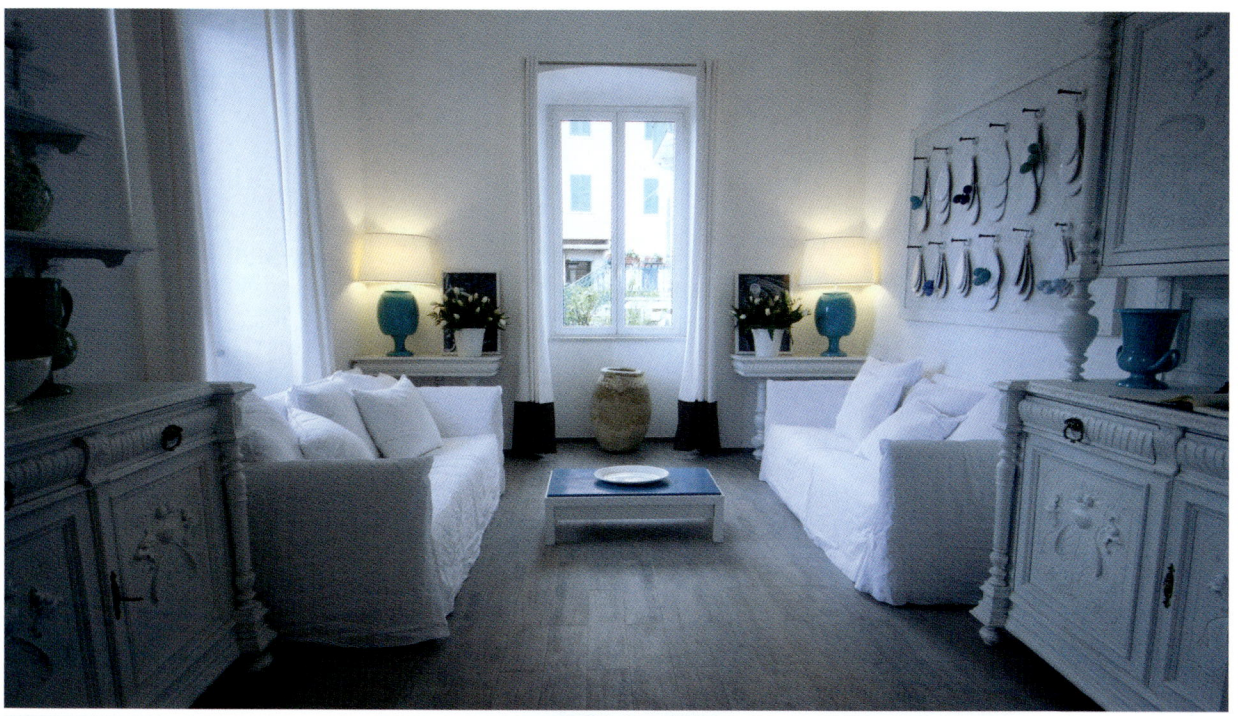

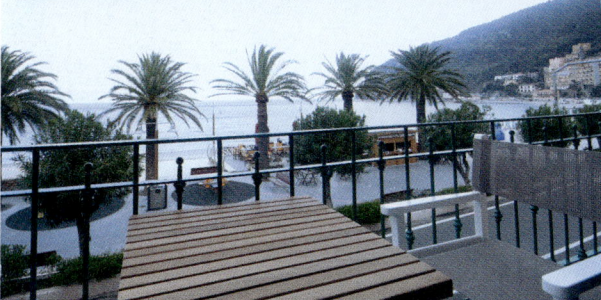
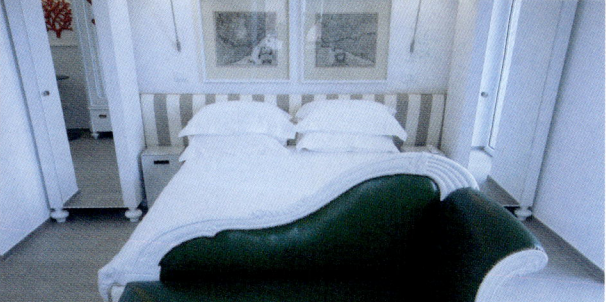

Cà de Tobia Luxury Guest House

Peaceful, luxury B&B on the Italian Riviera

No-one can deny the prettiness of the Italian Riviera. Long sandy beaches, charming fishing ports, hilly green backdrops and crystal clear water as far as the eye can see. Noli, on the stretch of Riviera di Ponente (the coast of the setting sun), is a fishing village of yesteryear where local fishermen still go out to sea at night on little engine-powered boats. Where maze-like narrow alleys and lanes have you weaving in and out of piazzas and the sunlight. The place where Mr Andrea Tobia took a seaside residence and reincarnated it into an intimate, designer enclave: Cà de Tobia, steps from Noli's promenade and beach. Andrea is an ever-present force, busying about in Ca' de Tobia, readily suggesting itineraries and whipping up gorgeous daily brunches (homemade cakes and biscuits! Fresh smoothies! Local meats!). He can also get you a coveted private beach spot at the exclusive Vittoria Club for a good price and organise picnics for your bike rides. The atmosphere is that of a private home, perhaps the special holiday home you always wished you had, decked out with antique dressers, exquisite pieces of porcelain, touches of whimsie and splashes of bold colours.

PRICE FROM:
€150

FEATURES:
Sea views

ACTIVITIES:
Fishing; Golf; Water sports

NEARBY:
Savona; Genova; Private beach; Hiking path; Genova Aquarium

GETTING THERE:
Genova Airport; Nice Airport, France

+39 346 992 3318 ☎
condenastjohansens.com/cadetobia 🌐
Via Aurelia 35, 17026 Noli (SV), Liguria, Italy 🏠

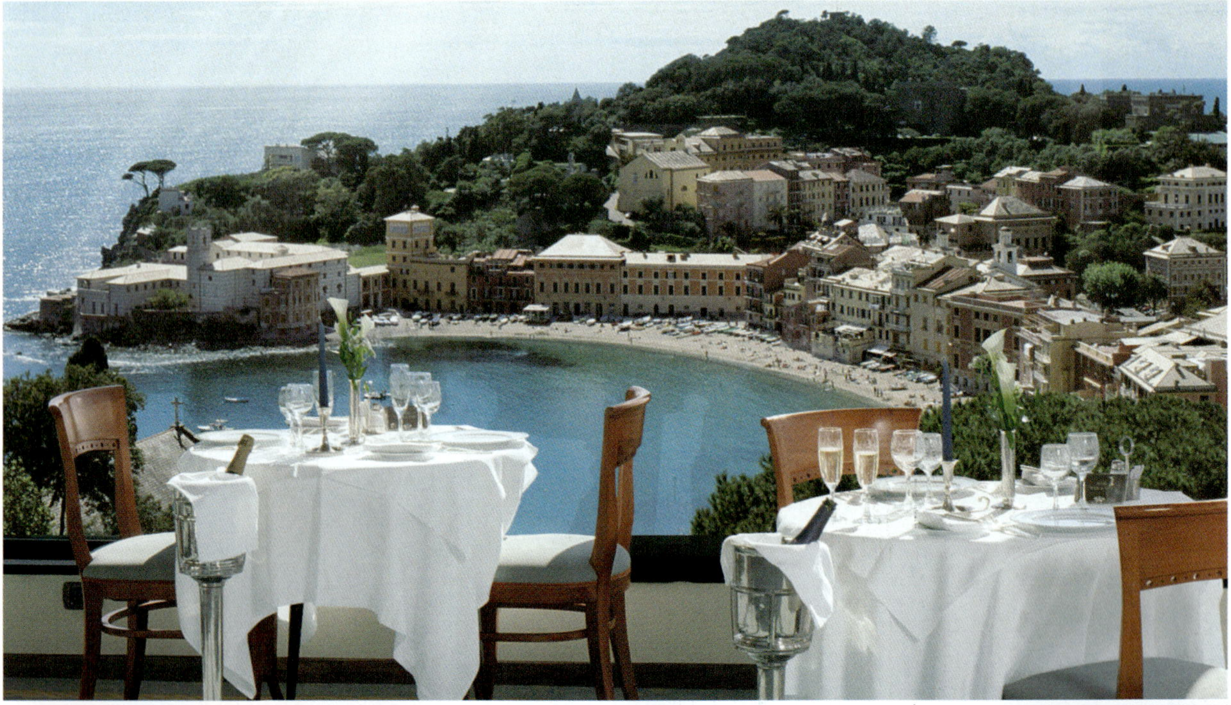

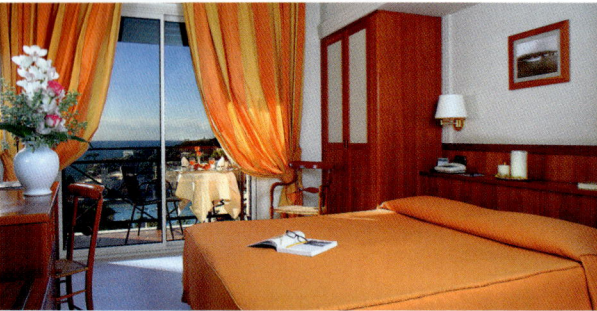

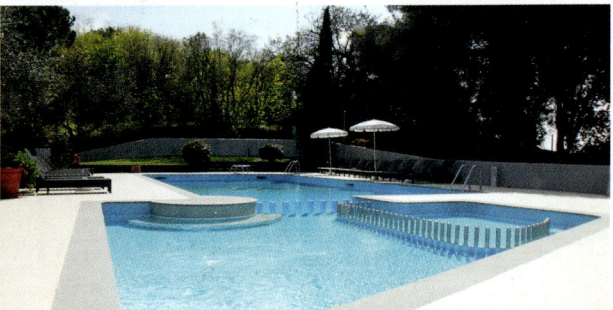

Hotel Vis à Vis

Family-run Italian Riviera bolthole for gastronomes

PRICE FROM:
€210

FEATURES:
Family friendly; Pet friendly; Pool; Restaurant; Sea views

ACTIVITIES:
Fishing; Golf; Horse riding

NEARBY:
Chiavari; Cinque Terre; Bay of Silence; Fairytale Bay; Portofino

GETTING THERE:
Genoa Airport; Pisa Airport; Milan Malpensa Airport

Top-notch food and wine, stunning scenery, ludicrously beautiful beaches. What's not to love about the Italian Riviera? And while Portofino and Cinque Terre are the top tourist hotspots, Sestri Levante, nestled between the two, is the place to go if you crave peace with your Prosecco. Perched on the top of a hill, looking down to the pretty former fishing village below (reached by a lift carved into the rocks) and Bay of Silence, Hotel Vis à Vis is pure Riviera magic. Jaw-dropping vistas abound from every terrace, while all of the 46 rooms come with a balcony or private garden; Junior Suites are divine with panoramas of the Gulf of Tigullio. Dining at Vis à Vis is pretty special too. The Olimpo restaurant is as one of the area's finest, dishing up first-rate, ultra-fresh Italian dishes against the rugged Ligurian coastline (floor-to-ceiling windows ensure you don't miss a thing). And the fourth-floor Ponte Giunone is where the style-set "do" lunch. When you're not cruising the Riviera, lazy days can be spent by the olive-tree fringed pool or in the super-luxe beauty centre before sundowners on the top-floor Ponte Zeus sky bar with, you've guessed it, more of those fabulous views. Magnifico!

☎ +39 0185 42661
🌐 condenastjohansens.com/visavis
🏠 Via della Chiusa 28, 16039 Sestri Levante (GE), Liguria, Italy

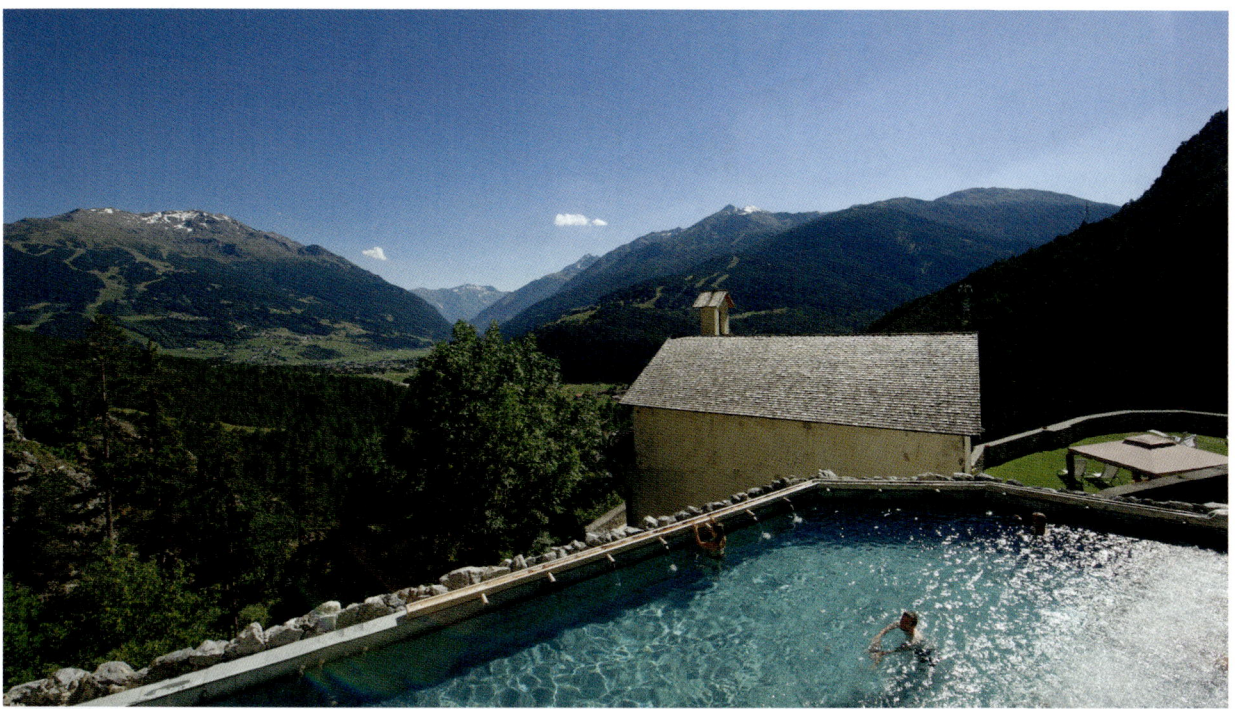

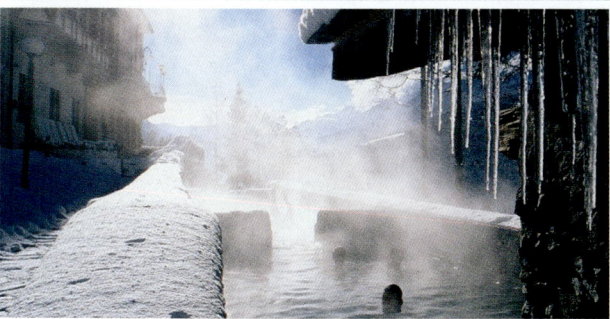

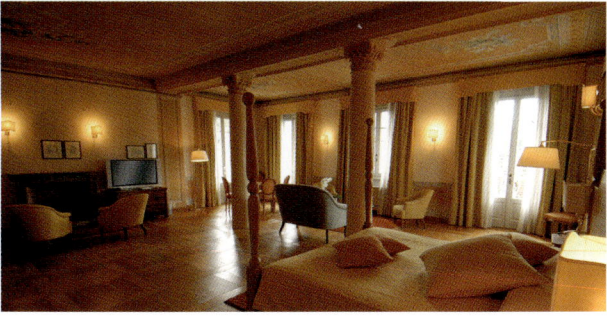

Bagni di Bormio Spa Resort

Invigorating, mountain-fresh Lombardy grande dame

At "the boot's" thigh-high point where Italy meets Switzerland and Austria, there's Bormio. A tourist hotspot for several reasons: its natural thermal springs; high mountain passes including the legendary Stelvio Pass; and year-round skiing. Visitors have been coming enmasse since the 1st-century BC seeking the therapeutic benefits of its waters. Waters that Bagni di Bormio Spa Resort has tapped into to offer an outstanding indoor/outdoor spa at its Grand Hotel Bagni Nuovi. Standing from on high in Stelvio National Park, the hotel looks down to the Valley of Bormio and beyond to an eye-popping mountain vista. A celebration of Belle Époque design, this genteel lady of a hotel is dressed with Venetian flair and has been entertaining guests since 1836. Following a major restoration after 27 years of closure it was brought back to life in 2003 to provide a variety of bedrooms and suites, many graced with a hydromassage bath fed from those magical thermal waters. The theatrical ballroom's restaurant, Ristorante Salone dei Balli, relaxed spa with extensive garden and Light Café (where you can dine in your bathrobe) are just some of Grand Hotel Bagni Nuovi's many stunning attributes. The Spa & Wellness Centre is another. Subdivided into four sections it spans the sunny Giardini di Venere, the undergound Grotta di Nettuno, revitalising Bagni di Giove and utterly tranquil Bagni di Ercole.

PRICE FROM:
€120 (per person)

FEATURES:
Pet friendly; Pool; Restaurant; Spa

ACTIVITIES:
Cycling; Golf; Skiing

NEARBY:
Livigno; Paso Stelvio; St Moritz, Switzerland; Bagni Vecchi's hot spring thermal baths; Stelvio National Park

GETTING THERE:
Milan Orio Airport; Milan Linate Airport; Milan Malpensa Airport

+39 0342 910131 ☎
condenastjohansens.com/bagnidibormio 🌐
Località Bagni Nuovi, 23038 Valdidentro (Sondrio), 🏠
Lombardy, Italy

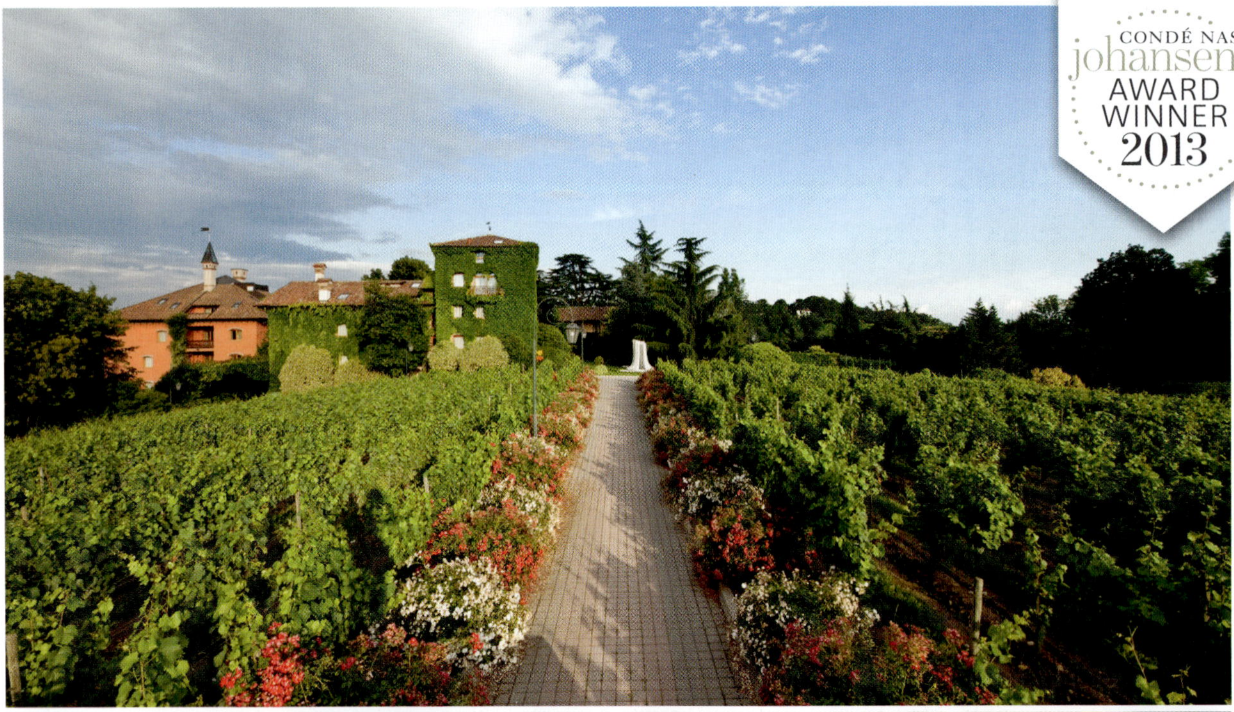

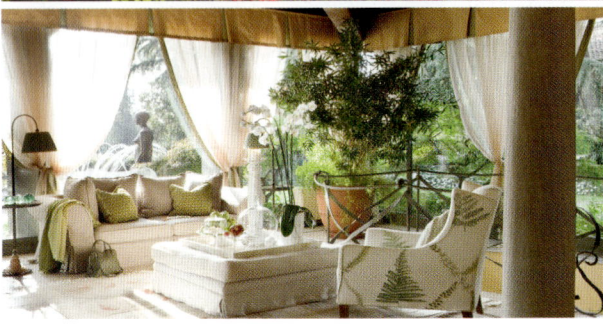

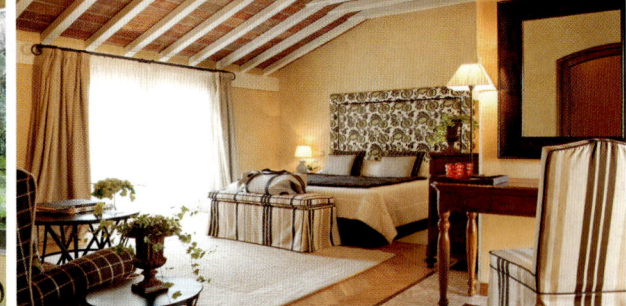

L'Albereta

Where all the finer things in life converge in the Franciacorta wine region

PRICE FROM:
€328

FEATURES:
Family friendly; Lake views; Pool; Restaurant; Spa

ACTIVITIES:
Golf; Sightseeing; Water sports

NEARBY:
Lake Iseo; Franciacorta fashion outlet; Lake Garda; Bergamo; Brescia

GETTING THERE:
Bergamo Airport; Milan Linate Airport; Milan Malpensa Airport

☎ +39 030 7760 550
🌐 condenastjohansens.com/albereta
🏠 Via Vittorio Emanuele 23, 25030 Erbusco (BS), Lombardy, Italy

Perched on a vineyard-strewn hilltop in leafy Lombardy, just an hour from Milan, exclusive L'Albereta is a lesson in Italian luxury. This 19th-century, ivy-veiled manor house is cocooned in 15,000 acres of patchwork parkland with views of the undulating countryside and Lake Iseo beyond. It's polaroid-perfection. Think arcaded passages fashioned with antique furniture, curios, designer lamps and tranquil verandas overlooking sculpture-peppered gardens. While guest rooms are huge and lavished with damask drapes, artworks, fireplaces and Jacuzzis - one even comes with a retractable roof (the Cabriolet Suite). Although the hotel's big draw is the Espace Vitalité Henri Chenot spa. It's a stunner. Italian design supremo Ettore Mocchetti is the man behind the 1,400m² (so much space!) temple to well-being kitted out with hydrotherapy pools, a Turkish bath, sauna, steam room and oodles of treatment booths dotted thoughout the botanical gardens. Light bites are available here, at the Wellness Restaurant, keeping those all-important energy levels up (but not the calories). However, if wine is your Achilles' heel, you won't be disappointed. With a vineyard on-site, L'Albereta's very own wines are top-notch. In fact, visits to the family cellars (Bellavista and Contadi Castaldi) are a special treat not to be missed.

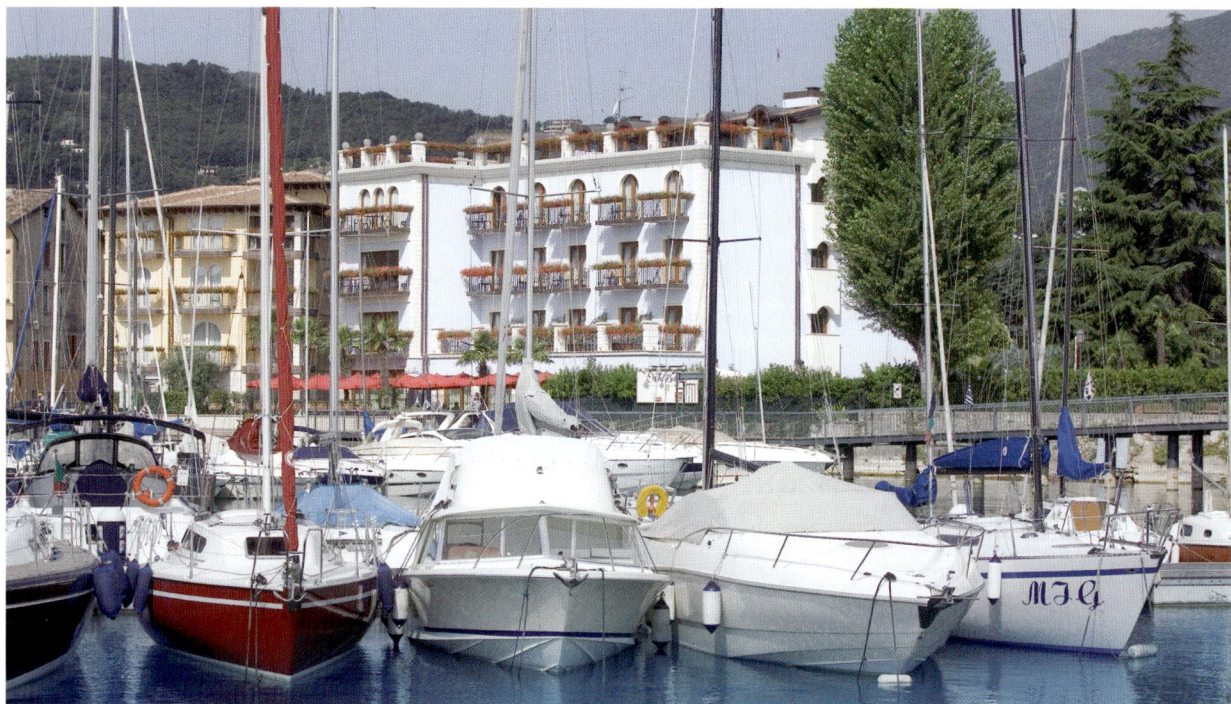

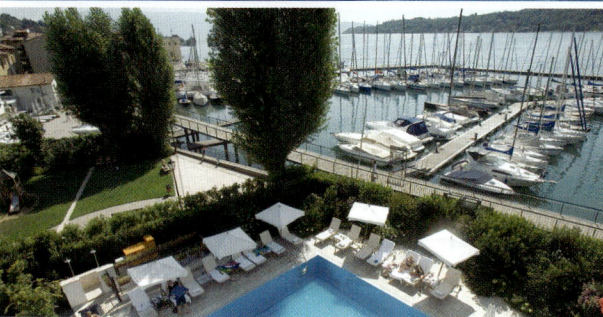
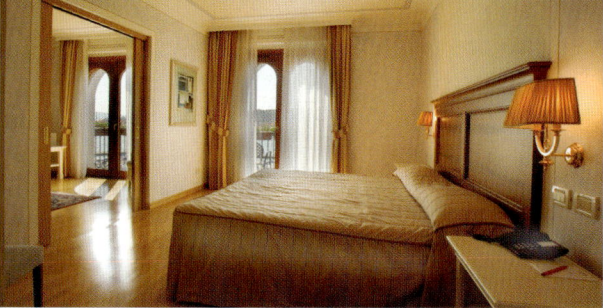

Hotel Bellerive

Warm and inviting Italian hospitality at Lake Garda

Dashing in white beside the marina of Salò, Hotel Bellerive beams across the hypnotically calm blue waters of Lake Garda dotted with bobbing sail boats. Inside, sophistication and tradition welcome you to an unadulterated Mediterranean experience. Rooms, suites and oh-so exclusive apartments in the Villa are fresh as a daisy, relaxed and inspired by the seasonal colours of Lake Garda. Days begin with a kick-start courtesy of a Bellerive breakfast that's a frenzy of baked goods featuring fresh sweet and savoury pastries. Taken on the terrace basked in morning sunlight, the blistering lake views are your backdrop, then, just when you think life couldn't get much better, come the evening there's the allure of Restaurant 100KM for dinner, so-called because it sources its ingredients from within a 100km radius. Its ingredient-led concept produces an elegant menu alongside fresh bread and pasta, freshly prepared each day. Hotel Bellerive's prime waterfront location means that sailing on Lake Garda and courses on the nautical pastime can be arranged before you can say "ahoy". But golfers will want to take advantage of the special guest rates at the local course. Take note food fans: don't go home without sampling the traditional flavours of the Mediterranean with the "Taste of Gardalake Experience".

PRICE FROM:
€190

FEATURES:
Family friendly; Lake views; Pet friendly; Pool; Restaurant

ACTIVITIES:
Shopping; Tennis; Walking

NEARBY:
Verona; Mantova; Lake Garda; Enogastronomic tours; Arena di Verona Opera

GETTING THERE:
Brescia Airport; Verona Airport; Bergamo Airport

+39 0365 520 410 ☎
condenastjohansens.com/bellerive 🌐
Via Pietro da Salò 11, 25087 Salò (BS), Lake Garda, Lombardy, 🏠
Italy

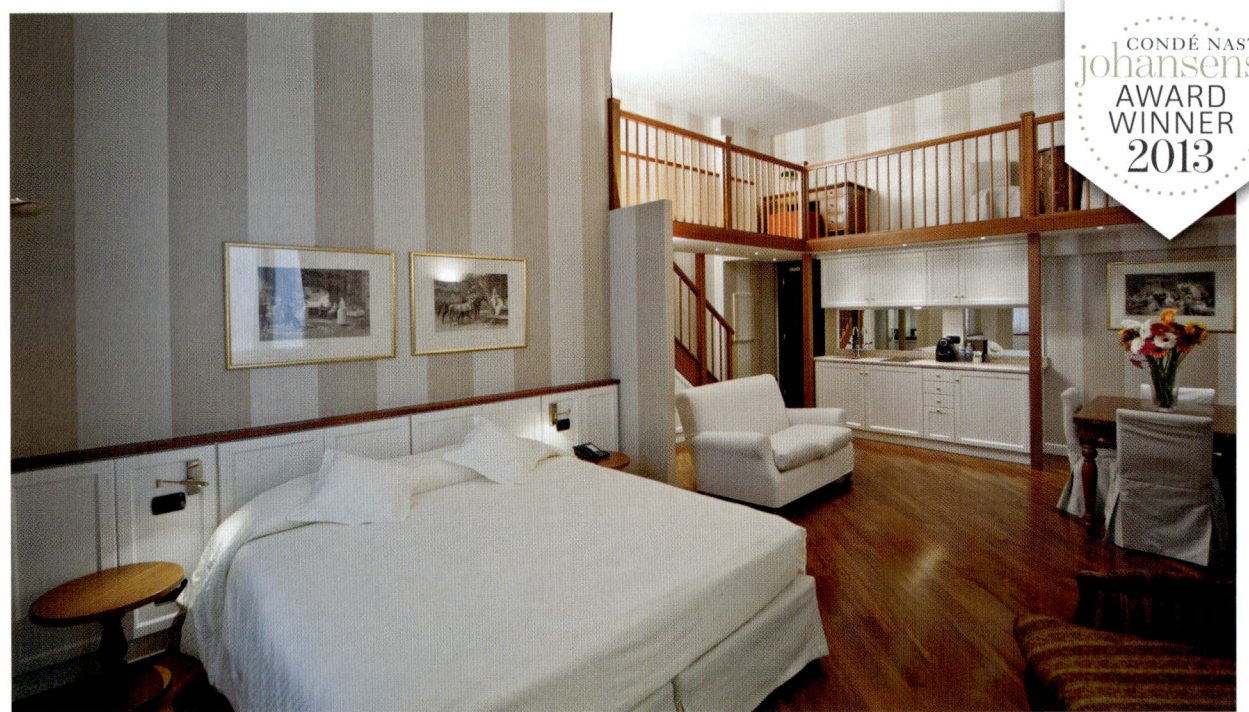

CONDÉ NAST
johansens
AWARD
WINNER
2013

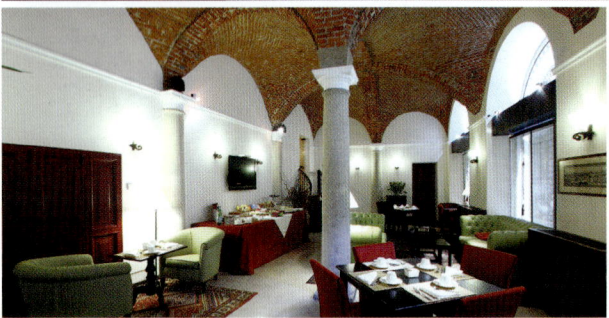

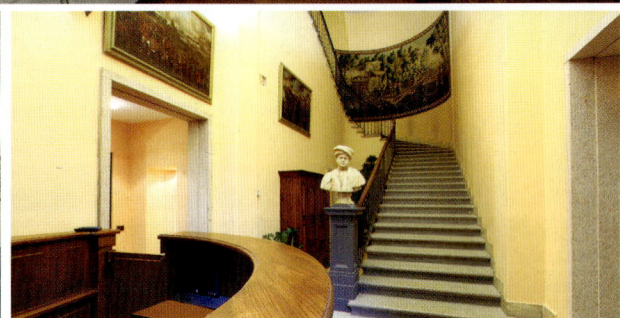

Camperio House Suites & Apartments

Exclusive, private suites with residential ambience in central Milan

PRICE FROM:
€180

FEATURES:
Family friendly; Gym; Pet friendly; Wheelchair access

ACTIVITIES:
Shopping; Sightseeing

NEARBY:
Bergamo; Sforza Castle; Milan Cathedral; La Scala Theatre

GETTING THERE:
Milan Linate Airport; Milan Malpensa Airport; Bergamo Orio al Serio Airport

☎ +39 02 303 22800
🌐 condenastjohansens.com/camperio
🏠 Via Camperio 9, 20123 Milan, Lombardy, Italy

You'll want to look your best when staying in Milan. You'll desire to be in the thick of it and immerse yourself into the fashion-conscious community. Cue: Camperio House Suites & Apartments, your very own glamorous home in prime estate flanked by major city sites. With Milan's glorious gothic cathedral a few minutes in one direction and the commanding Sforza Castle in the other, no epic walks are on the agenda so leave those comfortable (and ever-so-slightly ugly) walking shoes at home. The pedestrianised streets of Milan are your catwalk. Camperio House's entrance is so unassuming that it's easy to dismiss the gates that lead to this former convent and once aristocratic home. But as you enter into the shady cloister and through to the reception area dominated by the imposing, age-old stone staircase, it becomes apparent why Milan is known as a world-leader in design. As its name suggests, Camperio's accommodation is a suite and apartment affair, ideal for business travellers, families and the high-maintenance set. Fully kitted-out kitchenettes, marble bathrooms and bold, striking style are standard fixtures, although for those with no intention to cook, Classic Rooms are the perfect match free from kitchenettes, a butler service and fully-hosted options are available. Buffet breakfast is served each morning so the day starts with a light, fruity flavour.

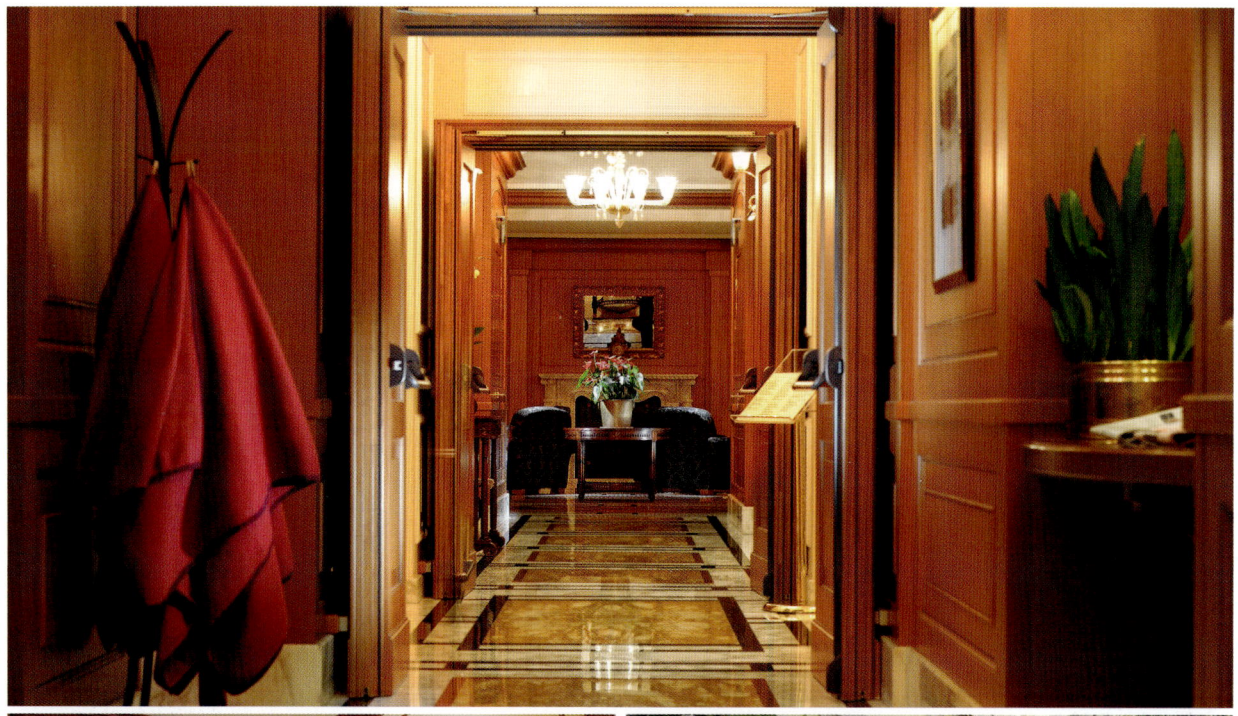

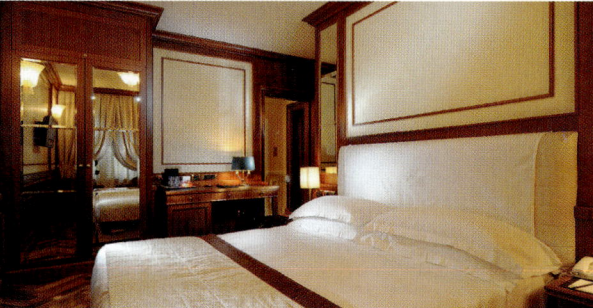
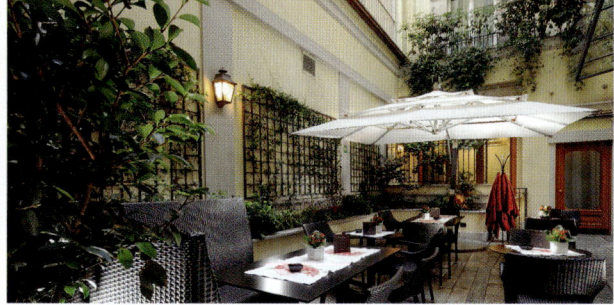

Hotel Manzoni

Quintessential Italian boutique hotel steps from Milan's fashion district

Shop 'til you drop! Amid the beating heart of a prestigious Milanese neighbourhood, Hotel Manzoni is only a short walk from the stunning high-end fashion stores of Via Montenapoleone. Combining irresistible comfort and historic character, this 18th-century jewel rocks all the charm of traditional Italian design: made-in-Italy marble finishes, parquet flooring and rich furnishings. These notes of elegance and luxury are just the ticket after a day of shopping and exploring the city with tech-savvy suites providing all the staple mod cons for relaxed downtime (WiFi, LCD tvs). Take advantage of Manzoni's spa treatments, hot tub and Turkish bath for 100% well-being. After all the shopping, your feet might just need it. With limo transfers and complimentary room gifts, Manzoni has the welcoming embrace of the archetypal Italian mamma - you'll want for nothing thanks to staff who go that extra mile. Breakfasts are cooked to order and the dining room has a homely quality that many city hotels often struggle to capture. Italian pastas, salads and wines take pride of place on the menu, although the Manzoni's passionate team will always create a variety of international dishes especially for you.

PRICE FROM:
€280

FEATURES:
Family friendly; Gym; Restaurant; Wheelchair access

ACTIVITIES:
Shopping; Sightseeing

NEARBY:
Via della Spiga; Via Montenapoleone; Piazza Duomo; Santa Maria delle Grazie; Mural of The Last Supper

GETTING THERE:
Milan Linate Airport; Milan Malpensa Airport; Bergamo Airport

+39 027 600 5700 ☎
condenastjohansens.com/hotelmanzoni 🌐
Via Santo Spirito 20, 20121 Milan, Lombardy, Italy 🏠

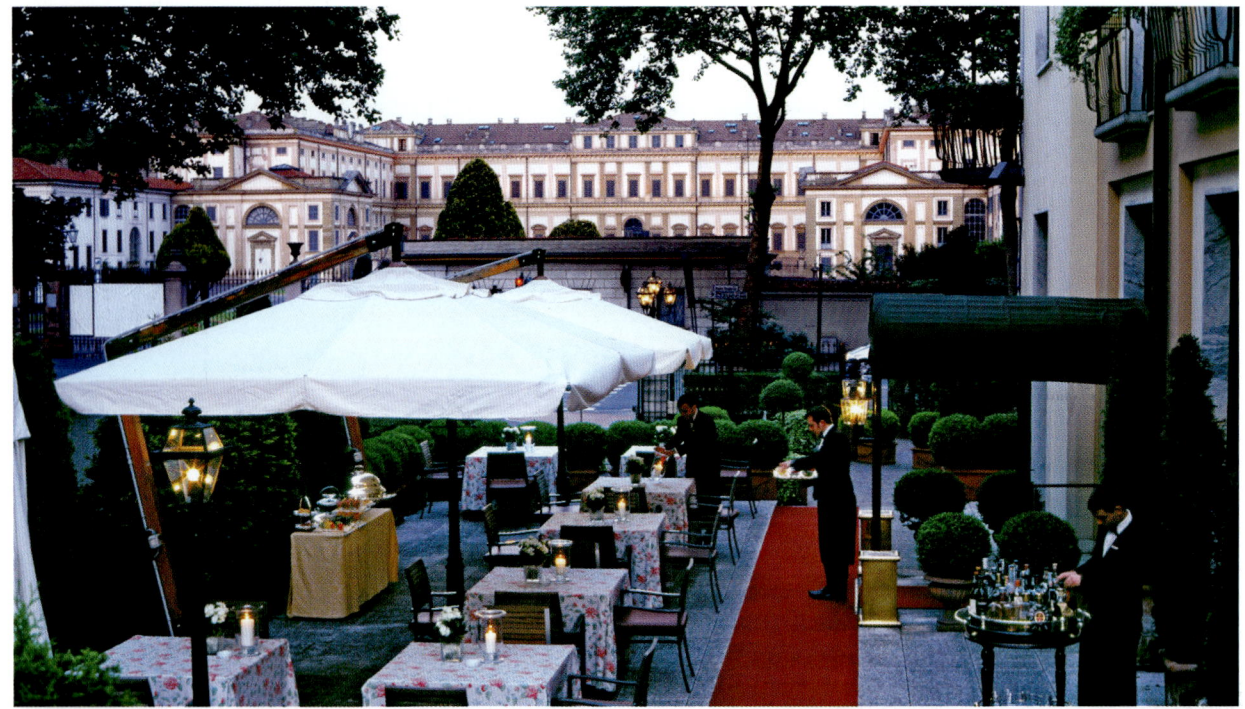

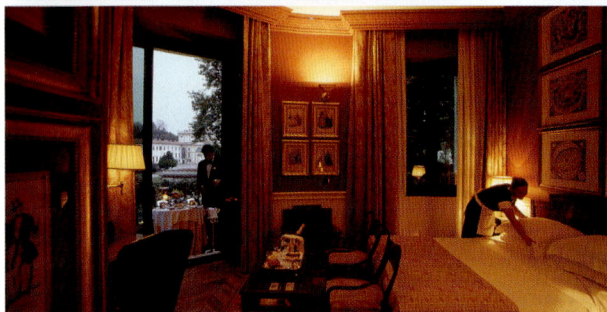
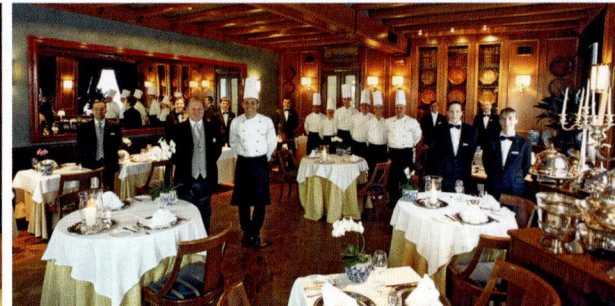

Hotel de la Ville & La Villa

Monza's most enchanting family-run luxury hotel with exclusive villa

PRICE FROM:
€134

FEATURES:
Gym; Restaurant; Wheelchair access

ACTIVITIES:
Cycling; Golf; Tennis

NEARBY:
Milan; Monza race circuit; Monza royal palace and park; Lake Como

GETTING THERE:
Milan Linate Airport; Bergamo Airport; Milan Malpensa Airport

☎ +39 039 39421
🌐 condenastjohansens.com/hoteldelaville
📍 Viale Regina Margherita di Savoia 15, 20900 Monza (MI), Lombardy, Italy

Splendid is the adjective best used to describe Hotel de la Ville & La Villa in Monza, Lombardy. This family-run luxury hotel and private villa has stood opposite Monza's Royal Palace (la Villa Reale) since 1800. Its spacious terrace faces the Neoclassical palace and its park, whilst the interior is a majesty of its own: polished wooden floorboards, oak panelling, Persian rugs, 18th-century Chinese porcelain and a myriad of exquisite antiques. The inviting bedrooms are adorned with plush fabrics, crisp linen-clad beds and marble bathrooms, and all have the technological comforts you could wish for. Unwinding with apéritifs and cocktails is encouraged in the intimate American Bar (a trip to the hotel's sauna beforehand will help set the relaxed mood) followed by dinner at Derby Grill, Hotel de la Ville's award-winning restaurant. Executive Chef Fabio Silva's mouth-watering menu has collected an impressive number of accolades. The close proximity of Hotel de la Ville to Monza's Formula 1 circuit is of course a big draw, and its short walk to Monza's historical city centre is a huge bonus. Milan is also tantalisingly close. Most impressive of all though, is the exceptional service at Hotel de la Ville. All whims are catered for thanks to the friendly and attentive staff. This is a hotel with character and lashings of charm.

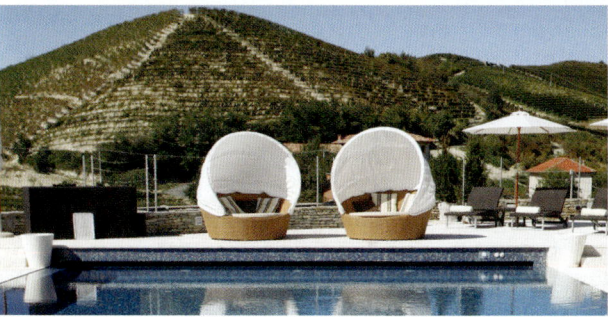

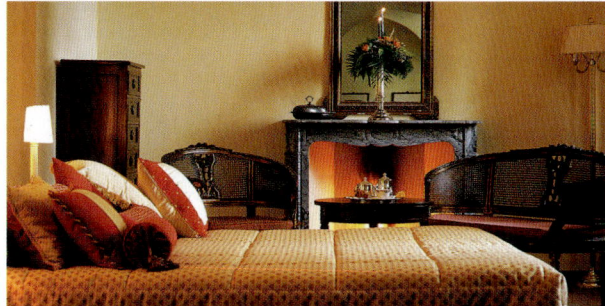

Relais San Maurizio Luxury Spa Resort

Utter tranquillity in the Piemonte hills

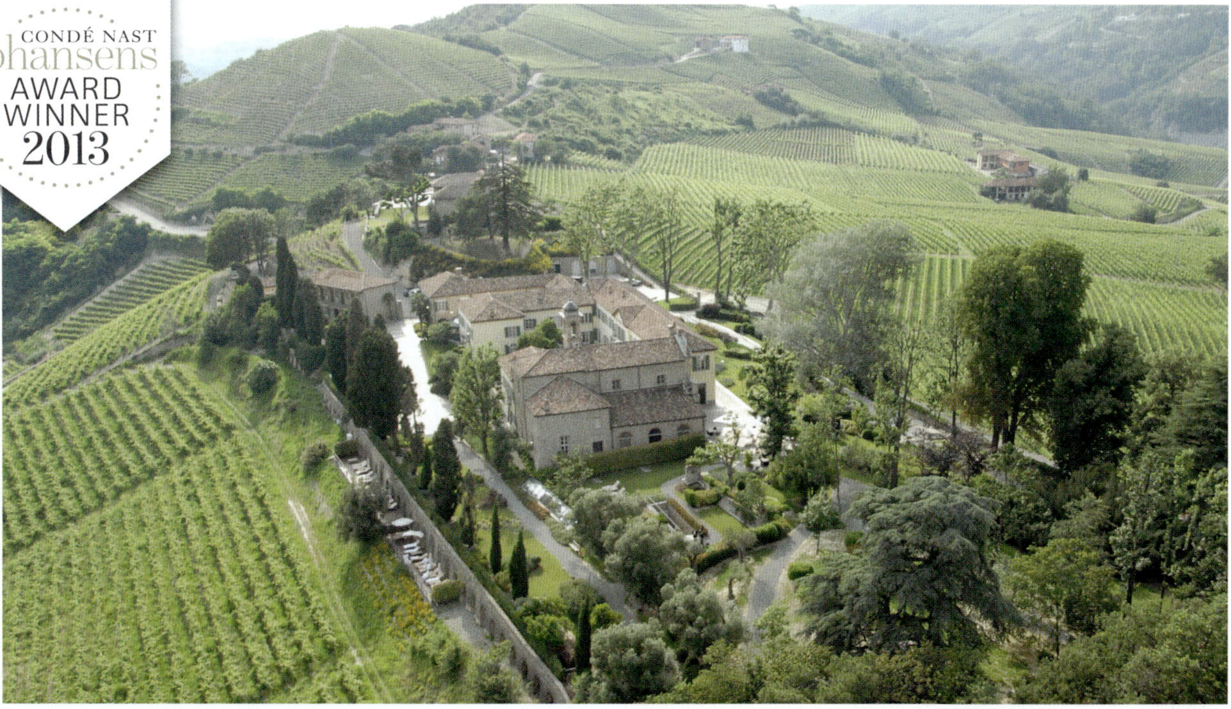

It's said that too much salt can be bad for you. But anyone visiting Relais San Maurizio Luxury Spa Resort, Italy, begs to differ. This completely secluded sanctuary in the Piemonte hills is the ultimate spa destination whose Grotta del Sale salt baths in ancient caves filled with mineral-rich water and salt, have invigorating properties. Soothing the senses, it's the perfect antidote to a hectic lifestyle. Nestled in Santa Stefano Belbo's vine-covered countryside, Relais San Maurizio is an old monastery. It has 31 exclusive rooms and suites, each uniquely decorated and located in various buildings. Choose a room in the stable conversion or a former monk's cell. Each is brimming with the charm of rich Italian history and embodies an all-encompassing quiet. Elegant simplicity and comfort are the key features of each one, enhanced by a view that's faultless. Trekking, biking and golfing are the favoured activities in these hills but let's not forget that this is Langhe Valley, an area renowned for its food and wine. At its heart of Langhe, Relais San Maurizio's Guido da Costigliole restaurant earned its Michelin Star by combining the abundance of local flavours with those from Provence.

PRICE FROM:
€318

FEATURES:
Gym; Michelin Starred restaurant; Pet friendly; Pool; Spa

ACTIVITIES:
Cycling; Golf; Walking

NEARBY:
Alba; Asti; Langhe wine cellars of Barolo and Barbaresco; White truffle fair; Royal residence in Turin

GETTING THERE:
Turin Airport; Genova Airport; Milan Malpensa Airport

+39 0141 841900 ☎
condenastjohansens.com/relaissanmaurizio 🌐
Località San Maurizio 39, 12058 Santo Stefano Belbo (CN), 🏠
Langhe Wine District, Piemonte, Italy

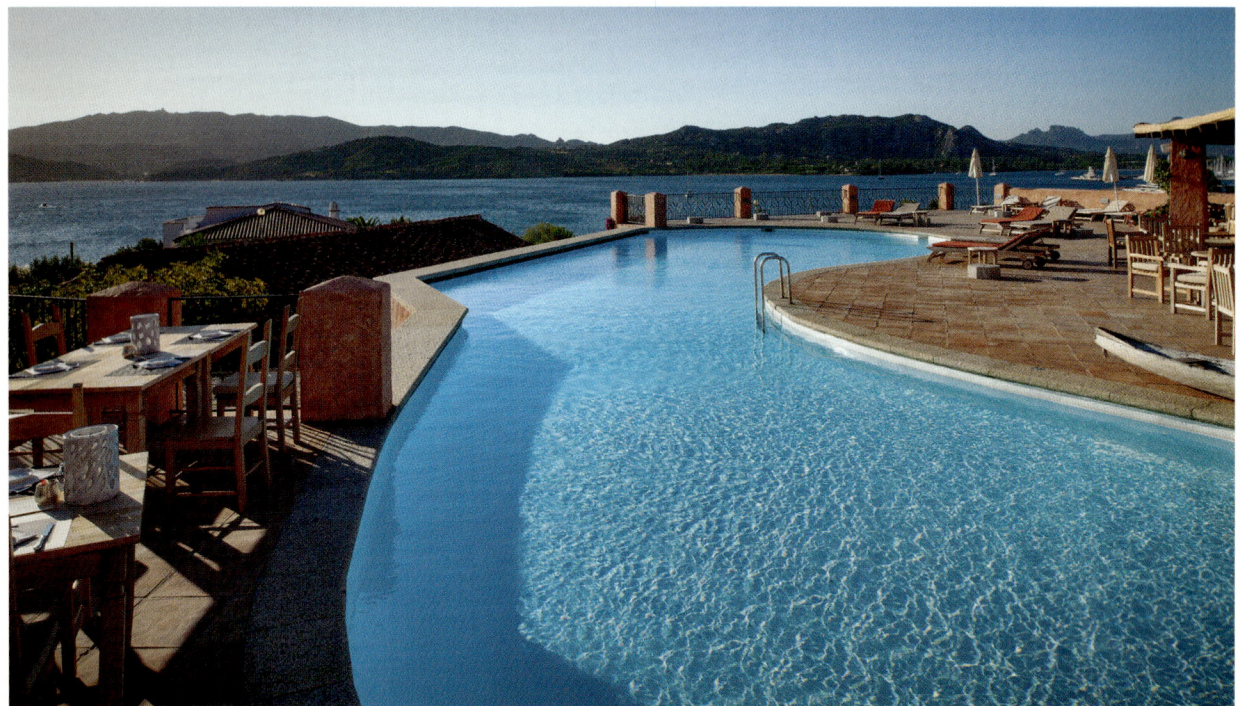

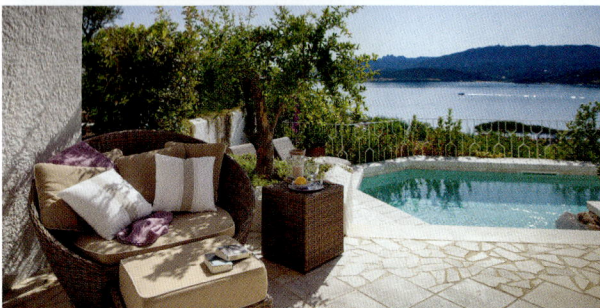

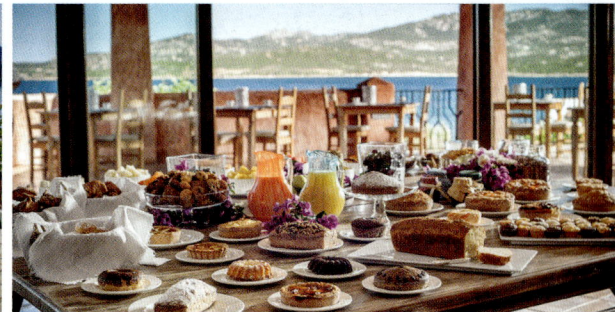

Hotel Relais Villa del Golfo & Spa

Stylish Sardinian seaside charmer

PRICE FROM:
€240

FEATURES:
Gym; Pool; Restaurant; Sea views; Spa

ACTIVITIES:
Golf; Sightseeing; Water sports

NEARBY:
San Pantaleo; Baia Sardinia; Porto Cervo; Emerald coast beaches; Marine park

GETTING THERE:
Olbia Airport; Alghero Airport

Sofas on tiled balconies, magnificent vistas and someone on hand to cater to your every whim. This is Hotel Relais Villa del Golfo & Spa on Sardinia's dazzling shore of Cannigione where kicking back has never been so luxurious, so spoiling and bewitching. But if sofa-surfing in the sun has you itching for some adventure, Hotel Relais Villa del Golfo's private yacht is readily available for exploring the Emerald Coast's impossibly beautiful beaches (reached via the hotel's private wooden deck). Bikes can also be hired for some two-wheeled Sicilian adventure. But before any water sport activities, tours by foot, horse or jeep, cooking and/or wine tasting courses, days begin with an incredible breakfast of home-made, freshly baked bread and cakes, just-picked fruit and veg, Italian cold meats and cheeses. Happy Hours follow on later at the bar each evening and then comes the grilled fare at Restaurant Miraluna's; the hotel prides itself on the locally sourced produce used in its dishes. No visit is complete without a trip to the indoor pool and Harmony Spa whose long, soothing massages, steam rooms and facial treatments are guaranteed to take every-day stresses away. Once in your jelly-like state of relaxation and contentment, there's nothing for it but to flop into your luxury suite that just happens to overlook a stunning bay (most rooms have sea views and a private garden).

☎ + 39 0789 892091
🌐 condenastjohansens.com/hotelvilladelgolfo
🏠 Via Monti Corru, Loc La Conia, 07020 Cannigione, Olbia-Tempio, Sardinia, Italy

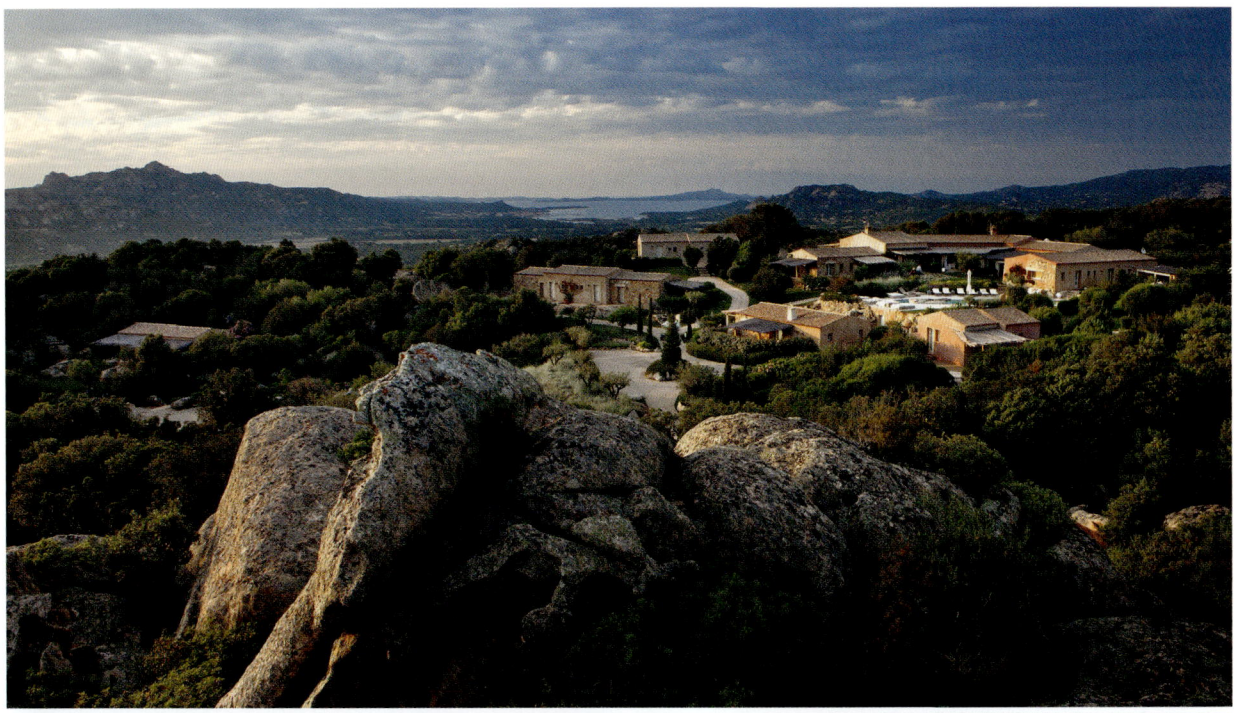

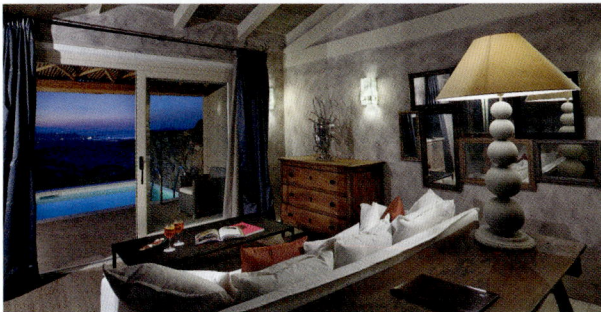

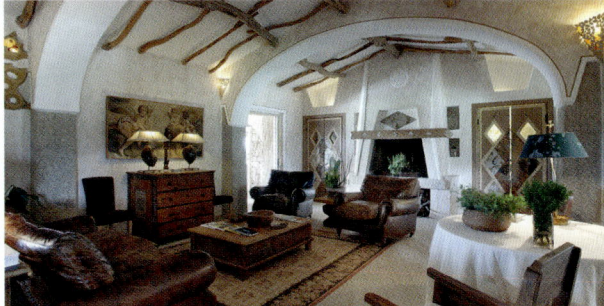

Petra Segreta Resort & Spa

Spectacular views from a spectacular Sardinian resort

Petra Segreta has you reaching for the camera and discovering an oasis of peace and harmony on the gorgeous northern coastline of Sardinia. In the wonderfully secluded village of San Pantaleo, famous for handmade wood crafts, iron works and ceramics, this luxury resort and spa lies in the region of Olbia whose incredible views of the Emerald Coast take your breath away. Private verandas from Petra Segreta's elegantly furnished suites take in these eye-popping vistas whose elegant farmhouse comfort is sumptuously simple and utterly relaxing. Each is scattered amidst the resort's greenery within quaint cottages filled with the scents of the surrounding Mediterranean vegetation. Located within the natural granite grottos of the resort, Petra Segreta's wellness centre specialises in Ayurvedic treatments with the added benefits of a Turkish bath and Roman sauna. And in the restaurant, understated perfection is the only standard owner and chef Luigi Bergeretto will accept. His talents extend beyond his Italian tv appearances to the cuisine to offer an excellent combination of locally grown flavours alongside the best of the region's wines. But you don't need to wait until dinner to sample his creations, picnics on the beach can be organised - simply ask.

PRICE FROM:
€250

FEATURES:
Gym; Pool; Restaurant; Sea views

ACTIVITIES:
Fishing; Golf; Water sports

NEARBY:
Cala di Volpe; Porto Cervo beach; Pevero Golf Course; Costa Smeralda beach; Marine Park of Tavolara and Molara

GETTING THERE:
Olbia Ferry Port; Olbia Airport

+39 0789 187 6441 ☎
condenastjohansens.com/petrasegretaresort 🌐
Strada Buddeu, CP 130, 07026 San Pantaleo, Olbia, Emerald 🏠
Coast, Sardinia, Italy

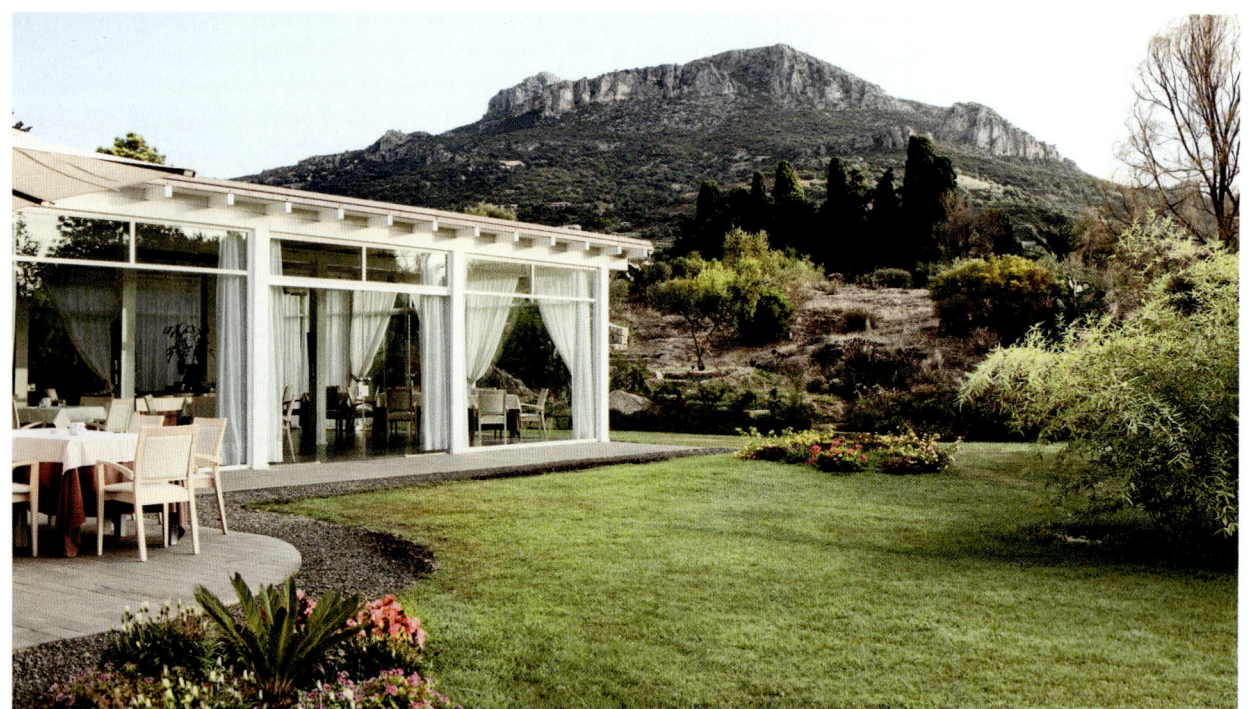

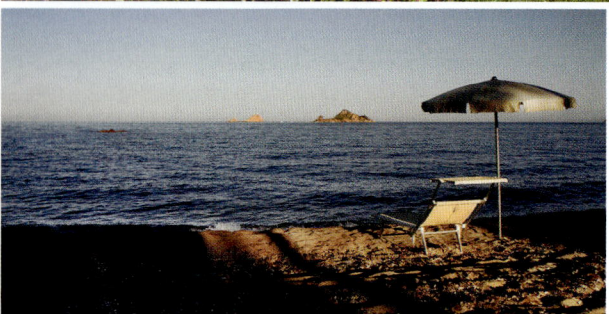

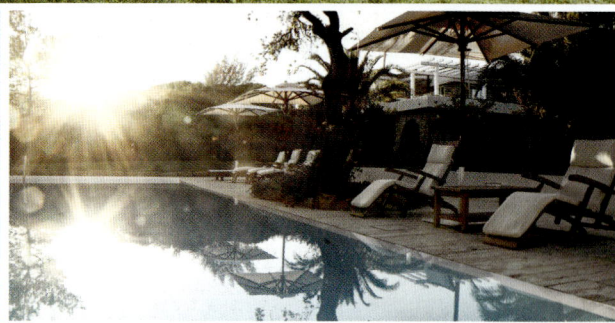

Lanthia Resort

Wild and wonderful Sardinia meets elegant design and hospitality

PRICE FROM:
€182

FEATURES:
Beach access; Pool; Restaurant; Sea views

ACTIVITIES:
Horse riding; Walking; Water sports

NEARBY:
Golfo di Orosei; Dorgali; Tortolì

GETTING THERE:
Olbia Airport; Cagliari Airport

☎ +39 0782 615103
🌐 condenastjohansens.com/lanthiaresort
🏠 Via Lungomare, 08040 Santa Maria Navarrese, Ogliastra, Sardinia, Italy

Sardinia's mountainous east coast province of Ogliastra is a scene-stealer of natural rich forest, fearsome granite rock and deepest blue sea. Off the tourist radar until recent years (still relatively unknown by many), the raw beauty of this undulating landscape is untouched and undamaged. And its coastal town of Santa Maria Navarrese remains an authentic Sardinian village where locals go about their day-to-day business unaffected by any lingering tourists. Protected by forests on one side and hugged by the Tyrrhenian Sea on the other (the beach is just 40 metres away), Lanthia Resort in Santa Maria Navarrese keeps matters elegantly simple with the purpose of allowing the surrounding natural wonderland to do all the talking. Materials from the island such as granite were used to build Lanthia Resort in the 1960s and following a recent revamp it's become a celebration of Sardinia and its artistic influence (ceramics, original artwork and hand-woven linens abound). Named after a Sardinian town, each of the 28 rooms and suites is indicative of the place they represent, each telling a story with their fabrics, paintings and colours. While at Lanthia Resort's restaurant the aim is to stimulate the senses with its creative spin on traditional local dishes prepared from Sardinian produce as the scents of juniper, fresh salty air and embracing forest fill the air.

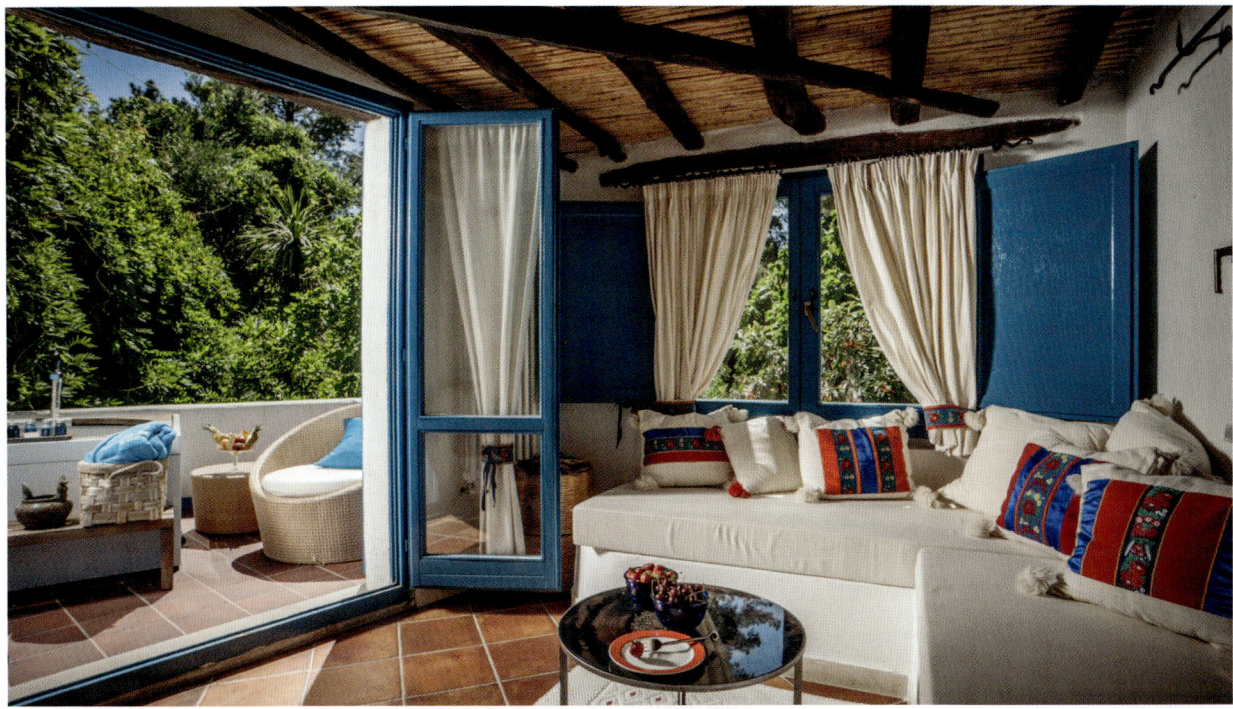

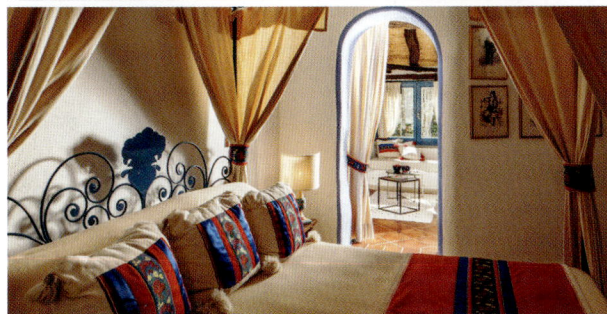

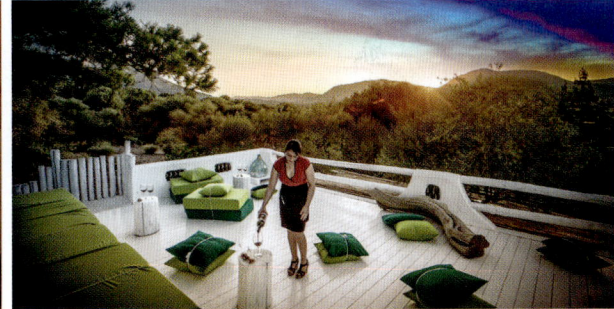

Su Gologone

Where memorable holidays in Sardinia are made

This is untouched Sardinia at its rugged best. Wild, mountainous and lush, peppered with remote villages, natural springs and ancient trails. Amid this highland wilderness, Su Gologone is a tranquil retreat in a lavender and rose-scented valley at the foot of the Supramonte. Food is a big deal here. When it opened in the 1960s it was just a simple restaurant but today, dishes such as suckling pig and ricotta-filled ravioli draw diners from across the world. However, Su Gologne isn't just a place for gourmands, there's much to delight art and spa lovers too. The focus is local, from the chefs to the arts and crafts (embroidered cushions, ceramics, sculpture, paintings) and even the swimming pool, which is filled with water from the nearby spring. Add in the fresh mountain air and fragrant gardens draped in bright bougainvillea and you'll wish you could stay forever. The rooms are divine, bordered by whitewashed walls set off by colourful Sardinian furnishings and there are tiled terraces, hot tubs and artworks aplenty. Feeling active? Then go cycling, horse riding and kayaking. Feeling arty? Take a craft class. But if you're feeling simply lazy, Sardinia's sun-kissed beaches are just half an hour away.

PRICE FROM:
€105

FEATURES:
Family friendly; Gym; Pet friendly; Pool; Restaurant

ACTIVITIES:
Cycling; Horse riding; Tennis

NEARBY:
Arts and crafts courses; Traditional bread making demonstrations; Oliena; Nuragic village; Lanaitto Valley

GETTING THERE:
Olbia Airport; Alghero Airport

+39 0784 287512 ☎
condenastjohansens.com/gologone 🌐
Località Su Gologone, Oliena (NU), 08025 Sardinia, Italy 🏠

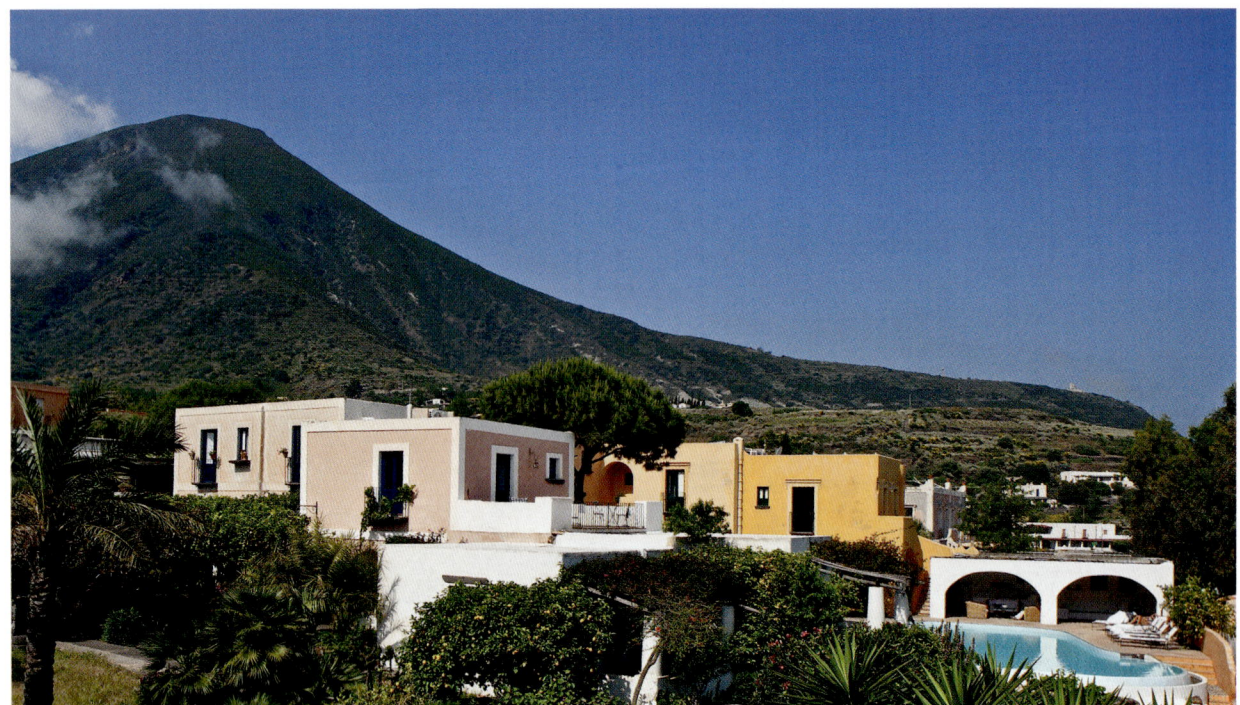

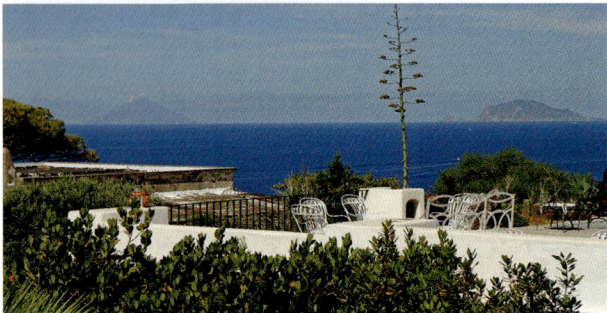

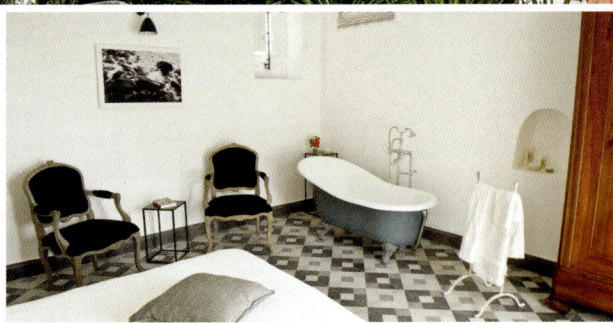

Hotel Signum

Secret Sicilian hideaway for the rich and famous

PRICE FROM:
€130

FEATURES:
Pet friendly; Pool; Restaurant; Sea views; Spa

ACTIVITIES:
Fishing; Tennis

NEARBY:
Vulcano Island; Lipari Island; Salina vineyards; Panarea; Volcano trekking

GETTING THERE:
Catania Fontanarossa Airport; Palermo Airport

☎ +39 090 9844222
🌐 condenastjohansens.com/signum
🏠 Via Scalo 15, 98050 Salina~Malfa, Aeolian Islands, Sicily, Italy

Tucked away in the lush green landscapes of the island of Salina hides Hotel Signum; a charming boutique hotel at the edge of the sea. Hotel Sigum was born when an ancient country hamlet was renovated to allow the public to experience the beauty and serenity that this naturally picturesque town offers. Inhabited since the Bronze Age, Salina is a breathtaking and beautiful volcanic island, dotted with vineyards and flowering capers. And from the hotel's chic antique-filled rooms you can look out over the crystal blue sea upon the silhouettes of Stromboli and Panarea and smell the scent of jasmine and citrus in the passing breeze. That's if you're not breathing in (in mouth-watering anticipation) the enticing aromas of the restaurant's seasonal, elegantly simple cuisine and sampling wines collected from every part of Italy and Europe kept in the impressive cellar. In-keeping with the traditional essence of the hotel, the spa offers the finest natural therapy techniques and has steam baths inspired by the very first thermal baths built over 3,500 years ago alongside numerous other harmonising treatments. Hotel Sigum is truly a haven of rest and relaxation perfect to revitalise your mind, body and soul. Top recommendation for: a honeymoon.

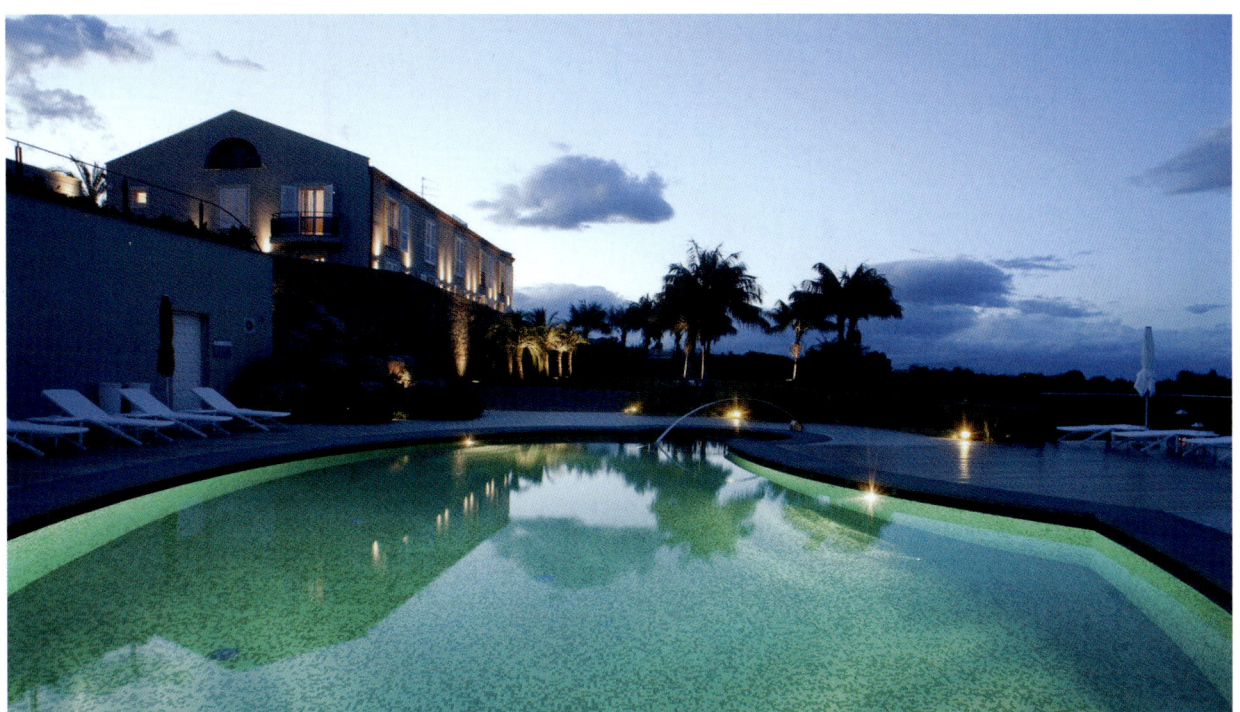

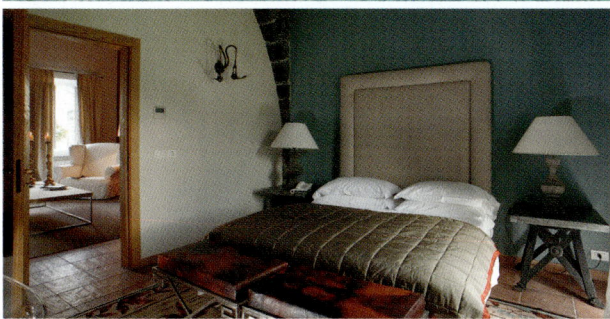

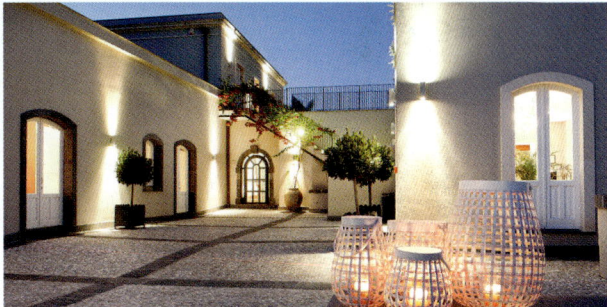

Donna Carmela Resort

Graceful Sicilian country residence and oenophile's paradise

Who knew that Mount Etna's volcanic explosions would create such a paradise for the 21st-century traveller? Donna Carmela Resort, a stunning boutique hotel in the foothills of Etna, nestles in the heart of Faro Nursery, the essence of a Mediterranean garden. The volcanic soil has almost magical properties, plants thrive on it, but more importantly, grape vines love it. This area boasts some of Italy's finest wines and the best place to sample them is Donna Carmela accompanied by top-notch Sicilian food from their restaurant, Cuisine of Donna Carmela; best described as a true flavour of everything that's great about this island. Donna Carmela's elegant walls host just 18 rooms and suites, which like Sicily, are a stylish mix of ancient meets cutting-edge modern. Rough hewn stone walls sit alongside sleek metallic satins and the dining room is a sophisticated blend of stone and linen; the perfect setting for the elegant dishes on the menu. If ancient history's your thing, check out nearby Taormina or the remains of Siracusa, while active types explore Etna. For something a little different: try drifting over Europe's largest active volcano by hot-air balloon.

PRICE FROM:
€140

FEATURES:
Family friendly; Pool; Restaurant; Sea views; Wheelchair access

ACTIVITIES:
Cycling; Golf; Skiing

NEARBY:
Acireale; Giarre; Siracusa; Etna Volcano villages; Taormina Greek Theatre

GETTING THERE:
Catania Airport

+39 095 809383 ☎
condenastjohansens.com/donnacarmela 🌐
Contrada Grotte 5, 95010 Carruba di Riposto, Catania, 🏠
Sicily, Italy

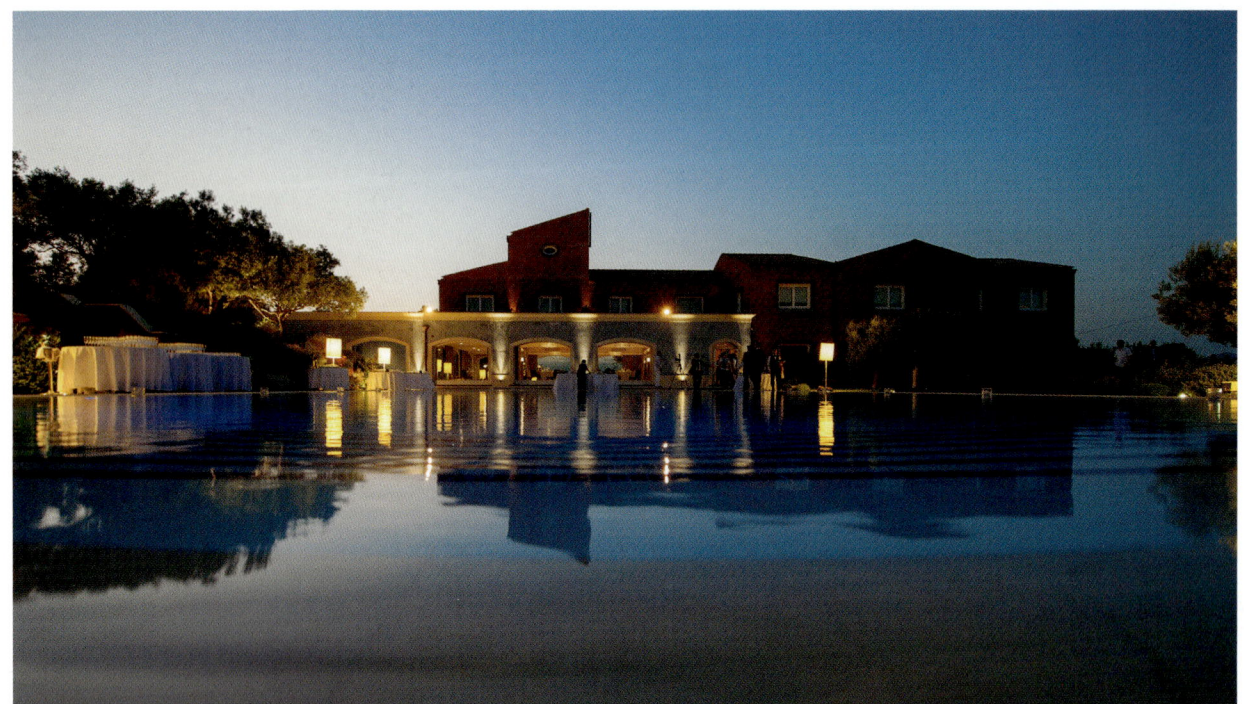

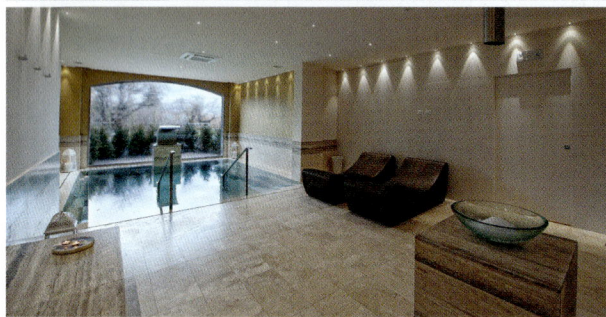

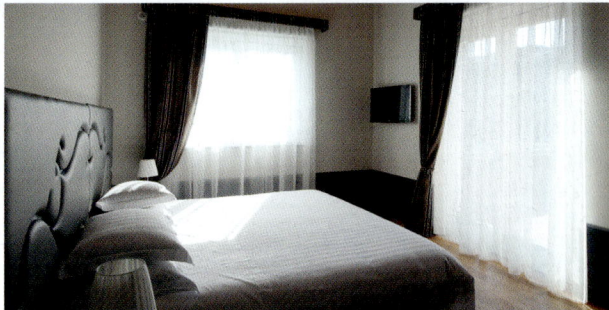

Villa Neri Resort & Spa

Fine wine and gourmet food plus Sicilian hospitality equals perfection

PRICE FROM:
€160

FEATURES:
Family friendly; Pet friendly; Pool; Restaurant; Spa

ACTIVITIES:
Golf; Horse riding; Skiing

NEARBY:
Piedimonte Etneo; Giarre; Taormina; Ortigia island; Aeolian Islands

GETTING THERE:
Catania–Fontanarossa Airport

Nestled in the volcanic region of Mount Etna sits the Silician sanctuary of Villa Neri Resort & Spa. Perched on a hillside in peaceful, stunningly dramatic landscape, it's secluded by vineyards and olive groves with the main focus on restful activity. A cool, tranquil atmosphere permeates throughout the 14 suites, each one elegant and roomy with rich fabrics, and gorgeous ceramic tiling in the bathrooms. Villa Neri's restaurant overlooks idyllic gardens and prepares a wide variety of mouth-watering local dishes. And its wine list is packed with fine examples including homegrown grapes, which can be sampled on a hotel tasting tour. (Test your wine knowledge and try to win "star pupil" status.) If you're more of a food lover, cooking lessons with the chef can be arranged and sampling the olive oil that's produced in-house (a great souvenir) is easily organised. Perfected over generations, Villa Neri's family-led hospitality is very special, which makes it the ideal spot for a weekend away, honeymoon or longer stay. It also means that unwinding comes easy and with a young vibe and the on-site spa it's a great choice for groups of friends to come and relax, use the facilities and leave rested and refreshed.

☎ +39 095 813 3002
🌐 condenastjohansens.com/villaneri
🏠 Contrada Arrigo, Linguaglossa (Catania), 95015 Sicily, Italy

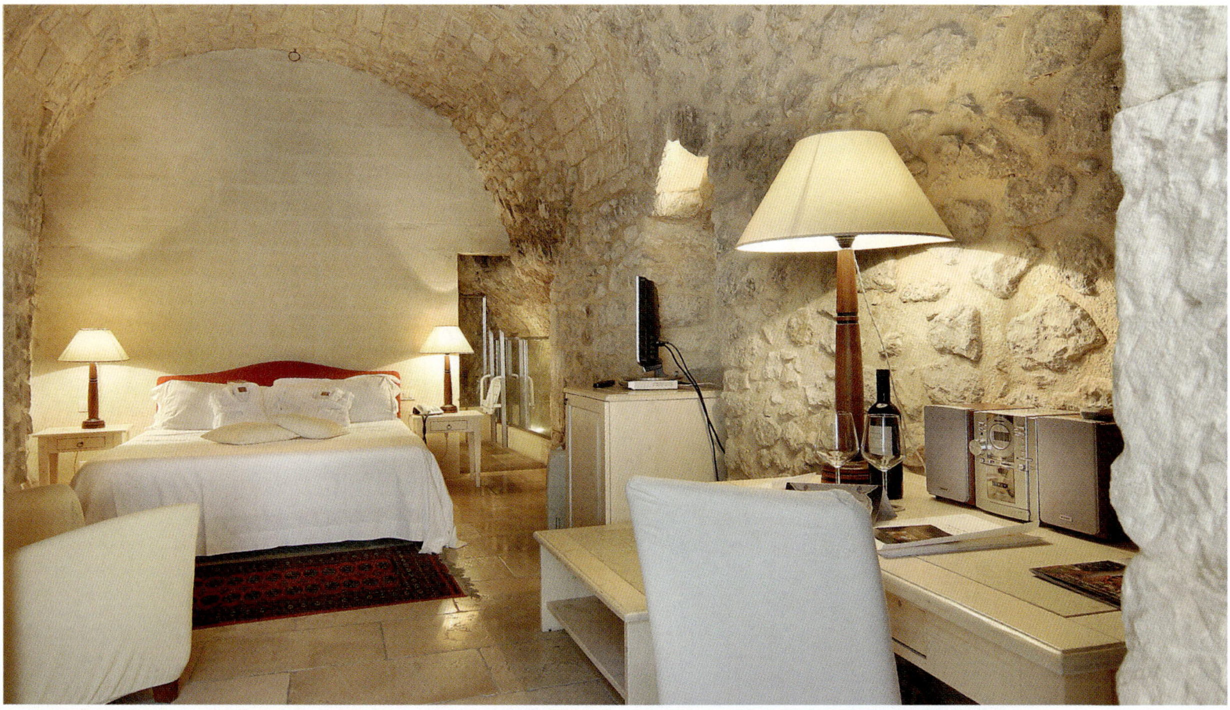

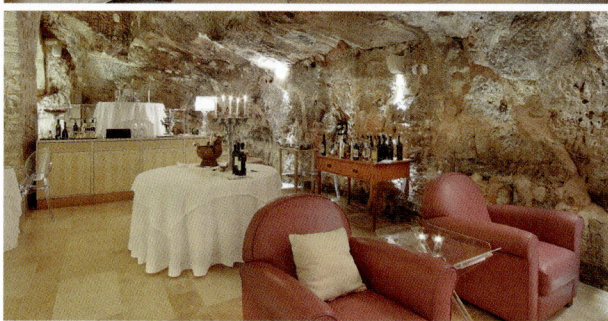

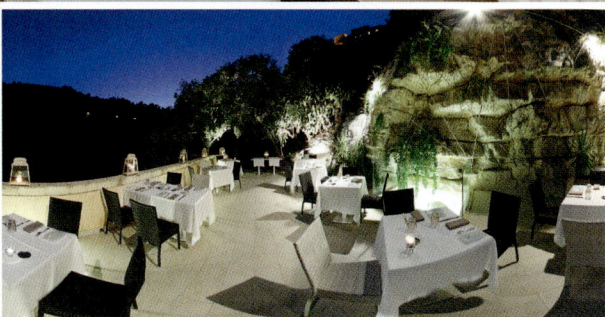

Locanda Don Serafino

Cavenous palatial den in the epicentre of Baroque Ragusa Ibla

Few places compare to Locanda Don Serafino in south-east Sicily. Right in the heart of Ragusa Ibla, a historic town dripping with Baroque gems, this 19th-century mansion-turned-10-room Italian inn is a terrific little sanctuary. A hideaway full of exposed limestone walls, vaulted rooms and narrow passageways. Antique furniture, hand-crafted wooden beds and embroidered rugs adorn the cave-like rooms and suites (book number 10 if you can with its medieval portals), and a reading room is carved into the rock. It's got character by the truckload with an informal, quirky atmosphere. Gourmet heaven is provided in two settings. In the centre of the town, a short walk away, is the eponymous 2 Michelin-Starred restaurant housed in former stables where the creative meals feature a twist on local specialities. Dishes aren't listed on a menu but publically displayed due to their daily freshness. 20km away on the beach-front there's Marina di Ragusa Lido Azzurro serving up fine fish fare; its well-stocked cellar completes the gastronomic experience. Exploring Ragusa Ibla's many sights and delights is a cinch. The narrow cobbled streets, 17th-century churches, picturesque piazzas and palm-lined gardens are right on the doorstep (make sure to pit stop at Gelati DiVini for wine-flavoured gelato). If you're after history and charm, Don Serafino is in a league of its own.

PRICE FROM:
€148

FEATURES:
Michelin Starred restaurant

ACTIVITIES:
Fishing; Sightseeing

NEARBY:
UNESCO Ragusa; Scicli; Hyblean beaches; UNESCO Baroque city of Modica

GETTING THERE:
Comiso Airport; Catania Airport

+39 0932 220065
condenastjohansens.com/serafino
Via XI Febbraio, 15 Ragusa Ibla, Sicily, Italy

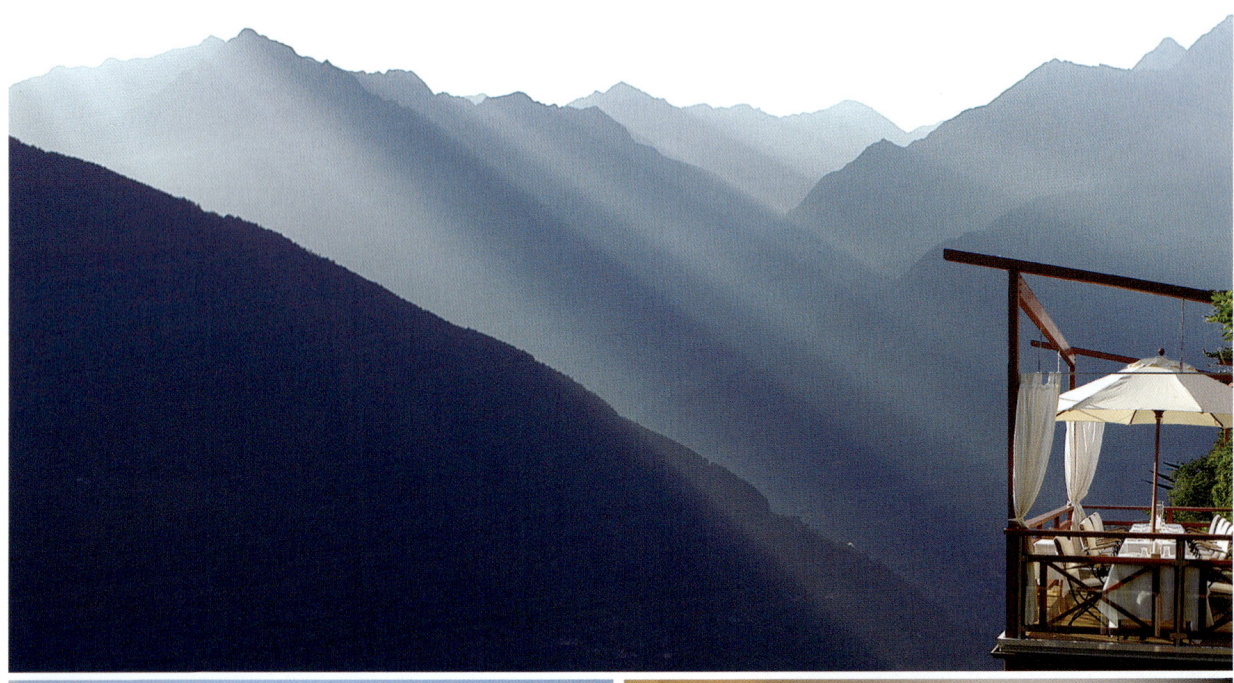

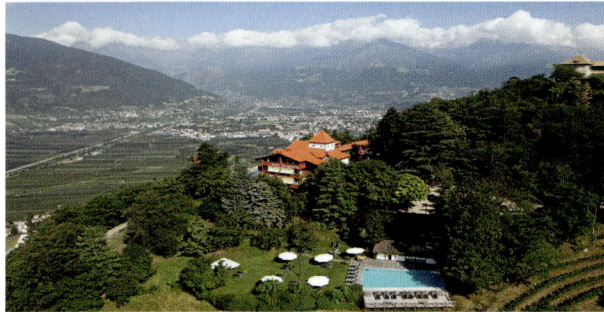

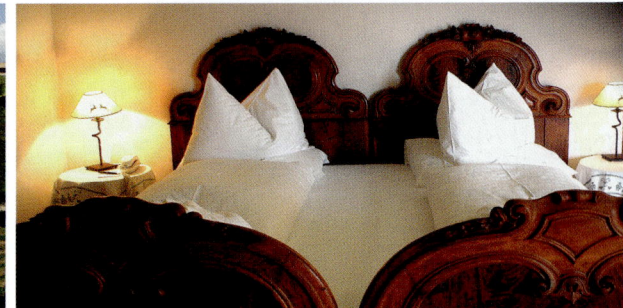

Castel Fragsburg

Tyrolean hunting lodge-turned-small luxury hotel and Michelin Starred restaurant

PRICE FROM:
€200

FEATURES:
Helipad; Michelin Starred restaurant; Pool; Restaurant; Spa

ACTIVITIES:
Golf; Horse riding; Walking

NEARBY:
Merano; Bolzano; Castel Trauttmansdorff Gardens; Golf Passeier; Ötzi, The Iceman Archeaology Museum

GETTING THERE:
Bolzano Airport; Innsbruck Airport; Verona Airport

If Heidi dreamed up a five-star boutique hotel in the South Tyrolean mountains it might come close to the alpine splendour of Castel Fragsburg. On the cliffside overlooking the unspoilt Dolomite mountains and this vineyard-filled Murano Valley, the 17th-century former hunting lodge has all the (von) trappings of luxury any self-respecting baroness could wish for. Castel Fragsburg's Dirndl and ledehosen-clad staff welcome you to your elegant Tyrolean suite complete with panoramic views of the mountains. Hungry after your trip up the winding mountain road? Castel Fragsburg's delicious food is famous for local specialities with a Mediterranean twist. Mr Michelin agrees and they are rightly proud of their 1 Star. Somehow food eaten at 700 metres in clean mountain air simply tastes better! Days may be spent enjoying an open-air concert at a nearby Schloss, sampling the local world-class tipple at the VinoCulti wine festival or relaxing in the sumptuous spa. Luxuriate in style with an alpine treatment or alfresco massage overlooking the stunning Dolomites. Then come the evening, head for the glassed veranda and test your vertigo while you enjoy a glass of the local vino straight from the vineyards below.

☎ +39 0473 244071
🌐 condenastjohansens.com/fragsburg
🏠 Via Fragsburg 3, 39012 Merano, Trentino - Alto Adige / Dolomites, Italy

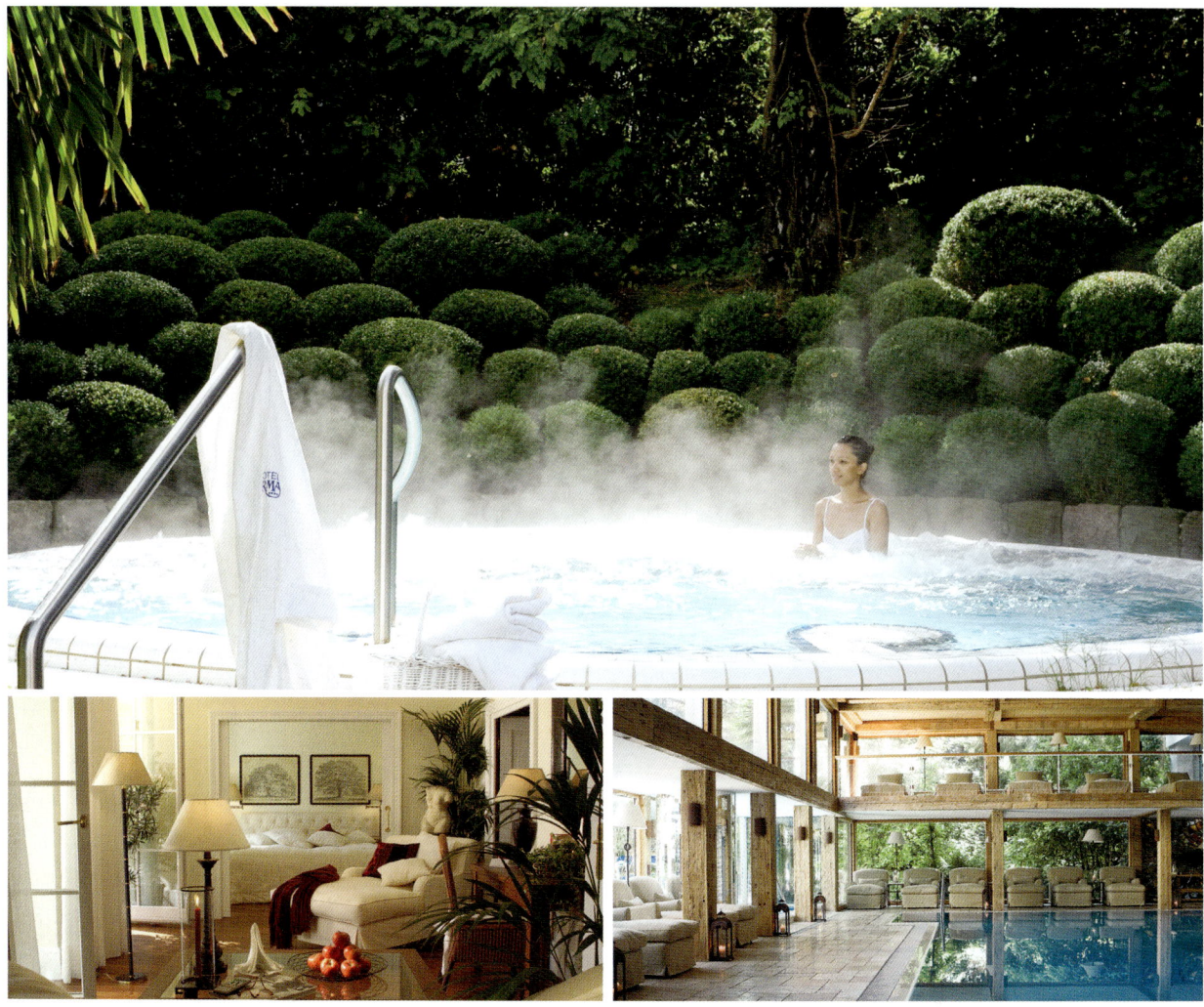

Meisters Hotel Irma - Villa Amore

The jewel in Meisters' crown, Merano

The spa town of Merano, in northern Italy's South Tyrol, ticks all the boxes for a relaxing Alpine escape. And if romance tops your wish list you won't be disappointed by Villa Amore, a grand three-suite house in the stunning grounds of the self-contained resort of Meisters Hotel Irma. Villa Amore overlooks a tranquil lake (hop on a rowing boat and glide around the swans) ensconced by a blanket of parkland home to fragrant herb and rose gardens, a pool, sun terrace and flower meadows. Your cares instantly float away in this peaceful place where an emphasis on good food is paramount. Opt for half-board (check out the snack buffet each afternoon) to fully enjoy the inventive Mediterranean dishes and excellent South Tyrolean wines. There's oodles of opportunity to realise those cheffy aspirations too, with gourmet events and cooking classes regularly on offer. Learn to make everything from fresh pasta to local specialities and take culinary tours and trips to wineries and farmers' markets. However, R&R is also high on the agenda with a host of spa treatments, beauty boosting therapies, saunas, baths and pools. At 12°C, the aptly named "killer pool" is not for the faint hearted! Back at Villa Amore where vast windows and sweeping balconies look out across the gardens, kick back in the penthouse suite, which spans no less than 80m², and admire the lake views from the huge roof terrace.

PRICE FROM:
€194 (per person, half board)

FEATURES:
Family friendly; Pet friendly; Pool; Restaurant; Spa

ACTIVITIES:
Golf; Skiing; Water sports

NEARBY:
Bolzano; Trauttmansdorff gardens; Merano wineries; Ötzi, The Iceman Archeaology Museum; The Dolomites

GETTING THERE:
Innsbruck Airport; Verona Airport

+39 0473 212 000 ☎
condenastjohansens.com/hotelirma 🌐
Via Belvedere 17, Bolzano, 39012 Merano - Meran (BZ), 🏠
Trentino - Alto Adige / Dolomites, Italy

100

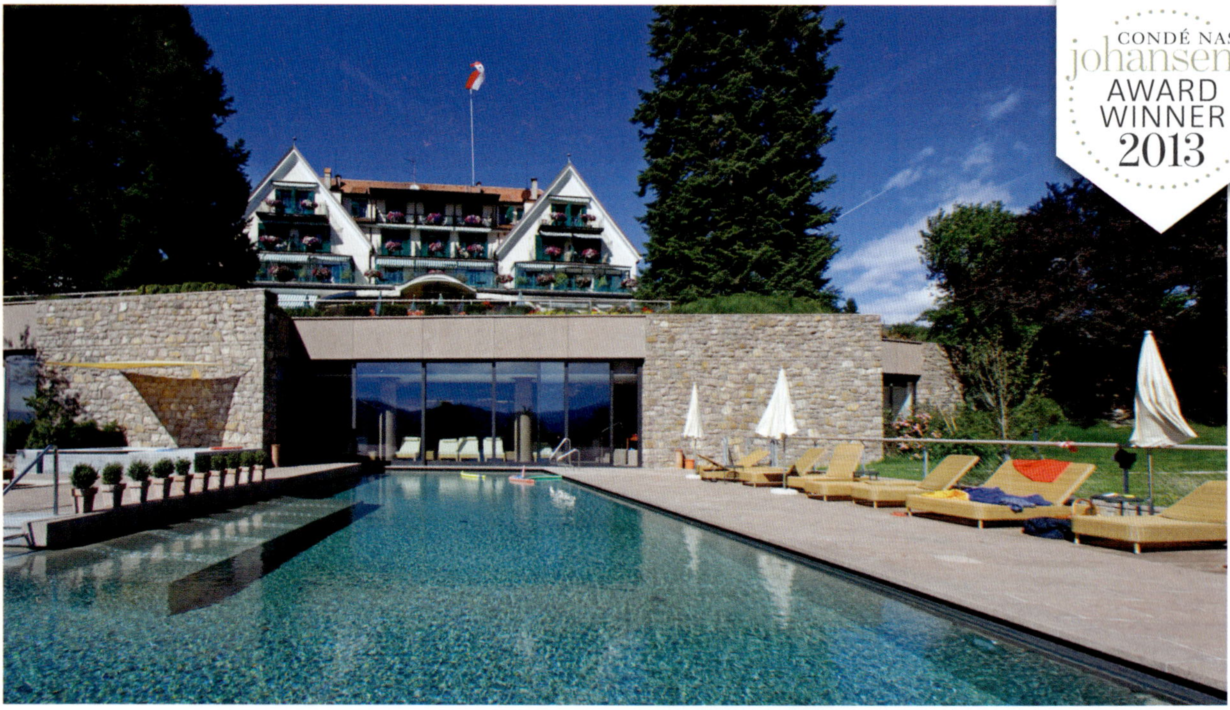

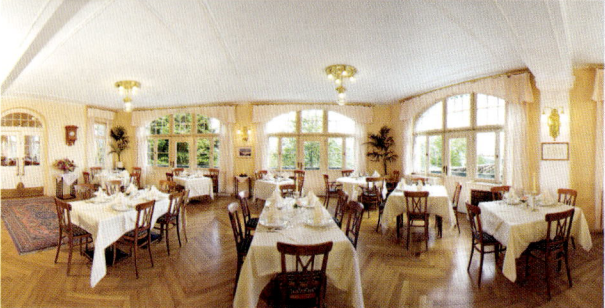

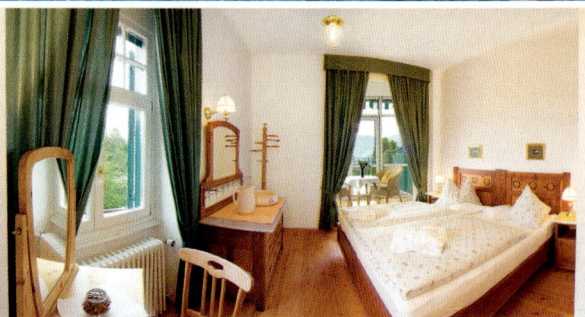

Parkhotel Holzner

Wholesome family fun in the Italian Alps

PRICE FROM:
€188

FEATURES:
Family friendly; Michelin Starred restaurant; Pool; Restaurant; Spa

ACTIVITIES:
Horse riding; Shooting; Walking

NEARBY:
Bolzano; Historic Rittner Railway; Earth Pyramids; Ötzi, The Iceman Archeaology Museum

GETTING THERE:
Bolzano Airport; Innsbruck Airport; Verona Airport

☎ +39 0471 345 231
🌐 condenastjohansens.com/parkhotelholzner
🏠 39054 Oberbozen Ritten/Soprabolzano Renon, Südtirol/Alto Adige, Trentino - Alto Adige / Dolomites, Italy

In 1908 it was cutting edge; today it's packed with character. Welcome to Parkhotel Holzner, a slice of art-nouveau history on the Renon Plateau, 1,200 metres high up in the Italian Dolomites. The scenery is pure mountain drama, and the view from the cable car as you approach from the town of Bolzano is jaw-dropping (Holzner is also reached by road and rail). The drama continues inside the hotel, where original features (Thonet chairs, turn-of-the-20th-century furniture, glistening chandeliers) effortlessly sit beside modern luxuries from gorgeous bathrooms and marshmallow-like beds with the softest duvets to a super spa (the Alpine herbs massage is divine). The restaurant is top presenting light Mediterranean cuisine matched by an impressive drinks list with an emphasis on South Tyrol wines. But a visit to Parkhotel Holzner is all about being outdoors. Besides the mountain backdrop, which you can marvel at while lounging by the sun-drenched pool or sipping Gewürztraminer on the terrace, there's the surrounding parkland to explore. Plus, depending on when you visit: hiking routes, cycling and skiing. When you've got your tourist hat on, hop on the train (cue more great vistas) to medieval Bolzano lined with arcaded streets, shops, castles and museums.

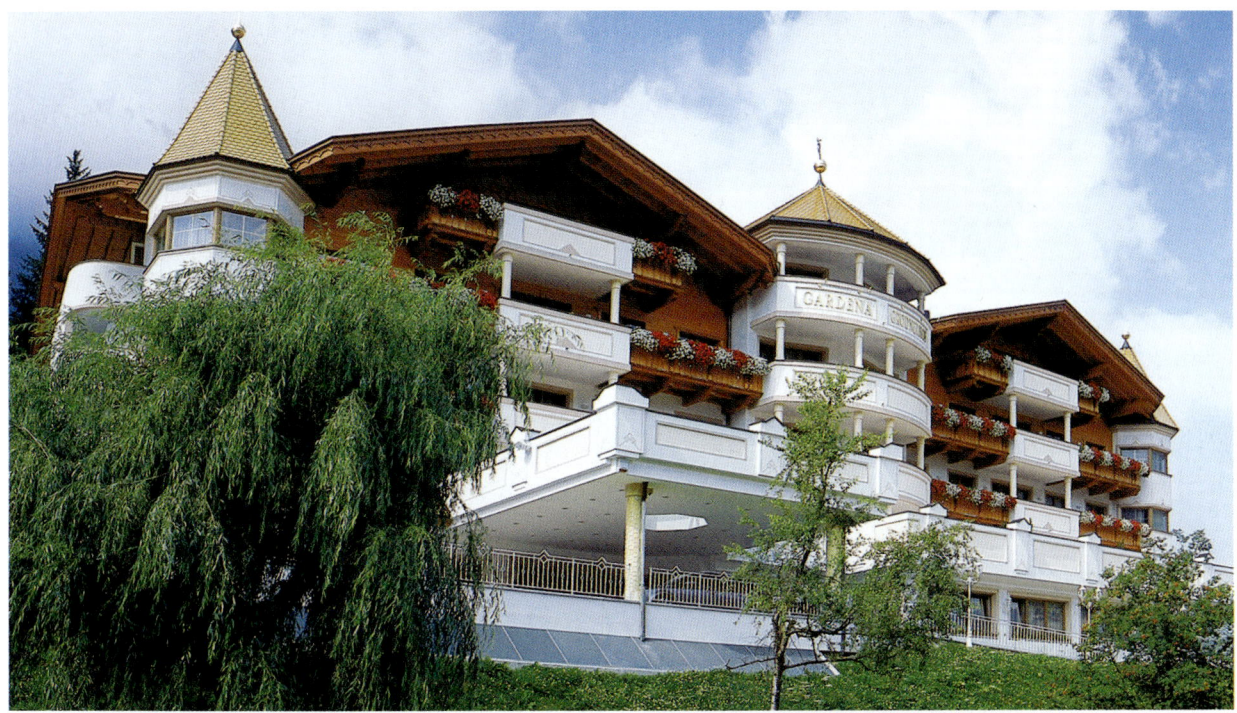

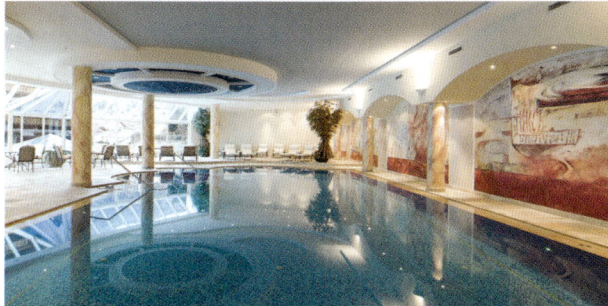
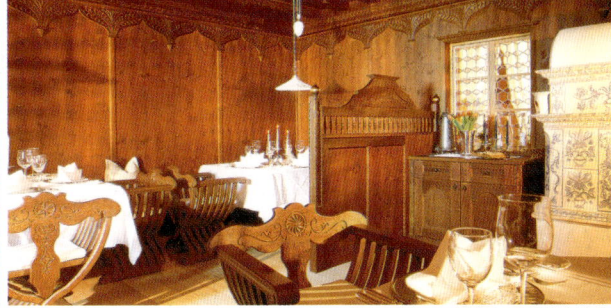

Hotel Gardena Grödnerhof

Classic Tyrolean mountain escape, serene spa and romantic restaurant

A slice of sublime mountain magic, Hotel Gardena Grödnerhof nestles amongst the spectacular pale peaks of the Dolomites. This turreted South Tyrolean lodge is a supersized sanctuary with a focus on regeneration where snow fans can get their fix of winter sports with ski lifts a blessed 200 metres away. (The in-house ski service will kit you out to conquer the myriad of slopes.) Spring brings hiking and biking opportunities with guided mountain excursions and free mountain bike rental as bonus add-ons. But if all this alpine air doesn't refresh you then the spa wellness centre will try. This soothing den of self-indulgence has various steam baths and saunas - Turkish bath and Finnish sauna included - and is accompanied by a first-class beauty farm offering numerous massages such as Ayurvedic and aromatic baths (the orange flower petal bath is a must-do). All guaranteed to send you into an utter jelly-like state. Simply reading the extensive treatment list will relax you! Even the smallest rooms at Gardena Grödnerhof are generous and all have balconies overlooking the hotel's extensive gardens or Ortisei's pretty town centre; the Gardena Deluxe Suite has a Tyrolean stove. Dine on top quality regional fare at the hotel's gourmet restaurant, Anna Stuben, and strike up a conversation with the expert sommelier to enjoy a glass (or few) of fine wine chosen by his very wise hand.

PRICE FROM:
€288

FEATURES:
Family friendly; Gym; Helipad; Michelin Starred restaurant; Spa

ACTIVITIES:
Golf; Skiing; Walking

NEARBY:
Bolzano; Bressanone; Cable gondola to Alpe di Siusi; Mountain hiking trails; Visits to local wineries

GETTING THERE:
Bolzano Airport; Innsbruck Airport; Verona Airport

+39 0471 796 315 ☎
condenastjohansens.com/gardena 🌐
Str Vidalong 3, 39046 Ortisei, Trentino - Alto Adige / 🏠
Dolomites, Italy

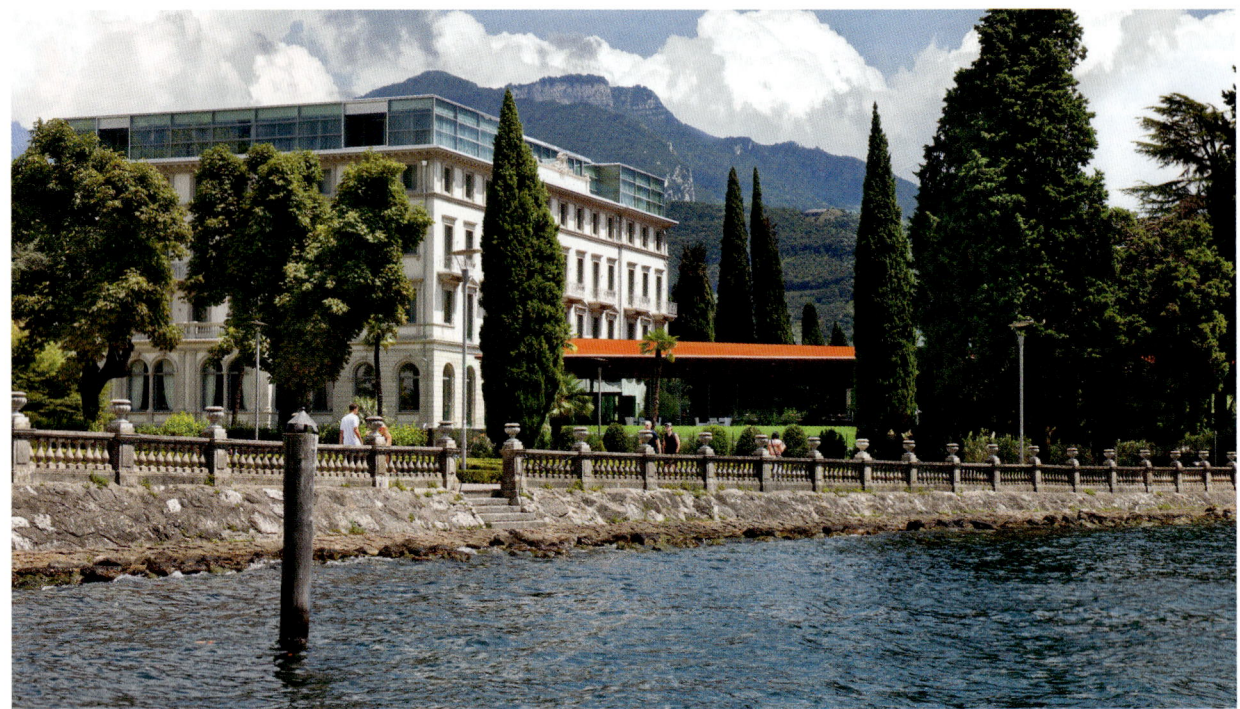

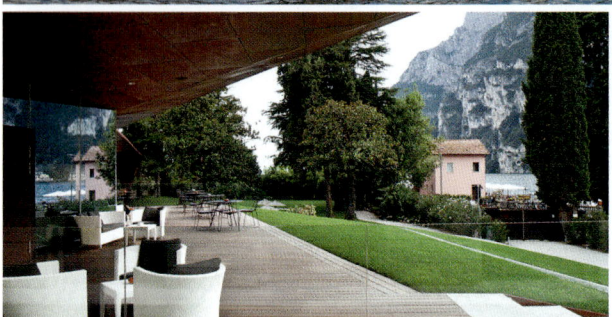
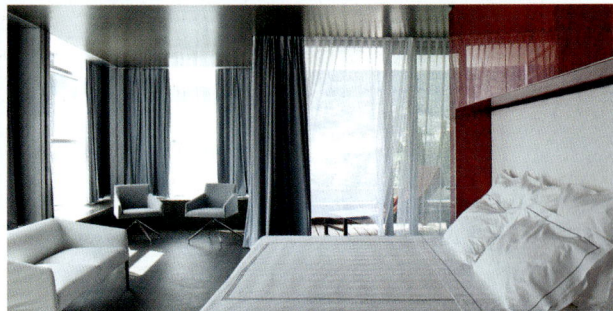

Lido Palace

Reincarnated Liberty-style hotel resort and spa in Riva del Garda

PRICE FROM:
€420

FEATURES:
Gym; Lake views; Pool; Restaurant; Spa

ACTIVITIES:
Cycling; Golf; Sightseeing

NEARBY:
Malcesine; Trento; Rovereto; Ponale Path; Mart Museum

GETTING THERE:
Brescia Airport; Verona Airport

Take one Imperial palazzo built for a royal family in 1899, place it in perfectly landscaped gardens with a view of Lake Garda to die for. Throw in a seriously cool, modern and sleek interior, and you have the Lido Palace where Belle Époque grandeur meets urban spa hideaway. Emperors came here to spoil themselves and now it's your turn. Outside, Lido Palace is an elegant, 19th-century palazzo. Inside, it's a beautifully modern, understated hotel carefully developed and designed so that old and new, the lake and interior coexist in effortless harmony. For example, take the stunning restaurant that juts out on to the lake like the bow of a ship and where huge glass windows fill the room with light. If you're watching the calories, you'll love Tremani's lighter cuisine that tastes much more fattening and fun than the usual spa fare. But for an indulgent blow-out head to Balì Bar for a pre-dinner cocktail and nibbles before sampling the gourmet delights at Il Re della Busa. Overseen by a Michelin-Starred chef, seafood and local produce are combined to deliver fabulous Italian cuisine of the highest order. Lido Palace's CXI SPA is also a monument to modern minimalism. Offering vinotherapy and acres of tranquillity, it's a retreat fit for an emperor.

☎ +39 0464 021899
🌐 condenastjohansens.com/lidopalace
🏠 Viale Carducci 10, 38066 Riva del Garda, Trentino - Alto Adige / Dolomites, Italy

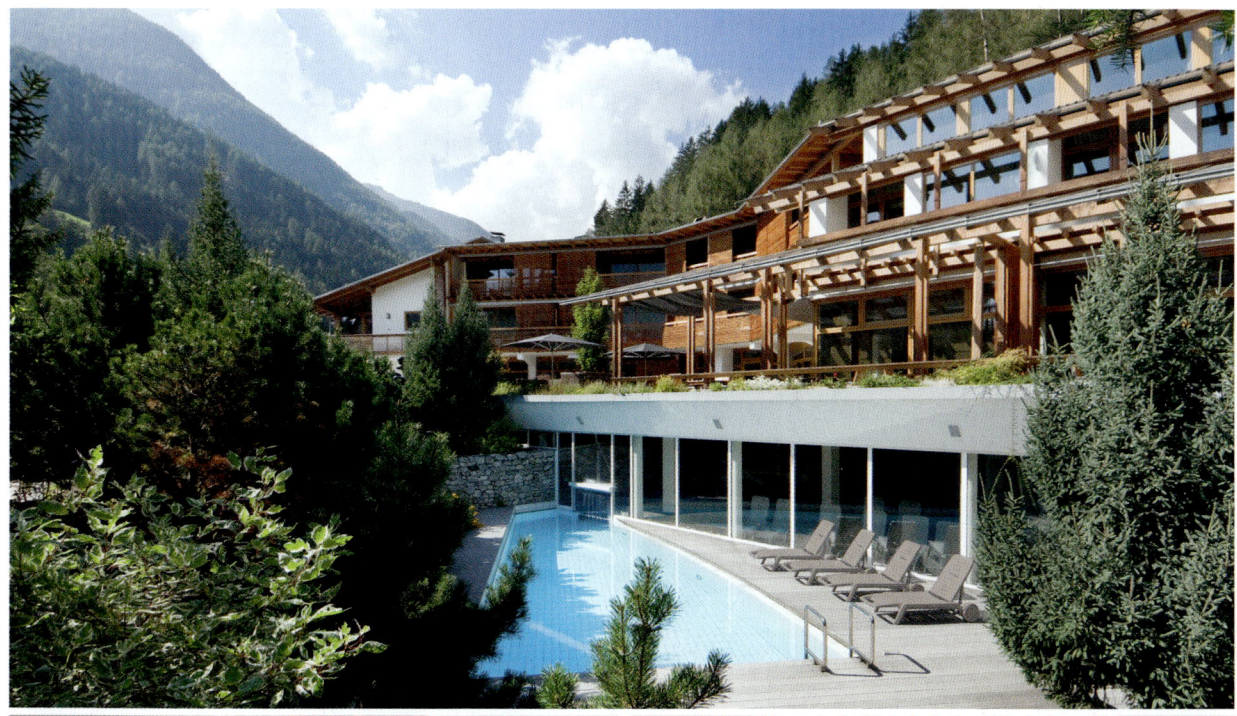

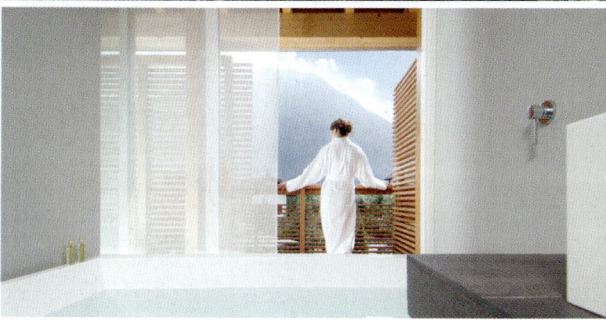

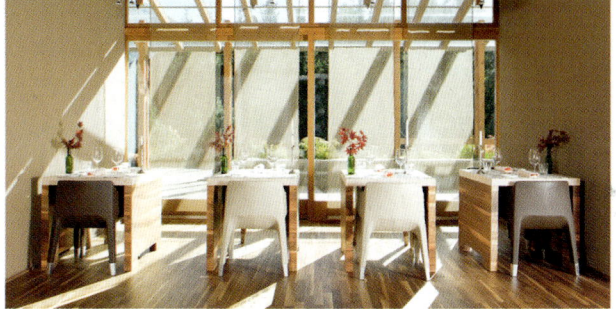

feldmilla. designhotel

Tyrolean cutting-edge, CO_2-free resort

The hospitality of feldmilla. designhotel, South Tyrol, is like no other. A unique climate-neutral property, each guest room and the apartment is an extraordinary haven of design with polished wood and crisp white beds enlivened with striking art and blasts of colour. For an utterly refreshing stay book the one-of-a-kind "clean air room" where environmental goodness (it's free of any volatile organic compounds) fuses with tasteful décor without compromising complete comfort. Restaurant toccorosso's gourmet menu sources locally grown produce and uses the wealth of Italian history to create simple, flavourful dishes. And a chic wood-burning fire adds an intimate glow to the lounge bar. However, the ultimate chill-out area is the spa's relax zone. Unwind here after a spa and/or beauty treatment (try an indoor and outdoor water therapy) but if an adrenaline rush is your desire the South Tyrolese mountains are for you. A host of year-round seasonal sports, feldmilla. designhotel is the ultimate base for outdoor pursuits such as mountain biking, trekking, paragliding, ice climbing, skiing, snowshoeing and golf. The little ones are encouraged to get involved too.

PRICE FROM:
€110

FEATURES:
Pool; Spa

ACTIVITIES:
Golf; Skiing; Walking

NEARBY:
Brunico; Castle of Tures; Three natural waterfalls, The Alps and three ski centres; UNESCO Dolomites

GETTING THERE:
Bolzano Airport; Innsbruck Airport; Verona Airport

+39 0474 677100 ☎
condenastjohansens.com/feldmilla 🌐
Schlossweg 9, 39032 Sand in Taufers, Trentino - Alto Adige / Dolomites, Italy 🏠

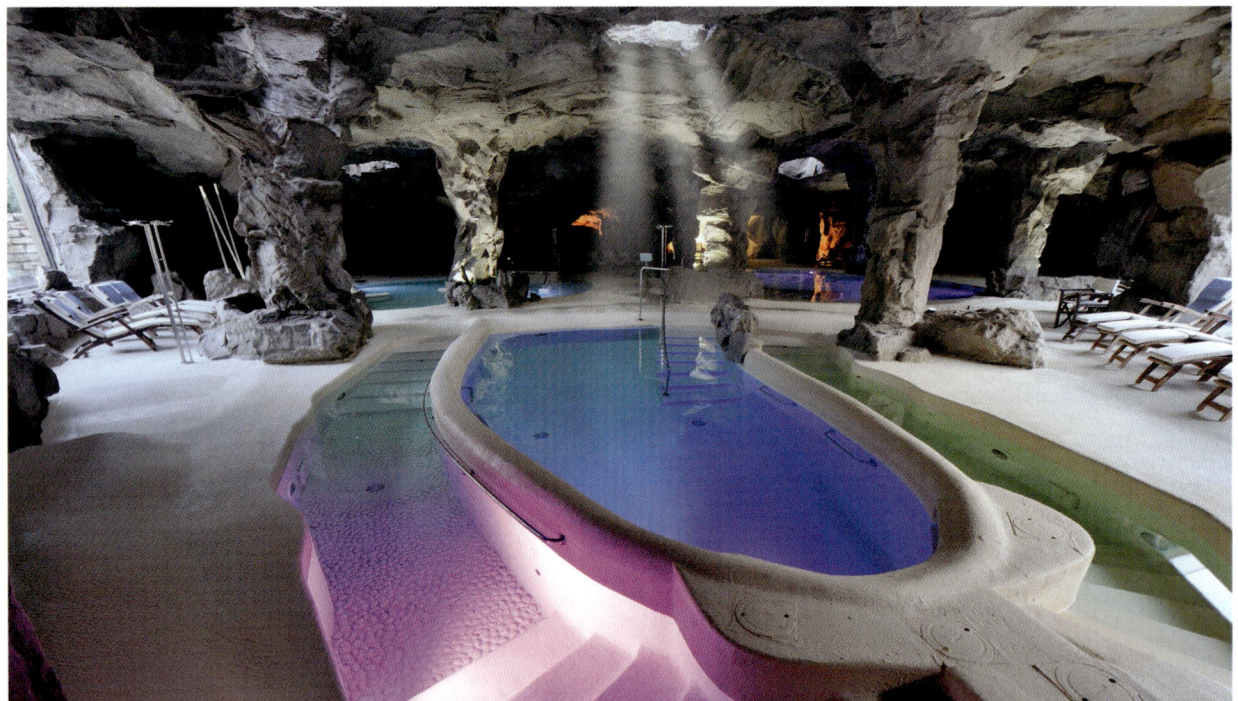

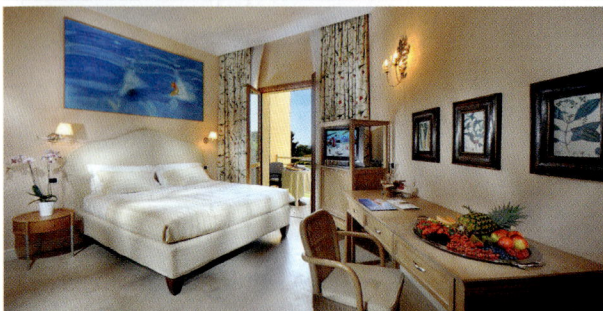

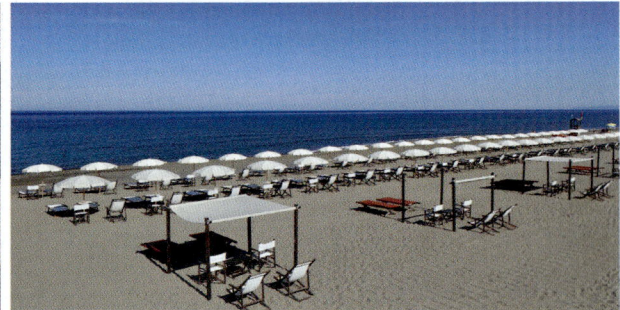

Tombolo Talasso Resort

Tuscany's must-visit beach-side spa resort

PRICE FROM:
€222

FEATURES:
Beach access; Family friendly; Restaurant; Sea views; Spa

ACTIVITIES:
Fishing; Golf; Water sports

NEARBY:
Siena; Pisa; Archaeological sites; Vineyards; Elba Island

GETTING THERE:
Pisa Airport

The spa at Tombolo Talasso Resort on Italy's Etruscan Coast is anything but ordinary. Sure, it's got treatments and therapies, saunas, steam rooms and Roman baths but add the "ooo" factor setting, a 1,000m^2 grotto of interconnecting caves with five pools and lagoons lit in magnificent jewel-like colours, and you've got pampering with an out-of-this-world edge. And the spa is only half of Tombolo Talasso's story because above ground there's the 96-room resort in the seaside town of Marina di Castagneto Carducci. Its big draw being the pristine private beach with water sports aplenty and unfurling views of the Tuscan archipelago with Corsica, Elba, Capraia and Sardinia in the distance. Then there are the sun-dappled decks, shaded terraces, tranquil gardens and the curvaceous, palm-fringed pool. As the sun sets, sink into a sofa on the Terrazza Mare with a chilled Aperol Spritz before heading to the restaurant for fresh fish and just-picked veg. Oenophiles enjoy the wine trail that meanders through the cypress and olive tree-lined hills nearby, however, you don't have to be a wine expert to appreciate its beauty featuring ancient churches, castles and the Tyrrhenian coastline. Tombolo Talasso's scenery is as intoxicating as the Super Tuscans it produces.

☎ +39 0565 74530
🌐 condenastjohansens.com/tombolo
🏠 Via del Corallo 3, 57022 Marina di Castagneto Carducci (LI), Tuscany, Italy

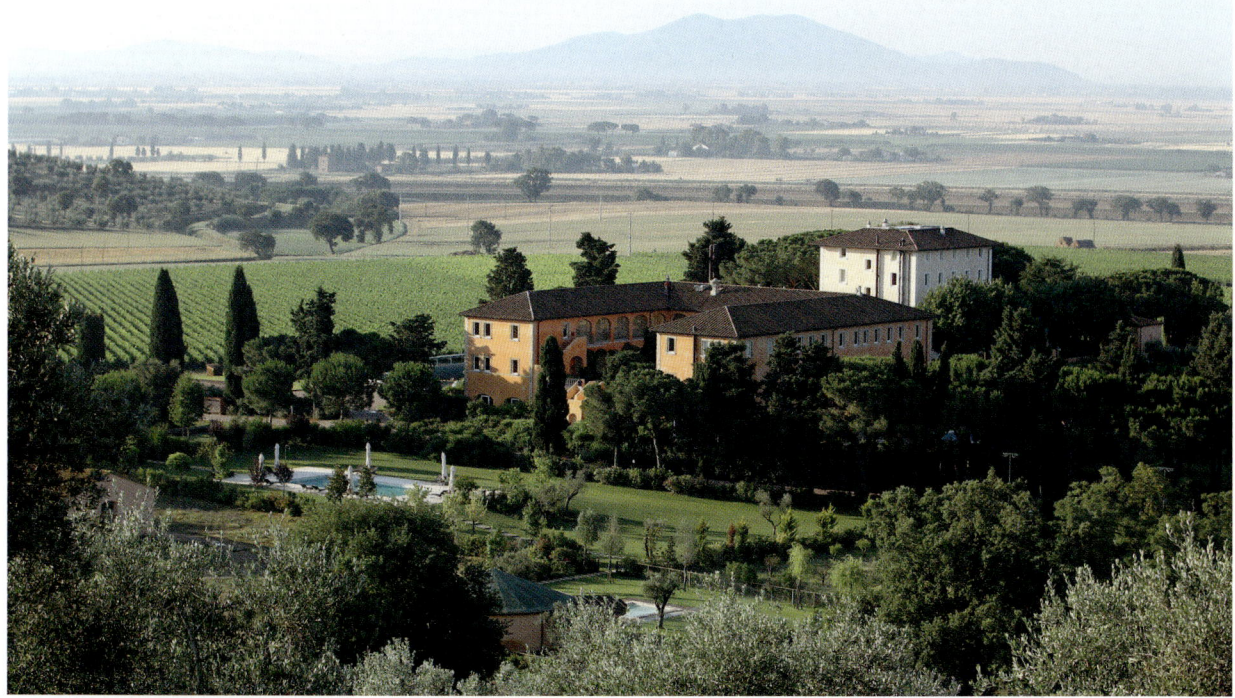

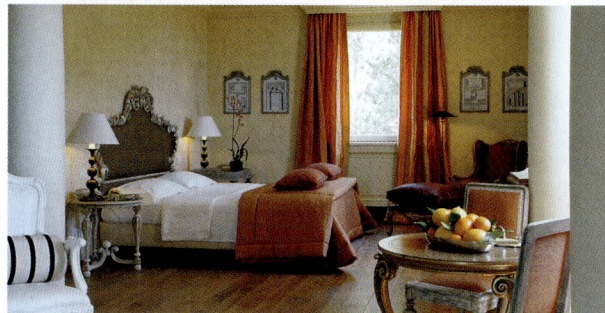

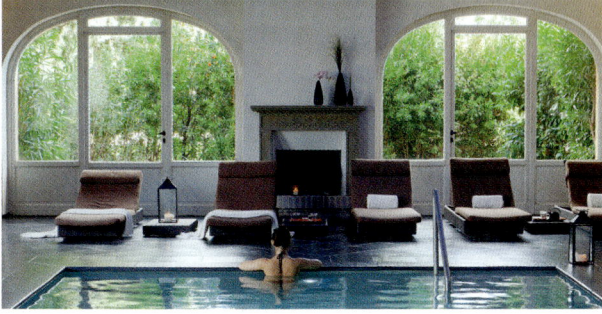

L'Andana

Most-spoiling Tuscan getaway in the Maremma hills

From the moment you turn into L'Andana's cypress and pine-tree lined driveway, you know you're in for a treat. Set on the Tenuta La Badiola estate spanning 1,200 acres of vineyards, olive groves and parkland in the undulating Maremma hills, this 19th-century Tuscan villa is a hideaway in every sense (switch on your sat-nav!). The warm pastel façade is the perfect foil for the richly decorated interiors lavished with gilt mirrors, cowhide sofas, antique furniture and silk drapes. The 33 rooms are split between the original lodge and a new wing, both equally spectacular with rustic-luxe décor, oak floors, stone fireplaces, chaise longues and objets d'art. The view from the epic (80m²) Prestige Suite, looking out across the vine-clad countryside to the Tyrrhenian Sea beyond, is the kind you don't easily forget. Neither is the fine breakfast spread served at the casual La Villa restaurant (Cinta Senese ham, orange-flower brioche). Gourmands love L'Andana. This is home to Alain Ducasse's only restaurant in Italy, (also co-owner of the hotel) Trattoria Toscana, recipient of a Michelin Star in 2007 whose seasonal dishes are inspired by Tuscan traditions. The estate is also home to a superb vaulted ESPA, a sun-drenched pool, golf course, wine cellar and chapel. And when the sea beckons, the gorgeous Maremma coast is just a few kilometres away.

PRICE FROM:
€440

FEATURES:
Family friendly; Gym; Michelin Starred restaurant; Pool; Spa

ACTIVITIES:
Golf; Horse riding; Water sports

NEARBY:
Castiglione; Grosseto; Siena; Maremma's sandy beaches; Maremma Natural Park

GETTING THERE:
Pisa Airport; Florence Airport; Rome Fiumicino Airport

+39 0564 944 800 ☎
condenastjohansens.com/andana 🌐
Tenuta La Badiola, Localitá Badiola, 58043 Castiglione della 🏠
Pescaia (Grosseto), Tuscany, Italy

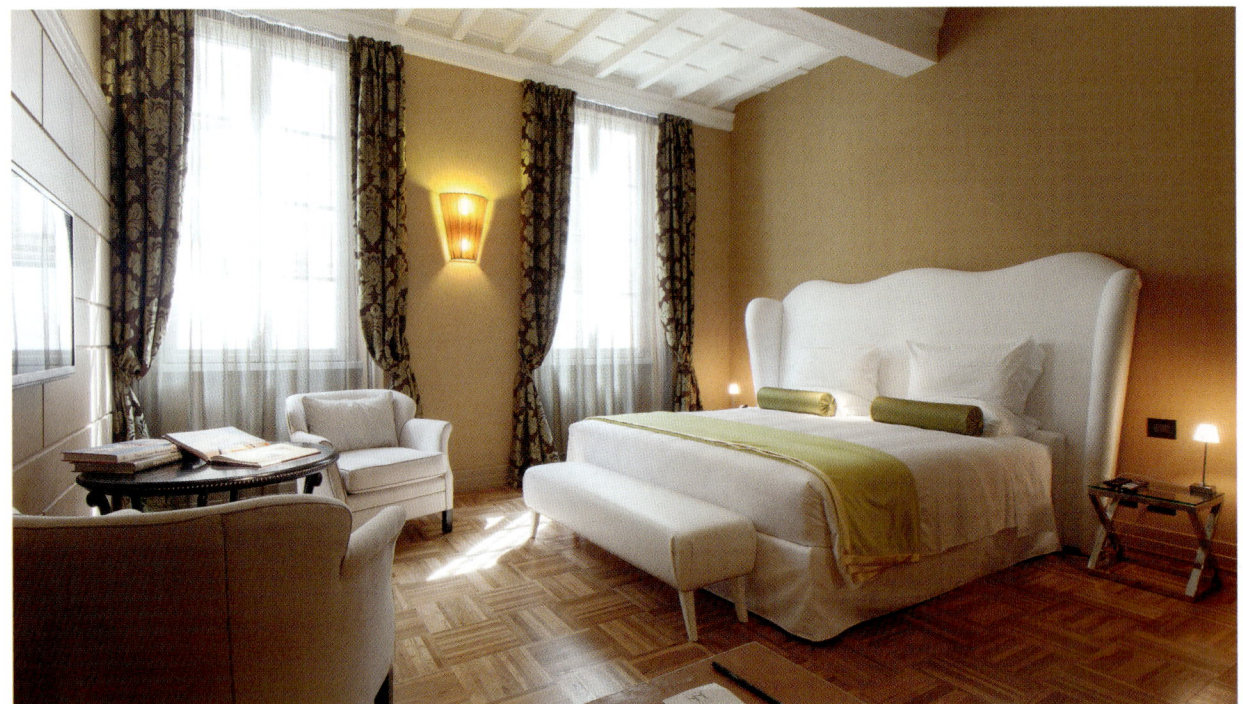

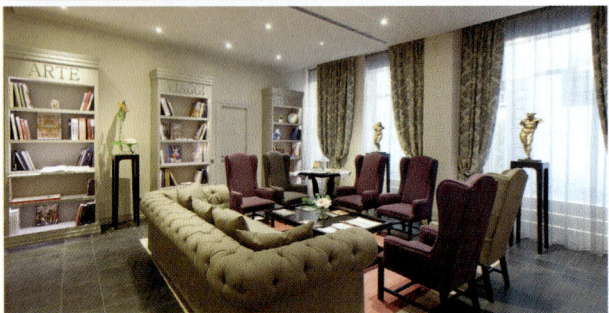
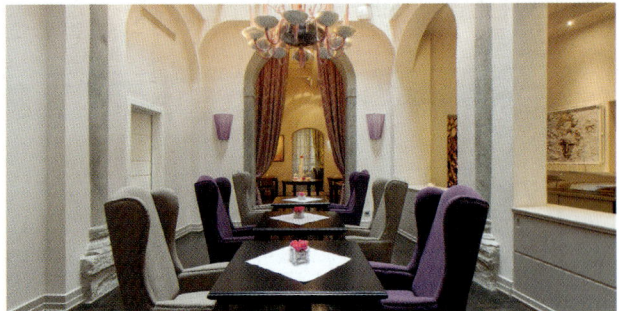

Firenze Number Nine Hotel and Spa

The jetset's hotel of choice in the pulsing heart of Florence

PRICE FROM:
€149

FEATURES:
Family friendly; Gym; Restaurant; Spa; Wheelchair access

ACTIVITIES:
Cycling; Shopping; Sightseeing

NEARBY:
San Lorenzo Church with Medici's Chapels; Duomo; Santa Maria Novella Church; Accademia and Uffizi Galleries; Ponte Vecchio

GETTING THERE:
Florence Santa Maria Novella Railway Station; Florence Airport; Pisa Airport

☎ +39 055 538 3583/6212
🌐 condenastjohansens.com/firenzenumbernine
📍 Via dei Conti 9, 50123 Florence, Tuscany, Italy

Firenze Number Nine Hotel and Spa is a chameleon of a hotel. To some it's a romantic retreat, for others it's an ideal base for business. For many it's a cool lounge-bar while the body-beautiful flock here for its fitness centre and spa. Number Nine's central location next to the Medici Chapels, just moments from the Duomo of Florence and Ponte Vecchio, means that all of the city's Renaissance glory is at your fingertips. Guided tours and excursions are regularly organised by the hotel so it's well worth asking what's on the agenda. Despite the central setting, Number Nine is an incredibly peaceful place. Brilliantly spacious for a city hotel, guest rooms and suites are enhanced by the light and airy décor that's fresh with a touch of funk. Number Nine refers to the bedrooms as "concept-rooms," each one different from the other with different features and services to suit the guests' needs. But all deliver upscale comfort with the use of hypoallergenic materials, top-class beds and high-tech entertainment systems. Works of original art are continually on display throughout the hotel creating a museum-like quality but there's no stuffiness here, as highlighted by Bar & Bistrot, Number Nine's popular hang-out for coffee, wine, romantic evenings and local specialities.

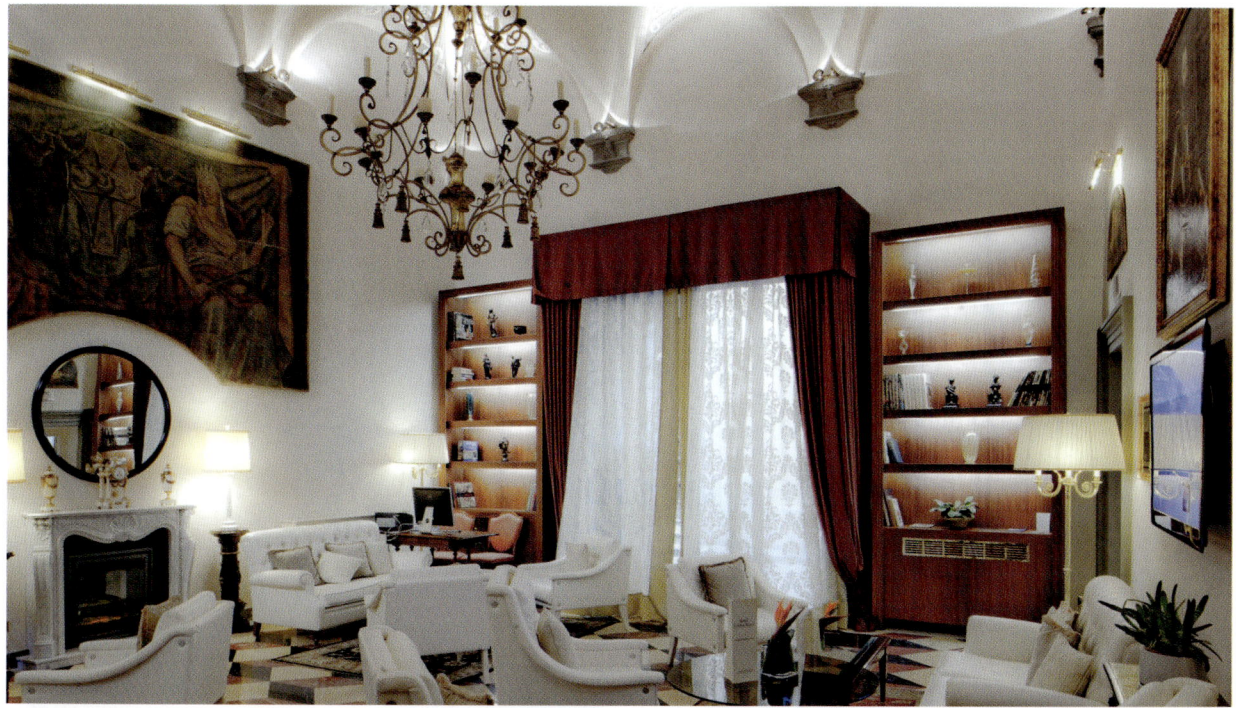

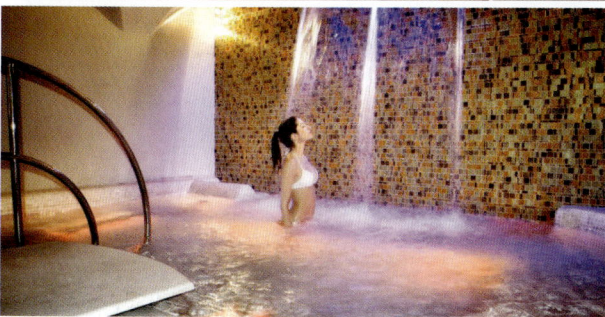

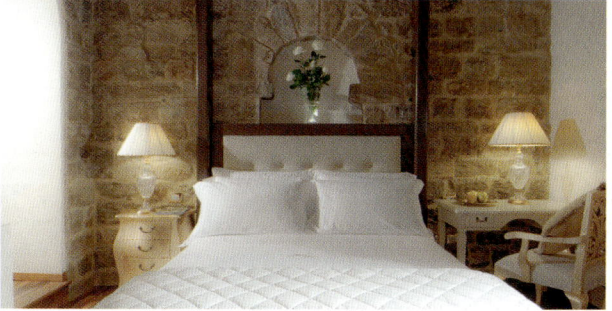

Golden Tower Hotel & Spa

Time out in timeless Florentine architecture

For total rejuvenation head for the new kid in town: Golden Tower Hotel & Spa. In the heart of Florence, no expense has been spared at this glitzy glamourpuss in a city where space comes at a premium. Golden Tower is a boutique hotel with an exceptional wellness centre offering escape from the city life that buzzes just outside its doors. Located minutes from the famous high-end Via Tornabuoni shopping district and many of Florence's popular tourist sites and restaurants, this urban hideaway delivers the best of both worlds: city centre convenience and peaceful seclusion. It also effortlessly combines history (Golden Tower's building and furnishings are a Renaissance masterpiece) with the modern technological world. Comprising a Beauty Centre and Spa Lounge, the wellness centre is a haven of luxury and tranquillity where a wide variety of massage treatments perfect for both city breaks and longer stays await you. Equipped with a Turkish bath, tropical showers and a Jacuzzi you'll feel pampered above and beyond the typical spa experience. Take to the Tower for an particularly special stay where sparkling marbles and techy gadgets go hand-in-hand. Their bathrooms of grey marble exude sumptuousness as you soak away any remnant of tension before an apéritif or tipple at the bar followed by a delicious dinner of dreamy Italian dishes.

PRICE FROM:
€250

FEATURES:
Restaurant; Wheelchair access

ACTIVITIES:
Shopping; Sightseeing

NEARBY:
Accademia and Uffizi Galleries; Ponte Vecchio; Duomo

GETTING THERE:
Florence Airport; Pisa Airport

+39 055 287 860 ☎
condenastjohansens.com/goldentowerhotel 🌐
Piazza Strozzi 11/R, 50123 Florence, Tuscany, Italy 🏠

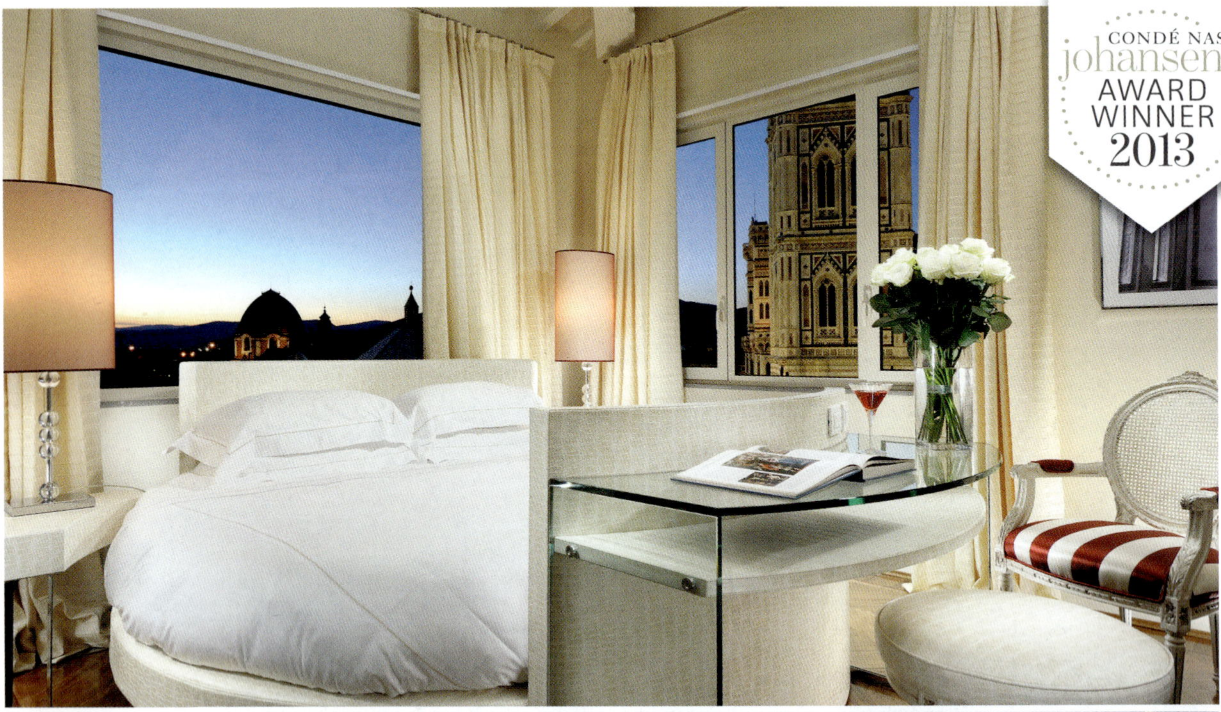

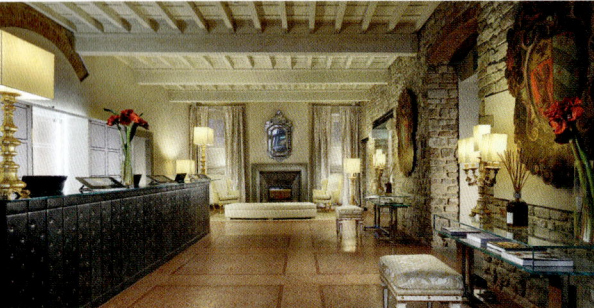

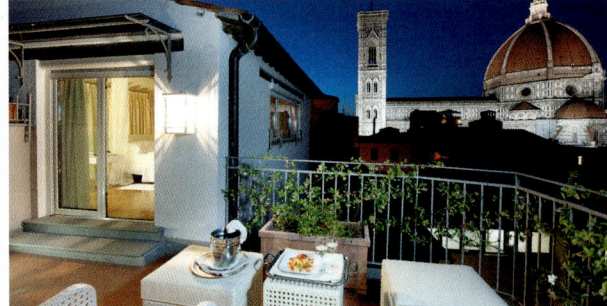

Hotel Brunelleschi

A fusion of historic Florentine architecture and contemporary opulence

PRICE FROM:
€204

FEATURES:
Gym; Restaurant; Wheelchair access

ACTIVITIES:
Golf; Shopping; Sightseeing

NEARBY:
Bologna; Uffizi Gallery; Bargello Museum; Ponte Vecchio;
Academy of Fine Arts

GETTING THERE:
Florence Airport; Pisa Airport; Bologna Airport

☎ +39 055 27370
🌐 condenastjohansens.com/hotelbrunelleschi
📍 Piazza Santa Elisabetta 3, 50122 Florence, Tuscany, Italy

Hotel Brunelleschi's biggest attraction is its unbeatable location. A stone's throw from Florence's spectacular cathedral, its terracotta-toned dome engineered by Filippo Brunelleschi is so close, you'll think you can touch it. Many of the rooms and suites afford bedside views of the Duomo; one has a rooftop terrace with Jacuzzi and skyline panorama. But all give you a heart-stirring glimpse of the historic city's buzzing life and breathtaking architecture. Poised in a peaceful piazza moments from the Uffizi Gallery, Piazza della Signoria and many other of Florence's Renaissance glories - not to mention the shopping stradas - Hotel Brunelleschi couldn't be more secluded and more central. This is a hotel of congruous contradictions. Housed within a 6th-century circular Byzantine tower and a medieval church (the hotel has a private museum that includes a Roman caldarium), the interior is a juxtaposition of contemporary design. Modern fixtures grace parquet floors and marble bathrooms adjoin discreetly decadent boudoirs. The silver basins and sleek four-poster beds are particularly fine. Every audio-visual amenity is available and speedy service is dispensed 24/7. Then there's Restaurant Santa Elisabetta and Osteria della Pagliazza serving up Tuscan food with soul that's so good it's a sin to miss.

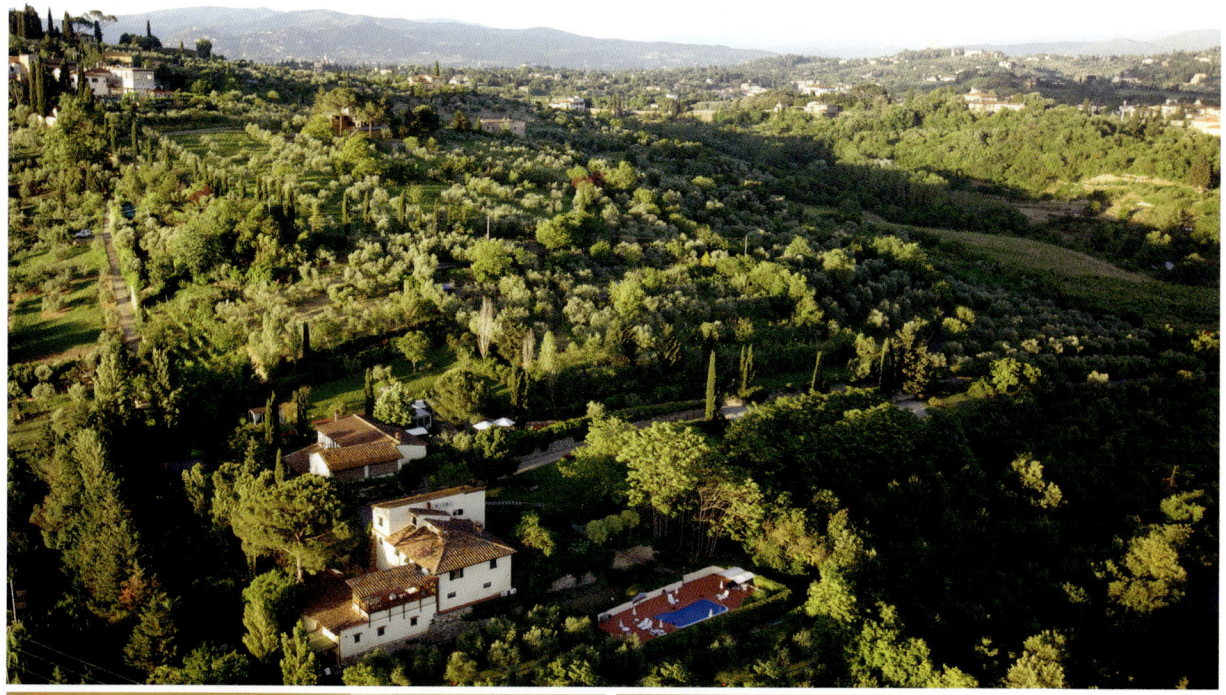

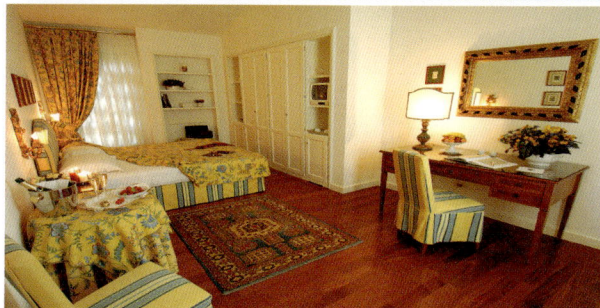
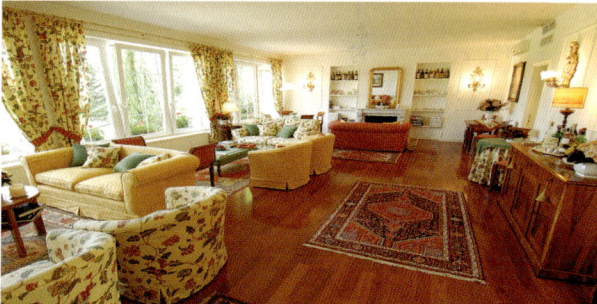

Marignolle Relais & Charme

Serenity found in the Certosa convent area of Tuscany

Channel your inner Medici and check into Marignolle Relais & Charme, a stunner of a villa in the hills overlooking Florence. Italian aristocrats built their country pads high in the hills to escape the overheated hustle and bustle of the city and Marignolle Relais & Charme is a retreat fit for royalty. Once a private house, it's been transformed into a top quality hotel while retaining the intimacy of a private home, and the atmosphere is one of peace and seclusion. With all the surrounding pastoral vistas it's hard to believe Florence is a mere five-minute drive away where you can take in the art, history, monuments, shops and restaurants. Nearby, there's the beautiful towns of San Gimignano and Siena, and the must-see Tower of Pisa, not to mention Chianti country. The hotel's friendly staff is always on hand to rustle up a legendary breakfast in the pretty gazebo, arrange a private tour of museums, galleries, wine cellars or designer outlets for the best of Italian fashion, and there's even a pool on the elegant terrace overlooking the green hills of Tuscany. Something for the fact file: the owner of Marignolle Relais & Charme is a keen golfer and member of the Florence Golf Course. He's won numerous golf tournaments.

PRICE FROM:
€195

FEATURES:
Family friendly; Pool

ACTIVITIES:
Golf; Horse riding; Tennis

NEARBY:
San Gimignano; Siena; Florence; Designer fashion outlet; Chianti

GETTING THERE:
Florence Airport; Pisa Airport; Bologna Airport

+39 055 228 6910 ☎
condenastjohansens.com/marignolle 🌐
Via di San Quirichino 16, 50124 Florence, Tuscany, Italy ▪

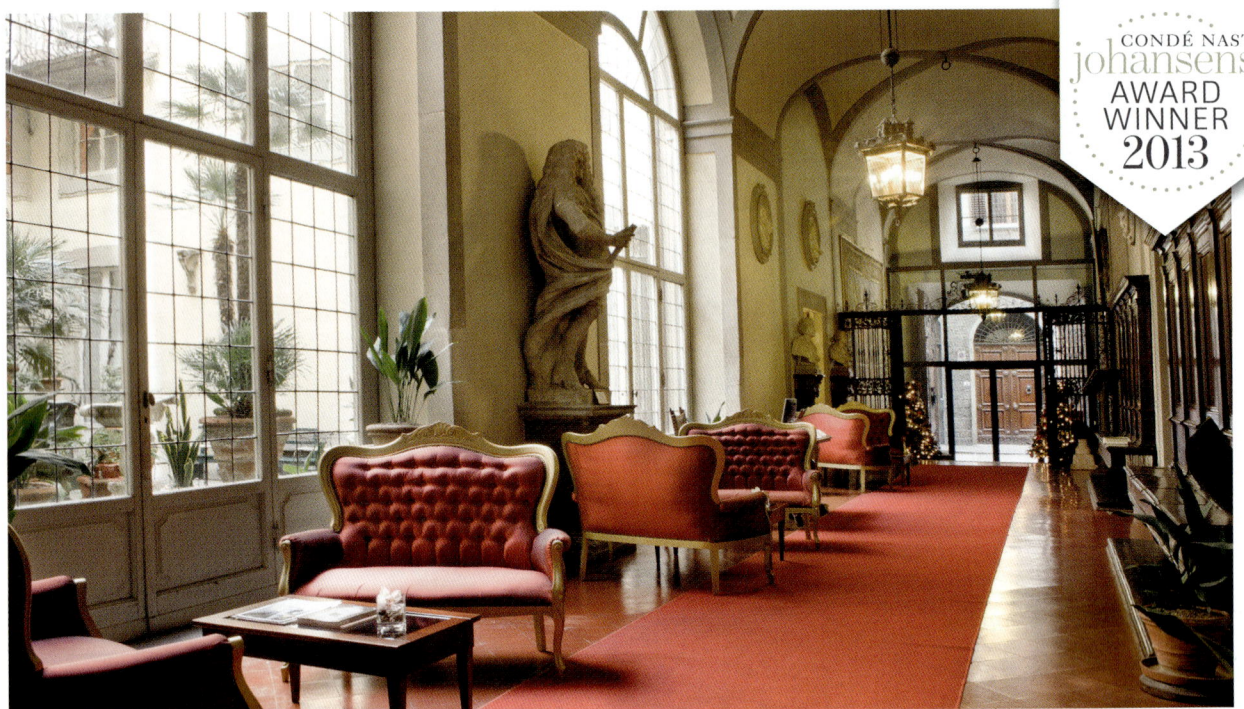

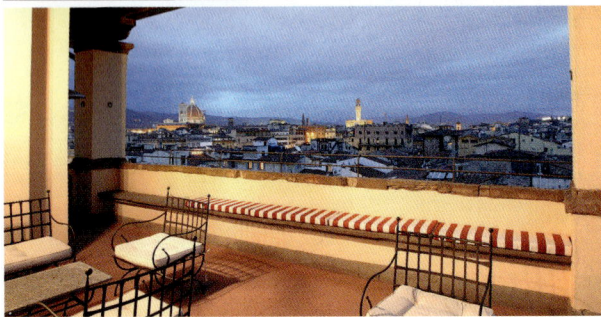
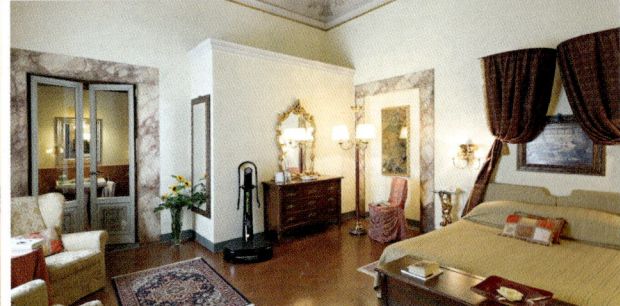

Palazzo Magnani Feroni - all-suites florence

Living as the noble Florentines used to

PRICE FROM:
€220

FEATURES:
Family friendly; Gym

ACTIVITIES:
Cycling; Golf; Shopping

NEARBY:
Medici's villas; Chianti wine region; Designer fashion outlet; Colle Val d'Elsa crystal production

GETTING THERE:
Florence Airport; Pisa Airport; Bologna Airport

Prepare to be seduced by Palazzo Magnani Feroni - all-suites florence, a brilliantly restored 16th-century noble residence-cum-eminent boutique retreat. Honeymooners flock to this city of romance and in turn, to this love nest in the heart of it. Each of its 12 suites is hugely spacious, decorated with elaborate works of art, antiques and ultra-modern surprises such as free WiFi. Some have hydro-shower cabins that play music and have mood lighting. Public spaces are positively palatial with statues, vaulted ceilings, intricate wood carvings, frescoes and more antiques; utterly sumptuous, regal and grandiose. Once you've recharged the energy levels with a lush Palazzo breakfast, there's the city's Renaissance art, culture and shopping to explore on your doorstep. Palazzo Magnani is brilliantly located for all of Florence's must-sees including the Uffizi and Ponte Vecchio. (There's great gelato served right outside the door too!) And if you do only one thing, ask the staff to organise a private tour for you. These are often unusual and fun ways to explore the cradle of the Renaissance, rolling hills of the Chianti region, the finest wines and traditional Tuscan recipes. They also have all the inside info on the best restaurants but take some time out with an apéritif or two on the Palazzo's rooftop bar and terrace. The image of the sun setting over the Duomo is one that stays with you forever.

☎ +39 055 2399544
🌐 condenastjohansens.com/florencepalace
🏠 Borgo San Frediano 5, 50124 Florence, Tuscany, Italy

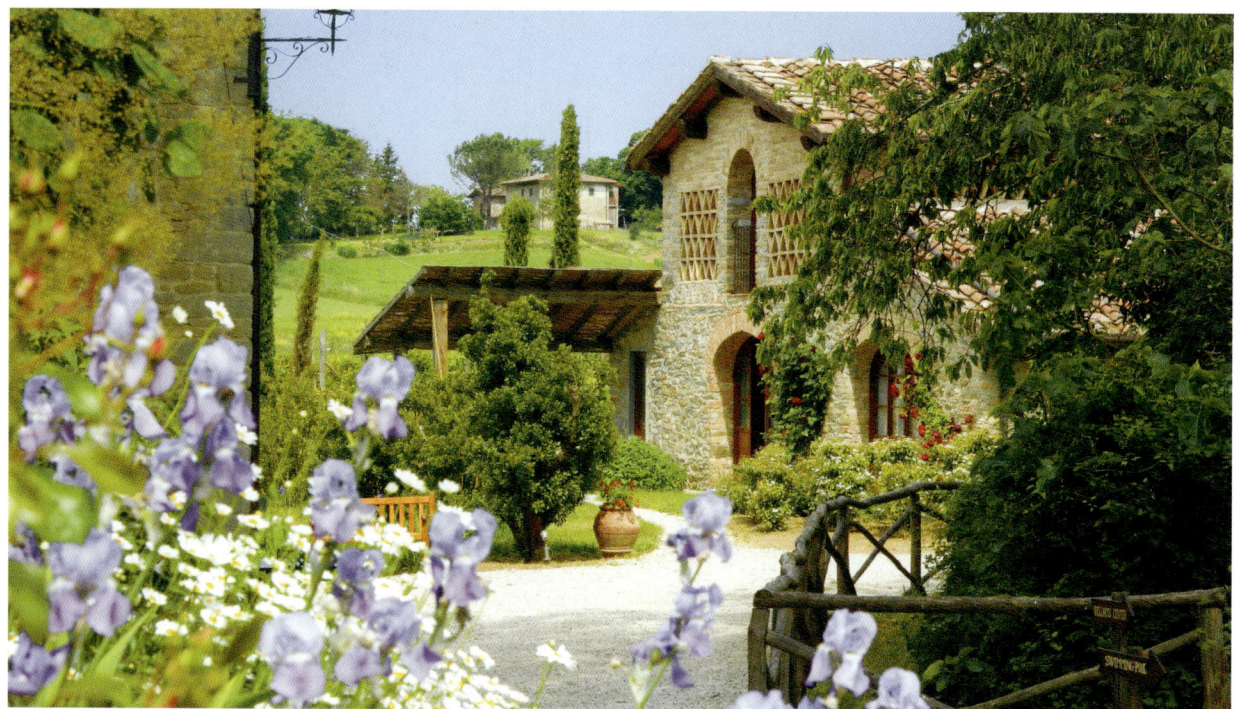

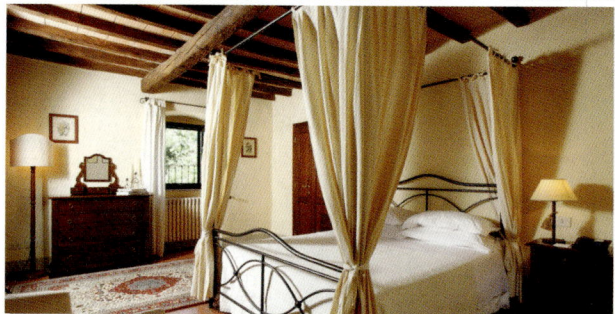

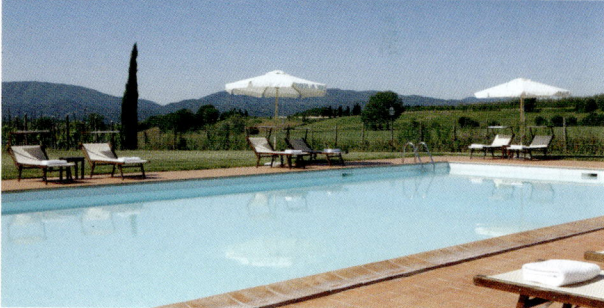

Monsignor Della Casa Country Resort & Spa

The heart of Tuscan adventure, romance and family fun

It's hard to pin down what makes Monsignor Della Casa Country Resort & Spa quite so special. There's so many highlights it's difficult to know where to start. Perhaps the location: Monsignor Della Casa is set in acres of undulating Tuscan countryside, just a short drive from the charms of Florence. Then there's the hotel itself, a beautifully restored Tuscan hamlet alongside wonderfully welcoming apartments and private villas that instantly feel like your pastoral home-from-home. Endless activities such as tennis, trekking, biking, volleyball and swimming have you working up an appetite while serious gourmands can join a local truffle tour to then enjoy their discoveries by candlelight shaved over some fresh pasta on the elegant terrace. The stock of local and national wines, freshly pressed olive oil and selection of regional cheeses are also well worth a try. If craving some peace and relaxation, Monsignor Della Casa is an expert in slowing down the pace. Try a cooking class or head to the spa housed in an old stone farmhouse bathed in light from the huge windows. Here you can relax with facial and body treatments that use local grapes and olive oil, before planning your next Tuscan adventure on this beautiful estate.

PRICE FROM:
€159

FEATURES:
Family friendly; Pool; Restaurant; Spa; Wheelchair access

ACTIVITIES:
Golf; Shopping; Sightseeing

NEARBY:
Florence; White truffle hunting; Mugello car and motorbike circuit; Chianti wine tasting; Designer fashion outlet

GETTING THERE:
Florence Airport; Bologna Airport; Pisa Airport

+39 055 840 821 ☎
condenastjohansens.com/monsignor 🌐
Via di Mucciano 16, 50032 Borgo San Lorenzo, Florence, 🏠
Tuscany, Italy

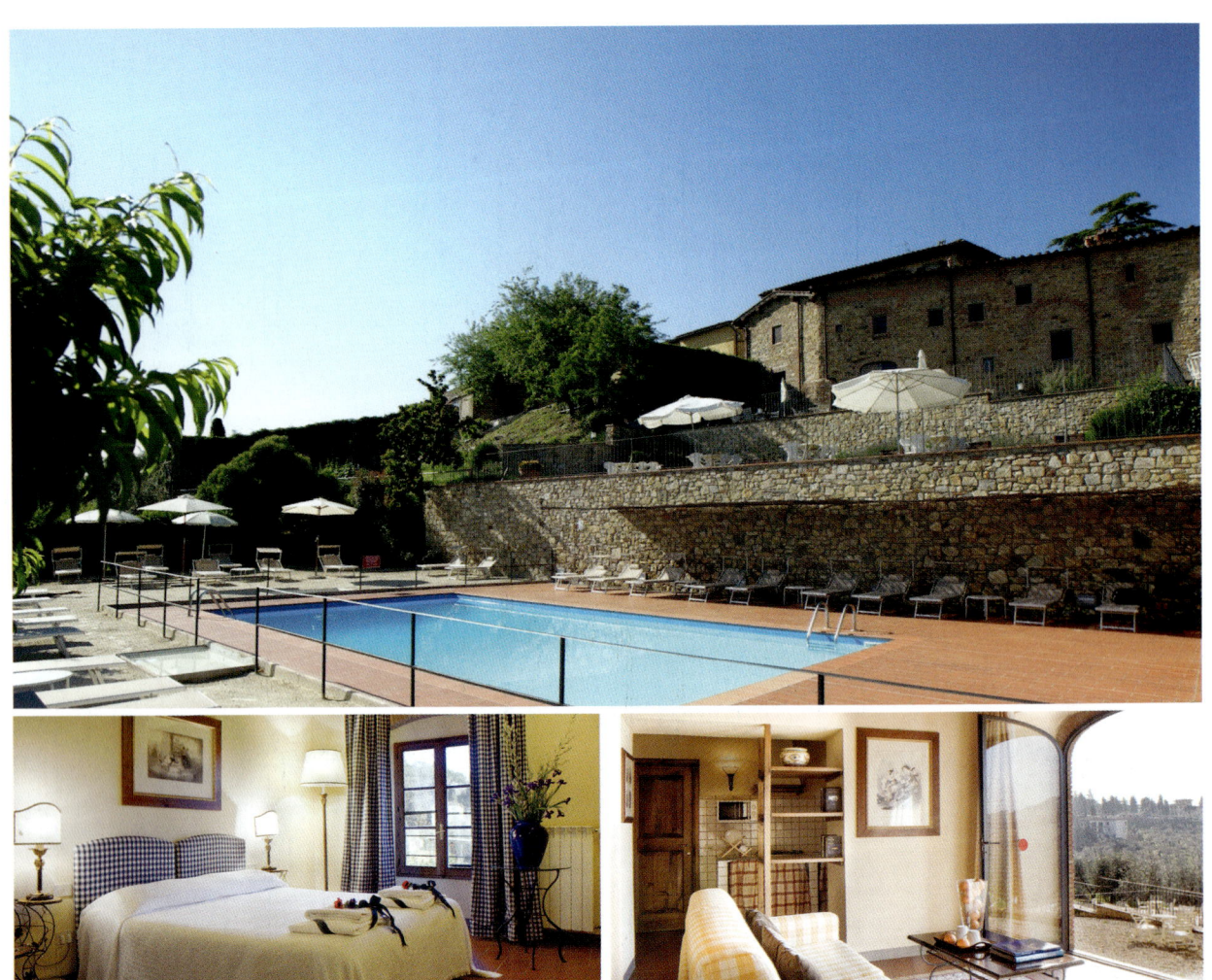

Country Relais Villa L'Olmo

Olive tree-laden hillside resort just outside Florence

PRICE FROM:
€80

FEATURES:
Family friendly; Gym; Pool

ACTIVITIES:
Golf; Horse riding

NEARBY:
Florence; San Gimignano; Estate vineyard and wine tasting; Impruneta terracotta and artistic ceramic workshops; Chianti food and wine tour

GETTING THERE:
Florence Airport; Pisa Airport; Bologna Airport

Deep in the Chianti region, Country Relais Villa L'Olmo is a bucolic beauty offering a true taste of rural Italy. The wine isn't bad either. Tucked away in the Florentine hills, Villa L'Olmo allows you to take a step back and recharge your batteries. (If you want to ramp it up a gear, shoot off to Florence just a drive away for a culture-shot or designer-fuelled foray into Gucci and Prada.) Made up of a collection of cobbled stone buildings naturally warmed by the sun and topped with earthy Impruneta terracotta tiles, there's a quirky, unexpected addition with the sand-edged pool amidst the vineyards and olive groves. Inside, a cheery country style decorates the cottages, apartments and rustic farmhouse, which is a great choice if visiting with chums. Cottages have their own private pools and the farmhouse has a spacious courtyard that's perfect for barbecues. Apartments have bijoux kitchens so you can rustle up something tasty any time, best accompanied by the Villa's very own olive oil and wine produced under their Diademia Wine & Champagne label. Tastings can be arranged but you can truly get to know the grape at the annual Festa Dell'Uva (Grape Festival) held every September.

☎ +39 055 23 11 311
🌐 condenastjohansens.com/relaisfarmholiday
🏠 Via Imprunetana per Tavarnuzze 19, I-50023 Impruneta, Florence, Tuscany, Italy

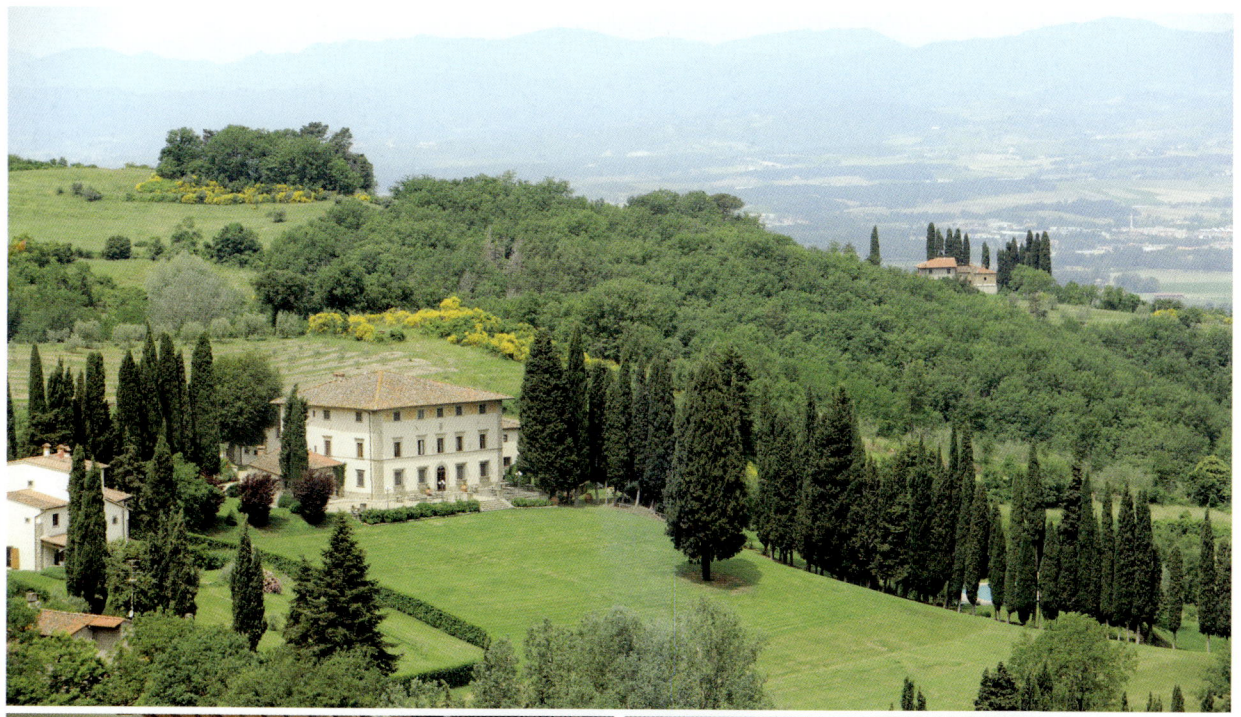

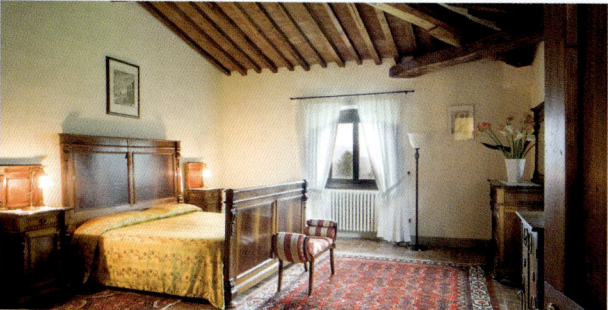
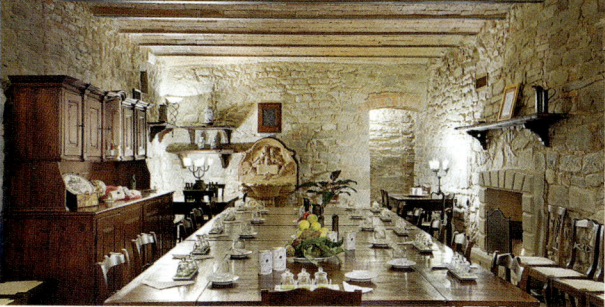

Villa Campestri Olive Oil Resort

Historic Tuscan villa in olive-tree filled countryside

The Renaissance Villa Campestri Olive Oil Resort in Tuscany's Mugello Valley is embarking on a cultural movement of its very own: the olive oil renaissance. Owner Paolo Pasquali is the force behind this olive oil resort (the only one of its kind) where the smooth sunny-yellow liquid is treated with reverence most commonly expressed for wine. Cultivated and produced on-site, the influence of the extra-virgin, cold-pressed potion filters into all aspects of the property. This is most apparent at L'Olivaia restaurant whose menu of elegant Tuscan dishes is led by the various oils' flavours. Try the four-course Olive Oil Menu as your initiation into this oily-world (the olive oil ice cream is surprisingly tasty). Then maybe sign up for a cooking class, have an olive oil massage and explore the surrounding rolling hills filled with olive trees on mountain bike. When Paolo purchased Villa Campestri from the noble Roti Michelozzi family 24 years ago, the subsequent renovation was utterly respectful and its original layout was kept intact. All villa, farmhouse and dairy house bedrooms remain in the their original centuries-old locations and ancient Manifattura Chini painted ceramics are in superb condition. Even the age-old Renaissance frescoes and designs created by celebrated artists Giotto and Fra Angelico are on display for admiration.

PRICE FROM:
€99

FEATURES:
Family friendly; Helipad; Pool; Restaurant

ACTIVITIES:
Fishing; Golf; Water sports

NEARBY:
Florence; Birthplace of Giotto; Museum of Beato Angelico; Car/motorbike Mugello race circuit; Barberino designer outlet

GETTING THERE:
Florence Airport; Bologna Airport; Pisa Airport

+39 055 849 0107
condenastjohansens.com/villacampestri
Via di Campestri 19/22, 50039 Vicchio di Mugello, Florence, Tuscany, Italy

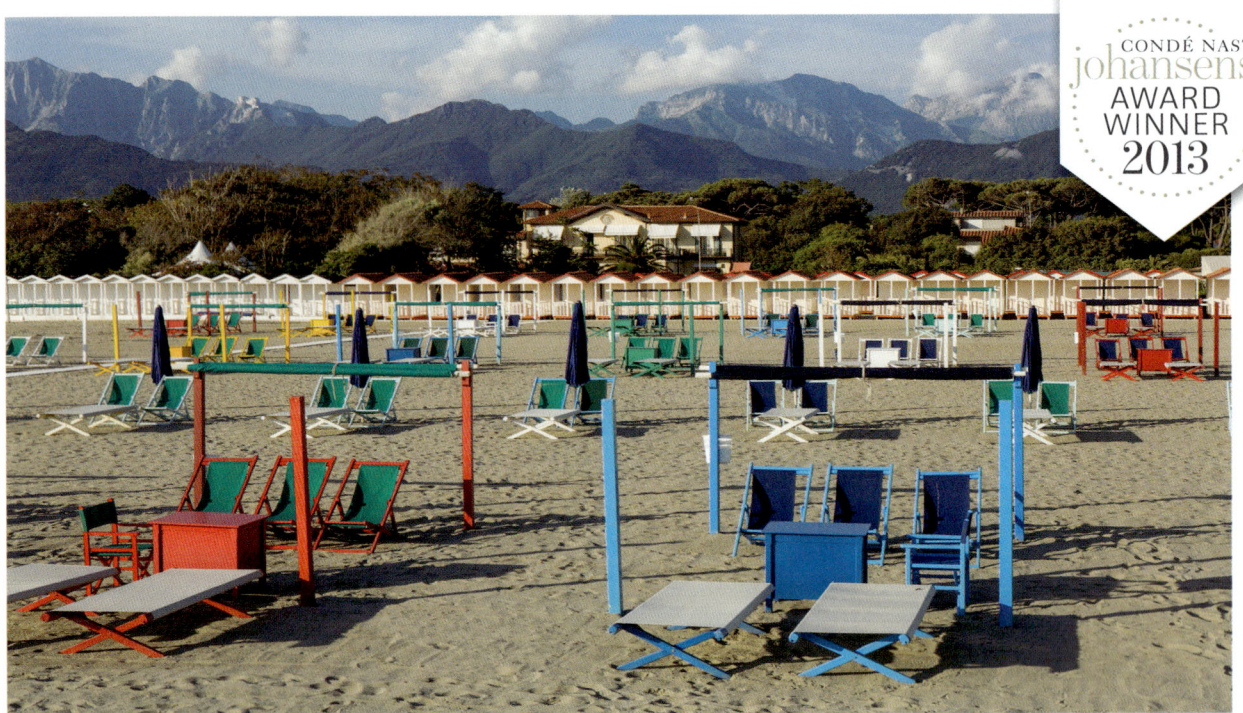

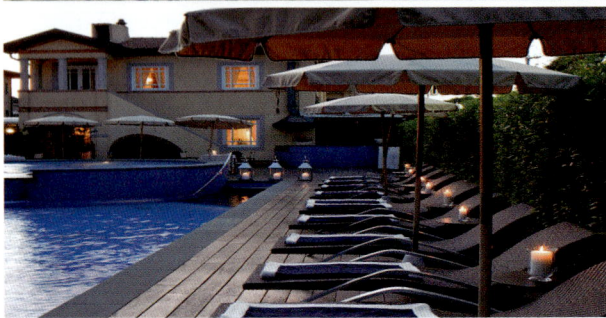

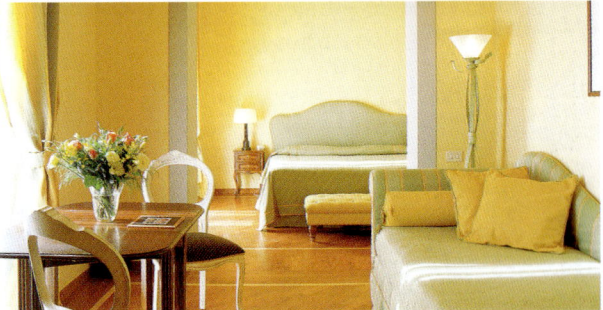

Hotel Byron

Liberty-style luxe and Michelin Star fodder on the Tuscan coast

PRICE FROM:
€280

FEATURES:
Family friendly; Michelin Starred restaurant; Pool; Sea views

ACTIVITIES:
Fishing; Golf; Water sports

NEARBY:
Lucca; Pisa; Puccini Opera Festival; Tour of Carrara marble caves

GETTING THERE:
Pisa Airport; Florence Airport

Dolce Vita. The phrase that could have been coined for Hotel Byron. Built over 100 years ago as a party pad for one of Italy's leading socialites, back then, you were no-one if you didn't have a villa in Forte dei Marmi. Today, the glamour is still here but without the showy glitz. This is old school elegance meets Italian charm and Forte dei Marmi is as equally loved for its woodlands and serenity as it is for its fabulous shopping and chic restaurants. Hotel Byron is a stately villa, built with style and comfort in equal measure and if you're looking for a hotel with star quality, this is for you. Moments from the Tyrrhenian Sea and beach, and with the Apuan Alps as a backdrop, it's a peaceful, beautiful retreat just a short walk from Forte dei Marmi. Rooms are high ceilinged, chic and simple, and the hotel's restaurant, Magnolia, is one of the best in town. Their chef holds a Michelin Star for his traditional, regional cooking that uses the best local produce to create food with creative flair. Easily reached from either Florence or Pisa, Hotel Byron is a hidden treasure on this stunning stretch of the Italian coast.

☎ +39 0584 787 052
🌐 condenastjohansens.com/byron
🏠 Viale A Morin 46, 55042 Forte dei Marmi (LU), Tuscany, Italy

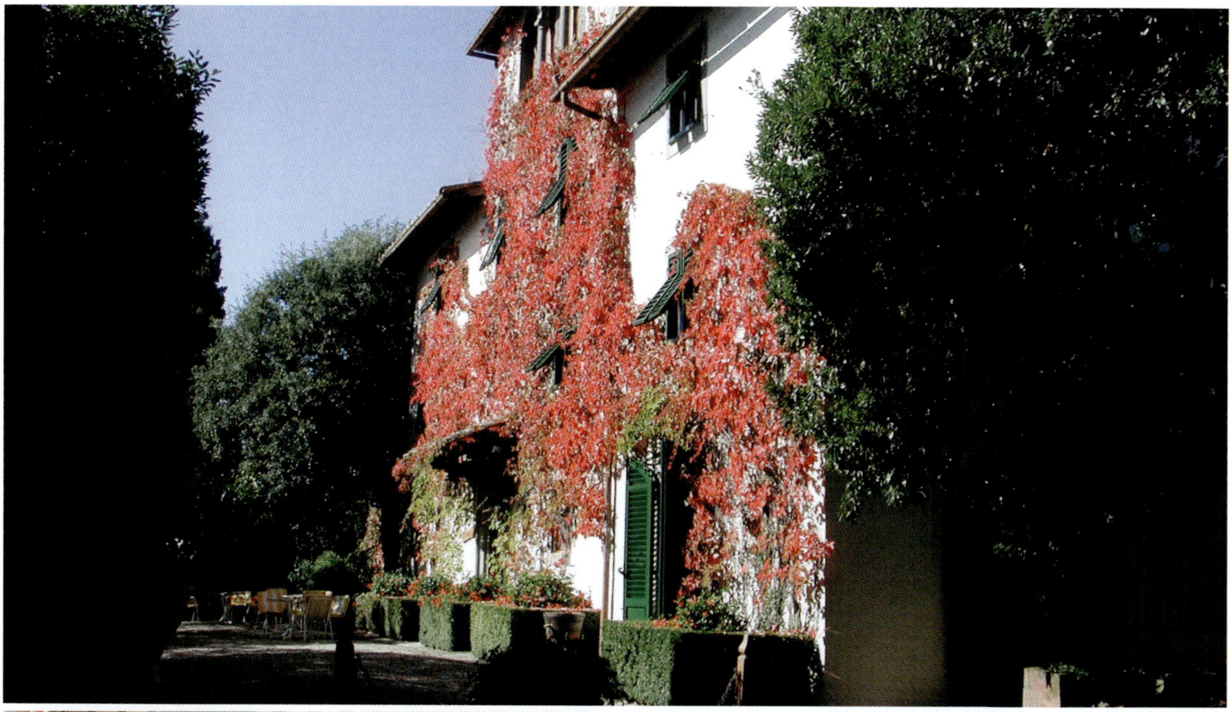

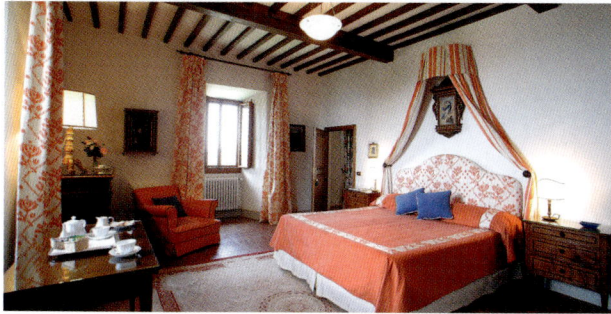
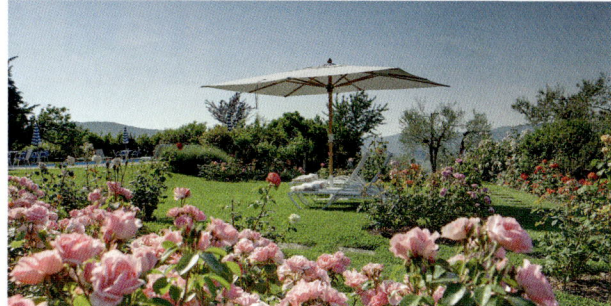

Villa le Barone

A taster of 16th-century aristocratic life in the Tuscan hills

Villa le Barone does grand: after all, it is the former summer house of Florentine nobility situated amid vineyards and cypress groves in rolling Chianti countryside. It does gourmet: just as you would hope excellent wines (dinner is a leisurely treat) and skilful Tuscan cooking classes (learning to make pasta was never more fun!) are on the agenda each day. It does Italian hospitality: so passionate and full of gusto. This handsome Renaissance manor house is big on character with endless nooks and crannies inside and out, a maze of rooms and staircases, and beautiful, fragrant rose and lavender gardens made for intimate afternoons. Add in the home-from-home vibe, fresh-cut flowers, log fires on chilly evenings and an honesty bar, and le Barone has laid-back escape written all over it. The Villa's 28 rooms brimming with paintings, antiques and country-chic fabrics are the essence of the rural high-life. Some are located in the main house, others in ivy-clad cottages. Some are big. Some are small. All adding to the irresistible charm. Wine-tasting tours, golf and culture are all within easy reach and there's an on-site tennis court. Florence and Siena are just a short drive away, however, one of the best journeys you'll make will be from your room to the pool and the candlelit terrace for dinner.

PRICE FROM:
€190

FEATURES:
Family friendly; Gym; Pool; Restaurant

ACTIVITIES:
Sightseeing; Tennis; Walking

NEARBY:
Florence; Siena; Cooking classes; Pieve di San Leolino's festivals, concerts and markets; Greve, Chianti

GETTING THERE:
Florence Airport; Pisa Airport

+39 055 852621 ☎
condenastjohansens.com/villalebarone 🌐
Via San Leolino 19, 50022 Panzano in Chianti (FI), Tuscany, 🏠
Italy

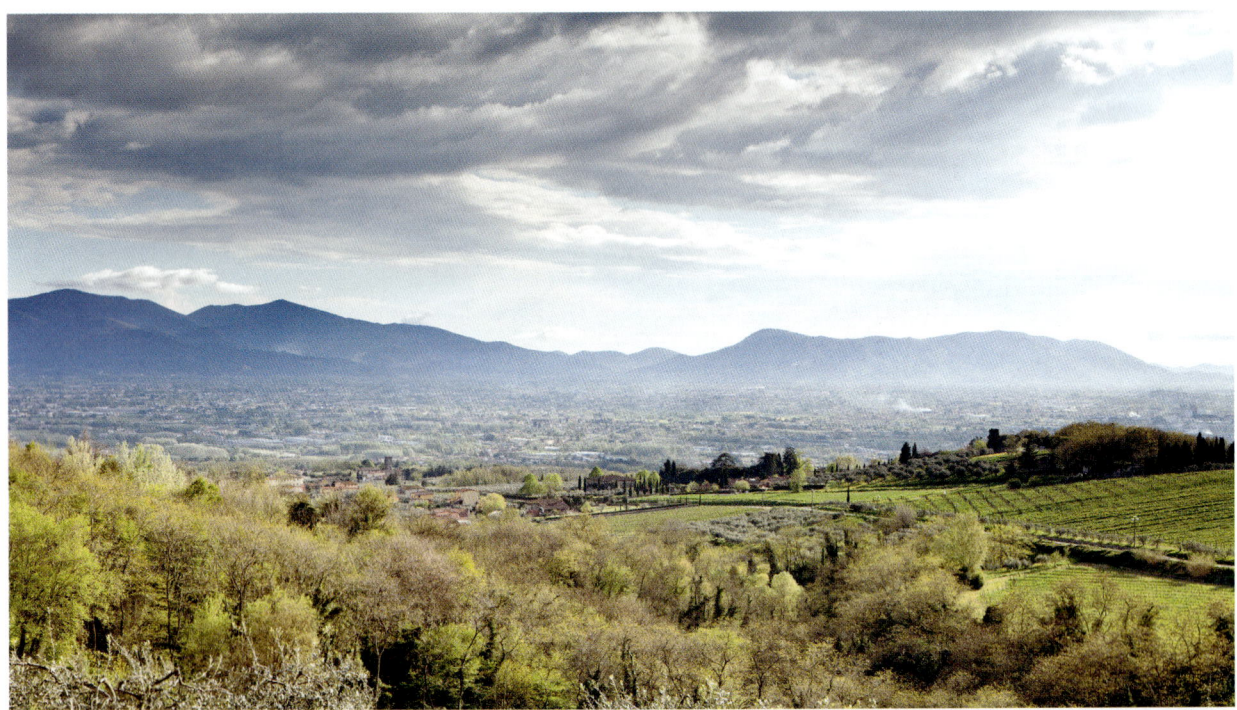

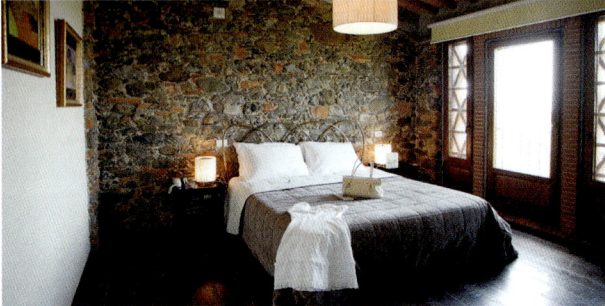
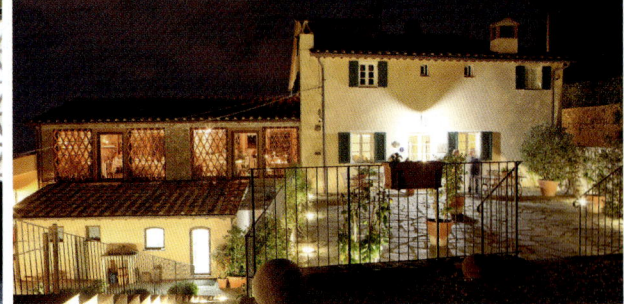

Tenuta San Pietro Luxury Hotel & Restaurant

Gourmet Tuscan estate in bucolic beauty

PRICE FROM:
€180

FEATURES:
Family friendly; Pet friendly; Pool; Restaurant

ACTIVITIES:
Cycling; Horse riding; Walking

NEARBY:
Pinocchio Park; Monte Carlo; Versilia beaches; Puccini's Museum; Lucca

GETTING THERE:
Pisa Airport; Florence Airport

Henry James described the Tuscan city of Lucca as "overflowing with everything." Behind its Renaissance walls, cobbled lanes and picturesque piazzas you'll uncover churches, art galleries, cafés and oodles of local flavour. A short drive into the hills above the town (sat-nav recommended) brings you to another little gem: Tenuta San Pietro Luxury Hotel & Restaurant, an eight-room, two-suite boutique bolthole with a private house feel. The restored 16th-century manor is quintessentially Tuscan with a sunset-hued stucco façade and terracotta-coloured barrel-tile roof. Inside, a stone and wood backdrop sets off the pared-back, rustic-luxe décor. If a terrific view tops your room wish list opt for Mille Fiori or Bella Vista. Both look out across the vineyards, olive groves and patchwork countryside beyond. Nothing however, can beat the twinkling night-time panorama from the candlelit restaurant terrace where delicate fish dishes and delicious gnocchi are enhanced by Chef Guido Lotti's signature flair. The perfect day: a morning cycle along the tree-lined avenues of Lucca followed by an afternoon at the Montechiari vineyard in medieval Montecarlo and a dip in Tenuta San Pietro's pool. Then time for an indulgent olive oil or chocolate massage before flopping into the restaurant for a gourmet dinner.

☎ +39 0583 926676
🌐 condenastjohansens.com/tenutasanpietro
📍 Via per San Pietro 22/26, San Pietro a Marcigliano, 55012 Capannori - Lucca, Tuscany, Italy

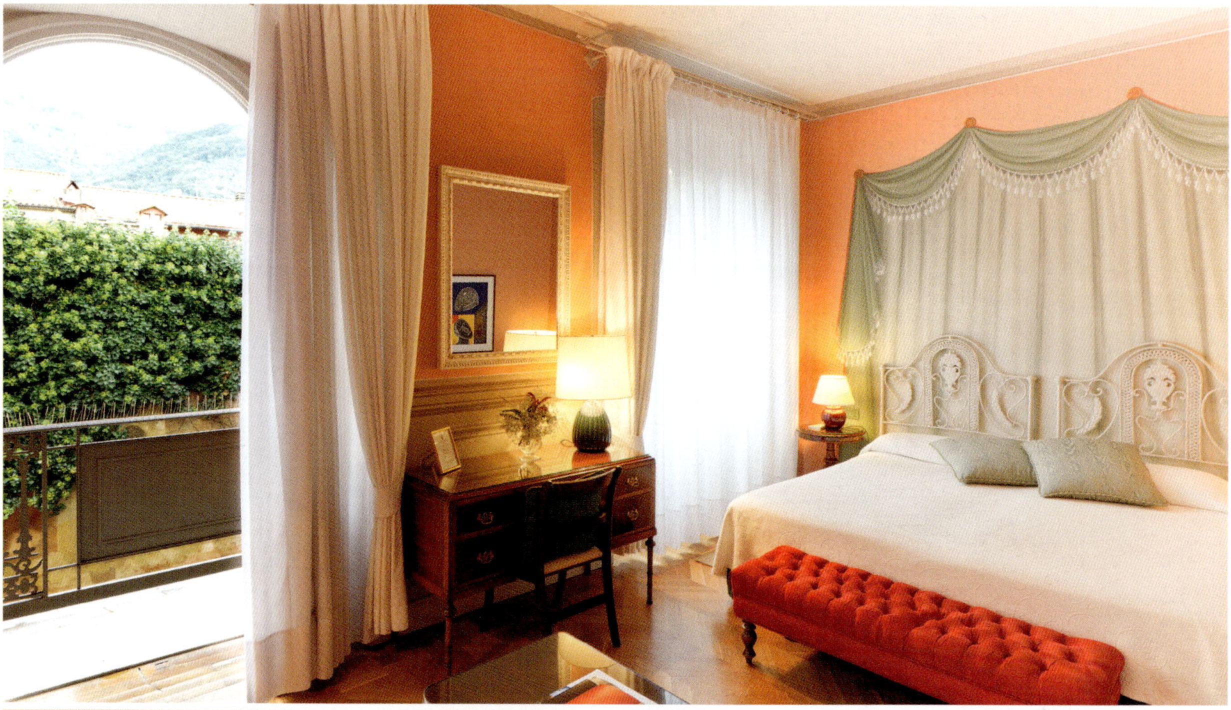

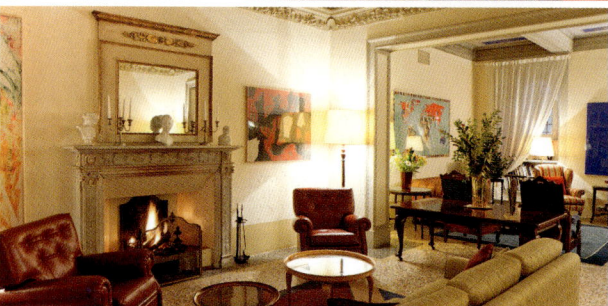
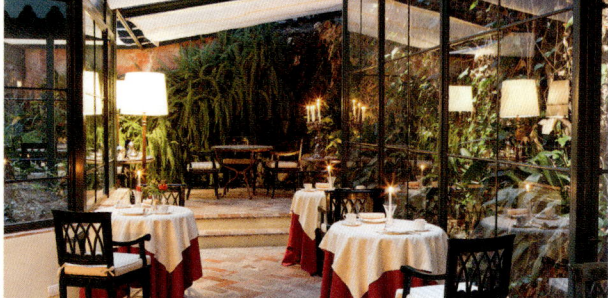

Albergo Pietrasanta - Palazzo Barsanti Bonetti

Ancestral Renaissance grandeur in Pietrasanta

Stop off during your grandiose Italian tour and discover THE room with a view at Albergo Pietrasanta - Palazzo Barsanti Bonetti, tucked away in Versilia, Tuscany. A well-kept secret, the Albergo remains undiscovered by many. For those in-the-know it's a country house retreat, Italian-style, whose 17th-century heart beats to a palatial rhythm within handsome walls adorned with lofty ceilings, frescoes and a green-fringed courtyard with pretty fountain. But the Albergo isn't afraid to mix it up with an enviable collection of bold modern artworks splashed across its immaculate walls. Choose a luxurious balcony-festooned courtyard room and watch the world go by or in the evening wander out to the beautiful cathedral square. Pietrasanta is magical by night. And it's surprisingly cosmopolitan with an artsy vibe, lots of good restaurants, bars and cafés. Manager Barbara Pardini and her attentive team are waiting to give you a great big hug (metaphorically speaking). They simply can't do enough for you, whether waving you off on a bicycle trip to nearby Fortei dei Marmi's sandy beaches, organising a private dinner party or mixing you a cocktail.

PRICE FROM:
€132

FEATURES:
Family friendly; Gym; Pet friendly; Wheelchair access

ACTIVITIES:
Fishing; Golf; Horse riding

NEARBY:
Carrara; Pisa; Cinque Terre; The most exclusive beach in Marina di Pietrasanta; Puccini Opera Festival

GETTING THERE:
Pisa Airport; Florence Airport

+39 0584 793 727 ☎
condenastjohansens.com/pietrasanta 🌐
Via Garibaldi 35, 55045 Pietrasanta (Lucca), Tuscany, Italy 🏠

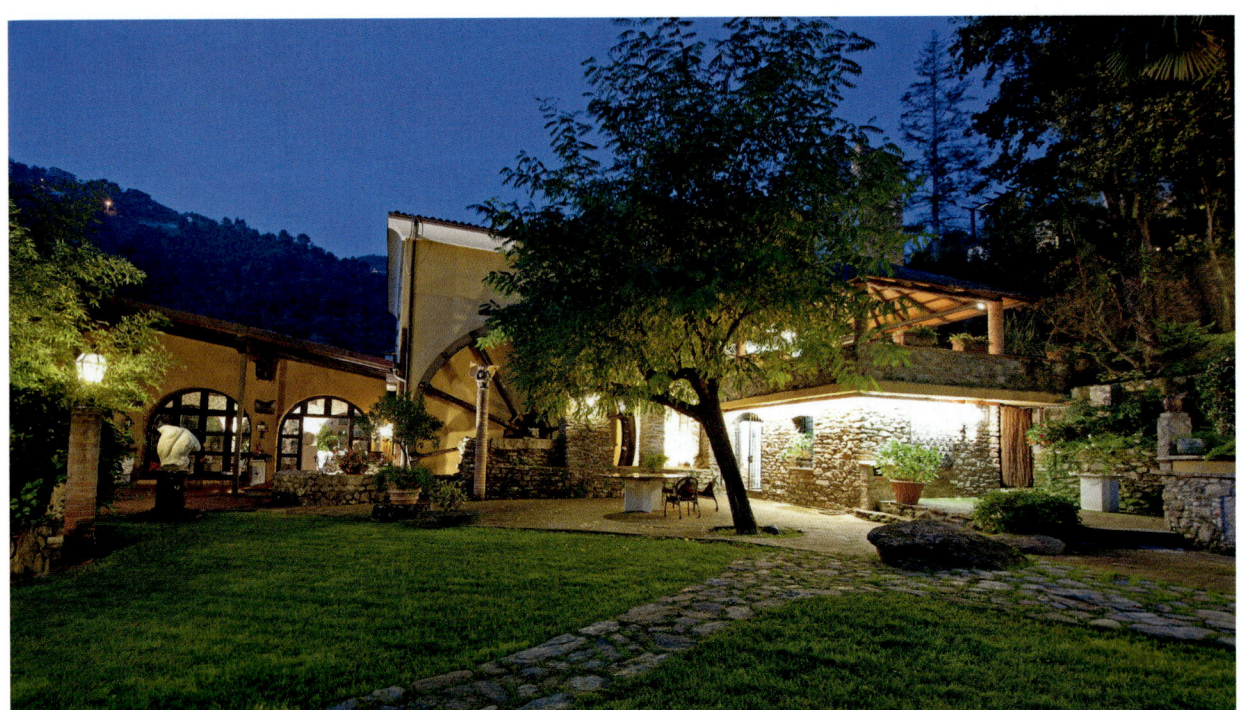

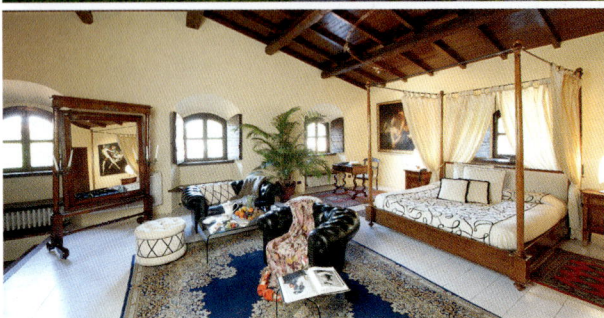

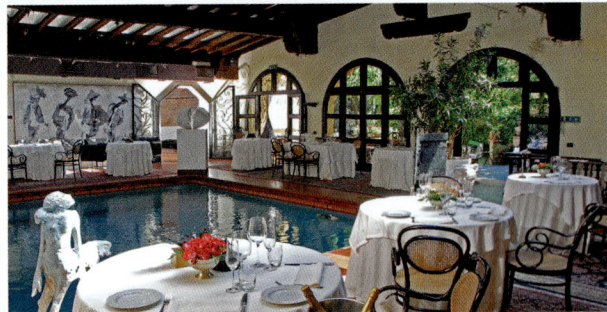

Il Bottaccio

An oasis of privacy and romance near Forte dei Marmi

PRICE FROM:
€280

FEATURES:
Beach access; Family friendly; Pet friendly; Restaurant; Spa

ACTIVITIES:
Golf; Shopping; Sightseeing

NEARBY:
Forte dei Marmi; Pisa; Florence; Five Lands; Carrara marble quarries

GETTING THERE:
Pisa Airport; Florence Airport

☎ +39 0585 340031
🌐 condenastjohansens.com/bottaccio
🏠 Via Bottaccio 1, 54038 Montignoso - Massa Carrara, Tuscany, Italy

Il Bottaccio is pure epicurean drama. A boutique bolthole housed in a 17th-century former oil mill in the foothills of the Apuan Alps in rural Tuscany, it delivers a killer trio of contemporary art, fine food and wine, and top-notch spa treatments. It just-so-happens to be phenomenally beautiful too. Imagine Florentine tiled floors, cathedral ceilings, grand fireplaces, Persian rugs, antiques and artworks aplenty with paintings and sculptures greeting you at every turn. In the eight huge suites, old and new mingle in perfect harmony alongside 18th-century paintings, antique bookcases and bas-reliefs, Versace lamps, Poltrona Frau sofas and Vietri ceramics. For something really special stay in the Royal Suite whose bathroom mosaics and two-metre-wide tub (one of the original olive vats) are stunning. Outside your private sanctuary, dazzling coastline (the Italian Riviera is within easy reach), mountains, national parks and medieval cities (Pisa, Lucca) await, while a visit to the hotel's divine Otzium spa is a must-do. But dinner is the main event here. Choose from the elegant Diana dining room or leafy poolside restaurant whose wooden portals look out onto the lush gardens. Both deliver artful Mediterranean cuisine. Complete your gastronomic getaway with a lesson at Il Bottaccio's excellent cooking school.

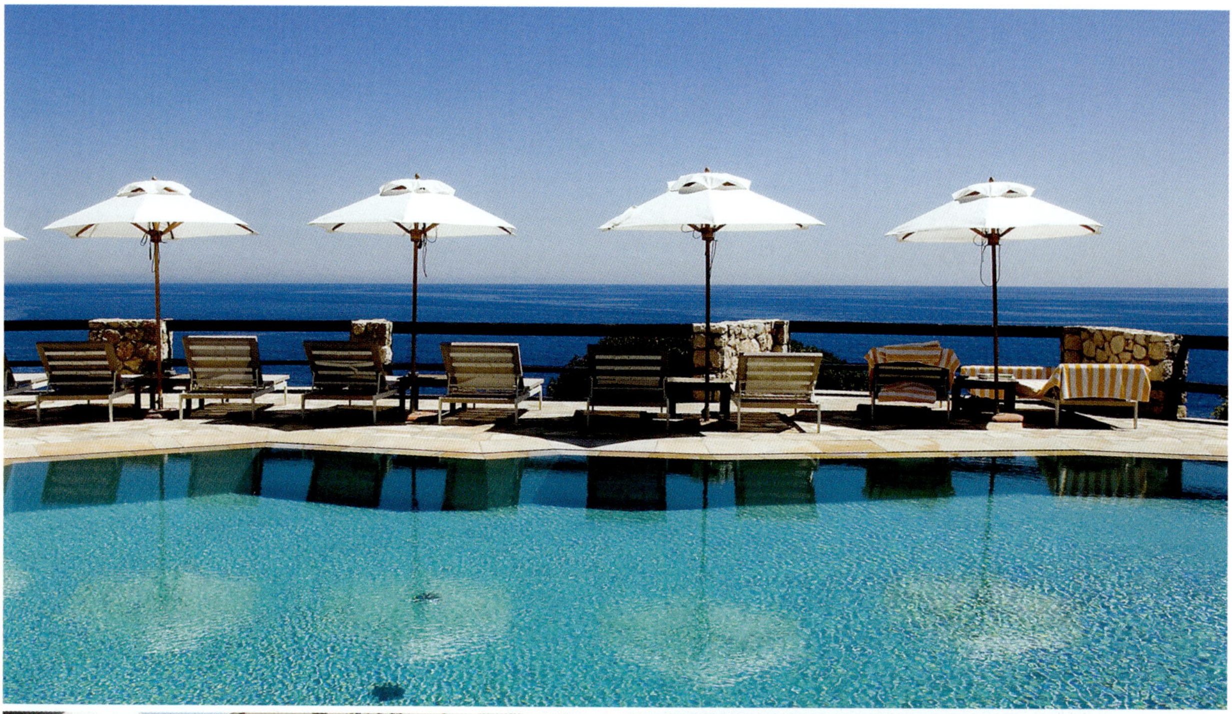

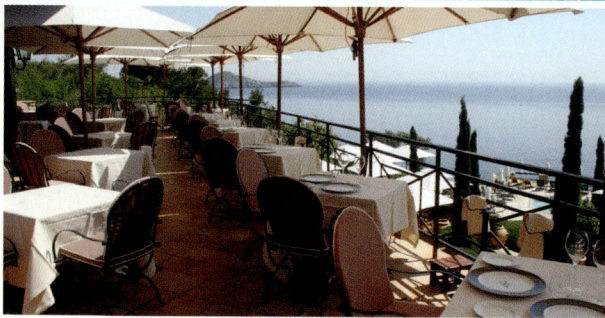
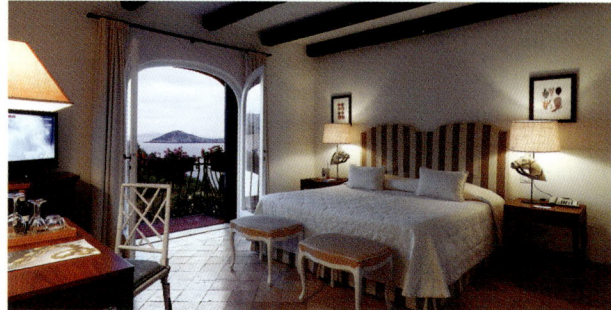

Il Pellicano Hotel

Seaside serenity enveloped by the olive trees of Argentario Peninsula

The hotel du jour of the 1960s jetset, Il Pellicano Hotel's star-studded 50-year history reads like a who's who of the great and the glamorous (Hollywood hot stars, fashionistas, European royalty). They all flocked here to sample a touch of "la dolce vita". And today, it remains one of the trendiest, most exclusive (though never pretentious) destinations in Maremma, south-west Tuscany. Hugging the hillside on the rugged Monte Argentario Peninsula, it's peaceful and pretty set among fragrant cypress and olive groves with stepped terraces. Winding stone pathways and immaculate gardens overlook a private rocky cove beyond which unfurls the glimmering Tyrrhenian Sea. The 50 rooms are spread across the main house and within cottages (go for the latter if you can). They're all individually decorated and universally beautiful, graced with spiffing marble bathrooms, hand-painted tiles, appliqué cushions, retro accents, terraces and balconies. Pampering heaven awaits at the Pelliclub where treatments take spa luxury to another level. Then there's mastering the art of a fantastic Bellini and Negroni during an afternoon cocktail class. Private sailing tours to enjoy too! But the real treat comes at sundown starting with a Pelican Martini on the terrace before heading to Il Pellicano Hotel's eponymous, not 1 but 2 Michelin-Starred restaurant. This is truly the high life.

PRICE FROM:
€428

FEATURES:
Beach access; Gym; Michelin Starred restaurant; Pool; Sea views

ACTIVITIES:
Fishing; Golf; Water sports

NEARBY:
Porto Ercole; Medieval towns; Tuscan islands; Vineyards

GETTING THERE:
Rome Fiumicino Airport; Pisa Airport

+39 0564 858111 ☎
condenastjohansens.com/ilpellicano 🌐
Località Sbarcatello, 58019 Porto Ercole (GR), Tuscany, Italy 🏠

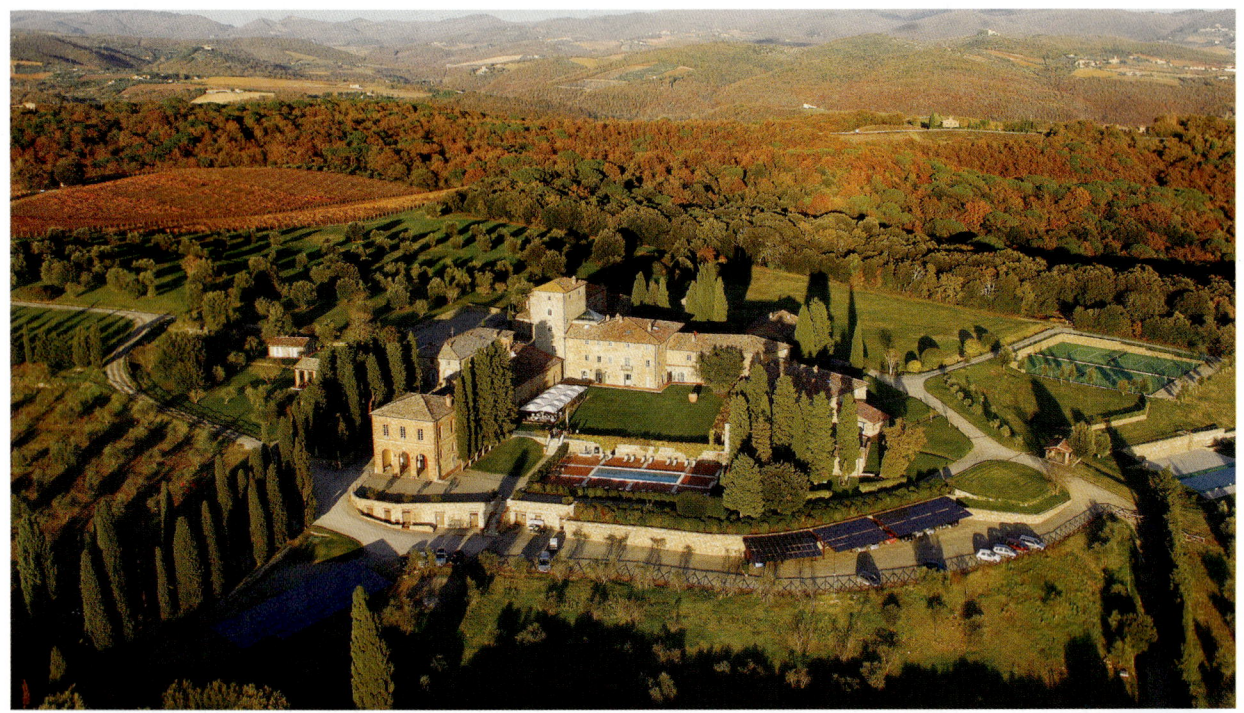

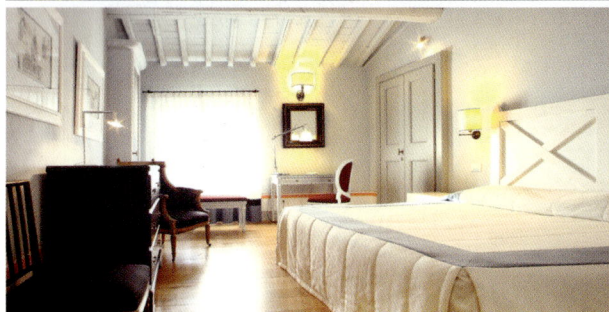
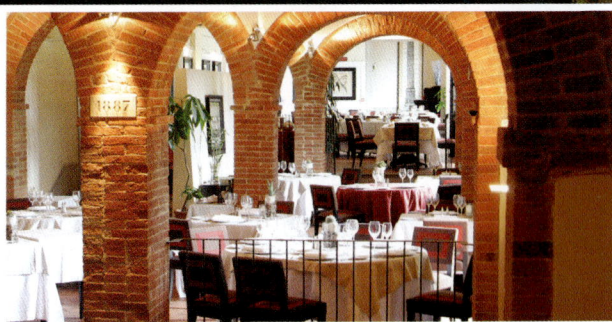

Borgo Scopeto Relais

The elegant Tuscan villa of your fantasies

PRICE FROM:
€240

FEATURES:
Family friendly; Helipad; Pool; Restaurant

ACTIVITIES:
Cycling; Tennis

NEARBY:
Siena; Florence; San Gimignano; Volterra; Chianti vineyards

GETTING THERE:
Florence Airport; Pisa Airport; Rome Airport

Majestic is a word that springs to mind when describing Borgo Scopeto Relais, a Tuscan knockout that gloriously straddles a hillside just a short drive from Siena. For rom-com fans, Borgo Scopeto Relais will look familiar as the dreamy Italian location in Hollywood's "Letters to Juliet". To all who visit, it's a dizzying concoction of ancient stone walls, terracotta roofs and cypress-lined avenues in a most wondrous bucolic setting. Choose your tipple from Borgo's wine list that includes Chianti Classicos from its very own vineyard and sample the extra virgin olive oil produced from the estate's 5,000 olive trees. Wellness treatments in the spa also make use of the grapes grown on-site in their vinotherapy treatments, so both your body and soul can truly capture the heady benefits of the fruit. Lofty rooms are classically elegant with sleek furnishings, marble baths and cool crisp cottons against rich details and contemporary prints on the walls. While top-notch restaurant La Tinaia located in the old cellars, keeps the Tuscan spirit alive on the plate. All in all, Borgo Scopeto Relais is the place to eat, sleep, drink and fall in love. Take to the road: standing to attention at the front door, glossy red Vespas are yours to hire for exploring this corner of rolling Chianti country.

☎ +39 0577 320001
🌐 condenastjohansens.com/borgoscopetorelais
📍 Strada Comunale 14, Siena Vagliagli No 18, Località Borgo Scopeto, 5301 Vagliagli - Siena, Tuscany, Italy

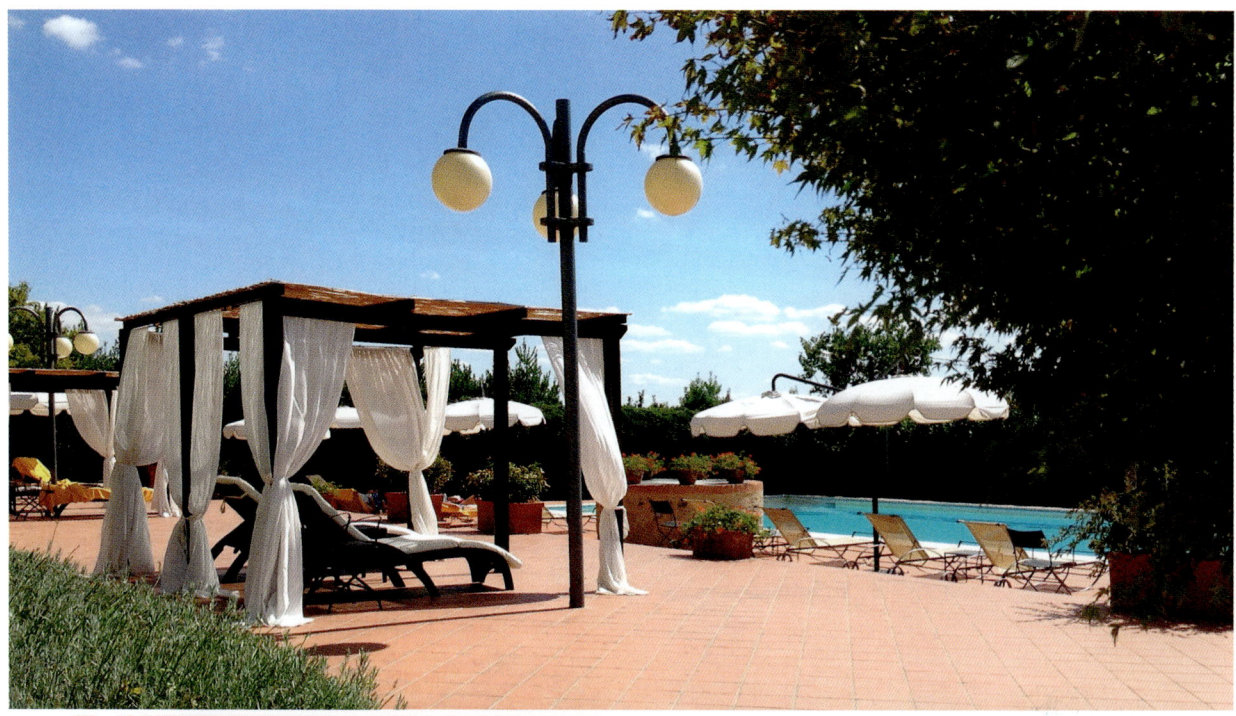

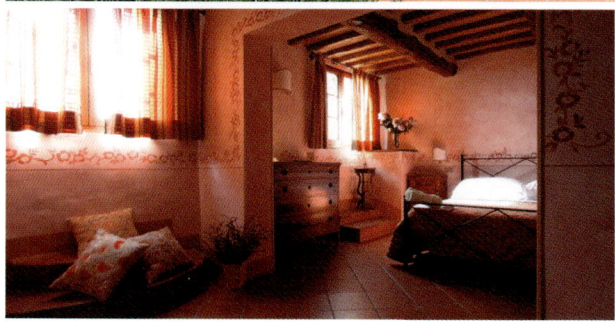

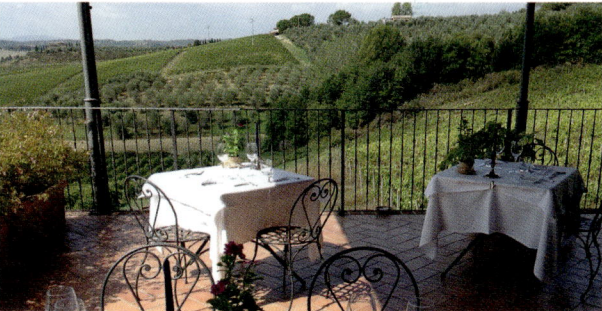

Villa Curina Resort

Romantic Tuscan villa in the rolling hills of Siena

Villa Curina Resort isn't your typical "resort". It's a re-imagined 16th-century hamlet. Located between Tuscany and Umbria, all the prerequisites of a resort are here: tip top accommodation, smart restaurant, pool and outdoor pursuits. However, this is a family-run business where everything expresses a genteel, rural Italian quality and style. Rooms and suites are achingly romantic with quaint nooks and crannies, odd shaped spaces, wooden beams and antiquities. And Il Convito di Curina restaurant is operated by husband and wife team Stefania and Andrea De Agostini. Stefania's homemade pasta dishes, breads and cakes appear on the menu alongside locally reared meat. But that's not all, Sommelier and champagne expert Andrea (the prestigious Ecole of Champagne have invited him to teach training courses), has compiled a wine list of approximately 400 bins including more than 120 varieties of hand-picked champagne. Both passionate oenologists, Stefania and Andrea's wine and champagne tasting sessions are always a big hit. Feel free to burn some off these delicious caolories on the grass tennis court located next to a vineyard where there's somewhat of a bygone-era feel (wooden rackets and all-white kits to the knee seem apt). Or head to the pool looking out to the oil-painting scene of rolling Tuscan hills with Siena in the distance.

PRICE FROM:
€153

FEATURES:
Pool; Restaurant

ACTIVITIES:
Cycling; Horse riding; Tennis

NEARBY:
Siena; Perugia; Chianti wine routes; Gastronomic tours

GETTING THERE:
Florence Airport; Perugia Airport; Pisa Airport

+39 0577 355630
condenastjohansens.com/villacurinaresort
Strada Provinciale 62, No 24, Località Curina, 53019
Castelnuovo Berardenga (Siena), Tuscany, Italy

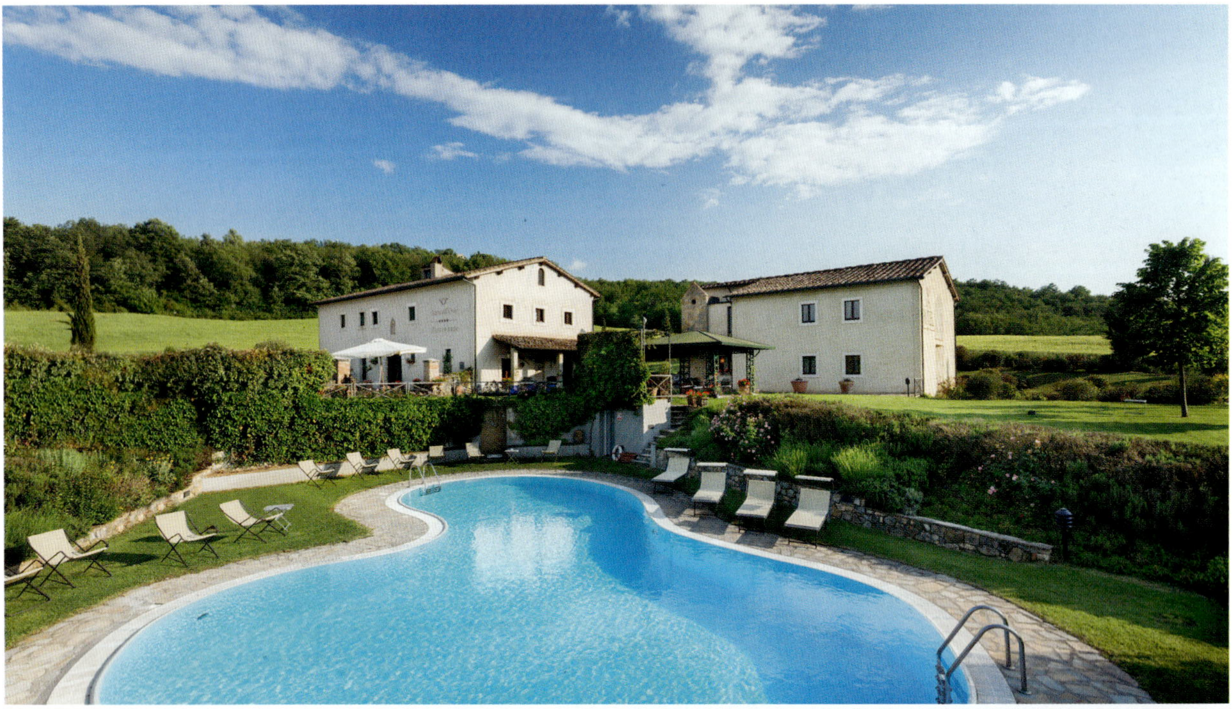

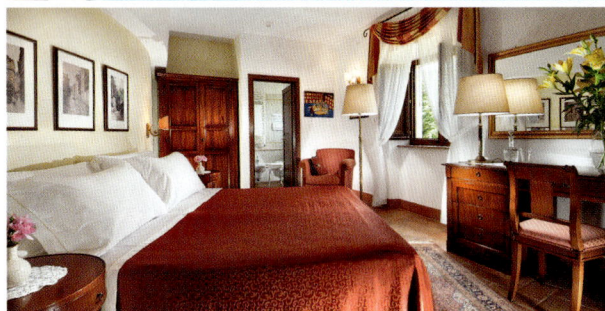

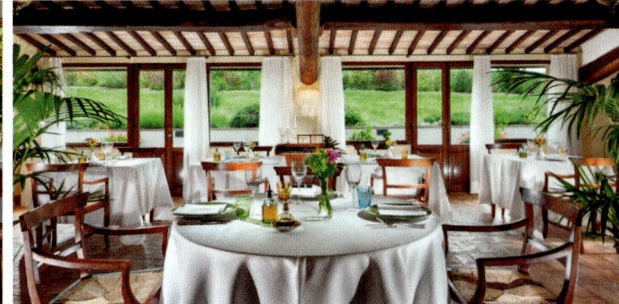

Relais Osteria dell'Orcia

Plush, iconic Tuscan country pad

PRICE FROM:
€130

FEATURES:
Family friendly; Pet friendly; Pool; Restaurant; Wheelchair access

ACTIVITIES:
Golf; Horse riding; Skiing

NEARBY:
San Quirico d'Orcia; Palio of Siena; Bagno Vignoni's thermal waters; Montalcino wineries and wine cellars; Archaeology Etruscan Museum of Chiusi

GETTING THERE:
Perugia Airport; Florence Airport

Relais Osteria dell'Orcia, Tuscany, lies in the heart of the vineyard-strewn Vallée Dell'Orcia World Heritage Site, aka the "sun valley". No surprise then to learn that it's the Relais' superb restaurant and wine selection that will have you wowing. Local specialities of olives, pastas and locally sourced meats brilliantly celebrate the quality produce in the area, each meal guaranteed to bring about food comas and grape-induced hazes. But for the health conscious contingent there's the thermal baths of Bagno Vignoni inducing jelly-like levels of relaxation in no time. Set in a fabulous medieval town bordered by lush green fields, Relais Osteria has gasp-worthy views from every room. A mass of exposed wooden beams, terracotta floors, plush furnishings and Tuscan style, they're every inch the luxe haven you desire on a getaway to the Italian countryside where comfort is paramount. Opt for a Junior Suite with canopy bed for something a little special. The romantic ambience of this beautifully restored 16th-century horse and carriage station is three-fold: secluded, indulgent and peaceful. Naturally, it's a wonderful venue for weddings, conferences and a much-needed escape. The Relais' historic charm never fails to win you over, neither does Zorro, the hotel's very own pet donkey!

☎ +39 0577 887111
🌐 condenastjohansens.com/osteriadellorcia
🏠 Podere Osteria 15, Località Bagno Vignoni, 53023 Castiglione d'Orcia, Siena, Tuscany, Italy

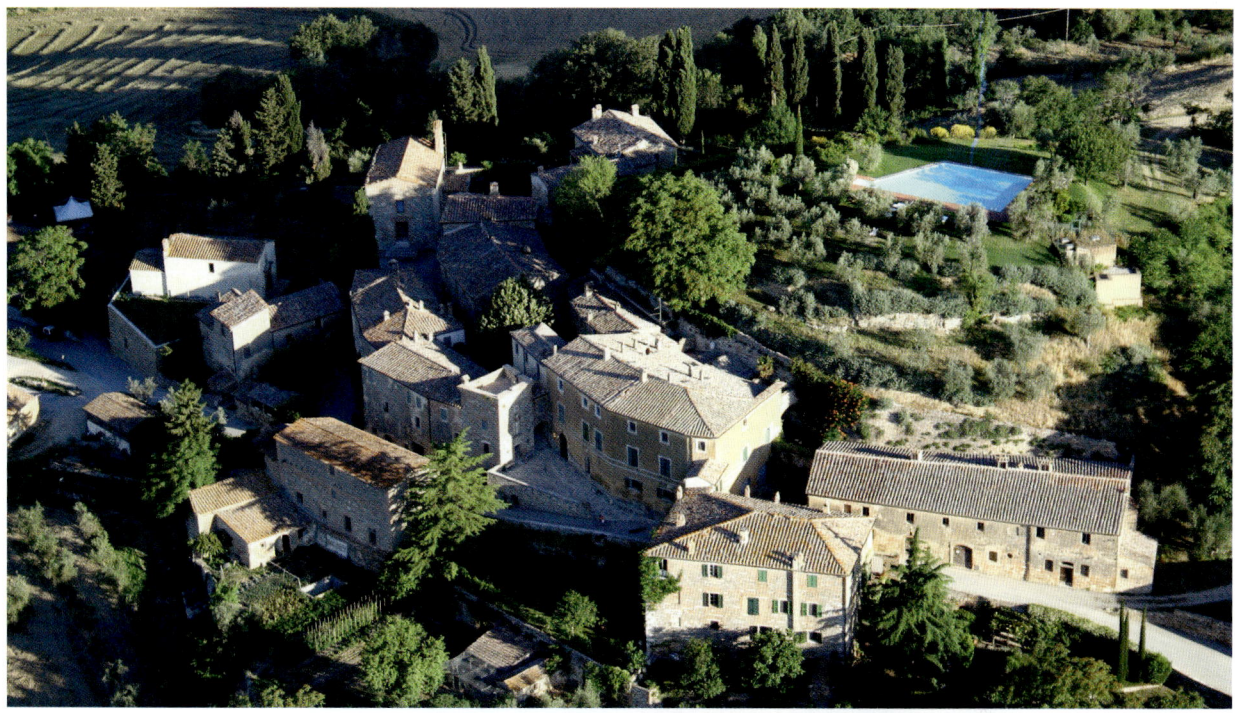

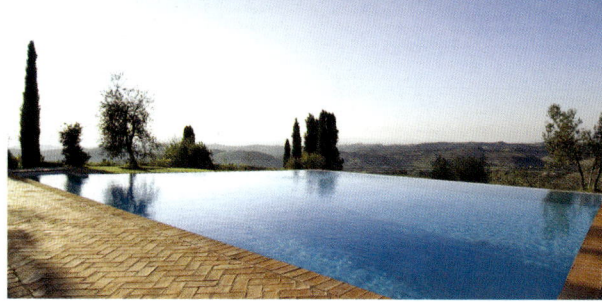
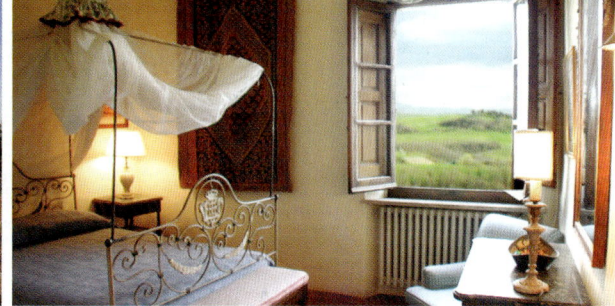

Borgo Lucignanello Bandini

Well-heeled Tuscan living in Lucignano d'Asso

Borgo Lucignanello is Tuscan heaven. Reached by winding roads past tiny villages and majestic cypresses, the miniature hamlet of Lucignano d'Asso is home to Borgo Lucignanello Bandini, a handful of beautiful retreats. The Piccolomini family has owned this enclave for over 600 years and you can feel the love that's been poured into every inch. It has everything you could want for the perfect Tuscan escape from an idyllic infinity pool looking out over the Tuscan plains to rustic yet elegant interiors oozing a cosy, welcoming atmosphere. Choosing where to rest your head isn't easy. Among your choices there's romantic honeymoon favourite, Casa Maria complete with rose decked pergola, or Casale Sarageto, a stunning 18th-century farmhouse with its own pool, garden and pizza oven. One thing's for sure, during a stay at Borgo Lucignanello Bandini you certainly won't go hungry. There's a different market for every day of the week in the nearby villages with local producers tempting you with everything from white truffles to the greenest and freshest olive oil you'll ever taste. While the foodies are salivating, oenophiles are swooning over the internationally renowned Brunello Montalcino wine. Before you know it, you'll be living like a true Italian and looking like one too; there's a Prada outlet just a short drive away.

PRICE FROM:
€240 (2-night min stay)

FEATURES:
Family friendly; Helipad; Pet friendly; Pool

ACTIVITIES:
Cycling; Horse riding; Walking

NEARBY:
Pienza; Montalcino and its Brunello wineries; Siena; Truffle hunting in the Crete Senesi; Hot-air ballooning

GETTING THERE:
Perugia Airport; Florence Airport; Pisa Airport

+39 0577 803 068 ☎
condenastjohansens.com/lucignanello 🌐
Località Lucignano d'Asso, 53020 San Giovanni d'Asso, Siena, 🏠
Tuscany, Italy

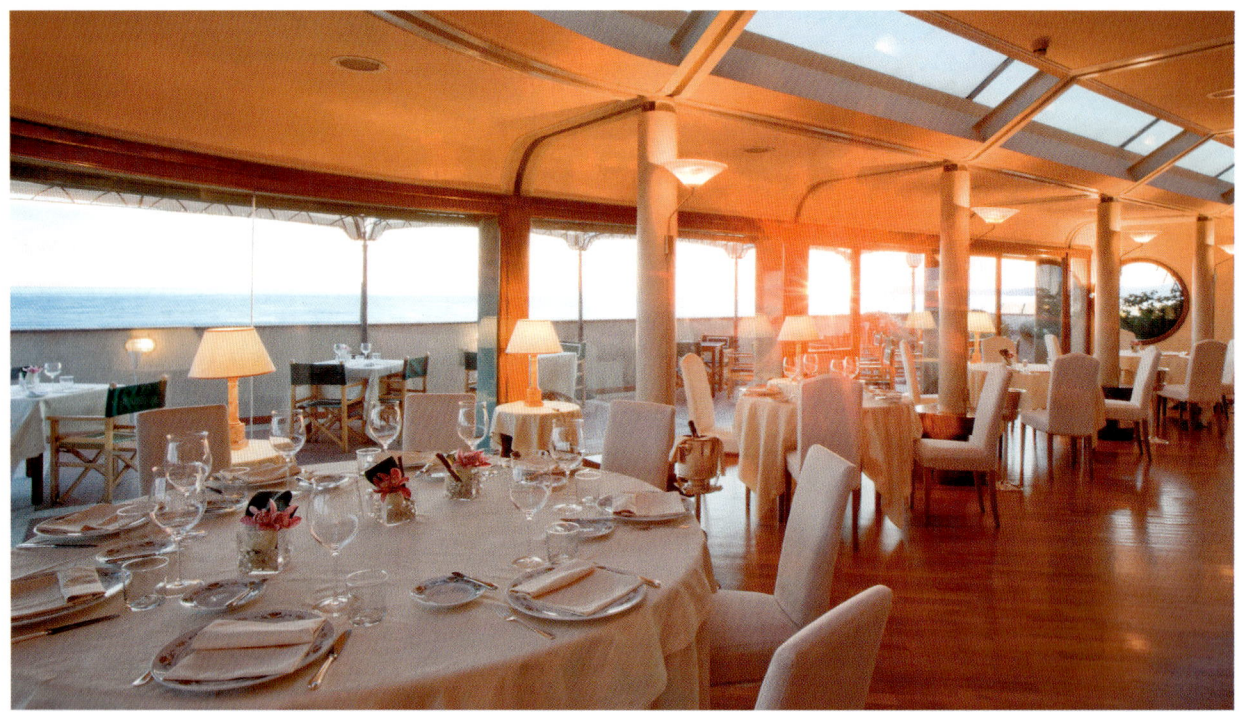

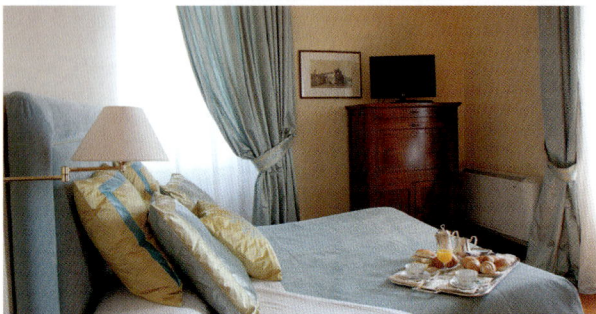

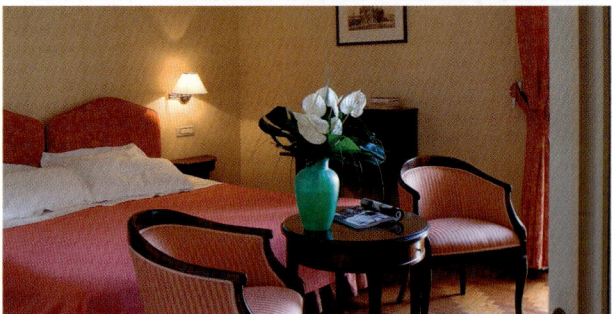

Hotel Plaza e de Russie

Stately elegance on the Tuscan Riviera

PRICE FROM:
€175

FEATURES:
Family friendly; Pet friendly; Restaurant; Sea views; Wheelchair access

ACTIVITIES:
Golf; Horse riding; Water sports

NEARBY:
Lucca; Pisa; Puccini Opera Festival; Tour of Carrara marble cave; Tour of Cinque Terre

GETTING THERE:
Pisa Airport; Florence Airport; Genova Airport

The Tuscan Riviera is a soothing scene of yellowstone canopies, wrought-iron verandas and colourfully patterned tiles. It's one of Italy's most popular tourist destinations and the charming Hotel Plaza e de Russie sits directly in one of its plazas where life happens at a relaxed pace and the sunshine feels like a warm embrace. You'll find yourself naturally easing into the carefree lifestyle and craving the Mediterranean flavours of La Terrazza, Plaza e de Russie's fine dining restaurant. Presiding high on the top floor, mouth-watering meals are devoured to a backdrop of phenomenal ocean views. Here, you'll be served a continental breakfast of fresh pastries, yoghurt and fruit each morning, setting you up for a healthy saunter to the fine sandy shoreline of Viareggio's stunning stretch of beach. A forest of fragrant pine trees lines the walk home back to the comfort of your room where well-deserved r&r involving a long-lingering bubble bath or a snooze before a pre-dinner cocktail in the American Bar will have you rejuvenated for another gastronomic feast. Top tip: reserve a room with balcony for the finest sea views.

☎ +39 0584 44449
🌐 condenastjohansens.com/russie
📍 Piazza d'Azeglio 1, 55049 Viareggio, Tuscany, Italy

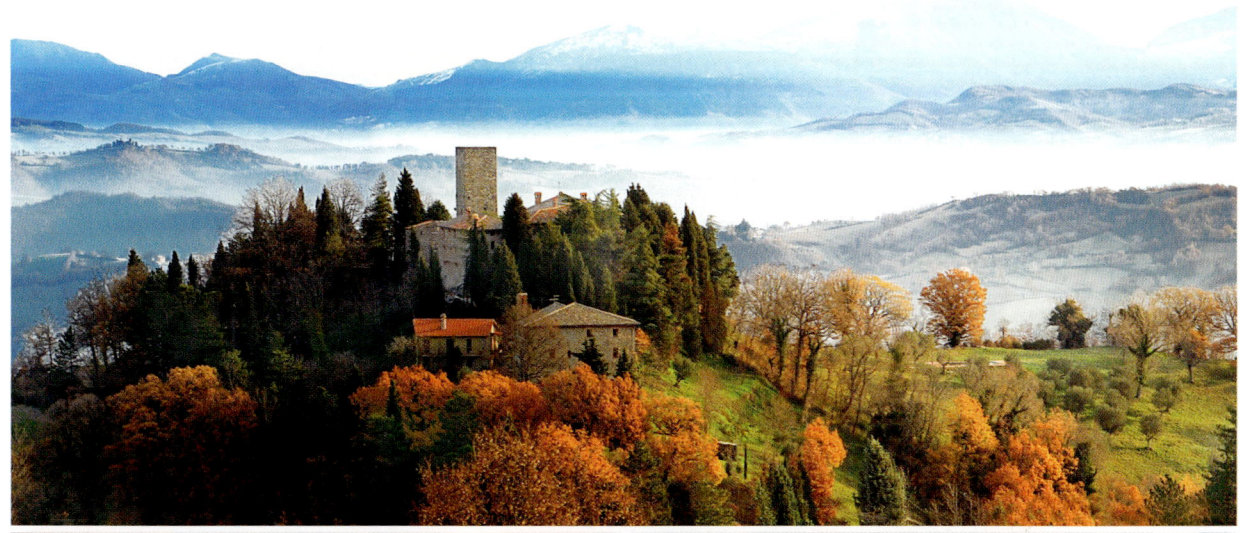

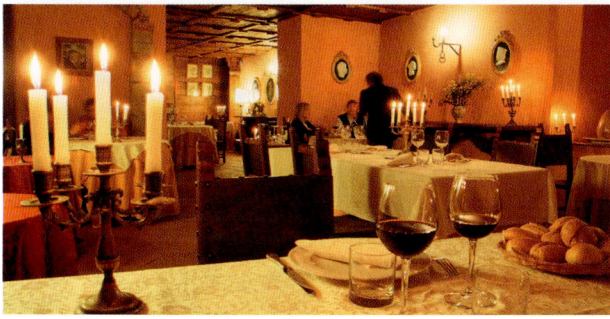
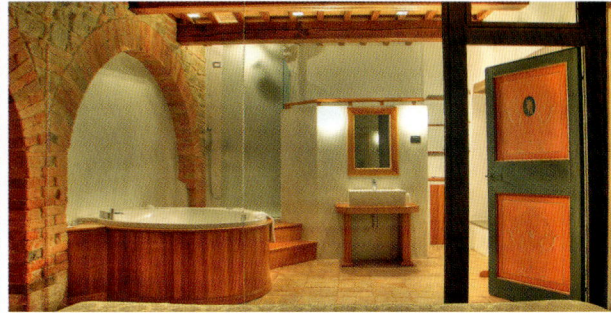

Castello di Petroia

Magical Umbrian medieval castle

It doesn't get more fairy tale than this: a honey-stone castle perched on an Umbrian hillside. Once the setting for the Montefeltro clan's juicy tales (think Henry VIII's court with an Italian twist) Castello di Petroia, Gubbio, is now home to a rustic-chic bolthole. So peaceful and snug with just 11 rooms amidst three ancient tower-hugging buildings, it's easy to imagine you are reigning supreme. Capturing an authentic castle mood, interiors are infused with warm woods, rich damasks and floaty four posters. Windows let in breathtaking views (autumn colours and misty mornings create sheer magic) and the scent of trees. Sleek modern touches stay politely discreet until you need them, though the spacious all-singing, all-dancing bathrooms of the Junior and Deluxe Suites feature whirlpool baths tucked beneath beamed or vaulted ceilings. Cheerful staff and kingly breakfasts of baked goodies with homemade fig jam set you up for the day. Come the evening, a table for two in Accumandugi Hall with candlelight bouncing off the walls works the Castello's magic all over again. Nothing but farm-fresh produce, including meat from the estate's very own land serves as the young chef's inspiration. Nearby are Gubbio, Assisi and Orvieto (all easy drives away) however, when the scenery is this spellbinding and the poolside is surrounded by olive tree prettiness it's tempting to kick back and drink it all in.

PRICE FROM:
€120

FEATURES:
Family friendly; Pet friendly; Pool; Restaurant

ACTIVITIES:
Cycling; Golf; Walking

NEARBY:
Gubbio; Perugia; Assisi; Siena; Umbria Jazz Festival

GETTING THERE:
Perugia Airport; Ancona Airport; Rome Fiumicino Airport

+39 075 92 02 87 ☎
condenastjohansens.com/castellodipetroia 🌐
Località Scritto di Gubbio, Petroia, 06024 Gubbio (PG), 🏠
Umbria, Italy

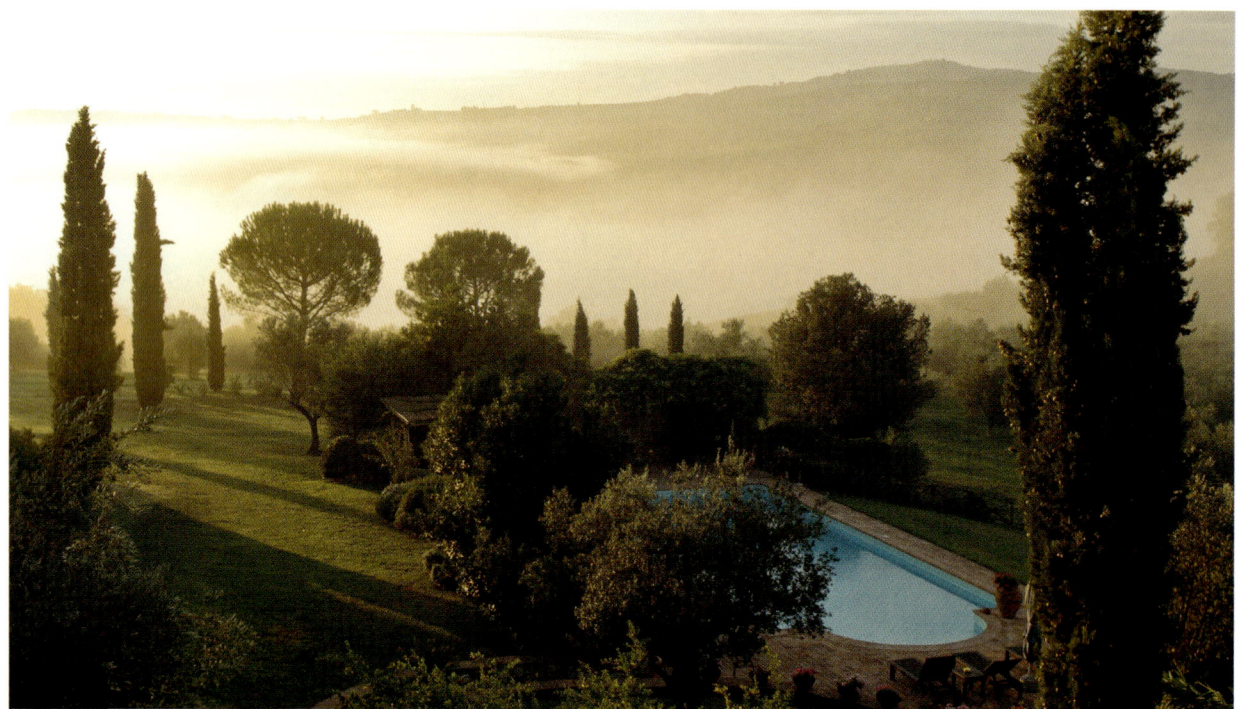

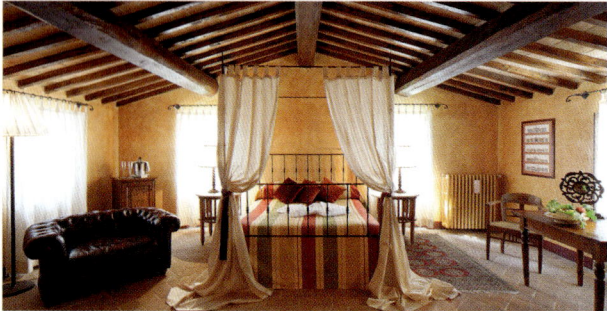
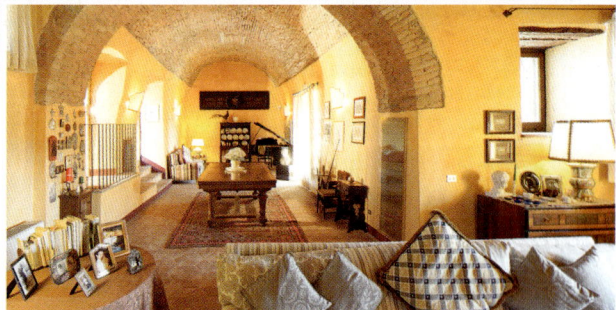

Romantik Hotel Tenuta di Canonica

Rural Umbrian charisma with a kooky kick

PRICE FROM:
€170

FEATURES:
Family friendly; Lake views; Pet friendly; Pool; Restaurant

ACTIVITIES:
Fishing; Golf; Horse riding

NEARBY:
Todi; Orvieto; Assisi; Spoleto; Civita di Bagnoregio ("the dying town");

GETTING THERE:
Perugia Airport; Rome Airport

Sitting on the edge of the Umbrian medieval town of Todi is Romantik Hotel Tenuta di Canonica. Its ancient stone structure may date back to the Roman era (original parts of the impressive Roman tower bring a real sense of authenticity) but the beautifully furnished suites are a mass of modern homely comfort oozing character. In this relaxed atmosphere you're surrounded by the unspoilt Umbrian countryside. Walk around the lush gardens (look out for the elves on the tree branches), check out the old well in the hall (it still works) and chat with Mozart, the multilingual parrot. Although this hotel appeals to travellers in search of tranquillity, there's no denying that its quirks make it an unforgettable experience. A stay here is more home-away-from-home than hotel. Ask Christin about Le Marmore Falls, an excursion through the spectacular scenery or remain closer to home with a swim in the outdoor pool. Returning ravenous, a spread of simple but delicious dishes by candlelight are yours to devour. The food is exceptional, with a mindfulness to health and well-being without compromising on flavour or local tradition.

☎ +39 075 8947545
🌐 condenastjohansens.com/tenutadicanonica
🏠 Località Canonica 75, 06059 Todi (PG), Umbria, Italy

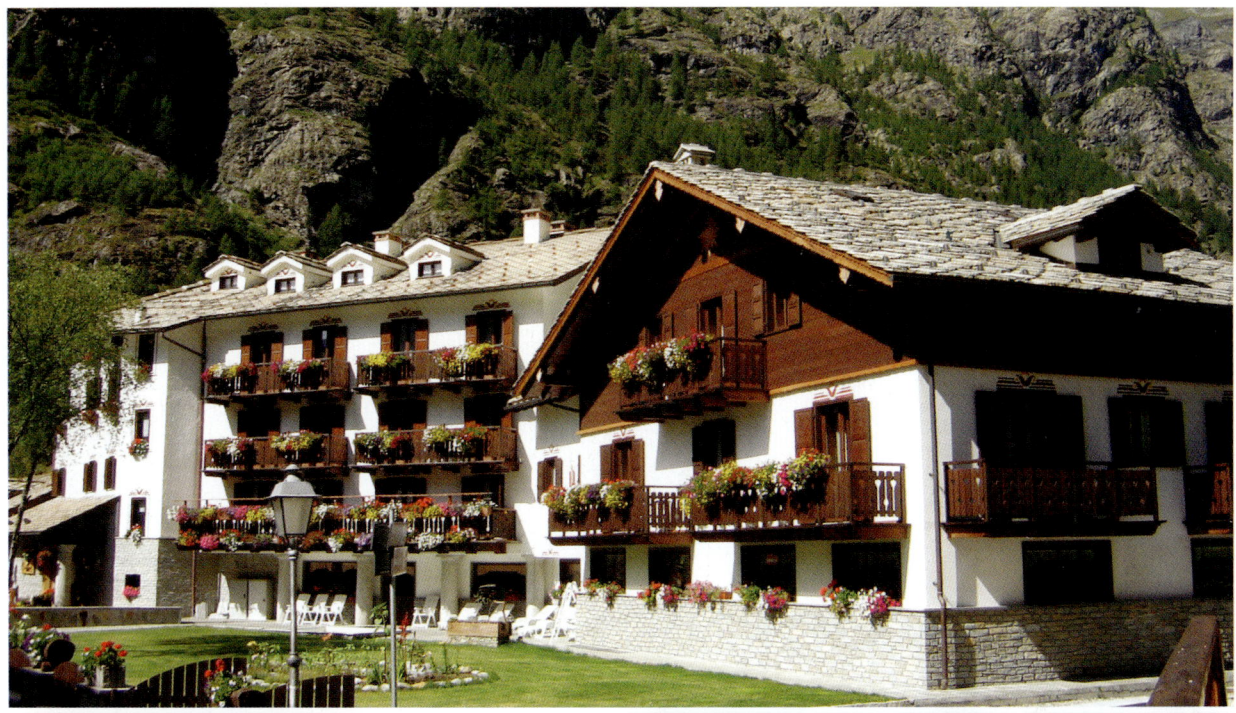

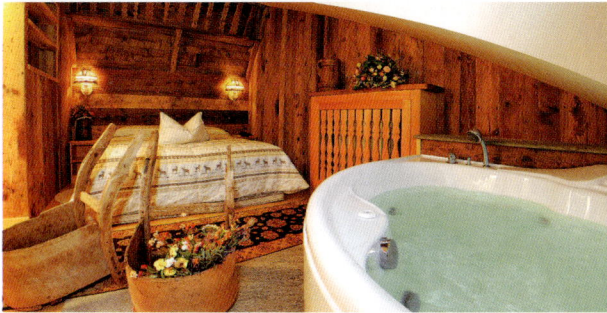

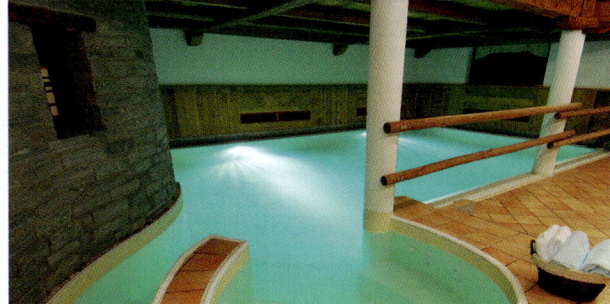

Romantik Hotel Jolanda Sport

Wood-tastic hideaway in the Monterosa ski resort

Located in the three valley Monterosa ski district, Romantik Hotel Jolanda Sport is THE destination for travellers who enjoy mountainous activities. It's the biggest ski resort in Europe. But when the waves of laziness wash over you, there's also plenty of opportunity to be indulgent. Bedecked in the warmth of natural wood and traditional embroideries, this inviting and friendly (great value for money too) hotel offers both summer and winter options. And with Jolanda Sport on the doorstep of the gondola, you can wave goodbye to carrying equipment around and focus on enjoying yourself. Whether it's the thrills of the downhills, the challenges of the summit or the opportunity to admire the breathtaking Monte Rosa vista, there's something for everyone. Featuring a hamman, selection of candlelit massages and Cornetta's cauldron (an aromatising bath), Jolanda Sport's intimate spa and sauna facilities await your weary return. As does your room or suite where wood and refined textiles combine for an Alpine welcome that's both stylish and comfortable; the bathrooms are particularly roomy. The motto of your host Annamaria and her team is "fresh air, healthy food," which means the cuisine of the lively restaurant is home-made and locally sourced. Served with the region's finest wines, those with a sweet tooth should leave some room: the desserts are sensational.

PRICE FROM:
€90 (per person)

FEATURES:
Family friendly; Helipad; Pool; Restaurant; Spa

ACTIVITIES:
Fishing; Golf; Skiing

NEARBY:
Aosta; Turin; Regina Margherita Alpine refuge; Heli-skiing; Climbing and tracking

GETTING THERE:
Turin Airport; Aosta Airport

+39 0125 366 140 ☎
condenastjohansens.com/jolandasport 🌐
Località Edelboden 31, 11020 Gressoney~La~Trinité, Valle d'Aosta, Italy 🏠

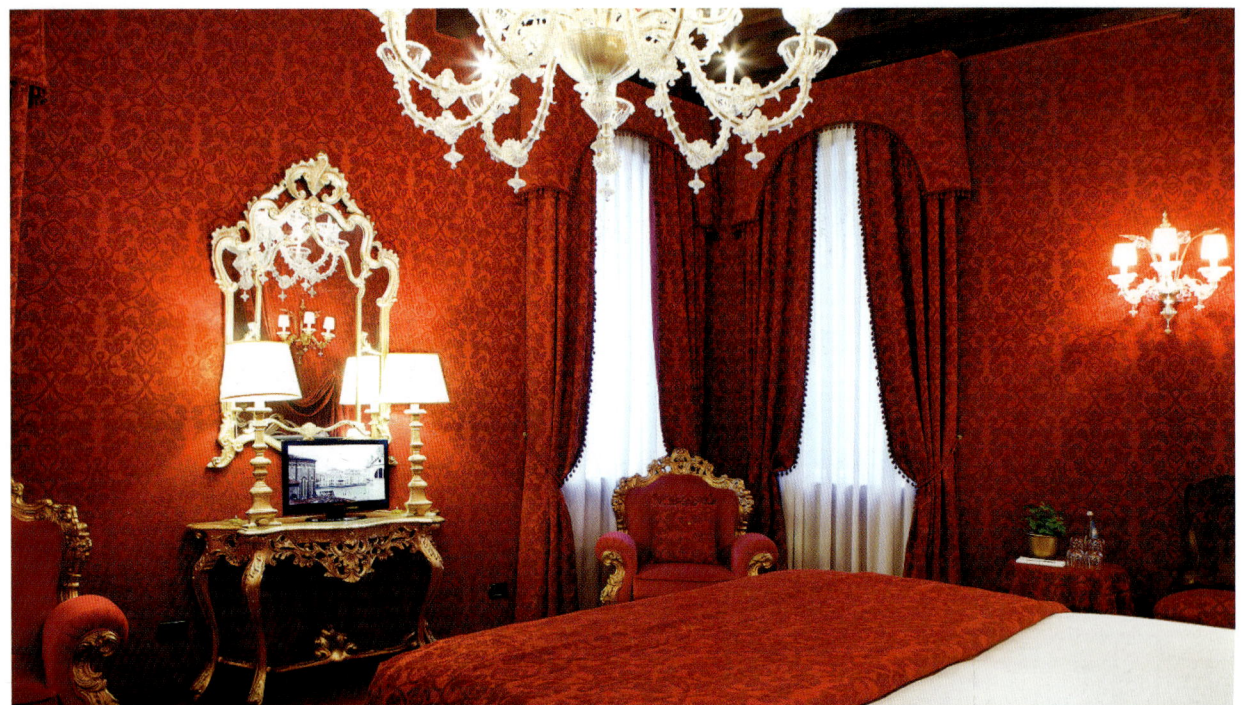

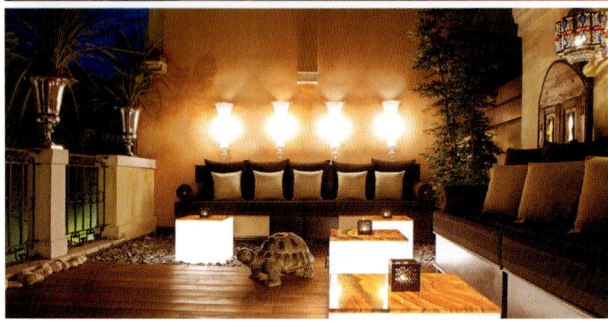

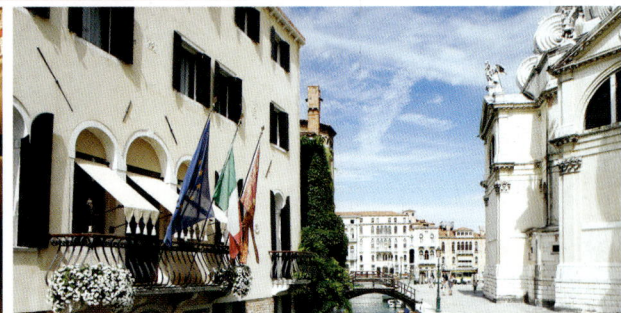

Ca Maria Adele

Discreet designer hideaway in Venice

PRICE FROM:
€363

FEATURES:
Pet friendly

ACTIVITIES:
Shopping; Sightseeing; Walking

NEARBY:
Gondola rides; Punta dalla Dogana Museum; St Mark's Square; Peggy Guggenheim Museum; Magazzini del Sale

GETTING THERE:
Treviso Airport; Venice Marco Polo Airport

☎ +39 041 52 03 078
🌐 condenastjohansens.com/camariaadele
🏠 Dorsoduro 111, 30123 Venice, Veneto, Italy

Ca Maria Adele, Venice, is an indulgent mix of two worlds. Lying within the walls of a 16th-century Venetian palazzo and hidden amongst the waterways of the city, it's a private bolthole of contrasts demonstrating old grandeur on the exterior with a modern, sleek and luxurious interior. It's lavish, quirky, intimate, romantic and utterly lovely. For an arrival that befits the Adele, hop on a vintage speedboat (à la Bond) direct from Marco Polo Airport to the hotel lobby where a cool glass of Prosecco awaits, along with the sublime breakfast policy: whenever, wherever and however! This is a grown-up getaway to make the honeymooners hallelujah; where 12 rooms are dressed-up-to-the-nines in swathes of velvety soft fabrics that hang floor-to-ceiling. Fur lines the walls as dazzling oversized Murano glass chandeliers hang from the ceiling to shine upon exotic teak wood furnishings. (Book the Noir Room whose black theme sets a highly dramatic scene.) Ca Maria Adele is 21st-century palazzo perfection and a hedonistic feast for all the senses where you'll find a Moroccan-styled terrace with couples whispering sweet-nothings at twilight and a beautifully laid-out honesty bar for a nightcap under the stars. Interesting tidbit: all the staff at Ca Maria Adele are male - welcoming and caring, they also happen to be very attractive!

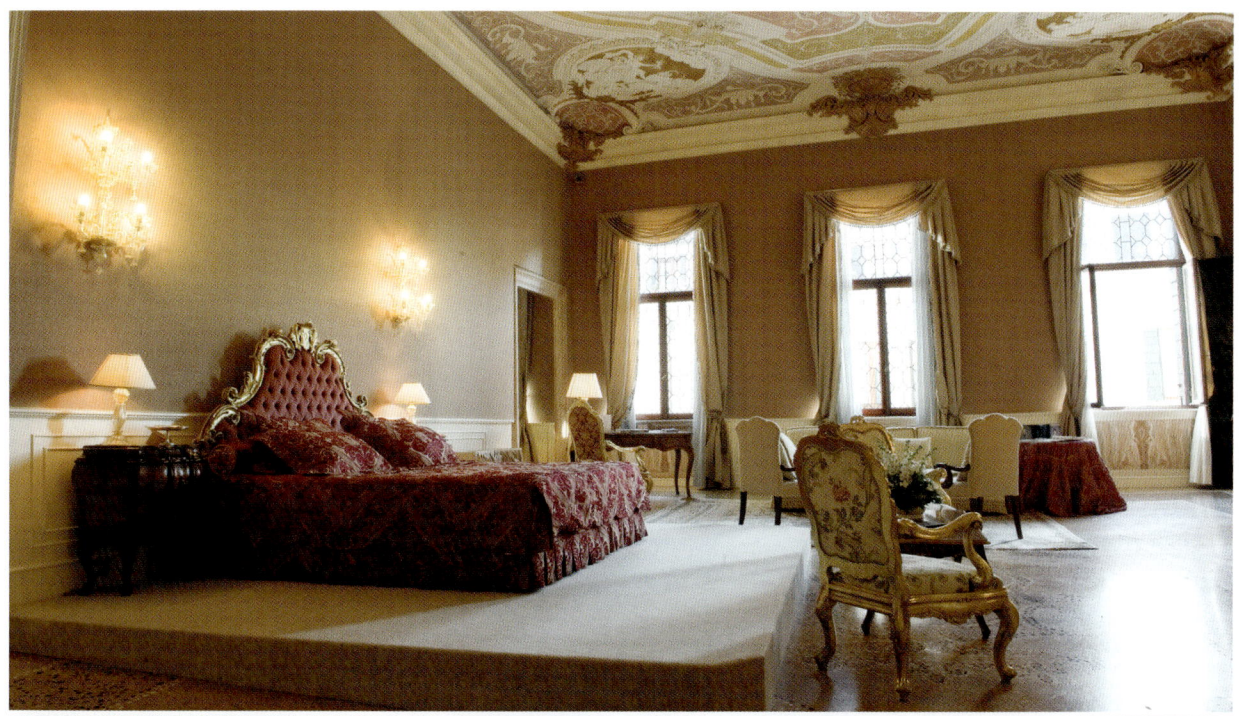

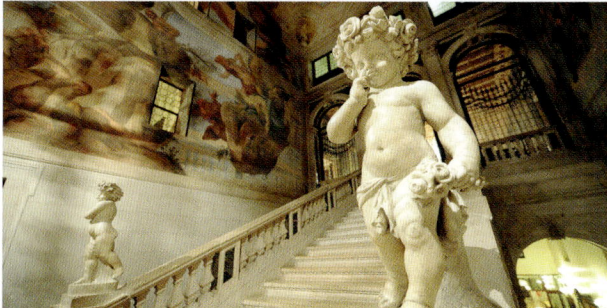
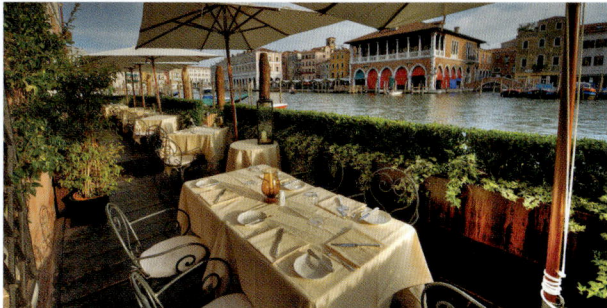

Ca' Sagredo Hotel

Venetian noble elegance on the world-famous Grand Canal

The sheer beauty of Ca' Sagredo Hotel is weep-with-joy wondrous. As you pull up alongside the Grand Canal, you'll need to pinch yourself, and again when you step inside. This 15th-century palazzo has been declared a National Monument and it's certainly a monument to decadence! It oozes romance while the opulently frescoed ballroom and lounge echoes with epic events of the past when Count Sagredo lived in this den of iniquity. Gliding up the imposing marble staircase (whilst resisting a tap on a cherub's cheek) is a grand affair in itself. Ca' Sagredo's views of the canal traffic and Rialto Market opposite are storybook scenes of old. And all rooms are a seriously sexy sight to behold with classic Venetian styling. The suite dedicated to art (the aptly named Arts Suite) is an ode to 18th-century artists such as Abbondio Stazio and Carpoforo Mazzetti. Art lovers be warned: there are so many treasures here, it's easy to forget the outside world. But there's always the hotel's panoramic waterside L'Alcova restaurant to remind you, whose dishes are a celebration of Italy on a plate and Grand Canal views add a flavour of their own.

PRICE FROM:
€450

FEATURES:
Family friendly; Restaurant; Wheelchair access

ACTIVITIES:
Shooting; Shopping; Sightseeing

NEARBY:
Ca' D'Oro; Grand Canal; Rialto Market; Rialto Bridge; St Mark's Square

GETTING THERE:
Venice Marco Polo Airport; Venice Train Station; Venice Cruise Terminal

+39 041 2413111 ☎
condenastjohansens.com/casagredo 🌐
Campo Santa Sofia 4198/99, 30121 Venice, Veneto, Italy 🏠

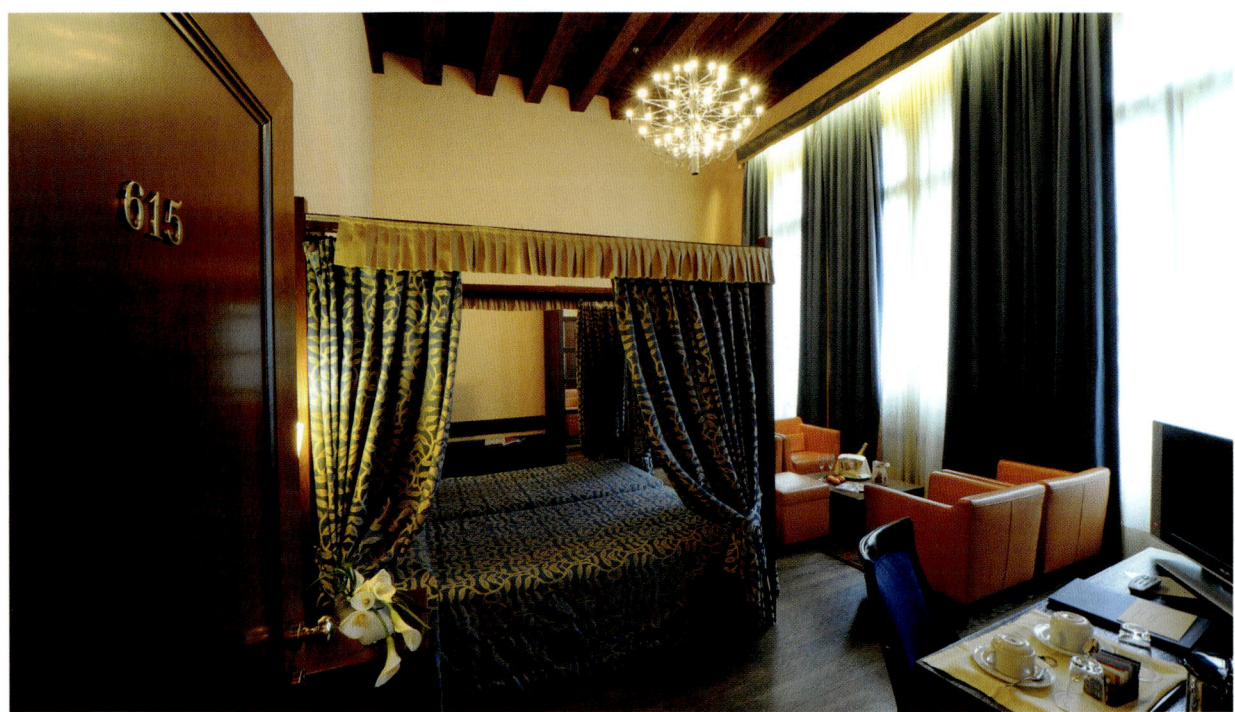

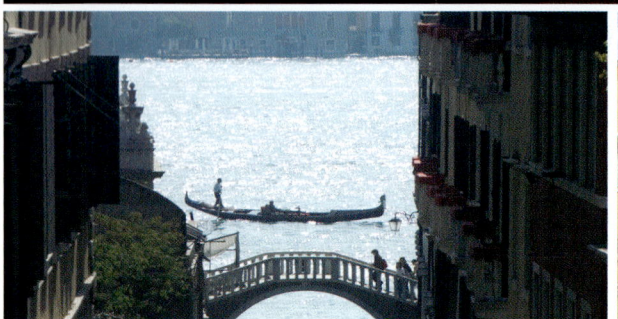
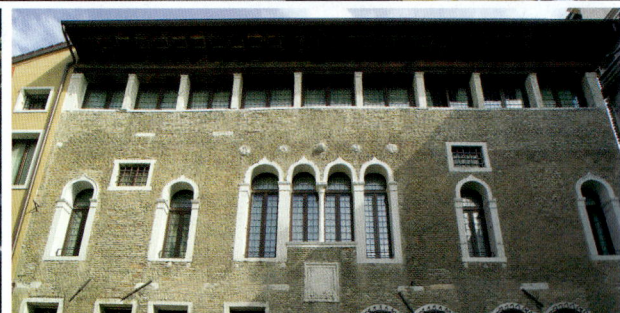

Palazzo Selvadego

A taste of 13th-century Venice with a 21st-century twist

PRICE FROM:
€160

FEATURES:
Sea views; Wheelchair access

ACTIVITIES:
Shopping; Sightseeing

NEARBY:
St Mark's Square; Rialto Bridge; Accademia; Peggy Gugenheim Museum; Theatre La Fenice

GETTING THERE:
Piazzale Roma car stop; Venezia Santa Lucia Railway Station; Venice Marco Polo Airport

Slip through the discreet door of Palazzo Selvadego, Venice, and the teeming hordes of Piazza San Marco and the lagoon will seem a world apart despite them being a mere whisper away. Arrive by water taxi, check-in at the Palazzo's sister property Hotel Monaco around the corner and you're in prime position for uncovering Venice's greatest attractions: the Basilica San Marco; the Bridge of Sighs; La Fenice... Intimate and charming are the best words to describe the late 13th-century Palazzo Selvadego. Its handsome Venetian Gothic façade has beautiful Byzantine windows like watchful eyes concealing the cool marble, exposed beams and parquet floors of the interior. Rooms are spacious, have access to free WiFi and look out to glimpses of the city's jumble of rooftops or a distant window box. If you have breakfast reservations head on over to Hotel Monaco where the canal-side views are simply amazing; from its terrace you can watch this unique city come to life. A peep into the Monaco also gives a glimpse of Venice's favourite ridollo (gaming hall), circa 1648. Ask Palazzo Selvadego's concierge desk for restaurant recommendations – they can direct you through the winding watery lined streets of Venice with their eyes closed.

☎ + 39 041 5200211
🌐 condenastjohansens.com/palazzoselvadego
🏠 San Marco 1124/B, 30124 Venice, Veneto, Italy

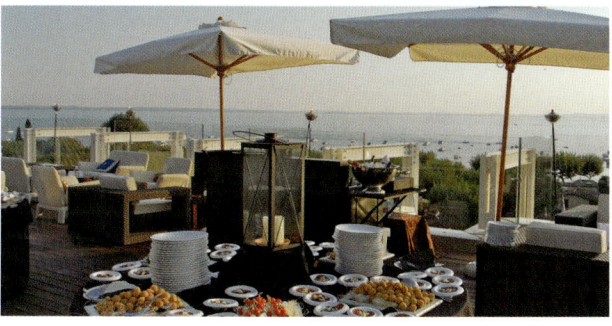

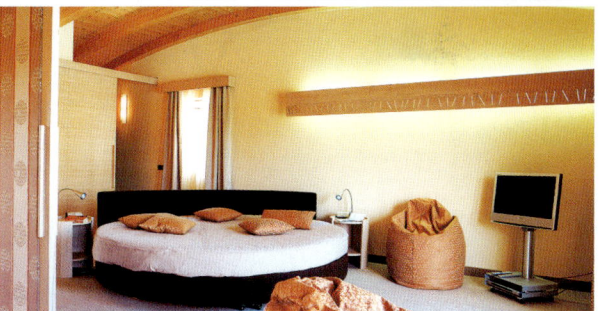

Color Hotel style & design

Lake Garda's most colourful designer resort hotel

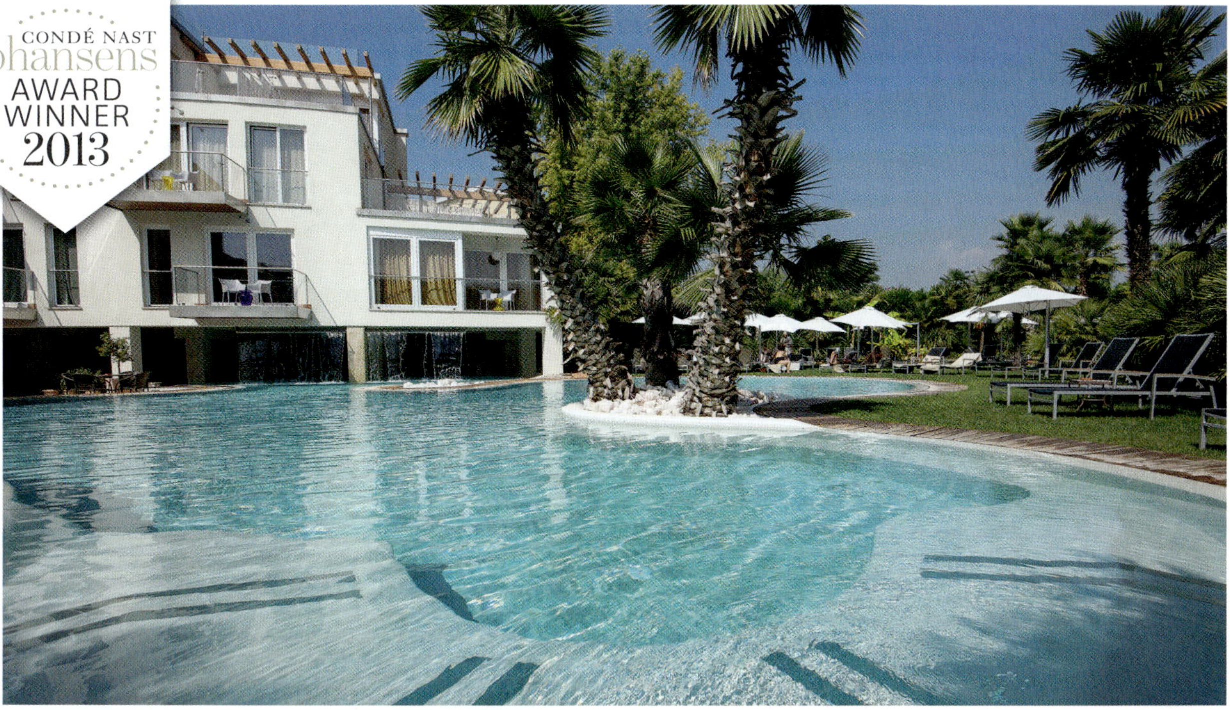

When the climate is mild year-round it does something to a place. Everything feels heightened and everyone is more pleasant. Lake Garda is the evidence for this and in its southeast corner, Color Hotel style & design is irrefutable confirmation. Set back from the water, Color Hotel is slightly off the tourist track, five minutes from Bardolino. Like a poster-boy for the archetypal Italian lakeside town, it resides below a swathe of green mountains, possesses ancient churches and sun-dappled piazzas. Color Hotel's intention is to harmonise guests' emotional and physical states by way of chrometherapy and clever design. Those on romantic breaks should reserve a red (red = passion) room or suite. Those in search of tranquillity should opt for one dressed in blue (blue = calm). Outside, the garden is a sea of green (green = relaxation) and there's more blue thanks to the four pools. Chances are, if you can't see the water, you'll hear it. And it's no coincidence that La Veranda restaurant is a colourful explosion of fresh, creative and simply delicious cuisine. However, the slaveringly good local dishes and wine can be enjoyed at Citronella or on the terrace. Must do: a special wine-tasting session at La Cantina.

PRICE FROM:
€112

FEATURES:
Family friendly; Lake views; Pool; Restaurant; Wheelchair access

ACTIVITIES:
Cycling; Water sports

NEARBY:
Bardolino Centre; Venice; Lake Garda; Opera; Juliet's Balcony

GETTING THERE:
Verona, Airport; Brescia Airport; Bergamo Airport

+39 045 621 0857 ☎
condenastjohansens.com/colorhotel 🌐
Via Santa Cristina 5, 37011 Bardolino (VR), Veneto, Italy 📍

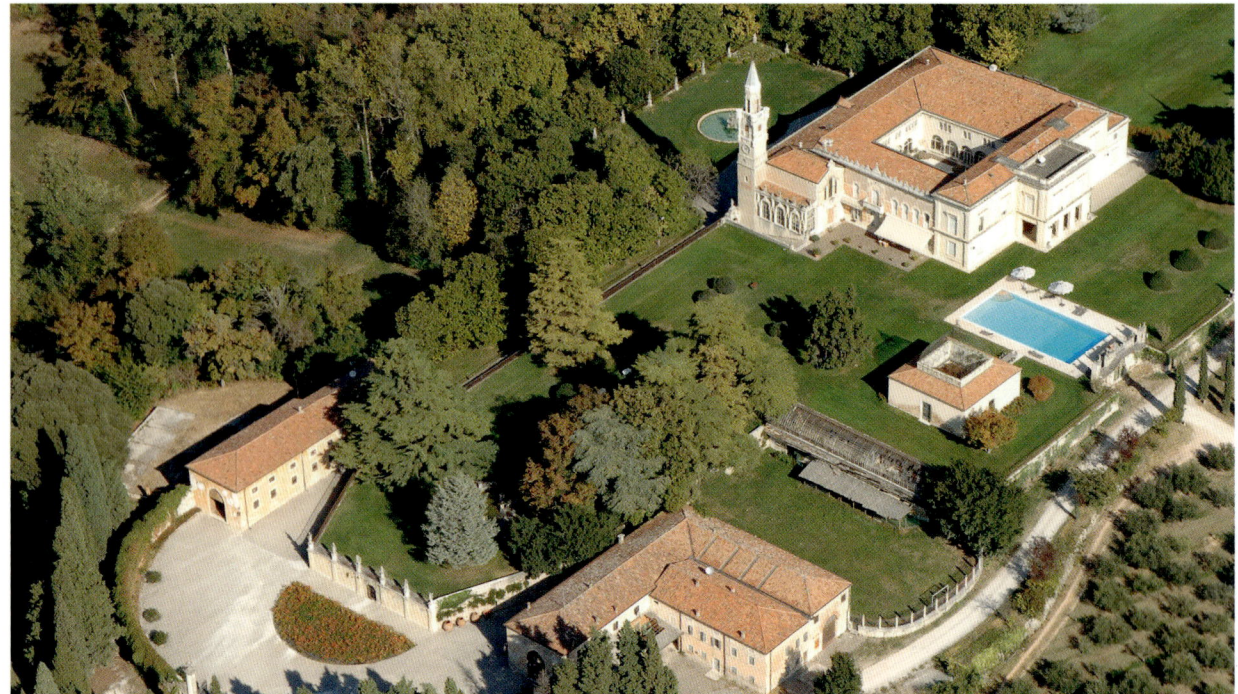

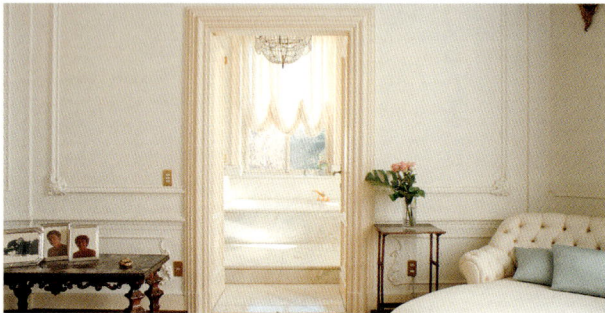
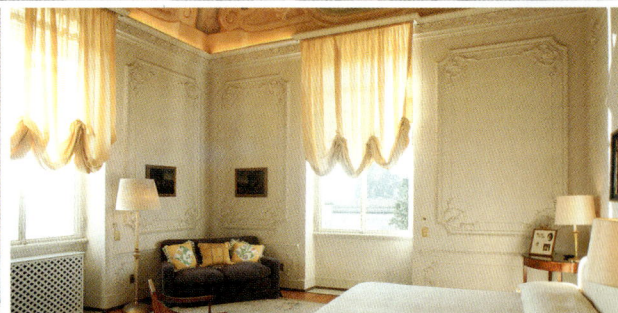

Villa d'Acquarone

Awe-inspiring ancient estate in the Verona hills

PRICE FROM:
€270

FEATURES:
Gym; Helipad; Pool; Wheelchair access

ACTIVITIES:
Cycling; Fishing; Walking

NEARBY:
Verona; Bardolino; Mantova; Lake Garda; Gardaland

GETTING THERE:
Verona Airport; Venice Marco Polo Airport; Bergamo Airport

When authors of fiction put pen to paper it's fantastical visions such as Villa d'Acquarone that spring from their imagination. Such architectural wonders and immaculate landscaped grounds seem too marvellous and grandiose to exist in real life. Yet here it is, just 10 minutes outside the city of Verona: Villa d'Acquarone on the Musella Hill in San Martino Buon Albergo. This impossibly beautiful aristocratic home has been in the d'Acquarone family for almost 100 years. And Brothers Zeno and Vittore now run it as an intimate, fully-hosted villa with just seven (well, eight if you include Gialla's and Rossa's interconnecting twin room) frescoed, silk-laden, marble bathroom-clad, antique-filled suites. For the ultimate noble experience hire the Villa in its entirety and enjoy the service of a private in-house chef. If staying with a group of friends or the family, add some fun to the proceedings and book some cooking lessons and wine tastings. That's if you can tear everyone away from the two-storey Library with more than 1,000 volumes piled high against a backdrop of Lodovico Dorigny frescoes dating to 1687. Outside, there's an aviary-turned-party space, pool and trails for walking, biking and jogging in the vast woodland.

☎ +39 342 782 8341
🌐 condenastjohansens.com/villadacquarone
🏠 via Pasubio 5, 37036 San Martino Buon Albergo, Verona, Veneto, Italy

Malta

Please go to condenastjohansens.com/malta

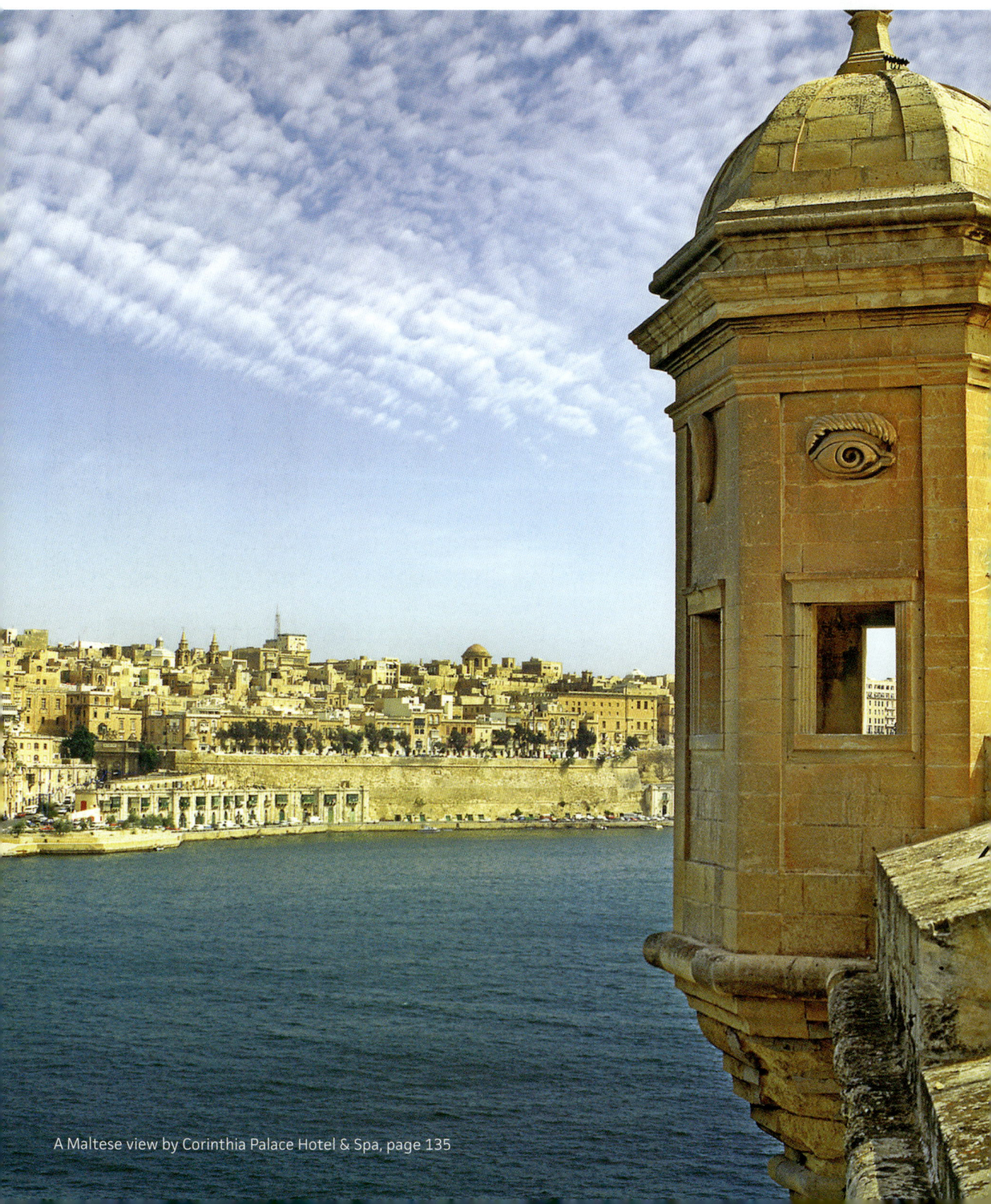

A Maltese view by Corinthia Palace Hotel & Spa, page 135

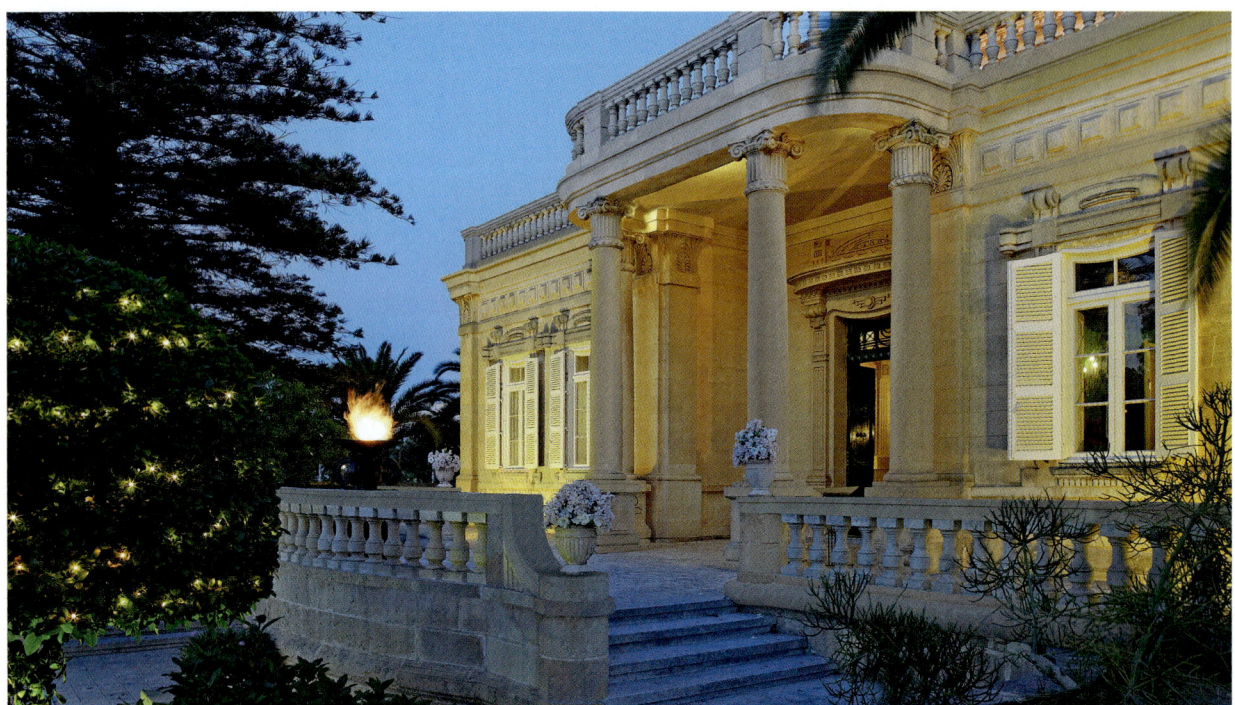

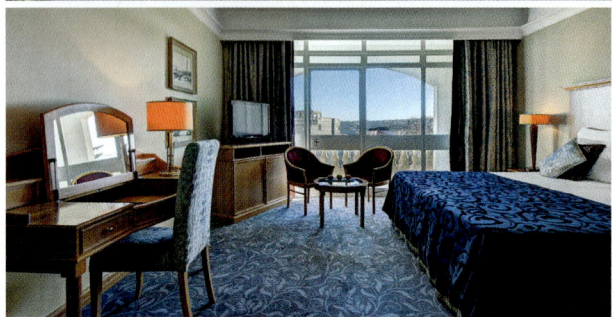

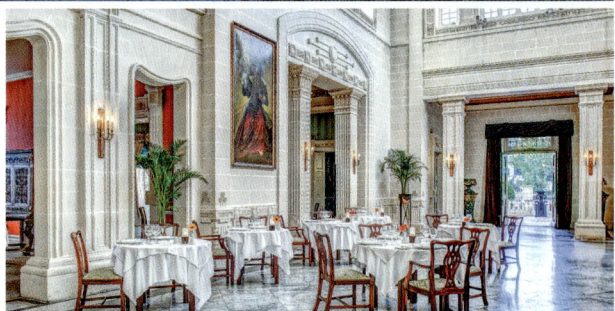

Corinthia Palace Hotel & Spa

A celebration of Maltese culture in San Anton

PRICE FROM:
€150

FEATURES:
Family friendly; Gym; Pool; Restaurant; Spa

ACTIVITIES:
Sightseeing; Tennis

NEARBY:
President's residential palace; San Anton gardens; Valletta; Mdina; The Royal Malta Golf Club

GETTING THERE:
Malta Airport

Corinthia Palace Hotel & Spa, San Anton, is a fabulous slice of history on the island of Malta. Built in 1920 as a private villa, it later became a restaurant before being transformed into a regal, first-class hotel opened in 1968 by the Duke of Edinburgh. Today, it remains a beacon of elegance on this small and beautiful island situated halfway between the Baroque capital of Valletta and the "silent city" of Mdina. It's pure old school drama. From the leafy landscaped gardens to the marble-decked Villa Corinthia restaurant (definitely worth getting dressed up for) it's fit for royalty. And yet, for all its stately splendour, the hotel is ultra friendly due in no small part to the staff who somehow manage to remember the names of the hundreds of guests (there are 152 rooms) that pass through its doors. For a touch of divine self-indulgence and pampering there's not only the Athenaeum Spa whose treatment list will make you stop and ponder for a while but also a fully-equipped gym, yoga classes, a sauna, tranquil gardens and Jacuzzi. Lazy days are spent lounging by the pool while a stroll through the San Anton gardens opposite the hotel is a must-do. Make sure to sample the Far Eastern fare at the hotel's Rickshaw Restaurant, Italian dishes at the poolside Pizza, Pasta & Co and Mediterranean magic of The Villa Corinthia too.

☎ +356 21 440301
🌐 condenastjohansens.com/corinthiapalace
🏠 De Paule Avenue, BZN 9023 San Anton, Malta

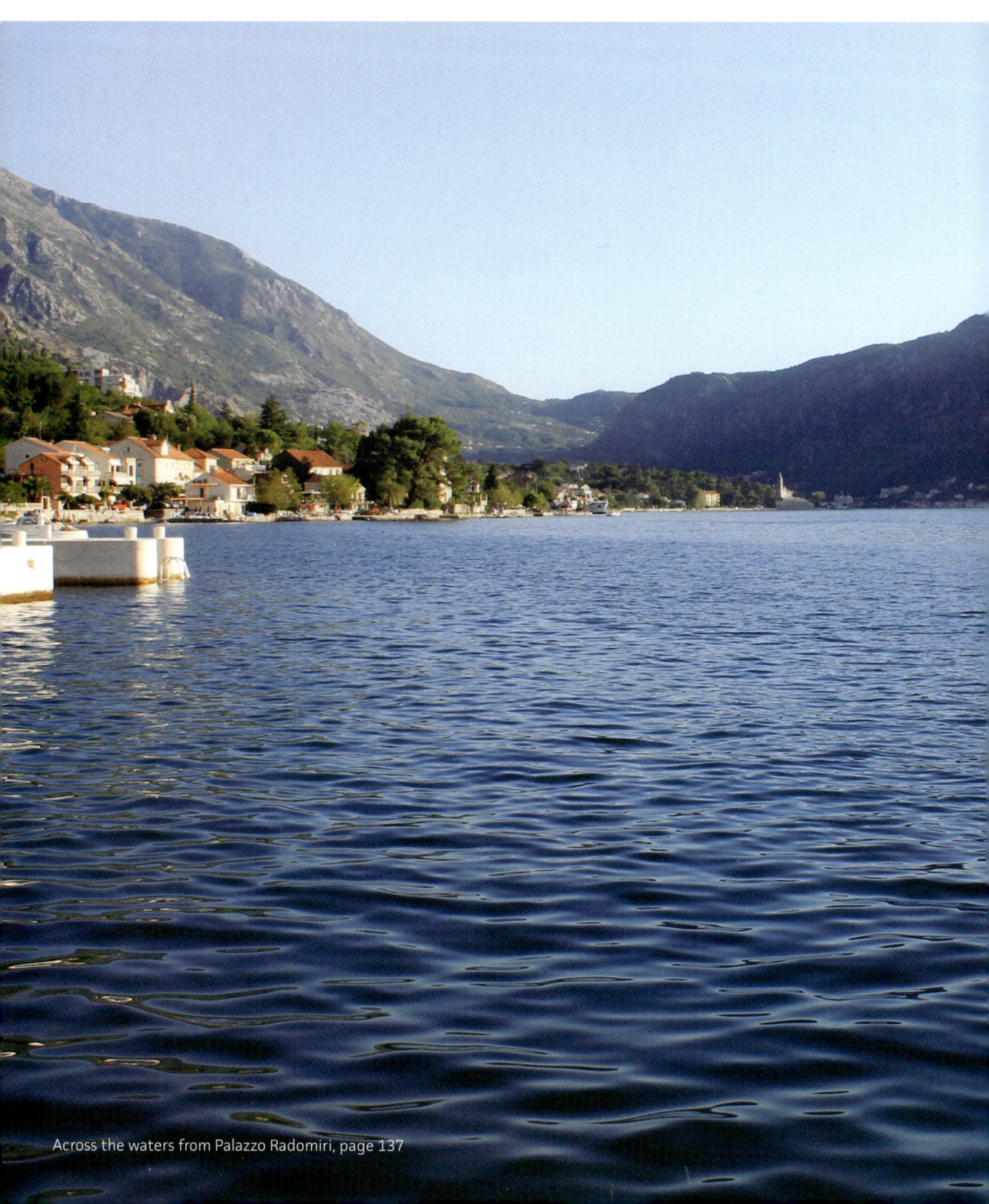

Montenegro

Please go to condenastjohansens.com/montenegro

Across the waters from Palazzo Radomiri, page 137

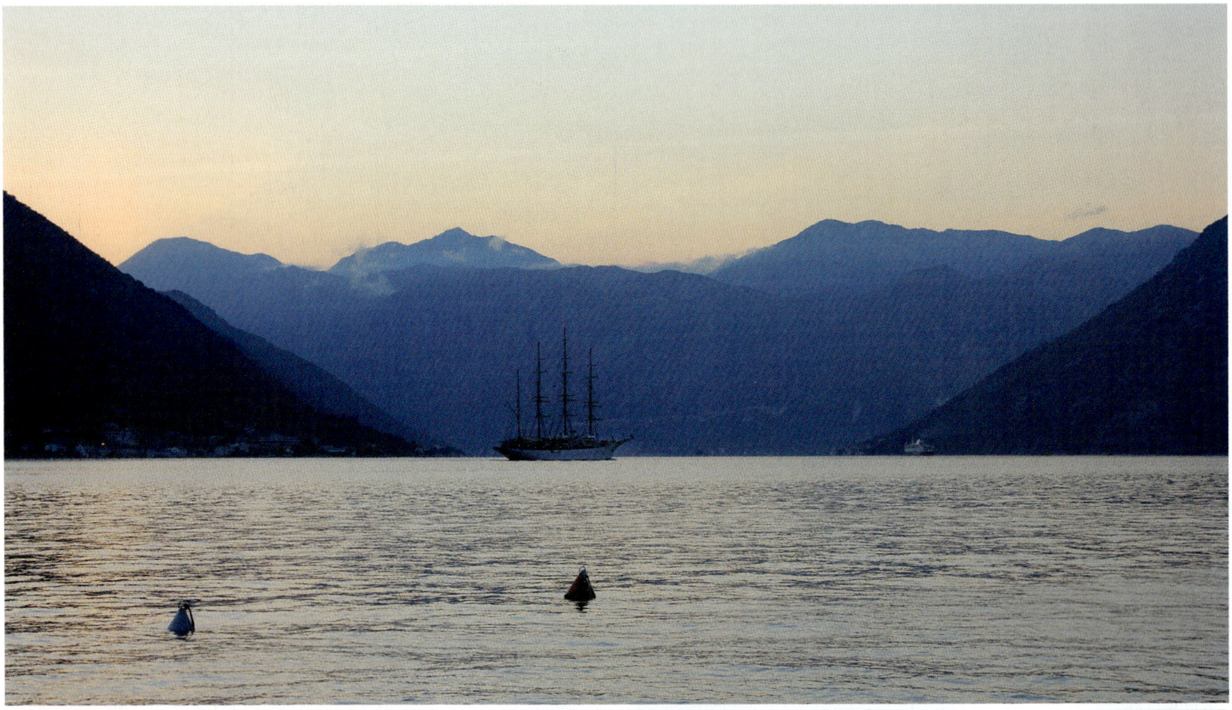

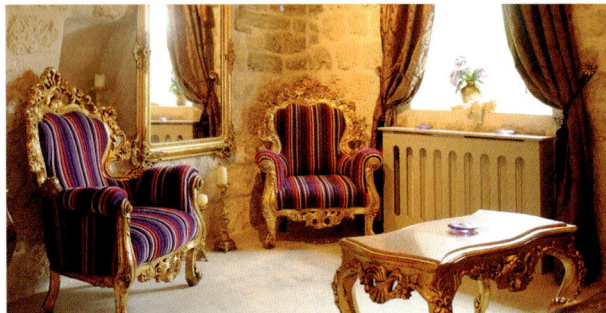

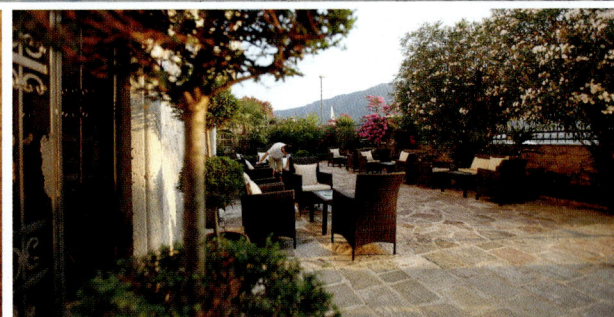

Palazzo Radomiri

Classic Venetian palace opulence in Montenegro's Kotor

PRICE FROM:
€120

FEATURES:
Beach access; Gym; Pool; Restaurant; Sea views

ACTIVITIES:
Cycling; Fishing; Water sports

NEARBY:
Perast; Tivat; Kotor's fortification; Summer festivals; Mamula Island's 19th-century Austro-Hungarian Fort

GETTING THERE:
Tivat Airport; Dubrovnik Airport, Croatia; Podgorica Airport

A master-class in unadulterated luxury, Palazzo Radomiri in Dobrota, Montenegro, is a hidden jewel that won't stay undiscovered for long. Tucked into a sheltered spot on Boka Kotorska bay its views are full of wondrous beauty and scenes of misty mornings over the fjord are otherwordly. Inside, Palazzo Radomiri effortlessly blends existing 18th-century quirks with contemporary elements to create a pared-down coolness. Think lots of exposed stone, subtle lighting and intense colour on feature walls and Rococo furniture. There are glimpses of Palazzo Radomiri's maritime history throughout too (each unique room is named after a Radomiri family ship) and fittingly you can arrive on your own boat thanks to the hotel's private mooring facilities. Stylish seafarers may book the Palazzo for exclusive use: the roof terrace overlooking the bay is a memorable spot for parties, and the market-fresh food to accompany the event is excellent. Montenegro's Kotor bay is gaining a reputation as the new Monte Carlo with visiting celebrities and oligarchs creating quite a buzz on the Adriatic in recent years. Kotor's Old Town, a short drive away, is an interesting spot with its ancient walls, Baroque architecture and elegant piazzas. Otherwise, catching rays on the private sun deck is an option!

☎ +382 32 333 172
🌐 condenastjohansens.com/palazzoradomiri
🏠 Dobrota 220, 85330 Kotor, Montenegro

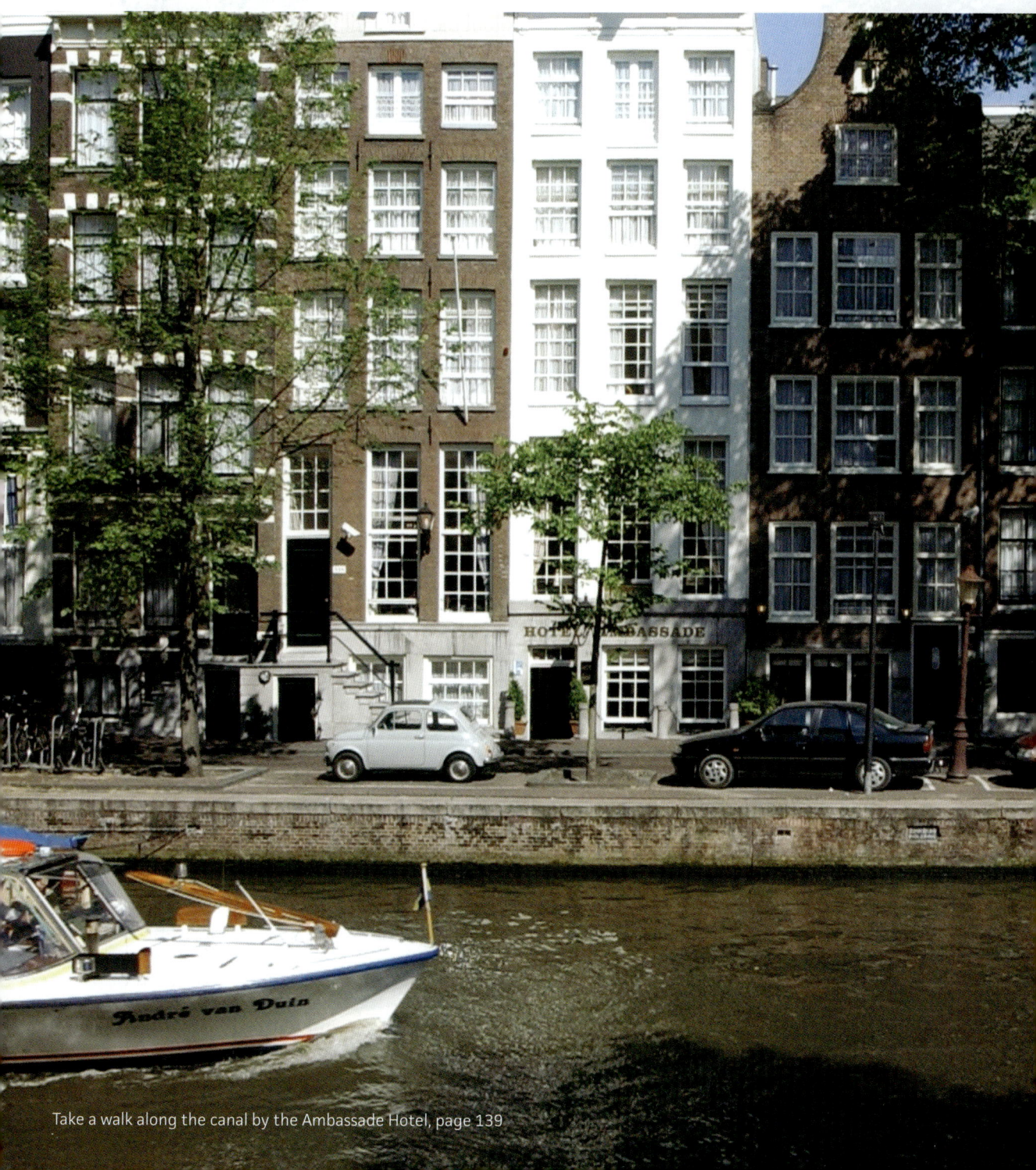

The Netherlands

Please go to condenastjohansens.com/the-netherlands

Take a walk along the canal by the Ambassade Hotel, page 139

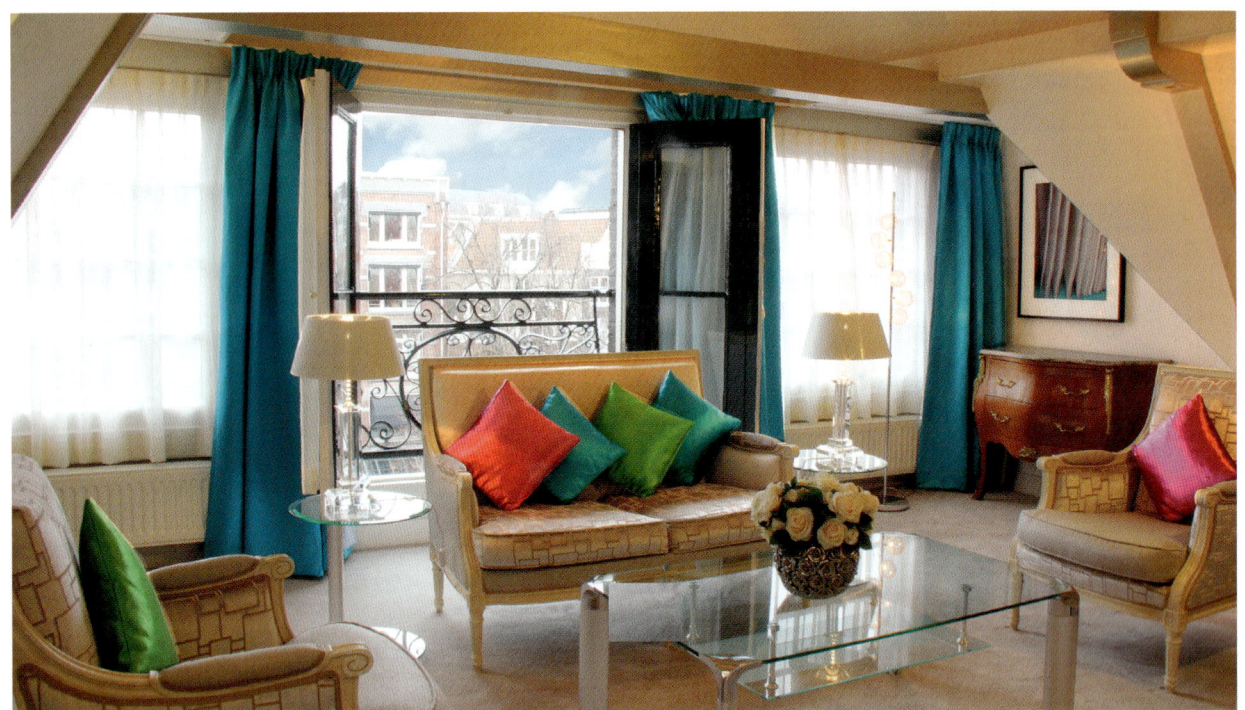

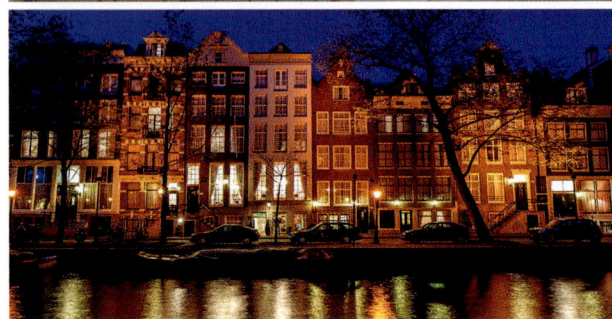

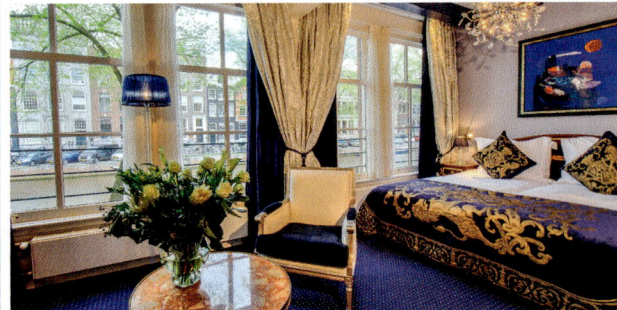

Ambassade Hotel

Canal-side Amsterdam at its quirky finest

PRICE FROM:
€185

FEATURES:
Pet friendly; Spa

ACTIVITIES:
Cycling; Shopping; Walking

NEARBY:
Royal Palace; Canal boat trips; Anne Frank's house

GETTING THERE:
Schiphol Airport

☎ +31 20 5550 222
🌐 condenastjohansens.com/ambassade
📍 Herengracht 341, 1016 AZ Amsterdam, The Netherlands

A house (well, nine interconnecting houses plus one next door) of artistic repute, Hotel Ambassade, Amsterdam, is a canal-side cracker. It's set beside Herengracht Canal, which translates to Patricians Canal (how very apt), in the 17th-century canal belt declared a UNESCO Heritage Site in 2010. During its evolution over 60 years Ambassade has become a master of personal service and has always been respectful of its age-old structure, maintaining its delightfully quaint stairways and unexpected nooks and crannies. From the moment you walk through the Van Vreden commissioned glass entranceway, owner Wouter Schopman's penchant for the CoBrA avant-garde art movement and Amsterdam's 19th-century impressionists is evident. And he's showing no signs of completing his collection any time soon. Wouter also owns a publishing house and it's common for authors to stay at Ambassade when visiting the city. To discover whose been here before you, mosey on over to The Library and seek out the countless signed copies. But before that, devour a traditional Dutch breakfast in the restaurant (available for brunch, lunch and high tea reservations), although if you're feeling especially unsociable you can always stay in the first-floor apartment complete with its very own kitchen and private entrance.

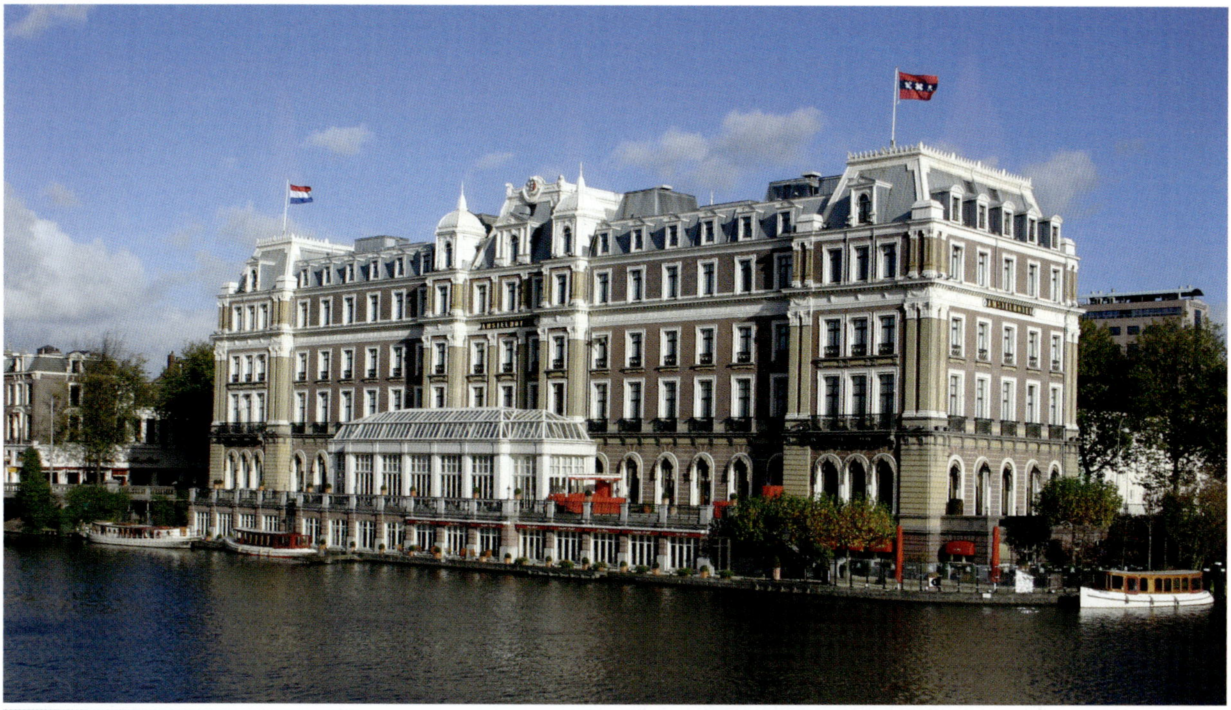

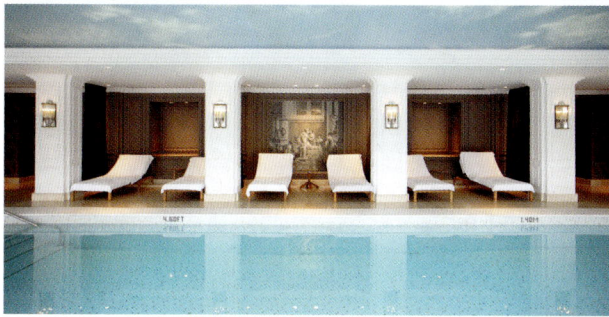

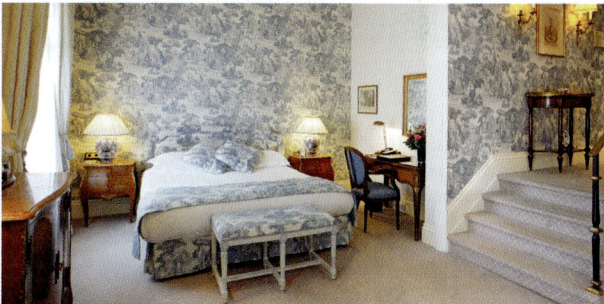

InterContinental Amstel Amsterdam

Classical city grandeur in Amsterdam's centre

Approaching 150 years since first opening her doors, this grand old dame hasn't lost any of her charms with age. From the Tsar and Tsarina of Russia and Her Majesty Queen Elizabeth II to Audrey Hepburn and the Rolling Stones, the glamorous InterContinental Amstel Amsterdam has played host to them all. Set alongside the Amstel River with Spiegelkwartier (the art and antiques district) and RAI Exhibition and Convention Centre on the doorstep, this is a prime spot for business types and leisure guests requiring city centre location whilst hankering authentic old school elegance. Nowhere is this more evident than in the original 19th-century entrance hall with cathedral-high ceiling, palatial chandelier, grand staircase and soaring arches. Here, you'll be welcomed by one of the Clefs d'Or concierges before being led to your room or suite. Whether staying in an Executive Room or the apartment-style Royal Suite, the theme is the same: classic opulence. In-room dining is available 24 hours but when a Michelin-Starred restaurant (the French Mediterranean La Rive) is on the premises it's a crime not to enjoy it. For more casual evenings there's Amstel Brasserie, the Amstel Lounge for a spot of afternoon tea and two summer terraces making the most of those river views and the new A bar for cocktails. Spoil yourself: hire the hotel's limousine to/from Schiphol International Airport.

PRICE FROM:
€395 (room only, excluding city tax)

FEATURES:
Gym; Michelin Starred restaurant; Pool; Sea views; Spa

ACTIVITIES:
Cycling; Shopping; Sightseeing

NEARBY:
Spiegelkwartier; RAI Exhibition and Convention Centre; Van Gogh Museum; Royal Theatre Carré; Rijksmuseum

GETTING THERE:
Amsterdam Central Station; Schiphol International Airport

+31 20 622 60 60 ☎
condenastjohansens.com/amstel 🌐
Professor Tulpplein 1, Amsterdam 1018 GX, The Netherlands ✉

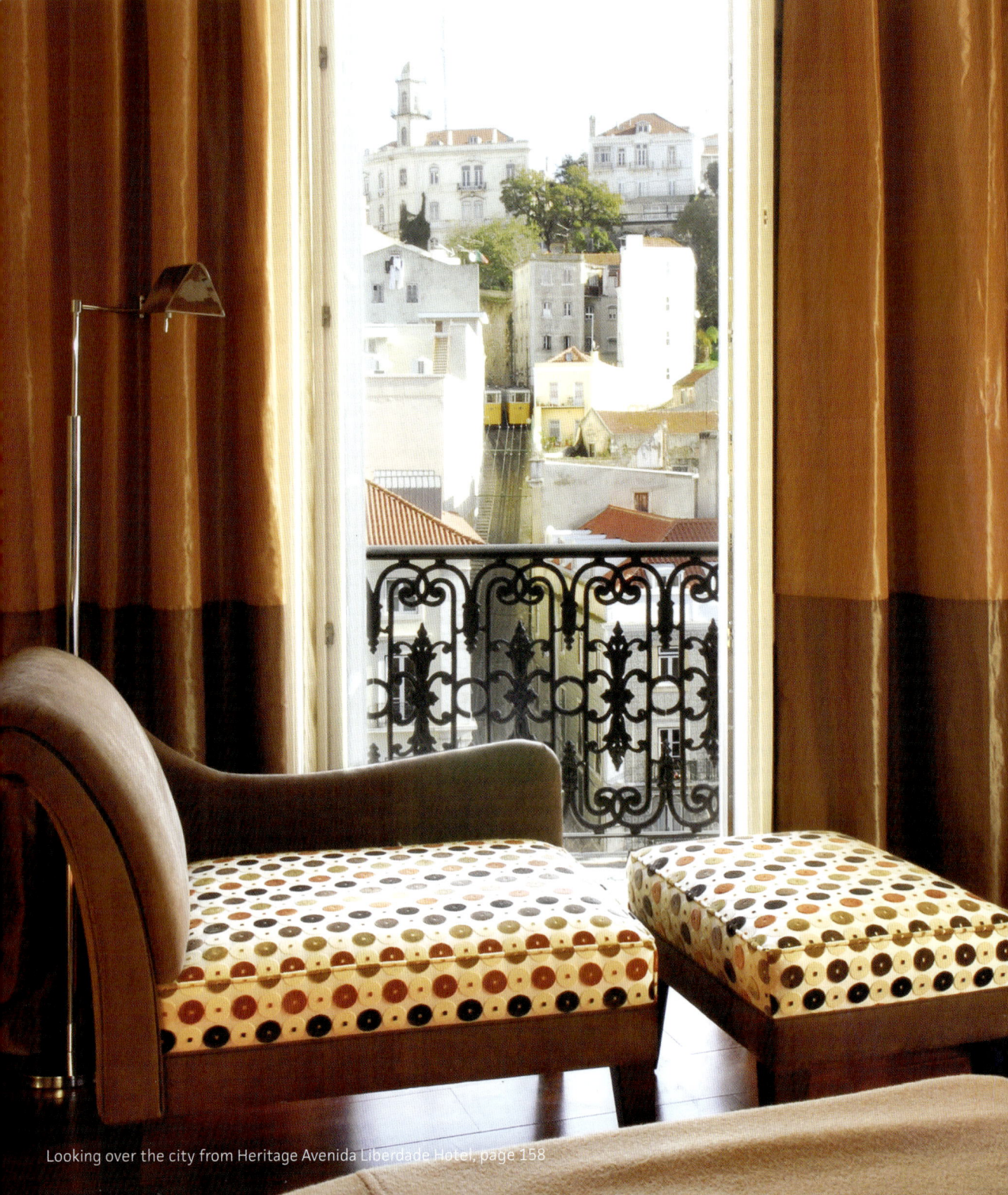

Portugal

Please go to condenastjohansens.com/portugal

Looking over the city from Heritage Avenida Liberdade Hotel, page 158

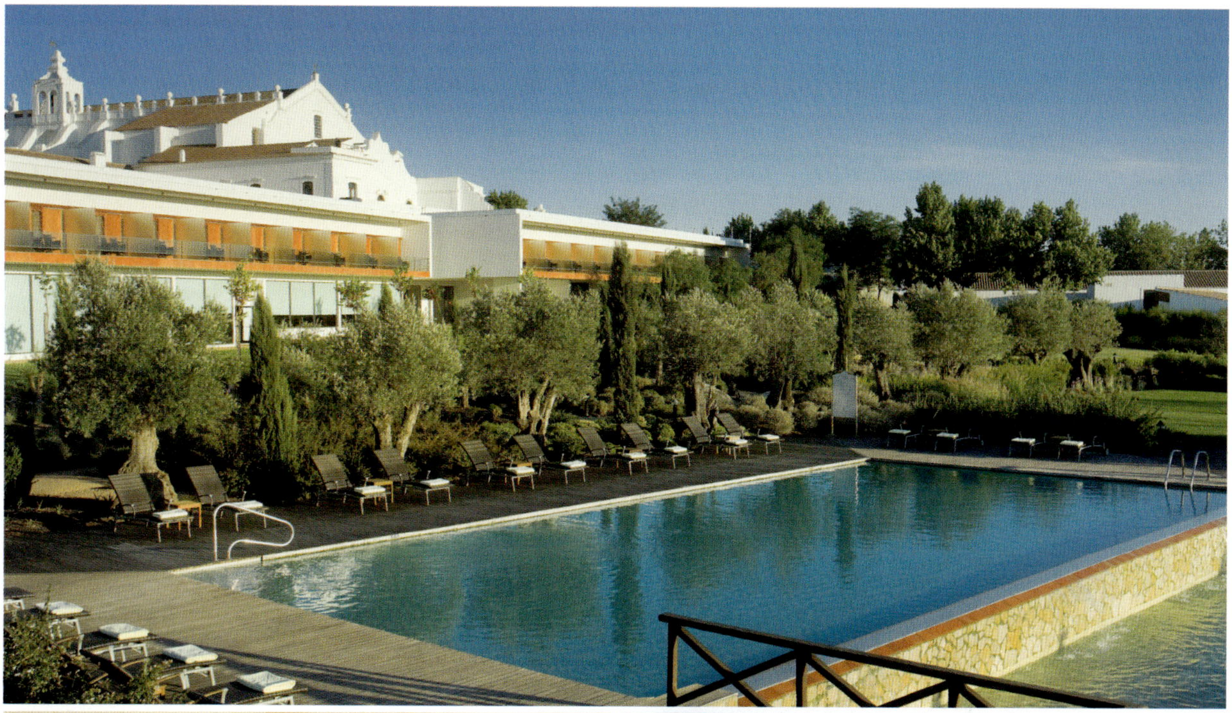

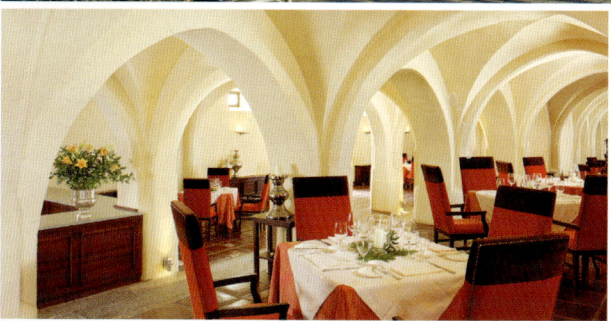

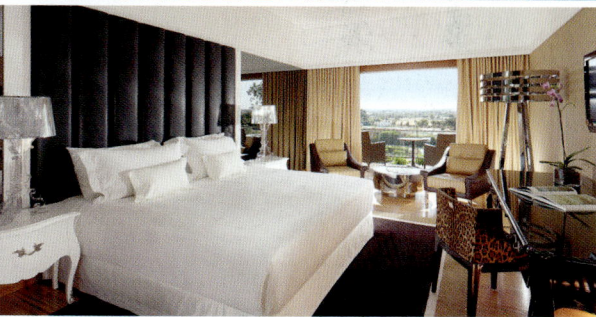

Convento do Espinheiro

21st-century comfort within 15th-century walls

Six centuries ago this majestic building echoed to the sound of chanting. Today, Convento do Epinheiro surrounds you with a similar sense of calm, with an opulent twist. A former convent, the original imposing, whitewashed building stands alongside a contemporary structure, which houses garden rooms and terraces. And despite its ancient and humble beginnings, Convento's facilities are upscale and up-to-date with high-end luxury as standard. Considered one of Portugal's leading hotels, Convento do Epinheiro feels remote for all the right reasons. Peaceful formal gardens encase the property and the rooms themselves are tastefully decorated in an opulent style with a nod to their past. Think plush marble bathrooms with hefty antique carved stone basins and fantastically ornate carved wooden headboards contrasting against the minimalist décor. Soothing the body and spirit is taken care at Diana Spa where treatments are a mix of ancient cures and modern therapies. The name pays homage to the Temple of Diana in nearby Évora, an ancient town, now a UNESCO Heritage Site, that's well worth a visit. Last but not least, take your pick of the Convento's wonderful restaurants. Try the chilled-out and cosy Claustro or put your glad rags on and enjoy the delicious local Alentejo cuisine at the elegant Divinus.

PRICE FROM:
€184

FEATURES:
Helipad; Pool; Restaurant; Spa

ACTIVITIES:
Cycling; Horse riding; Tennis

NEARBY:
Estremoz; Borba; Horse-drawn carriage rides; Alentejo vineyards; Vila Viçosa

GETTING THERE:
Lisbon Airport

+351 266 788 200 ☎
condenastjohansens.com/espinheiro 🌐
Canaviais, 7005-839 Évora, Alentejo, Portugal 🏢

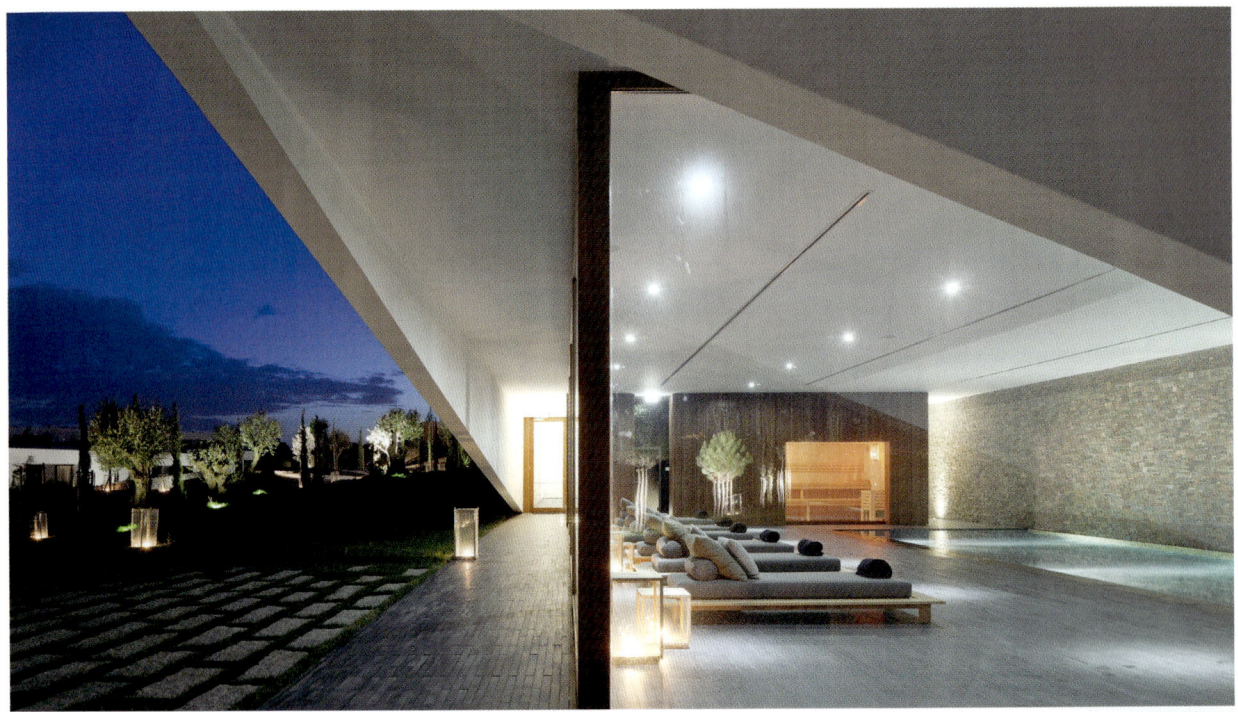

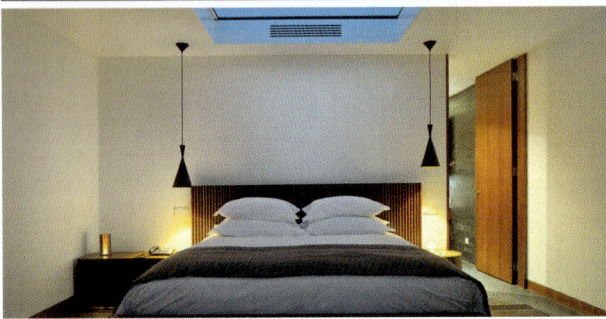

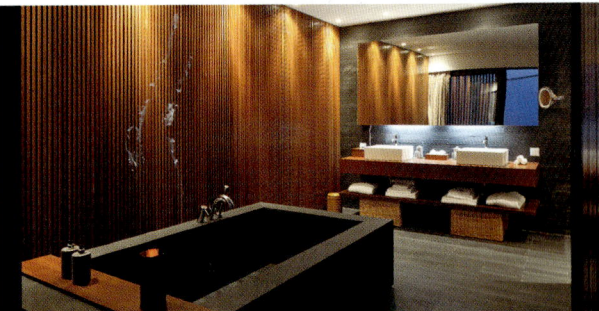

L'AND Vineyards Resort

Innovative, boldly designed wine resort in Alentejo countryside

PRICE FROM:
€170

FEATURES:
Lake views; Pool; Restaurant; Spa; Wheelchair access

ACTIVITIES:
Cycling; Tennis; Walking

NEARBY:
Évora; Estremoz; Monsaraz

GETTING THERE:
Lisbon Airport

45 minutes from Portugal's capital, Alentejo holds a surprising card. Somewhat unexpected but nevertheless a winner - L'AND Vineyards Resort is an oenology retreat in the epicentre of this rural region known for its agricultural, livestock farming and wood producing prowess. It demands your attention. A bright white beast of a building in meticulous, landscaped grounds. The odd lines and bare, neutral coloured walls should create a stark setting but bizarrely they have the opposite effect. Maybe it's the come-hither lighting, the use of warm woods and natural materials as well as fires on each suite terrace that lure you in. Whatever it is, it works. Just outside each suite is the formal vine garden, a constant reminder that this is a noteworthy vineyard estate that beckons you to decide how to hone your taste-testing skills; perhaps attend a viniculture course. But to Sky View or L'AND View, that is the question. These two types of suites are both insanely stylish and spacious, however, stargazes should book a Sky View Suite whose party trick is its retractable bedroom ceiling. Take to the spa for some vinotherapy and then the courtyard restaurant and lobby lounge area for some authentic local flavours.

☎ +351 266 242 400
🌐 condenastjohansens.com/landvineyards
🏠 Herdade das Valadas, EN 4, Apartado 122, 7050-031
Montemor~o~Novo, Alentejo, Portugal

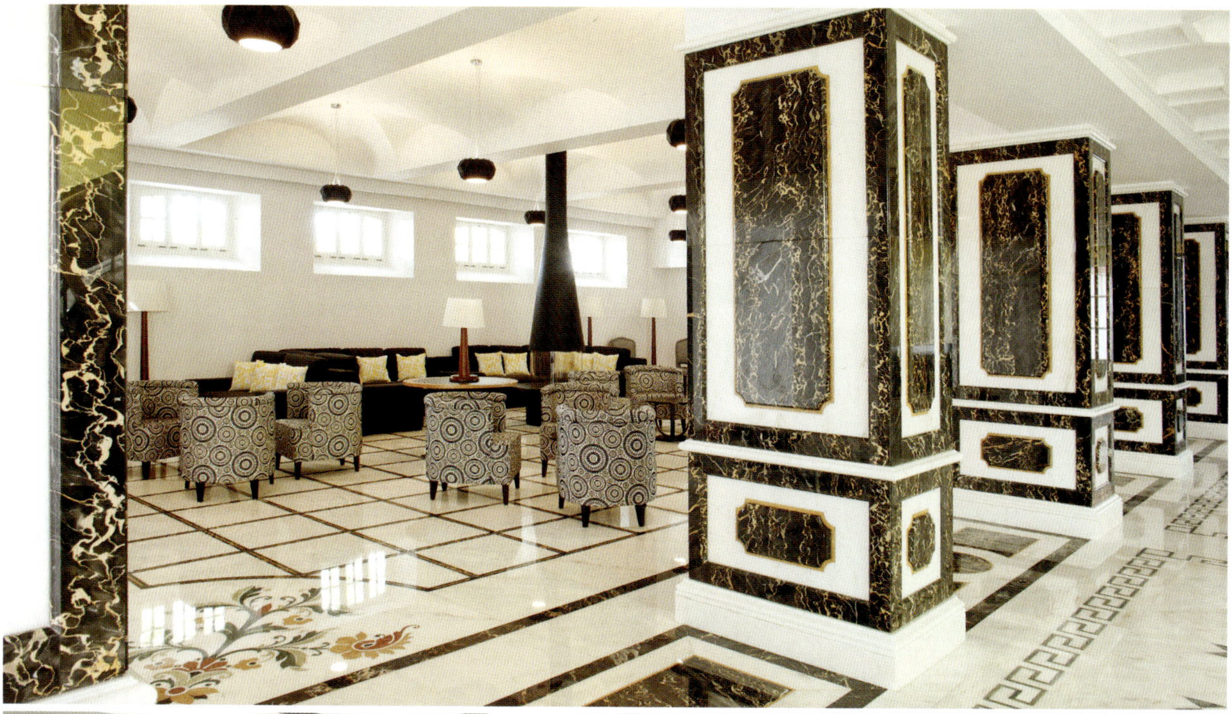

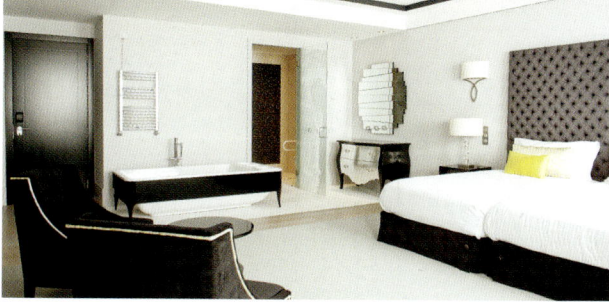
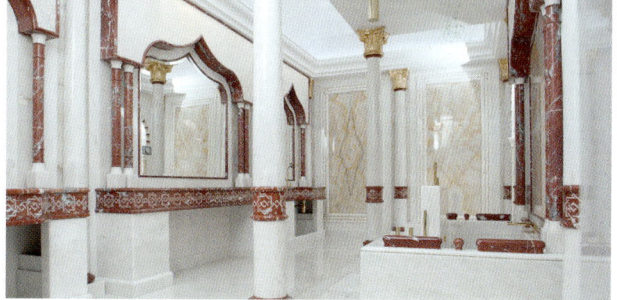

Alentejo Marmòris Hotel & SPA

Interior design at its most artistic in Vila Viçosa

It's all a bit marble-mad at Vila Viçosa; like a life-size Legoland but with... marble. This is Portugal's marble capital of the world, and it's utterly enchanting. The dukes of Bragança thought so too. In fact, the nearby Paço Ducal Palace was the last residence of the Portuguese monarchy. And like the town's palace, Moorish castles, churches and houses, Alentejo Marmòris Hotel & Spa has tapped into the readily available source of shiny stone to create an innovative work of art. Glossy with reflection, what strikes you upon entering Alentejo Marmòris Hotel is the rousing design that has your eyes darting from one feature to the next. Elegant geometric lines are juxtaposed with palatial pillars and the grandiose, all set against a palette of black, white, yellow and gold with splashes of red. It all feels new and fresh, clever and progressive: put simply, it's different. Each bedroom and suite is further testament to this with an en-suite (marble!) bathroom connected through an open wall. A visit to Stone Spa, Alentejo Marmòris Hotel's (marble!) temple to well-being, is a highlight of anyone's stay, as is dining at Narcissus Fernandesii where Alexander Silva places a distinctive mark on regional dishes prepared from local produce.

PRICE FROM:
€104

FEATURES:
Family friendly; Gym; Pool; Restaurant; Spa

ACTIVITIES:
Horse riding; Sightseeing; Water sports

NEARBY:
Borba; Estremoz; Wine routes of Alentejo; Évora; Elvas, Spain

GETTING THERE:
Lisbon Airport

+351 268 887 010 ☎
condenastjohansens.com/alentejomarmoris 🌐
Largo Gago Coutinho 11, 7160-214 Vila Viçosa, Alentejo, 🏠
Portugal

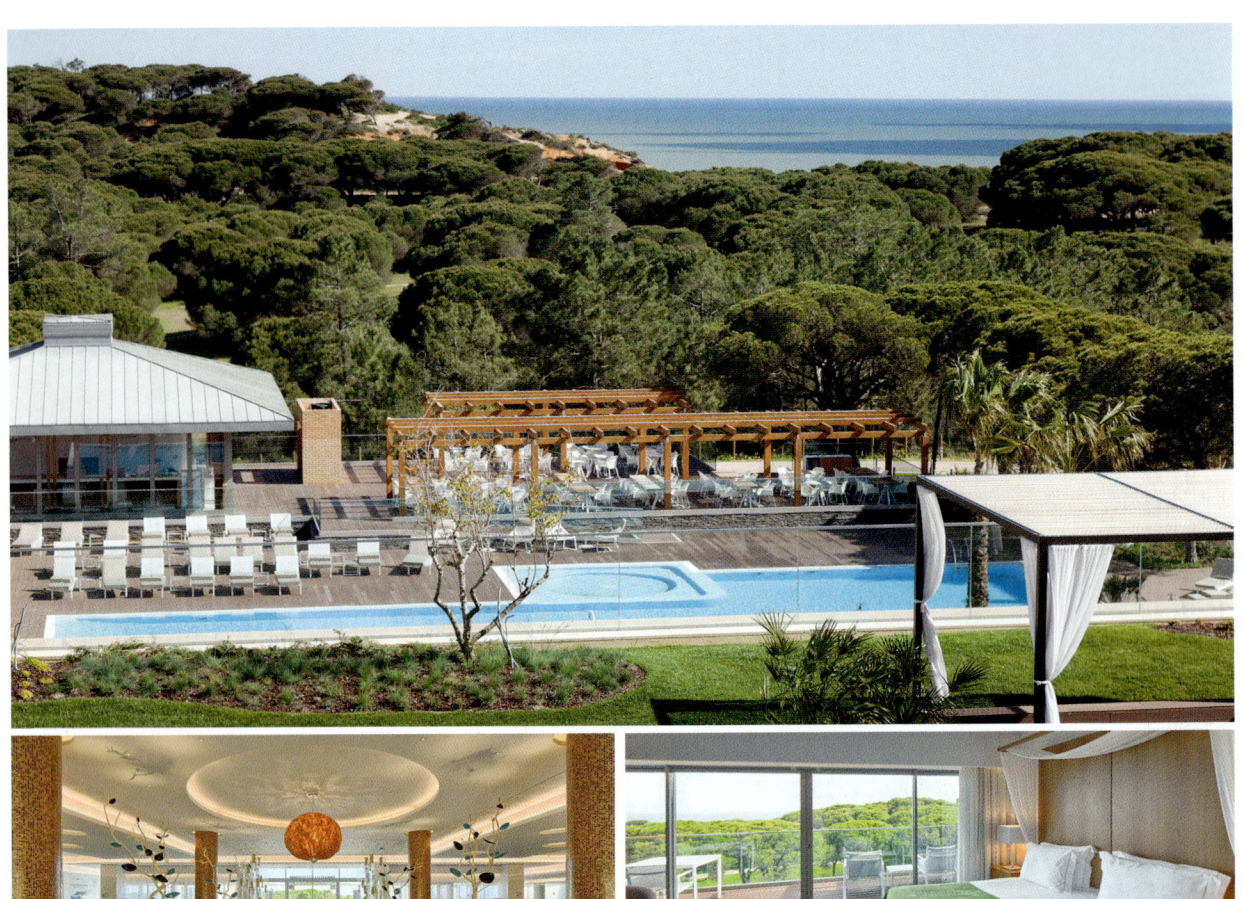

EPIC SANA Algarve Hotel

Relaxing in style by Albufeira's Falésia beach

PRICE FROM:
€110

FEATURES:
Beach access; Restaurant; Sea views; Spa

ACTIVITIES:
Fishing; Sightseeing; Walking

NEARBY:
Albufeira; Marina of Vilamoura, Loulé markets; Quinta do Lago; Vale do Lobo Golf Courses

GETTING THERE:
Faro Airport

Spread across private acres of pine forest and gardens above the golden Falésia beach, EPIC SANA Algarve Hotel is where memories are made. The holiday children boast about and the time parents refer to with a fond smile. For it's all here: days filled with poolside antics (five outside and one inside); sandcastle building on the beach just a few minutes' walk away; relaxation at Sayanna Wellness spa and fitness centre; and active fun including water sports and various games on EPIC SANA Algarve's multi-purpose sports field. Entertainment of the food and drink variety is a highlight at EPIC SANA with no less than three restaurants and two bars. Al Quimia is the gourmet option focused on Portuguese cuisine and wine while the international Abyad Restaurant and seasonal, typically Algarvian Open Deck (try the fresh grilled fish) keep matters casual. By EPIC bar also serves snacks but for some live music and a cheeky cocktail head to Bluum Bar. Whether you're retreating to a bedroom in the main hotel, an apartment with kitchenette or family-friendly suite, there'll be a private terrace and huge sink-into bed waiting for you.

☎ +351 289 104 300
🌐 condenastjohansens.com/epicsanaalgarve
🏠 Pinhal do Concelho, Praia da Falésia, Olhos de Água 8200-593 Albufeira, Algarve, Portugal

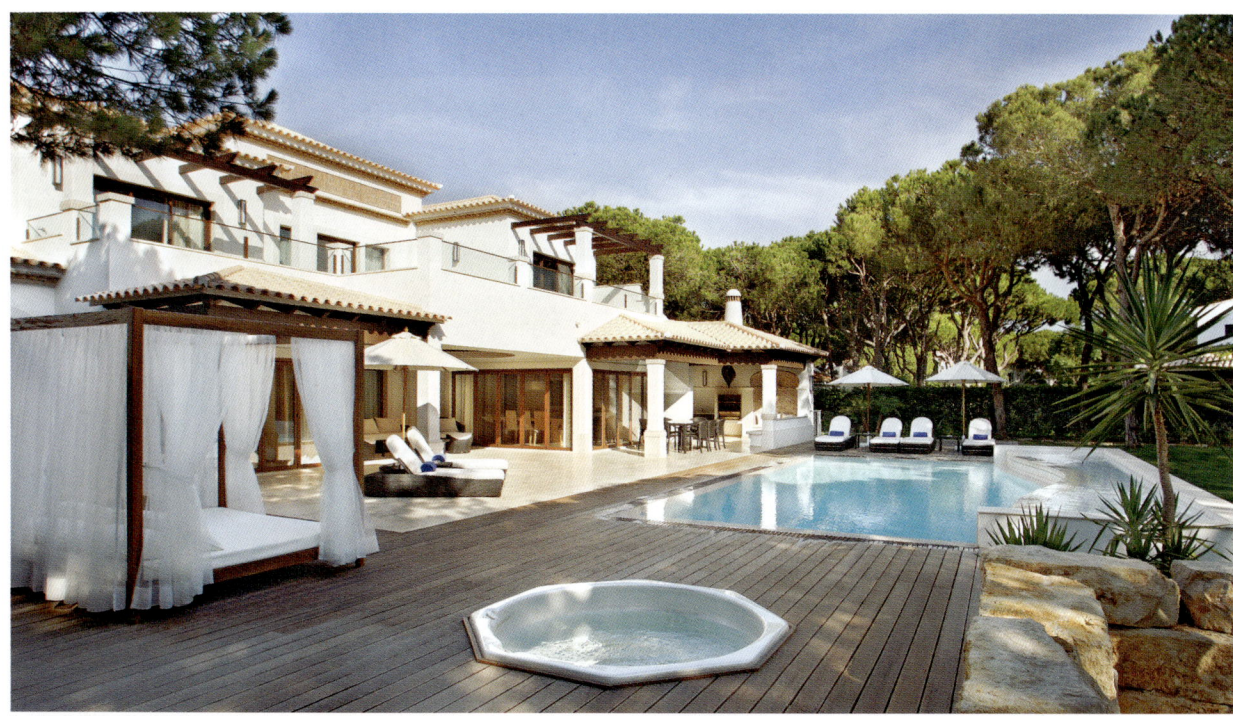

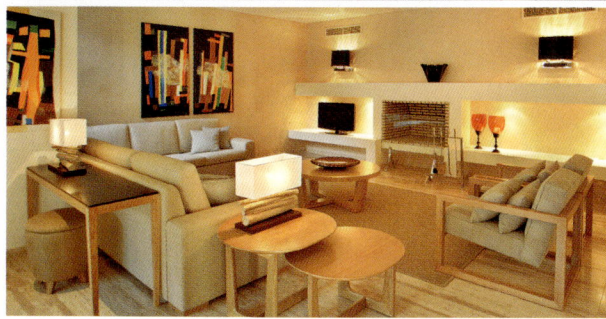
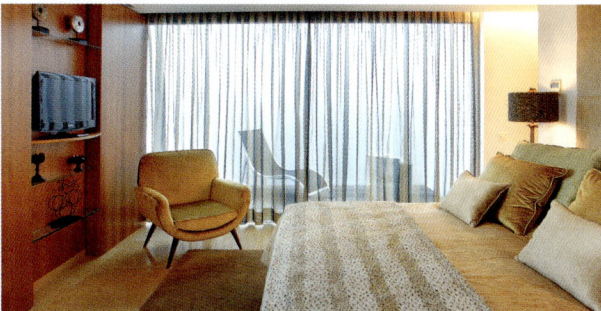

Pine Cliffs Terraces and Villas

Action-packed Algarve vacation experience

The mighty Pine Cliffs Resort, Albufeira, is an idyllic location. Run by friendly staff with dedicated childcare facilities that provide peace of mind from the get-go, it's the resort's unique town house Terraces and deluxe Villas that attract a discerning crowd. Not least because each is a spacious home-from-home that's utterly secluded but they're also impeccably pristine and comfortable with all the techie requirements of modern life and high quality self-catering facilities you could possibly desire - perfect for a family getaway or an exclusive retreat with friends. If you're not in the mood for playing chef on holiday, Pine Cliffs has 11 bars and restaurants to choose from, catering for every taste. And thank goodness because you're going to work up an appetite! The resort's cliff-top nine-hole golf course is a constant distraction but first, take a visit to The Pine Cliffs Golf Academy to work on that handicap with the aid of the latest technology. For those who prefer swinging a racket rather than a club, The Tennis Academy offers 24/7 play and tuition across five courts. In addition to the in-resort facilities, Pine Cliffs works closely with a number of partner companies to offer wild boat rides, adventures in the tree tops and water sports including swimming with dolphins; a sure-fire winner with the children. Worth noting: some bars, restaurants and facilities are seasonal so check in advance.

PRICE FROM:
€275

FEATURES:
Beach access; Family friendly; Gym; Pool; Restaurant

ACTIVITIES:
Fishing; Golf; Water sports

NEARBY:
Faro; Vilamoura; Albufeira; Fishing villages; Sardine restaurants

GETTING THERE:
Faro Airport

+351 289 500 100 ☎
condenastjohansens.com/pinecliffs 🌐
Praia da Falésia, Apt 644, 8200-909 Albufeira, Algarve, 🏠
Portugal

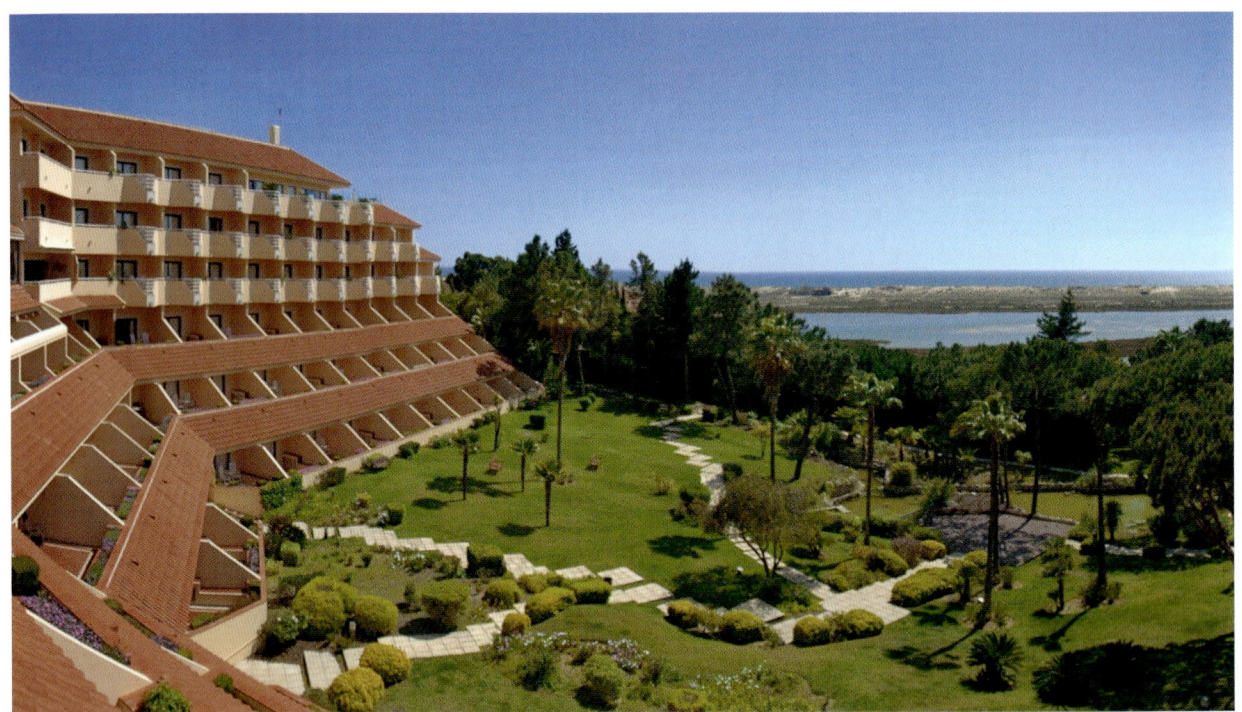

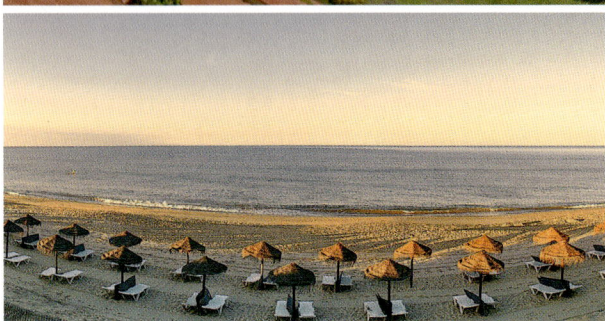

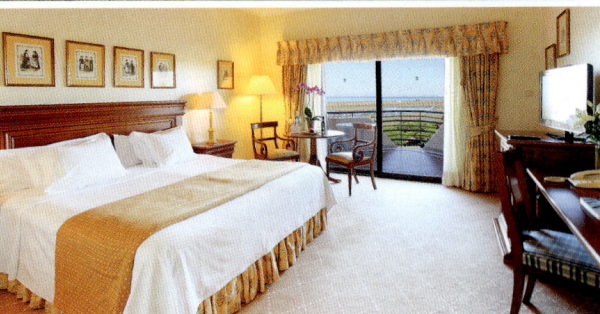

Hotel Quinta do Lago

High-end hospitality in the centre of the Algarve's natural beauty

PRICE FROM:
€190

FEATURES:
Beach access; Family friendly; Restaurant; Sea views; Spa

ACTIVITIES:
Golf; Horse riding; Walking

NEARBY:
Quinta do Lago golf courses; Vilamoura Marina; Loulé; Gigi Restaurant; Faro

GETTING THERE:
Faro Airport; Lisbon Airport

☎ +351 289 350 350
⊕ condenastjohansens.com/hotelquintadolago
▪ Quinta do Lago, 8135-024 Almancil, Algarve, Portugal

Not your average Algarve getaway but a rural idyll with lush green views of Ria Formosa Natural Park. This is Hotel Quinta do Lago at the southern tip of Portugal wrapped in blossoming gardens inhabited by an abundance of birdlife beside the sandy shores of Quinta do Lago beach, and it's easy to get to, just a short drive from Faro's airport. A slick operation, Hotel Quinta do Lago is family owned, with a personal service that goes the extra mile. Everyone here will know your name and it's this friendly, professional attitude that keeps travellers coming back time and again. Whether you're a golf lover, a water sports fan or a beach babe, it's all here to enjoy on the doorstep. Plus, children aged 2-12 have the Kids Club to keep them amused. Guest rooms are pleasingly roomy and all have ample balconies to soak up those vistas of the lagoon or dreamy umbrella dotted beach, while the two restaurants serve tasty seafood and international dishes. Book early for the smart Italian option, Ca' d'Oro, or try Brisa Do Mar's Portuguese specialities such as its famous salt-crusted fish and Algarvean black pig cataplana. The spa and excellent golf facilities keep you close to home, although nearby local markets and monuments may temporarily tempt you away for a dose of culture.

147

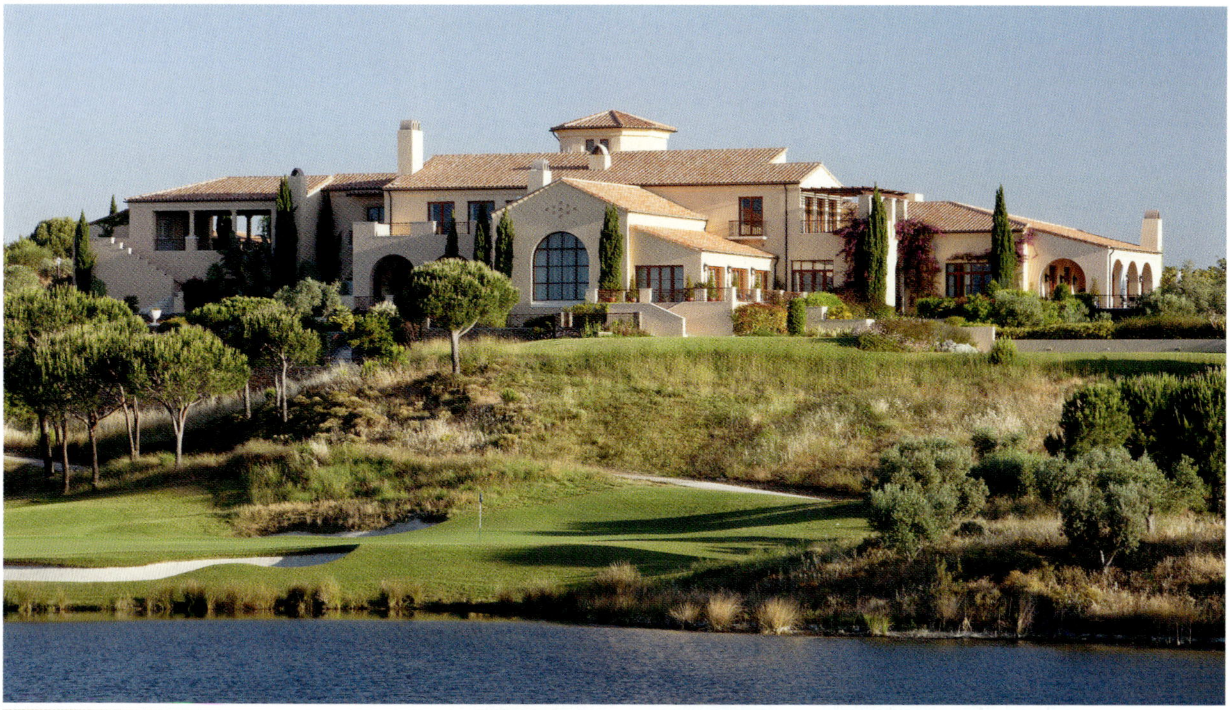

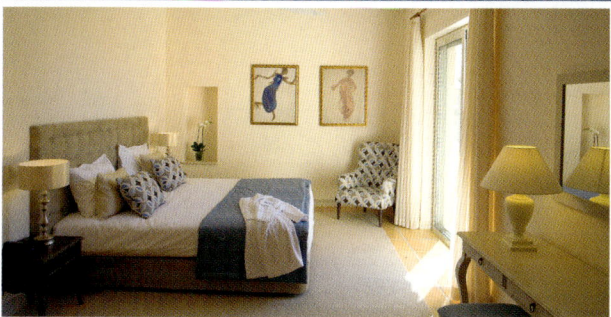
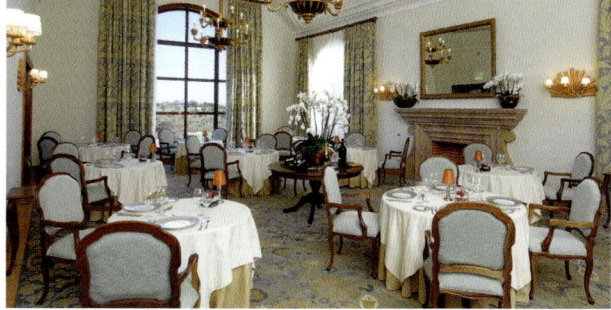

Monte Rei Golf & Country Club

Golfy pleasures, class and sophistication on the Algarve

There are few places on Portugal's Eastern Algarve quite as impressive as Monte Rei Golf & Country Club. A stunning resort, its fantastic Jack Nicklaus Signature golf course offers rack rates and lessons to any level of player. However, there's much more to Monte Rei than golf with many outdoor pursuits on the doorstep. At the heart of the villa complex (known as Miradouro Village), there is Veranda where you'll find the Veranda Restaurant, a bar, gym, tennis courts, pools and spa facilities. The Kid's Villa (unsupervised playroom) is also just steps away. A short distance from Miradouro Village is Monte Rei's Clubhouse (housing Vistas Restaurant and Grill Restaurant), Golf Academy and golf course. After a long day on the challenging stadium green, top Chef Jaime Perez's fine dining Vistas Restaurant delivers gourmet food packed with local flavours. His creations are an exciting combination of Catalonian, Andalucían and Basque cuisine. Each one, two and three-bedroom classically-styled villa, which has access to a communal pool at Veranda, is complete with a fully-equipped kitchen and spacious bathroom. Offering a little more space are detached four-bedroom villas featuring their own private gardens and pools. Every villa benefits from a daily cleaning service and turndown each evening, and have flatscreen tvs, dvd players and free WiFi.

PRICE FROM:
€170

FEATURES:
Family friendly; Gym; Helipad; Pool; Restaurant

ACTIVITIES:
Horse riding; Tennis; Walking

NEARBY:
Tavira; Vila Real de Santo António; River Guadiana; Ayamonte, Spain; Seville, Spain

GETTING THERE:
Faro Airport; Seville Airport

+351 281 950 950 ☎
condenastjohansens.com/monterei 🌐
Sitio do Pocinho, Sesmarias, 8901-907 Vila Nova de Cacela, Algarve, Portugal

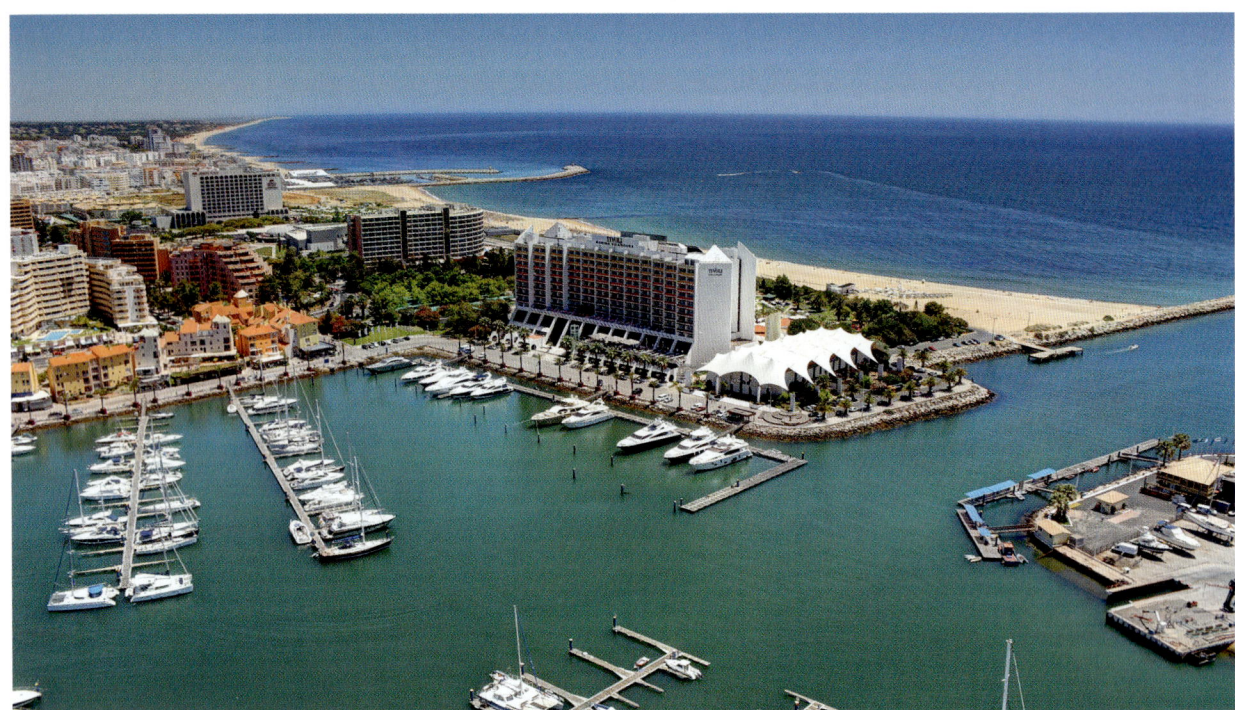

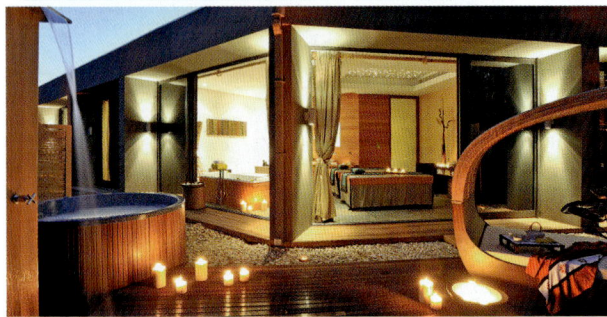
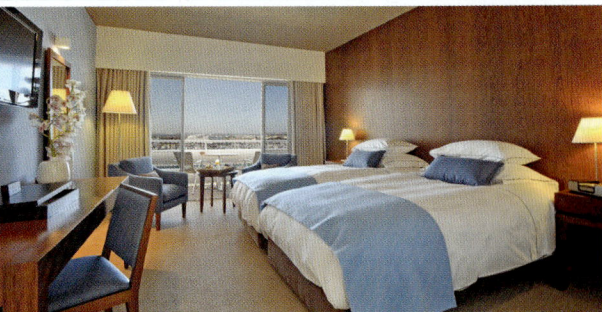

Tivoli Marina Vilamoura

The Algarve at its glitzy, swanky best

PRICE FROM:
€150

FEATURES:
Family friendly; Pool; Restaurant; Sea views; Spa

ACTIVITIES:
Fishing; Golf; Water sports

NEARBY:
Falésia beach; Loulé market; Faro shopping; Historic Silves; Almancil

GETTING THERE:
Faro Airport

☎ +351 218 507 708
🌐 condenastjohansens.com/tivolimarina
🏠 Marina de Vilamoura, 8125-901 Vilamoura, Algarve, Portugal

As well as being home to some of the world's most beautiful beaches, the Algarve is a magnet for golfers, spa lovers and foodies. And this is most certainly the case at the resort town of Vilamoura known for its nightlife and bars, a short drive west of Faro. Overlooking the yacht-rich marina, Tivoli Marina Vilamoura is right in the heart of town delivering glamour by the bucketload. A lesson in contemporary cool with minimalist décor, retro-chic furniture and pops of colour, most of the 383 rooms have a sink-into bed, rain shower and high-tech touches aplenty. Activities of the lively variety include water sports, football, tennis and golf (a fully staffed Golf Desk helps with bookings at the 31 courses in the area). Lazier options include lounging (ice-lolly in hand) by the shapely pool, on the beach (powder-soft sand) or at the sublime Angsana Spa by Banyan Tree. All the while the children (aged 2 - 10) are kept occupied with excursions and activities organised by T/Kids. The siren call of Pepper's Steakhouse draws carnivores from across Vilamoura while the fresh Portuguese fare at Chili restaurant and the relaxed-luxe Menta vie for your stomach's attention. When you want to up the glamour ante even higher, head to Side Bar for cocktails overlooking the marina or the hot nightspot Purobeach Villamoura set beside the sea with restaurant, bar, DJ performances and great lounge beds on the beach.

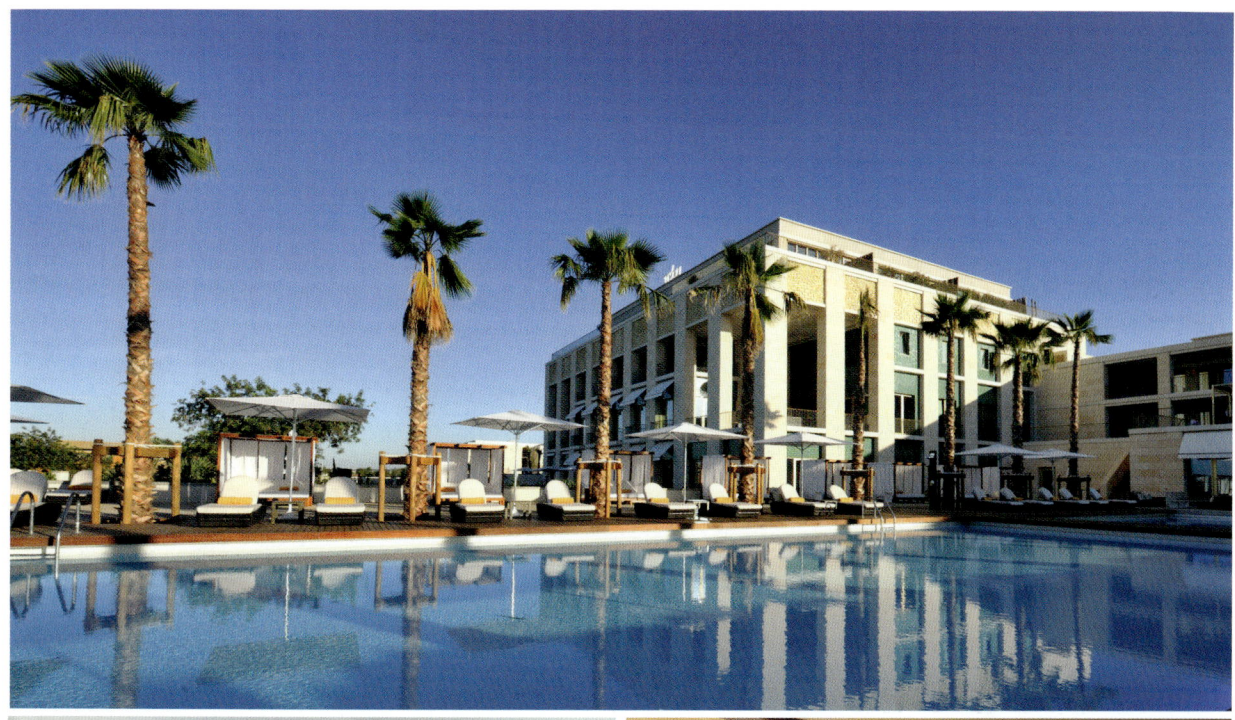

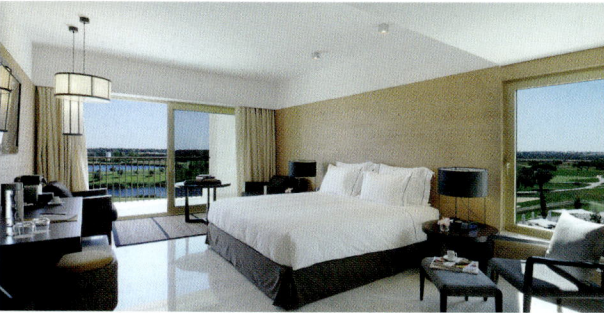

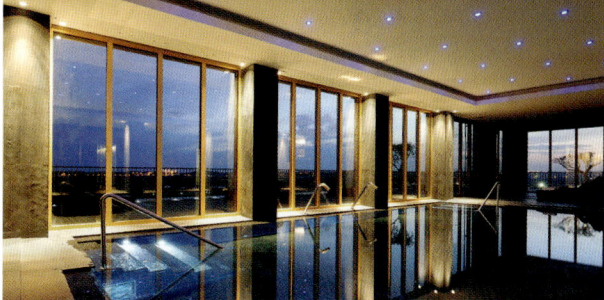

Tivoli Victoria

The Algarve's premier golfing, spa-ing and relaxing hotspot

Love golf? Then you'll love Tivoli Victoria, a stylish and sophisticated resort in Vilamoura on the Algarve overlooking the sprawling Arnold Palmer-designed Oceanico Victoria Golf Course. But if getting in the swing isn't your thing, there's much more besides fairways and fringes at Tivoli Victoria. For starters there's Elements Spa by Banyan Tree, a heavenly hideaway with to-die-for Asian massages and indulgent treatment rituals. The pool is pretty sweet too. Imagine sweeping sundecks, palm trees, posh loungers and icy refreshers on demand (served by seriously smart staff). Tivoli is vast, with 280 rooms and suites, all marble and minimalist décor. But if you want to impress, choose the huge Presidential Suite with terrace, hot tub and Bang & Olufsen music systems. Of its two restaurants, glamour is on the agenda at top-floor Emo whose inventive dishes and gorgeous views are served in a plush setting (monochrome palette, designer chandeliers). It's dining at its most refined. By contrast, Sensorial restaurant is all about laid-back buffet fare. Want a change of scenery? Head to the buzzing marina where seafood and sea views will have you mmming and wowing in unison.

PRICE FROM:
€150

FEATURES:
Family friendly; Pool; Restaurant; Spa; Wheelchair access

ACTIVITIES:
Fishing; Golf; Water sports

NEARBY:
Loulé market; Faro shopping; Vilamoura Marina; Oceânico Victoria Golf Course

GETTING THERE:
Faro Airport

+ 351 218 507 708 ☎
condenastjohansens.com/tivolivictoria 🌐
Avenida dos Descobrimentos, 8125 - 309 Vilamoura, Algarve, 🏠
Portugal

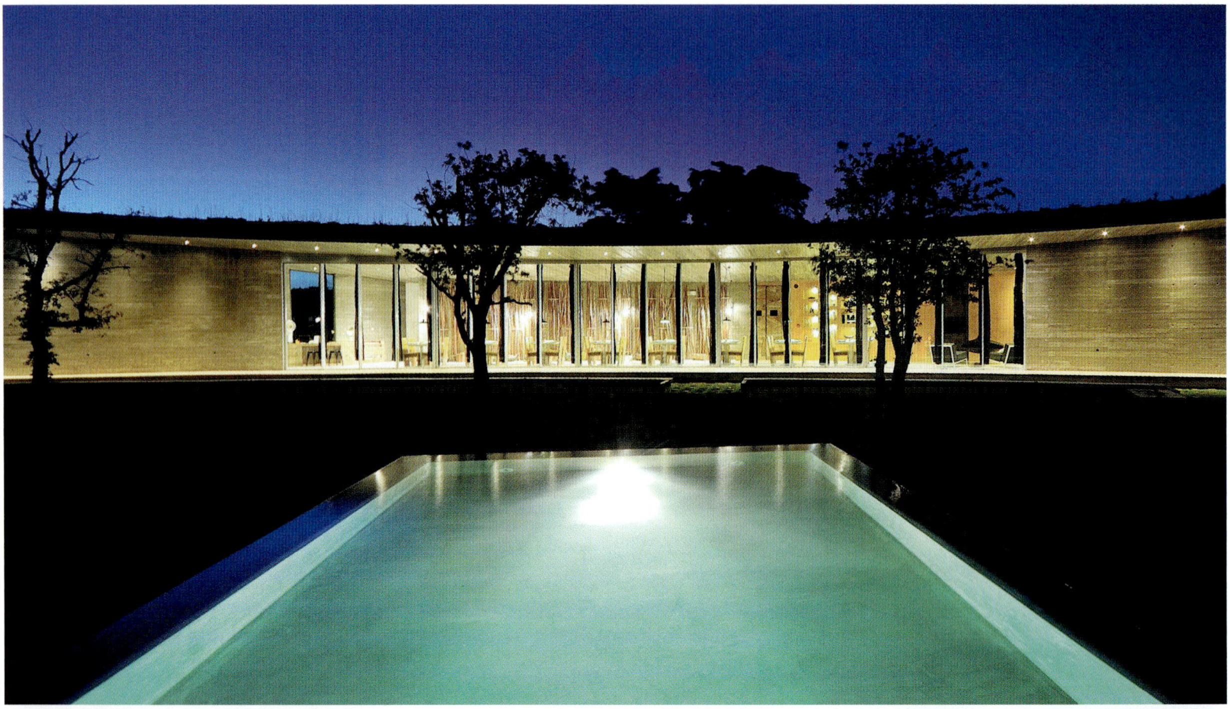

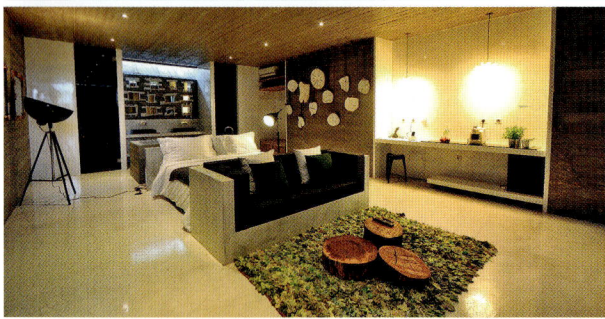

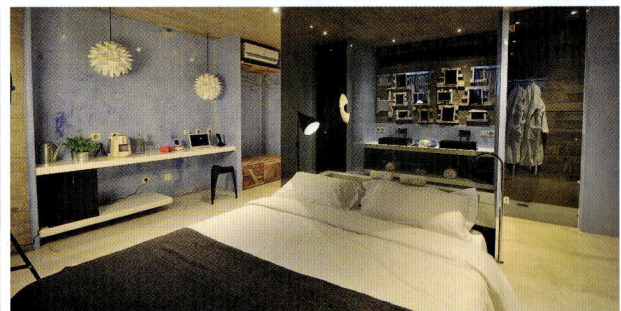

Rio do Prado

Boundary breaking eco-tourism and forward thinking design in Óbidos

PRICE FROM:
€170

FEATURES:
Lake views; Pool; Restaurant; Wheelchair access

ACTIVITIES:
Cycling; Golf; Walking

NEARBY:
Óbidos Lagoon; "Meadow of the Queen" (Várzea da Rainha); Bird-watching; Low carbon farming experiences; Organic bread making classes

GETTING THERE:
Lisbon Airport

☎ +351 262 959 623
🌐 condenastjohansens.com/riodoprado
🏠 Rua das Poças, Arelho (Óbidos Lagoon) 2510-191 Óbidos, Estremadura, Portugal

Scrupulously eco-friendly, sci-fi stylish and altogether alternative, Rio do Prado, close to Óbidos Lagoon, is part of a new wave in hospitality. Placing paramount importance on eco-design, sustainable tourism and respecting the rural land it's surrounded by, Rio do Prado is the answer to the Green Party's prayers. But don't think there's any compromise on comfort. It's all a clever lesson on how to be green in luxury with an avant-garde approach. For instance, each of the (15) suites has all the hallmarks of a first-rate hotel yet recycled eucalyptus wood provides artistic shade, a carefully planted tree flanks the doorway, stumps of trees act as tables and an outside fireplace has you kicking-back alfresco in the evening. In interesting contrast to these natural elements, oversized standalone lamps and the square concrete structure of each suite add an industrial touch. Maria Batata Restaurant provides a surprise or two also. An advocate of seasonal produce, its menus are decided on a daily basis prepared from the vegetables, fruit, herbs and preserves supplied from Rio do Prado's very own organic farm. At the restaurant there's the Bookstore (why not?!) that operates as a library. Nice touch: the small Black Spa whose Float Room has you weightless in warm Epsom salt solution.

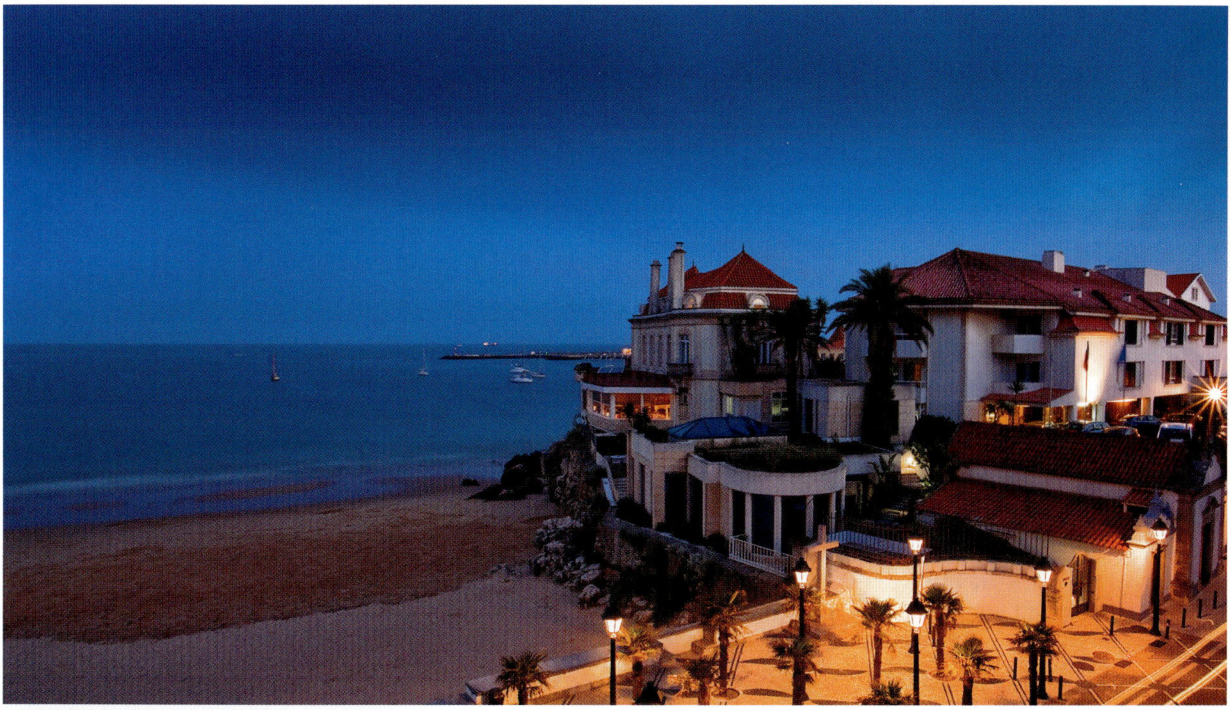

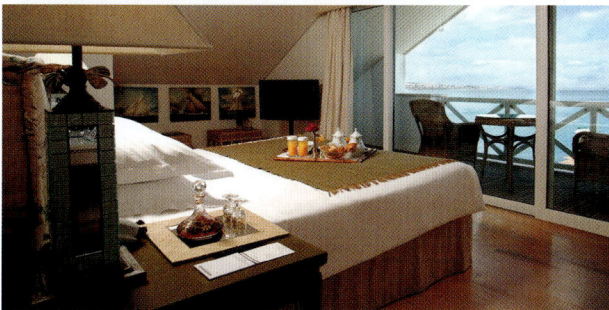
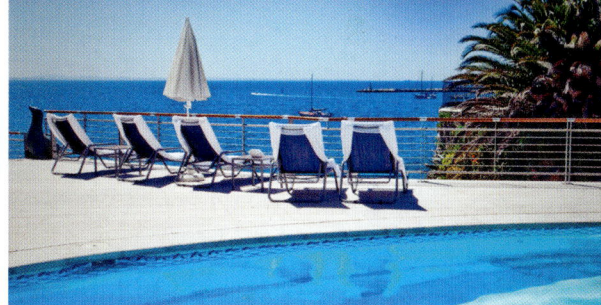

The Albatroz Seafront Hotel

Former seaside royal retreat now boutique retreat for all in Cascais

The name says it all: Seafront. Like a vessel on the sea, The Albatroz Seafront Hotel beside the bay of Cascais rises majestically from a promontory overlooking the azure blue sea. Just 30 minutes from Lisbon, the family-run Albatroz is coastal living at its glamorous best. Elegant and relaxed, guests typically return time and again and often strike up longstanding relationships with the owners and staff. The tan-limbed set head for the sun terrace with its 180^0 views of the sea while water babies hone their swimming techniques in the sea-facing pool, admiring the view as they glide. When thirst kicks in, there's the seafront bar serving fruity cocktails and local gourmet snacks, and The Albatroz restaurant to satisfy the gourmand. Carefully designed to maximise the stunning vista, the dining room is a Mediterranean-inspired affair dominated by fabulously fresh fish and seafood with a Portuguese twist. After dinner nothing beats watching the twinkling lights of the Estoril coast over a glass of local Port. Although, if feeling a little curious about the local scene, a saunter into Cascais (just a two-minute stroll away) might be more the ticket. And at the end of a day, comfort awaits in your room, which is guaranteed to differ from your neighbour next door; all 44 have been thoughtfully and individually designed. And their views, well, let's just say they're full of watery wonder.

PRICE FROM:
€150

FEATURES:
Pool; Restaurant; Sea views; Wheelchair access

ACTIVITIES:
Golf; Walking; Water sports

NEARBY:
Cascais; Estoril; Sintra; Lisbon

GETTING THERE:
Lisbon Airport

+351 21 484 73 80
condenastjohansens.com/albatroz
Rua Frederico Arouca 100, 2750-353 Cascais, Lisbon & Tagus Valley, Portugal

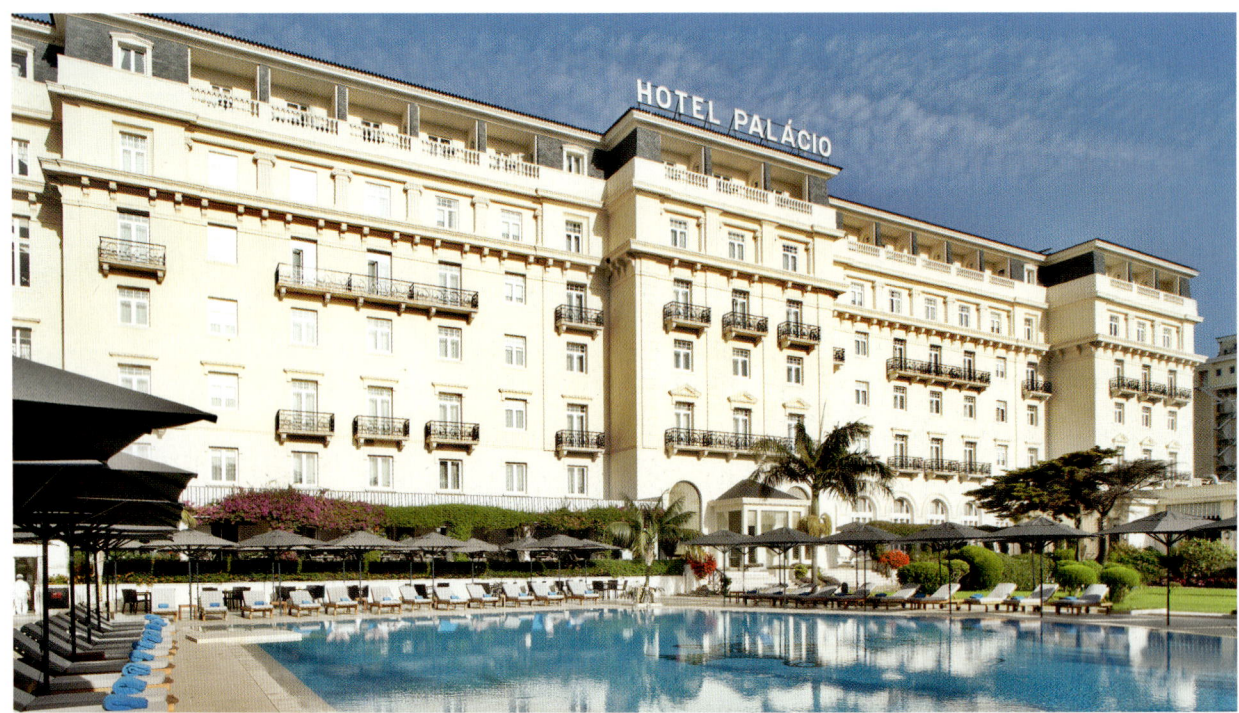

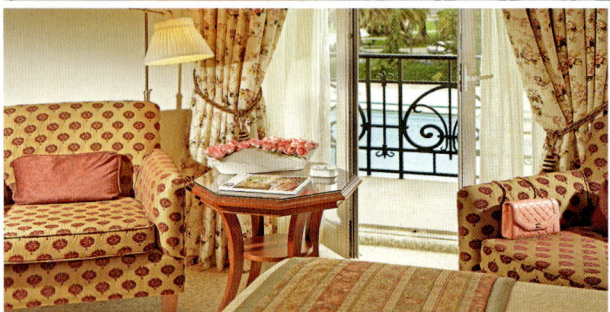

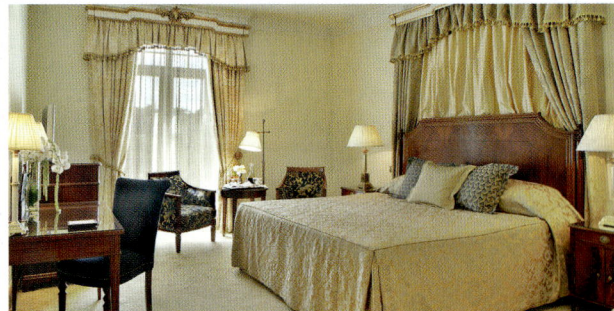

Palácio Estoril, Hotel, Golf & Spa

Estoril's glamourpuss whose recent facelift really has worked wonders

PRICE FROM:
€280

FEATURES:
Family friendly; Gym; Pool; Restaurant; Sea views

ACTIVITIES:
Fishing; Golf; Water sports

NEARBY:
Cascais; Sintra; Lisbon; Guincho beach and restaurants

GETTING THERE:
Lisbon Airport

Behind the impossibly grand white façade of this fabulous 1930s palace are romantic stories of royalty in exile, espionage and none other than James Bond himself. During World War II, European heads of state flocked to neutral Portugal and the elegant Palácio Estoril was their HQ. Just 20 minutes from Lisbon, these days Palácio Estoril, Hotel, Golf & Spa combines its old world charm with 21st-century touches including a Banyan Tree spa. Rooms and suites are classically styled, supremely comfortable and many have views of the stunning Estoril coast located a minute away. Golfers love it here. Spoiled for choice, the internationally renowned Estoril Golf, one of the oldest and smartest in Portugal, is right on the doorstep and there are six more within putting distance. But if you simply wish to relax and soak up the sun, head to Palácio Estoril's alluring pool next to the Bougainvillea Terrace restaurant, which also overlooks the verdant garden. The Four Seasons Grill gives a sophisticated, modern take on traditional Portuguese and international cuisines and should you feel like exploring the local scene it's lined with top quality bars and cafés representing every corner of the globe. It's easy to see why Estoril is known as the Coast of Kings.

☎ +351 21 464 80 00
🌐 condenastjohansens.com/estoril
🏠 Rua Particular, 2769-504 Estoril, Lisbon & Tagus Valley, Portugal

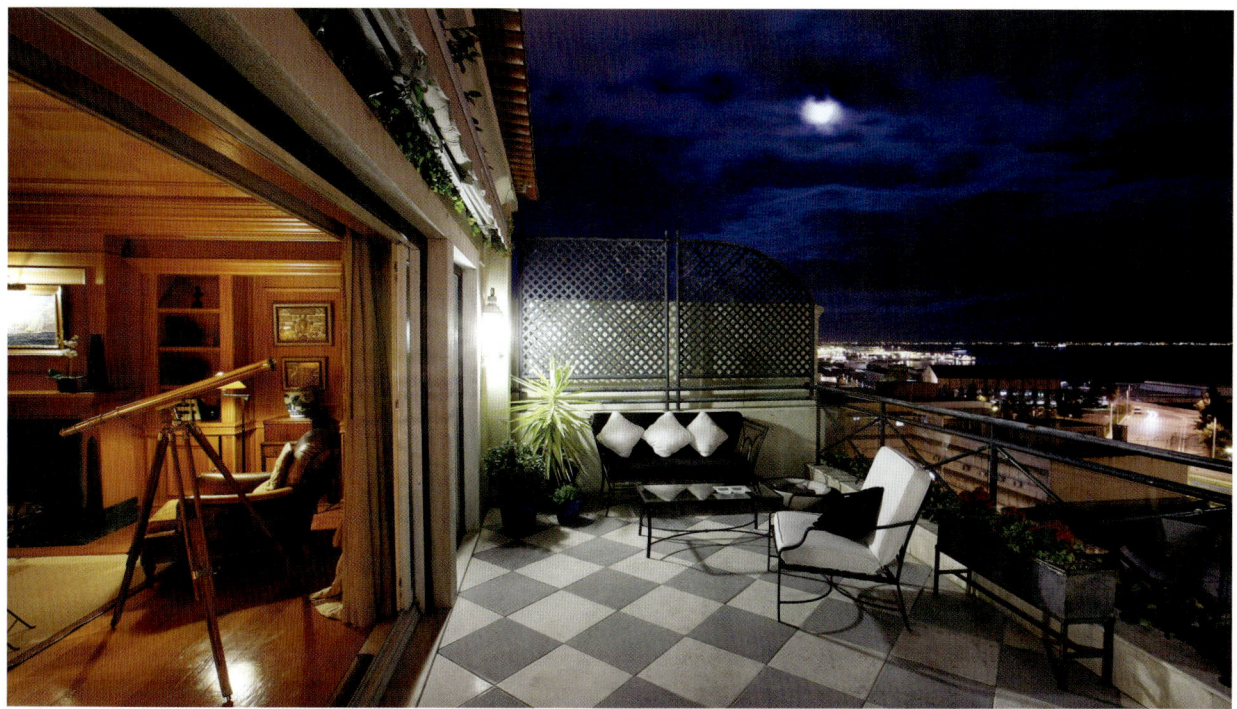

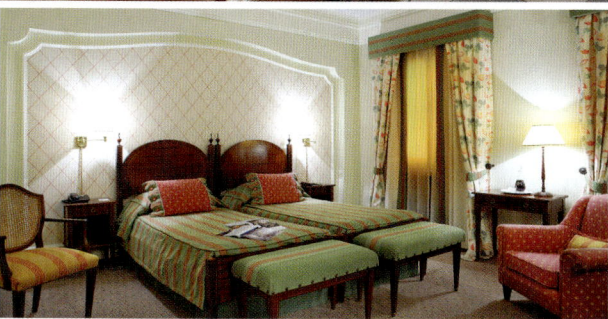

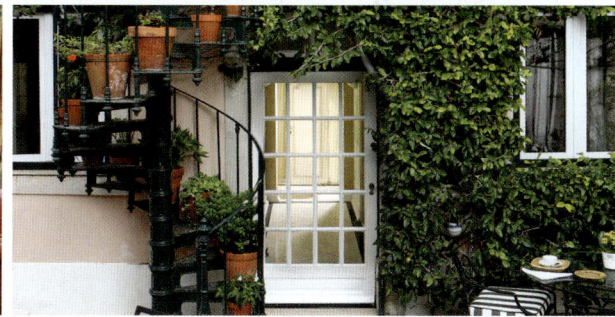

As Janelas Verdes

Neoclassical Lisbon palace-come-chic guest house overlooking the River Tagus

The handsome As Janelas Verdes, Lisbon, stands in the quieter Lapa/Santos area alongside the Museum of Ancient Art. Full of character, the hotel's eye-like "green windows" have undoubtably witnessed many dramas since its 18th-century palace days. Bewitching you with its reassuringly warm atmosphere, much like a deep soak in a tub, one minute you might be taking tea (accompanied by the stupendous custard tarts Portugal is known for) in the secluded courtyard garden, then in the next, cosying up by the fireplace and helping yourself to drinks at the Library's honesty bar. That's if you can tear yourself away from gazing across the bay from the brass telescope overlooking the roof terrace. It's the little touches that make all the difference here. Rooms blend flawlessly with elegant interiors and crisp linens. But you must step out to explore Lisbon's tram-filled streets and colourful cityscape. Staff at As Janelas Verdes will happily point you in the right direction for culture, chic shopping and the best nightlife. Then, back to the hotel for more of those pastries…

PRICE FROM:
€147

FEATURES:
Sea views

ACTIVITIES:
Golf; Sightseeing; Walking

NEARBY:
Museum of Ancient Art; Basilica da Estrela; Parliament; Docks; World Heritage monuments

GETTING THERE:
Lisbon Airport

+351 21 39 68 143 ☎
condenastjohansens.com/janelasverdes 🌐
Rua das Janelas Verdes 47, 1200-690 Lisbon, Lisbon & Tagus Valley, Portugal 🏠

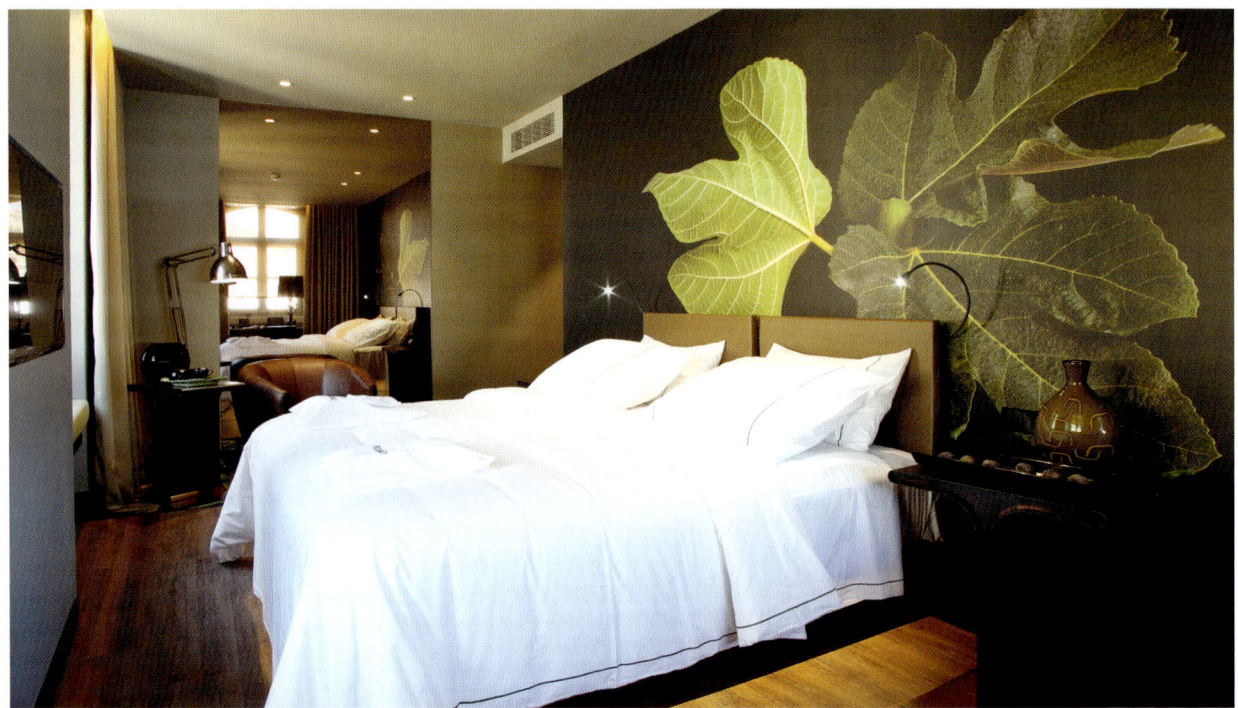

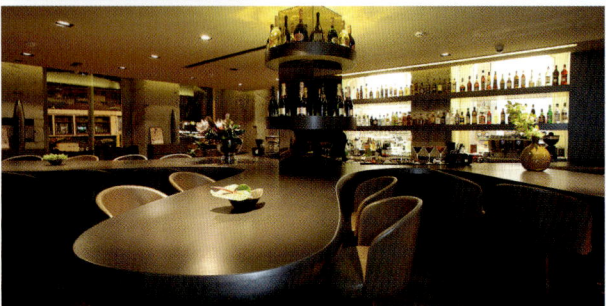
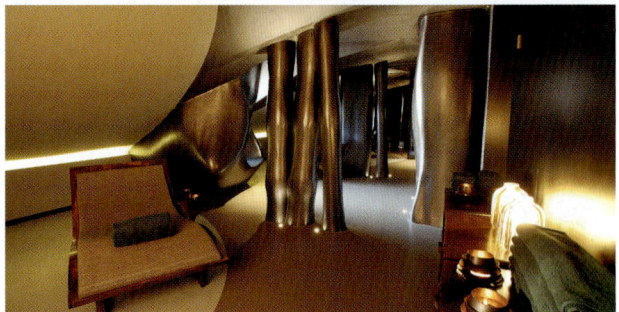

The Beautique Hotels Figueira

Quirky designer flair and relaxation in Lisbon

PRICE FROM:
€135

FEATURES:
Gym; Restaurant; Spa; Wheelchair access

ACTIVITIES:
Shopping; Sightseeing

NEARBY:
Alfama; Cascais; Estoril; Sintra

GETTING THERE:
Lisbon Airport

The Beautique Hotels Figueira is the hot new spot on the Lisbon hotel scene, a grown-up urban tree-house in Figueira Square in the historic heart of the city. Anyone who has been to this magnificent plaza will know there are very few trees here but as you step inside this 50-room retreat, prepare to be enveloped in its magical, forest-like interior. As you wind your way up through the eight cavernous floors, it feels like you're climbing a giant fig tree, thanks to interior designer Nini Andrade Silva's ingenious use of shape, texture and colour. Glossy gold walls and columns form the trunk from which rooms and spaces extend like branches, decked out in earthy tones and adorned with murals of leaves and fruit (that look good enough to eat). Don't miss the washbasins in the public bathrooms, which resemble a fig that's been cut in half. The large, beautiful rooms have astonishing attention to detail while Honra restaurant is rapidly becoming the dining place of choice in this smart part of town. But the cherry on the cake is right at the top of the "tree": a super-sweet spa that you'll be loath to leave.

☏ +351 21 049 2940
🌐 condenastjohansens.com/beautiquehotels
🏠 Praça da Figueira 16, 1100-241 Lisbon, Lisbon & Tagus Valley, Portugal

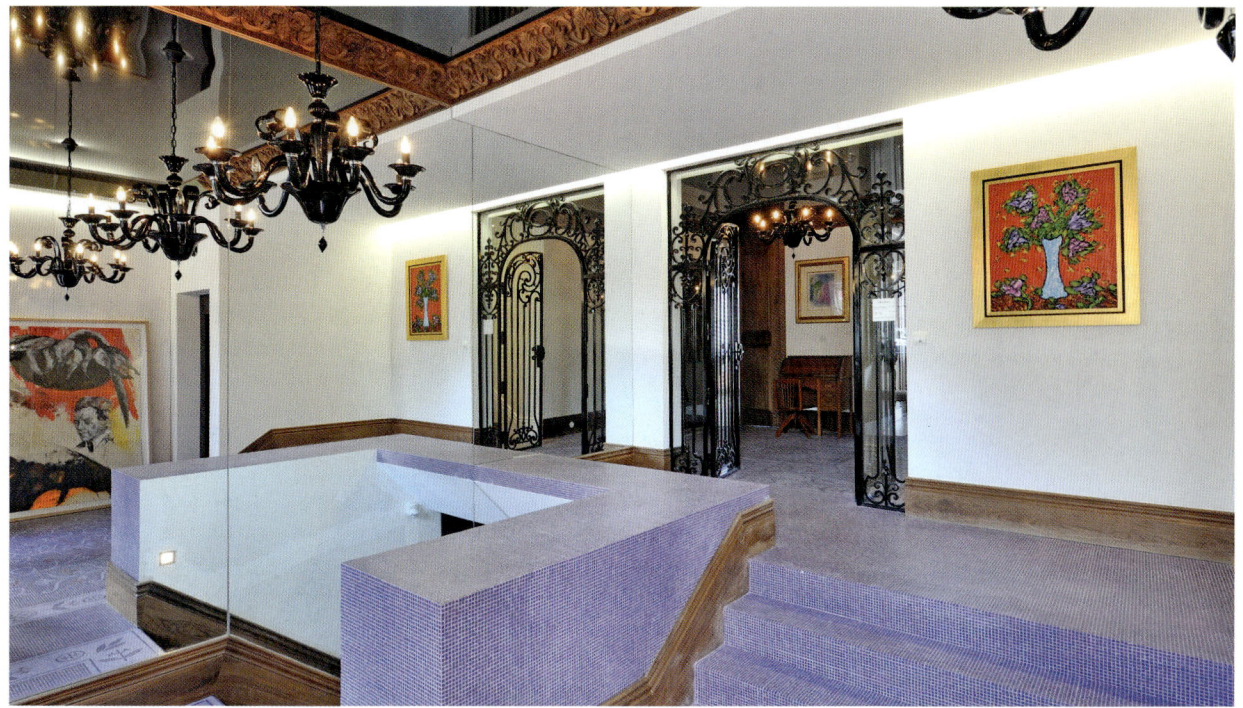

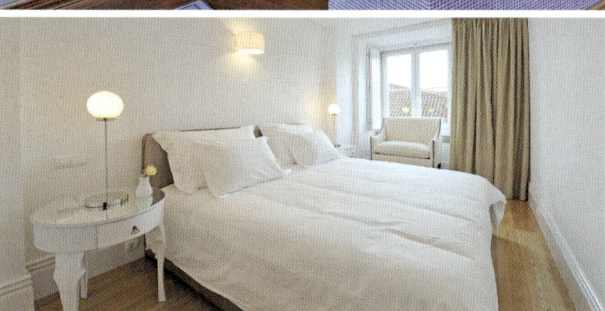
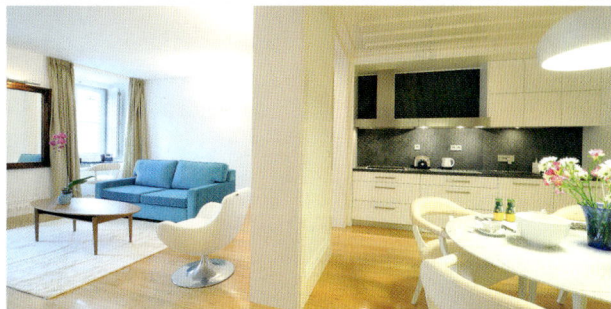

Chiado16-Premium Accommodation

Sumptuous suites and guest rooms in Lisbon's historic centre

Perched atop one of Lisbon's many hills is Chiado16-Premium Accommodation in, you've guessed it, the Chiado district. This is where the Hermes-toting crowd, theatre-going gang, cool café cats and band of bookworms all converge. Where the roads are paved with sophistication. A little shinier and newer than other parts of Lisbon, Chiado was the subject of a 10-year renovation programme (completed in 1998) following a devastating fire. Although unaffected, this 17th-century town house underwent a huge revamp and its entire interior was gutted and rebuilt into the swish Chiado16 that's now known and loved. Waiting for you inside is resident owner Heleen and her knowledgeable staff who'll equip you with helpful local info before leading you to your fuss-free, gracefully styled suite or room. Suites are so large (each spans an entire floor) they're more like apartments with kitchens, living areas and laundry rooms, with every one looking out to a picture-postcard view. If the thought of a tasty continental breakfast gets you up and at 'em in the morning then let Heleen know and she'll arrange for delivery to your door. And for a taste of Portuguese flavours, some tapas and local wine, take the few steps next door to Tágide restaurant.

PRICE FROM:
€156

FEATURES:
Family friendly; Sea views

ACTIVITIES:
Golf; Shopping; Sightseeing

NEARBY:
Belém Theatre; Alfama Old City; Estoril; Cascais; Sintra

GETTING THERE:
Lisbon Airport

+351 394 1616 ☎
condenastjohansens.com/chiado16 🌐
Largo da Academia Nacional das Belas Artes No 16 & 17, 🏠
1200-005 Lisbon, Lisbon & Tagus Valley, Portugal

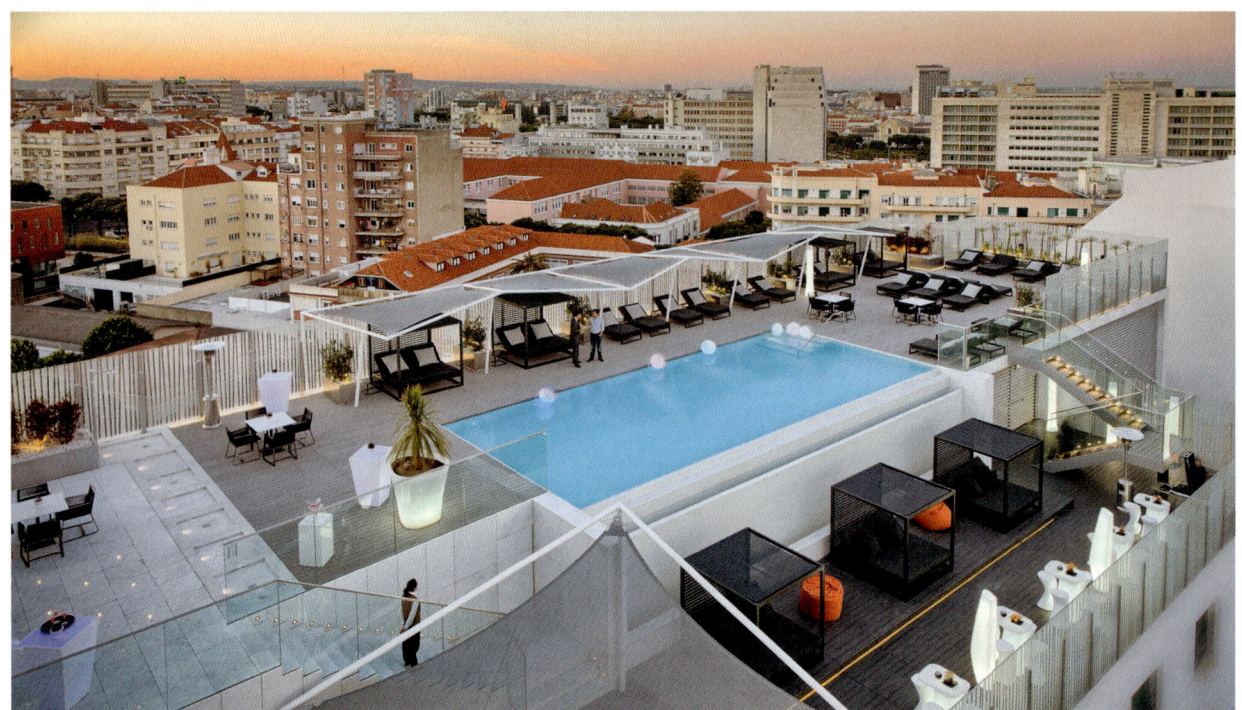

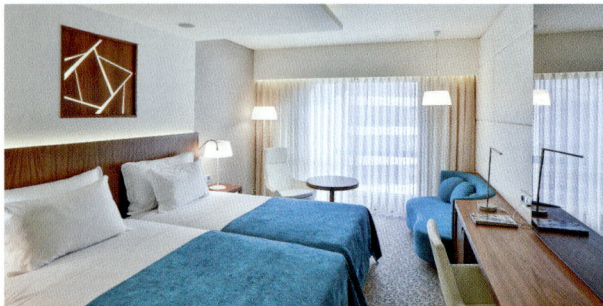
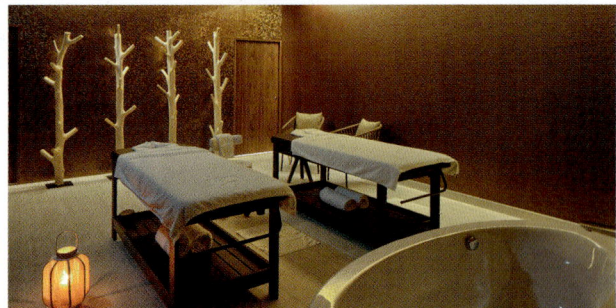

EPIC SANA Lisboa Hotel

On the cutting-edge of design and service in Lisbon

PRICE FROM:
€311

FEATURES:
Pool; Restaurant; Spa

ACTIVITIES:
Golf; Shopping; Sightseeing

NEARBY:
Amoreiras Shopping Centre; Eduardo VII Park; Avenida da Liberdade; Marquês de Pombal; Baixa-Chiado

GETTING THERE:
Lisbon International Airport; Rossio Railway Station; Parque Metro Station

EPIC SANA Lisboa Hotel is a breath of fresh air: edgy and glamorous. Setting new heights in personal service and comfort to Lisbon's luxury hotel scene, a smart crowd is attracted here for business and pleasure. The close proximity to the city's action, specifically the Eduardo VII Park and Amoreiras Shopping Centre, means that Lisbon's at your fingertips. Avenida da Liberdade is a hop, skip and jump away with São Jorge Castle just a five-minute drive. Inside, a retro-futurist design of muted colours, polished marble and gleaming glass are given warmth with artful dashes of blues, velvet seating and clever lighting. This is also the case in the Deluxe Rooms and Suites where neutral palettes are creatively contrasted against dark wood furnishings and electric blue elements. Added extras include an integrated sound system that can connect to your MP3 player. For a seriously spoiling stay opt for the Presidential Suite with kitchenette, two bedrooms and two bathrooms and visit the Sayanna Wellness spa and fitness centre. Mealtimes at EPIC SANA's Flor-de-Lis restaurant are an international affair and no stay is complete without a trip to the rooftop Upscale Bar, also home to the outdoor pool. Views from up here on the ninth floor stretch across to the River Tagus.

☎ +351 211 597 330
🌐 condenastjohansens.com/epicsanalisbon
🏠 Avenida Engenheiro Duarte Pacheco 15, 1070-100 Lisbon, Lisbon & Tagus Valley, Portugal

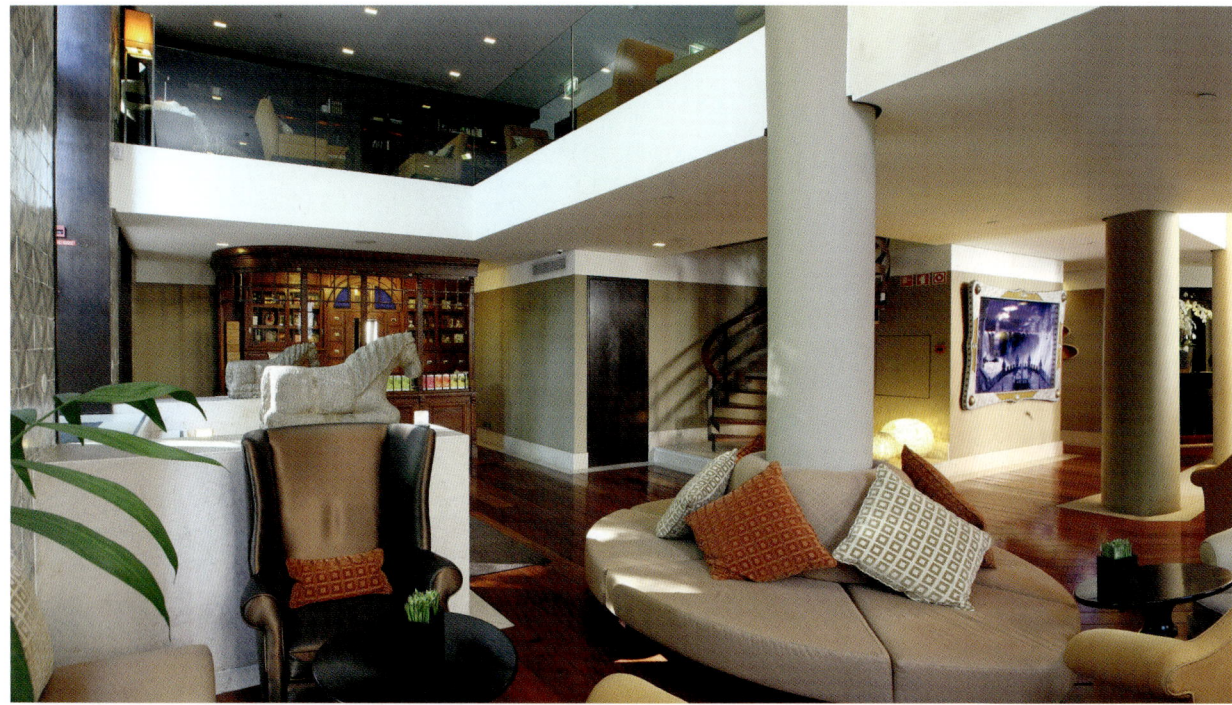

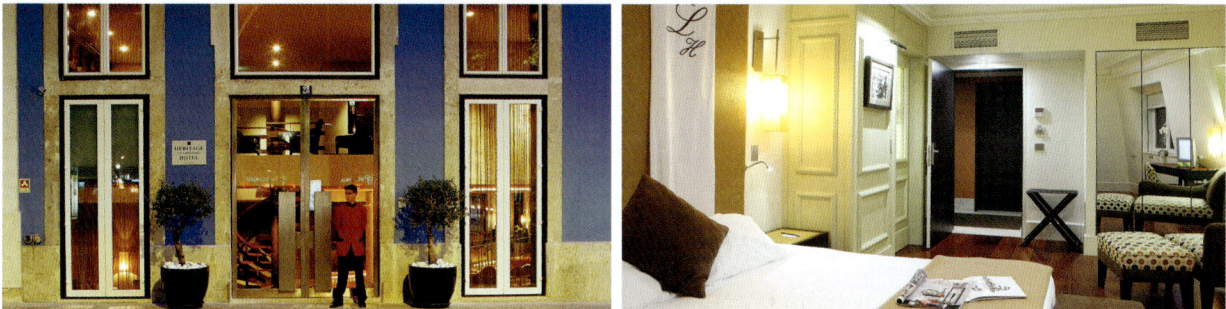

Heritage Avenida Liberdade Hotel

Lisbon palace turned refined 21st-century town house accommodation

You'll find this boutique gem hidden away in the heart of Lisbon. A bustling city packed with fun bars, great restaurants and museums, Heritage Avenida Liberdade Hotel is the perfect base from which to explore this historic hotspot. Step inside the antique wooden door and you'll find a smart, modern town house hidden behind the elegant 18th-century façade. Painstakingly restored with modern touches, this is a smart, contemporary, yet distinctly Portuguese idyll right on Avenida da Liberdade dotted with sculptures. The hotel couldn't be more central. From here you can effortlessly reach the city's museums, shops and all the must-see tourist sites. And come the evening, Heritage Avenida Liberdade Hotel is the ultimate comfortable retreat (and surprisingly good value) whose antique wooden tea station and attentive, discreet staff are on hand to brew up the perfect cup. Or you might prefer to prop up against the bar before exploring the fantastic range of Lisbon's restaurants and bars right on your doorstep.

PRICE FROM:
€167

FEATURES:
Pool; Wheelchair access

ACTIVITIES:
Golf; Shopping; Sightseeing

NEARBY:
Avenida da Liberdade; Restauradores Square and tram to Bairro Alto; Alfama

GETTING THERE:
Lisbon Airport

+351 213 404 040 ☎
condenastjohansens.com/avliberdade 🌐
Avenida da Liberdade 28, 1250-145 Lisbon, Lisbon & Tagus Valley, Portugal 🏠

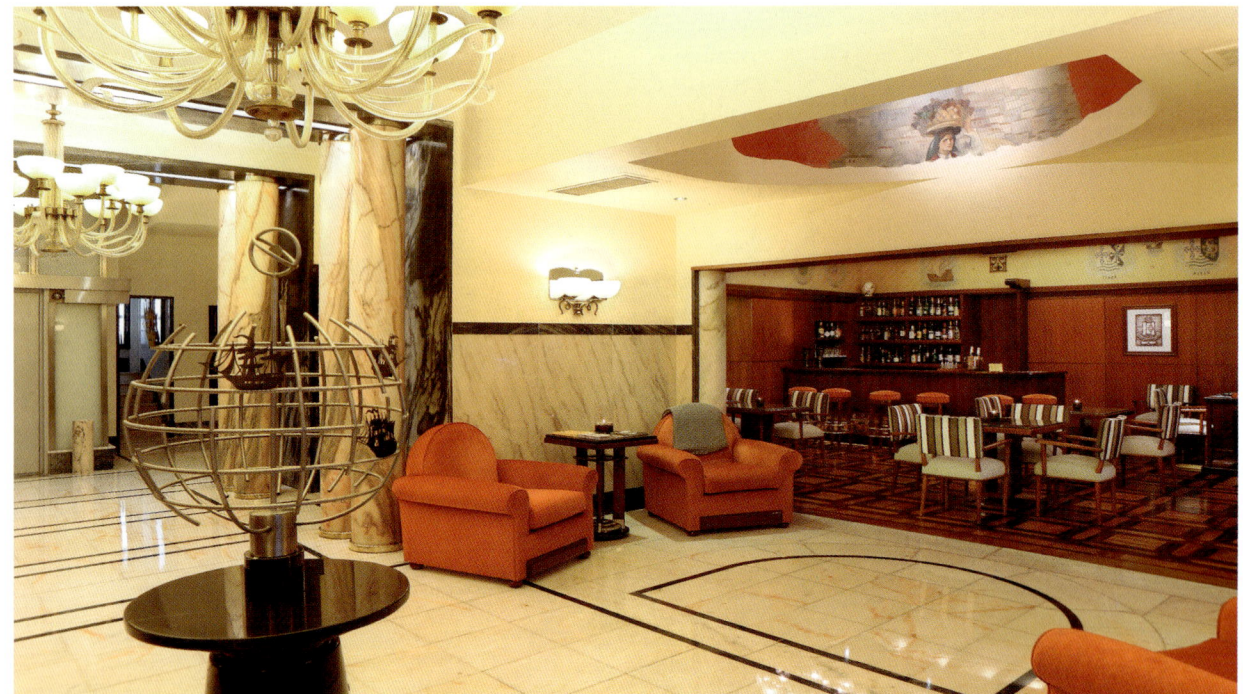

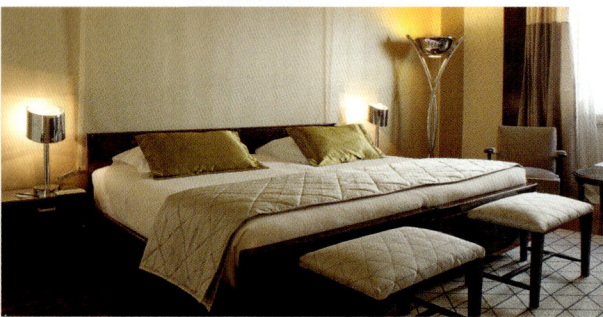

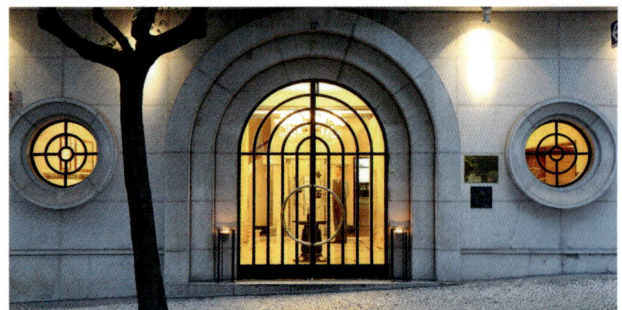

Hotel Britania

Fabulous art deco blast from the past in the heart of Lisbon

PRICE FROM:
€147

ACTIVITIES:
Golf; Shopping; Sightseeing

NEARBY:
Alfama; Avenida da Liberdade; Restauradores Square and tram to Bairro Alto

GETTING THERE:
Lisbon Airport

Tucked away on a quiet Lisbon street, yet moments from the buzz of Avenida da Liberdade, is the art deco brilliance of Hotel Britania. It's a museum piece and the only art deco building left standing in the city. Lovingly and carefully restored to all its 1940s glory, the marble sparkles in the lobby and the elegant, warm tones of the spacious bedrooms hark back to yesteryear. Hotel Britania is traditional, old fashioned and conservative in all the most charming of ways. Service is discreet and excellent, and the bar is the perfect place to sip a cocktail before heading out to Lisbon's hotspots. By day, Hotel Britania's location is hard to beat: Avenida da Liberdade, the city's main boulevard, world-class shopping, art galleries, museums and funicular railways waiting to whisk you to Lisbon's prettiest gardens and town squares, are all here. By night, Hotel Britania really comes into its own. Bairro Alto is only a few minutes away and come nightfall, this sleepy street turns into the vibrant heart of Lisbon's nightlife with every imagined type of entertainment on display including Fado. This hauntingly beautiful song will stay with you long after you leave.

☎ +351 21 31 55 016
🌐 condenastjohansens.com/britania
🏠 Rua Rodrigues Sampaio 17, 1150-278 Lisbon, Lisbon & Tagus Valley, Portugal

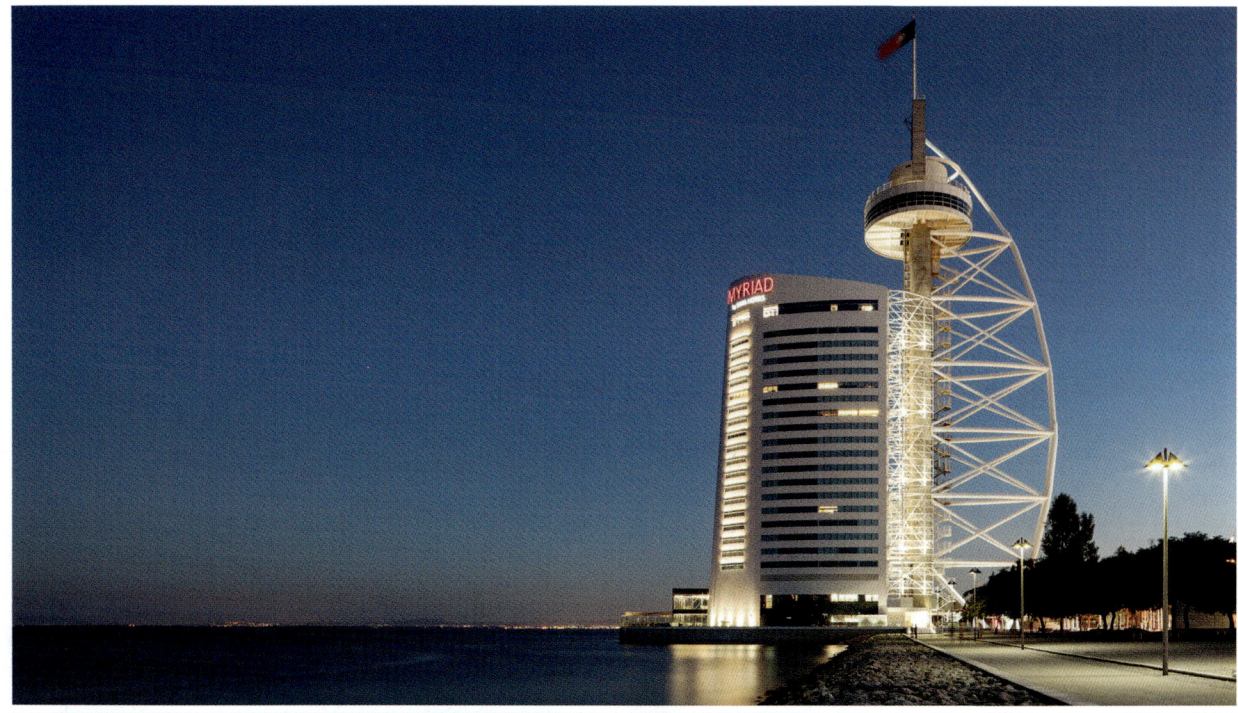

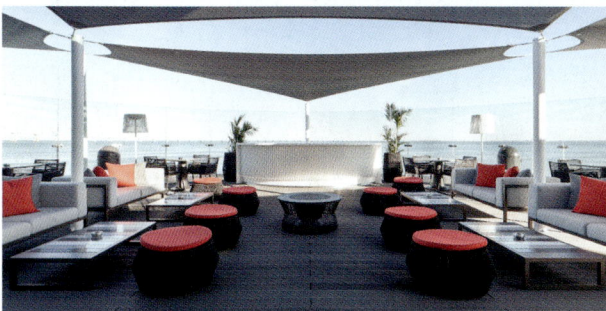
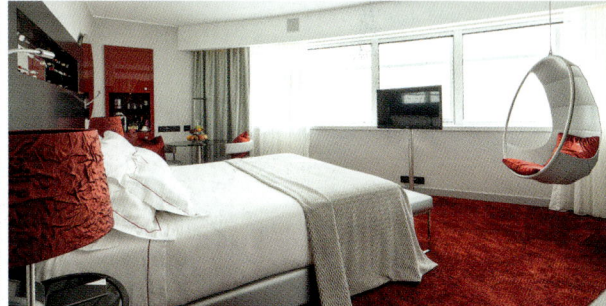

Myriad by SANA Hotels

Architectural and design innovation on the River Tagus

Myriad by SANA Hotels has you stepping back and looking up. Towering high beside, and partially on, Lisbon's River Tagus, it's a whacking-great feat of engineering brilliance that grabs your full attention. All at once glamorous and glossy, futuristic and artistic, its hallmark is matchless hospitality and spellbinding comfort. It's also an alternative Lisbon scene to the norm located within eastern Lisbon's Parque das Nações; a pleasure (and business) playground complete with gardens, a huge aquarium, casino, funicular and Virtual Reality Pavilion. The city's historical district is a just short drive away. As you first step into Myriad, the ground-breaking interior design has your eyes involuntarily darting upwards yet again (sorry neck) to the seemingly endless glass atrium dotted with light fixtures shaped like jellyfish. Up there (23-floors high) is the downright fabulous Sayanna Wellness SPA with panoramic views and techy accommodations ranging from deluxe rooms to the presidential suite. Try and book high and river viewing. But don't bypass the ground floor completely. This is where the fashionable River Lounge Restaurant & Bar is, at-the-ready to mix a cocktail and serve dishes with a Mediterranean flavour. Keep posted for: the hotly anticipated restaurant located at the top of the adjacent Vasco da Gama Tower promising a 360° view of the city.

PRICE FROM:
€210

FEATURES:
Family friendly; Gym; Restaurant; Sea views; Spa

ACTIVITIES:
Golf; Shopping; Sightseeing

NEARBY:
Lisbon International Fair; Pavilhão Atlântico; Vasco da Gama Shopping Centre; Lisbon Oceanarium; Lisbon Casino

GETTING THERE:
Moscavide Underground Station; Lisbon Orient Railway Station; Lisbon Airport

+351 211 107 600 ☎
condenastjohansens.com/myriad 🌐
Cais das Naus, Lote 2.21.01, 1990-173 Lisbon, Lisbon & Tagus Valley, Portugal 🏠

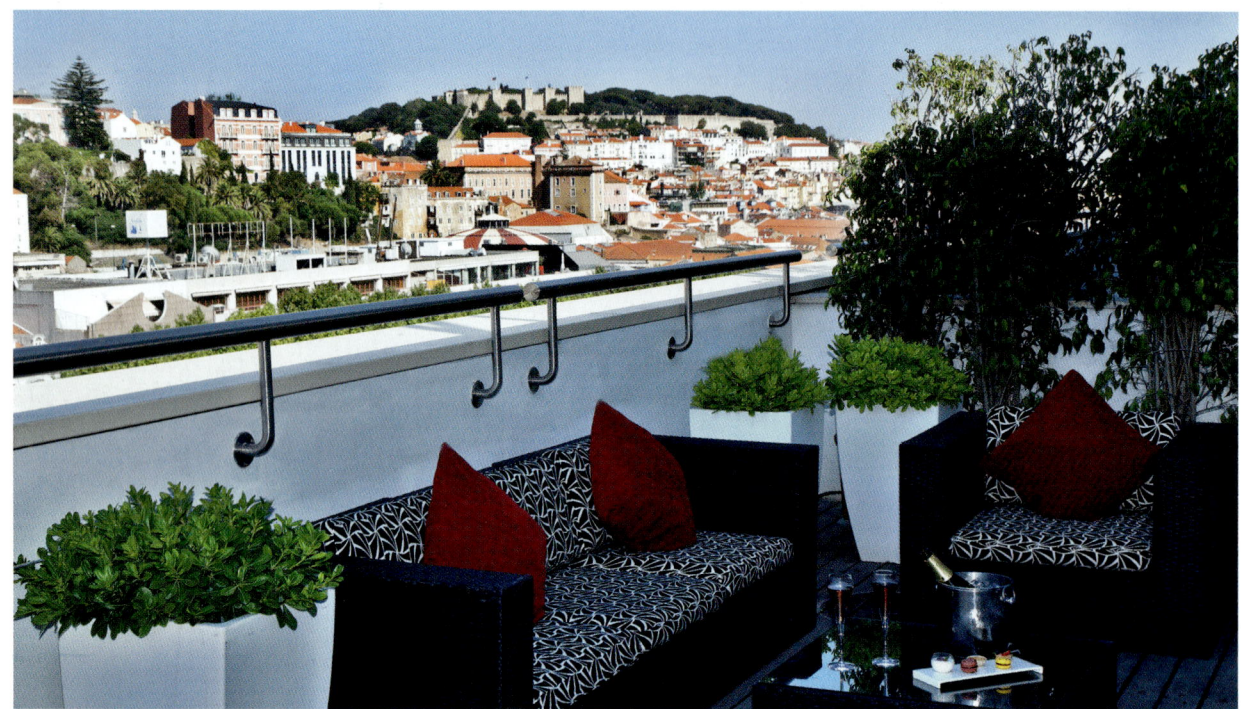

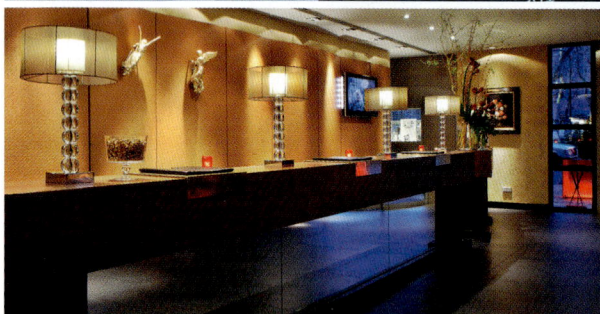

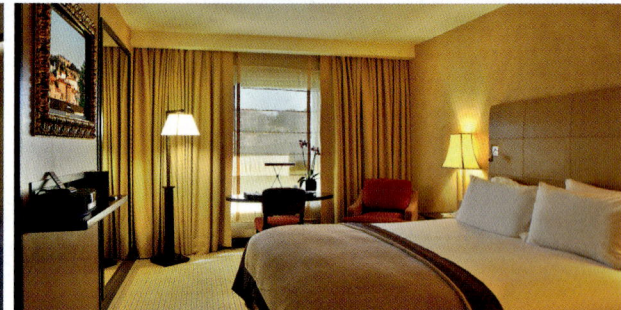

Sofitel Lisbon Liberdade

Lisbon does contemporary cool and city chic

PRICE FROM:
€160

FEATURES:
Gym; Restaurant; Wheelchair access

ACTIVITIES:
Golf; Shopping; Sightseeing

NEARBY:
Alfama Old City; Belém Tower; Estoril; Cascais; Sintra

GETTING THERE:
Lisbon Airport

From the moment you step into the handsome lobby of Sofitel Lisbon Liberdade you know you're in for a treat. Situated on the elegant, tree-lined Avenida da Liberdade in the heart of the city, its sleek and sexy palettes of scarlet, black and gold set against dark wood furnishings create a totally cool atmosphere. A cosiness permeates throughout the guest rooms (163 including 12 suites), each packed with personality and funky touches such as framed silhouettes by local artists. The trendy guest rooms are all high-tech, high style, kitted out in Bose sound systems, luxurious bathroom goodies and fit-for-royalty beds, which have proved so popular that there's now a brochure from which you can order your own. Situated in the smart part of town, Liberdade is steps from upscale stores such as Prada, Armani and Gucci (refuel with a wicked pastry from one of the area's many beckoning cafés) and within walking distance of top cultural spots including the 16th-century São Roque Church. Evenings are all about AdLib restaurant where Chef Daniel Schlaipfer presents Portuguese classics with a French twist with nights ending on a (cocktail) high at the welcoming lobby bar.

☎ +351 21 322 83 00
🌐 condenastjohansens.com/sofitellisbon
🏠 Avenida da Liberdade 127, 1269-038 Lisbon, Lisbon & Tagus Valley, Portugal

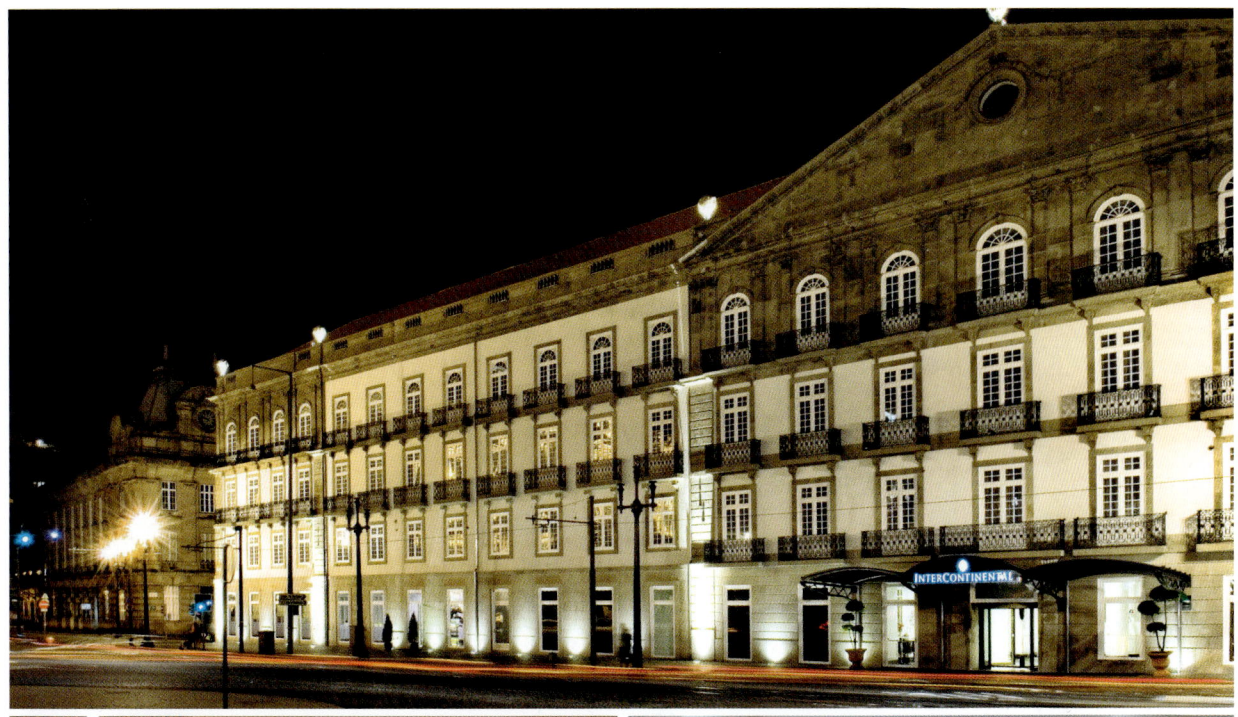

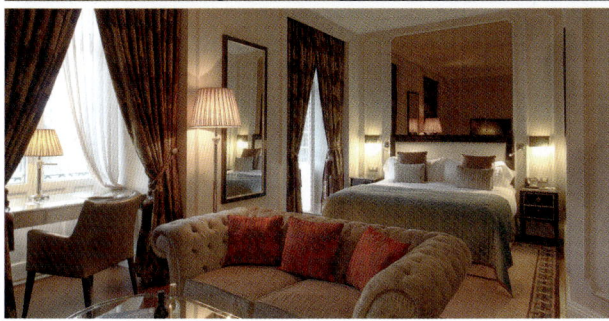
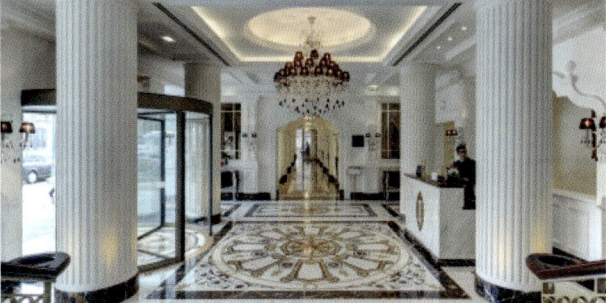

InterContinental Porto-Palácio das Cardosas

Palatial grandeur and professional hotel service in fascinating Porto

Once a sleepy city best known for the River Douro and its port production, today, Porto is a vibrant, cosmopolitan playground brimming with outstanding collections of contemporary art, imposing architecture and delectable cuisine. Right in the beating heart of the old town, the InterContinental Porto-Palácio das Cardosas occupies a block on the majestic Praça da Liberdade. Built as a monastery in the 15th century and converted into a palace three centuries later, it's surely one of the grandest places to stay in the city with unfurling views of the tree-lined Avenida dos Aliados (some of the best of which are found at the hotel's fine dining restaurant, Astoria). The elegant interiors are predominantly white with swathes of marble, crystal chandeliers and parquet floors, and the 105 rooms have high ceilings, damask drapes and, if you're lucky, framed glass doors that open onto a terrace overlooking the square. Call on Porto-Palácio das Cardosas's switched-on concierge for sightseeing suggestions, which may include a boat ride down the river, a francesinha (steak and cured ham toastie oozing with melted cheese and boozy tomato sauce) or strolls through the vertiginous streets at sundown.

PRICE FROM:
€135

FEATURES:
Family friendly; Gym; Restaurant; Wheelchair access

ACTIVITIES:
Shopping; Sightseeing; Walking

NEARBY:
Ribeira District; Boat trips on Douro; Bolhão market; Port and wine tastings

GETTING THERE:
São Bento Railway Station; Leixões Port; Porto - Francisco Sá Carneiro Airport

+351 22 003 5600 ☎
condenastjohansens.com/portopalacio 🌐
Praça da Liberdade 25, 4000-322 Oporto, Oporto & Northern 🏠
Portugal, Portugal

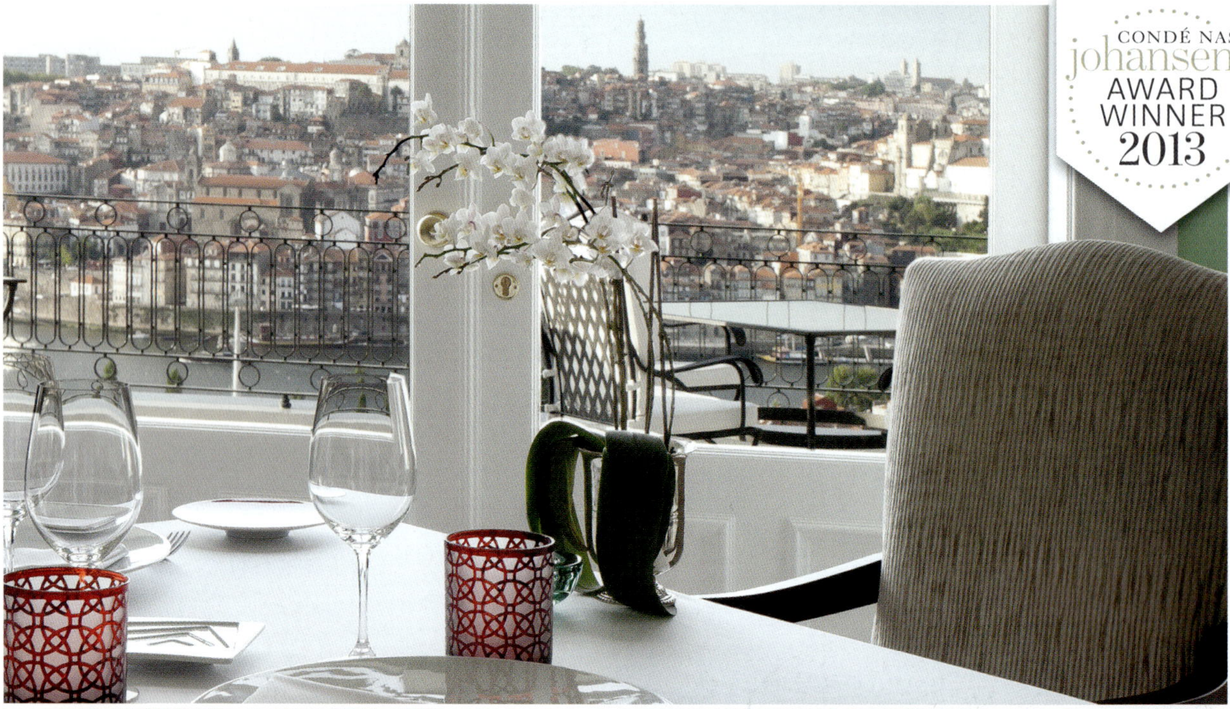

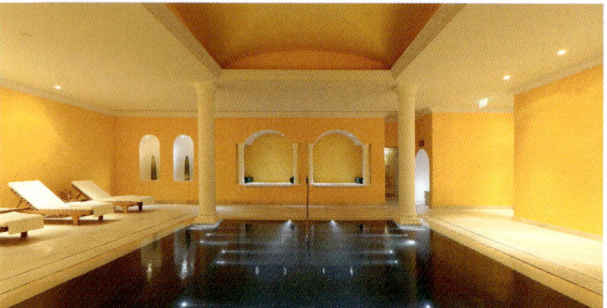

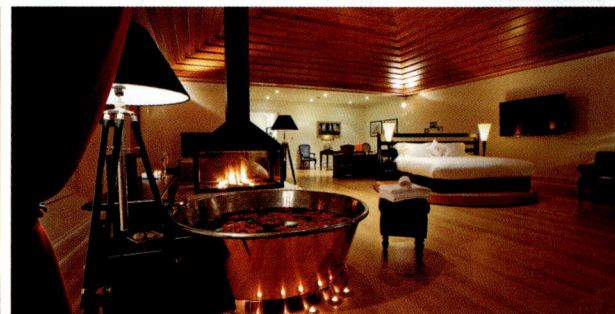

The Yeatman Hotel

Unique wine hotel overlooking buzzing Porto

PRICE FROM:
€195

FEATURES:
Family friendly; Gym; Michelin Starred restaurant; Pool; Spa

ACTIVITIES:
Cycling; Golf; Sightseeing

NEARBY:
Pinhão; Viana do Castelo; Boat trips on Douro; UNESCO historic city of Porto; UNESCO Guimarães

GETTING THERE:
Devesas Railway Station; Leixões Port; Porto - Francisco Sá Carneiro Airport

☎ +351 220 133 100
🌐 condenastjohansens.com/theyeatman
🏠 Rua do Choupelo (Santa Marinha), Vila Nova de Gaia
4400-088, Oporto & Northern Portugal, Portugal

UNESCO protected Porto may be a lesser-known Portuguese tourist hub than say the Algarve or Lisbon but not to the Port aficionado. Porto is a significant plot on the vineyard map. From the mountainous upper Douro Valley (also a World Heritage Site) barrels of the sweet elixir are brought to Porto's neighbouring city, Vila Nova de Gaia, where it's stored in lodges for ageing and blending. Standing amidst these Port lodges on the steep bank above the River Douro is The Yeatman, a wine hotel and spa. Wine hospitality is at The Yeatman's core, expressed in its Michelin-Starred gourmet restaurant, 24-hour wine bar, vinotherapy spa and staggeringly stylish bedrooms where paintings and objets d'art pertaining to specific wineries adorn the spaces. Every room looks out to the city of Porto and river below with terraces opening out to the scene. Quirky touches such as Master Suites 007 and 008's barrel beds add some individual style. Mesmerising views accompany meals at the restaurant whose menu is a celebration of traditional Portuguese flavours enhanced with an innovative twist and wine pairings. Try the tasting menus to discover Portugal's finest flavours, and grace Caudalie's Vinothérapie® Spa to benefit from the grape by-products in extensive treatments.

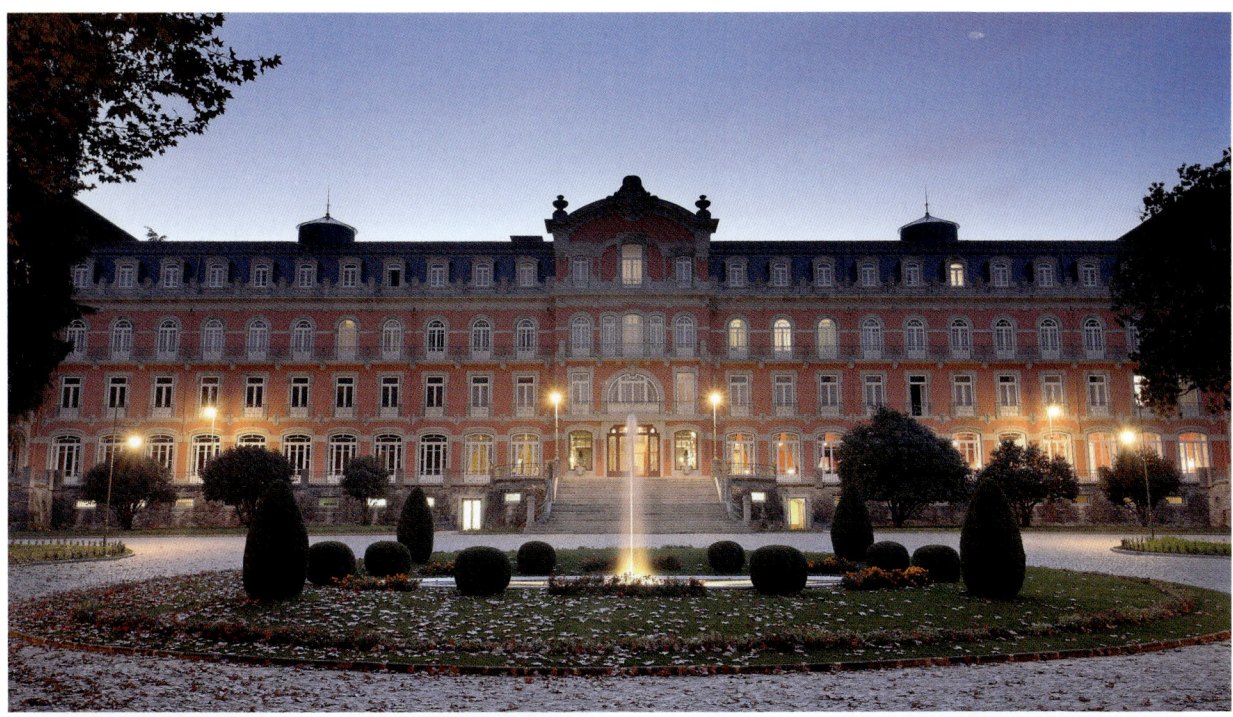

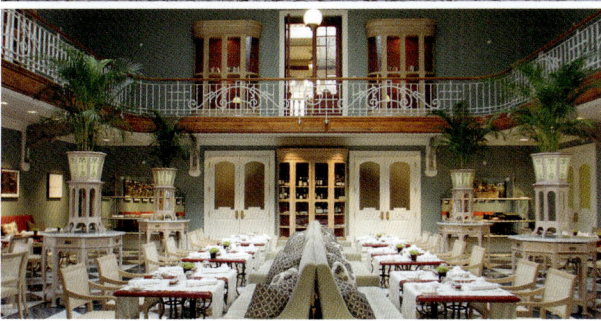

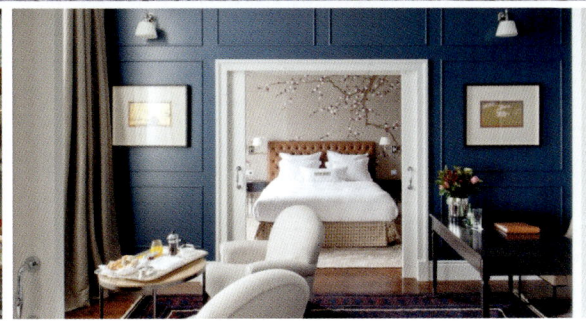

Vidago Palace

Restored grand palace in the peaceful town of Vidago

Three years since Vidago Palace's mammoth revamp was completed, its five-star reputation is unquestionably re-established. The spa loving and golf mad sophisticates' palatial playground surpassed many expectations when it re-opened in 2010. The Palace's 20th-century glory days set the bar high but with the creative minds of interior architects Jose Pedro Lopes Vieira and Diogo Rosa Lã, and heralded architect Alvaro Siza Vieira (mastermind behind the spa and Club House), the challenge was met with gusto. By propelling the Palace's existing attributes into the 21st-century, everything feels fresh whilst remaining authentic. Everything's meticulously finished yet sumptuously comfortable. But it was possibly the re-invention of Vidago's spa that caused most excitement and like an unexpected curveball, the winning strike went left field: no Belle Époque traditions here but futuristic, pure-white minimalism. Also hotly anticipated, the injection of new life into the Mackenzie Ross-designed golf course became an expansion: a par 72 course with golf academy, driving range and putting greens. Its informal Club House Bar & Restaurant is one of four culinary options including Salão Nobre Dining Room where traditional northern Portuguese (organic) fare is served in the former grandiose ballroom. Breakfasts are an elaborate buffet affair in the light and airy Winter Garden.

PRICE FROM:
€135

FEATURES:
Family friendly; Gym; Pool; Restaurant; Spa

ACTIVITIES:
Golf; Tennis; Walking

NEARBY:
Chaves; Porto; Vidago natural spring water fountain; Old city of Chaves; Douro River

GETTING THERE:
Porto - Francisco Sá Carneiro Airport

+351 276 990 920 ☎
condenastjohansens.com/vidago 🌐
Parque de Vidago, 5425-307 Vidago, Oporto & Northern Portugal, Portugal 🏠

Spain

Please go to condenastjohansens.com/spain

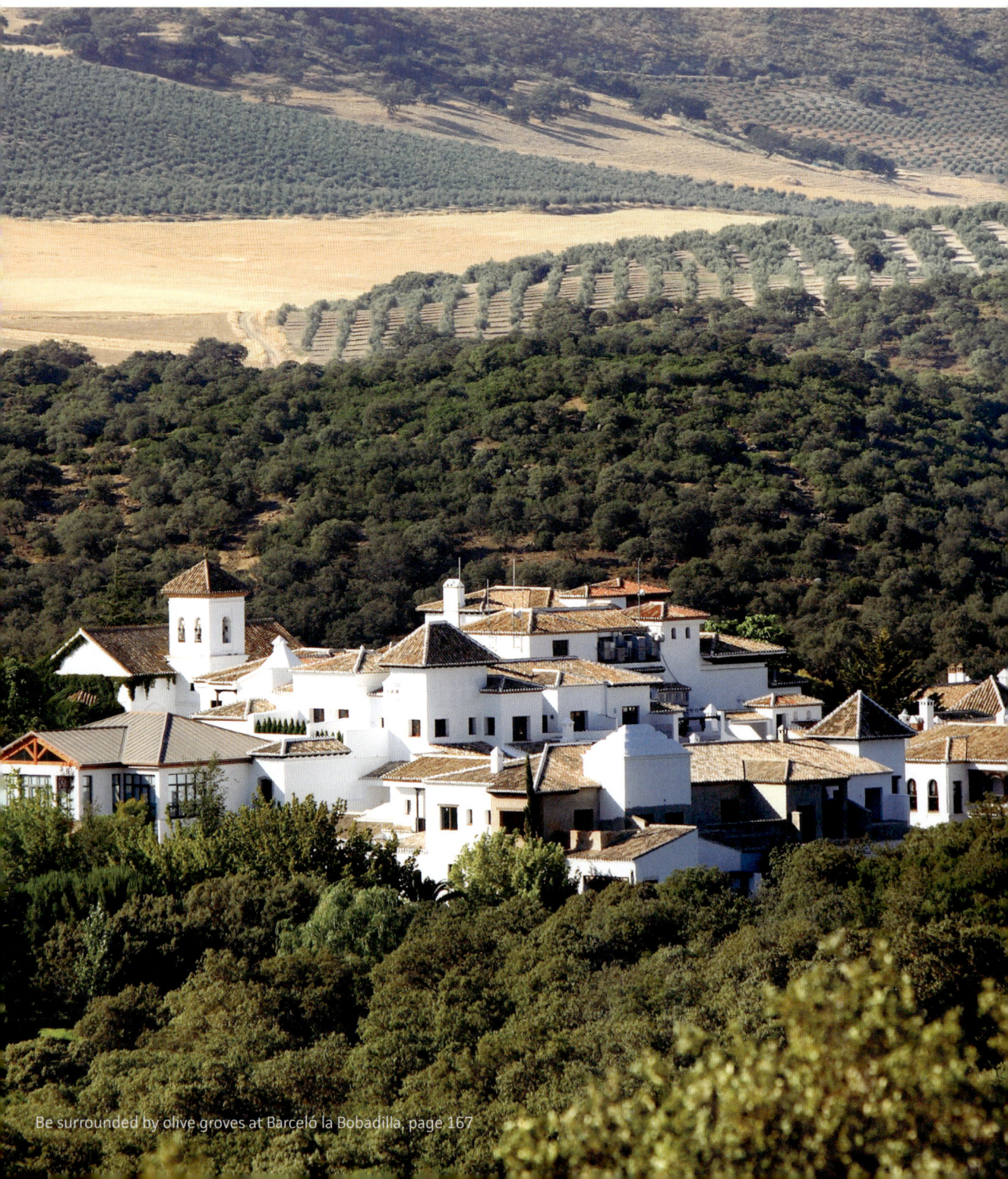

Be surrounded by olive groves at Barceló la Bobadilla, page 167

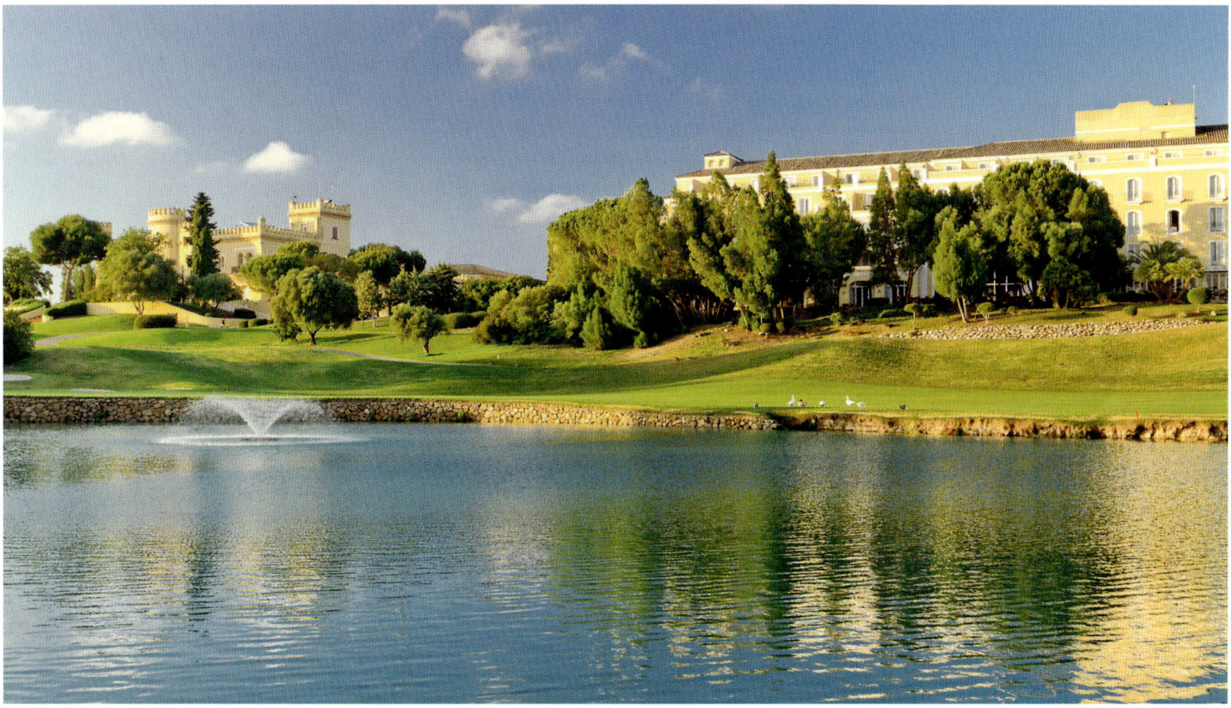

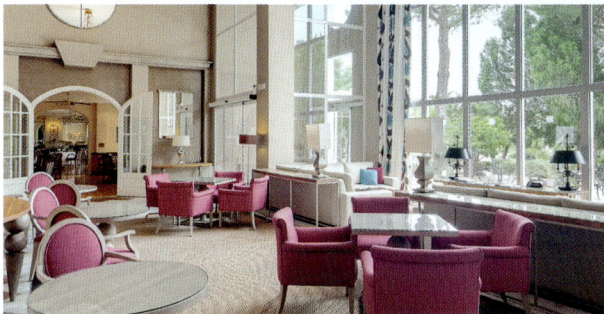

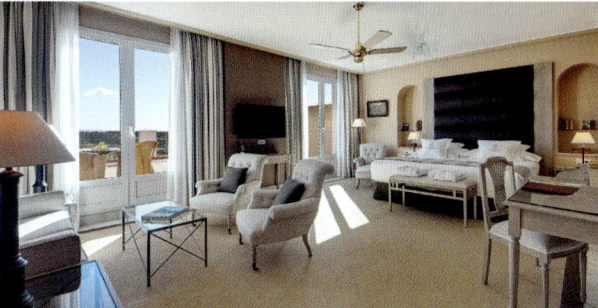

Barceló Montecastillo Golf & Sports Resort

The premier resort hotel in Cádiz with it all

Rising from the hills, 10 minutes outside the Spanish city of Jerez, you can't miss Barceló Montecastillo Golf & Sports Resort: just look for the ochre-coloured castle that anchors this 400-acre estate. And keep your eyes peeled for the 18-hole Jack Nicklaus-designed golf course that unfurls before it. Or perhaps the race circuit next door, which hosts the Spanish MotoGP will be the first thing you see. Yes, sports are a big deal here and as a guest you enjoy free, unlimited time on the challenging golf course. The hotel also has pools, tennis courts, a running track and two football pitches and don't be surprised if you spot an international footballer sitting next to you at dinner in the El Lagar restaurant (many train here) possibly tucking into a meal from the healthy gourmet menu created from the finest flavour-packed ingredients. Recently given a grand facelift, Barceló is beautiful, outside and in, with swathes of marble, designer lighting and pared-down décor throughout with 124 rooms and suites, and secluded villas scattered within the grounds. Activities aside, Barceló has r&r in the bag. Peace pervades the hotel and there's a tranquil spa (and the curiously sounding "sleep-enhancing bedding"). Don't miss: the flamenco dancing and bullfighting in the city and a trip to the sherry bodegas.

PRICE FROM:
€99

FEATURES:
Family friendly; Pet friendly; Pool; Restaurant; Spa

ACTIVITIES:
Golf; Horse riding; Tennis

NEARBY:
Jerez de la Frontera; Pueblos Blancos; El Puerto de Sabnta María; Sanlúcar de Barrameda; Sevilla

GETTING THERE:
Jerez Airport; Seville Airport; Gibraltar Airport

+34 956 151 200 ☎
condenastjohansens.com/barcelomontecastillo 🌐
Ctra Arcos Km 9.6, 11406 Jerez de la Frontera, Cádiz, 🏠
Andalucía, Spain

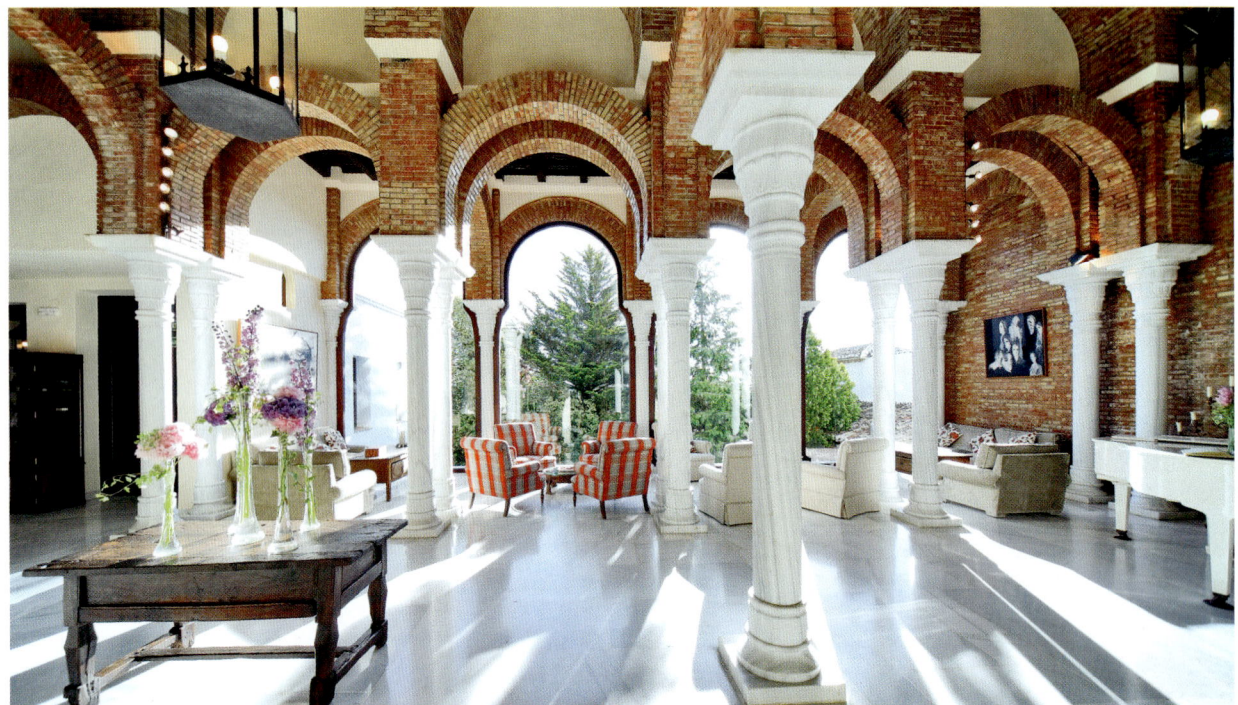

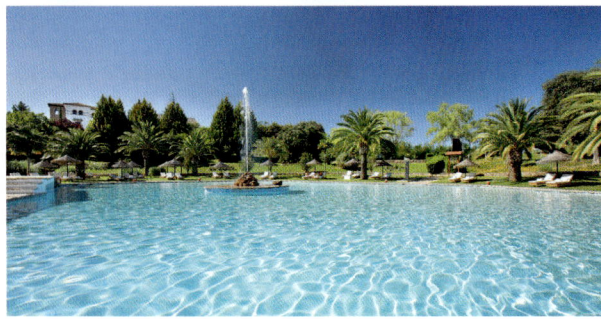

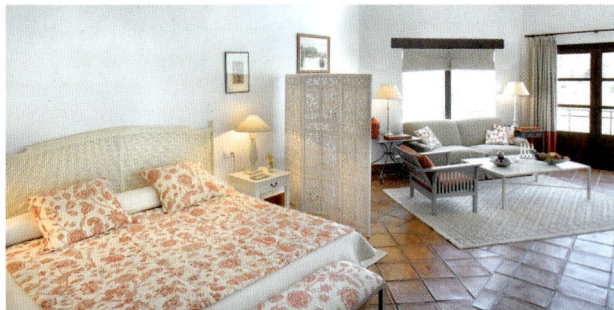

Barceló la Bobadilla

Whitewashed village-style resort in the pretty Granada Hills

PRICE FROM:
€210

FEATURES:
Family friendly; Pool; Restaurant; Spa

ACTIVITIES:
Cycling; Horse riding

NEARBY:
Picasso Museum; Alhambra de Granada; Mezquita de Córdoba; Seville; Costa del Sol

GETTING THERE:
Granada Airport; Málaga Airport

☎ +34 958 32 18 61
🌐 condenastjohansens.com/bobadilla
🏠 Finca La Bobadilla, Ctra Salinas - Villanueva de Tapia, (A-333) Km 65.5, 18300 Loja, Granada, Andalucía, Spain

The Alhambra in Granada has been wowing travellers for centuries and is a must-visit when staying in your very own palatial enclave: Barceló la Bobadilla. High in the Andalucían hills surrounded by a verdant Edenic setting, la Bobadilla is an elegant, Nazari-style retreat with sun-drenched rooms, fabulous food and top-notch facilities. No two guest rooms and suites are alike, however, all have gardens or balconies that provide extra space for families and private outdoor space for romancing couples. Children are particularly well looked after at Barceló la Bobadilla in the Mini Club or children's pool while parents take full advantage of the U-Spa. A spacious collection of peaceful rooms, Turkish baths and Finnish saunas, the spa practises a varied range of therapies from water to steam treatments. Come mealtime and three equally wonderful restaurants provide differing atmospheres and cuisines: informal, relaxed lunches by the pool at Mirador; delicious Spanish and regional cuisine at El Cortijo; and international and traditional flavours at the formal La Finca. Plus, a new gourmet healthy option full of goodnes is now available, designed by a nutrionist (more about pure and simple balanced food rather than low-calorie food).

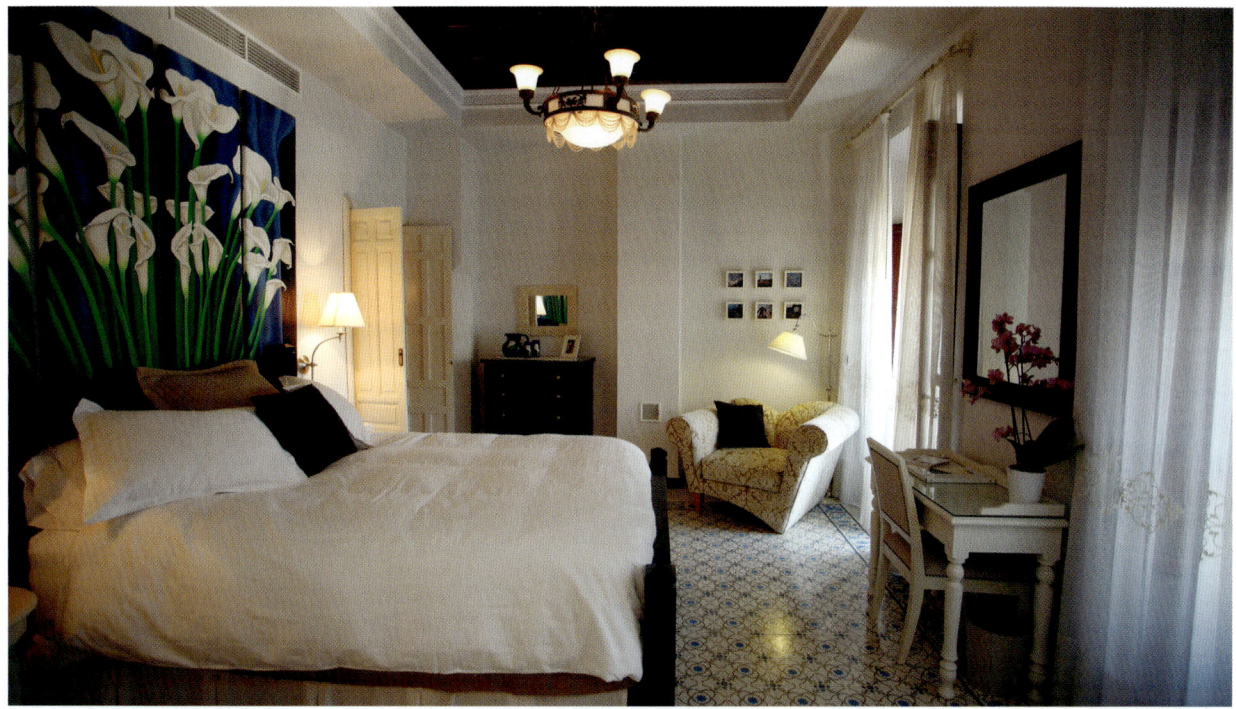

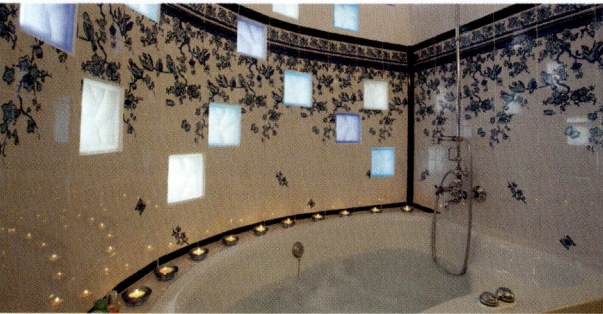
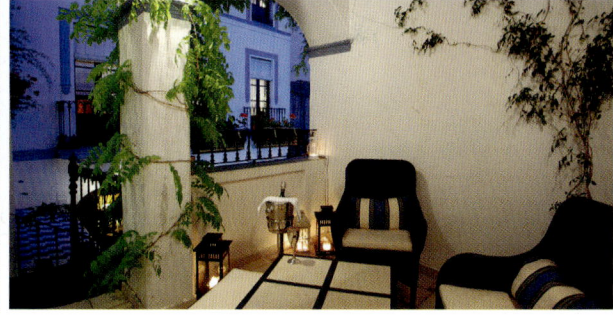

La Casa Noble

Adults-only Andalucían B&B packed with cosy corners

An hour north of Seville, the town of Aracena is a beautiful base for exploring Andalucía. And at its centre is La Casa Noble, a turn-of-the-century, art-nouveau bolthole - the super-cosy, ultra-comfortable second home you dream of. Its individually decorated rooms are simply gorgeous with standout features such as original fireplaces and superb reproduction furniture. (Mariposa, a romantic suite complete with Jacuzzi, hand-painted tiles and leafy arcaded patio is the one to book for the ultimate sexy sojourn.) However, there are NO tvs in sight because it's all about the art of conversation here, meeting fellow guests over evening tapas and making new friends. Breakfasts of pancakes dripping with maple syrup are served on a terrace with the hilltop castle and church in the distance. Head to Obra, the basement bar, for an apéritif before hitting a restaurant in town - just ask owner Melanie Denny to give you the insider's scoop on the best places to go. Beyond La Casa Noble, there's horse riding, mountain biking and hiking on offer, and a visit to the Cavern of the Marvels; Aracena's underground system of caves and lakes must be on your "to do" list. Add to that: sampling jamón Iberico in the local bodegas, taking cooking and cheese-making classes, and visiting the local art galleries and historical places of interest. The only problem is fitting it all in!

PRICE FROM:
€195

FEATURES:
Wheelchair access

ACTIVITIES:
Horse riding; Walking

NEARBY:
Seville; Natural Park - Sierras of Aracena & Peaks of Aroche; Gruta de las Maravillas (limestone caves); Original Rio Tinto Mine

GETTING THERE:
Seville Airport; Faro Airport

+34 959 127 778 ☎
condenastjohansens.com/lacasanoble 🌐
Calle Campito 35, 21200 Aracena (Huelva), Andalucía, Spain 📮

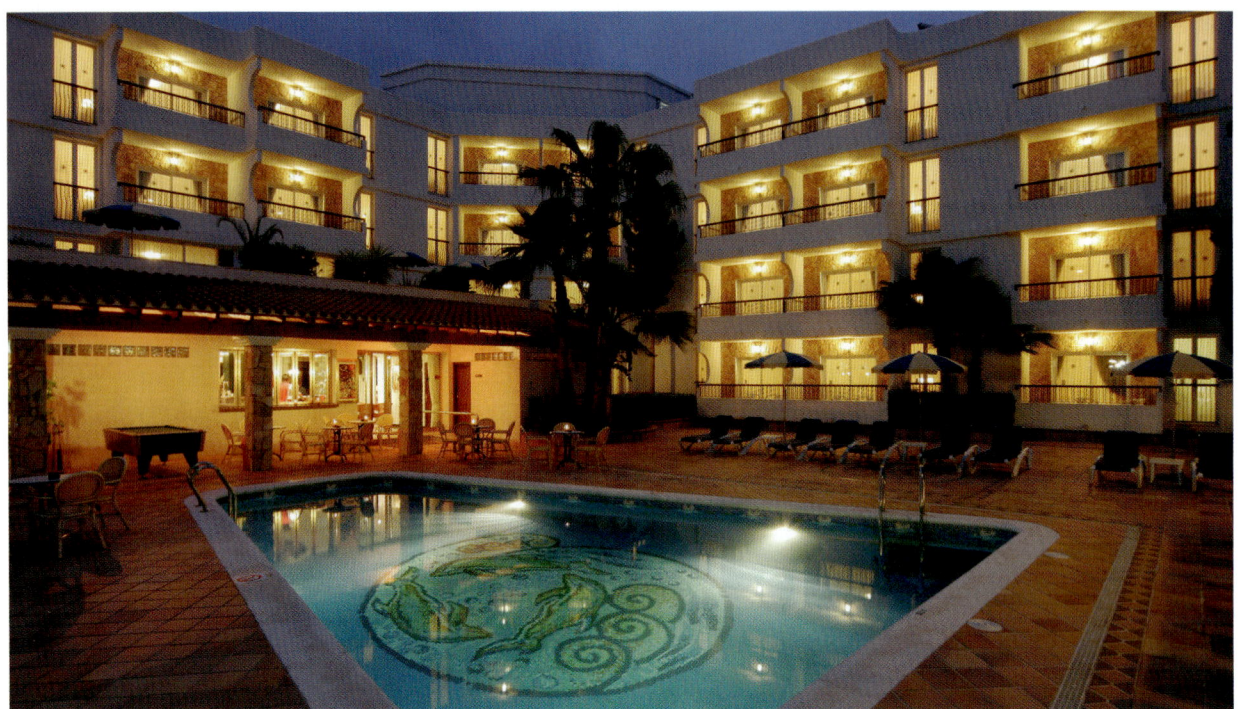

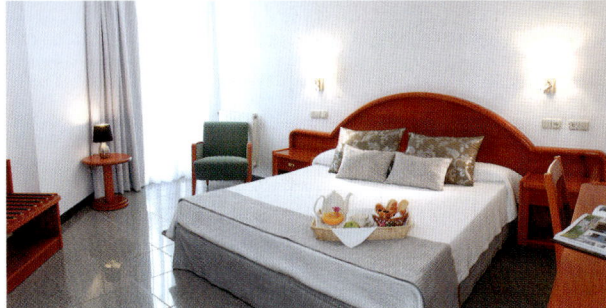

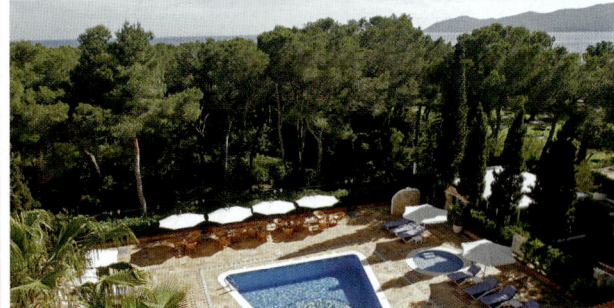

S'Argamassa Palace Suite Hotel

All-suite retreat in Ibiza's enchanting pine forest

PRICE FROM:
€135

FEATURES:
Gym; Pool; Restaurant; Sea views; Spa

ACTIVITIES:
Golf; Horse riding; Water sports

NEARBY:
Old Town; Golf Club of Ibiza; Cala Pada beach; Nightclubs

GETTING THERE:
Ibiza Airport

Set against the royal blue backdrop of cloudless skies, S'Argamassa Palace Suite Hotel, Ibiza, is the ideal destination for exploring this stunning island. Only a few minutes from the bustling city of Santa Eulalia (and great shops), pine trees surround this oasis of calm with just 24 blissfully luxurious suites, each one naturally lit and with their own terrace or balcony. Go for a stroll after your buffet breakfast, enjoyed as you bask in the warming sun, then head to Cala Pada beach located just moments away. But for some adventure further afield just ask the staff who are always full of useful suggestions. Personal service that's all about attention to detail is their forte. Recently, the hotel underwent an extensive renovation with nothing but comfort and relaxation in mind. And the new addition of Nikki Beach Club is its exclusive adults-only facility offering pure white sunbeds and exotic cocktails on tap while the children are occupied with their own separate pool and entertainer with boundless energy. Come mealtimes, the à la carte restaurant whips up a medley of mouth-watering Mediterranean dishes whose mini ensaimadas are unmissable.

☎ +34 971 330 271
🌐 condenastjohansens.com/sargamassa
🏠 Avenida S'Argamassa 82, 07840 Santa Eulalia del Río, Ibiza, Balearic Islands, Spain

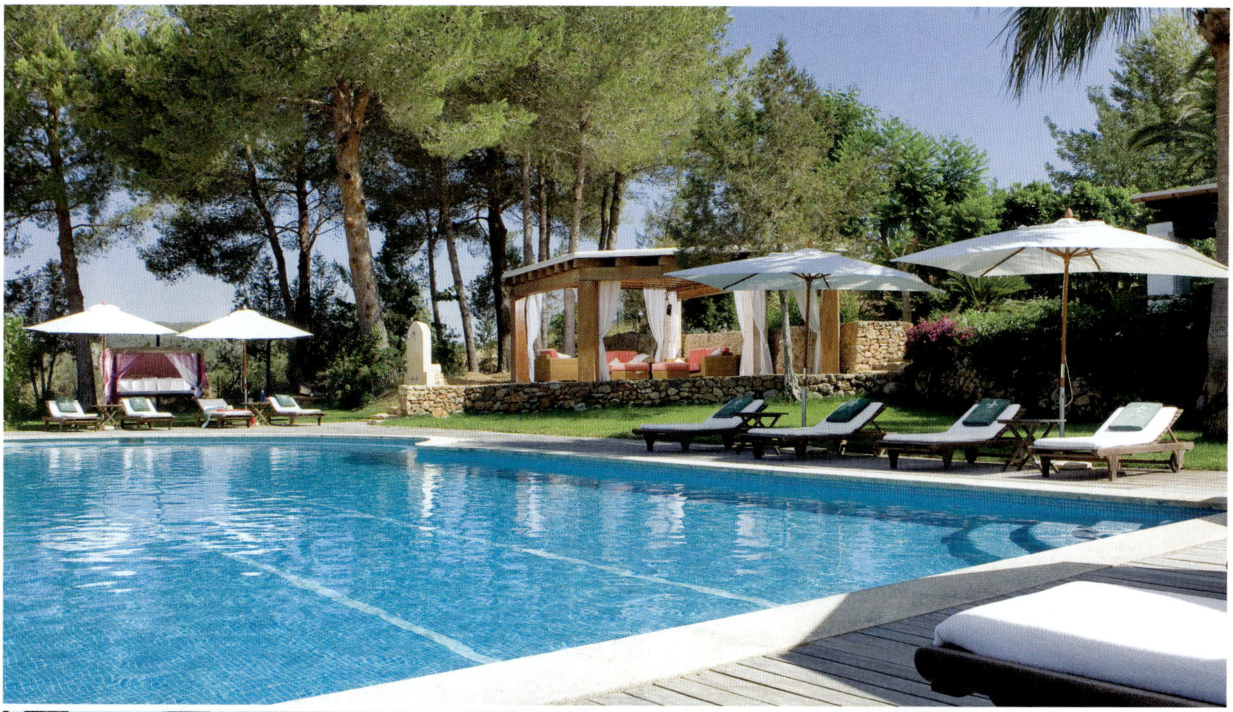

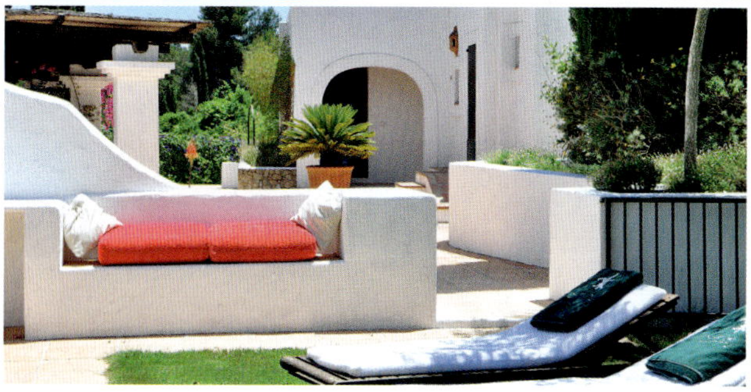

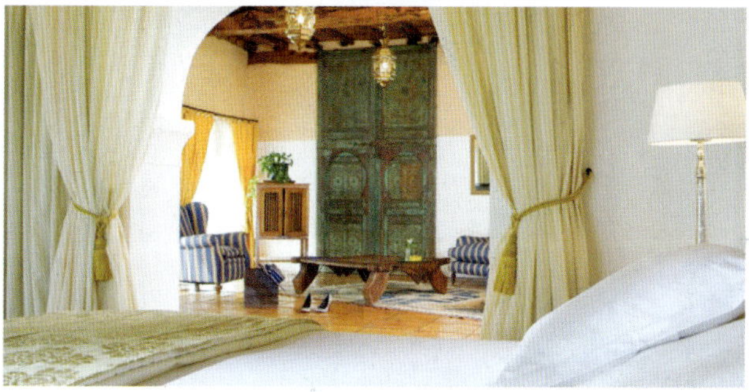

Cas Gasi

Ibizan colour, sizzle and luxury

A former country house turned boutique hotel, Cas Gasi in Santa Gertrudis, Ibiza, is one of those up-your-sleeve places you save for the end of the summer (but tell very few about). It's low key loveliness nested right in the thick of this beautiful island is totally discreet. Get off the beaten track, up into the hills and flop by the pool of this chilled-out escape to hear your body sing with relief and your skin glow a little more. Surrounded by pine forests, olive groves and organically-fed veggie patches with almond, fig and carob trees trickling down the hillside, Ibiza's Cas Gasi is bursting with all the best spoils of the Med. Nowhere is this more true than in the utterly exclusive restaurant where the ingredients are seasonal, packed with flavour and determined by produce grown at Cas Gasi's very own organic plot. The relaxed and at-home vibe is a favourite among celebrity guests - when not in Balearics' boltholes of their own, Jade Jagger and Kate Moss are huge fans of it here - and no wonder when the intimate 10 rooms and suites are this cosy and comfortable. Each one with their own character, uniquely decorated in a rustic Spanish theme filled with cool terracotta-tiled flooring, striking fabrics and warming chintz-a-copia.

PRICE FROM:
€303.60

FEATURES:
Pet friendly; Pool; Restaurant

ACTIVITIES:
Cycling; Golf; Water sports

NEARBY:
Santa Gertrudis; St Rafael; Santa Eulàlia; San Antonio; Hippy market in San Carlos

GETTING THERE:
Ibiza Airport

+34 971 197 700 ☎
condenastjohansens.com/casgasi 🌐
Camino Viejo de Sant Mateu s/n, 07814 Santa Gertrudis, 🏠
Ibiza, Balearic Islands, Spain

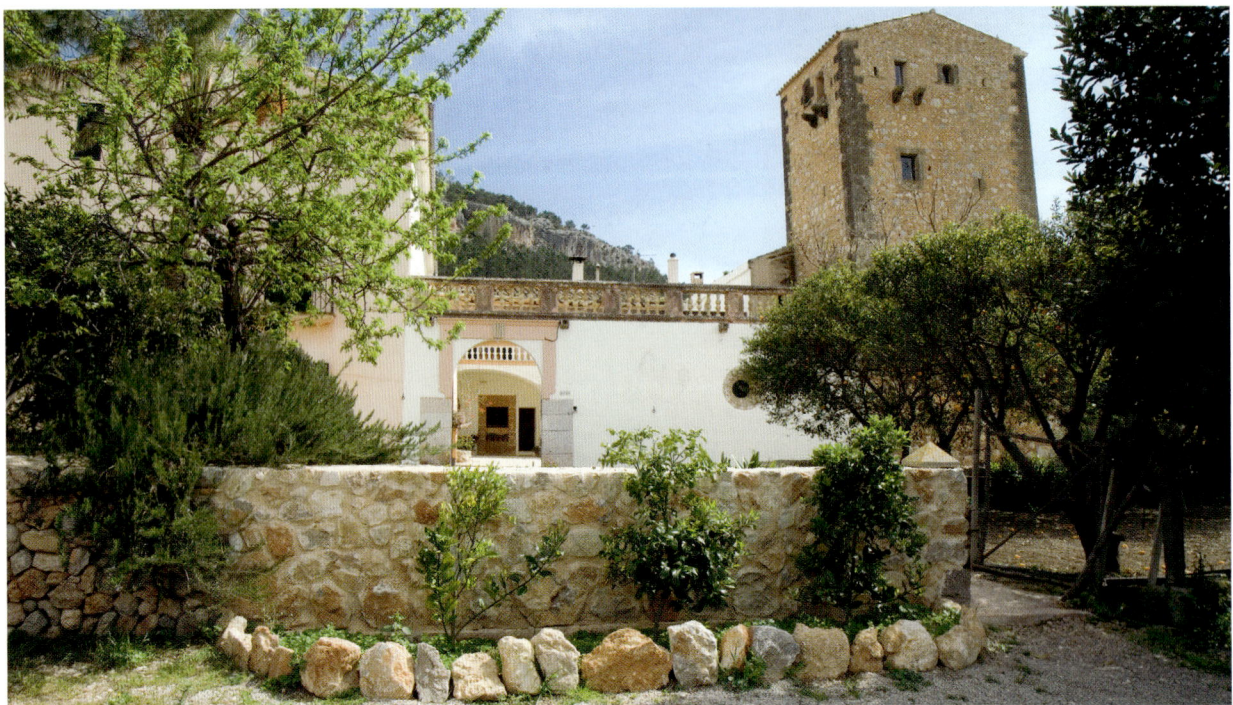

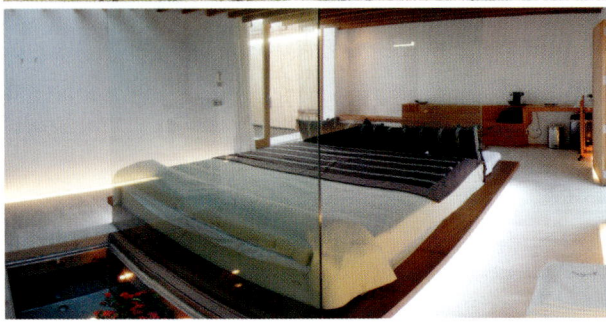

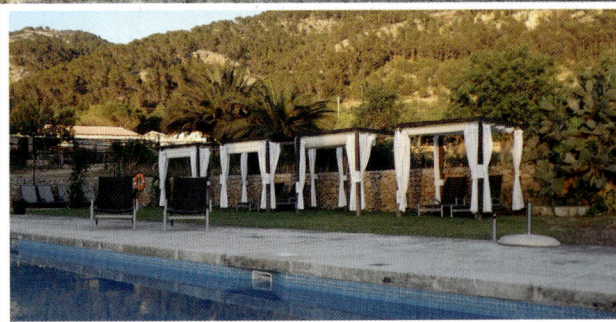

Hotel Son Esteve

Rural Mallorca at its peaceful best

PRICE FROM:
€185

FEATURES:
Family friendly; Pool; Restaurant

ACTIVITIES:
Fishing; Golf; Walking

NEARBY:
Golf Andratx; Sant Elm beach; Camp de Mar beach; Mini Folies Beach Club; Santa Ponsa Golf Club

GETTING THERE:
Palma de Mallorca Airport

There's no mistaking you're in the Mallorcan countryside at Hotel Son Esteve, Andratx. Almond trees, roaming sheep and birdsong surround this gorgeous finca. Serene, rural chic interiors behind the thick stone walls are equally as delightful while suites in the converted outhouse are jaw-droppingly beautiful. Beg, steal or borrow to stay in one! You'll love the minimal Japanese-inspired aesthetic with glass walls, slatted teak and outdoor showers on secluded terraces. Your host Bernat is rightly proud of his rustic abode and greets you like a personal guest. Epic tapas-style breakfasts of cheeses, meat pies, fruit and custard tarts set you up for the day and be sure not to miss the chance of Bernat cooking for you. He loves the land and embraces the slow pace of life here, and keeps his dishes (served in the vaulted dining room) earthy and delicious. Teaming up with two prestigious Mallorcan cellars means that the wine is remarkable too. Should you feel in the mood for some adrenaline-pumping action, you can scoot off to play tennis or some golf, or hang out with the yachting fraternity at Port Andratx. Otherwise, pull up a sun lounger and lie back to relax and become as ripe and luscious as a Son Esteve olive!

☎ +34 655 572 630
🌐 condenastjohansens.com/sonesteve
🏠 Camí C'as Vidals 42, 07150 Andratx - Mallorca, Balearic Islands, Spain

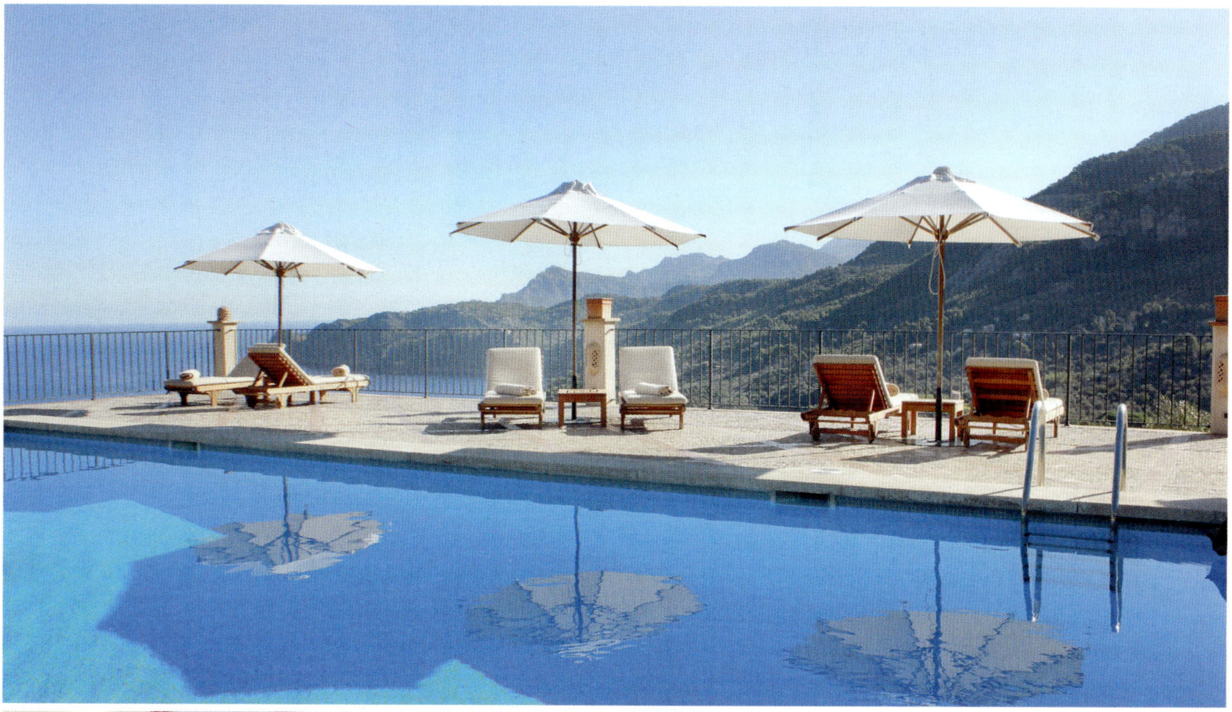

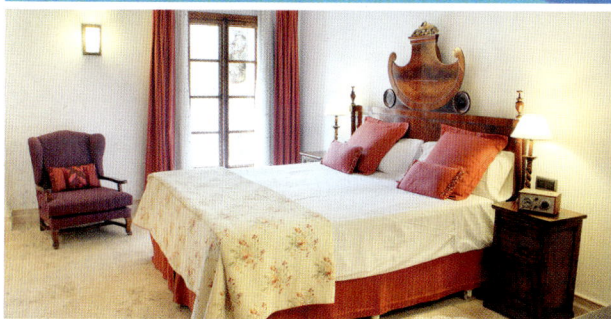
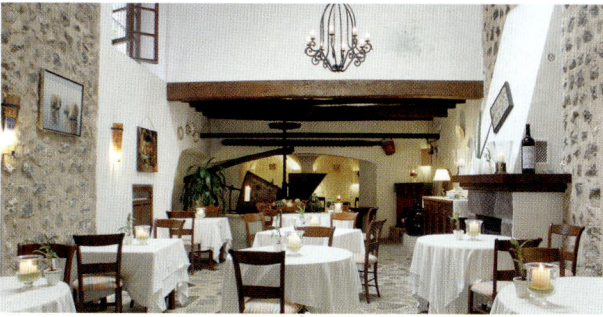

SA Pedrissa

Going green with Spanish finesse in Deià, Mallorca

Attracting literary, artistic and musical talents for decades, Deià village on Mallorca's northern cliff edge is inherently inspiring. English poet, novelist and scholar Robert Graves certainly thought so (a resident for many years) and from the moment you catch sight of the Balearic Sea views, rugged Deià Cove and strategically placed casas along the cliffside, there's no stopping the superlatives from flowing. SA Pedrissa looks out to all this beauty, tucked in between Deià and Valldemosa (Mallorca's two most visited villages) and secluded by olive and pine trees. It's an adults-only retreat (16 and over) with traces of its previous life as farm and home to the Archduke Ludwig Salvator of Austria still intact. The Archduke was a passionate conservationist and his visionary principles continue to be upheld by SA Pedrissa; a staunch advocate of sustainability and eco-tourism. The water you'll use will be heated by solar energy and reused to water the garden. Organic waste fertilises the soil and local purveyors supply both the hotel and restaurant. Ingredients are so fresh that Chef's Mediterranean flavours (seafood/fish from the sea below, fine wines from Mallorca and the mainland) will have your taste buds in a frenzy. So, to your suite or double room for some R&R where natural light fills the airy spaces splashed with bright colours; some have a whirlpool bath and panoramic views.

PRICE FROM:
€375

FEATURES:
Pool; Restaurant; Sea views

ACTIVITIES:
Cycling; Sightseeing; Walking

NEARBY:
Deià; Valldemosa; Port de Sóller; Palma de Mallorca

GETTING THERE:
Palma de Mallorca Airport

+34 971 63 91 11 ☎
condenastjohansens.com/sapedrissa 🌐
Carretera Valldemossa – Deià, 07179 Deià, Mallorca, Balearic 🏠
Islands, Spain

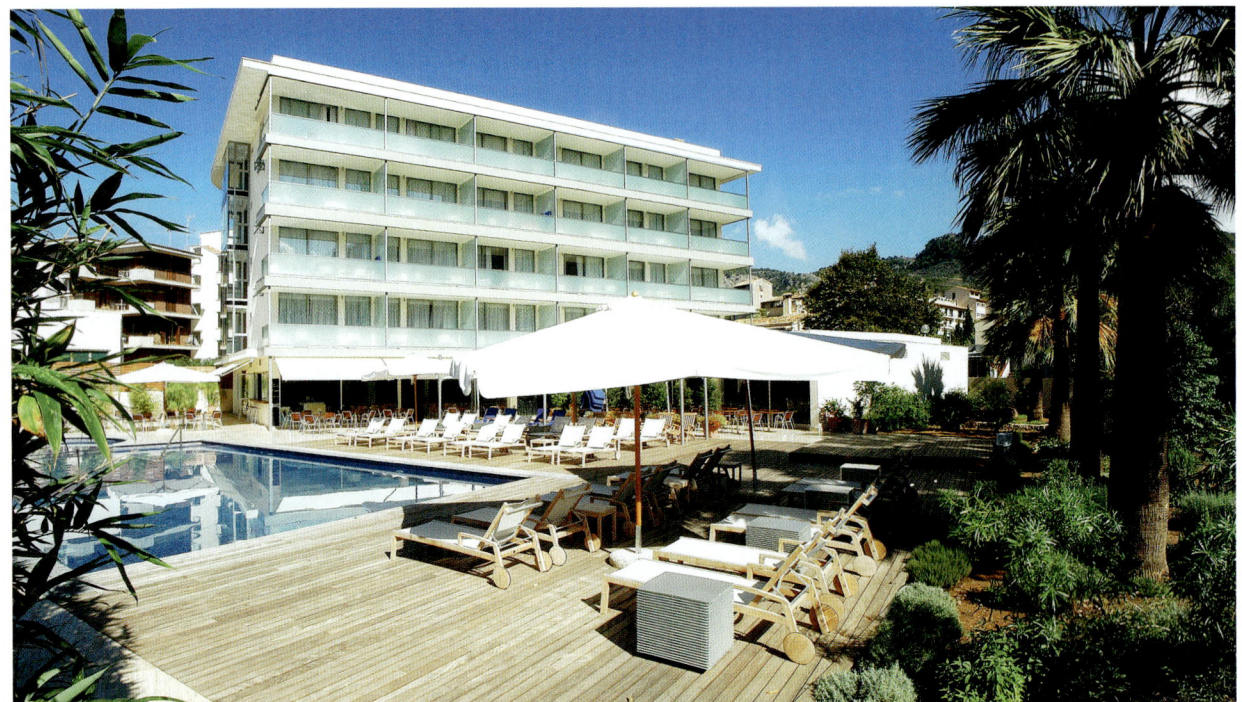

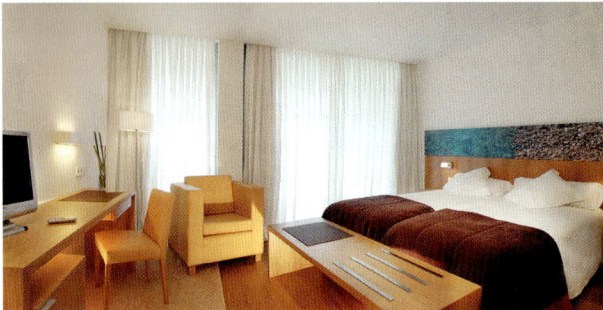

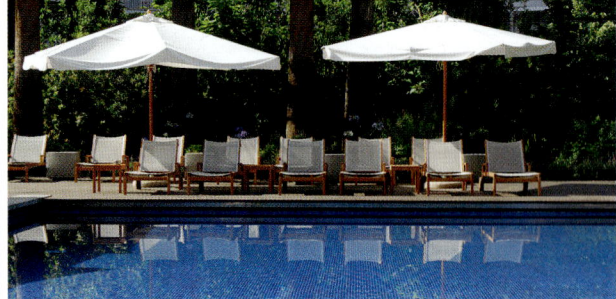

Aimia Hotel

Minimalist Mallorcan beach-side retreat

PRICE FROM:
€195

FEATURES:
Gym; Pool; Restaurant; Sea views; Wheelchair access

ACTIVITIES:
Sightseeing; Walking; Water sports

NEARBY:
Sóller; Deià; Valldemossa; Palma; Hiking

GETTING THERE:
Palma Airport

☎ +34 971 631 200
🌐 condenastjohansens.com/aimia
🏠 Santa Maria del Camí, 1 07108 Puerto de Sóller, Mallorca, Balearic Islands, Spain

Puerto de Sóller is one of Mallorca's lesser-known treasures. A wonderfully quiet village resort in a beautiful horseshoe bay at the base of the verdant Serra de Tramuntana. The marvellously modern Aimia Hotel sits confidently in this enviable location, minutes from the beach and metres from its main esplanade. Rooms at Aimia are spacious, smart and pleasingly unfussy. All clean lines, muted tones and clever lighting with glorious views of the mountains and the sparkling Mediterranean Sea (many have balconies). Perfect for peace-seekers, this is a place for alfresco living: breakfasting on the impressive poolside terrace, lazing on a sunbed, taking a siesta in the sun, walking along white-sand beaches and amidst citrus groves. A trip on the 100-year-old tramway to Sóller is a worthwhile day out too. (Knowledgeable staff will happily recommend treks, cultural spots and gastronomic delights). But back at the hotel, business meetings are in session and pampering is in process at Aimia Hotel's Spa. Equipped with a sauna, Turkish bath, gym, Jacuzzi, cyclonic showers and treatment rooms, pure bliss is the order of the day here. The hotel's Airecel Restaurant offers up an excellent blend of traditional Mallorcan cuisine and contemporary Mediterranean flavours.

CONDÉ NAST johansens AWARD WINNER 2013

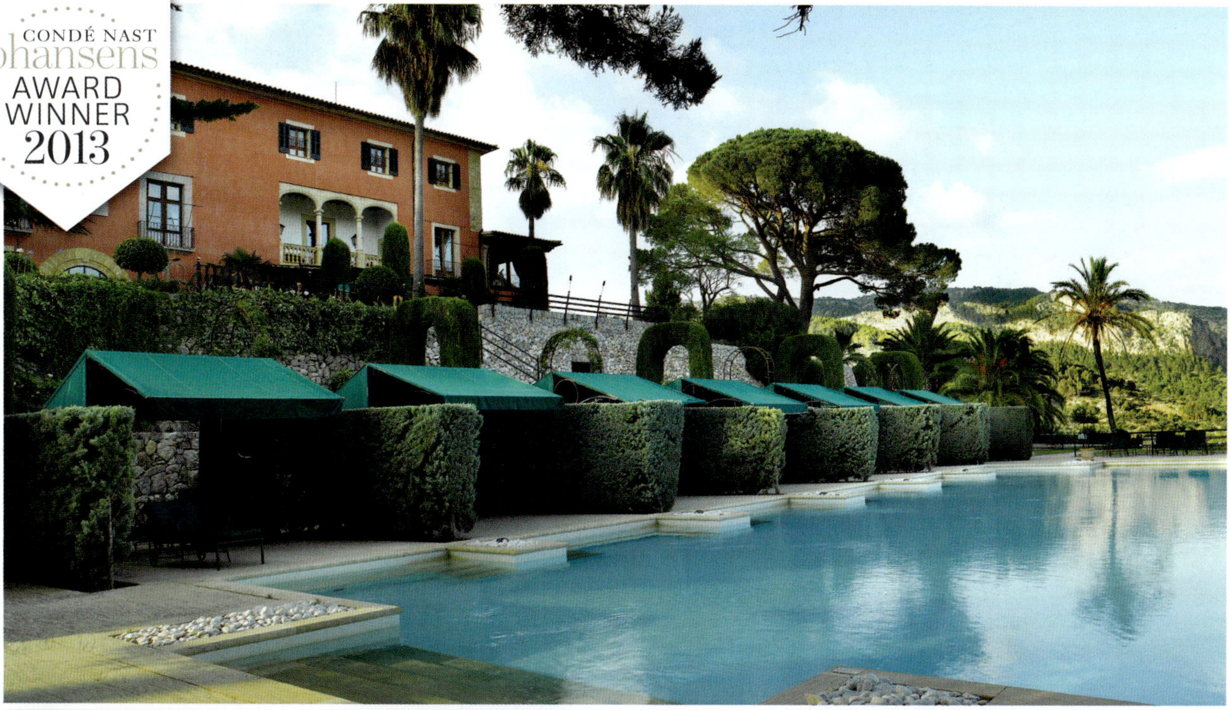

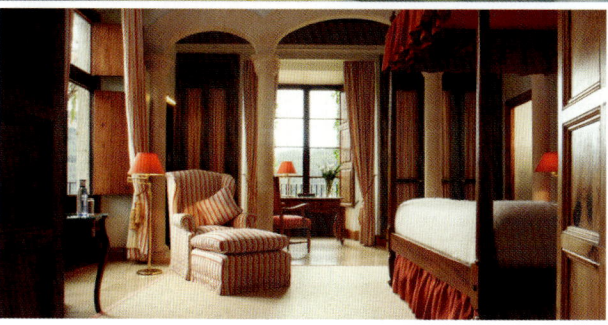

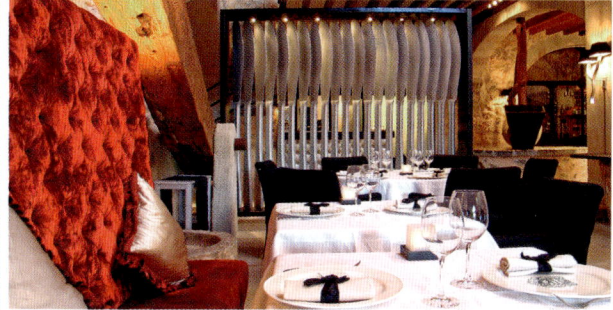

Gran Hotel Son Net

Modernity meets Mallorcan country house finesse

Fashioning its very own vineyard, Son Net Estate dates back to 1672 and screams quintessential Mallorca. Gran Hotel Son Net's rooms and suites are awash with colonial influences; beautiful four-poster beds and immaculate marble bathrooms big enough to party in! While outside, the wild Sierra Tramuntana mountains majestically shape the skyline, seen in all their glory from the casual El Gazebo restaurant. In fact, the resort is so superbly located you could find yourself chilling in La Fuente beauty centre within 30 minutes of landing at Mallorca Airport. It's all about peace and tranquillity at this Spanish bolthole, encouraging you to contemplate and rejuvenate, aided by the second-to-none staff. Be sure to ask them about the rooms and suites because the choice is varied. Some include private pools and/or breathtaking views. Some have a private entrance, twin beds and/or Jacuzzi tubs. When deciding whether to eat at the casual, alfresco poolside El Gazebo or Oleum restaurant where gourmet cooking uses fresh local produce, Bar Son Net will shake you up a pre-dinner cocktail apéritif.

PRICE FROM:
€205

FEATURES:
Family friendly; Gym; Helipad; Pool; Restaurant

ACTIVITIES:
Cycling; Golf; Walking

NEARBY:
Palma de Mallorca; Beaches; Sierra Tramuntana mountains

GETTING THERE:
Palma de Mallorca Airport

+34 971 14 70 00
condenastjohansens.com/sonnet
07194 Puigpunyent, Mallorca, Balearic Islands, Spain

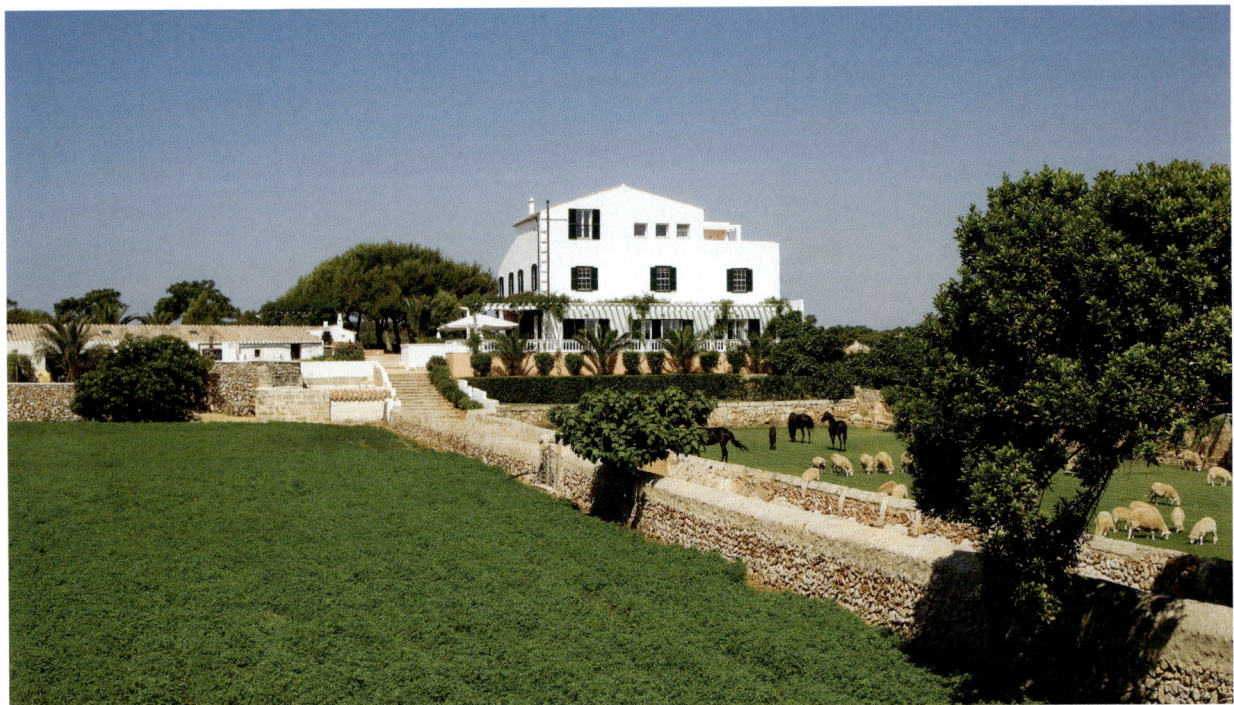

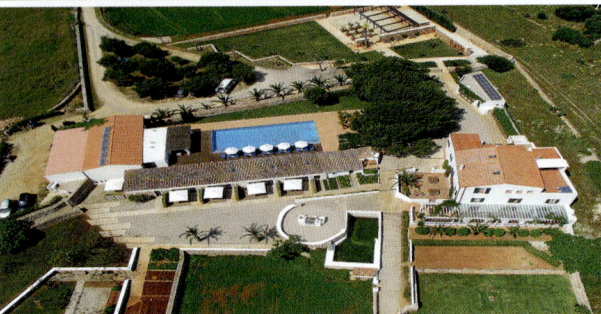

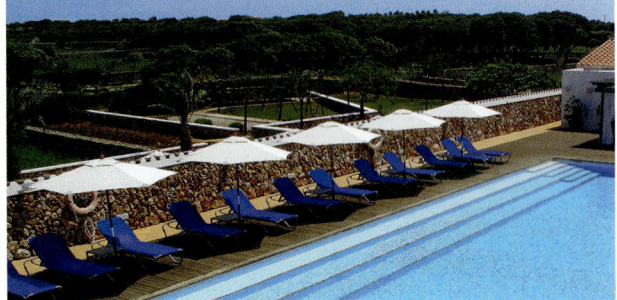

Hotel Sant Joan de Binissaida

Graceful modernity and eco-conscious hospitality in Menorca

PRICE FROM:
€140

FEATURES:
Beach access; Family friendly; Pool; Restaurant; Sea views

ACTIVITIES:
Golf; Horse riding; Water sports

NEARBY:
Es Castell; Sant Lluis; Mahon

GETTING THERE:
Mahon Airport

Menorca remains one of the most tranquil islands of the Balearics. Partly because 20 years ago UNESCO declared it a biosphere reserve for its unique flora and fauna, wildlife and archaeological sites. And with meandering coastal paths, deserted beaches and untouched countryside all within reach, Hotel Sant Joan de Binissaida is the quintessential laid-back Med escape where boutique chic meets rural cool. An 18th-century former farmhouse on Menorca's east coast, it's only a 10-minute hop from the capital Mahon, packed with character in its own acres of tranquil gardens with views of the sea in the distance. The 12 rooms, named after composers (one of Spain's oldest opera houses is just down the road), are a modern-rustic mix. Think minimalist décor, sandstone flooring, carved wooden headboards and designer lamps. The pièce de résistance is the vast Rossini Suite with soaring beamed ceilings, leather armchairs, a marble bathroom and fabulous four poster. The restaurant is run by the team behind Ses Forquilles in Mahon, one of the island's top dining spots and they're achieving great culinary heights here at Hotel Sant Joan de Binissaida. Expect updated Mediterranean classics, fresh fish and vegetables grown on-site. Hopeless romantics should book the table under the pergola but a terrace and several cosy dining rooms offer alternative options.

☎ +34 971 35 55 98
🌐 condenastjohansens.com/binissaida
🏠 Cami de Binissaida 108, Es Castell, 07720 Menorca, Balearic Islands, Spain

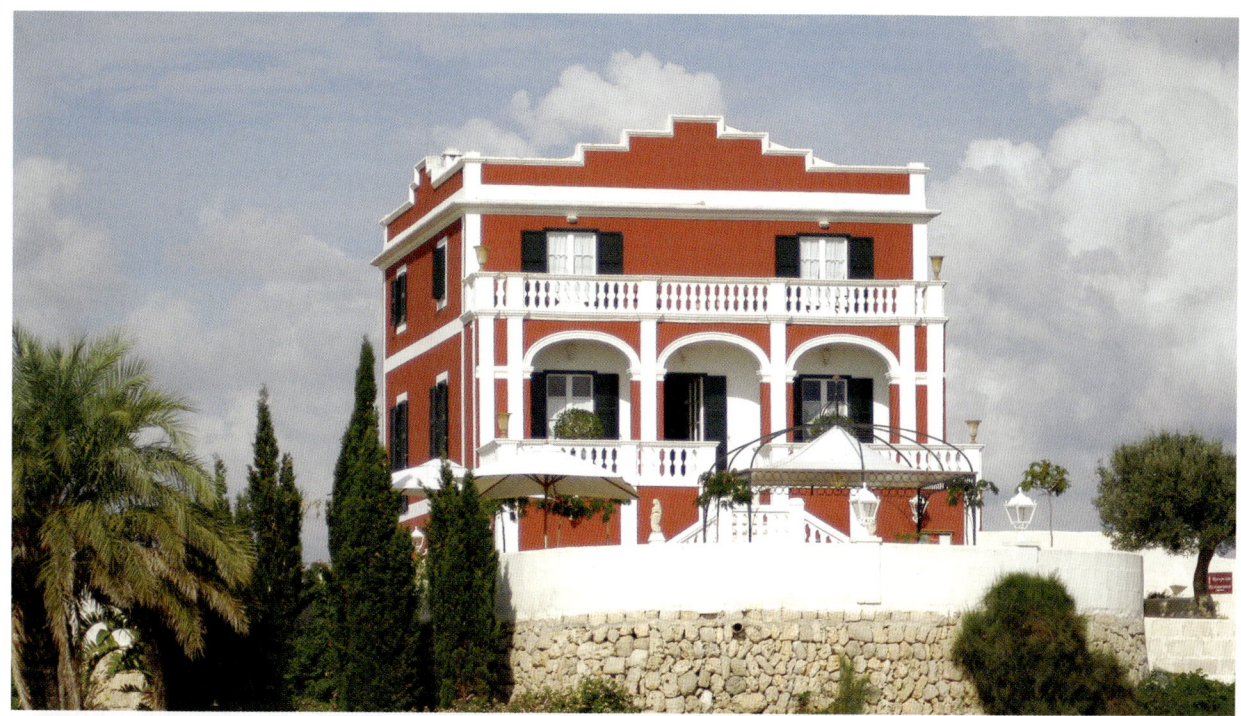

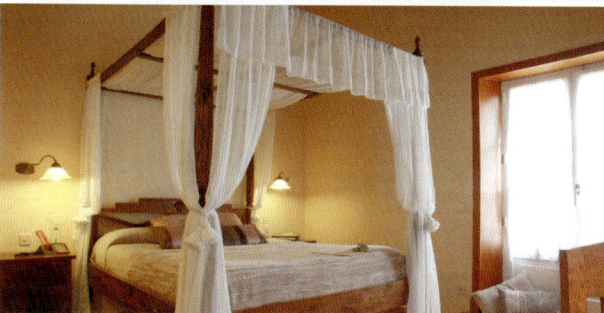

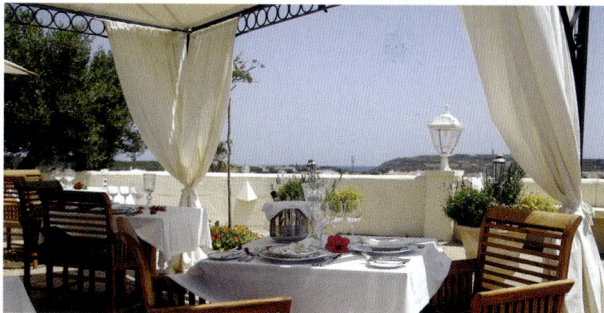

Son Granot

The ultimate country sojourn on the Menorcan coast

UNESCO-protected Menorca is the untouched Balearic Island rich with hidden gems. One of them is Son Granot, an 18th-century, Georgian-style mansion perched on a hill overlooking pine and fig tree-strewn countryside, close to the port of Mahon. The former home of Colonel Patrick Mackellar, a British military engineer who designed and constructed the town of Es Castell (which is just a short walk away), today it's an eight-room, two-suite rural retreat. Behind the pillar-box red façade, the country-cool rooms are flush with colonial-style furniture, four-poster beds, terracotta-tiled floors and wooden beamed ceilings. (Ask for one of the two rooms located at the front of the main house where you'll wake up to views across the hillside and Mahon beyond.) Lazy days are spent relaxing in the terraced botanical gardens or by the pool, while activities include golf, diving, horse-riding and cycling. Gourmet nights take place at Son Granot's exceptional restaurant. What isn't grown or produced on-site (be sure to try the sobrasada; imagine chorizo packed with paprika) is sourced locally and seasonally. Each dish is a work of art and delicious. When you want to mix it up, stroll to Es Castell and onto Mahon for seafood on the seafront.

PRICE FROM:
€200

FEATURES:
Family friendly; Pet friendly; Pool; Restaurant; Sea views

ACTIVITIES:
Fishing; Golf; Water sports

NEARBY:
Es Castell; Mahon

GETTING THERE:
Menorca Airport

+34 971 355 555
condenastjohansens.com/songranot
Ctra de Sant Felip s/n, 07720 Es Castell, Menorca, Balearic Islands, Spain

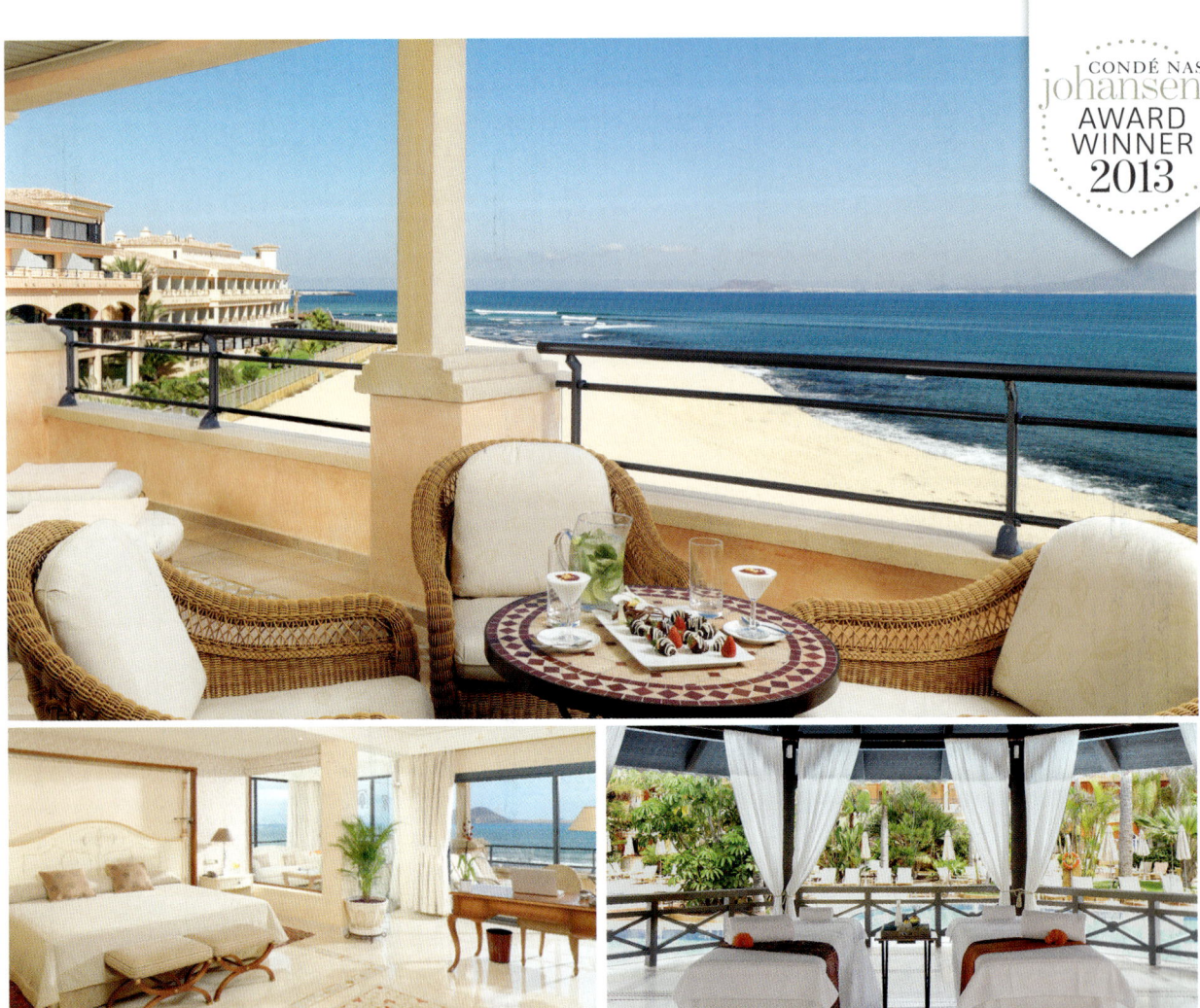

Gran Hotel Atlantis Bahía Real

Top-notch resort on Fuerteventura's coast

PRICE FROM:
€307

FEATURES:
Beach access; Family friendly; Restaurant; Sea views; Spa

ACTIVITIES:
Sightseeing; Tennis; Water sports

NEARBY:
Natural Sand Dune Park of Corralejo; Island of Lobos; Lanzarote; Fishing village and resort of Corralejo; La Oliva

GETTING THERE:
Fuerteventura Airport

☎ +34 928 537 153
🌐 condenastjohansens.com/bahiareal
🏠 Avenida Grandes Playas s/n, 35660 Corralejo, Fuerteventura, Canary Islands, Spain

Wrapped up by Blue Ribbon beaches, Gran Hotel Atlantis Bahía Real, Fuerteventura, is a luxury seaside gift. Utopian white sands and turquoise seas provide breathtaking views from this family-friendly hotel resort, which is part of UNESCO's biosphere. This protected habitat hosts a wonder of natural wildlife. Ask the Atlantis team to organise a trip to explore these volcanic shores. That's if you can tear yourself away from the spa and its spectacular views. Returning from a day of enjoyment and excursion, Gran Hotel Atlantis Bahía Real's private gym is there if you need it but some "me time" in your opulent room may be more appealing. Rooms and suites are decorated with a timeless elegance and combine space and comfort. And there's fine dining to be enjoyed at La Cúpula de Carles Gaig whose menu of mouth-watering delights is overseen by Gaig's Michelin-Starred expertise. For something a little different Yamatori presents a fusion of Japanese sushi and teppanyaki whilst the Piano Bar El Mirador is a pocket of romance with a view of the stars and a sky as crystal clear as your champagne flute. Top tip: for stunning sunset views and stellar star-gazing nights choose a sea-view room or suite - you won't be disappointed.

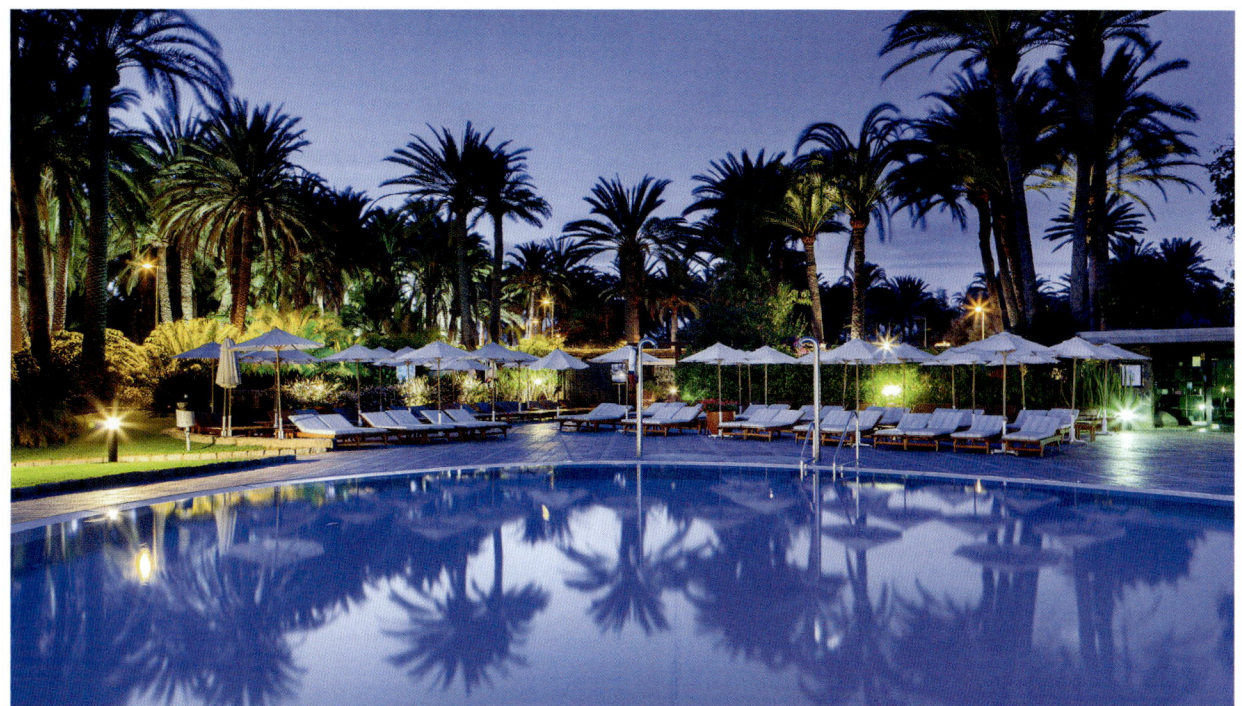

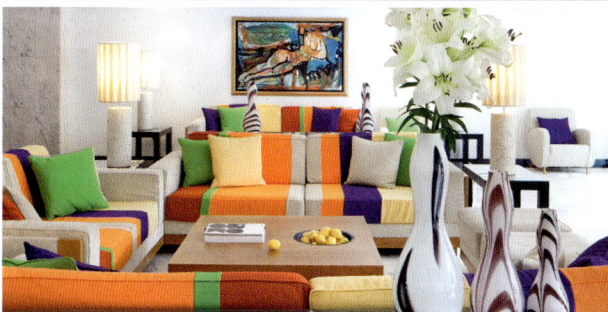
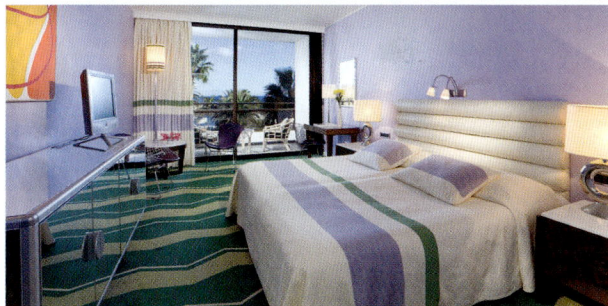

Seaside Hotel Palm Beach

Progressive design with a retro 1970s twist in Maspalomas

Year-round temperate Maspalomas, Gran Canaria, stands apart from its Canary Island neighbours and Caribbean peers for its resort-town vibe. Chock-full with restaurants, nightlife, outdoor pursuits and hotels alongside a university campus, hospitals and schools, this thriving area's most important landmark of all is the nature reserve: Dunes of Maspalomas. Beside which stands the kooky Seaside Hotel Palm Beach. Satisfying the beach-loving brood, water-sport nut and sun-seeking pack, this palm-tree haven is also one for interior design enthusiasts. Parisian architect and designer Alberto Pinto's 21st-century perspective on 1970s colour and shaping is a kaleidoscopic explosion. Inspired by Gran Canaria's natural and vibrant colour palette, rooms and suites feature striking colour pairings (eg violet and green, coral and blue); some have balconies looking out to the golden dunes. However, the view of a smooth green blanket of a grassy golf course might be more to your taste and there are no less than eight on the island, four of which are close to the hotel. With its sunny disposition all year, this is the ideal spot for some winter practise. All-day dining is available in two restaurants and a pool bar. Options include à la carte, buffet, barbecue, Italian and gourmet. Too good to miss: cocktails and baked goods made at Seaside Palm Beach's very own bakery.

PRICE FROM:
€214

FEATURES:
Gym; Pool; Restaurant; Sea views; Spa

ACTIVITIES:
Golf; Tennis; Water sports

NEARBY:
Las Palmas; Maspalomas sand dunes; Campo de Golf de Maspalomas; Tejeda; Arucas

GETTING THERE:
Gran Canaria Airport

+34 928 063 200 ☎
condenastjohansens.com/hotelpalmbeach 🌐
Avenida del Oasis s/n, 35100 Maspalomas, Gran Canaria, 🏠
Canary Islands, Spain

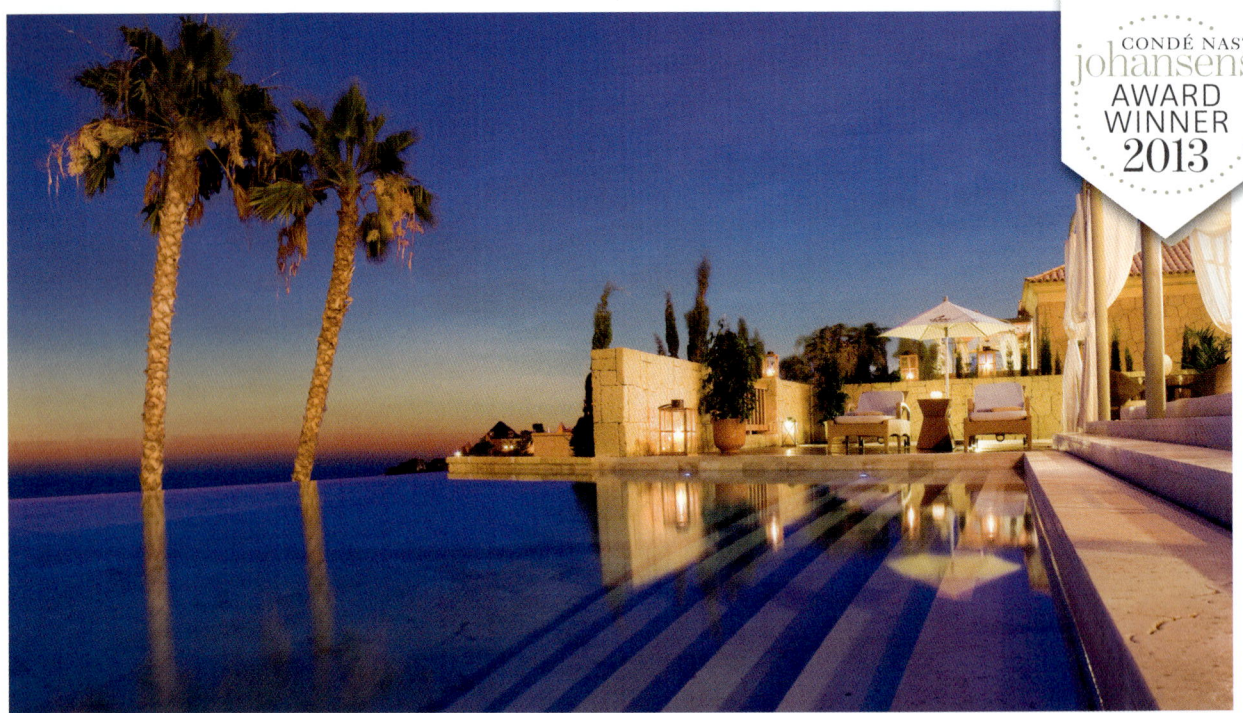

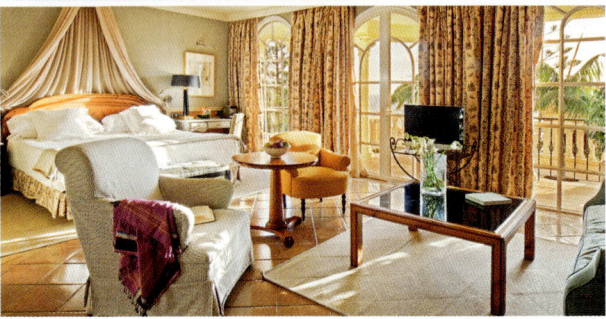

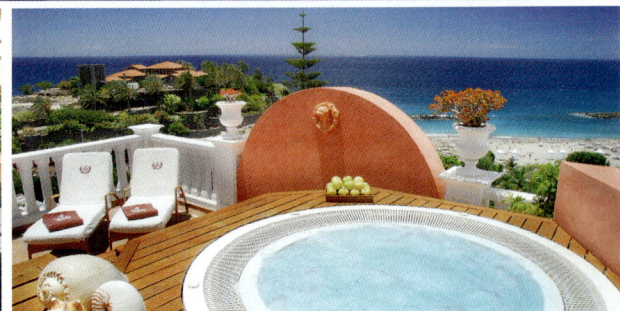

Gran Hotel Bahía del Duque Resort

Private, refined resort beside Tenerife's beautiful Duque beach

PRICE FROM:
€372

FEATURES:
Beach access; Pool; Restaurant; Sea views; Spa

ACTIVITIES:
Fishing; Golf; Water sports

NEARBY:
La Caleta; Adeje; Puerto Colon Marina; Siam Park; Las Cañadas National Park

GETTING THERE:
Tenerife South (Reina Sofia) Airport; Tenerife North (Los Rodeos) Airport

☎ +34 922 746 932
🌐 condenastjohansens.com/bahiaduque
🏠 Avenida de Bruselas s/n, Costa Adeje 38660, Tenerife, Canary Islands, Spain

A testament to colonial architecture, Gran Hotel Bahía del Duque Resort in Tenerife is a cluster of impeccable villas. So sublimely luxurious, you needn't step out of the resort into the "Island Of The Eternal Spring". At a consistent 20°C+, this UNESCO protected plot of forests, majestic cliffs and utopic beaches cries out for exploration. However, in-resort you can relax in the reading lounge or enjoy a plethora of high-adrenaline or family-friendly activities such as sailing on del Duque's very own yacht, Pámpano. Younger children love the dedicated Ents team while older siblings can relax in their own surf-style beach lounge complete with video consoles and table football. The casas ducales and villas, decorated by prestigious interior designer Pascua Ortega, mix the latest technology with maximum comfort and views of the spectacular Playa del Duque. But for a particularly opulent stay casas ducales include independent receptions and are complete with butler service. Tired muscles? Soothe them with exclusive thalassotherapy treatments at the L'Occitane spa. And when hunger strikes, a choice of eight restaurants featuring a medley of global cuisines are available to satisfy the most discerning rumbling tum (and any fussy younger ones too). An adults-only lounge bar offers quiet sanctuary.

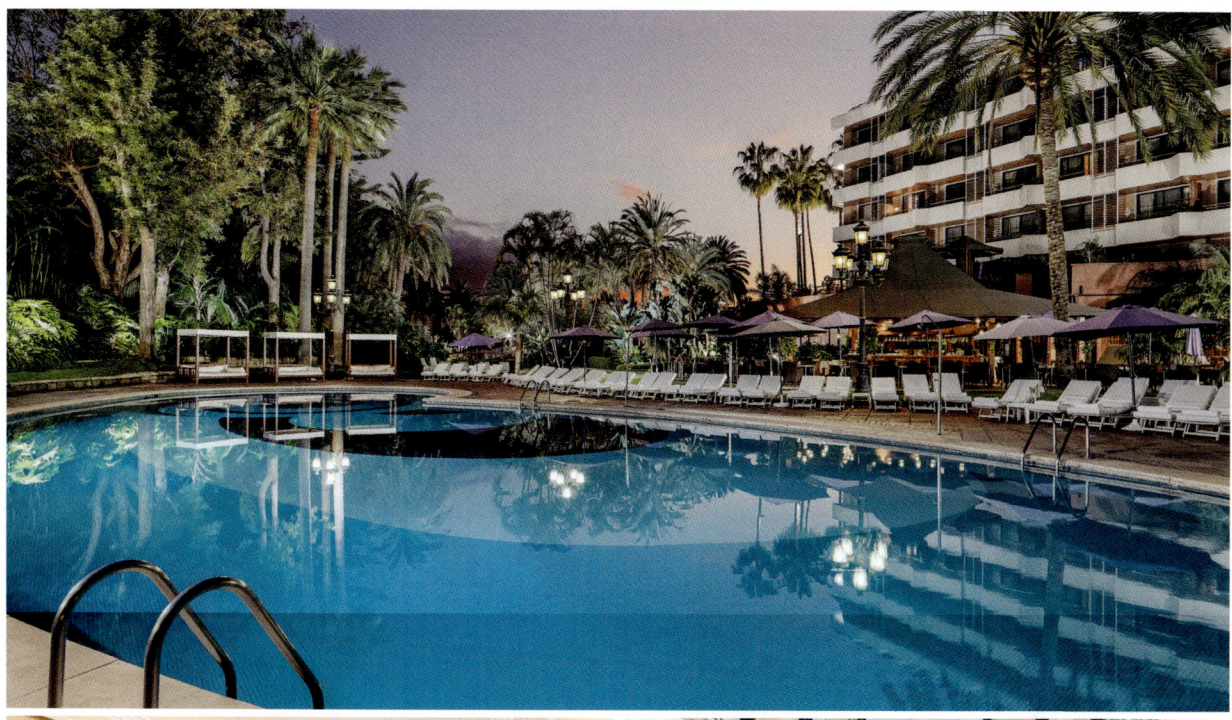

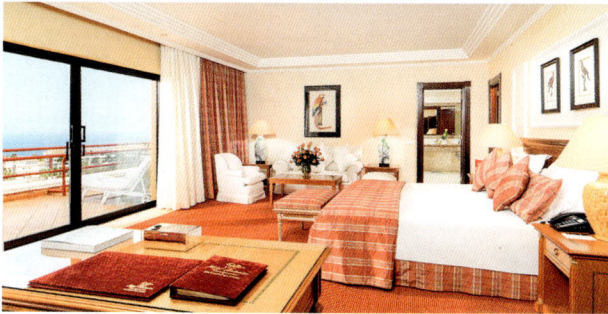

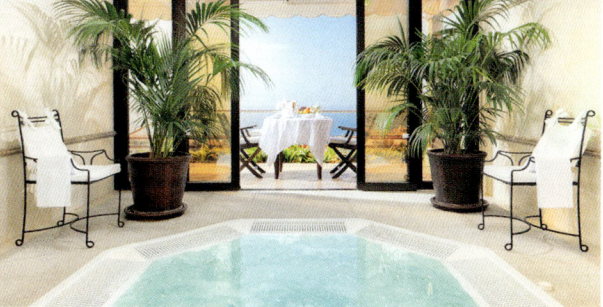

Hotel Botánico & The Oriental Spa Garden

Year-round R&R on the lush slopes of north Tenerife

An ultimate go-to for relaxation, Tenerife's Hotel Botánico & The Oriental Spa Garden is located in the north of the island. Surrounding its unfussy 1970s architecture are subtropical gardens and a lake packed with koi carp giving a taster of the volcanic high drama beyond the hotel's borders. Views of which (the ocean, mountains or gardens) are seen through oversized windows from each room and suite, sumptuously designed as an oasis of escape. Be as lazy as you like or as active as you please. Tennis courts, a driving range and numerous tours beckon to be joined but it's the stonking-great, child-free spa that makes you step back and behold. Decorated with a Far Eastern vibe, it has a pool, Jacuzzi, ice temple, sauna, fitness centre and an eye-popping list of treatments. Four à la carte restaurants serve regional and Asian menus as well as a super-healthy option known as the Essence of Wellbeing suitable for vegetarians, those that wish to lose weight, simply feel virtuous or have specific dietary requirements. A 10-minute walk away is the chilled town of Puerto de la Cruz with colonial buildings and traces of its former fishing village life in narrow, bustling streets to explore (visit during the annual sardine festival!).

PRICE FROM:
€270

FEATURES:
Pet friendly; Pool; Restaurant; Sea views; Spa

ACTIVITIES:
Fishing; Golf; Water sports

NEARBY:
Puerto de la Cruz; La Orotava; Santa Cruz; Loro Parque; Buenavista Golf

GETTING THERE:
Tenerife South (Reina Sofia) Airport

+34 922 38 14 00 ☎
condenastjohansens.com/hotelbotanico 🌐
Avenida Richard J Yeoward 1, 38400 Puerto de La Cruz, 🏠
Tenerife, Canary Islands, Spain

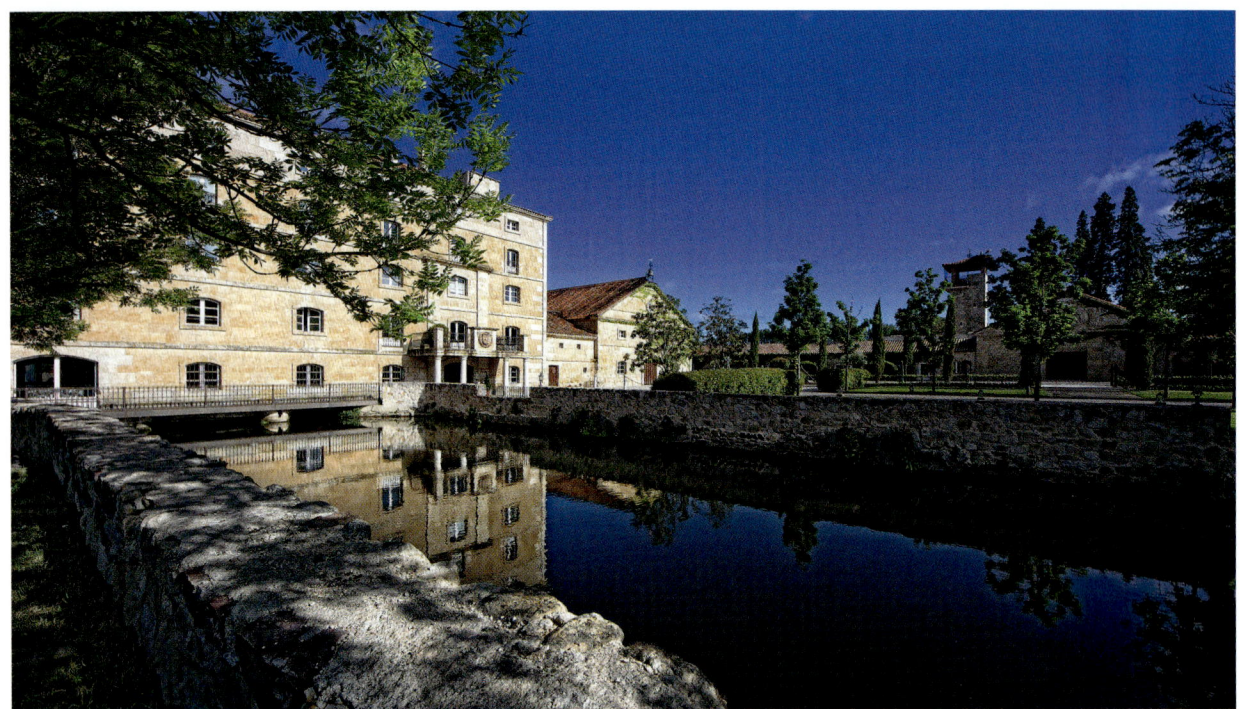

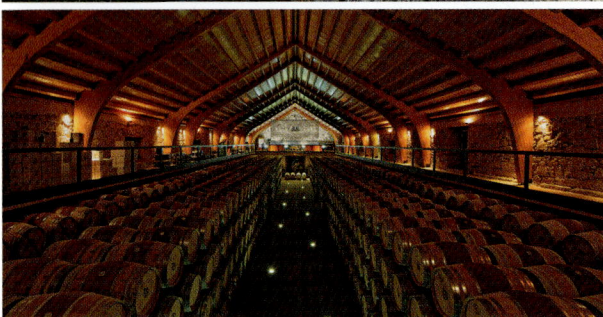

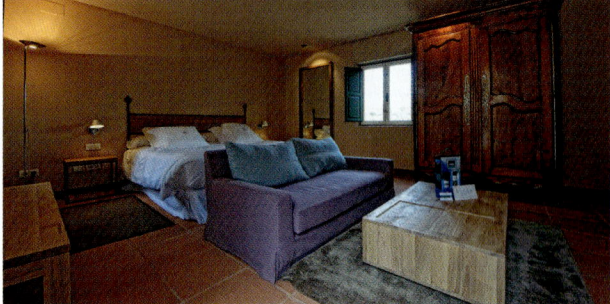

Hacienda Zorita Wine Hotel & Spa

Groundbreaking wine and spa hotel near Salamanca

PRICE FROM:
€150

FEATURES:
Family friendly; Pool; Restaurant; Spa; Wheelchair access

ACTIVITIES:
Golf; Horse riding; Sightseeing

NEARBY:
Salamanca; Avila; Zamora

GETTING THERE:
Madrid Barajas Airport; Oporto Airport

Welcome to the Land of Bread and Wine. Yes, it's as good as it sounds and Hacienda Zorita Wine Hotel & Spa is right in the mouth-watering middle of it. For hundreds of years the Duero Valley has been known as a culinary hotspot with just the right climate for some of the world's best wine. Hacienda Zorita promises food, wine and adventure. It's a huge 14th-century former monastery, a short drive from Salamanca built as a farm and vineyard by monks who clearly knew a thing or two about hospitality. Columbus himself is said to have stayed here (maybe if he hadn't, the Americas would have been discovered sooner) and the current owners have transformed this ancient building into Spain's first luxury wine hotel. Rooms are chic and simple with local antiques sitting alongside cool, contemporary décor, and even the spa uses wine in its treatments. Book in for a few days and sample produce from Hacienda Zorita's farm at a simple farm-to-table restaurant under the direction of Michelin-Starred Chef Victor Gutierrez. The idea here is simple, understated luxury with the best produce available. They do it well.

☎ +34 923 129 400
🌐 condenastjohansens.com/zorita
🏠 Carretera Salamanca-Ledesma, Km 8.7, 37115 Valverdón, Salamanca, Castilla y León, Spain

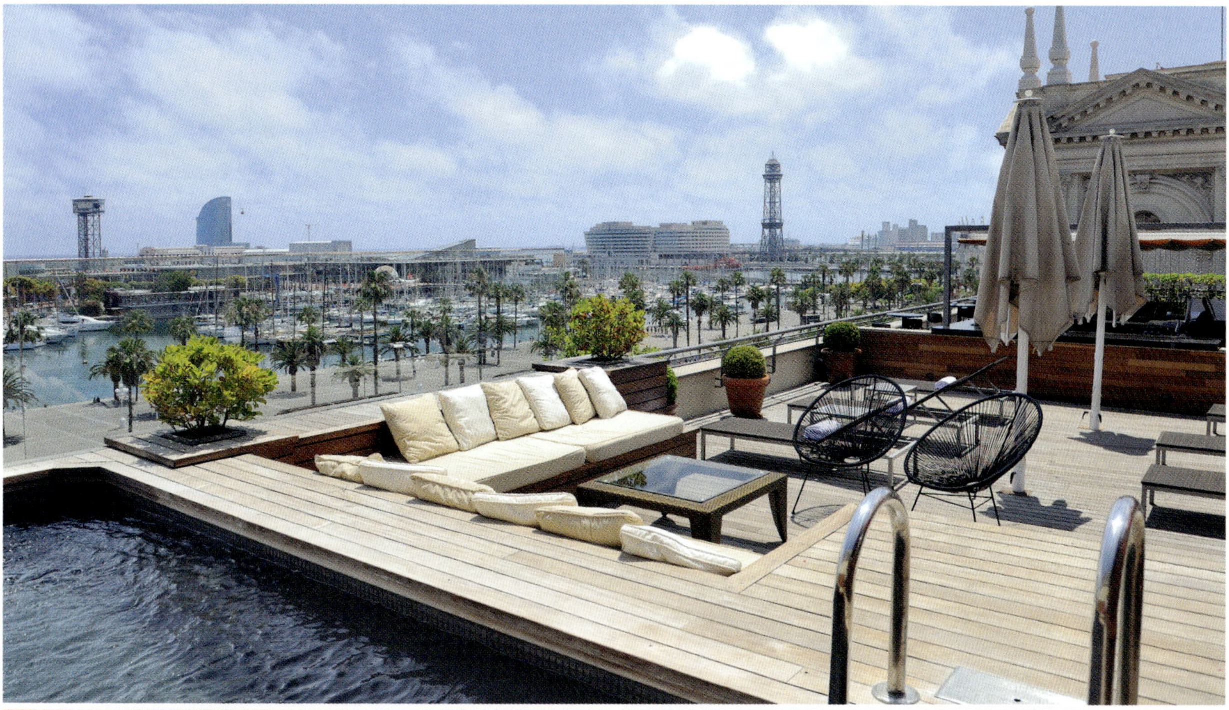

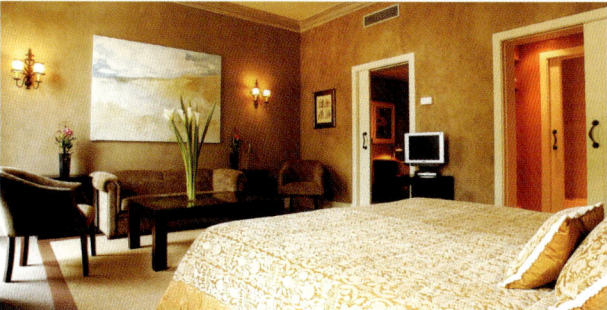
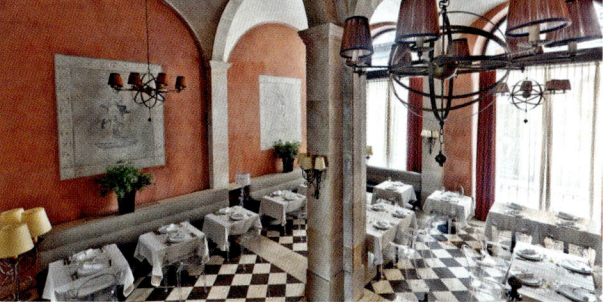

Hotel Duquesa de Cardona

Chic, sleek, city boutique hotel beside Barcelona's port

When you've had enough of Barcelona's tourist trail there's Hotel Duquesa de Cardona offering respite from the hustle and bustle. Barcelona's city streets below seem a million miles away when you're hanging out on the roof terrace despite the fact that this marina-front hotel is slap bang in the middle of the action. Las Ramblas and the Gothic Quarter are so close you're in the thick of their pulsing streets in no time. Everything you could want from a city hotel, the Duquesa delivers. Cool, sophisticated and full of character, a glass of Cava upon arrival sets the tone. Rooms are light and airy with a crisp modern boutique feel and fear not if your room is located roadside because windows are quadruple glazed so you don't hear one car horn. Hotel Duquesa's 16th-century building was once home to kings and noble types and much of its grandeur remains. Columns, vaulted ceilings and art deco windows fuse with wrought iron, contemporary banquettes and Philippe Starck ghost chairs in the restaurant where you can enjoy great à la carte menus. Alfresco tapas at the rooftop bar is also a must. It's all about location and luxury here, and the Hotel Duquesa does it with effortless style.

PRICE FROM:
€215

FEATURES:
Pool; Restaurant; Sea views; Wheelchair access

ACTIVITIES:
Shopping; Sightseeing; Water sports

NEARBY:
Port; Gothic Quarter; Las Ramblas; La Boquería market; Picasso Museum

GETTING THERE:
Barcelona Airport; Gerona Airport

+34 93 268 90 90 ☎
condenastjohansens.com/duquesadecardona 🌐
Paseo Colon 12, 08002 Barcelona, Cataluña, Spain 🏠

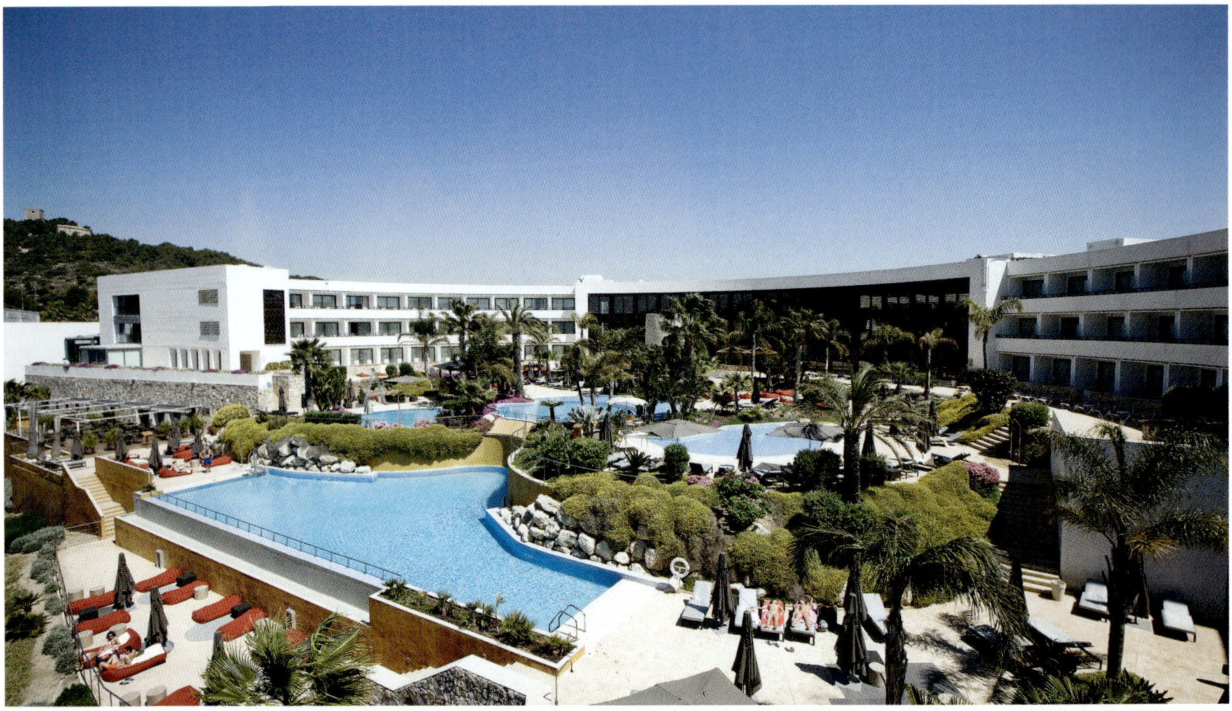

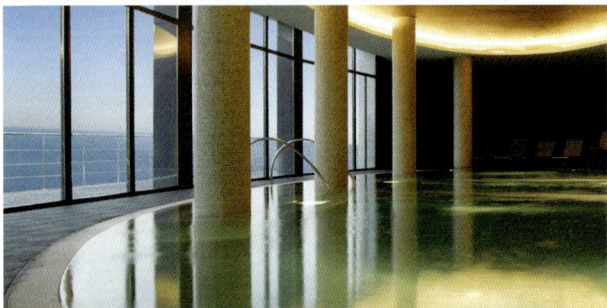

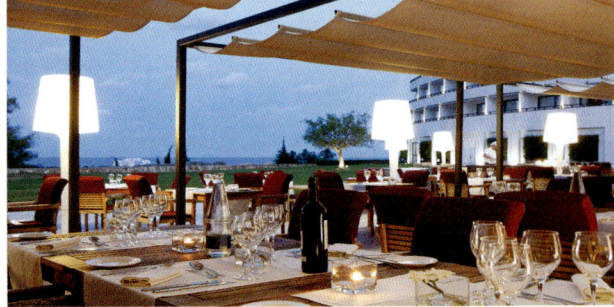

Dolce Sitges

Business mixes with pleasure at big and beautiful Sitges resort

PRICE FROM:
€169

FEATURES:
Family friendly; Pool; Restaurant; Sea views; Spa

ACTIVITIES:
Golf; Sightseeing; Water sports

NEARBY:
Sitges; Barcelona; Garraf Natural Park; Wine routes; Tarragona

GETTING THERE:
Sitges Railway Station; Barcelona Airport

☎ +34 938 109 000
🌐 condenastjohansens.com/dolcesitges
🏠 Av Cami de Miralpeix 12, Sitges 08870, Barcelona, Cataluña, Spain

Modern, stylish and spacious, Dolce Sitges exudes the cosmopolitan attitude of Barcelona yet offers the intimacy and peace of a Mediterranean seaside village. Commanding an elevated position on a hillside in Sitges, this magnificent beast looks out to golden beaches and conveniently neighbours cool night spots. (Visit during October and attend the world-renowned Sitges annual film festival and carnival.) Reflecting the town's vibrancy, Dolce Sitges is a veritable pleasure/leisure resort with all the luxe trappings you could hope for. Inside, it's a clean-lined and smart affair but far from dull with each room harbouring an individual twist and mood-enhancing lighting. To match its exhaustive facilities, Dolce Sitges' assortment of dining options cater for the entire range of discerning palatte. Fine dining, modern buffet, Mediterranean, local favourites and a delicatessen all deliver something a little different. Which means socialising and entertaining is a breeze; simply choose how and where you like. Drinks poolside, at the cool Alea Lounge and sophisticated Bar Malvasia are just three options of many. When a touch of pampering is required, there's Dolce Vital Spa whose theme of pure indulgence is complemented by the state-of-the-art fitness centre. For those visiting on business (Dolce Sitges is a big player in the corporate world), impressing clients is a guaranteed promise.

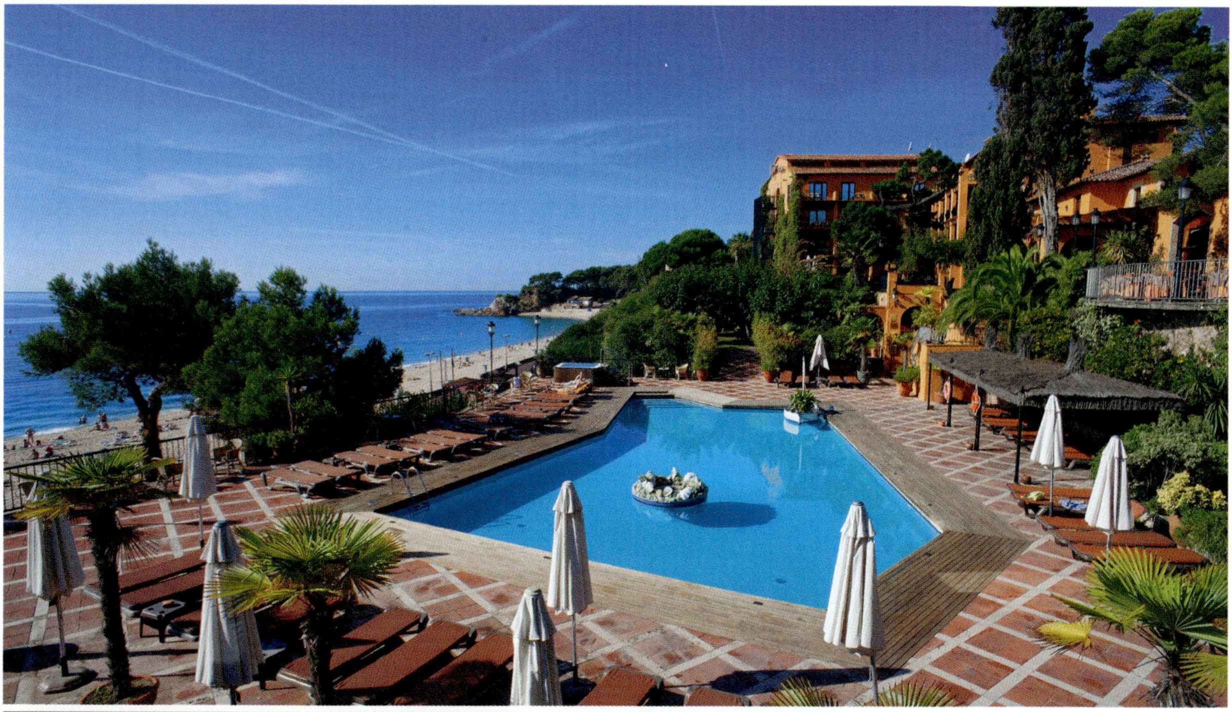

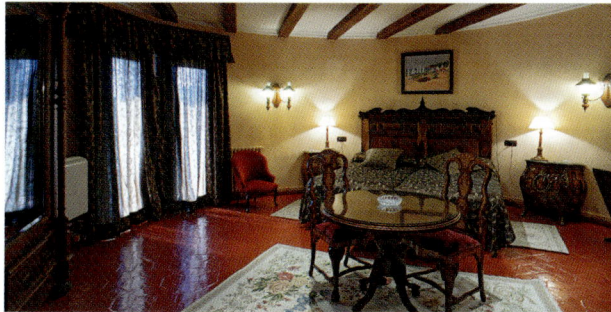
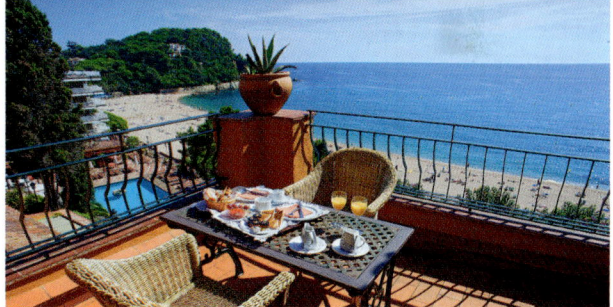

Hotel Rigat Park & Spa Beach Hotel

Traditional beach-side holidaying on the Gerona coast

One man's Costa Bravan dream became a reality in 1956 when the Hotel Rigat Park & Spa Beach Hotel opened. Still a family-run operation, the son of ski champion Fillipo Rigat keeps the hotel's traditional spirit alive with cosy, antique-packed interiors and lovingly collected paintings and ceramics. Perfect for a classic beachy break, its large terrace and pool area are an extension of the ocean whose glorious sheer blue waters are are in constant view. Vivid bougainvillea cascades down terracotta-hued hacienda walls and a 300-year-old tamarind tree growing in the bar area brings the tropical vibe inside. If you like subtle bling with your dining, check out the gold ceiling in Hotel Rigat's Baroque-style restaurant. Here, Catalan influences mix rice, fish and lots of Mediterranean veggies but the dessert trolley is truly the star. (Tumbling towers of profiteroles, cupcakes and tantalising tartlets!) Of course, eating outdoors is a must and Hotel Rigat serves a mean breakfast alfresco. Eggs as you like them and coffee any expert barista would be proud of. Soothe kinks or strains in the bijou spa or whizz off on a boat trip to nearby Tossa del Mar for a little culture and shopping.

PRICE FROM:
€192 (excluding VAT)

FEATURES:
Beach access; Gym; Pool; Restaurant; Sea views

ACTIVITIES:
Fishing; Golf; Water sports

NEARBY:
Santa Clotilde Gardens; Catamaran trips; Golf PGA; Gerona; Barcelona

GETTING THERE:
Gerona Airport; Barcelona Airport

+34 972 36 52 00 ☎
condenastjohansens.com/rigat 🌐
Av Amèrica 1, Playa de Fenals, 17310 Lloret de Mar, Costa 🏠
Brava, Gerona, Cataluña, Spain

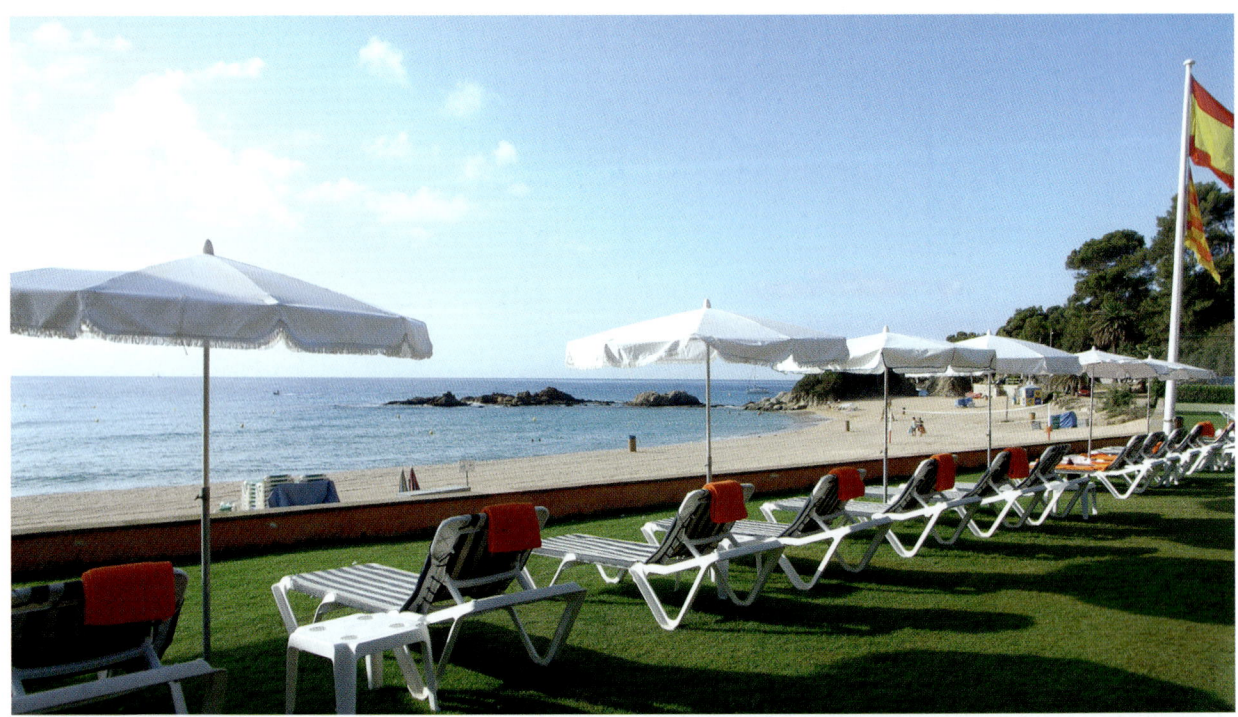

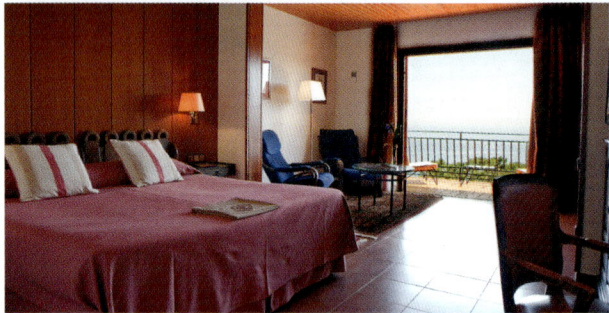

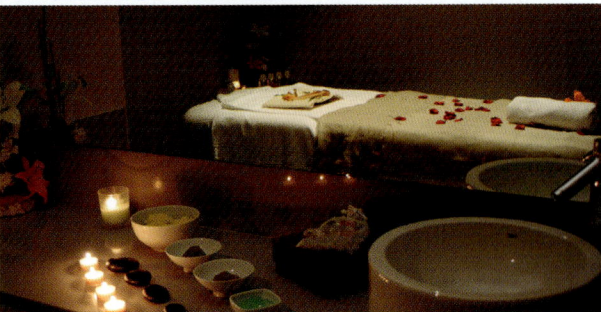

Hotel Santa Marta

Classic seaside luxury just on the edge of vibrant Lloret de Mar

PRICE FROM:
€182.50

FEATURES:
Beach access; Family friendly; Pool; Restaurant; Spa

ACTIVITIES:
Fishing; Golf; Water sports

NEARBY:
Santa Clotilde Gardens; Tossa del Mar; Gerona; Barcelona; Cadaqués

GETTING THERE:
Gerona Airport; Barcelona Airport

A popular stop-off for fun-seekers, families, active types and cyclists thanks to its great views and peachy beach, Hotel Santa Marta in Lloret de Mar oozes old school charm. You can pause, dust off your lycra and drink in the ocean air or purely pull up a sun lounger and relax poolside. Cosseted by the lush Santa Cristina cove, Hotel Santa Marta is blissfully secluded. There's even a golf buggy to ferry you back and forth to the beach. Staff are eager to please and the top-rated food enhances the high standard of service in the restaurant. The freshest Mediterranean produce is plucked from local markets and suppliers so Chef Francisco Saez and team can whip up Costa Bravan classics in no time. How about lunch, a bowl of gazpacho and glass of zingy white while overlooking the sea? With something to please everyone there's a spa and up-to-the-minute fitness centre, with the craziness of Lloret de Mar's nightlife close by and the quaint Tossa de Mar just along the coast. Top tip: opt for an ocean-view room with balcony if you can. It's worth it.

☎ +34 972 364 904
🌐 condenastjohansens.com/santamarta
🏠 Playa de Santa Cristina, 17310 Lloret de Mar, Costa Brava, Gerona, Cataluña, Spain

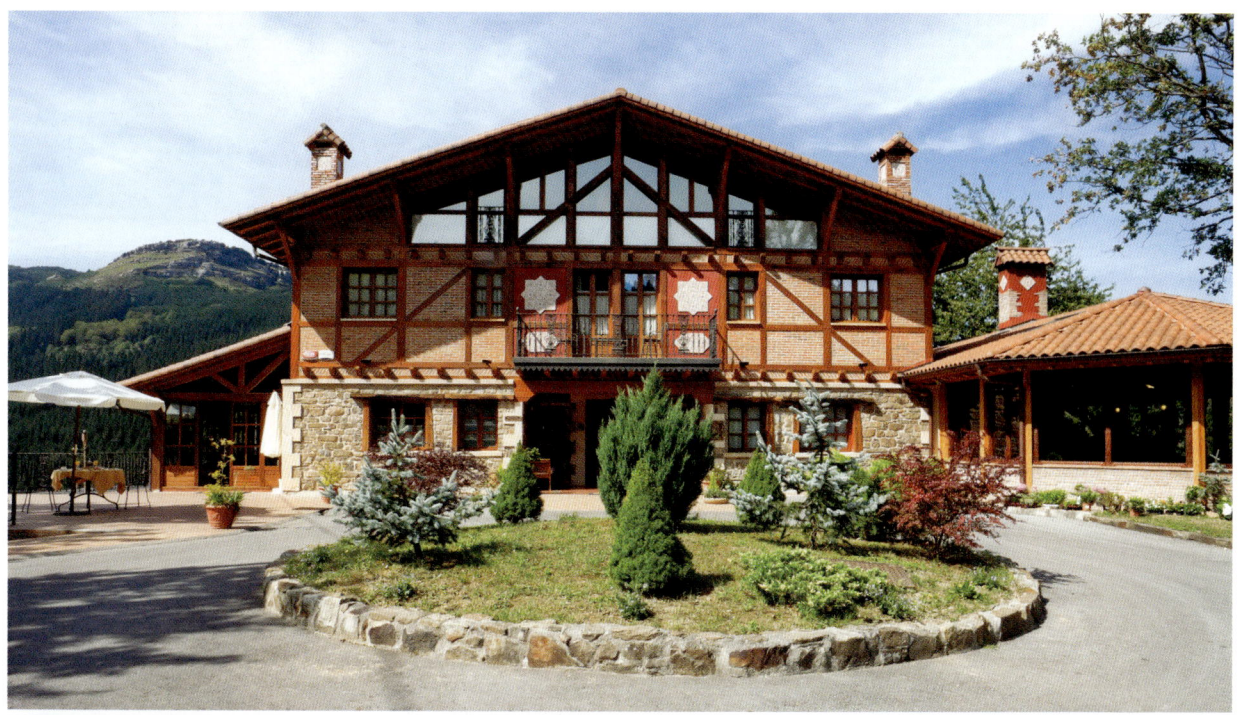

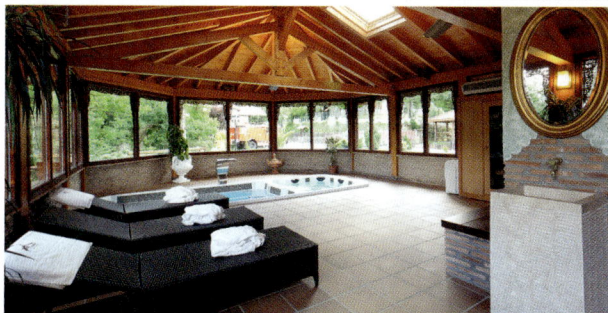
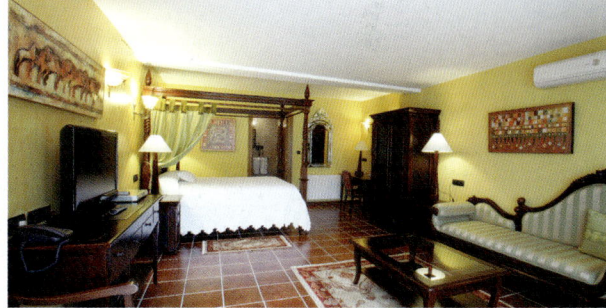

Hotel Etxegana

Basque beauty with an exotic flair in Gorbeia Natural Park

Finding Hotel Etxegana in northern Spain's Basque Country is half the fun. Nestled in Gorbeia Natural Park, a 30-minute drive from Bilbao and Vitoria, this rustic-luxe retreat is all about the scenery: mountains, valleys and undulating countryside. And the silence – it's pin-drop peaceful only interrupted by some vocal farm animals. The 18-room lodge is a super base from which to explore the area. Hike up Mount Gorbeia (at 1,480 metres it's the highest peak in Basque Country) uncover rich flora and fauna (Pyrenean oak and chestnut woods), discover wildlife (peregrine falcons, bobcats and deer) and visit craft studios, limestone caves and wetlands. Don't miss the towering Gujuli Waterfall and Sanctuary of Virgen de Oro, a 16th-century chapel with a breathtaking Baroque altarpiece and unfurling views of the Zuia Valley and be sure to unwind in Etxegana's spa whose treatments, hammam, sauna and Jacuzzi hit the spot after a day in the hills. Or relax on the huge deck that was made for nothing more than lazing on sundowners. Inside, you'll discover a treasure trove of artefacts, objets d'art and curios from around the world plus local art and hand-carved furniture; it's all so delightful. Dining is an experience in itself. The inventive Basque cuisine is top-rate while floor-to-ceiling windows ensure you don't miss a moment of the drama outside.

PRICE FROM:
€125

FEATURES:
Gym; Pet friendly; Pool; Restaurant; Spa

ACTIVITIES:
Fishing; Golf; Horse riding

NEARBY:
Bilbao; Vitoria; Gorbeia Natural Park; Guggenheim Bilbao Museum; Reserva de la Biosfera (Urdaibai)

GETTING THERE:
Bilbao (Loiu) Airport; Vitoria (Foronda) Airport

+34 946 338 448 ☎
condenastjohansens.com/etxegana 🌐
Ipiñaburu 38, Zeanuri, 48144 Bizkaia, Vizcaya, País Vasco, 🏠
Spain

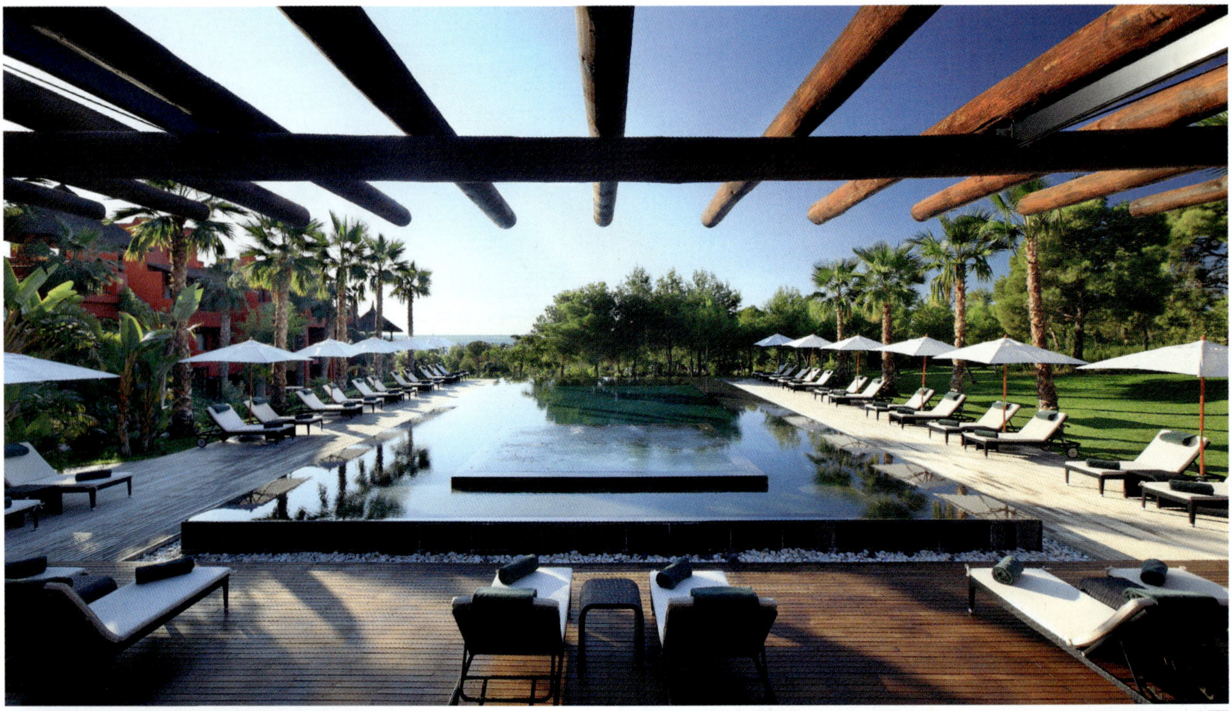

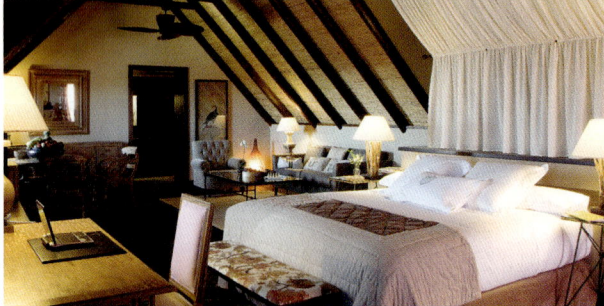

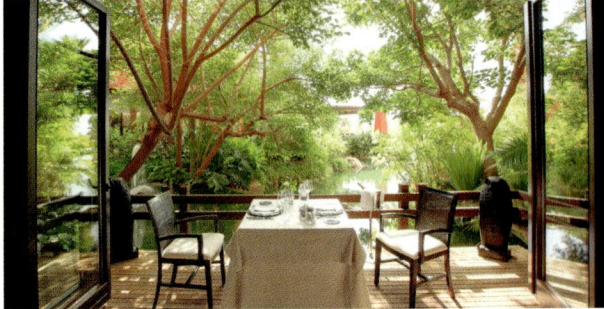

Barceló Asia Gardens Hotel & Thai Spa

Thailand and Bali converge on Spain's Costa Blanca

PRICE FROM:
€240

FEATURES:
Family friendly; Pool; Restaurant; Sea views; Spa

ACTIVITIES:
Cycling; Golf; Water sports

NEARBY:
Finestrat; Benidorm; Altea; Terra Natura and Aqua Natura Water Theme Parks; Terra Mítica Theme Park

GETTING THERE:
Alicante Airport; Valencia Airport

☎ +34 966 818 400
🌐 condenastjohansens.com/asiagardens
📍 Rotonda del Fuego s/n, Terra Mítica, Costa Blanca, 03502 Alicante, Valencia, Spain

Ever imagine stumbling upon a Thai-infused resort on the ever-popular Costa Blanca? No? Meet Barceló Asia Gardens Hotel & Thai Spa, Alicante, an inspired concept that works like a dream. Taking the finest elements of an Asian resort: a Zen-calm atmosphere, above-and-beyond service and friendly professionalism, Barceló Asia Gardens looks and acts the part. The stunning reception area and atrium (dark wood and woven ceilings with a Chesterfield twist) leads you to Thai-luxe rooms dressed in modernist Balinese-style furnishings beside sleek, glamorous bathrooms and dazzling Mediterranean light. Beds are heavenly and the higher the room, the better the view. Techno-fittings, WiFi and iPod docks are standard. A wander around the resort takes in the hot chilli-pink buildings set among a tapestry of lush gardens with a number of meandering infinity pools full of private little inlets. Two of the pools are heated and there's a children's pool for the little scamps. The kiddies are also spoilt with fun at the pirate-themed Miniclub. Feast on Asian-fused Mediterranean cuisine at Udaipur Grand Buffet and reserve a table at restaurant Koh Samui or the sophisticated In Black (over 12s only). Don't miss out on a Thai massage within one of the traditional Thai stilt houses - the spa staff have honed their skills to perfection!

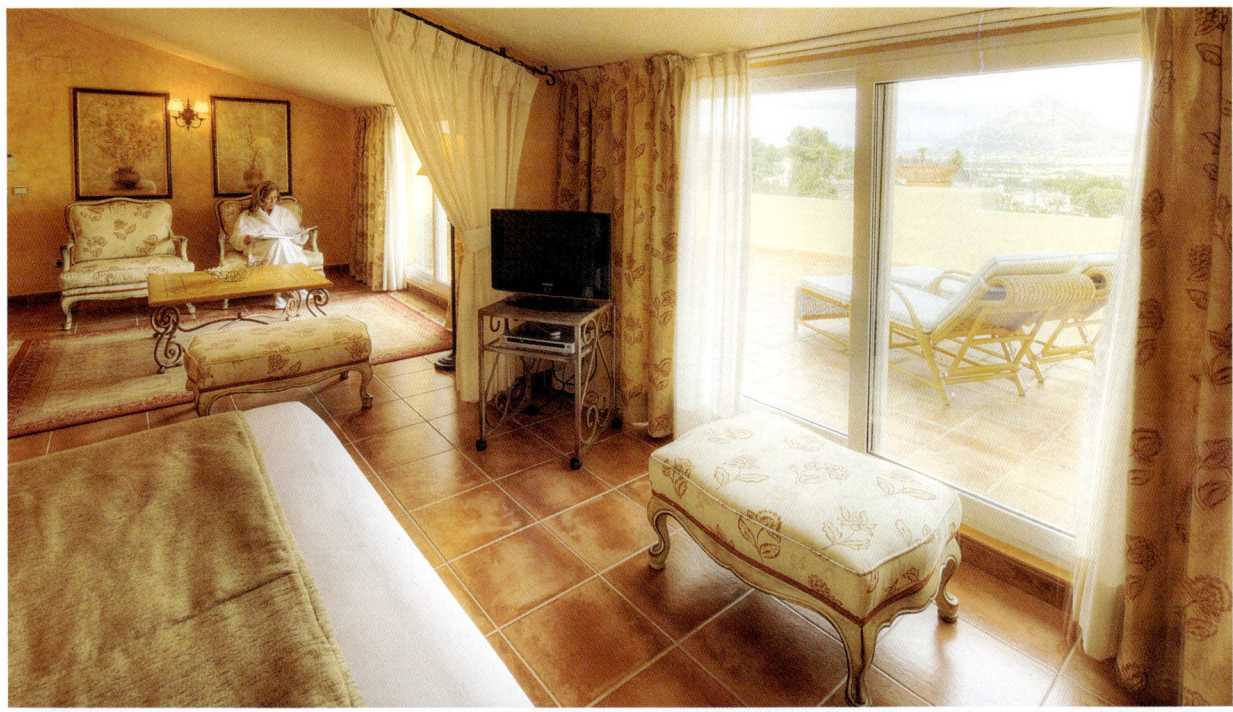

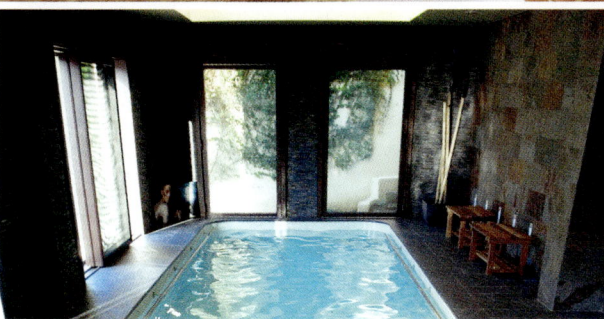

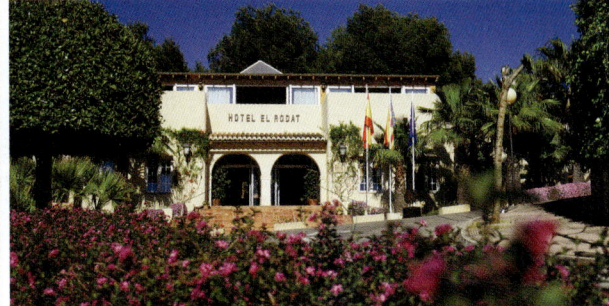

El Rodat Hotel Village & Spa

Relaxed bolthole overlooking the coastal town of Jávea

Radiating scents of jasmine and lavender, the gardens of El Rodat Hotel, Alicante, have you instantly relaxed and yearning for a Spanish siesta. But don't be too hasty to rest your head. Once greeted by the friendly Mediterranean hospitality, check out the chromotherapy fitness pool and spa and surrender to treatments such as gold-dust rehydration. You'll be left feeling fully relaxed, feeling head-to-toe fantastic. Then there's nothing to it but to flop into your room - Gran, Junior or Doble – with spacious living area, delicate drapes and traditionally tiled flooring, each designed to keep the cool in and the Alicante heat out. Keen golfers are kept occupied by El Rodat's very own fairway while foodies find seventh heaven at the hotel's restaurant where a feast of seasonal tapas, fresh seafood, paella and other Spanish delights fill the menu. Catering to families, parties of friends and business functions, El Rodat's conference facilities are also workshops for gastronomes and photographers. Papping and snapping poolside bougainvillea will put you in the pink for the hotel's photography contest. But if this isn't adventurous enough for you, chat with a member of staff who will be only too happy to organise a diving, riding or hiking expedition on your behalf. They know all the best spots. Make sure you're back at the hotel in time for sundown and sangria though. Salud!

PRICE FROM:
€118

FEATURES:
Pool; Restaurant; Sea views; Spa

ACTIVITIES:
Golf; Horse riding; Water sports

NEARBY:
Denia; Valencia; Jávea old town, Port and fish market; El Montgo Natural Park

GETTING THERE:
Alicante Airport; Valencia Airport

+34 966 470 710 ☎
condenastjohansens.com/elrodat 🌐
C/La Murciana 9, Jávea 03730, Alicante, Valencia, Spain 🏠

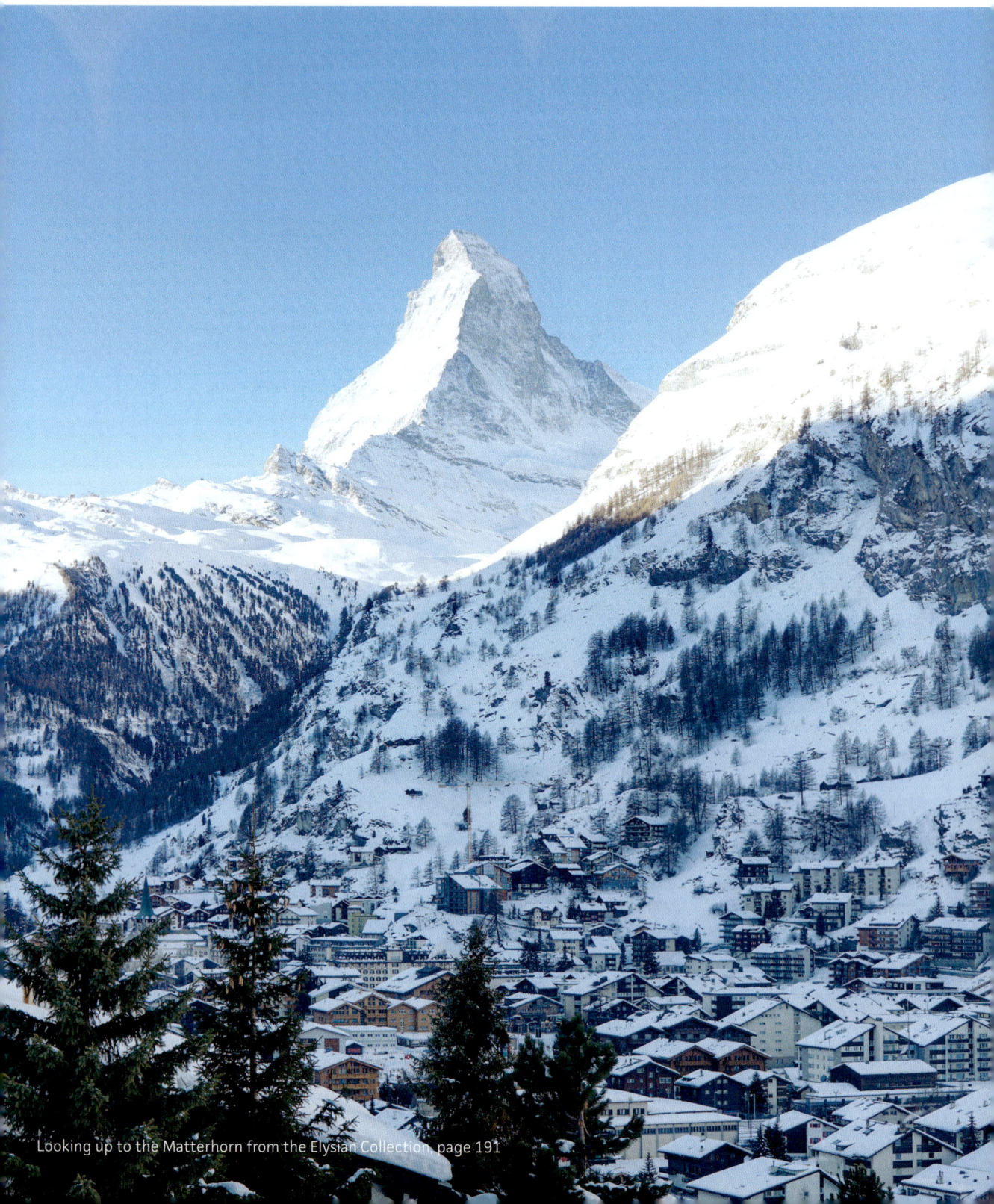

Switzerland

Please go to condenastjohansens.com/switzerland

Looking up to the Matterhorn from the Elysian Collection, page 191

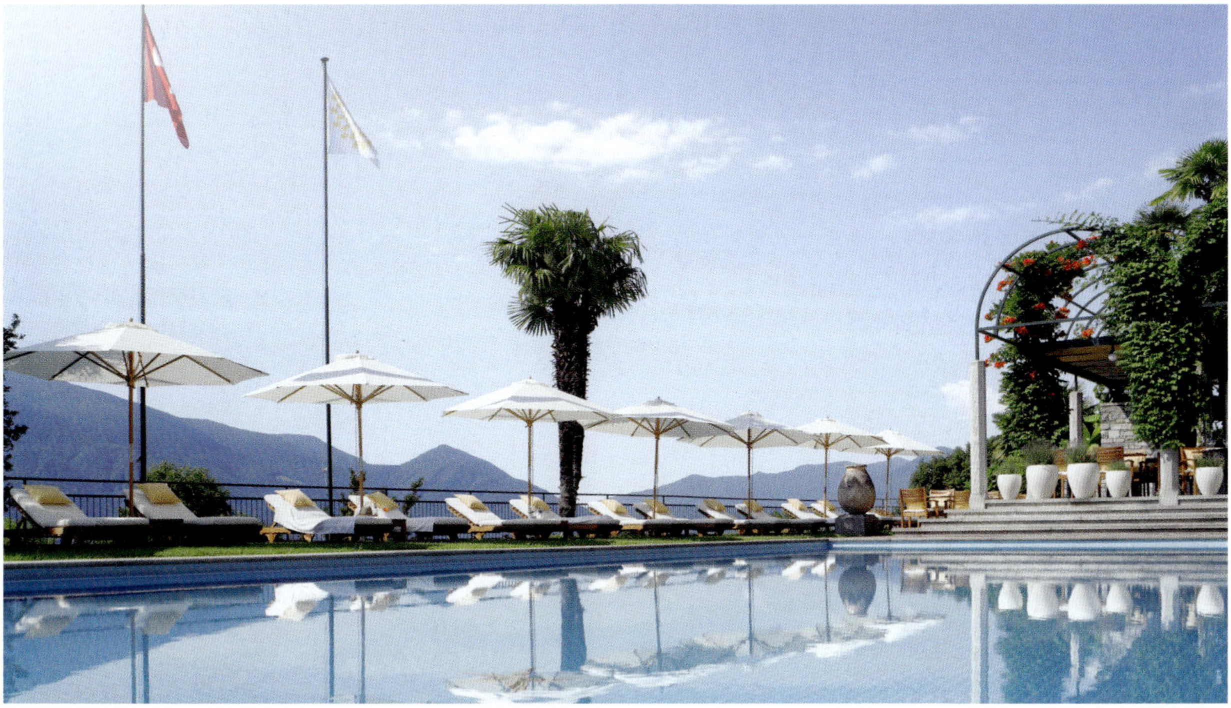

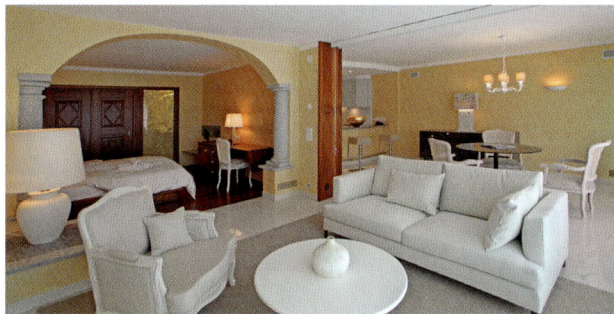

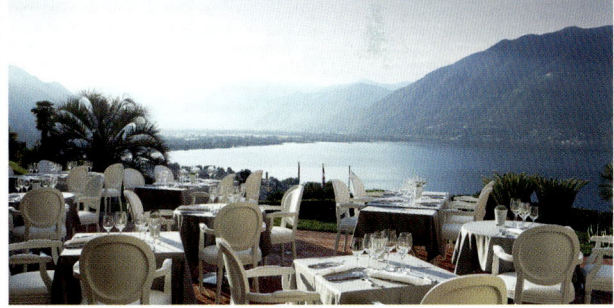

Villa Orselina

Tasteful, stylish Lake Maggiore hilltop hotel

Where Italy meets Switzerland, the Swiss Alps tower over Lake Maggiore and the highest point in Switzerland coincides with the lowest, there's Villa Orselina. Above on high, minutes from the city of Locarno and charming Ascona, it's nigh-on impossible to find a more captivating spot. You'll be snap-happy with photogenic scenes at every turn. Every room and suite faces south and looks across to the lake; most have balconies (with binoculars). The Italian eatery, Il Ristorante has a picture-perfect panoramic vista. And the alfresco La Pergola restaurant's poolside/subtropical garden setting provides yet more lakeside perspectives. Even the chilled Grand Bar has an intimate terrace leading out to the mesmerising sight. Villa Orselina's interior design is as pretty as its surroundings, bedecked in warm neutral colours with intricate woodwork and inviting fireplaces. Special high-tech touches such as bathrooms with starlit ceilings and showers with rainbow-coloured lighting add a funky element. However, it's all about Italian traditions at Il Ristorante whose humungous wine cellar complements each course of antipasti, primo, secondo piatta and dolce followed by an espresso. If this leaves you feeling decidedly decadent each evening, take a trip to the new spa and feel fresh as a daisy in no time.

PRICE FROM:
CHF300

FEATURES:
Lake views; Pool; Restaurant; Spa

ACTIVITIES:
Golf; Skiing; Water sports

NEARBY:
Ascona; Como, Italy; Locarno Film Festival; Ascona Jazz Festival; Ticino Natural Park

GETTING THERE:
Lugano Airport; Milan Malpensa Airport, Italy; Milan Linate Airport, Italy

+41 91 735 73 73 ☎
condenastjohansens.com/villaorselina 🌐
Via Santuario 10, 6644 Locarno - Orselina, Switzerland 🏠

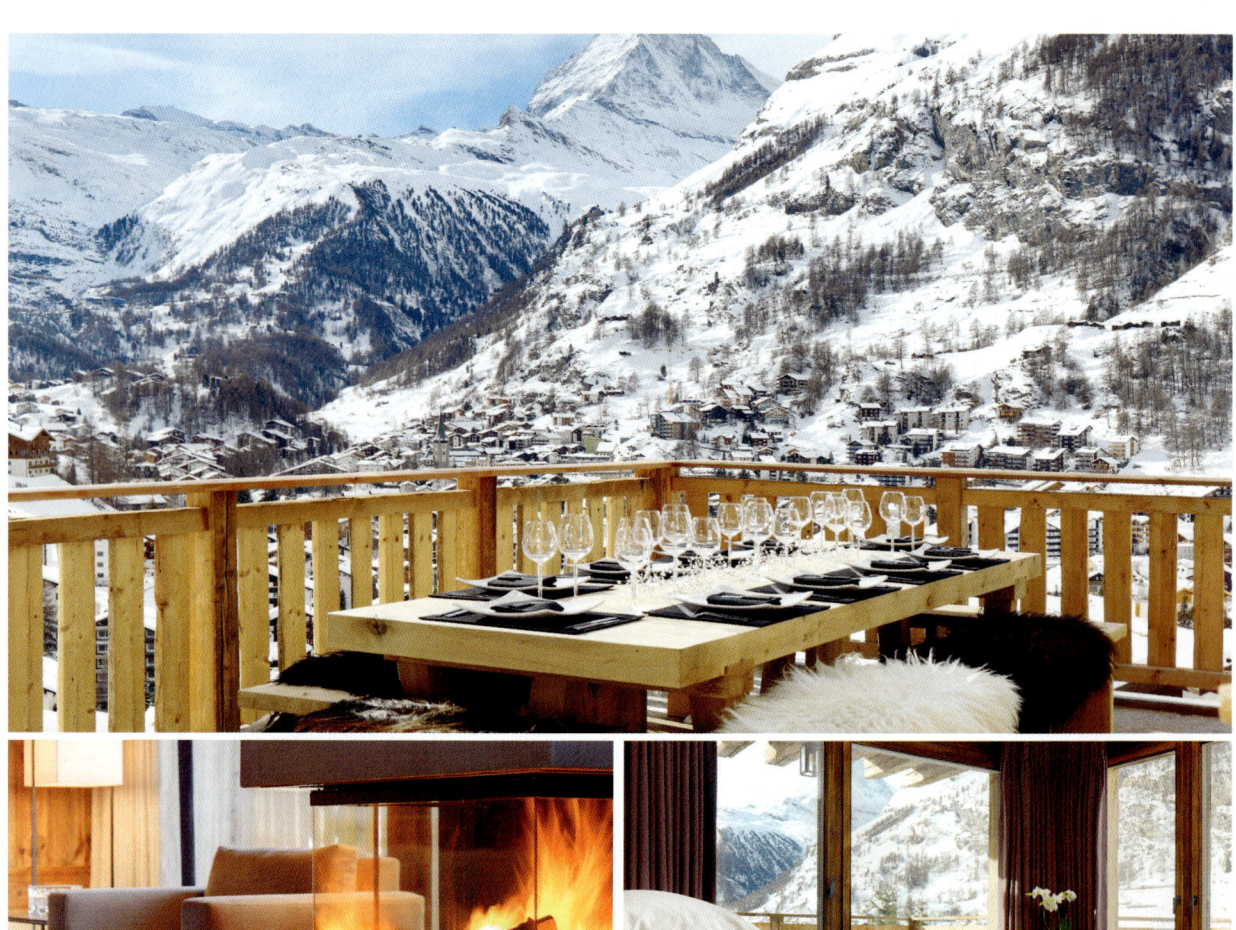

Elysian Collection

Über-private, ultra-stylish Swiss ski chalets

PRICE FROM:
CHF14,500 (per week)

FEATURES:
Family friendly; Pet friendly

ACTIVITIES:
Golf; Shopping; Skiing

NEARBY:
Year-round snow and alpine sports; Gourmet mountain restaurants; Matterhorn helicopter tours; Glacier Express

GETTING THERE:
Zürich Airport; Geneva Airport; Milan Malpensa Airport, Italy

Elysian Collection's four über-private chalets do not belong to this mortal world. They're in a super league of their own. Surrounded by swoonworthy scenery, the year-round skiing/snowboarding opportunities are fit for a king – quite literally: Klosters is a favourite of The Prince of Wales. The service (fully catered or B&B) is beyond compare with Michelin Star-trained chefs and expert sommeliers serve you each day. One of the four chalets (Chesa Falcun) is located in the pretty village of Klosters. Consider it a wooden mini-palace with six bedrooms (plus one designated for travelling staff). And the cherry on this indulgent cake? The wellness area. Several hours south, dominated by the mighty Matterhorn in Zermatt, are Elysian Collection's three other chalets: Grace, Chalet Les Anges and Chalet Maurice. Reached via private funicular railway, the six-bedroom Chalet Maurice is the stuff dreams are made of. The largest chalet of them all is Chalet Les Anges: a seven en-suite beauty with spa, ornamental pool and black marble plunge pool. Then there's Grace and its five bedrooms. With a wellness area, games room and cinema there's a sense of playfulness about this chalet. The sort of place a young prince could get into trouble…

☎ +44 (0)20 3468 2235
🌐 condenastjohansens.com/elysiancollection
🏠 3920 Zermatt, Switzerland

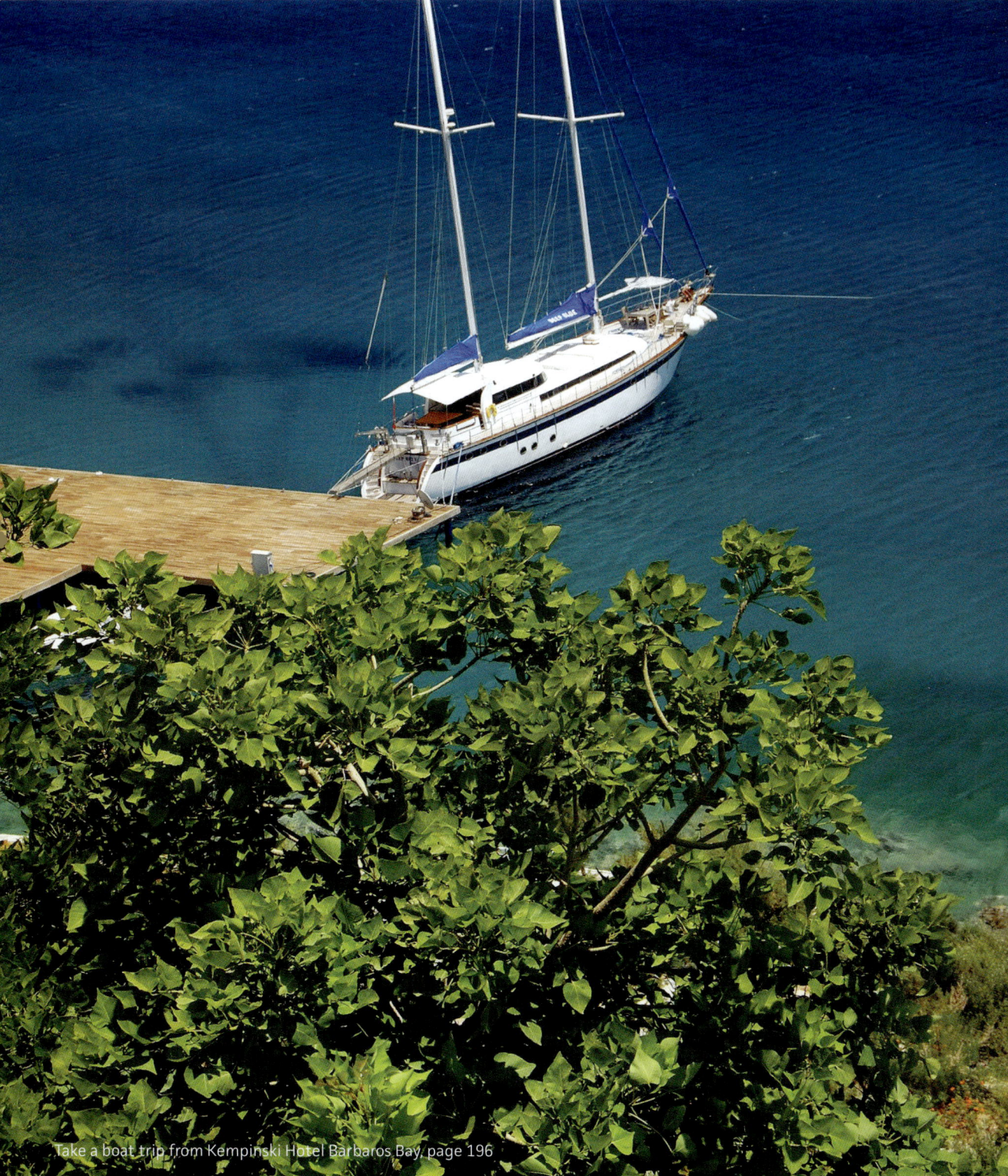

Turkey

Please go to condenastjohansens.com/turkey

Take a boat trip from Kempinski Hotel Barbaros Bay, page 196

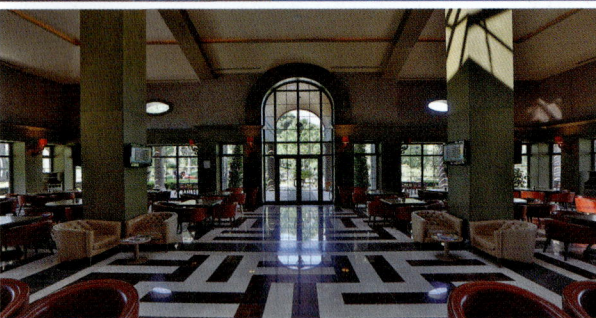

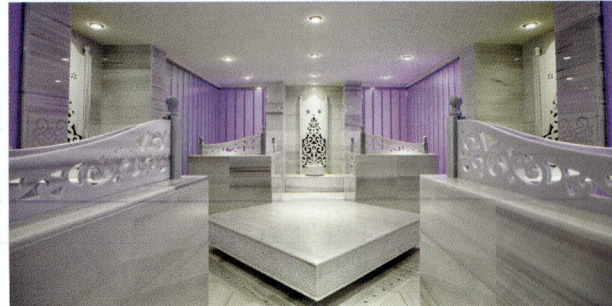

CONDÉ NAST johansens AWARD WINNER 2013

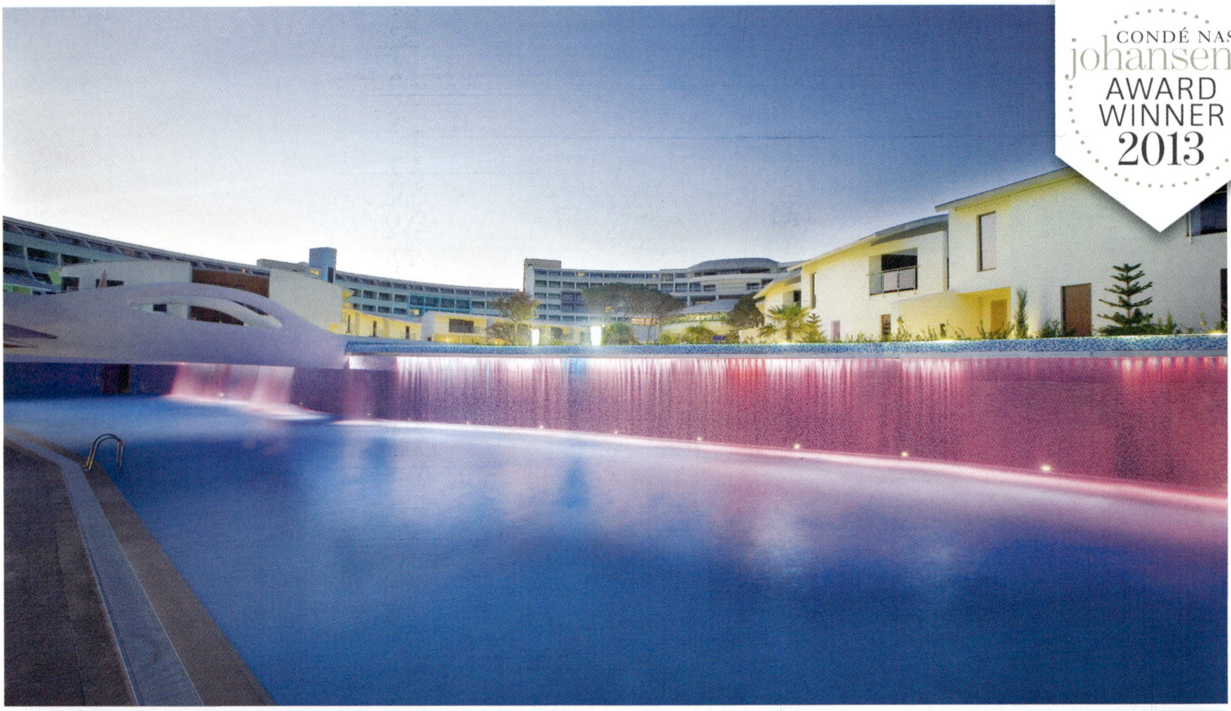

Cornelia Diamond Golf Resort & Spa

Enormous beach-side pleasure centre on Antalya's coast

PRICE FROM:
€400

FEATURES:
Beach access; Family friendly; Restaurant; Sea views; Spa

ACTIVITIES:
Fishing; Golf; Water sports

NEARBY:
Belek; Side; ESPA Crassula Spa Centre; Nick Faldo Championship Golf Course; Aspendos Theatre

GETTING THERE:
Antalya Airport

Cornelia Diamond Golf Resort & Spa, Belek, is a decadent dream that's been made a reality. Less resort, more miniature kingdom, there's a refreshing emphasis on nature and the environment at this green and pleasant place with accommodation to suit everyone from spacious garden facing family rooms to sleek Lake Houses (connected to the main hotel by a space-age tunnel). Crassula Spa is a watery playground of Jacuzzis, pools, relaxation areas and traditional hammam and hosts the most indulgent haven of all: the Spa King Suite. Available for private hire, its Turkish bath, sauna, pool, Asian massage and garden can all be exclusively yours. As if this wasn't enough, Cornelia Diamond provides alternative activities such as golf, entertainment at the hotel's amphitheatre and water sports at the resort's beach. Younger guests haven't been forgotten either thanks to Children's Heaven where there's a cinema and waterpark. After all this fun and exercise, room service might be tempting but then you'd be missing out on the taste explosion offered at the nine restaurants offering everything from traditional Turkish kebabs to the finest seafood.

☎ +90 242 710 1600
condenastjohansens.com/corneliadiamond
Iskele Mevkii, Belek, Antalya, Turkey

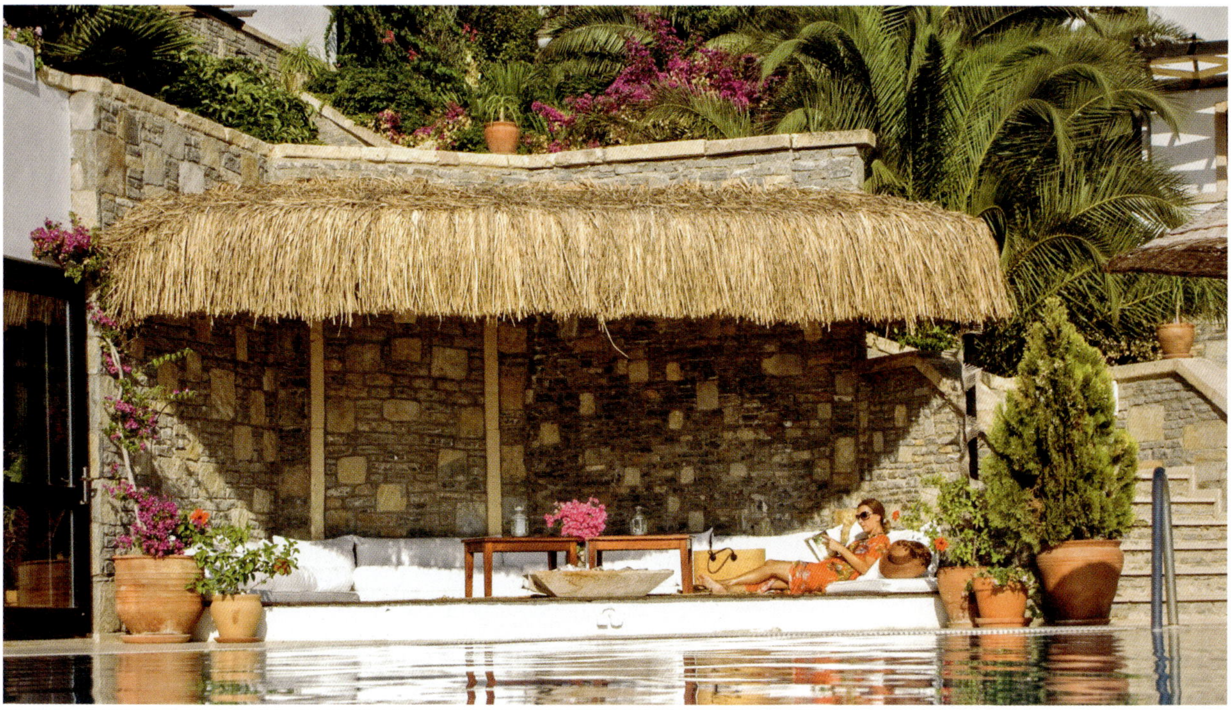

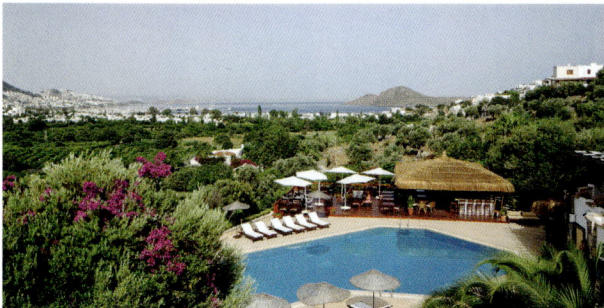
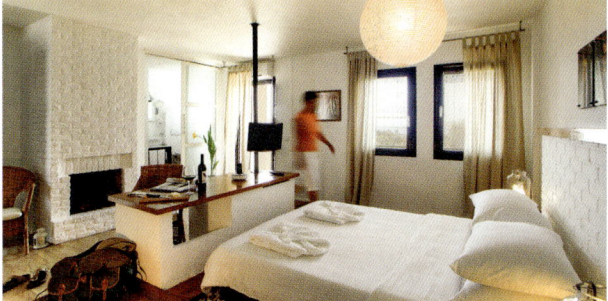

4reasons hotel+bistro

Relaxed family-run resort in the peaceful hills of Yalikavak

A true Turkish delight with achingly good views, this is laid-back luxury at its best. Perched high on a hilltop, tickling Anatolia's west coast, the 4reasons haven-on-earth offers an escape from the madding crowds of nearby bustling Bodrum just a hop, skip and a jump from the charming fishing port of Yalikavak. Overlooking the azure Aegean Sea, 4reasons hotel+bistro in Turkey provides a zen-like paradise nestled amongst olive groves. It's a small and perfectly formed oasis of calm designed to take your breath away, lift the spirits, get your groove on and deliver you swiftly into a restorative state of just letting it be. Go get cocooned in the balmy environment of your surrounds and tune in to the rhythm of nature. Eat, breathe, chill and savour it all. Dine at the magical hands of 4reasons bistro's creative chefs then retire to one of the rooms or suites, each elegantly simple in their décor with whitewashed and wood interiors; the perfect antidote to those hot pink, eye-popping sunsets.

PRICE FROM:
€110

FEATURES:
Family friendly; Pool; Restaurant; Sea views

ACTIVITIES:
Fishing; Horse riding; Water sports

NEARBY:
Bodrum; Gumusluk; Beaches; Gullet cruise; Sailing

GETTING THERE:
Milas-Bodrum Airport

+90 252 385 3212 ☎
condenastjohansens.com/4reasonshotel 🌐
Bakan Caddesi 2, Yalikavak, 48430 Bodrum, Turkey 🏠

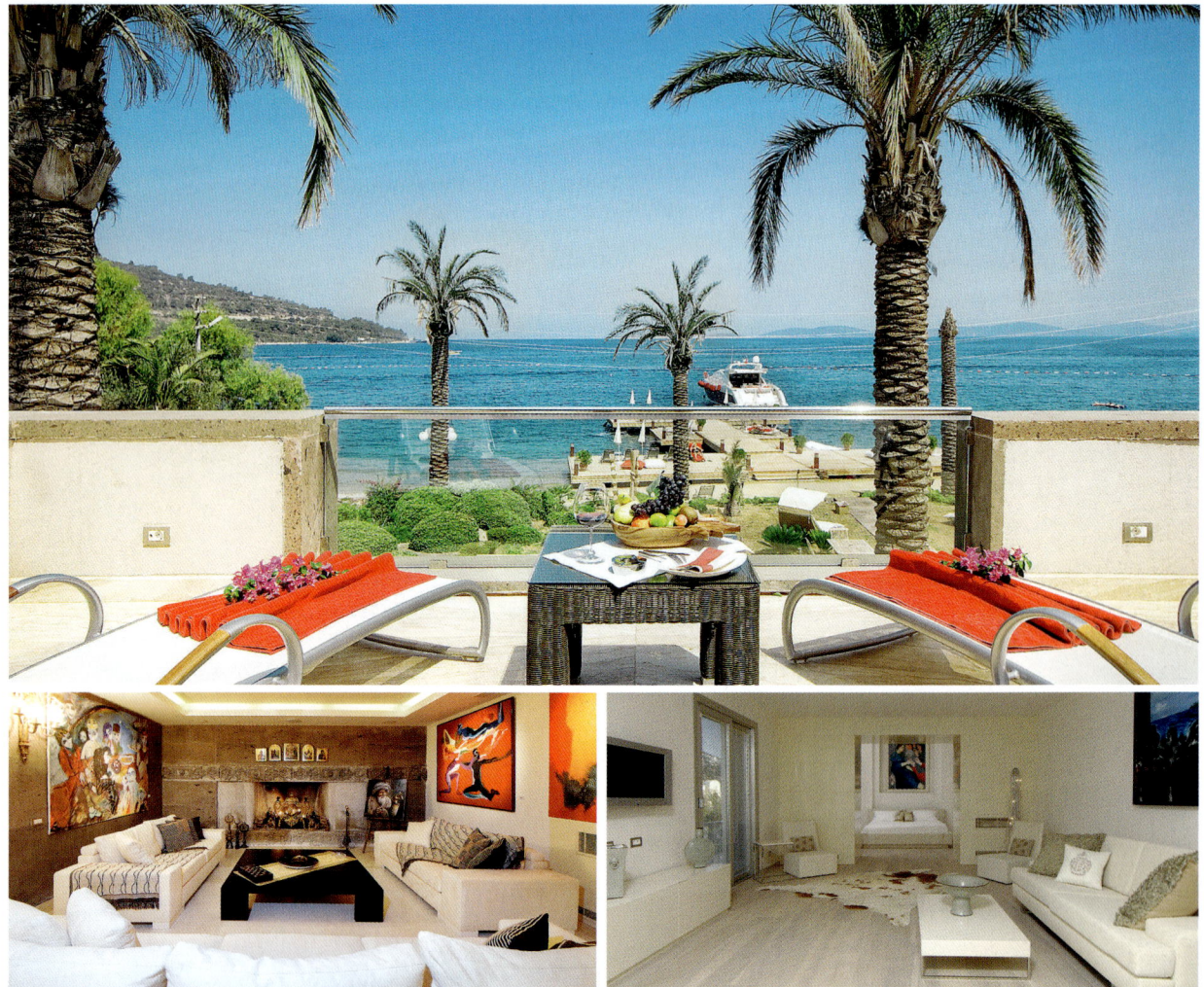

Casa Dell'Arte Residence

Funky art hotel in the fishing village of Torba

PRICE FROM:
€300

FEATURES:
Beach access; Gym; Pool; Restaurant; Spa

ACTIVITIES:
Fishing; Tennis; Water sports

NEARBY:
Türkbüks; Marmaris; Private gullet cruises; Bodrum Knights Castle; Bodrum Underwater Archaeology Museum and Mauseleum

GETTING THERE:
Milas-Bodrum Airport; Dalaman Airport

Lovingly created by a prolific Turkish art collector, Casa Dell'Arte Residence on the Bodrum Peninsula's Torba Bay is a masterclass in hip. A sleek minimalist cube – flanked by vintage cars – it unfolds like Pandora's Box as you walk through the ornate doors. There's a definite touch of Liberace-esque bonkers to it: chandeliers cascade above the exterior courtyard and a grand piano sits below a glass staircase. But the eccentricity is expertly reigned in within the zodiac-themed suites where art is the main focus. Each displays carefully chosen contemporary Turkish pieces highlighted by sexy, stylish furniture (all custom designed) and subtle cream tones. Lofty duplex boltholes channel Sagittarian or Scorpio energy and the earthy, fiery vibe of the Taurus and Leo is present in the sea-view suites designed with bedroom and sitting areas looking out to the ocean. The dining experience at Casa Dell'Arte restaurant is a rustic, charming one with a choice of beach-side tables laden with meze and catch of the day. Don't forget to book a private art tour of Casa Dell'Arte's masterpieces or become a living, breathing work of art yourself and strike a pose on the sunbathing jetty or private beach overlooking the Aegean.

☎ +90 252 367 1848
🌐 condenastjohansens.com/casadellarte
🏠 Torba Mahallesi, Ismet İnönü Caddesi No 64-66, 48400 Bodrum, Turkey

Kempinski Hotel Barbaros Bay

Turkish hospitality at its warmest, just outside bustling Bodrum

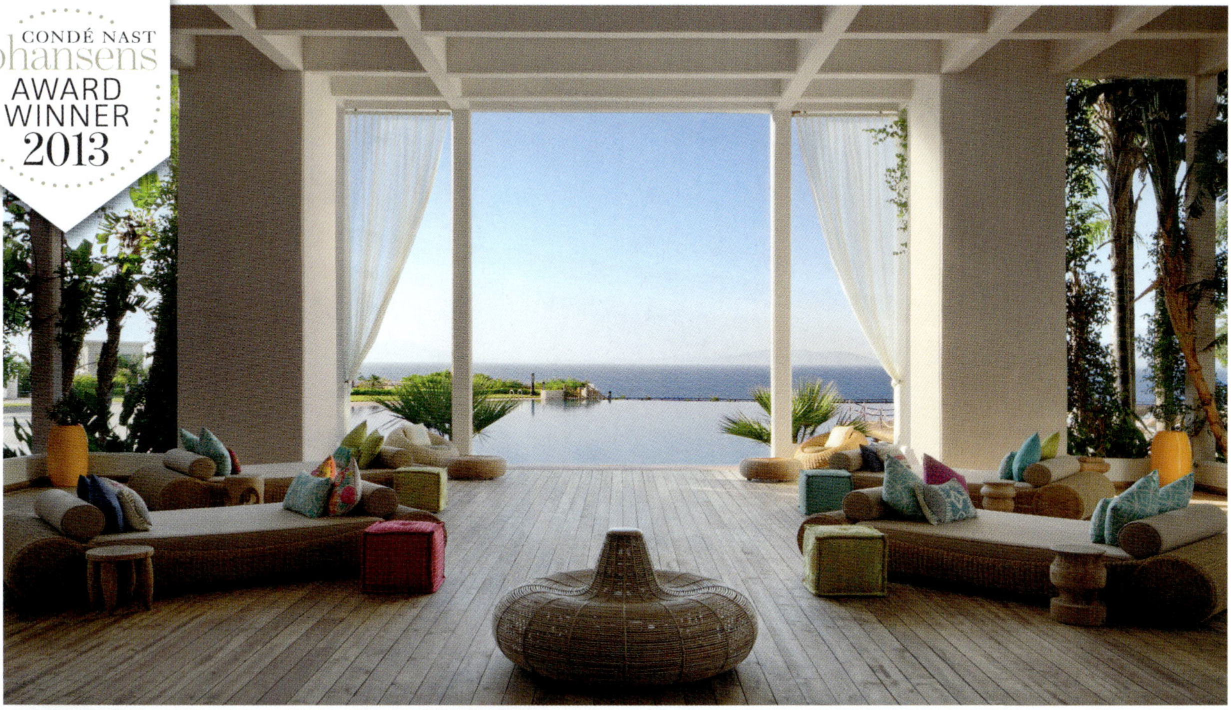

From The Spa to the private marina and on-site helipad, everything about Kempinski Hotel Barbaros Bay screams pure, unadulterated luxury. But it's the views that will send your jaw to the floor. Perched on the cliff side in the rocky Gokova Gulf (Turkey's St Tropez), the hotel delivers knockout panoramas of the unfurling Aegean Sea over a private bay from every room, terrace and sun-lounger. A contemporary complex of columns, all white and laden with glass, the hotel rises from the hillside like a mini city and yet the über-chilled vibe belies its vast size. Outside, the huge, curvaceous infinity pool is the scene-stealer; inside, you'll find a haven of easy-breezy elegance with sweeping lounges strewn with overstuffed sofas, muted tones, wooden floors and floor-to-ceiling windows (did we mention the views?). Days spent cruising the rugged coastline by catamaran are only matched by hitting the spa – a whopping 5,500m² sanctuary of pools, Turkish baths, steam and treatment rooms. Like everything else at Barbaros Bay, the food is seriously good. Four excellent restaurants serve everything from Italian to Asian cuisine but seafood under the stars at the beach-front dining spot, Barbarossa, is where memory-making moments are made.

PRICE FROM:
€160

FEATURES:
Beach access; Family friendly; Restaurant; Sea views; Spa

ACTIVITIES:
Fishing; Golf; Water sports

NEARBY:
Bodrum; Turkbuku; Kos; Ephesus; Gulet cruise

GETTING THERE:
Milas-Bodrum Airport

+90 252 311 03 03 ☎
condenastjohansens.com/barbaros 🌐
Kizilagac Koyu, Gerenkuyu Mevkii, Yaliciftlik, 48400 Bodrum, 🏠
Turkey

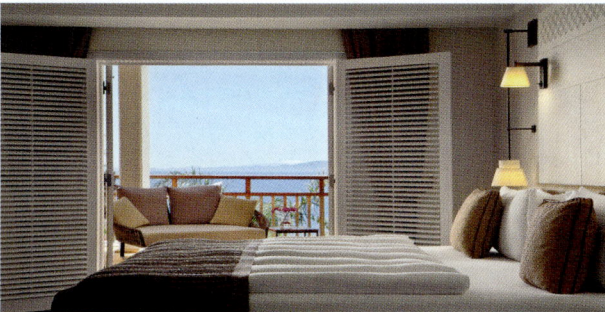
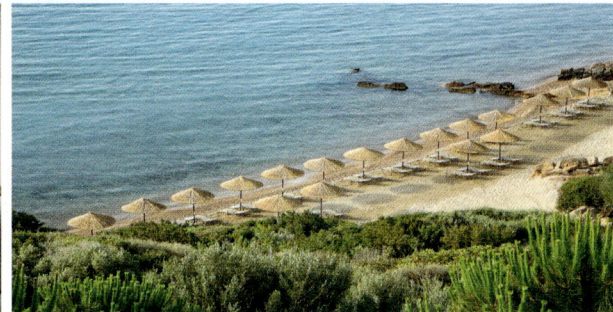

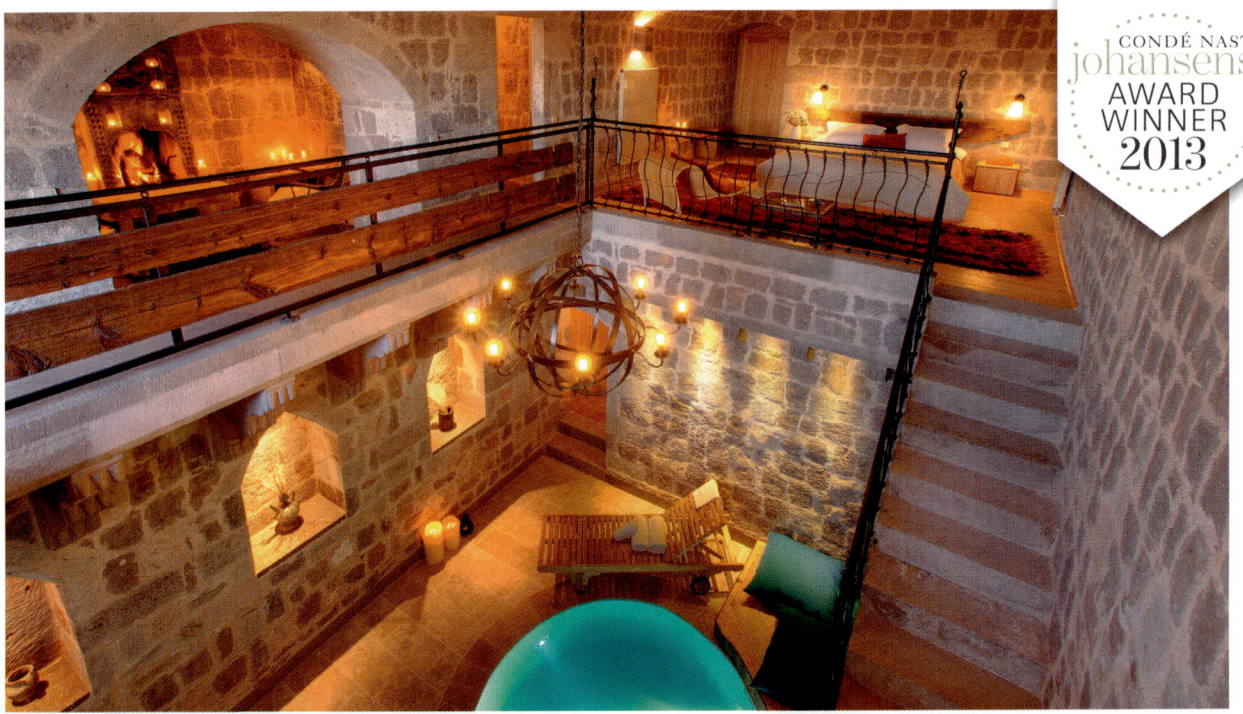

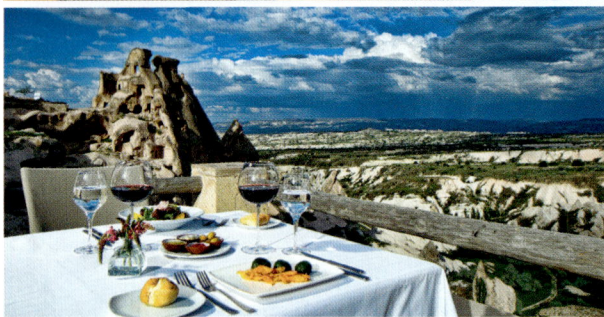

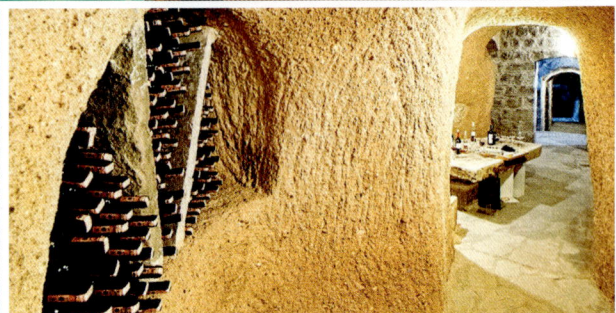

argos in Cappadocia

Monkish serenity in Cappadocia's age-old stone caves

PRICE FROM:
€150

FEATURES:
Pet friendly; Restaurant

ACTIVITIES:
Cycling; Horse riding; Walking

NEARBY:
Göreme; Nevşehir; Hiking in valleys; UNESCO Göreme Open-Air Museum; Uçhisar Castle

GETTING THERE:
Nevsehir Airport; Kayseri Airport

☎ +90 384 2193130
⊕ condenastjohansens.com/argos
⌂ Uçhisar, 50240 Nevşehir (Cappadocia), Turkey

Your very own ivory tower, argos in Cappadocia (one-time monastery and Silk Road stop-off) is an inspired hotel hewn from volcanic stone. A maze of caves and underground tunnels housing a devilishly decadent wine cellar, argos in Cappadocia is located in the ancient village of Uçhisar. Carved from the volcanic lava emitted from the nearby Mount Erciyes, the city is a spectacular focus for the sunrises and sunsets that illuminate the Cappadocian terrain. Blanketed in snow during the winter and strewn with roses and birdsong come summer, this is about as dramatic as hotel locations get. Rooms have been crafted, rather than built from the local stone and are elegantly simple and stylish with Seljuk and Ottoman touches as a reminder of the centuries-old civilisation surrounding you. Most have views of the lush gardens or sun terraces and some suites have their own underground cave pool for secret subterranean swimming. Above ground, enjoy a drink on the terrace overlooking Pigeon Valley before experiencing argos in Cappadocia's fabulous food. Chefs work their magic with fresh local ingredients combined with cutting-edge techniques giving you a unique flavour of the best of a cuisine that's been a thousand years in the making.

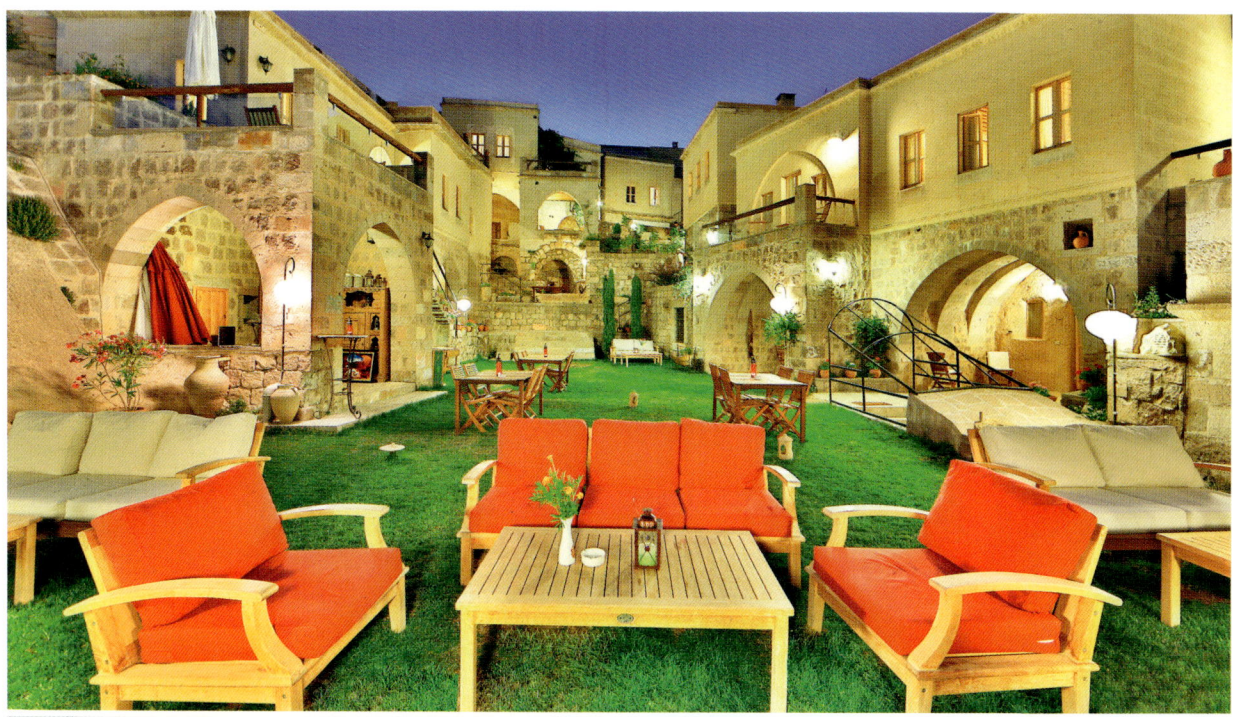

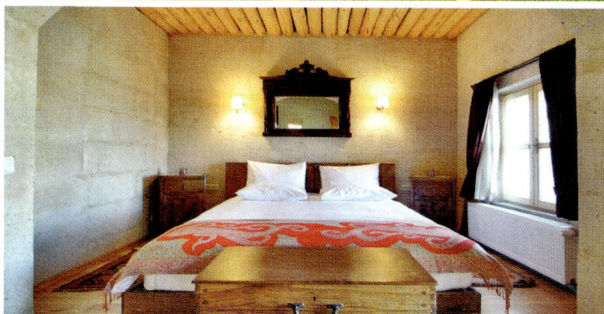
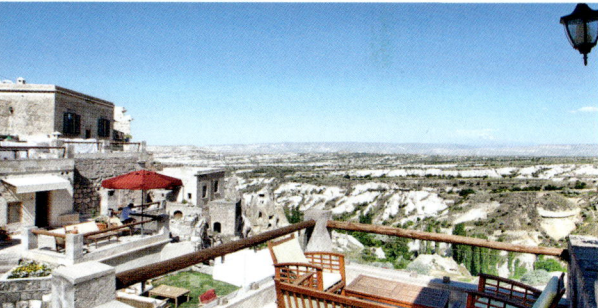

Taskonaklar Rocky Palace

Fantasy meets luxurious reality in Cappadocia

The science fiction landscape of centuries-old Cappadocia in central Turkey has to be seen to be believed. And nothing beats soaring above it in a hot-air balloon. It's pure adventure drama looking down on the honeycomb of subterranean villages, troglodyte dwellings and cave churches with meringue-like peaks and mushroom-shaped "fairy chimneys" (huge pinnacles that stand up to 40 metres tall). For a window onto this fantastical world, check into Taskonaklar Rocky Palace in the citadel of Uçhisar. Carved from the volcanic rock, this cavernous retreat is brimming with history and character with domed ceilings, arched windows, hidden alcoves and antique-stuffed nooks and crannies. For total melodrama book Suite 119 whose vast, vaulted rooms are lined with Persian rugs, or Royal Suite 101 complete with wow-factor terrace featuring an LED-lit hot tub looking out to jaw-dropping panoramas. With so many steep streets and hills, you'll be walking up an appetite in no time (make sure to head through the tunnels to Uçhisar Castle with unfurling views of the Göreme Valley below). Your much needed energy boost in the form of Taskonaklar's traditional Turkish fare, is the order of the day with just-baked breakfast pastries hitting the spot each morning.

PRICE FROM:
€120

FEATURES:
Restaurant

ACTIVITIES:
Horse riding; Sightseeing; Walking

NEARBY:
Göreme; Ürgüp; Pigeon Valley; Trekking; Hot-air ballooning

GETTING THERE:
Nevşehir Airport; Kayseri Airport

+90 384 219 3001 ☎
condenastjohansens.com/taskonaklar 🌐
Gedik Sokak No 8, Uçhisar, Nevşehir (Cappadocia), Turkey 🏠

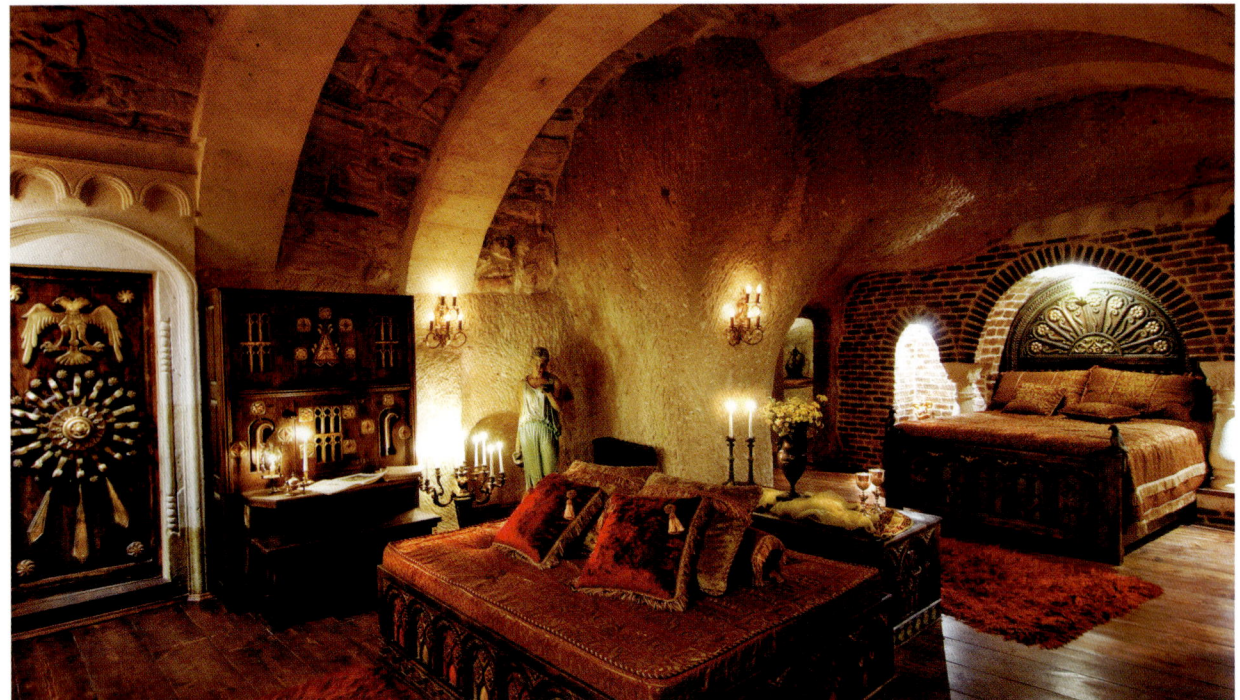

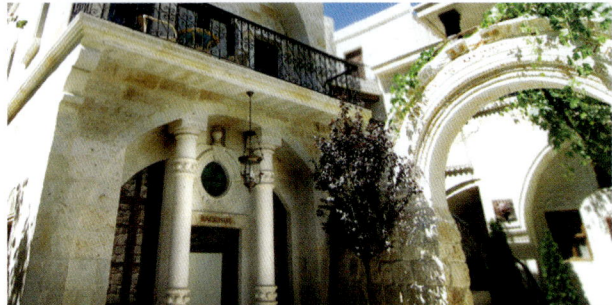
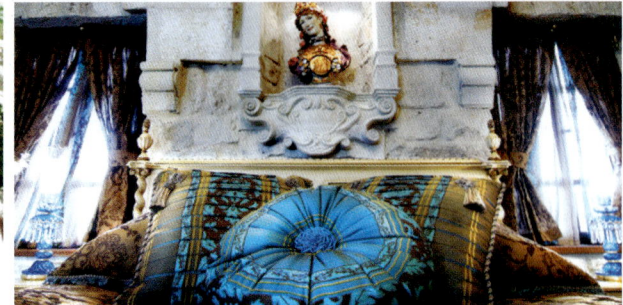

Sacred House

Fairy tales are brought to life in Cappadocia

PRICE FROM:
€200

FEATURES:
Restaurant

ACTIVITIES:
Fishing; Golf; Skiing

NEARBY:
Göreme; Avanos; Nevşehir; Wineries; UNESCO Göreme Open-Air Museum

GETTING THERE:
Nevşehir Airport; Kayseri Airport

A stunning design coup in the heart of the Cappadocia's UNESCO World Heritage Site, Sacred House is something from a parallel universe. An ambitious restoration and interior design project, it's the brainchild of host Turan Gulcuoglu, a big romantic with a talent for combining medieval art and contemporary luxury. Each of his 23 rooms is exquisitely and uniquely decorated with a specific theme. Choose from The King's Ego, a stately tale of dark wooden beams and golden goblets. Or perhaps Anka's Lair with its richly coloured linens set against a backdrop of stone. They're all spacious with a theatrical sense of comfort - forget tv, it's time to let your imagination run wild. Wining and dining takes place in the intimacy of the cellar (the sweet cherry liquor wins many over) and the restaurant where the menu features both Turkish and European dishes (each selected for their bold and unusual flavours). The breakfast is worth waking up early for. Sacred House is your very own fairy tale, a boutique hotel that's so cosy you'll never want this story to end. Listen out: Sacred House is due to re-open in early 2014 following a revamp that's set to add a touch more drama. The Roman underground spa is hotly anticipated.

☎ +90 384 341 7102
🌐 condenastjohansens.com/sacredhouse
🏠 Dutlucami Mahallesi, Barbaros Hayrettin Sokak, No 25, 50400 Ürgüp - Nevşehir (Cappadocia), Turkey

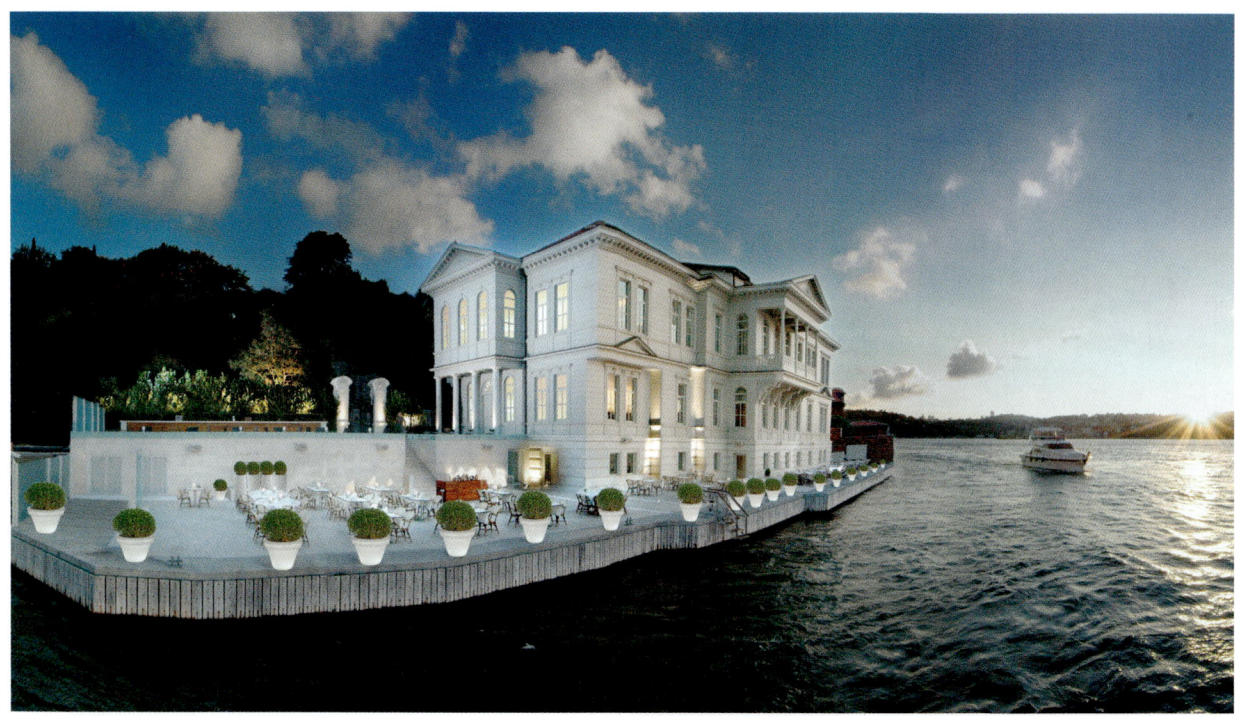

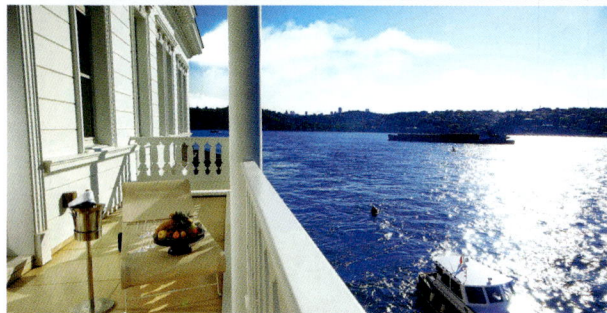
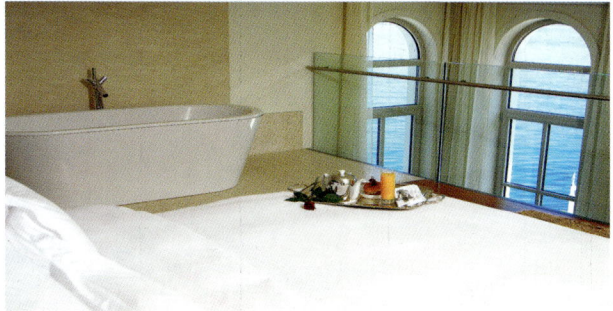

A'jia Hotel

Classic Ottoman architecture meets minimal design on Istanbul's Bosphorus

Seemingly floating on the Asian waters of the Bosphorus, you arrive by speed boat to Istanbul's A'jia Hotel. Away from the hustle and bustle of Sultanhamet's old city, this grand mansion captures the essence of contemporary chic alongside traditional Ottoman grandeur. Soothing cool white interiors with creamy leather, shiny floors and flowing drapes set the minimalist scene where modern gizmos and gadgets keep matters very 21st century in this masterpiece of 19th-century design. After staff warmly welcome you, they fade discreetly into the background leaving you to relish in your lofty room full of low key glamour. Request a river view to catch the amazing sunsets over the water and wake up to the Straits' sights and sounds as it revs up into its daily rhythm. Dining at A'jia's smart restaurant is a refined affair of Mediterranean dishes where you can also enjoy drinks and breakfast on the terrace (more views!). Pile up indulgent pancakes or tuck into traditional Turkish breakfasts of cheeses, olives, honey and fresh bread each morning before exploring Istanbul's markets, minarets and hammams (essential!) knowing that A'jia's calm, cocooning walls await your return at the end of a busy day.

PRICE FROM:
€275

FEATURES:
Family friendly; Restaurant; Sea views; Wheelchair access

ACTIVITIES:
Fishing; Shopping; Sightseeing

NEARBY:
Istanbul old city; Bosphorus; European side of Istanbul

GETTING THERE:
Istanbul Sabiha Gökçen Airport; Istanbul Ataturk Airport

+90 216 413 9300
condenastjohansens.com/ajiahotel
Ahmet Rasim Pasa Yalisi, Çubuklu Caddesi, No 27, Kanlica, Istanbul, Turkey

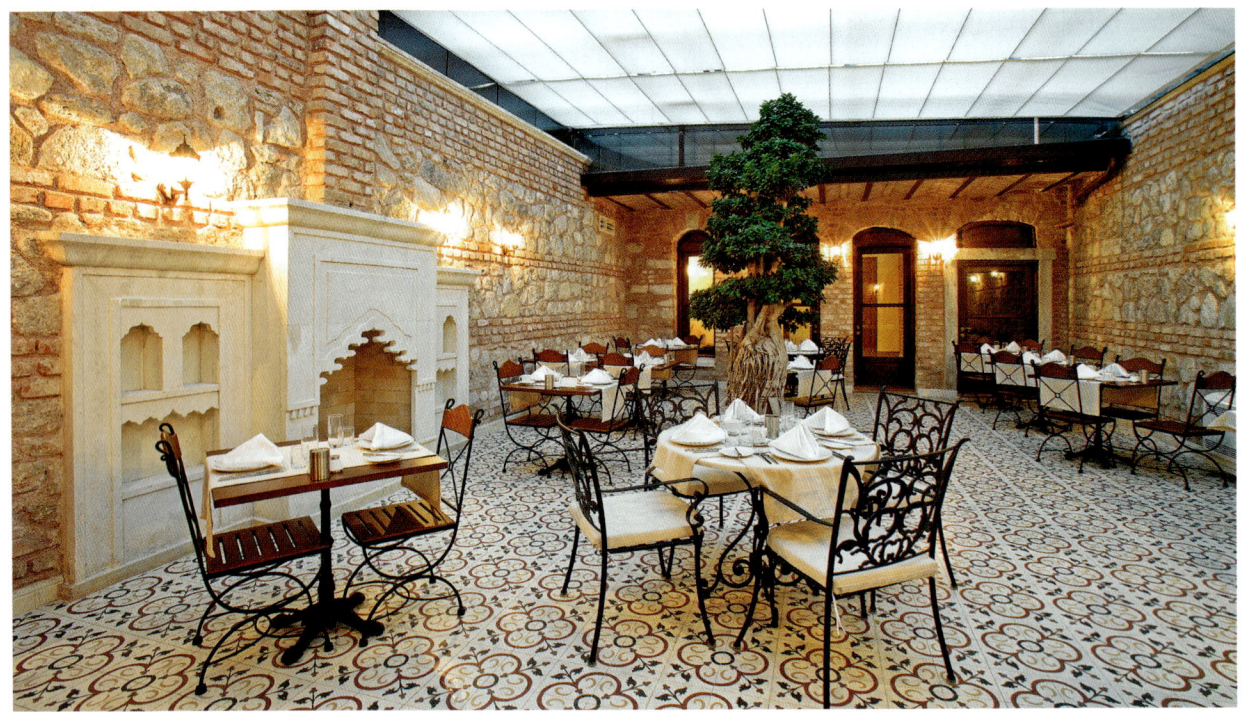

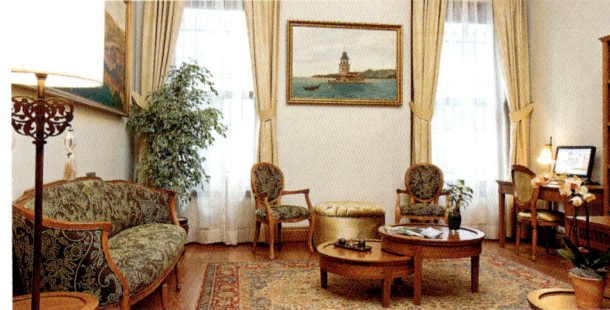
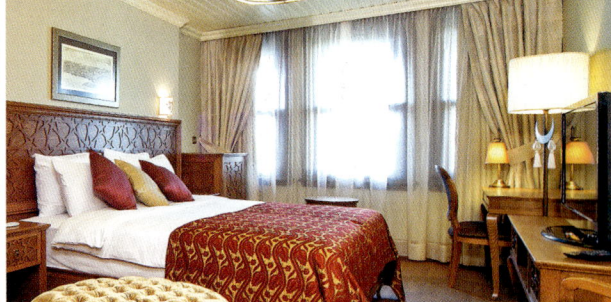

Celine Hotel

A dash of modernity in old Istanbul

PRICE FROM:
€158

FEATURES:
Family friendly; Sea views

ACTIVITIES:
Shopping; Sightseeing

NEARBY:
Topkapi Palace; Janissary barracks; Hagia Sophia Museum; Blue Mosque; Grand Bazaar

GETTING THERE:
Istanbul Atatürk Airport; Istanbul Sabiha Gökçen Airport

Perfectly located in the beating heart of Turkey's fascinating capital, Celine Hotel resides within Istanbul's ancient Sultanahmet district. A charming bijou hotel, it's just a minute away from the ancient Roman Hippodrome of Constantinople and neighbours the Blue Mosque, yet offers a tranquil sanctuary from the wonderfully frantic hustle and bustle on the street. Warm hospitality is the top priority here with 14 plush suites complete with chic modern bathrooms kitted out with heated marble flooring and Jacuzzis for relaxing me-time. Tastefully decorated in luxury soft furnishings with an authentic Ottoman style, they are spacious and designed with sheer comfort in mind. They're also dens of high-techery with motion-sensitive lights, iPod docking stations and various other gizmos for the utmost entertainment and convenience. A colourful hot and cold breakfast buffet is laid out in the light, airy and exquisitely tiled conservatory each morning. And after a day of exploring the city and sampling the local fare head to Celine's Irish-style bar where you'll find the owner and his colourful team (all speak great English) offering gems of advice on where to go and what to do next. Istanbul is divine by moonlight and Celine's views from its higher floors take full advantage of the mesmorising scene. Glimpses of the blue Bosphorus waters can be seen up here.

☎ +90 212 517 19 19
🌐 condenastjohansens.com/celinehotel
🏠 Peykhane Cad No 28, 34122 Sultanahmet - Istanbul, Turkey

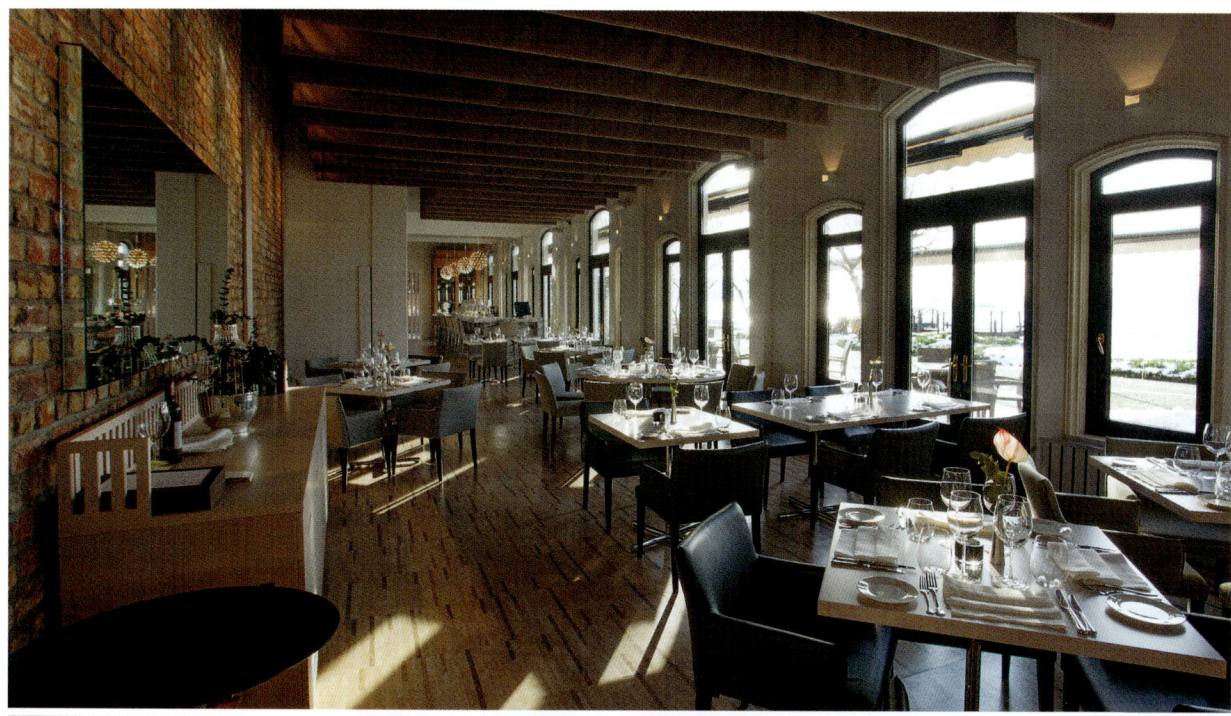

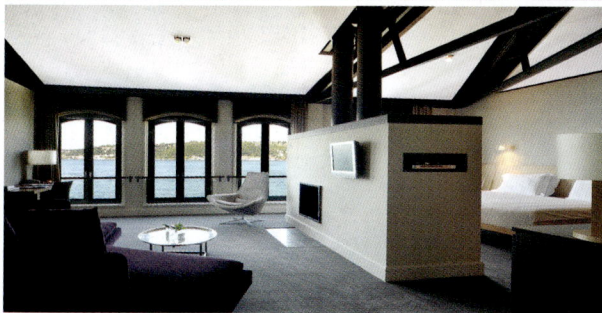
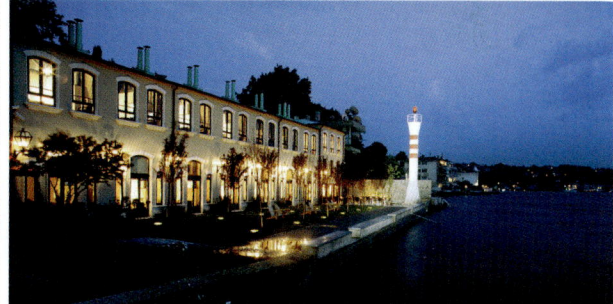

Sumahan On The Water

Utter serenity beside the Bosphorus Straits

What the Asian side of Istanbul lacks in sightseeing hotspots (the magnificent mosques, museums and palaces are all on the European side), it more than makes up for in peace and charm. And it's here that you'll find fashionable Sumahan On The Water. Right on the banks of the Bosphorus, this boutique retreat has buzz without the bustle. Industrial touches (exposed brickwork, steel girders) hint at the 19th-century building's former life as a raki distillery (raki is Turkey's equivalent of ouzo), while the 24 rooms have a New-York-loft-apartment feel with polished wood floors, marble bathrooms, picture windows (what a view to wake up to!) and Eames chairs. The seven loft suites come with a private water-front garden and a mini-hammam. Tapasuma is Sumahan's glamorous Turkish and Mediterranean restaurant whose mezzes (small dishes) include just-caught fish, while the Waterfront Cafe's light Turkish and international menu is best enjoyed on the seaside terrace. The nearby neighbourhood of Çengelköy with its wooden houses, seaside mansions, fish stands and pastry shops, is the ideal spot for a stroll to burn off those gloriously consumed calories. And when you feel like switching sides, hop on the private boat to the heart of the city action. Before you head out though, book a Bosphorus Dream Massage at the hotel spa for your return.

PRICE FROM:
€175

FEATURES:
Family friendly; Gym; Restaurant; Sea views; Wheelchair access

ACTIVITIES:
Fishing; Shopping; Tennis

NEARBY:
Old City; Bosphorus; Beylerbeyi Palace; Istanbul's nightclubs

GETTING THERE:
Istanbul Atatürk Airport; Istanbul Sabiha Gökçen Airport

+90 216 422 8000 ☎
condenastjohansens.com/sumahan ⊕
Kuleli Caddesi No 43, Çengelköy, 34684 Istanbul, Turkey ⌂

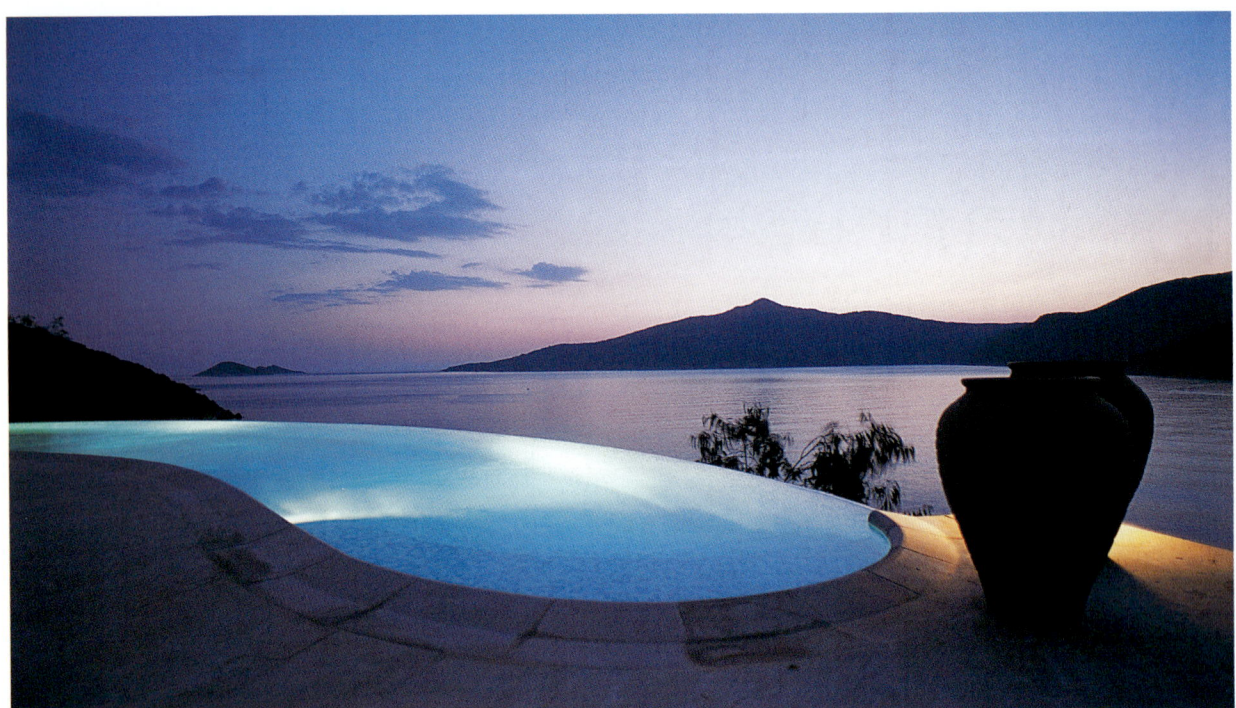

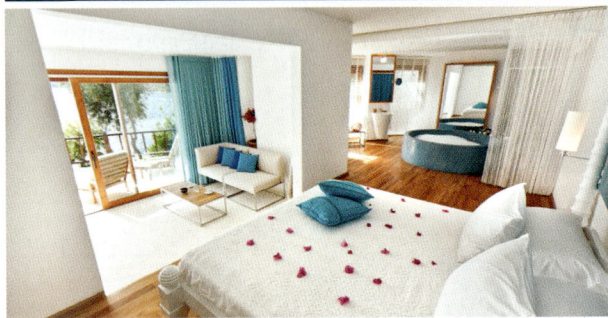

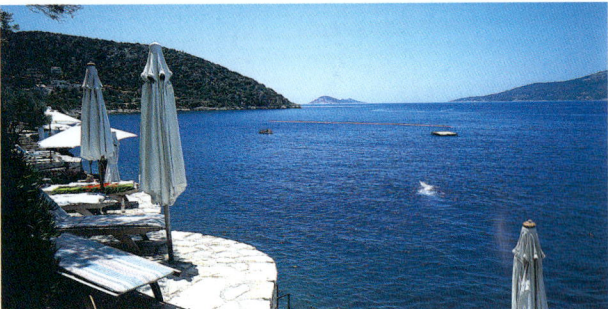

Villa Mahal

An ocean lover's paradise in quiet Kalkan

PRICE FROM:
€300

FEATURES:
Beach access; Pool; Restaurant; Sea views; Spa

ACTIVITIES:
Fishing; Walking; Water sports

NEARBY:
Kas; Fethiye; Daily gulet cruise; Yacht harbour; Patara beach

GETTING THERE:
Dalaman Airport

☎ +90 242 844 32 68
🌐 condenastjohansens.com/villamahal
🏠 Kalkan, 07960 Antalya, Turkey

This little patch of the Lycian Coast honours the few known facts about the ancient Lycian civilisation. Just like these fascinating, mysterious people (who were also perhaps very fit considering this steep mountainous land), Kalkan is enigmatic, independent and terrifically free spirited. It remains unspoilt by towering concrete and swarms of tourists and retains its rugged, natural beauty. Approached from an inconspicuous dusty track, Villa Mahal in Kalkan Bay suddenly materialises as a welcome mirage in the blinding sun. Instantaneously it's evident that Villa Mahal's world is all about kicking-back, relaxing and rejuvenating. This is a refuge from the daily grind where decisions revolve around the rooftop restaurant's Turkish/Mediterranean menu, beach restaurant's à la carte options, the perfect sunbathing spot (Beach Club? Infinity pool? Private terrace?) and water sport pursuits (sailing? Kayaking? Scuba diving?). If the lack of stress doesn't have you in a zombie-like state then time spent glassy-eyed staring at the twinkling emerald green and dark blue water assuredly will. Full-height windows from bedrooms and suites bring the meditative powers of the setting in; all have terraces making most of the view. Indulgent tip: book one of the Sunset Rooms or the two-storey Pool Room with its very own pool and unbeatable view.

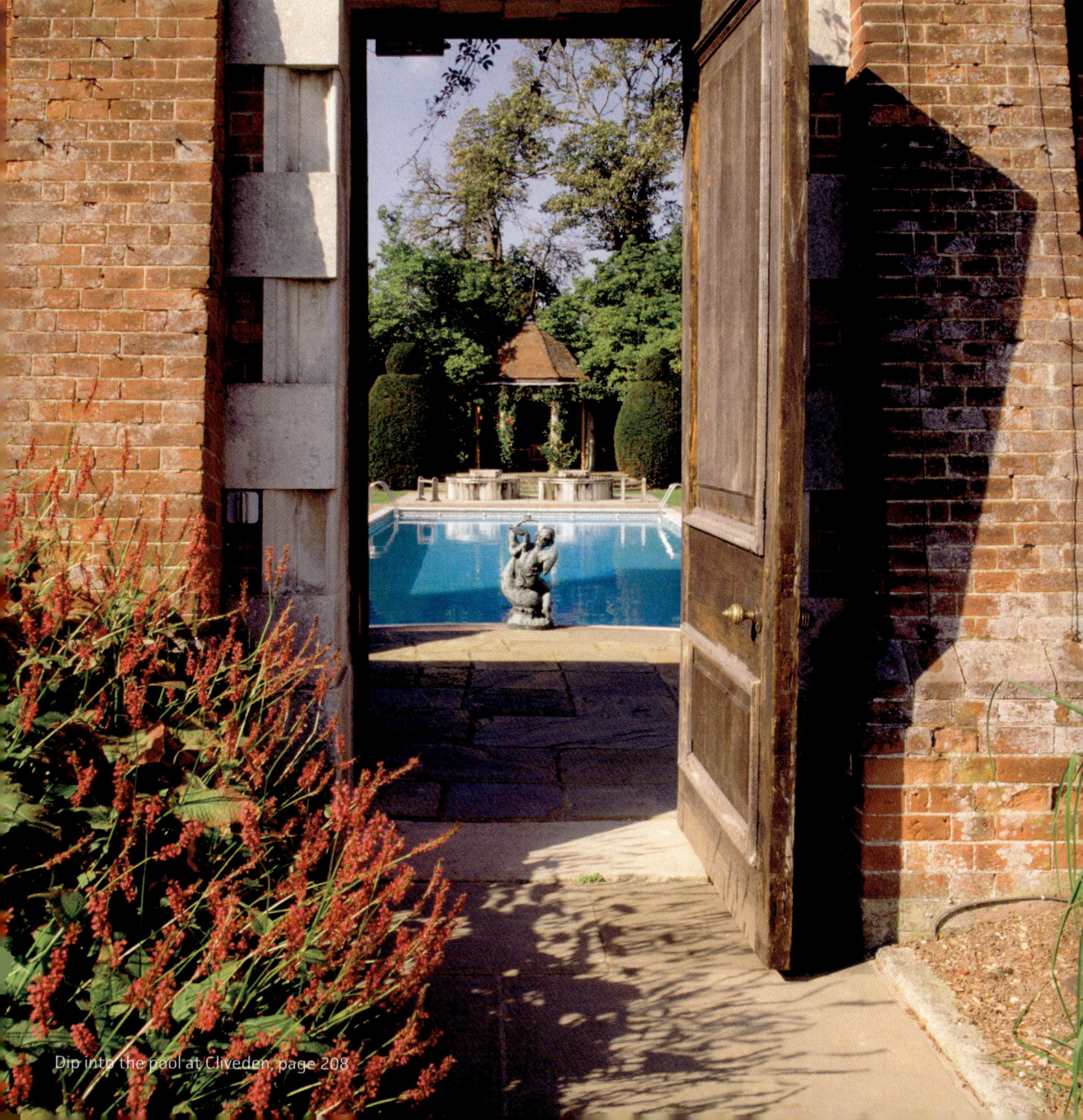

UK/ England

Please go to condenastjohansens.com/england

Dip into the pool at Cliveden, page 208

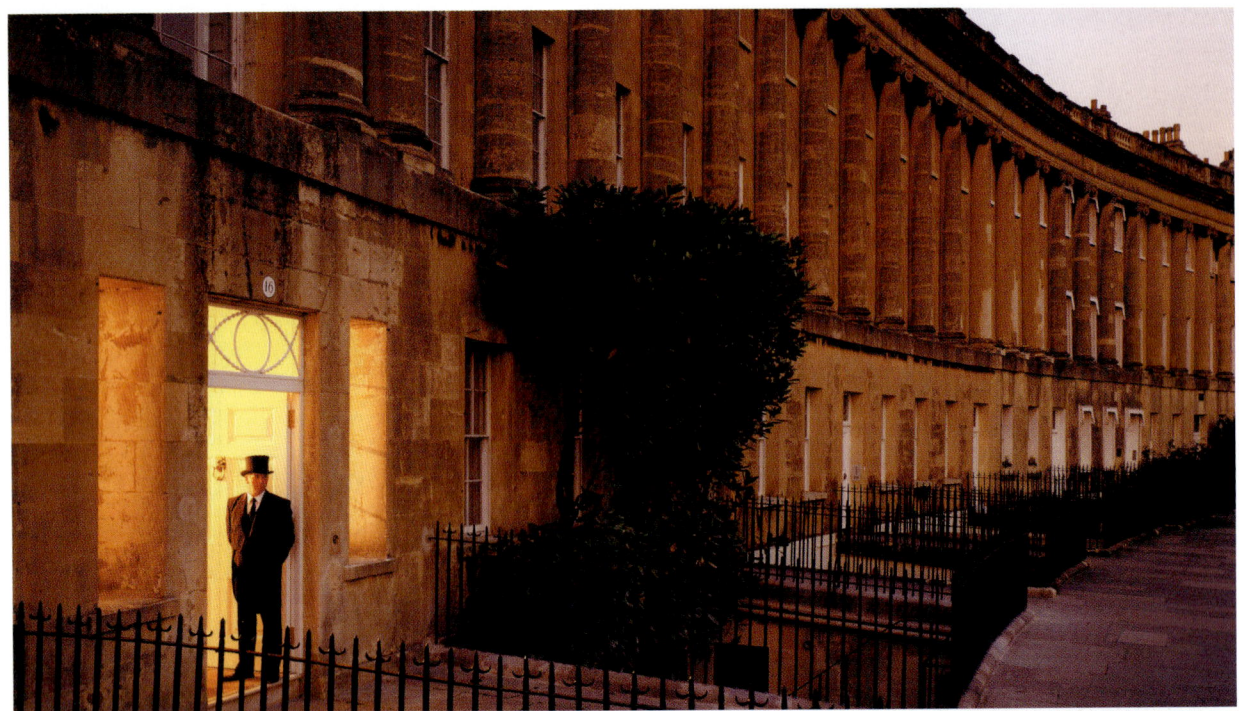

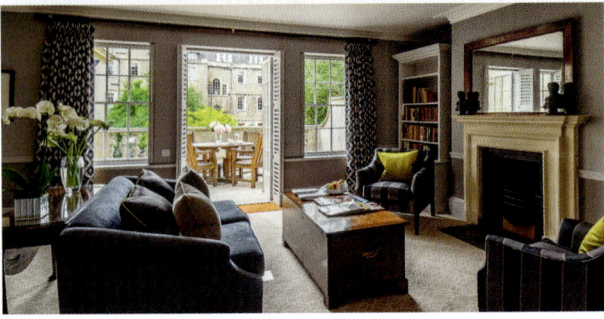

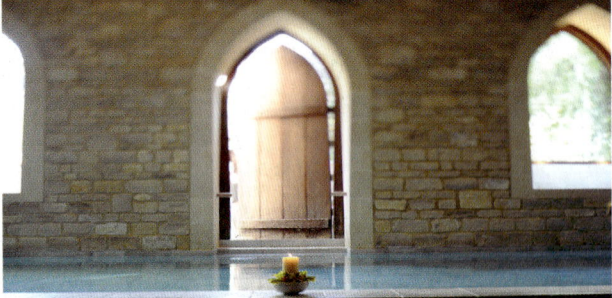

The Royal Crescent Hotel & Spa

Bath's Georgian splendour leads to ultra luxurious living

PRICE FROM:
£249

FEATURES:
Family friendly; Gym; Pet friendly; Restaurant; Spa

ACTIVITIES:
Golf; Horse riding; Sightseeing

NEARBY:
Lady Sophina River Launch; Thermae Bath Spa; The Roman Baths; Prior Park National Trust landscaped gardens; Lacock Abbey

GETTING THERE:
M4 jct 18; Bath Spa Railway Station; Bristol Airport

Escape, romance, spa and dine at The Royal Crescent Hotel & Spa, Bath. It's all made so very easy at this Georgian masterpiece. John Wood the Younger's eye-popping semi-circle of 30 terraced houses has hardly altered since its completion in 1774 and in the centre of it: The Royal Crescent Hotel providing an opportunity to experience gracious living from the age when Bath was the centre of the civilised world. As one of the Grade I listed collection of buildings, The Royal Crescent Hotel has been carefully restored to its original splendour. Individually styled bedrooms are rich in period features alongside 21st-century comforts with spoiling touches such as roll top baths, working fireplaces and balconies. Beyond the main mansion stretches an acre of hidden garden and four original coach houses where The Dower House fine dining restaurant and The Spa, specialising in holistic treatments, are located. In this surprisingly open space, a sun dappled terrace and landscaped lawns allow guests to eat alfresco during the summer months (afternoon tea comes highly recommended). For something a little bit different, The Royal Crescent Hotel can arrange Champagne cruises along the Kennet and Avon waterway in the hotel's private 1920s River Launch, Lady Sophina.

☎ +44 (0)1225 823333
🌐 condenastjohansens.com/royalcrescent
🏠 16 Royal Crescent, Bath, Bath & North East Somerset
BA1 2LS, England

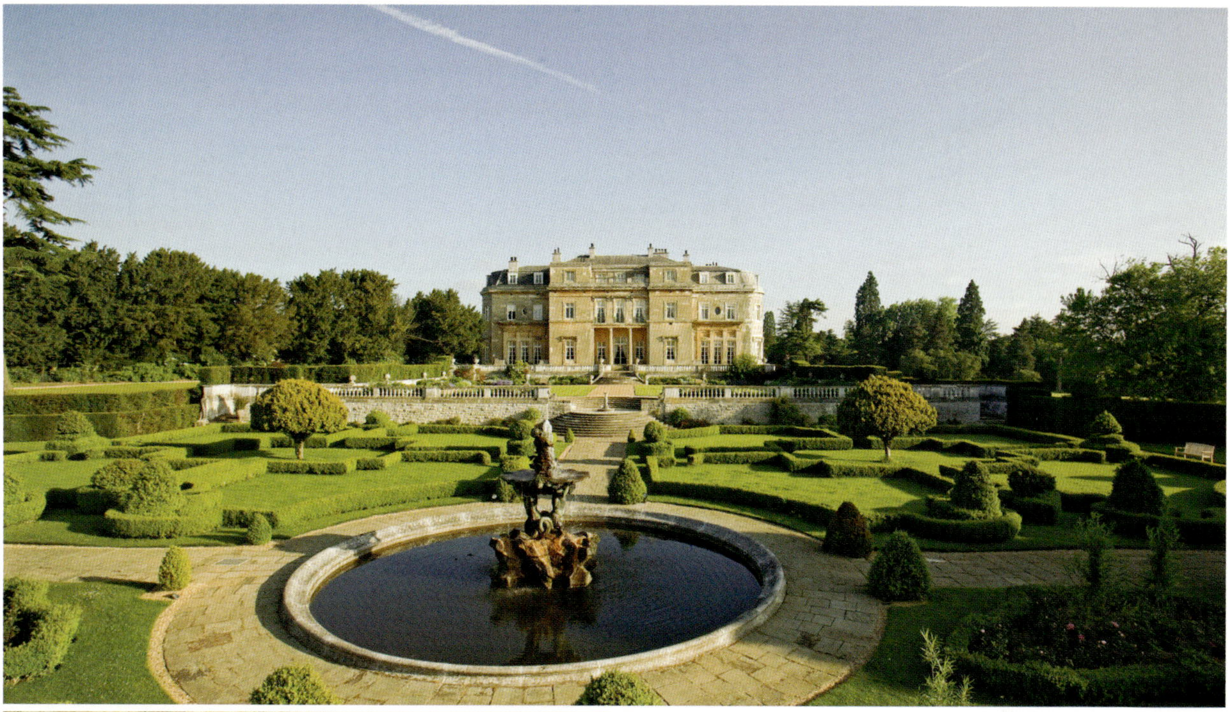

![Luton Hoo Hotel exterior and formal gardens with fountain]

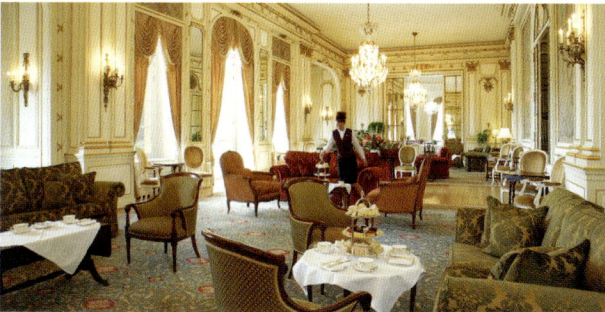

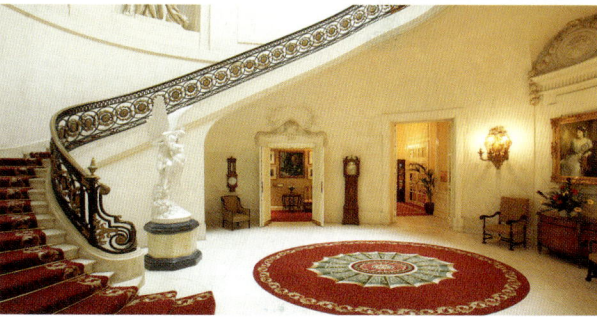

Luton Hoo Hotel, Golf & Spa

Grade I listed, grade 1 hotel in endless acres of Hertfordshire/Bedfordshire parkland

Where horse-drawn carriages and chugging automobiles once stood, golf buggies and London-style cabs come and go transporting guests around Luton Hoo Hotel, Golf & Spa's 1,000-acre estate. Famed architect Robert Adam and landscaper "Capability" Brown designed this masterpiece in the late 18th century that today gives a glimpse into the aristocratic life of yesteryear. As you step into the imposing Grand Hall and through to the elegant lounges (where afternoon tea is a boom) take time to soak up the details. Towering ceilings; chandeliers; precious paintings; tapestries; restored stonework; and marquetry. Then there's the views out to the green Hertfordshire/Bedfordshire parkland, lake, rock garden, 18-hole golf course and immaculate formal gardens. Staying at The Mansion House is a taster of a bygone high-life while more contemporary rooms are next door in The Parkland wing. A short stroll away are The Flower Garden rooms beside the spa, and The Club House (former stables) popular with the golfing set. This is also where you'll find the Adam's Brasserie offering an informal alternative from The Mansion's fine dining Wernher Restaurant whose menus offer exciting flavours (ham hock with apricot, fillet of beef with purple Arran potatoes) and carefully selected wines from both internationally renowned and smaller, boutique vineyards.

PRICE FROM:
£280

FEATURES:
Gym; Helipad; Pool; Restaurant; Spa

ACTIVITIES:
Golf; Tennis; Walking

NEARBY:
Cathedral city of St Albans; Hitchin; Hatfield House and Gardens; Knebworth House; Woburn Safari Park

GETTING THERE:
M1 jct 10; Luton Parkway Railway Station; Luton Airport

+44 (0)1582 734437 ☎
condenastjohansens.com/lutonhoo 🌐
The Mansion House, Luton Hoo, Luton, Bedfordshire 🏠
LU1 3TQ, England

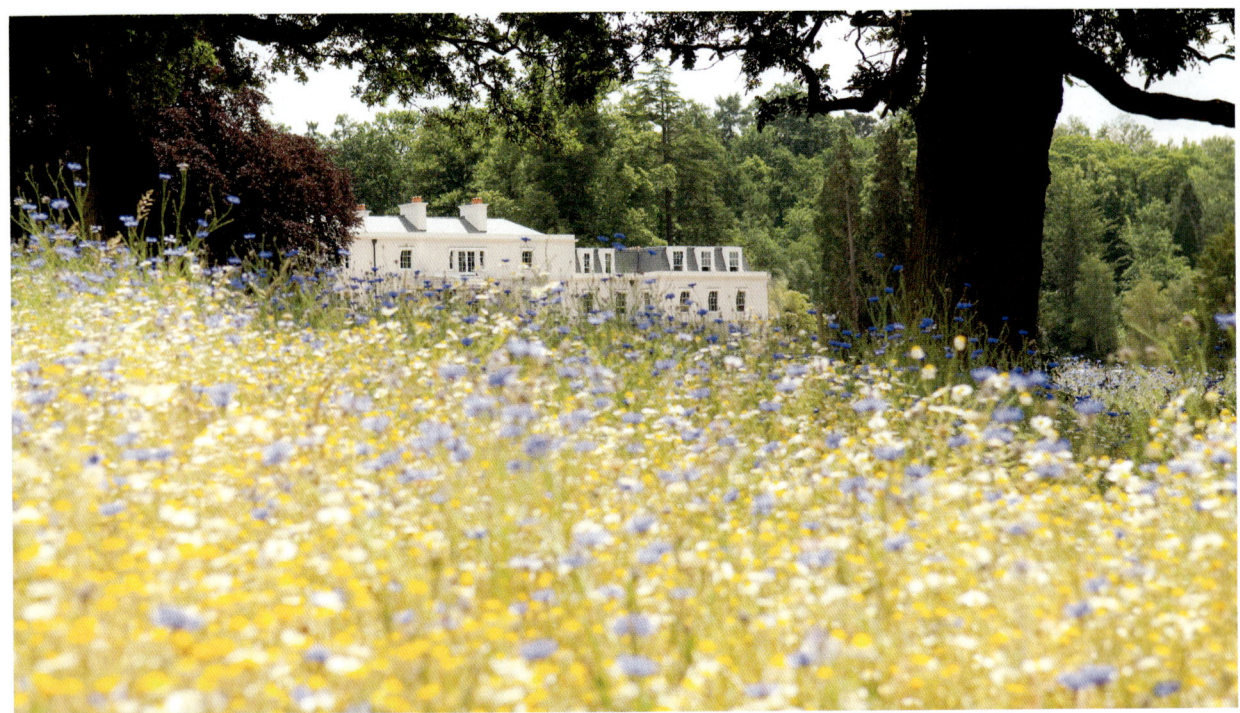

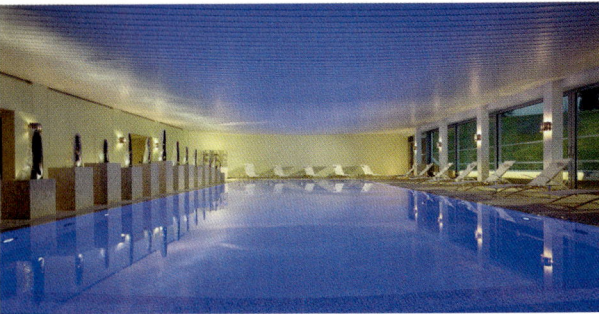

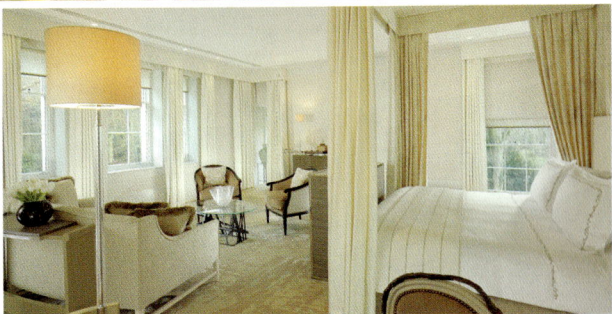

Coworth Park

A British charmer through and through in Berkshire's fair countryside

PRICE FROM:
£215 (room only, excluding VAT)

FEATURES:
Family friendly; Gym; Helipad; Restaurant; Spa

ACTIVITIES:
Golf; Horse riding; Walking

NEARBY:
Windsor Great Park; Legoland; Windsor Castle; Ascot Racecourse

GETTING THERE:
A30; M3 jct 3; London Heathrow Airport

☎ +44 (0)1344 876600
🌐 condenastjohansens.com/coworthpark
🏠 Blacknest Road, Ascot, Berkshire SL5 7SE, England

Coworth Park, just outside Ascot, is redefining the country house hotel for the 21st century. While upholding all that's great about the English countryside, Coworth's estate (The Mansion House, The Stables, The Cottages, The Dower House, Polo Centre) is a fresh take on the luxury country house hotel where nothing is formulaic. Peppered with surprises, this is a country retreat for the discerning tribe hankering for something out of the ordinary. Idyllically set within far-reaching, photo-pretty parkland (visit during the spring to see those beautiful blooming flowers for yourself) including a polo field on the borders of Windsor Great Park, Coworth is also home to an eco-luxury spa and three restaurants. And perhaps most interestingly, a Chocolate Room. Situated within the kitchens Coworth has its very own Chocolatier who creates sweet treats of the heavenly variety alongside one of the UK's most talented chefs, Brian Hughson (equipped with more than 20 years' culinary experience at top London restaurants) who rustles up classic British dishes with a twist at Restaurant Coworth Park. For more casual dinners The Barn is ideal or there's The Spatisserie in The Spa where bathrobe wearing guests enjoy a little indulgence. Noteworthy credential: Coworth is a member of the Dorchester Collection.

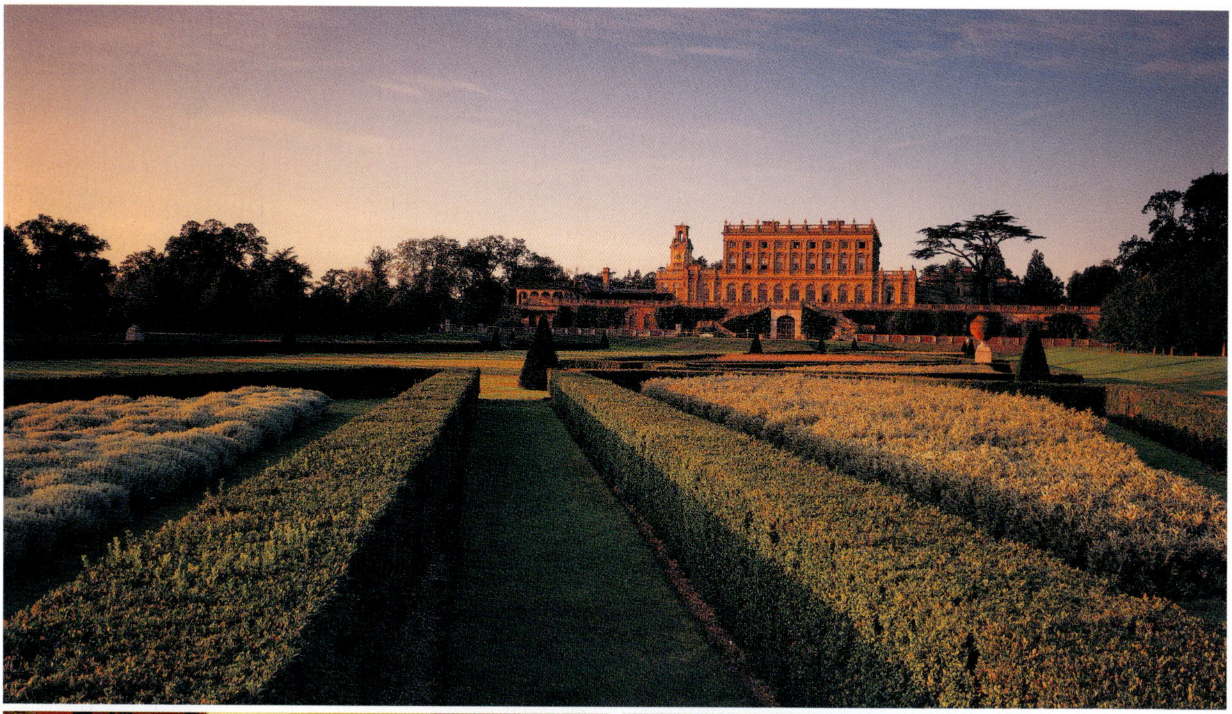

![Cliveden house and formal gardens at dusk]

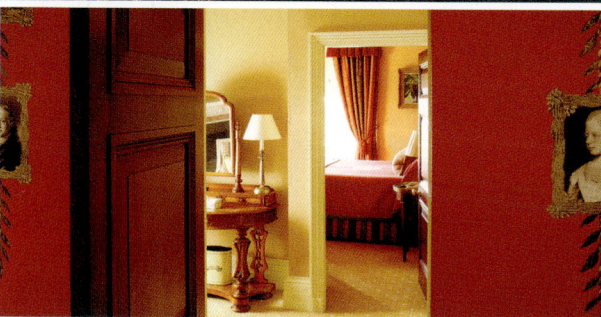

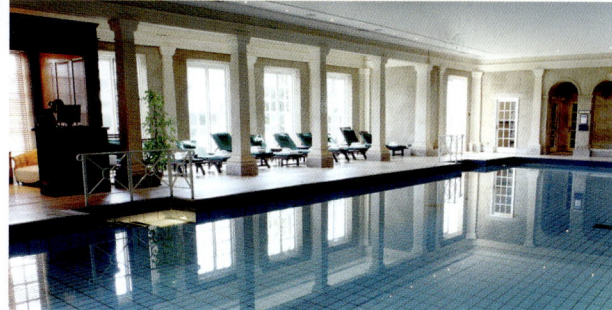

Cliveden

One of Britain's best presiding above the River Thames in Berkshire

Cliveden is epic. Almost SO grand, extremely opulent and irrepressibly English it seems too fantastic to believe but here it is, in Berkshire, beside the River Thames to be precise, conveniently near to London and Heathrow Airport. During Cliveden's 300-year history, royal guests from George I to Queen Victoria have graced its stately walls. As home to the wealthy American family, the Astors, celebrities and artists including Charlie Chaplin and George Bernard Shaw have also visited (scenes from The Beatles' movie "Help" were filmed here too). Today, Cliveden's hundreds of surrounding acres and impossibly immaculate formal gardens belong to the National Trust. Inside, the equally mind-blowing Great Hall sets an imposing welcome with incredibly ornate fireplace, oak panelling and priceless artworks. But despite all this extravagance, there's a refreshing absence of pretension, mainly due to the warm, friendly staff instantly placing you at ease and making you feel like a treasured, personal guest. If the occasion requires some fine dining treatment, The Terrace Dining Room doesn't disappoint (traditional and elegant with a dash of romance) whilst The Club Room restaurant located in the house's former stables, which keeps things more casual. Don't forget: there's a luxury spa, idyllic river cruises and meeting room facilities too.

PRICE FROM:
£252

FEATURES:
Family friendly; Gym; Pet friendly; Pool; Spa

ACTIVITIES:
Horse riding; Tennis; Walking

NEARBY:
Windsor Castle; Windsor Great Park; Ascot Racecourse; Henley; Legoland

GETTING THERE:
M4 jct 7; Taplow/Burnham Railway Stations; London Heathrow Airport

+44 (0)1628 668561 ☎
condenastjohansens.com/cliveden 🌐
Taplow, Berkshire SL6 0JF, England 🏠

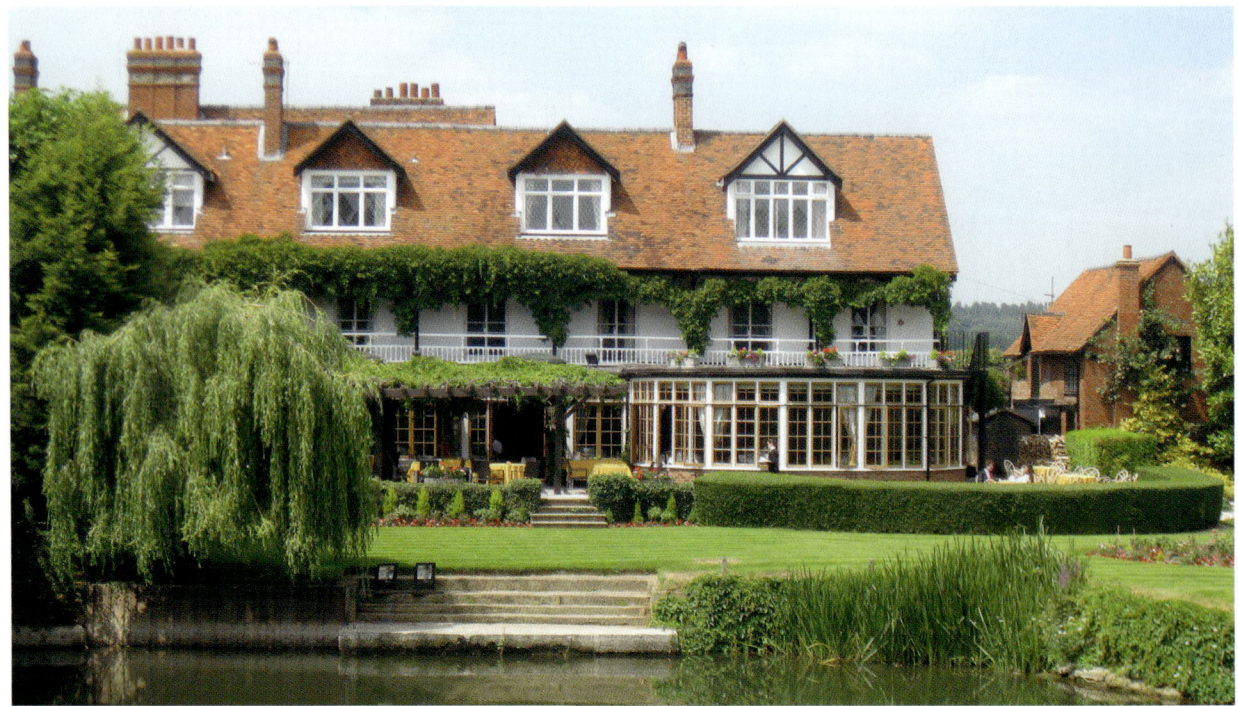

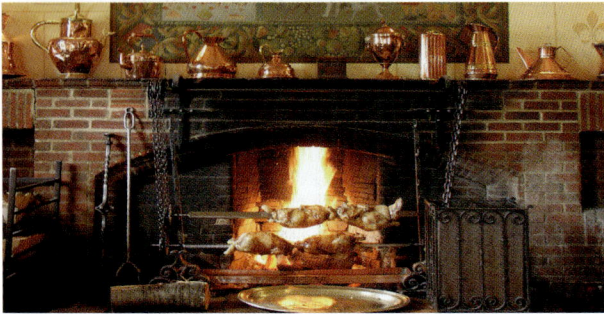

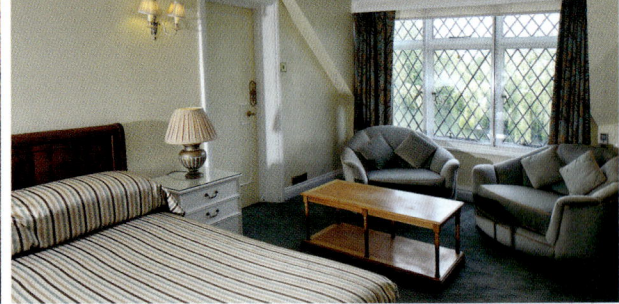

The French Horn

Sonning-on-Thames' ravishing riverside restaurant with rooms

PRICE FROM:
£160

FEATURES:
Helipad; Restaurant

ACTIVITIES:
Fishing; Golf; Horse riding

NEARBY:
Reading; Henley; Mapledurham House; Windsor Castle; Ascot

GETTING THERE:
London Heathrow Airport; London Gatwick Airport

To quote Jerome K Jerome's Three Men in a Boat, this riverside stretch of Sonning-on-Thames is "the most fairy-like little nook on the whole river." Written in 1889, this is just as true today of this blessedly beautiful spot and since its days as a coaching inn some 200 years ago, The French Horn continues to charm guests. Comfortable accommodation, excellent service and gourmet food is what you get at The French Horn; a first-rate restaurant with rooms. Bedrooms and suites are located within the main house but for longer stays the riverside cottages are just the ticket. (Make sure you ask for a River Thames view. When the view's this good, you want to see it as much as possible.) Get the taste buds whirring with pre-dinner drinks at the intimate, old panelled bar before taking your pew in the award-winning river-viewing restaurant. This is where you'll find the finest Aylesbury roast duck, cooked daily on a spit over an open fire and an exceptional wine list with bins dating back to 1945. Expertly chosen by owner Michael Emmanuel, his enthusiasm for burgundies means some rare examples have made the grade on the list alongside the menu celebrating French and English cooking.

☎ +44 (0)1189 692204
🌐 condenastjohansens.com/frenchhorn
🏠 Sonning~on~Thames, Berkshire RG4 6TN, England

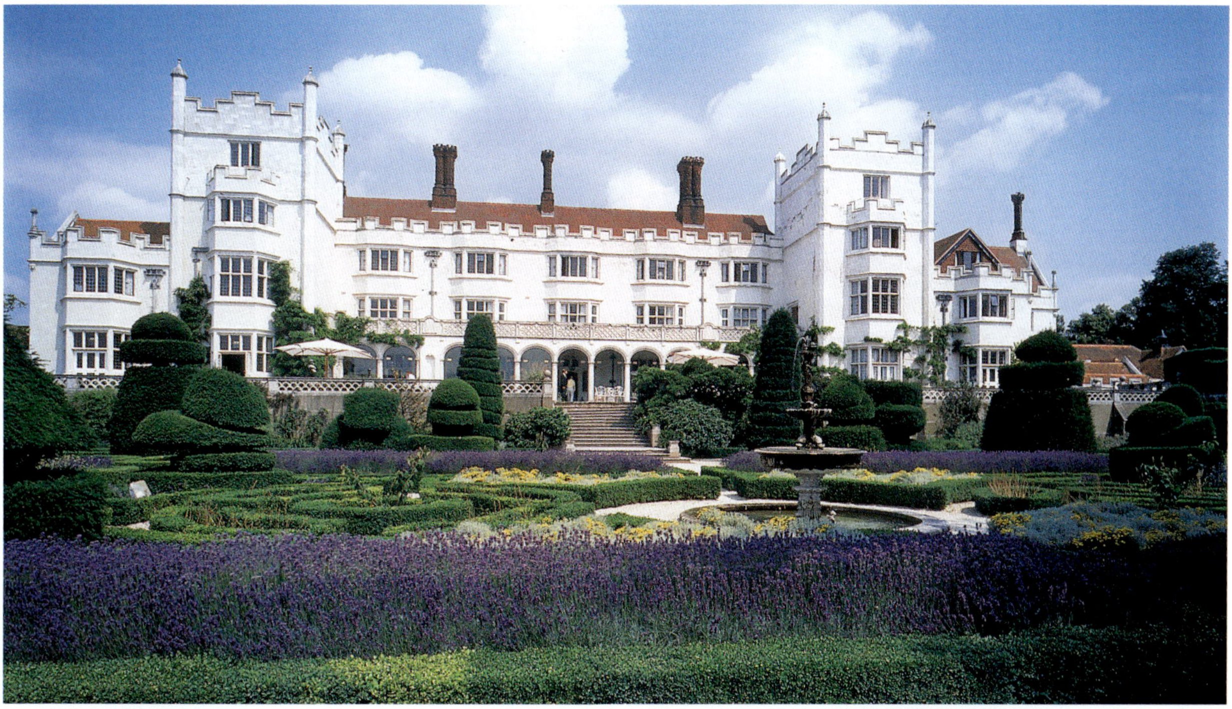

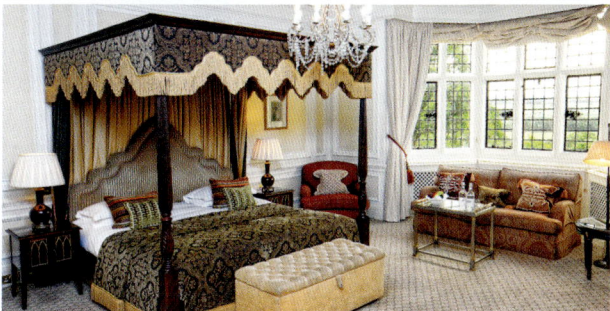
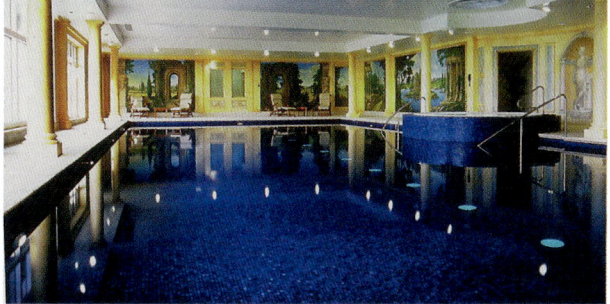

Danesfield House Hotel and Spa

Victorian proportions in rural Buckinghamshire

The Victorians knew a thing or two about show-stopping architecture. Cue: the wedding-cake white Danesfield House Hotel and Spa, Buckinghamshire. Built at the end of the 19th century, its arresting beauty is matched by the swathes of stunning gardens that encase it and the views out to the River Thames and Chiltern Hills beyond. For a special occasion book the most-spoiling Tower Suite set within the clock tower of the house spanning three floors. Or there's the Executive Rooms richly decorated and furnished in a classic style. The only rooms not in-keeping with the timeless, traditional design favoured throughout Danesfield are the two Feature Rooms where modernity rules the day. Before taking dinner in one of Danesfield's two restaurants it's pleasant to soak up your surroundings and suppress pre-dinner hunger pains with a drink in the chandelier-clad Grand Hall with minstrels' gallery, the sun-lit atrium or comfortable bar. Sublime modern European cuisine is rustled up at the Michelin-Starred restaurant but for something a little less formal, The Orangery's seasonal menu is a great alternative. If you feel the need to burn off some of these well-worth-it calories, leisure facilities include a spa with 20-metre ozone-cleansed pool, sauna, steam room and gym.

PRICE FROM:
£164

FEATURES:
Family friendly; Helipad; Michelin Starred restaurant; Pool; Spa

ACTIVITIES:
Golf; Shooting; Tennis

NEARBY:
Marlow; Henley; Windsor; Ascot; River walks

GETTING THERE:
A4155; M40 jct 4; London Heathrow Airport

+44 (0)1628 891010 ☎
condenastjohansens.com/danesfieldhouse 🌐
Henley Road, Marlow-on-Thames, Buckinghamshire SL7 2EY, 🏠
England

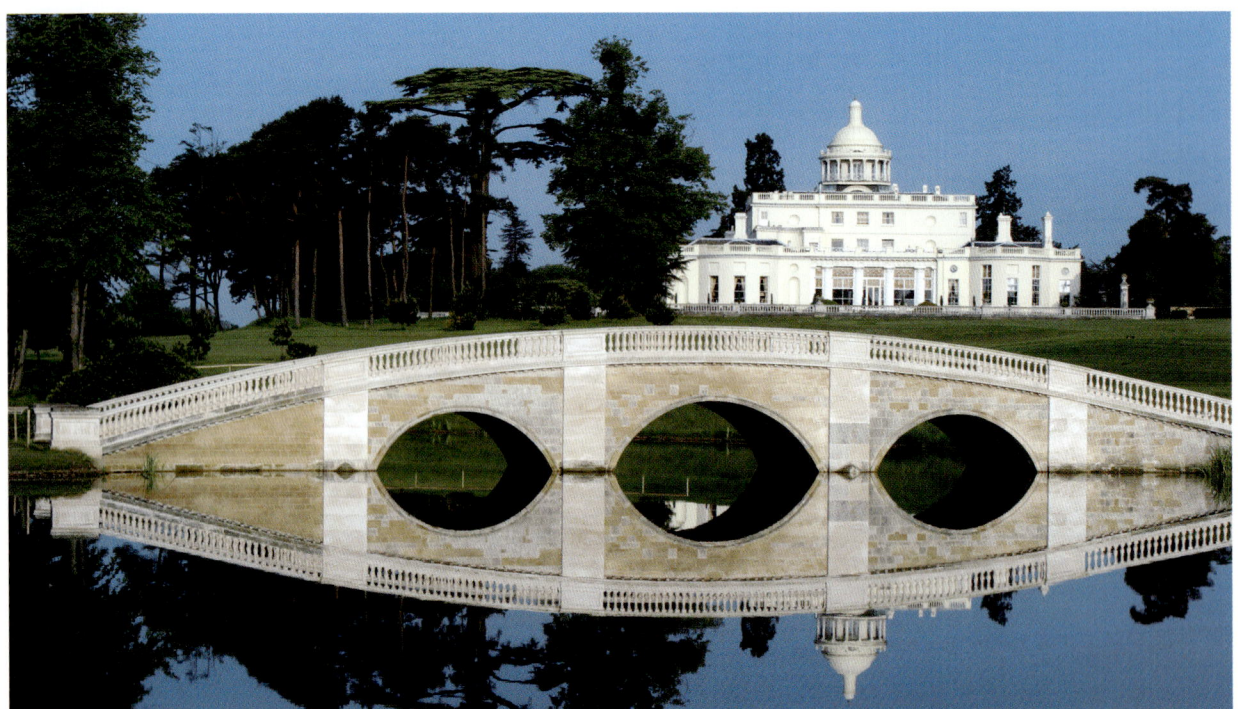

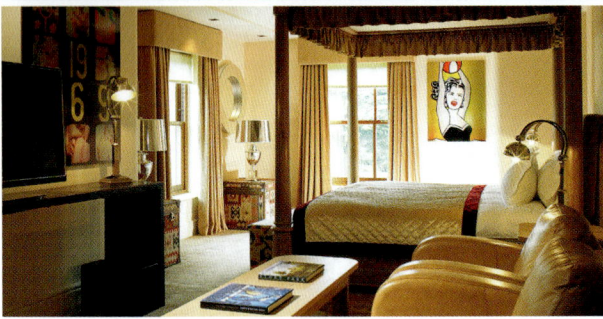
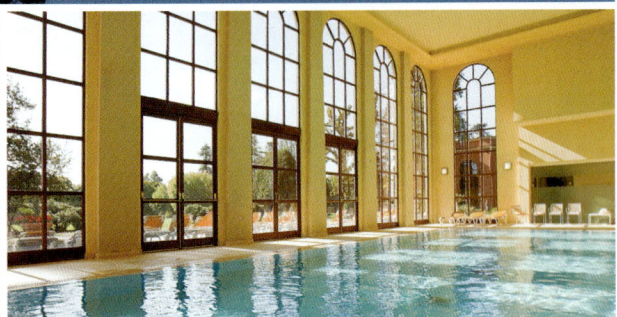

Stoke Park Country Club, Spa & Hotel

Members' club exclusivity and leading hotel standards in Bucks countryside

PRICE FROM:
£285

FEATURES:
Family friendly; Helipad; Pool; Restaurant; Spa

ACTIVITIES:
Fishing; Golf; Tennis

NEARBY:
Windsor Castle; Ascot; Henley; Legoland

GETTING THERE:
Off the B416; M4 jct 6; London Heathrow Airport

☎ +44 (0)1753 717171
🌐 condenastjohansens.com/stokepark
🏠 Park Road, Stoke Poges, Buckinghamshire SL2 4PG, England

Instantly recognisable as the backdrop for a variety of British films (Goldfinger, Bridget Jones's Diary, Layer Cake…), Stoke Park Country Club, Spa & Hotel in Buckinghamshire is a leader in England's luxury hotel scene. Set amidst hundreds of acres of parkland, Stoke Park has been at the pulsing heart of English heritage for over 900 years playing host to numerous members of royalty and aristocracy, plus the annual Boodles tennis event. Today, guests are drawn to this leisure playground for many reasons. Just 35 minutes outside of London, it's both convenient for Heathrow Airport and a sojourn from the capital. Private bars, cosy lounges, eight function rooms and the finest restaurants outside of London are all available for entertaining and special events. Be sure to sample the 3 AA Rosette-awarded, modern British cuisine at Humphry's fine dining restaurant. Since 1908 Stoke Park has been home to one of the world's finest 27-hole championship golf courses and is now also a go-to spa destination with endless pampering packages available at Stoke Park Spa. Located above the spa and health pavilion are 28 of the 49 bedrooms designed with contemporary panache while the Palladian house contains another 21, each one mirroring the Grade I building's style dressed with antiques, fine fabrics and an eclectic selection of abstract, good-humoured art. All overlook the awesome grounds.

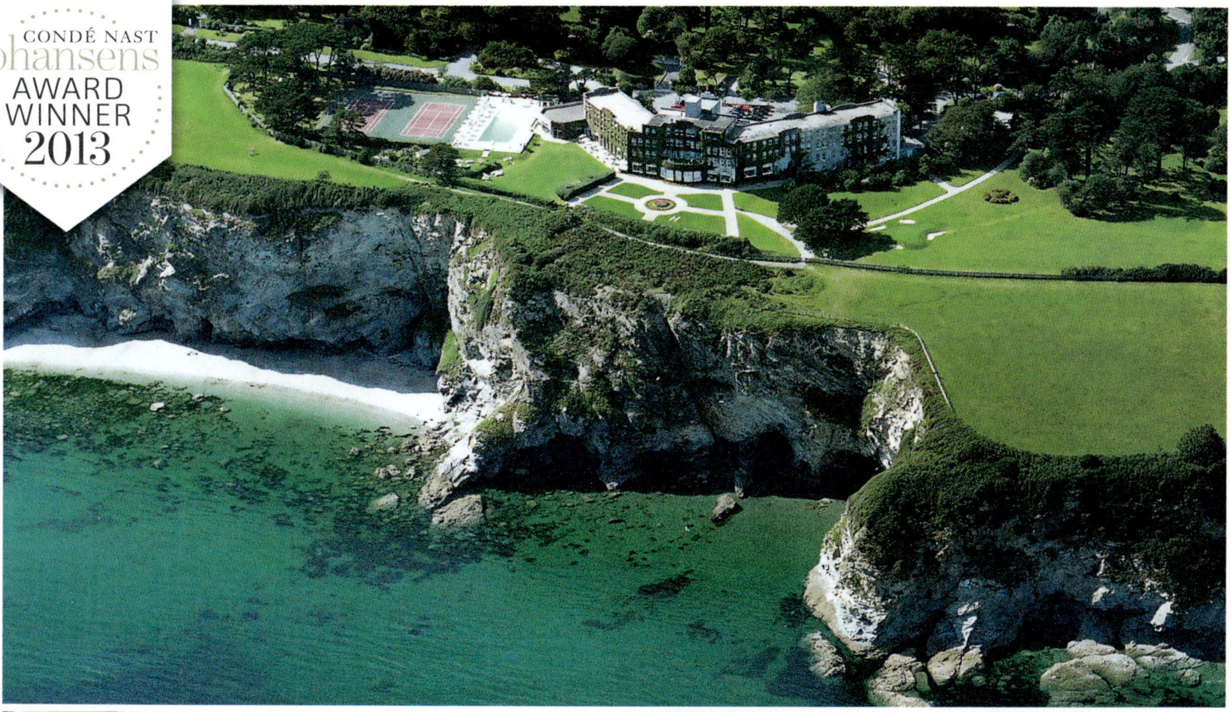

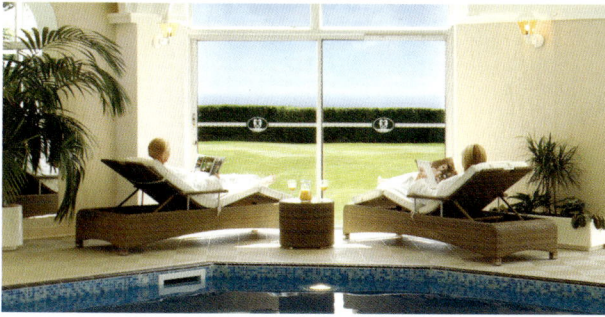

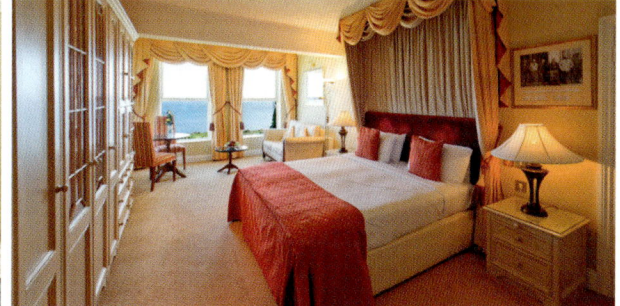

Carlyon Bay Hotel

Fun for all the family on Cornwall's coast, St Austell

When Percy Brend opened a butcher's shop in Barnstaple in the 1920s it was a seemingly ordinary event. But it marked the beginning of the Brend family's presence in England's South West, who are now the owners of a hotel empire based in Cornwall and Devon. Perched above the cliffs of St Austell, Carlyon Bay Hotel is their pride and joy. As a family-run property, families are very welcome at Carlyon. They're so welcome that children enjoy free lunches, drinks and ice creams throughout their stay; free buckets and spades for use at the hotel's private sandy Carlyon Cove too. While the little ones are being entertained by the holiday club or in the supervised playroom, mums and dads can spend time on the cliff-side 18-hole championship golf course complete with Club House serving meals and drinks. That's if they can drag themselves away from the holistic spa. (With over 40 treatments it's an idea to choose in advance to save deliberation time.) Bedrooms range from singles to super-sized state rooms, however, it's well worth opting for a panoramic sea view room. And for more of those hypnotic views, the fine dining Bay View Restaurant doesn't disappoint, although for more informal evenings try Taste brasserie.

PRICE FROM:
£145

FEATURES:
Family friendly; Pool; Restaurant; Sea views; Spa

ACTIVITIES:
Fishing; Golf; Walking

NEARBY:
The Eden Project; Lost Gardens of Heligan; The Minack Theatre; Fowey

GETTING THERE:
A391; St Austell Railway Station; Newquay Airport

+44 (0)1726 812304 ☎
condenastjohansens.com/carlyonbay 🌐
Sea Road, St Austell, Cornwall PL25 3RD, England 🏠

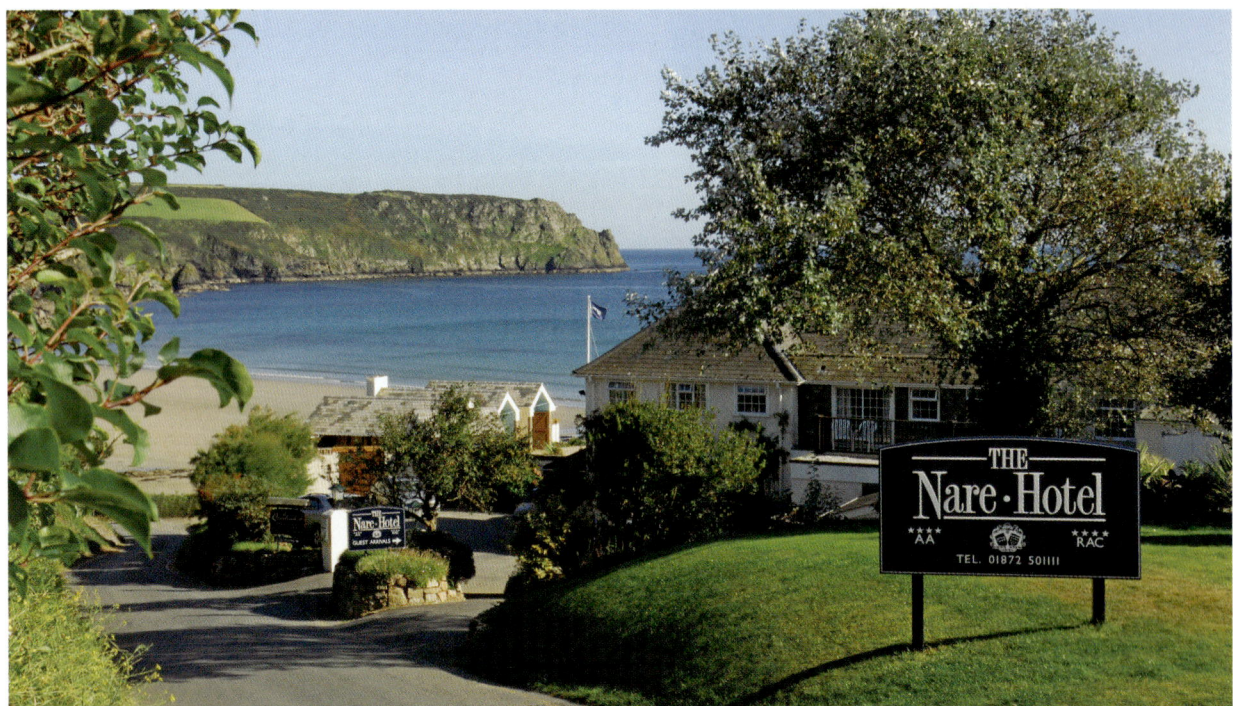

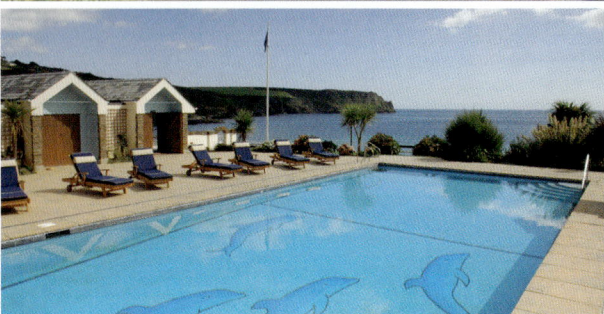

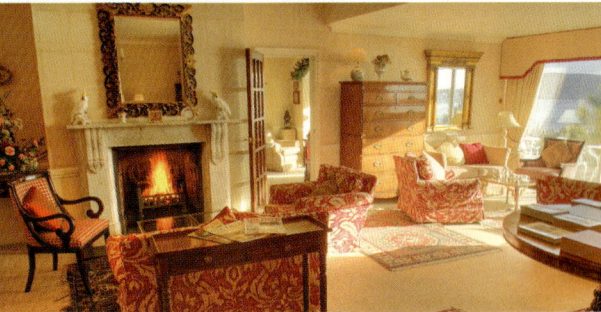

The Nare

Beach-side getaway on Cornwall's south coast

PRICE FROM:
£270

FEATURES:
Beach access; Family friendly; Pet friendly; Spa; Wheelchair access

ACTIVITIES:
Fishing; Tennis; Walking

NEARBY:
Many of The Great Gardens of Cornwall including Lost Gardens of Heligan; National Maritime Museum; St Mawes; Truro; Lanhydrock country house and estate

GETTING THERE:
M5; Truro Railway Station; Newquay Airport

Hailing from a well-respected family in Cornish hospitality, it's second nature for owner Toby Ashworth to be a hands-on host at The Nare. His grandmother Bettye Gray purchased this characterful house in 1989 and since then it's evolved into one of Cornwall's most comfortable hotels. In a prime position, The Nare is situated beside the endless sandy beach of Gerrans Bay. Most bedrooms look out to this idyllic scene and have patios and balconies where you can while away the hours. More sea views are the backdrop to The Nare's two restaurants. The main Dining Room is the more traditional with table d'hôte menus that specialise in classic English cuisine. Local seafood dishes such as Portloe lobster and crab, and delicious home-made puddings with lashings of Cornish cream also make a welcome appearance. Meals are available throughout the day in the informal Quarterdeck where families can dine early on the terrace or inside where floor-to-ceiling windows bring the scenic views to your table. Make the most of your time in Cornwall and explore the glorious Roseland Peninsula's coastline and villages, as well as local houses and gardens.

☎ +44 (0)1872 501111
🌐 condenastjohansens.com/nare
🏠 Carne Beach, Veryan-in-Roseland, Truro, Cornwall TR2 5PF, England

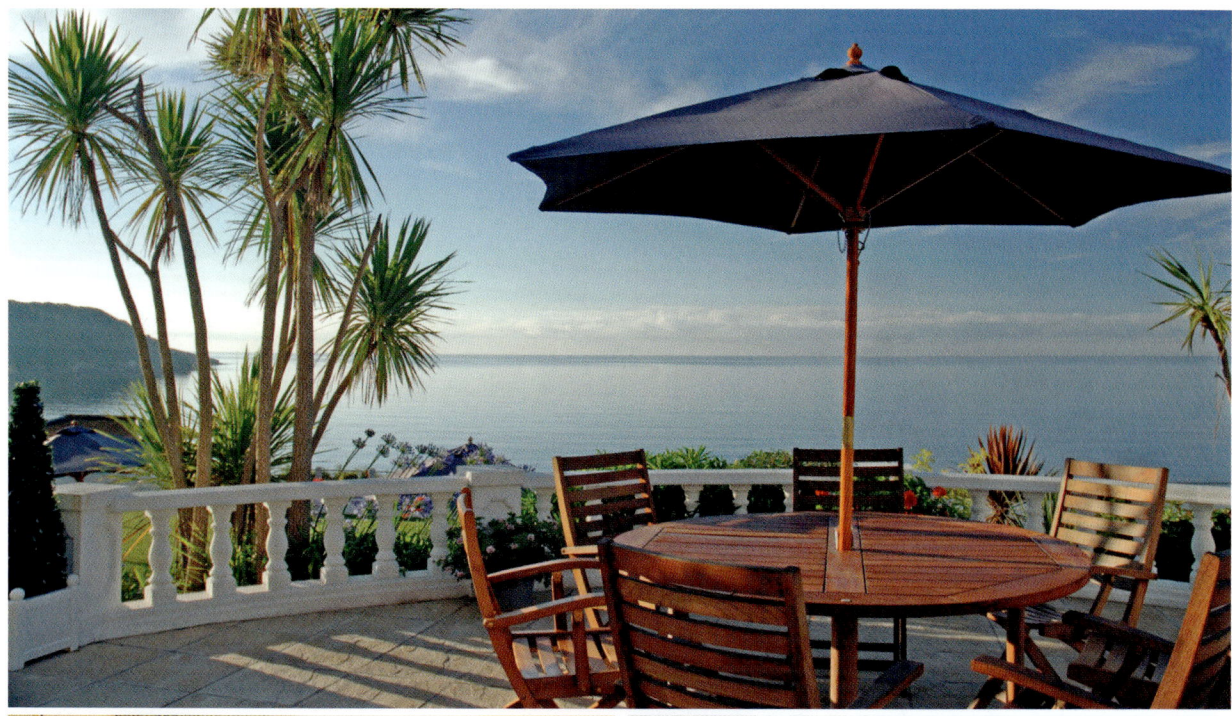

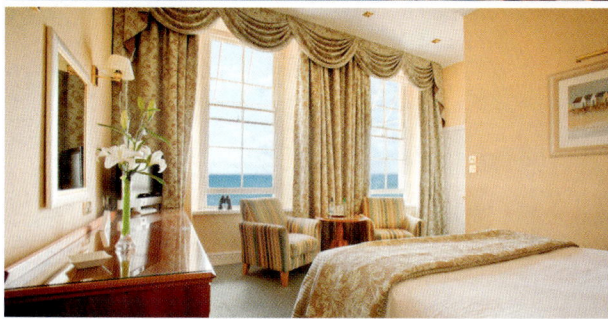
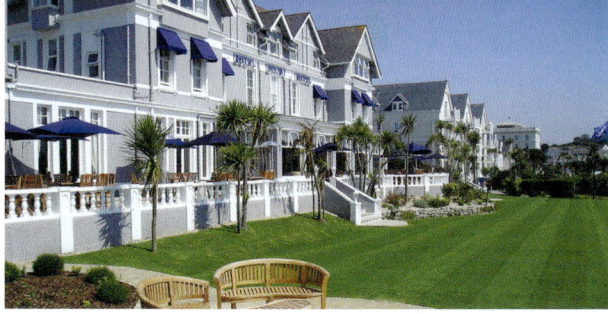

The Royal Duchy Hotel

Seaside relaxation on Falmouth Bay

Popular for its polished service, cosseting comfort and sea views across Falmouth Bay and to Pendennis Castle, The Royal Duchy promises a relaxing getaway. However, there's plenty of active pursuits in surrounding Cornwall and the West Country such as deep-sea fishing, fly-fishing, yachting, sailing, pony trekking and numerous water sports to keep days interesting if and when you feel sprightly. Families are more than welcome to The Royal Duchy with specific family rooms and large interconnecting rooms as well as deluxe with sea-front views. Thoughtful touches include binoculars, fresh flowers, slippers and chocolates, and careful consideration is made for those requiring extra beds, cots and bunk beds. On-site there's ample to keep you (and the children) busy with an indoor heated pool, snooker room, sauna and treatment room, not to mention an entertainment programme during the school holidays. Then, come mealtimes, The Terrace Restaurant offers up an eclectic mix of classic and inventive dishes alongside a children's menu, all prepared from fresh Cornish produce. For a less formal affair, meals and snacks can be served to you in the Terrace Lounge or bar (try a Duchy cocktail or local beer while you're here). It's entirely up to you.

PRICE FROM:
£160

FEATURES:
Family friendly; Pool; Restaurant; Sea views

ACTIVITIES:
Golf; Walking; Water sports

NEARBY:
National Maritime Museum; Pendennis Castle; The Eden Project; Lost Gardens of Heligan; St Ives

GETTING THERE:
A39; Falmouth Railway Station; Newquay Airport

+44 (0)1326 313042 ☎
condenastjohansens.com/royalduchy 🌐
Cliff Road, Falmouth, Cornwall TR11 4NX, England 🏠

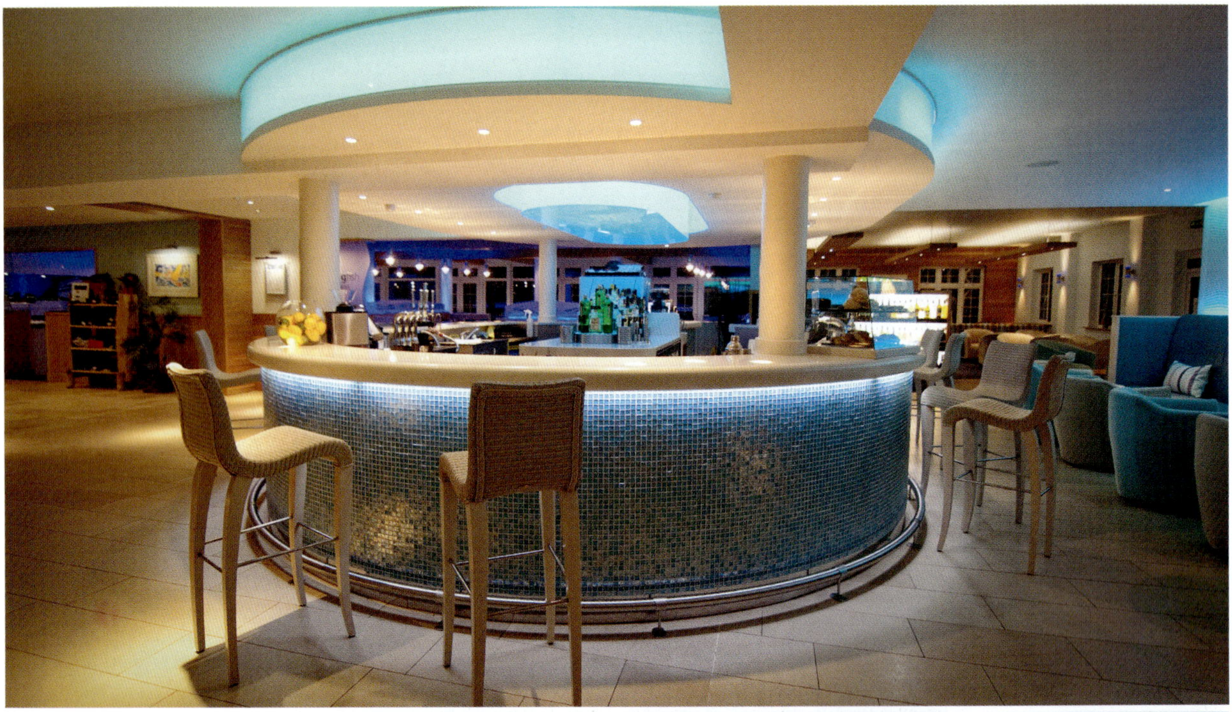

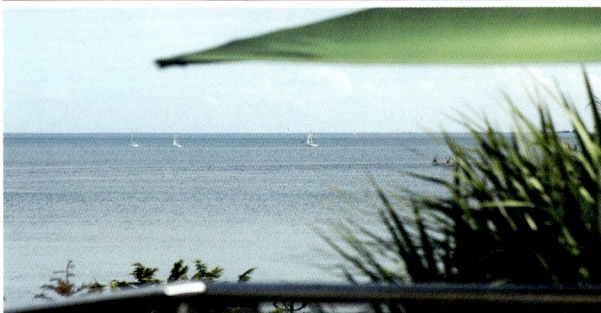
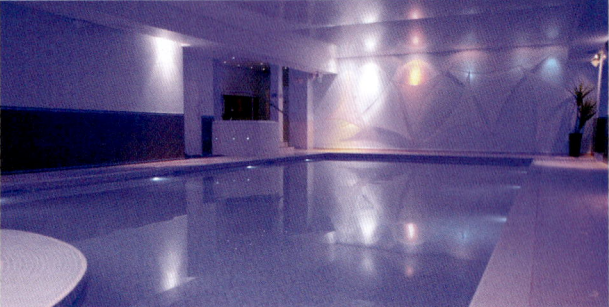

St Michael's Hotel & Spa

Cornish coastal trend-setter

PRICE FROM:
£59 (per person)

FEATURES:
Beach access; Gym; Restaurant; Sea views; Spa

ACTIVITIES:
Golf; Tennis; Walking

NEARBY:
Eden Project; Trebah Garden; National Maritime Museum; Blue flag beach; Pendennis Castle

GETTING THERE:
Just off A39; Falmouth Railway Station; Newquay Airport

On the golden-sand Cornish coast, St Michael's Hotel & Spa in Falmouth has been the subject of a careful and extensive refurbishment. The results are incredible. Fashioned with a contemporary gloss, St Michael's is now a state-of-the-art health club, spa and first-class restaurant with fresh, on-trend bedrooms, bars and conference suites. The Flying Fish Restaurant provides the chance to sample Cornwall's finest fish, seafood and seasonal produce. Its regularly changing menus are created by Executive Head Chef Nick Hodges, a staunch advocate of using local produce with a mindful respect for sustainable fishing. Views of the sea and hotel gardens from the restaurant enhance the experience even further, and weather permitting, its sun terrace is the blessedly idyllic spot for some alfresco dining. Surrounded by sub-tropical gardens, St Michael's Spa has an impressive range of health and relaxation treatments. There's also an indoor pool and large fitness suite when feeling a little more active or the attractions of Falmouth to while away the hours. Feel the sand between your toes on the blue flag beach located directly opposite the hotel, go surfing, sailing, golfing or visit the Eden Project within an hour's drive.

☎ +44 (0)1326 312707
🌐 condenastjohansens.com/stmichaelsfalmouth
🏠 Gyllyngvase Beach, Falmouth, Cornwall TR11 4NB, England

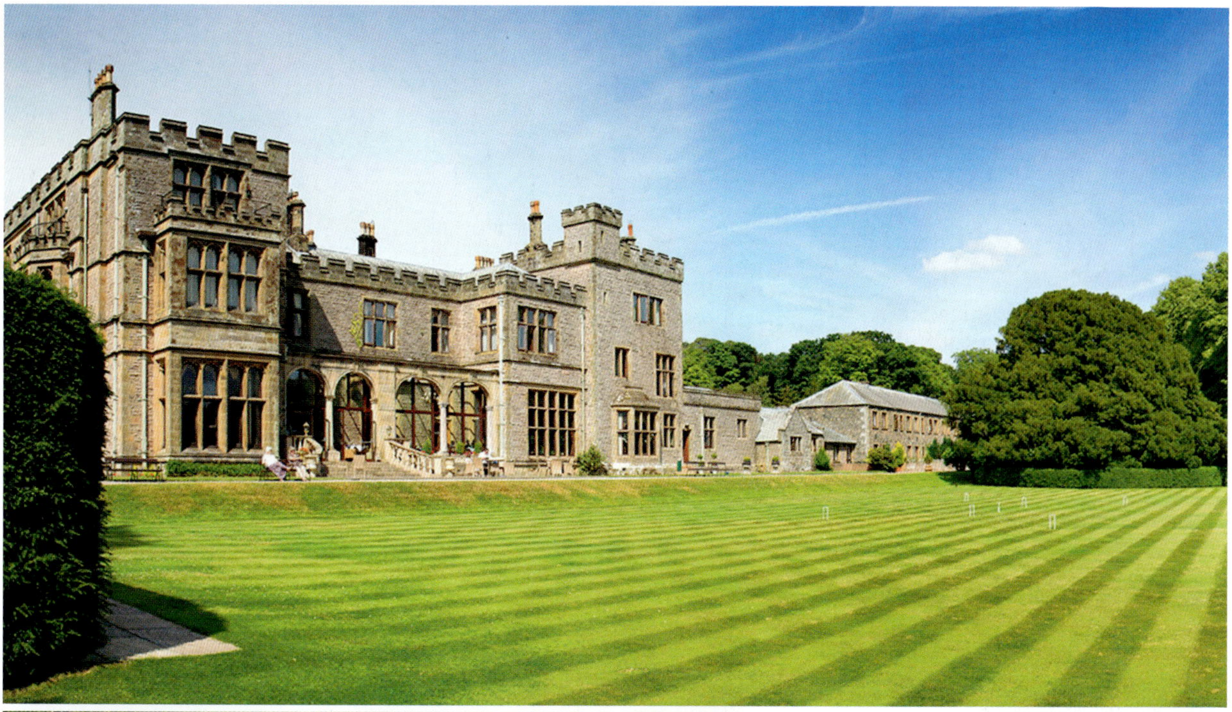

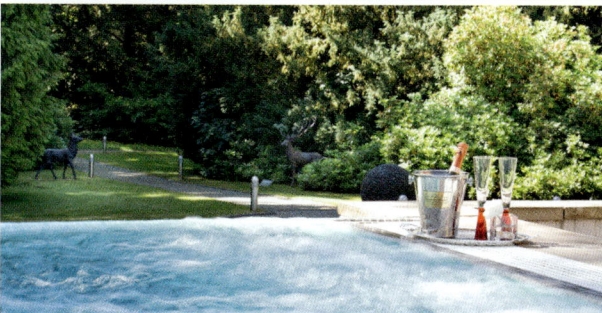

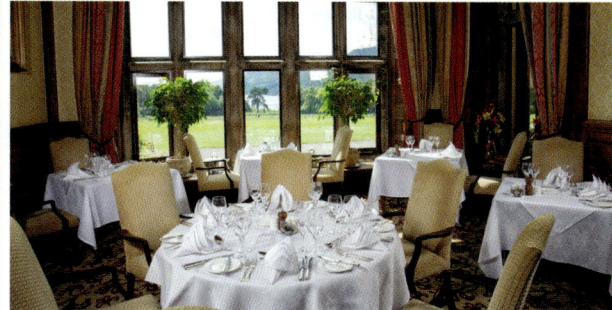

Armathwaite Hall Country House Hotel and Spa

The Lake District manor with its very own wildlife park

At first sight Armathwaite Hall Country House and Spa in the English Lake District is an impressive grand hotel where aficionados of fine dining and discerning spa lovers escape to. However, beyond these stately home walls lies a 400-acre estate encompassing The Lake District Wildlife Park. What started as the resident Graves family's farm park has become an attraction in its own right dedicated to the conservation of endangered species including lar gibbons, mandrills and Grant's zebras (special ticket rates are given to families staying at the Hall). Armathwaite is also the perfect base for uncovering the nearby Bassenthwaite Lake and Skiddaw Mountain, and an outdoor playground for quad biking, archery, falconry and coarse fishing. Guest rooms are full of individuality and character from the most indulgent Studio Suites to Spa and Club Rooms. The common theme throughout is comfort and relaxation with rooms in the main house dressed in a traditional, country home style and Spa Rooms reflecting a more contemporary feel. For some pampering, Armathwaite's spa has all the therapeutic answers with infinity-edge pool, aroma room, exercise classes and treatment rooms. While the Lake View Restaurant's English and classical French cuisine offers up local seasonal produce and Cumbrian specialities by the skilled hand of Master Chef Kevin Dowling.

PRICE FROM:
£200

FEATURES:
Family friendly; Lake views; Pet friendly; Pool; Spa

ACTIVITIES:
Fishing; Golf; Shooting

NEARBY:
The Lake District Wildlife Park; Bassenthwaite Lake; Lake District National Park; Wordsworth Museum; Beatrix Potter Museum

GETTING THERE:
M6 jct 40; Carlisle Railway Station; Newcastle Airport

+44 (0)17687 76551 ☎
condenastjohansens.com/armathwaite 🌐
Bassenthwaite Lake, Keswick, Cumbria CA12 4RE, England 🏠

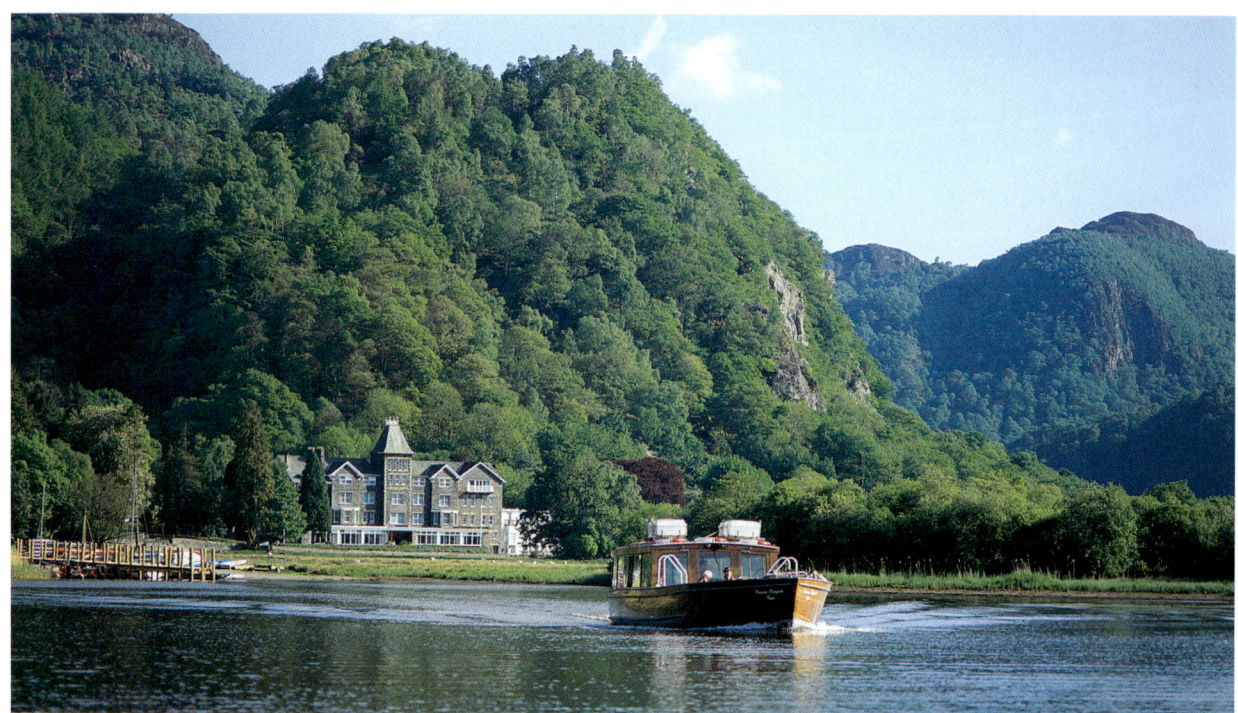

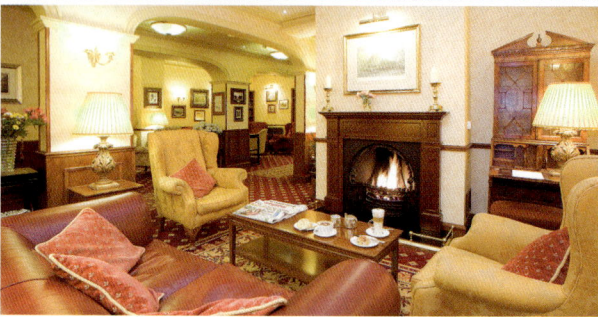

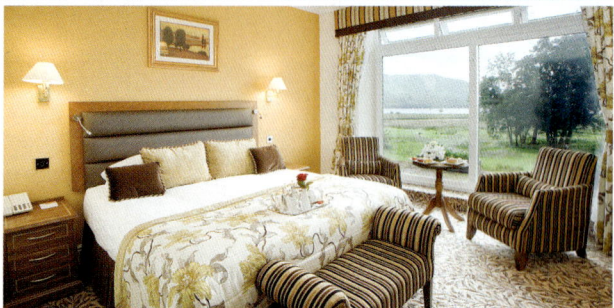

The Lodore Falls Hotel

The Lake District at its dramatic best

PRICE FROM:
£126

FEATURES:
Family friendly; Lake views; Pool; Restaurant; Spa

ACTIVITIES:
Golf; Tennis; Walking

NEARBY:
Keswick; Derwentwater Launch; Keswick Golf Club; Trotters World of Animals; Honistor Slate Mine with new Via ferrata walk/climb

GETTING THERE:
A66; M6 jct 40; Newcastle Airport

☎ +44 (0)17687 77285
🌐 condenastjohansens.com/lodorefalls
🏠 Borrowdale, Keswick, Cumbria CA12 5UX, England

Looking out to Lake Derwentwater from one side and thick wooded fells from the other, The Lodore Falls Hotel is a scenic showstopper. There's even a waterfall in the landscaped gardens. This is the heart of the Lake District, specifically the centre of Borrowdale Valley near Keswick, a go-to getaway for avid walkers, water sport lovers (March to November) and anyone looking for some escape with a dash of pampering thrown in. Owned and run by the Graves family, service is personalised and friendly, and as a family-owned property The Lodore is a family-friendly hotel. Special family breaks including discount vouchers to local attractions are often available. Recently the subject of a facelift that's pushed Lodore's plush quota and comfort scale to new heights, each of the 69 Fell Side and Lake View rooms, family rooms and suites is a lesson in tasteful design. And at the The Lake View Lounge Bar and garden the philosophy is total relaxation. Here, light bites, coffee and afternoon tea are on the menu. It's also a perfect spot for a pre-dinner drink before dining at Lake View Restaurant whose creative cuisine (lots of local produce, lots of flavour) is only matched by those Lakeland views. Pamper alert: The Falls Beauty Salon is a four-treatment room sanctuary of indulgence.

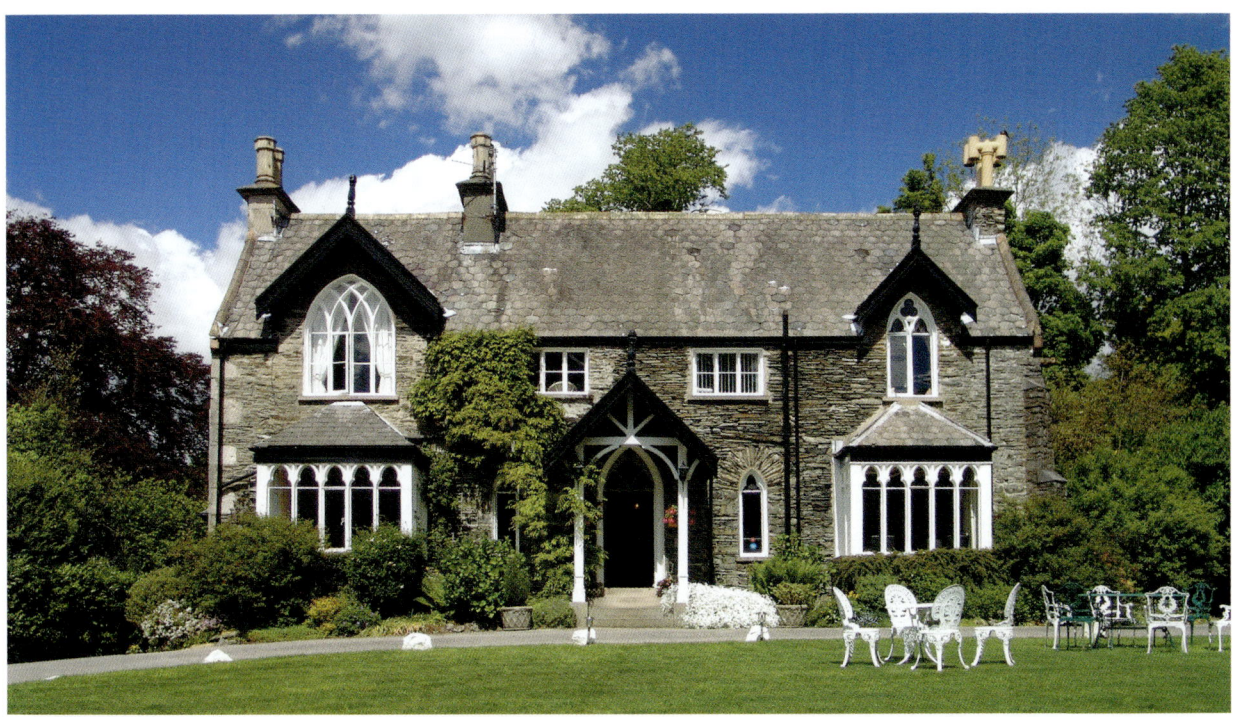

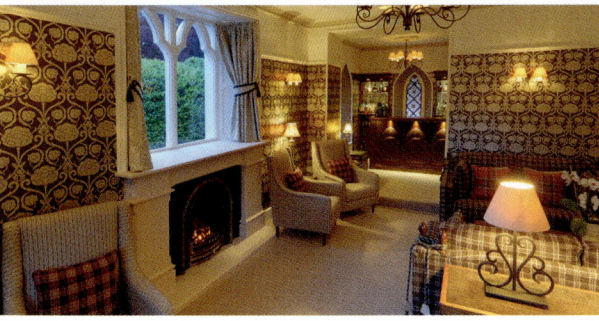
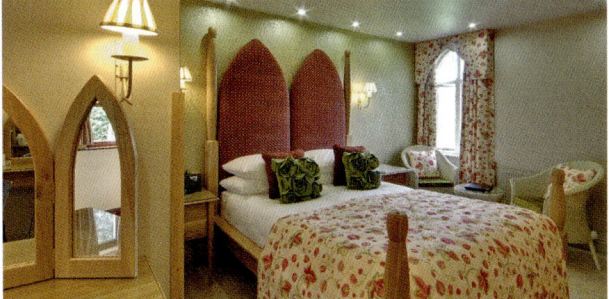

Cedar Manor Hotel and Restaurant

Rural elegance in Cumbria's Windermere

Cedar Manor Hotel and Restaurant in the Lake District may be chocolate-box-pretty from the outside but inside there's nothing twee or cutesy about it. Everything is just-so and country home chic, in-keeping with its original Victorian Gothic-style yet refreshingly smart. It's easy to imagine the original Victorian gentleman of the house mulling about in his garden and resting by the dominating cedar tree; perhaps admiring the brickwork and tall arched windows. Today, it's owners Jonathan and Caroline Kaye who love and (continually) invest in this boutique retreat with 10 elegant bedrooms just ½ mile from Lake Windermere. Like every great country pad, the sofas are sink-into cosy, the armchairs are reading-the-paper-perfection and each room is graced with locally crafted furnishings; some even have views to the Lake and Langdale Pikes. Considered one of the finest suites in the Lake District, Cedar Manor's two-storey Coach House Suite is packed with "wow" factors (super-king-size bed, huge double bathroom with stand-alone air bath and walk-in wet room) whilst special touches (spa baths) in rooms and suites located within the main house make for a difficult decision. However, there's no debating the venue for breakfast, lunch or dinner. It has to be Cedar Manor's fine dining restaurant whose seasonally changing menus are a local attraction.

PRICE FROM:
£110

FEATURES:
Family friendly; Lake views; Restaurant

ACTIVITIES:
Fishing; Golf; Walking

NEARBY:
Windermere town and lake; Blackwell Arts & Crafts House; Beatrix Potter Centre; Dove Cottage

GETTING THERE:
A591; M6 jct 36; Windermere Railway Station

+44 (0)1539 443192 ☎
condenastjohansens.com/cedarmanor 🌐
Ambleside Road, Windermere, Cumbria LA23 1AX, England 🏠

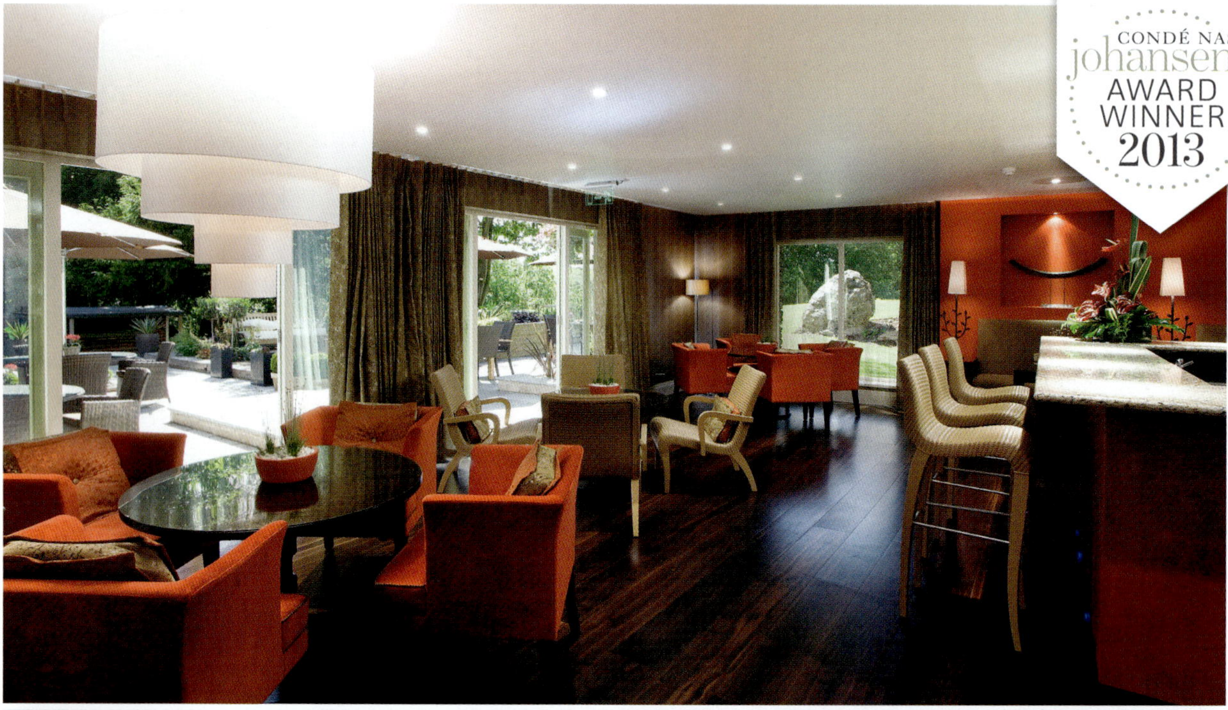

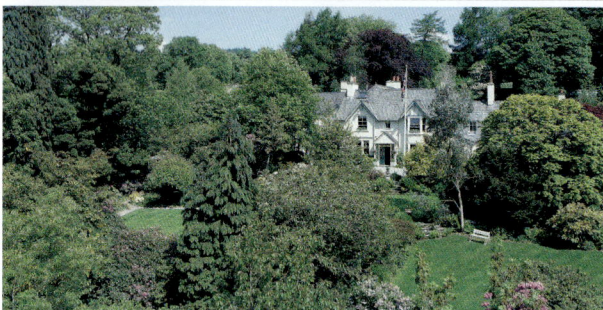

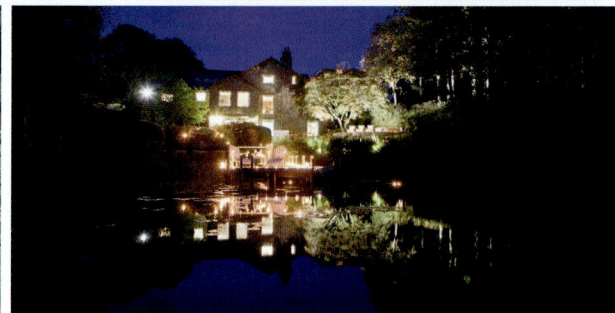

Gilpin Hotel & Lake House

Two outstanding country houses - one family's gift to Cumbria

PRICE FROM:
£335 (including 5-course dinner)

FEATURES:
Helipad; Lake views*; Pool*; Restaurant; Spa*

ACTIVITIES:
Fishing; Golf; Walking

NEARBY:
Windermere; Beatrix Potter Museum; Holker Hall; Levens Hall; Blackwell, The Arts & Crafts House

GETTING THERE:
M6 jct 36; Oxenholme or Windermere Railway Station; Manchester Airport

*Lake House only

☎ +44 (0)15394 88818
🌐 condenastjohansens.com/thegilpin
🏠 Crook Road, Windermere, Cumbria LA23 3NE, England

When a property is run with the unwavering passion that's expressed by the Cunliffes, it shows in every detail. Owned and managed by the family for over 25 years, Gilpin Hotel & Lake House in Windermere comprises two country houses spanning across two estates. The Georgian Gilpin Hotel is where you'll find 14 country-chic bedrooms and suites and six deluxe Garden Suites (complete with private cedar-wood hot tubs in their own decked gardens). Set in 100 acres of grounds, one mile from Gilpin Hotel, the six-suite Lake House stands on the shore of a private lake with boat house and jetty. Opened in 2010, this new addition has been a much talked about success not least because of its secluded Swedish-style Jetty Lake House Spa exclusively for Lake House guests. Designed with couples in mind, the spa is raised three metres into the tree canopy with floor-to-ceiling windows overlooking the lake. Each evening a chauffeur can ferry Lake House guests to and from the restaurant located in Gilpin Hotel. There are four dining rooms to choose from here, each one serving Head Chef Dan Grigg's British dishes prepared from Lake District produce and West Coast seafood. 200 wines from 13 countries accompany his foodie delights. Take note wedding planners: small weddings of 25 guests can be arranged at the Lake House.

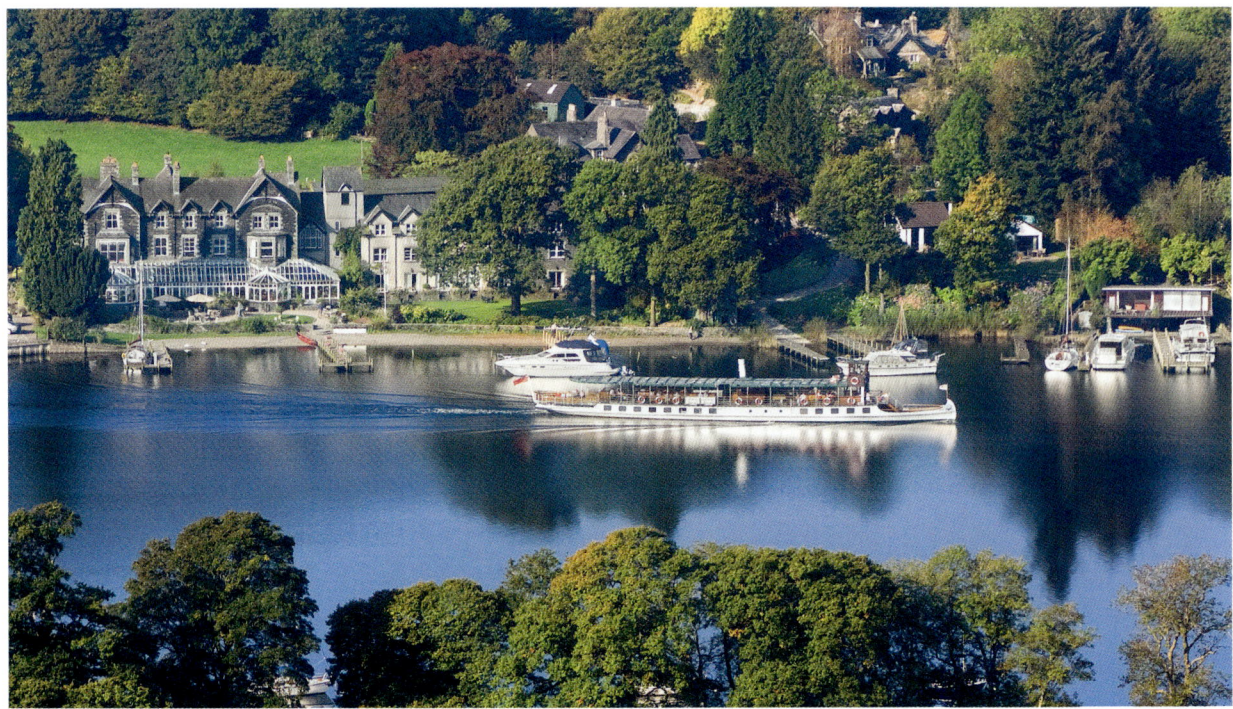

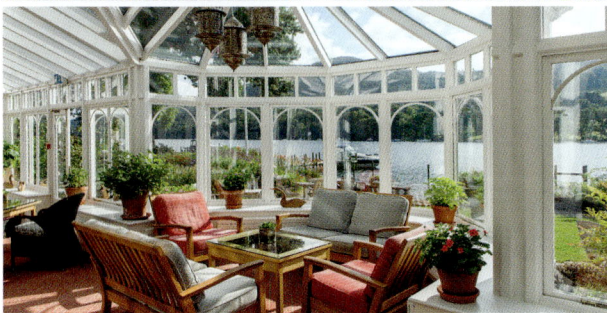

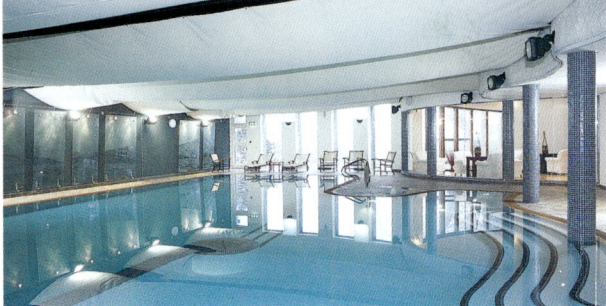

Lakeside Hotel & Spa

Overlooking nothing but Lake Windermere

Sensationally picturesque and uniquely located, Lakeside Hotel & Spa on the edge of Lake Windermere is a reassuringly classic and relaxed English Lake District hotel. From the moment you step through the doors its enchanting spell is cast and lingers long after your visit is over. Many of the bedrooms and suites look out to the lovely lake vistas and ground floor rooms open onto private patios. Children are welcome here, with a selection of family-friendly rooms containing bunk beds or sofa beds (interconnecting rooms too). While in the kitchen, Cumbrian favourites are the order of the day served in both the highly-applauded Lakeview restaurant and casual John Ruskin's Brasserie. Dishes in John Ruskin's Bar also showcase traditional fare. To achieve an authentic Lake District experience, cruisers are berthed adjacent to the hotel ready for your exploration and adventure but in case of inclement weather, Lakeside Hotel's pool and spa (exclusive to hotel residents) provides a pampering alternative. The huge indoor pool, gym, sauna, steam room and Aveda treatment rooms complete the picture. For business travellers: the Lakeside's Windermere Suite is a business and events centre located opposite the hotel available for private use offering delegates discreet privacy and first-rate hotel services.

PRICE FROM:
£165

FEATURES:
Family friendly; Gym; Pool; Spa

ACTIVITIES:
Fishing; Walking; Water sports

NEARBY:
Windermere lake cruisers; Lake District Aquarium; Lakeland Motor Museum; Lakeside and Haverthwaite Steam Railway; Holker Hall and Gardens

GETTING THERE:
M6 jct 36; Oxenholme Railway Station; Manchester Airport

+44 (0)15395 30001 ☎
condenastjohansens.com/lakeside 🌐
Lakeside, Newby Bridge, Cumbria LA12 8AT, England 🏠

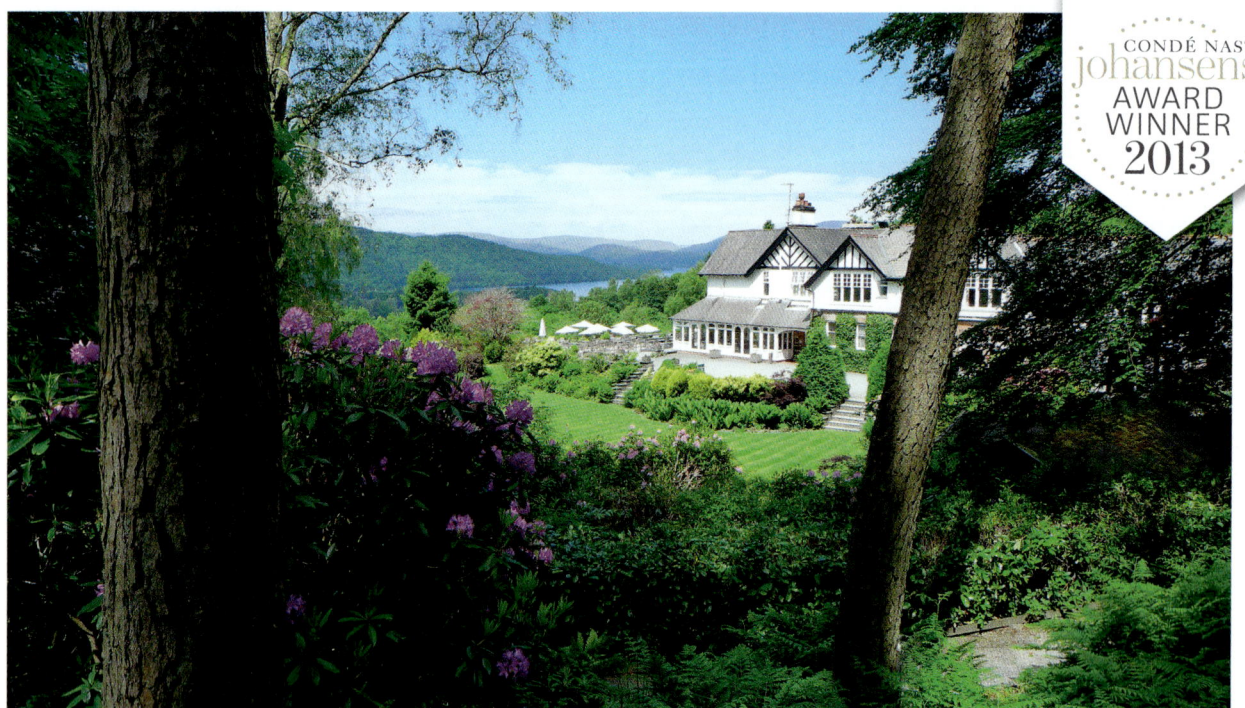

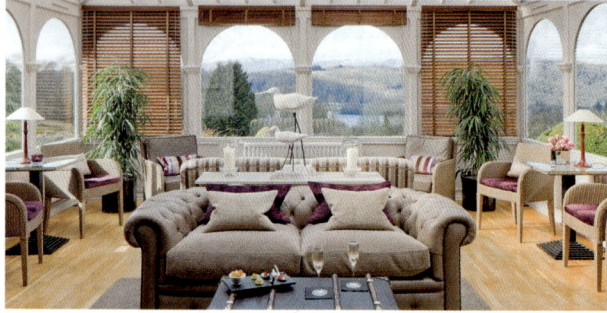

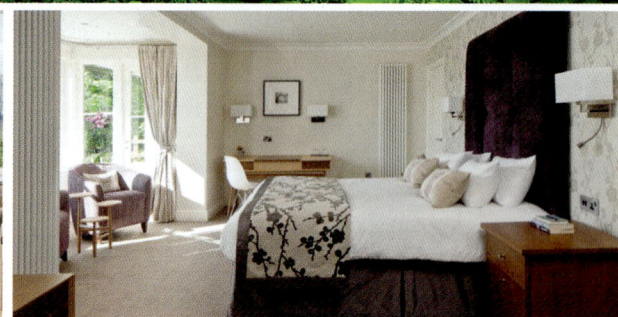

Linthwaite House

Getting country house hospitality perfectly right in the Lake District

PRICE FROM:
£99

FEATURES:
Family friendly; Helipad; Lake views; Pet friendly; Restaurant

ACTIVITIES:
Fishing; Golf; Walking

NEARBY:
Windermere; Beatrix Potter Museum; Dove Cottage; Lake District National Park; Brantwood

GETTING THERE:
A591; M6 jct 36; Manchester Airport

☎ +44 (0)15394 88600
🌐 condenastjohansens.com/linthwaitehouse
🏠 Crook Road, Windermere, Cumbria LA23 3JA, England

Something that strikes you about Linthwaite House in the Lake District is the unyielding passion owner Mike Bevans has for his 30-bedroom slice of the dream. And it's infectious! There's those Lake Windermere vistas (over to Belle Isle) for starters and endless acres of flowering garden and woodland as well as a nine-hole putting green and par three practice hole. Inside, showroom-perfect bedrooms and a seriously good restaurant seal the deal. So centrally located at the heart of England, Linthwaite is a prime spot. Walkers love it here (fell trails begin from the front door) while culture vultures can follow in the footsteps of William Wordsworth and Beatrix Potter. But stepping out of Linthwaite's cosseting world isn't easy. By marrying on-trend interior fashions with homely comfort (very House & Garden) and providing the best of traditional hospitality, you never want to leave! The implausibly pretty lake, garden and fell views from most of the bedrooms keep you rooted to the cushioned spot too. If you've reserved the popular Luxury Lake View Room with outside hot tub, just try and remember to keep a check on the time. It would be a crying shame to miss out on Linthwaite's modern British food prepared from nothing but fresh, local produce. The list of fine wines is equally impressive.

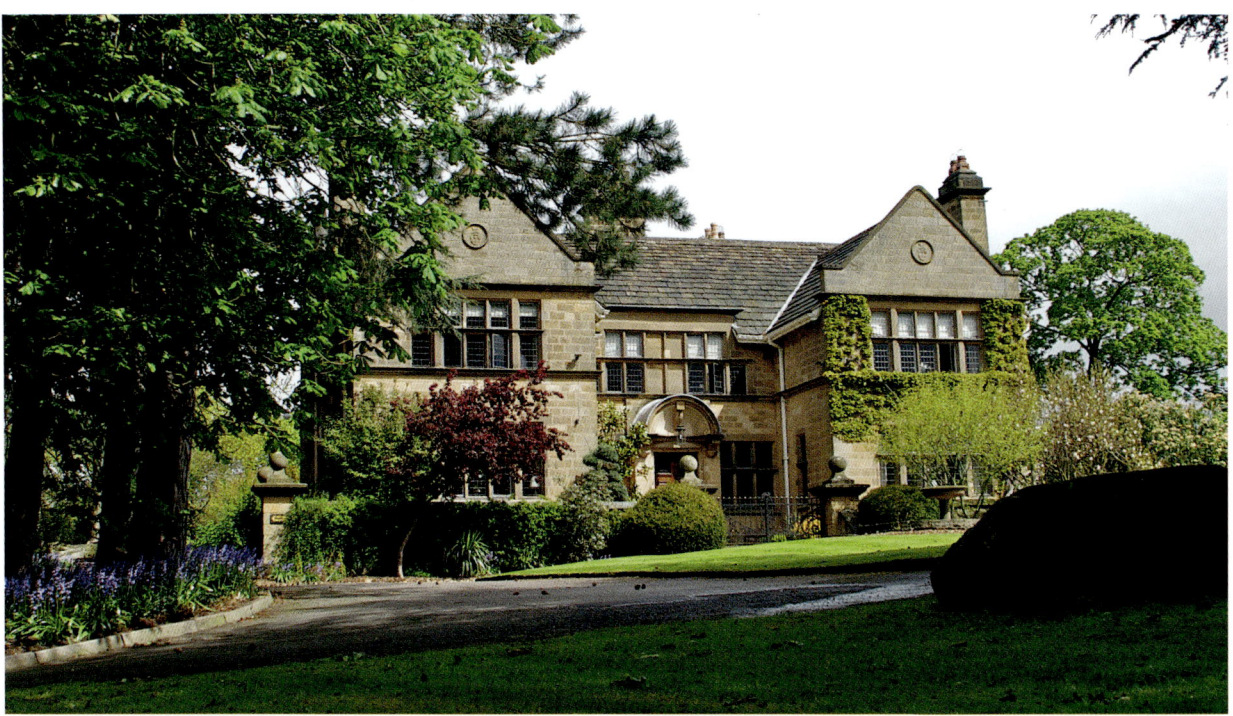

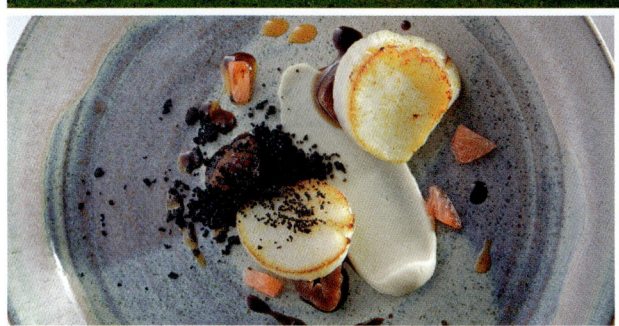

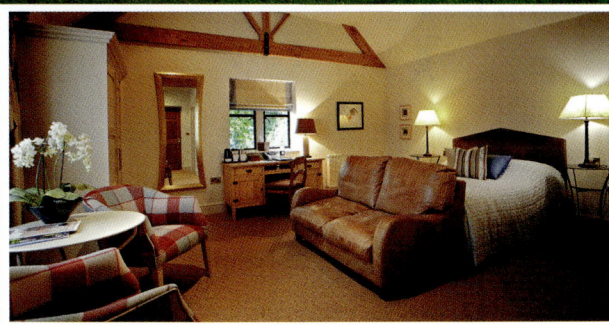

Fischer's Baslow Hall

Michelin-Starred restaurant with rooms on the edge of Chatsworth House Estate

As scrumptiously delightful as a Bakewell tart, Fischer's Baslow Hall sits only four miles from where the teatime fancy originates. A beautiful Edwardian manor house, this is an intimate, pleasure-inducing, cosy country house a-flurry with soft furnishings, plump pillows and fluffy white towels. Gorgeous floral prints, parquet flooring and pretty leaded windows embrace the character and warmth of this listed building with the charming Susan and Max at the helm. Having renovated the property with pride and invested with love, their hospitality is unparalleled alongside a carefully chosen team of dedicated staff. They all go to great lengths to ensure your visit is memorable. This is most evidently true for Head Chef Rupert Rowley whose instinctive approach creates Michelin Starred, locally sourced dishes (some of which is grown in the hotel's garden). In honour of its highly commended success, Baslow Hall offers "foodie" packages that are out-of-this-world. And private dining options perfect for wedding and business receptions. With other packages including tickets to Chatsworth House (home to the Duke and Duchess of Devonshire), your stay will be a satisfying mix of English heritage and traditions.

PRICE FROM:
£105

FEATURES:
Michelin Starred restaurant

ACTIVITIES:
Fishing; Golf; Walking

NEARBY:
Bakewell; Chatsworth; Haddon Hall; Market towns of Bakewell and Buxton; Peak District National Park

GETTING THERE:
A623; M1 jct 29; Manchester Airport

+44 (0)1246 583259 ☎
condenastjohansens.com/fischers 🌐
Calver Road, Baslow, Derbyshire DE45 1RR, England 🏠

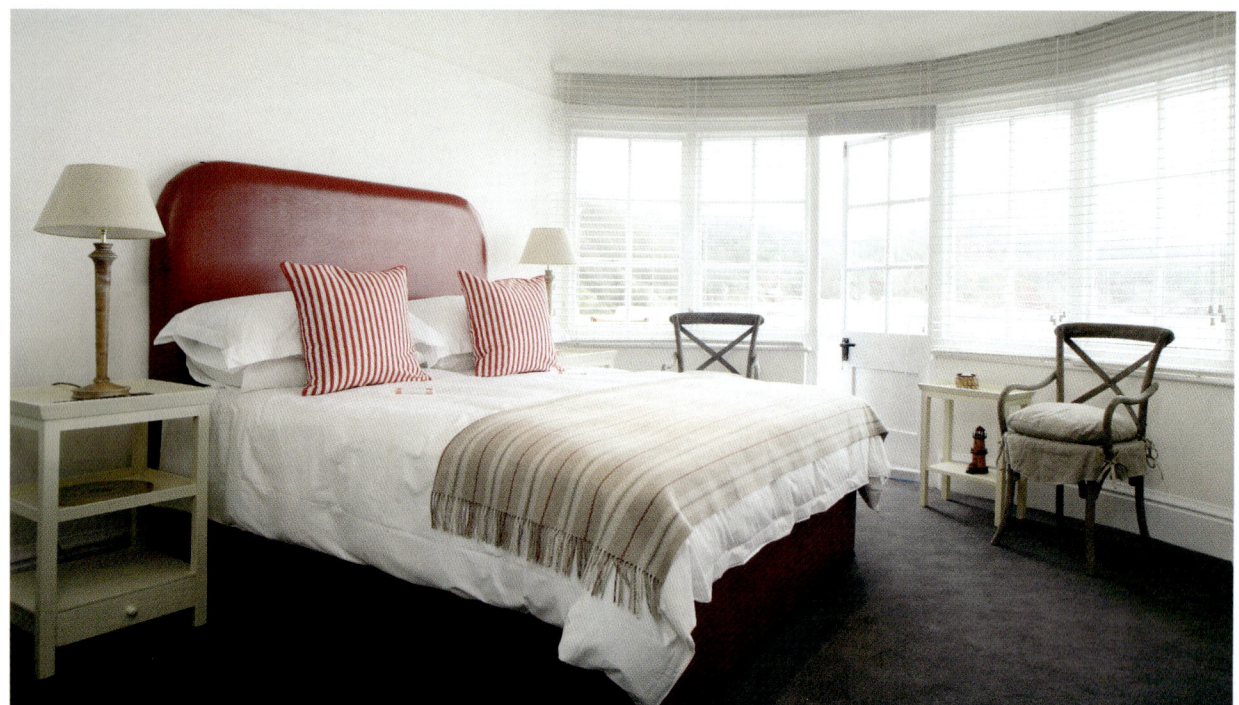

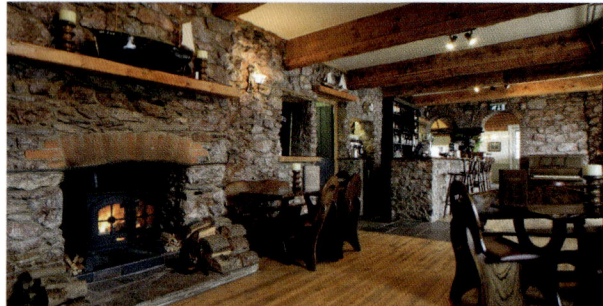

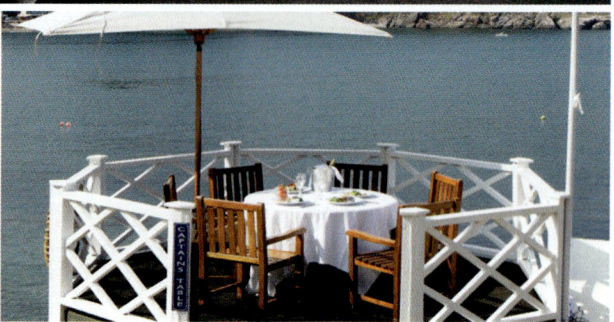

The Cary Arms

Seaside adventure for everyone on South Devon's coast

PRICE FROM:
£175

FEATURES:
Family friendly; Pet friendly; Restaurant; Sea views; Spa

ACTIVITIES:
Fishing; Walking; Water sports

NEARBY:
Babbacombe Cliff Railway; Cockington Court; Torre Abbey; Greenway, former home of Agatha Christie

GETTING THERE:
M5; Newton Abbot Railway Station; Plymouth Airport

☎ +44 (0)1803 327110
🌐 condenastjohansens.com/caryarms
🏠 Babbacombe Beach, South Devon TQ1 3LX, England

Lana de Savary's passion and talent for establishing high quality hotels, clubs and resorts with her husband Peter led her to the picturesque Babbacombe Bay on the South West Coast Path. Based on the concept of creating a place of fun for everyone whilst maintaining the essence of a quintessential English pub and luxury of a boutique hotel, The Cary Arms was born. Celebrating all that's great about the British seaside, it's wholesome, hearty and comforting. It's also a hotspot for water sport enthusiasts (currently there's a large grey seal swimming in these waters, known affectionately as The Cary Arms' resident seal). The whole family is welcome here, including the dog. There's not only a family room but a dog friendly one too complete with dog bed and bowl. Each guest room is an expression of international designer Kathleen Fraser whose chic seaside living décor brings a freshness and New England flavour. They all overlook the sea and luxury rooms have a private balcony or terrace. For those hankering utter seclusion there are one to five-bedroom cottages within the grounds. When the weather's fine, dinner is taken alfresco otherwise the Conservatory is a wonderful viewing point whose ever-changing menus present simple, seasonal, gastro-pub cuisine created from local produce and line-caught seafood.

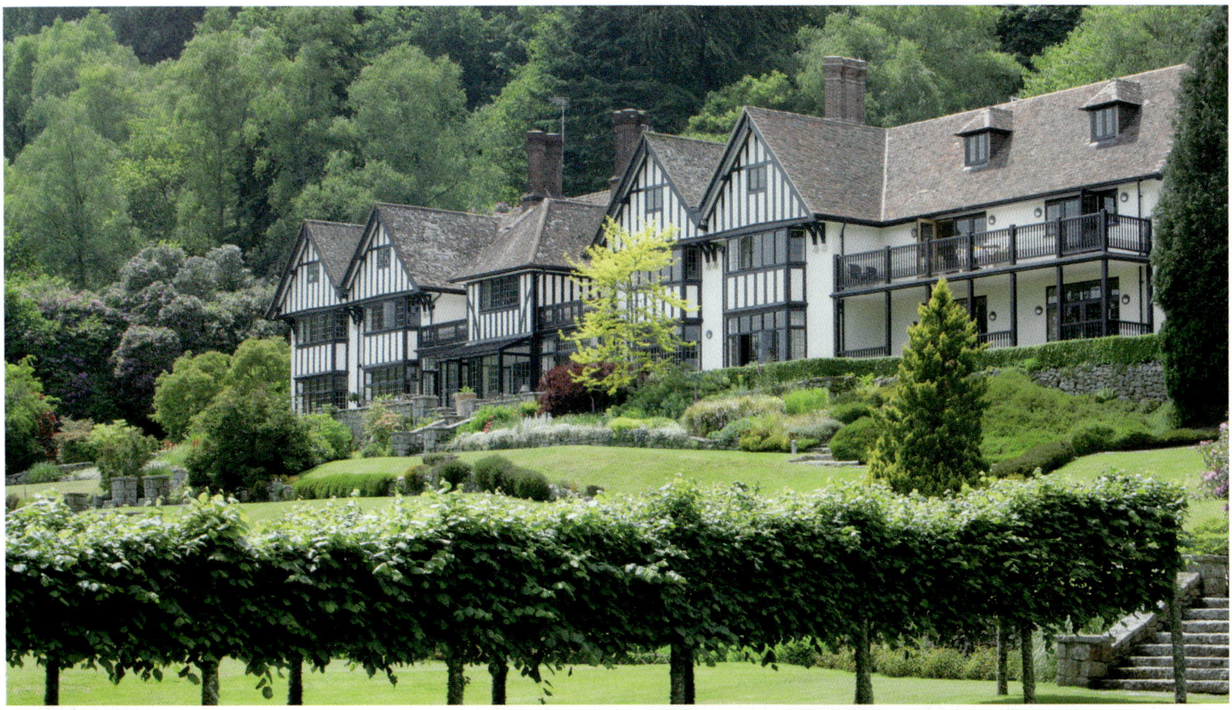

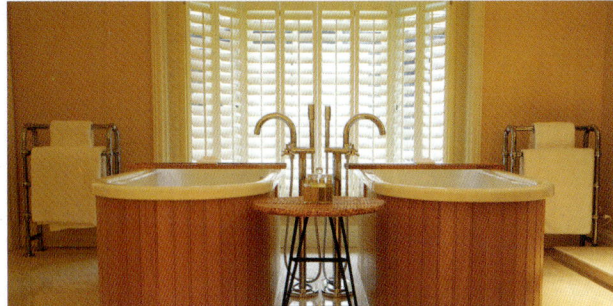

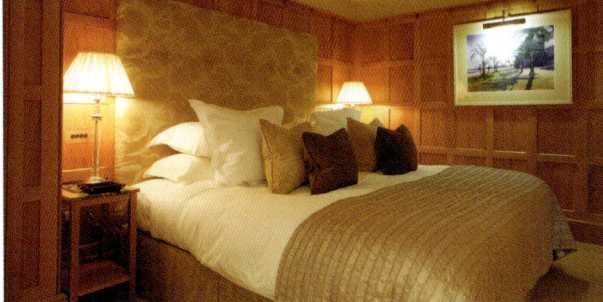

Gidleigh Park

Gourmet delights and natural wonder in Dartmoor National Park

At the heart of Dartmoor's astonishing untamed beauty, Gidleigh Park is the ultimate country house escape. In over 100 acres of woodland featuring the River Teign, colourful gardens, a croquet lawn and an 18-hole Peter Allis designed golf course, it's difficult to imagine a more peaceful scene. A walker's paradise, Gidleigh Park is a great base for exploring the surrounding archaeologically rich land (muddy Wellingtons and walking boots in the boot room please!). However, the family-run Gidleigh isn't just a scenic countryside getaway, it's the internationally applauded residence for Michael Caines MBE's 2 Michelin-Starred cuisine accompanied by one of Britain's finest wine lists of 1,300 bins (13,000 bottles!). Michael's modern European cuisine is also a celebration of West Country produce with meat and fish sourced from local suppliers and herbs and veggies picked from Gidleigh's Kitchen Garden. Continuing the starry high standards set in the restaurant, seriously chic bedrooms are equally above par, furnished with original antiques and paintings from the owners' private collection. For total seclusion book the thatched two-bedroom Pavilion with kitchen and club room located in the grounds. Thoughtful touches: the complimentary pantry offering fruit, yogurts and hot drinks; the warming open fire in the lounge; and the heated dog kennels.

PRICE FROM:
£350

FEATURES:
Family friendly; Michelin Starred restaurant; Pet friendly; Wheelchair access

ACTIVITIES:
Fishing; Golf; Walking

NEARBY:
Castle Drogo; Dartmouth; Exeter Cathedral; Dartmoor National Park; RHS Rosemoor

GETTING THERE:
M5 jct 31; Exeter St Davids Railway Station; Exeter International Airport

+44 (0)1647 432367 ☎
condenastjohansens.com/gidleighpark 🌐
Chagford, Devon TQ13 8HH, England 🏠

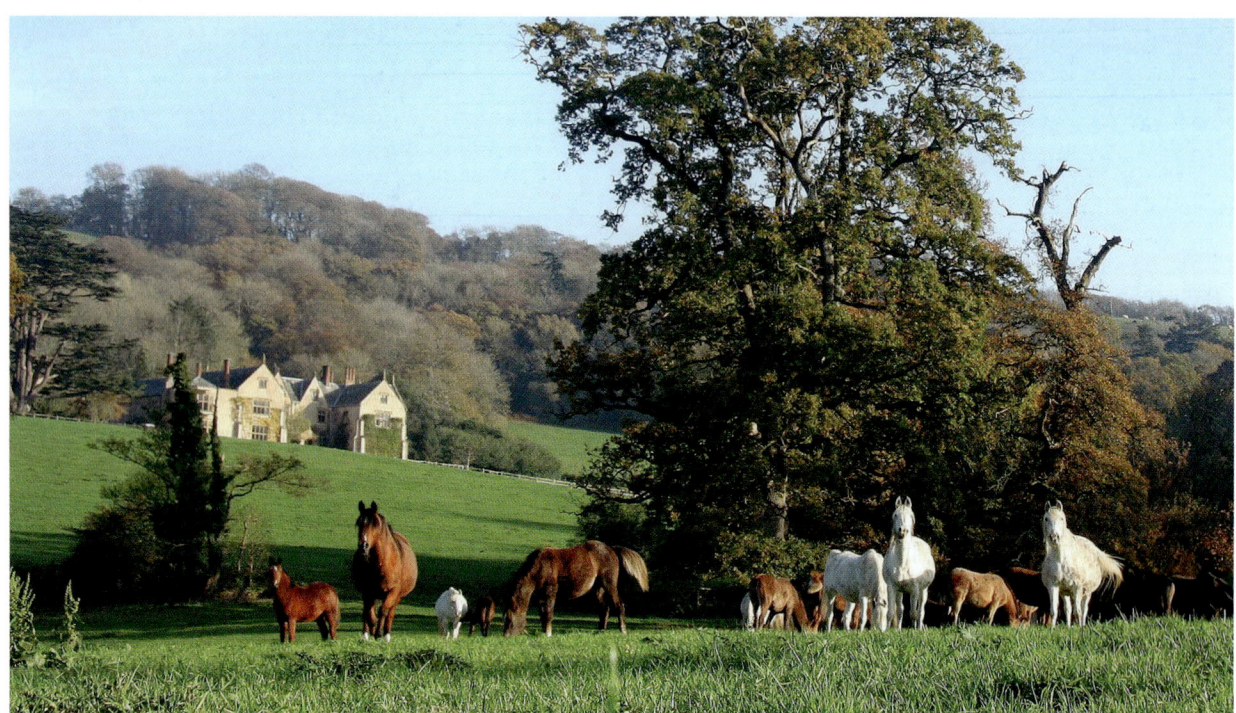

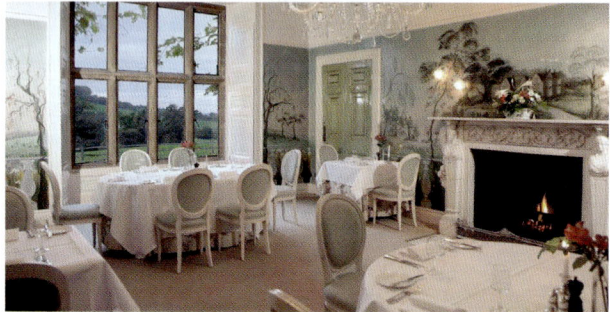

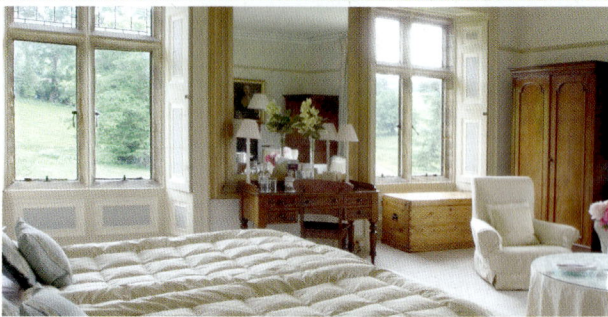

Combe House Devon

Elegant Elizabethan manor near Exeter, in Devon's stunning countryside

PRICE FROM:
£215

FEATURES:
Family friendly; Helipad; Pet friendly; Restaurant

ACTIVITIES:
Shopping; Sightseeing; Walking

NEARBY:
South West Coast Sidmouth to Lyme Regis; Dartmoor; Exeter Cathedral City; Honiton antiques shopping; Darts Farm Village, Topsham

GETTING THERE:
M5 jct 29/A30/A303; Honiton Railway Station; Exeter Airport

☎ +44 (0)1404 540400
🌐 condenastjohansens.com/combehousedevon
🏠 Gittisham, Near Honiton, Exeter, Devon EX14 3AD, England

Discover this wildly romantic and achingly luxurious 450-year-old Elizabethan manor, Combe House Devon offering stunning views, great food, wine and hospitality. One of Devon's finest estates, the House is set in tranquil gardens surrounded by 3,500 acres of country estate where Arabian horses roam freely. It's also home to charming owners Ken and Ruth Hunt who are justly proud of their friendly yet professional team whose aim is to enhance each guest's stay in every way. A welcoming huge log fire awaits as you enter the oak-panelled Great Hall where portraits of the previous owners hang and comfy sofas are piled high with cushions. Décor in the 15 bedrooms is stylishly elegant, tones are soft and muted, and comfort rules, whether it's a fabulous four-poster bed or a gleaming copper bathtub for two. For hopeless romantics there's the picture-postcard pretty Cottage tucked away in the woods, whilst families or friends should book the new Combe Thatch House with its own garden, stream and ancient orchard plus a large Aga kitchen. However, forget the pots and pans and sample the famous restaurant's delights whipped up by two Master Chefs of Great Britain from seasonal ingredients sourced from Combe House's restored Victorian kitchen gardens. The next evening, celebrate that special occasion in the wonderfully restored Georgian kitchen.

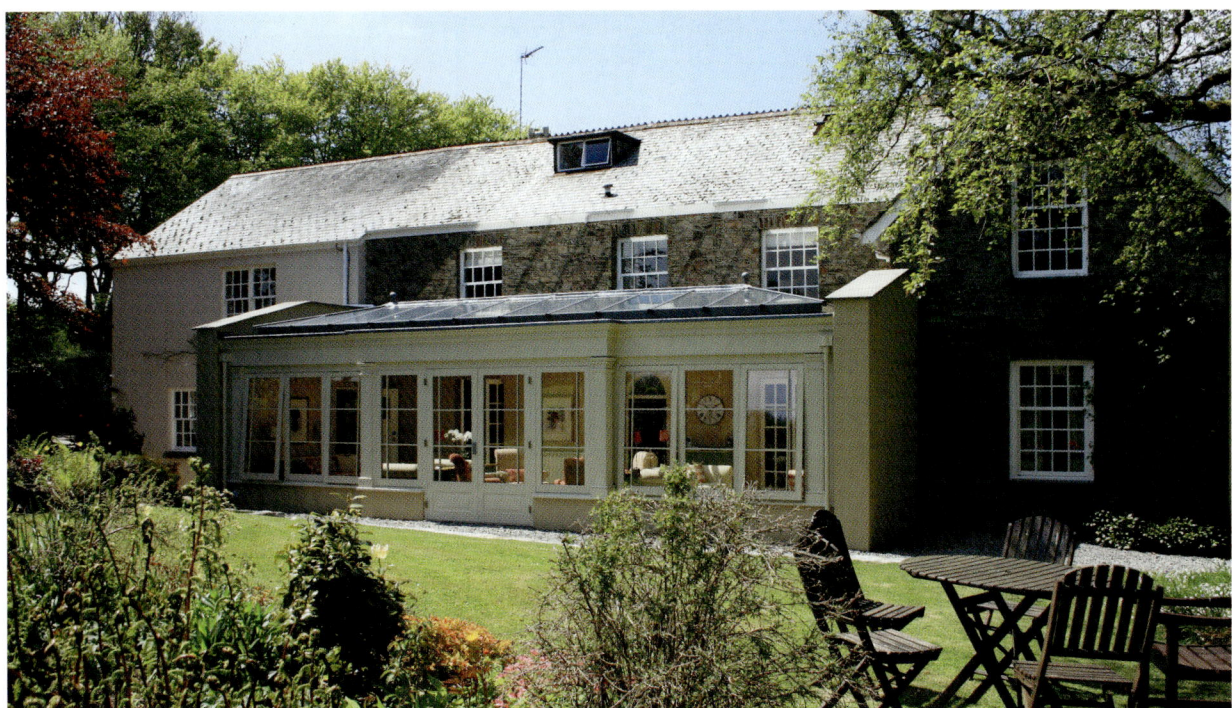

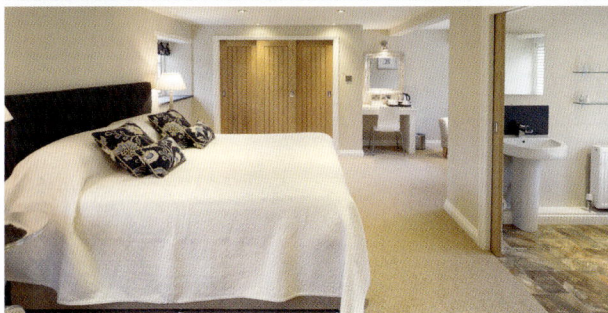

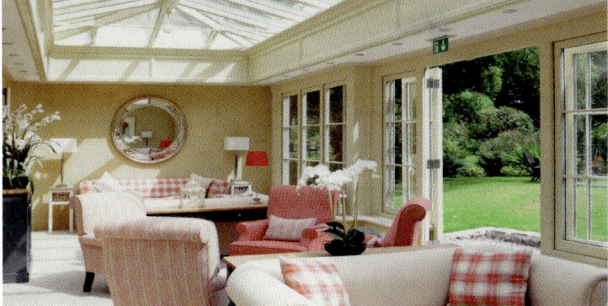

The Old Rectory Hotel

A North Devon escape from the daily grind

A place for contemplation, relaxation and rejuvenation, The Old Rectory Hotel, North Devon, keeps things uncomplicated. Caring hospitality, stylish elegance and great cuisine are its hallmarks run by perfectionists Huw Rees and Sam Prosser. High up on the cliffs of Exmoor National Park on North Devon's coast, The Old Rectory looks out to undulating National Trust land from acres of an impossibly immaculate garden with trout pond and Victorian maze. The hotel was originally a Georgian rectory and has undergone a beautifully executed refurbishment to provide all the modern comforts discerning travellers expect (free super fast WiFi for one). Each bedroom has a character of its own and a tasteful country chic style. Eight are located in The Old Rectory while three new, exceptionally spoiling suites are next door in the Coach House. When it comes to mealtimes, Huw and Sam's ethos of doing things well is never more evident. The excellent dishes are created from local seasonal produce (North Coast fish and seafood, meat from an ethical local farm) served alongside an expertly chosen wine list that's won high acclaim. If you feel the need to burn off some of these calories, The Old Rectory's garden leads to the Coastal Path where some of the most spectacular scenery England has to offer is found.

PRICE FROM:
£210

FEATURES:
Restaurant; Wheelchair access

ACTIVITIES:
Fishing; Golf; Walking

NEARBY:
South West Coastal Path; Lynmouth; Woolacombe; Exmoor; Lundy Island

GETTING THERE:
M5 jct 25; Barnstaple Railway Station; Bristol Airport

+44 (0)1598 763368 ☎
condenastjohansens.com/oldrectoryexmoor 🌐
Martinhoe, Exmoor National Park, Devon EX31 4QT, England 🏠

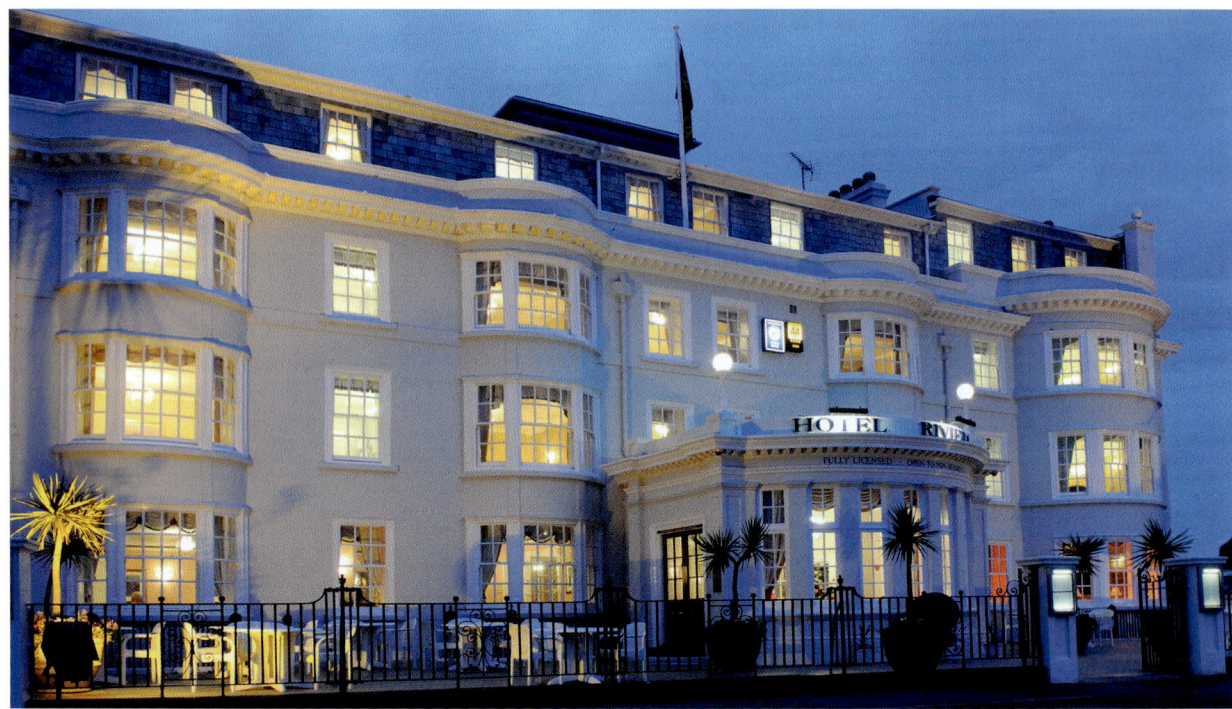

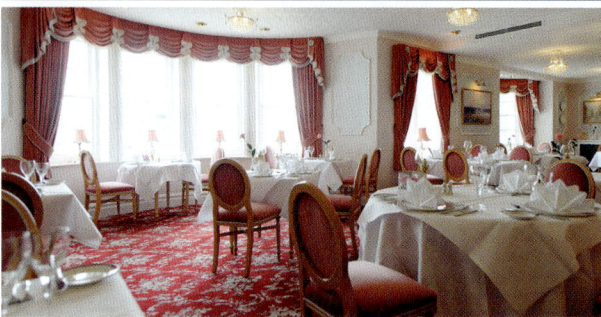
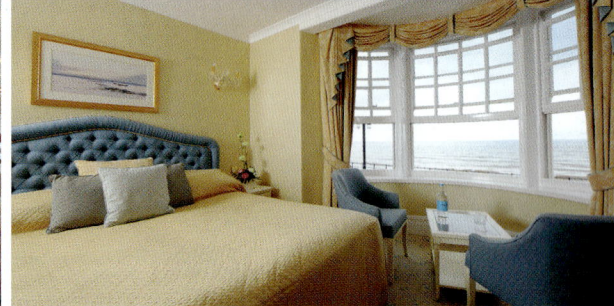

Hotel Riviera

The pride of Sidmouth's Regency England

PRICE FROM:
£228

FEATURES:
Beach access; Family friendly; Restaurant; Sea views;
Wheelchair access

ACTIVITIES:
Golf; Tennis; Walking

NEARBY:
Killerton House and Gardens; Exeter Cathedral; Powderham
Castle; Dartmoor

GETTING THERE:
M5 jct 30; Honiton/Exeter St David's Railway Stations; Exeter
Airport

☎ +44 (0)1395 515201
🌐 condenastjohansens.com/riviera
🏠 The Esplanade, Sidmouth, Devon EX10 8AY, England

Poet Laureate John Betjeman described Sidmouth as "a town caught still in a timeless charm." Full of Regency splendour, seaside fun and dramatic (protected Jurassic) red cliff coastline, his words still ring true today. Perfectly located at the centre of Sidmouth's historic Georgian esplanade is Hotel Riviera overlooking Lyme Bay. Its bright Regency façade with bow-fronted windows foretells the elegance within whose handsome public rooms and classically appointed bedrooms (many with sea views) are arguably some of the most comfortable and hospitable in the region. This prestigious and welcoming coastal hotel - awarded 4 Stars by both the AA and Visit Britain - is also a proven success story of traditional service and know-how. Owned and run by the Wharton family for more than 40 years, Hotel Riviera places comfort and professional hospitality above all else, committed to providing the very highest standards of excellence. Nowhere is this more evident than in the fine dining salon where cuisine prepared by English and French trained chefs is paired with exceptional wines from the cellar. The newly refurbished Cocktail Bar is open till midnight most evenings where the resident pianist can be found playing for your pleasure. Look out for: Hotel Riviera's annually anticipated festive programme and seasonal breaks.

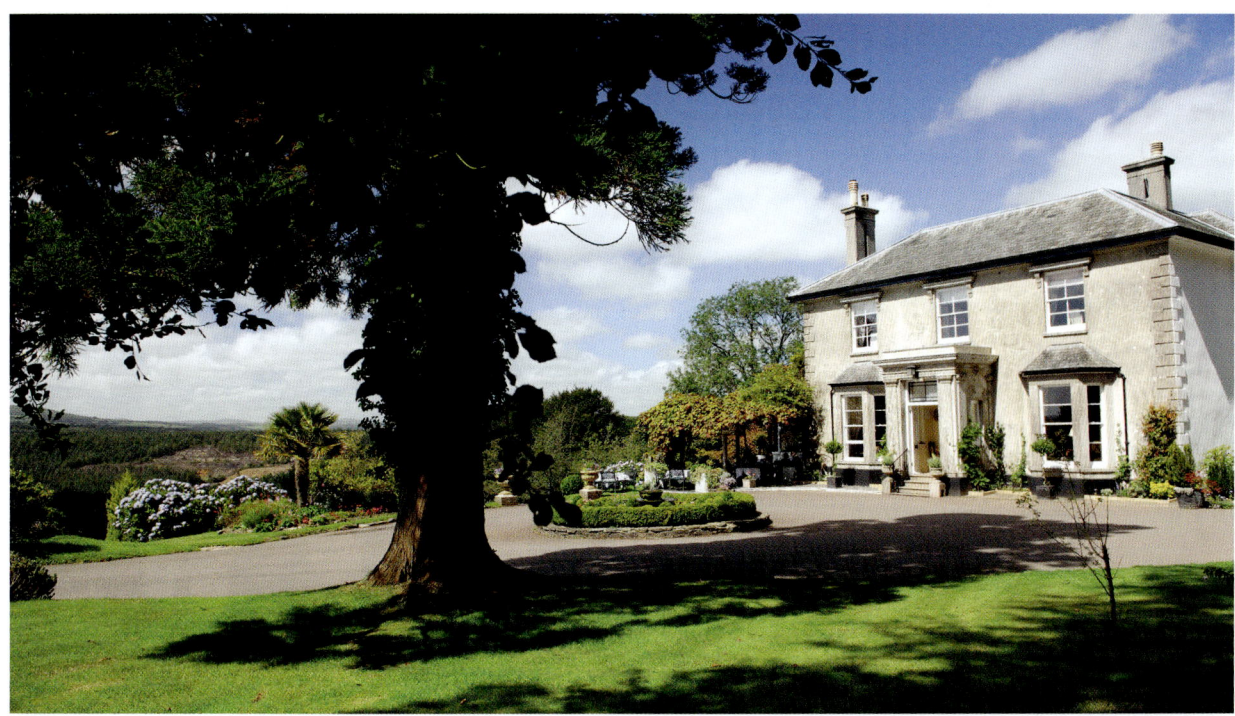

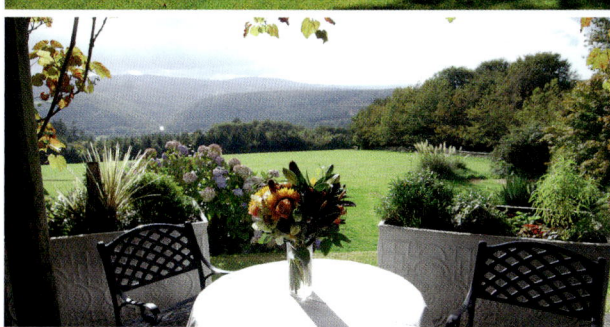

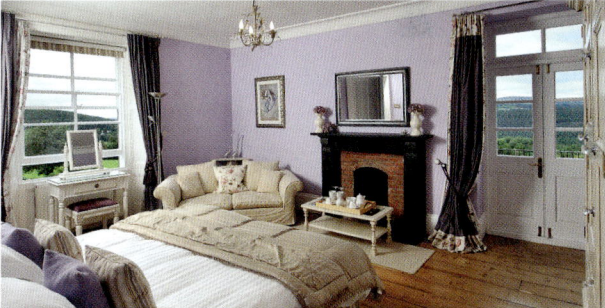

The Horn of Plenty

Tavistock proves that the best things really do come in small packages

The Horn of Plenty Country House Hotel & Restaurant in Devon is somewhere to escape to, nestle in and breathe out. You're not far from Tavistock, Dartmoor and The Eden Project here but the surrounding five acres of skilfully crafted gardens allow you to hole up with a lover, retreat for a well-deserved break or simply drink in the natural beauty around you with uninterrupted tranquillity. The refinement of the house is perfectly matched by its setting with breathtaking views of Tamar Valley below. Foodies come to The Horn of Plenty for the fine dining restaurant whose impeccable reputation has been upheld for more than 40 years. Genuinely passionate about creating superb food from seasonal produce that's locally sourced whenever possible, the kitchen creates menus that often include Newlyn crab, rump of Devonshire lamb and Cornish turbot. It's known as one of the best in Devon, if not the South West. As for the 10 guest rooms, each individually styled refuge is decorated to showroom perfection. Those in the main house are classic in character whilst Garden House rooms reflect a more contemporary design. Brides-to-be take note: this is a great venue for bespoke, truly memorable weddings.

PRICE FROM:
£95

FEATURES:
Helipad; Pet friendly; Restaurant; Wheelchair access

ACTIVITIES:
Golf; Sightseeing; Walking

NEARBY:
Plymouth; Dartmoor National Park; Buckland Abbey; Devon coastline; The Eden Project

GETTING THERE:
Just off A390; M5 jct 31; Exeter Airport

+44 (0)1822 832528 ☎
condenastjohansens.com/thehornofplenty 🌐
Gulworthy, Tavistock, Devon PL19 8JD, England 🏠

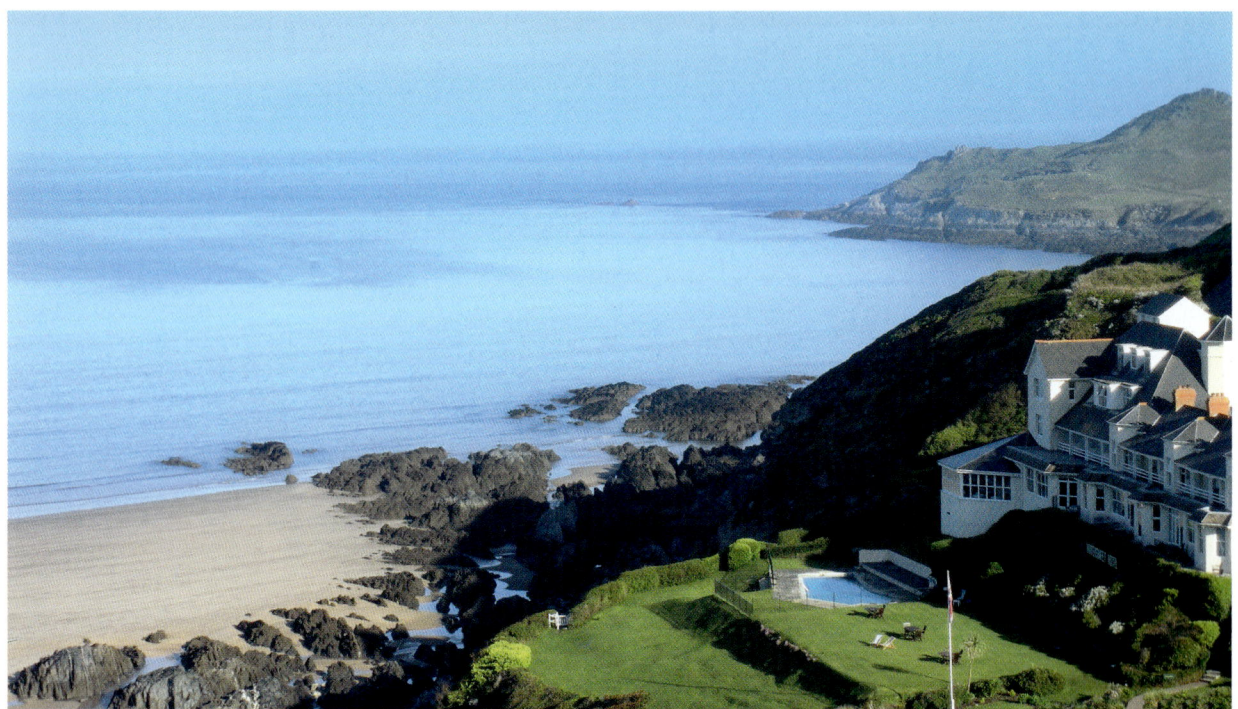

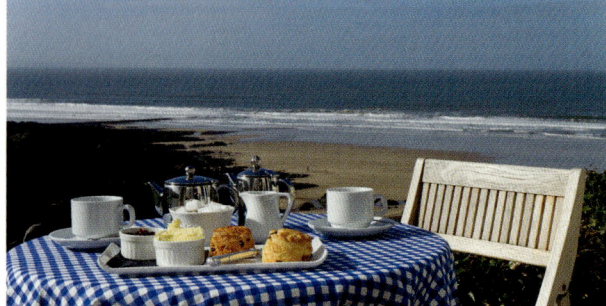

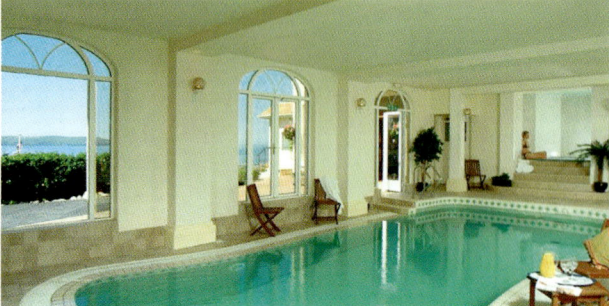

Watersmeet Hotel & Restaurant

North Devon's premier coastal escape

PRICE FROM:
£150

FEATURES:
Family friendly; Pool; Restaurant; Spa; Wheelchair access

ACTIVITIES:
Fishing; Golf; Walking

NEARBY:
Barnstaple; National Trust coastal walks; Arlington Court;
Saunton Sands Championship Golf Course; Watermouth Castle

GETTING THERE:
A361; M5 jct 27; Newquay Cornwall Airport

Grab your surfboard, walking boots and golf clubs (the bucket and spade too) and head to Combesgate Beach. For this is a North Devon beachy hotspot for surfing, National Trust coastal walks and challenging golf (Saunton Sands Championship Golf Course). From an elevated position at the water's edge of the beach, Watersmeet Hotel & Restaurant has direct access to the sandy shore via a set of steps and oversees the incomparable natural beauty from on high, considered one of the finest and most dramatic locations in the South West. Ever-changing, the rugged coastline across to Lundy Island is a staggeringly picturesque site best viewed from oversized windows in Watersmeet's reception rooms. Many guest rooms have balconies with these sea views, one of which has a four poster and the suite on the top floor is a cosy, romantic option. If visiting with the family, Watersmeet has a selection of rooms suitable – just ask. Weather permitting, a spot of lunch and tea alfresco on the terrace or in the tea garden is a must and dining by candlelight while watching the sunset at the pavilion restaurant is an essential treat to anyone's stay. Dishes are well balanced, imaginative and contain local ingredients. Alternatively, there's the new Bistro restaurant serving elegantly presented classic British favourites. Additional facilities: a heated outdoor pool, indoor pool with hot spa and steam room.

☎ +44 (0)1271 870333
🌐 condenastjohansens.com/watersmeet
🏠 Mortehoe, Woolacombe, Devon EX34 7EB, England

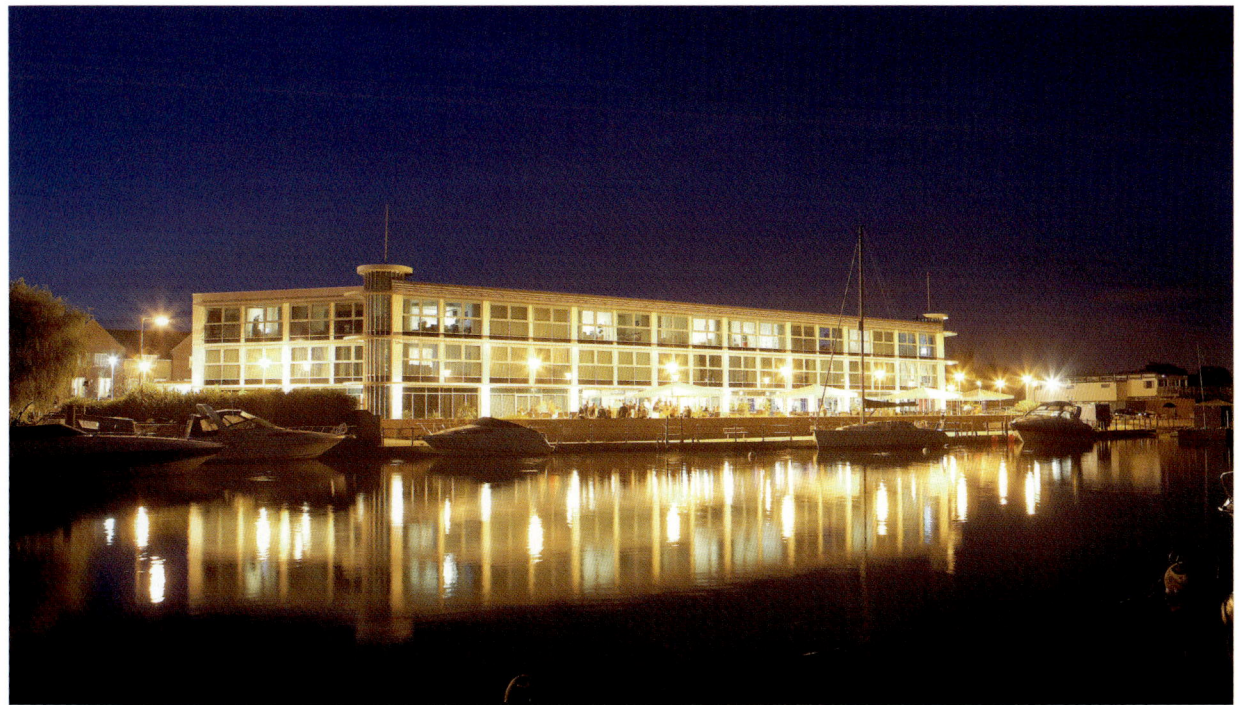

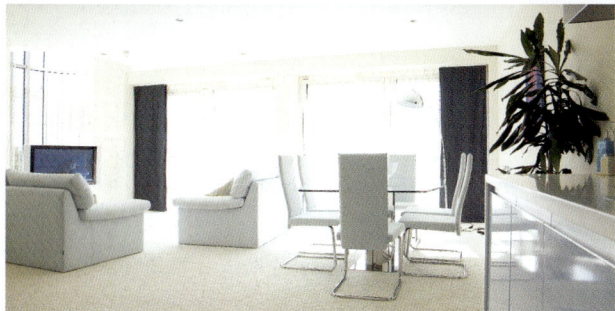
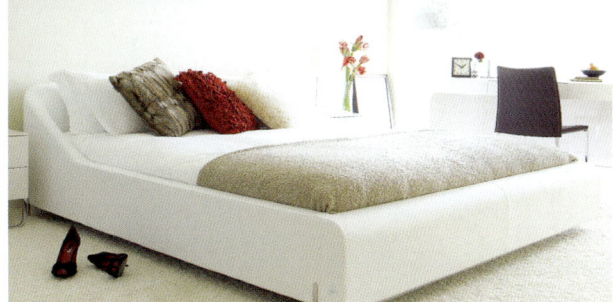

Captains Club Hotel & Spa

Timeless nautical style near Christchurch, Dorset

Maritime fever at Captain's Club Hotel & Spa is contagious. If the nautically themed bedrooms and suites, fresh fish at the aptly named Tides Restaurant and natural marine products in CCSpa fail to have you reaching for your deck shoes, then the riverside views from every room just might. Trips on Captain's Club's private 34-foot cruiser, *Nauti Girl*, most certainly will. For this is where the Rivers Avon and Stour meet, a short stroll from the age-old coastal town of Christchurch (whose Priory Church has choir stalls older than those in Westminster Abbey). Captain's Club Hotel moors alongside the river like a mighty cruise liner overseeing its active comings and goings. Inside, it's sleek and contemporary, awash with neutral colour schemes and ever-present watery-related elements in each of the State Rooms (doubles) and suites. For longer stays, or visits with the family, the two and three-bedroom, two-bathroom suites (kitchen too!) are perfect. And just as the hotel's style is elegantly uncomplicated, fresh and innovative, so too is Tide Restaurant's cuisine. Full of traditional favourites, just-caught shellfish and grilled fare, there's something for everyone. Chef will even prepare baby food on request. The Lounge's cocktails also draw a crowd but it's the afternoon Tea@Club selections that are a must.

PRICE FROM:
£179

FEATURES:
Family friendly; Pet friendly; Restaurant; Spa; Wheelchair access

ACTIVITIES:
Fishing; Golf; Walking

NEARBY:
Christchurch Priory; Christchurch Harbour; River and sea cruise; New Forest National Park

GETTING THERE:
A35; Christchurch Railway Station; Bournemouth International Airport

+44 (0)1202 475111 ☎
condenastjohansens.com/captainsclubhotel 🌐
Wick Ferry, Wick Lane, Christchurch, Dorset BH23 1HU, 🏠
England

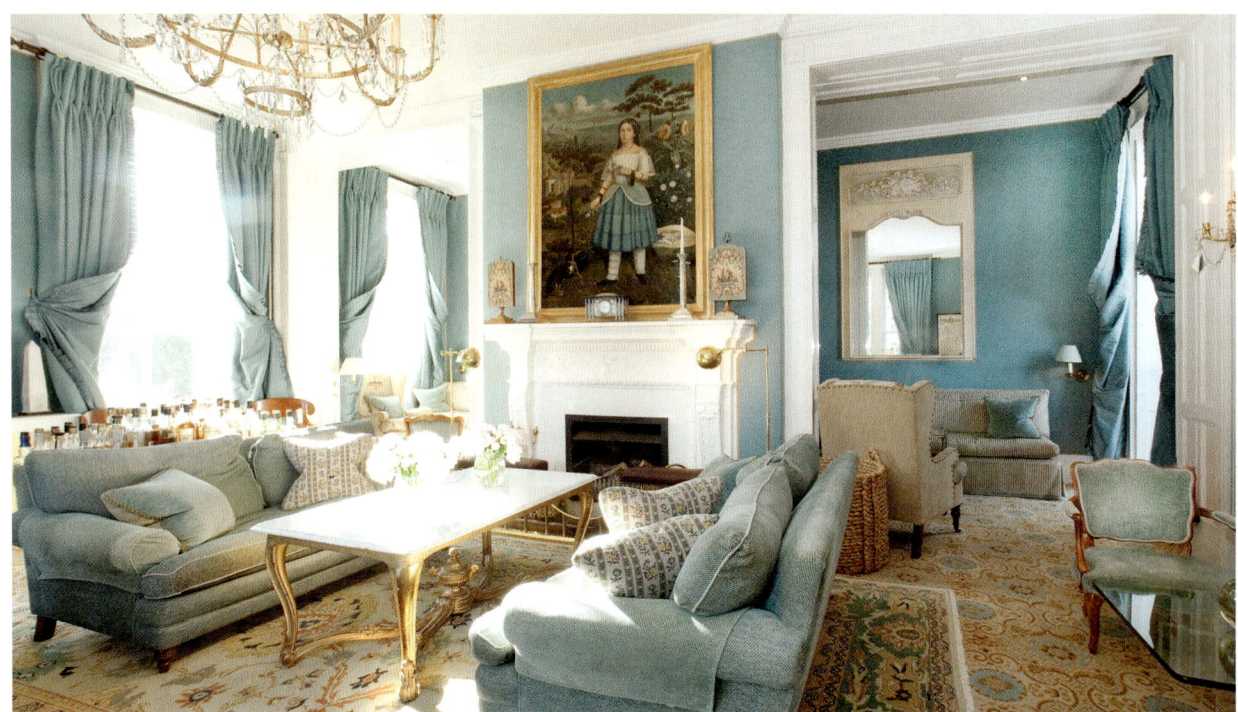
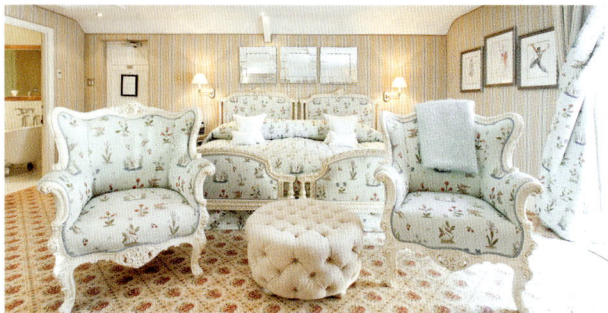
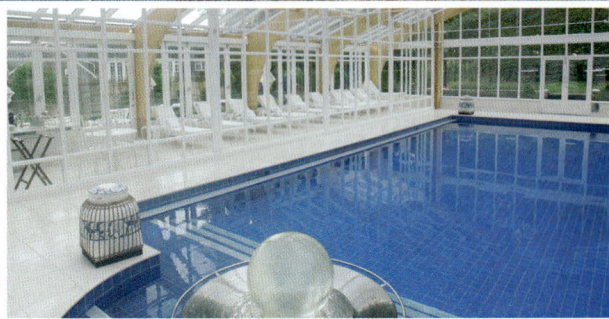

Summer Lodge Country House Hotel

Traditional English charm in pretty Evershot village

PRICE FROM:
£235

FEATURES:
Family friendly; Pet friendly; Pool; Restaurant; Spa

ACTIVITIES:
Fishing; Golf; Walking

NEARBY:
Thomas Hardy country; Cerne Abbas; Abbotsbury; Heritage Coast; Sherborne

GETTING THERE:
A37; M5 jct 25; Bristol Airport

For an escape to the English countryside in distinguished style, it's got to be Summer Lodge Country House Hotel in Evershot, West Dorset. Complete with a pretty English garden spanning four acres, this idyllic scene borders a deer park teeming with wildlife and natural beauty all year-round. A private residence for almost 200 years, Summer Lodge was built as a dower house in 1798 for the second Earl of Ilchester. (Local architect and novelist Thomas Hardy was commissioned to extend the house in 1893.) And it wasn't until 1979 that Summer's charms opened up to the public. Now, it's a small country house hotel setting new heights in comfort, style, relaxation, courteous hospitality and exceptional cuisine; it feels more like a (genteel) home than a hotel. The bedrooms, suites and cottages are exceptionally tasteful and combine the finest English furnishings with all the modern amenities you would expect, including free WiFi. Meals in the restaurant (whose credentials are too many to list) are the creation of Head Chef Steven Titman, and world-renowned Sommelier Eric Zwiebel lends his expertise to proceedings. Steven's lip-smacking cuisine uses an abundance of fresh local produce and herbs grown on-site. His traditional Dorset cream teas are legendary. For active guests: a conservatory-style pool, spa, gym, croquet lawn, tennis court and bicycles are all at your disposal.

☎ +44 (0)1935 482000
🌐 condenastjohansens.com/summerlodge
🏠 9 Fore Street, Evershot, Dorset DT2 0JR, England

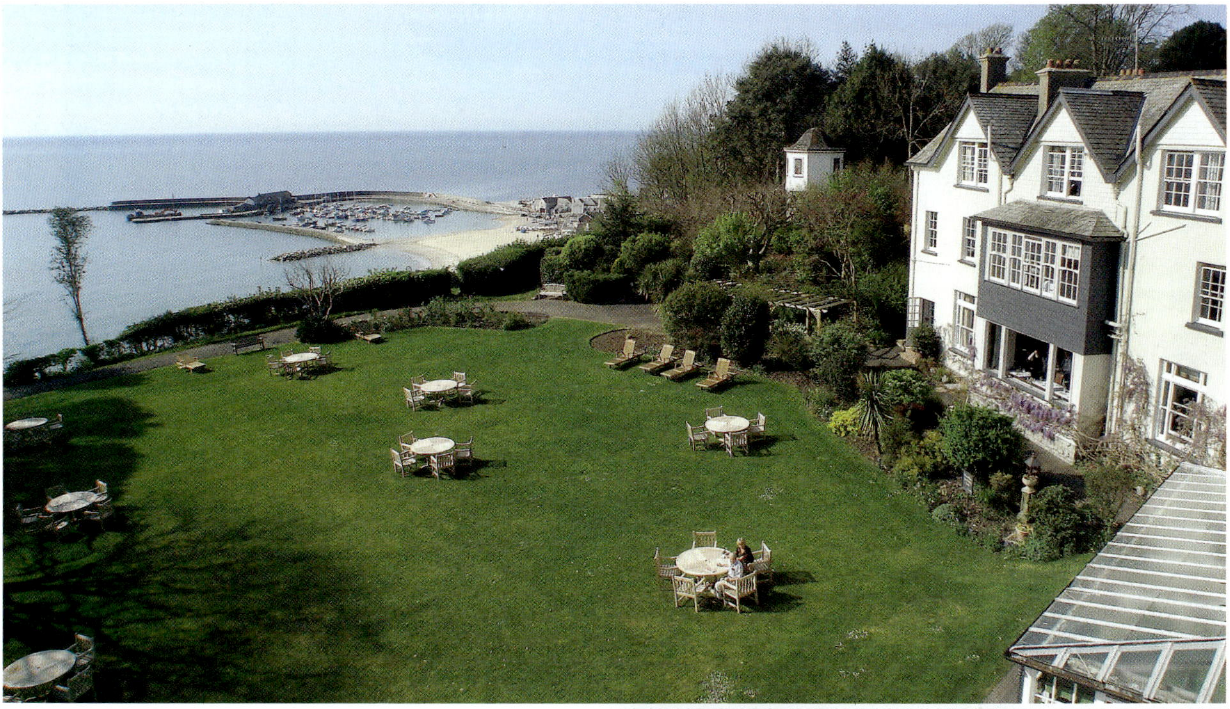

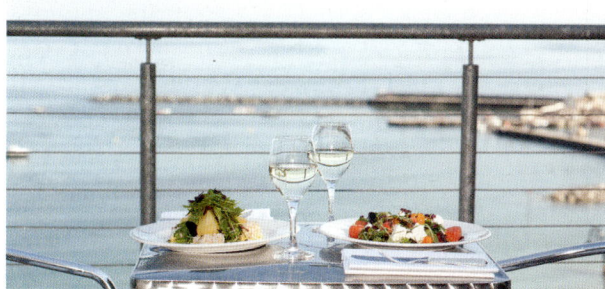

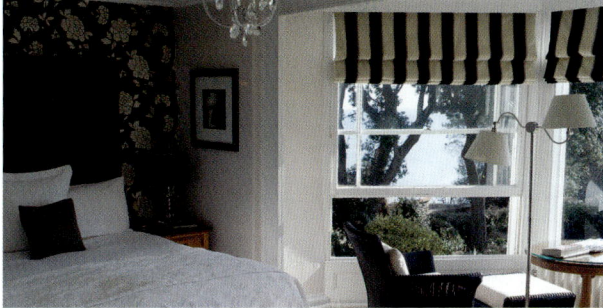

Alexandra Hotel and Restaurant

Reassuringly traditional Dorset seaside hotel and foodie favourite

A breath of fresh air, Alexandra Hotel and Restaurant in Lyme Regis is poised on the Jurassic Coast overlooking the picturesque Cobb Harbour. Distinctly devoid of any pretention or formality, Alexandra has found a balance between comfortable seaside holiday home and charming boutique hotel. Like the countess for whom the residence was built in 1735, this grande dame is reassuringly old fashioned, elegant and well maintained with just a hint of eccentricity. The place eeks of windswept romance and is set in beautiful gardens that lead you down to the beach; the perfect place to unfurl. The fresh sea air, rock-pooling and sandcastle building, coupled with treats such as beer crab and cucumber sandwiches are the stuff innocent Enid Blyton-esque childhood memories are made of. But Alexandra is a foodie destination at heart with Chef Ian Grant keeping it simple. Local and in-season, the menus are always a recipe for success. The recurring scallops with roasted cauliflower purée and truffle oil, and exceedingly good Dorset apple cake bear speak for themselves. Seemingly a million miles away from it all, the essence of Alexandra is so good you'll want to bottle it up and take it home with you.

PRICE FROM:
£177

FEATURES:
Family friendly; Gym; Restaurant; Spa

ACTIVITIES:
Fishing; Golf; Horse riding

NEARBY:
South West Coast Path; Beaches; Fossil walks

GETTING THERE:
On the A3052; M25 jct 25; Exeter Airport

+44 (0)1297 442010 ☎
condenastjohansens.com/hotelalexandra 🌐
Pound Street, Lyme Regis, Dorset DT7 3HZ, England 🏠

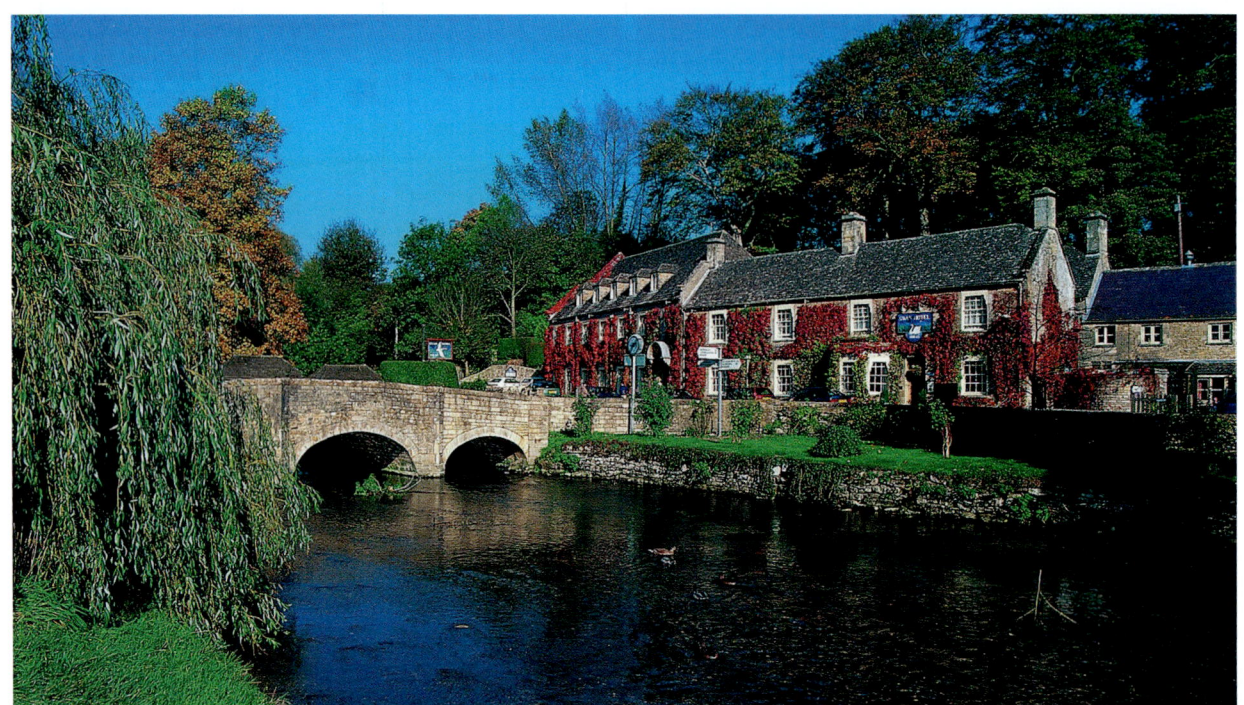

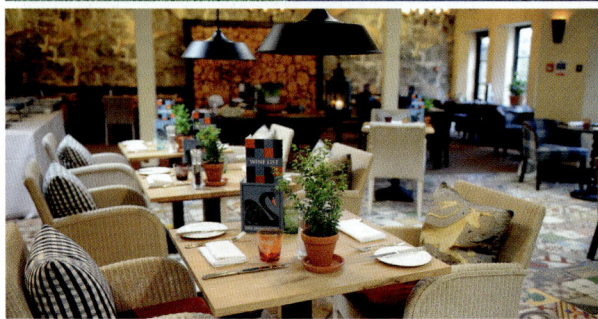

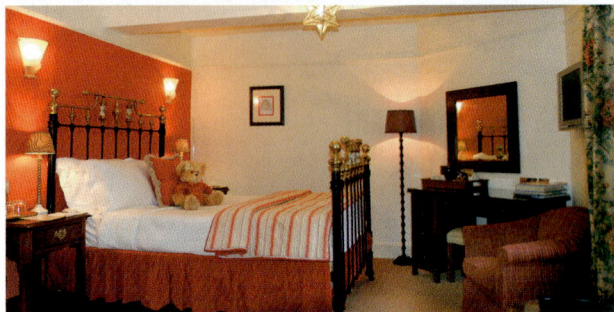

The Swan Hotel

Smart, stylish and ever-so "Cotswolds" village inn

PRICE FROM:
£170

FEATURES:
Family friendly; Pet friendly; Restaurant; Wheelchair access

ACTIVITIES:
Fishing; Horse riding; Walking

NEARBY:
Cheltenham; Bath; Oxford; Cotswold Wildlife Park; Bibury Trout Farm

GETTING THERE:
A429; M4 jct 15/M5 jct 11; Birmingham International Airport

☎ +44 (0)1285 740695
🌐 condenastjohansens.com/swanhotelbibury
📍 Bibury, Gloucestershire GL7 5NW, England

Bibury is the archetypal Cotswolds village. Honey-hued terraced cottages, hilly green scenery and a tranquil riverside location all sound too perfect to be true yet this is Bibury, home to The Swan Hotel, a 17th-century coaching inn. Recommended by Condé Nast Johansens for 30 years, The Swan always delivers the perfect Cotswolds experience for country lovers, anglers (fishing on the trout-filled River Coln can be arranged) and walkers. It's also an unashamedly romantic spot where winding down comes easy. Understanding the desires of the modern-day traveller, The Swan's interiors are an inspired mix of classic country living and dynamic contemporary flair. Oak panelling, plush carpets and sumptuous fabrics dress the eclectic rooms whose fine paintings, artwork and antiques add additional special touches. If you're bringing the family, choose the two-bedroom Family Suite but if some romancing is on the agenda, Superior Four Poster Rooms and the secluded Garden Cottage Suites (situated a short walk from the main hotel) are perfect. Warm and graceful, The Swan Brasserie is the inn's trump card. Dictated by fresh local produce, the seasonally influenced menu features European-style favourites alongside fine wines. If it's a lighter bite you're craving, the convivial Swan Bar is at your disposal all day. Their afternoon teas are something to write home about.

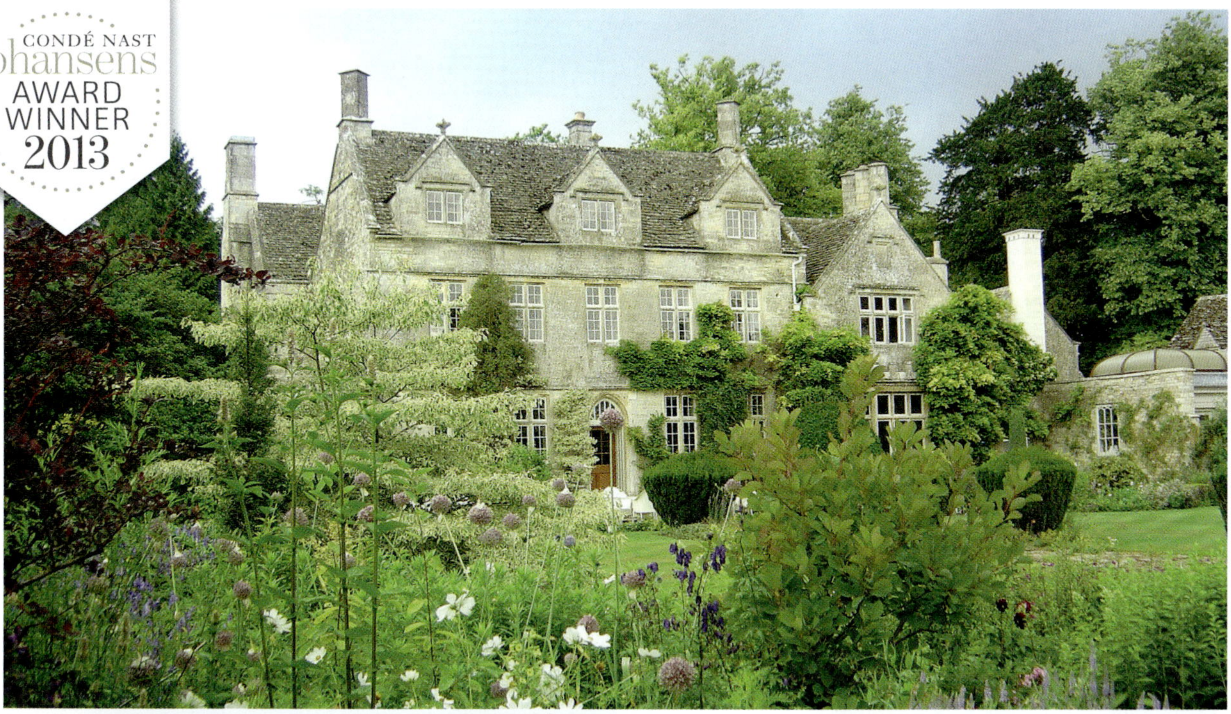

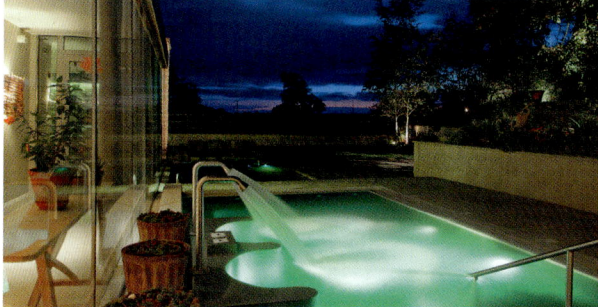

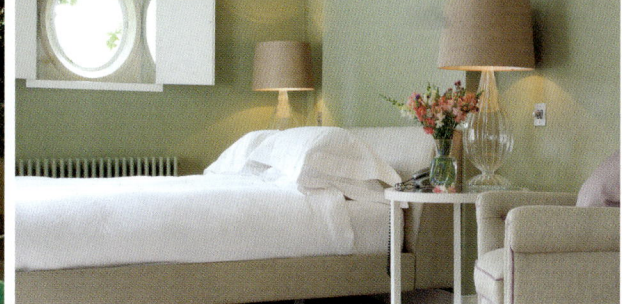

Barnsley House

Designer interiors and legendary gardens in Barnsley, the Cotswolds

Placing the Cotswolds village of Barnsley on the map with its enchanting gardens and ancient meadows, Barnsley House's setting is a hard one to beat. Designed by former owner Rosemary Verey, OBE, VMH, the gardens' collection of intimate, artistic nooks and crannies met with admiration upon its opening to the public in 1970. Notably from HRH the Prince of Wales and Sir Elton John (who subsequently employed Rosemary) and they continue to attract thousands of paying visitors today. Inside, an original approach to the traditional concept of comfort and luxury has resulted in unfussy, soothing rooms whose 17th-century origins have been given a 21st-century transformation. Stone fireplaces, wooden floors and exposed beams add authenticity to the country atmosphere whilst high-tech equipment such as cinema surround-sound hi-fi systems and wide-screen plasmas make Barnsley House an incredibly spoiling escape. The Barnsley Spa & Skincare Centre is well worth a visit for the ultimate stress-busting break and to complete the pampering, meals at The Potager Restaurant are a must. Head Chef Graham Grafton can often be seen picking vegetables from the gardens to produce English classics with Italian inspiration. Calling all film lovers: Barnsley House has its very own big screen cinema room showing films at selected times.

PRICE FROM:
£290

FEATURES:
Helipad; Pet friendly; Restaurant; Spa

ACTIVITIES:
Golf; Tennis; Walking

NEARBY:
Bibury village; Cirencester; Cheltenham

GETTING THERE:
M4 jct 15; Kemble Railway Station; Bristol Airport

+44 (0)1285 740000 ☎
condenastjohansens.com/barnsleyhouse 🌐
Barnsley, Cirencester, Gloucestershire GL7 5EE, England 🏠

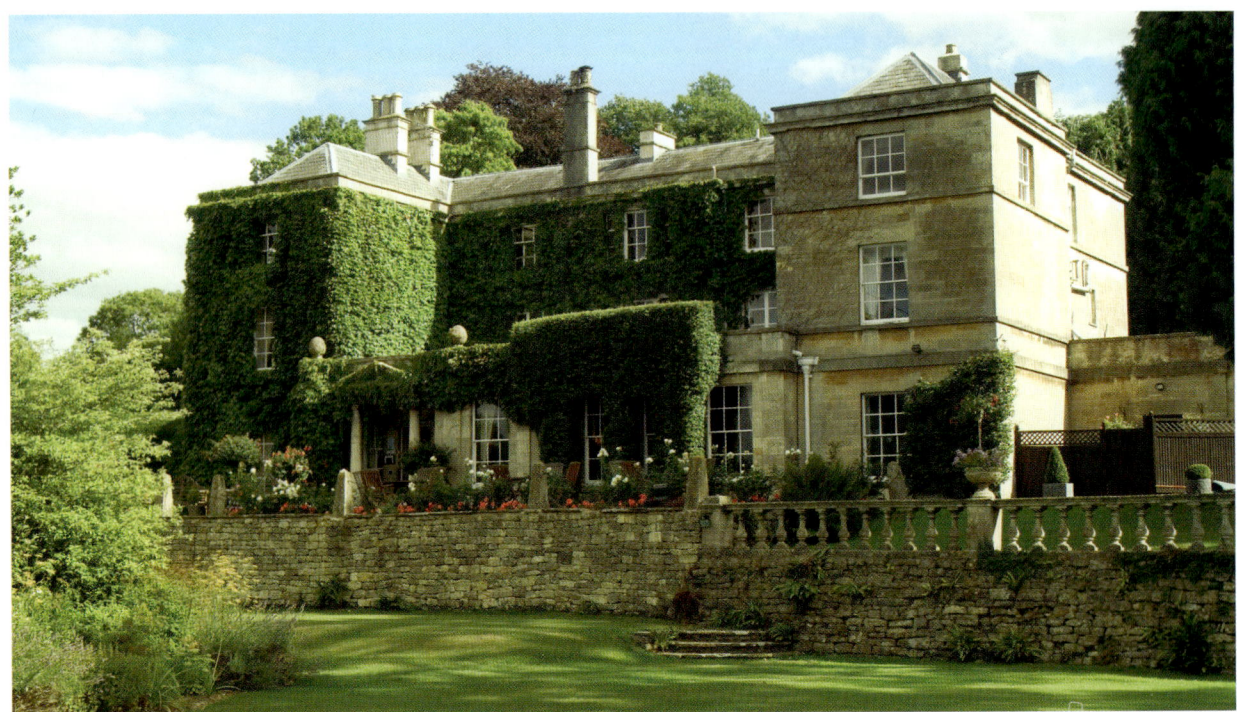

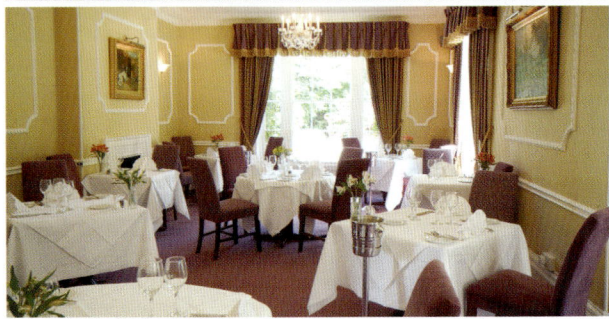

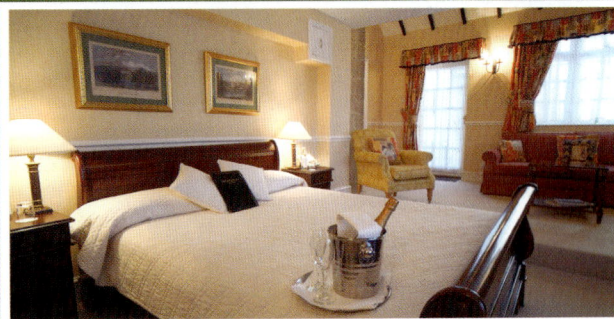

Burleigh Court Hotel

Gentleman's manor-turned-charming Cotswolds hotel

PRICE FROM:
£150

FEATURES:
Family friendly; Pet friendly; Pool; Restaurant; Wheelchair access

ACTIVITIES:
Fishing; Golf; Shooting

NEARBY:
Cirencester; Cheltenham; Bath; Slimbridge Wildfowl Trust; Westonbirt Arboretum

GETTING THERE:
A419; M4; Heathrow Airport

Swashbuckling vistas from every room of Burleigh Court Hotel's elegantly dressed rooms take in the Cotswolds and Golden Valley. This is a country retreat of a bygone era - a hidden gem in the truest sense: hard to find but utterly worth the search. Near Stroud, Burleigh Court Hotel is a small but perfectly formed and divinely serviced hotel with romantic country weekend written all over it. Located within an equestrian triangle of Gatcombe Park, Badminton and Cheltenham, it's a horse lover's haven minus the pomp and ceremony. Following a countryside outing, sashay onto the terrace and tuck into a very English afternoon tea looking out to more of those views. At the restaurant, Burleigh Court's Mediterranean/French fusion food is packed with local produce including rainbow trout if you're lucky (courtesy of Chef Adrian Jarrad, a keen fisherman). And room for dessert is not just advisable but absolutely necessary! Red apple cheesecake anyone? After dinner, curl up into a deep leather sofa or armchair and unwind by the roaring log fire with an after-dinner brandy. Special bonus: superior room and suite guests will find a complimentary decanter of sherry waiting for them upon arrival.

☎ +44 (0)1453 883804
🌐 condenastjohansens.com/burleighgloucestershire
🏠 Burleigh, Minchinhampton, Near Stroud, Gloucestershire GL5 2PF, England

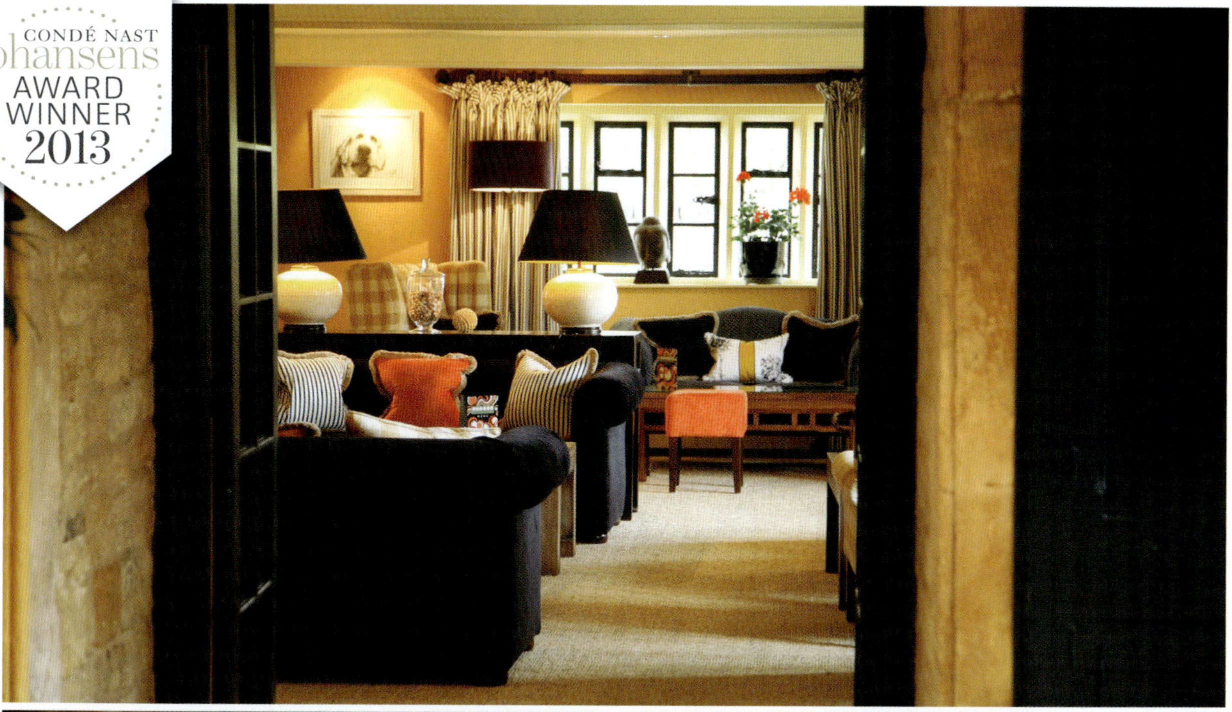

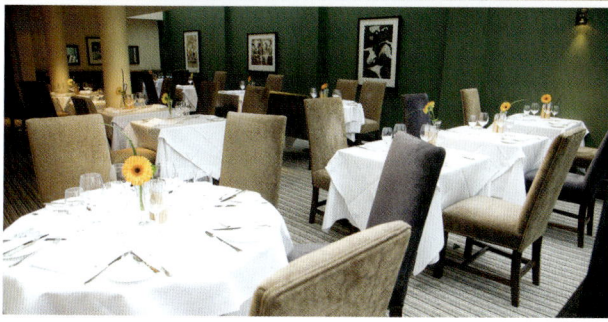
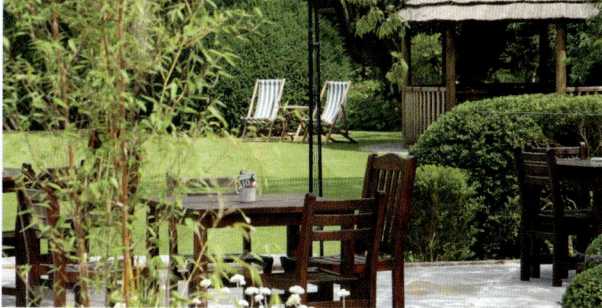

The Manor House Hotel

A Cotswolds treasure highlighting the finer things in life

Market day at the 13th-century market town of Moreton-in-Marsh is a Tuesday. The goods on sale may have altered since trading began in 1227 but the buzz is undoubtedly the same. And at the pulsing heart of this historic High Street is the 16th-century Manor House Hotel, a former coaching inn turned upscale boutique escape charming guests with tales of yesteryear. King George VI and Queen Elizabeth The Queen Mother stayed here during World War II and the town itself inspired scenes in J R R Tolkien's Lord of the Rings. Sensitively refurbished with plush fabrics, elegant furnishings and contemporary convenience, The Manor House's atmosphere is informal and friendly. Its rooms and suites are the essence of chic country style with views to the picturesque High Street or The Manor's pretty garden, at the bottom of which is the Apple Cottage Suite with private hot tub. Filled with sweet scented flowers and meandering pathways, the garden features a 300-year-old mulberry tree and mature evergreen oak complete with a sun terrace. This is a favourite spot for afternoon teas, drinks and small gatherings. Breakfasts, lunches and dinners highlighting local produce with seasonal twists are served in The Mulberry Restaurant whilst the laid-back Beagle Bar & Brasserie whips up equally fine fare but snacks too.

PRICE FROM:
£158

FEATURES:
Family friendly; Pet friendly; Restaurant; Wheelchair access

ACTIVITIES:
Golf; Sightseeing; Walking

NEARBY:
Cheltenham Races, Blenheim Palace; Bath; Oxford; Stratford-upon-Avon

GETTING THERE:
On the A429; M40, jct 8/15; Birmingham International Airport

+44 (0)1608 650501 ☎
condenastjohansens.com/manorhousemoreton 🌐
Moreton-in-Marsh, Gloucestershire GL56 0LJ, England 🏠

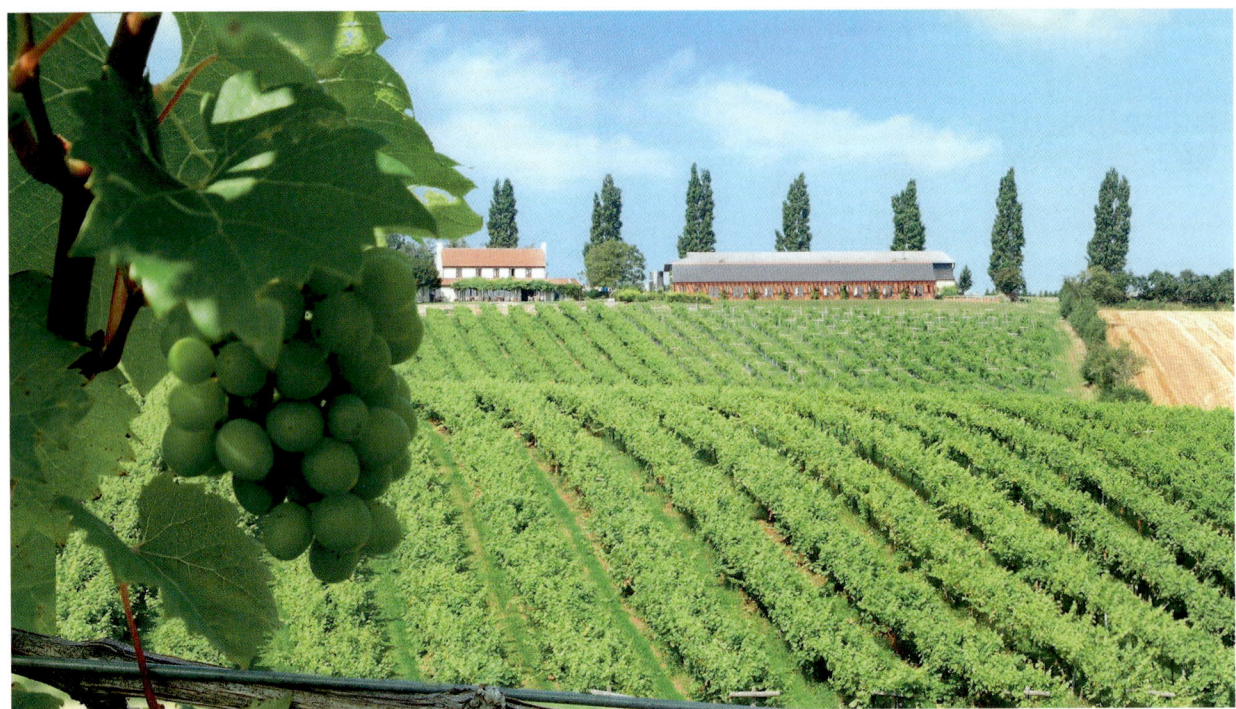

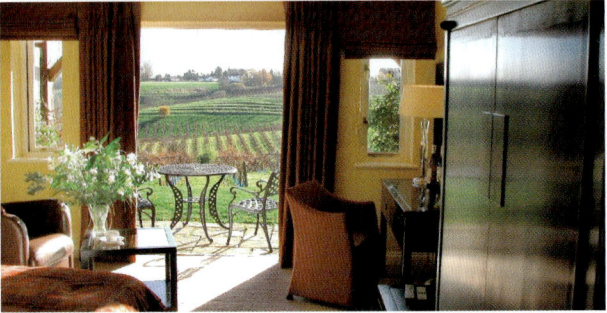
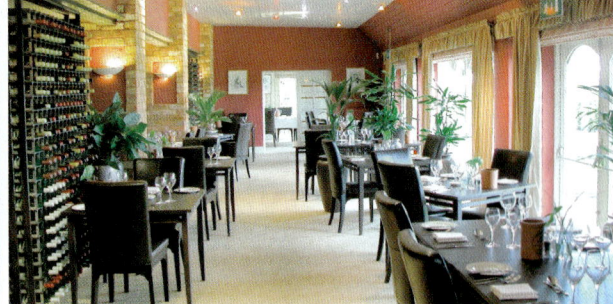

Three Choirs Vineyards Estate

Gloucestershire vineyard estate with quality rooms

PRICE FROM:
£125

FEATURES:
Family friendly; Restaurant; Wheelchair access

ACTIVITIES:
Fishing; Golf; Walking

NEARBY:
Newent; Gloucester; Malvern Hills; Cheltenham; The Dean Heritage Museum

GETTING THERE:
B4215; M5, jct 3; Bristol Airport

☎ +44 (0)1531 890223
🌐 condenastjohansens.com/threechoirs
🏠 Newent, Gloucestershire GL18 1LS, England

On the edge of the Forest of Dean, between Gloucestershire's market town of Newent and the village of Dymock, resides a surprise in waiting: the Three Choirs Vineyards Estate. One of England's best known vineyards, this hidden escape stands amidst acres of unspoilt countryside and copses. Presiding above the militarily precise vines below is the Three Choirs Vineyard Restaurant, eight bedrooms and the Vine Room. Three additional and extremely private rooms are situated between the vines away from the main house in elegant lodges (king-size beds, stunning bathrooms and large verandas overlooking the crops). A fresh breakfast hamper can be delivered to your lodge if requested and if you'd like your own private barbecue, no problem, just ask and all the ingredients shall be provided. Hearty cooked breakfasts are served in the highly rated restaurant where Head Chef Siobhan Hartley also dishes up mouth-watering modern English meals at lunch and dinner from nothing but fresh ingredients. Of course, its wine list showcases the estate's produce. Strolling around the vineyard is permitted and while visiting why not learn about the wine-making process and relax in the Vine Room with a glass or two and simply immerse yourself in the peaceful surroundings.

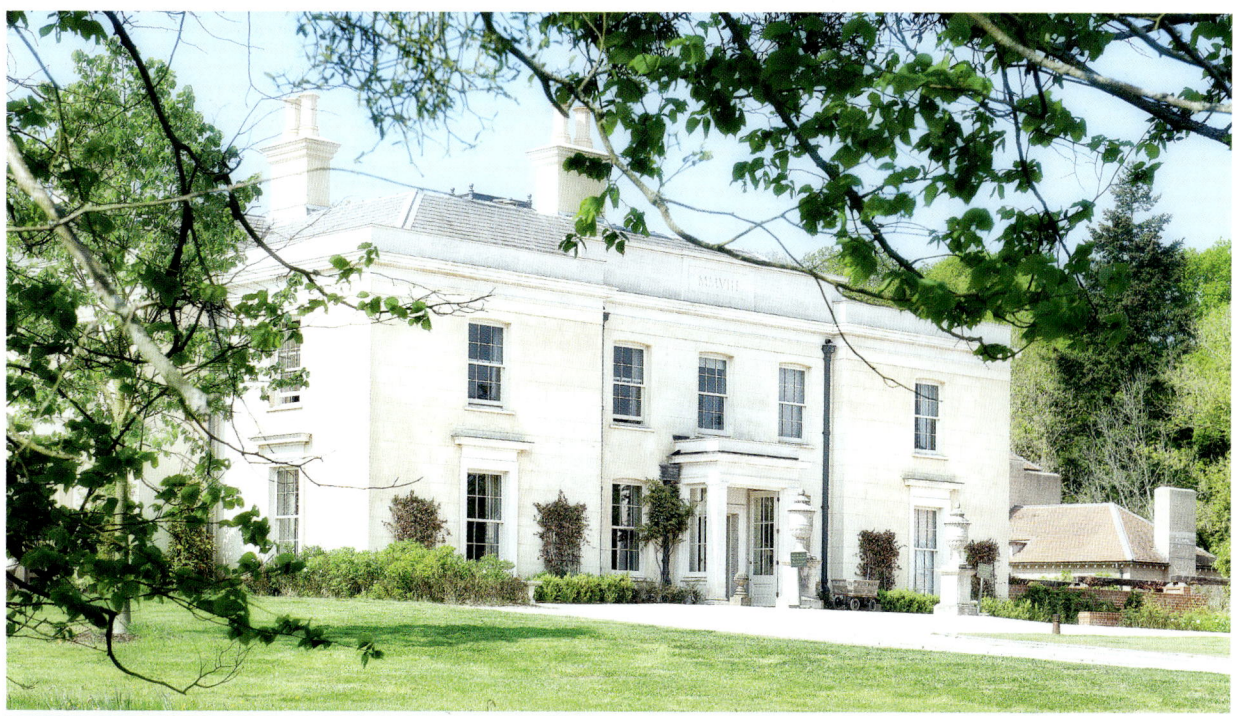

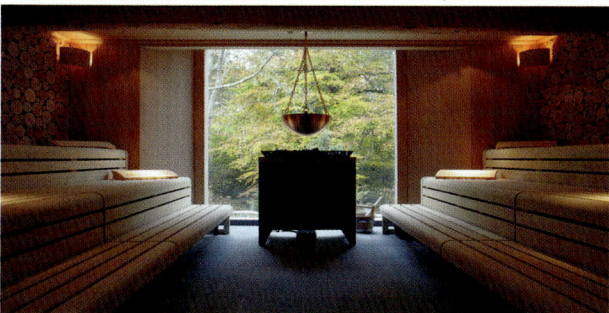

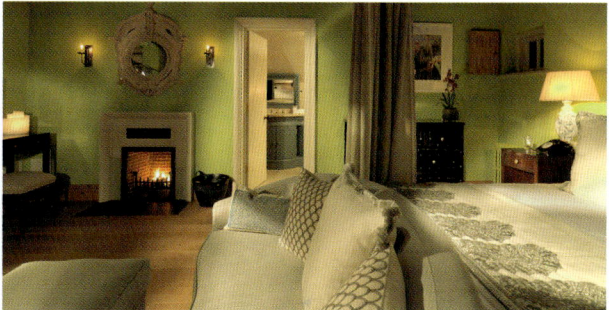

Lime Wood

The New Forest's fresh, new spin on the traditional English country house hotel

The secret behind Lime Wood's brilliance is simple: source and acquire the best. Thanks to the creative juices of sought-after architects and interior designers such as Martin Brudnizki, Lime Wood in the New Forest has become a byword for deft design. And in the kitchen, Luke Holder and Angela Hartnett (yes, the once protégée of Gordon Ramsay) are creating exciting foodie waves with their home-cooked style that's all about fine English fodder with an Italian attitude of sharing and provenance. Likewise, the three-storey Herb House Spa leads the way in sophisticated spa-ing alongside cutting-edge technology and healthy cuisine at the Raw & Cured food bar. All this is an easy drive from London, so city slickers and their families often retreat here for some fresh country air. Beyond the bedrooms and suites available in the main Regency-style country house (17th-century charm and character still intact alongside high-end amenities, hand-picked artwork, some log fires and wood-burning stoves), the Coach House, Crescent and self-contained Forest Lodges, Cottages and Cabin are alternative locations for family-friendly breaks, romantic getaways and good old fashioned relaxation. If you find yourself invited to the Kitchen Table, go! It's a chance to chat with the chefs and taste the highlights of Hartnett Holder & Co's seasonal menu.

PRICE FROM:
£255

FEATURES:
Family friendly; Pet friendly; Pool; Restaurant; Spa

ACTIVITIES:
Fishing; Golf; Walking

NEARBY:
Lyndhurst; London; New Forest National Park; Highcliffe beach; Lymington

GETTING THERE:
A31; M27; Southampton/Bournemouth Airports

+44 (0)23 8028 7177 ☎
condenastjohansens.com/limewood 🌐
Beaulieu Road, Lyndhurst, Hampshire SO43 7FZ, England 🏠

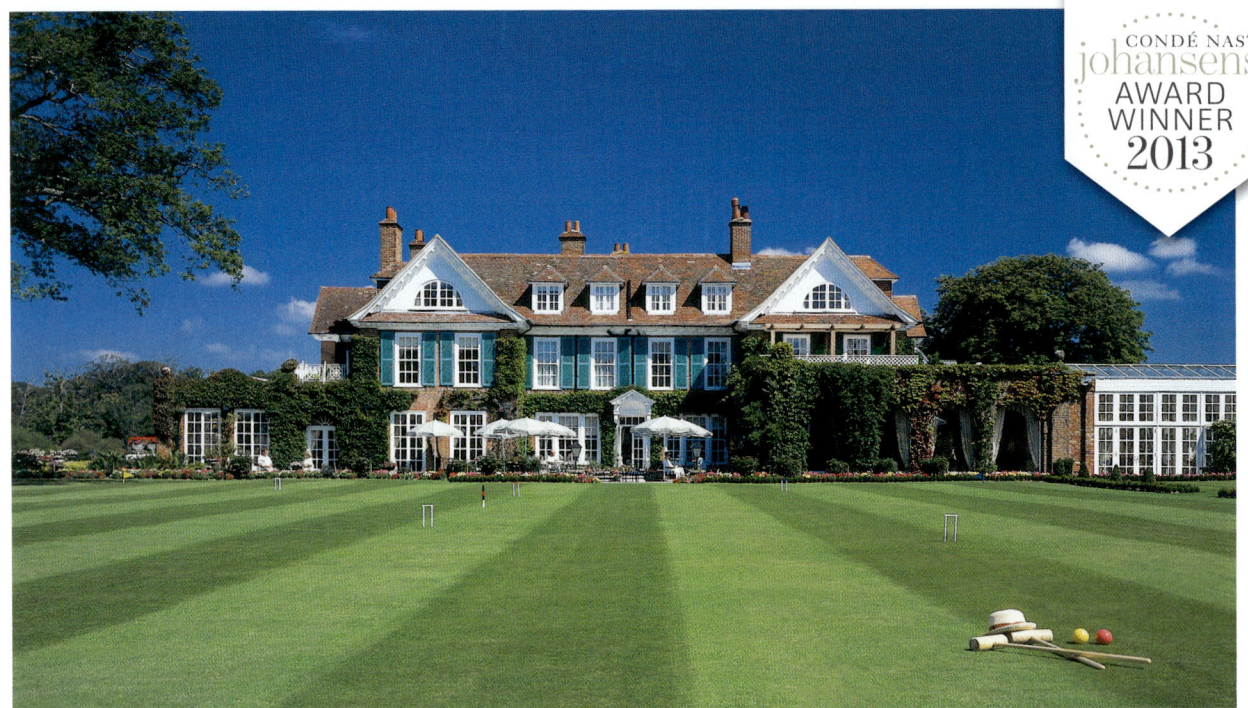

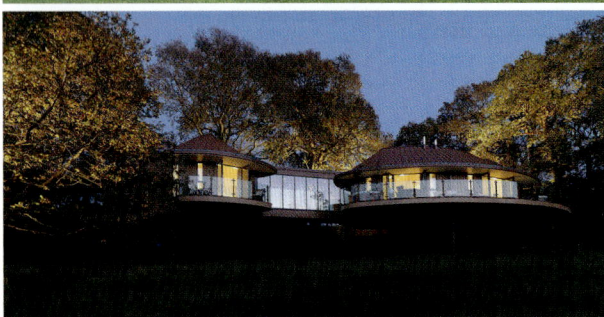

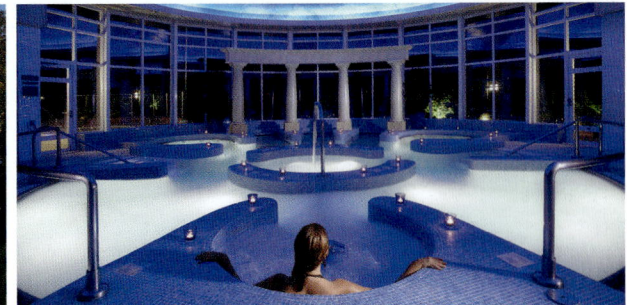

Chewton Glen

Ultimate luxury and on-trend style on the edge of the New Forest

PRICE FROM:
£280

FEATURES:
Family friendly; Helipad; Pool; Restaurant; Spa

ACTIVITIES:
Fishing; Golf; Shooting

NEARBY:
New Forest National Park; Isle of Wight; Bournemouth; Lymington

GETTING THERE:
M27 jct 1; Southampton Central Railway Station; Southampton Airport

☎ +44 (0)1425 275341
🌐 condenastjohansens.com/chewtonglen
🏠 New Forest, Hampshire BH25 6QS, England

When a hotel's received as many accolades as Chewton Glen in Hampshire, expectations run high on arrival. But despite this, you'll still be blown away, even if you're a returning guest because Chewton Glen is always improving (even when it doesn't seem possible) and evolving. There's certainly no restriction with space thanks to the acres of gardens and parkland at the edge of the New Forest; the sea's only a gentle 10-minute stroll away too. (Bring your camera for those awesome seascapes across to the Isle of Wight.) Inside, each bedroom and suite is nothing short of utter luxury with marble bathrooms and views over the grounds. Recently opened eco-conscious Treehouses offer alternative accommodation tucked away in Chewton Glen's wooded valley. These spacious suites are set on stilts, and are hugely private complete with kitchenettes; both romantic for couples and fun for the family. However, you're missing out if you bypass Vetiver restaurant where Executive Chef Luke Matthews whips up clever dishes from fresh local produce alongside an impressive wine list. That's if you can haul yourself away from the heavenly spa with steam room, sauna and hydrotherapy pool. Outside there's another pool, sun terrace, croquet lawn, tennis and a 9-hole par 3 course.

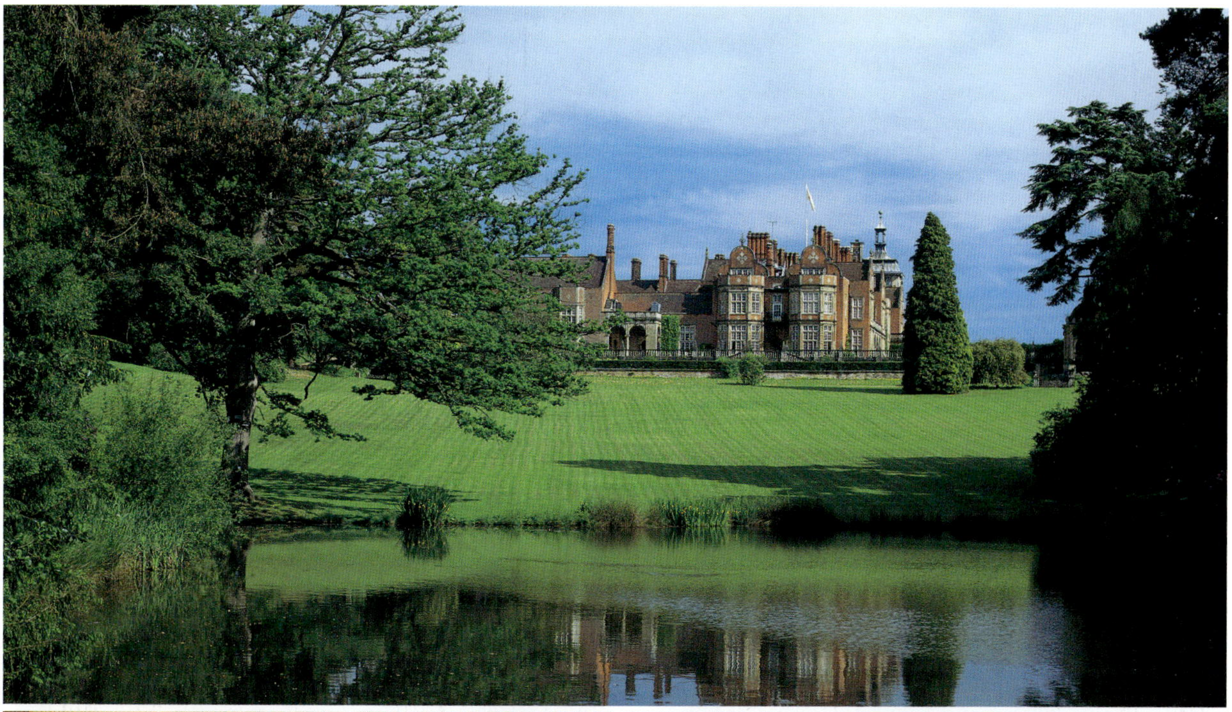

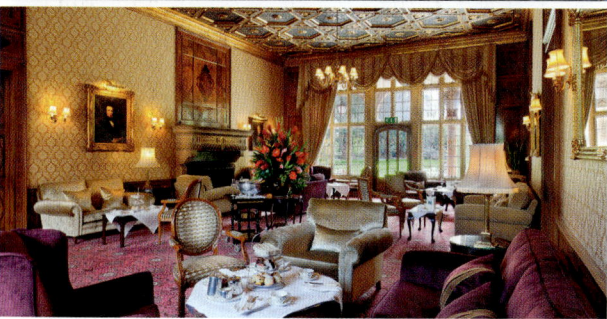
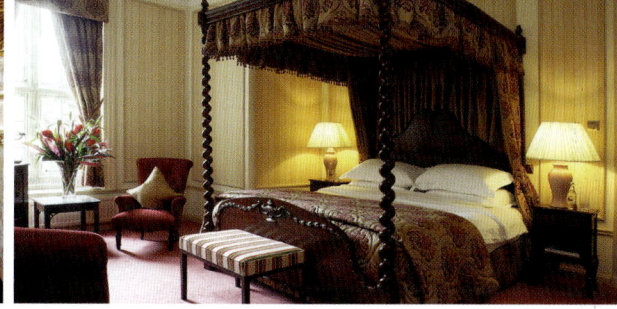

Tylney Hall

Endless fun to be had at this Hampshire country estate

Romantics love Tylney Hall's red brick beauty. Historians relish in the period details. Foodies flock to the Oak Room Restaurant while pleasure-seekers head to the Spa (five treatment rooms, a gym, saunas and a whirlpool). Golfers mosey on over to the adjacent 18-hole course. Even the children and teenagers are occupied (treasure hunts, board games, swimming, a dvd film library…). The family dog too, with walking routes within the estate. So, looking beyond its grand façade and acres of ornamental gardens and parkland, this impressive Grade II listed Mansion is more resort-hotel than stately home. Yes, traditional comfort of squishy sofas, panelled walls and shelves stacked with books maintain Tylney's classic style, yet a modern gloss keeps this Hampshire escape slick and fresh. Luxuriously appointed, some bedrooms and suites have four-poster beds and spa baths, but all are filled with masses of natural light and old school elegance. For lunch and dinner, the much-talked-about Oak Room Restaurant is Head Chef Stephen Hine's gift to the world. Placing a modern twist on classic dishes, it's become a leader in Hampshire's dining scene and during the summer a terrace opens up for alfresco dining looking out to where the wooded trails, lake, orchard and Victorian greenhouses are hidden. Note to party planners: Tylney has 12 private banqueting rooms.

PRICE FROM:
£250

FEATURES:
Gym; Pet friendly; Pool; Restaurant; Spa

ACTIVITIES:
Fishing; Golf; Tennis

NEARBY:
Antiquing at Hartley Wintney and West Green House and Gardens; Jane Austen's house; Winchester Cathedral; Watercress Line Steam Railway; Basingstoke

GETTING THERE:
M3 jct 5; Farnborough Airport; London Heathrow Airport

+44 (0)1256 764881 ☎
condenastjohansens.com/tylneyhall 🌐
Rotherwick, Hook, Hampshire RG27 9AZ, England 🏠

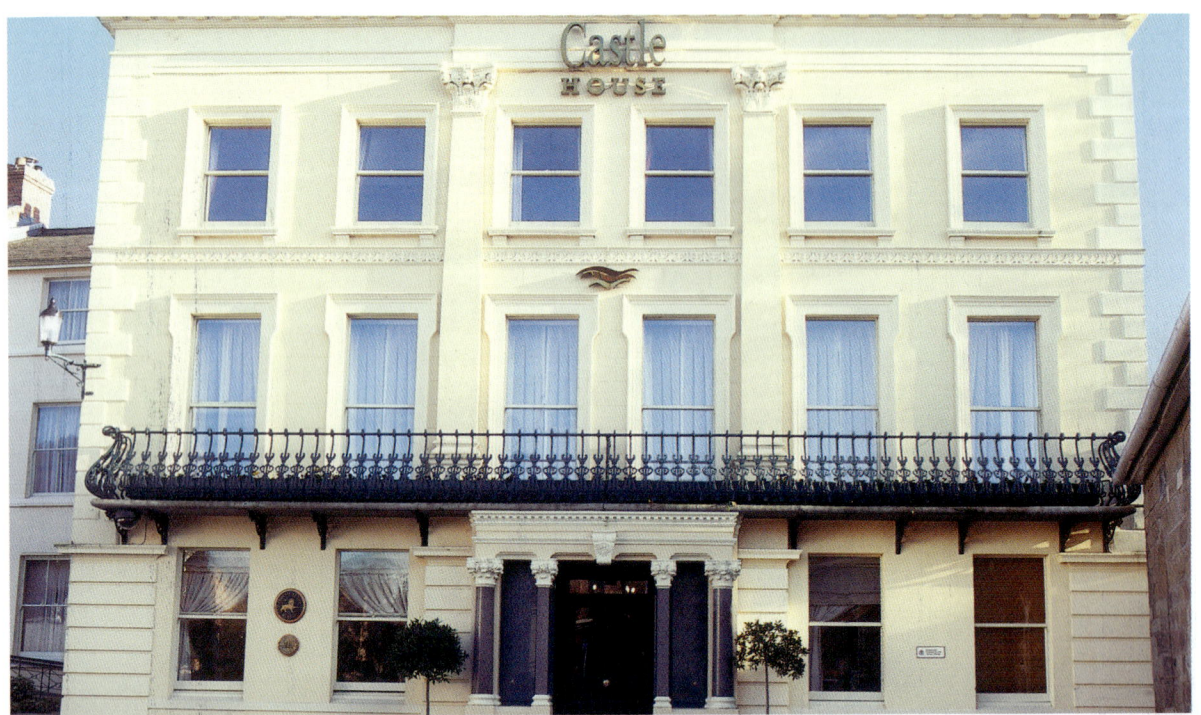

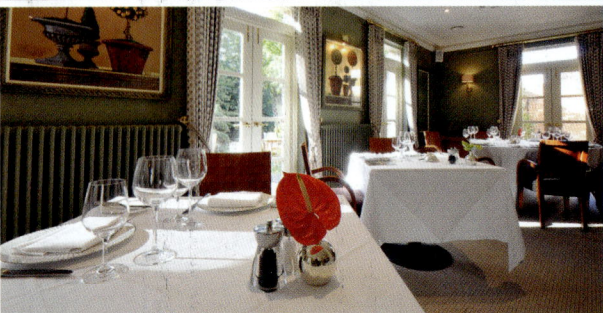

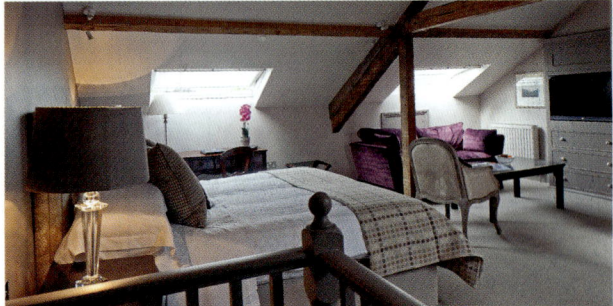

Castle House

Make-yourself-at-home Hereford town house hotel

PRICE FROM:
£150

FEATURES:
Family friendly; Restaurant; Wheelchair access

ACTIVITIES:
Golf; Sightseeing; Walking

NEARBY:
Mappa Mundi; Chained Library at Hereford Cathedral; Ludlow; Hay on Wye; Cheltenham

GETTING THERE:
M4 jct 15; Hereford Railway Station; Birmingham Airport

☎ +44 (0)1432 356321
🌐 condenastjohansens.com/castlehse
🏠 Castle Street, Hereford, Herefordshire HR1 2NW, England

In the middle of Hereford, just a hop, skip and a jump from Hereford Cathedral, Castle House is a smart town house hotel with a 2 AA Rosette-awarded restaurant to match. A testament to luxury boutique style, the Castle's immaculate Georgian façade gives way to a warm welcome and bright lobby area. From here, a dominating grand staircase leads you to individually designed luxury suites and bedrooms while eight more guest rooms, suites and a penthouse family room are located in Castle House's additional town house known as Number 25, a few yards from the main hotel. Here, the rooms uphold the refined ambience but feature a more contemporary feel. The restaurant, overseen by Head Chef Claire Nicholls, is predominantly an English affair, however, an international twist brings an interesting element to the dishes (Claire loves Asian flavours). Locally sourced produce and home grown vegetables have a huge role to play on the menu. In fact, some of the beef and lamb that appear on it have been reared on the owner's nearby farm (tours of the farm can be easily arranged). Lighter bites, pastries and cocktails are the Castle Bar & Bistro's speciality. The hotel's pretty terraced garden runs beside the old Hereford Castle's moat and is the perfect spot for a relaxed traditional afternoon tea - brewed from tea leaves of course.

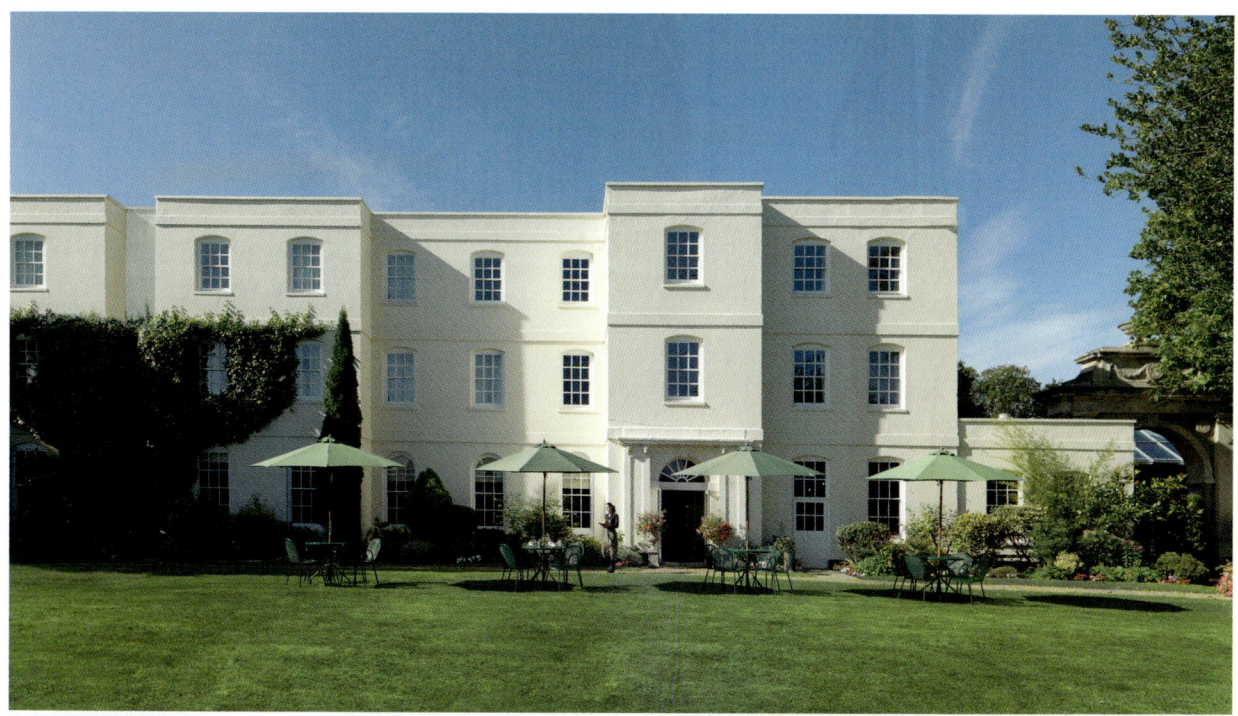

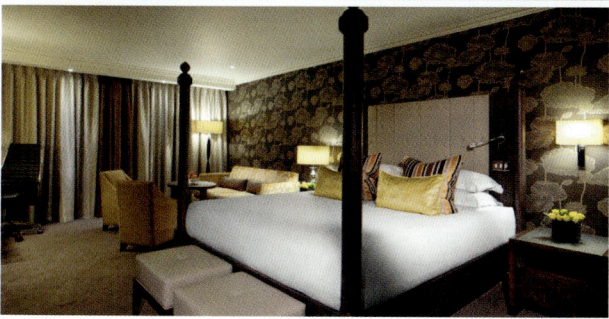

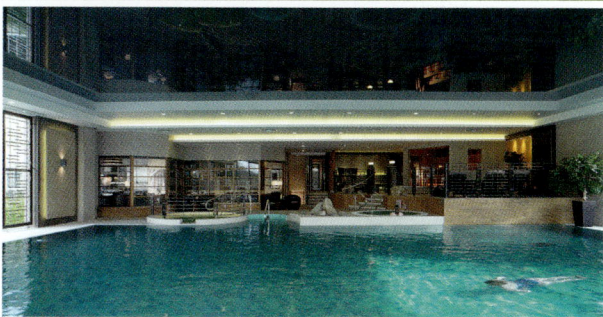

Sopwell House

Dashing Georgian splendour meets modern-luxe in historic St Albans

Illustrious characters Francis Bacon, Anne Boleyn, King Henry VIII, Edward Strong and Lord Mountbatten all play a part in Sopwell House's history. Today, notable guests include national/international football teams hosted by the Bejerano family who bought this 129-room hotel in 1986. Just five minutes from St Albans, Sopwell House stands in acres of private Hertfordshire countryside and has become a sought-after venue for weddings, special events and business meetings. It's also gained a reputation as a leisure break destination thanks to its formidable day spa, extensive Country Club (Technogym equipment, weights gym, state-of-the-art studio with classes including Zumba and Pilates) and par 72 golf course on its doorstep. The fine dining restaurant offers a contemporary British and European menu showcasing Paris-trained Executive Chef James Chapman's talents. While the all-day, more casual Brasserie serves simple, flavour-packed classics and worldwide-inspired dishes. Relaxing in the Cocktail Lounge is popular (try the signature Lord Mountbatten cocktail) and the garden-viewing Conservatory filled with light is ideal for an drink. Maintaining the traditional ambience of its Georgian heritage, each bedroom, suite and apartment is a fusion of classic British style and modern comfort. If privacy is the top priority, stay in a spacious Mews Apartment set apart from the main hotel.

PRICE FROM:
£124

FEATURES:
Gym; Pool; Restaurant; Spa; Wheelchair access

ACTIVITIES:
Golf; Walking

NEARBY:
St Albans Cathedral; Butterfly World Project; Willows Farm Village and Park; Warner Bros Studio Tour London – The Making of Harry Potter

GETTING THERE:
M1 jct 8; St Albans Railway Station; London Luton Airport

+44 (0)1727 864477 ☎
condenastjohansens.com/sopwellhouse 🌐
Cottonmill Lane, Sopwell, St Albans, Hertfordshire AL1 2HQ, 🏠
England

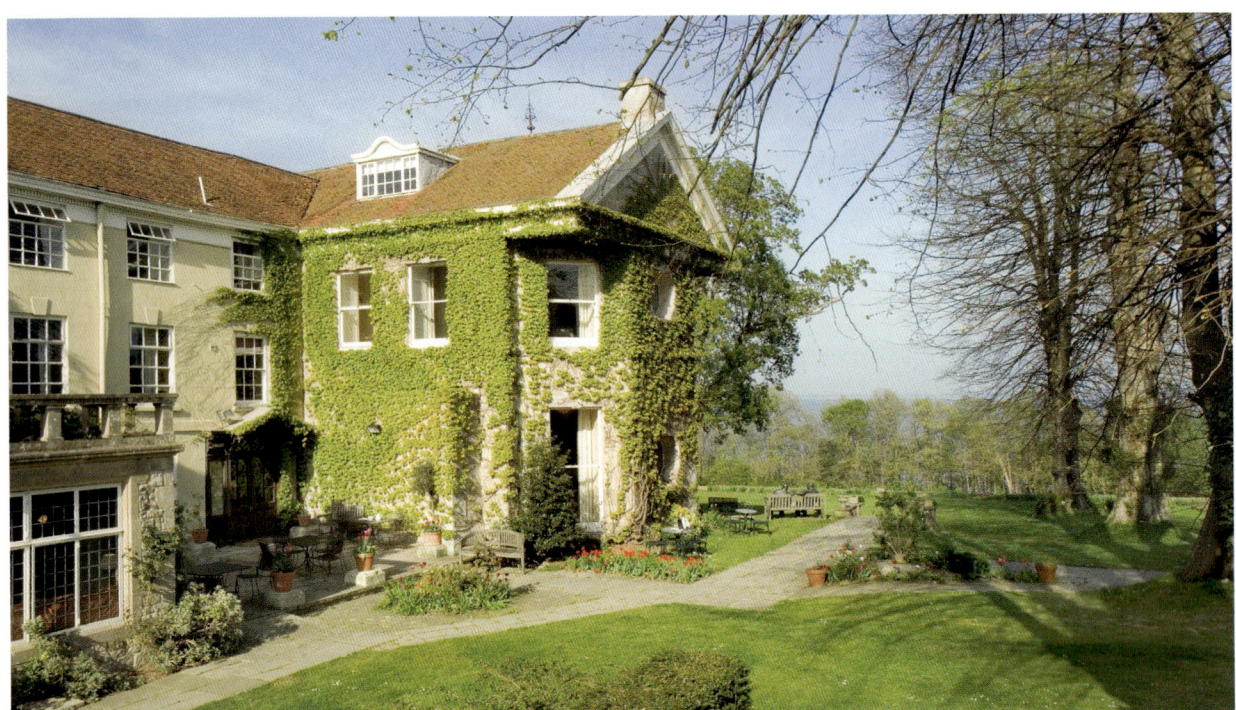

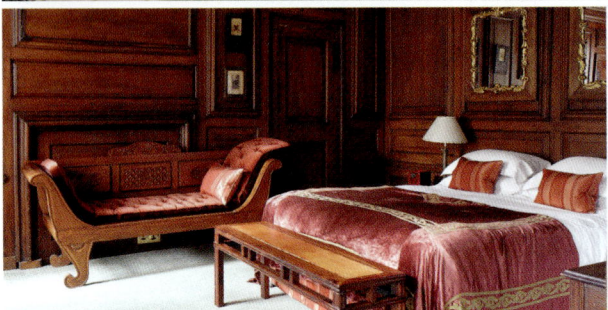

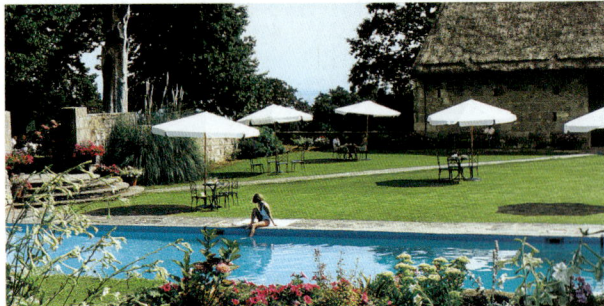

The Priory Bay Hotel

Timeless Isle of Wight retreat

PRICE FROM:
£160

FEATURES:
Beach access; Family friendly; Pool; Restaurant; Sea views

ACTIVITIES:
Golf; Tennis; Walking

NEARBY:
Ryde; Ventnor Botanic Garden; Osborne House; Carisbrooke Castle; Sailing at Seaview and Bembridge

GETTING THERE:
A3055; Cowes (Southampton) Ferry Terminal; Fishbourne (Portsmouth) Ferry Terminal, Hovertravel

☎ +44 (0)1983 613146
🌐 condenastjohansens.com/priorybayiow
🏠 Priory Drive, Seaview, Isle of Wight PO34 5BU, England

Overlooking the sea from atop a small valley, Priory Bay Hotel, Isle of Wight, is a charming Virginia creeper-clad hideaway. Secluded between the eastern coastal towns of Bembridge and Seaview, this is an idyllic year-round escape for a country break in 60 acres of private gardens and woodland (teeming with wildlife and birds of prey) that lead to the hotel's golden, sandy beach. Inside, through the medieval arched stone entrance, public rooms are framed by tall windows and warmed by roaring log fires. Comfortable, classically-styled bedrooms look out to the grounds or sea, and two family rooms allow mum and dad to sleep peacefully with the children in the next room. For something a little different, Priory Bay has luxury yurts within its grounds, available April to October, surrounded by the woodland and flower-filled gardens close to coastal paths (perfect for long autumn walks) and the private beach. With not one but two restaurants showcasing seasonal cuisine that specialises in local and foraged produce, choose from the tasting menu in The Island Room or brasserie-style dining in The Priory Oyster and sample organic and bio-dynamic wines from the innovative wine list. Highlights: coastal walks, private beach, outdoor pool, adjoining six-hole golf course, tennis courts, tree climbing, falconry courses, seasonal boating and yachting plus a wedding pavilion on the beach.

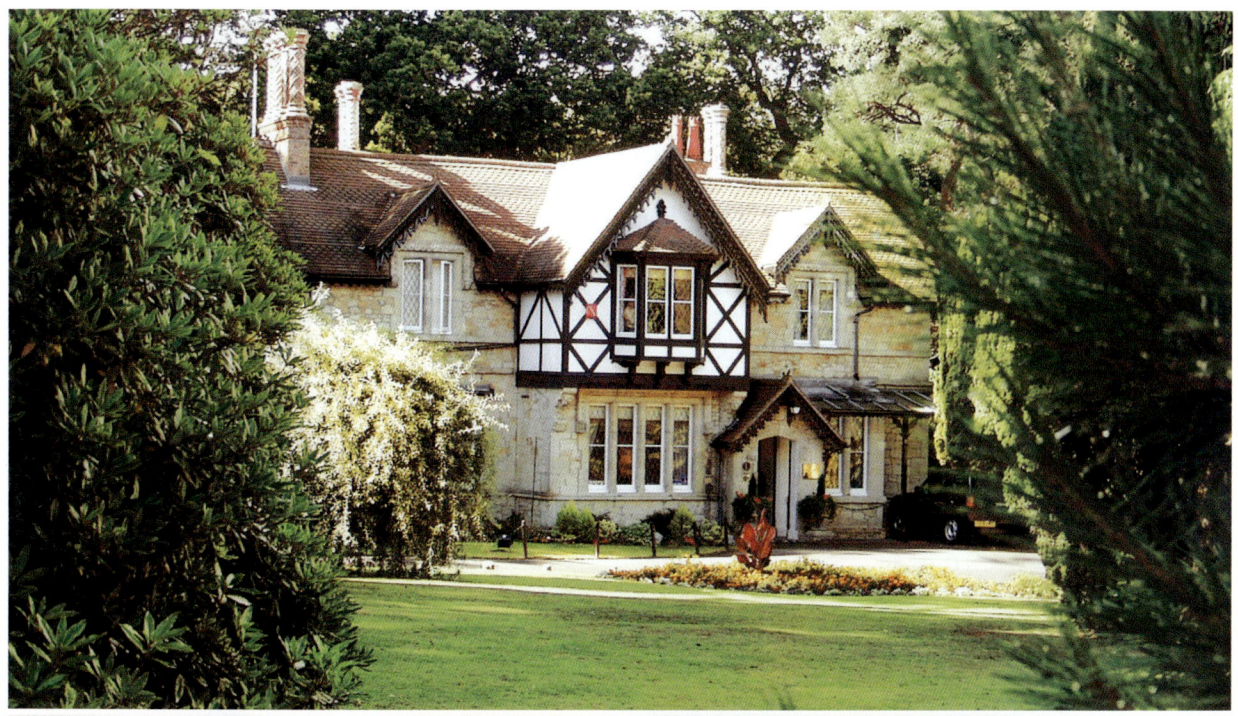

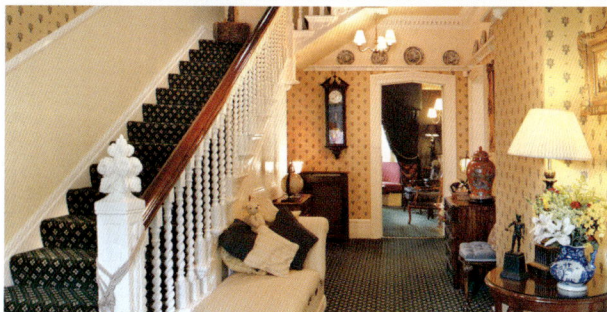
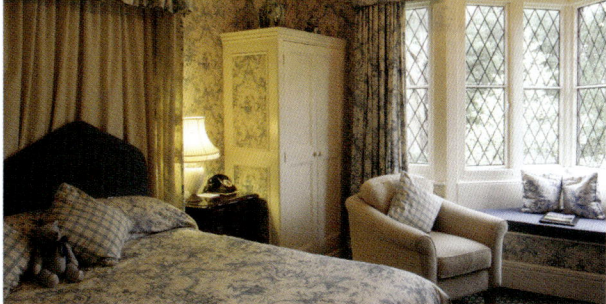

Rylstone Manor Hotel

A cliff-top charmer overlooking Shanklin Bay

Mike and Carole Hailston are the proud owners of Rylstone Manor Hotel, Isle of Wight, on the edge of the popular seaside town of Shanklin. (The town where Charles Darwin wrote his Origin of Species during an 18 month-long visit.) A handsome manor house hotel hidden away in acres of its own tranquil mature gardens, this former gentleman's residence is a traditional Isle of Wight treasure perfect for a break away from the stresses of everyday life. You can catch a glimpse of the sea from some of the charming bedrooms, and the stylish day rooms are just the ticket for a good book and afternoon tea. Of course, in good weather you'll hanker for some of that fresh sea air and from the Rylstone's cliff-top gardens you can take in stunning views of Shanklin Bay. A two-minute walk and you're at the promenade and beach. After a day's exploring, Mike's daily-changing menus provide delicious sustenance determined by the best produce available alongside a well considered wine list, which includes some interesting local vintages. Passionate about his craft, Mike likes to talk to his diners after service in the drawing room - just one example of the personalised treatment Mike and Carole provide.

PRICE FROM:
£140

FEATURES:
Restaurant; Sea views

ACTIVITIES:
Fishing; Golf; Walking

NEARBY:
Osborne House; Ventnor Botanic Gardens; Old village of Godshill; Carisbrooke Castle

GETTING THERE:
A3055; Cowes (Southampton) Ferry Terminal; Fishbourne (Portsmouth) Ferry Terminal

+44 (0)1983 862806 ☎
condenastjohansens.com/rylstonemanor 🌐
Rylstone Gardens, Shanklin, Isle of Wight PO37 6RG, England 🏠

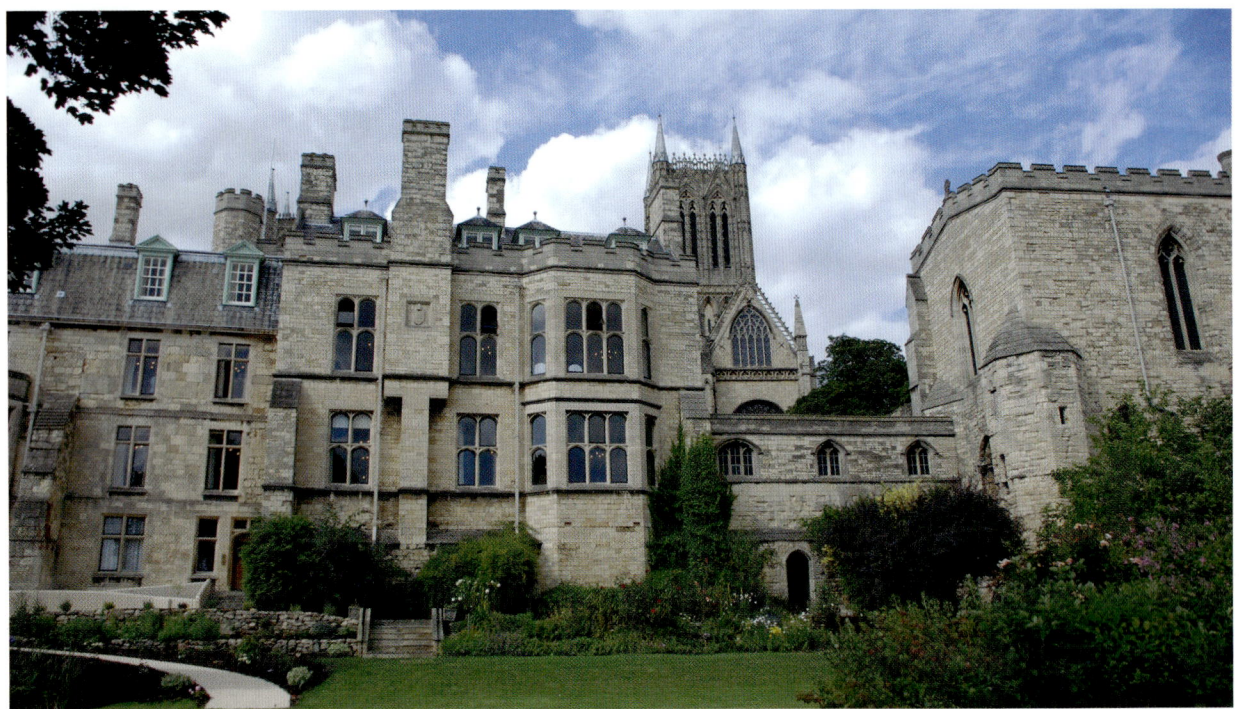

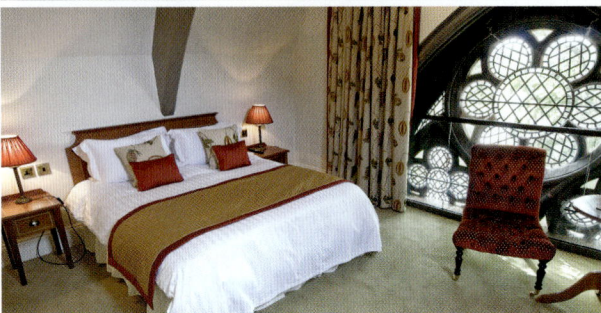
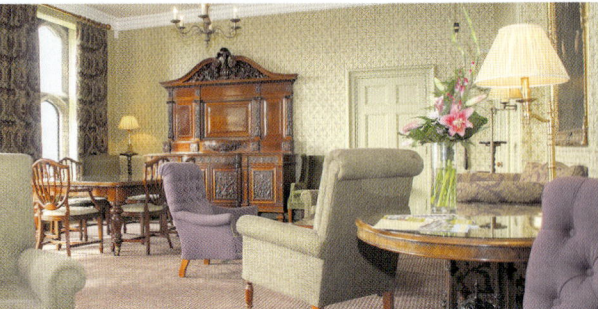

The Old Palace

Serenity found in Lincoln's historic quarter

PRICE FROM:
£75

FEATURES:
Family friendly; Pet friendly; Restaurant; Wheelchair access

ACTIVITIES:
Fishing; Golf; Horse riding

NEARBY:
Lincoln Cathedral; Lincoln Castle; Medieval Bishop's Palace; Doddington Hall; Lincolnshire Showground

GETTING THERE:
A46; Lincoln Railway Station; Humberside Airport

☎ +44 (0)1522 580000
🌐 condenastjohansens.com/oldpalace
🏠 Minster Yard, Lincoln, Lincolnshire LN2 1PU, England

Set apart from the bustling streets of Lincoln at the heart of its historic centre, The Old Palace discreetly nestles in seclusion beside the towering Lincoln Cathedral. Delivering 21st-century comfort with a bygone elegance, a sense of tranquillity and contemplation when the Bishops of Lincoln lived here is still present. In total, The Old Palace has 32 guest rooms and suites spread across the Palace itself and an adjacent converted church. Breathing new life into the buildings (dating back to the Victorian and Georgian periods), many rooms take in the views of the Cathedral and Lincoln. Some have connecting doors perfect for families but it's the Tower and Lodge Suites that are particularly plush. Dressed in neutral colour schemes with rich red and purple accents, their original stone windows, generous bathrooms and unrivalled views of Lincoln Cathedral are regally resplendent. Evening drinks in The Drawing Room (the former library) are a great way to begin an evening before dining in the new informal restaurant where Head Chef Paul Newton cooks up classic British dishes with a modern continental twist. Always fresh, seasonal and locally sourced, Paul's use of farm-fresh Lincolnshire ingredients brings extra flavour to his creations. Private dinners for groups can be arranged, wedding receptions and parties also.

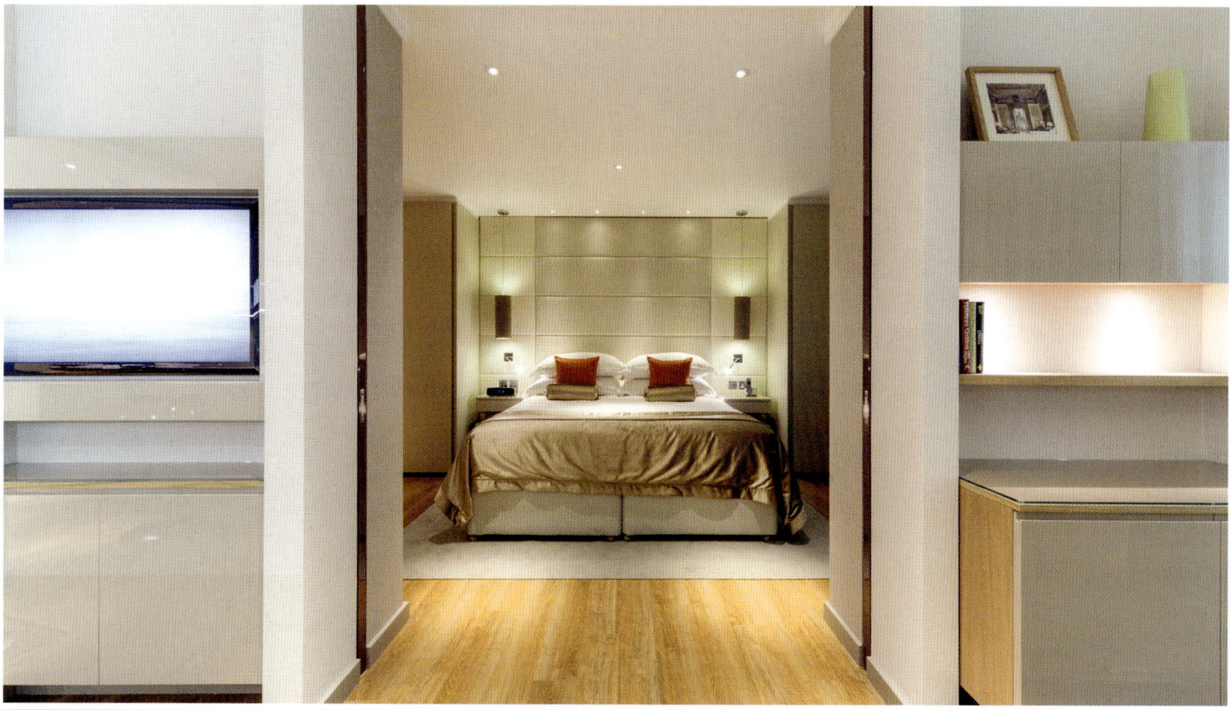

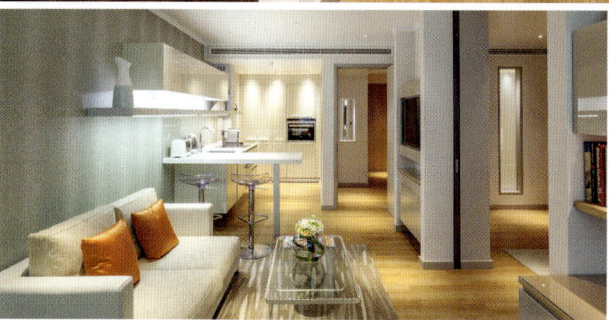
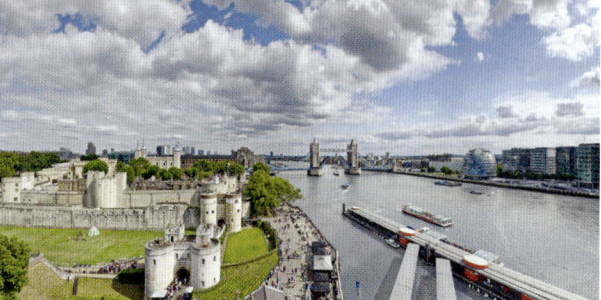

Cheval Three Quays at the Tower of London

Luxury lifestyle apartments on London's River Thames

The leaders in luxury serviced apartments, Cheval Residences is arriving in London's Square Mile in March 2014. Beside the Tower of London overlooking the River Thames with unrivalled views of Tower Bridge and City Hall, Cheval Three Quays is a great base for exploring The City of London's ancient history and landmarks. It's also ideal for discovering the copious attractions and exhibitions of the South Bank. Cheval Three Quays will include studios, one, two and three-bedroom apartments and penthouses for both short and extended stays whether visiting for business or a city getaway. Each one a celebration of cutting-edge interior design with clever lighting, shiny surfaces, clean lines and geometric shapes. Original artworks by Barnaby Gorton and an elegant water feature by the renowned William Pye add an artistic grace. At the heart of Cheval Three Quays lies exceptional management and service, which will be delivered through a dedicated team of Concierge, Housekeeping and Maintenance. Facilities include a state-of-art fitness room while those who prefer to sit back and relax can enjoy the café and restaurant facilities on the ground floor. Getting around couldn't be easier with Tower Hill Underground Station just minutes away and the Thames Clipper at Cheval Three Quays provides transport along the river from Greenwich and the O2 Arena to Putney and Chelsea Harbour.

PRICE FROM:
£240

FEATURES:
Family friendly; Gym; Pet friendly; Restaurant; Wheelchair access

ACTIVITIES:
Shopping; Sightseeing; Walking

NEARBY:
Tower of London; Tower Bridge; South Bank; Canary Wharf; Westminster Abbey

GETTING THERE:
Tower Hill Underground Station; London Liverpool Street Railway Station; London City Airport

+44 (0)20 3597 3000 ☎
condenastjohansens.com/chevalthreequays 🌐
40 Lower Thames Street, EC3R 6AG London, England 🏠

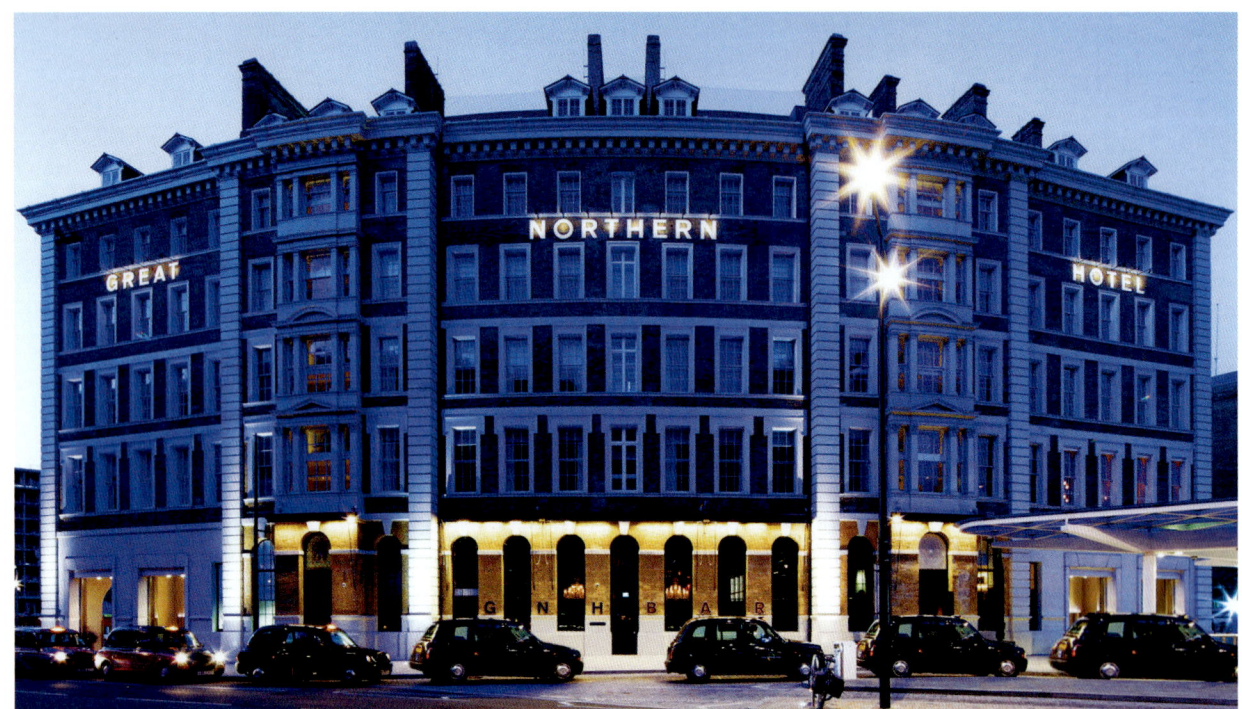

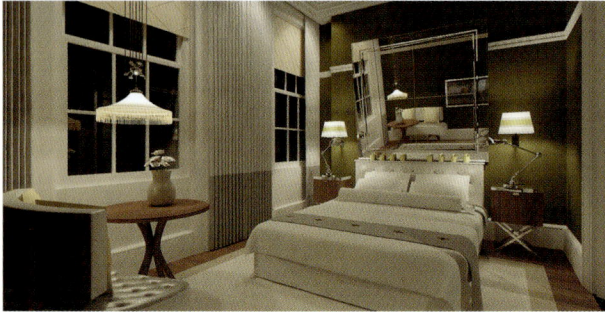

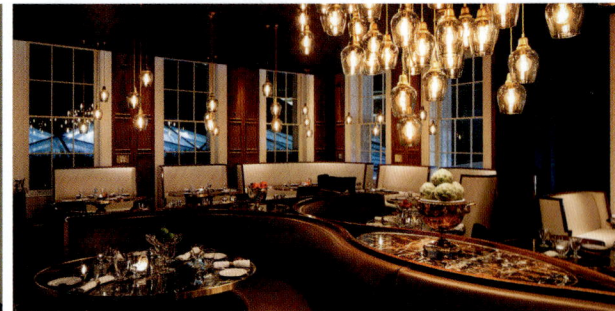

Great Northern Hotel

King's Cross St Pancras' first luxury boutique hotel

PRICE FROM:

£250

FEATURES:

Family friendly; Restaurant; Wheelchair access

ACTIVITIES:

Shopping; Sightseeing; Walking

NEARBY:

Gagosian Gallery; King's Place; The British Library; King's Cross Square; Granary Square

GETTING THERE:

King's Cross St Pancras Railway Station - Eurostar; London Luton Airport; London City Airport

☎ +44 (0)20 3388 0800

🌐 condenastjohansens.com/gnhlondon

⌂ King's Cross St Pancras Station, Pancras Road, London N1C 4TB, England

Forming an intergral part of the exciting London King's Cross St Pancras regeneration, Great Northern Hotel is located 25 metres from Eurostar's terminal with the King's Cross western concourse dome fitting into its curved shape. Inside, tunnel-like corridors lead to 91 rooms with custom furnishings, high ceilings, tall windows, Farrow & Ball colours and extras such as Nespresso machines. There are three categories: Couchette, Wainscot and Cubitt. Couchette rooms are evocative of a train's sleeping berth with a luxury twist while at the top, Wainscot rooms are sexy dens covered in American walnut. For total serenity, reserve a Cubitt room, many of which have views of the station's western concourse dome. On each floor a complimentary Pantry stocked with home-made cakes, iconic candies, hot drinks and reading material are all at guests' disposal. At no extra charge, in-room entertainment includes 20 audio books, 96 tv channels including Sky, a film library of 70 movies and super-fast 500mg WiFi connection. (Crank up the volume, all rooms are excellently sound-proofed.) On the first floor is highly acclaimed Chef Mark Sargeant's Plum + Spilt Milk all-day restaurant. Formerly Head Chef at the Gordon Ramsay Restaurant at Claridge's, Mark brings excitement to classic British dishes, while directly on the station's concourse, GNH Bar whips up breakfast, lunch and irresistible cocktails.

247

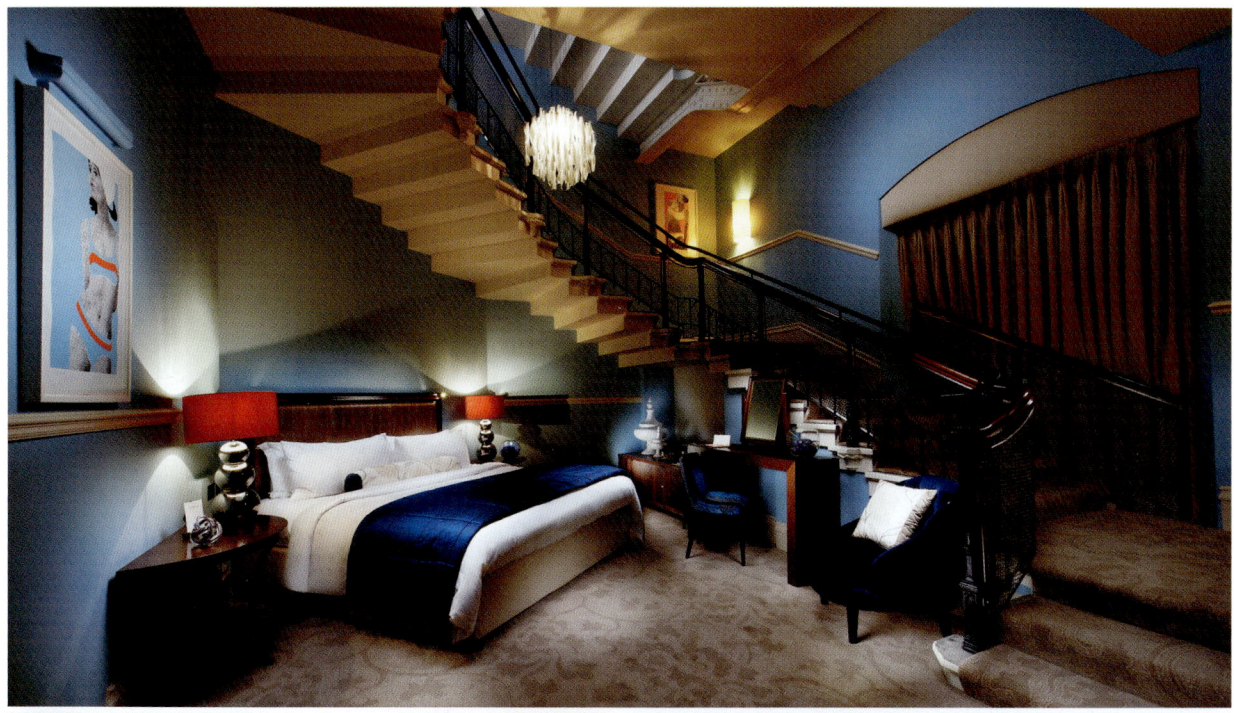

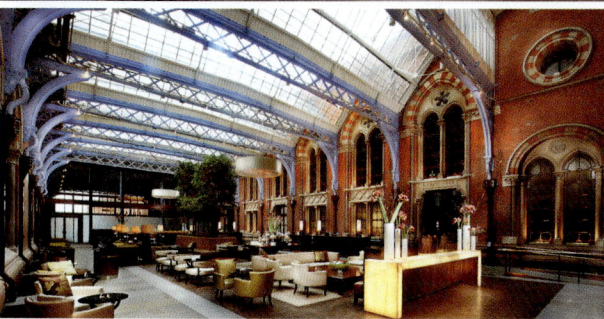
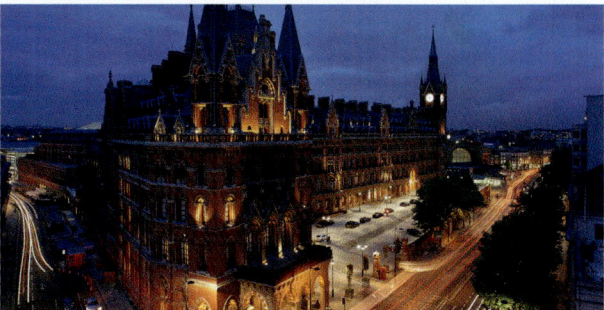

St Pancras Renaissance Hotel

Flamboyant Victorian grandiose meets contemporary London

Victorian brilliance meets 21st-century extravagance at St Pancras Renaissance Hotel, London; a bastion of Gothic Revival design from the illustrious architect George Gilbert Scott. Scott's interpretation of the brief: "add lustre to St Pancras Train Station," was the grand cathedral-like, red brick icon that stands today (140 years on) alongside the international Eurostar station. After 78 years closed as a hotel, St Pancras Renaissance has had the ultimate comeback. Now an established member of London's elite, its ornate opulent magnificence has returned with additional grandeur and comfort gracing every inch. Whilst respectful of the original structure and period details (see: the main lobby's Barlow Blue ironwork, recreated 1870s décor of the Sir Gilbert Scott Suite and Gothic Grand Staircase), there's also an on-trend element running through St Pancras Renaissance. For a taste of upscale Victoriana, reserve a Chamber Suite (exclusive hospitality and butler service included), otherwise there's elegant, contemporary-styled bedrooms in the newly built extension. Like the station it occupies, the hotel is abuzz with activity. From socialising in the Hansom Lobby, pampering at the spa, dining at The Gilbert Scott restaurant run by Marcus Wareing (an attraction in its own right) to drinking at the Booking Office and Platform overlooking the Eurostar platforms.

PRICE FROM:
£245

FEATURES:
Family friendly; Gym; Pool; Restaurant; Spa

ACTIVITIES:
Shopping; Sightseeing

NEARBY:
Regent's Park; The Foundling Museum; Platform 9 and ¾; British Library; Paris by Eurostar

GETTING THERE:
King's Cross St Pancras Railway Station - Eurostar; London Heathrow Airport; London Gatwick Airport

+44 (0)20 7841 3540 ☎
condenastjohansens.com/stpancras 🌐
Euston Road, NW1 2AR London, England 🏠

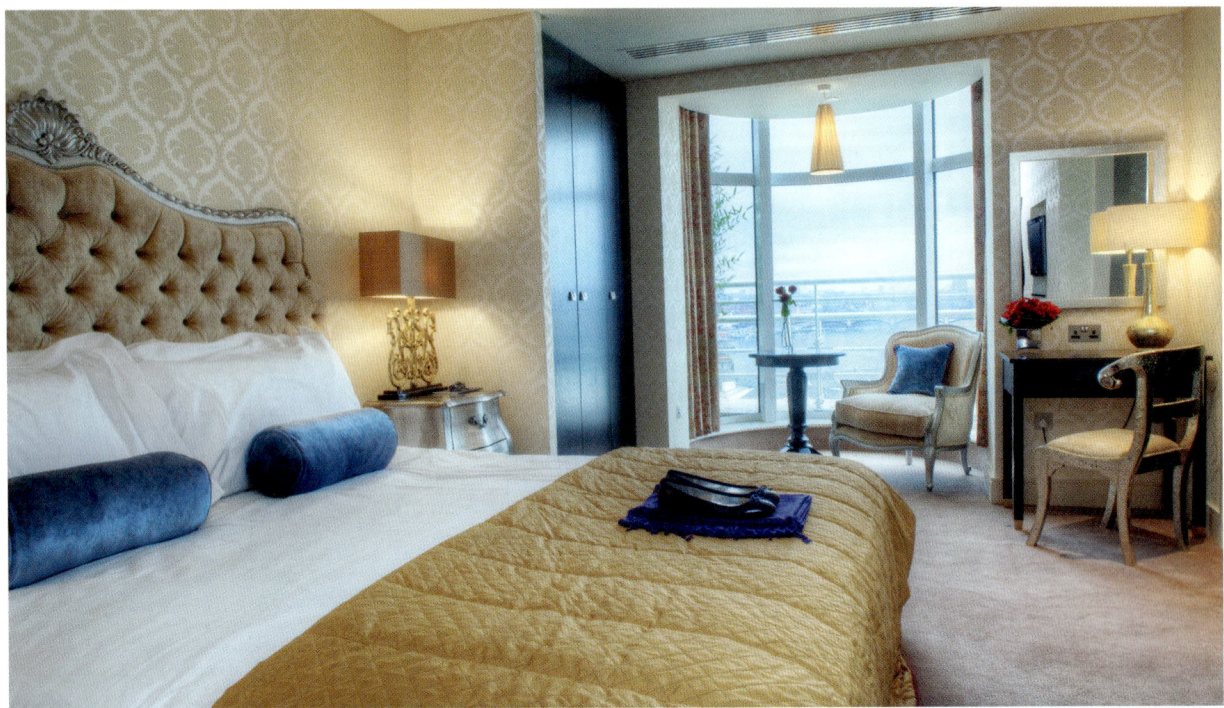

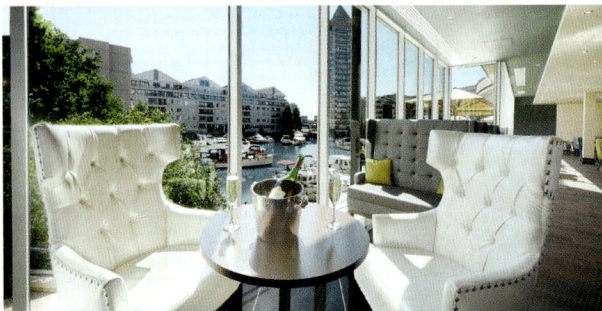
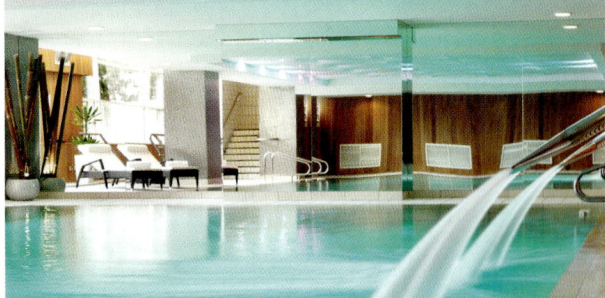

Wyndham Grand London Chelsea Harbour

West London's harbourside retreat

PRICE FROM:
£220

FEATURES:
Family friendly; Gym; Pool; Restaurant; Spa

ACTIVITIES:
Shopping; Sightseeing

NEARBY:
Chelsea Harbour Design Centre; Harrods; Harvey Nichols; King's Road; Westfield Shopping Centre

GETTING THERE:
Imperial Wharf Railway Station; King's Cross St Pancras Railway Station - Eurostar; London Heathrow Airport

Wyndham Grand London Chelsea Harbour is a rare breed of hotel. Glamorously located beside a yacht-filled marina on the north bank of the River Thames, it's only a short boat ride from the heart of the Docklands and a convenient chauffeur-driven jaunt to the centre of fashion-conscious Knightsbridge. The West London location means you're in prime position for exploring all of central London's sites and high-end shopping on King's Road and Sloane Street. Yet the peaceful setting has you convinced you're a world apart. An all-suite hotel, Wyndham's spacious (heightened by the oversized windows), immaculate rooms are flush with luxuries such as Egyptian cotton linen, espresso machines and balconies. For elevated luxury there's the four Penthouse Suites whose panoramic views take in the Thames and city skyline. Eating at Wyndham Grand is an informal affair at Chelsea Riverside Brasserie where the dishes of seasonal produce, locally sourced ingredients and prime-cut steaks are matched by fine wines. On warm days, the alfresco terrace is a popular spot while The Harbour Bar draws a lunchtime crowd for sushi, Thai dishes and British classics. The Blue Harbour Health Club and Spa provides the essential combination of luxury, comfort and relaxation for guests and local residents alike.

☎ +44 (0)20 7823 3000
🌐 condenastjohansens.com/wyndhamlondon
🏠 Chelsea Harbour, London SW10 0XG, England

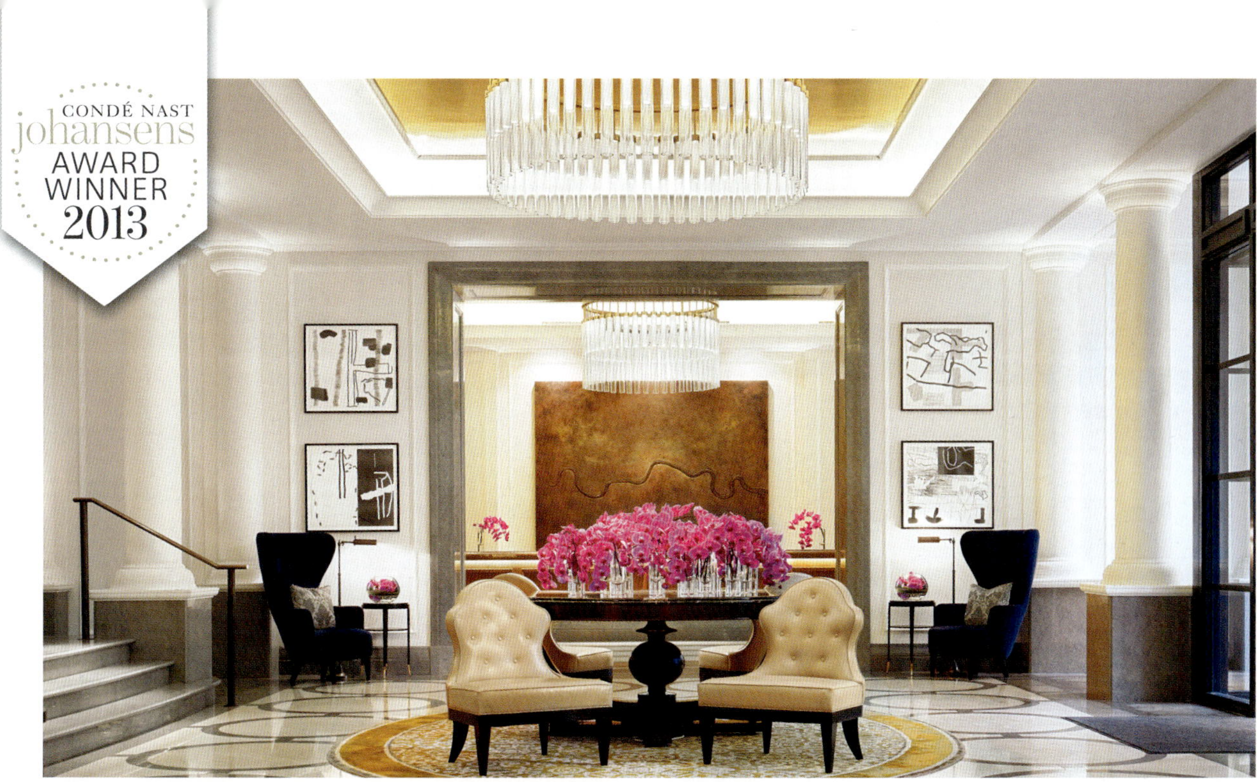

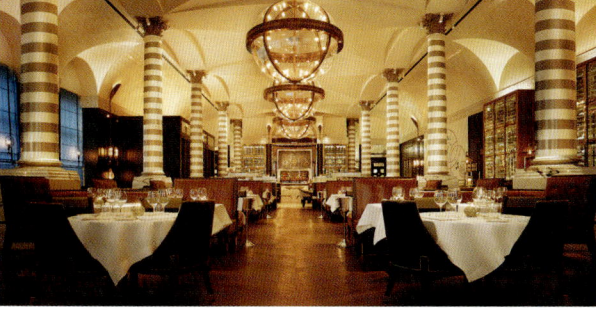

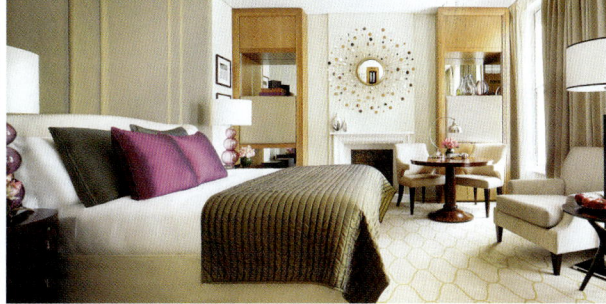

Corinthia Hotel London

Central London five-star stunner

Opulent Corinthia Hotel London is the jewel in the family-owned collection's crown. After a hotly anticipated opening in 2011, this dynamo of a hotel holds its place in the upper echelon of five-star fabulousness and old school glamour. Upon entering the marble lobby you'll be struck by the natural light streaming through a huge skylight that's refracted through an even bigger Baccarat chandelier. The world's best designers were called in to dress Corinthia London and it shows, from the elegant, generously sized bedrooms to the black and white marble and mosaic spa. Corinthia London is, quite simply, cool. The city's hottest destination, its bars and restaurants spoil guests and outsiders alike for choice. Spend an evening listening to some chilled live music in the low-lit Bassoon Bar or head over to Massimo Restaurant & Oyster Bar for some Italian cuisine and fresh oysters. Home cooking your joy? Try The Northall for the best of British. You'd be forgiven for not stepping out the front door but you'd be missing out on the fantastic setting right in the heart of London's Whitehall. Trafalgar Square and the Thames are on your doorstep. Mayfair is moments away. Corinthia London wins on location hands down.

PRICE FROM:
£360

FEATURES:
Family friendly; Pool; Restaurant; Spa

ACTIVITIES:
Shopping; Sightseeing

NEARBY:
Trafalgar Square; National Gallery; London Eye; West End theatres

GETTING THERE:
Charing Cross Station; King's Cross St Pancras Railway Station - Eurostar; London Heathrow Airport

+44 (0)20 7321 3000 ☎
condenastjohansens.com/corinthialondon ⊕
Whitehall Place, London, SW1A 2BD, England 🏠

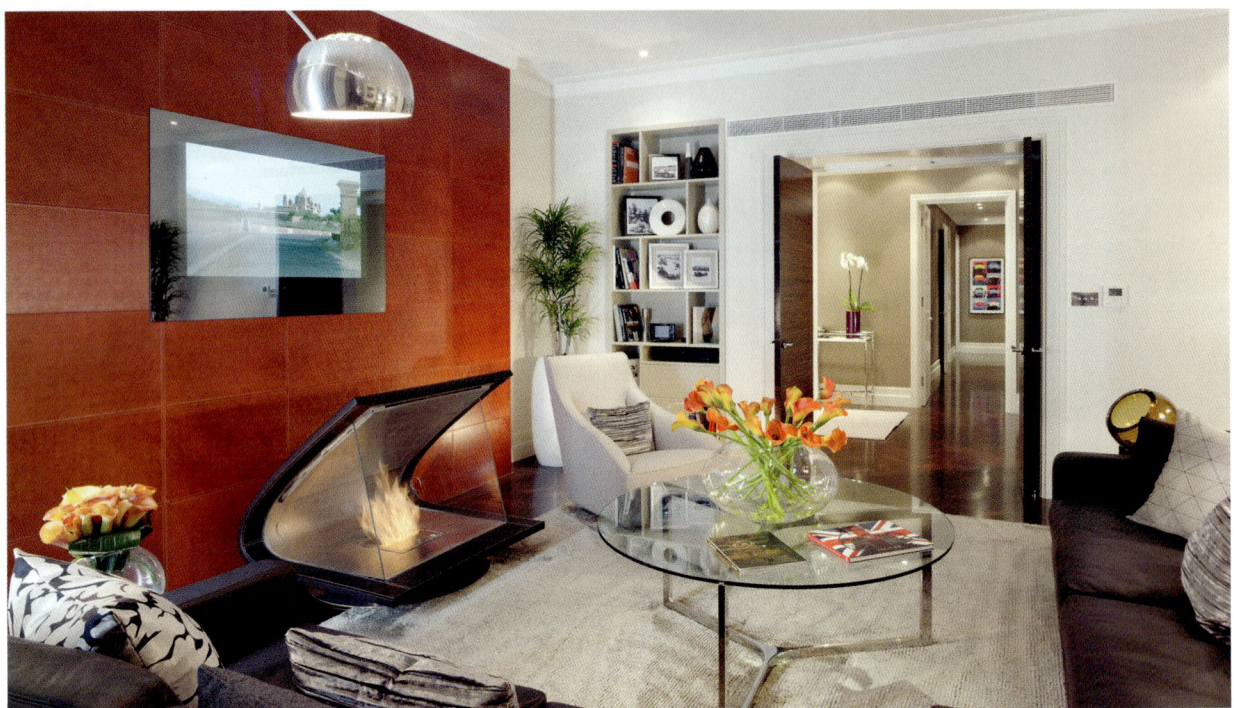

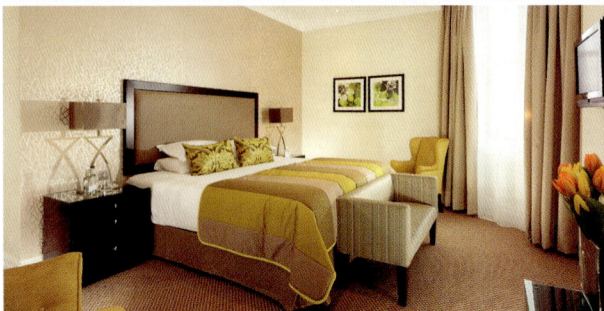

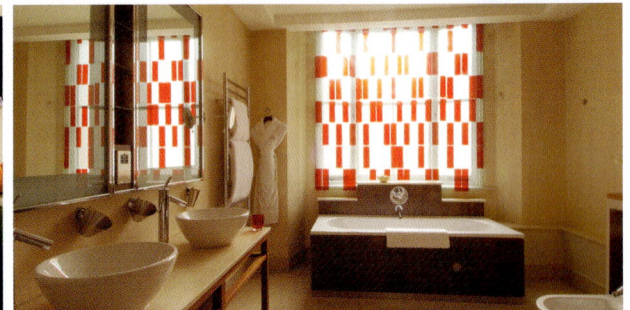

Taj 51 Buckingham Gate Suites and Residences

Avant-garde town houses in Westminster's epicentre

PRICE FROM:
£255

FEATURES:
Family friendly; Gym; Michelin Starred restaurant; Spa

ACTIVITIES:
Horse riding; Shopping; Sightseeing

NEARBY:
Buckingham Palace; St James's Park; Houses of Parliament; London Eye

GETTING THERE:
Victoria Station; King's Cross St Pancras Railway Station - Eurostar; London Heathrow Airport

☎ +44 (0)20 7769 7766
🌐 condenastjohansens.com/buckinghamgate
🏠 51 Buckingham Gate, Westminster, London SW1E 6AF, England

A palace by The Palace. Taj 51 Buckingham Gate Suites and Residences in London does a regal job of balancing splendour, sophistication and modern elegance with more than enough comfort to keep you living the life of luxury in your central London home-away-from-home. A polished butler service will pander to your every gastronomic whim, either in or out of your very own kitchen-en-suite, while fellow resident, the Michelin-Starred Quilon (sister to the famous Bombay Brasserie) offers some of the finest curry-leafed, ginger-infused and delicately coconut-flavoured south-west coastal Indian fare the city has to offer. You may be living like a prince or princess but here, you'll feast like a king. Uncover the secret utopia Taj 51 Buckingham Gate holds within its walls: a romantic alfresco courtyard setting where city-living seclusion is unrivalled. Escaping the hustle and bustle of London, soak up the Midsummer Night's Dreamy atmosphere, complete with a refreshingly good chilli vodka Qojito in one hand and a cool mint shisha in the other. Stretch out in any one of the beautifully designed suites - maybe the Jaguar Suite dressed by Jaguar's Design Director or the two-bedroom Cinema Suite decorated as a tribute to the history of film - and feel totally at home-suite-home.

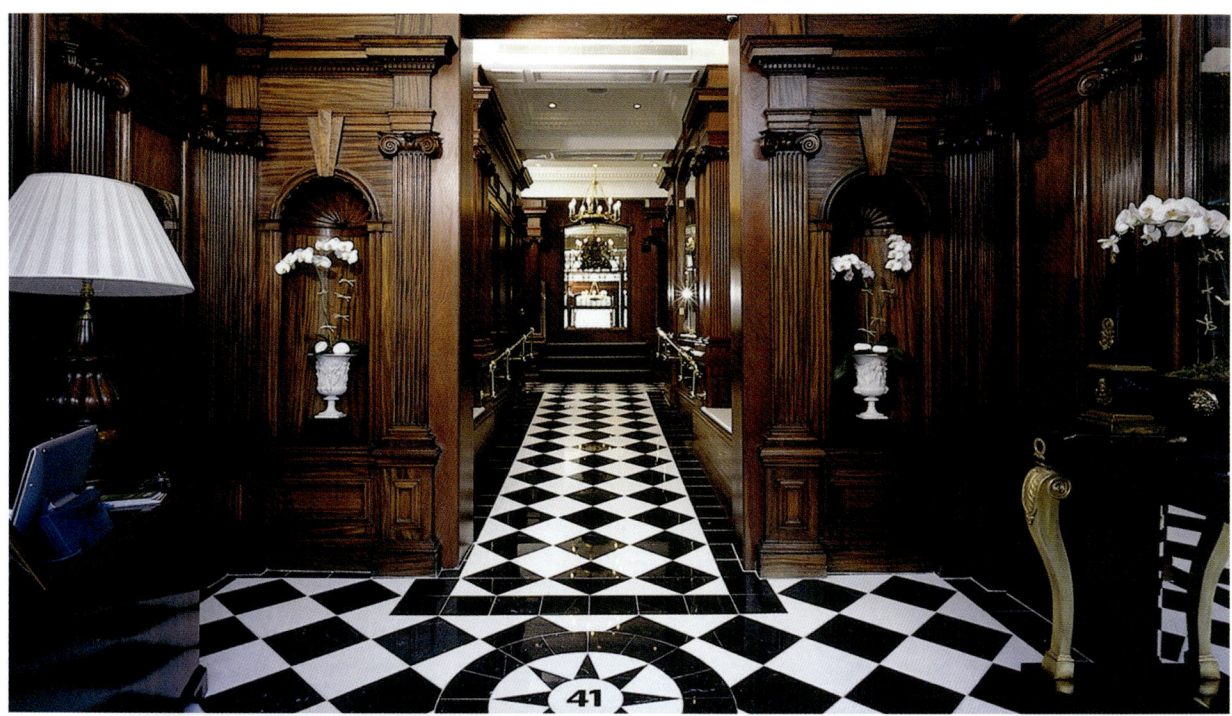

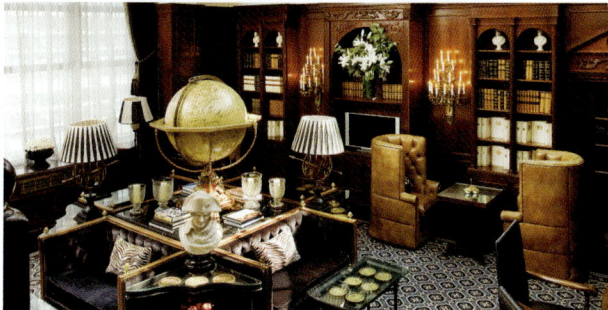
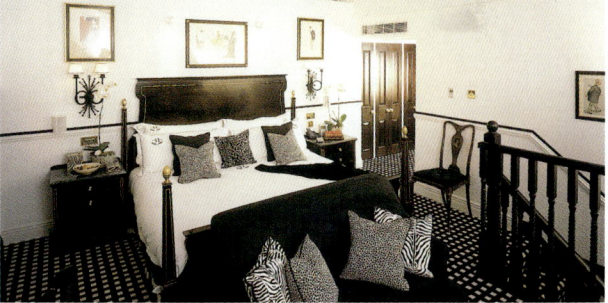

41

The pad you wished you had in London's royal district

Talking about getting the royal treatment is irresistible when discussing 41. On the doorstep of Buckingham Palace with views of The Royal Mews, it's a two-minute dash to the Queen's Gallery or the Changing of The Guard. From the guest-preference forms to the aromatherapy pillow menu, in-room treatments and even Pet Concierge, nothing is too big an ask for the exceptionally attentive staff. In the heart of London's sovereign quarter, 41 presents a home-away-from-home experience. And what a home it is! A boutique retreat from the frenzy of the Big Smoke. The discreet private entrance, stylish monochrome décor, opulent rooms and apartments (all crisp white linen and welcoming fireplaces), smart technology and elegant mahogany-panelled Executive Lounge, all give this little gem the air of a private members' club. The Executive Lounge's "Plunder The Pantry" invitation (complimentary snacks are laid out from 8pm each evening) sums up 41's character: thoughtful, clever and classy. Diamond-sharp service is always on the agenda, however, the location is the jewel in the crown. Step outside and London's parks, palaces and parades are at your feet.

PRICE FROM:
£329

FEATURES:
Family friendly; Pet friendly

ACTIVITIES:
Horse riding; Shopping; Sightseeing

NEARBY:
Buckingham Palace; London Eye; Houses of Parliament; Hyde Park; Green Park

GETTING THERE:
Victoria Underground Station; London Heathrow Airport; London Gatwick Airport

+44 (0)20 7300 0041 ☎
condenastjohansens.com/41buckinghampalaceroad 🌐
41 Buckingham Palace Road, London SW1W 0PS, England 🏠

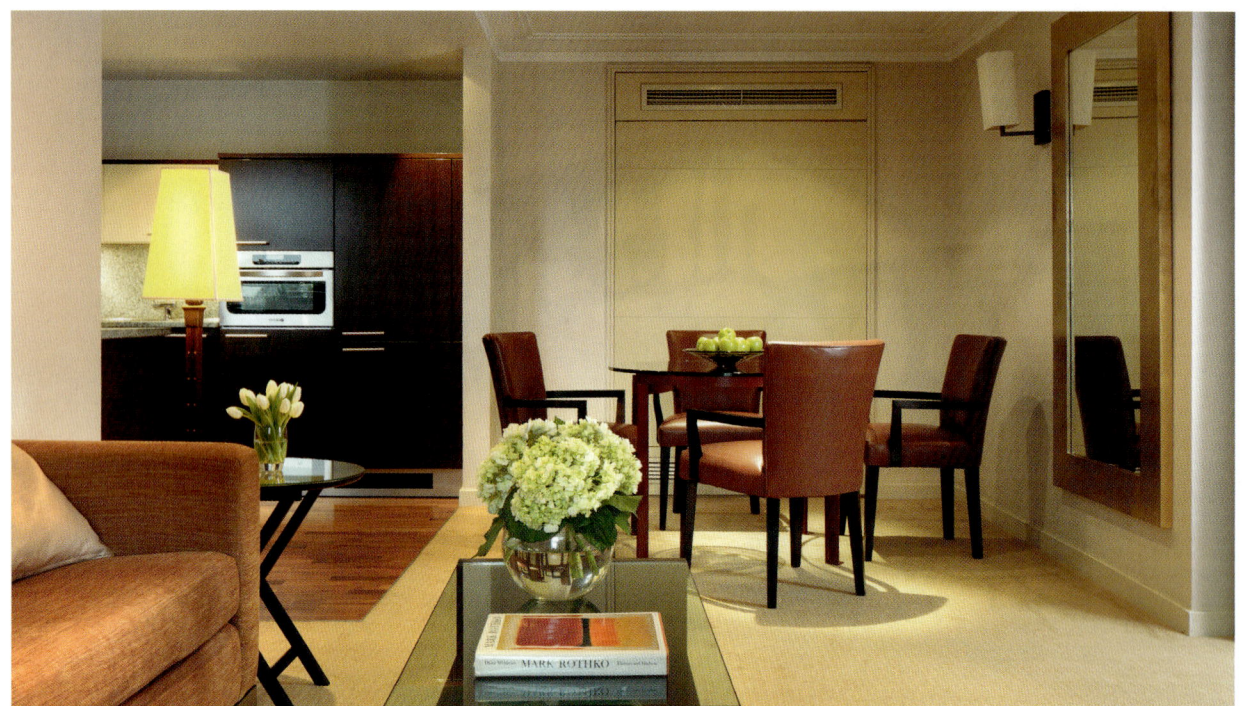

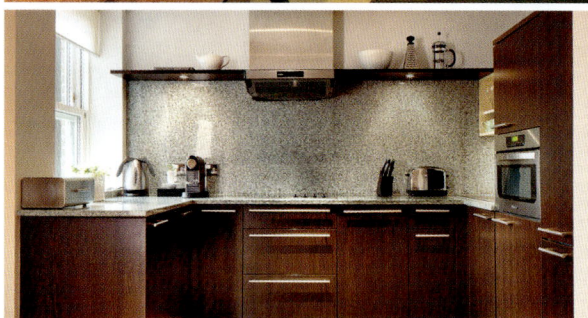

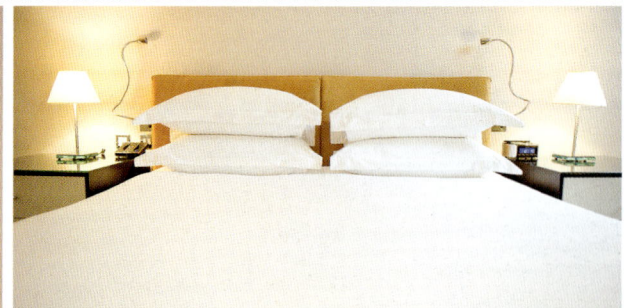

Cheval Phoenix House

Exclusive fully-serviced apartments with luxury hotel style in Chelsea

PRICE FROM:
£214 (excluding VAT, min 3-day stay)

FEATURES:
Family friendly; Gym

ACTIVITIES:
Shopping; Sightseeing

NEARBY:
Royal Court Theatre; Sloane Square; Saatchi Gallery; Le Cercle restaurant

GETTING THERE:
Sloane Square Underground Station; Victoria Railway Station; London Heathrow Airport

☎ +44 (0)20 7259 8222
🌐 condenastjohansens.com/phoenixhouse
🏠 1 Wilbraham Place, Sloane Street, London SW1X 9AE, England

Home to the well-heeled and a film star or two, London's affluent Chelsea is a rare mix of high-end and high-street shopping, artistic influence (Saatchi Gallery) and football (home to the Premier League's Chelsea Football Club). Aiming and succeeding to charm whomever walks through its doors, Cheval Phoenix House is at the core of everything Chelsea has to offer. Located minutes from the boutiques and galleries of Sloane Square, the pedestrianised Duke of York Square and Chelsea Harbour, Cheval Phoenix is your exclusive gateway to one of the capital's most desirable neighbourhoods. Extremely private, it houses 33 fully-serviced apartments with fully-equipped kitchens, ranging from studios, one and two-bedroom apartments and duplexes. Attentive 24-hour concierge service and security, housekeeping Monday through to Friday and private chef services (from neighbouring modern French Le Cercle restaurant) means that not only is this your London home-from-home but also a spoiling retreat delivering world-class hotel services. There'll even be a Well-Being Welcome Tray to greet you upon arrival. Ideal for short breaks and longer stays for individuals, couples and families, Cheval Phoenix is smart, modern and stylish where you can just as easily entertain guests as kick back and relax in comfort.

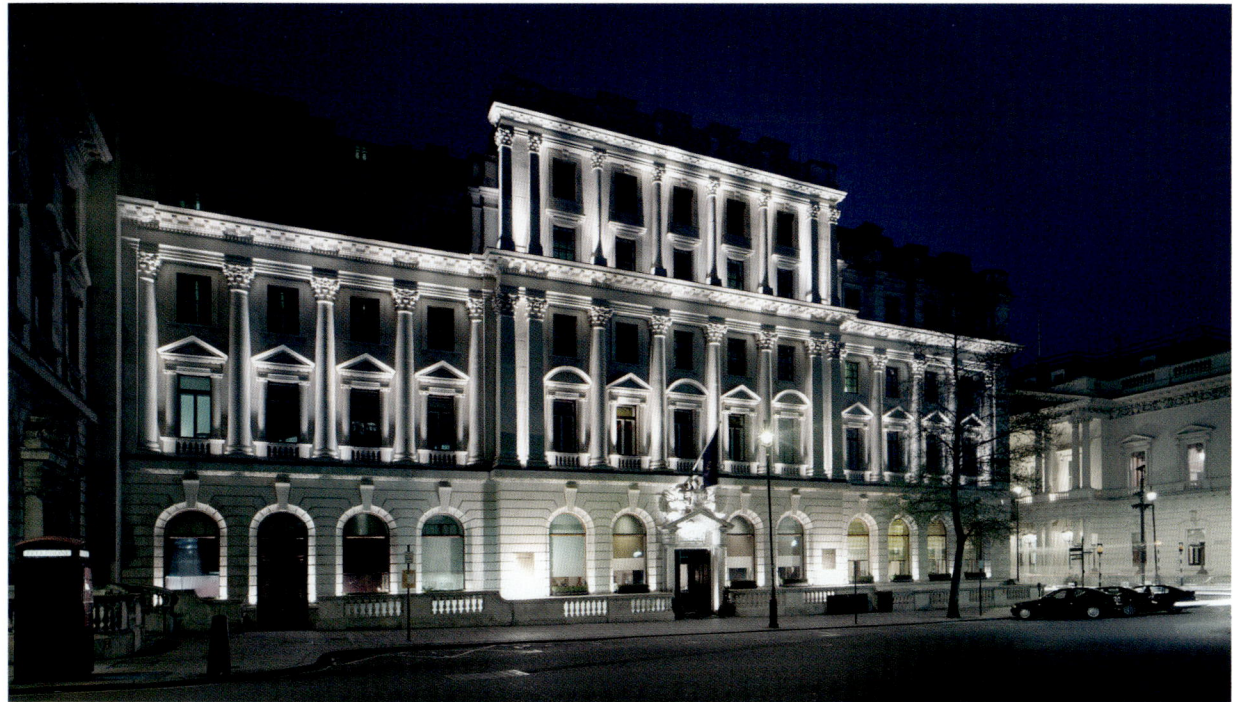

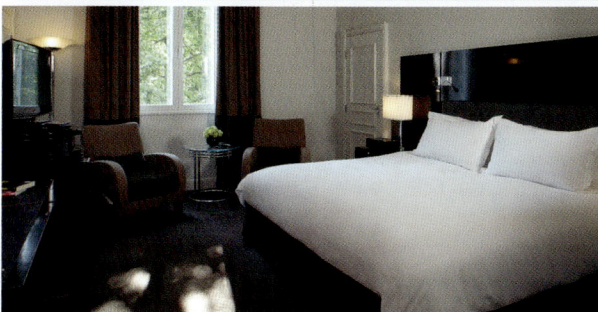
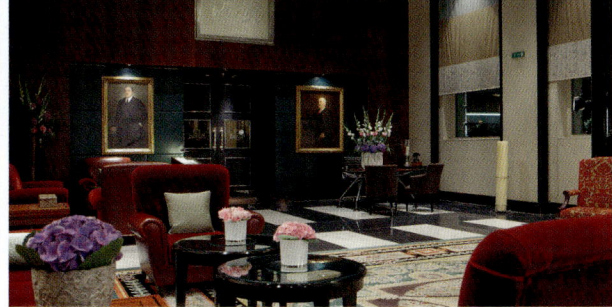

Sofitel London St James

A fusion of British class and French finesse in London's elite St James

On the corner of Waterloo Place and Pall Mall, Sofitel London St James proudly stands in prime City of Westminster position. Moments from the flashing lights of Piccadilly Circus and the lions guarding Nelson's Column in Trafalgar Square, this is London's buzzing St James's area known for its high-end and popular commercial appeal. As with many buildings in this area, the Sofitel London's imposing Grade II listed structure is owned by the Crown Estate (Buckingham Palace is a five-minute walk away), and behind its regal façade is a stylish interior blending classic British design with contemporary French flair. Formerly the headquarters to the Cox's & King's bank (whose original artwork still hangs on the walls today), you're led through the smart lobby and into your plush room or suite. Each is utterly serene decorated in tones of chocolate, almond and olive fitted with high-def tvs (110 channels!), WiFi and sleek black and white marble bathrooms. French-British cuisine is the trademark of the brasserie, The Balcon, while sultry St James Bar is where you'll find a large selection of Champagnes and vintage cocktails. For afternoon tea with a French twist head to The Rose Lounge. Don't miss: the stunning Sofitel So SPA and Technogym-equipped So FIT gym.

PRICE FROM:
£425

FEATURES:
Family friendly; Gym; Pet friendly; Restaurant; Spa

ACTIVITIES:
Shopping; Sightseeing; Walking

NEARBY:
Trafalgar Square; Buckingham Palace; London Eye; National Gallery; Bond Street shopping

GETTING THERE:
Piccadilly Underground Station; King's Cross St Pancras Railway Station - Eurostar; London Heathrow Airport

+44 (0)20 7747 2200 ☎
condenastjohansens.com/stjames 🌐
6 Waterloo Place, London SW1Y 4AN, England 🏠

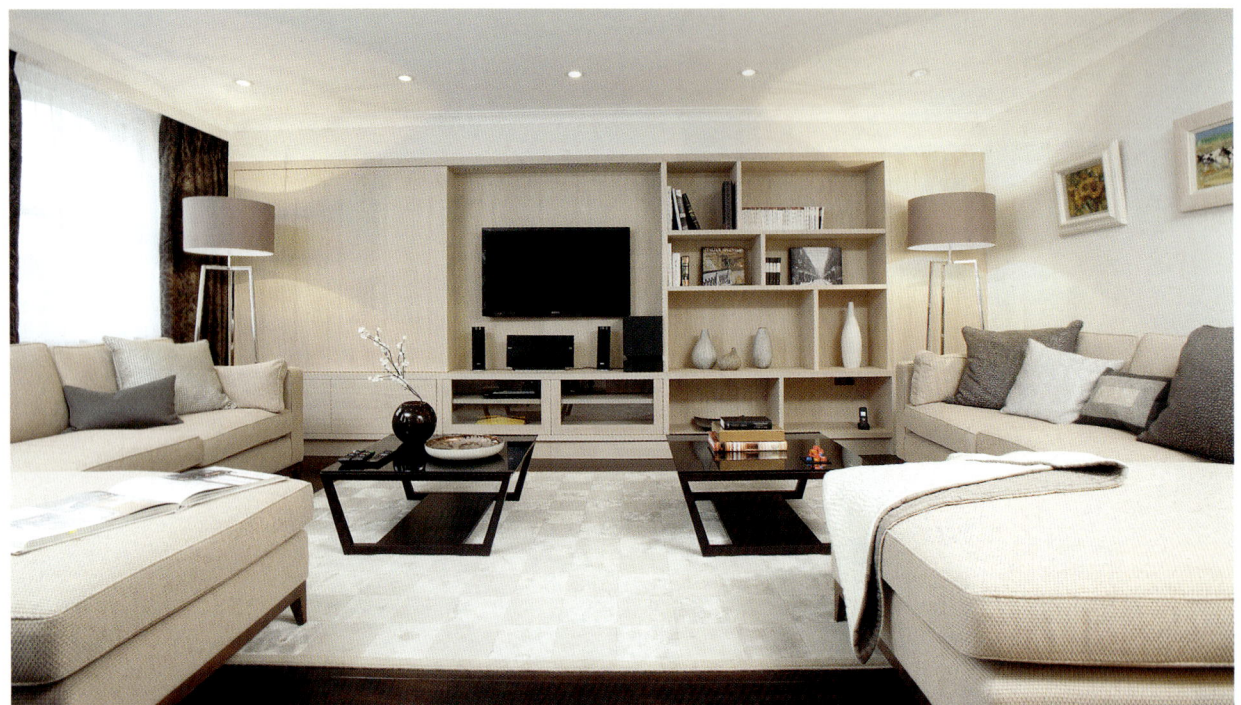

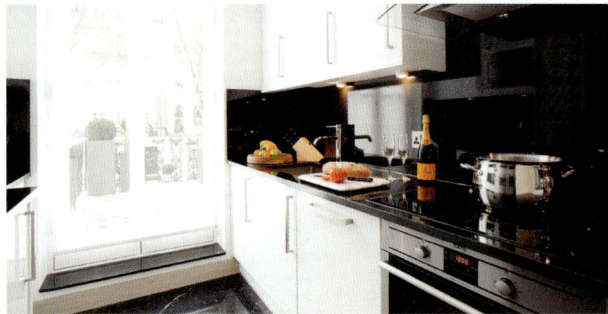

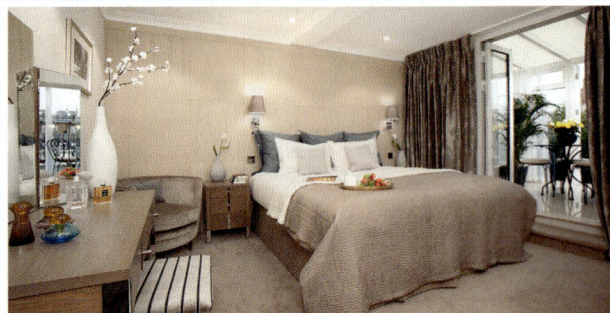

Claverley Court

Fashionable apartments in upscale Knightsbridge

PRICE FROM:
£252

FEATURES:
Family friendly

ACTIVITIES:
Shopping; Sightseeing

NEARBY:
Hyde Park; Science Museum; Victoria and Albert Museum

GETTING THERE:
Knightsbridge Underground Station; London Heathrow Airport

Dreaming of the ultimate London pied-à-terre? Welcome to Claverley Court. Spacious, chic apartments in a quiet, tree-lined Knightsbridge square but with all the benefits of a five-star London hotel, this is London living at its five-star best. Potter the pavements in your new Jimmy Choos (the boutique is seconds from Claverley Court's elegant front door) or pop into Harvey Nichols for the best designer ware this side of Milan. After a hard day's shopping, relax in the Beaufort Suite, a beautifully designed, marble and walnut-clad penthouse before making your evening plans. Will it be a short taxi hop to the West End for world-class theatre? Or a trip to one of Knightbridge's acclaimed restaurants? Families will find their home-from-home in Claverley Court's Knightsbridge Suite, a split level, three-bed, three-bathroom apartment sumptuously furnished, complete with Jacuzzi in the master suite. Travelling solo or à deux? Choose a one-bed apartment finished to the highest standard. Whatever you choose, take your pick of an east or west facing pad; early birds can watch the sunrise, night owls can toast the sunset before hitting the glamorous clubs and bars moments from your own front door.

☎ +44 (0)20 7938 5930
🌐 condenastjohansens.com/claverleycourt
🏠 Beaufort Gardens, London SW3 1PS, England

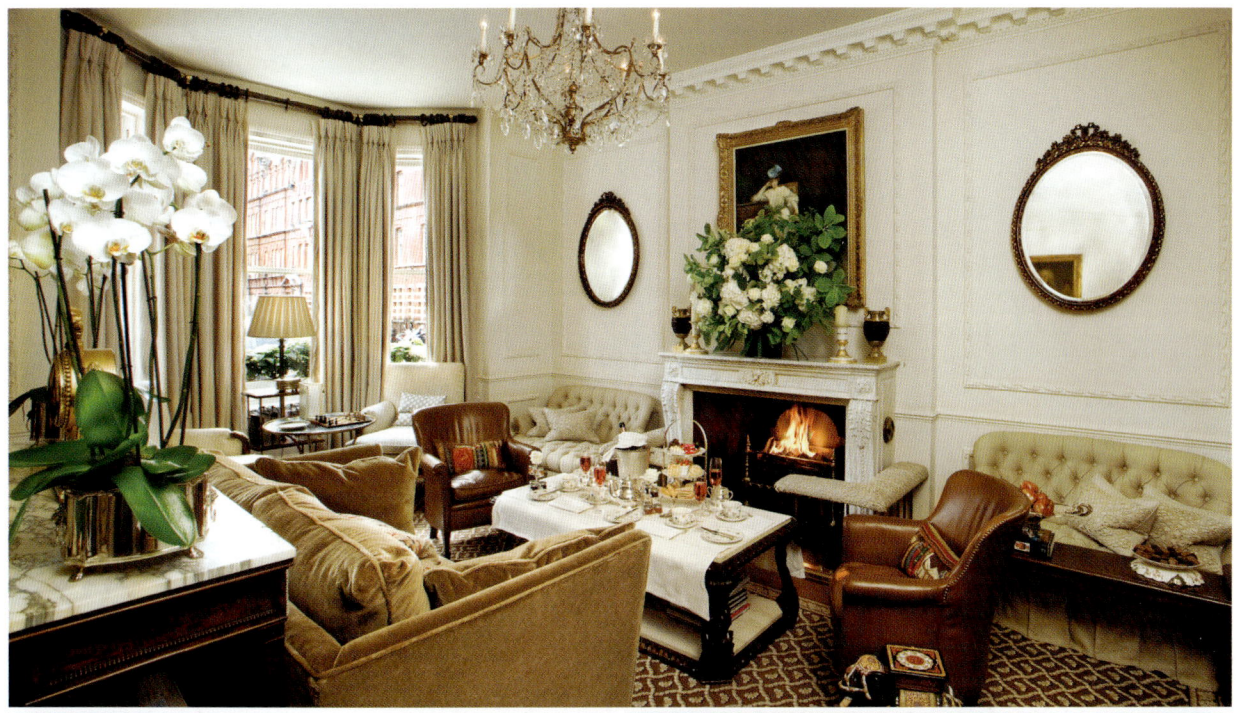

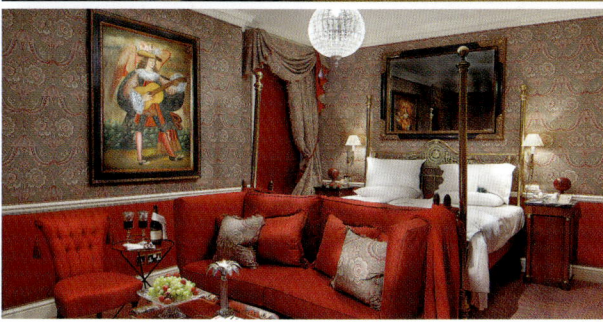
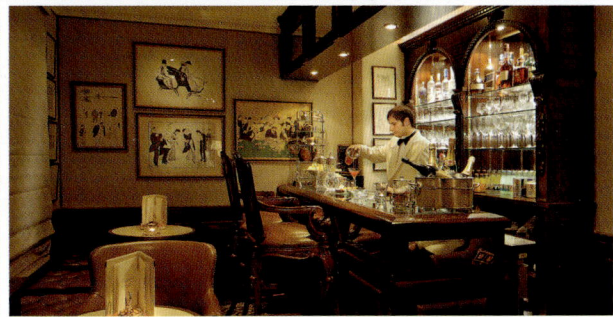

The Egerton House Hotel

Enchanting Victorian house in residential Knightsbridge

The Egerton House Hotel, London, has an incredible back story dating to the 1820s. Learn about its history as you indulge on the first-class breakfasts in the intimate dining area inspired by the recipes in Bea Tollman's cookbook, A Life In Food (Bea is founder of the elite Red Carnation Hotels group, owner of Egerton). But a healthy kick-start to the day is only one focus at this charmingly understated but beautifully decorated boutique hotel. The well-being of visiting children and pets are a high priority too; at turndown they'll discover wonderfully thoughtful touches such as a teddy bear book and doggie treat. With so many nearby London attractions and Kensington Gardens on the doorstep it's easy to fill your days, although it's equally tempting to unwind in Egerton House's regal Drawing Room with a traditional afternoon tea of warm scones, clotted cream and perhaps a cheeky glass of Champagne. Or if you prefer, one of Antonio's (barman extraordinaire) memorable martinis, lauded as the best in London. Before sinking into your bed's exceptionally soft pillows and under the snuggle-cosy duvet for some well-deserved shuteye, the in-room interactive infotainment system, with on-demand services, Bose audio and high-speed internet, provides some relaxing downtime.

PRICE FROM:
£330

FEATURES:
Family friendly; Pet friendly

ACTIVITIES:
Shopping; Sightseeing; Walking

NEARBY:
Harrods; Victoria and Albert Museum; Hyde Park; Buckingham Palace

GETTING THERE:
Knightsbridge Underground Station; Victoria Railway Station; London Heathrow Airport

+44 (0)20 7589 2412 ☎
condenastjohansens.com/egertonhouse 🌐
17-19 Egerton Terrace, Knightsbridge, London SW3 2BX, 🏠
England

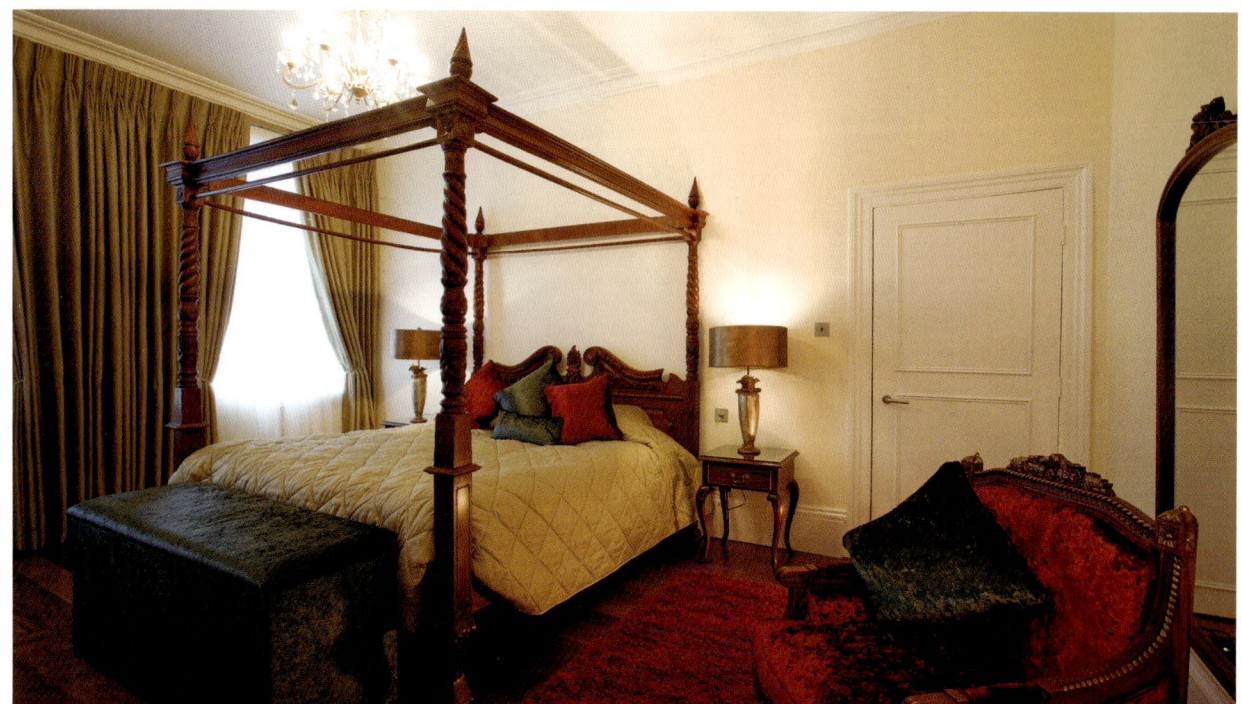

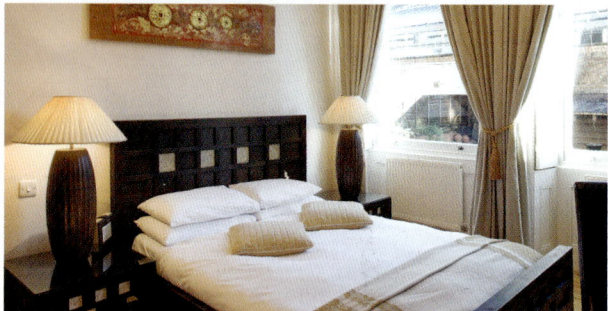

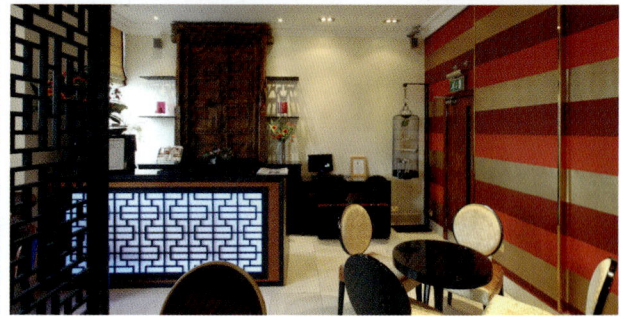

Mayflower Hotel

Your swanky West London home

PRICE FROM:
£120

FEATURES:
Family friendly; Pet friendly

ACTIVITIES:
Shopping; Sightseeing; Walking

NEARBY:
Earls Court Exhibition Centre; Harrods; Hyde Park; Madame Tussauds; London Eye

GETTING THERE:
London Heathrow Airport; London Gatwick Airport; London Stansted Airport

☎ +44 (0)20 7370 0991
🌐 condenastjohansens.com/mayflower
🏠 26-28 Trebovir Road, London SW5 9NJ, England

Full of originality, Mayflower Hotel is the convenient West London crash pad you wish you had. Located in the favoured neighbourhood for a string of the rich and rare over the years (Freddie Mercury, Alfred Hitchcock and currently Gary Barlow, even a young Diana, Princess of Wales), this boutique town house hotel marries vibrant Eastern design with Western contemporary comfort. It's the perfect retreat if travelling alone or on business, not to mention great value for money. Earls Court Exhibition Centre, Knightsbridge, Chelsea and various attractions such as the Natural History and Science Museums are all nearby. It's worth noting that Mayflower's guest rooms located on the ground floor are small but stylish, rich in pale stone, vibrant fabrics and Indian and Oriental antiques. Upstairs on the first floor, larger bedrooms are refurbished in light fresh colours with sparkling glass lighting and mirrors. Each has a smart bathroom of sparkling marble, slate and chrome complete with a walk-in shower. Continental buffet breakfast is laid out in the downstairs dining room every morning and when the weather is fine, Mayflower's extended patio garden opens out for some alfresco action. The dining room also provides an endless flow of coffee and juice throughout the day.

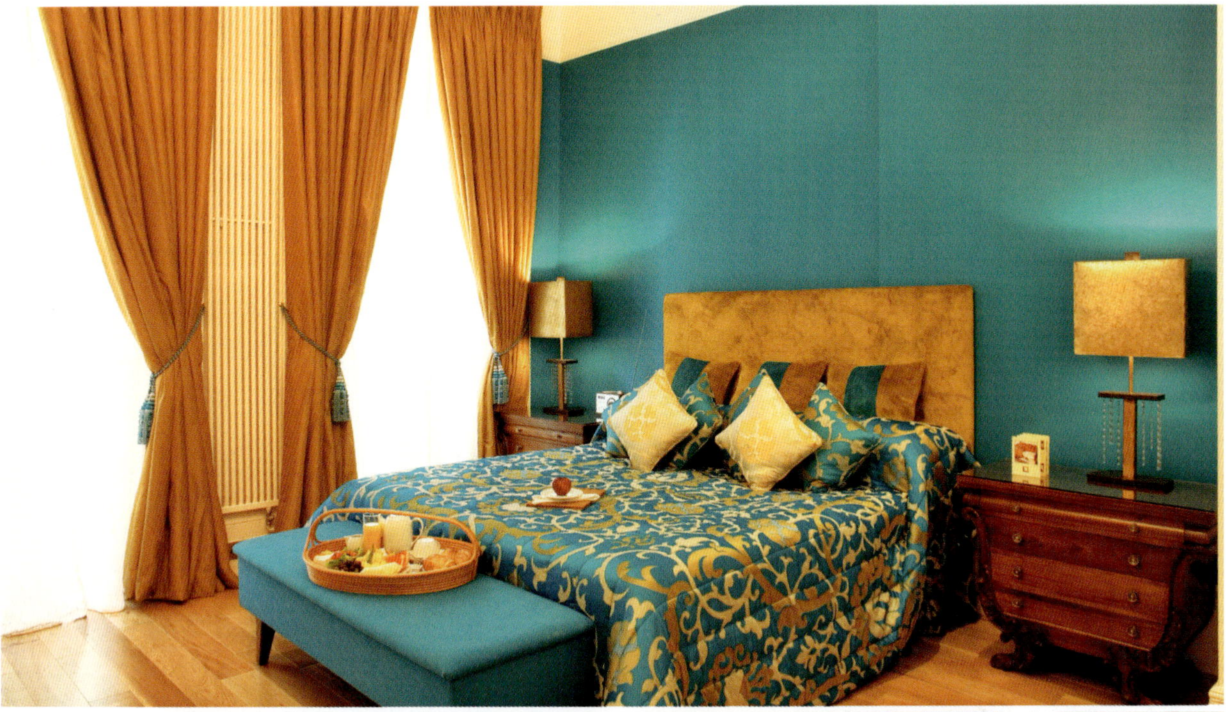

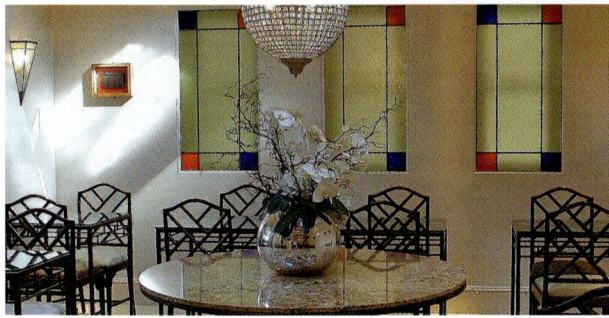

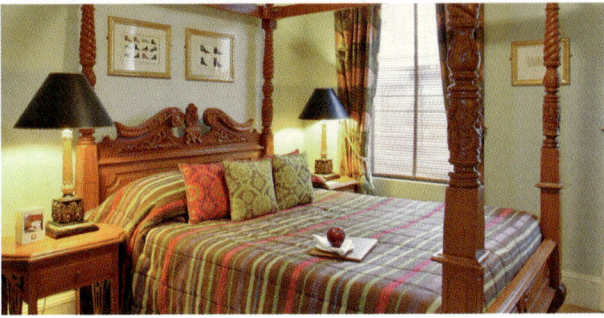

Twenty Nevern Square

Discreet chic residence in the centre of London's Earls Court

Twenty Nevern Square in London's Earls Court is a town house home-hotel with a residential vibe. Set beside the very smart Nevern Square Garden (privately owned by Garden Members from neighbouring town houses), Earls Court and Olympia Exhibition Centres are minutes away. Harrods, Harvey Nichols, King's Road and High Street Kensington are a short walk, as are theatres and attractions such as the Victoria and Albert Museum and Science Museum. Inside, European and Oriental furnishings harmoniously fuse together to furnish the irregularly shaped rooms with surprising nooks and crannies cleverly made into sumptuous features (see: the Mezzanine Double Room's cushioned snug). The bedrooms may be compact but with clever use of neutral coloured walls set against delicate silks, bold patterns and intricate touches such as hand-carved headboards, the quirkiness and designer flair of each room has you settling in and cosying up. Book one of the three suites for some extra space and if you're looking to really spoil someone, then the grandeur of the Ottoman Suite with free-standing bath beside a log fire and private balcony looking across to the manicured Nevern Square Garden is the perfect treat. Breakfast is served in the light, bright Conservatory opening onto a decked balcony area, and gym facilities are available by arrangement.

PRICE FROM:
£130

FEATURES:
Family friendly

ACTIVITIES:
Shopping; Sightseeing; Walking

NEARBY:
Victoria and Albert Museum; Natural History Museum; Harrods; Hyde Park

GETTING THERE:
Earls Court Underground Station; London Heathrow Airport; London Gatwick Airport

+44 (0)20 7565 9555 ☎
condenastjohansens.com/twentynevernsquare 🌐
20 Nevern Square, London SW5 9PD, England 🏠

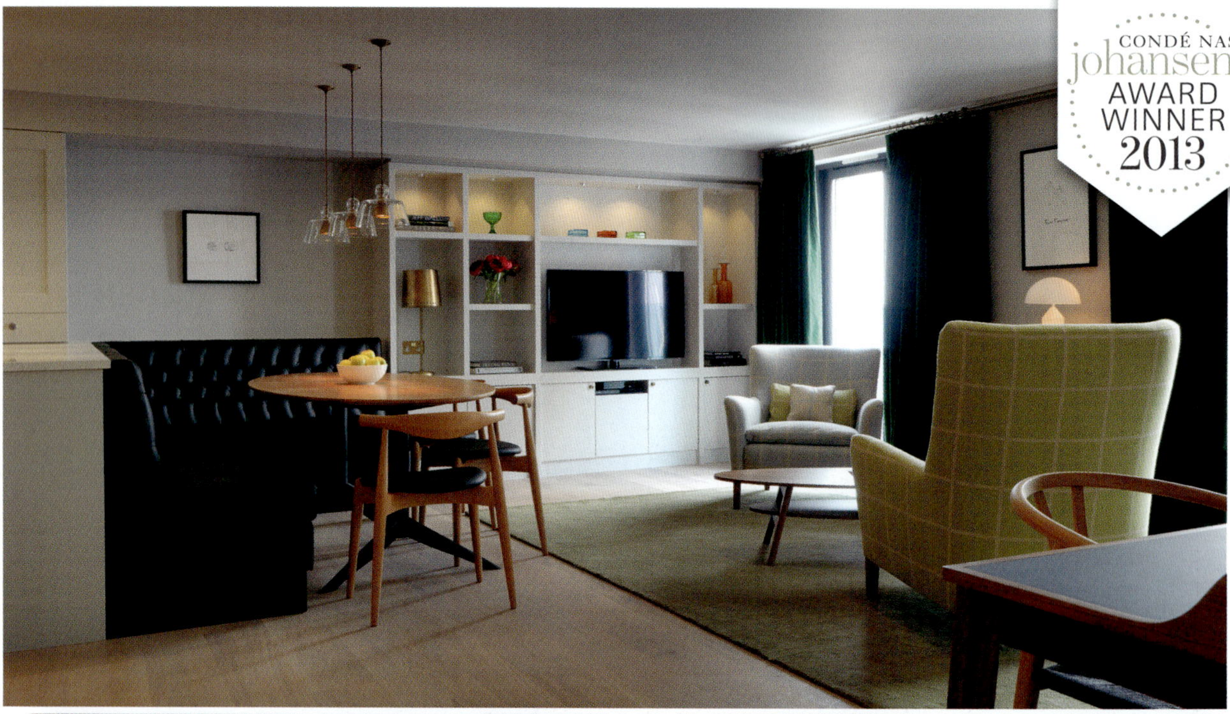

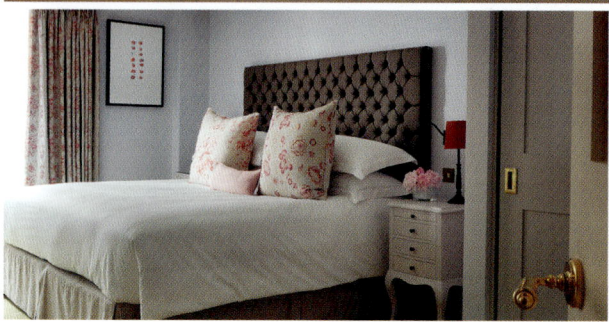
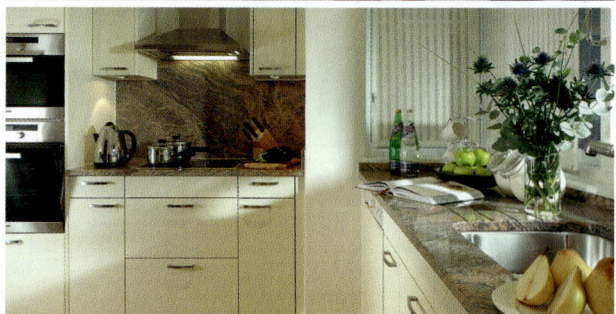

Cheval Knightsbridge

Fully-serviced apartment living, Knightsbridge style

PRICE FROM:
£393 (excluding VAT, min 5-day stay)

FEATURES:
Family friendly

ACTIVITIES:
Horse riding; Shopping; Sightseeing

NEARBY:
Harrods; Harvey Nichols; Victoria and Albert Museum;
Kensington Gardens

GETTING THERE:
Knightsbridge Underground Station; Victoria Railway Station;
London Heathrow Airport

With Harrods, Harvey Nichols and the flagship stores of Manolo Blahnik and Jimmy Choo, London's Knightsbridge is serious shopping territory. It's also an essential stop on London's tourist trail for Hyde Park and the Victoria & Albert Museum. In plum position for exploring this assembly of attractions, the residences of Cheval Knightsbridge allow you to temporarily reside in this exclusive neighbourhood on extended stays. Spread across several sought-after locations in the highly exclusive Brompton Road, Montpelier Mews (just off Brompton Road) and Cheval Place (parallel to Brompton Road), Cheval Knightsbridge is a collection of two and three-bedroom mews houses, apartments, town houses and a city cottage (which is available for three months or more). Created with families, groups of friends and corporate trips in mind, each accommodation has been designed as a private home with the added benefits of spoiling hotel services including maid service Monday to Friday, a 24-hour concierge, CCTV and health club membership. Designed for week-long, monthly or even longer stays, each one is full of individual style and character fitted with modern kitchens and the latest techy gizmos. So, as your luxury London pad, do as the local rich-set do and immerse in the city high life.

☎ +44 (0)20 7225 3325
🌐 condenastjohansens.com/chevalknightsbridge
🏠 15 Cheval Place, London SW7 1EW, England

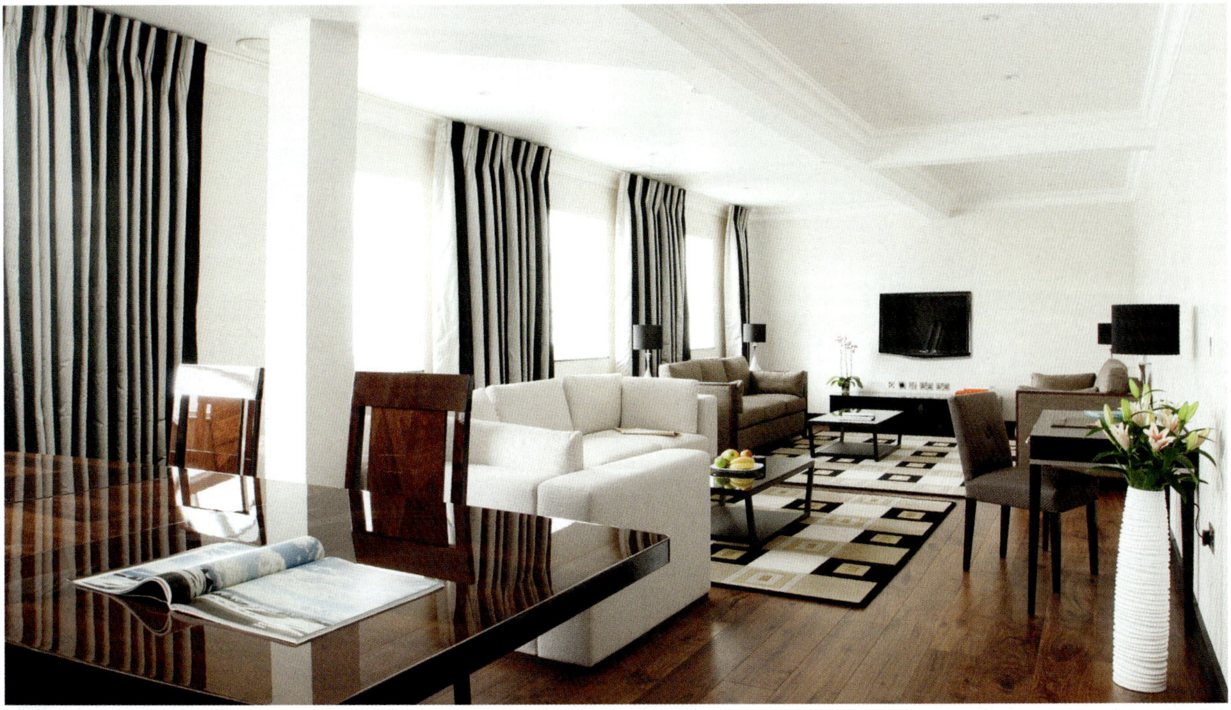

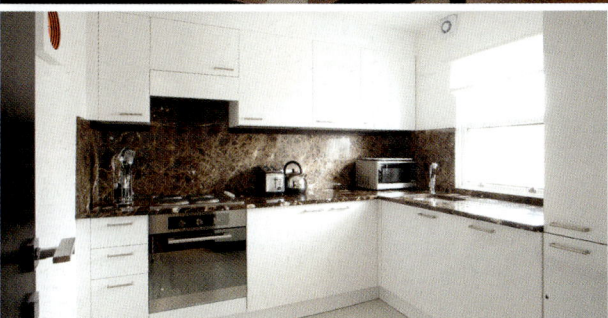

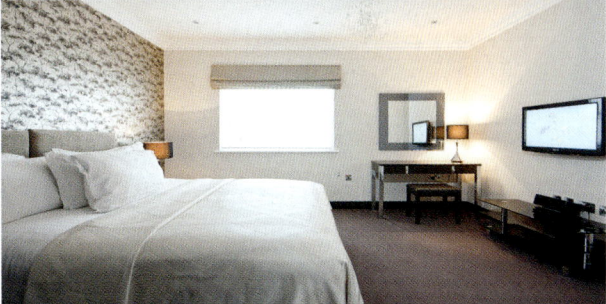

130 Queen's Gate Apartments

South Kensington super-luxe town house apartments

One thirty isn't the time but rather the place for the ultimate city getaway. Surrounded by top London attractions, this is the capital's Royal Borough of Kensington and Chelsea, all leafy streets lined with 19th-century town houses. Mary Poppins territory. There's a continental vibe to the neighbourhood that wows fashionistas and foodies alike and 130 Queen's Gate Apartments is very much part of this ever-so European high-end style. Shiny Italian marbles and ergonomically-friendly soft furnishings fill each apartment, which have one, two, three or four bedrooms. And modern amenities such as dishwashers and washer dryers are standard conveniences (you can simply ignore them of course – the housekeeper will blitz the apartment daily Monday to Saturday). At 130 Queen's Gate Apartments, London, the emphasis is on home comforts with 24-hour multi-lingual staff on hand to take the stress of planning away from you. It's also more than prepared for England's typically inclement weather. If the rain sets in, root yourself to the sumptuous spot and enjoy the apartment's state-of-the-art audio-visual system, Jacuzzi bath and services of a private chef in your very own kitchen. Don't forget, if you need anything, anything at all, there's the all-knowing concierge at your service.

PRICE FROM:
£280

FEATURES:
Family friendly; Gym

ACTIVITIES:
Shopping; Sightseeing

NEARBY:
London Eye; Royal Albert Hall; Hyde Park

GETTING THERE:
South Kensington Underground Station; Gloucester Road Underground Station; London Heathrow International Airport

+44 (0)20 793 85930 ☎
condenastjohansens.com/queensgate 🌐
130 Queen's Gate, Kensington, London SW7 5LE, England 🏠

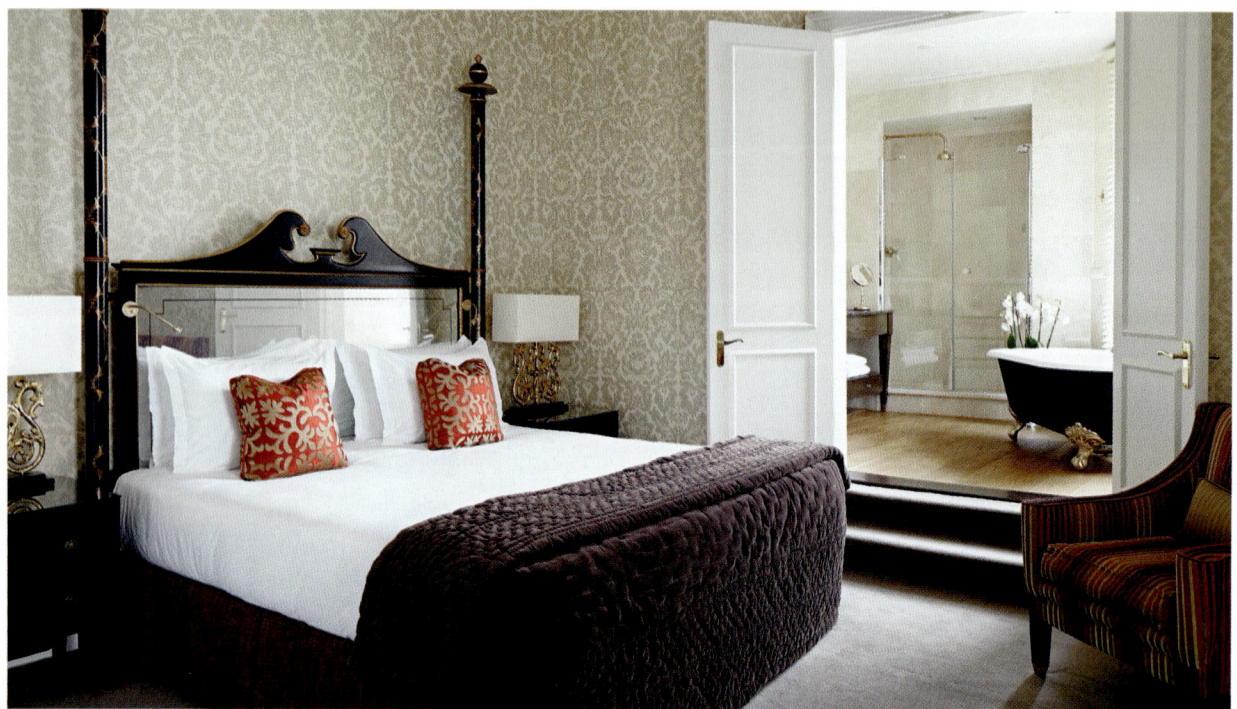

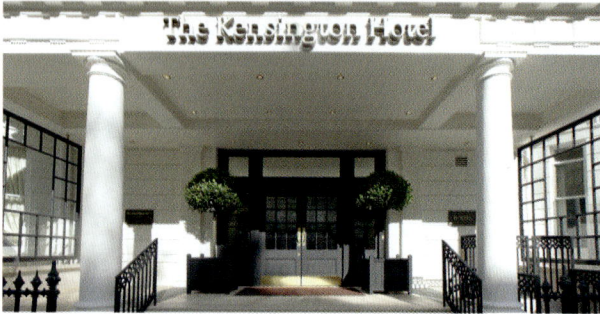

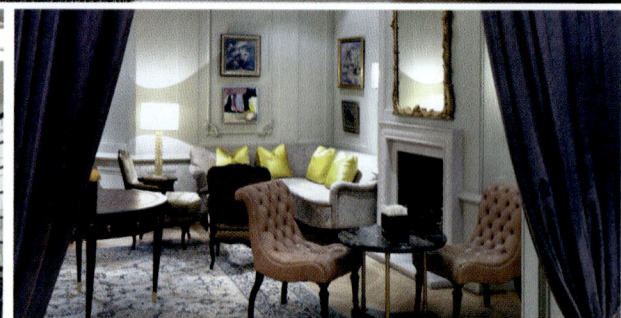

The Kensington Hotel

Your South Kensington base for days filled with afternoon teas and museum trips

PRICE FROM:
£235

FEATURES:
Family friendly; Gym; Restaurant; Wheelchair access

ACTIVITIES:
Shopping; Sightseeing

NEARBY:
Natural History Museum; Victoria and Albert Museum; Science Museum; Christie's Auction House; Hyde Park

GETTING THERE:
South Kensington Undergound Station; Victoria Railway Station; London Heathrow Airport

☎ +44 (0)20 7589 6300
🌐 condenastjohansens.com/kensington
🏠 109-113 Queen's Gate, South Kensington, SW7 5LR London, England

Around the corner from the Natural History, Victoria & Albert and Science Museums (all free!), The Kensington Hotel is perfectly situated to enjoy them all. The Royal Albert Hall, Hyde Park, Kensington Palace, Harrods and Harvey Nichols are all within walking distance too. One of London's most elite addresses, South Kensington, is the savvy choice for culture vultures. Spanning across several Regency town houses, The Kensington Hotel offers a taste of London's affluent urban lifestyle. Inside, the dazzling chandelier above and red velvet reception alcove in front of you appear like the inside of a jewellery box, all at once glam and cosseting. From here to the Morning Room, along to the Drawing Room (afternoon teas are a boom here), varying colour schemes and eclectic furnishings create distinctive atmospheres as you pass through one town house to the next. Artwork from all over the world dresses the walls alongside objets d'art, which also appear in the guest rooms and suites, which come in all shapes and sizes; many have oversized windows (sound-proofed) bringing in rays of natural light. Back downstairs and through the original doors of Dublin's post office, the low-ceilinged, speakeasy-esque Aubrey Bar is ever-ready to mix a cocktail or two while its neighbouring all-day Aubrey Restaurant serves British fare with an international twist. Added bonus: complimentary WiFi is available.

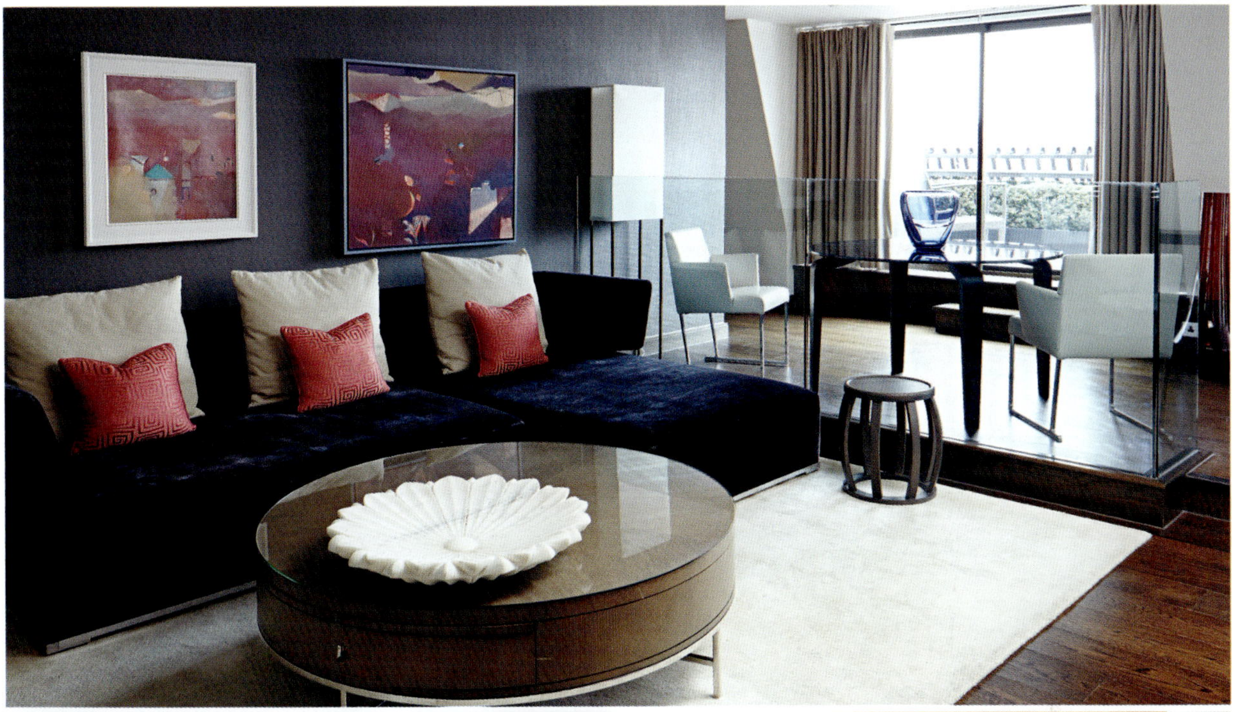

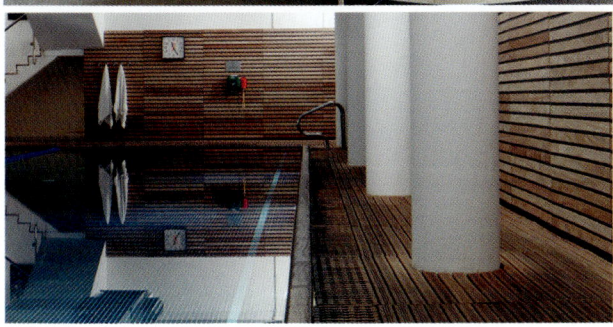
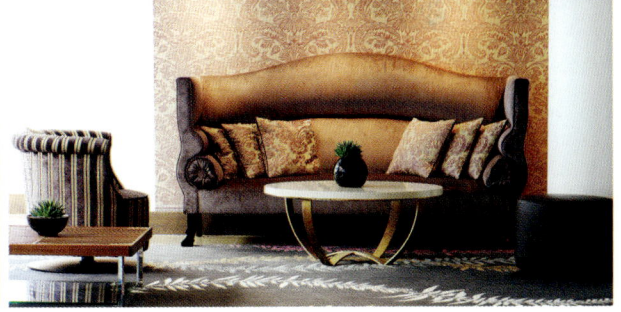

The Marylebone Hotel

Urban cool and cosmopolitan flair in the heart of fashionable Marylebone village

London's district of Marylebone is where village-style character meets vibrant city life. With Theatreland, Madame Tussauds, Regent's and Hyde Parks, high-street and high-end shopping at Oxford and Bond Streets all close by, it offers the best of both worlds: a brilliant base for the tourist trail and a fashionable residential address. Spanning across an entire block of the neighbourhood, The Marylebone Hotel is a reflection of its affluent location. Despite its vast size (257 bedrooms, restaurant and bar, six conference suites, business centre, health club, pool and spa all under its roof), an intimate atmosphere travels through The Marylebone whose service is instantly welcoming. This is apparent as soon as you enter the glamorous lobby where Parisian furnishings, Italian ceramics and a hand-laid mosaic floor set the scene. All at once exclusive yet comfortable, it doesn't matter if you're travelling with the family (check out the children's concierge service), on business (WiFi is complimentary) or for pleasure, The Marylebone Hotel's resort facilities cater for all. The impressive Third Space Gym with 18-metre pool and spa is an attraction in its own right. So too is 108 Marylebone Lane where the menu features traditional favourites, fine wines, spirits and cocktails. No stay is complete without an afternoon tea in the lounge with a glass of English sparkling wine.

PRICE FROM:
£235

FEATURES:
Family friendly; Gym; Pool; Restaurant; Spa

ACTIVITIES:
Shopping; Sightseeing

NEARBY:
Oxford Street; Bond Street; Hyde Park; Theatreland; Madame Tussauds

GETTING THERE:
Bond Street Underground Station; Paddington Railway Station; London City Airport

+44 (0)20 7486 6600 ☎
condenastjohansens.com/marylebone 🌐
47 Welbeck Street, Marylebone, W1G 8DN London, England 🏠

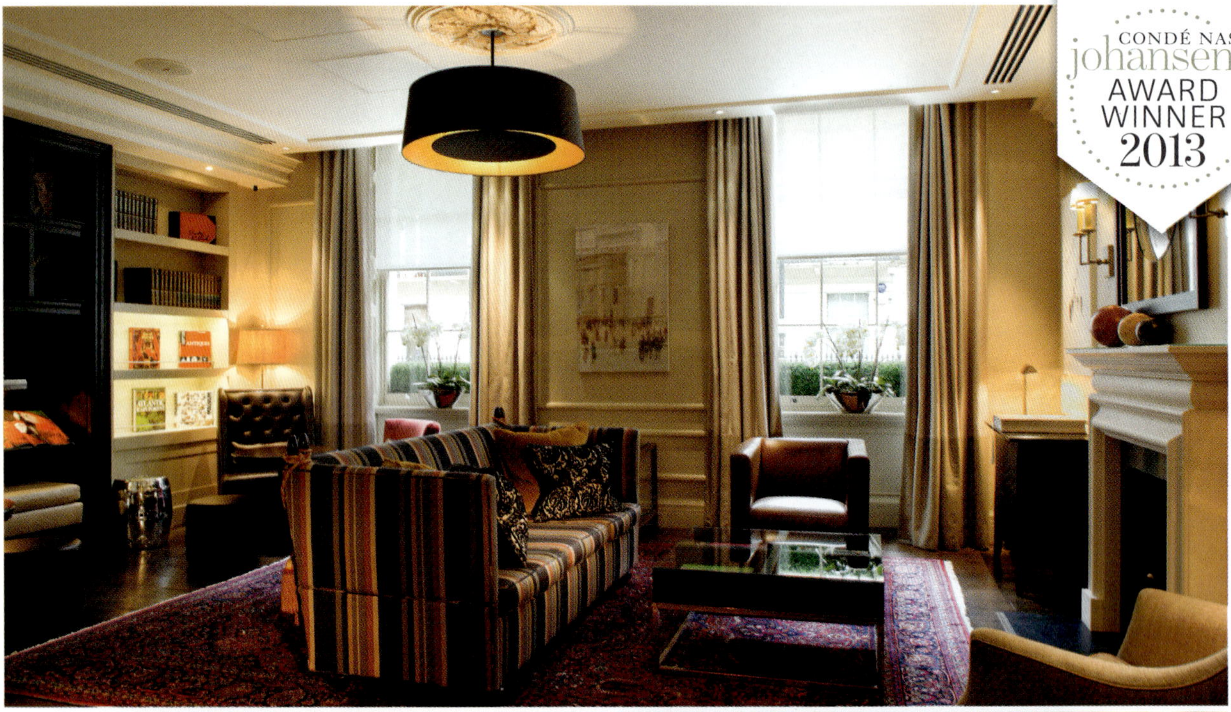

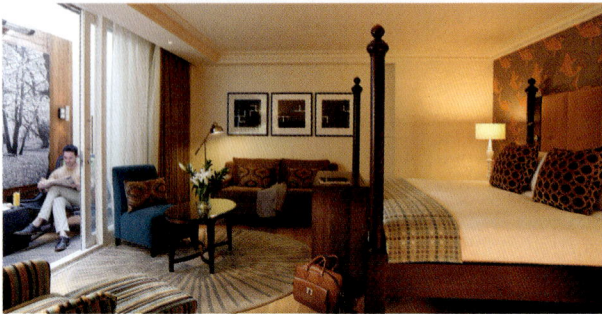

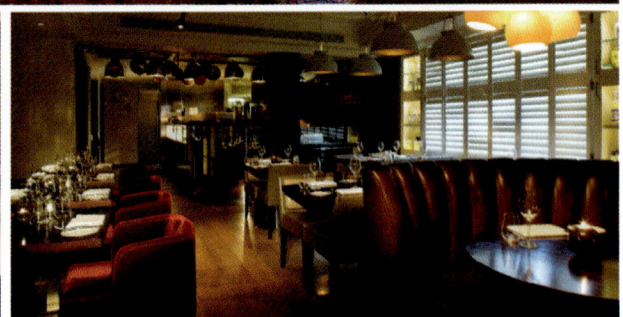

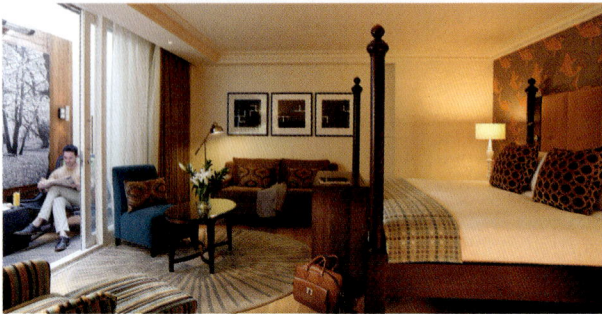

The Arch London

London lifestyle at its finest

PRICE FROM:
£235

FEATURES:
Gym; Restaurant; Wheelchair access

ACTIVITIES:
Shopping; Sightseeing

NEARBY:
Selfridges; Hyde Park; Oxford Street; Bond Street; Kensington High Street

GETTING THERE:
King's Cross St Pancras Railway Station - Eurostar; London Heathrow Airport; London Gatwick Airport

The Arch London at Marble Arch gets it just right in every way: West End location; knockout design; superior hospitality; and sublime food and drink. It's London at its swanky (yet never pretentious) best. Sleek and on-trend, The Arch throws a curveball at the meaning of boutique hotel with the result being a sophisticated, intimate and highly stylish retreat. And despite its central location, the quiet residential address means that noisy traffic and the day-to-day buzz of city life isn't a concern from your peaceful room. However, the damage you'll do to your wallet might be. The three-pronged attack from Oxford (Selfridges!), Regent (Liberty!) and Bond (Fenwicks!) Streets will leave you defenceless. So, back to your guest room or suite to assess the damage to your credit cards where maybe the bespoke colour scheme, ultra-sumptuous bathroom, high-techery, vibrant art, crisp linens and rich textiles and furnishings will help soften the blow. To start an evening off in style, there's the glam Bar whose cocktail menu is only matched by the elegance of Le Salon de Champagne and open kitchen of the lively HUNter 486 Restaurant (named after the 1950s district dialling code for Marylebone).

☎ +44 (0)20 7724 4700
🌐 condenastjohansens.com/thearchlondon
🏠 50 Great Cumberland Place, Marble Arch, London W1H 7FD, England

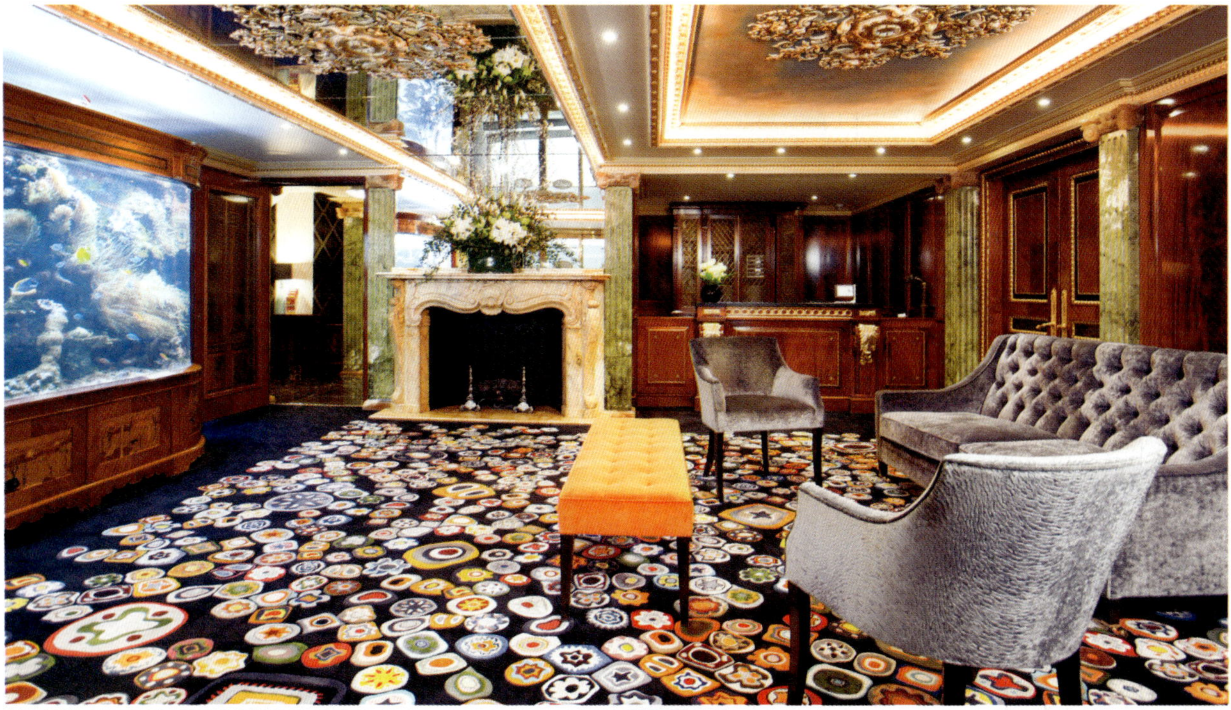

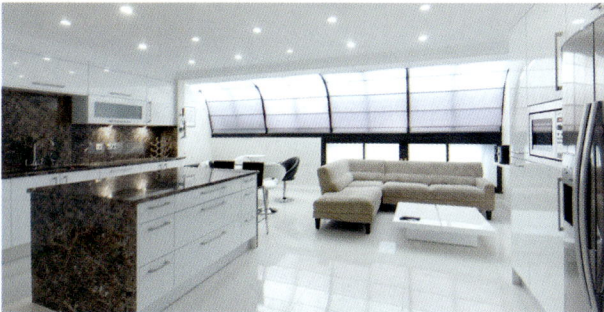
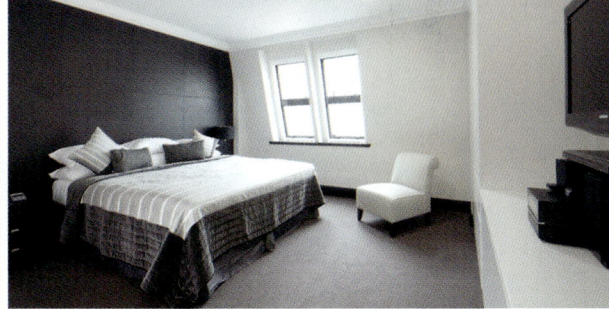

Mayfair House

Serviced apartments/suite accommodation in London Mayfair grandeur

Location is everything in London therefore Mayfair House has it all. Hyde Park in one direction, Bond Street shopping in the other, Green Park this way and Berkeley Square that. Then there's Mayfair House's address in the Shepherd Market neighourhood; a London hotspot tucked between Piccadilly and Curzon Street. This was the site of the annual fifteen-day "May Fair" that took place during the 17th and 18th centuries. Today, it attracts a well-heeled, in-the-know, diverse crowd seeking out the eclectic eateries, pubs and boutique shops that line its narrow streets and alleyways. For those requiring a luxury crash pad for seven nights or more (three months max), Mayfair House's assortment of apartments and suites are the sublime solution. On the top floor is the whopping Presidential Penthouse Suite, a four-double bedroom, four-bathroom beast with private entrance and rooftop terrace. The glossy, just-revamped three-bedroom, two-bathroom Executive Suite also has a private entrance. And one and two-bedroom apartments offer a choice of Classic, Contemporary and Executive. Call on the obliging concierge if you need help deciding and if you need a parking space during your stay, mention this prior to arrival and one shall magically be reserved on-site.

PRICE FROM:
£332

FEATURES:
Family friendly; Gym; Wheelchair access

ACTIVITIES:
Shopping; Sightseeing; Walking

NEARBY:
Green Park; Upscale Bond Street shopping; Piccadilly Circus; Oxford Street shopping; Royal Academy of Arts

GETTING THERE:
Green Park Underground Station; King's Cross St Pancras Railway Station - Eurostar; London Heathrow Airport

+44 (0)20 7491 0000 ☎
condenastjohansens.com/mayfairhouse 🌐
22-28 Shepherd Street, Mayfair, London W1J 7JH, England 🏠

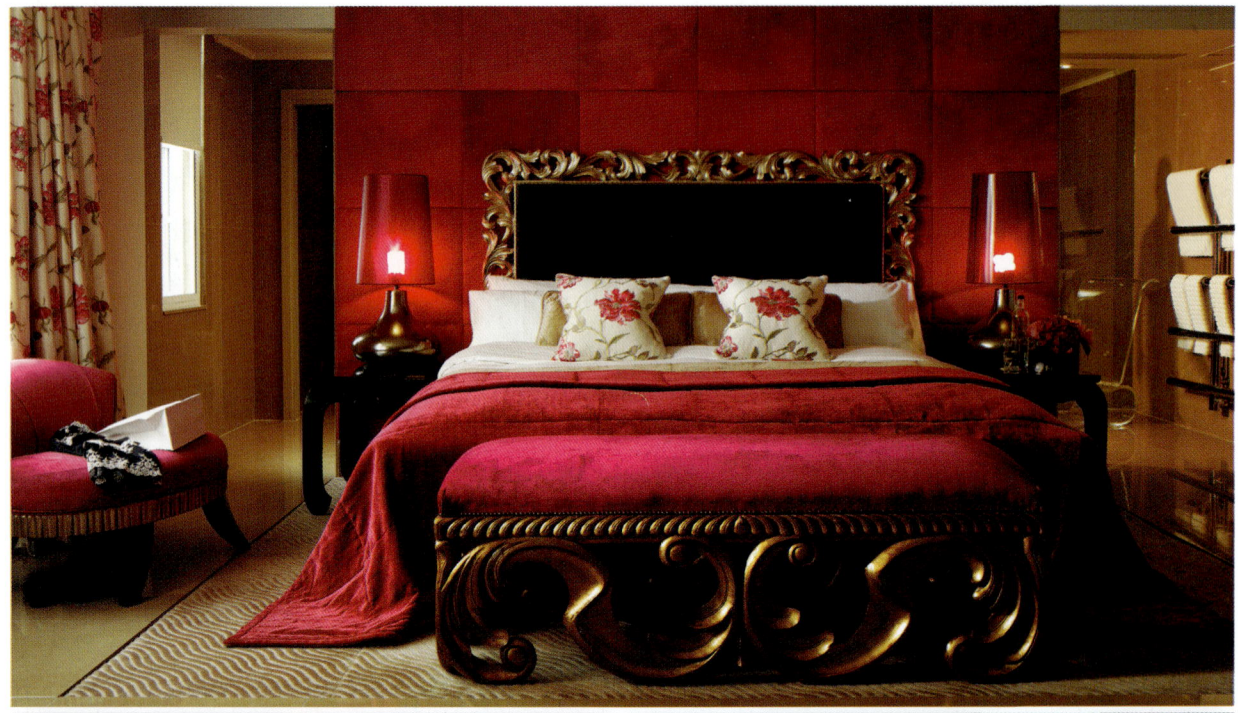

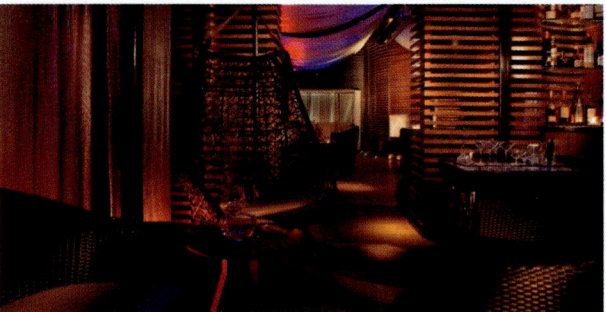 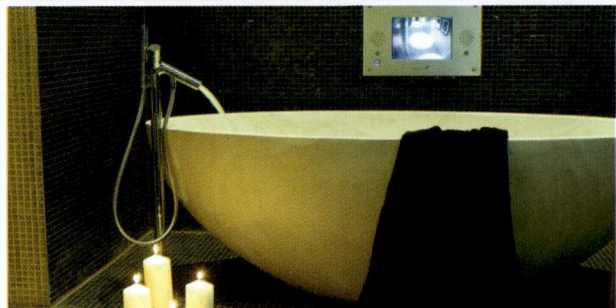

The May Fair Hotel

London Mayfair's stylish and spirited trend-setter

PRICE FROM:
£240

FEATURES:
Gym; Restaurant; Spa; Wheelchair access

ACTIVITIES:
Shopping; Sightseeing

NEARBY:
Green Park; Bond Street shopping; Royal Academy;
Buckingham Palace; Piccadilly Circus

GETTING THERE:
Green Park Underground Station; Victoria Railway Station;
London Heathrow Airport

☎ +44 (0)20 7769 4041
🌐 condenastjohansens.com/mayfair
🏠 Stratton Street, Mayfair, London W1J 8LT, England

Mayfair is the London neighbourhood where designer label junkies come to shop, where food fans enjoy fine eateries and art aficionados flock for the galleries and world-famous Christies and Sotheby's. And in the thick of it is The May Fair Hotel, totally in-keeping with its grand, high-styling London setting. It also offers that other very British trait: a touch of eccentricity. As you would expect, all the staple services of a leading city hotel are here, however, The May Fair stands apart for many reasons. Yes, the suites are bag-swinging spacious but it's their vibrant colour schemes, surprising detail and good old fashioned decadence that all come together to make even the most moneyed oil baron happy. Then there's May Fair Bar. On the surface, it's an extremely hip watering hole but look a little closer to uncover its seriously fine selection of vintage wines and champagnes. Quince restaurant is similarly surprising. Alongside its 21st-century take on age-old Eastern Mediterranean recipes, there's also an original cocktails and cupcakes afternoon tea option. Let's not forget the Cigar Room - an exclusive enclave at the heart of the hotel that recreates the outdoors - the Italian leather trimmed 201-seat private cinema, the exclusive casino and poker room, and inner sanctum that is the spa.

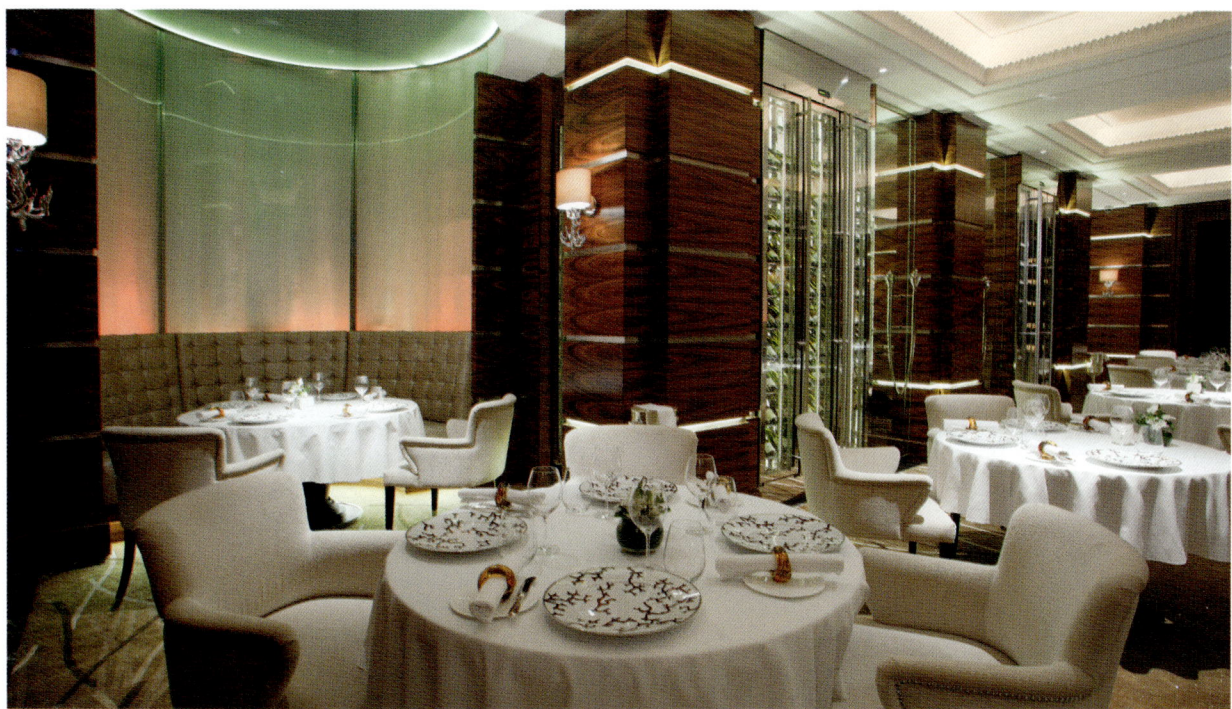

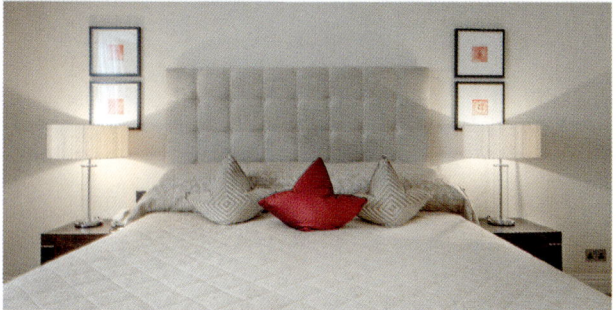

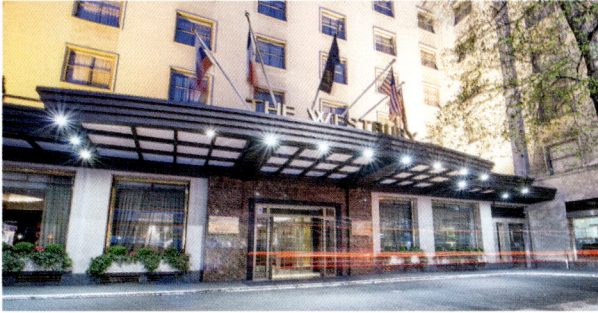

The Westbury

Central London location with worldwide appeal

London's your oyster at The Westbury, Mayfair. A matter of moments and you're in Bond Street, Regent Street, Oxford Street and Piccadilly Circus. With Soho, Leicester Square, Covent Garden, Green Park and Buckingham Palace a short walk away. Simply put, The Westbury is central. In the beating heart of the capital's fashionable Mayfair, it's a five-star sophisticate in an enviable location. Personal service (often lacking in large city hotels) is a trademark of The Westbury where each and every member of staff displays a marked passion to ensure every guest has a memorable stay. Complete with expert concierge and extremely knowledgeable, multi-lingual staff, guests from around the world each receive the star treatment and stay in bedrooms or suites graced with luxury touches at every turn. Each is an interior design masterclass on how to create a warm, comforting, homely space with the finest of fabrics, elegant muted colour schemes and on-trend fashion. Since 2011, Alyn Williams at The Westbury has been drawing a crowd for its fine dining feats of flavour, while the civilised Polo Bar with its impressive cocktail list and bar menu keep matters a little more informal. But for something alternative, there's the Japanese Tsukji Sushi Restaurant where all the ingredients are organic.

PRICE FROM:
£439

FEATURES:
Gym; Michelin Starred restaurant; Restaurant

ACTIVITIES:
Cycling; Sightseeing; Walking

NEARBY:
Mayfair shopping; West End theatres; Royal Academy of Arts; National Gallery; London Eye

GETTING THERE:
Bond Street Underground Station; King's Cross St Pancras Railway Station - Eurostar; London Heathrow Airport

+44 (0)20 7629 7755
condenastjohansens.com/westburymayfair
Bond Street, Mayfair, London W1S 2YF, England

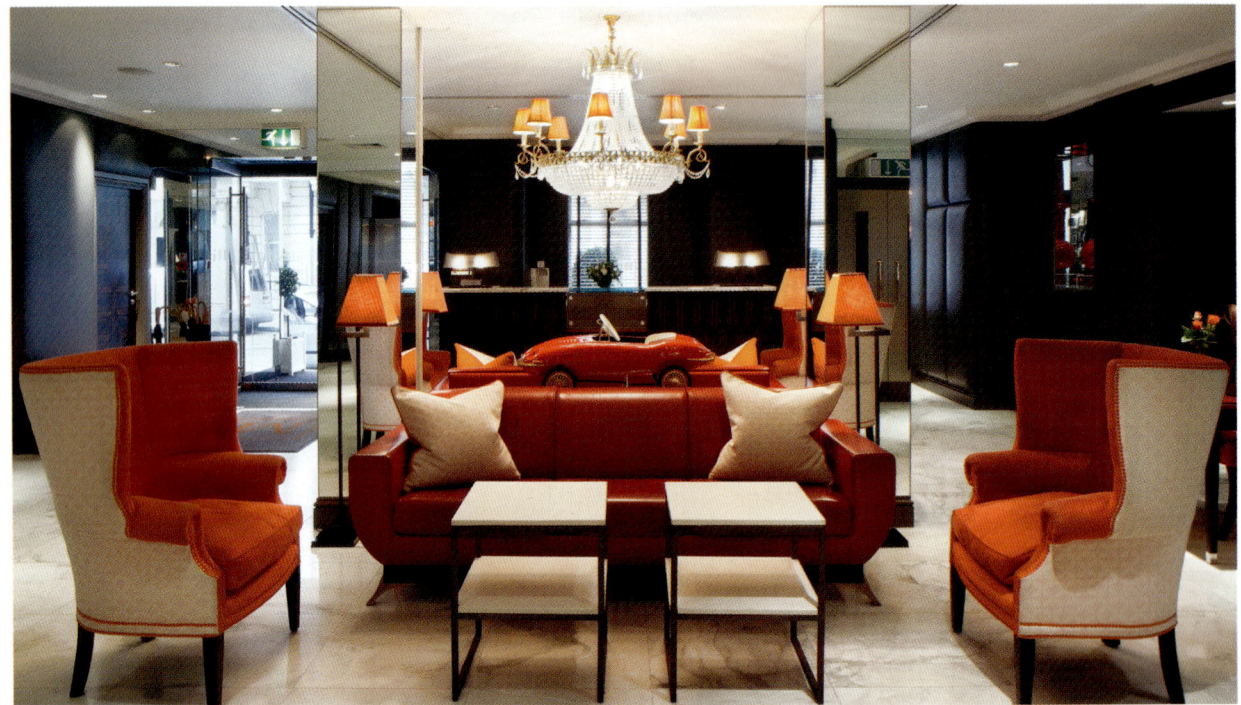

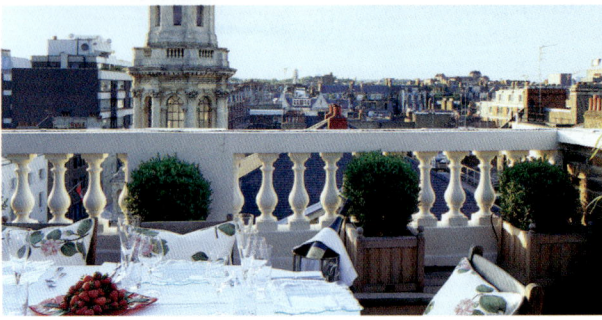

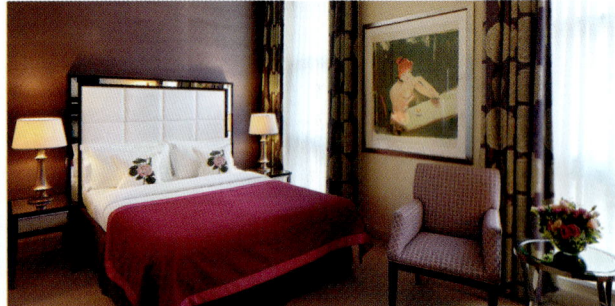

The Mandeville Hotel

Boutique panache in London's Marylebone

PRICE FROM:
£270

FEATURES:
Family friendly; Restaurant; Wheelchair access

ACTIVITIES:
Shopping; Sightseeing

NEARBY:
The Wallace Collection; Selfridges; Wigmore Hall; Regent's Park; Hyde Park

GETTING THERE:
Bond Street Underground Station; Victoria Railway Station; London Heathrow Airport

☎ +44 (0)20 7935 5599
🌐 condenastjohansens.com/mandeville
🏠 Mandeville Place, Marylebone, London W1U 2BE, England

Quirky yet sophisticated, progressive whilst old school, blissfully quiet but centrally located, The Mandeville Hotel in London's Marylebone Village cleverly manages it all. Funky enough for the fashionistas and retro glam enough for the traditionalists, The Mandeville is a central London hotel for everyone offering a highly personalised service. Harley, Oxford, Bond and Regent Streets are all within walking distance; Regent's and Hyde Parks too. Back inside, the expertly furnished guest rooms and suites are dressed in nothing but the finest fabrics put together by some of the leading London design houses. From the town house apartment-style terrace suite with its indulgent pink bathroom and roof terrace to each stylish single room, the superior level of quality remains the same. Achieving an equally high level of hospitality is The Mandeville's Reform Social and Grill. Channelling a gentleman's club vibe, its typically British menu includes classic favourites alongside elegant dishes for breakfast, Sunday brunch, lunch and dinner. No visit is complete without enjoying a superb Vintage or Gentleman's Afternoon Tea (Festive Afternoon Teas from November too) and browse through the cocktail list of British classics made with some of the finest spirits distilled in the UK. For your next event: book the Red Room. Coloured red for vitality and ambition, it positively encourages success.

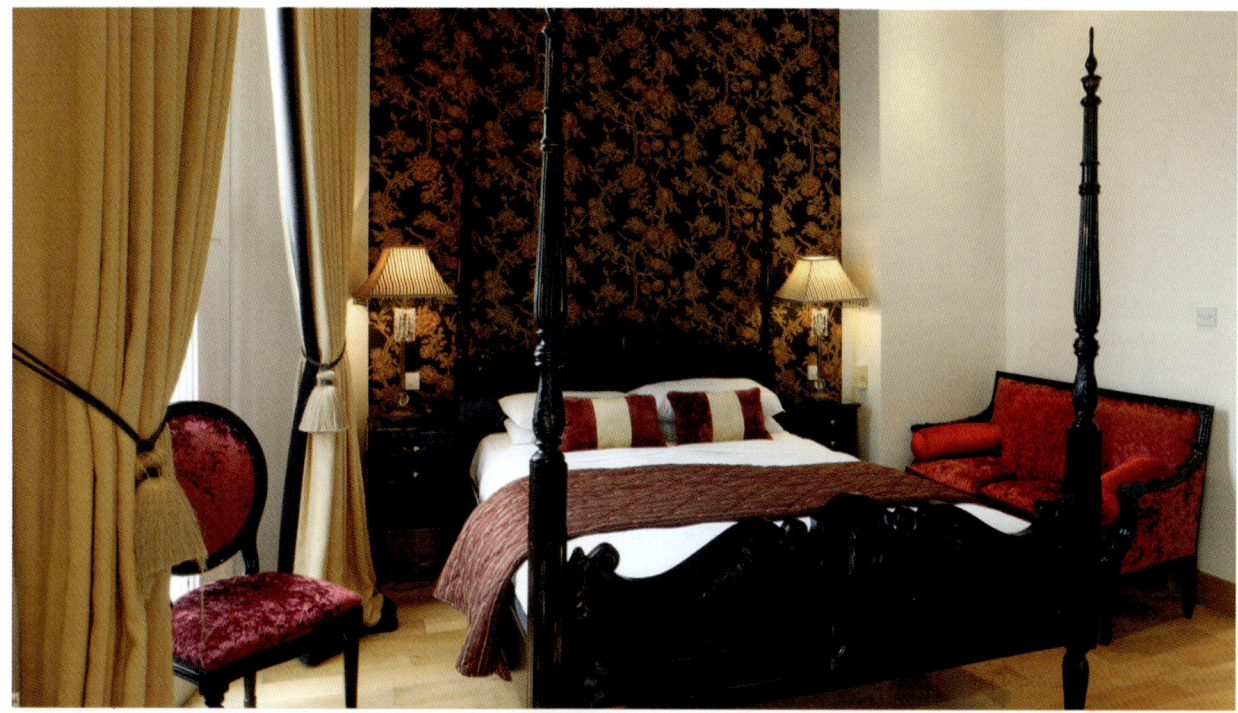

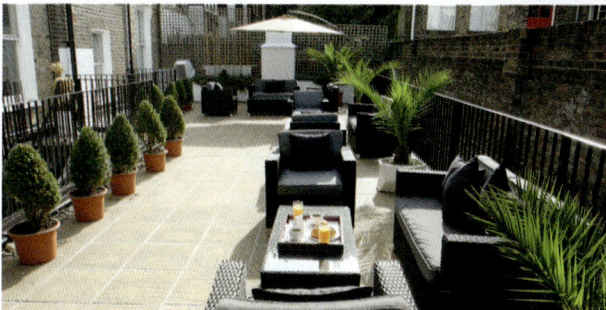
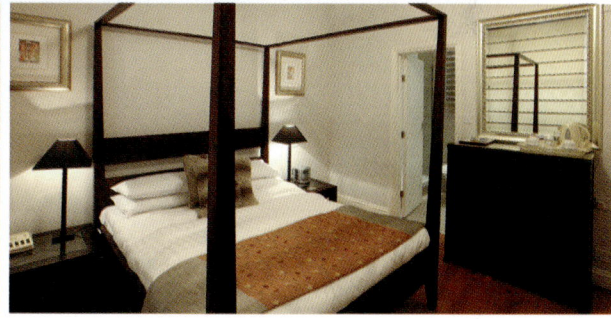

New Linden Hotel

Your Notting Hill home with an Oriental flair

The New Linden Hotel in Notting Hill is a little gem with instant appeal. Set within one of London's pretty white town houses in a peaceful residential street, you're in the heart of the cosmopolitan Notting Hill neighbourhood, a short walk from Portobello Road Market and within easy reach of various tourist hot spots. You're also just a few steps from the fashionable Westbourne Grove where the annual Notting Hill Carnival passes through. Transformed into a 50-bedroom bolthole, none of the building's Victorian charm has been lost. Beyond the ornate entrance pillars are stylish bedrooms and suites in palettes of cream, brown, red and black with an Oriental panache alongside trendy minimal furnishings, high-tech entertainment units and stunning marble, limestone and slate bathrooms. Clever interior design uses every inch of the building with some bedrooms particularly cosy, however, the high-end finishes and use of lavish fabrics and materials such as silk, velvet and the finest cotton create an incredibly lavish and comfortable setting. If staying with friends or the children, Triple and Family rooms are ideal while the Honeymoon Suite is The New Linden's crowning glory complete with Jacuzzi bath and private terrace. Head on down to the lower ground floor for a freshly prepared breakfast each morning or weather permitting, go outside to the communal terrace.

PRICE FROM:
£120

FEATURES:
Family friendly

ACTIVITIES:
Shopping; Sightseeing

NEARBY:
Madame Tussauds; Whiteleys of Bayswater; Hyde Park; Kensington Palace Gardens

GETTING THERE:
Notting Hill Underground Station; Paddington Railway Station; London Heathrow Airport

+44 (0)20 7221 4321 ☎
condenastjohansens.com/newlindenhotel 🌐
58-60 Leinster Square, Notting Hill, London W2 4PS, England 🏠

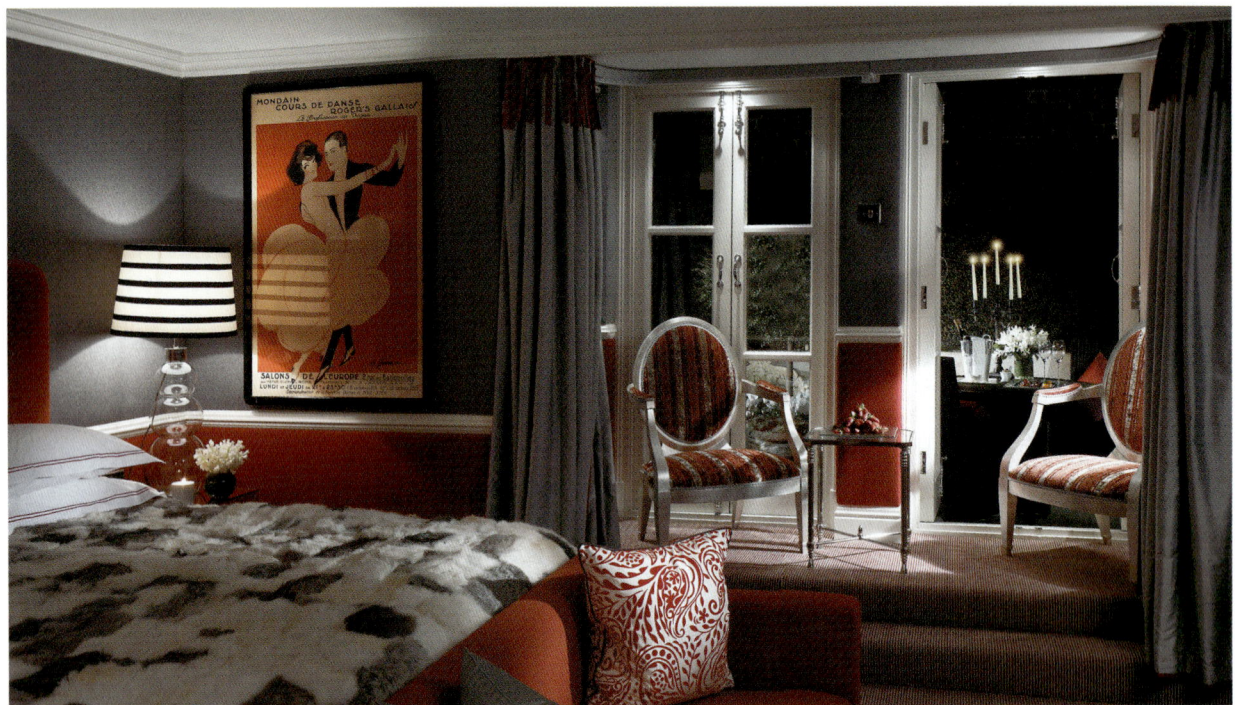

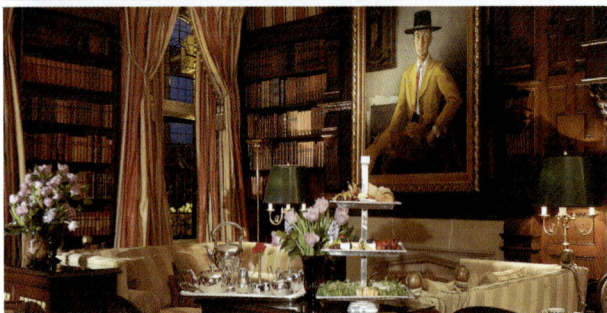
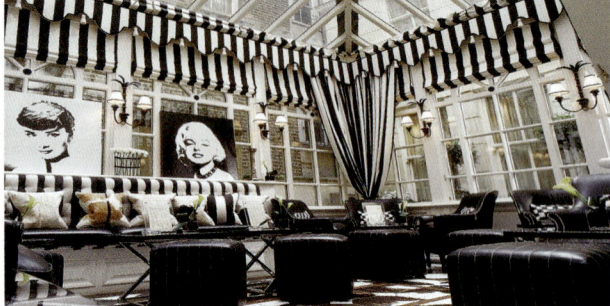

The Milestone Hotel and Apartments

London Kensington's premier address and premier hotel

PRICE FROM:
£354

FEATURES:
Family friendly; Gym; Pet friendly; Pool; Spa

ACTIVITIES:
Horse riding; Shopping; Sightseeing

NEARBY:
Kensington Palace and Gardens; Royal Albert Hall; Buckingham Palace; Harrods

GETTING THERE:
Paddington Railway Station; London Heathrow Airport; London Gatwick Airport

☎ +44 (0)20 7917 1000
🌐 condenastjohansens.com/milestone
🏠 1 Kensington Court, London W8 5DL, England

Opposite Kensington Palace & Gardens (the London residence of the Duke and Duchess of Cambridge and son Prince George), just a five-minute walk from the Royal Albert Hall and around the corner from Harrods and Harvey Nichols, is The Milestone Hotel and Apartments. The throbbing heart of London's most exclusive neighbourhood, this is the Royal Borough of Kensington with Hyde Park, upscale shopping, popular museums and endless tourist attractions on its doorstep. The Milestone's blend of personal service (complete a guest preference form prior to arrival to receive all your favourite treats), family and pet-friendly policies, opulent comfort and inspired cuisine see it winning accolades year after year. With a staff to guest ratio of 2:1 it's no wonder. Each room, suite and apartment is utterly different, fashioned with fine fabrics, fresh flowers, antique furnishings and rare works of art. The club-like Stables Bar is a cosy spot for a drink (try one of Markus' cocktails) and the chic black and white conservatory is ideal for intimate meetings, teas and light snacks while the sophisticated Cheneston's Restaurant rustles up some of the finest cuisine in the city. Burn off all this indulgence with a trip to the fitness centre complete with resistance pool, sauna and therapy treatments. The Milestone's philosophy: "no request is too large, no detail too small."

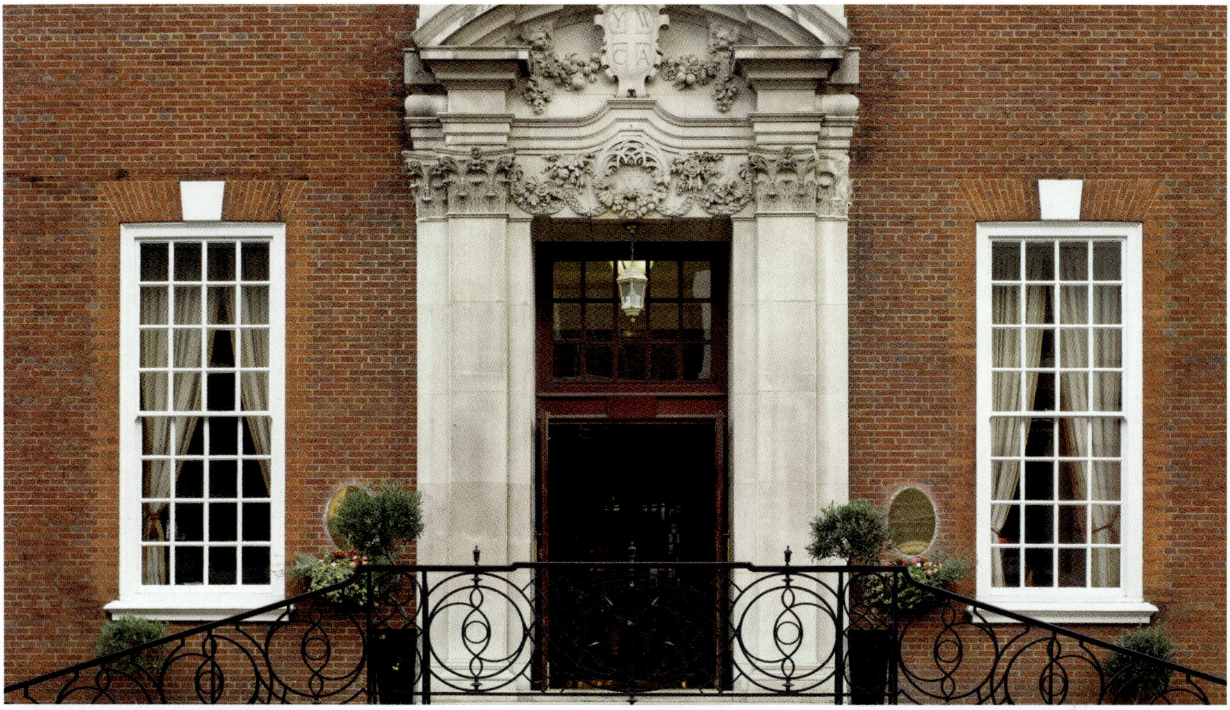

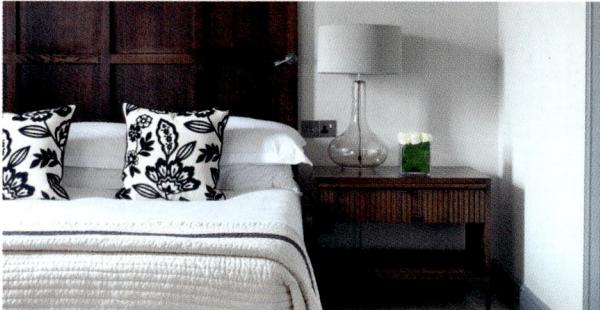
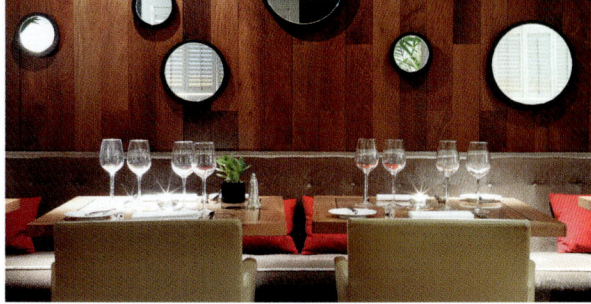

The Bloomsbury Hotel

Neo-Georgian timeless elegance in central London's leafy Bloomsbury

Reassuringly traditional whilst refreshingly fashionable, The Bloomsbury Hotel is minutes from London's Theatreland, Covent Garden and Oxford Street. It's also around the corner from The British Museum in the district of Bloomsbury, a mass of formal green squares and architectural significance. The Bloomsbury Hotel is located within a neo-Georgian building designed by the renowned British architect, Sir Edwin Landseer Lutyens (best known for the Cenotaph in Whitehall). As such, an essence of orderliness and classic British style permeates throughout but there's nothing stuffy or pretentious about it with an interior that's all about refined yet comfortable living accompanied by friendly, unfussy service. Bold fabrics, striking colours and geometric lines in the rooms and suites lend a contemporary edge with luxury details such as duck down pillows and duvets, 300-count linen, underfloor bathroom heating and complimentary WiFi. Studio Suites are the spacious, king-size option for the ultimate experience. Just like the traditional spirit of the building itself, the Landseer Bar and Restaurant is a celebration of traditional British dishes given the gourmet treatment with Executive Chef Paul O'Brien. Afternoon tea in Lutyens Lounge is the quintessential English treat. Check out: the hidden chapel that can be booked for special events.

PRICE FROM:
£235

FEATURES:
Family friendly; Gym; Restaurant; Wheelchair access

ACTIVITIES:
Shopping; Sightseeing

NEARBY:
British Museum; Oxford Street; Covent Garden; West End theatres; Trafalgar Square

GETTING THERE:
Tottenham Court Road Undergound Station; King's Cross St Pancras Railway Station - Eurostar; London City Airport

+44 (0)20 7347 1000 ☎
condenastjohansens.com/bloomsbury 🌐
16-22 Great Russell Street, Bloomsbury, London WC1B 3NN, 🏠
England

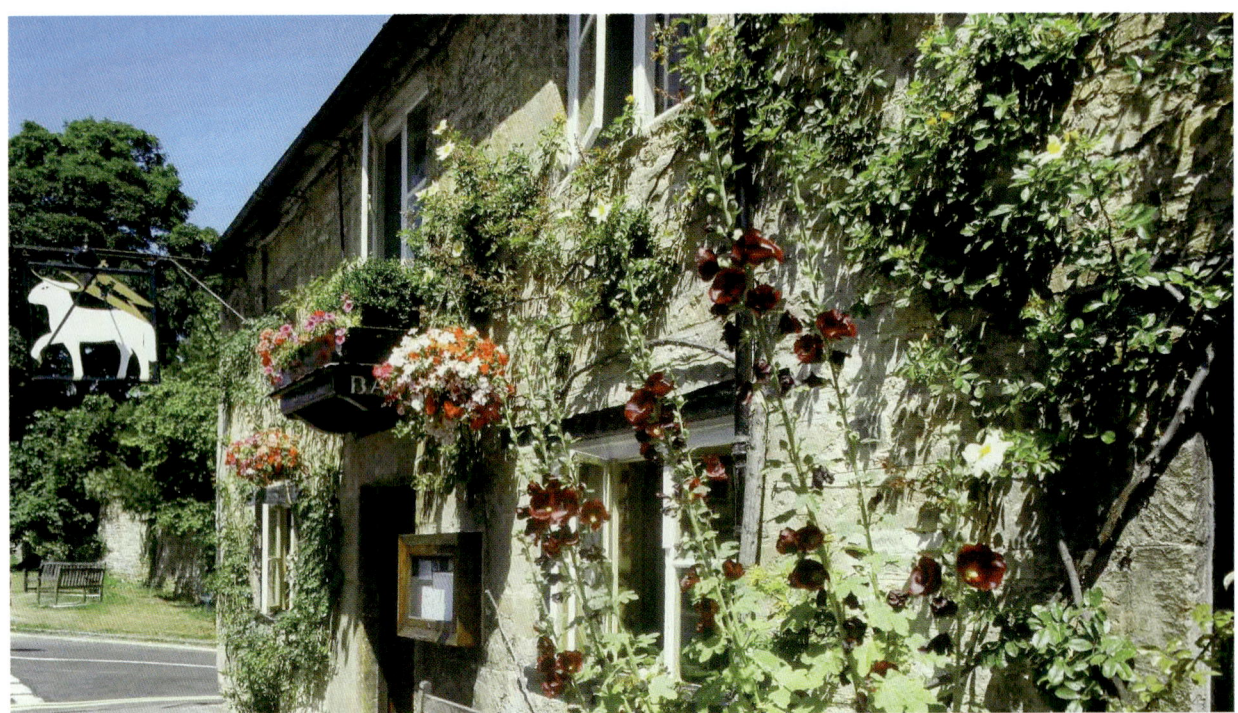

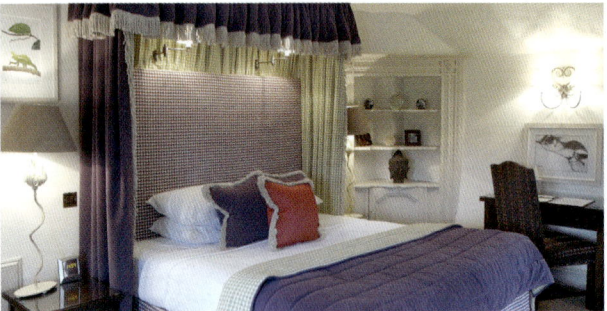

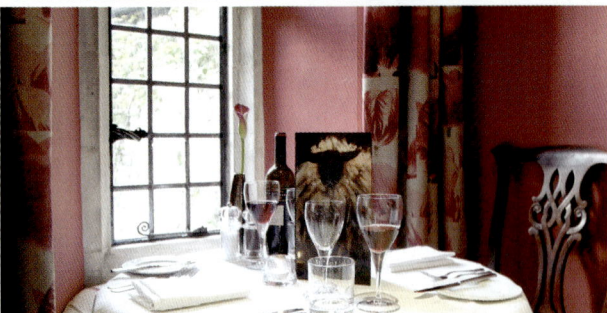

The Lamb Inn

The quintessential English inn within the archetypal Cotswolds village

PRICE FROM:
£160

FEATURES:
Pet friendly; Restaurant

ACTIVITIES:
Fishing; Golf; Horse riding

NEARBY:
River Windrush; Oxford, Cheltenham, Stow-on-the-Wold; Cheltenham Racecourse

GETTING THERE:
A40; M40; London Heathrow Airport

☎ +44 (0)1993 823155
🌐 condenastjohansens.com/lambinnburford
🏠 Sheep Street, Burford, Oxfordshire OX18 4LR, England

It doesn't take too much imagination to picture Burford in its 15th-century sheep market town heyday. Little has changed to its medieval streets lined with distinctive Cotswolds stone cottages and green lawns, except maybe the antique shops and exclusive boutiques that now trade their wares instead. On Sheep Street, a collection of former weavers' cottages has provided the setting for the picture-postcard Lamb Inn since 1718. And today, it's the embodiment of what a top-rate inn should be: cosy comfort, historic nuance, good food, fine drink and outstanding service. A contemporary punch complements the original features such as centuries-old flagstone flooring, antiques and beckoning log fires, with a fresh, chic country home style of bold colour pairings and richly patterned fabrics. Each of the 17 bedrooms is a romantic spot, however, families or groups of friends, perhaps visiting for a party or special occasion, are wise to reserve The Allium Room and connecting Rosie Room to create a two-floor apartment. Facing the pretty courtyard, The Lamb Inn Bar celebrates locally sourced produce (don't forget to sample its English real ales on tap) while the coveted, more formal Lamb Restaurant specialises in fresh fish and offers a fantastic vegetarian menu option. In the summer you can eat outside in the walled garden.

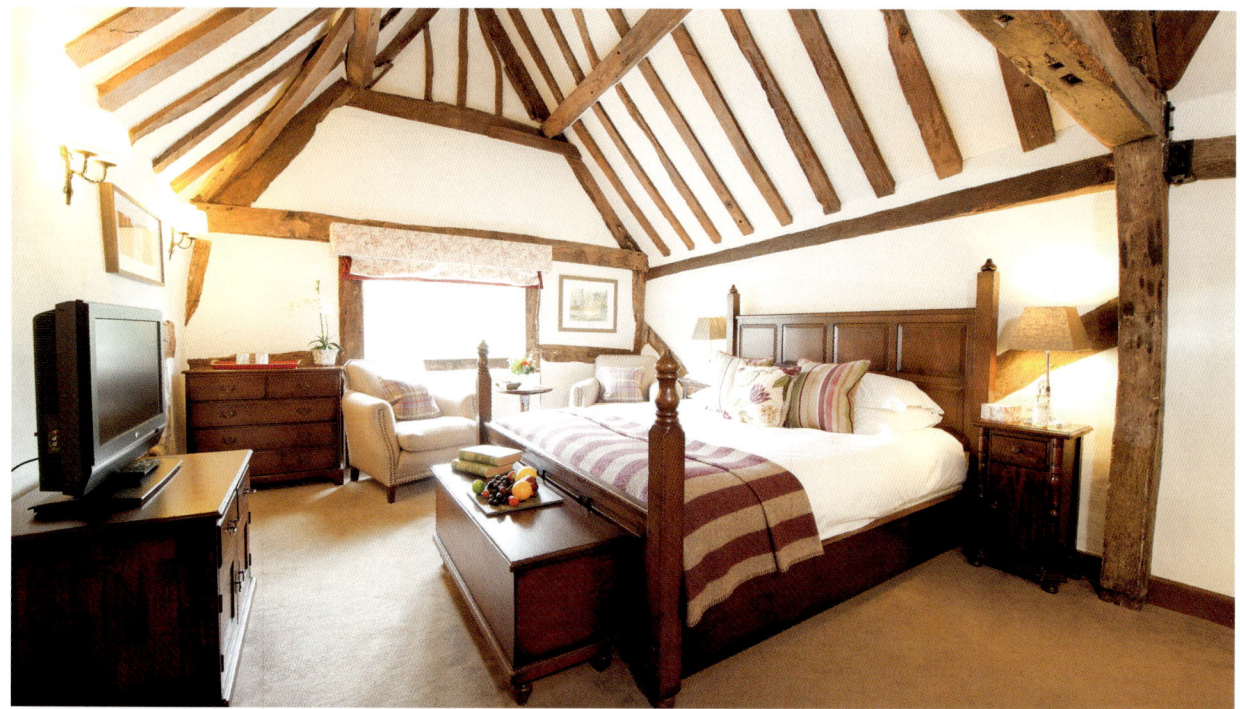

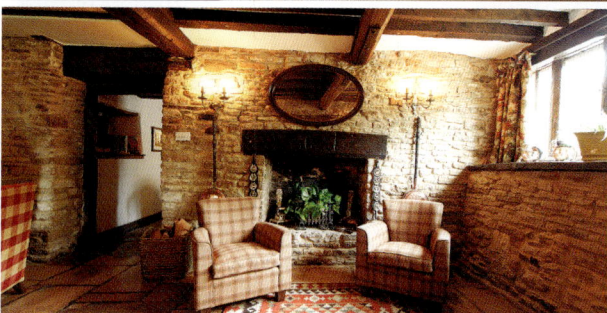

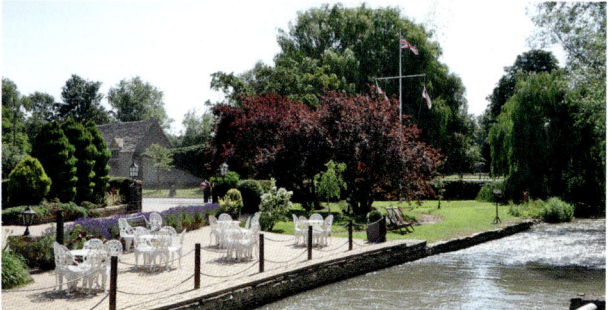

Old Swan & Minster Mill

Charm of the past and convenience of the present meet at Minster Lovell

The de Savary family's latest gift to the boutique hotel scene is the Cotswolds treasure: Old Swan & Minster Mill. With the de Savary's authority on unpretentious, upscale hospitality, the idyllic setting of Old Minster and the Old Swan's inherent charm, this centuries-old inn is setting new standards in traditional English accommodation and gastro-pub dining. Oak beams, log fires and the essence of bygone years create the archetypal Cotswolds scene while a touch of modern grace keeps matters fresh and unstuffy. Set alongside the River Windrush (fishing can be arranged here), the Old Swan stands within tens of acres of prize-winning floral and kitchen gardens and wild-flower meadows. An apiary, tennis court, children's activity area, playroom and two spa treatment rooms offering Yon-Ka treatments complete the picture alongside the 16 guest rooms and suites. Draped in rich fabrics, bedrooms are relaxed and romantic; some overlook the gardens and meadows beyond. A laid-back vibe permeates through the various dining rooms and bars, of which there are four private areas to choose from depending on the size of the party, plus numerous snugs for couples. (The Malt House located in the gardens can host up to 100.) Whichever you choose you'll enjoy fresh local ingredients crafted into hearty dishes. Note to dog lovers: canine companions are welcome in allocated rooms.

PRICE FROM:
£155

FEATURES:
Family friendly; Helipad; Pet friendly; Restaurant; Wheelchair access

ACTIVITIES:
Fishing; Horse riding; Tennis

NEARBY:
Oxford; Blenheim Palace; Cheltenham Racecourse; Cotswold Wildlife Park and Gardens; Sudeley Castle and Gardens

GETTING THERE:
A40; M40 jct 8 and 9; London Heathrow Airport

+44 (0)1993 774441
condenastjohansens.com/milloldswan
Minster Lovell, Near Burford, Oxfordshire OX29 0RN, England

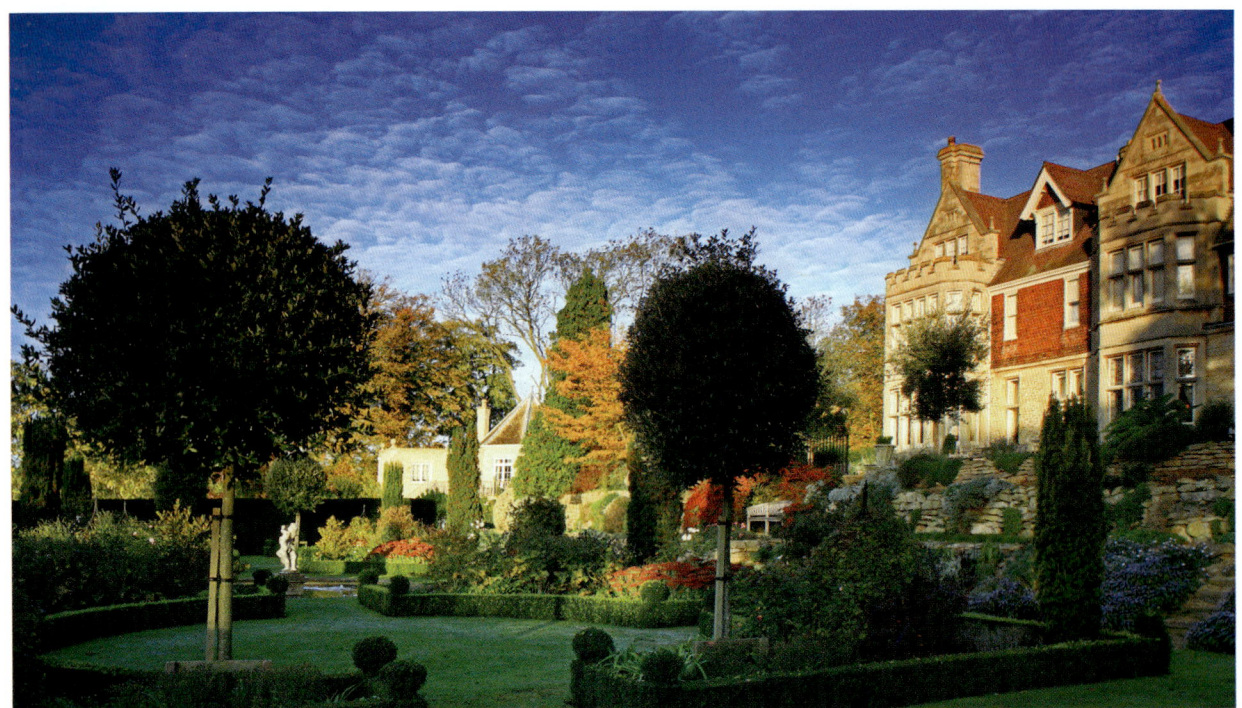

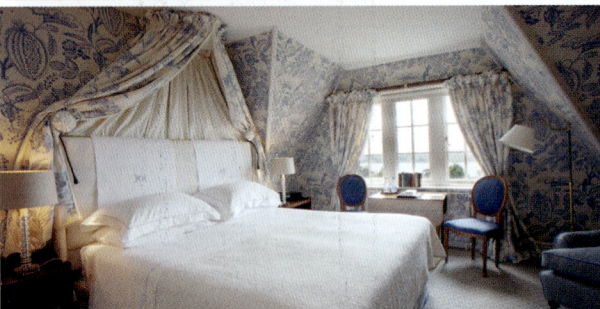

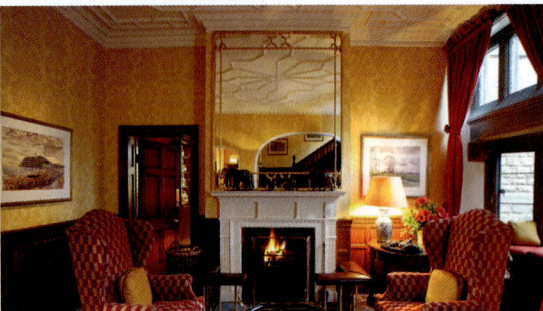

Hambleton Hall

Where comfort, food and wine rule the day at Rutland Water

PRICE FROM:
£265

FEATURES:
Helipad; Michelin Starred restaurant; Pet friendly; Pool; Wheelchair access

ACTIVITIES:
Fishing; Golf; Walking

NEARBY:
Oakham; Hambleton Bakery; Rutland Water; Burghley House; Rockingham Castle

GETTING THERE:
A606; A1(M); East Midlands International Airport

☎ +44 (0)1572 756991
🌐 condenastjohansens.com/hambletonhall
🏠 Hambleton, Oakham, Rutland LE15 8TH, England

Hambleton Hall, overlooking Rutland Water, started its life as a hunting lodge for Walter Marshall in 1881, whose penchant for socialising and enjoying the high life gained him a reputation for fine dinner parties. Following his death, younger sister Mrs Astley-Cooper continued the convivial hospitality at Hambleton Hall hosting guests such as Noël Coward and today, it is owners Tim and Stefa Hart who uphold Hambleton's welcoming reception. With more than 30 years at the helm, the Harts have established Hambleton Hall as an exceptional lakeside hotel that continues to attact acclaim for achieving near perfection. Artful displays of flowers from local hedgerows and the garden add splashes of colour to the plush bedrooms. And for extra privacy there's the Croquet Pavilion, a two-bedroom cottage complete with lake-viewing terrace, living and breakfast rooms. With a restaurant that would make Walter proud, Chef Aaron Patterson and his brigade's Michelin-Starred food offers strongly seasonal menus. Grouse, Scottish ceps, chanterelles, partridge and woodcock all appear when they're supposed to, alongside vegetables, herbs and salads from Hambleton's garden. Equally as fine as the food, the award-winning wine list is a varied selection from boutique vineyards at an impossibly reasonable price. Each must pass the owners' taste-test to make the grade.

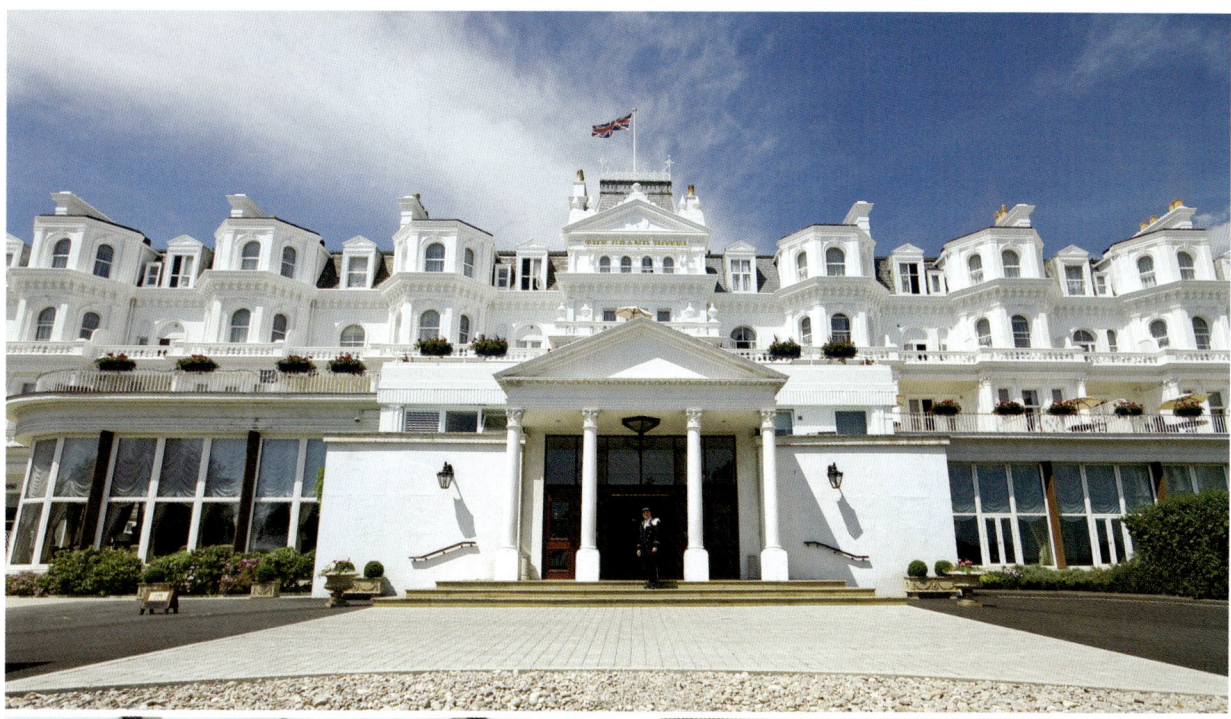

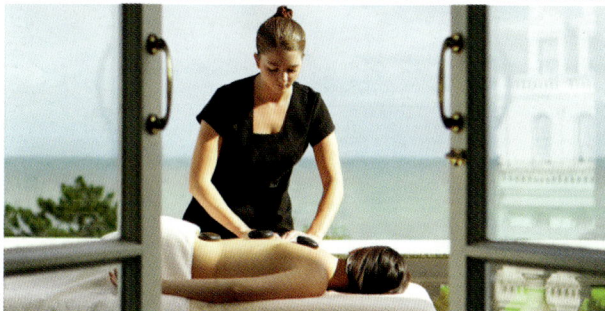
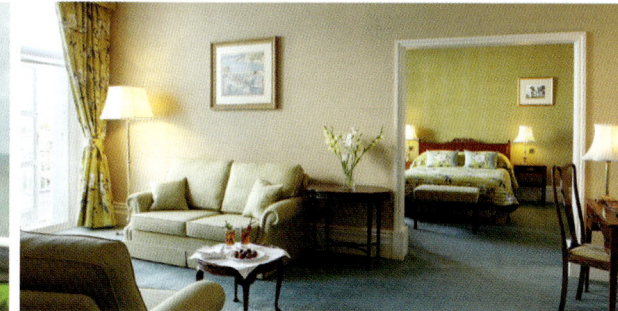

The Grand Hotel

Seaside high life on Eastbourne's Victorian parade

Officially Britain's "sunniest place" thanks to its sheltered south-easterly position, Eastbourne is a go-to destination for a spot of sea air. It's also a fascinating illustration of a Victorian seaside town as commissioned by wealthy landowner William Cavendish in 1859. The idea of a resort built "for gentlemen by gentlemen" resulted in grand, sprawling feats of architecture such as The Grand Hotel along Eastbourne's seafront. Behind The Grand's crisp-white façade lies an interior filled with natural light (thank you oversized windows and tall ceilings), flush with rich fabrics, fresh flowers and antique furnishings that appear brand new. Many of the 152 bedrooms are nothing less than vast, each one refurbished to include every comfort the demanding guest requires. But there are so many places within The Grand where you can simply kick back and while away the hours, not just in your room. The choice of mealtime options is impressive too. Try The Mirabelle Restaurant for fine dining at its modern European best; The Garden Restaurant for British classics with a modern twist. Cocktails, afternoon tea, private dining… it's all here. The opportunity to burn off some of those devoured calories also: The Grand's Health Club and Spa facilities include indoor and outdoor pools, a gym, sauna, spa bath, steam room, snooker tables, hair salon and eight treatment rooms.

PRICE FROM:
£230

FEATURES:
Family friendly; Pool; Restaurant; Sea views; Spa

ACTIVITIES:
Fishing; Golf; Horse riding

NEARBY:
South Downs Way National Park; The English Wine Centre; Theatres; Glyndebourne Opera

GETTING THERE:
A22; M23 jct 11; London Gatwick Airport

+44 (0)1323 412345
condenastjohansens.com/grandeastbourne
King Edward's Parade, Eastbourne, East Sussex BN21 4EQ, England

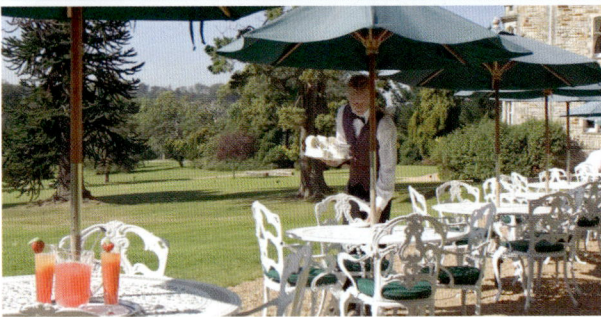

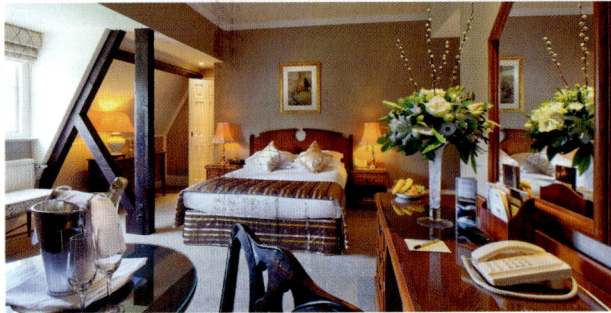

Ashdown Park Hotel and Country Club

The ultimate de-stresser in East Sussex countryside

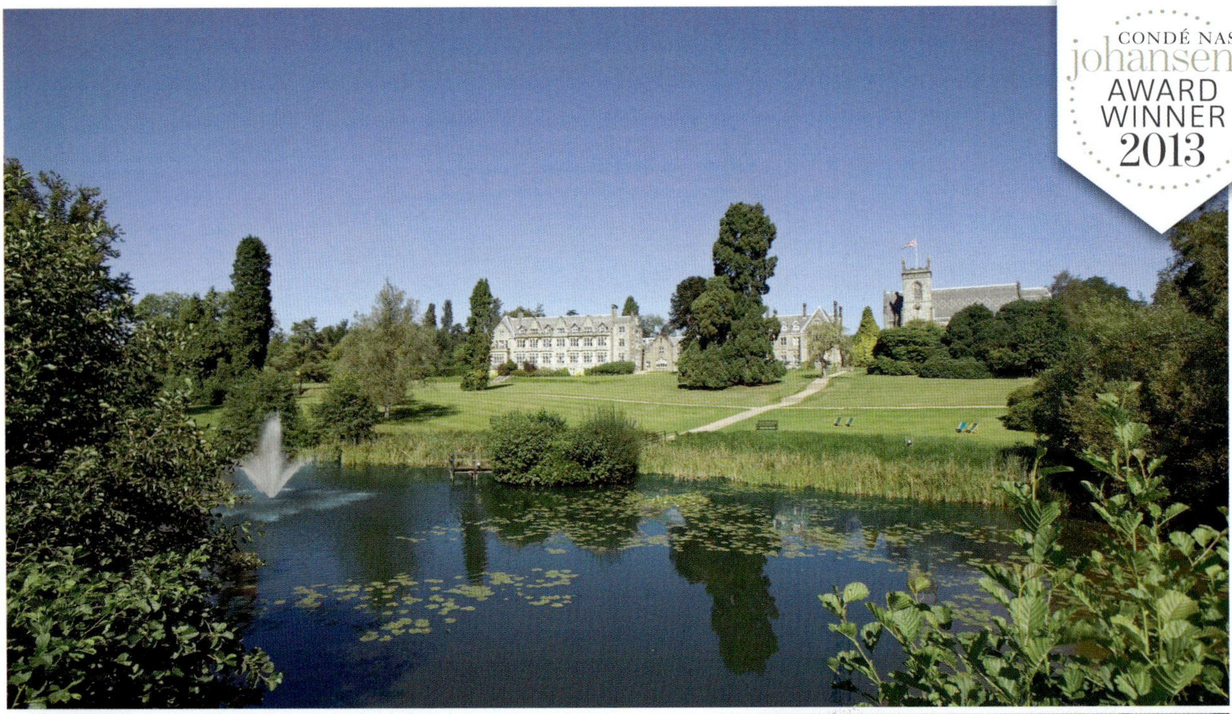

PRICE FROM:
£230

FEATURES:
Lake views; Pet friendly; Pool; Restaurant; Spa

ACTIVITIES:
Fishing; Golf; Tennis

NEARBY:
Bluebell Railway; Lingfield Park Racecourse; Wakehurst Place; Hever Castle

GETTING THERE:
M23 jct 10; East Grinstead Railway Station; London Gatwick Airport

☎ +44 (0)1342 824988
🌐 condenastjohansens.com/ashdownpark
🏠 Wych Cross, Forest Row, East Sussex RH18 5JR, England

Ashdown Park Hotel and Country Club, East Sussex, breaks the mould of the traditional, grand country hotel. Yes, it has all the hallmarks of a stately, plush, sprawling estate but it's also somehow intimate, comfortable and unpretentious. It's a clever balancing act pleasing those seeking classic British hospitality and others hankering for up-to-the-minute spa and leisure facilities. The setting alone, of everlasting green countryside (where deer roam freely), is enough to place a content smile on anyone's face. In fact, regaining perspective and finding inner calm comes easy with woodland walks (or jogging trails if feeling athletic) in the surrounding Ashdown Forest whose meditative powers are strong. Whether visiting with family or getting away with a loved one, Ashdown's eight room categories suit every occasion; each one an immaculate country chic retreat. But head to the Country Club for some adrenaline pumping action where the gym, tennis courts and aerobics studio reside alongside The Spa that takes the edge off. Here, treatments have been specifically created for men and women. Complimentary amenities include a heated indoor pool, steam room, sauna and 18 hole par 3 golf course. Perfect days end with dinners at the Anderida Restaurant where a resident pianist and wonderful views set the scene.

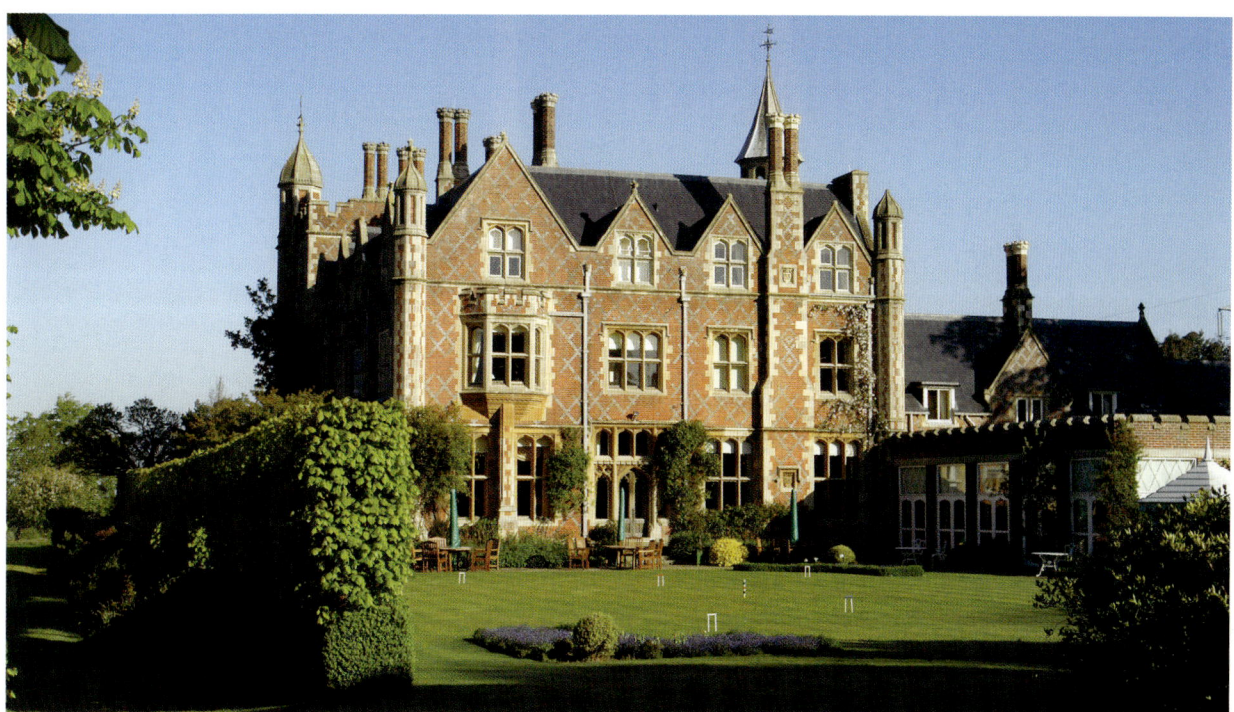

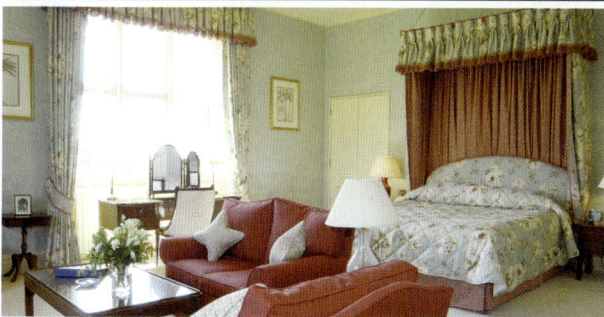

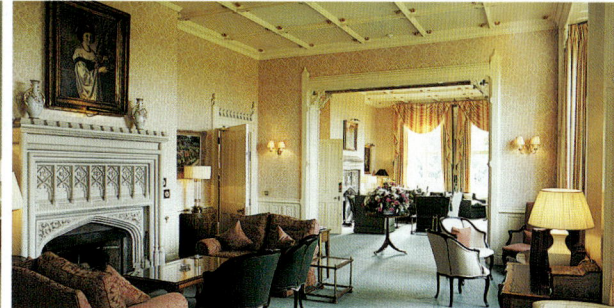

Horsted Place Country House Hotel

Serene Sussex Downs country estate

Horsted Place Country House Hotel is a splendid Victorian Gothic house built in 1850. Set in rolling Sussex countryside, on the edge of the South Downs, it's perfectly placed for two championship golf courses and the 600-year-old Glyndebourne. The enchanting grounds and formal gardens offer tennis and croquet and a nugget of royal history: a myrtle tree grown from a sprig of Queen Victoria's wedding bouquet. You'll also be walking in the steps of Queen Elizabeth II and Prince Philip who have frequented this once-private estate. Horsted is a country house hotel with all the accoutrements one would expect from a sumptuous period drama. 24-hour room service, silver cloches and Egyptian cotton sheets, a log fire in the Drawing Room, canapés on the terrace and a pianist at dinner being just some of the luxuries available. Complimentary use of Horsted Health Club, just a two-minute drive away, allows you to keep to your fitness regime before tucking into traditional afternoon tea guilt-free. This is certainly something to write home about: lavish and elegantly indulgent with finger sandwiches, crumbly scones and the lightest meringues. Everything is home-made (the restaurant's award-winning chef changes the à la carte menu daily). That's the key to Horsted: the extra touch.

PRICE FROM:
£145

FEATURES:
Helipad; Restaurant

ACTIVITIES:
Golf; Tennis; Walking

NEARBY:
Lewes; Glyndebourne Opera; Sheffield Park gardens; Bluebell Railway; East Sussex National Golf Course

GETTING THERE:
On the A26; M23 jct 10; London Gatwick Airport;

+44 (0)1825 750581 ☎
condenastjohansens.com/horstedplace 🌐
Little Horsted, East Sussex TN22 5TS, England 🏠

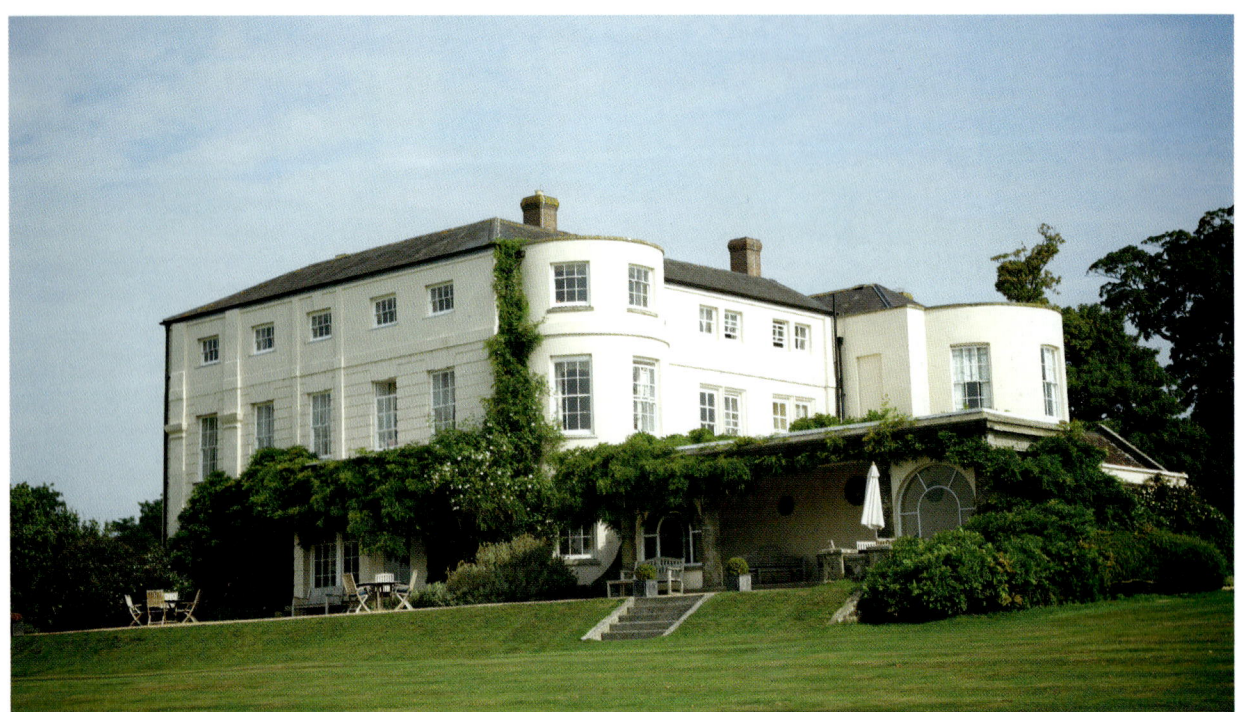

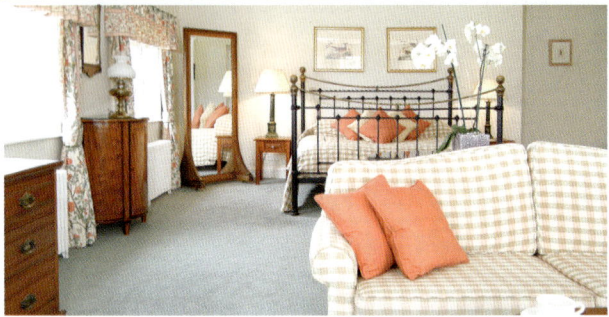

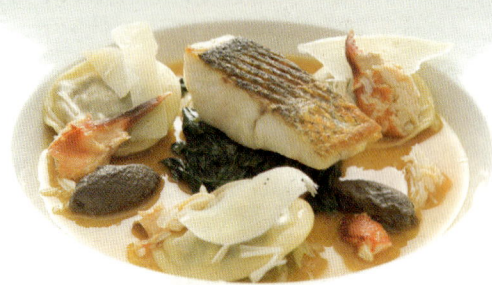

Newick Park Hotel & Country Estate

Upholding English country traditions in East Sussex

PRICE FROM:
£165

FEATURES:
Family friendly; Pet friendly; Pool; Restaurant; Wheelchair access

ACTIVITIES:
Golf; Shooting; Walking

NEARBY:
Lewes; Sheffield Park and Garden; Wakehurst Place; Opera at Glyndebourne; Bluebell Railway

GETTING THERE:
M23 jct 11; Uckfield Railway Station; London Gatwick Airport

☎ +44 (0)1825 723633
🌐 condenastjohansens.com/newickpark
🏠 Newick, Near Lewes, East Sussex BN8 4SB, England

Newick Park Hotel & Country Estate is a magnificent example of (Grade II* listed) Georgian splendour. Set to a beautiful backdrop of hundreds of acres of parkland and landscaped gardens, views take in the Longford River and South Downs National Park. This is the quintessential English countryside scene, however, Newick Park is conveniently close to the main road and rail routes (London Gatwick Airport is only 30 minutes away). Utterly tranquil and private with nothing but birdsong interrupting the silence, bedrooms are located in the Main House. Each looks out to the serene setting and expresses a classic country-chic style peppered with elegant antiques. For a touch of romance book one of the four-poster rooms, one of which is eight-foot wide, or one of the three double bedrooms located in The Granary situated two minutes from the Main House. In the dining room Head Chef Chris Moore presents a modern European menu prepared from ingredients grown in the hotel's Victorian Walled Garden (whenever possible). This is just one of the historical gardens on the estate. There is also The Dell, which was primarily planted in Victorian times containing a rare collection of royal ferns. The Dell provides a picture-perfect setting for dream weddings and private parties – business events too. Exclusive hire of Newick Park is available by appointment.

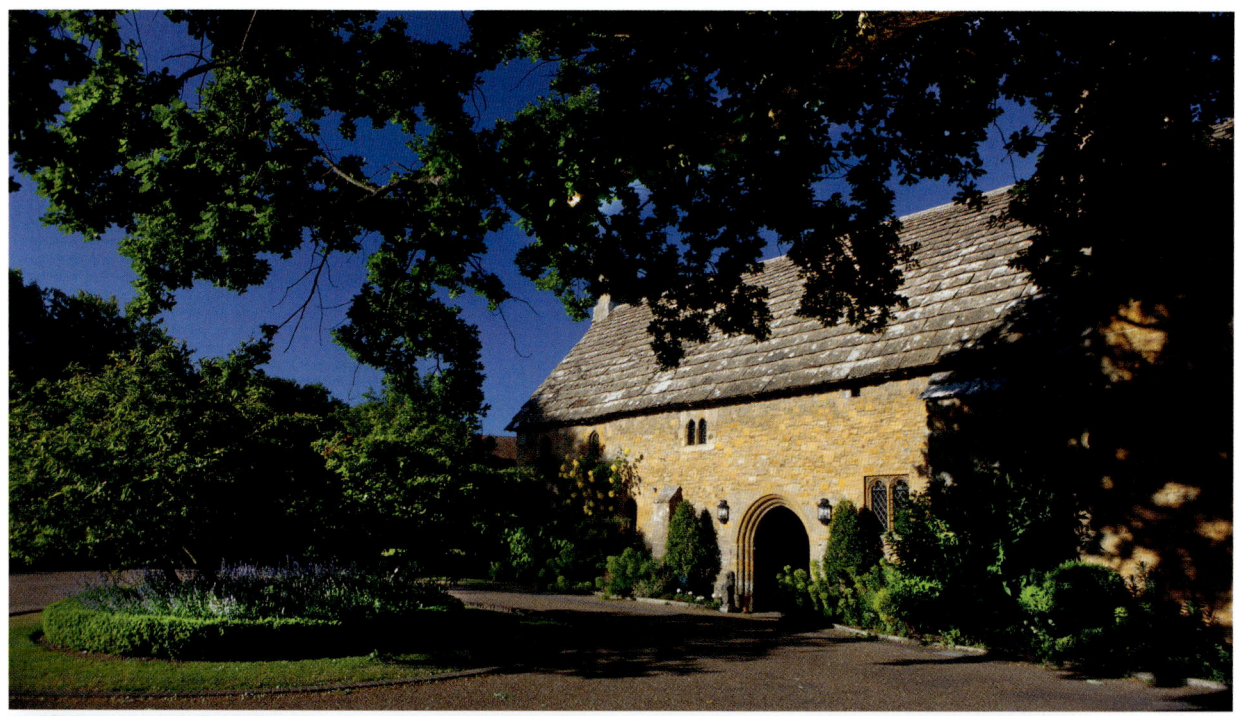

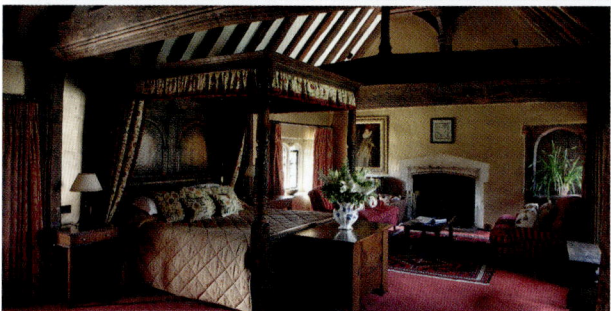
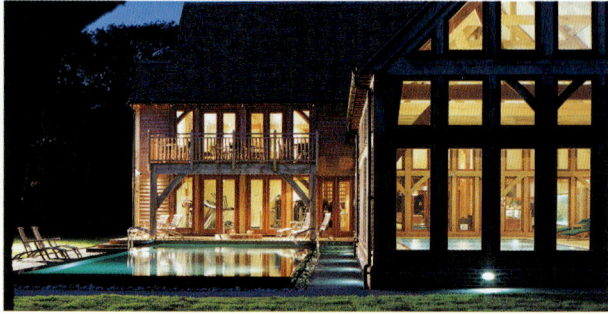

Bailiffscourt Hotel & Spa

The Middle Ages meets fanciful decadence near the Sussex Coast

Time travel is possible after all, or at least it is at Bailiffscourt Hotel & Spa in Climping. However, before you brush up on your flux-capacitor knowledge, it's worthwhile knowing that Baillifscourt was the vision of Lady Moyne (wife of Lord Moyne, aka Walter Guinness of the famed stout empire). Brought to reality by Amyas Phillips in 1933. By using authentic material salvaged from age-old buildings, this most-convincing Medieval House with six outbuildings (complete with gnarled 15th-century beams, gothic mullioned windows) and private parkland featuring a moat, resulted in a playground for the rich and famous of its day. Host to many a-bopping party, Baillifscourt was also attractive to many Bright Young Things (and perhaps some of Lord Moyne's political friends) because of its close proximity to Goodwood and unspoilt Climping beach. When the natural transition to luxurious hotel took place in 1948, the appeal of Baillifscourt remained as popular as ever. Now the four posters, open log fires, purpose-built spa, two tennis courts, croquet lawn and beautiful views across the countryside draw in a new generation of BYTs seeking good hospitality and great food. Menus at Tapestry Restaurant are eclectic, and in summer you can eat out in the rose-clad courtyard or walled garden.

PRICE FROM:
£259

FEATURES:
Family friendly; Pet friendly; Pool; Restaurant; Spa

ACTIVITIES:
Fishing; Golf; Tennis

NEARBY:
Arundel Castle; Goodwood Estate; Chichester Festival Theatre; Climping beach; Golf

GETTING THERE:
A259; M27 jct 1; London Gatwick Airport

+44 (0)1903 723511 ☎
condenastjohansens.com/bailiffscourt 🌐
Climping, Arundel, West Sussex BN17 5RW, England 🏠

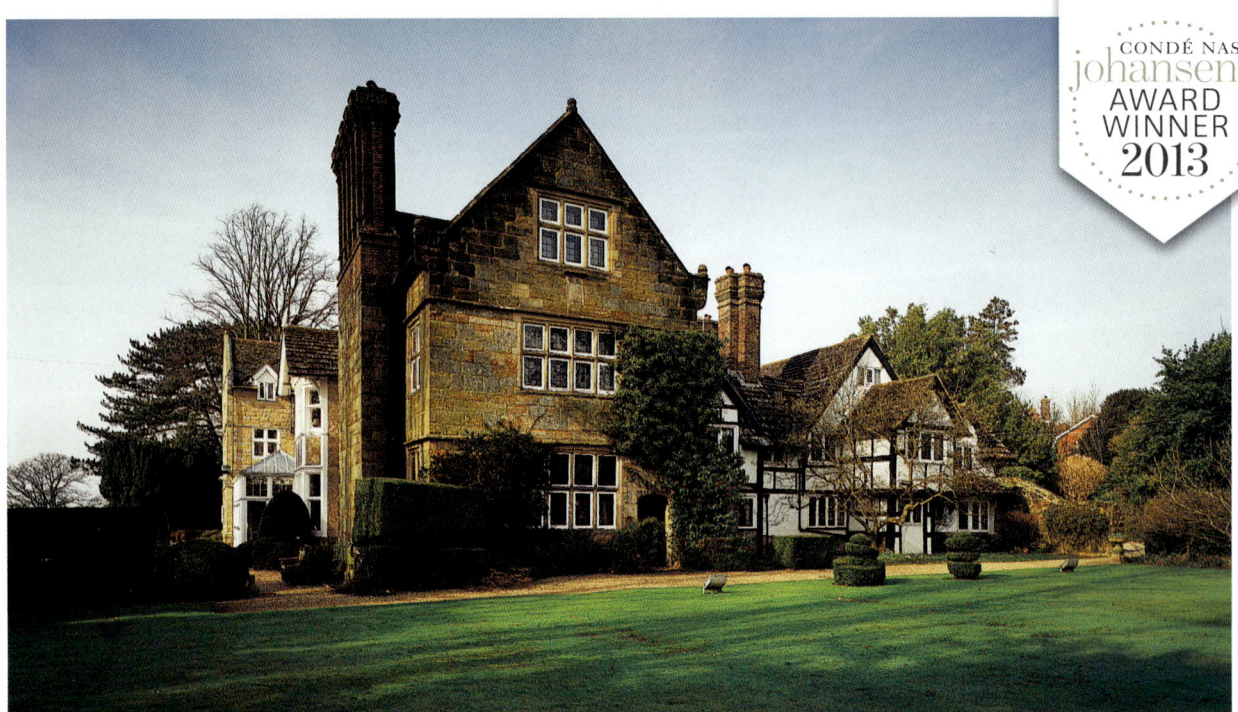

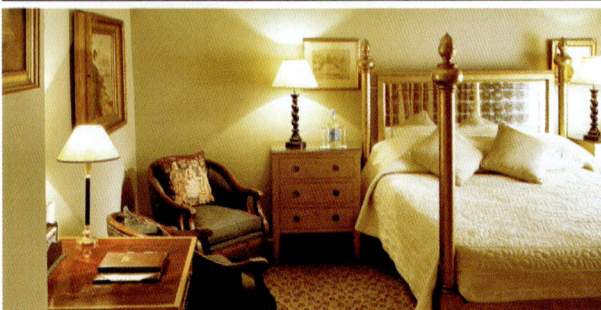

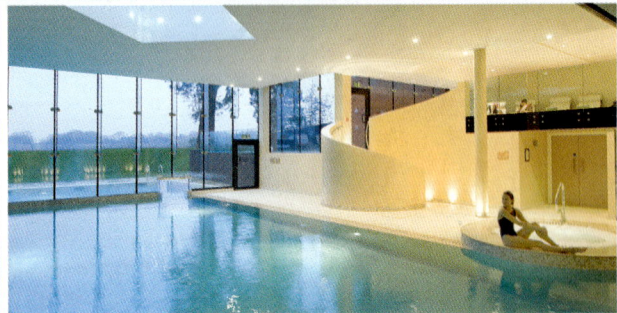

Ockenden Manor Hotel

Enchanting West Sussex Elizabethan manor house

PRICE FROM:
£190

FEATURES:
Family friendly; Michelin Starred restaurant; Pet friendly; Pool; Spa

ACTIVITIES:
Fishing; Golf; Horse riding

NEARBY:
Haywards Heath; Brighton; Bluebell Railway; Wakehurst and Nymans Gardens; Glyndebourne Opera

GETTING THERE:
A272; M23 jct 10; London Gatwick Airport

☎ +44 (0)1444 416111
🌐 condenastjohansens.com/ockendenmanor
⌂ Ockenden Lane, Cuckfield, West Sussex RH17 5LD, England

Brimming with tales of yore and packed with personality, Ockenden Manor Hotel snuggles within acres of private gardens and parkland in the oil-painting pretty Tudor village of Cuckfield. An Elizabethan manor house, Ockenden's history has been traced back as far as 1520. Initially a family home, then a Jewish boys school and residence for Canadian troops during WWII, Ockenden's life as a hotel began in the late 1940s. Ideally positioned for exploring Sussex and Kent (the chalky hills of the South Downs, Cuckmere Valley, Brighton and Lewes), the manor looks out to far-reaching West Sussex countryside and from the minute you step through its doors you're swept away by warm hospitality and culinary delights. The 28 distinctive bedrooms and suites (named after family members who once lived here) have fascinating quirks and nooks and crannies at every turn. Climb the private staircase to Elizabeth, indulge in a Victorian-style bath in Hugh or enjoy the huge four-poster bed in Charles. No visit to Ockenden is complete without sampling the creative Michelin-Starred cuisine of Head Chef Stephen Crane. Choose from fixed price menus or the seven-course Tasting Menu in this utterly romantic restaurant looking out to sweeping vistas of the garden and beyond. Must do: a trip to Ockenden's luxury spa set within the walled gardens.

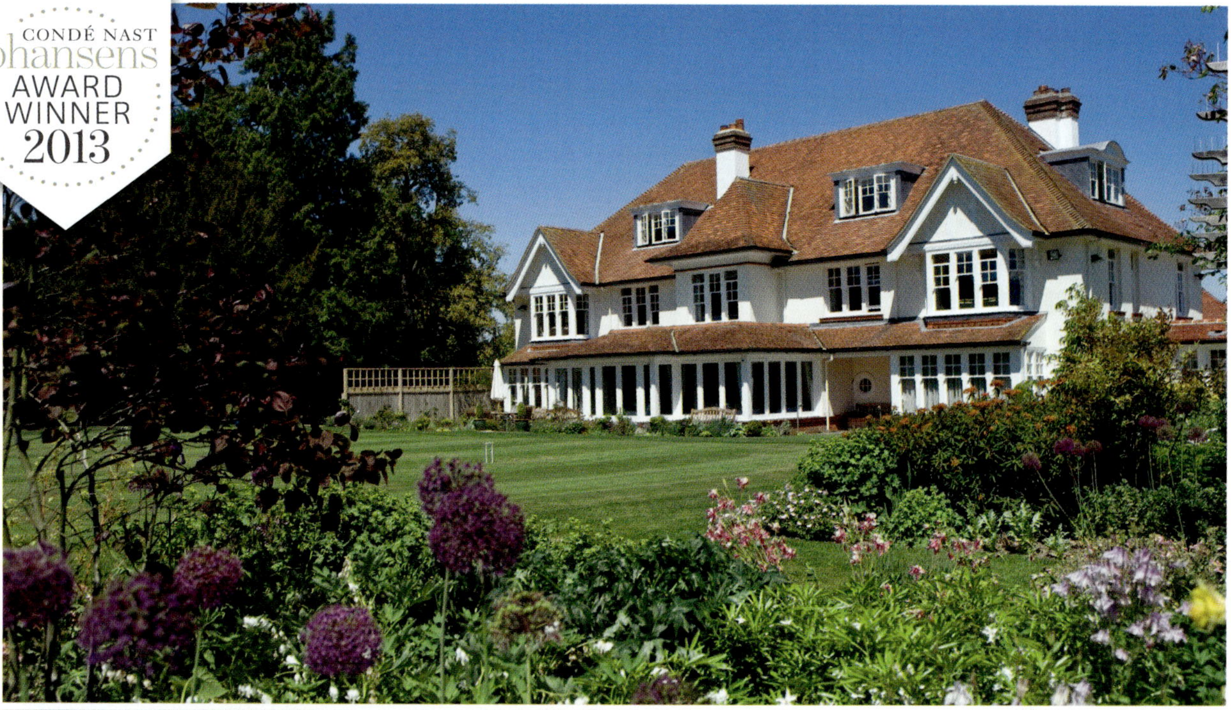

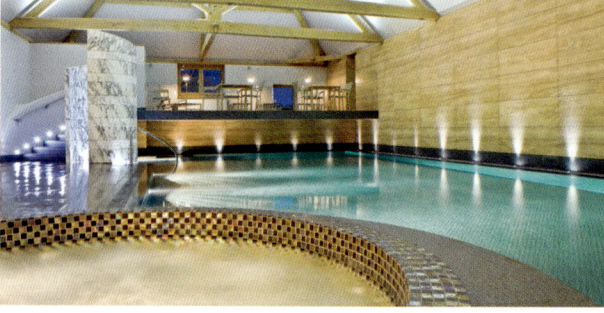

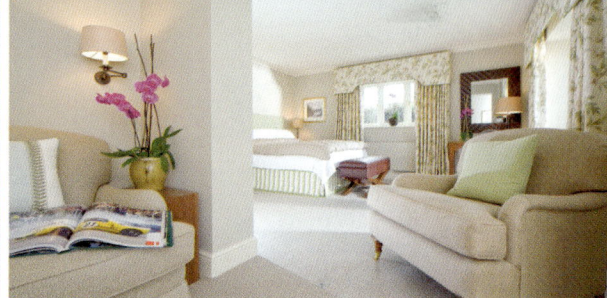

Park House

Soaking up the natural beauty in South Downs' countryside

Get the camera charged and paint brushes at the ready. Park House's scenic setting in private acres of South Downs National Park (an official Area of Outstanding Natural Beauty) is one that you'll want to capture. The archetypal English countryside scene, Park House is in the quaint village of Bepton, a short drive from the historic market town of Midhurst. A family-run hotel with a welcoming atmosphere and home-from-home quality, Park House is as warm as it is stylish with a designer finesse to the interiors whose classic country chic style has been given a contemporary interpretation that brings everything up-to-date and on-trend. Guest rooms are located in the main hotel or there are three cottages nestled in the grounds. Most main hotel rooms look out to the pretty rose garden and grounds (these include grass tennis courts, croquet and bowls lawns, a six-hole golf course and summer outdoor pool). While the more private, exclusive-use cottages are well-equipped sanctuaries great for long-term stays, groups of friends, families or romantic sojourns. Two have their own kitchen although the seasonal, locally sourced dishes at the restaurant are irresistible and promise English classics. Two bonus features: Park House has a restored barn available for parties/business events; plus the PH2O Spa, a state-of-the-art therapeutic facility.

PRICE FROM:
£135

FEATURES:
Gym; Pool; Restaurant; Spa

ACTIVITIES:
Fishing; Golf; Horse riding

NEARBY:
Weald and Downland Open Air Museum; Petworth House; Goodwood Racecourse and Estate; Cowdray ruins

GETTING THERE:
A3; London Gatwick Airport; London Heathrow Airport

+44 (0)1730 819 000 ☎
condenastjohansens.com/parkhousehotel 🌐
Bepton, Midhurst, West Sussex GU29 0JB, England 🏠

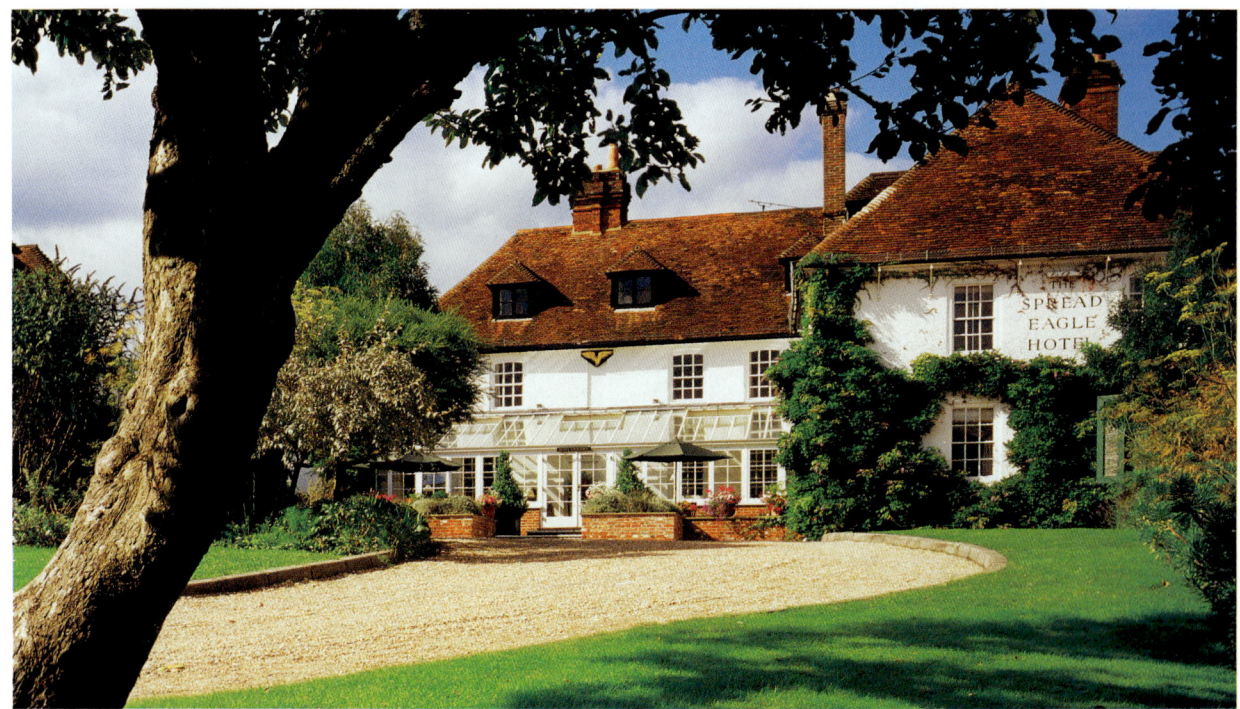

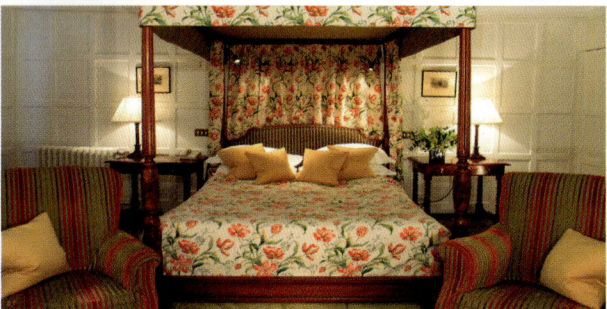

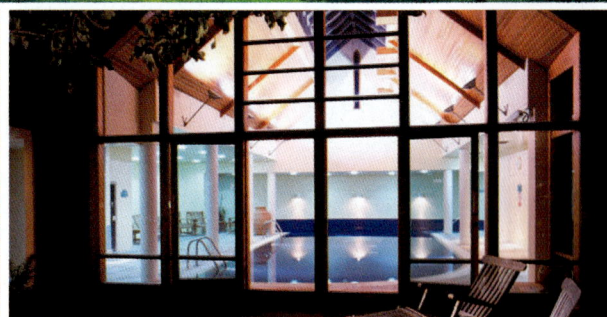

The Spread Eagle Hotel & Spa

A charming step back in time in the market town of Midhurst

PRICE FROM:
£190

FEATURES:
Family friendly; Pet friendly; Pool; Restaurant; Spa

ACTIVITIES:
Fishing; Golf; Horse riding

NEARBY:
Petworth House; Cowdray Park; Goodwood House and Estate; Chichester Cathedral; West Dean Gardens

GETTING THERE:
Just off A272/286; M25 jct 9; London Gatwick Airport

☎ +44 (0)1730 816911
🌐 condenastjohansens.com/spreadeaglemidhurst
🏠 South Street, Midhurst, West Sussex GU29 9NH, England

Rich in charm and period features, The Spread Eagle Hotel & Spa in Midhurst is one of England's oldest coaching inns. Dating from 1430, age-old oak beams, original open fireplaces and stained-glass windows generate an atmosphere of centuries past while modern comforts such as pampering spa services and gourmet meals bring it right up-to-date. Perhaps The Spread Eagle's most unexpected card is its Scandinavian-inspired luxury spa. Wonderfully contemporary with an impressive vaulted glass ceiling and plenty of wet areas, it also has a fitness suite. But back in the 15th-century walls of The Spread Eagle, the restaurant's new Head Chef Richard Cave-Toye whips up a modern classic menu using seasonal flavours and plenty of local produce to tempt you. As you would expect, the bedrooms are peppered with antiques and some have four-poster beds. The White Room has a secret passage and is said to have been used by smugglers to evade the king's men. Queen Elizabeth I reputedly stayed in the Queen's Suite in 1591. With easy access to Sussex and the South Downs, this is a great base for exploring the area with one of The Spread Eagle's cream teas waiting for you on your return - children's high teas too. Note to dog owners: well-behaved four-legged friends are allowed in some bedrooms.

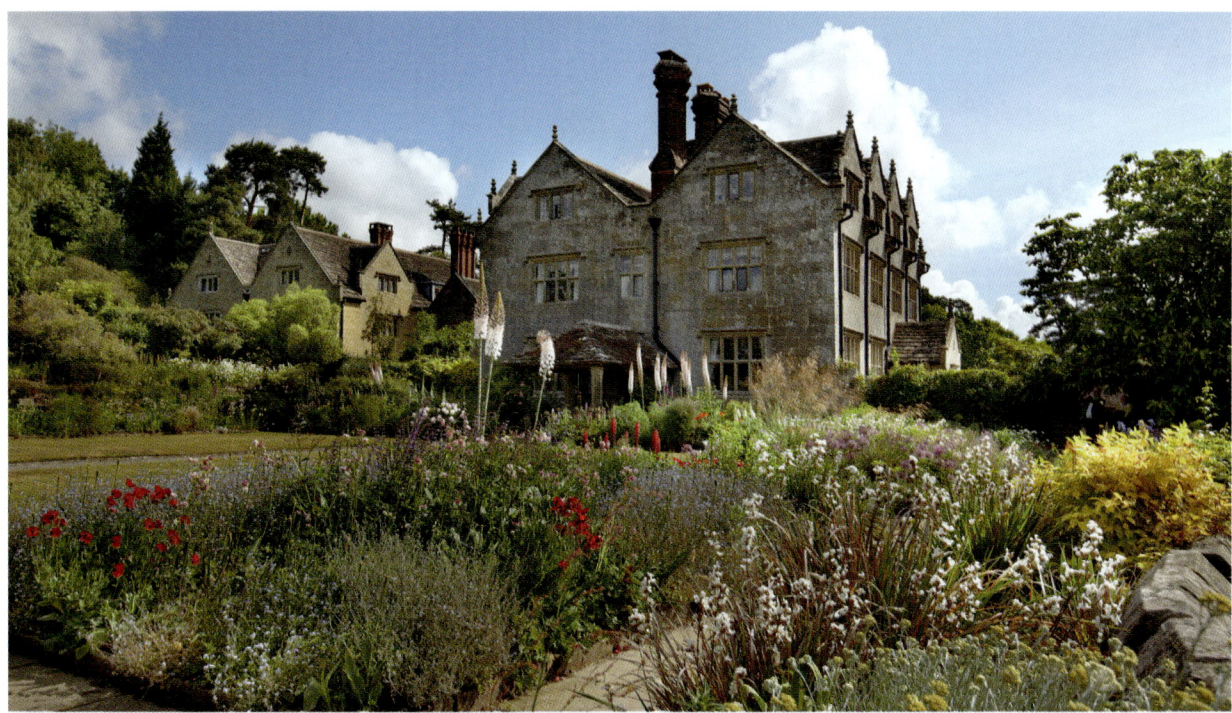

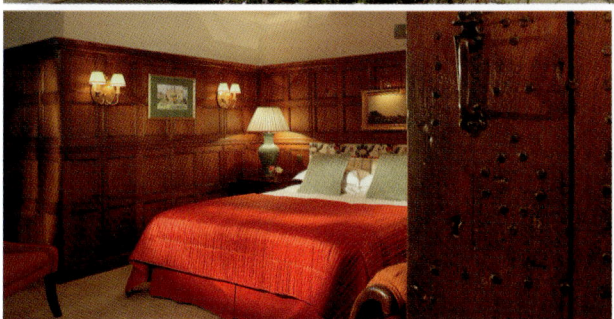
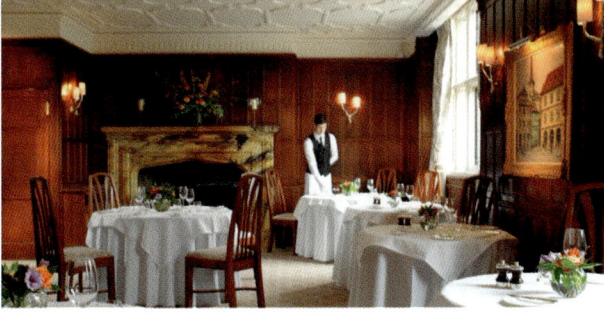

Gravetye Manor

Elizabethan manor house enveloped by Sussex woodland

In the quaint English village of West Hoathly on Vowels Lane, Gravetye Manor conjures a barrage of "ooo"s and Harry Potter-esque imagery. Home to the late William Robinson (father of the English flower garden), his world-famous horticultural work draws attention to exquisite blooms, colours and textures. Book a garden-view room to gaze upon the carefully crafted designs and take time to notice the classical furnishings and floral influences. You'll feel as fresh as a daisy as you awake from a satisfying slumber in these panelled dens of relaxation. Feel all Elizabeth Bennet with walks in the garden, reading by the fire and afternoon tea in the Sitting Room; simple, quintessential English living. More into croquet than crochet? Speak to the Gravetye staff if you need something a little more exciting. Deer stalking and riding the Bluebell Railway come highly recommended. The team can also arrange tickets to the widely acclaimed Glyndebourne music events. Gravetye Manor in West Sussex was originally built for a bride and like the best honeymoon destinations, it provides a great beginning to a happy ever after.

PRICE FROM:
£240

FEATURES:
Family friendly; Restaurant

ACTIVITIES:
Golf; Horse riding; Walking

NEARBY:
Royal Ashdown Golf Course; Wakehurst Place; Hever Castle; Standen (National Trust)

GETTING THERE:
M25 jct 6; East Grinstead Railway Station; London Gatwick Airport

+44 (0)1342 810567 ☎
condenastjohansens.com/gravetyemanor 🌐
Vowels Lane, Near West Hoathly, West Sussex 🏠
RH19 4LJ, England

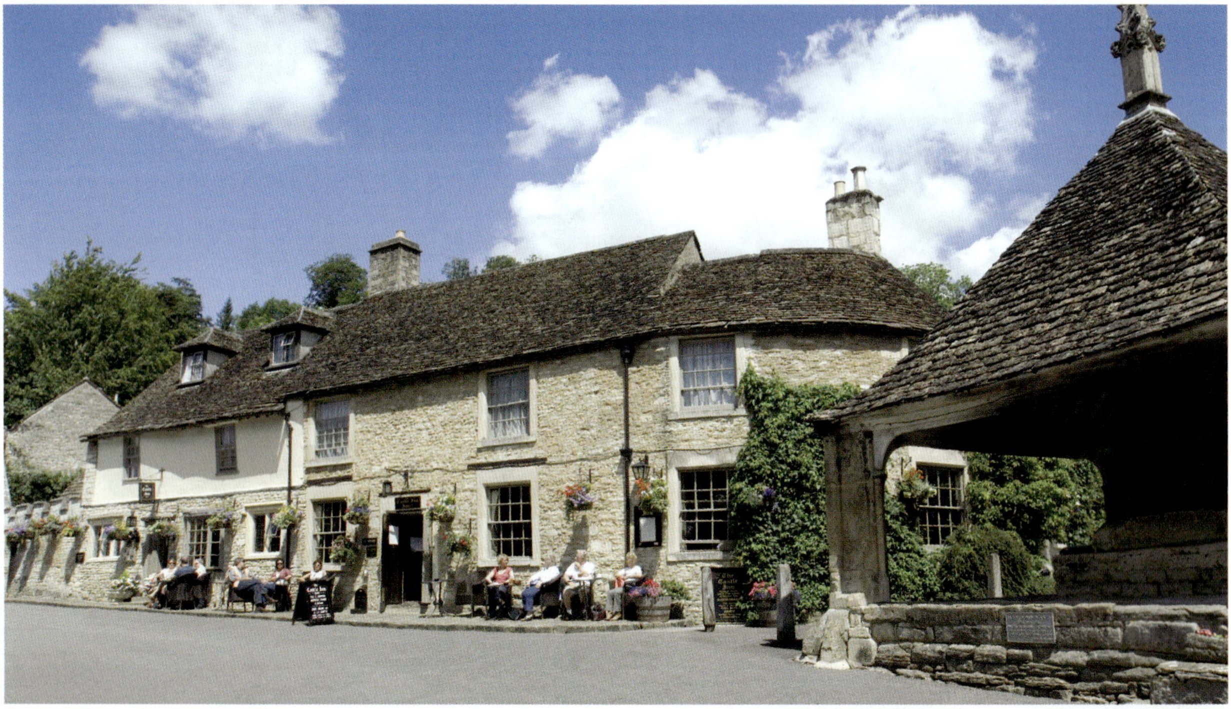

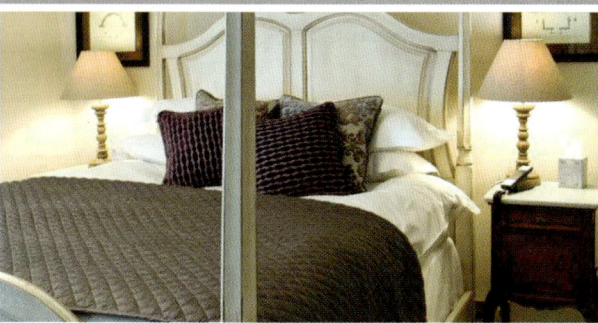

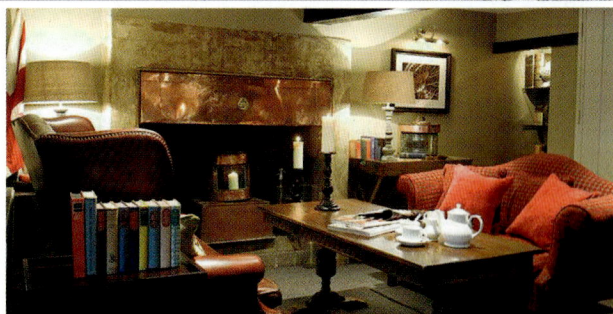

The Castle Inn

Medieval timepiece in the heart of the Cotswolds

PRICE FROM:
£125

FEATURES:
Family friendly; Restaurant

ACTIVITIES:
Fishing; Golf; Walking

NEARBY:
Bath; Lacock; Cotswolds villages; Bradford-on-Avon

GETTING THERE:
M4 jct 17; Chippenham Railway Station; Bristol Airport

☎ +44 (0)1249 783030
🌐 condenastjohansens.com/castleinn
🏠 Castle Combe, Wiltshire SN14 7HN, England

Castle Combe is the Cotswolds village that time forgot. A perfectly preserved 15th-century piece of history in Wiltshire's north-west corner - often referred to as the "prettiest village in England". There's not one street light, overhead cable or tv aerial in sight, just rows of yellow Cotswolds stone houses along narrow roads leading to a medieval church and 14th-century Market Cross. If it all looks a little familiar it's possibly because Hollywood has immortalised the village most recently in Steven Speilberg's War Horse, and perhaps most famously as Puddleby-on-the-Marsh in the 1967 adaptation of Dr Doolittle. Facing the Market Cross is The Castle Inn whose origins trace as far back as the 12th century. However, there's nothing antiquated about its standard of service or facilities despite its respectful preservation of unique historic character and features that remain true to its setting. In fact, The Castle Inn has a surprisingly contemporary flair with 11 bedrooms dressed in sumptuous fabrics alongside swish bathrooms. No English inn is complete without a cosy bar with open fire and The Castle Inn doesn't disappoint. Dishing up traditional favourites and an à la carte menu for dinner, there's also the private Oak Room and relaxed, alfresco Terrace Patio when the weather permits.

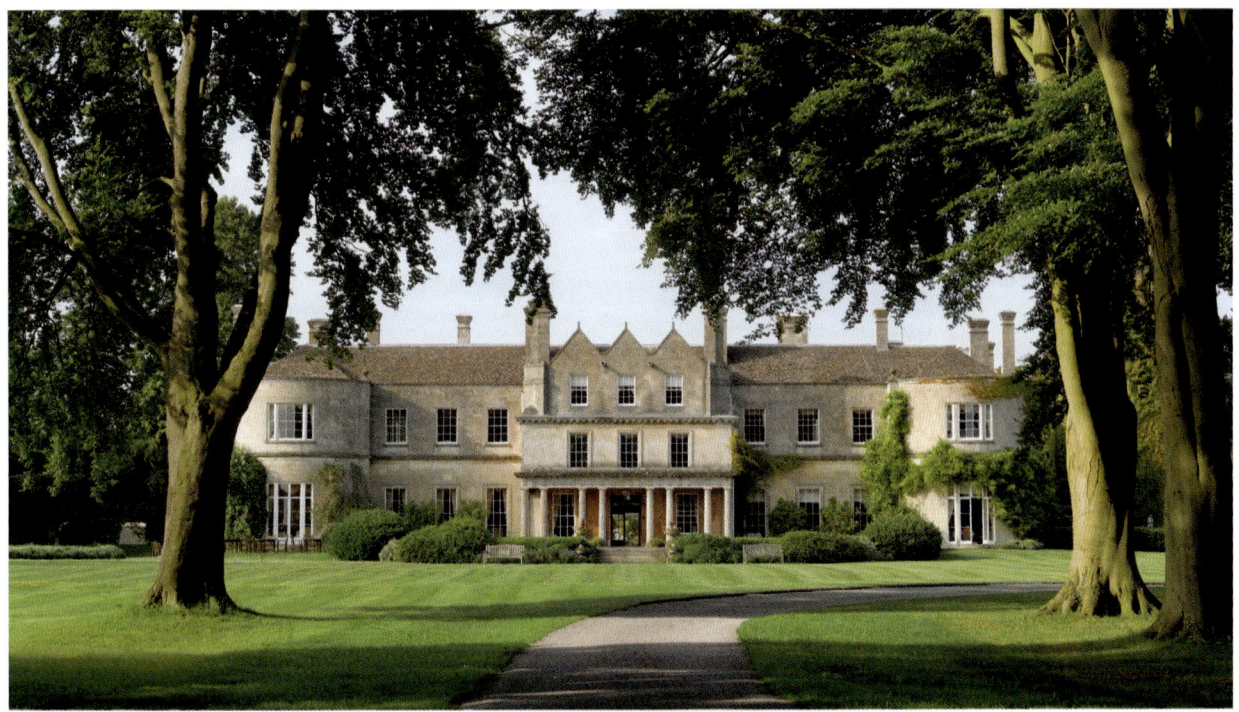

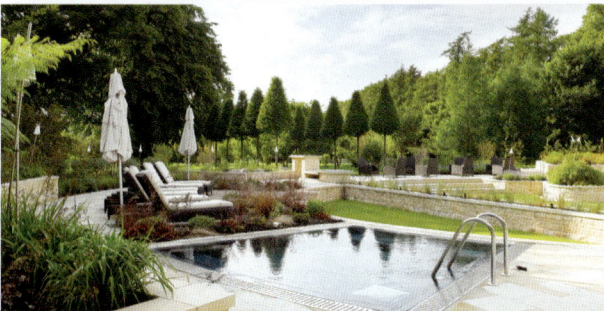

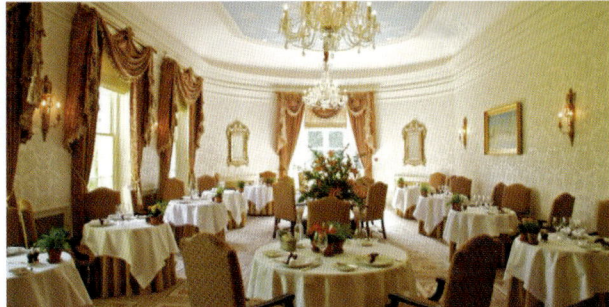

Lucknam Park Hotel & Spa

Spectacular Palladian mansion in picturesque, private Wiltshire estate

Lucknam Park Hotel & Spa, Wiltshire is an authority on the high-life. A Palladian mansion in hundreds of private green acres, a short drive from historic Bath. Beyond the imposing exterior resides a collection of suites and bedrooms dressed in fine fabrics with antiques reflecting each room's personality; bathrooms are a flawless sweep of marble. Book in advance to guarantee a table at The Park restaurant whose Michelin-Starred dishes are a celebration of organic ingredients, local produce and garden-grown herbs that result in eyes-closed appreciation. Or there's the relaxed Brasserie (next to the spa so why not enjoy the facilities of one then the other), complete with open kitchen and wood-fired oven that's a hub of activity with lounge area, bar and restaurant serving all day. But who can resist traditional afternoon tea of home-made scones, clotted cream, cakes and tea in the Drawing Room or wood-panelled Library? If feeling a little guilty after all this indulgence, head to The Spa at Lucknam Park for a health kick (with the just-opened Well Being at Lucknam Park Spa promising instant results), the Equestrian Centre, tennis courts or football pitch. Foodie bonus: Lucknam's Cookery School hosts courses led by Head Chef Hrishikesh Desai. A Master Class with Michelin-Starred Chef Hywel Jones is also available. Even the children can join in during the school holidays.

PRICE FROM:
£345

FEATURES:
Family friendly; Helipad; Pool; Spa

ACTIVITIES:
Horse riding; Walking

NEARBY:
Bath; Lacock; Castle Combe; The Cotswolds; Longleat

GETTING THERE:
A420; M4 jct 18; Bristol Airport

+44 (0)1225 742777 ☎
condenastjohansens.com/lucknampark 🌐
Colerne, Chippenham, Wiltshire SN14 8AZ, England 🏠

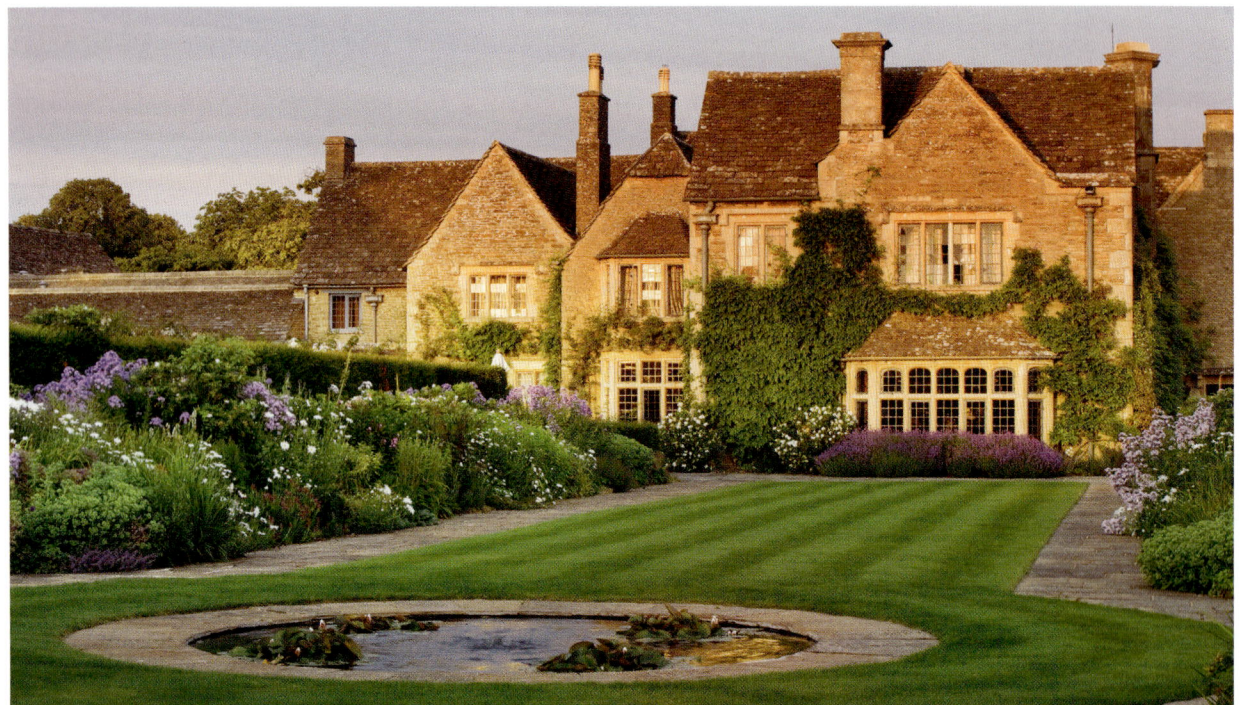

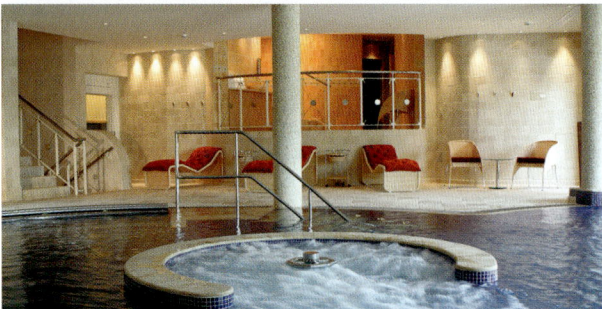
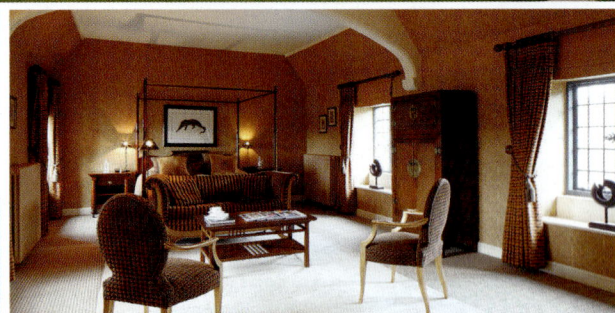

Whatley Manor Hotel & Spa

Cosseting Cotswolds manor set in wonderful English countryside

PRICE FROM:
£305

FEATURES:
Gym; Helipad; Michelin Starred restaurant; Pet friendly; Spa

ACTIVITIES:
Golf; Horse riding; Shooting

NEARBY:
Malmesbury Abbey and Gardens; Westonbirt Arboretum; Tetbury; Castle Combe; Bath

GETTING THERE:
B4040; M4 jct 17; London Heathrow Airport

☎ +44 (0)1666 822888
🌐 condenastjohansens.com/whatley
🏠 Easton Grey, Malmesbury, Wiltshire SN16 0RB, England

Down the road from Malmesbury, Whatley Manor is the country retreat that will revive, restore and send you home feeling a different person. Embraced by 26 distinct gardens and Wiltshire countryside, this is a gateway to the Cotswolds. To some, Whatley Manor is known as a luxury spa destination. To others, it's a gastronomic show-stopper. For everyone who visits, it's an utterly relaxing retreat in cosseting surrounds. Those who come here for the highly-acclaimed Aquarias spa feel the benefits of its hydrotherapy pool, thermal cabins, tepidarium, luxurious La Prairie beauty treatments and "beyond organic" spa treatments by ila. Foodies seeking out its exceptional restaurant embark on a heavenly gastronomic journey including amuse bouches to petit fours intercepted by meticulously prepared 2 Michelin-Starred dishes in The Dining Room. The brasserie, Le Mazot, with its refreshingly alternative Swiss interior, offers an informal dining experience and the option to eat alfresco on the kitchen garden terrace. It's all about very careful attention to detail throughout the 15 bedrooms and eight suites furnished with Italian furniture and handmade French wallpaper. Completely welcoming with the ambience of a family-owned country home. A note to film buffs: Whatley Manor has a private cinema (seats 40), popcorn included. Bring your favourite film or choose from the hotel's library.

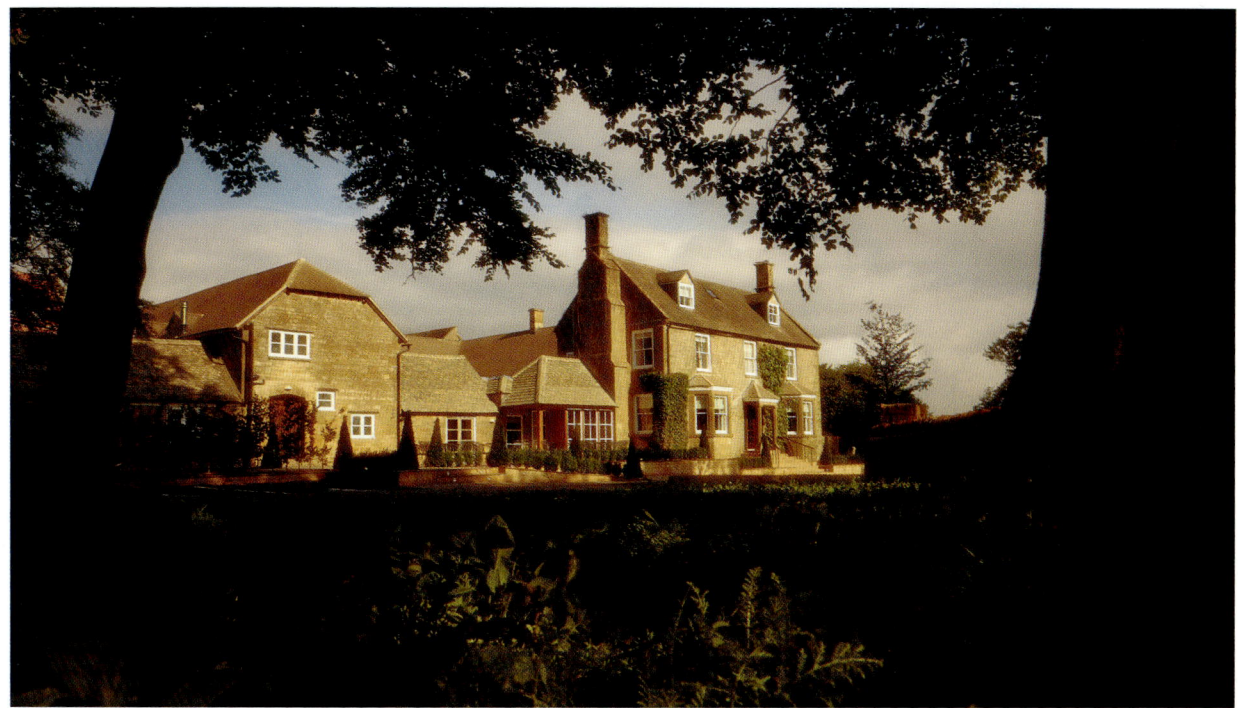

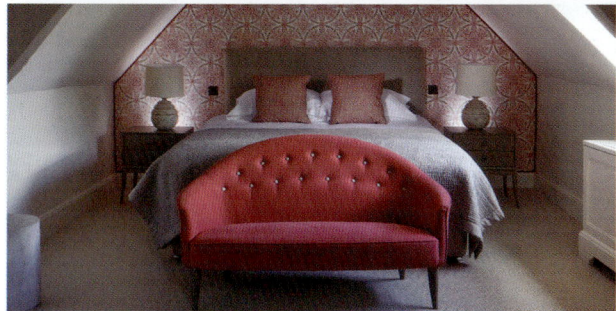
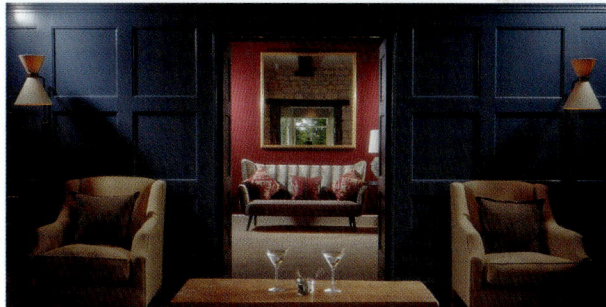

Dormy House Hotel

Setting new heights of hospitality in Worcestershire

Broadway in Worcestershire is a charming slice of yore known as the "jewel of the Cotswolds". Lined with red chestnut trees and 16th-century Cotswolds limestone buildings, the nickname tells it how it is. Numerous artistic talents including Elgar, J M Barrie and William Morris chose Broadway as their home – clearly no lack of inspiration here – and it's now a hub for the art, antique and outdoor loving enthusiast. Standing high on Willersey Hill, the 17th-century farmhouse that's now the utterly chic and charming Dormy House Hotel, has undergone a revitalising revamp following a multi-million pound investment and six months of intense work by leading designers, landscapers, spa developers and a Michelin–Starred chef. The result is a hotel that's like home - only better. The Main House rooms and private Rose Cottage uphold Dormy's traditional essence while The Emily Wing rooms are a vision of the 1950s. When it comes to food, Dormy House has always been a forerunner and now, with the aid of Michelin-Starred Executive Chef John Wood, Head Chef Paul Napper is dishing up classic flavours with an exciting punch in The Garden Room (alfresco in summer) and in the casual Potting Shed. Watch out for: the opening of Dormy's House Spa. It's planned to be a knockout.

PRICE FROM:
£250

FEATURES:
Family friendly; Helipad; Restaurant; Wheelchair access

ACTIVITIES:
Shopping; Sightseeing; Walking

NEARBY:
The Cotswolds; Cheltenham; Stratford-upon-Avon; Hidcote Manor; Kiftsgate Gardens

GETTING THERE:
A44; M40 jct 8/15; Birmingham International Airport

+44 (0)1386 852711 ☎
condenastjohansens.com/dormyhouse 🌐
Willersey Hill, Broadway, Worcestershire WR12 7LF, England 🏠

UK/Scotland

Please go to condenastjohansens.com/scotland

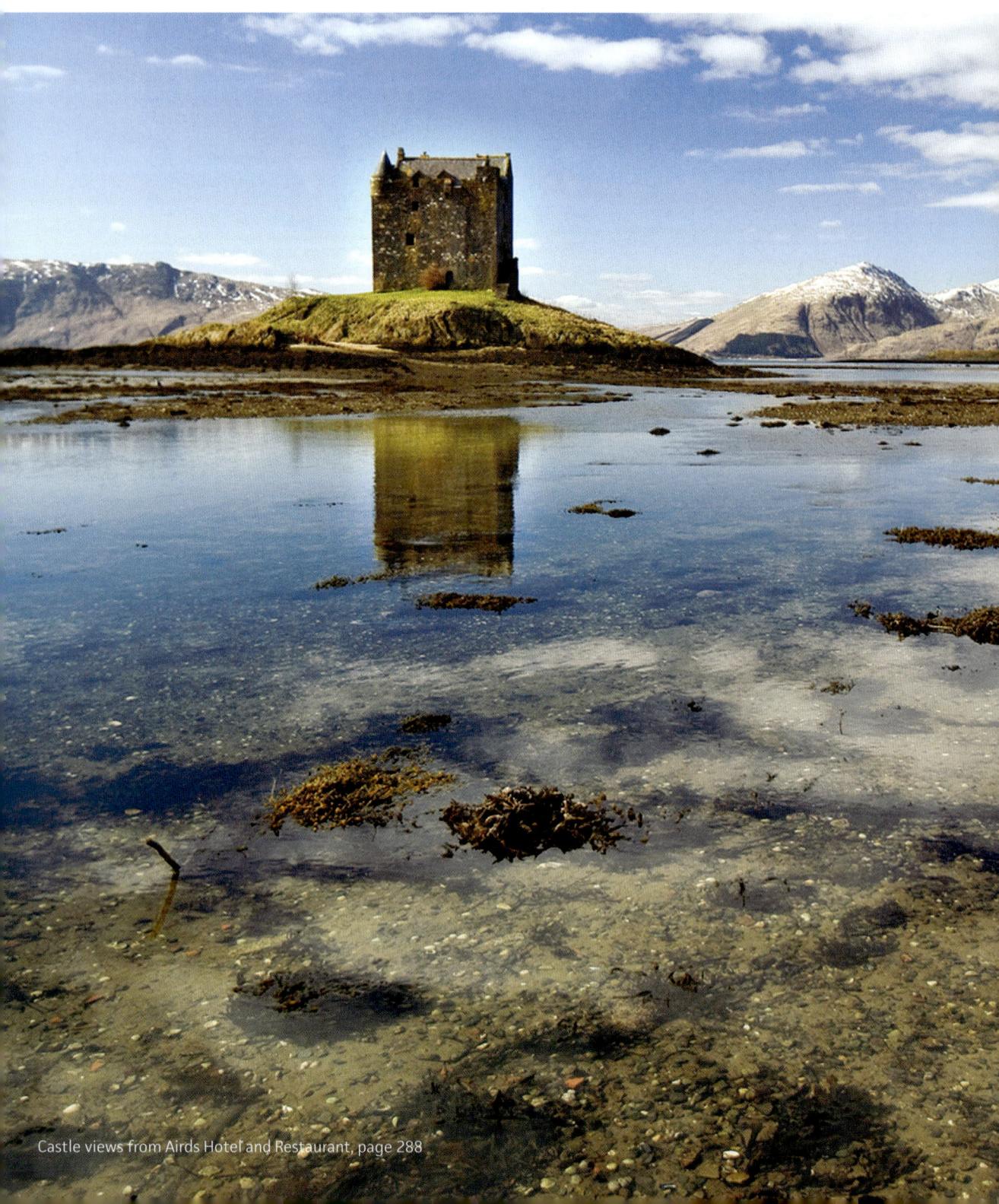

Castle views from Airds Hotel and Restaurant, page 288

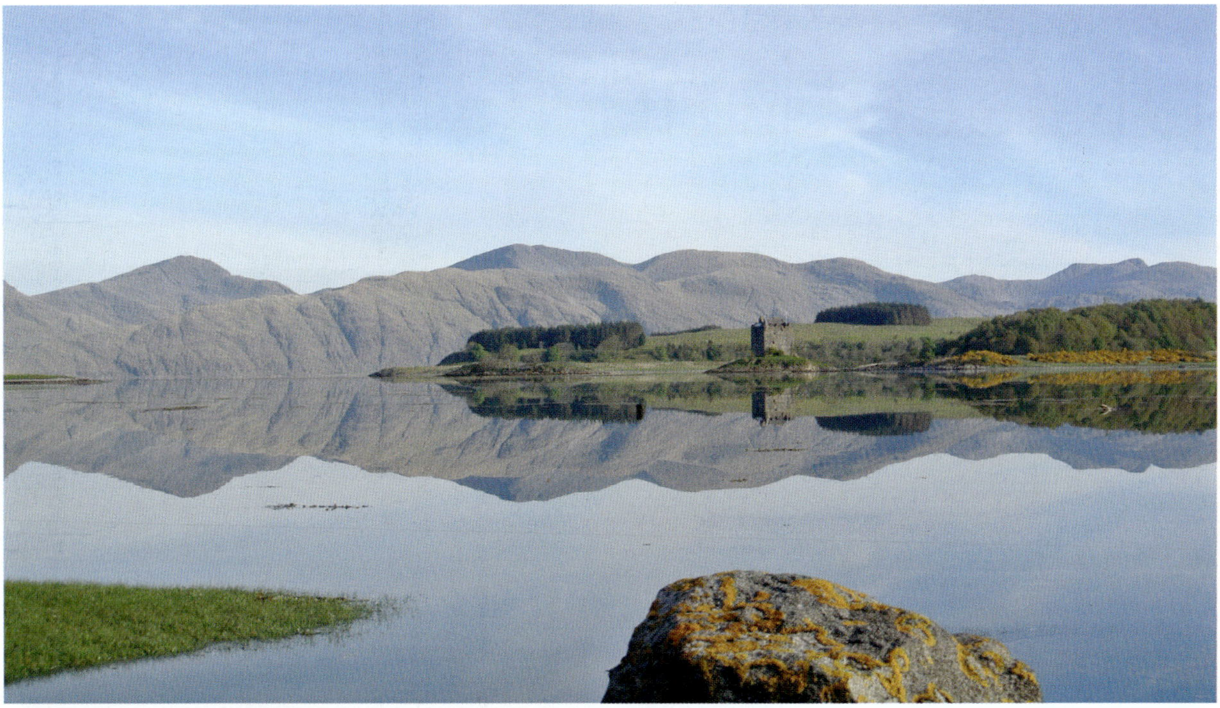

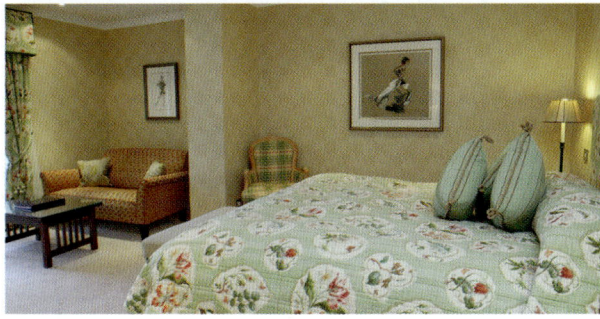

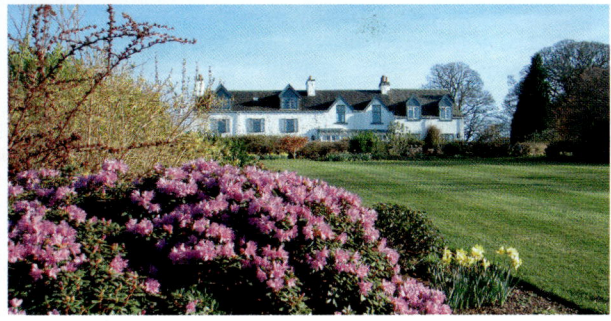

Airds Hotel and Restaurant

Loch-side romance on the West Coast of Scotland

Whatever you do, bring your camera on a visit to Airds Hotel and Restaurant. For the scenery surrounding this understated treasure with gourmet restaurant is an image you'll want to capture and take home with you. Like the otherwordly scenery that fades in and out on your computer's screensaver, here it is in reality, in the stunning hamlet of Port Appin beside Loch Linnhe on the West Coast of Scotland, near Oban. Airds began its life as an 18th-century ferry inn before establishing itself as a noteworthy romantic hotel whose relaxed yet professional staff raises the level of charm and welcoming atmosphere to an exceptional level. (The owners are previous guests who couldn't resist its allure.) The eight bedrooms, three suites and two-bedroom self-catering cottage within the grounds, have all recently been refurbished to offer sophisticated, charming rooms that further enhance the intimate warmth and atmosphere of tranquillity. Some have awe-inspiring views across Loch Linnhe with the Morvern mountains behind. Renowned as one of the finest in Scotland, the restaurant sources only the best local ingredients, including world-class fish and seafood, to produce award-winning cuisine.

PRICE FROM:
£290

FEATURES:
Helipad; Lake views; Pet friendly; Restaurant

ACTIVITIES:
Cycling; Horse riding; Water sports

NEARBY:
Isle of Lismore; Oban; Glencoe; Ben Nevis; Isle of Mull

GETTING THERE:
Oban Airport; Glasgow International Airport; Edinburgh International Airport

+44 (0)1631 730236 ☎
condenastjohansens.com/airdshotel 🌐
Port Appin, Appin, Argyll PA38 4DF, Scotland 🏠

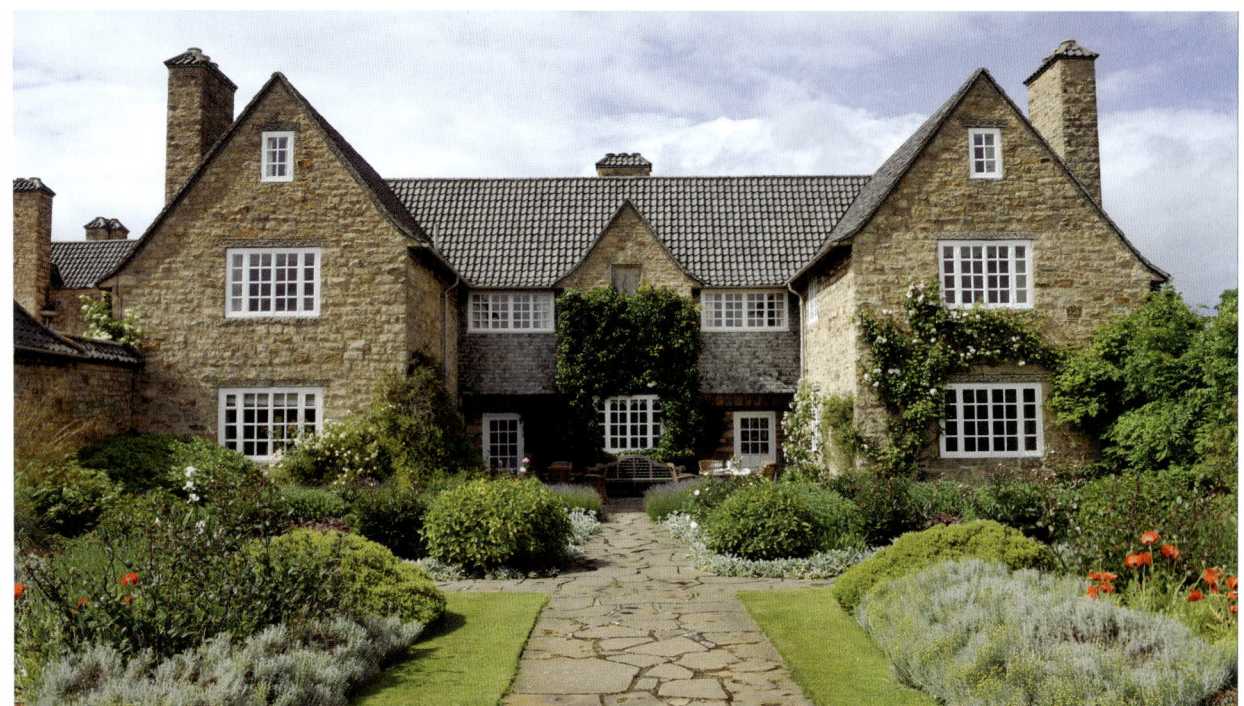

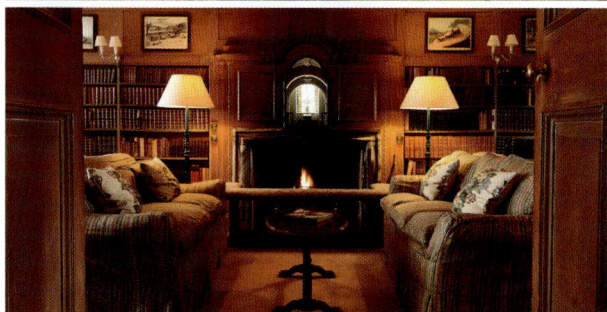
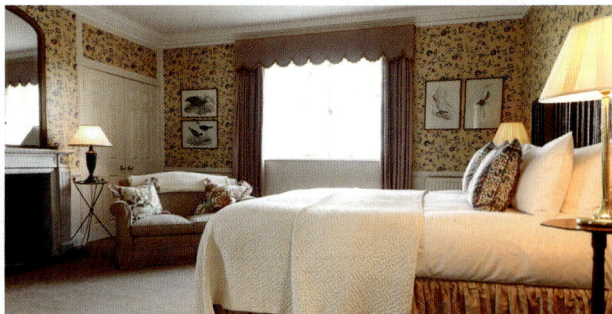

Greywalls and Chez Roux

Elegant Edwardian retreat on the edge of Muirfield Championship Golf Course

Minutes from the world-famous Muirfield Championship Golf Course (15-time host to The British Open) and an impressive 10 golf courses within a five-mile radius, Greywalls Hotel is a golfer's dream. However, it would be unfair to confine this delightful retreat to a single glory. A handsome 1901 Edwardian country house designed by Sir Edwin Lutyens, Greywalls Hotel and Chez Roux in East Lothian is seductively charming. Bedrooms are full of Edwardian character with modern luxuries (dados and padded headboards meet plush pillows and en-suite bathrooms), all with superb views of the verdant Scottish countryside. There's excellent cuisine to be had at Chez Roux under the direction of Chef Albert Roux OBE, KFO, head of the Roux cooking dynasty. Not to mention boundless opportunities to ease away any stresses with pleasant strolls in the acres of walled gardens encompassing a putting green, croquet lawn, tennis courts, herbaceous borders, beehives and chicken coops. Visits to the Whisky Room will relax you to your toes. This is also a fabulous venue for large parties, well catered for in the Colonel's House, a self-catering lodge perfect for a family holiday or golfing group. For fact fans: Greywalls and Chez Roux is managed by Inverlochy Castle Management International (ICMI).

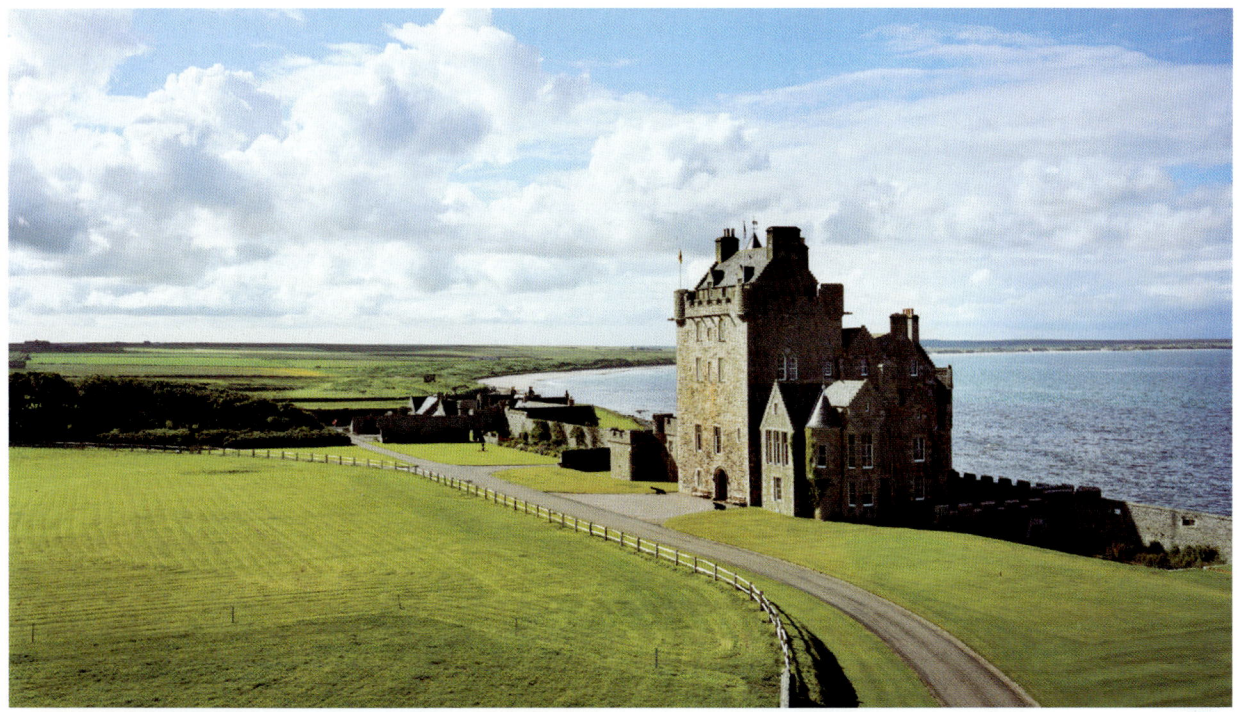

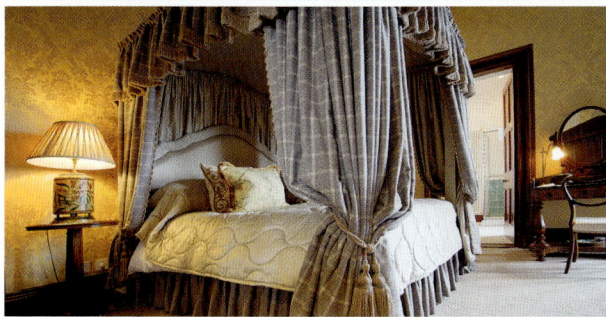

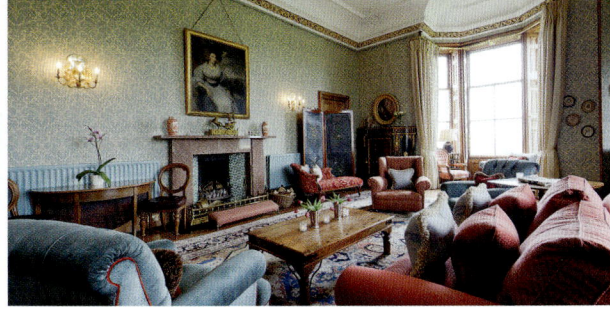

Ackergill Tower

Fantastical Highland castle on guard beside the North Sea

It's not breaking news to learn that Scotland's north coastline has a theatrical beauty like no other. It's common knowledge that The Northern Lights, John O' Groats and the Orkney Islands are attractions of rarefied wonder. But what's less known is that 30 minutes south of John O' Groats is the remote, fortified 15th-century castle of Ackergill Tower, Wick. Keeping watch out to the North Sea on one side and beautiful formal gardens on the other, Ackergill is a warm and welcoming corner of isolation (yes to tasteful tartan fabrics, log fires and wood panelling). It has 35 guest rooms in total, 17 located in the main tower and an additional 18 rooms spread across one to five-bedroom self-catering cottages and a wonderfully romantic circular treehouse within the endless grounds. (For a special get-together with family or friends book the five-bedroom Beach House.) Memorable meals, courtesy of the seriously sumptuous Grand Hall menu, is a celebration of local produce from nearby estates, rivers and the coast; don't forget to call on Martin, the expert Sommelier whose know-how is unrivalled, when selecting your accompanying wines. A meal is not complete without a cheeky "wee dram" from the Old Pulteney Distillery. Good to know: the entire property can be exclusively hired.

PRICE FROM:
£225

FEATURES:
Beach access; Helipad; Pet friendly; Restaurant; Sea views

ACTIVITIES:
Fishing; Shooting; Walking

NEARBY:
John O' Groats; Castle of Mey; Old Pulteney distillery; Wick Heritage Centre

GETTING THERE:
Wick Airport; Inverness Airport

+44 (0)1955 603556 ☎
condenastjohansens.com/ackergilltower 🌐
By Wick, Caithness KW1 4RG, Highland, Scotland 🏠

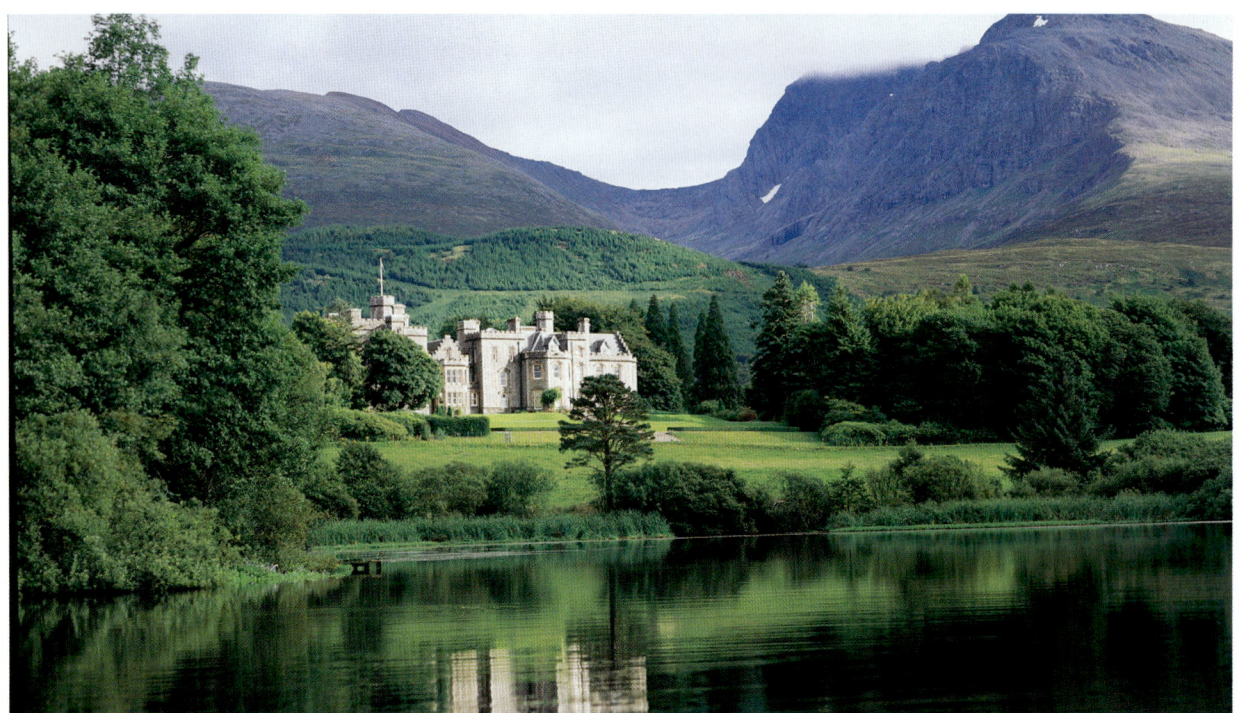

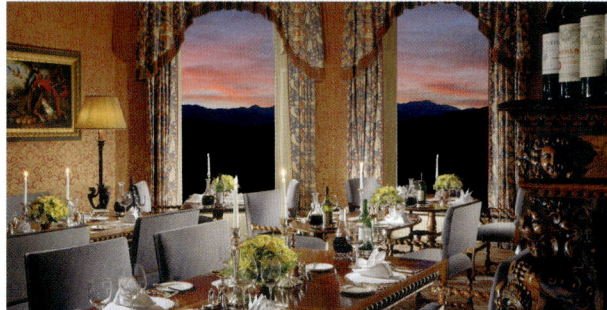

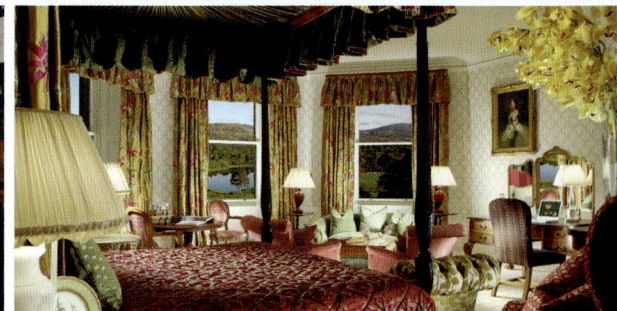

Inverlochy Castle

Fairy-tale castle romance in the foothills of Ben Nevis

PRICE FROM:
£480

FEATURES:
Family friendly; Helipad; Michelin Starred restaurant; Pet friendly

ACTIVITIES:
Fishing; Golf; Walking

NEARBY:
Ben Nevis; Glencoe; Glenfinnan; Loch Ness; The Jacobite steam train - aka Hogwarts Express

GETTING THERE:
On the A82; Fort William Railway Station; Inverness Airport

☎ +44 (0)1397 702177
🌐 condenastjohansens.com/inverlochy
📍 Torlundy, Fort William PH33 6SN, Highland, Scotland

After a week of sketching and painting at Lord Abinger's Inverlochy Castle in 1873, Queen Victoria wrote, "I never saw a lovelier or more romantic spot." Built 10 years prior to her visit, not far from its original 13th-century fort namesake, (the first) Lord Abinger could not have picked a more scenic location in the foothills of Ben Nevis, the Western Highlands. Today, the mighty castle is one of Scotland's finest hotels managed with passion and professionalism by Jane Watson. Jane and her staff make every effort to put each guest completely at ease in this most grandiose of settings whose imposing reception room displays Venetian crystal chandeliers, a Michaelangelo-style ceiling and handsome staircase leading to three elaborately decorated dining rooms. In contrast, whilst being spacious and in-keeping with the essence of the Castle, Inverlochy's rooms and suites unveil a fresh, modern take on the traditional floral and tartan-clad theme alongside incredibly stylish bathrooms. High-tech touches such as mirror tvs and laptops on request keep matters very 21st century. Maintaining high standards in the kitchen is Chef Philip Carnegie whose Michelin-Starred modern British cuisine uses local game, hand-picked wild mushrooms and scallops from the Isle of Skye. Worth noting: Inverlochy Castle Management International runs the show here.

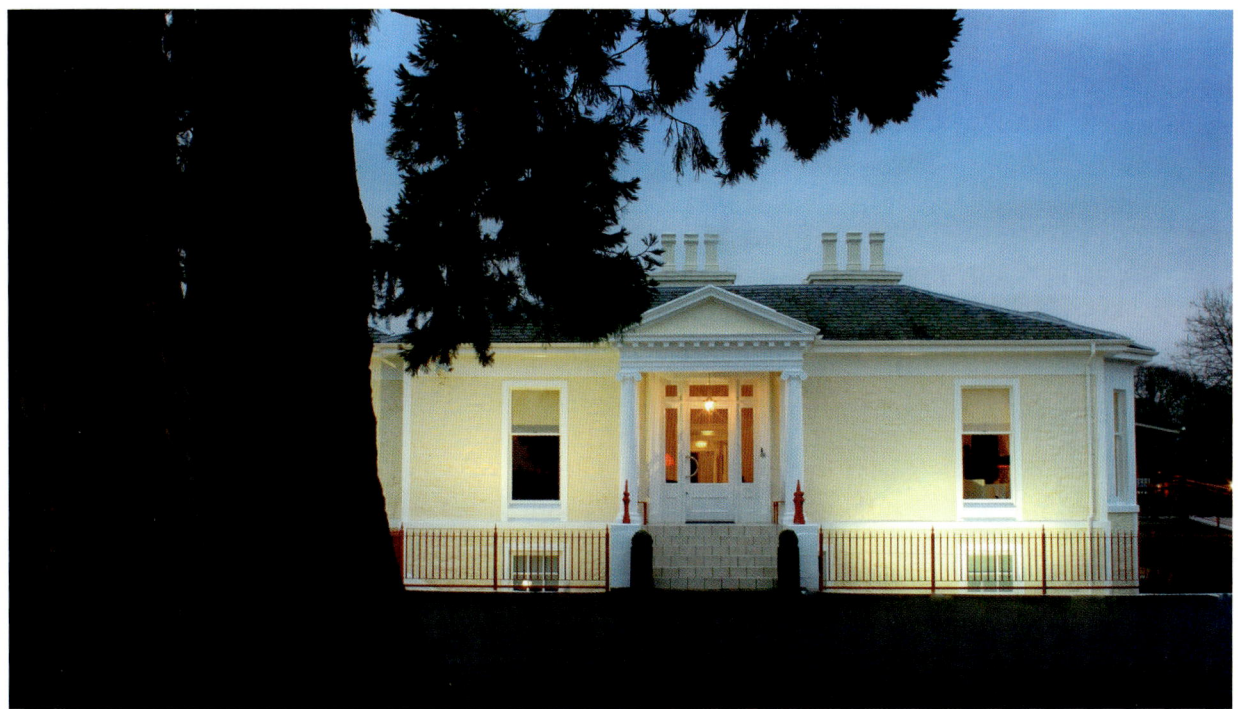

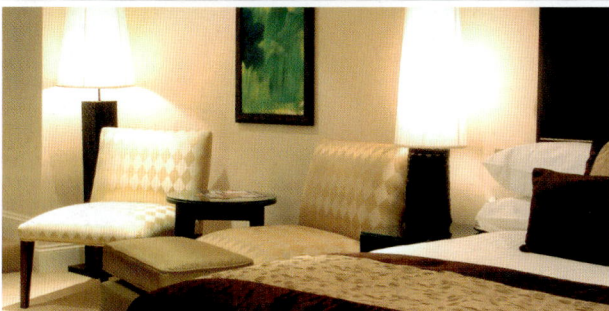

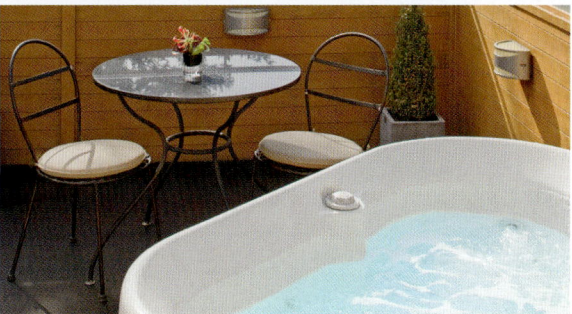

Rocpool Reserve and Chez Roux

Inverness retreat leading the way in interior design and cuisine

In the UK's northernmost city of Inverness, the 11-room boutique Rocpool Reserve and Chez Roux is making waves in the hospitality scene. Just a quick dash from the High Street and Inverness Castle, this city centre retreat looks out to the River Ness. Designer rooms exemplify classic elegance and contemporary grace while the superb staff demonstrates first-class service and phenomenal attention to detail. The seriously stylish bedrooms come in four categories (Hip, Chic, Decadent and Extra Decadent) but all have emperor-size beds and fixtures such as plasma tvs, dvd players and luxuries such as Egyptian linens and Italian ceramics in the bathrooms. Two have hot tubs on private terraces. Unwinding at r Bar at Reserve is made exceptionally easy during cocktail hour before dining in the triumphant Chez Roux. Facing the river, menus (choose from à la carte or a set menu) include local Scottish produce blended with classic French country cuisine, all overseen by multi award-winning Chef Albert Roux OBE, KFO, head of the famous cooking dynasty behind such establishments as Le Gavroche, which was the first ever restaurant in the UK to be awarded 3 Michelin Stars. Worthy note: Rocpool Reserve and Chez Roux is managed by Inverlochy Castle Management International.

PRICE FROM:
£195

FEATURES:
Restaurant; Wheelchair access

ACTIVITIES:
Fishing; Golf; Sightseeing

NEARBY:
Inverness High Street; Castle Stuart Golf Course; Loch Ness; Caledonian Canal; Culloden Battlefield

GETTING THERE:
Inverness Railway Station; Inverness Airport

+44 (0)1463 240089 ☎
condenastjohansens.com/rocpool 🌐
Culduthel Road, Inverness IV2 4AG, Scotland 🏠

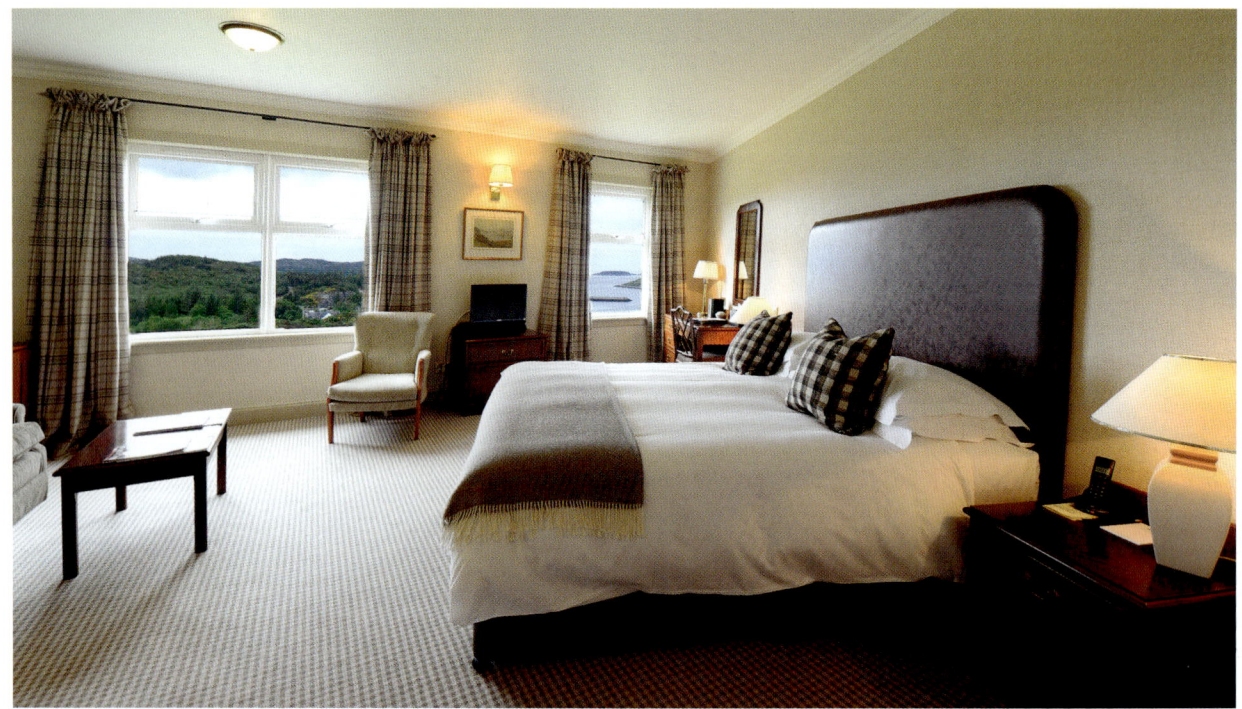

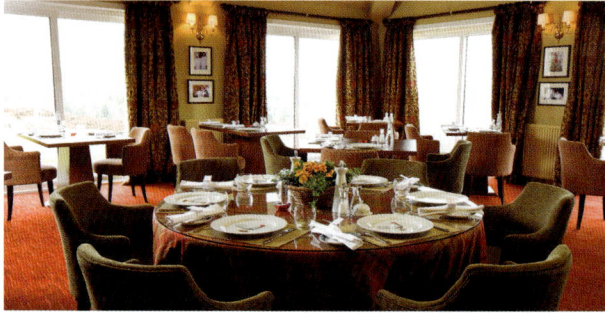
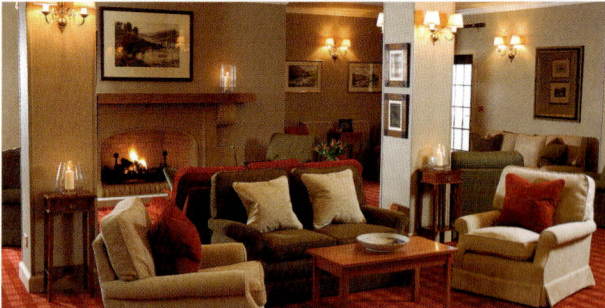

Inver Lodge Hotel and Chez Roux

Handsome, charming and tasteful Highland belter

PRICE FROM:
£215

FEATURES:
Family friendly; Helipad; Lake views; Pet friendly; Restaurant

ACTIVITIES:
Fishing; Shooting; Walking

NEARBY:
Bird-watching; Rugged Sutherland coastline; Assynt Hills; Ardveck Castle; The Rein stone caves of Alt-nan-uamh

GETTING THERE:
Inverness Railway Station; Lairg Railway Station; Inverness Airport

An inspired location for a first-class hotel, Inver Lodge Hotel and Chez Roux in the Scottish Highlands has it all. Remote enough to feel out-of-the-way yet accessible to Inverness (two hours by car, and what a drive!), Inver Lodge has more than a dram or two of Scottish charm plus a world-class restaurant. Utterly serene, this hilltop retreat looks down to the sleepy fishing village of Lochinver, across the waters of Loch Inver and over to the Western Isles. You'll be grabbing your hiking boots before you know it and wading on in the nearby river and/or loch for a spot of trout or salmon fishing. Inside, it's all about muted colours and clean lines with a splash of elegant tartan. Bedrooms are oversized so the whole family are comfortable here (superior rooms come with even more space). However, when the views are this spectacular and the log fires are roaring, romance is always in the air. Before relishing the hearty country cooking at the exquisite Chez Roux restaurant - overseen by Chef Albert Roux OBE, KFO – time spent in the foyer lounge sets you up for the gourmet delights ahead. Worth noting: highly respected Inverlochy Castle Management International runs Inver Lodge.

☎ +44 (0)1571 844496
🌐 condenastjohansens.com/inverlodge
🏠 Lochinver, Sutherland IV27 4LU, Highland, Scotland

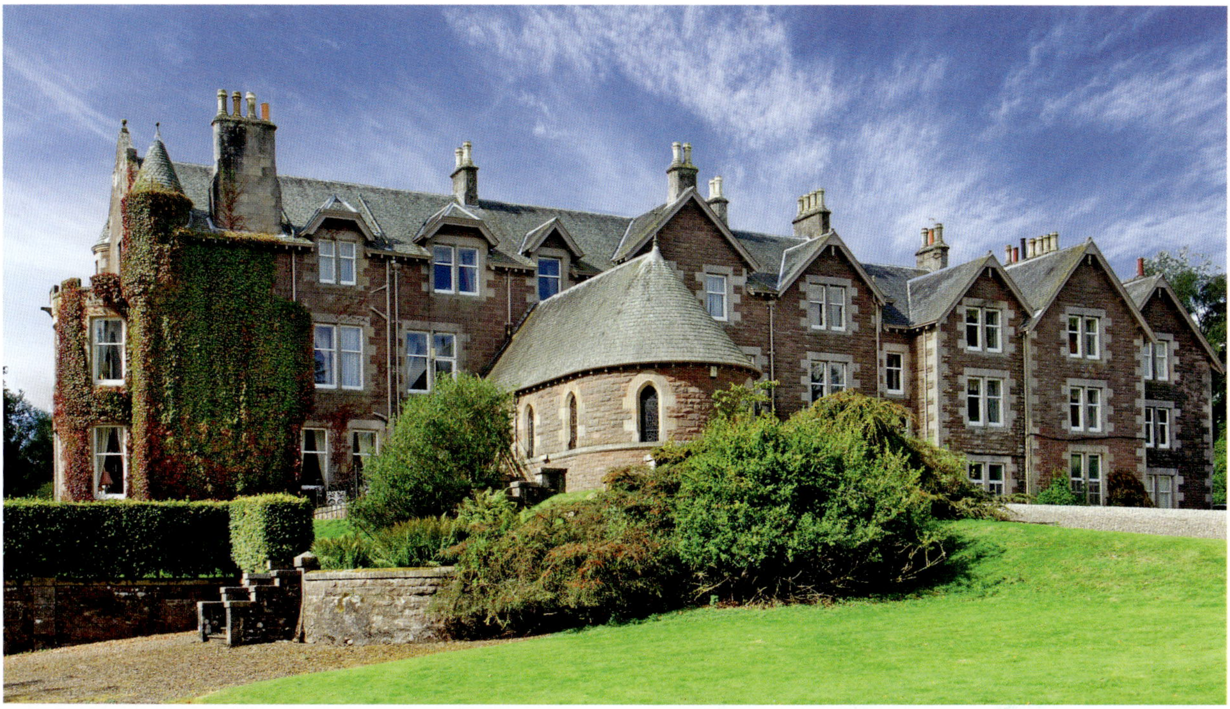

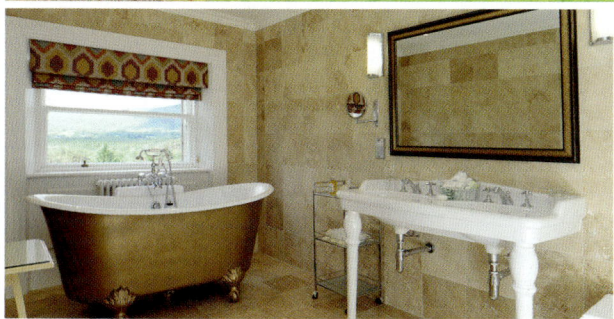
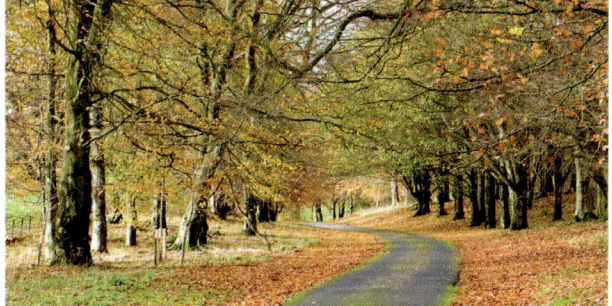

Cromlix and Chez Roux

Picturesque Perthshire's Victorian grande dame

Proving that he's just as savvy off the tennis court as he is on it, 2013 Wimbledon Champion Andy Murray is now owner of Cromlix and Chez Roux, Perthshire. Opening in April 2014 before the Ryder Cup takes place a short drive away at Gleneagles in September 2014, Cromlix's revitalising overhaul is hugely exciting. Directed by the professional team at Inverlochy Castle Management International (Inverlochy Castle and Rocpool Reserve are just two of nine first-class properties in their dependable hands), a modern injection into this Victorian mansion is just what the doctor ordered. Not only will Cromlix provide 10 bedrooms, five suites, a billiards room, bar, lounge, drawing room and restaurant, but meeting facilities at an executive level for day and 24-hour delegate rates too. Plus there's approximately 34 acres of parkland surrounding the estate complete with four lochs and two mineral springs. But the ace that's going to secure its success? Scotland's sixth Chez Roux dining establishment overseen by Chef Albert Roux OBE, KFO. The convenient location near Stirling, Edinburgh and Glasgow as well as attractions such as Stirling Castle, Wallace Monument and Bannockburn certainly seal the deal.

PRICE FROM:
£210

FEATURES:
Family friendly; Restaurant

ACTIVITIES:
Fishing; Tennis; Walking

NEARBY:
Dunblane; Stirling; The Trossachs

GETTING THERE:
Edinburgh International Airport; Glasgow International Airport

condenastjohansens.com/cromlix
Kinbuck, By Dunblane, Near Stirling FK15 9JT, Perth &
Kinross, Scotland

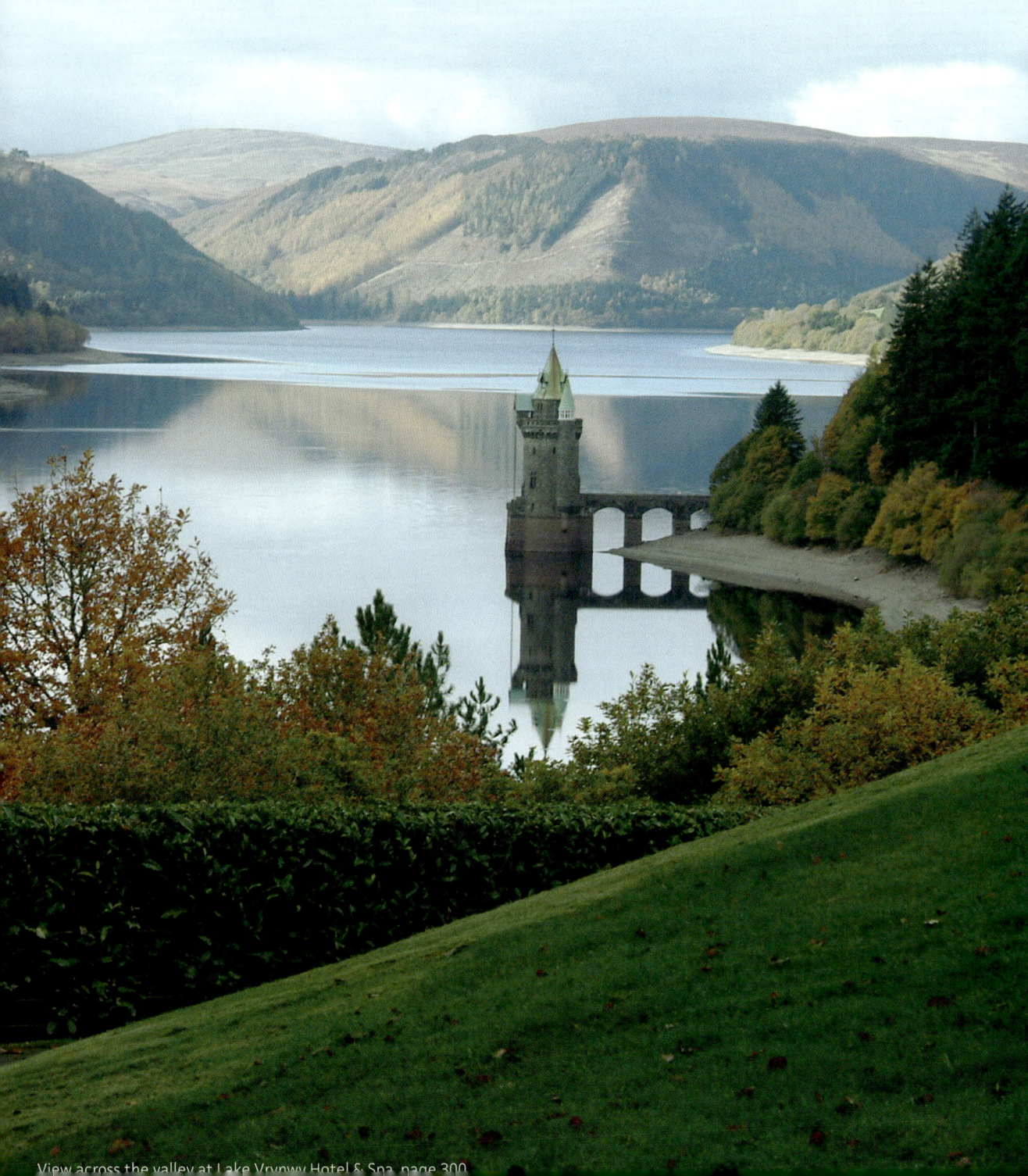

UK/Wales

Please go to condenastjohansens.com/wales

View across the valley at Lake Vyrnwy Hotel & Spa, page 300

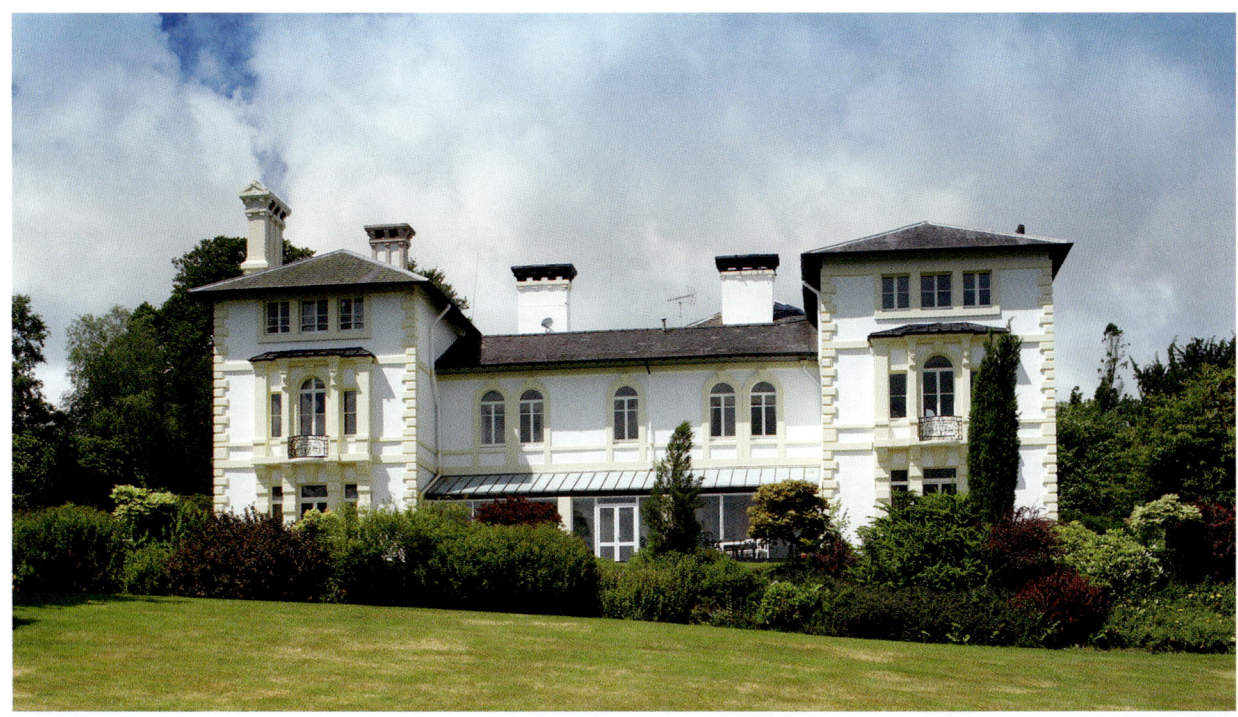

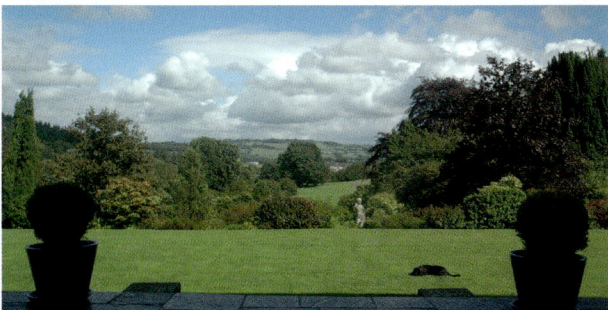
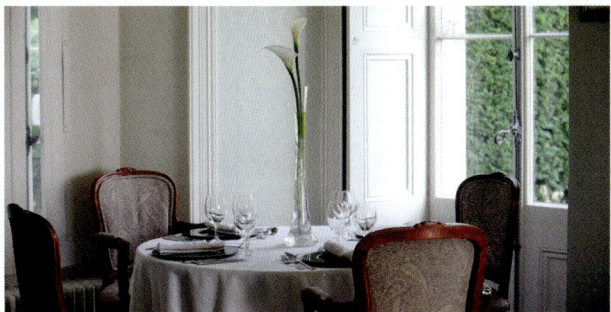

The Falcondale Hotel & Restaurant

A touch of Italian flair in South West Wales

Peaking out above rich green woodland, The Falcondale Hotel & Restaurant, just outside Lampeter, surveys spectacular Teifi Valley from on high. Originally built in 1859 as a distinguished private home, this Victorian Italianate villa is a South West Wales treasure whose acres of peaceful ornamental woods and lawns are set to a stunning backdrop of the Cambrian Mountains and Cardigan Bay. Owned by Chris and Lisa, a warm welcome greets each guest to their remote country escape, which is a wonderful choice for weddings or business events. As a Victorian house, The Falcondale's guest rooms vary in shape and size, each affectionately categorised into Small, Standard, Better and Best indicative of their size and grandeur. Small and Standard rooms are perfect for those travelling on business or visiting for a short break, while the Better or Best rooms are more spacious and look out to the rolling green pastures of the Valley. Food at Falcondale is seriously good with a reputation for getting the best out of the region's rich larder (lobster, crab, Welsh lamb and beef, speciality cheeses…) under the direction of Head Chef Mike Green. Watch out for: The Falcondale's year-round themed packages such as Romantic Getaways and Dog Training courses.

PRICE FROM:
£140

FEATURES:
Family friendly; Pet friendly; Restaurant; Wheelchair access

ACTIVITIES:
Fishing; Golf; Walking

NEARBY:
Llanerchaeron (National Trust); Dolaucothi gold mines (National Trust); University of Wales; National Botanic Garden of Wales

GETTING THERE:
M4; Carmarthen/Aberystwyth Railway Stations; Cardiff Airport

+44 (0)1570 422910 ☎
condenastjohansens.com/falcondale 🌐
Falcondale Drive, Lampeter, Ceredigion SA48 7RX, Wales 🏠

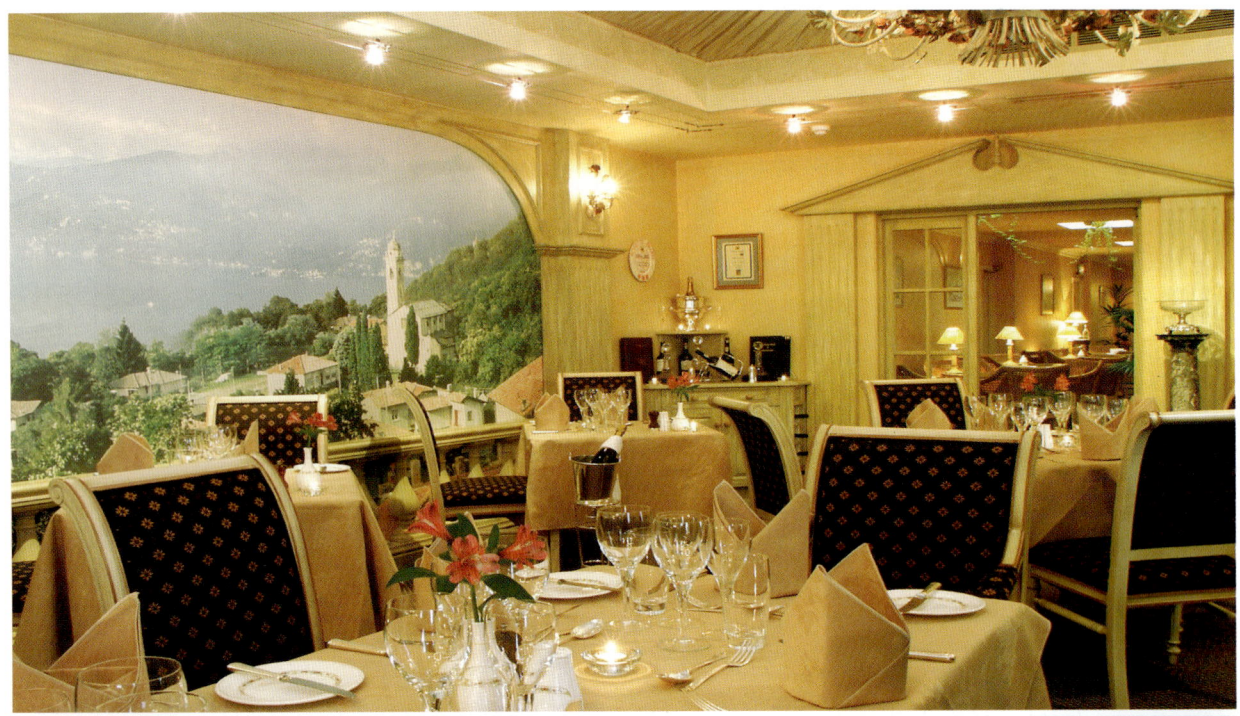

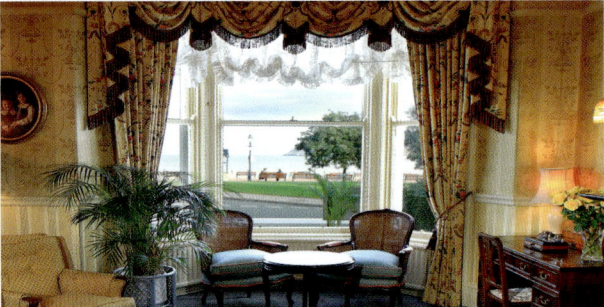

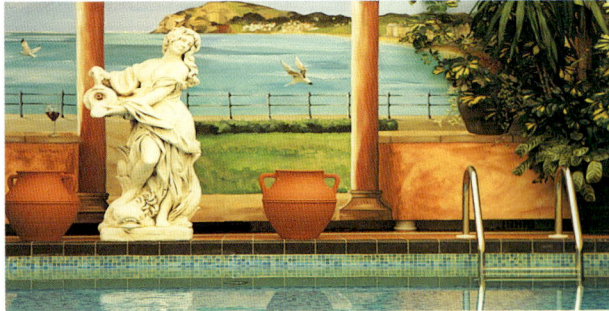

St Tudno Hotel & Restaurant

Llandudno Promenade's most welcoming Victorian seaside hotel

PRICE FROM:
£98

FEATURES:
Family friendly; Pet friendly; Pool; Restaurant; Sea views

ACTIVITIES:
Fishing; Golf; Walking

NEARBY:
Theatre at Llandudno; Bodnant Gardens; Dry ski slope and toboggan run on the Great Orme; Conwy Castle; Caernarfon Castle; Snowdonia National Park

GETTING THERE:
On the A470; Llandudno Railway Station; Manchester Airport

☎ +44 (0)1492 874411
🌐 condenastjohansens.com/sttudno
🏠 North Promenade, Llandudno, North Wales LL30 2LP, Wales

With more than 40 years of hospitality to its name, St Tudno Hotel & Restaurant in Llandudno is one of Wales' most charming small hotels. Superbly located on the seafront, you're in prime position for enjoying the promenade, pier and sandy beach. Intimate and cosseting with just 18 bedrooms, this lovingly refurbished hotel (complete with passenger lift) provides a particularly warm welcome only found in smaller hotels. Owner Martin Bland and his staff take special care to enhance each guest's stay from the individuality of the bedrooms featuring thoughtful extras such as complimentary WiFi, to the special dining experience in the 2 AA Rosette-awarded Terrace Restaurant. Regarded as one of Wales' leading places to eat, its seasonal menus highlight Welsh favourites and local meats, while St Tudno's afternoon teas are gaining well-deserved attention for their outstanding quality of pastries and sandwiches. Reached via the Secret Garden, St Tudno's indoor heated swimming pool is a restful sanctuary surrounded by plants with a mural of Llandudno Bay at one end. However, there's a whole host of attractions outside to explore such as Snowdonia National Park, the world-famous Bodnant Gardens, Anglesey and glorious walks on the Great Orme. Previous awards include: Johansens Hotel Award for Excellence; Best Seaside Resort Hotel in Great Britain (Good Hotel Guide); Welsh Hotel of the Year.

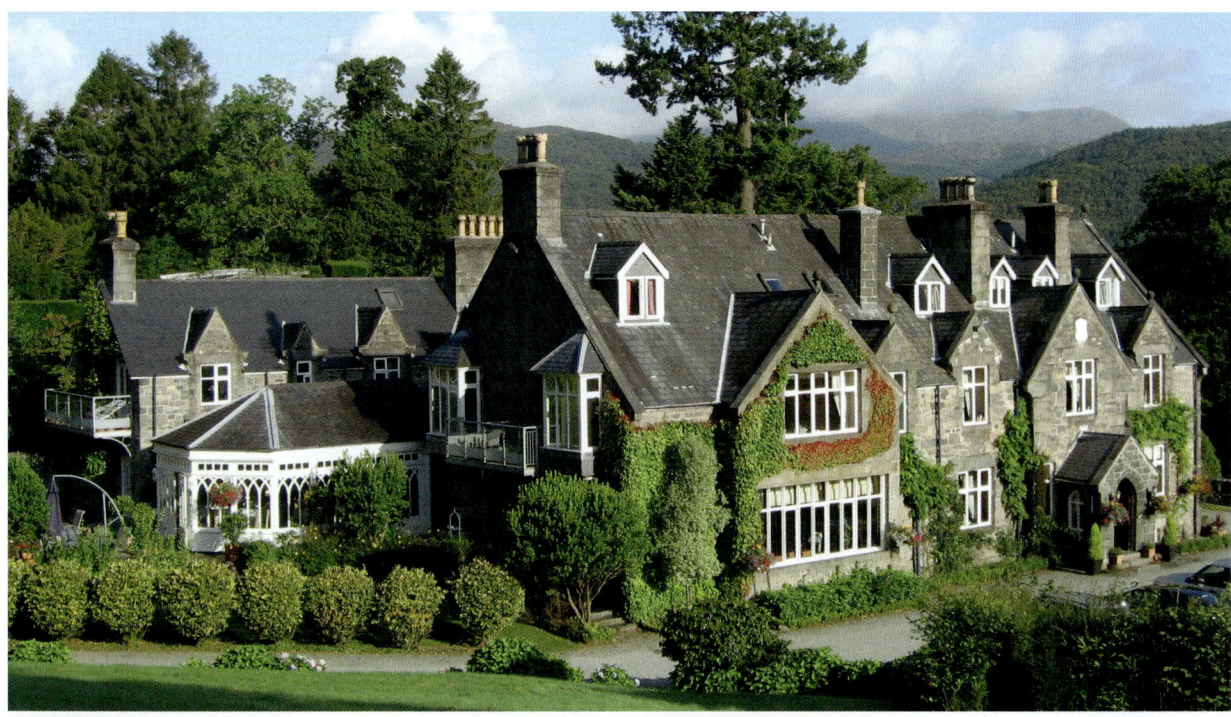

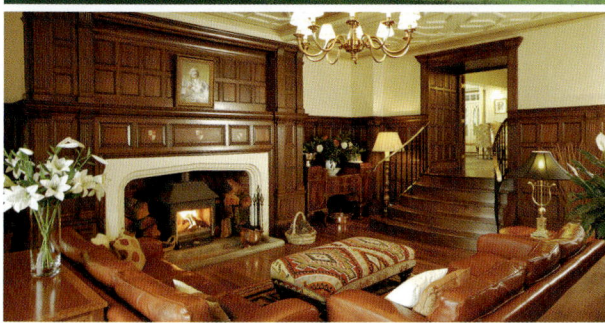

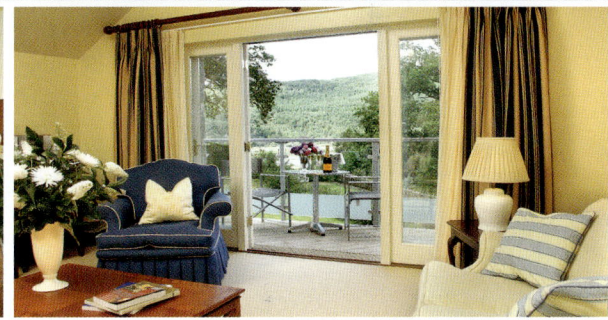

Penmaenuchaf Hall

Grand Victorian mansion proudly presiding over Snowdonia National Park

In the south of the Snowdonia National Park where Mid and North Wales meet, the handsome Victorian Penmaenuchaf Hall stands. Presiding over arresting scenery across the Mawddach Estuary and to distant wooded mountain slopes, it's near the market town of Dolgellau. From the moment you reach the end of the long tree-lined drive you're in a state of relaxation for Penmaenuchaf's all-encompassing comfort has you captive from the get-go. Original oak and mahogany panelling, stained-glass windows, slate floors, squishy sofas and log fires in winter set the scene, keeping you rooted to the soothing spot. Bedrooms have you hypnotised with views from their balconies. However, move you must, for a natural playground alive with sporting adventure is all around you. Fishing along the Mawddach River (or llyn Penmaenuchaf) is within the hotel's grounds and mountain biking, off-roading, sandy beaches, walking/hiking routes, bird-watching and championship golf are all on the doorstep. The hotel's very own acres of private manicured lawns featuring both a water and lavender garden and woodland, are particularly peaceful and the ideal spot for a stroll after a meal at the garden room restaurant. Contemporary British food is the theme here, packed with flavour from local produce and home-grown herbs, salads and vegetables.

PRICE FROM:
£170

FEATURES:
Helipad; Pet friendly; Restaurant

ACTIVITIES:
Fishing; Golf; Walking

NEARBY:
Snowdonia National Park; Narrow Guage Railways; Bodnant Gardens; Portmeirion; Shrewsbury

GETTING THERE:
Manchester Airport; Birmingham Airport; Morfa Mawddach Railway Station

+44 (0)1341 422129 ☎
condenastjohansens.com/penmaenuchafhall 🌐
Penmaenpool, Dolgellau, Gwynedd LL40 1YB, Wales 🏠

298

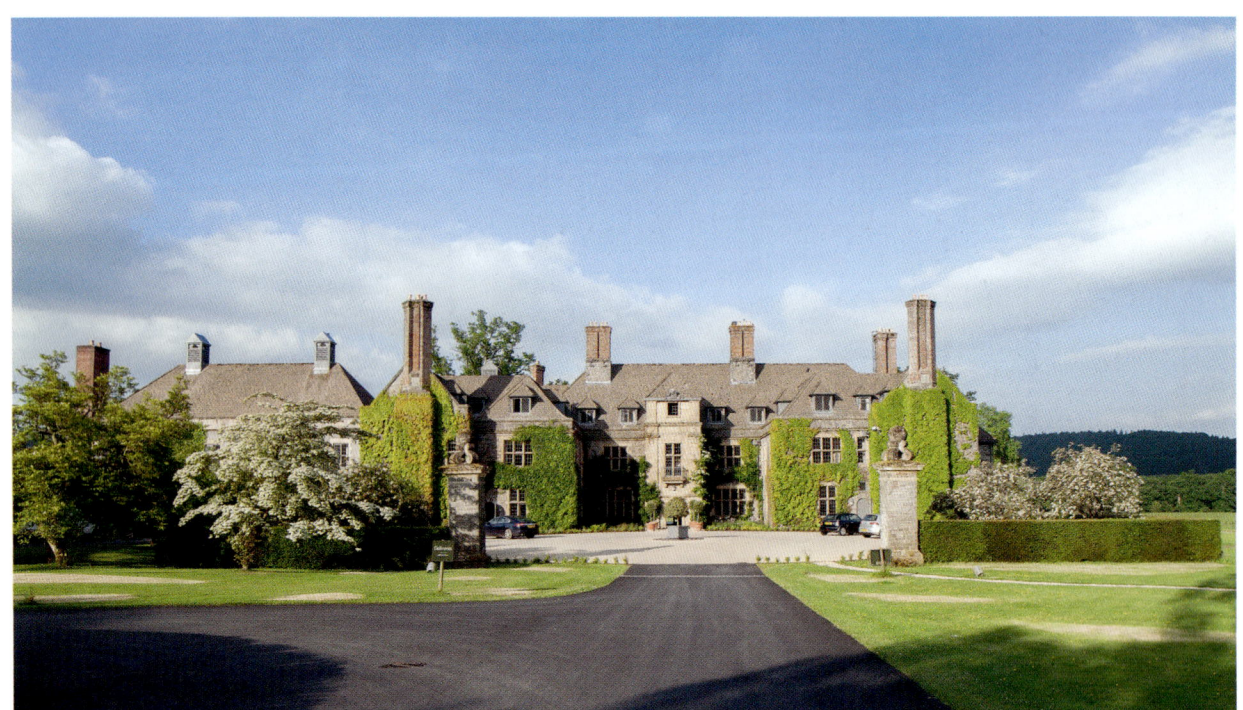

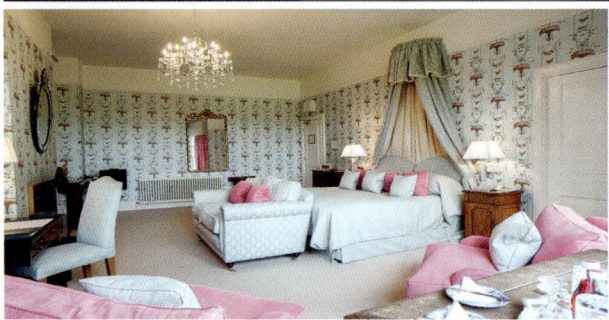
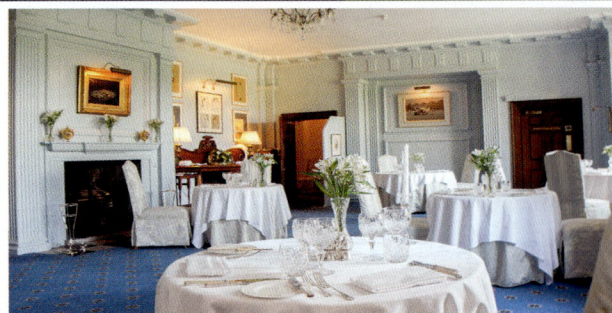

Llangoed Hall

A celebration of Welsh countryside and Edwardian architecture

PRICE FROM:
£150

FEATURES:
Helipad; Pet friendly; Restaurant

ACTIVITIES:
Fishing; Sightseeing; Walking

NEARBY:
Brecon Beacons National Park; Black Mountains; Hay-on-Wye specialist book shops; Hereford Cathedral; Tretower Court

GETTING THERE:
A470; M4 jct 24; Cardiff Airport

Left for ruin in the 1980s, the saviour of centuries-old Llangoed Hall in Wye Valley's designated Area of Outstanding Natural Beauty was Sir Bernard Ashley. Armed with an artistic flair, dogged determination, his children's professional expertise and the memory of late wife and business partner (Laura Ashley of chic country-style fame), the resurrection of Llangoed Hall took three years. Architect Sir Bertram Clough Williams-Ellis's 1912 redesign had been preserved. 23 years on and Llangoed is under new ownership determined to continue the rural home ambience Sir Bernard created. Although sensitive to Llangoed's Jacobean legacy (specifically the south wing's arched porch), the Hall is a mass of Edwardian style exhibiting many of the era's artistic greats. Antiques and artworks fashioned by Walter Sickert, Augustus John and Rex Whistler adorn the interiors. It's all a very British affair. In fact, only products with The Royal Warrant Holders Association stamp will do. Timeless and elegant, the formal Dining Room is a testament to local Welsh produce (black beef and Radnorshire lamb) seasoned to perfection with herbs from Llangoed's gardens.

☎ +44 (0)1874 754525
🌐 condenastjohansens.com/llangoedhall
🏠 Llyswen, Brecon, Powys LD3 0YP, Wales

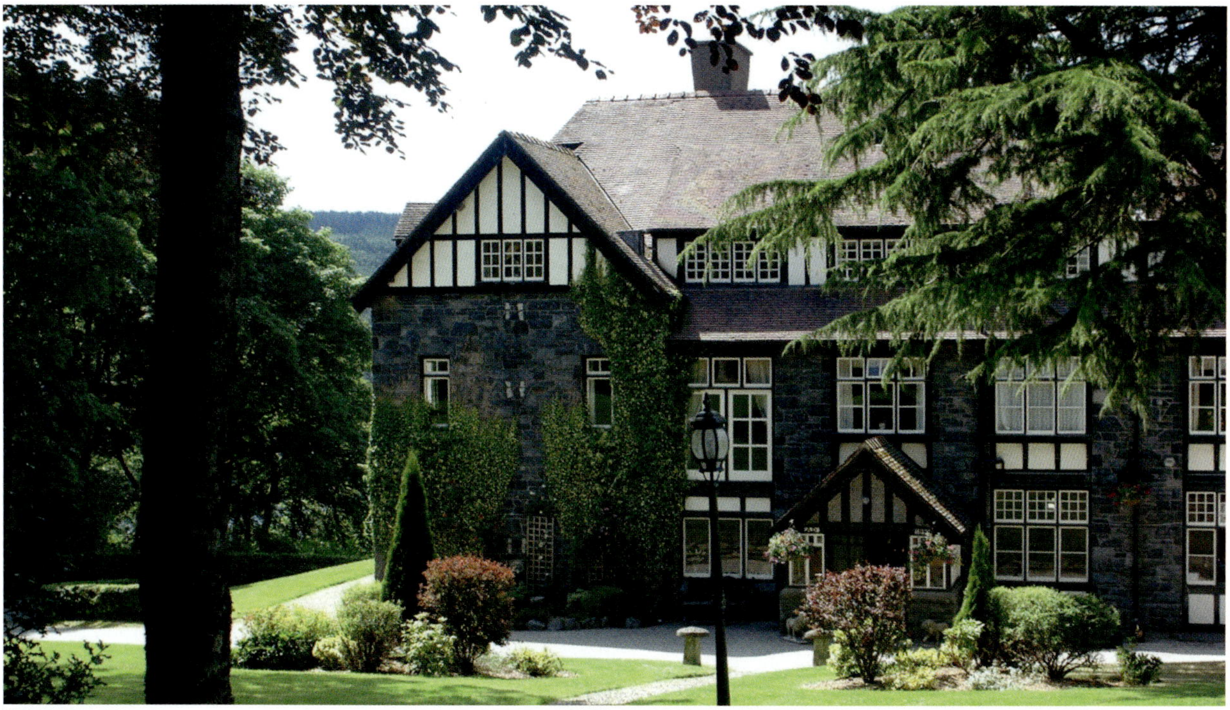

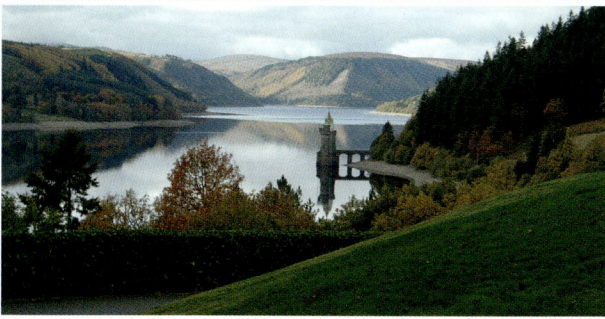
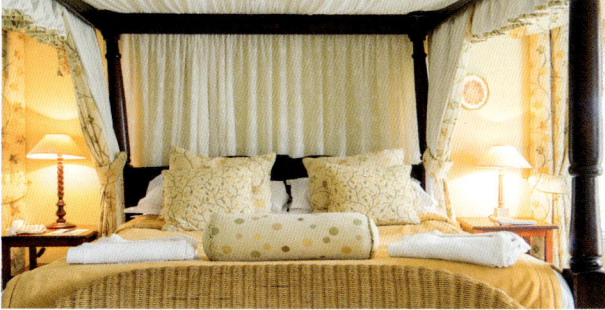

Lake Vyrnwy Hotel & Spa

The Mid Wales secret that needs to be told

The location of Lake Vyrnwy Hotel & Spa, Mid Wales, is simply magical. Overlooking the stunning lake surrounded by wild moorland, forest and the rugged Berwyn mountains, the natural beauty of this special place is designated a protected Natural Nature Reserve. It's also a Site of Special Scientific Interest and a Special Area of Conservation, which means this picturesque getaway is an outdoor enthusiast's dream. Fantastic walking trails and opportunities for clay shooting, fly-fishing, water sports and cycling are all on the doorstep. Jaw-dropping vistas can be admired from the warm ambience of Lake Vyrnwy Hotel's drawing room where sumptuous sofas invite you to while away the hours. Balconies located off most bedrooms also take in the intoxicating view. As the sun goes down, the Tower Bar Lounge's balcony is the perfect spot to savour a glass of wine before enjoying dinner in the restaurant where the menus reflect a genuine enthusiasm for food prepared from as much local produce as possible. The contemporary Tavern Bar is ideal for more informal dining. For the complete Lake Vyrnwy Hotel experience, a touch of pampering in the luxury spa and thermal suite; its extensive range of therapies and array of facilities include an Arabian rasul mud therapy chamber and Monsoon shower.

PRICE FROM:
£144

FEATURES:
Gym; Helipad; Lake views; Pet friendly; Spa

ACTIVITIES:
Fishing; Shooting; Walking

NEARBY:
Powis Castle; Snowdonia National Park; Portmeirion; Centre for Alternative Technology; Little Railways of Wales

GETTING THERE:
A490; Shrewsbury/Welshpool Railway Stations; Mid Wales Airport

+44 (0)1691 870692 ☎
condenastjohansens.com/lakevyrnwy 🌐
Lake Vyrnwy, Llanwddyn, Powys SY10 0LY, Wales 🏠

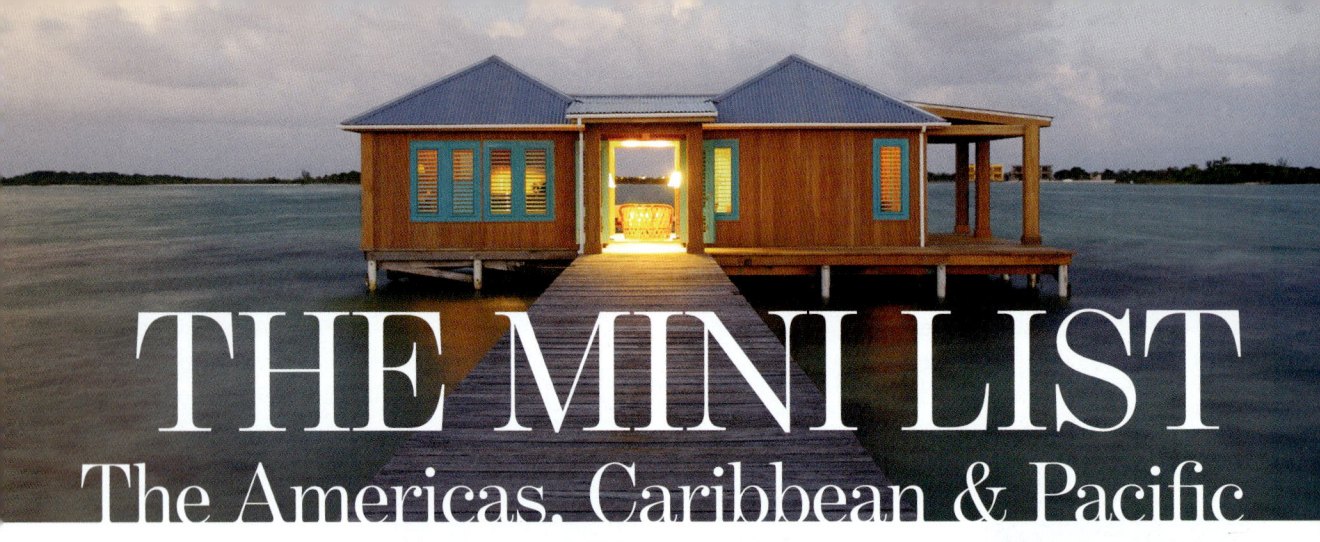

THE MINI LIST
The Americas, Caribbean & Pacific

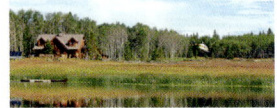

CANADA - BRITISH COLUMBIA (BANFF)

Siwash Lake Ranch

Box 39, 70 Mile House, British Columbia V0K 2K0, Canada

Tel: +1 250 395 6541
condenastjohansens.com/siwashlakeranch

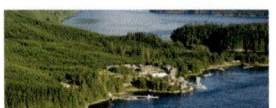

CANADA - BRITISH COLUMBIA (SONORA ISLAND)

Sonora Resort

Sonora Island, British Columbia, Canada

Tel: +1 604 233 0460
condenastjohansens.com/sonoraresort

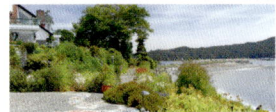

CANADA - BRITISH COLUMBIA (SOOKE)

Sooke Harbour House

1528 Whiffen Spit Road, Sooke, British Columbia V9Z 0T4, Canada

Tel: +1 250 642 3421
condenastjohansens.com/sookeharbour

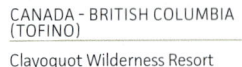

CANADA - BRITISH COLUMBIA (TOFINO)

Clayoquot Wilderness Resort

Tofino, British Columbia V0R 2Z0, Canada

Tel: +1 250 726 8235
condenastjohansens.com/clayoquot

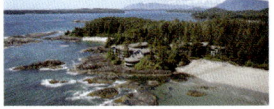

CANADA - BRITISH COLUMBIA (TOFINO)

Wickaninnish Inn

Osprey Lane at Chesterman Beach, Tofino, British Columbia V0R 2Z0, Canada

Tel: +1 250 725 3100
condenastjohansens.com/wickaninnish

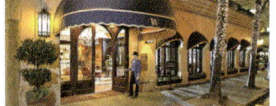

CANADA - BRITISH COLUMBIA (VANCOUVER)

Wedgewood Hotel & Spa

845 Hornby Street, Vancouver, British Columbia V6Z 1V1, Canada

Tel: +1 604 689 7777
condenastjohansens.com/wedgewoodbc

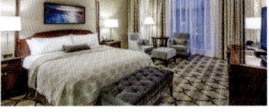

CANADA - BRITISH COLUMBIA (VICTORIA)

The Magnolia Hotel & Spa

623 Courtney Street, Victoria, British Columbia V8W 1B8, Canada

Tel: +1 250 381 0999
condenastjohansens.com/magnoliahotel

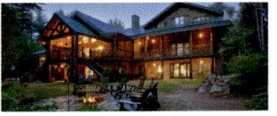

CANADA - NOVA SCOTIA (EAST KEMPTVILLE)

Trout Point Lodge of Nova Scotia

189 Trout Point Road, Off the East Branch Road and Highway 203, East Kemptville, Nova Scotia B0W 1Y0, Canada

Tel: +1 902 761 2142
condenastjohansens.com/troutpoint

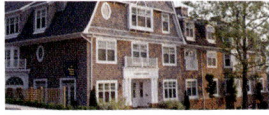

CANADA - ONTARIO (NIAGARA-ON-THE-LAKE)

Harbour House

85 Melville Street, Box 760, Niagara-on-the-Lake, Ontario L0S 1J0, Canada

Tel: +1 905 468 4683
condenastjohansens.com/harbourhouseca

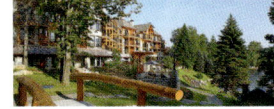

CANADA - QUÉBEC (MONT-TREMBLANT)

Hôtel Quintessence

3004 chemin de la chapelle, Mont-Tremblant, Québec J8E 1E1, Canada

Tel: +1 819 425 3400
condenastjohansens.com/quintessence

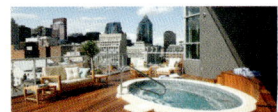

CANADA - QUÉBEC (MONTRÉAL)

Hotel le Crystal

1100 rue de la Montagne, Montréal, Québec H3G 0A1, Canada

Tel: +1 877 861 5550
condenastjohansens.com/hotellecrystal

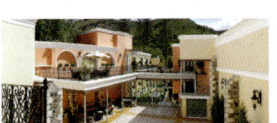

MÉXICO - GUANAJUATO (GUANAJUATO)

Villa María Cristina

Paseo de La Presa de la Olla No 76 Centro, Guanajuato, Guanajuato 36000, México

Tel: +52 473 731 2182
condenastjohansens.com/villamariacristina

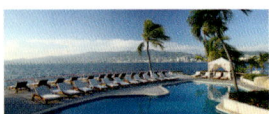

MÉXICO - GUERRERO (ACAPULCO)

Las Brisas Acapulco

Carretera Escenica 5255, Acapulco, Guerrero 39867, México

Tel: +52 744 469 6900
condenastjohansens.com/brisasacapulco

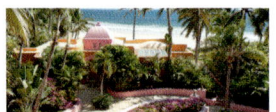

MÉXICO - JALISCO (COSTALEGRE - PUERTO VALLARTA)

Las Alamandas Resort

Carretera Federal 200, Km 83.5, Costalegre, Jalisco 48850, México

Tel: +52 322 285 5500
condenastjohansens.com/alamandas

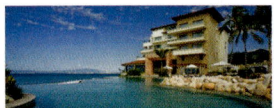

MÉXICO - JALISCO (PUERTO VALLARTA)

Garza Blanca Preserve Resort & Spa

Km 7.5 Carretera a Barra de Navidad, Puerto Vallarta, Jalisco 48390, México

Tel: +52 322 176 0700
condenastjohansens.com/garzablancaresort

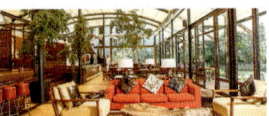

MÉXICO - MÉXICO (VALLE DE BRAVO)

Hotel Rodavento

Km 3.5 Carretera Valle de Bravo - Los Saucos, Valle de Bravo, México 51200, México

Tel: +52 726 251 4182
condenastjohansens.com/rodavento

Properties listed here can be found in our 2014 The Americas, Caribbean & Pacific Guide and online at condenastjohansens.com

Top image: Cayo Espanto a private island, Belize, Caribbean

THE MINI LIST
The Americas, Caribbean & Pacific

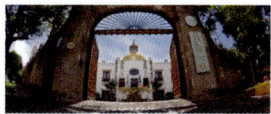

MÉXICO - MORELOS (CUERNAVACA)

Anticavilla Hotel, Restaurante & Spa

Rio Amacuzac No 10, Esquina Chilpancingo, Col Vista Hermosa, Cuernavaca, Morelos 62290, México

Tel: +52 777 313 3131
condenastjohansens.com/anticavillahotel

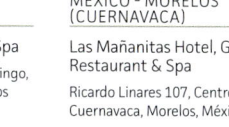

MÉXICO - MORELOS (CUERNAVACA)

Las Mañanitas Hotel, Garden Restaurant & Spa

Ricardo Linares 107, Centro 62000, Cuernavaca, Morelos, México

Tel: +52 777 362 00 00
condenastjohansens.com/lasmananitas

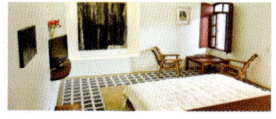

MÉXICO - MORELOS (TEPOZTLÁN)

Hostal de La Luz

Carretera Federal Tepoztlán, Amatlan Km 4, Tepoztlán, Morelos 62524, México

Tel: +1 739 393 3076
condenastjohansens.com/hostaldelaluz

MÉXICO - OAXACA (OAXACA)

Azul de Oaxaca Hotel + Galeria

Abasolo 313, Centro, 68000 Oaxaca, Oaxaca, México

Tel: +52 951 501 0016
condenastjohansens.com/hotelazuloaxaca

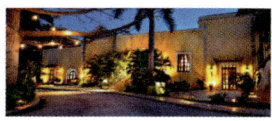

MÉXICO - YUCATÁN (MÉRIDA)

Hacienda Xcanatún - Casa de Piedra

Calle 20 S/N, Comisaría Xcanatún, Km 12 Carretera Mérida - Progreso, Mérida, Yucatán 97302, México

Tel: +52 999 930 2140
condenastjohansens.com/xcanatun

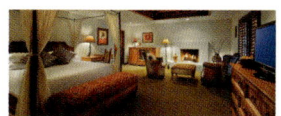

USA - ARIZONA (PARADISE VALLEY)

The Hermosa Inn

5532 North Palo Cristi Road, Paradise Valley, Arizona 85253, USA

Tel: +1 602 955 8614
condenastjohansens.com/hermosa

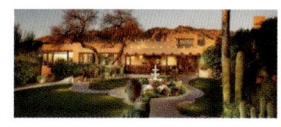

USA - ARIZONA (PARADISE VALLEY - SCOTTSDALE)

Sanctuary Camelback Mountain Resort & Spa

5700 East McDonald Drive, Scottsdale, Arizona 85253, USA

Tel: +1 480 948 2100
condenastjohansens.com/sanctuaryaz

USA - ARIZONA (TUCSON)

Hacienda del Sol Guest Ranch Resort

5501 North Hacienda del Sol Road, Tucson, Arizona 85718, USA

Tel: +1 520 299 1501
condenastjohansens.com/haciendadelsol

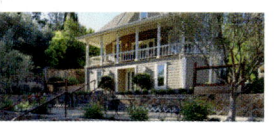

USA - CALIFORNIA (CALISTOGA)

The Chanric Inn

1805 Foothill Boulevard, Calistoga, California 94515, USA

Tel: +1 707 942 4535
condenastjohansens.com/chanricinn

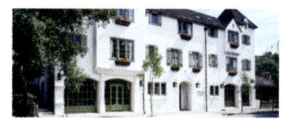

USA - CALIFORNIA (CARMEL-BY-THE-SEA)

L'Auberge Carmel

Monte Verde at Seventh, Carmel-by-the-Sea, California 93921, USA

Tel: +1 831 624 8578
condenastjohansens.com/laubergecarmel

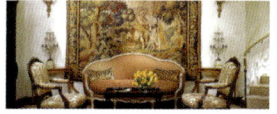

USA - CALIFORNIA (CARMEL VALLEY)

Bernardus Lodge

415 West Carmel Valley Road, Carmel Valley, California 93924, USA

Tel: +1 888 648 9463
condenastjohansens.com/bernardus

USA - CALIFORNIA (HEALDSBURG)

Hotel Les Mars

27 North Street, Healdsburg, California 95448, USA

Tel: +1 707 433 4211
condenastjohansens.com/lesmarshotel

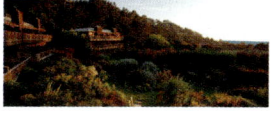

USA - CALIFORNIA (MENDOCINO)

The Stanford Inn By The Sea

Coast Highway One & Comptche-Ukiah Road, Mendocino, California 95460, USA

Tel: +1 707 937 5615
condenastjohansens.com/stanfordinn

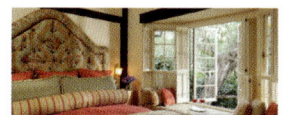

USA - CALIFORNIA (MONTEREY)

Old Monterey Inn

500 Martin Street, Monterey, California 93940, USA

Tel: +1 831 375 8284
condenastjohansens.com/oldmontereyinn

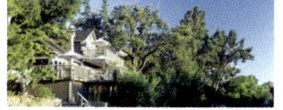

USA - CALIFORNIA (NAPA)

Milliken Creek Inn and Spa

1815 Silverado Trail, Napa, California 94558, USA

Tel: +1 707 255 1197
condenastjohansens.com/milliken

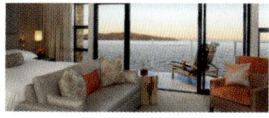

USA - CALIFORNIA (SAN FRANCISCO BAY AREA)

Inn Above Tide

30 El Portal, Sausalito, California 94965, USA

Tel: +1 415 332 9535
condenastjohansens.com/innabovetide

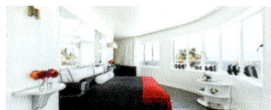

USA - CALIFORNIA (SANTA MONICA)

Hotel Shangri-La

1301 Ocean Avenue, Santa Monica, California 90401, USA

Tel: +1 310 394 2791
condenastjohansens.com/shangrilaca

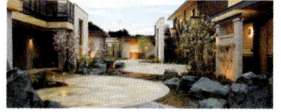

USA - CALIFORNIA (YOUNTVILLE)

Bardessono Hotel & Spa

6526 Yount Street, Yountville, California 94599, USA

Tel: +1 707 204 6000
condenastjohansens.com/bardessono

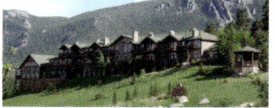

USA - COLORADO (ESTES PARK)

Taharaa Mountain Lodge

3110 S Saint Vrain Avenue, Estes Park, Colorado 80517, USA

Tel: +1 970 577 0098
condenastjohansens.com/taharaa

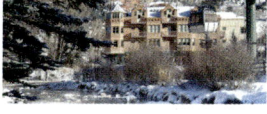

USA - COLORADO (TELLURIDE)

Hotel Columbia

301 West San Juan Avenue, Telluride, Colorado 81435, USA

Tel: +1 970 728 0660/6294
condenastjohansens.com/columbiatelluride

Properties listed here can be found in our 2014 The Americas, Caribbean & Pacific Guide and online at condenastjohansens.com

THE MINI LIST
The Americas, Caribbean & Pacific

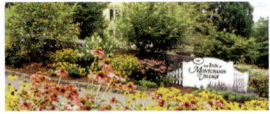

USA - DELAWARE (WILMINGTON)

Inn at Montchanin Village & Spa

Route 100 & Kirk Road, Montchanin,
Wilmington, Delaware 19710, USA

Tel: +1 302 888 2133
condenastjohansens.com/montchanin

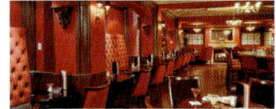

USA - DISTRICT OF COLUMBIA (WASHINGTON D.C.)

The Hay-Adams

Sixteenth & H Streets NW, Washington D.C.,
District of Columbia 20006, USA

Tel: +1 202 638 6600
condenastjohansens.com/hayadams

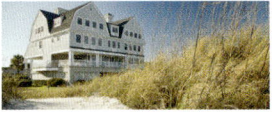

USA - FLORIDA (AMELIA ISLAND)

Elizabeth Pointe Lodge

98 South Fletcher Avenue, Amelia Island,
Florida 32034, USA

Tel: +1 800 112 3359
condenastjohansens.com/elizabethpointelodge

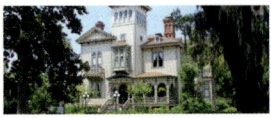

USA - FLORIDA (AMELIA ISLAND)

The Fairbanks House

227 South 7th Street, Amelia Island, Florida
32034, USA

Tel: +1 904 277 0500
condenastjohansens.com/fairbankshouse

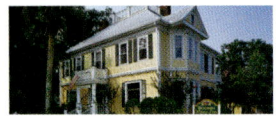

USA - FLORIDA (APALACHICOLA)

Coombs House Inn

80 Sixth Street, Corner of Avenue E & 6th
Street, Apalachicola, St George Island,
Florida 32320, USA

Tel: +1 850 653 9199
condenastjohansens.com/coombshouse

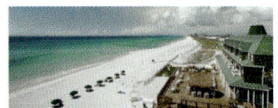

USA - FLORIDA (DESTIN)

Henderson Park Inn

2700 Scenic Highway 98, Destin, Florida
32541, USA

Tel: +1 866 398 4432
condenastjohansens.com/henderson

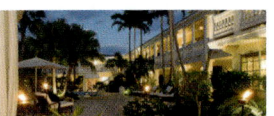

USA - FLORIDA (FORT LAUDERDALE)

The Pillars Hotel

111 North Birch Road, Fort Lauderdale,
Florida 33304, USA

Tel: +1 954 467 9639
condenastjohansens.com/pillarshotel

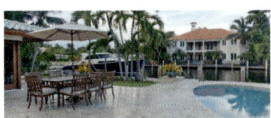

USA - FLORIDA (FORT LAUDERDALE)

The Pillars Villa

111 North Birch Road, Fort Lauderdale,
Florida 33304, USA

Tel: +1 954 467 9639
condenastjohansens.com/pillarsvilla

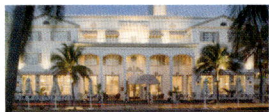

USA - FLORIDA (MIAMI BEACH)

The Betsy - South Beach

1440 Ocean Drive, Miami Beach, Florida
33139, USA

Tel: +1 305 531 6100
condenastjohansens.com/thebetsyhotel

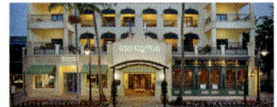

USA - FLORIDA (NAPLES)

The Inn On Fifth

699 5th Avenue South, Naples, Florida
34102, USA

Tel: +1 239 403 8777
condenastjohansens.com/innonfifth

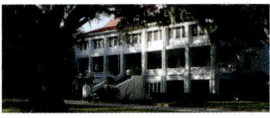

USA - GEORGIA (CUMBERLAND ISLAND)

Greyfield Inn

Cumberland Island, Georgia, USA

Tel: +1 904 261 6408
condenastjohansens.com/greyfieldinn

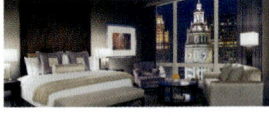

USA - ILLINOIS (CHICAGO)

Trump International Hotel & Tower®
Chicago

401 North Wabash Avenue, Chicago, Illinois
60611, USA

Tel: +1 312 588 8000
condenastjohansens.com/trumpchicago

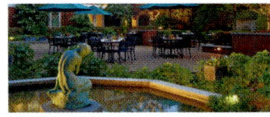

USA - MAINE (PORTLAND)

Portland Harbor Hotel

468 Fore Street, Portland, Maine 04101,
USA

Tel: +1 207 775 9090
condenastjohansens.com/portlandharbor

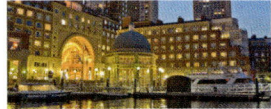

USA - MASSACHUSETTS (BOSTON)

Boston Harbor Hotel

70 Rowes Wharf, Boston, Massachusetts
02110, USA

Tel: +1 617 439 7000
condenastjohansens.com/bhh

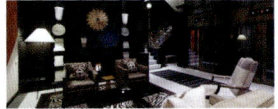

USA - MASSACHUSETTS (BOSTON)

Fifteen Beacon

15 Beacon Street, Boston, Massachusetts
02108, USA

Tel: +1 617 670 1500
condenastjohansens.com/xvbeacon

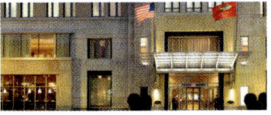

USA - MASSACHUSETTS (BOSTON)

Mandarin Oriental, Boston

776 Boylston Street, Boston, Massachusetts
02199, USA

Tel: +1 617 535 8888
condenastjohansens.com/mandarinorientalboston

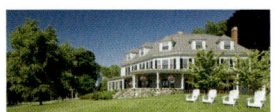

USA - MASSACHUSETTS (IPSWICH)

The Inn at Castle Hill

280 Argilla Road, Ipswich, Massachusetts
01938, USA

Tel: +1 978 412 2555
condenastjohansens.com/castlehill

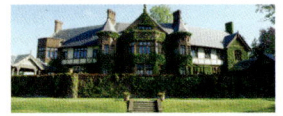

USA - MASSACHUSETTS (LENOX)

Blantyre

16 Blantyre Road, PO Box 995, Lenox,
Massachusetts 01240, USA

Tel: +1 413 637 3556
condenastjohansens.com/blantyre

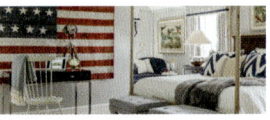

USA - MASSACHUSETTS (LEXINGTON)

The Inn at Hastings Park

2027 Massachusetts Avenue, Lexington,
Massachusetts 02421, USA

Tel: +1 781 301 6660
condenastjohansens.com/innathastingspark

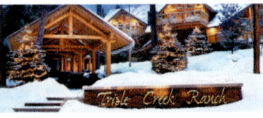

USA - MONTANA (DARBY)

Triple Creek Ranch

5551 West Fork Road, Darby, Montana
59829, USA

Tel: +1 406 821 4600
condenastjohansens.com/triplecreek

Properties listed here can be found in our 2014 The Americas, Caribbean & Pacific Guide and online at condenastjohansens.com

THE MINI LIST
The Americas, Caribbean & Pacific

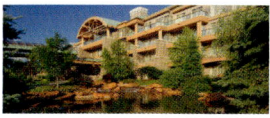

USA - NEW YORK (VERONA)

The Lodge at Turning Stone

5218 Patrick Road, Verona, New York 13478, USA

Tel: +1 315 361 8525
condenastjohansens.com/turningstone

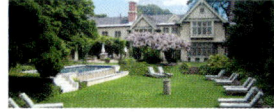

USA - NEW YORK/LONG ISLAND (EAST HAMPTON)

The Baker House 1650

181 Main Street, East Hampton, New York 11937, USA

Tel: +1 631 324 4081
condenastjohansens.com/bakerhouse

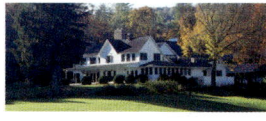

USA - NORTH CAROLINA (HIGHLANDS)

Inn at Half Mile Farm

PO Box 2769, 214 Half Mile Drive, Highlands, North Carolina 28741, USA

Tel: +1 828 526 8170
condenastjohansens.com/halfmilefarm

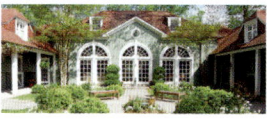

USA - VIRGINIA (MIDDLEBURG)

Goodstone Inn & Restaurant

36205 Snake Hill Road, Middleburg, Virginia 20117, USA

Tel: +1 540 687 3333
condenastjohansens.com/goodstoneinn

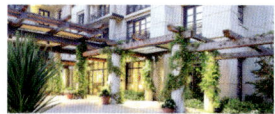

USA - WASHINGTON (BELLEVUE)

Hotel Bellevue

11200 South East 6th Street, Bellevue, Washington 98004, USA

Tel: +1 425 454 4424
condenastjohansens.com/bellevue

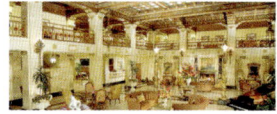

USA - WASHINGTON (SPOKANE)

The Davenport Hotel and Tower

10 South Post Street, Spokane, Washington 99201, USA

Tel: +1 509 455 8888
condenastjohansens.com/davenport

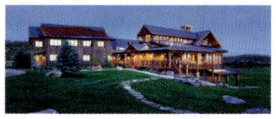

USA - WYOMING (SARATOGA)

The Lodge and Spa at Brush Creek Ranch

66 Brush Creek Ranch Road, Saratoga, Wyoming 82331, USA

Tel: +1 307 327 5284
condenastjohansens.com/brushcreekranch

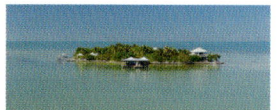

BELIZE - AMBERGRIS CAYE (CAYO ESPANTO)

Cayo Espanto a private island

Ambergris Caye, Cayo Espanto, Belize

Tel: +910 323 8355
condenastjohansens.com/cayoespanto

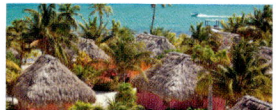

BELIZE - AMBERGRIS CAYE (SAN PEDRO)

Matachica Resort & Spa

5 Miles North of San Pedro, Ambergris Caye, Belize

Tel: +501 226 5010/1
condenastjohansens.com/matachica

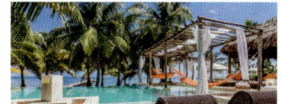

BELIZE - AMBERGRIS CAYE (SAN PEDRO)

El Secreto

11 Miles North of San Pedro, Ambergris Caye, Belize

Tel: +501 236 5111
condenastjohansens.com/elsecreto

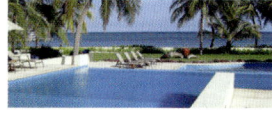

BELIZE - AMBERGRIS CAYE (SAN PEDRO)

The Phoenix Resort

San Pedro, Ambergris Caye, Belize

Tel: +501 226 2083
condenastjohansens.com/thephoenixbelize

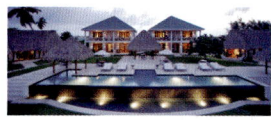

BELIZE - AMBERGRIS CAYE (SAN PEDRO)

Victoria House

San Pedro, Ambergris Caye, Belize

Tel: +501 226 2067
condenastjohansens.com/victoriahouse

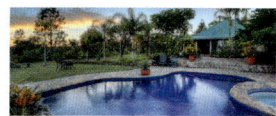

BELIZE - CAYO DISTRICT (MOUNTAIN PINE RIDGE)

Hidden Valley Inn & Reserve

Mountain Pine Ridge, Belmopan, Belize

Tel: +501 822 3320
condenastjohansens.com/hiddenvalleyinn

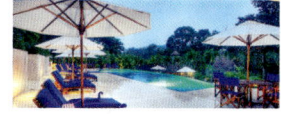

BELIZE - CAYO DISTRICT (SAN IGNACIO)

The Lodge at Chaa Creek

San Ignacio, Cayo District, Belize

Tel: +501 834 4009/10
condenastjohansens.com/chaacreek

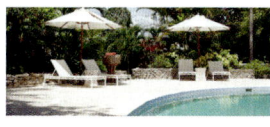

BELIZE - TOLEDO DISTRICT (PUNTA GORDA)

Belcampo Lodge Belize

Punta Gorda, Toledo District, Belize

Tel: +501 722 0050
condenastjohansens.com/belcampo

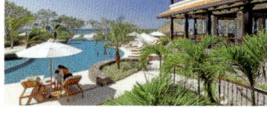

COSTA RICA - GUANACASTE (PINILLA)

Hacienda Pinilla Villas

Pinilla, Guanacaste, Costa Rica

Tel: +506 26 81 43 18
condenastjohansens.com/haciendapinilla

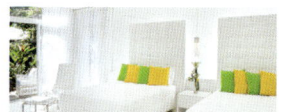

COSTA RICA - LIMÓN (PUERTO VIEJO)

Le Caméléon Boutique Hotel

Cocles Beach, Puerto Viejo, Limón, Costa Rica

Tel: +506 2272 7056/7036
condenastjohansens.com/lecameleon

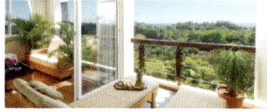

COSTA RICA - PUNTARENAS (MANUEL ANTONIO)

Gaia Hotel & Reserve

Km 2.7 Ctra Quepos, Manuel Antonio, Puntarenas, Costa Rica

Tel: +506 2777 9797
condenastjohansens.com/gaiahr

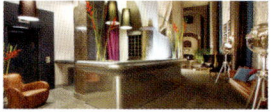

COSTA RICA - SAN JOSÉ (SANTA ANA)

alta hotel

Alto de las Palomas, Old Road Escazu, Santa Ana, Costa Rica

Tel: +506 2282 4160
condenastjohansens.com/altahotel

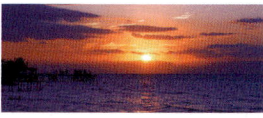

GUATEMALA - IZABAL (LAKE IZABAL)

G Boutique Hotel at Mariscos

Lake Izabal, Mariscos, Izabal, Guatemala

Tel: +502 2441 8795
condenastjohansens.com/gguatemala

Properties listed here can be found in our 2014 The Americas, Caribbean & Pacific Guide and online at condenastjohansens.com

THE MINI LIST
The Americas, Caribbean & Pacific

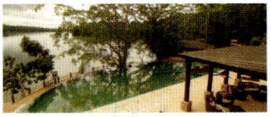

GUATEMALA - PETÉN (FLORES)

Las Lagunas Boutique Hotel

Laguna Quexil, Desarrollo Tayasal, Km 1 Carretera a San Miguel, Flores, Petén, Guatemala

Tel: +502 3009 4800

condenastjohansens.com/laslagunashotel

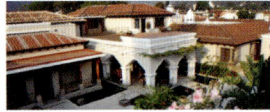

GUATEMALA - SACATEPÉQUEZ (LA ANTIGUA GUATEMALA)

Casa Rosal

4a Avenida Sur # 24, La Antigua Guatemala, Sacatepéquez, Guatemala

Tel: +502 7955 5353

condenastjohansens.com/casarosal

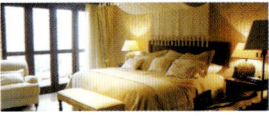

GUATEMALA - SACATEPÉQUEZ (LA ANTIGUA GUATEMALA)

El Convento Boutique Hotel

2a Avenue Norte 11, La Antigua Guatemala, Sacatepéquez, Guatemala

Tel: +502 7720 7272

condenastjohansens.com/elconventoantigua

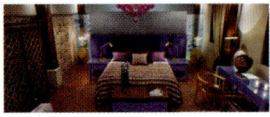

GUATEMALA - SACATEPÉQUEZ (LA ANTIGUA GUATEMALA)

Mil Flores Luxury Design Hotel

3a Calle Oriente 16, La Antigua Guatemala, Sacatepéquez, Guatemala

Tel: +502 7832 9715/6

condenastjohansens.com/hotelmilflores

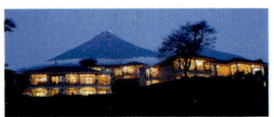

GUATEMALA - SACATEPÉQUEZ (SAN JUAN ALOTENANGO - ANTIGUA GUATEMALA)

La Reunión Golf Resort & Residences

Km 91.5 Ruta Nacional 14, San Juan Alotenango, Sacatepéquez, Guatemala

Tel: +502 7873 1400

condenastjohansens.com/lareunion

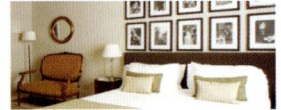

ARGENTINA - BUENOS AIRES (CIUDAD DE BUENOS AIRES)

Legado Mitico

Gurruchaga 1848, C1414DIL Ciudad de Buenos Aires, Buenos Aires, Argentina

Tel: +54 11 4833 1300

condenastjohansens.com/legadomitico

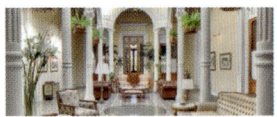

ARGENTINA - BUENOS AIRES (SAN ISIDRO)

Hotel Del Casco

Avenida del Libertador 16,170, B1642CKV, San Isidro, Buenos Aires, Argentina

Tel: +54 11 4732 3993/3553

condenastjohansens.com/hoteldelcasco

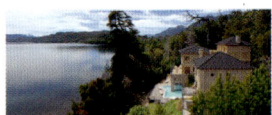

ARGENTINA - NEUQUÉN (PATAGONIA - VILLA LA ANGOSTURA)

Luma Casa de Montaña

Avenida Siete Lagos 2369 - 8407 Villa La Angostura, Neuquén, Patagonia, Argentina

Tel: +54 294 4495611

condenastjohansens.com/lumapatagonia

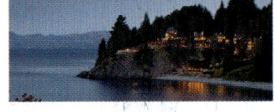

ARGENTINA - RÍO NEGRO (PATAGONIA - SAN CARLOS DE BARILOCHE)

Charming - Luxury Lodge & Private Spa

Km 7.5 Bustillo Avenue, San Carlos de Bariloche, Río Negro, Patagonia, Argentina

Tel: +54 2944 462889

condenastjohansens.com/charmingbariloche

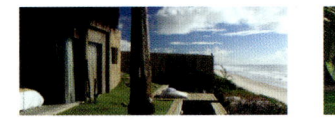

ARGENTINA - RÍO NEGRO (PATAGONIA - SAN CARLOS DE BARILOCHE)

Llao Llao Hotel & Resort Golf - Spa

Avenida Ezequiel Bustillo Km 25, San Carlos de Bariloche, Río Negro, Patagonia, Argentina

Tel: +54 294 444 5700

condenastjohansens.com/llaollao

BRAZIL - ALAGOAS (BARRA DE SÃO MIGUEL)

Kenoa - Exclusive Beach Spa & Resort

Rua Escritor Jorge Lima 58, Barra de São Miguel, Alagoas 57180-000, Brazil

Tel: +55 82 3272 1285

condenastjohansens.com/kenoaresort

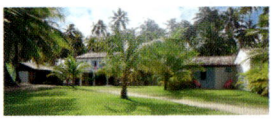

BRAZIL - ALAGOAS (PORTO DE PEDRAS)

Pousada Patacho

Praia do Patacho s/n, Porto de Pedras, Alagoas 57945-000, Brazil

Tel: +55 82 3298 1253

condenastjohansens.com/pousadapatacho

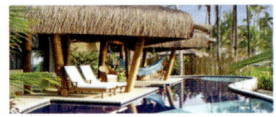

BRAZIL - ALAGOAS (SÃO MIGUEL DOS MILAGRES)

Pousada do Toque

Rua Felisberto de Ataíde, Povoado do Toque, São Miguel dos Milagres, Alagoas 57940-000, Brazil

Tel: +55 82 3295 1127

condenastjohansens.com/pousadadotoque

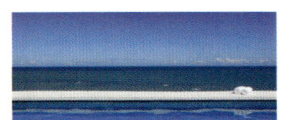

BRAZIL - BAHIA (ARRAIAL D'AJUDA)

Maitei Hotel

Estrada do Mucugê 475, Arraial D'Ajuda, Porto Seguro, Bahia 45816-000, Brazil

Tel: +55 73 3575 3877/3799

condenastjohansens.com/maitei

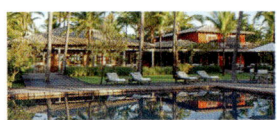

BRAZIL - BAHIA (CORUMBAU)

Fazenda São Francisco

Ponta do Corumbau s/n, Prado, Bahia, Brazil

Tel: +55 11 3078 4411

condenastjohansens.com/fazenda

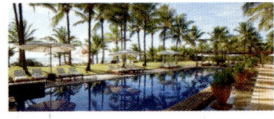

BRAZIL - BAHIA (ITACARÉ)

Txai Resort

Rod Ilhéus-Itacaré km 48, Itacaré, Bahia 45530-000, Brazil

Tel: +55 73 2101 5000

condenastjohansens.com/txairesort

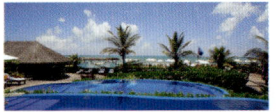

BRAZIL - BAHIA (PENÍNSULA DE MARAÚ - MARAÚ)

Kiaroa Eco-Luxury Resort

Loteamento da Costa, área SD6, Distrito de Barra Grande, Municipio de Maraú, Bahia, CEP 45 520-000, Brazil

Tel: +55 71 3272 1320

condenastjohansens.com/kiaroa

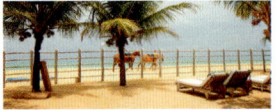

BRAZIL - BAHIA (TRANCOSO)

Estrela D'Água

Estrada Arraial d'Ajuda/Trancoso, 1011, Trancoso, Porto Seguro, Bahia 45818-000, Brazil

Tel: +55 73 3668 1030

condenastjohansens.com/estreladagua

BRAZIL - BAHIA (TRANCOSO)

Etnia Clube de Mar

Estrada Trancoso, Itaquena No 300, Km 02, Trancoso, Bahia 45818-000, Brazil

Tel: +55 73 3668 1137

condenastjohansens.com/etniaclube

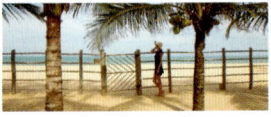

BRAZIL - BAHIA (TRANCOSO)

Etnia Pousada and Boutique

Trancoso, Bahia 45818-000, Brazil

Tel: +55 73 3668 1137

condenastjohansens.com/etnia

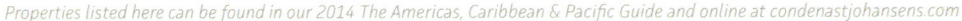

Properties listed here can be found in our 2014 The Americas, Caribbean & Pacific Guide and online at condenastjohansens.com

305

THE MINI LIST
The Americas, Caribbean & Pacific

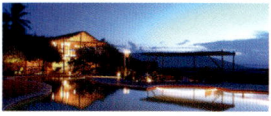

BRAZIL - CEARÁ (JERICOACOARA)

Vila Kalango

Rua das Dunas 30, Jericoacoara, Ceará 62598-000, Brazil

Tel: +55 88 3669 2290/2289
condenastjohansens.com/vilakalango

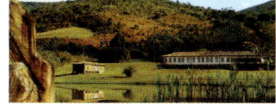

BRAZIL - MINAS GERAIS (LIMA DUARTE)

Reserva do Ibitipoca

Fazenda do Engenho, s/n Conceição do Ibitipoca, Lima Duarte, Minas Gerais 36140-000, Brazil

Tel: +55 32 2101 5103
condenastjohansens.com/reservadoibitipoca

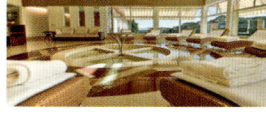

BRAZIL - PARANÁ (LAPA)

Lapinha Spa

Estrada da Lapa, Rio Negro, Km 16, Lapa, Paraná 83750-000, Brazil

Tel: +55 41 3622 1044
condenastjohansens.com/lapinha

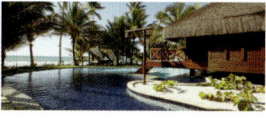

BRAZIL - PERNAMBUCO (PORTO DE GALINHAS)

Nannai Resort & Spa

Rodovia PE-09, acesso à Muro Alto, Km 3, Ipojuca, Pernambuco 55590-000, Brazil

Tel: +55 81 3552 0100
condenastjohansens.com/nannaibeach

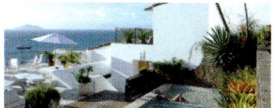

BRAZIL - RIO DE JANEIRO (BÚZIOS)

Casas Brancas Boutique-Hotel & Spa

Alto do Humaitá 10, Armação dos Búzios, Rio de Janeiro 28950-000, Brazil

Tel: +55 22 2623 1458/1603
condenastjohansens.com/casasbrancas

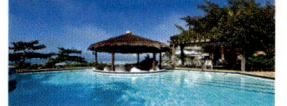

BRAZIL - RIO DE JANEIRO (BÚZIOS)

Hotel Le Relais La Borie

1374 Rua dos Gravatás, Praia de Geribá, Armação dos Búzios, Rio de Janeiro 28950-000, Brazil

Tel: +55 22 2620 8504
condenastjohansens.com/laborie

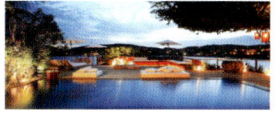

BRAZIL - RIO DE JANEIRO (BÚZIOS)

Insólito Boutique Hotel

Rua E1 - Lotes 3 and 4, Condomínio Atlântico, Armação de Búzios, Rio de Janeiro 28950-000, Brazil

Tel: +55 22 2623 2172
condenastjohansens.com/insolitohotel

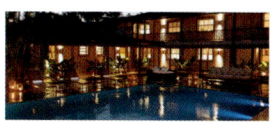

BRAZIL - RIO DE JANEIRO (PARATY)

Pousada Literária Ltda

Rua Tenente, Francisco Antônio, 362, Paraty, Rio de Janeiro 23970-000, Brazil

Tel: +55 24 3371 1460
condenastjohansens.com/pousadaliteraria

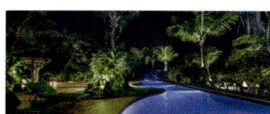

BRAZIL - RIO GRANDE DO NORTE (PRAIA DA PIPA)

Toca da Coruja

Avenida Baia dos Golfinhos 464, Praia da Pipa, Tibau do Sul, Rio Grande do Norte 59179-000, Brazil

Tel: +55 84 3246 2226/2225
condenastjohansens.com/tocadacoruja

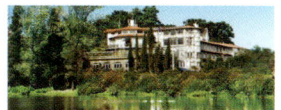

BRAZIL - RIO GRANDE DO SUL (GRAMADO)

Estalagem St. Hubertus

Rua Carrieri, 974, Gramado, Rio Grande do Sul, Cep: 95670-000, Brazil

Tel: +55 54 3286 1273
condenastjohansens.com/sthubertus

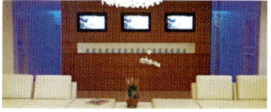

BRAZIL - RIO GRANDE DO SUL (GRAMADO)

Kurotel - Longevity Medical Center and Spa

Rua Nacões Unidas 533, PO Box 65, Gramado, Rio Grande do Sul 95670-000, Brazil

Tel: +55 54 3295 9393
condenastjohansens.com/kurotel

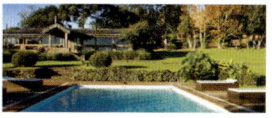

BRAZIL - RIO GRANDE DO SUL (GRAMADO)

La Hacienda Inn and Restaurant

Estrada da Serra Grande 4200, Gramado, Rio Grande do Sul 95670-000, Brazil

Tel: +55 54 3295 3025/88
condenastjohansens.com/lahacienda

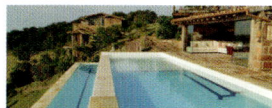

BRAZIL - SANTA CATARINA (IMBITUBA)

Ponta da Piteira

Ibiraquera, Imbituba, Santa Catarina, Brazil

Tel: +55 48 3356 0232
condenastjohansens.com/pontadapiteira

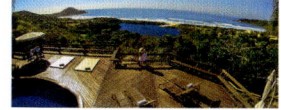

BRAZIL - SANTA CATARINA (PRAIA DO ROSA)

Solar Mirador Exclusive Resort

Estrada Geral do Rosa s/n, Praia do Rosa, Imbituba, Santa Catarina 88780-000, Brazil

Tel: +55 48 3355 6144/6004
condenastjohansens.com/solarmirador

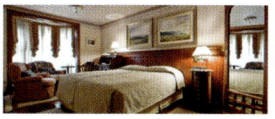

BRAZIL - SÃO PAULO (CAMPOS DO JORDÃO)

Hotel Frontenac

Av Dr Paulo Ribas, 295 Capivari, Campos do Jordão, São Paulo 12460-000, Brazil

Tel: +55 12 3669 1000
condenastjohansens.com/frontenac

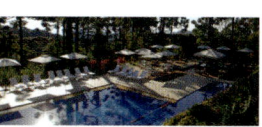

BRAZIL - SÃO PAULO (CAMPOS DO JORDÃO)

Hotel Toriba

Avenida Ernesto Diederichsen 2962, Campos do Jordão, São Paulo 12460-000, Brazil

Tel: +55 12 3668 5000
condenastjohansens.com/toriba

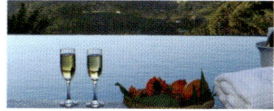

BRAZIL - SÃO PAULO (SANTO ANTÔNIO DO PINHAL)

Pousada Quinta dos Pinhais

Estrada do Pico Agudo, Km 3, Santo Antônio do Pinhal, São Paulo 12450-000, Brazil

Tel: +55 12 3666 2030/2463/1731
condenastjohansens.com/quintadospinhais

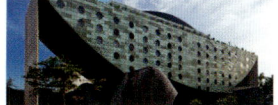

BRAZIL - SÃO PAULO (SÃO PAULO)

Hotel Unique

Avenida Brigadeiro Luis Antonio, 4.700 São Paulo, São Paulo 01402-002, Brazil

Tel: +55 11 3055 4710/00
condenastjohansens.com/hotelunique

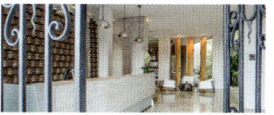

COLOMBIA - BOLÍVAR (CARTAGENA DE INDIAS)

Bóvedas de Santa Clara Hotel Boutique

Calle del Torno No. 39-29, Barrio San Diego, Cartagena de Indias, Bolívar, Colombia

Tel: +57 5 650 44 65
condenastjohansens.com/bovedasdesantaclara

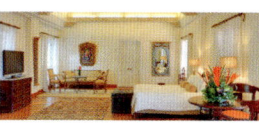

COLOMBIA - BOLÍVAR (CARTAGENA DE INDIAS)

Casa Pestagua

Calle Santo Domingo No 33-63, Cartagena de Indias, Bolívar, Colombia

Tel: +57 5 664 9510/6286
condenastjohansens.com/casapestagua

Properties listed here can be found in our 2014 The Americas, Caribbean & Pacific Guide and online at condenastjohansens.com

306

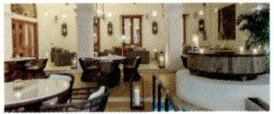

COLOMBIA - BOLÍVAR (CARTAGENA DE INDIAS)

Casa San Agustín

Centro, Calle de la Universidad No 36-44 Cartagena de Indias, Bolívar, Colombia

Tel: +575 681 0000
condenastjohansens.com/casasanagustin

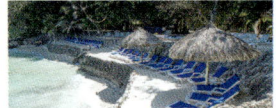

COLOMBIA - BOLÍVAR (CARTAGENA DE INDIAS)

Hotel San Pedro de Majagua

Isla Grande, Islas del Rosario, Cartagena de Indias, Bolívar, Colombia

Tel: +57 5 650 44 65
condenastjohansens.com/hotelmajagua

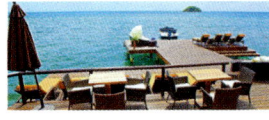

COLOMBIA - ISLA DE PROVIDENCIA (MARACAIBO BAY)

Deep Blue

Maracaibo Bay, Isla de Providencia, Colombia

Tel: +57 8 514 8423
condenastjohansens.com/deepblue

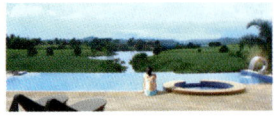

COLOMBIA - RISARALDA (PEREIRA)

Visus Hotel Boutique & Spa

Kilómetro 6 vía Cerrito, Vereda Pavas, Hacienda Malabar, Pereira, Risaralda, Colombia

Tel: +317 6 317 0060
condenastjohansens.com/visus

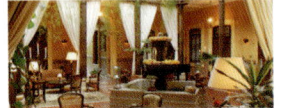

ECUADOR - AZUAY (CUENCA)

Mansión Alcázar Boutique Hotel

Calle Bolívar 12-55 Y Tarqui, Cuenca, Azuay, Ecuador

Tel: +593 72823 918
condenastjohansens.com/mansionalcazar

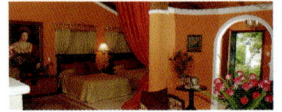

ECUADOR - IMBABURA (COTACACHI)

La Mirage Garden Hotel & Spa

Cotacachi, Imbabura, Ecuador

Tel: +593 6 291 5237
condenastjohansens.com/mirage

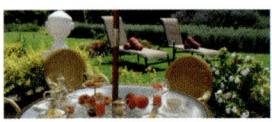

ECUADOR - PICHINCHA (QUITO)

Boutique Hotel Mansión del Ángel

Calle Los Ríos N13-134 y Pasaje Ascencio Gándara, Quito, Pichincha, Ecuador

Tel: +593 2 2557721
condenastjohansens.com/mansiondelangel

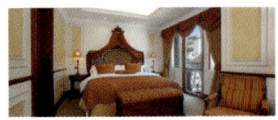

ECUADOR - PICHINCHA (QUITO)

Hotel Plaza Grande

Calle García Moreno, N5-16 y Chile, Quito, Pichincha, Ecuador

Tel: +593 2 2528 700
condenastjohansens.com/plazagrandequito

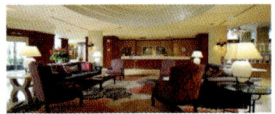

PERÚ - LIMA (LIMA)

Swissôtel Lima

Via Central 150, Centro Empresarial Real, San Isidro, Lima 27, Perú

Tel: +511 421 4400
condenastjohansens.com/swissotellima

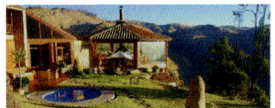

PERÚ - LIMA (SANTIAGO DE VIÑAK)

Refugio Viñak-Sierra de Lunahuaná

Santiago de Viñak, Yauyos, Lima, Perú

Tel: +511 421 6952 ext 105
condenastjohansens.com/refugiosdelperu

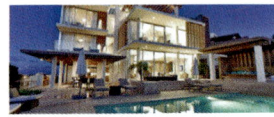

CARIBBEAN - ANGUILLA (LITTLE BAY)

Àni Villas

Little Bay, Anguilla

Tel: +1 264 497 7888
condenastjohansens.com/anivillas

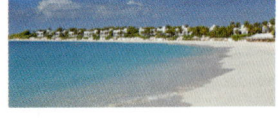

CARIBBEAN - ANGUILLA (MAUNDAYS BAY)

Cap Juluca

Maundays Bay, AI-2640, Anguilla

Tel: +1 264 497 6666
condenastjohansens.com/capjuluca

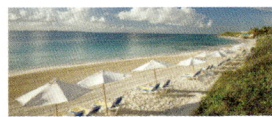

CARIBBEAN - ANGUILLA (RENDEZVOUS BAY)

CuisinArt Golf Resort & Spa

Rendezvous Bay, Anguilla

Tel: +1 264 498 2000
condenastjohansens.com/cuisinartresort

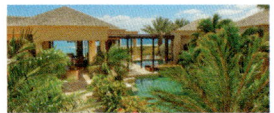

CARIBBEAN - ANGUILLA (SANDY HILL BAY BEACH)

Bird of Paradise

Sandy Hill Bay Beach, Anguilla

Tel: +1 414 791 9461
condenastjohansens.com/birdofparadise

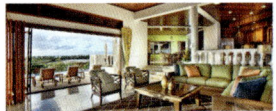

CARIBBEAN - ANGUILLA (WEST END)

Sheriva Boutique Villa Hotel

Maundays Bay Road, West End AI-2640, Anguilla

Tel: +1 264 498 9898
condenastjohansens.com/sheriva

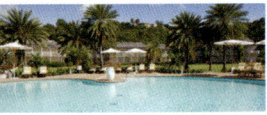

CARIBBEAN - ANTIGUA (SAINT PAUL)

The Inn at English Harbour

187 Dockyard Drive, English Harbour, Saint Paul, Antigua

Tel: +1 268 460 1014
condenastjohansens.com/innatenglishharbour

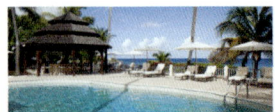

CARIBBEAN - ANTIGUA (ST JOHN'S)

Blue Waters

St John's, Antigua

Tel: +44 (0)870 360 1245
condenastjohansens.com/bluewaters

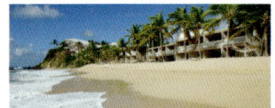

CARIBBEAN - ANTIGUA (ST JOHN'S)

Curtain Bluff

St John's, Antigua

Tel: +1 268 462 8400
condenastjohansens.com/curtainbluff

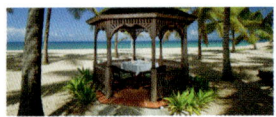

CARIBBEAN - ANTIGUA (ST JOHN'S)

Galley Bay Resort

Five Islands, St John's, Antigua

Tel: +1 954 481 8787
condenastjohansens.com/galleybay

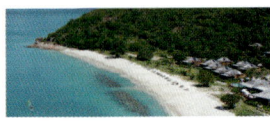

CARIBBEAN - ANTIGUA (ST JOHN'S)

Hermitage Bay

St John's, Antigua

Tel: +1 268 562 5500
condenastjohansens.com/hermitagebay

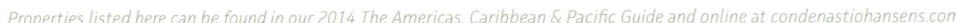

Properties listed here can be found in our 2014 The Americas, Caribbean & Pacific Guide and online at condenastjohansens.com

THE MINI LIST
The Americas, Caribbean & Pacific

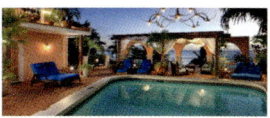

CARIBBEAN - BARBADOS (CHRIST CHURCH)

Little Arches Boutique Hotel

Enterprise Beach Road, Christ Church, Barbados

Tel: +1 246 420 4689
condenastjohansens.com/littlearches

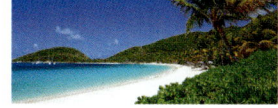

CARIBBEAN - BRITISH VIRGIN ISLANDS (PETER ISLAND)

Peter Island Resort & Spa

Peter Island, British Virgin Islands

Tel: +616 458 6767
condenastjohansens.com/peterislandresort

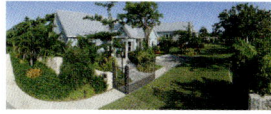

CARIBBEAN - CAYMAN ISLANDS (GRAND CAYMAN)

Cotton Tree

375 Conch Point Road, PO Box 31324, Grand Cayman KY1-1206, Cayman Islands

Tel: +1 345 943 0700
condenastjohansens.com/caymancottontree

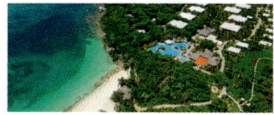

CARIBBEAN - CUBA (CAIBARIÉN)

Meliá Buenavista All Inclusive Royal Service & Spa

Punta Madruguilla, Oeste Cayo Santa María, Caibarién, Villa Clara, Cuba

Tel: +53 24 204 55 77 ext 1442
condenastjohansens.com/royalservicebuenavista

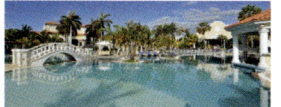

CARIBBEAN - CUBA (HOLGUÍN)

Royal Service Paradisus Río de Oro

Playa Esmeralda, Carretera Guardalavaca, Holguín, Rafael Freyre, Cuba

Tel: +53 24 204 55 77 ext 1442
condenastjohansens.com/royalserviceriodeoro

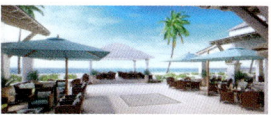

CARIBBEAN - CUBA (VARADERO)

Royal Service Paradisus Princesa del Mar

Autopista Sur, Carretera Las Morlas, Km 19½, Varadero, Matanzas, Cuba

Tel: +53 24 204 55 77 ext 1442
condenastjohansens.com/royalserviceprincesa

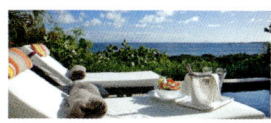

CARIBBEAN - GRENADA (ST GEORGE'S)

Spice Island Beach Resort

Grand Anse Beach, St George's, Grenada

Tel: +1 473 444 4258/4423
condenastjohansens.com/spiceisland

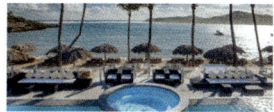

CARIBBEAN - SAINT-BARTHÉLEMY (ANSE DE TOINY)

Hôtel Le Toiny

Anse de Toiny, Saint-Barthélemy

Tel: +590 590 27 88 88
condenastjohansens.com/letoiny

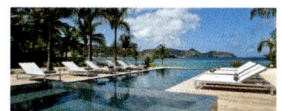

CARIBBEAN - SAINT-BARTHÉLEMY (GRAND CUL DE SAC)

Hotel Guanahani & Spa

Grand Cul de Sac, Saint-Barthélemy

Tel: +590 590 52 90 00
condenastjohansens.com/guanahani

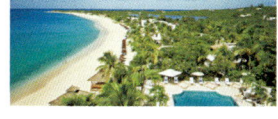

CARIBBEAN - SAINT-BARTHÉLEMY (LORIENT BAY)

The Palm Beach Villa

Lorient Bay, Saint-Barthélemy

Tel: +33 664 170970
condenastjohansens.com/palmbeachvilla

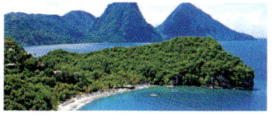

CARIBBEAN - SAINT-MARTIN (BAIE LONGUE)

La Samanna

Baie Longue Saint-Martin, French West Indies

Tel: +590 590 87 64 00
condenastjohansens.com/lasamanna

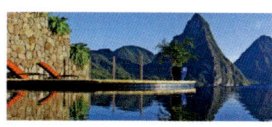

CARIBBEAN - SAINT LUCIA (SOUFRIÈRE)

Anse Chastanet

Soufrière, Saint Lucia

Tel: +1 758 459 7000/6100
condenastjohansens.com/ansechastanet

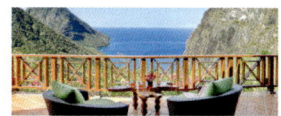

CARIBBEAN - SAINT LUCIA (SOUFRIÈRE)

Jade Mountain

Soufrière, Saint Lucia

Tel: +1 758 459 4000/6100
condenastjohansens.com/jademountain

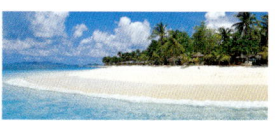

CARIBBEAN - SAINT LUCIA (SOUFRIÈRE)

Ladera

Soufrière, Saint Lucia

Tel: +1 866 290 0978
condenastjohansens.com/ladera

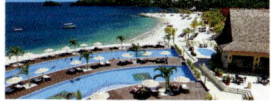

CARIBBEAN - SAINT VINCENT & THE GRENADINES (PALM ISLAND)

Palm Island

Palm Island, The Grenadines

Tel: +1 954 481 8787
condenastjohansens.com/palmisland

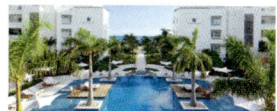

CARIBBEAN - SAINT VINCENT & THE GRENADINES (KINGSTOWN)

Buccament Bay Resort

Kingstown, Saint Vincent, Saint Vincent & The Grenadines

Tel: +1 855 212 1972
condenastjohansens.com/buccamentbay

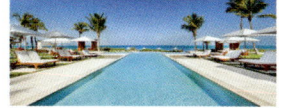

CARIBBEAN - TURKS & CAICOS ISLANDS (PROVIDENCIALES)

Gansevoort Turks + Caicos, a Wymara Resort

Lower Bight Road, Grace Bay Beach, Providenciales, Turks & Caicos Islands

Tel: +1 649 941 7555
condenastjohansens.com/gansevoorttc

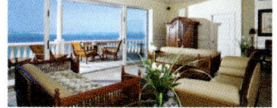

CARIBBEAN - TURKS & CAICOS ISLANDS (PROVIDENCIALES)

Grace Bay Club

Grace Bay Circle Road, Grace Bay, Providenciales, Turks & Caicos Islands

Tel: +1 649 946 5050
condenastjohansens.com/gracebayclub

CARIBBEAN - TURKS & CAICOS ISLANDS (PROVIDENCIALES)

Point Grace

Grace Bay Beach, Providenciales, Turks & Caicos Islands

Tel: +1 649 946 5096
condenastjohansens.com/pointgrace

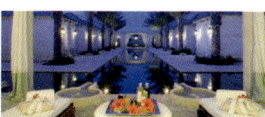

CARIBBEAN - TURKS & CAICOS ISLANDS (PROVIDENCIALES)

Regent Palms, Turks & Caicos

16 Princess Drive, Grace Bay Beach, Providenciales, Turks & Caicos Islands

Tel: +649 946 8666
condenastjohansens.com/regentpalms

Properties listed here can be found in our 2014 The Americas, Caribbean & Pacific Guide and online at condenastjohansens.com

THE MINI LIST
The Americas, Caribbean & Pacific

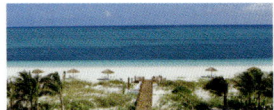

CARIBBEAN - TURKS & CAICOS ISLANDS (PROVIDENCIALES)

West Bay Club

Lower Bight Road, Providenciales, Turks & Caicos Islands

Tel: +1 649 946 8550
condenastjohansens.com/thewestbayclub

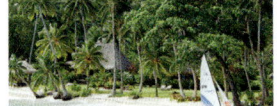

PACIFIC - FIJI ISLANDS (TAVEUNI ISLAND)

Qamea Resort & Spa

PA Matei, Qamea Island, Fiji Islands

Tel: +64 9 360 0858
condenastjohansens.com/qamea

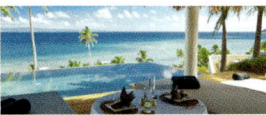

PACIFIC - FIJI ISLANDS (MATEI)

Taveuni Palms Resort

Matei, Taveuni, Fiji Islands

Tel: +679 888 0032
condenastjohansens.com/taveunipalms

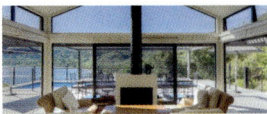

PACIFIC - NEW ZEALAND (NORTH ISLAND)

The Point Villas

24A & B The Point Villas, The Point (Whakameoenga Point), Taupo, North Island, New Zealand

Tel: +64 7 377 8002
condenastjohansens.com/thepointvillas

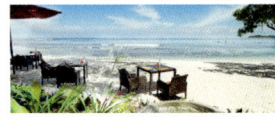

PACIFIC - VANUATU (EFATE ISLAND)

Eratap Beach Resort

Eratap Point, Port Vila, Efate Island, Vanuatu

Tel: +678 554 5007
condenastjohansens.com/eratap

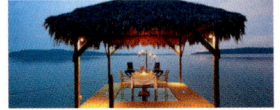

PACIFIC - VANUATU (EFATE ISLAND)

The Havannah Vanuatu

Samoa Point, Port Vila, Efate Island, Vanuatu

Tel: + 678 551 8060
condenastjohansens.com/thehavannah

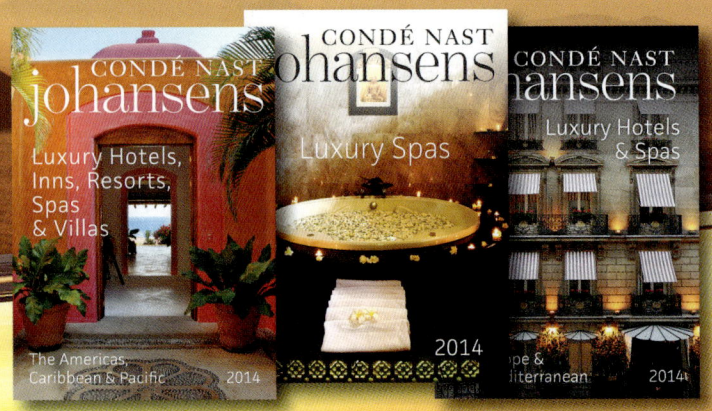

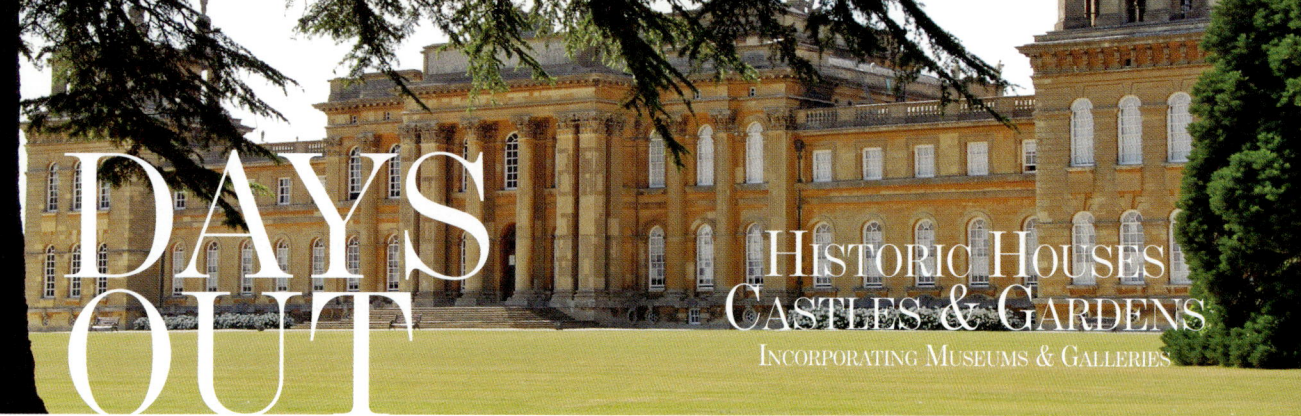

DAYS OUT

HISTORIC HOUSES CASTLES & GARDENS
INCORPORATING MUSEUMS & GALLERIES

FRANCE

Loire Valley

Château de Chenonceau - 37150 Chenonceaux, Loire Valley 37150.
Tel: +33 2 47 23 44 06

IRELAND

Cork

Blarney Castle, House and Garden - Blarney, Cork. Tel: +353 21 4385252

Kildare

The Irish National Stud & Gardens - The Irish National Stud, Tully, Kildare
Town, Kildare. Tel: +353 45 521617

Westmeath

Tullynally Castle and Gardens - Tullynally Estate, Castlepollard,
Westmeath. Tel: +353 44 966 1159

Wicklow

Mount Usher Gardens - Ashford, Wicklow. Tel: +353 40440205

ITALY

Veneto

Ridotto Ball Room - Hotel Monaco & Grand Canal, San Marco 1332, 30124
Venezia, Veneto. Tel: +39 04 15200211

UK/ENGLAND

Bath & North East Somerset

Maunsel House - North Newton, Nr Taunton, Bath & North East Somerset
TA7 0BU. Tel: +44 (0)1278 661076

Bedfordshire

Queen Anne's Summerhouse - Shuttleworth Estate, Old Warden,
Bedfordshire SG18 9EP. Tel: +44 (0)1628 825925
Moggerhanger Park - Park Road, Moggerhanger, Bedfordshire MK44 3RW.
Tel: +44 (0)1767 641007

Buckinghamshire

Nether Winchendon House - Nr Aylesbury, Buckinghamshire HP18 0DY.
Tel: +44 (0)1844 290101
Waddesdon Manor - Waddesdon, Nr Aylesbury, Buckinghamshire
HP18 0JH. Tel: +44 (0)1296 653226

Cambridgeshire

The Manor - Hemingford Grey, Huntingdon, Cambridgeshire PE28 9BN.
Tel: +44 (0)1480 463134

Cheshire

Dorfold Hall - Nantwich, Cheshire CW5 8LD. Tel: +44 (0)1270 625245
Peover Hall and Gardens - Peover Estate, Over Peover, Knutsford, Cheshire
WA16 9HW. Tel: +44 (0)1565 724 220
Rode Hall - Scholar Green (by Stoke-on-Trent), Cheshire ST7 3QP.
Tel: +44 (0)1270 882961/873237
Tabley House Collection - Knutsford, Cheshire WA16 0HB.
Tel: +44 (0)1565 750151

Cornwall

Burncoose Nurseries and Garden - Gwennap, Redruth, Cornwall TR16 6BJ.
Tel: +44 (0)1209 861112
Caerhays Castle and Estate - Estate Office, Gorran, St Austell, Cornwall
PL26 6LY. Tel: +44 (0)1872 501310/501144
Pencarrow House and Gardens - Washway, Bodmin, Cornwall PL30 3AG.
Tel: +44 (0)1208 841369
Prideaux Place - Padstow, Cornwall PL28 8RP. Tel: +44 (0)1841 532411

Cumbria

The Beatrix Potter Gallery - Main Street, Hawkshead, Cumbria LA22 0NS.
Tel: +44 (0)15394 36355
Isel Hall - Cockermouth, Cumbria CA13 0QG. Tel: +44 (0)1900 826127

Derbyshire

Melbourne Hall & Gardens - Melbourne, Derbyshire DE73 8EN.
Tel: +44 (0)1332 862502
Renishaw Hall and Gardens - Nr Sheffield, Derbyshire S21 3WB.
Tel: +44 (0)1246 432210

Devon

Downes - Crediton, Devon EX17 3PL. Tel: +44 (0)1363 775142
Powderham Castle - Kenton, Exeter, Devon EX6 8JQ.
Tel: +44 (0)1626 890243
Torre Abbey - The Kings Drive, Torquay, Devon TQ2 5JE.
Tel: +44 (0)1803 293593

Dorset

Chiffchaffs - Chaffeymoor, Bourton, Gillingham, Dorset SP8 5BY.
Tel: +44 (0)1747 840841
Clavell Tower - Kimmeridge, Nr Wareham, Dorset.
Tel: +44 (0)1628 825925
Moignes Court - Owermoigne, Dorchester, Dorset DT2 8HY.
Tel: +44 (0)1305 853300

Durham

Auckland Castle - Bishop Auckland, Durham DL14 7NR.
Tel: +44 (0)1388 601627
The Bowes Museum - Barnard Castle, Durham DL12 8NP.
Tel: +44 (0)1833 690606
Raby Castle - Staindrop, Darlington, Durham DL2 3AH.
Tel: +44 (0)1833 660 202

Essex

Ingatestone Hall - Hall Lane, Ingatestone, Essex CM4 9NR.
Tel: +44 (0)1277 353010

Top image: Blenheim Palace, Oxfordshire, UK/England

Gloucestershire

Berkeley Castle - Berkeley, Gloucestershire GL13 9BQ.
Tel: +44 (0)1453 810332
Cheltenham Art Gallery & Museum - Clarence Street, Cheltenham,
Gloucestershire GL50 3JT. Tel: +44 (0)1242 237431
Hardwicke Court - Nr Gloucester, Gloucestershire GL2 4RS.
Tel: +44 (0)1452 720212
Sezincote House & Garden - Nr Moreton-in-Marsh, Gloucestershire
GL56 9AW. Tel: +44 (0)1386 700444

Hampshire

Avington Park - Winchester, Hampshire SO21 1DB.
Tel: +44 (0)1962 779260
Greywell Hill House - Greywell, Hook, Hampshire RG29 1DG.
Tel: +44 (0)1256 703565

Hertfordshire

Gorhambury - St Albans, Hertfordshire AL3 6AH. Tel: +44 (0)1727 854051

Kent

Belmont House and Gardens - Belmont Park, Throwley, Faversham, Kent
ME13 0HH. Tel: +44 (0)1795 890202
The Grange - Ramsgate, Kent CT11 9NY. Tel: +44 (0)1628 825925
Hever Castle and Gardens - Nr Edenbridge, Kent TN8 7NG.
Tel: +44 (0)1732 861710
Mount Ephraim Gardens - Staple Street, Hernhill, Nr Faversham, Kent
ME13 9TX. Tel: +44 (0)1227 751496
The New College of Cobham - Cobhambury Road, Cobham, Nr Gravesend,
Kent DA12 3BG. Tel: +44 (0)1474 812503
Penshurst Place and Gardens - Penshurst, Nr Tonbridge, Kent TN11 8DG.
Tel: +44 (0)1892 870307
Riverhill Himalayan Gardens - Riverhill, Sevenoaks, Kent TN15 0RR.
Tel: +44 (0)1732 459777

Lincolnshire

Elsham Hall Country and Wildlife Park - The Estate Office, Brigg,
Lincolnshire DN20 0QZ. Tel: +44 (0)1652 688698

London

18 Stafford Terrace - 18 Stafford Terrace, London W8 7BH.
Tel: +44 (0)20 7612 3306
Burgh House & Hampstead Museum - New End Square, Hampstead,
London NW3 1LT. Tel: +44 (0)20 7431 0144
Chelsea Physic Garden - 66 Royal Hospital Road, Chelsea, London
SW3 4HS. Tel: +44 (0)20 7352 5646
Handel House Museum - 25 Brook Street, London W1K 4HB.
Tel: +44 (0)20 7495 1685
Leighton House - 12 Holland Park Road, London W14 8LZ.
Tel: +44 (0)20 7602 3316
Pitzhanger Manor House - Walpole Park, Mattock Lane, Ealing, London
W5 5EQ. Tel: +44 (0)20 8567 1227
Spencer House - 27 St James's Place, London SW1A 1NR.
Tel: +44 (0)20 7514 1958
Strawberry Hill House - 268 Waldegrave Road, Twickenham, London
TW1 4ST. Tel: +44 (0)20 8744 1241

Merseyside

Meols Hall - Churchtown, Southport, Merseyside PR9 7LZ.
Tel: +44 (0)1704 228326

West Midlands

The Barber Institute of Fine Arts - University of Birmingham, Edgbaston,
Birmingham, West Midlands B15 2TS. Tel: +44 (0)121 414 7333
The Birmingham Botanical Gardens & Glasshouses - Westbourne Road,
Edgbaston, Birmingham, West Midlands B15 3TR.
Tel: +44 (0)121 454 1860

Norfolk

South Elmham Hall - Hall Lane, St Cross, Harleston, Norfolk IP20 0PY.
Tel: +44 (0)1986 782526
Walsingham Abbey Grounds and Shirehall Museum - Common Place,
Walsingham, Norfolk NR22 6BP. Tel: +44 (0)1328 820510

Northumberland

Chipchase Castle & Gardens - Wark on Tyne, Hexham, Northumberland
NE48 3NT. Tel: +44 (0)1434 230203

Oxfordshire

Blenheim Palace - Woodstock, Oxfordshire OX20 1PX.
Tel: +44 (0)1993 810510
Kingston Bagpuize House - Abingdon, Oxfordshire OX13 5AX.
Tel: +44 (0)1865 820259
Mapledurham House & Watermill - Nr Reading, Oxfordshire RG4 7TR.
Tel: +44 (0)1189 723350
Stonor Park - Nr Henley-on-Thames, Oxfordshire RG9 6HF.
Tel: +44 (0)1491 638587
Wallingford Castle Gardens - Castle Street, Wallingford, Oxfordshire
OX10 8DL. Tel: +44 (0)1491 835373

Shropshire

Hodnet Hall Gardens - Hodnet, Market Drayton, Shropshire TF9 3NN.
Tel: +44 (0)1630 685786
The White House - Aston Munslow, Shropshire. Tel: +44 (0)1628 825925

Somerset

Kentsford - Washford, Watchet, Somerset TA23 0JD.
Tel: +44 (0)1984 632309
Orchard Wyndham - Williton, Taunton, Somerset TA4 4HH.
Tel: +44 (0)1984 632309
Robin Hood's Hut - Halswell, Goathurst, Somerset.
Tel: +44 (0)1628 825925
Woodlands Castle - Woodlands, Ruishton, Taunton, Somerset TA3 5LU.
Tel: +44 (0)1823 444955

Staffordshire

Whitmore Hall - Whitmore, Newcastle-under-Lyme, Staffordshire
ST5 5HW. Tel: +44 (0)1782 680478

Suffolk

Freston Tower - Nr Ipswich, Suffolk IP9 1AD. Tel: +44 (0)1628 825925
Glemham Hall - Little Glemham, Woodbridge, Suffolk IP13 0BT.
Tel: +44 (0)1728 748289
Kentwell Hall - Long Melford, Sudbury, Suffolk CO10 9BA.
Tel: +44 (0)1787 310207
Newbourne Hall - Newbourne, Nr Woodbridge, Suffolk IP12 4NP.
Tel: +44 (0)1473 736764

Surrey

Goddards - Abinger Common, Dorking, Surrey. Tel: +44 (0)1628 825920
Titsey Place and Gardens - Titsey, Oxted, Surrey RH8 0SD.
Tel: +44 (0)1273 715356

East Sussex

Charleston - Nr Firle, Lewes, East Sussex BN8 6LL. Tel: +44 (0)1323 811626
Firle Place - Firle, Nr Lewes, East Sussex BN8 6LP. Tel: +44 (0)1273 858307
Pashley Manor Gardens - Ticehurst, Nr Wadhurst, East Sussex TN5 7HE.
Tel: +44 (0)1580 200888
Wilmington Priory - Wilmington, Nr Eastbourne, East Sussex BN26 5SW.
Tel: +44 (0)1628 825925

West Sussex

Arundel Castle - Arundel, West Sussex BN18 9AB. Tel: +44 (0)1903 882173

INDEX

Days Out incorporating Historic Houses, Castles & Gardens, Museums & Galleries

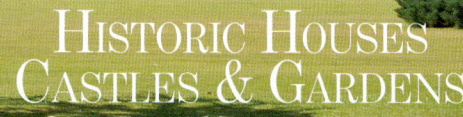

historichouses.co.uk

**HISTORIC HOUSES
CASTLES & GARDENS**
INCORPORATING MUSEUMS & GALLERIES

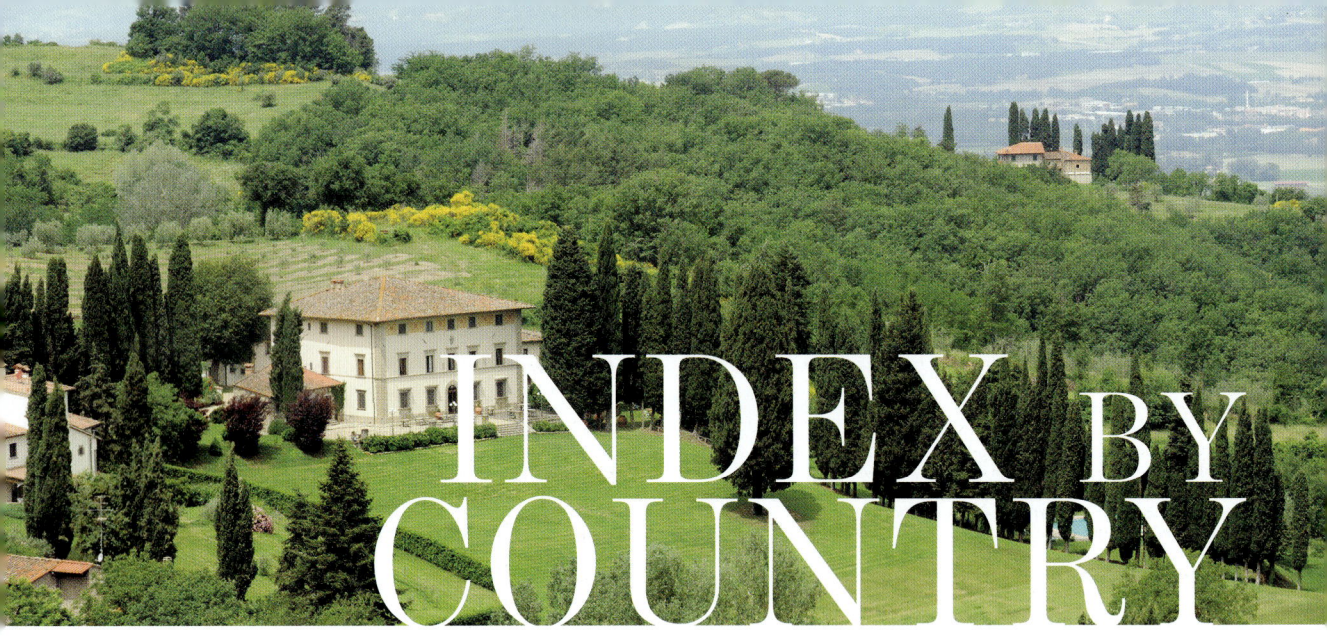

INDEX BY COUNTRY

Top image: Villa Campestri Olive Oil Resort, Italy, page 114

313

INDEX
by Country

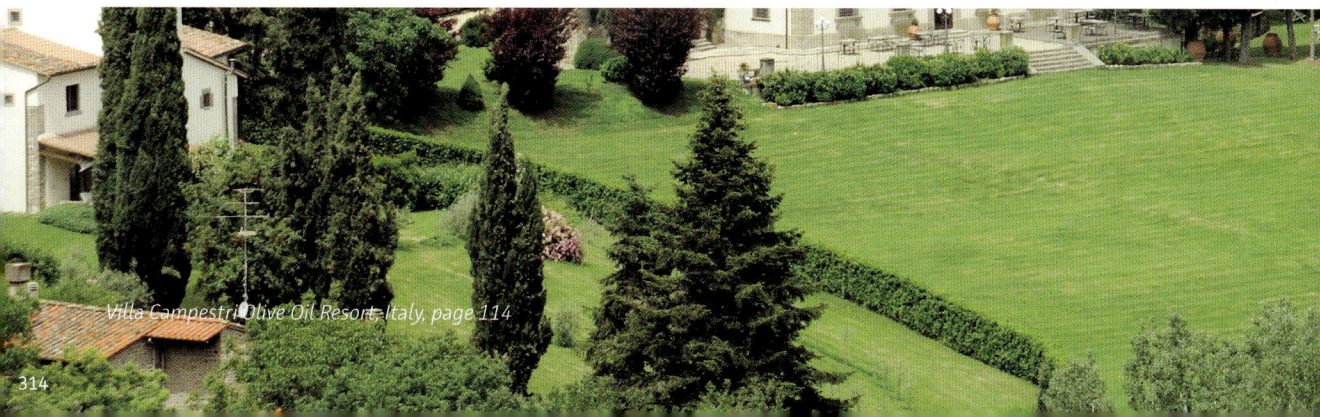

Villa Campestri Olive Oil Resort - Italy, page 114

INDEX
by Country

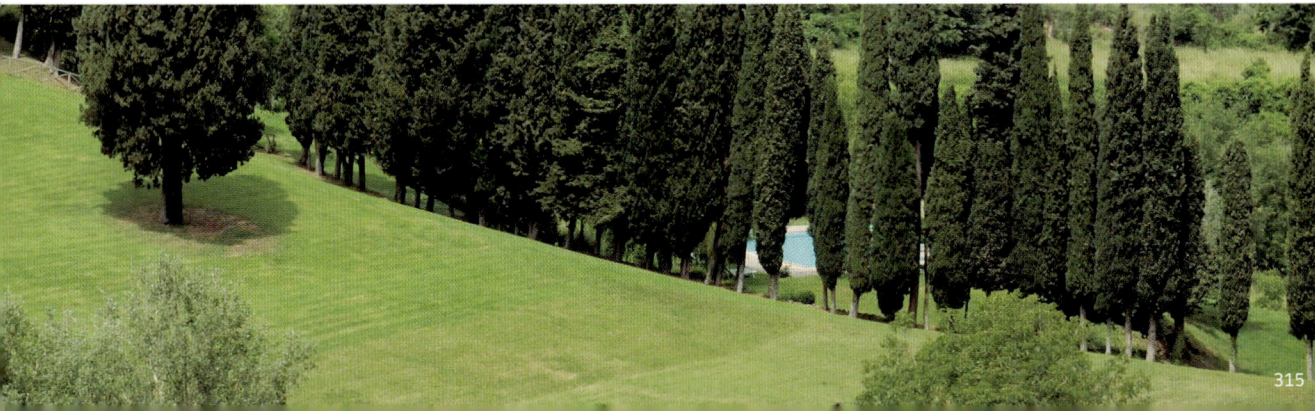

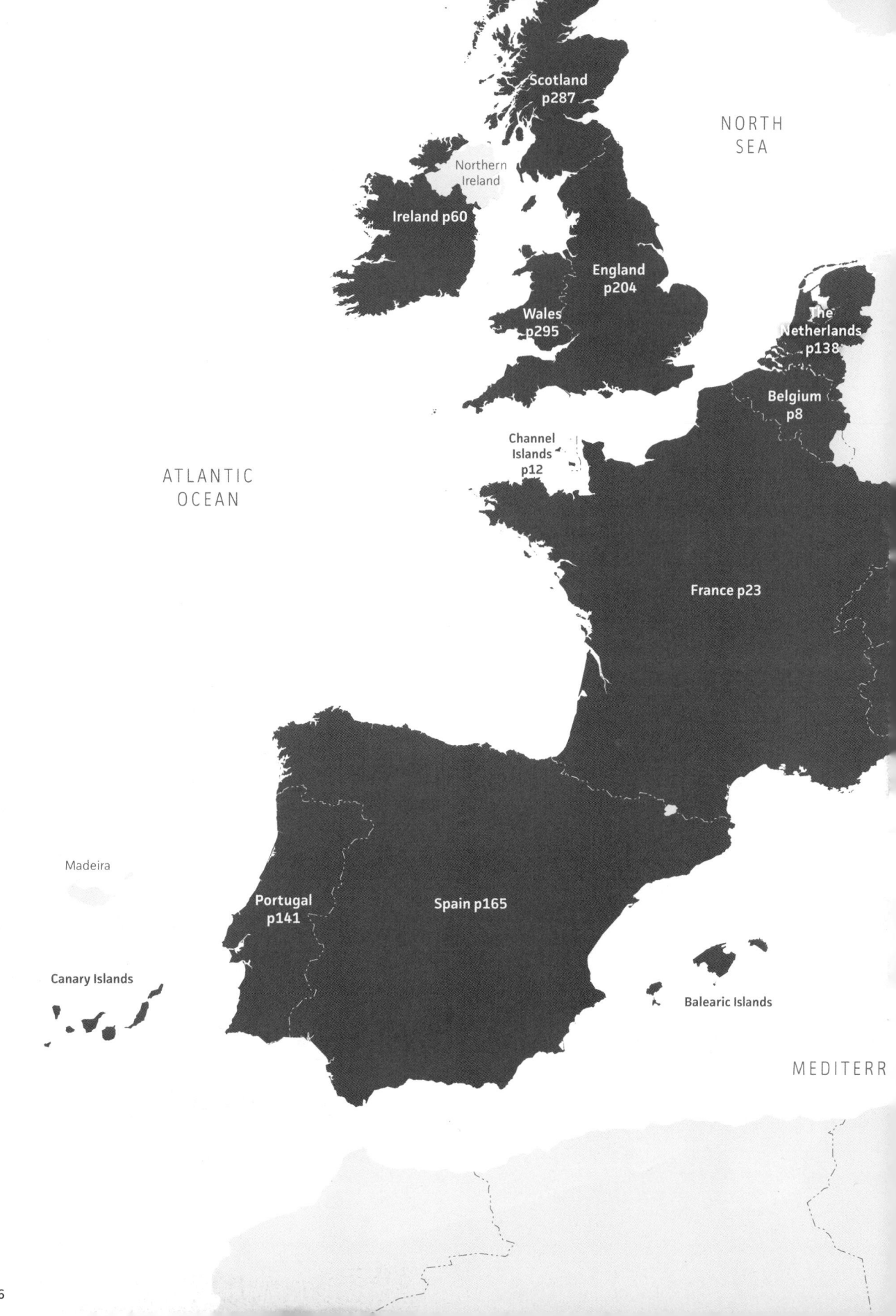

NORTH
SEA

Scotland
p287

Northern
Ireland

Ireland p60

England
p204

The
Netherlands
p138

Wales
p295

Belgium
p8

ATLANTIC
OCEAN

Channel
Islands
p12

France p23

Madeira

Portugal
p141

Spain p165

Canary Islands

Balearic Islands

MEDITERR

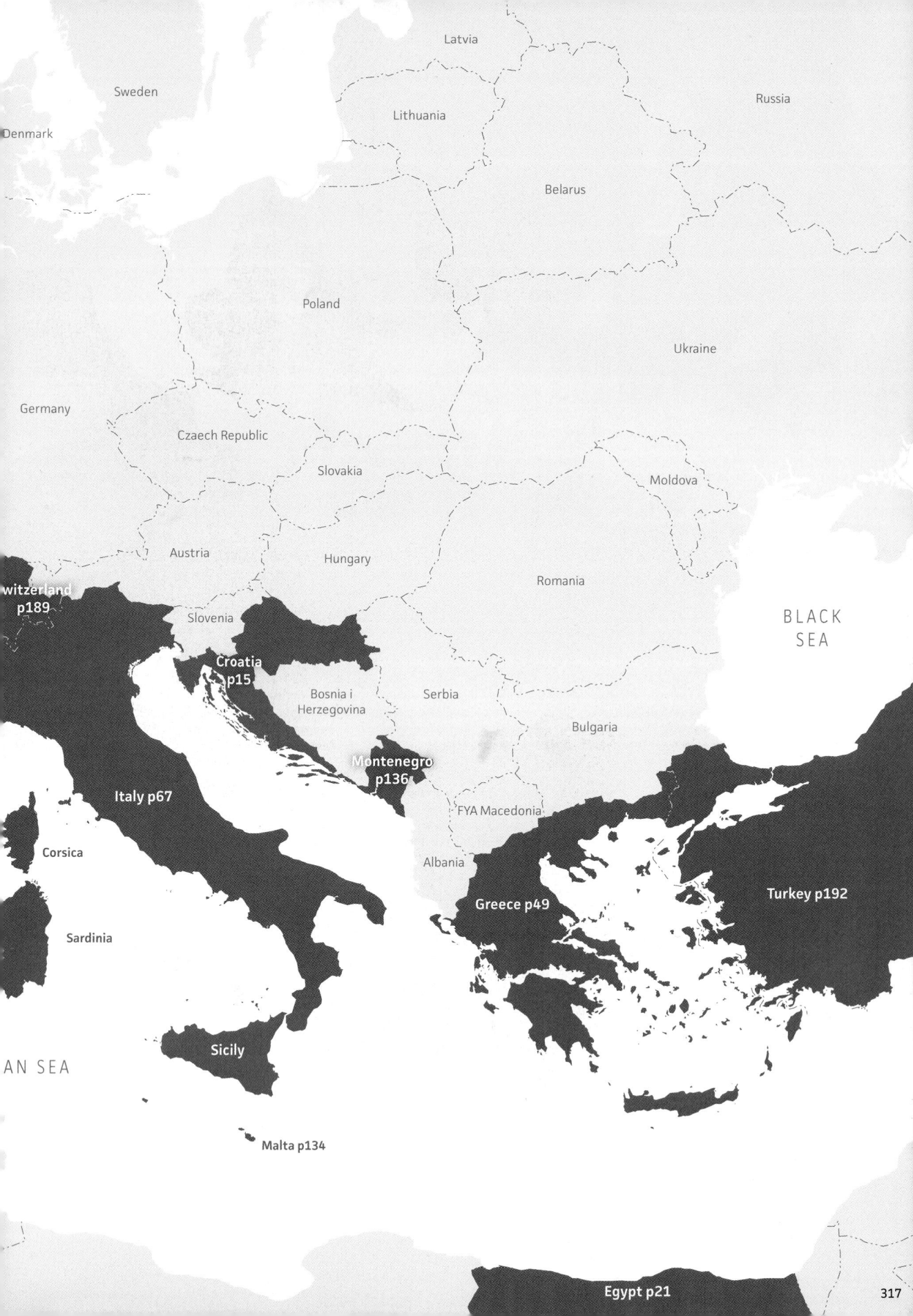

Sweden

Denmark

Latvia

Lithuania

Russia

Belarus

Poland

Ukraine

Germany

Czaech Republic

Slovakia

Moldova

Austria

Hungary

Romania

BLACK
SEA

Switzerland
p189

Slovenia

Croatia
p15

Bosnia i
Herzegovina

Serbia

Bulgaria

Italy p67

Montenegro
p136

FYA Macedonia

Corsica

Albania

Turkey p192

Sardinia

Greece p49

AN SEA

Sicily

Malta p134

Egypt p21

317

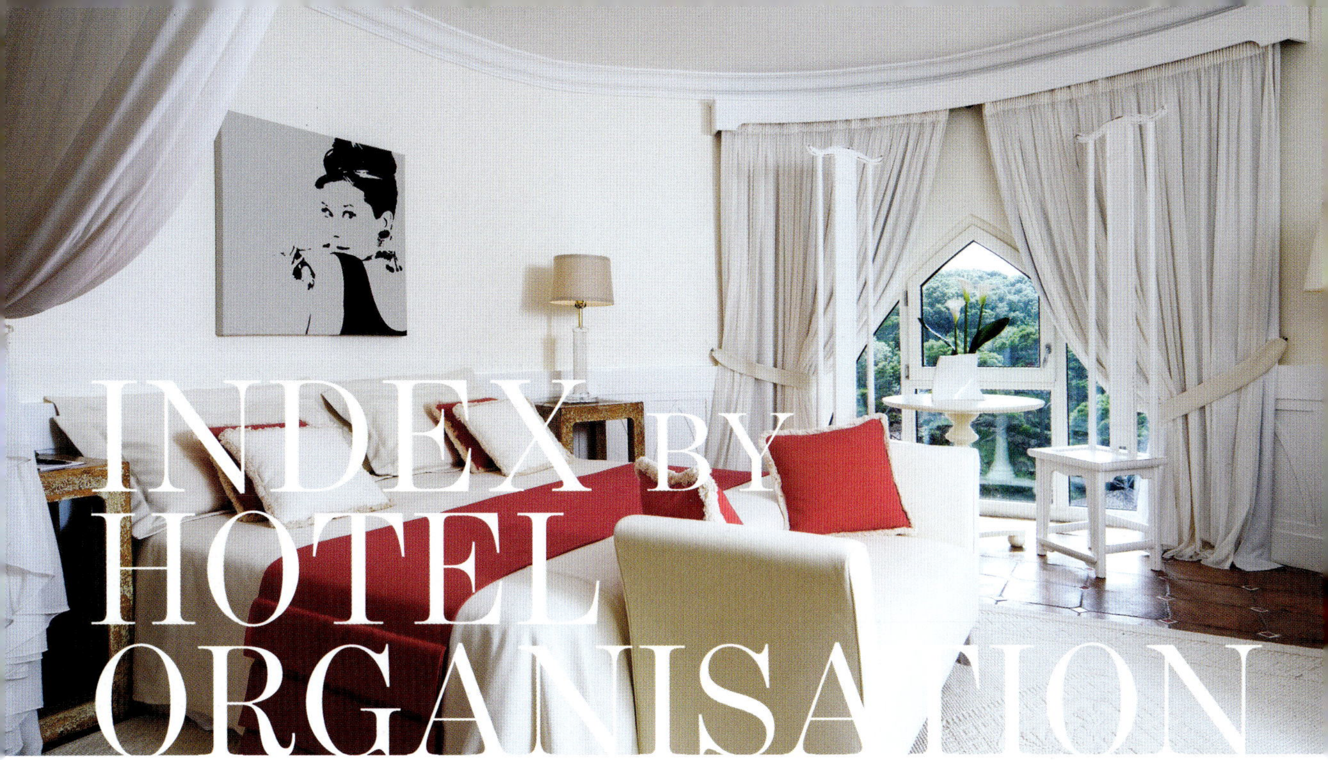

INDEX BY HOTEL ORGANISATION

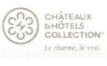
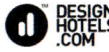

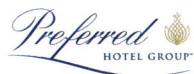
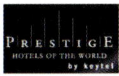

Top image: Mezzatorre Resort & Spa, Italy, page 68

Relais & Châteaux

 Small Luxury Hotels of the World

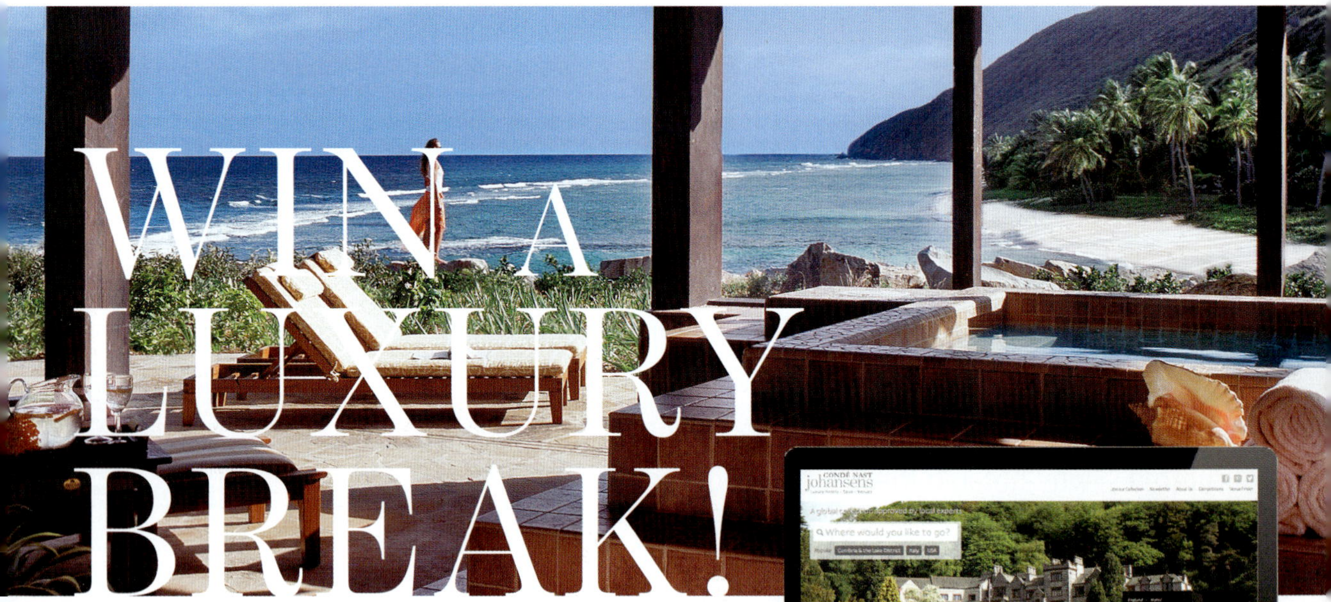

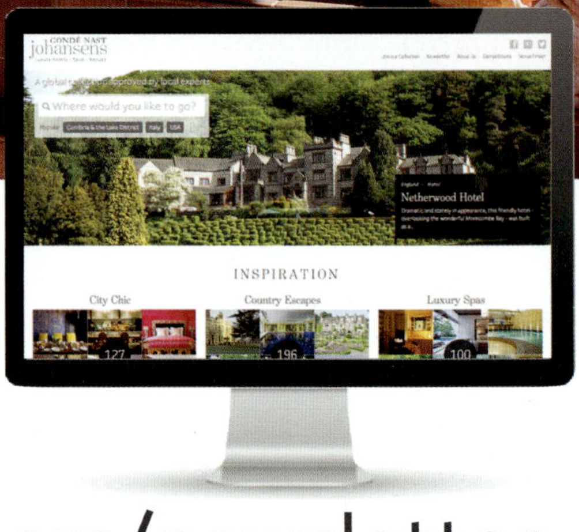

required by **professionals**, desired by **enthusiasts**

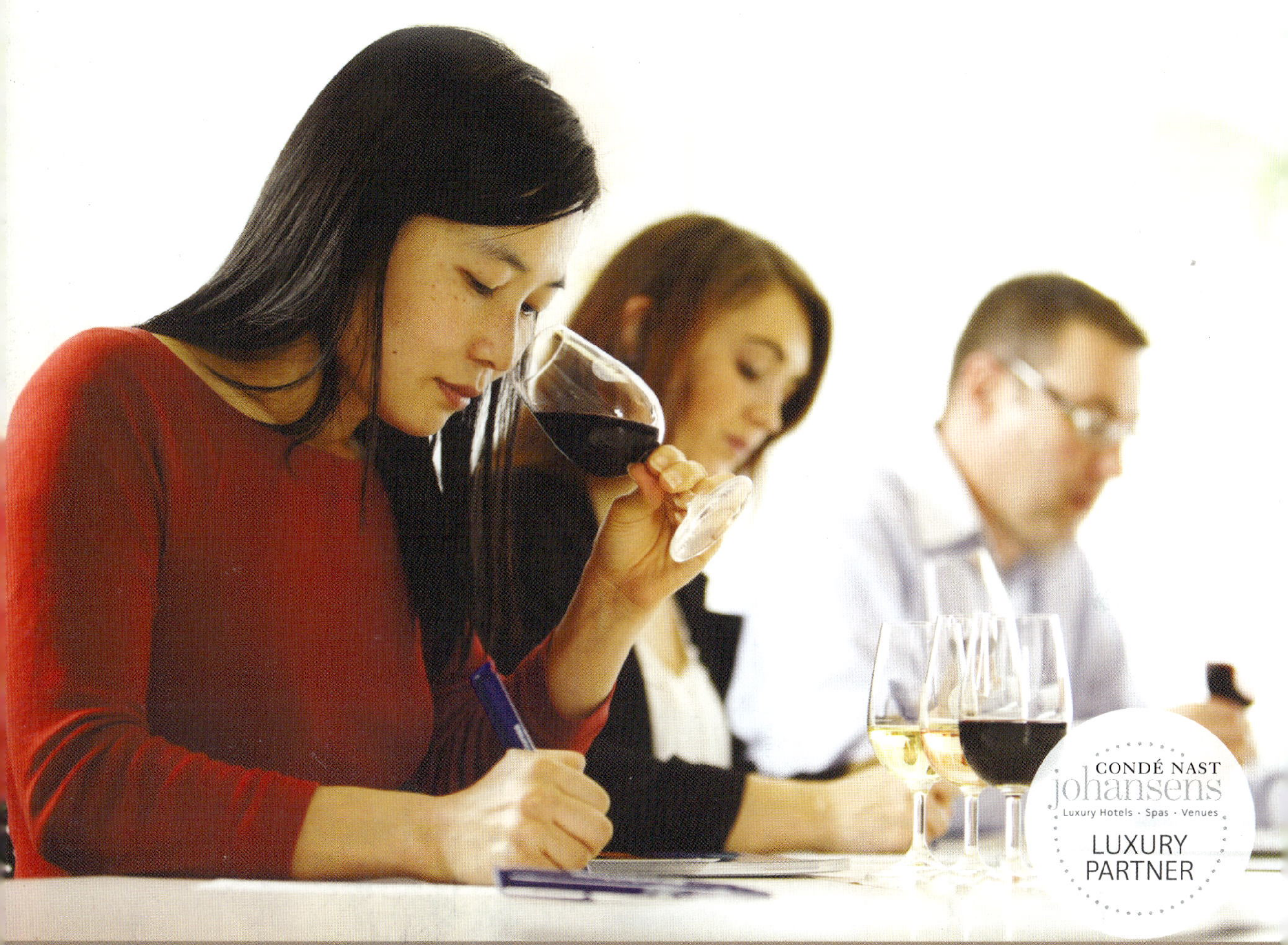

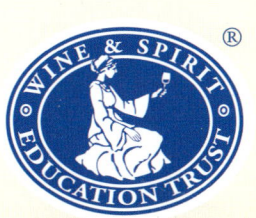